ROC

4-1-43

GEOMETRY

Ron Larson

Laurie Boswell

Lee Stiff

REASONING

APPLYING

MEASURING

McDougal Littell

A HOUGHTON MIFFLIN COMPANY

Evanston, Illincis • Boston • Dallas

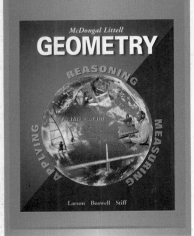

About the Cover

Geometry brings math to life with many real-life applications. The cover illustrates some of the applications used in this book. Examples of mathematics in sports, engineering, and carpentry are shown on pages 127, 152, 191, and 234. Circling the globe are three key aspects of Geometry—*measuring, reasoning,* and *applying* geometrical ideas. As you explore the applications presented in the book, try to make your own connections between mathematics and the world around you!

ISBN: 0-395-93777-9   89–DWO–03 02

Internet Web Site: http://www.mcdougallittell.com

About the Authors

▶ **Ron Larson** is a professor of mathematics at Penn State University at Erie. He is the author of a broad range of mathematics textbooks for middle school, high school, and college students. He is one of the pioneers in the use of multimedia and the Internet to enhance the learning of mathematics. Dr. Larson is a member of the National Council of Teachers of Mathematics and is a frequent speaker at NCTM and other national and regional mathematics meetings.

▶ **Laurie Boswell** is a mathematics teacher at Profile Junior-Senior High School in Bethlehem, New Hampshire. She is active in NCTM and local mathematics organizations. A recipient of the 1986 Presidential Award for Excellence in Mathematics Teaching, she is also the 1992 Tandy Technology Scholar and the 1991 recipient of the Richard Balomenos Mathematics Education Service Award presented by the New Hampshire Association of Teachers of Mathematics.

▶ **Lee Stiff** is a professor of mathematics education in the College of Education and Psychology of North Carolina State University at Raleigh and has taught mathematics at the high school and middle school levels. He served on the NCTM Board of Directors and was elected President of NCTM for the years 2000–2002. He is the 1992 recipient of the W. W. Rankin Award for Excellence in Mathematics Education presented by the North Carolina Council of Teachers of Mathematics.

▶ REVIEWERS

Jose Anaya
Mathematics Teacher
Juarez High School
Chicago, IL

Pamela W. Coffield
Mathematics Teacher
Brookstone School
Columbus, GA

Tom Griffith
Mathematics Teacher
Scripps Ranch High School
San Diego, CA

Judy Hicks
Mathematics Teacher
Ralston Valley High School
Arvada, CO

Viola Okoro
Mathematics Teacher
Laguna Creek High School
Elk Grove, CA

Carol Sander
Mathematics Resource Teacher
Rockville High School
Rockville, MD

▶ CALIFORNIA TEACHER PANEL

Marianne Clarke
Mathematics Teacher
Westminster High School
Westminster, CA

Janet Eichsteadt
Mathematics Teacher
Woodbridge High School
Irvine, CA

Tom Griffith
Mathematics Teacher
Scripps Ranch High School
San Diego, CA

Jerry Hickman
Mathematics Teacher
El Camino Real Senior High School
Woodland Hills, CA

Roger Hitchcock
Mathematics Teacher
The Clovis Center
Clovis, CA

Jerry Lewin
Mathematics Department Chair
Alhambra High School
Alhambra, CA

Viola Okoro
Mathematics Teacher
Laguna Creek High School
Elk Grove, CA

Patricia Schubert
Mathematics Teacher
Capistrano Valley High School
Mission Viejo, CA

Gary Smith
Mathematics Teacher
Mira Costa High School
Manhattan Beach, CA

Jeff Speranza
Mathematics Department Chair
Westmoor High School
Daly City, CA

▶ PENNSYLVANIA TEACHER PANEL

Bill Garrett
Mathematics Department Chair
Norristown High School
Norristown, PA

Adrienne Kapisak
Mathematics Teacher
Gateway High School
Monroeville, PA

Patricia Klagholz
Mathematics Department Chair
Lamberton School
Philadelphia, PA

Ed Lorinchak
Mathematics Teacher
Pittsburgh School for the Performing Arts
Pittsburgh, PA

Kathryn Nalevanko
Mathematics Teacher
Scranton High School
Scranton, PA

Ben Preddy
Mathematics Teacher
Haverford High School
Havertown, PA

Cerise Sawyer
Mathematics Teacher
Cumberland Valley High School
Mechanicsburg, PA

Don Stark
Mathematics Teacher
Baldwin High School
Pittsburgh, PA

Brenda Williams
Mathematics Teacher
Abington Heights High School
Clarks Summit, PA

▶ STUDENT REVIEW PANEL

Racquel Allen
Watertown High School
Massachusetts

Kristin Biedinger
Gateway Senior High School
Pennsylvania

Brett Brown
El Camino Real High School
California

James Bruce DeMark
Lakota West High School
Ohio

Anthony Espinoza
Thomas A. Edison High School
Texas

Jessica Langton
Danbury High School
Connecticut

Molly McClure
William Henry Harrison High School
Indiana

Kevin W. Mechtley
Topeka High School
Kansas

Andy Nichols
Brandon High School
Mississippi

Annie Phare
Ferndale High School
Washington

Andrew J. Polsky
Parkway North High School
Missouri

Malavika Prabhu
Riverside High School
South Carolina

Lauren Reed
Naperville North High School
Illinois

Kelly Riordan
Cherry Creek High School
Colorado

Cecilia Serna
South Forsyth High School
Georgia

B. J. Singletary
Clinch County High School
Georgia

Jaclyn Stancu
Lower Moreland High School
Pennsylvania

Dustin Stuflick
Montgomery High School
California

Julie Testerman
Memorial High School
New Hampshire

Angel Nicole Todd
Harrison High School
Michigan

Van Tran
Montgomery Blair High School
Maryland

Steven L. White
Mandarin High School
Florida

Basics of Geometry

CHAPTER 2

Reasoning and Proof

APPLICATION HIGHLIGHTS

Robotics *69, 93*
Advertising *77*
Research Buggy *77*
Winds at Sea *84*
Zoology *90*
Fitness *97*
Auto Racing *98*
Wind-Chill Factor *99*
Pay Raises *100*
Optical Illusion *106*
Wall Trim *115*

MATH & HISTORY

Recreational
Logic Puzzles *95*

INTERNET CONNECTIONS

www.mcdougallittell.com
Application Links
69, 84, 95
Student Help
72, 76, 88, 93, 97, 114
Career Links
77, 90, 106
Extra Challenge
78, 85, 94, 101, 107

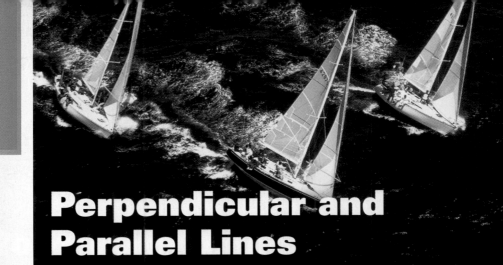

CHAPTER
3

Perpendicular and Parallel Lines

Congruent Triangles

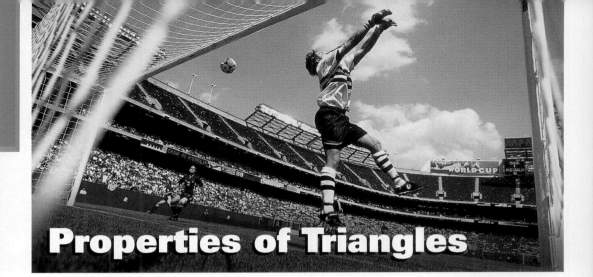

Properties of Triangles

CHAPTER
6

Quadrilaterals

CHAPTER

7

Transformations

Similarity

CHAPTER
9

Right Triangles and Trigonometry

CHAPTER
10

Circles

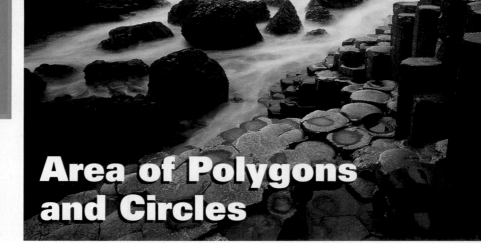

CHAPTER

11

Area of Polygons and Circles

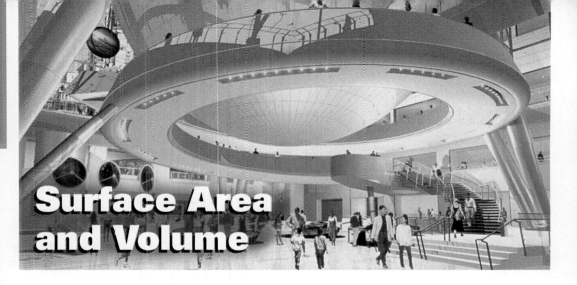

Surface Area and Volume

▶ Student Resources

▶ Who Uses Mathematics in Real Life?

Here are some careers that use the mathematics you will study in Geometry.

EMTs *p. 609*
Some Emergency Medical Technicians (EMTs) train specifically for wilderness emergencies. These EMTs must be able to improvise with materials they have on hand.

CIVIL ENGINEERING *p. 170*
Civil engineers design and supervise the construction of roads, buildings, tunnels, bridges, and water supply systems.

ADVERTISING COPYWRITER *p. 77*
Advertising copywriters write the advertisements you see and hear every day. These ads appear in many forms including Internet home pages.

LOGO DESIGNERS *p. 415*
Logo designers create symbols that represent the name of a company or organization. The logos appear on packaging, letterheads, and Web sites.

GEOSCIENTISTS *p. 644*
Geoscientists do a variety of things, including locating earthquakes, searching for oil, studying fossils, and mapping the ocean floor.

STUDENT HELP

▶ *Your textbook contains* many special elements to help you learn. It provides several study helps that may be new to you. For example, every chapter begins with a Study Guide.

Chapter Preview The Study Guide starts with a short description of what you will be learning.

Key Vocabulary This list highlights important new terms that will be introduced in the chapter as well as reviewing terms that you already know.

Skill Review These exercises review key skills that you'll apply in the chapter. They will help you identify any topics that you need to review.

Study Strategy The study strategies suggest ideas to help you better understand the math you are learning as well as help you prepare for tests.

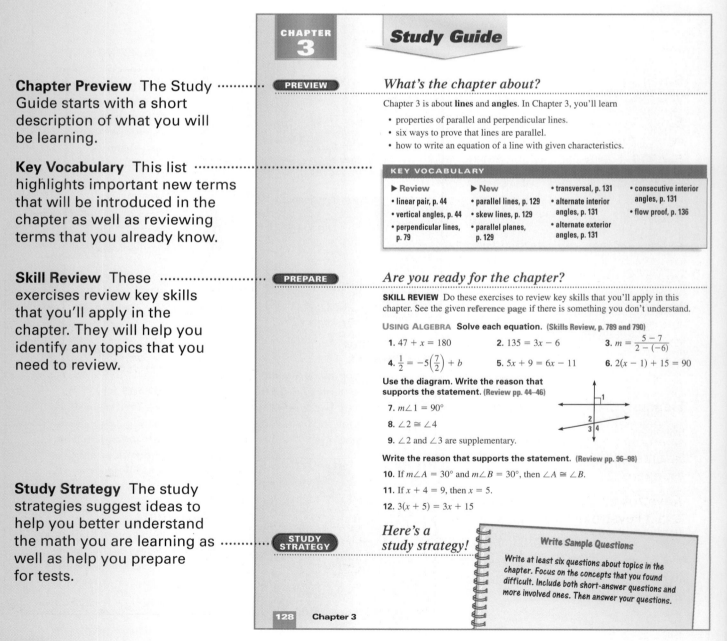

CHAPTER 3

Study Guide

PREVIEW

What's the chapter about?

Chapter 3 is about **lines** and **angles**. In Chapter 3, you'll learn

- properties of parallel and perpendicular lines.
- six ways to prove that lines are parallel.
- how to write an equation of a line with given characteristics.

KEY VOCABULARY

▶ **Review**
- linear pair, p. 44
- vertical angles, p. 44
- perpendicular lines, p. 79

▶ **New**
- parallel lines, p. 129
- skew lines, p. 129
- parallel planes, p. 129

- transversal, p. 131
- alternate interior angles, p. 131
- alternate exterior angles, p. 131

- consecutive interior angles, p. 131
- flow proof, p. 136

PREPARE

Are you ready for the chapter?

SKILL REVIEW Do these exercises to review key skills that you'll apply in this chapter. See the given **reference page** if there is something you don't understand.

USING ALGEBRA Solve each equation. (Skills Review, p. 789 and 790)

1. $47 + x = 180$ **2.** $135 = 3x - 6$ **3.** $m = \dfrac{5 - 7}{2 - (-6)}$

4. $\dfrac{1}{2} = -5\left(\dfrac{7}{2}\right) + b$ **5.** $5x + 9 = 6x - 11$ **6.** $2(x - 1) + 15 = 90$

Use the diagram. Write the reason that supports the statement. (Review pp. 44–46)

7. $m\angle 1 = 90°$

8. $\angle 2 \cong \angle 4$

9. $\angle 2$ and $\angle 3$ are supplementary.

Write the reason that supports the statement. (Review pp. 96–98)

10. If $m\angle A = 30°$ and $m\angle B = 30°$, then $\angle A \cong \angle B$.

11. If $x + 4 = 9$, then $x = 5$.

12. $3(x + 5) = 3x + 15$

STUDY STRATEGY

Here's a study strategy!

Write Sample Questions

Write at least six questions about topics in the chapter. Focus on the concepts that you found difficult. Include both short-answer questions and more involved ones. Then answer your questions.

128   Chapter 3

Also, in every lesson you will find a variety of Student Help notes.

STUDENT HELP

📖 In the Book

Study Tip The study tips will help you avoid common errors.

Skills Review Here you can find where to review skills you've studied in earlier math classes.

Look Back Here are references to material in earlier lessons that may help you understand the lesson.

Extra Practice Your book contains more exercises to practice the skills you are learning.

Homework Help Here you can find suggestions about which Examples may help you solve Exercises.

🌐 On the Internet

Homework Help: These are places where you can find additional examples on the Web site, and additional suggestions for solving an exercise.

Keystroke Help These provide the exact keystroke sequences for many different kinds of calculators.

Software Help These provide the instructions for geometry software applications.

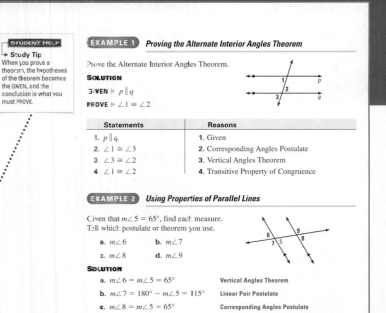

STUDENT HELP
▶ Study Tip
When you prove a theorem, the hypotheses of the theorem becomes the GIVEN, and the conclusion is what you must PROVE.

EXAMPLE 1 *Proving the Alternate Interior Angles Theorem*

Prove the Alternate Interior Angles Theorem.

SOLUTION

GIVEN ▶ $p \parallel q$

PROVE ▶ $\angle 1 \cong \angle 2$

Statements	Reasons
1. $p \parallel q$	1. Given
2. $\angle 1 \cong \angle 3$	2. Corresponding Angles Postulate
3. $\angle 3 \cong \angle 2$	3. Vertical Angles Theorem
4. $\angle 1 \cong \angle 2$	4. Transitive Property of Congruence

EXAMPLE 2 *Using Properties of Parallel Lines*

Given that $m\angle 5 = 65°$, find each measure. Tell which postulate or theorem you use.

  a. $m\angle 6$ **b.** $m\angle 7$

  c. $m\angle 8$ **d.** $m\angle 9$

SOLUTION

  a. $m\angle 6 = m\angle 5 = 65°$ **Vertical Angles Theorem**

  b. $m\angle 7 = 180° - m\angle 5 = 115°$ **Linear Pair Postulate**

  c. $m\angle 8 = m\angle 5 = 65°$ **Corresponding Angles Postulate**

  d. $m\angle 9 = m\angle 7 = 115°$ **Alternate Exterior Angles Theorem**

GUIDED PRACTICE

Vocabulary Check ✓
Concept Check ✓
Skill Check ✓

1. Define *slope of a line*.

2. The slope of line m is $-\frac{1}{5}$. What is the slope of a line perpendicular to m?

3. In the coordinate plane shown at the right, is $\overleftrightarrow{AC}$ perpendicular to $\overleftrightarrow{BD}$? Explain.

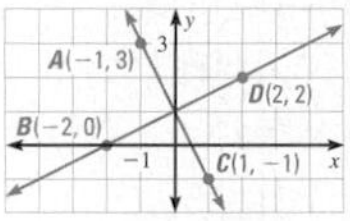

4. Decide whether the lines with the equations $y = 2x - 1$ and $y = -2x + 1$ are perpendicular.

5. Decide whether the lines with the equations $5y - x = 15$ and $y + 5x = 2$ are perpendicular.

6. The line ℓ_1 has the equation $y = 3x$. The line ℓ_2 is perpendicular to ℓ_1 and passes through the point $P(0, 0)$. Write an equation of ℓ_2.

PRACTICE AND APPLICATIONS

STUDENT HELP
▶ Extra Practice
to help you master skills is on p. 808.

SLOPES OF PERPENDICULAR LINES The slopes of two lines are given. Are the lines perpendicular?

7. $m_1 = 2, m_2 = -\frac{1}{2}$ 8. $m_1 = \frac{2}{3}, m_2 = \frac{3}{2}$ 9. $m_1 = \frac{1}{4}, m_2 = -4$

10. $m_1 = \frac{5}{7}, m_2 = -\frac{7}{5}$ 11. $m_1 = -\frac{1}{2}, m_2 = -\frac{1}{2}$ 12. $m_1 = -1, m_2 = 1$

SLOPES OF PERPENDICULAR LINES Lines j and n are perpendicular. The slope of line j is given. What is the slope of line n? Check your answer.

13. 2   14. 5   15. -3 16. -7

17. $\frac{2}{3}$ 18. $\frac{1}{5}$ 19. $-\frac{1}{3}$ 20. $-\frac{4}{3}$

IDENTIFYING PERPENDICULAR LINES Find the slope of $\overleftrightarrow{AC}$ and $\overleftrightarrow{BD}$. Decide whether $\overleftrightarrow{AC}$ is perpendicular to $\overleftrightarrow{BD}$.

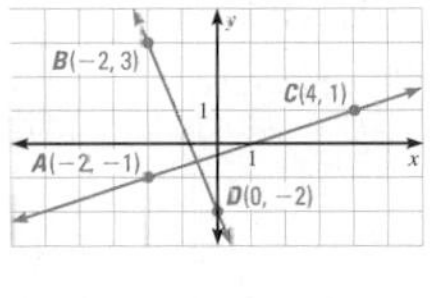

21.   22.

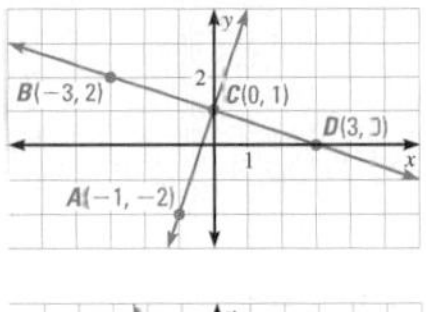

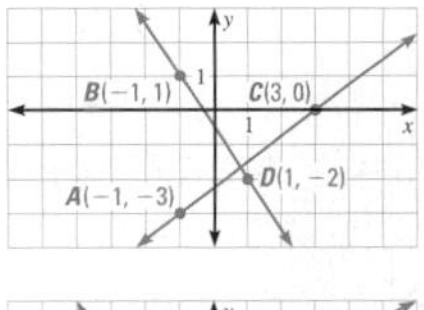

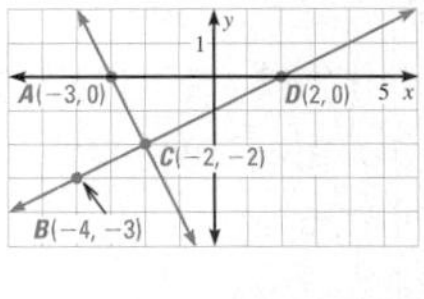

STUDENT HELP
▶ HOMEWORK HELP
Example 1: Exs. 7–20
Example 2: Exs. 21–24, 33–37
Example 3: Exs. 25–28, 47–50
Example 4: Exs. 29–32
Example 5: Exs. 38–41
Example 6: Exs. 42–46

23.   24.

BASICS OF GEOMETRY

▶ *How are airport runways named?*

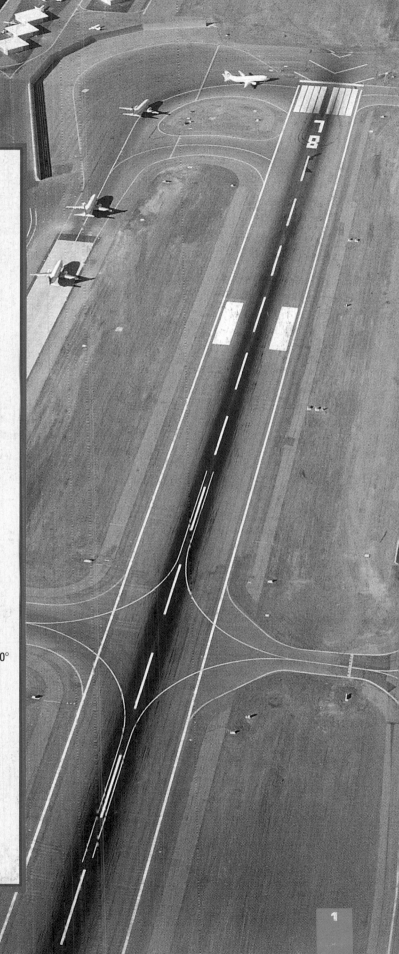

APPLICATION: Runways

Air traffic controllers and pilots need a way to refer to runways that is consistent among different airports.

Runways are named based on the angles they form with due north, measured in a clockwise direction. These angles are called *bearings*.

The bearing of a runway is divided by 10 to find the runway number.

Approach	Bearing	Runway
from west to east	90°	9
from north to south	180°	18
from east to west	270°	27
from south to north	360°	36

Think & Discuss

1. Why is it important to use a consistent runway naming scheme?

2. The bearing of the unlabeled runway in the diagram is 50°. What are the missing runway numbers?

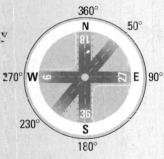

Learn More About It

You will learn more about angles of intersecting runways in Exercises 55–60 on p. 32.

You will learn more about angles of intersecting runways in Exercises 55–60 on p. 32.

APPLICATION LINK Visit www.mcdougallittell.com for more information about airport runways.

Study Guide

PREVIEW

What's the chapter about?

Chapter 1 is about the **basic elements of geometry**. In Chapter 1, you'll learn

- how to measure segments and angles.
- how to divide a segment or angle into two equal parts.
- relationships among special pairs of angles.

KEY VOCABULARY

▶ **New**

- conjecture, p. 4
- point, line, plane, p. 10
- segment, ray, p. 11
- postulate, p. 17
- length of a segment, p. 17

- congruent segments, p. 19
- congruent angles, p. 26
- measure of an angle, p. 27
- acute angle, p. 28
- right angle, p. 28
- obtuse angle, p. 28

- straight angle, p. 28
- segment bisector, p. 34
- angle bisector, p. 36
- vertical angles, p. 44
- complementary angles, p. 46
- supplementary angles, p. 46

PREPARE

Are you ready for the chapter?

SKILL REVIEW Do these exercises to review key skills that you'll apply in this chapter. See the given **reference page** if there is something you don't understand.

Subtract the integers. (Skills Review, p. 785)

1. $17 - 9$ **2.** $9 - 17$ **3.** $5 - (-3)$ **4.** $3 - (-5)$

5. $-7 - 2$ **6.** $-7 - (-2)$ **7.** $-6 - (-5)$ **8.** $-5 - (-6)$

Evaluate the sum. (Skills Review, p. 786)

9. $2^2 + 4^2$ **10.** $5^2 + (-2)^2$ **11.** $(-1)^2 + 1^2$ **12.** $(-5)^2 + 0^2$

Evaluate the radical expression. Round your answer to two decimal places. (Skills Review, p. 799)

13. $\sqrt{36 + 4}$ **14.** $\sqrt{1 + 49}$ **15.** $\sqrt{225 + 100}$ **16.** $\sqrt{9 + 9}$

STUDY STRATEGY

Here's a study strategy!

Learning Vocabulary

Important words in this book are in bold type and are highlighted in yellow.

- Keep a section in your notebook for writing down definitions of new words.
- Draw and label sketches near your definitions, if this helps you.
- Use your vocabulary pages to review for quizzes and tests.

Patterns and Inductive Reasoning

What you should learn

GOAL 1 Find and describe patterns.

GOAL 2 Use inductive reasoning to make **real-life** conjectures, as in **Ex. 42**.

Why you should learn it

▼ To make predictions based on observations, such as predicting full moons in **Example 6**.

GOAL 1 FINDING AND DESCRIBING PATTERNS

Geometry, like much of mathematics and science, developed when people began recognizing and describing patterns. In this course, you will study many amazing patterns that were discovered by people throughout history and all around the world. You will also learn to recognize and describe patterns of your own. Sometimes, patterns allow you to make accurate predictions.

EXAMPLE 1 *Describing a Visual Pattern*

Sketch the next figure in the pattern.

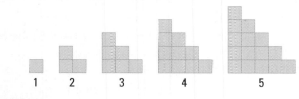

SOLUTION

Each figure in the pattern looks like the previous figure with another row of squares added to the bottom. Each figure looks like a stairway.

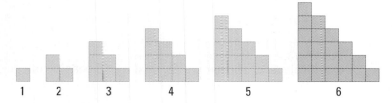

▶ The sixth figure in the pattern has six squares in the bottom row.

EXAMPLE 2 *Describing a Number Pattern*

Describe a pattern in the sequence of numbers. Predict the next number.

  a. 1, 4, 16, 64, . . .   **b.** $-5, -2, 4, 13, . . .$

SOLUTION

  a. Each number is four times the previous number. The next number is 256.

  b. You add 3 to get the second number, then add 6 to get the third number, then add 9 to get the fourth number. To find the fifth number, add the next multiple of 3, which is 12.

    ▶ So, the next number is $13 + 12$, or 25.

GOAL 2 USING INDUCTIVE REASONING

Much of the reasoning in geometry consists of three stages.

❶ Look for a Pattern Look at several examples. Use diagrams and tables to help discover a pattern.

❷ Make a Conjecture Use the examples to make a general *conjecture*. A **conjecture** is an unproven statement that is based on observations. Discuss the conjecture with others. Modify the conjecture, if necessary.

❸ Verify the Conjecture Use logical reasoning to verify that the conjecture is true in all cases. (You will do this in Chapter 2 and throughout this book.)

Looking for patterns and making conjectures is part of a process called **inductive reasoning**.

Logical Reasoning

EXAMPLE 3 *Making a Conjecture*

Complete the conjecture.

Conjecture: The sum of the first *n* odd positive integers is __?__ .

SOLUTION

List some specific examples and look for a pattern.

Examples:

first odd positive integer:	$1 = 1^2$
sum of first **two** odd positive integers:	$1 + 3 = 4 = 2^2$
sum of first **three** odd positive integers:	$1 + 3 + 5 = 9 = 3^2$
sum of first **four** odd positive integers:	$1 + 3 + 5 + 7 = 16 = 4^2$

Conjecture: The sum of the first *n* odd positive integers is n^2.

. . . .

To prove that a conjecture is true, you need to prove it is true in *all* cases. To prove that a conjecture is false, you need to provide a single *counterexample*. A **counterexample** is an example that shows a conjecture is false.

EXAMPLE 4 *Finding a Counterexample*

Show the conjecture is false by finding a counterexample.

Conjecture: For all real numbers *x*, the expression x^2 is greater than or equal to *x*.

SOLUTION

The conjecture is false. Here is a counterexample: $(0.5)^2 = 0.25$, and 0.25 is *not* greater than or equal to 0.5. In fact, any number between 0 and 1 is a counterexample.

Not every conjecture is known to be true or false. Conjectures that are not known to be true or false are called *unproven* or *undecided*.

EXAMPLE 5 *Examining an Unproven Conjecture*

In the early 1700s a Prussian mathematician named Goldbach noticed that many even numbers greater than 2 can be written as the sum of two primes.

Specific Cases:

$4 = 2 + 2$	$10 = 3 + 7$	$16 = 3 + 13$
$6 = 3 + 3$	$12 = 5 + 7$	$18 = 5 + 13$
$8 = 3 + 5$	$14 = 3 + 11$	$20 = 3 + 17$

Conjecture: Every even number greater than 2 can be written as the sum of two primes.

This is called *Goldbach's Conjecture*. No one has ever proved that this conjecture is true or found a counterexample to show that it is false. As of the writing of this book, it is unknown whether this conjecture is true or false. It is known, however, that all even numbers up to 4×10^{14} confirm Goldbach's Conjecture.

EXAMPLE 6 *Using Inductive Reasoning in Real Life*

MOON CYCLES A full moon occurs when the moon is on the opposite side of Earth from the sun. During a full moon, the moon appears as a complete circle.

New moon | Waxing crescent | First quarter | Waxing gibbous | Full moon | Waning gibbous | Last quarter | Waning crescent

Use inductive reasoning and the information below to make a conjecture about how often a full moon occurs.

Specific Cases: In 2005, the first six full moons occur on January 25, February 24, March 25, April 24, May 23, and June 22.

SOLUTION

Conjecture: A full moon occurs every 29 or 30 days.

This conjecture is true. The moon revolves around Earth once approximately every 29.5 days.

. . . .

Inductive reasoning is important to the study of mathematics: you look for a pattern in specific cases and then you write a conjecture that you think describes the general case. Remember, though, that just because something is true for several specific cases does not *prove* that it is true in general.

GUIDED PRACTICE

Vocabulary Check ✔
Concept Check ✔
Skill Check ✔

1. Explain what a *conjecture* is.

2. How can you prove that a conjecture is false?

Sketch the next figure in the pattern.

3.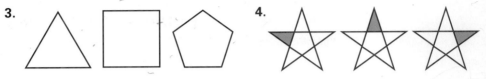

4.

Describe a pattern in the sequence of numbers. Predict the next number.

5. 2, 6, 18, 54, . . .

6. 0, 1, 4, 9, . . .

7. 256, 64, 16, 4, . . .

8. 3, 0, −3, 0, 3, 0, . . .

9. 7.0, 7.5, 8.0, 8.5, . . .

10. 13, 7, 1, −5, . . .

11. Complete the conjecture based on the pattern you observe.

$3 + 4 + 5 = 4 \cdot 3$	$6 + 7 + 8 = 7 \cdot 3$	$9 + 10 + 11 = 10 \cdot 3$
$4 + 5 + 6 = 5 \cdot 3$	$7 + 8 + 9 = 8 \cdot 3$	$10 + 11 + 12 = 11 \cdot 3$
$5 + 6 + 7 = 6 \cdot 3$	$8 + 9 + 10 = 9 \cdot 3$	$11 + 12 + 13 = 12 \cdot 3$

Conjecture: The sum of any three consecutive integers is ___?___.

PRACTICE AND APPLICATIONS

STUDENT HELP

▶ **Extra Practice**
to help you master
skills is on p. 803.

SKETCHING VISUAL PATTERNS Sketch the next figure in the pattern.

12.

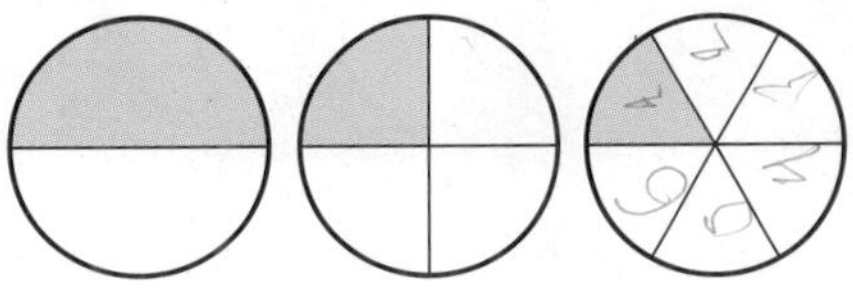

13.

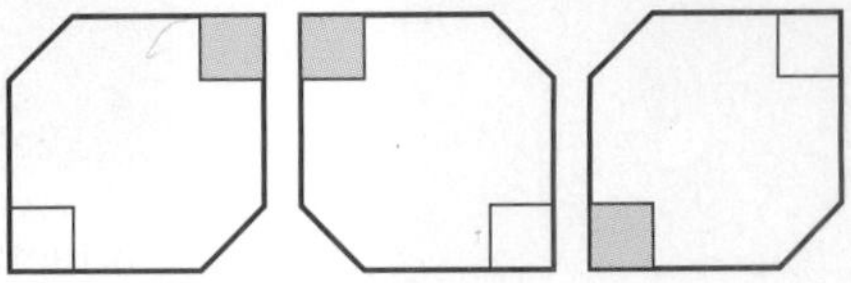

14.

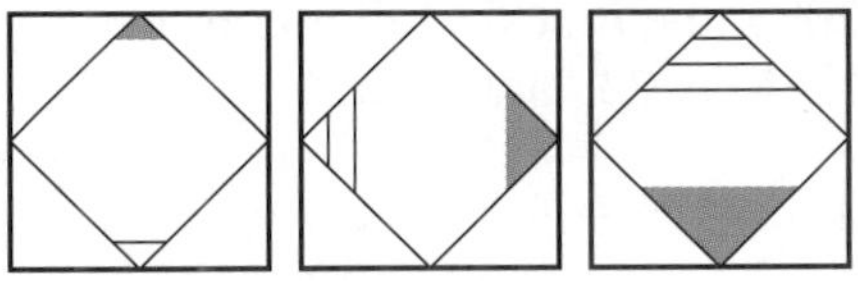

15.

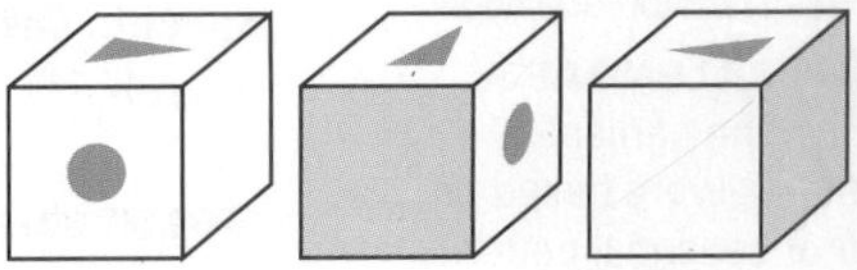

STUDENT HELP

▶ **HOMEWORK HELP**
Example 1: Exs. 12–15,
24, 25
Example 2: Exs. 16–23,
26–28
Example 3: Exs. 29–33
Example 4: Exs. 34–39
Example 5: Exs. 40, 41
Example 6: Exs. 42, 43

DESCRIBING NUMBER PATTERNS Describe a pattern in the sequence of numbers. Predict the next number.

16. 1, 4, 7, 10, . . .

17. 10, 5, 2.5, 1.25, . . .

18. 1, 11, 121, 1331, . . .

19. 5, 0, −5, −10, . . .

20. 7, 9, 13, 19, 27, . . .

21. 1, 3, 6, 10, 15, . . .

22. 256, 16, 4, 2, . . .

23. 1.1, 1.01, 1.001, 1.0001, . . .

VISUALIZING PATTERNS The first three objects in a pattern are shown. How many blocks are in the next object?

24.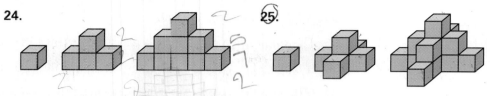

25.

MAKING PREDICTIONS In Exercises 26–28, use the pattern from Example 1 shown below. Each square is 1 unit × 1 unit.

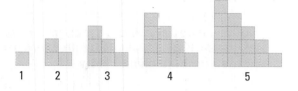

1   2   3   4   5

26. Find the distance around each figure. Organize your results in a table.

27. Use your table to describe a pattern in the distances.

28. Predict the distance around the twentieth figure in this pattern.

MAKING CONJECTURES Complete the conjecture based on the pattern you observe in the specific cases.

29. **Conjecture:** The sum of any two odd numbers is ____?____ .

$1 + 1 = 2$ $7 + 11 = 18$

$1 + 3 = 4$ $13 + 19 = 32$

$3 + 5 = 8$ $201 + 305 = 506$

30. **Conjecture:** The product of any two odd numbers is ____?____ .

$1 \times 1 = 1$ $7 \times 11 = 77$

$1 \times 3 = 3$ $13 \times 19 = 247$

$3 \times 5 = 15$ $201 \times 305 = 61,305$

31. **Conjecture:** The product of a number $(n - 1)$ and the number $(n + 1)$ is always equal to ____?____ .

$3 \cdot 5 = 4^2 - 1$ $6 \cdot 8 = 7^2 - 1$

$4 \cdot 6 = 5^2 - 1$ $7 \cdot 9 = 8^2 - 1$

$5 \cdot 7 = 6^2 - 1$ $8 \cdot 10 = 9^2 - 1$

CALCULATOR Use a calculator to explore the pattern. Write a conjecture based on what you observe.

32. $101 \times 34 = $ ____?____

$101 \times 25 = $ ____?____

$101 \times 97 = $ ____?____

$101 \times 49 = $ ____?____

33. $11 \times 11 = $ ____?____

$111 \times 111 = $ ____?____

$1111 \times 1111 = $ ____?____

$11,111 \times 11,111 = $ ____?____

FINDING COUNTEREXAMPLES Show the conjecture is false by finding a counterexample.

34. All prime numbers are odd.

35. The sum of two numbers is always greater than the larger number.

36. If the product of two numbers is even, then the two numbers must be even.

37. If the product of two numbers is positive, then the two numbers must both be positive.

38. The square root of a number x is always less than x.

39. If m is a nonzero integer, then $\dfrac{m+1}{m}$ is always greater than 1.

GOLDBACH'S CONJECTURE In Exercises 40 and 41, use the list of the first prime numbers given below.

$$\{2, 3, 5, 7, 11, 13, 17, 19, 23, 29, 31, 37, \ldots\}$$

40. Show that Goldbach's Conjecture (see page 5) is true for the even numbers from 20 to 40 by writing each even number as a sum of two primes.

41. Show that the following conjecture is not true by finding a counterexample.

Conjecture: All *odd* numbers can be expressed as the sum of two primes.

42. 🌐 **BACTERIA GROWTH** Suppose you are studying bacteria in biology class. The table shows the number of bacteria after n doubling periods.

n (periods)	0	1	2	3	4	5
Billions of bacteria	3	6	12	24	48	96

Your teacher asks you to predict the number of bacteria after 8 doubling periods. What would your prediction be?

43. SCIENCE ▸ CONNECTION Diagrams and formulas for four molecular compounds are shown. Draw a diagram and write the formula for the next two compounds in the pattern.

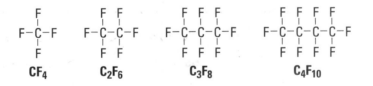

USING ALGEBRA Find a pattern in the coordinates of the points. Then use the pattern to find the *y*-coordinate of the point (3, ?).

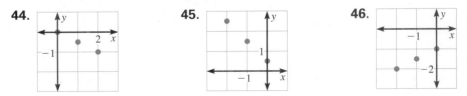

44. **45.** **46.**

47. **MULTIPLE CHOICE** Which number is next in the sequence?

45, 90, 135, 180, . . .

(A) 205   (B) 210   (C) 215   (D) 220   (E) 225

48. **MULTIPLE CHOICE** What is the next figure in the pattern?

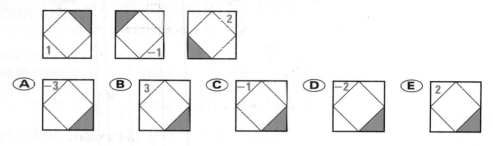

★ **Challenge**

DIVIDING A CIRCLE In Exercises 49–51, use the information about regions in a circle formed by connecting points on the circle.

If you draw points on a circle and then connect every pair of points, the circle is divided into a number of regions, as shown.

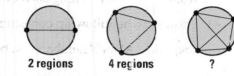

2 regions   4 regions   ?

49. Copy and complete the table for the case of 4 and 5 points.

Number of points on circle	2	3	4	5	6
Maximum number of regions	2	4	?	?	?

50. Make a conjecture about the relationship between the number of points on the circle and number of regions in the circle.

51. Test your conjecture for the case of 6 points. What do you notice?

MIXED REVIEW

PLOTTING POINTS Plot in a coordinate plane. (Skills Review, p. 792, for 1.2)

52. $(5, 2)$ **53.** $(3, -8)$ **54.** $(-4, -6)$ **55.** $(1, -10)$

56. $(-2, 7)$ **57.** $(-3, 8)$ **58.** $(4, -1)$ **59.** $(-2, -6)$

EVALUATING EXPRESSIONS Evaluate the expression. (Skills Review, p. 786)

60. 3^2 **61.** 5^2 **62.** $(-4)^2$ **63.** -7^2

64. $3^2 + 4^2$ **65.** $5^2 + 12^2$ **66.** $(-2)^2 + 2^2$ **67.** $(-10)^2 + (-5)^2$

FINDING A PATTERN Write the next number in the sequence. (Review 1.1)

68. 1, 5, 25, 125, . . .   **69.** 4.4, 40.4, 400.4, 4000.4, . . .

70. 3, 7, 11, 15, . . .   **71.** $-1, +1, -2, +2, -3, . . .$

1.2

Points, Lines, and Planes

GOAL 1 USING UNDEFINED TERMS AND DEFINITIONS

A **definition** uses known words to describe a new word. In geometry, some words, such as *point*, *line*, and *plane*, are **undefined terms**. Although these words are not formally defined, it is important to have general agreement about what each word means.

A **point** has no dimension. It is usually represented by a small dot.

A **line** extends in one dimension. It is usually represented by a straight line with two arrowheads to indicate that the line extends without end in two directions. In this book, lines are always straight lines.

A **plane** extends in two dimensions. It is usually represented by a shape that looks like a tabletop or wall. You must imagine that the plane extends without end, even though the drawing of a plane appears to have edges.

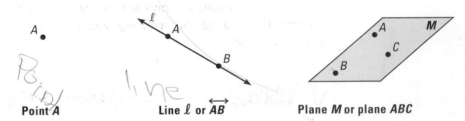

Point *A*   Line *ℓ* or $\overleftrightarrow{AB}$ Plane *M* or plane *ABC*

A few basic concepts in geometry must also be commonly understood without being defined. One such concept is the idea that a point *lies on* a line or a plane.

Collinear points are points that lie on the same line.

Coplanar points are points that lie on the same plane.

EXAMPLE 1   *Naming Collinear and Coplanar Points*

a. Name three points that are collinear.

b. Name four points that are coplanar.

c. Name three points that are not collinear.

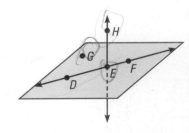

SOLUTION

a. Points *D*, *E*, and *F* lie on the same line, so they are collinear.

b. Points *D*, *E*, *F*, and *G* lie on the same plane, so they are coplanar. Also, *D*, *E*, *F*, and *H* are coplanar, although the plane containing them is not drawn.

c. There are many correct answers. For instance, points *H*, *E*, and *G* do not lie on the same line.

Another undefined concept in geometry is the idea that a point on a line *is between* two other points on the line. You can use this idea to define other important terms in geometry.

Consider the **line** AB (symbolized by $\overleftrightarrow{AB}$).
The **line segment** or **segment** AB (symbolized by $\overline{AB}$) consists of the **endpoints** A and B, and all points on $\overleftrightarrow{AB}$ that are between A and B.

The **ray** AB (symbolized by $\overrightarrow{AB}$) consists of the **initial point** A and all points on $\overleftrightarrow{AB}$ that lie on the same side of A as point B.

Note that $\overleftrightarrow{AB}$ is the same as $\overleftrightarrow{BA}$, and $\overline{AB}$ is the same as $\overline{BA}$. However, $\overrightarrow{AB}$ and $\overrightarrow{BA}$ are *not* the same. They have different initial points and extend in different directions.

If C is between A and B, then $\overrightarrow{CA}$ and $\overrightarrow{CB}$ are **opposite rays**.

Like points, segments and rays are collinear if they lie on the same line. So, any two opposite rays are collinear. Segments, rays, and lines are coplanar if they lie on the same plane.

EXAMPLE 2 Drawing Lines, Segments, and Rays

Draw three noncollinear points, J, K, and L. Then draw $\overleftrightarrow{JK}$, $\overline{KL}$ and $\overrightarrow{LJ}$.

SOLUTION

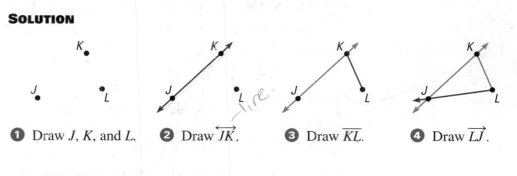

① Draw J, K, and L. ② Draw $\overleftrightarrow{JK}$. ③ Draw $\overline{KL}$. ④ Draw $\overrightarrow{LJ}$.

EXAMPLE 3 Drawing Opposite Rays

Draw two lines. Label points on the lines and name two pairs of opposite rays.

SOLUTION

Points M, N, and X are collinear and X is between M and N. So, $\overrightarrow{XM}$ and $\overrightarrow{XN}$ are opposite rays.

Points P, Q, and X are collinear and X is between P and Q. So, $\overrightarrow{XP}$ and $\overrightarrow{XQ}$ are opposite rays.

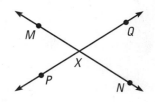

GOAL 2 **SKETCHING INTERSECTIONS OF LINES AND PLANES**

Two or more geometric figures **intersect** if they have one or more points in common. The **intersection** of the figures is the set of points the figures have in common.

▶ **ACTIVITY**
Developing
Concepts

Modeling Intersections

Use two index cards. Label them as shown and cut slots halfway along each card.

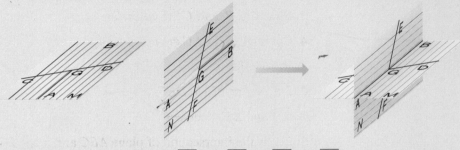

1. What is the intersection of $\overline{AB}$ and $\overline{CD}$? of $\overline{AB}$ and $\overline{EF}$?

2. Slide the cards together. What is the intersection of $\overline{CD}$ and $\overline{EF}$?

3. What is the intersection of planes M and N?

4. Are $\overleftrightarrow{CD}$ and $\overleftrightarrow{EF}$ coplanar? Explain.

EXAMPLE 4 *Sketching Intersections*

STUDENT HELP

INTERNET
HOMEWORK HELP
Visit our Web site
www.mcdougallittell.com
for extra examples.

Sketch the figure described.

a. a line that intersects a plane in one point

b. two planes that intersect in a line

SOLUTION

a.

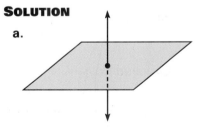

b.

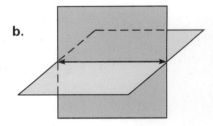

Draw a plane and a line.

Emphasize the point where they meet.

Dashes indicate where the line is hidden by the plane.

Draw two planes.

Emphasize the line where they meet.

Dashes indicate where one plane is hidden by the other plane.

GUIDED PRACTICE

Vocabulary Check ✓

1. Describe what each of these symbols means: $\overline{PQ}$, $\overrightarrow{PQ}$, $\overleftrightarrow{PQ}$, $\overrightarrow{QP}$.

Concept Check ✓

2. Sketch a line that contains point R between points S and T. Which of the following are true?

    A. $\overrightarrow{SR}$ is the same as $\overrightarrow{ST}$.
    B. $\overleftrightarrow{SR}$ is the same as $\overleftrightarrow{RT}$.

    C. $\overrightarrow{RS}$ is the same as $\overrightarrow{TS}$.
    D. $\overrightarrow{RS}$ and $\overrightarrow{RT}$ are opposite rays.

    E. $\overline{ST}$ is the same as $\overline{TS}$.
    F. $\overrightarrow{ST}$ is the same as $\overrightarrow{TS}$.

Skill Check ✓

Decide whether the statement is *true* or *false*.

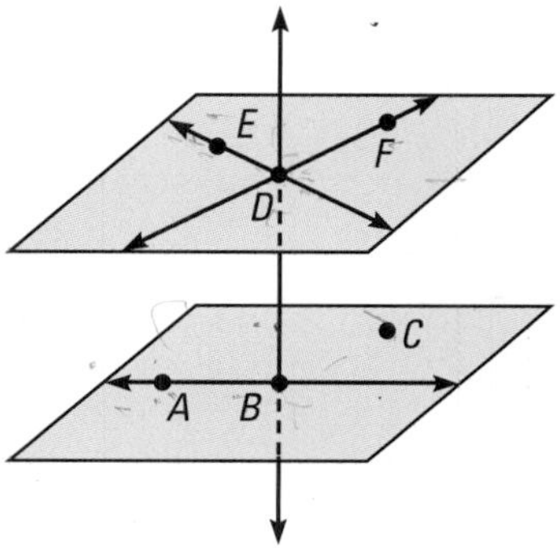

3. Points A, B, and C are collinear.

4. Points A, B, and C are coplanar.

5. Point F lies on $\overleftrightarrow{DE}$.

6. $\overleftrightarrow{DE}$ lies on plane DEF.

7. $\overleftrightarrow{BD}$ and $\overleftrightarrow{DE}$ intersect.

8. $\overleftrightarrow{BD}$ is the intersection of plane ABC and plane DEF.

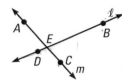

PRACTICE AND APPLICATIONS

STUDENT HELP

► **Extra Practice**
to help you master
skills is on p. 803.

EVALUATING STATEMENTS **Decide whether the statement is *true* or *false*.**

9. Point A lies on line ℓ.
10. A, B, and C are collinear.

11. Point B lies on line ℓ.
12. A, B, and C are coplanar.

13. Point C lies on line m.
14. D, E, and B are collinear.

15. Point D lies on line m.
16. D, E, and B are coplanar.

NAMING COLLINEAR POINTS **Name a point that is collinear with the given points.**

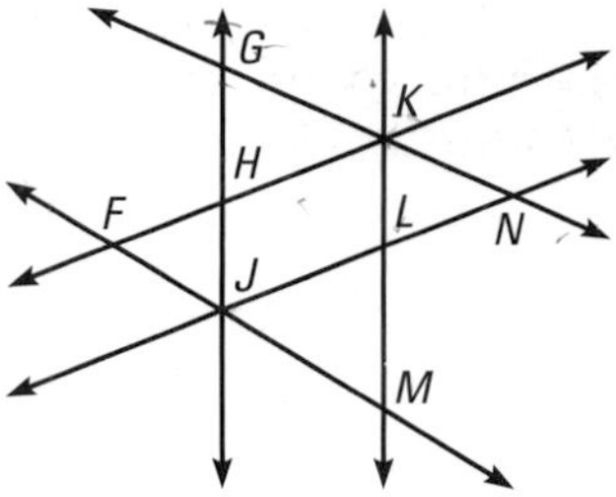

17. F and H
18. G and K

19. K and L
20. M and J

21. J and N
22. K and H

23. H and G
24. J and F

STUDENT HELP

► **HOMEWORK HELP**
Example 1: Exs. 9–43
Example 2: Exs. 44–49
Example 3: Exs. 50, 51
Example 4: Exs. 52–67

NAMING NONCOLLINEAR POINTS **Name three points in the diagram that are not collinear.**

25.
26.
27.

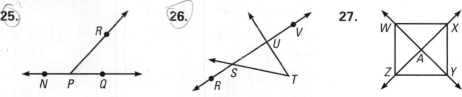

NAMING COPLANAR POINTS Name a point that is coplanar with the given points.

28. *A*, *B*, and *C*

29. *D*, *C*, and *F*

30. *G*, *A*, and *D*

31. *E*, *F*, and *G*

32. *A*, *B*, and *H*

33. *B*, *C*, and *F*

34. *A*, *B*, and *F*

35. *B*, *C*, and *G*

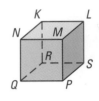

NAMING NONCOPLANAR POINTS Name all the points that are not coplanar with the given points.

36. *N*, *K*, and *L*

37. *S*, *P*, and *M*

38. *P*, *Q*, and *N*

39. *R*, *S*, and *L*

40. *P*, *Q*, and *R*

41. *R*, *K*, and *N*

42. *P*, *S*, and *K*

43. *Q*, *K*, and *L*

COMPLETING DEFINITIONS Complete the sentence.

44. $\overline{AB}$ consists of the endpoints *A* and *B* and all the points on the line $\overleftrightarrow{AB}$ that lie ___?___.

45. $\overrightarrow{CD}$ consists of the initial point *C* and all points on the line $\overleftrightarrow{CD}$ that lie ___?___.

46. Two rays or segments are collinear if they ___?___.

47. $\overrightarrow{CA}$ and $\overrightarrow{CB}$ are opposite rays if ___?___.

SKETCHING FIGURES Sketch the lines, segments, and rays.

48. Draw four points *J*, *K*, *L*, and *M*, no three of which are collinear. Then sketch $\overrightarrow{JK}$, $\overline{KL}$, $\overleftrightarrow{LM}$, and $\overrightarrow{MJ}$.

49. Draw five points *P*, *Q*, *R*, *S*, and *T*, no three of which are collinear. Then sketch $\overleftrightarrow{PQ}$, $\overleftrightarrow{RS}$, $\overline{QR}$, $\overline{ST}$, and $\overrightarrow{TP}$.

50. Draw two points, *X* and *Y*. Then sketch $\overleftrightarrow{XY}$. Add a point *W* between *X* and *Y* so that $\overrightarrow{WX}$ and $\overrightarrow{WY}$ are opposite rays.

51. Draw two points, *A* and *B*. Then sketch $\overrightarrow{AB}$. Add a point *C* on the ray so that *B* is between *A* and *C*.

🌎 **EVERYDAY INTERSECTIONS** What kind of geometric intersection does the photograph suggest?

52.

53.

54.

COMPLETING SENTENCES Fill in each blank with the appropriate response based on the points labeled in the photograph.

55. $\overleftrightarrow{AB}$ and $\overrightarrow{BC}$ intersect at __?__.

56. $\overleftrightarrow{AD}$ and $\overleftrightarrow{AE}$ intersect at __?__.

57. $\overleftrightarrow{HG}$ and $\overleftrightarrow{DH}$ intersect at __?__.

58. Plane *ABC* and plane *DCG* intersect at __?__.

59. Plane *GHD* and plane *DHE* intersect at __?__.

60. Plane *EAD* and plane *BCD* intersect at __?__.

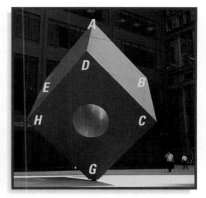

Red Cube, by sculptor Isamu Noguchi

SKETCHING FIGURES Sketch the figure described.

61. Three points that are coplanar but not collinear.

62. Two lines that lie in a plane but do not intersect.

63. Three lines that intersect in a point and all lie in the same plane.

64. Three lines that intersect in a point but do not all lie in the same plane.

65. Two lines that intersect and another line that does not intersect either one.

66. Two planes that do not intersect.

67. Three planes that intersect in a line.

TWO-POINT PERSPECTIVE In Exercises 68–72, use the information and diagram below.

In *perspective drawing*, lines that do not intersect in real life are represented in a drawing by lines that appear to intersect at a point far away on the horizon. This point is called a *vanishing point*.

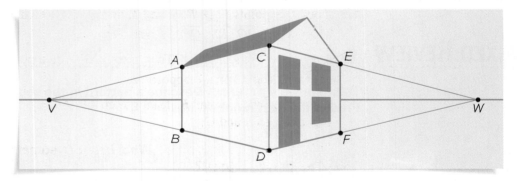

The diagram shows a drawing of a house with two vanishing points. You can use the vanishing points to draw the hidden parts of the house.

68. Name two lines that intersect at vanishing point *V*.

69. Name two lines that intersect at vanishing point *W*.

70. Trace the diagram. Draw $\overleftrightarrow{EV}$ and $\overleftrightarrow{AW}$. Label their intersection as *G*.

71. Draw $\overleftrightarrow{FV}$ and $\overleftrightarrow{BW}$. Label their intersection as *H*.

72. Draw the hidden edges of the house: $\overline{AG}$, $\overline{EG}$, $\overline{BH}$, $\overline{FH}$, and $\overline{GH}$.

73. MULTIPLE CHOICE Which statement(s) are true about the two lines shown in the drawing to the right?

   I. The lines intersect in one point.

   II. The lines do not intersect.

   III. The lines are coplanar.

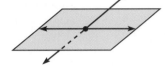

   Ⓐ I only   **Ⓑ** I and II only   **Ⓒ** I and III only

   Ⓓ II and III only **Ⓔ** I, II, and III

74. MULTIPLE CHOICE What is the intersection of $\overrightarrow{PQ}$ and $\overrightarrow{QP}$?

   Ⓐ $\overrightarrow{PQ}$ **Ⓑ** $\overline{PQ}$ **Ⓒ** P and Q **Ⓓ** P only   **Ⓔ** Q only

75. MULTIPLE CHOICE Points K, L, M, and N are not coplanar. What is the intersection of plane KLM and plane KLN?

   Ⓐ K and L **Ⓑ** M and N **Ⓒ** $\overline{KL}$ **Ⓓ** $\overleftrightarrow{KL}$

   Ⓔ The planes do not intersect.

★ **Challenge**

76. INTERSECTING LINES In each diagram below, every line intersects all the other lines, but only two lines pass through each intersection point.

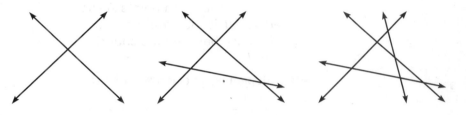

Can you draw 5 lines that intersect in this way? 6 lines? Is there a pattern to the number of intersection points?

MIXED REVIEW

DESCRIBING PATTERNS Describe a pattern in the sequence of numbers. Predict the next number. (Review 1.1)

77. 1, 6, 36, 216, . . .   **78.** 2, −2, 2, −2, 2, . . .

79. 8.1, 88.11, 888.111, 8888.1111, . . .   **80.** 0, 3, 9, 18, 30, . . .

OPERATIONS WITH INTEGERS Simplify the expression. (Skills Review, p.785)

81. $0 - 2$ **82.** $3 - 9$ **83.** $9 - (-4)$ **84.** $-5 - (-2)$

85. $5 - 0$ **86.** $4 - 7$ **87.** $3 - (-8)$ **88.** $-7 - (-5)$

RADICAL EXPRESSIONS Simplify the expression. Round your answer to two decimal places. (Skills Review, p. 799, for 1.3)

89. $\sqrt{21 + 100}$ **90.** $\sqrt{40 + 60}$ **91.** $\sqrt{25 + 144}$ **92.** $\sqrt{9 + 16}$

93. $\sqrt{5^2 + 7^2}$ **94.** $\sqrt{3^2 + (-2)^2}$ **95.** $\sqrt{(-3)^2 + 3^2}$ **96.** $\sqrt{(-5)^2 + 10^2}$

1.3

Segments and Their Measures

What you should learn

GOAL 1 Use segment postulates.

GOAL 2 Use the Distance Formula to measure distances, as applied in **Exs. 45–54**.

Why you should learn it

▼ To solve **real-life** problems, such as finding distances along a diagonal city street in **Example 4**.

GOAL 1 USING SEGMENT POSTULATES

In geometry, rules that are accepted without proof are called **postulates** or **axioms**. Rules that are proved are called *theorems*. In this lesson, you will study two postulates about the lengths of segments.

POSTULATE

POSTULATE 1 *Ruler Postulate*

The points on a line can be matched one to one with the real numbers. The real number that corresponds to a point is the **coordinate** of the point.

The **distance** between points A and B, written as AB, is the absolute value of the difference between the coordinates of A and B.

AB is also called the **length** of $\overline{AB}$.

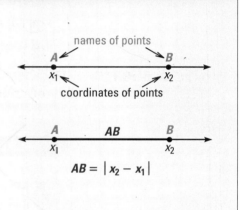

names of points

coordinates of points

$$AB = |x_2 - x_1|$$

EXAMPLE 1 *Finding the Distance Between Two Points*

Measure the length of the segment to the nearest millimeter.

SOLUTION

Use a metric ruler. Align one mark of the ruler with A. Then estimate the coordinate of B. For example, if you align A with 3, B appears to align with 5.5.

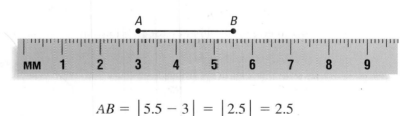

$$AB = |5.5 - 3| = |2.5| = 2.5$$

▶ The distance between A and B is about 2.5 cm.

· · · · · · · · · ·

It doesn't matter how you place the ruler. For example, if the ruler in Example 1 is placed so that A is aligned with 4, then B aligns with 6.5. The difference in the coordinates is the same.

When three points lie on a line, you can say that one of them is **between** the other two. This concept applies to collinear points only. For instance, in the figures below, point *B* is between points *A* and *C*, but point *E* is not between points *D* and *F*.

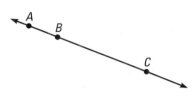

Point *B* is between points *A* and *C*.   **Point *E* is not between points *D* and *F*.**

POSTULATE

POSTULATE 2 *Segment Addition Postulate*

If *B* is between *A* and *C*, then *AB* + *BC* = *AC*.

If *AB* + *BC* = *AC*, then *B* is between *A* and *C*.

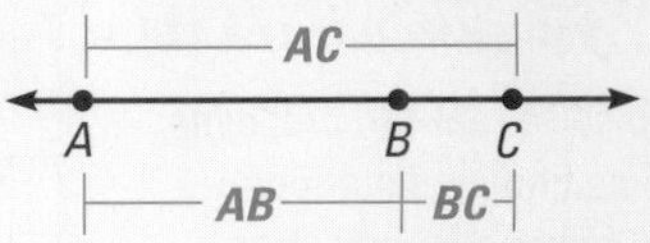

EXAMPLE 2 *Finding Distances on a Map*

MAP READING Use the map to find the distances between the three cities that lie on a line.

SOLUTION

Using the scale on the map, you can estimate that the distance between Athens and Macon is

   AM = 80 miles.

The distance between Macon and Albany is

   MB = 90 miles.

Knowing that Athens, Macon, and Albany lie on the same line, you can use the Segment Addition Postulate to conclude that the distance between Athens and Albany is

   AB = *AM* + *MB* = 80 + 90 = 170 miles.

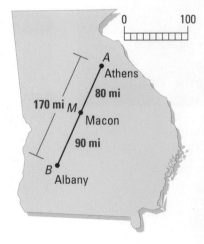

· · · · · · · · · ·

The Segment Addition Postulate can be generalized to three or more segments, as long as the segments lie on a line. If *P*, *Q*, *R*, and *S* lie on a line as shown, then

   PS = *PQ* + *QR* + *RS*.

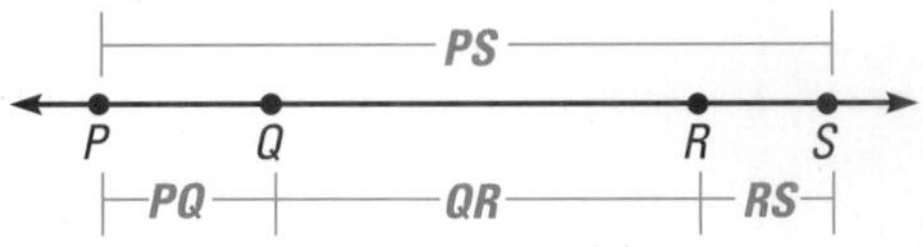

GOAL 2 **USING THE DISTANCE FORMULA**

STUDENT HELP

↳ **Study Tip**
The small numbers in x_1 and x_2 are called *subscripts*. You read them as "*x* sub 1" and "*x* sub 2."

The **Distance Formula** is a formula for computing the distance between two points in a *coordinate* plane.

THE DISTANCE FORMULA

If $A(x_1, y_1)$ and $B(x_2, y_2)$ are points in a coordinate plane, then the distance between A and B is

$$AB = \sqrt{(x_2 - x_1)^2 + (y_2 - y_1)^2}.$$

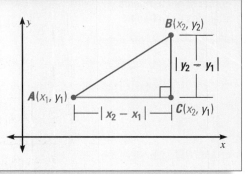

Using Algebra

EXAMPLE 3 *Using the Distance Formula*

Find the lengths of the segments. Tell whether any of the segments have the same length.

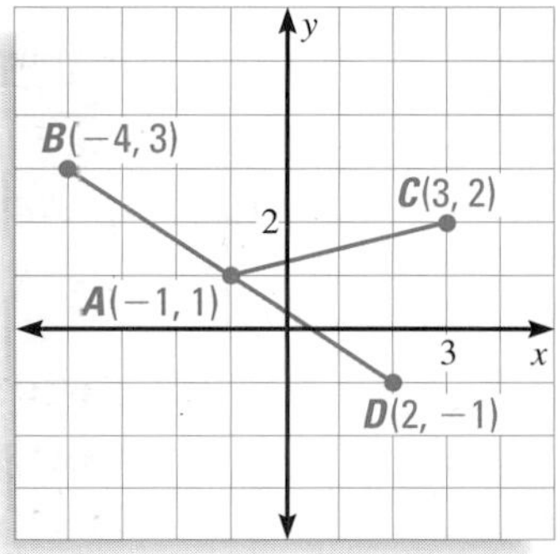

SOLUTION

Use the Distance Formula.

$$AB = \sqrt{[(-4) - (-1)]^2 + (3 - 1)^2}$$
$$= \sqrt{(-3)^2 + 2^2} = \sqrt{9 + 4} = \sqrt{13}$$

$$AC = \sqrt{[3 - (-1)]^2 + (2 - 1)^2}$$
$$= \sqrt{4^2 + 1^2} = \sqrt{16 + 1} = \sqrt{17}$$

$$AD = \sqrt{[2 - (-1)]^2 + (-1 - 1)^2}$$
$$= \sqrt{3^2 + (-2)^2} = \sqrt{9 + 4} = \sqrt{13}$$

▶ So, $\overline{AB}$ and $\overline{AD}$ have the same length, but $\overline{AC}$ has a different length.

· · · · · · · · · ·

Segments that have the same length are called **congruent segments**. For instance, in Example 3, $\overline{AB}$ and $\overline{AD}$ are congruent because each has a length of $\sqrt{13}$. There is a special symbol, $\cong$, for indicating *congruence*.

LENGTHS ARE EQUAL. **SEGMENTS ARE CONGRUENT.**

$$AB = AD$$ $$\overline{AB} \cong \overline{AD}$$

"is equal to" "is congruent to"

The Distance Formula is based on the *Pythagorean Theorem,* which you will see again when you work with right triangles in Chapter 9.

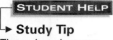

STUDENT HELP

→ **Study Tip**
The red mark at one corner of each triangle indicates a right angle.

CONCEPT SUMMARY **DISTANCE FORMULA AND PYTHAGOREAN THEOREM**

DISTANCE FORMULA

$$(AB)^2 = (x_2 - x_1)^2 + (y_2 - y_1)^2$$

$B(x_2, y_2)$

$|y_2 - y_1|$

$A(x_1, y_1)$ $|x_2 - x_1|$ $C(x_2, y_1)$

PYTHAGOREAN THEOREM

$$c^2 = a^2 + b^2$$

c b

a

EXAMPLE 4   *Finding Distances on a City Map*

MAP READING On the map, the city blocks are 340 feet apart east-west and 480 feet apart north-south.

a. Find the walking distance between A and B.

b. What would the distance be if a diagonal street existed between the two points?

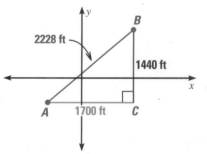

$B(1020, 960)$

480

340

$A(-680, -480)$

SOLUTION

a. To walk from A to B, you would have to walk five blocks east and three blocks north.

$$5 \text{ blocks} \cdot 340 \, \frac{\text{feet}}{\text{block}} = 1700 \text{ feet}$$

$$3 \text{ blocks} \cdot 480 \, \frac{\text{feet}}{\text{block}} = 1440 \text{ feet}$$

▶ So, the walking distance is $1700 + 1440$, which is a total of **3140** feet.

2228 ft

1440 ft

A 1700 ft C

B

b. To find the diagonal distance between A and B, use the Distance Formula.

$$AB = \sqrt{[1020 - (-680)]^2 + [960 - (-480)]^2}$$

$$= \sqrt{1700^2 + 1440^2}$$

$$= \sqrt{4,963,600} \approx 2228 \text{ feet}$$

▶ So, the diagonal distance would be about 2228 feet, which is 912 feet less than the walking distance.

→ **Study Tip**
If you use a calculator to compute distances, use the parenthesis keys to group what needs to be squared.

GUIDED PRACTICE

Vocabulary Check ✓

1. What is a *postulate*?

Concept Check ✓

2. Draw a sketch of three collinear points. Label them. Then write.the Segment Addition Postulate for the points.

3. Use the diagram. How can you determine *BD* if you know *BC* and *CD*? if you know *AB* and *AD*?

Skill Check ✓

Find the distance between the two points.

4. $C(0, 0)$, $D(5, 2)$

5. $G(3, 0)$, $H(8, 10)$

6. $M(1, -3)$, $N(3, 5)$

7. $P(-8, -6)$, $Q(-3, 0)$

8. $S(7, 3)$, $T(1, -5)$

9. $V(-2, -6)$, $W(1, -2)$

Use the Distance Formula to decide whether $\overline{JK} \cong \overline{KL}$.

10. $J(3, -5)$
    $K(-1, 2)$
    $L(-5, -5)$

11. $J(0, -8)$
    $K(4, 3)$
    $L(-2, -7)$

12. $J(10, 2)$
    $K(7, -3)$
    $L(4, -8)$

PRACTICE AND APPLICATIONS

STUDENT HELP

▶ **Extra Practice**
to help you master
skills is on p. 803.

MEASUREMENT **Measure the length of the segment to the nearest millimeter.**

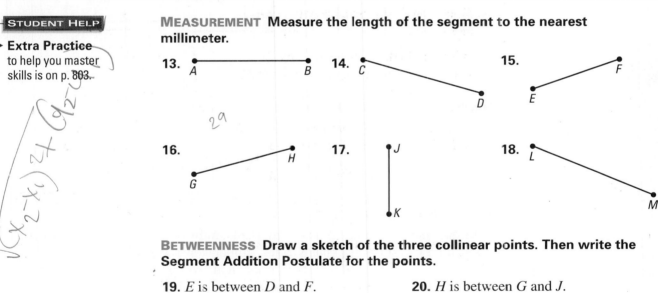

BETWEENNESS **Draw a sketch of the three collinear points. Then write the Segment Addition Postulate for the points.**

19. *E* is between *D* and *F*.

20. *H* is between *G* and *J*.

21. *M* is between *N* and *P*.

22. *R* is between *Q* and *S*.

🧩 **LOGICAL REASONING** **In the diagram of the collinear points, *PT* = 20, *QS* = 6, and *PQ* = *QR* = *RS*. Find each length.**

23. *QR*

24. *RS*

25. *PQ*

26. *ST*

27. *RP*

28. *RT*

29. *SP*

30. *QT*

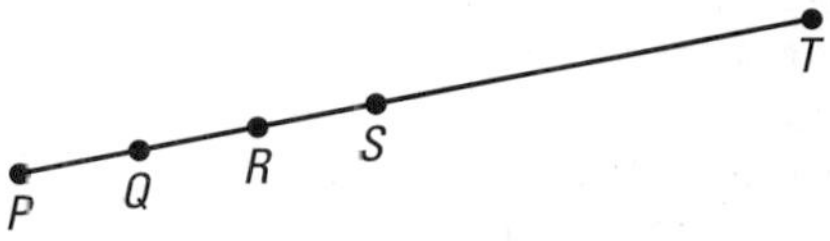

STUDENT HELP

▶ **HOMEWORK HELP**
Example 1: Exs. 13–18
Example 2: Exs. 19–33
Example 3: Exs. 34–43
Example 4: Exs. 44–54

USING ALGEBRA Suppose *M* is between *L* and *N*. Use the Segment Addition Postulate to solve for the variable. Then find the lengths of $\overline{LM}$, $\overline{MN}$, and $\overline{LN}$.

31. $LM = 3x + 8$
$MN = 2x - 5$
$LN = 23$

32. $LM = 7y + 9$
$MN = 3y + 4$
$LN = 143$

33. $LM = \frac{1}{2}z + 2$
$MN = 3z + \frac{3}{2}$
$LN = 5z + 2$

DISTANCE FORMULA Find the distance between each pair of points.

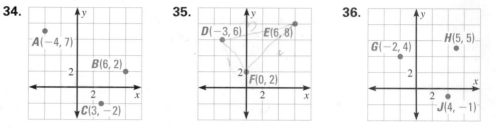

34. *A*(−4, 7) *B*(6, 2) *C*(3, −2)

35. *D*(−3, 6) *E*(6, 8) *F*(0, 2)

36. *G*(−2, 4) *H*(5, 5) *J*(4, −1)

DISTANCE FORMULA Find the lengths of the segments. Tell whether any of the segments have the same length.

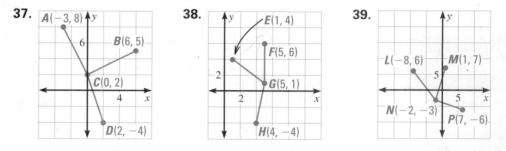

37. *A*(−3, 8) *B*(6, 5) *C*(0, 2) *D*(2, −4)

38. *E*(1, 4) *F*(5, 6) *G*(5, 1) *H*(4, −4)

39. *L*(−8, 6) *M*(1, 7) *N*(−2, −3) *P*(7, −6)

CONGRUENCE Use the Distance Formula to decide whether $\overline{PQ} \cong \overline{QR}$.

40. $P(4, -4)$
$Q(1, -6)$
$R(-1, -3)$

41. $P(-1, -6)$
$Q(-8, 5)$
$R(3, -2)$

42. $P(5, 1)$
$Q(-5, -7)$
$R(-3, 6)$

43. $P(-2, 0)$
$Q(10, -14)$
$R(-4, -2)$

CAMBRIA INCLINE In Exercises 44 and 45, use the information about the incline railway given below.

In the days before automobiles were available, railways called "inclines" brought people up and down hills in many cities. In Johnstown, Pennsylvania, the Cambria Incline was reputedly the steepest in the world when it was completed in 1893. It rises about 514 feet vertically as it moves 734 feet horizontally.

44. On graph paper, draw a coordinate plane and mark the axes using a scale that allows you to plot (0, 0) and (734, 514). Plot the points and connect them with a segment to represent the incline track.

45. Use the Distance Formula to estimate the length of the track.

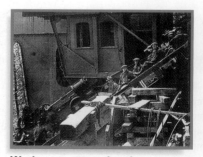

Workers constructing the Cambria Incline

DRIVING DISTANCES In Exercises 46 and 47, use the map of cities in Louisiana shown below. Coordinates on the map are given in miles.

The coordinates of Alexandria, Kinder, Eunice, Opelousas, Ville Platte, and Bunkie are $A(26, 56)$, $K(0, 0)$, $E(26, 1)$, $O(46, 5)$, $V(36, 12)$, and $B(40, 32)$.

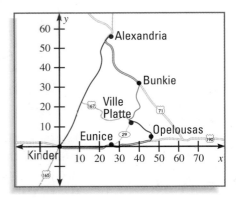

46. What is the shortest flying distance between Eunice and Alexandria?

47. Using only roads shown on the map, what is the approximate shortest driving distance between Eunice and Alexandria?

LONG-DISTANCE RATES In Exercises 48–52, find the distance between the two cities using the information given in the table, which is from a coordinate system used for calculating long-distance telephone rates.

Buffalo, NY	(5075, 2326)	Omaha, NE	(6687, 4595)
Chicago, IL	(5986, 3426)	Providence, RI	(4550, 1219)
Dallas, TX	(8436, 4034)	San Diego, CA	(9468, 7629)
Miami, FL	(8351, 527)	Seattle, WA	(6336, 8896)

48. Buffalo and Dallas

49. Chicago and Seattle

50. Miami and Omaha

51. Providence and San Diego

52. The long-distance coordinate system is measured in units of $\sqrt{0.1}$ mile. Convert the distances you found in Exs. 48–51 to miles.

CAMPUS PATHWAYS In Exercises 53 and 54, use the campus map below. Sidewalks around the edge of a campus quadrangle connect the buildings. Students sometimes take shortcuts by walking across the grass along the pathways shown. The coordinate system shown is measured in yards.

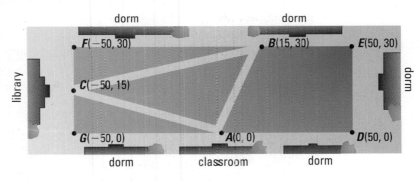

53. Find the distances from A to B, from B to C, and from C to A if you have to walk around the quadrangle along the sidewalks.

54. Find the distances from A to B, from B to C, and from C to A if you are able to walk across the grass along the pathways.

55. MULTIPLE CHOICE Points K and L are on $\overline{AB}$. If $AK > BL$, then which statement must be true?

(**A**) $AK < KB$ (**B**) $AL < LB$ (**C**) $AL > BK$

(**D**) $KL < LB$ (**E**) $AL + BK > AB$

56. MULTIPLE CHOICE Suppose point M lies on $\overline{CD}$, $CM = 2 \cdot MD$, and $CD = 18$. What is the length of MD?

(**A**) 3   (**B**) 6   (**C**) 9   (**D**) 12   (**E**) 36

★ **Challenge**

THREE-DIMENSIONAL DISTANCE In Exercises 57–59, use the following information to find the distance between the pair of points.

In a three-dimensional coordinate system, the distance between two points (x_1, y_1, z_1) and (x_2, y_2, z_2) is

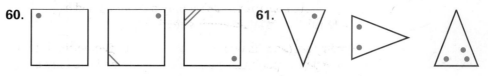

$$\sqrt{(x_2 - x_1)^2 + (y_2 - y_1)^2 + (z_2 - z_1)^2}.$$

EXTRA CHALLENGE
www.mcdougallittell.com

57. $P(0, 20, -32)$
    $Q(2, -10, -20)$

58. $A(-8, 15, -4)$
    $B(10, 1, -6)$

59. $F(4, -42, 60)$
    $G(-7, -11, 38)$

MIXED REVIEW

SKETCHING VISUAL PATTERNS Sketch the next figure in the pattern.
(Review 1.1)

60. **61.**

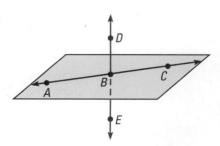

EVALUATING STATEMENTS Determine if the statement is _true_ or _false_.
(Review 1.2)

62. E lies on $\overleftrightarrow{BD}$.

63. E lies on $\overrightarrow{BD}$.

64. A, B, and D are collinear.

65. $\overrightarrow{BD}$ and $\overrightarrow{BE}$ are opposite rays.

66. B lies in plane ADC.

67. The intersection of $\overleftrightarrow{DE}$ and $\overleftrightarrow{AC}$ is B.

NAMING RAYS Name the ray described. (Review 1.2 for 1.4)

68. Name a ray that contains M.

69. Name a ray that has N as an endpoint.

70. Name two rays that intersect at P.

71. Name a pair of opposite rays.

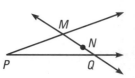

Write the next number in the sequence. (Lesson 1.1)

1. 10, 9.5, 9, 8.5, . . .

2. 0, 2, −2, 4, −4, . . .

Sketch the figure described. (Lesson 1.2)

3. Two segments that do not intersect.

4. Two lines that do not intersect, and a third line that intersects each of them.

5. Two lines that intersect a plane at the same point.

6. Three planes that do not intersect.

7. 🌐 MINIATURE GOLF At a miniature golf course, a water hazard blocks the direct shot from the tee at $T(0, 0)$ to the cup at $C(−1, 7)$. If you hit the ball so it bounces off an angled wall at $B(3, 4)$, it will go into the cup. The coordinate system is measured in feet. Draw a diagram of the situation. Find TB and BC. (Lesson 1.3)

MATH & History

Geometric Constructions

APPLICATION LINK
www.mcdougallittell.com

THEN

MORE THAN 2000 YEARS AGO, the Greek mathematician Euclid published a 13 volume work called *The Elements*. In his systematic approach, figures are *constructed* using only a *compass* and a *straightedge* (a ruler without measuring marks).

NOW

TODAY, geometry software may be used to construct geometric figures. Programs allow you to perform constructions as if you have only a compass and straightedge. They also let you make measurements of lengths, angles, and areas.

1. Draw two points and use a *straightedge* to construct the line that passes through them.

2. With the points as centers, use a *compass* to draw two circles of different sizes so that the circles intersect in two points. Mark the two points of intersection and construct the line through them.

3. Connect the four points you constructed. What are the properties of the shape formed?

An early printed edition of *The Elements*

Euclid develops The Elements.

c. 300 B.C.

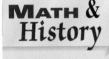

1796

Gauss proves constructing a shape with 17 congruent sides and 17 congruent angles is possible.

1990s

Geometry software duplicates the tools for construction on screen.

1.4

Angles and Their Measures

What you should learn

GOAL 1 Use angle postulates.

GOAL 2 Classify angles as acute, right, obtuse, or straight.

Why you should learn it

▼ To solve **real-life** problems about angles, such as the field of vision of a horse wearing blinkers in **Example 2.**

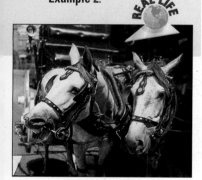

GOAL 1 USING ANGLE POSTULATES

An **angle** consists of two different rays that have the same initial point. The rays are the **sides** of the angle. The initial point is the **vertex** of the angle.

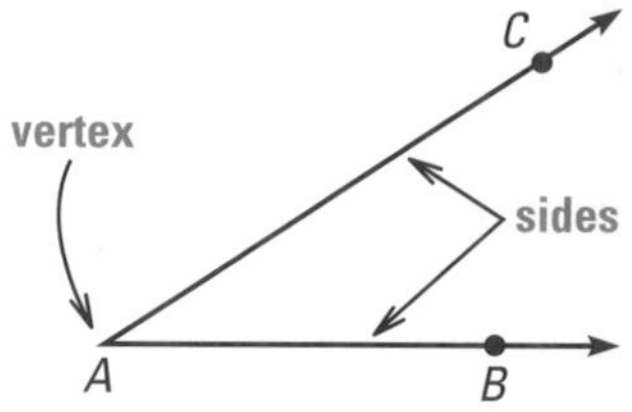

The angle that has sides $\overrightarrow{AB}$ and $\overrightarrow{AC}$ is denoted by $\angle BAC$, $\angle CAB$, or $\angle A$. The point A is the vertex of the angle.

EXAMPLE 1 Naming Angles

Name the angles in the figure.

SOLUTION

There are three different angles.

• $\angle PQS$ or $\angle SQP$

• $\angle SQR$ or $\angle RQS$

• $\angle PQR$ or $\angle RQP$

You should not name any of these angles as $\angle Q$ because all three angles have Q as their vertex. The name $\angle Q$ would not distinguish one angle from the others.

· · · · · · · · ·

The *measure* of $\angle A$ is denoted by $m\angle A$. The measure of an angle can be approximated with a protractor, using units called *degrees* (°). For instance, $\angle BAC$ has a measure of 50°, which can be written as

$$m\angle BAC = 50°.$$

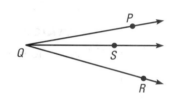

Angles that have the same measure are called **congruent angles.** For instance, $\angle BAC$ and $\angle DEF$ each have a measure of 50°, so they are congruent.

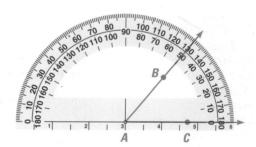

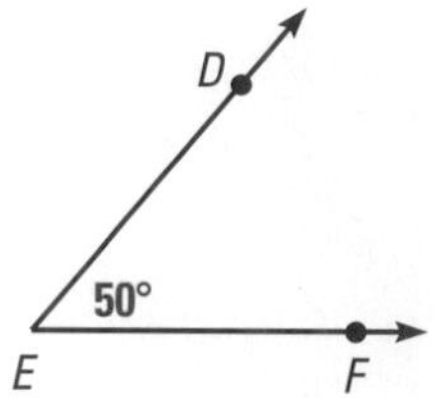

MEASURES ARE EQUAL.	ANGLES ARE CONGRUENT.
$m\angle BAC = m\angle DEF$	$\angle BAC \cong \angle DEF$
"is equal to"	"is congruent to"

Logical Reasoning

POSTULATE 3 *Protractor Postulate*

Consider a point A on one side of $\overrightarrow{OB}$. The rays of the form $\overrightarrow{OA}$ can be matched one to one with the real numbers from 0 to 180.

The **measure** of $\angle AOB$ is equal to the absolute value of the difference between the real numbers for $\overrightarrow{OA}$ and $\overrightarrow{OB}$.

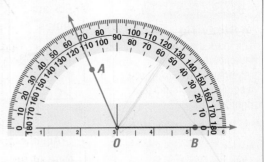

A point is in the **interior** of an angle if it is between points that lie on each side of the angle.

A point is in the **exterior** of an angle if it is not on the angle or in its interior.

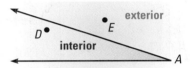

POSTULATE 4 *Angle Addition Postulate*

If P is in the interior of $\angle RST$, then

$$m\angle RSP + m\angle PST = m\angle RST.$$

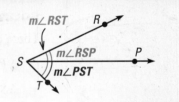

EXAMPLE 2 *Calculating Angle Measures*

VISION Each eye of a horse wearing blinkers has an angle of vision that measures 100°. The angle of vision that is seen by both eyes measures 60°.

Find the angle of vision seen by the left eye alone.

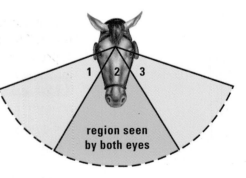

region seen by both eyes

SOLUTION

You can use the Angle Addition Postulate.

$m\angle 2 + m\angle 3 = 100°$	Total vision for left eye is 100°.
$m\angle 3 = 100° - m\angle 2$	Subtract $m\angle 2$ from each side.
$m\angle 3 = 100° - 60°$	Substitute 60° for $m\angle 2$.
$m\angle 3 = 40°$	Subtract.

▶ So, the vision for the left eye alone measures 40°.

GOAL 2 CLASSIFYING ANGLES

> **STUDENT HELP**
>
> **Study Tip**
> The mark used to indicate a right angle resembles the corner of a square, which has four right angles.

Angles are classified as **acute**, **right**, **obtuse**, and **straight**, according to their measures. Angles have measures greater than 0° and less than or equal to 180°.

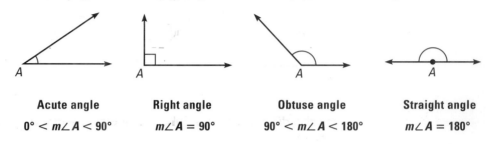

Acute angle	Right angle	Obtuse angle	Straight angle
$0° < m\angle A < 90°$	$m\angle A = 90°$	$90° < m\angle A < 180°$	$m\angle A = 180°$

EXAMPLE 3 *Classifying Angles in a Coordinate Plane*

Plot the points $L(-4, 2)$, $M(-1, -1)$, $N(2, 2)$, $Q(4, -1)$, and $P(2, -4)$. Then measure and classify the following angles as acute, right, obtuse, or straight.

a. $\angle LMN$ **b.** $\angle LMP$ **c.** $\angle NMQ$ **d.** $\angle LMQ$

SOLUTION

Begin by plotting the points. Then use a protractor to measure each angle.

MEASURE	CLASSIFICATION
a. $m\angle LMN = 90°$	right angle
b. $m\angle LMP = 180°$	straight angle
c. $m\angle NMQ = 45°$	acute angle
d. $m\angle LMQ = 135°$	obtuse angle

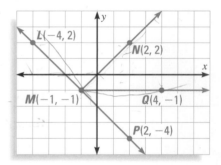

Two angles are **adjacent angles** if they share a common vertex and side, but have no common interior points.

EXAMPLE 4 *Drawing Adjacent Angles*

Use a protractor to draw two adjacent acute angles $\angle RSP$ and $\angle PST$ so that $\angle RST$ is (**a**) acute and (**b**) obtuse.

SOLUTION

a.

b.

> **STUDENT HELP**
>
> **INTERNET HOMEWORK HELP**
> Visit our Web site www.mcdougallittell.com for extra examples.

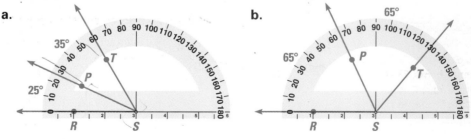

GUIDED PRACTICE

Vocabulary Check ✓

Match the angle with its classification.

A. acute **B.** obtuse **C.** right **D.** straight

1.

2.

3.

4.

Concept Check ✓

Use the diagram at the right to answer the questions. Explain your answers.

5. Is $\angle DEF \cong \angle FEG$?

6. Is $\angle DEG \cong \angle HEG$?

7. Are $\angle DEF$ and $\angle FEH$ adjacent?

8. Are $\angle GED$ and $\angle DEF$ adjacent?

Skill Check ✓

Name the vertex and sides of the angle. Then estimate its measure.

9.

10.

11.

12.

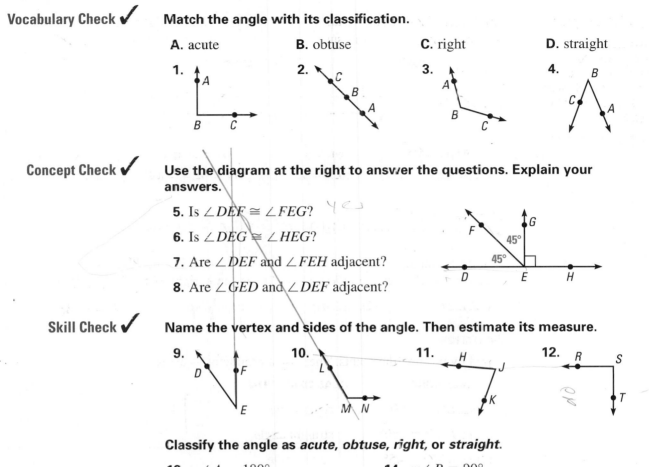

Classify the angle as *acute, obtuse, right,* or *straight*.

13. $m\angle A = 180°$

14. $m\angle B = 90°$

15. $m\angle C = 100°$

16. $m\angle D = 45°$

PRACTICE AND APPLICATIONS

STUDENT HELP

Extra Practice to help you master skills is on pp. 803 and 804.

NAMING PARTS **Name the vertex and sides of the angle.**

17.

18.

19.

STUDENT HELP

HOMEWORK HELP
Example 1: Exs. 17–22
Example 2: Exs. 23–34
Example 3: Exs. 35–43
Example 4: Exs. 38, 39

NAMING ANGLES **Write two names for the angle.**

20.

21.

22.

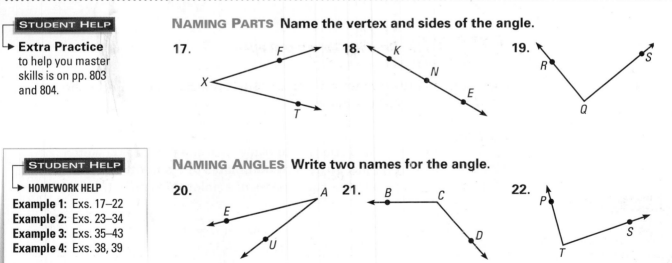

MEASURING ANGLES Copy the angle, extend its sides, and use a protractor to measure it to the nearest degree.

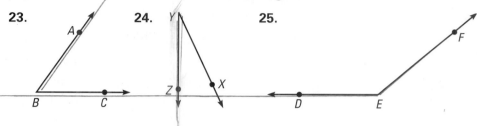

23.   24.   25.

ANGLE ADDITION Use the Angle Addition Postulate to find the measure of the unknown angle.

26. $m\angle ABC = \underline{\ ?\ }$ 27. $m\angle DEF = \underline{\ ?\ }$ 28. $m\angle PQR = \underline{\ ?\ }$

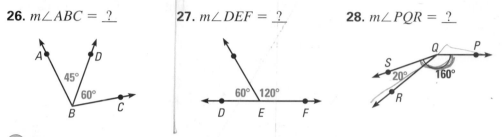

🧩 **LOGICAL REASONING** Draw a sketch that uses all of the following information.

D is in the interior of $\angle BAE$. $m\angle BAC = 130°$
E is in the interior of $\angle DAF$. $m\angle EAC = 100°$
F is in the interior of $\angle EAC$. $m\angle BAD = m\angle EAF = m\angle FAC$

29. Find $m\angle FAC$.   30. Find $m\angle BAD$.   31. Find $m\angle FAB$.

32. Find $m\angle DAE$.   33. Find $m\angle FAD$.   34. Find $m\angle BAE$.

CLASSIFYING ANGLES State whether the angle appears to be *acute*, *right*, *obtuse*, or *straight*. Then estimate its measure.

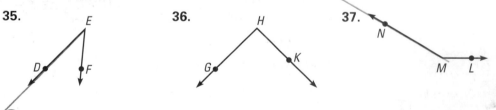

35.   36.   37.

🧩 **LOGICAL REASONING** Draw five points, *A, B, C, D,* and *E* so that all three statements are true.

38. $\angle DBE$ is a straight angle.
    $\angle DBA$ is a right angle.
    $\angle ABC$ is a straight angle.

39. C is in the interior of $\angle ADE$.
    $m\angle ADC + m\angle CDE = 120°$.
    $\angle CDB$ is a straight angle.

🔵 **USING ALGEBRA** In a coordinate plane, plot the points and sketch $\angle ABC$. Classify the angle. Write the coordinates of a point that lies in the interior of the angle and the coordinates of a point that lies in the exterior of the angle.

40. $A(3, -2)$
    $B(5, -1)$
    $C(4, -4)$

41. $A(5, -1)$
    $B(3, -2)$
    $C(4, -4)$

42. $A(5, -1)$
    $B(3, -2)$
    $C(0, -1)$

43. $A(-3, 1)$
    $B(-2, 2)$
    $C(-1, 4)$

🌐 **GEOGRAPHY** For each city on the polar map, estimate the measure of ∠*BOA*, where *B* is on the Prime Meridian (0° longitude), *O* is the North Pole, and *A* is the city.

44. Clyde River, Canada **45.** Fairbanks, Alaska **46.** Angmagssalik, Greenland

47. Old Crow, Canada **48.** Reykjavik, Iceland **49.** Tuktoyaktuk, Canada

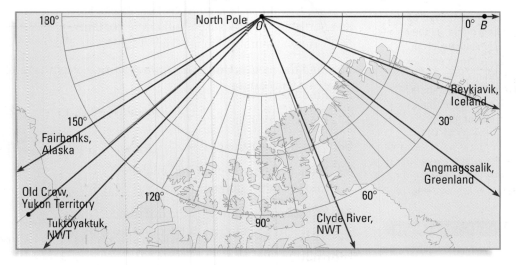

🎯 **PLAYING DARTS** In Exercises 50–53, use the following information to find the score for the indicated dart toss landing at point *A*.

A dartboard is 18 inches across. It is divided into twenty wedges of equal size. The score of a toss is indicated by numbers around the board. The score is doubled if a dart lands in the *double ring* and tripled if it lands in the *triple ring*. Only the top half of the dart board is shown.

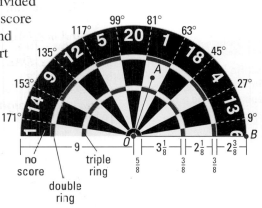

50. $m\angle BOA = 160°; AO = 3$ in.

51. $m\angle BOA = 35°; AO = 4$ in.

52. $m\angle BOA = 60°; AO = 5$ in.

53. $m\angle BOA = 90°; AO = 6.5$ in.

Test Preparation

54. MULTI-STEP PROBLEM Use a piece of paper folded in half three times and labeled as shown.

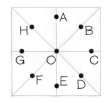

a. Name eight congruent acute angles.

b. Name eight right angles.

c. Name eight congruent obtuse angles.

d. Name two adjacent angles that combine to form a straight angle.

★ **Challenge**

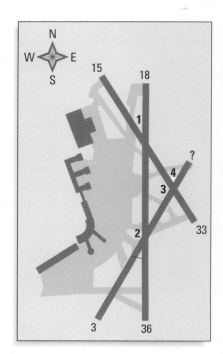

🌐 **AIRPORT RUNWAYS** In Exercises 55–60, use the diagram of Ronald Reagan Washington National Airport and the information about runway numbering on page 1.

An airport runway is named by dividing its *bearing* (the angle measured clockwise from due north) by 10. Because a full circle contains 360°, runway numbers range from 1 to 36.

STUDENT HELP

➡ **HOMEWORK HELP**
Bearings are measured around a circle, so they can have values larger than 180°. You can think of bearings between 180° and 360° as angles that are "bigger" than a straight angle.

55. Find the measure of ∠1.

56. Find the measure of ∠2.

57. Find the measure of ∠3.

58. Find the measure of ∠4.

59. What is the number of the unlabeled runway in the diagram?

60. *Writing* Explain why the difference between the numbers at the opposite ends of a runway is always 18.

EXTRA CHALLENGE

➡ www.mcdougallittell.com

MIXED REVIEW

STUDENT HELP

➡ **Skills Review**
For help solving equations, see p.790.

🆇🆈 **USING ALGEBRA** Solve for *x*. (Skills Review, p. 790, for 1.5)

61. $\dfrac{x + 3}{2} = 3$

62. $\dfrac{5 + x}{2} = 5$

63. $\dfrac{x + 4}{2} = -4$

64. $\dfrac{-8 + x}{2} = 12$

65. $\dfrac{x + 7}{2} = -10$

66. $\dfrac{-9 + x}{2} = -7$

67. $\dfrac{x + (-1)}{2} = 7$

68. $\dfrac{8 + x}{2} = -1$

69. $\dfrac{x + (-3)}{2} = -4$

EVALUATING STATEMENTS Decide whether the statement is *true* or *false*. (Review 1.2)

70. *U*, *S*, and *Q* are collinear.

71. *T*, *Q*, *S*, and *P* are coplanar.

72. $\overleftrightarrow{UQ}$ and $\overleftrightarrow{PT}$ intersect.

73. $\overrightarrow{SR}$ and $\overrightarrow{TS}$ are opposite rays.

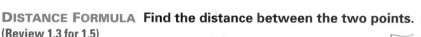

DISTANCE FORMULA Find the distance between the two points. (Review 1.3 for 1.5)

74. *A*(3, 10), *B*(−2, −2)

75. *C*(0, 8), *D*(−8, 3)

76. *E*(−3, 11), *F*(4, 4)

77. *G*(10, −2), *H*(0, 9)

78. *J*(5, 7), *K*(7, 5)

79. *L*(0, −3), *M*(−3, 0)

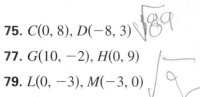

◖ ACTIVITY 1.5

Developing Concepts

Folding Bisectors

GROUP ACTIVITY
Work with a partner.

MATERIALS
- rulers
- paper
- protractor
- pencils

▶ **QUESTION** How can you divide a segment or an angle into two equal parts?

You can fold a piece of paper so that one half of a segment or angle lies exactly on the other half.

▶ **EXPLORING THE CONCEPT: SEGMENT BISECTOR**

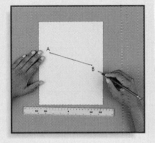

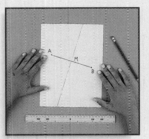
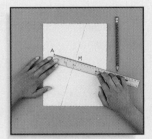

1 On a piece of paper, draw $\overline{AB}$.

2 Fold the paper so that B is on top of A.

3 Label the point where the fold intersects $\overline{AB}$ as point M.

4 Use a ruler to measure $\overline{AM}$ and $\overline{MB}$.

▶ **EXPLORING THE CONCEPT: ANGLE BISECTOR**

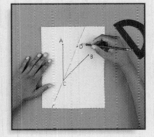
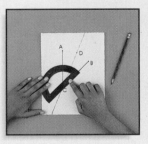

5 On a piece of paper, draw $\angle ACB$.

6 Fold the paper so $\overrightarrow{CB}$ is on top of $\overrightarrow{CA}$.

7 Draw any point on the fold and label the point D.

8 Use a protractor to measure $\angle ACD$ and $\angle BCD$.

▶ **DRAWING CONCLUSIONS**

1. What do you notice about the segments you measured in Step 4?

2. What do you notice about the angles you measured in Step 8?

EXTENSION

CRITICAL THINKING Is it possible to fold congruent angles from a straight angle if you are given the vertex of the angle? Explain.

Segment and Angle Bisectors

What you should learn

GOAL 1 Bisect a segment.

GOAL 2 Bisect an angle, as applied in **Exs. 50–55**.

Why you should learn it

▼ To solve **real-life** problems, such as finding the angle measures of a kite in **Example 4.**

GOAL 1 **BISECTING A SEGMENT**

The **midpoint** of a segment is the point that divides, or **bisects**, the segment into two congruent segments. In this book, matching red *congruence marks* identify congruent segments in diagrams.

A **segment bisector** is a segment, ray, line, or plane that intersects a segment at its midpoint.

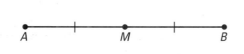

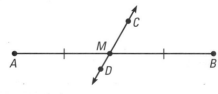

M is the midpoint of $\overline{AB}$ if M is on $\overline{AB}$ and AM = MB.

$\overleftrightarrow{CD}$ is a bisector of $\overline{AB}$.

You can use a **compass** and a **straightedge** (a ruler without marks) to **construct** a segment bisector and midpoint of $\overline{AB}$. A **construction** is a geometric drawing that uses a limited set of tools, usually a compass and a straightedge.

▶ **ACTIVITY**

Construction

Segment Bisector and Midpoint

Use the following steps to construct a bisector of $\overline{AB}$ and find the midpoint M of $\overline{AB}$.

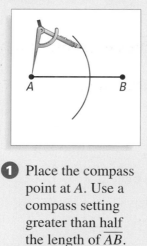

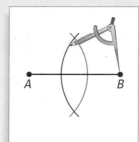

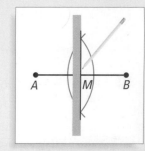

1 Place the compass point at *A*. Use a compass setting greater than half the length of $\overline{AB}$. Draw an arc.

2 Keep the same compass setting. Place the compass point at *B*. Draw an arc. It should intersect the other arc in two places.

3 Use a straightedge to draw a segment through the points of intersection. This segment bisects $\overline{AB}$ at *M*, the midpoint of $\overline{AB}$.

If you know the coordinates of the endpoints of a segment, you can calculate the coordinates of the midpoint. You simply take the mean, or average, of the *x*-coordinates and of the *y*-coordinates. This method is summarized as the **Midpoint Formula**.

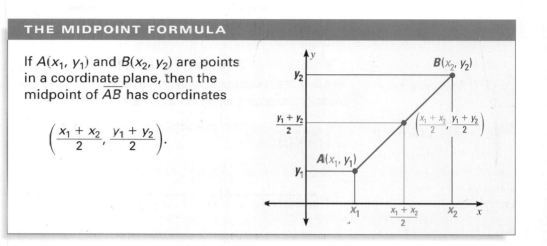

THE MIDPOINT FORMULA

If $A(x_1, y_1)$ and $B(x_2, y_2)$ are points in a coordinate plane, then the midpoint of $\overline{AB}$ has coordinates

$$\left(\frac{x_1 + x_2}{2}, \frac{y_1 + y_2}{2} \right).$$

EXAMPLE 1 *Finding the Coordinates of the Midpoint of a Segment*

Find the coordinates of the midpoint of $\overline{AB}$ with endpoints $A(-2, 3)$ and $B(5, -2)$.

SOLUTION

Use the Midpoint Formula as follows.

$$M = \left(\frac{-2 + 5}{2}, \frac{3 + (-2)}{2} \right)$$

$$= \left(\frac{3}{2}, \frac{1}{2} \right)$$

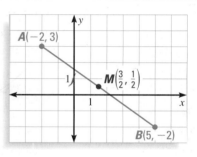

EXAMPLE 2 *Finding the Coordinates of an Endpoint of a Segment*

Using Algebra

The midpoint of $\overline{RP}$ is $M(2, 4)$. One endpoint is $R(-1, 7)$. Find the coordinates of the other endpoint.

SOLUTION

Let (x, y) be the coordinates of P. Use the Midpoint Formula to write equations involving x and y.

$$\frac{-1 + x}{2} = 2 \qquad\qquad \frac{7 + y}{2} = 4$$

$$-1 + x = 4 \qquad\qquad 7 + y = 8$$

$$x = 5 \qquad\qquad y = 1$$

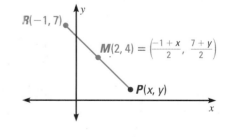

▶ So, the other endpoint of the segment is $P(5, 1)$.

STUDENT HELP

▶ **Study Tip**
Sketching the points in a coordinate plane helps you check your work. You should sketch a drawing of a problem even if the directions don't ask for a sketch.

An **angle bisector** is a ray that divides an angle into two adjacent angles that are congruent. In the diagram at the right, the ray $\overrightarrow{CD}$ bisects $\angle ABC$ because it divides the angle into two congruent angles, $\angle ACD$ and $\angle BCD$.

In this book, matching *congruence arcs* identify congruent angles in diagrams.

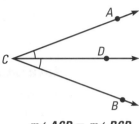

$m\angle ACD = m\angle BCD$

▶ **ACTIVITY**

Construction

Angle Bisector

Use the following steps to construct an angle bisector of $\angle C$.

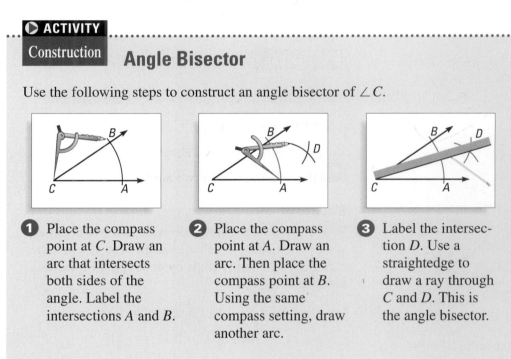

1 Place the compass point at C. Draw an arc that intersects both sides of the angle. Label the intersections A and B.

2 Place the compass point at A. Draw an arc. Then place the compass point at B. Using the same compass setting, draw another arc.

3 Label the intersection D. Use a straightedge to draw a ray through C and D. This is the angle bisector.

After you have constructed an angle bisector, you should check that it divides the original angle into two congruent angles. One way to do this is to use a protractor to check that the angles have the same measure.

Another way is to fold the piece of paper along the angle bisector. When you hold the paper up to a light, you should be able to see that the sides of the two angles line up, which implies that the angles are congruent.

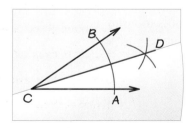

Fold on $\overrightarrow{CD}$.

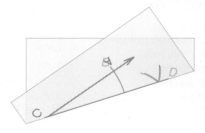

The sides of angles $\angle BCD$ and $\angle ACD$ line up.

EXAMPLE 3 *Dividing an Angle Measure in Half*

The ray $\overrightarrow{FH}$ bisects the angle $\angle EFG$.
Given that $m\angle EFG = 120°$, what are the
measures of $\angle EFH$ and $\angle HFG$?

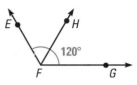

SOLUTION

An angle bisector divides an angle into two congruent angles, each of which has
half the measure of the original angle. So,

$$m\angle EFH = m\angle HFG = \frac{120°}{2} = 60°.$$

EXAMPLE 4 *Doubling an Angle Measure*

KITE DESIGN In the kite, two angles are bisected.

$\angle EKI$ is bisected by $\overrightarrow{KT}$.

$\angle ITE$ is bisected by $\overrightarrow{TK}$.

Find the measures of the two angles.

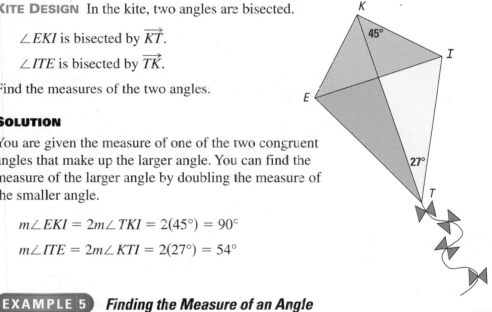

SOLUTION

You are given the measure of one of the two congruent
angles that make up the larger angle. You can find the
measure of the larger angle by doubling the measure of
the smaller angle.

$$m\angle EKI = 2m\angle TKI = 2(45°) = 90°$$
$$m\angle ITE = 2m\angle KTI = 2(27°) = 54°$$

EXAMPLE 5 *Finding the Measure of an Angle*

*Using
Algebra*

In the diagram, $\overrightarrow{RQ}$ bisects $\angle PRS$. The
measures of the two congruent angles
are $(x + 40)°$ and $(3x - 20)°$. Solve for x.

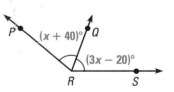

SOLUTION

$m\angle PRQ = m\angle QRS$	Congruent angles have equal measures.
$(x + 40)° = (3x - 20)°$	Substitute given measures.
$x + 60 = 3x$	Add 20° to each side.
$60 = 2x$	Subtract x from each side.
$30 = x$	Divide each side by 2.

▶ So, $x = 30$. You can check by substituting to see that each of the congruent
angles has a measure of $70°$.

GUIDED PRACTICE

Vocabulary Check ✓

1. What kind of geometric figure is an *angle bisector*?

Concept Check ✓

2. How do you indicate congruent segments in a diagram? How do you indicate congruent angles in a diagram?

3. What is the simplified form of the Midpoint Formula if one of the endpoints of a segment is (0, 0) and the other is (*x*, *y*)?

Skill Check ✓

Find the coordinates of the midpoint of a segment with the given endpoints.

4. $A(5, 4)$, $B(-3, 2)$ **5.** $A(-1, -9)$, $B(11, -5)$ **6.** $A(6, -4)$, $B(1, 8)$

Find the coordinates of the other endpoint of a segment with the given endpoint and midpoint M.

7. $C(3, 0)$
$M(3, 4)$

8. $D(5, 2)$
$M(7, 6)$

9. $E(-4, 2)$
$M(-3, -2)$

10. Suppose $m\angle JKL$ is 90°. If the ray $\overrightarrow{KM}$ bisects $\angle JKL$, what are the measures of $\angle JKM$ and $\angle LKM$?

$\overrightarrow{QS}$ **is the angle bisector of** $\angle PQR$**. Find the two angle measures not given in the diagram.**

11.   **12.**   **13.**

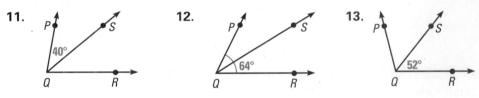

PRACTICE AND APPLICATIONS

STUDENT HELP

► **Extra Practice**
to help you master
skills is on p. 804.

⊿ **CONSTRUCTION** Use a ruler to measure and redraw the line segment on a piece of paper. Then use construction tools to construct a segment bisector.

14.   **15.**   **16.**

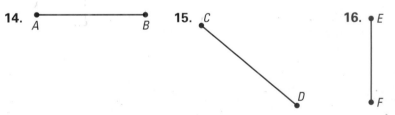

STUDENT HELP

► HOMEWORK HELP
Example 1: Exs. 17–24
Example 2: Exs. 25–30
Example 3: Exs. 37–42
Example 4: Exs. 37–42
Example 5: Exs. 44–49

FINDING THE MIDPOINT Find the coordinates of the midpoint of a segment with the given endpoints.

17. $A(0, 0)$
$B(-8, 6)$

18. $J(-1, 7)$
$K(3, -3)$

19. $C(10, 8)$
$D(-2, 5)$

20. $P(-12, -9)$
$Q(2, 10)$

21. $S(0, -8)$
$T(-6, 14)$

22. $E(4, 4)$
$F(4, -18)$

23. $V(-1.5, 8)$
$W(0.25, -1)$

24. $G(-5.5, -6.1)$
$H(-0.5, 9.1)$

USING ALGEBRA Find the coordinates of the other endpoint of a segment with the given endpoint and midpoint *M*.

25. $R(2, 6)$ $M(-1, 1)$

26. $T(-8, -1)$ $M(0, 3)$

27. $W(3, -12)$ $M(2, -1)$

28. $Q(-5, 9)$ $M(-8, -2)$

29. $A(6, 7)$ $M(10, -7)$

30. $D(-3.5, -6)$ $M(1.5, 4.5)$

RECOGNIZING CONGRUENCE Use the marks on the diagram to name the congruent segments and congruent angles.

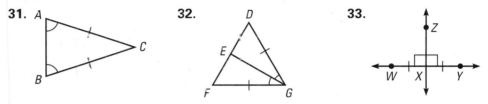

31.

32.

33.

CONSTRUCTION Use a protractor to measure and redraw the angle on a piece of paper. Then use construction tools to find the angle bisector.

34.

35.

36.

ANALYZING ANGLE BISECTORS $\overrightarrow{QS}$ is the angle bisector of $\angle PQR$. Find the two angle measures not given in the diagram.

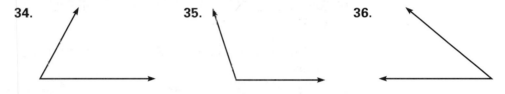

37.

38.

39.

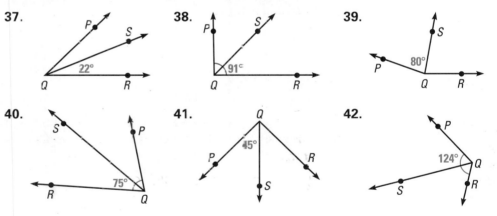

40.

41.

42.

STUDENT HELP

SOFTWARE HELP Visit our Web site www.mcdougallittell.com to see instructions for several software applications.

43. **TECHNOLOGY** Use geometry software to draw a triangle. Construct the angle bisector of one angle. Then find the midpoint of the opposite side of the triangle. Change your triangle and observe what happens.

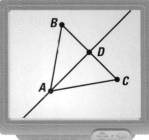

Does the angle bisector *always* pass through the midpoint of the opposite side? Does it *ever* pass through the midpoint?

STUDENT HELP

HOMEWORK HELP
Visit our Web site
www.mcdougallittell.com
for help with Ex. 44–49.

USING ALGEBRA $\overrightarrow{BD}$ bisects $\angle ABC$. **Find the value of x.**

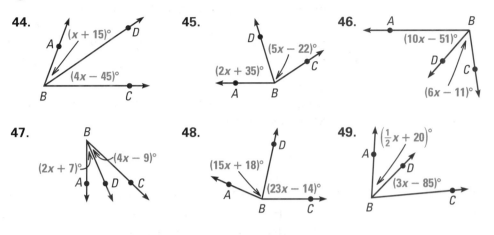

44. $(x + 15)°$, $(4x - 45)°$

45. $(5x - 22)°$, $(2x + 35)°$

46. $(10x - 51)°$, $(6x - 11)°$

47. $(2x + 7)°$, $(4x - 9)°$

48. $(15x + 18)°$, $(23x - 14)°$

49. $\left(\frac{1}{2}x + 20\right)°$, $(3x - 85)°$

STRIKE ZONE **In Exercises 50 and 51, use the information below. For each player, find the coordinate of *T*, a point on the top of the strike zone.**
In baseball, the "strike zone" is the region a baseball needs to pass through in order for an umpire to declare it a strike if it is not hit. The *top of the strike zone* is a horizontal plane passing through the midpoint between the top of the hitter's shoulders and the top of the uniform pants when the player is in a batting stance.

▶ Source: Major League Baseball

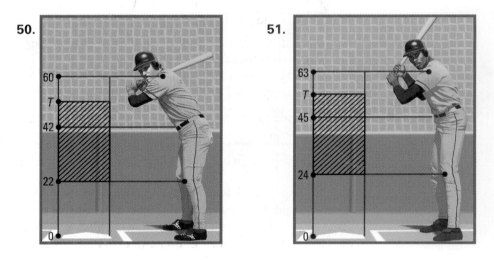

50.

51.

AIR HOCKEY **When an air hockey puck is hit into the sideboards, it bounces off so that $\angle 1$ and $\angle 2$ are congruent. Find $m\angle 1$, $m\angle 2$, $m\angle 3$, and $m\angle 4$.**

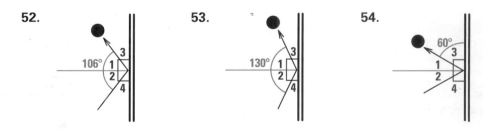

52. $106°$

53. $130°$

54. $60°$

55. 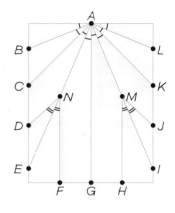 **PAPER AIRPLANES** The diagram represents an unfolded piece of paper used to make a paper airplane. The segments represent where the paper was folded to make the airplane.

Using the diagram, name as many pairs of congruent segments and as many congruent angles as you can.

56. *Writing* Explain, in your own words, how you would divide a line segment into four congruent segments using a compass and straightedge. Then explain how you could do it using the Midpoint Formula.

57. MIDPOINT FORMULA REVISITED Another version of the Midpoint Formula, for $A(x_1, y_1)$ and $B(x_2, y_2)$, is

$$M\left[x_1 + \frac{1}{2}(x_2 - x_1), y_1 + \frac{1}{2}(y_2 - y_1)\right].$$

Redo Exercises 17–24 using this version of the Midpoint Formula. Do you get the same answers as before? Use algebra to explain why the formula above is equivalent to the one in the lesson.

Test Preparation

58. MULTI-STEP PROBLEM Sketch a triangle with three sides of different lengths.

a. Using construction tools, find the midpoints of all three sides and the angle bisectors of all three angles of your triangle.

b. Determine whether or not the angle bisectors pass through the midpoints.

c. *Writing* Write a brief paragraph explaining your results. Determine if your results would be different if you used a different kind of triangle.

★ **Challenge**

INFINITE SERIES A football team practices running back and forth on the field in a special way. First they run from one end of the 100 yd field to the other. Then they turn around and run half the previous distance. Then they turn around again and run half the previous distance, and so on.

59. Suppose the athletes continue the running drill with smaller and smaller distances. What is the coordinate of the point that they approach?

60. What is the total distance that the athletes cover?

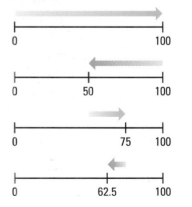

MIXED REVIEW

SKETCHING VISUAL PATTERNS **Sketch the next figure in the pattern.**
(Review 1.1)

61.  **62.**

DISTANCE FORMULA **Find the distance between the two points.** (Review 1.3)

63. $A(3, 12), B(-5, -1)$ **64.** $C(-6, 9), D(-2, -7)$ **65.** $E(8, -8), F(2, 14)$

66. $G(3, -8), H(0, -2)$ **67.** $J(-4, -5), K(5, -1)$ **68.** $L(-10, 1), M(-4, 9)$

MEASURING ANGLES **Use a protractor to find the measure of the angle.**
(Review 1.4 for 1.6)

69. 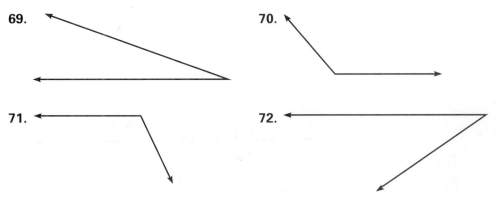 **70.**

71. **72.**

QUIZ 2

1. State the Angle Addition Postulate
for the three angles shown at the right.
(Lesson 1.4)

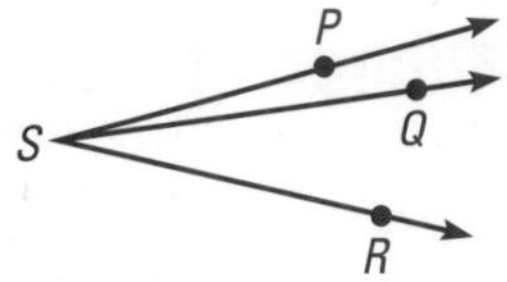

In a coordinate plane, plot the points and sketch $\angle DEF$. **Classify the**
angle. Write the coordinates of a point that lies in the interior of the
angle and the coordinates of a point that lies in the exterior of the angle.
(Lesson 1.4)

2. $D(-2, 3)$ **3.** $D(-6, -3)$ **4.** $D(-1, 8)$ **5.** $D(1, 10)$
 $E(4, -3)$ $E(0, -5)$ $E(-4, 0)$ $E(1, 1)$
 $F(2, 6)$ $F(8, -5)$ $F(4, 0)$ $F(8, 1)$

6. In the diagram, $\overrightarrow{KM}$ is the angle bisector
of $\angle JKL$. Find $m\angle MKL$ and $m\angle JKL$.
(Lesson 1.5)

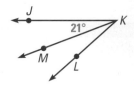

▶ ACTIVITY 1.6

Using Technology

Angles and Intersecting Lines

You can use geometry software to construct intersecting lines and measure the angles formed by the lines.

▶ **CONSTRUCT** **Construct intersecting lines.**

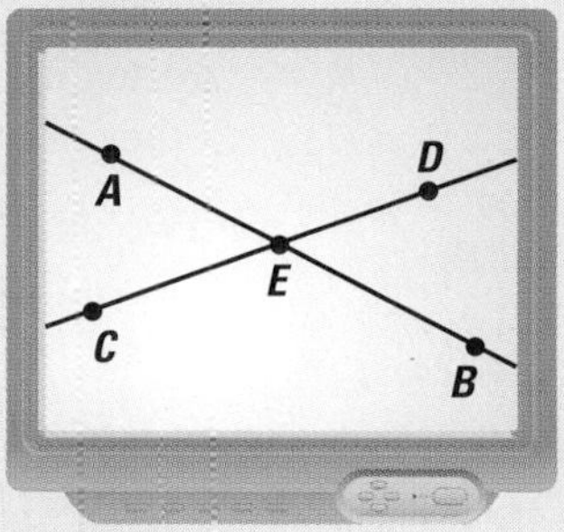

① Draw a line. Label two points *A* and *B* on the line.

② Draw a second line that intersects the first line. Label two points *C* and *D* on the line.

③ Select the two lines and construct their point of intersection. Label the point *E*.

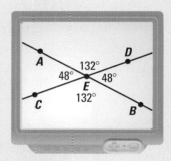

▶ **INVESTIGATE**

1. Measure the four angles formed by the intersecting lines: ∠*AEC*, ∠*AED*, ∠*BEC*, and ∠*BED*. When measuring angles, select the points *in order,* with the vertex as the second point. Record the measures.

2. Move the lines into different positions by dragging the points. Record the measures of the four angles again.

▶ **MAKE A CONJECTURE**

3. What do you notice about the angle measures?

▶ **INVESTIGATE**

You can use geometry software to perform calculations with measures.

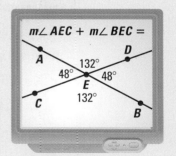

4. Select all four angle measures you have made. Calculate the sum of the measures of any two adjacent angles.

5. Move the lines into different positions by dragging the points. Then find the sum of the two angle measures again.

▶ **MAKE A CONJECTURE**

6. What do you notice about the sum of the measures of adjacent angles formed by intersecting lines?

1.6

Angle Pair Relationships

What you should learn

GOAL 1 Identify vertical angles and linear pairs.

GOAL 2 Identify complementary and supplementary angles.

Why you should learn it

▼ To solve **real-life** problems, such as finding the measures of angles formed by the cables of a bridge in **Ex. 53**.

GOAL 1 VERTICAL ANGLES AND LINEAR PAIRS

In Lesson 1.4, you learned that two angles are *adjacent* if they share a common vertex and side but have no common interior points. In this lesson, you will study other relationships between pairs of angles.

Two angles are **vertical angles** if their sides form two pairs of opposite rays. Two adjacent angles are a **linear pair** if their noncommon sides are opposite rays.

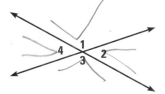
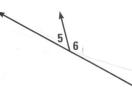

∠1 and ∠3 are vertical angles.   ∠5 and ∠6 are a linear pair.
∠2 and ∠4 are vertical angles.

In this book, you can assume from a diagram that two adjacent angles form a linear pair if the noncommon sides appear to lie on the same line.

EXAMPLE 1   *Identifying Vertical Angles and Linear Pairs*

a. Are ∠2 and ∠3 a linear pair?

b. Are ∠3 and ∠4 a linear pair?

c. Are ∠1 and ∠3 vertical angles?

d. Are ∠2 and ∠4 vertical angles?

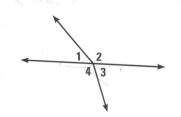

SOLUTION

a. No. The angles are adjacent but their noncommon sides are not opposite rays.

b. Yes. The angles are adjacent and their noncommon sides are opposite rays.

c. No. The sides of the angles do not form two pairs of opposite rays.

d. No. The sides of the angles do not form two pairs of opposite rays.

· · · · · · · · · ·

In Activity 1.6 on page 43, you may have discovered two results:

• *Vertical angles are congruent.*

• *The sum of the measures of angles that form a linear pair is 180°.*

Both of these results will be stated formally in Chapter 2.

Logical Reasoning

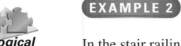

EXAMPLE 2 Finding Angle Measures

In the stair railing shown at the right, $\angle 6$ has a measure of $130°$. Find the measures of the other three angles.

SOLUTION

$\angle 6$ and $\angle 7$ are a linear pair. So, the sum of their measures is $180°$.

$$m\angle 6 + m\angle 7 = 180°$$
$$130° + m\angle 7 = 180°$$
$$m\angle 7 = 50°$$

$\angle 6$ and $\angle 5$ are also a linear pair. So, it follows that $m\angle 5 = 50°$.

$\angle 6$ and $\angle 8$ are vertical angles. So, they are congruent and have the same measure.

$$m\angle 8 = m\angle 6 = 130°$$

Using Algebra

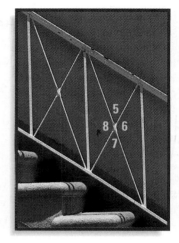

EXAMPLE 3 Finding Angle Measures

Solve for x and y.
Then find the angle measures.

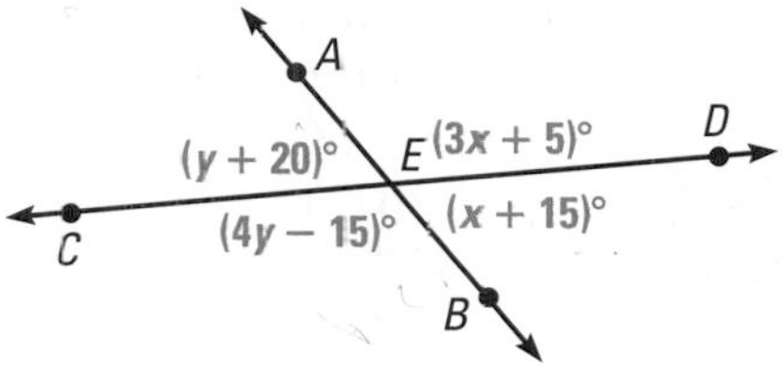

SOLUTION

Use the fact that the sum of the measures of angles that form a linear pair is $180°$.

$$m\angle AED + m\angle DEB = 180°$$
$$(3x + 5)° + (x + 15)° = 180°$$
$$4x + 20 = 180$$
$$4x = 160$$
$$\mathbf{x = 40}$$

$$m\angle AEC + m\angle CEB = 180°$$
$$(y + 20)° + (4y - 15)° = 180°$$
$$5y + 5 = 180$$
$$5y = 175$$
$$\mathbf{y = 35}$$

Use substitution to find the angle measures.

$$m\angle AED = (3x + 5)° = (3 \cdot 40 + 5)° = 125°$$
$$m\angle DEB = (x + 15)° = (40 + 15)° = 55°$$
$$m\angle AEC = (y + 20)° = (35 + 20)° = 55°$$
$$m\angle CEB = (4y - 15)° = (4 \cdot 35 - 15)° = 125°$$

▶ So, the angle measures are $125°$, $55°$, $55°$, and $125°$. Because the vertical angles are congruent, the result is reasonable.

STUDENT HELP

INTERNET
HOMEWORK HELP
Visit our Web site www.mcdougallittell.com for extra examples.

GOAL 2 COMPLEMENTARY AND SUPPLEMENTARY ANGLES

Two angles are **complementary angles** if the sum of their measures is 90°. Each angle is the **complement** of the other. Complementary angles can be adjacent or nonadjacent.

Two angles are **supplementary angles** if the sum of their measures is 180°. Each angle is the **supplement** of the other. Supplementary angles can be adjacent or nonadjacent.

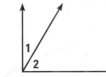
complementary
adjacent

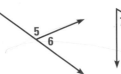
complementary
nonadjacent

supplementary
adjacent

supplementary
nonadjacent

EXAMPLE 4 *Identifying Angles*

State whether the two angles are complementary, supplementary, or neither.

SOLUTION

The angle showing 4:00 has a measure of 120° and the angle showing 10:00 has a measure of 60°. Because the sum of these two measures is 180°, the angles are supplementary.

EXAMPLE 5 *Finding Measures of Complements and Supplements*

a. Given that $\angle A$ is a complement of $\angle C$ and $m\angle A = 47°$, find $m\angle C$.

b. Given that $\angle P$ is a supplement of $\angle R$ and $m\angle R = 36°$, find $m\angle P$.

SOLUTION

a. $m\angle C = 90° - m\angle A = 90° - 47° = 43°$

b. $m\angle P = 180° - m\angle R = 180° - 36° = 144°$

EXAMPLE 6 *Finding the Measure of a Complement*

Using Algebra

$\angle W$ and $\angle Z$ are complementary. The measure of $\angle Z$ is five times the measure of $\angle W$. Find $m\angle W$.

SOLUTION

Because the angles are complementary, $m\angle W + m\angle Z = 90°$. But $m\angle Z = 5(m\angle W)$, so $m\angle W + 5(m\angle W) = 90°$. Because $6(m\angle W) = 90°$, you know that $m\angle W = 15°$.

GUIDED PRACTICE

Vocabulary Check ✔

1. Explain the difference between *complementary angles* and *supplementary angles*.

Concept Check ✔

2. Sketch examples of acute vertical angles and obtuse vertical angles.

3. Sketch examples of adjacent congruent complementary angles and adjacent congruent supplementary angles.

Skill Check ✔

FINDING ANGLE MEASURES **Find the measure of ∠1.**

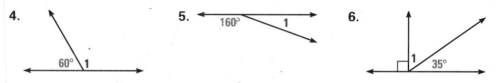

4.

60° 1

5.

160° 1

6.

1 35°

7. 🌐 **OPENING A DOOR** The figure shows a doorway viewed from above. If you open the door so that the measure of ∠1 is 50°, how many more degrees would you have to open the door so that the angle between the wall and the door is 90°?

PRACTICE AND APPLICATIONS

STUDENT HELP

▶ **Extra Practice**
to help you master
skills is on p. 804.

IDENTIFYING ANGLE PAIRS **Use the figure at the right.**

8. Are ∠5 and ∠6 a linear pair? No

9. Are ∠5 and ∠9 a linear pair? Yes

10. Are ∠5 and ∠8 a linear pair? No

11. Are ∠5 and ∠8 vertical angles? yes

12. Are ∠5 and ∠7 vertical angles? No

13. Are ∠9 and ∠6 vertical angles? No

Pair = 2

5 6 7
9 8

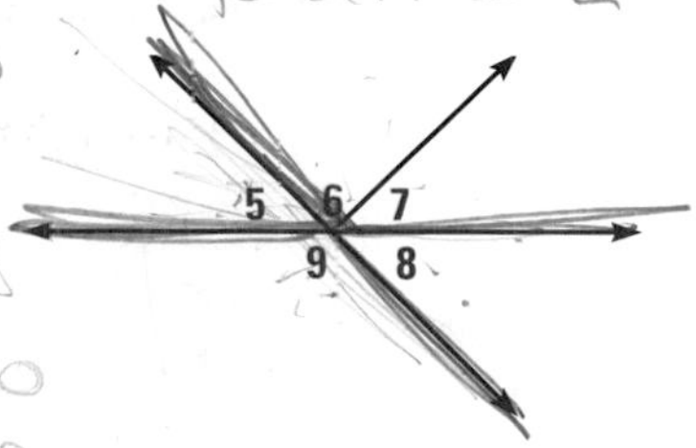

EVALUATING STATEMENTS **Decide whether the statement is *always*, *sometimes*, or *never* true.**

14. If $m\angle 1 = 40°$, then $m\angle 2 = 140°$. Never true

15. If $m\angle 4 = 130°$, then $m\angle 2 = 50°$. always

16. ∠1 and ∠4 are congruent. Sometimes

17. $m\angle 2 + m\angle 3 = m\angle 1 + m\angle 4$ always true

18. $\angle 2 \cong \angle 1$ Yes

19. $m\angle 2 = 90° - m\angle 3$ Never true

1 4
3 2

150
110
No

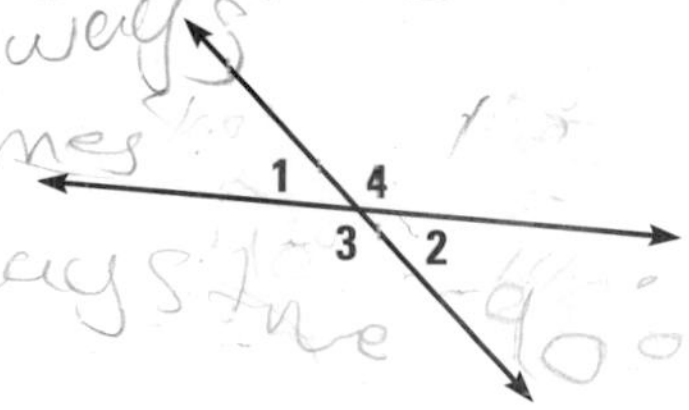

STUDENT HELP

▶ **HOMEWORK HELP**
Example 1: Exs. 8–13
Example 2: Exs. 14–27
Example 3: Exs. 28–36
Example 4: Exs. 37–40
Example 5: Exs. 41, 42
Example 6: Exs. 43, 44

FINDING ANGLE MEASURES Use the figure at the right.

20. If $m\angle 6 = 72°$, then $m\angle 7 = \underline{\quad?\quad}$.

21. If $m\angle 8 = 80°$, then $m\angle 6 = \underline{\quad?\quad}$.

22. If $m\angle 9 = 110°$, then $m\angle 8 = \underline{\quad?\quad}$.

23. If $m\angle 9 = 123°$, then $m\angle 7 = \underline{\quad?\quad}$.

24. If $m\angle 7 = 142°$, then $m\angle 8 = \underline{\quad?\quad}$.

25. If $m\angle 6 = 13°$, then $m\angle 9 = \underline{\quad?\quad}$.

26. If $m\angle 9 = 170°$, then $m\angle 6 = \underline{\quad?\quad}$.

27. If $m\angle 8 = 26°$, then $m\angle 7 = \underline{\quad?\quad}$.

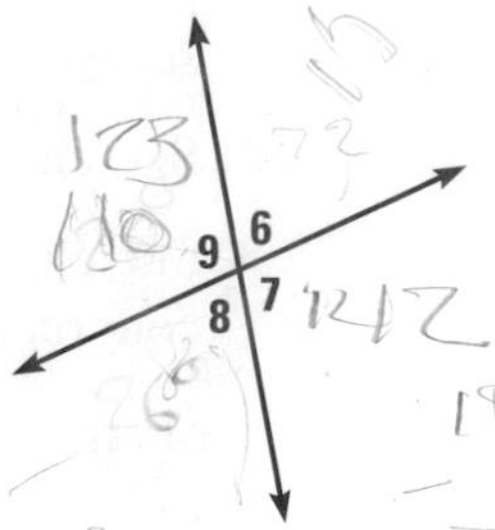

USING ALGEBRA Find the value(s) of the variable(s).

28. $105°$, $(2x - 11)°$

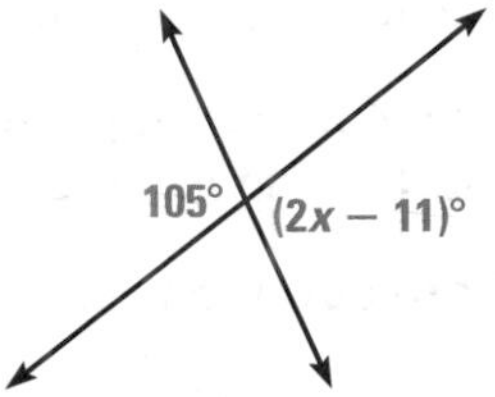

29. $(6x + 19)°$, $x°$

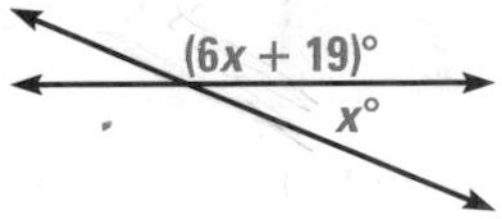

30. $78°$, $(5x - 2)°$

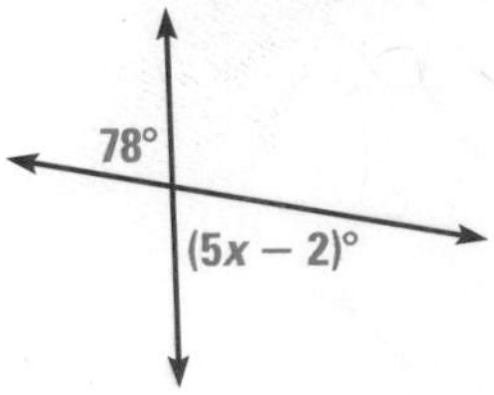

31. $(y - 12)°$, $(6x - 32)°$, $(3y - 8)°$, $(2x - 20)°$

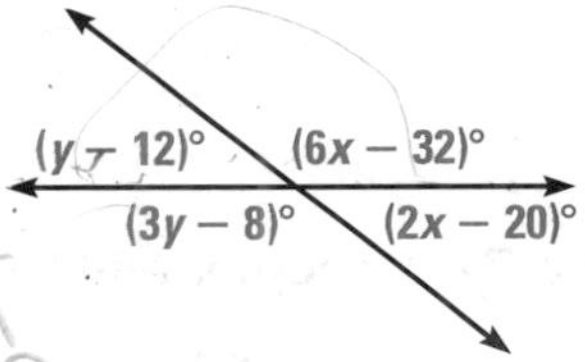

32. $(2y + 28)°$, $(4x + 10)°$, $(4y + 26)°$, $(3x - 5)°$

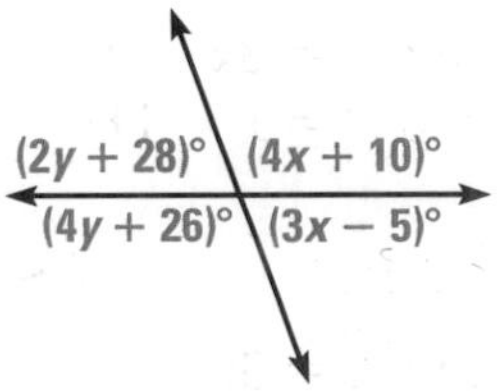

33. $(9y - 187)°$, $(7x - 248)°$, $(11y - 253)°$, $(x + 44)°$

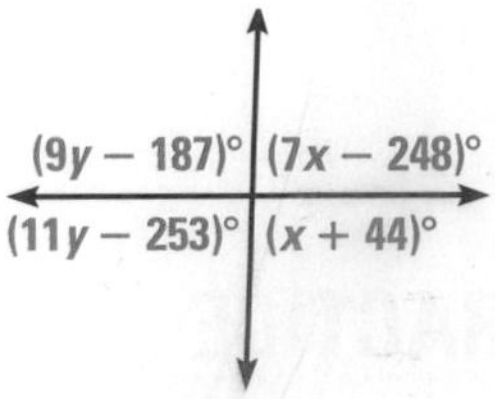

34. $(3x + 20)°$, $y°$, $(5x - 50)°$

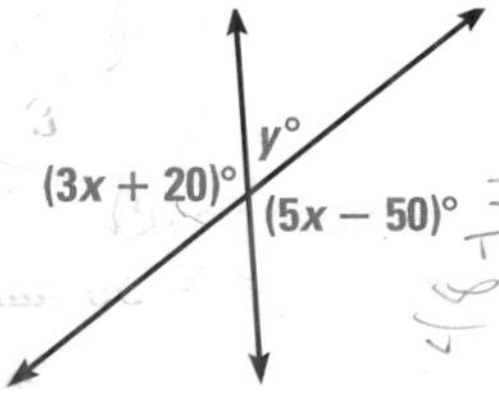

35. $6x°$, $(4x + 16)°$, $11y°$

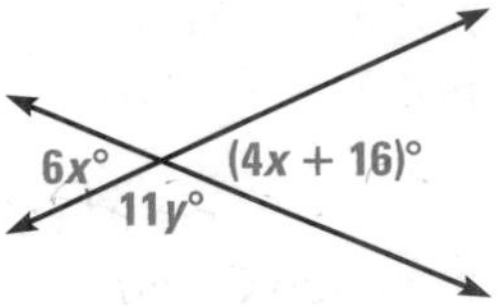

36. $7x°$, $y°$, $56°$, $2x°$

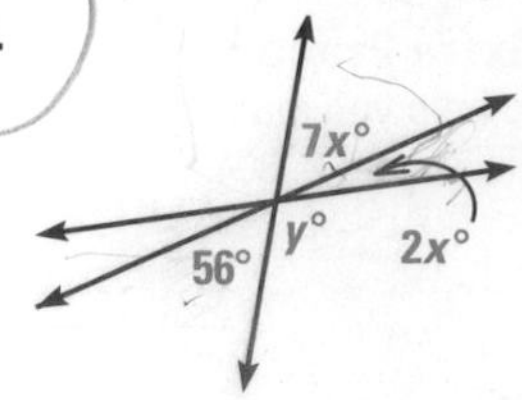

IDENTIFYING ANGLES State whether the two angles shown are *complementary*, *supplementary*, or *neither*.

37.

38.

39.

40.

41. FINDING COMPLEMENTS In the table, assume that $\angle 1$ and $\angle 2$ are complementary. Copy and complete the table.

$m\angle 1$	2°	10°	25°	33°	40°	49°	55°	62°	76°	86°
$m\angle 2$	?	?	?	?	?	?	?	?	?	?

42. FINDING SUPPLEMENTS In the table, assume that $\angle 1$ and $\angle 2$ are supplementary. Copy and complete the table.

$m\angle 1$	4°	16°	48°	72°	90°	99°	120°	152°	169°	178°
$m\angle 2$	?	?	?	?	?	?	?	?	?	?

43. (xy) **USING ALGEBRA** $\angle A$ and $\angle B$ are complementary. The measure of $\angle B$ is three times the measure of $\angle A$. Find $m\angle A$ and $m\angle B$.

44. (xy) **USING ALGEBRA** $\angle C$ and $\angle D$ are supplementary. The measure of $\angle D$ is eight times the measure of $\angle C$. Find $m\angle C$ and $m\angle D$.

FINDING ANGLES $\angle A$ and $\angle B$ are complementary. Find $m\angle A$ and $m\angle B$.

45. $m\angle A = 5x + 8$
$m\angle B = x + 4$

46. $m\angle A = 3x - 7$
$m\angle B = 11x - 1$

47. $m\angle A = 8x - 7$
$m\angle B = x - 11$

48. $m\angle A = \frac{3}{4}x - 13$
$m\angle B = 3x - 17$

FINDING ANGLES $\angle A$ and $\angle B$ are supplementary. Find $m\angle A$ and $m\angle B$.

49. $m\angle A = 3x$
$m\angle B = x + 8$

50. $m\angle A = 6x - 1$
$m\angle B = 5x - 17$

51. $m\angle A = 12x + 1$
$m\angle B = x + 10$

52. $m\angle A = \frac{3}{8}x + 50$
$m\angle B = x + 31$

53. 🌐 **BRIDGES** The Alamillo Bridge in Seville, Spain, was designed by Santiago Calatrava. In the bridge, $m\angle 1 = 58°$ and $m\angle 2 = 24°$. Find the supplements of both $\angle 1$ and $\angle 2$.

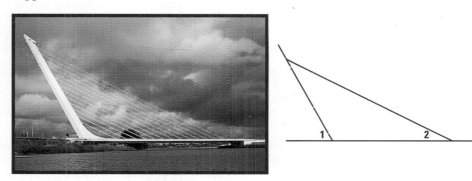

54. 🌐 **BASEBALL** The foul lines of a baseball field intersect at home plate to form a right angle. Suppose you hit a baseball whose path forms an angle of 34° with the third base foul line. What is the angle between the first base foul line and the path of the baseball?

55. PLANTING TREES To support a young tree, you attach wires from the trunk to the ground. The obtuse angle the wire makes with the ground is supplementary to the acute angle the wire makes, and it is three times as large. Find the measures of the angles.

56. *Writing* Give an example of an angle that *does not* have a complement. In general, what is true about an angle that has a complement?

57. MULTIPLE CHOICE In the diagram shown at the right, what are the values of x and y?

(A) $x = 74, y = 106$

(B) $x = 16, y = 88$

(C) $x = 74, y = 16$

(D) $x = 18, y = 118$

(E) $x = 18, y = 94$

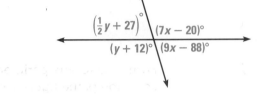

58. MULTIPLE CHOICE $\angle F$ and $\angle G$ are supplementary. The measure of $\angle G$ is six and one half times the measure of $\angle F$. What is $m\angle F$?

(A) $20°$ (B) $24°$ (C) $24.5°$ (D) $26.5°$ (E) $156°$

★ Challenge

59. USING ALGEBRA Find the values of x and y in the diagram shown at the right.

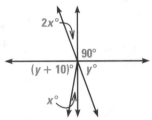

MIXED REVIEW

SOLVING EQUATIONS Solve the equation. (Skills Review, p. 802, for 1.7)

60. $3x = 96$

61. $\frac{1}{2} \cdot 5 \cdot h = 20$

62. $\frac{1}{2} \cdot b \cdot 6 = 15$

63. $s^2 = 200$

64. $2 \cdot 3.14 \cdot r = 40$

65. $3.14 \cdot r^2 = 314$

FINDING COLLINEAR POINTS Use the diagram to find a third point that is collinear with the given points. (Review 1.2)

66. A and J

67. D and F

68. H and E

69. B and G

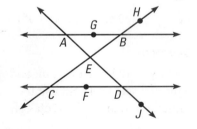

FINDING THE MIDPOINT Find the coordinates of the midpoint of a segment with the given endpoints. (Review 1.5)

70. $A(0, 0), B(-6, -4)$ **71.** $F(2, 5), G(-10, 7)$ **72.** $K(8, -6), L(-2, -2)$

73. $M(-14, -9), N(0, 11)$ **74.** $P(-1.5, 4), Q(5, -9)$ **75.** $S(-2.4, 5), T(7.6, 9)$

Introduction to Perimeter, Circumference, and Area

What you should learn

GOAL 1 Find the perimeter and area of common plane figures.

GOAL 2 Use a general problem-solving plan.

Why you should learn it

▼ To solve **real-life** problems about perimeter and area, such as finding the number of bags of seed you need for a field in **Example 4**.

In this lesson, you will review some common formulas for perimeter, circumference, and area. You will learn more about area in Chapters 6, 11, and 12.

PERIMETER, CIRCUMFERENCE, AND AREA FORMULAS

Formulas for the perimeter P, area A, and circumference C of some common plane figures are given below.

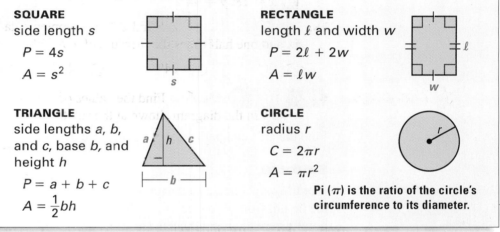

SQUARE
side length s

$P = 4s$

$A = s^2$

RECTANGLE
length ℓ and width w

$P = 2\ell + 2w$

$A = \ell w$

TRIANGLE
side lengths a, b, and c, base b, and height h

$P = a + b + c$

$A = \frac{1}{2}bh$

CIRCLE
radius r

$C = 2\pi r$

$A = \pi r^2$

Pi (π) is the ratio of the circle's circumference to its diameter.

The measurements of perimeter and circumference use units such as centimeters, meters, kilometers, inches, feet, yards, and miles. The measurements of area use units such as square centimeters (cm^2), square meters (m^2), and so on.

EXAMPLE 1   *Finding the Perimeter and Area of a Rectangle*

Find the perimeter and area of a rectangle of length 12 inches and width 5 inches.

SOLUTION

Begin by drawing a diagram and labeling the length and width. Then, use the formulas for perimeter and area of a rectangle.

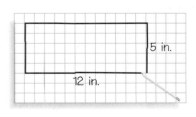

$$P = 2\ell + 2w \qquad A = \ell w$$

$$= 2(12) + 2(5) \qquad = (12)(5)$$

$$= 34 \qquad\qquad = 60$$

▶ So, the perimeter is 34 inches and the area is 60 square inches.

EXAMPLE 2   *Finding the Area and Circumference of a Circle*

Find the diameter, radius, circumference, and area of the circle shown at the right. Use 3.14 as an approximation for π.

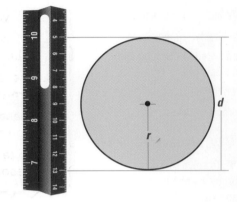

SOLUTION

From the diagram, you can see that the diameter of the circle is

$$d = 13 - 5 = 8 \text{ cm.}$$

The radius is one half the diameter.

$$r = \frac{1}{2}(8) = 4 \text{ cm}$$

Using the formulas for circumference and area, you have

$$C = 2\pi r \approx 2(3.14)(4) \approx 25.1 \text{ cm}$$

$$A = \pi r^2 \approx 3.14(4^2) \approx 50.2 \text{ cm}^2.$$

STUDENT HELP

▸ **Study Tip**
Some approximations for $\pi = 3.141592654\ldots$ are 3.14 and $\frac{22}{7}$.

EXAMPLE 3   *Finding Measurements of a Triangle in a Coordinate Plane*

Find the area and perimeter of the triangle defined by $D(1, 3)$, $E(8, 3)$, and $F(4, 7)$.

SOLUTION

Plot the points in a coordinate plane. Draw the height from F to side $\overline{DE}$. Label the point where the height meets $\overline{DE}$ as G. Point G has coordinates $(4, 3)$.

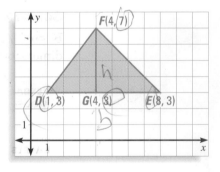

base: $DE = 8 - 1 = 7$

height: $FG = 7 - 3 = 4$

$$A = \frac{1}{2}(\text{base})(\text{height})$$

$$= \frac{1}{2}(7)(4)$$

$$= 14 \text{ square units}$$

To find the perimeter, use the Distance Formula.

$$EF = \sqrt{(4 - 8)^2 + (7 - 3)^2} \qquad DF = \sqrt{(4 - 1)^2 + (7 - 3)^2}$$

$$= \sqrt{(-4)^2 + 4^2} \qquad\qquad\quad = \sqrt{3^2 + 4^2}$$

$$= \sqrt{32} \qquad\qquad\qquad\quad\;\; = \sqrt{25}$$

$$= 4\sqrt{2} \text{ units} \qquad\qquad\quad = 5 \text{ units}$$

▸ So, the perimeter is $DE + EF + DF = (7 + 4\sqrt{2} + 5)$, or $12 + 4\sqrt{2}$, units.

STUDENT HELP

▸ **Skills Review**
For help with simplifying radicals, see page 799.

A problem-solving plan can help you organize solutions to geometry problems.

A PROBLEM-SOLVING PLAN

1. Ask yourself what you need to solve the problem. Write a **verbal model** or **draw a sketch** that will help you find what you need to know.

2. **Label known and unknown facts** on or near your sketch.

3. Use labels and facts to **choose related definitions**, **theorems**, **formulas**, or other results you may need.

4. **Reason logically** to link the facts, using a proof or other written argument.

5. Write a **conclusion** that answers the original problem. **Check** that your reasoning is correct.

EXAMPLE 4 *Using the Area of a Rectangle*

SOCCER FIELD You have a part-time job at a school. You need to buy enough grass seed to cover the school's soccer field. The field is 50 yards wide and 100 yards long. The instructions on the seed bags say that one bag will cover 5000 square feet. How many bags do you need?

SOLUTION

Begin by rewriting the dimensions of the field in feet. Multiplying each of the dimensions by 3, you find that the field is 150 feet wide and 300 feet long.

PROBLEM SOLVING STRATEGY

| **VERBAL MODEL** | $\boxed{\text{Area of field}} = \boxed{\text{Bags of seed}} \cdot \boxed{\text{Coverage per bag}}$ |

LABELS

Area of field = $150 \cdot 300$ (square feet)

Bags of seed = n (bags)

Coverage per bag = 5000 (square feet per bag)

REASONING

$150 \cdot 300 = n \cdot 5000$ Write model for area of field.

$\dfrac{150 \cdot 300}{5000} = n$ Divide each side by 5000.

$9 = n$ Simplify.

▶ You need 9 bags of seed.

✓ **UNIT ANALYSIS** You can use *unit analysis* to verify the units of measure.

$$\text{ft}^2 = \text{bags} \cdot \frac{\text{ft}^2}{\text{bag}}$$

EXAMPLE 5 *Using the Area of a Square*

 SWIMMING POOL You are planning a deck along two sides of a pool. The pool measures 18 feet by 12 feet. The deck is to be 8 feet wide. What is the area of the deck?

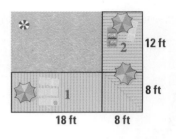

SOLUTION

PROBLEM SOLVING STRATEGY

DRAW A SKETCH From your diagram, you can see that the area of the deck can be represented as the sum of the areas of two rectangles and a square.

VERBAL MODEL

Area of deck	=	Area of rectangle 1	+	Area of rectangle 2	+	Area of square

LABELS

Area of deck $= A$ (square feet)

Area of rectangle 1 $= 8 \cdot 18$ (square feet)

Area of rectangle 2 $= 8 \cdot 12$ (square feet)

Area of square $= 8 \cdot 8$ (square feet)

REASONING

$A = 8 \cdot 18 + 8 \cdot 12 + 8 \cdot 8$ **Write model for deck area.**

$= 304$ **Simplify.**

▶ The area of the deck is 304 square feet.

EXAMPLE 6 *Using the Area of a Triangle*

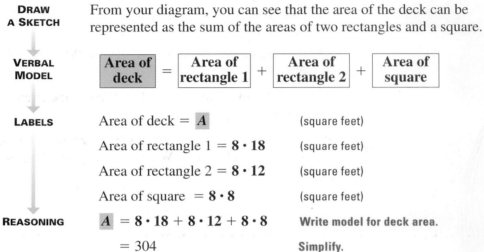 **FLAG DESIGN** You are making a triangular flag with a base of 24 inches and an area of 360 square inches. How long should it be?

24 in.

$A = 360$ in.^{2}

SOLUTION

PROBLEM SOLVING STRATEGY

VERBAL MODEL

Area of flag	$= \frac{1}{2} \cdot$	Base of flag	$\cdot$	Length of flag

LABELS

Area of flag $= \textbf{360}$ (square inches)

Base of flag $= \textbf{24}$ (inches)

Length of flag $= L$ (inches)

REASONING

$360 = \frac{1}{2}(24)L$ **Write model for flag area.**

$360 = 12L$ **Simplify.**

$30 = L$ **Divide each side by 12.**

▶ The flag should be 30 inches long.

GUIDED PRACTICE

Vocabulary Check ✔

Concept Check ✔

Skill Check ✔

1. The perimeter of a circle is called its ___?___.

2. Explain how to find the perimeter of a rectangle.

In Exercises 3–5, find the area of the figure. (Where necessary, use $\pi \approx 3.14$.)

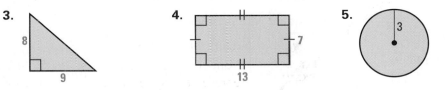

3.

4.

5.

6. The perimeter of a square is 12 meters. What is the length of a side of the square?

7. The radius of a circle is 4 inches. What is the circumference of the circle? (Use $\pi \approx 3.14$.)

8. 🌐 **FENCING** You are putting a fence around a rectangular garden with length 15 feet and width 8 feet. What is the length of the fence that you will need?

PRACTICE AND APPLICATIONS

STUDENT HELP

▶ **Extra Practice**
to help you master
skills is on p. 804.

FINDING PERIMETER, CIRCUMFERENCE, AND AREA Find the perimeter (or circumference) and area of the figure. (Where necessary, use $\pi \approx 3.14$.)

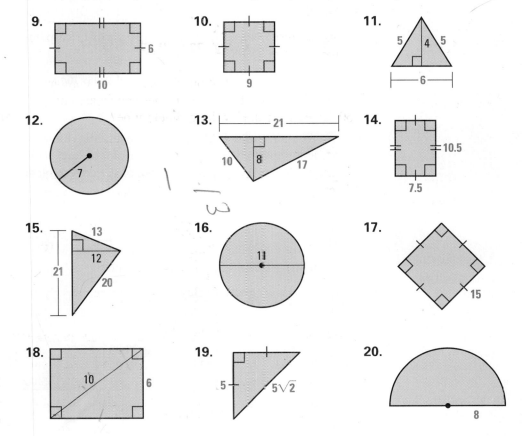

9.

10.

11.

12.

13.

14.

15.

16.

17.

18.

19.

20.

STUDENT HELP

▶ **HOMEWORK HELP**
Example 1: Exs. 9–26
Example 2: Exs. 9–26
Example 3: Exs. 27–33
Example 4: Exs. 34–40
Example 5: Exs. 34–40
Example 6: Exs. 41–48

STUDENT HELP

HOMEWORK HELP
Visit our Web site
www.mcdougallittell.com
for help with problem
solving in Exs. 21–26.

FINDING AREA Find the area of the figure described.

21. Triangle with height 6 cm and base 5 cm

22. Rectangle with length 12 yd and width 9 yd

23. Square with side length 8 ft

24. Circle with radius 10 m (Use $\pi \approx 3.14$.)

25. Square with perimeter 24 m

26. Circle with diameter 100 ft (Use $\pi \approx 3.14$.)

FINDING AREA Find the area of the figure.

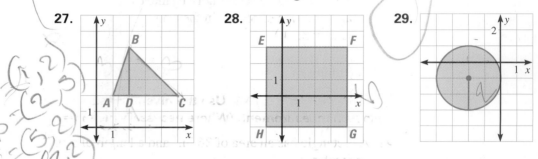

27.

28.

29.

FINDING AREA Draw the figure in a coordinate plane and find its area.

30. Triangle defined by $A(3, 4)$, $B(7, 4)$, and $C(5, 7)$

31. Triangle defined by $R(-2, -3)$, $S(6, -3)$, and $T(5, 4)$

32. Rectangle defined by $L(-2, -4)$, $M(-2, 1)$, $N(7, 1)$, and $P(7, -4)$

33. Square defined by $W(5, 0)$, $X(0, 5)$, $Y(-5, 0)$, and $Z(0, -5)$

34. CARPETING How many square yards of carpet are needed to carpet a room that is 15 feet by 25 feet?

35. WINDOWS A rectangular pane of glass measuring 12 inches by 18 inches is surrounded by a wooden frame that is 2 inches wide. What is the area of the window, including the frame?

36. MILLENNIUM DOME The largest fabric dome in the world, the Millennium Dome covers a circular plot of land with a diameter of 320 meters. What is the circumference of the covered land? What is its area? (Use $\pi \approx 3.14$.)

37. SPREADSHEET Use a spreadsheet to show many different possible values of length and width for a rectangle with an area of 100 m². For each possible rectangle, calculate the perimeter. What are the dimensions of the rectangle with the smallest perimeter?

FOCUS ON APPLICATIONS

MILLENNIUM DOME
Built for the year 2000, this dome in Greenwich, England, is over 50 m tall and is covered by more than 100,000 square meters of fabric.

APPLICATION LINK
www.mcdougallittell.com

	A	B	C	D	E	F	G	H
				Perimeter of Rectangle				
		A	B	C	D	E	F	G	H
1	Length	1.00	2.00	3.00	4.00	5.00	6.00	...
2	Width	100.00	50.00	33.33	25.00	20.00	16.67	...
3	Area	100.00	100.00	100.00	100.00	100.00	100.00	...
4	Perimeter	202.00	104.00	72.67	58.00	50.00	45.33	...
5								

38. 🌐 **CRANBERRY HARVEST** To harvest cranberries, the field is flooded so that the berries float. The berries are gathered with an inflatable boom. What area of cranberries can be gathered into a circular region with a radius of 5.5 meters? (Use $\pi \approx 3.14$.)

39. 🌐 **BICYCLES** How many times does a bicycle tire that has a radius of 21 inches rotate when it travels 420 inches? (Use $\pi \approx 3.14$.)

40. 🌐 **FLYING DISC** A plastic flying disc is circular and has a circular hole in the middle. If the diameter of the outer edge of the ring is 13 inches and the diameter of the inner edge of the ring is 10 inches, what is the area of plastic in the ring? (Use $\pi \approx 3.14$.)

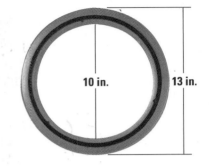

10 in.   13 in.

🧩 **LOGICAL REASONING** Use the given measurements to find the unknown measurement. (Where necessary, use $\pi \approx 3.14$.)

41. A rectangle has an area of 36 in.^{2} and a length of 9 in. Find its perimeter.

42. A square has an area of 10,000 m^2. Find its perimeter.

43. A triangle has an area of 48 ft^2 and a base of 16 ft. Find its height.

44. A triangle has an area of 52 yd^2 and a height of 13 yd. Find its base.

45. A circle has an area of 200π cm^2. Find its radius.

46. A circle has an area of 1 m^2. Find its diameter.

47. A circle has a circumference of 100 yd. Find its area.

48. A right triangle has sides of length 4.5 cm, 6 cm, and 7.5 cm. Find its area.

Test Preparation

49. MULTI-STEP PROBLEM Use the following information.
Earth has a radius of about 3960 miles at the equator. Because there are 5280 feet in one mile, the radius of Earth is about 20,908,800 feet.

a. Suppose you could wrap a cable around Earth to form a circle that is snug against the ground. Find the length of the cable in feet by finding the circumference of Earth. (Assume that Earth is perfectly round. Use $\pi \approx 3.14$.)

b. Suppose you add 6 feet to the cable length in part (a). Use this length as the circumference of a new circle. Find the radius of the larger circle.

c. Use your results from parts (a) and (b) to find how high off of the ground the longer cable would be if it was evenly spaced around Earth.

d. Would the answer to part (c) be different on a planet with a different radius? Explain.

★ Challenge

50. DOUBLING A RECTANGLE'S SIDES The length and width of a rectangle are doubled. How do the perimeter and area of the new rectangle compare with the perimeter and area of the original rectangle? Illustrate your answer.

MIXED REVIEW

SKETCHING FIGURES **Sketch the points, lines, segments, and rays.**
(Review 1.2 for 2.1)

51. Draw opposite rays using the points *A*, *B*, and *C*, with *B* as the initial point for both rays.

52. Draw four noncollinear points, *W*, *X*, *Y*, and *Z*, no three of which are collinear. Then sketch $\overleftrightarrow{XY}$, $\overrightarrow{YW}$, $\overline{XZ}$ and $\overleftrightarrow{ZY}$.

USING ALGEBRA **Plot the points in a coordinate plane and sketch ∠*DEF*. Classify the angle. Write the coordinates of one point in the interior of the angle and one point in the exterior of the angle.** (Review 1.4)

53. *D*(2, −2)
  E(4, −3)
  F(6, −2)

54. *D*(0, 0)
  E(−3, 0)
  F(0, −2)

55. *D*(0, 1)
  E(2, 3)
  F(4, 1)

56. *D*(−3, −2)
  E(3, −4)
  F(1, 3)

FINDING THE MIDPOINT **Find the coordinates of the midpoint of a segment with the given endpoints.** (Review 1.5)

57. *A*(0, 0), *B*(5, 3)

58. *C*(2, −3), *D*(4, 4)

59. *E*(−3, 4), *F*(−2, −1)

60. *G*(−2, 0), *H*(−7, −6)

61. *J*(0, 5), *K*(14, 1)

62. *M*(−44, 9), *N*(6, −7)

QUIZ 3

Self-Test for Lessons 1.6 and 1.7

In Exercises 1–4, find the measure of the angle. (Lesson 1.6)

1. Complement of ∠*A*; *m*∠*A* = 41°

2. Supplement of ∠*B*; *m*∠*B* = 127°

3. Supplement of ∠*C*; *m*∠*C* = 22°

4. Complement of ∠*D*; *m*∠*D* = 35°

5. ∠*A* and ∠*B* are complementary. The measure of ∠*A* is five times the measure of ∠*B*. Find *m*∠*A* and *m*∠*B*. (Lesson 1.6)

In Exercises 6–9, use the given information to find the unknown measurement. (Lesson 1.7)

6. Find the area and circumference of a circle with a radius of 18 meters. (Use $\pi \approx 3.14$.)

7. Find the area of a triangle with a base of 13 inches and a height of 11 inches.

8. Find the area and perimeter of a rectangle with a length of 10 centimeters and a width of 4.6 centimeters.

9. Find the area of a triangle defined by *P*(−3, 4), *Q*(7, 4), and *R*(−1, 12).

10. **WALLPAPER** You are buying rolls of wallpaper to paper the walls of a rectangular room. The room measures 12 feet by 24 feet and the walls are 8 feet high. A roll of wallpaper contains 28 ft². About how many rolls of wallpaper will you need? (Lesson 1.7)

Chapter Summary

WHAT did you learn?

Find and describe patterns. **(1.1)**

Use inductive reasoning. **(1.1)**

Use defined and undefined terms. **(1.2)**

Sketch intersections of lines and planes. **(1.2)**

Use segment postulates and the Distance Formula. **(1.3)**

Use angle postulates and classify angles. **(1.4)**

Bisect a segment and bisect an angle. **(1.5)**

Identify vertical angles, linear pairs, complementary angles, and supplementary angles. **(1.6)**

Find the perimeter, circumference, and area of common plane figures. **(1.7)**

Use a general problem-solving plan. **(1.7)**

WHY did you learn it?

Use a pattern to predict a figure or number in a sequence. **(p. 3)**

Make and verify conjectures such as a conjecture about the frequency of full moons. **(p. 5)**

Understand the basic elements of geometry.

Visualize the basic elements of geometry and the ways they can intersect.

Solve real-life problems, such as finding the distance between two points on a map. **(p. 20)**

Solve problems in geometry and in real life, such as finding the measure of the angle of vision for a horse wearing blinkers. **(p. 27)**

Solve problems in geometry and in real life, such as finding an angle measure of a kite. **(p. 37)**

Find the angle measures of geometric figures and real-life structures, such as intersecting metal supports of a stair railing. **(p. 45)**

To solve problems related to measurement, such as finding the area of a deck for a pool. **(p. 54)**

To solve problems related to mathematics and real life, such as finding the number of bags of grass seed you need for a soccer field. **(p. 53)**

How does Chapter 1 fit into the BIGGER PICTURE of geometry?

In this chapter, you learned a basic reasoning skill—inductive reasoning. You also learned many fundamental terms—*point, line, plane, segment,* and *angle,* to name a few. Added to this were four basic postulates. These building blocks will be used throughout the remainder of this book to develop new terms, postulates, and theorems to explain the geometry of the world around you.

STUDY STRATEGY

How did you use your vocabulary pages?

The definitions of vocabulary terms you made, using the **Study Strategy** on page 2, may resemble this one.

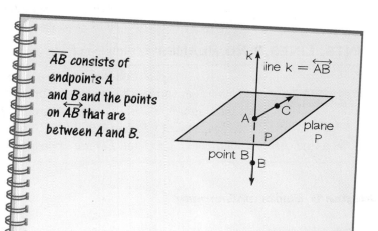

$\overline{AB}$ consists of endpoints A and B and the points on $\overleftrightarrow{AB}$ that are between A and B.

line k = $\overleftrightarrow{AB}$

plane P

point B

Chapter Review

VOCABULARY

- conjecture, p. 4
- inductive reasoning, p. 4
- counterexample, p. 4
- definition, undefined, p. 10
- point, line, plane, p. 10
- collinear, coplanar, p. 10
- line segment, p. 11
- endpoints, p. 11
- ray, p. 11
- initial point, p. 11

- opposite rays, p. 11
- intersect, intersection, p. 12
- postulates, or axioms, p. 17
- coordinate, p. 17
- distance, length, p. 17
- between, p. 18
- Distance Formula, p. 19
- congruent segments, p. 19
- angle, p. 26
- sides, vertex of an angle, p. 26

- congruent angles, p. 26
- measure of an angle, p. 27
- interior of an angle, p. 27
- exterior of an angle, p. 27
- acute, obtuse angles, p. 28
- right, straight angles, p. 28
- adjacent angles, p. 28
- midpoint, p. 34
- bisect, p. 34
- segment bisector, p. 34

- compass, straightedge, p. 34
- construct, construction, p. 34
- Midpoint Formula, p. 35
- angle bisector, p. 36
- vertical angles, p. 44
- linear pair, p. 44
- complementary angles, p. 46
- complement of an angle, p. 46
- supplementary angles, p. 46
- supplement of an angle, p. 46

1.1   PATTERNS AND INDUCTIVE REASONING

Examples on pp. 3–5

EXAMPLE   Make a conjecture based on the results shown.

Conjecture: Given a 3-digit number, form a 6-digit number by repeating the digits. Divide the number by 7, then 11, then 13. The result is the original number.

$$456,456 \div 7 \div 11 \div 13 = 456$$
$$562,562 \div 7 \div 11 \div 13 = 562$$
$$109,109 \div 7 \div 11 \div 13 = 109$$

In Exercises 1–3, describe a pattern in the sequence of numbers.

1. 5, 12, 19, 26, 33, . . .   **2.** 0, 2, 6, 14, 30, . . .   **3.** 4, 12, 36, 108, 324, . . .

4. Sketch the next figure in the pattern.

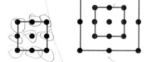

5. Make a conjecture based on the results.

$$4 \cdot 5 \cdot 6 \cdot 7 + 1 = 29 \cdot 29$$
$$5 \cdot 6 \cdot 7 \cdot 8 + 1 = 41 \cdot 41$$
$$6 \cdot 7 \cdot 8 \cdot 9 + 1 = 55 \cdot 55$$

7·8·9·10+1=

6. Show the conjecture is false by finding a counterexample:

Conjecture: *The cube of a number is always greater than the number.*

1.2   POINTS, LINES, AND PLANES

Examples on pp. 10–12

EXAMPLE

C, E, and D are collinear. A, B, C, D, and E are coplanar.
$\overleftrightarrow{CD}$ is a line. $\overline{AB}$ is a segment. $\overrightarrow{EC}$ and $\overrightarrow{ED}$ are opposite rays.

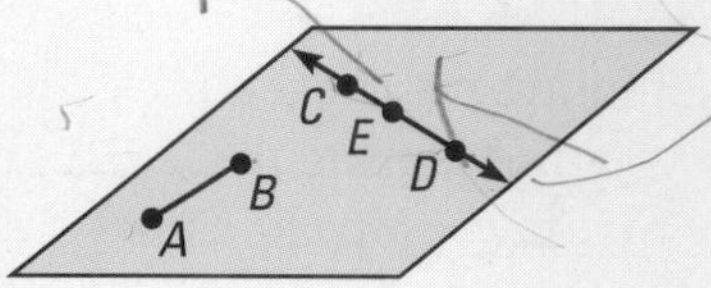

7. Draw five coplanar points, A, B, C, D, and E so that $\overrightarrow{BA}$ and $\overrightarrow{EC}$ are opposite rays, and $\overline{DE}$ intersects $\overleftrightarrow{AC}$ at B.

8. Sketch three planes that do not intersect.

9. Sketch two lines that are not coplanar and do not intersect.

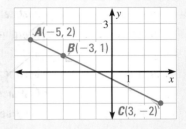

SEGMENTS AND THEIR MEASURES

Examples on pp. 17–20

> **EXAMPLE** B is between A and C, so $AB + BC = AC$.
> Use the Distance Formula to find AB and BC.
>
> $AB = \sqrt{[-3 - (-5)]^2 + (1 - 2)^2} = \sqrt{2^2 + (-1)^2} = \sqrt{5}$
>
> $BC = \sqrt{[3 - (-3)]^2 + (-2 - 1)^2} = \sqrt{6^2 + (-3)^2} = \sqrt{45}$
>
> Because $AB \neq BC$, $\overline{AB}$ and $\overline{BC}$ are *not* congruent segments.

10. Q is between P and S. R is between Q and S. S is between Q and T. $PT = 30$, $QS = 16$, and $PQ = QR = RS$. Find PQ, ST, and RP.

Use the Distance Formula to decide whether $\overline{PQ} \cong \overline{QR}$.

11. $P(-4, 3)$
    $Q(-2, 1)$
    $R(0, -1)$

12. $P(-3, 5)$
    $Q(1, 3)$
    $R(4, 1)$

13. $P(-2, -2)$
    $Q(0, 1)$
    $R(1, 4)$

ANGLES AND THEIR MEASURES

Examples on pp. 26–28

> **EXAMPLE**
>
> $m\angle ACD + m\angle DCB = m\angle ACB$
>
> $\angle ACD$ is an acute angle: $m\angle ACD < 90°$.
>
> $\angle DCB$ is a right angle: $m\angle DCB = 90°$.
>
> $\angle ACB$ is an obtuse angle: $m\angle ACB > 90°$.

Classify the angle as *acute, right, obtuse,* or *straight*. Sketch the angle. Then use a protractor to check your results.

14. $m\angle KLM = 180°$ straight

15. $m\angle A = 150°$ obtuse

16. $m\angle Y = 45°$ Acute

Use the Angle Addition Postulate to find the measure of the unknown angle.

17. $m\angle DEF$

105
obtuse

18. $m\angle HJL$

19. $m\angle QNM$

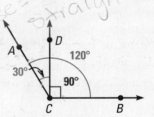

1.5 SEGMENT AND ANGLE BISECTORS

Examples on pp. 35–37

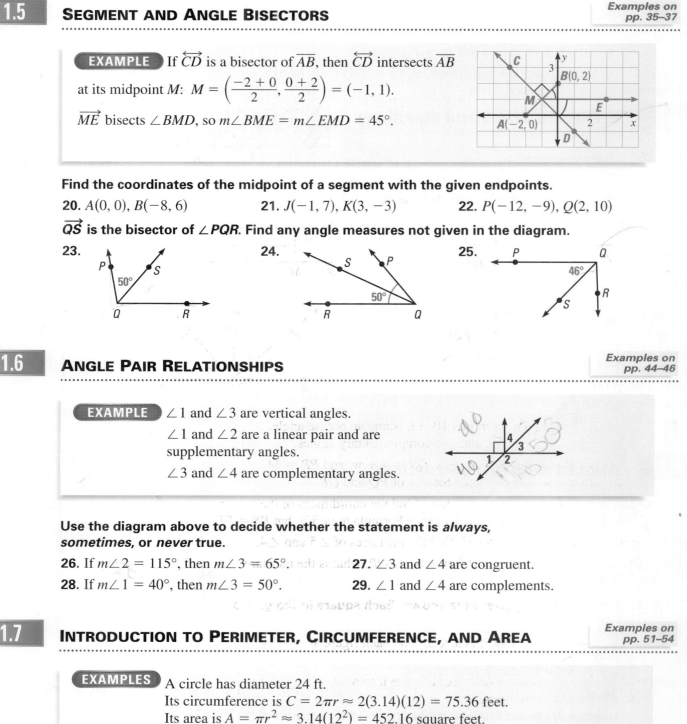

EXAMPLE If $\overleftrightarrow{CD}$ is a bisector of $\overline{AB}$, then $\overleftrightarrow{CD}$ intersects $\overline{AB}$ at its midpoint M: $M = \left(\dfrac{-2 + 0}{2}, \dfrac{0 + 2}{2}\right) = (-1, 1)$.

$\overrightarrow{ME}$ bisects $\angle BMD$, so $m\angle BME = m\angle EMD = 45°$.

Find the coordinates of the midpoint of a segment with the given endpoints.

20. $A(0, 0)$, $B(-8, 6)$ **21.** $J(-1, 7)$, $K(3, -3)$ **22.** $P(-12, -9)$, $Q(2, 10)$

$\overrightarrow{QS}$ **is the bisector of** $\angle PQR$**. Find any angle measures not given in the diagram.**

23.   **24.**   **25.**

1.6 ANGLE PAIR RELATIONSHIPS

Examples on pp. 44–46

EXAMPLE $\angle 1$ and $\angle 3$ are vertical angles.

$\angle 1$ and $\angle 2$ are a linear pair and are supplementary angles.

$\angle 3$ and $\angle 4$ are complementary angles.

Use the diagram above to decide whether the statement is _always_, _sometimes_, or _never_ true.

26. If $m\angle 2 = 115°$, then $m\angle 3 = 65°$.   **27.** $\angle 3$ and $\angle 4$ are congruent.

28. If $m\angle 1 = 40°$, then $m\angle 3 = 50°$.   **29.** $\angle 1$ and $\angle 4$ are complements.

1.7 INTRODUCTION TO PERIMETER, CIRCUMFERENCE, AND AREA

Examples on pp. 51–54

EXAMPLES A circle has diameter 24 ft.

Its circumference is $C = 2\pi r \approx 2(3.14)(12) = 75.36$ feet.

Its area is $A = \pi r^2 \approx 3.14(12^2) = 452.16$ square feet.

Find the perimeter (or circumference) and area of the figure described.

30. Rectangle with length 10 cm and width 4.5 cm

31. Circle with radius 9 in. (Use $\pi \approx 3.14$.)

32. Triangle defined by $A(-6, 0)$, $B(2, 0)$, and $C(-2, -3)$

33. A square garden has sides of length 14 ft. What is its perimeter?

Chapter Test

Use the diagram to name the figures.

1. Three collinear points
2. Four noncoplanar points
3. Two opposite rays
4. Two intersecting lines
5. The intersection of plane *LMN* and plane *QLS*

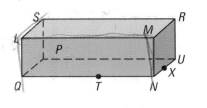

Find the length of the segment.

6. $\overline{MP}$
7. $\overline{SM}$
8. $\overline{NR}$
9. $\overline{MR}$

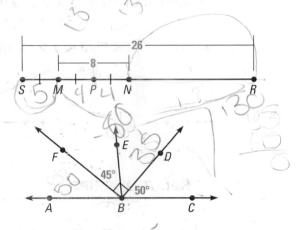

Find the measure of the angle.

10. $\angle DBE$
11. $\angle FBC$
12. $\angle ABF$
13. $\angle DBA$

14. Refer to the diagram for Exercises 10–13. Name an obtuse angle, an acute angle, a right angle, and two complementary angles.

15. *Q* is between *P* and *R*. $PQ = 2w - 3$, $QR = 4 + w$, and $PR = 34$. Find the value of *w*. Then find the lengths of $\overline{PQ}$ and $\overline{QR}$.

16. $\overline{RT}$ has endpoints $R(-3, 8)$ and $T(3, 6)$. Find the coordinates of the midpoint, *S*, of $\overline{RT}$. Then use the Distance Formula to verify that $RS = ST$.

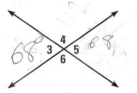

17. Use the diagram. If $m\angle 3 = 68°$, find the measures of $\angle 5$ and $\angle 4$.

18. Suppose $m\angle PQR = 130°$. If $\overrightarrow{QT}$ bisects $\angle PQR$, what is the measure of $\angle PQT$?

The first five figures in a pattern are shown. Each square in the grid is 1 unit × 1 unit.

19. Make a table that shows the distance around each figure at each stage.

20. Describe the pattern of the distances and use it to predict the distance around the figure at stage 20.

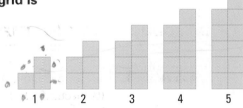

A center pivot irrigation system uses a fixed water supply to water a circular region of a field. The radius of the watering system is 560 feet long. (Use $\pi \approx 3.14$.)

21. If some workers walked around the circumference of the watered region, how far would they have to walk? Round to the nearest foot.

22. Find the area of the region watered. Round to the nearest square foot.

🔵 **TEST-TAKING STRATEGY** Work as quickly as you can through the easier sections, but avoid making careless errors on easy questions.

1. **MULTIPLE CHOICE** What is the next number in the sequence?

   4488; 44,088; 440,088; 4,400,088; . . .

   (A) 400,008   (B) 40,000,088

   (C) 44,000,088   (D) 440,000,088

   (E) 44,000,008

2. **MULTIPLE CHOICE** Which of the following statements is *false*?

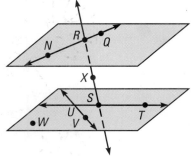

   (A) S, T, V, and W are coplanar.

   (B) X, T, S, and U are coplanar.

   (C) Q, N, and R are collinear.

   (D) S, R, and X are collinear.

   (E) $\overrightarrow{TS}$ and $\overrightarrow{TU}$ are opposite rays.

3. **MULTIPLE CHOICE** Which of the line segments shown in the coordinate plane are congruent?

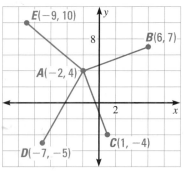

   (A) $\overline{AC}$ and $\overline{AE}$ (B) $\overline{AB}$ and $\overline{AE}$

   (C) $\overline{AD}$ and $\overline{AC}$ (D) $\overline{AD}$ and $\overline{AB}$

   (E) $\overline{AB}$ and $\overline{AC}$

4. **MULTIPLE CHOICE** B is between A and C, D is between B and C, and C is between B and E. $AE = 28$, $BC = 10$, and $AB = DB = DC$. What is the length of $\overline{CE}$?

   (A) 5   (B) 10   (C) 12

   (D) 13   (E) 15

5. **MULTIPLE CHOICE** If $\angle 4$ and $\angle 5$ are complementary and $m\angle 4 = 19°$, find $m\angle 5$.

   (A) 19°   (B) 71°   (C) 109°

   (D) 161°   (E) cannot be determined

6. **MULTIPLE CHOICE** $\angle 1$ and $\angle 2$ in the diagram are ___?___.

   (A) complementary

   (B) supplementary

   (C) congruent

   (D) vertical angles

   (E) a linear pair

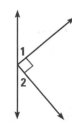

7. **MULTIPLE CHOICE** The midpoint of $\overline{BC}$ is $M(-10, -16)$. One endpoint is $B(-1, 8)$. What are the coordinates of C?

   (A) $(-21, -40)$ (B) $(-20, -40)$

   (C) $(-19, -40)$ (D) $(-21, -24)$

   (E) $(8, 32)$

8. **MULTIPLE CHOICE** If $\overrightarrow{QS}$ bisects $\angle PQR$, find the measure of $\angle PQR$.

   (A) 17°

   (B) 56°

   (C) 21°

   (D) 39°

   (E) 78°

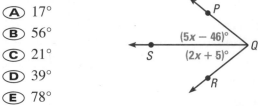

9. **MULTIPLE CHOICE** Two angles are complementary and one angle has a measure that is 9 times the measure of the other angle. What is the angle measure of the larger angle?

   (A) 9°

   (B) 18°

   (C) 81°

   (D) 90°

   (E) 162°

10. QUANTITATIVE COMPARISON Consider the areas of the two triangles that are described below.

COLUMN A	COLUMN B
The area of a triangle defined by $A(-6, 7)$, $B(-6, -1)$, and $C(-3, 2)$	The area of a triangle defined by $D(0, 4)$, $E(6, 4)$, and $F(6, 0)$

Choose the statement that is true.

(A) The quantity in column A is greater.

(B) The quantity in column B is greater.

(C) The two quantities are equal.

(D) The relationship cannot be determined from the information given.

MULTI-STEP PROBLEM In Exercises 11–14, use the figure at the right.

11. Name an angle that is (a) acute, (b) obtuse, (c) straight, and (d) right.

12. Classify each pair of angles as *complementary*, *supplementary*, or *vertical* angles.

    a. $\angle ABS$ and $\angle SBC$

    b. $\angle BAH$ and $\angle GAH$

    c. $\angle BEF$ and $\angle FEM$

    d. $\angle ABS$ and $\angle EBC$

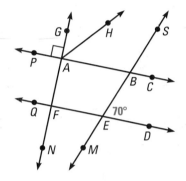

13. If $\overrightarrow{AH}$ bisects $\angle GAB$, find the measures of $\angle GAH$ and $\angle BAH$

14. If $m\angle QFN = x°$, express the measures of $\angle QFA$, $\angle AFE$, and $\angle EFN$ in terms of x.

MULTI-STEP PROBLEM Consider some rectangles with a perimeter of 24 inches.

15. Copy and complete the table below.

Width (in.)	Perimeter (in.)	Length (in.)	Area (in.²)
1	?	?	?
2	?	?	?
3	?	?	?
4	?	?	?
5	?	?	?
6	?	?	?
7	?	?	?

16. Which rectangle in the table has the greatest area?

17. Look at the entries in the table. Describe a pattern in the widths and lengths. Use the pattern to predict the length of a rectangle with a width of 3.5 inches.

18. Make a conjecture about the dimensions of a rectangle with greatest area if the perimeter of the rectangle is known. Describe a way to test your conjecture.

Taxicab Geometry

OBJECTIVE Compare distances in taxicab geometry to distances in Euclidean geometry.

Materials: ruler, graph paper, colored pencils, poster paper

In *taxicab geometry*, distances are measured along paths that are made of horizontal and vertical segments. Diagonal paths are not allowed. This simulates the movement of taxicabs in a city, which can travel only on streets, never through buildings.

FINDING TAXICAB DISTANCES

Follow these steps to learn more about distance in taxicab geometry.

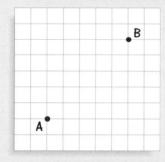
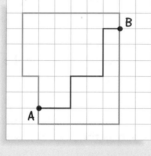
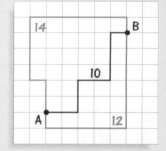

1 Copy points *A* and *B* on a piece of graph paper.

2 Trace paths from *A* to *B* using the grid lines. You may move horizontally and vertically but not diagonally.

3 Calculate the distances covered by your paths.

INVESTIGATION

Repeat Steps 2 and 3 above several times, then answer the exercises.

1. Compare your paths and those of your classmates. Are the distances always the same? What is the length of the shortest possible path from *A* to *B*?

2. The length of the shortest path from *A* to *B* is called the *taxicab distance* from *A* to *B*. Can you find other paths from *A* to *B* that have the same distance?

3. Use the Distance Formula to find the Euclidean distance from *A* to *B*. Which is greater, the taxicab distance from *A* to *B* or the Euclidean distance?

4. On another piece of graph paper, plot a new pair of points. Find the taxicab distance and Euclidean distance for the points. Repeat this for several pairs of points. Write a general statement that compares taxicab distance and Euclidean distance.

5. Write a general formula for the taxicab distance from $A(x_1, y_1)$ to $B(x_2, y_2)$.

TAXICAB CIRCLES

Suppose you are in a city with a square grid and want to find all the places you can reach if you walk 4 blocks along the streets. This forms a figure in taxicab geometry in the same way that a circle is formed in Euclidean geometry.

INVESTIGATION

6. On a piece of graph paper, plot a point $O(0, 0)$. Plot all the points that have a taxicab distance of 4 units from point O. How are the points arranged?

7. To find the circumference of your taxicab circle, imagine that you are walking a shortest taxicab path that passes through all the points you drew in Investigation Exercise 6. Draw one such path. What is its total length? (Remember that all distances in taxicab geometry are horizontal or vertical.)

8. To find the diameter of your taxicab circle, draw a shortest taxicab path that joins two points on the circumference and also passes through the center O. What is its length?

9. In Euclidean geometry, the constant π is defined as the ratio of a circle's circumference to its diameter. If π is defined in the same way in taxicab geometry, does it have a constant value? If so, what is the value?

PRESENT YOUR RESULTS

Gather your work and present it as a poster.

- Include your answers to the Investigation Exercises.

- Include your calculations and drawings you used to find the value of π in taxicab geometry.

- Summarize how taxicab geometry and Euclidean geometry are different.

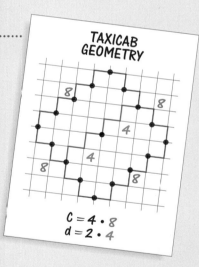

EXTENSIONS

In Euclidean geometry, the points that lie between two points A and B form a segment. In taxicab geometry, what kind of region do the points that lie *between* two points A and B form? (*Hint:* A point C lies *between* A and B in taxicab geometry if this equation is true for the taxicab distances: $AC + CB = AB$.)

In Euclidean geometry, the midpoint of $\overline{AB}$ *bisects* the segment into two parts. All the points in one part are closer to A than to B, and all the points in the other part are closer to B than to A. Is there a set of points that *bisects* the set of points between A and B in taxicab geometry? What does it look like?

REASONING
AND PROOF

▶ *How do robots use reasoning?*

APPLICATION: Robotics

Dante II is a robot that investigates live volcanoes. It processes data collected from sensors to choose a path to follow.

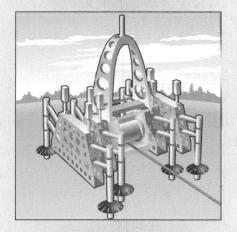

Think & Discuss

1. Dante II has to travel 700 feet to reach the bottom of a crater. Dante II has an average stride of 45 inches. The robot concludes that it will take about 187 steps to reach the bottom. Explain the reasoning Dante II used to reach this conclusion.

2. Instruct Dante II how to calculate the amount of steps needed to reach the bottom of any crater. Start your instructions with "If the distance to the bottom of the crater is x feet and your stride is y inches, then __?__."

Learn More About It

You will explore reasoning in robots in Exercise 49 on p. 93.

APPLICATION LINK Visit www.mcdougallittell.com for more information about reasoning and robots.

Study Guide

PREVIEW

What's the chapter about?

Chapter 2 is about **reasoning** and developing **proof**. Reasoning and proof are important tools used in geometry. In Chapter 2, you'll learn how to

- write a two-column proof and a paragraph proof.

- prove segment and angle relationships.

KEY VOCABULARY

▶ **Review**
- conjecture, p. 4
- inductive reasoning, p. 4
- counterexample, p. 4
- definition, p. 10
- postulates, p. 17

- vertical angles, p. 44
- linear pair, p. 44
▶ **New**
- if-then form, p. 71
- converse, p. 72
- inverse, p. 72

- contrapositive, p. 72
- biconditional statement, p. 80
- theorem, p. 102
- two-column proof, p. 102
- paragraph proof, p. 102

PREPARE

Are you ready for the chapter?

SKILL REVIEW Do these exercises to review skills that you'll apply in this chapter. See the given **reference page** if there is something you don't understand.

STUDENT HELP

▶ **Study Tip**
"Student Help" boxes throughout the chapter give you study tips and tell you where to look for extra help in this book and on the Internet.

Use the diagram below to name the point. (Review Example 1, p. 10)

1. A fourth point coplanar with points A, B, and C

2. A fourth point coplanar with points A, E, and F

3. A fourth point coplanar with points B, C, and G

4. A fourth point coplanar with points D, C, and F

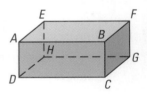

Find the measure of the angle, given that $m\angle 7 = 38°$. (Review Example 2, p. 45)

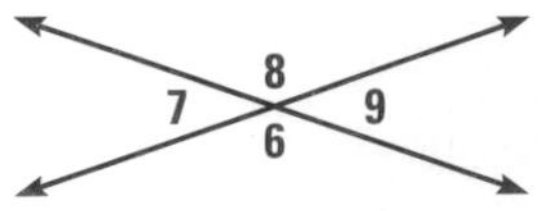

5. $m\angle 6$ 6. $m\angle 8$ 7. $m\angle 9$

STUDY
STRATEGY

Here's a study strategy!

Previewing Lessons

Preview each lesson of the chapter. Knowing what you are about to learn can help you make the mental connections to what you already know. When previewing a lesson, look for the following:

- terms defined in a previous lesson

- properties that have been introduced in a previous lesson

2.1

Conditional Statements

What you should learn

GOAL 1 Recognize and analyze a conditional statement.

GOAL 2 Write postulates about points, lines, and planes using conditional statements.

Why you should learn it

▼ Point, line, and plane postulates help you analyze **real-life** objects, such as the research buggy below and in **Ex. 54**.

Coastal Research Amphibious Buggy

GOAL 1   RECOGNIZING CONDITIONAL STATEMENTS

In this lesson you will study a type of logical statement called a conditional statement. A **conditional statement** has two parts, a *hypothesis* and a *conclusion*. When the statement is written in **if-then form**, the "if" part contains the **hypothesis** and the "then" part contains the **conclusion**. Here is an example:

If **it is noon in Georgia**, then **it is 9 A.M. in California**.

Hypothesis   Conclusion

EXAMPLE 1   *Rewriting in If-Then Form*

Rewrite the conditional statement in *if-then form*.

a. Two points are collinear if they lie on the same line.

b. All sharks have a boneless skeleton.

c. A number divisible by 9 is also divisible by 3.

SOLUTION

a. If two points lie on the same line, then they are collinear.

b. If a fish is a shark, then it has a boneless skeleton.

c. If a number is divisible by 9, then it is divisible by 3.

· · · · · · · · · ·

Conditional statements can be either true or false. To show that a conditional statement is true, you must present an argument that the conclusion follows for *all* cases that fulfill the hypothesis. To show that a conditional statement is false, describe a single counterexample that shows the statement is not always true.

EXAMPLE 2   *Writing a Counterexample*

Write a counterexample to show that the following conditional statement is false.

If $x^2 = 16$, then $x = 4$.

SOLUTION

As a counterexample, let $x = -4$. The hypothesis is true, because $(-4)^2 = 16$. However, the conclusion is false. This implies that the given conditional statement is false.

The **converse** of a conditional statement is formed by switching the hypothesis and conclusion. Here is an example.

Statement: If you see lightning, then you hear thunder.

Converse: If you hear thunder, then you see lightning.

EXAMPLE 3 *Writing the Converse of a Conditional Statement*

STUDENT HELP

INTERNET

HOMEWORK HELP
Visit our Web site
www.mcdougallittell.com
for extra examples.

Write the converse of the following conditional statement.

Statement: If two segments are congruent, then they have the same length.

SOLUTION

Converse: If two segments have the same length, then they are congruent.

· · · · · · · · · ·

A statement can be altered by **negation,** that is, by writing the negative of the statement. Here are some examples.

STATEMENT	NEGATION
$m\angle A = 30°$	$m\angle A \neq 30°$
$\angle A$ is acute.	$\angle A$ is not acute.

When you negate the hypothesis and conclusion of a conditional statement, you form the **inverse.** When you negate the hypothesis and conclusion of the converse of a conditional statement, you form the **contrapositive.**

Original	If $m\angle A = 30°$, then $\angle A$ is acute.	
Inverse	If $m\angle A \neq 30°$, then $\angle A$ is not acute.	**Both false** / **Both true**
Converse	If $\angle A$ is acute, then $m\angle A = 30°$.	
Contrapositive	If $\angle A$ is not acute, then $m\angle A \neq 30°$.	

When two statements are both true or both false, they are called **equivalent statements.** A conditional statement is equivalent to its contrapositive. Similarly, the inverse and converse of any conditional statement are equivalent. This is shown in the table above.

EXAMPLE 4 *Writing an Inverse, Converse, and Contrapositive*

FOCUS ON APPLICATIONS

REAL LIFE

CROCUS There are
some exceptions to
the statement in Example 4.
For instance, crocuses can
bloom when snow is on
the ground.

Write the (**a**) inverse, (**b**) converse, and (**c**) contrapositive of the statement.

If there is snow on the ground, then flowers are not in bloom.

SOLUTION

a. Inverse: If there is no snow on the ground, then flowers are in bloom.

b. Converse: If flowers are not in bloom, then there is snow on the ground.

c. Contrapositive: If flowers are in bloom, then there is no snow on the ground.

GOAL 2 USING POINT, LINE, AND PLANE POSTULATES

In Chapter 1, you studied four postulates.

Ruler Postulate	(Lesson 1.3, page 17)
Segment Addition Postulate	(Lesson 1.3, page 18)
Protractor Postulate	(Lesson 1.4, page 27)
Angle Addition Postulate	(Lesson 1.4, page 27)

Remember that postulates are assumed to be true—they form the foundation on which other statements (called *theorems*) are built.

STUDENT HELP
▶ **Study Tip** There is a list of all the postulates in this course at the end of the book beginning on page 827.

POINT, LINE, AND PLANE POSTULATES

POSTULATE 5   Through any two points there exists exactly one line.

POSTULATE 6   A line contains at least two points.

POSTULATE 7   If two lines intersect, then their intersection is exactly one point.

POSTULATE 8   Through any three noncollinear points there exists exactly one plane.

POSTULATE 9   A plane contains at least three noncollinear points.

POSTULATE 10 If two points lie in a plane, then the line containing them lies in the plane.

POSTULATE 11 If two planes intersect, then their intersection is a line.

EXAMPLE 5 *Identifying Postulates*

Logical Reasoning

Use the diagram at the right to give examples of Postulates 5 through 11.

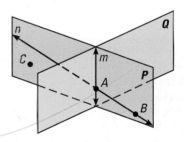

SOLUTION

a. Postulate 5: There is exactly one line (line *n*) that passes through the points *A* and *B*.

b. Postulate 6: Line *n* contains at least two points. For instance, line *n* contains the points *A* and *B*.

c. Postulate 7: Lines *m* and *n* intersect at point *A*.

d. Postulate 8: Plane *P* passes through the noncollinear points *A, B,* and *C*.

e. Postulate 9: Plane *P* contains at least three noncollinear points, *A, B,* and *C*.

f. Postulate 10: Points *A* and *B* lie in plane *P*. So, line *n*, which contains points *A* and *B*, also lies in plane *P*.

g. Postulate 11: Planes *P* and *Q* intersect. So, they intersect in a line, labeled in the diagram as line *m*.

2.1 Conditional Statements **73**

EXAMPLE 6 *Rewriting a Postulate*

a. Rewrite Postulate 5 in if-then form.

b. Write the inverse, converse, and contrapositive of Postulate 5.

SOLUTION

a. Postulate 5 can be rewritten in if-then form as follows:

> If two points are distinct, then there is exactly one line that passes through them.

b. Inverse: If two points are not distinct, then it is not true that there is exactly one line that passes through them.

Converse: If exactly one line passes through two points, then the two points are distinct.

Contrapositive: If it is not true that exactly one line passes through two points, then the two points are not distinct.

Logical Reasoning

EXAMPLE 7 *Using Postulates and Counterexamples*

Decide whether the statement is *true* or *false*. If it is false, give a counterexample.

a. A line can be in more than one plane.

b. Four noncollinear points are always coplanar.

c. Two nonintersecting lines can be noncoplanar.

SOLUTION

a. In the diagram at the right, line *k* is in plane *S* and line *k* is in plane *T*.

So, it is *true* that a line can be in more than one plane.

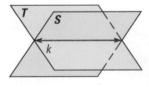

b. Consider the points *A*, *B*, *C*, and *D* at the right. The points *A*, *B*, and *C* lie in a plane, but there is no plane that contains all four points.

So, as shown in the counterexample at the right, it is *false* that four noncollinear points are always coplanar.

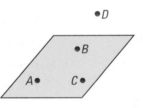

c. In the diagram at the right, line *m* and line *n* are nonintersecting and are also noncoplanar.

So, it is *true* that two nonintersecting lines can be noncoplanar.

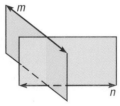

STUDENT HELP

↳ **Study Tip**
A box can be used to help visualize points and lines in space. For instance, the diagram shows that $\overleftrightarrow{AE}$ and $\overleftrightarrow{DC}$ are noncoplanar.

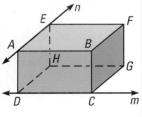

GUIDED PRACTICE

Vocabulary Check ✓

1. The ___?___ of a conditional statement is found by switching the hypothesis and conclusion.

Concept Check ✓

2. State the postulate described in each diagram.

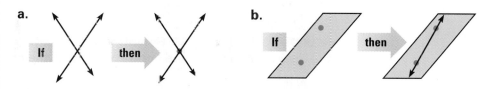

a. If then

b. If then

Skill Check ✓

3. Write the hypothesis and conclusion of the statement, "If the dew point equals the air temperature, then it will rain."

In Exercises 4 and 5, write the statement in if-then form.

4. When threatened, the African ball python protects itself by coiling into a ball with its head in the middle.

5. The measure of a right angle is 90°.

6. Write the inverse, converse, and contrapositive of the conditional statement, "If a cactus is of the *cereus* variety, then its flowers open at night."

Decide whether the statement is *true* or *false*. Make a sketch to help you decide.

7. Through three noncollinear points there exists exactly one line.

8. If a line and a plane intersect, and the line does not lie in the plane, then their intersection is a point.

PRACTICE AND APPLICATIONS

STUDENT HELP

► **Extra Practice**
to help you master
skills is on p. 805.

REWRITING STATEMENTS **Rewrite the conditional statement in if-then form.**

9. An object weighs one ton if it weighs 2000 pounds.

10. An object weighs 16 ounces if it weighs one pound.

11. Three points are collinear if they lie on the same line.

12. Blue trunkfish live in the waters of a coral reef.

13. Hagfish live in salt water.

STUDENT HELP

► HOMEWORK HELP
Example 1: Exs. 9–13
Example 2: Exs. 14–17
Example 3: Exs. 18–21
Example 4: Exs. 46–52
Example 5: Exs. 25–34
Example 6: Exs. 22–24
Example 7: Exs. 35–38

ANALYZING STATEMENTS **Decide whether the statement is *true* or *false*. If false, provide a counterexample.**

14. A point may lie in more than one plane.

15. If x^4 equals 81, then x must equal 3.

16. If it is snowing, then the temperature is below freezing.

17. If four points are collinear, then they are coplanar.

WRITING CONVERSES Write the converse of the statement.

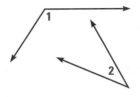

18. If ∠1 measures 123°, then ∠1 is obtuse.

19. If ∠2 measures 38°, then ∠2 is acute.

20. I will go to the mall if it is not raining.

21. I will go to the movies if it is raining.

REWRITING POSTULATES Rewrite the postulate in if-then form. Then write the inverse, converse, and contrapositive of the conditional statement.

22. A line contains at least two points.

23. Through any three noncollinear points there exists exactly one plane.

24. A plane contains at least three noncollinear points.

ILLUSTRATING POSTULATES Fill in the blank. Then draw a sketch that helps illustrate your answer.

25. If two lines intersect, then their intersection is ___?___ point(s).

26. Through any ___?___ points there exists exactly one line.

27. If two points lie in a plane, then the ___?___ containing them lies in the plane.

28. If two planes intersect, then their intersection is ___?___.

LINKING POSTULATES Use the diagram to state the postulate(s) that verifies the truth of the statement.

29. The points *U* and *T* lie on line *ℓ*.

30. Line *ℓ* contains points *U* and *T*.

31. The points *W*, *S*, and *T* lie in plane *A*.

32. The points *S* and *T* lie in plane *A*. Therefore, line *m* lies in plane *A*.

33. The planes *A* and *B* intersect in line *ℓ*.

34. Lines *m* and *ℓ* intersect at point *T*.

USING POSTULATES In Exercises 35–38, state the postulate that shows that the statement is false.

35. A line contains only one point.

36. Two planes intersect in exactly one point.

37. Three points, *A*, *B*, and *C*, are noncollinear, and two planes, *M* and *N*, each contain points *A*, *B*, and *C*.

38. Two points, *P* and *Q*, are collinear and two different lines, $\overleftrightarrow{RS}$ and $\overleftrightarrow{XY}$, each pass through points *P* and *Q*.

39. *Writing* Give an example of a true conditional statement with a true converse.

POINTS AND LINES IN SPACE Think of the intersection of the ceiling and the front wall of your classroom as line *k*. Think of the center of the floor as point *A* and the center of the ceiling as point *B*.

40. Is there more than one line that contains both points *A* and *B*?

41. Is there more than one plane that contains both points *A* and *B*?

42. Is there a plane that contains line *k* and point *A*?

43. Is there a plane that contains points *A*, *B*, and a point on the front wall?

(xy) USING ALGEBRA Find the inverse, converse, and contrapositive of the statement.

44. If $x = y$, then $5x = 5y$.

45. $6x - 6 = x + 14$ if $x = 4$.

QUOTES OF WISDOM Rewrite the statement in if-then form. Then (a) determine the hypothesis and conclusion, and (b) find the inverse of the conditional statement.

46. "If you tell the truth, you don't have to remember anything."   — Mark Twain

47. "One can never consent to creep when one feels the impulse to soar."
                                                                    — Helen Keller

48. "Freedom is not worth having if it does not include the freedom to make mistakes."   — Mahatma Ghandi

49. "Early to bed and early to rise, makes a man healthy, wealthy, and wise."
                                                                    — Benjamin Franklin

ADVERTISING In Exercises 50–52, use the following advertising slogan: "You want a great selection of used cars? Come and see Bargain Bob's Used Cars!"

50. Write the slogan in if-then form. What are the hypothesis and conclusion of the conditional statement?

51. Write the inverse, converse, and contrapositive of the conditional statement.

52. *Writing* Find a real-life advertisement or slogan similar to the one given. Then repeat Exercises 50 and 51 using the advertisement or slogan.

53. **TECHNOLOGY** Use geometry software to draw a segment with endpoints *A* and *C*. Draw a third point *B* not on $\overline{AC}$. Measure $\overline{AB}$, $\overline{BC}$, and $\overline{AC}$. Move *B* closer to $\overline{AC}$ and observe the measures of $\overline{AB}$, $\overline{BC}$, and $\overline{AC}$.

54. **RESEARCH BUGGY** The diagram at the right shows the 35 foot tall Coastal Research Amphibious Buggy, also known as CRAB. This vehicle moves along the ocean floor collecting data that are used to make an accurate map of the ocean floor. Using the postulates you have learned, make a conjecture about why the CRAB was built with three legs instead of four.

55. MULTIPLE CHOICE Use the conditional statement "If the measure of an angle is 44°, then the angle is acute" to decide which of the following are true.

   I. The statement is true.
   II. The converse of the statement is true.
   III. The contrapositive of the statement is true.

  Ⓐ I only   **Ⓑ** II only   **Ⓒ** I and II   **Ⓓ** I and III   **Ⓔ** I, II, and III

56. MULTIPLE CHOICE Which one of the following statements is *not* true?

  Ⓐ If $x = 2$, then $x^2 = 4$.

  Ⓑ If $x = -2$, then $x^2 = 4$.

  Ⓒ If $x^3 = -8$, then $x = -2$.

  Ⓓ If $x^2 = 4$, then $x = 2$.

  Ⓔ If $x = -2$, then $x^3 = -8$.

★ **Challenge**

MAKING A CONJECTURE **Sketch a line *k* and a point *P* not on line *k*. Make a conjecture about how many planes can be drawn through line *k* and point *P*, and then answer the following questions.**

57. Which postulate allows you to state that there are two points, R and S, on line k?

58. Which postulate allows you to conclude that exactly one plane X can be drawn to contain points P, R, and S?

59. Which postulate guarantees that line k is contained in plane X?

60. Was your conjecture correct?

EXTRA CHALLENGE
www.mcdougallittell.com

MIXED REVIEW

DRAWING ANGLES **Plot the points in a coordinate plane. Then classify** $\angle ABC$. **(Review 1.4 for 2.2)**

61. $A(0, 7), B(2, 2), C(6, -1)$ **62.** $A(-1, 0), B(-6, 4), C(-6, -1)$

63. $A(1, 3), B(1, -5), C(-5, -5)$ **64.** $A(-3, -1), B(2, 5), C(3, -2)$

FINDING THE MIDPOINT **Find the coordinates of the midpoint of the segment joining the two points.** **(Review 1.5)**

65. $A(-2, 8), B(4, -12)$ **66.** $A(8, 8), B(-6, 1)$

67. $A(-7, -4), B(4, 7)$ **68.** $A(0, -9), B(-8, 5)$

69. $A(1, 4), B(11, -6)$ **70.** $A(-10, -10), B(2, 12)$

FINDING PERIMETER AND AREA **Find the area and perimeter (or circumference) of the figure described. (Use $\pi \approx 3.14$ when necessary.)** **(Review 1.7 for 2.2)**

71. circle, radius = 6 m   **72.** square, side = 11 cm

73. square, side = 38.75 mm   **74.** circle, diameter = 23 ft

2.2

Definitions and Biconditional Statements

What you should learn

GOAL 1 Recognize and use definitions.

GOAL 2 Recognize and use biconditional statements.

Why you should learn it

▼ You can use biconditional statements to help analyze geographic relations, such as whether three cities in Florida lie on the same line, as in **Ex. 50**.

GOAL 1 RECOGNIZING AND USING DEFINITIONS

In Lesson 1.2 you learned that a *definition* uses known words to describe a new word. Here are two examples.

Two lines are called **perpendicular lines** if they intersect to form a right angle. A **line perpendicular to a plane** is a line that intersects the plane in a point and is perpendicular to every line in the plane that intersects it. The symbol ⊥ is read as "is perpendicular to."

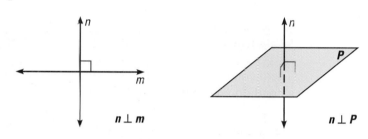

All definitions can be interpreted "forward" and "backward." For instance, the definition of perpendicular lines means (1) if two lines are perpendicular, then they intersect to form a right angle, *and* (2) if two lines intersect to form a right angle, then they are perpendicular.

EXAMPLE 1 *Using Definitions*

Decide whether each statement about the diagram is true. Explain your answer using the definitions you have learned.

  a. Points D, X, and B are collinear.

  b. $\overleftrightarrow{AC}$ is perpendicular to $\overleftrightarrow{DB}$.

  c. $\angle AXB$ is adjacent to $\angle CXD$.

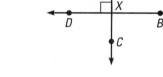

SOLUTION

  a. This statement is true. Two or more points are *collinear* if they lie on the same line. The points D, X, and B all lie on line $\overleftrightarrow{DB}$ so they are collinear.

  b. This statement is true. The right angle symbol in the diagram indicates that the lines $\overleftrightarrow{AC}$ and $\overleftrightarrow{DB}$ intersect to form a right angle. So, the lines are perpendicular.

  c. This statement is false. By definition, adjacent angles must share a common side. Because $\angle AXB$ and $\angle CXD$ do not share a common side, they are not adjacent.

STUDENT HELP

→ **Study Tip**
When a conditional statement contains the word "if," the hypothesis does not always follow the "if." This is shown in the "only-if" statement at the right.

GOAL 2 **USING BICONDITIONAL STATEMENTS**

Conditional statements are not always written in if-then form. Another common form of a conditional statement is *only-if* form. Here is an example.

It is Saturday, only if **I am working at the restaurant**.

⎵ Hypothesis ⎵ ⎵ Conclusion ⎵

You can rewrite this conditional statement in if-then form as follows:

If **it is Saturday**, then **I am working at the restaurant**.

A **biconditional statement** is a statement that contains the phrase "if and only if." Writing a biconditional statement is equivalent to writing a conditional statement *and* its converse.

EXAMPLE 2 *Rewriting a Biconditional Statement*

The biconditional statement below can be rewritten as a conditional statement and its converse.

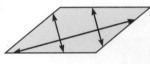

   Three lines are coplanar if and only if they lie in the same plane.

Conditional statement: If three lines are coplanar, then they lie in the same plane.

Converse: If three lines lie in the same plane, then they are coplanar.

· · · · · · · · · ·

A biconditional statement can be either true or false. To be true, *both* the conditional statement and its converse must be true. This means that a true biconditional statement is true both "forward" and "backward." All definitions can be written as true biconditional statements.

EXAMPLE 3 *Analyzing a Biconditional Statement*

Using Algebra

Consider the following statement: $x = 3$ if and only if $x^2 = 9$.

   a. Is this a biconditional statement?

   b. Is the statement true?

SOLUTION

   a. The statement is biconditional because it contains "if and only if."

   b. The statement can be rewritten as the following statement and its converse.

   Conditional statement: If $x = 3$, then $x^2 = 9$.

   Converse: If $x^2 = 9$, then $x = 3$.

   ▶ The first of these statements is true, but the second is false.
   So, the biconditional statement is false.

EXAMPLE 4 *Writing a Biconditional Statement*

Each of the following statements is true. Write the converse of each statement and decide whether the converse is *true* or *false*. If the converse is true, combine it with the original statement to form a true biconditional statement. If the converse is false, state a counterexample.

a. If two points lie in a plane, then the line containing them lies in the plane.

b. If a number ends in 0, then the number is divisible by 5.

SOLUTION

a. Converse: If a line containing two points lies in a plane, then the points lie in the plane.

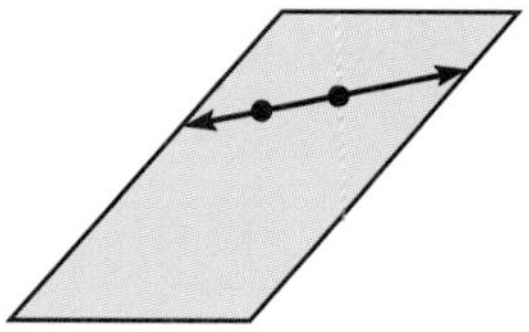

The converse is true, as shown in the diagram. So, it can be combined with the original statement to form the true biconditional statement written below.

Biconditional statement: Two points lie in a plane if and only if the line containing them lies in the plane.

b. Converse: If a number is divisible by 5, then the number ends in 0.

The converse is false. As a counterexample, consider the number 15. It is divisible by 5, but it does not end in 0, as shown at the right.

$$10 \div 5 = 2$$
$$\blacktriangleright 15 \div 5 = 3$$
$$20 \div 5 = 4$$

· · · · · · · · · ·

Knowing how to use true biconditional statements is an important tool for reasoning in geometry. For instance, if you can write a true biconditional statement, then you can use the conditional statement or the converse to justify an argument.

EXAMPLE 5 *Writing a Postulate as a Biconditional*

The second part of the Segment Addition Postulate is the converse of the first part. Combine the statements to form a true biconditional statement.

SOLUTION

The first part of the Segment Addition Postulate can be written as follows:

If B lies between points A and C, then $AB + BC = AC$.

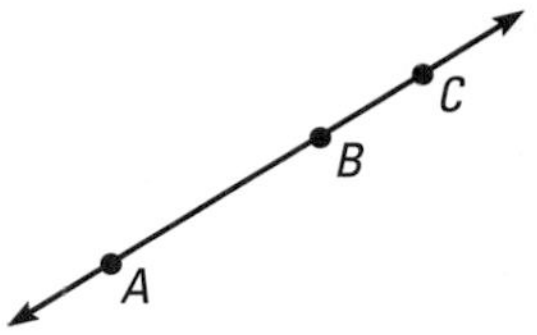

The converse of this is as follows:

If $AB + BC = AC$, then B lies between A and C.

Combining these statements produces the following true biconditional statement:

Point B lies between points A and C if and only if $AB + BC = AC$.

GUIDED PRACTICE

Vocabulary Check ✔   1. Describe in your own words what a *true biconditional statement* is.

Concept Check ✔   2. **ERROR ANALYSIS** What is wrong with Jared's argument below?

The statements "I eat cereal only if it is morning" and "If I eat cereal, then it is morning" are not equivalent.

Skill Check ✔   **Tell whether the statement is a biconditional.**

3. I will work after school only if I have the time.

4. An angle is called a right angle if and only if it measures 90°.

5. Two segments are congruent if and only if they have the same length.

Rewrite the biconditional statement as a conditional statement and its converse.

6. The ceiling fan runs if and only if the light switch is on.

7. You scored a touchdown if and only if the football crossed the goal line.

8. The expression $3x + 4$ is equal to 10 if and only if x is 2.

🌐 **WINDOWS** **Decide whether the statement about the window shown is true. Explain your answer using the definitions you have learned.**

9. The points D, E, and F are collinear.

10. $m\angle CBA = 90°$

11. $\angle DBA$ and $\angle EBC$ are not complementary.

12. $\overline{DE} \perp \overline{AC}$

PRACTICE AND APPLICATIONS

STUDENT HELP

▶ **Extra Practice**
to help you master
skills is on p. 805.

PERPENDICULAR LINES **Use the diagram to determine whether the statement is *true* or *false*.**

13. Points A, F, and G are collinear.

14. $\angle DCJ$ and $\angle DCH$ are supplementary.

15. $\overline{DC}$ is perpendicular to line ℓ.

16. $\overline{FB}$ is perpendicular to line n.

17. $\angle FBJ$ and $\angle JBA$ are complementary.

18. Line m bisects $\angle JCH$.

19. $\angle ABJ$ and $\angle DCH$ are supplementary.

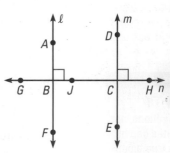

STUDENT HELP

→ HOMEWORK HELP
Example 1: Exs. 13–19
Example 2: Exs. 20–23
Example 3: Exs. 28–31
Example 4: Exs. 32–37
Example 5: Exs. 44–46

BICONDITIONAL STATEMENTS Rewrite the biconditional statement as a conditional statement and its converse.

20. Two angles are congruent if and only if they have the same measure.

21. A ray bisects an angle if and only if it divides the angle into two congruent angles.

22. Two lines are perpendicular if and only if they intersect to form right angles.

23. A point is a midpoint of a segment if and only if it divides the segment into two congruent segments.

FINDING COUNTEREXAMPLES Give a counterexample that demonstrates that the converse of the statement is false.

24. If an angle measures 94°, then it is obtuse.

25. If two angles measure 42° and 48°, then they are complementary.

26. If Terry lives in Tampa, then she lives in Florida.

27. If a polygon is a square, then it has four sides.

ANALYZING BICONDITIONAL STATEMENTS Determine whether the biconditional statement about the diagram is *true* or *false*. If false, provide a counterexample.

28. $\overrightarrow{SR}$ is perpendicular to $\overline{QR}$ if and only if $\angle SRQ$ measures 90°.

29. *PQ* and *PS* are equal if and only if *PQ* and *PS* are both 8 centimeters.

30. $\angle PQR$ and $\angle QRS$ are supplementary if and only if $m\angle PQR = m\angle QRS = 90°$.

31. $\angle PSR$ measures 90° if and only if $\angle PSR$ is a right angle.

FOCUS ON APPLICATIONS

REWRITING STATEMENTS Rewrite the true statement in if-then form and write the converse. If the converse is true, combine it with the if-then statement to form a true biconditional statement. If the converse is false, provide a counterexample.

32. Adjacent angles share a common side.

33. Two circles have the same circumference if they have the same diameter.

34. The perimeter of a triangle is the sum of the lengths of its sides.

35. All leopards have spots.

36. Panthers live in the forest.

37. A leopard is a snow leopard if the leopard has pale gray fur.

SNOW LEOPARDS
The pale coat of the snow leopard, as mentioned in Ex. 37, allows the animal to blend in with the snow 3960 meters (13,000 feet) high in the mountains of Central Asia.

USING ALGEBRA Determine whether the statement can be combined with its converse to form a true biconditional.

38. If $3u + 2 = u + 12$, then $u = 5$.   **39.** If $v = 1$, then $9v - 4v = 2v + 3v$.

40. If $w^2 - 10 = w + 2$, then $w = 4$.   **41.** If $x^3 - 27 = 0$, then $x = 3$.

42. If $y = -3$, then $y^2 = 9$.   **43.** If $z = 3$, then $7 + 18z = 5z + 7 + 13z$.

44. REWRITING A POSTULATE Write the converse of the Angle Addition Postulate and decide whether the converse is *true* or *false*. If true, write the postulate as a true biconditional. If false, provide a counterexample.

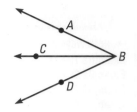

Angle Addition Postulate: If C is in the interior of $\angle ABD$, then $m\angle ABC + m\angle CBD = m\angle ABD$.

45. *Writing* Give an example of a true biconditional statement.

46. 🌐 **MUSICAL GROUPS** The table shows four different groups, along with the number of instrumentalists in each group. Write your own definitions of the musical groups and verify that they are true biconditional statements by writing each definition "forward" and "backward." The first one is started for you.

> **Sample**: A musical group is a *piano trio* if and only if it contains exactly one pianist, one violinist, and one cellist.

Musical group	Pianist	Violinist	Cellist	Violist
Piano trio	1	1	1	—
String quartet	—	2	1	1
String quintet	—	2	1	2
Piano quintet	1	2	1	1

🔺 **TECHNOLOGY** In Exercises 47–49, use geometry software to complete the statement.

47. If the sides of a square are doubled, then the area is ____?____.

48. If the sides of a square are doubled, then the perimeter is ____?____.

49. Decide whether the statements in Exercises 47 and 48 can be written as true biconditionals. If not, provide a counterexample.

50. 🌐 **AIR DISTANCES** The air distance between Jacksonville, Florida, and Merritt Island, Florida, is 148 miles and the air distance between Merritt Island and Fort Pierce, Florida, is 70 miles. Given that the air distance between Jacksonville and Fort Pierce is 218 miles, does Merritt Island fall on the line connecting Jacksonville and Fort Pierce?

🌐 **WINDS AT SEA** Use the portion of the Beaufort wind scale table shown to determine whether the biconditional statement is *true* or *false*. If false, provide a counterexample.

51. A storm is a hurricane if and only if the winds of the storm measure 64 knots or greater.

52. Winds at sea are classified as a strong gale if and only if the winds measure 34–40 knots.

53. Winds are classified as 10 on the Beaufort scale if and only if the winds measure 41–55 knots.

Beaufort Wind Scale for Open Sea		
Number	Knots	Description
8	34–40	gale winds
9	41–47	strong gale
10	48–55	storm
11	56–63	violent storm
12	64+	hurricane

FOCUS ON APPLICATIONS

REAL LIFE **WINDS AT SEA** Along with wind speed, sailors need to know the direction of the wind. Flags, also known as telltales, help sailors determine wind direction.

🌐 **APPLICATION LINK** www.mcdougallittell.com

54. MULTIPLE CHOICE Which one of the following statements cannot be written as a true biconditional statement?

   Ⓐ Any angle that measures between 90° and 180° is obtuse.

   Ⓑ $2x - 5 = x + 1$ only if $x = 6$.

   Ⓒ Any angle that measures between 0° and 90° is acute.

   Ⓓ If two angles measure 110° and 70°, then they are supplementary.

   Ⓔ If the sum of the measures of two angles equals 180°, then they are supplementary.

55. MULTIPLE CHOICE Which of the following statements about the conditional statement "If two lines intersect to form a right angle, then they are perpendicular" is true?

  I. The converse is true.
  II. The statement can be written as a true biconditional.
  III. The statement is false.

   Ⓐ I only   Ⓑ I and II only   Ⓒ II and III only
   Ⓓ III only   Ⓔ I, II, and III

★ **Challenge**

WRITING STATEMENTS In Exercises 56 and 57, determine (a) whether the contrapositive of the true statement is *true* or *false* and (b) whether the true statement can be written as a true biconditional.

56. If I am in Des Moines, then I am in the capital of Iowa.

57. If two angles measure 10° and 80°, then they are complementary.

58. 🧩 **LOGICAL REASONING** You are given that the contrapositive of a statement is true. Will that help you determine whether the statement can be written as a true biconditional? Explain. (*Hint:* Use your results from Exercises 56 and 57.)

EXTRA CHALLENGE
www.mcdougallittell.com

MIXED REVIEW

STUDYING ANGLES Find the measures of a complement and a supplement of the angle. (Review 1.6 for 2.3)

59. 87°   **60.** 73°   **61.** 14°   **62.** 29°

FINDING PERIMETER AND AREA Find the area and perimeter, or circumference of the figure described. (Use $\pi \approx 3.14$ when necessary.) (Review 1.7 for 2.3)

63. rectangle: $w = 3$ ft, $l = 12$ ft   **64.** rectangle: $w = 7$ cm, $l = 10$ cm

65. circle: $r = 8$ in.   **66.** square: $s = 6$ m

CONDITIONAL STATEMENTS Write the converse of the statement. (Review 2.1 for 2.3)

67. If the sides of a rectangle are all congruent, then the rectangle is a square.

68. If $8x + 1 = 3x + 16$, then $x = 3$.

ACTIVITY 2.3

Developing Concepts

Logic Puzzle

▶ **QUESTION** How can deductive reasoning be used to solve a logic puzzle?

▶ **EXPLORING THE CONCEPT**

Using the clues below, determine the favorite hobbies and hometowns of five students: Maynard, Tamara, Dave, Marie, and Brad. They live in Hart's Location, Grand Rapids, Stockton, Ravenna, and Springdale. Their favorite hobbies are playing basketball, reading, playing computer games, playing the guitar, and in-line skating.

To keep track of the information given in the clues, record it in a grid like the one shown. For each clue, shade the appropriate boxes in the grid. The unshaded boxes show the solution of the puzzle.

CLUES

1. Brad lives in Grand Rapids.

2. Marie does not live in Hart's Location.

3. If Maynard lives in Ravenna, then his favorite hobby is playing the guitar.

4. Tamara's favorite hobby is playing basketball.

5. The favorite hobby of the person who lives in Grand Rapids is in-line skating.

6. Tamara, Dave, and Marie do not live in Ravenna.

7. The person whose favorite hobby is reading does not live in Stockton or Hart's Location.

8. Neither Marie nor Dave lives in Stockton.

Brad lives in Grand Rapids, so he doesn't live elsewhere, and none of the others live in Grand Rapids.

▶ **DRAWING CONCLUSIONS**

1. Write Clue 2 as a conditional statement in if-then form. Then write the contrapositive of the statement. Explain why the contrapositive of this statement is a helpful clue.

2. Using Clue 3, what additional information do you need to conclude that Maynard's favorite hobby is playing the guitar?

3. Explain how you can use Clue 1 and Clue 5 to conclude that Brad's favorite hobby is in-line skating.

4. **CRITICAL THINKING** Make up a logic puzzle similar to the one shown above. Be sure that the clues you give make the puzzle solvable. Then trade puzzles with your partner and solve each other's puzzles.

2.3

Deductive Reasoning

What you should learn

GOAL 1 Use symbolic notation to represent logical statements.

GOAL 2 Form conclusions by applying the laws of logic to true statements, such as statements about a trip to Alabama in **Example 6**.

Why you should learn it

▼ The laws of logic help you with classification. For instance, the Law of Syllogism is used to determine true statements about birds in **Example 5**.

GOAL 1   USING SYMBOLIC NOTATION

In Lesson 2.1 you learned that a conditional statement has a hypothesis and a conclusion. Conditional statements can be written using symbolic notation, where p represents the hypothesis, q represents the conclusion, and $\rightarrow$ is read as "implies." Here are some examples.

If **the sun is out**, then **the weather is good**.
$\underbrace{\phantom{\text{If the sun is out}}}_{p}\qquad\underbrace{\phantom{\text{the weather is good}}}_{q}$

This conditional statement can be written symbolically as follows:

$$\text{If } p, \text{ then } q\qquad\text{or}\qquad p \rightarrow q.$$

To form the converse of an "If p, then q" statement, simply switch p and q.

If **the weather is good**, then **the sun is out**.
$\underbrace{\phantom{\text{the weather is good}}}_{q}\qquad\underbrace{\phantom{\text{the sun is out}}}_{p}$

The converse can be written symbolically as follows:

$$\text{If } q, \text{ then } p\qquad\text{or}\qquad q \rightarrow p.$$

A biconditional statement can be written using symbolic notation as follows:

$$\text{If } p, \text{ then } q \text{ and if } q, \text{ then } p\qquad\text{or}\qquad p \leftrightarrow q.$$

Most often a biconditional statement is written in this form:

$$p \text{ if and only if } q.$$

EXAMPLE 1   *Using Symbolic Notation*

Let p be "the value of x is -5" and let q be "the absolute value of x is 5."

a. Write $p \rightarrow q$ in words.

b. Write $q \rightarrow p$ in words.

c. Decide whether the biconditional statement $p \leftrightarrow q$ is true.

SOLUTION

a. If the value of x is -5, then the absolute value of x is 5.

b. If the absolute value of x is 5, then the value of x is -5.

c. The conditional statement in part (a) is true, but its converse in part (b) is false. So, the biconditional statement $p \leftrightarrow q$ is false.

To write the inverse and contrapositive in symbolic notation, you need to be able to write the negation of a statement symbolically. The symbol for negation (~) is written before the letter. Here are some examples.

STATEMENT	SYMBOL	NEGATION	SYMBOL
∠3 measures 90°.	p	∠3 does not measure 90°.	$\sim p$
∠3 is not acute.	q	∠3 is acute.	$\sim q$

The inverse and contrapositive of $p \rightarrow q$ are as follows:

Inverse: $\sim p \rightarrow \sim q$

If ∠3 does not measure 90°, then ∠3 is acute.

Contrapositive: $\sim q \rightarrow \sim p$

If ∠3 is acute, then ∠3 does not measure 90°.

Notice that the inverse is false, but the contrapositive is true.

EXAMPLE 2   *Writing an Inverse and a Contrapositive*

Let p be "it is raining" and let q be "the soccer game is canceled."

a. Write the contrapositive of $p \rightarrow q$.

b. Write the inverse of $p \rightarrow q$.

SOLUTION

a. Contrapositive: $\sim q \rightarrow \sim p$

If the soccer game is not canceled, then it is not raining.

b. Inverse: $\sim p \rightarrow \sim q$

If it is not raining, then the soccer game is not canceled.

· · · · · · · · · ·

Recall from Lesson 2.1 that a conditional statement is equivalent to its contrapositive and that the converse and inverse are equivalent.

Equivalent Statements	Equivalent Statements
Conditional Statement $p \rightarrow q$ If the car will start, then the battery is charged.	**Converse** $q \rightarrow p$ If the battery is charged, then the car will start.
Contrapositive $\sim q \rightarrow \sim p$ If the battery is not charged, then the car will not start.	**Inverse** $\sim p \rightarrow \sim q$ If the car will not start, then the battery is not charged.

In the table above the conditional statement and its contrapositive are true. The converse and inverse are false. (Just because a car won't start does not imply that its battery is dead.)

USING THE LAWS OF LOGIC

Deductive reasoning uses facts, definitions, and accepted properties in a logical order to write a **logical argument**. This differs from *inductive reasoning*, in which previous examples and patterns are used to form a conjecture.

EXAMPLE 3 *Using Inductive and Deductive Reasoning*

The following examples show how inductive and deductive reasoning differ.

  a. Andrea knows that Robin is a sophomore and Todd is a junior. All the other juniors that Andrea knows are older than Robin. Therefore, Andrea reasons *inductively* that Todd is older than Robin based on past observations.

  b. Andrea knows that Todd is older than Chan. She also knows that Chan is older than Robin. Andrea reasons *deductively* that Todd is older than Robin based on accepted statements.

· · · · · · · · · ·

There are two *laws of deductive reasoning*. The first is the **Law of Detachment**, shown below. The **Law of Syllogism** follows on the next page.

LAW OF DETACHMENT

If $p \rightarrow q$ is a true conditional statement and p is true, then q is true.

EXAMPLE 4 *Using the Law of Detachment*

State whether the argument is valid.

  a. Jamal knows that if he misses the practice the day before a game, then he will not be a starting player in the game. Jamal misses practice on Tuesday so he concludes that he will not be able to start in the game on Wednesday.

  b. If two angles form a linear pair, then they are supplementary; $\angle A$ and $\angle B$ are supplementary. So, $\angle A$ and $\angle B$ form a linear pair.

SOLUTION

  a. This logical argument is a valid use of the Law of Detachment. It is given that both a statement $(p \rightarrow q)$ and its hypothesis (p) are true. So, it is valid for Jamal to conclude that the conclusion (q) is true.

  b. This logical argument is not a valid use of the Law of Detachment. Given that a statement $(p \rightarrow q)$ and its conclusion (q) are true does not mean the hypothesis (p) is true. The argument implies that all supplementary angles form a linear pair.

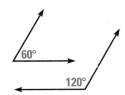

  The diagram shows that this is not a valid conclusion.

LAW OF SYLLOGISM

If $p \rightarrow q$ and $q \rightarrow r$ are true conditional statements, then $p \rightarrow r$ is true.

EXAMPLE 5   *Using the Law of Syllogism*

ZOOLOGY Write some conditional statements that can be made from the following true statements using the Law of Syllogism.

1. If a bird is the fastest bird on land, then it is the largest of all birds.
2. If a bird is the largest of all birds, then it is an ostrich.
3. If a bird is a bee hummingbird, then it is the smallest of all birds.
4. If a bird is the largest of all birds, then it is flightless.
5. If a bird is the smallest bird, then it has a nest the size of a walnut half-shell.

SOLUTION

Here are the conditional statements that use the Law of Syllogism.

a. If a bird is the fastest bird on land, then it is an ostrich. (Use 1 and 2.)

b. If a bird is a bee hummingbird, then it has a nest the size of a walnut half-shell. (Use 3 and 5.)

c. If a bird is the fastest bird on land, then it is flightless. (Use 1 and 4.)

EXAMPLE 6   *Using the Laws of Deductive Reasoning*

*Logical
Reasoning*

Over the summer, Mike visited Alabama. Given the following true statements, can you conclude that Mike visited the Civil Rights Memorial?

If Mike visits Alabama, then he will spend a day in Montgomery.

If Mike spends a day in Montgomery, then he will visit the Civil Rights Memorial.

SOLUTION

Let *p*, *q*, and *r* represent the following.

p: Mike visits Alabama.

q: Mike spends a day in Montgomery.

r: Mike visits the Civil Rights Memorial.

Because $p \rightarrow q$ is true and $q \rightarrow r$ is true, you can apply the Law of Syllogism to conclude that $p \rightarrow r$ is true.

**Civil Rights Memorial in
Montgomery, Alabama**

If Mike visits Alabama, then he will visit the Civil Rights Memorial.

▶ You are told that Mike visited Alabama, which means *p* is true. Using the Law of Detachment, you can conclude that he visited the Civil Rights Memorial.

GUIDED PRACTICE

Vocabulary Check ✓

1. If the statements $p \to q$ and $q \to r$ are true, then the statement $p \to r$ is true by the Law of ___?___. If the statement $p \to q$ is true and p is true, then q is true by the Law of ___?___.

Concept Check ✓

2. State whether the following argument uses inductive or deductive reasoning: "If it is Friday, then Kendra's family has pizza for dinner. Today is Friday, therefore, Kendra's family will have pizza for dinner."

Skill Check ✓

3. Given the notation for a conditional statement is $p \to q$, what statement is represented by $q \to p$?

4. A conditional statement is defined in symbolic notation as $p \to q$. Use symbolic notation to write the inverse of $p \to q$.

5. Write the contrapositive of the following statement: "If you don't enjoy scary movies, then you wouldn't have liked this one."

6. If a ray bisects a right angle, then the congruent angles formed are complementary. In the diagram, $\angle ABC$ is a right angle. Are $\angle ABD$ and $\angle CBD$ complementary? Explain your reasoning.

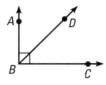

7. If $f \to g$ and $g \to h$ are true statements, and f is true, does it follow that h is true? Explain.

PRACTICE AND APPLICATIONS

STUDENT HELP

► **Extra Practice**
to help you master skills is on p. 805.

WRITING STATEMENTS Using *p* and *q* below, write the symbolic statement in words.

    p: Points *X, Y,* and *Z* are collinear.

    q: Points *X, Y,* and *Z* lie on the same line.

8. $q \to p$ 9. $\sim q$ 10. $\sim p$

11. $\sim p \to \sim q$ 12. $p \leftrightarrow q$ 13. $\sim q \to \sim p$

WRITING INVERSE AND CONTRAPOSITIVE Given that the statement is of the form $p \to q$, write *p* and *q*. Then write the inverse and the contrapositive of $p \to q$ both symbolically and in words.

14. If Jed gets a C on the exam, then he will get an A for the quarter.

STUDENT HELP

► **HOMEWORK HELP**
Example 1: Exs. 8–13
Example 2: Exs. 14–20
Example 3: Exs. 21, 22
Example 4: Exs. 23–25
Example 5: Exs. 30–48
Example 6: Exs. 30–48

15. If Alberto finds a summer job, then he will buy a car.

16. If the fuse has blown, then the light will not go on.

17. If the car is running, then the key is in the ignition.

18. If you dial 911, then there is an emergency.

19. If Gina walks to the store, then she will buy a newspaper.

20. If it is not raining, then Petra will ride her bike to school.

LOGICAL REASONING Decide whether *inductive* or *deductive* reasoning is used to reach the conclusion. Explain your reasoning.

21. For the past three Wednesdays the cafeteria has served macaroni and cheese for lunch. Dana concludes that the cafeteria will serve macaroni and cheese for lunch this Wednesday.

22. If you live in Nevada and are between the ages of 16 and 18, then you must take driver's education to get your license. Marcus lives in Nevada, is 16 years old, and has his driver's license. Therefore, Marcus took driver's education.

USING THE LAW OF DETACHMENT State whether the argument is valid. Explain your reasoning.

23. If the sum of the measures of two angles is 90°, then the two angles are complementary. Because $m\angle A + m\angle C = 90°$, $\angle A$ and $\angle C$ are complementary.

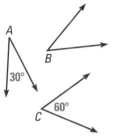

24. If two adjacent angles form a right angle, then the two angles are complementary. Because $\angle A$ and $\angle C$ are complementary, $\angle A$ and $\angle C$ are adjacent.

25. If $\angle A$ and $\angle C$ are acute angles, then any angle whose measure is between the measures of $\angle A$ and $\angle C$ is also acute. In the diagram above it is shown that $m\angle A \leq m\angle B \leq m\angle C$, so $\angle B$ must be acute.

USING ALGEBRA State whether any conclusions can be made using the true statement, given that $x = 3$.

26. If $x > 2x - 10$, then $x = y$.

27. If $2x + 3 < 4x < 5x$, then $y \leq x$.

28. If $4x \geq 12$, then $y = 6x$.

29. If $x + 3 = 10$, then $y = x$.

MAKING CONCLUSIONS Use the Law of Syllogism to write the statement that follows from the pair of true statements.

30. If the sun is shining, then it is a beautiful day.

If it is a beautiful day, then we will have a picnic.

31. If the stereo is on, then the volume is loud.

If the volume is loud, then the neighbors will complain.

32. If Ginger goes to the movies, then Marta will go to the movies.

If Yumi goes to the movies, then Ginger will go to the movies.

USING DEDUCTIVE REASONING Select the word that makes the concluding statement true.

33. The Oak Terrace apartment building does not allow dogs. Serena lives at Oak Terrace. So, Serena (must, may, may not) keep a dog.

34. The Kolob Arch is the world's widest natural arch. The world's widest arch is in Zion National Park. So, the Kolob Arch (is, may be, is not) in Zion.

35. Zion National Park is in Utah. Jeremy spent a week in Utah. So, Jeremy (must have, may have, never) visited Zion National Park.

The Kolob Arch mentioned in Ex. 34, spans 310 feet.

36. p_1: $m\angle 2 = 115°$

37. $p_1 \rightarrow p_2$: If $m\angle 2 = 115°$, then $m\angle 1 = 65°$.

38. $p_2 \rightarrow p_3$: If $m\angle 1 = 65°$, then $m\angle 4 = 65°$.

39. $p_3 \rightarrow p_4$: If $m\angle 4 = 65°$, then $m\angle 3 = 65°$.

40. $p_4 \rightarrow p_5$: If $m\angle 3 = 65°$, then $m\angle 5 = 65°$.

41. $p_5 \rightarrow p_6$: If $m\angle 5 = 65°$, then $m\angle 6 = 115°$.

42. $p_1 \rightarrow p_6$: If $m\angle 2 = 115°$, then $m\angle 6 = 115°$.

43. *Writing* Describe a time in your life when you use deductive reasoning.

44. CRITICAL THINKING Describe an instance where inductive reasoning can
lead to an incorrect conclusion.

LOGICAL REASONING In Exercises 45–48, use the true statements to
determine whether the conclusion is *true* or *false*. Explain your reasoning.

• If Diego goes shopping, then he will buy a pretzel.

• If the mall is open, then Angela and Diego will go shopping.

• If Angela goes shopping, then she will buy a pizza.

• The mall is open.

45. Diego bought a pretzel.　　　　　**46.** Angela and Diego went shopping.

47. Angela bought a pretzel.　　　　　**48.** Diego had some of Angela's pizza.

49. **ROBOTICS** Because robots can withstand higher temperatures than
humans, a fire-fighting robot is under development. Write the following
statements about the robot in order. Then use the Law of Syllogism to
complete the statement, "If there is a fire, then ___?___."

　A. If the robot sets off a fire alarm, then it concludes there is a fire.

　B. If the robot senses high levels of smoke and heat, then it sets off a fire
　　　alarm.

　C. If the robot locates the fire, then the robot extinguishes the fire.

　D. If there is a fire, then the robot senses high levels of smoke and heat.

　E. If the robot concludes there is a fire, then it locates the fire.

50. **DOGS** Use the true statements to form other conditional statements.

　A. If a dog is a gazehound, then it hunts by sight.

　B. If a hound bays (makes long barks while hunting), then it is a scent hound.

　C. If a dog is a foxhound, then it does not hunt primarily by sight.

　D. If a dog is a coonhound, then it bays when it hunts.

　E. If a dog is a greyhound, then it is a gazehound.

51. MULTI-STEP PROBLEM Let *p* be "Jana wins the contest" and *q* be "Jana gets two free tickets to the concert."

    a. Write $p \rightarrow q$ in words.

    b. Write the converse of $p \rightarrow q$, both in words and symbols.

    c. Write the contrapositive of $p \rightarrow q$, both in words and symbols.

    d. Suppose Jana gets two free tickets to the concert but does not win the contest. Is this a counterexample to the converse or to the contrapositive?

    e. What do you need to know about the conditional statement from part (a) so the Law of Detachment can be used to conclude that Jana gets two free tickets to the concert?

    f. *Writing* Use the statement in part (a) to write a second statement that uses the Law of Syllogism to reach a valid conclusion.

★ **Challenge**   **CONTRAPOSITIVES** **Use the true statements to answer the questions.**

    • If a creature is a fly, then it has six legs.

    • If a creature has six legs, then it is an insect.

52. Use symbolic notation to describe the statements.

53. Use the statements and the Law of Syllogism to write a conditional statement, both in words and symbols.

54. Write the contrapositive of each statement, both in words and symbols.

55. Using the contrapositives and the Law of Syllogism, write a conditional statement. Is the statement true? Does the Law of Syllogism work for contrapositives?

MIXED REVIEW

NAMING POINTS **Use the diagram to name a point.** (Review 1.2)

56. A third point collinear with *A* and *C*

57. A fourth point coplanar with *A*, *C*, and *E*

58. A point coplanar with *A* and *B*, but not coplanar with *A*, *B*, and *C*

59. A point coplanar with *A* and *C*, but not coplanar with *E* and *F*

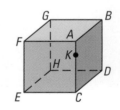

FINDING ANGLE MEASURES **Find $m\angle ABD$ given that $\angle ABC$ and $\angle CBD$ are adjacent angles.** (Review 1.4 for 2.4)

60. $m\angle ABC = 20°, m\angle CBD = 10°$

61. $m\angle CBD = 13°, m\angle ABC = 28°$

62. $m\angle ABC = 3y + 1, m\angle CBD = 12 - y$

63. $m\angle CBD = 11 + 2f - g, m\angle ABC = 5g - 4 + f$

Write the true statement in if-then form and write its converse. Determine whether the statement and its converse can be combined to form a true biconditional statement. (Lesson 2.1 and Lesson 2.2)

1. If today is June 4, then tomorrow is June 5.

2. A century is a period of 100 years.

3. Two circles are congruent if they have the same diameter.

LOGICAL REASONING **Use the true statements to answer the questions.** (Lesson 2.3)

* If John drives into the fence, then John's father will be angry.

* If John backs the car out, then John will drive into the fence.

* John backs the car out.

4. Does John drive into the fence?   **5.** Is John's father angry?

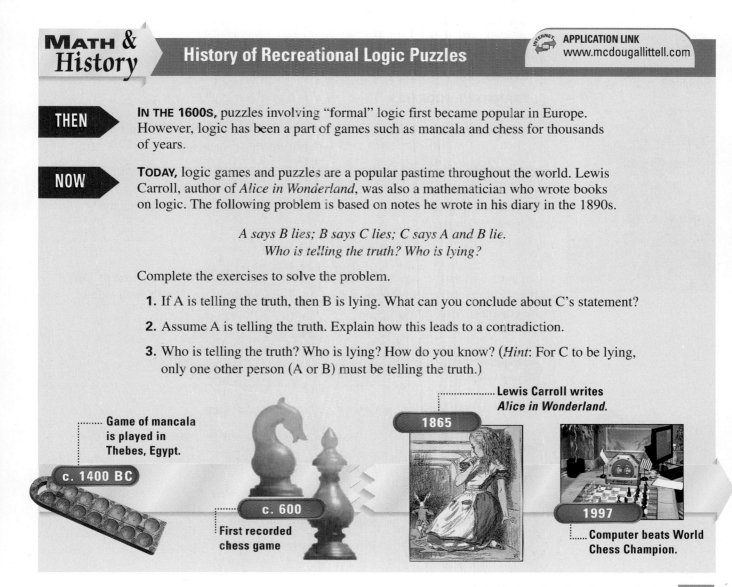

MATH &
History

History of Recreational Logic Puzzles

APPLICATION LINK
www.mcdougallittell.com

THEN

IN THE 1600S, puzzles involving "formal" logic first became popular in Europe. However, logic has been a part of games such as mancala and chess for thousands of years.

NOW

TODAY, logic games and puzzles are a popular pastime throughout the world. Lewis Carroll, author of *Alice in Wonderland*, was also a mathematician who wrote books on logic. The following problem is based on notes he wrote in his diary in the 1890s.

A says B lies; B says C lies; C says A and B lie.
Who is telling the truth? Who is lying?

Complete the exercises to solve the problem.

1. If A is telling the truth, then B is lying. What can you conclude about C's statement?

2. Assume A is telling the truth. Explain how this leads to a contradiction.

3. Who is telling the truth? Who is lying? How do you know? (*Hint*: For C to be lying, only one other person (A or B) must be telling the truth.)

Game of mancala is played in Thebes, Egypt.

c. 1400 BC

c. 600
First recorded chess game

1865

Lewis Carroll writes
Alice in Wonderland.

1997
Computer beats World Chess Champion.

2.4 Reasoning with Properties from Algebra

What you should learn

GOAL 1 Use properties from algebra.

GOAL 2 Use properties of length and measure to justify segment and angle relationships, such as the angles at the turns of a racetrack, as in **Example 5** and **Ex. 28**.

Why you should learn it

▼ Using algebraic properties helps you when rewriting a formula, such as the formula for an athlete's target heart rate in **Example 3**.

GOAL 1 USING PROPERTIES FROM ALGEBRA

Many properties from algebra concern the equality of real numbers. Several of these are summarized in the following list.

ALGEBRAIC PROPERTIES OF EQUALITY

Let a, b, and c be real numbers.

ADDITION PROPERTY	If $a = b$, then $a + c = b + c$.
SUBTRACTION PROPERTY	If $a = b$, then $a - c = b - c$.
MULTIPLICATION PROPERTY	If $a = b$, then $ac = bc$.
DIVISION PROPERTY	If $a = b$ and $c \neq 0$, then $a \div c = b \div c$.
REFLEXIVE PROPERTY	For any real number a, $a = a$.
SYMMETRIC PROPERTY	If $a = b$, then $b = a$.
TRANSITIVE PROPERTY	If $a = b$ and $b = c$, then $a = c$.
SUBSTITUTION PROPERTY	If $a = b$, then a can be substituted for b in any equation or expression.

Properties of equality along with other properties from algebra, such as the *distributive property*,

$$a(b + c) = ab + ac$$

can be used to solve equations. For instance, you can use the subtraction property of equality to solve the equation $x + 3 = 7$. By subtracting 3 from each side of the equation, you obtain $x = 4$.

EXAMPLE 1 *Writing Reasons*

Using Algebra

Solve $5x - 18 = 3x + 2$ and write a reason for each step.

SOLUTION

$5x - 18 = 3x + 2$	**Given**
$2x - 18 = 2$	**Subtraction property of equality**
$2x = 20$	**Addition property of equality**
$x = 10$	**Division property of equality**

EXAMPLE 2 *Writing Reasons*

STUDENT HELP

HOMEWORK HELP
Visit our Web site
www.mcdougallittell.com
for extra examples.

Solve $55z - 3(9z + 12) = -64$ and write a reason for each step.

SOLUTION

$55z - 3(9z + 12) = -64$	**Given**
$55z - 27z - 36 = -64$	**Distributive property**
$28z - 36 = -64$	**Simplify.**
$28z = -28$	**Addition property of equality**
$z = -1$	**Division property of equality**

EXAMPLE 3 *Using Properties in Real Life*

FITNESS Before exercising, you should find your target heart rate. This is the rate at which you achieve an effective workout while not placing too much strain on your heart. Your target heart rate r (in beats per minute) can be determined from your age a (in years) using the equation $a = 220 - \frac{10}{7}r$.

a. Solve the formula for r and write a reason for each step.

b. Use the result to find the target heart rate for a 16 year old.

c. Find the target heart rate for the following ages: 20, 30, 40, 50, and 60. What happens to the target heart rate as a person gets older?

SOLUTION

a.

$a = 220 - \frac{10}{7}r$	**Given**
$a + \frac{10}{7}r = 220$	**Addition property of equality**
$\frac{10}{7}r = 220 - a$	**Subtraction property of equality**
$r = \frac{7}{10}(220 - a)$	**Multiplication property of equality**

b. Using $a = 16$, the target heart rate is:

$r = \frac{7}{10}(220 - a)$	**Given**
$r = \frac{7}{10}(220 - 16)$	**Substitute 16 for a.**
$r = 142.8$	**Simplify.**

▶ The target heart rate for a 16 year old is about 143 beats per minute.

c. From the table, the target heart rate appears to decrease as a person ages.

Age	20	30	40	50	60
Rate	140	133	126	119	112

GOAL 2 USING PROPERTIES OF LENGTH AND MEASURE

The algebraic properties of equality can be used in geometry.

CONCEPT SUMMARY	PROPERTIES OF EQUALITY	
	SEGMENT LENGTH	**ANGLE MEASURE**
REFLEXIVE	For any segment AB, $AB = AB$.	For any angle A, $m\angle A = m\angle A$.
SYMMETRIC	If $AB = CD$, then $CD = AB$.	If $m\angle A = m\angle B$, then $m\angle B = m\angle A$.
TRANSITIVE	If $AB = CD$ and $CD = EF$, then $AB = EF$.	If $m\angle A = m\angle B$ and $m\angle B = m\angle C$, then $m\angle A = m\angle C$.

EXAMPLE 4 *Using Properties of Length*

In the diagram, $AB = CD$. The argument below shows that $AC = BD$.

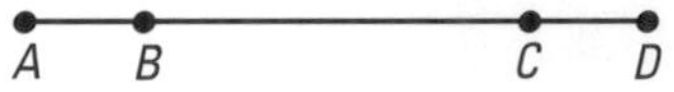

$AB = CD$	**Given**
$AB + BC = BC + CD$	**Addition property of equality**
$AC = AB + BC$	**Segment Addition Postulate**
$BD = BC + CD$	**Segment Addition Postulate**
$AC = BD$	**Substitution property of equality**

EXAMPLE 5 *Using Properties of Measure*

banking angle

AUTO RACING
Banked turns help the cars travel around the track at high speeds. The angles provide an inward force that helps keep the cars from flying off the track.

AUTO RACING The Talladega Superspeedway racetrack in Alabama has four banked turns, which are described in the diagram at the left. Use the given information about the maximum banking angle of the four turns to find $m\angle 4$.

$m\angle 1 + m\angle 2 = 66°$
$m\angle 1 + m\angle 2 + m\angle 3 = 99°$
$m\angle 3 = m\angle 1$
$m\angle 1 = m\angle 4$

SOLUTION

$m\angle 1 + m\angle 2 = 66°$	**Given**
$m\angle 1 + m\angle 2 + m\angle 3 = 99°$	**Given**
$66° + m\angle 3 = 99°$	**Substitution property of equality**
$m\angle 3 = 33°$	**Subtraction property of equality**
$m\angle 3 = m\angle 1, m\angle 1 = m\angle 4$	**Given**
$m\angle 3 = m\angle 4$	**Transitive property of equality**
$m\angle 4 = 33°$	**Substitution property of equality**

GUIDED PRACTICE

Vocabulary Check ✓

1. Name the property that makes the following statement true:
"If $m\angle 3 = m\angle 5$, then $m\angle 5 = m\angle 3$."

Concept Check ✓ **Use the diagram at the right.**

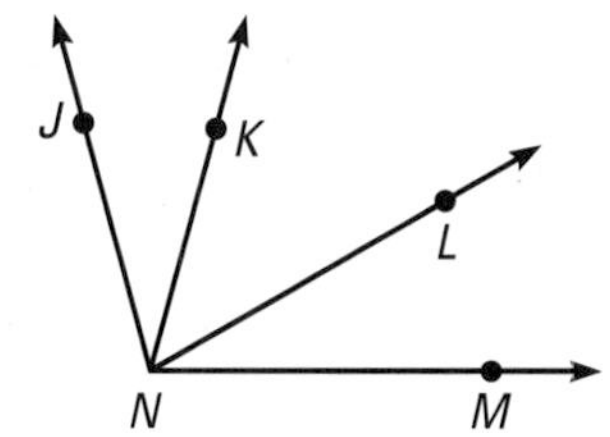

2. Explain how the addition property of equality supports this statement: "If $m\angle JNK = m\angle LNM$, then $m\angle JNL = m\angle KNM$."

3. Explain how the subtraction property of equality supports this statement: "If $m\angle JNL = m\angle KNM$, then $m\angle JNK = m\angle LNM$."

Skill Check ✓ **In Exercises 4–8, match the conditional statement with the property of equality.**

4. If $JK = PQ$ and $PQ = ST$, then $JK = ST$. **A.** Addition property

5. If $m\angle S = 30°$, then $5° + m\angle S = 35°$. **B.** Substitution property

6. If $ST = 2$ and $SU = ST + 3$, then $SU = 5$. **C.** Transitive property

7. If $m\angle K = 45°$, then $3(m\angle K) = 135°$. **D.** Symmetric property

8. If $m\angle P = m\angle Q$, then $m\angle Q = m\angle P$. **E.** Multiplication property

9. 🌐 **WIND-CHILL FACTOR** If the wind is blowing at 20 miles per hour, you can find the wind-chill temperature W (in degrees Fahrenheit) by using the equation $W = 1.42T - 38.5$, where T is the actual temperature (in degrees Fahrenheit). Solve this equation for T and write a reason for each step. What is the actual temperature if the wind chill temperature is $-24.3°F$ and the wind is blowing at 20 miles per hour?

PRACTICE AND APPLICATIONS

STUDENT HELP

▸ **Extra Practice**
to help you master
skills is on p. 806.

COMPLETING STATEMENTS In Exercises 10–14, use the property to complete the statement.

10. Symmetric property of equality: If $m\angle A = m\angle B$, then __?__.

11. Transitive property of equality: If $BC = CD$ and $CD = EF$, then __?__.

12. Substitution property of equality: If $LK + JM = 12$ and $LK = 2$, then __?__.

13. Subtraction property of equality: If $PQ + ST = RS + ST$, then __?__.

14. Division property of equality: If $3(m\angle A) = 90°$, then $m\angle A =$ __?__.

STUDENT HELP

▸ **HOMEWORK HELP**
Example 1: Exs. 10–23
Example 2: Exs. 15–23
Example 3: Exs. 29–31
Example 4: Exs. 24–27
Example 5: Ex. 28

15. Copy and complete the argument below, giving a reason for each step.

$2(3x + 1) = 5x + 14$	Given
$6x + 2 = 5x + 14$	__?__
$x + 2 = 14$	__?__
$x = 12$	__?__

SOLVING EQUATIONS In Exercises 16–23, solve the equation and state a reason for each step.

16. $p - 1 = 6$

17. $q + 9 = 13$

18. $2r - 7 = 9$

19. $7s + 20 = 4s - 13$

20. $3(2t + 9) = 30$

21. $-2(-w + 3) = 15$

22. $26u + 4(12u - 5) = 128$

23. $3(4v - 1) - 8v = 17$

24. **LOGICAL REASONING** In the diagram, $m\angle RPQ = m\angle RPS$. Verify each step in the argument that shows $m\angle SPQ = 2(m\angle RPQ)$.

$m\angle RPQ = m\angle RPS$

$m\angle SPQ = m\angle RPQ + m\angle RPS$

$m\angle SPQ = m\angle RPQ + m\angle RPQ$

$m\angle SPQ = 2(m\angle RPQ)$

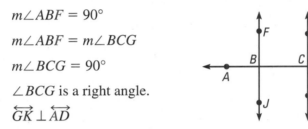

25. **LOGICAL REASONING** In the diagram, $m\angle ABF = m\angle BCG$ and $m\angle ABF = 90°$. Verify each step in the argument that shows $\overleftrightarrow{GK} \perp \overleftrightarrow{AD}$.

$m\angle ABF = 90°$

$m\angle ABF = m\angle BCG$

$m\angle BCG = 90°$

$\angle BCG$ is a right angle.

$\overleftrightarrow{GK} \perp \overleftrightarrow{AD}$

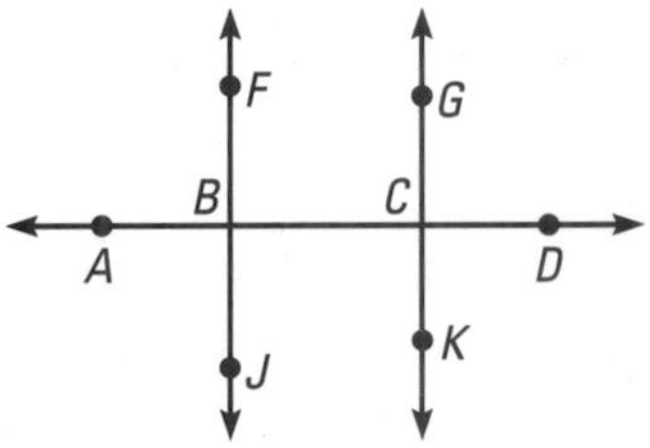

DEVELOPING ARGUMENTS In Exercises 26 and 27, give an argument for the statement, including a reason for each step.

26. If $\angle 1$ and $\angle 2$ are right angles, then they are supplementary.

27. If B lies between A and C and $AB = 3$ and $BC = 8$, then $AC = 11$.

FOCUS ON PEOPLE

REAL LIFE **BILL ELLIOTT** holds the qualifying record at Daytona International Speedway with a speed of 210.364 miles per hour.

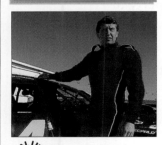

28. **AUTO RACING** Some facts about the maximum banking angles of Daytona International Speedway at corners 1, 2, 3, and 4 are at the right. Find $m\angle 3$. Explain your steps. (Banked corners are described on page 98.)

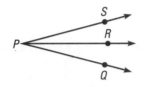

$m\angle 1 + m\angle 3 + m\angle 4 = 93°$

$m\angle 2 + m\angle 4 = 62°$

$m\angle 2 = m\angle 3$

$m\angle 1 = m\angle 2$

PAY RAISES In Exercises 29–31, suppose you receive a raise at work. You can calculate your percent increase by using the pay raise formula $c(r + 1) = n$, where c is your current wage (in dollars per hour), r is your percent increase (as a decimal), and n is your new wage (in dollars per hour).

29. Solve the formula for r and write a reason for each step.

30. Use the result from Exercise 29 to find your percent increase if your current wage is \$10.00 and your new wage will be \$10.80.

31. Suppose Donald gets a 6% pay raise and his new wage is \$12.72. Find Donald's old wage. Explain the steps you used to find your answer.

32. MULTI-STEP PROBLEM State a reason that makes the statement true.

a. If $4(x - 5 - 2x) = 0.5(12x - 16)$, then $4x - 20 + 8x = 6x - 8$.

b. If $4x - 20 + 8x = 6x - 8$, then $12x - 20 = 6x - 8$.

c. If $12x - 20 = 6x - 8$, then $6x - 20 = -8$.

d. If $6x - 20 = -8$, then $6x = 12$.

e. If $6x = 12$, then $x = 2$.

f. *Writing* Use parts (a) through (e) to provide an argument for "If $4(x - 5 + 2x) = 0.5(12x - 16)$, then $x = 2$."

★ **Challenge**

DETERMINING PROPERTIES Decide whether the relationship is *reflexive*, *symmetric*, or *transitive*. When the relationship does not have any of these properties, give a counterexample.

33. Set: students in a geometry class
Relationship: "earned the same grade as"
Example: Jim earned the same grade as Mario.

34. Set: letters of the alphabet
Relationship: "comes after"
Example: H comes after G.

MIXED REVIEW

USING THE DISTANCE FORMULA Find the distance between the two points. Round your result to two decimal places. **(Review 1.3 for 2.5)**

35. $A(4, 5)$, $B(-3, -2)$ **36.** $E(-7, 6)$, $F(2, 0)$ **37.** $J(1, 1)$, $K(-1, 11)$

38. $P(8, -4)$, $Q(1, -4)$ **39.** $S(9, -1)$, $T(2, -6)$ **40.** $V(7, 10)$, $W(1, 5)$

DETERMINING ENDPOINTS In Exercises 41–44, you are given an endpoint and the midpoint of a line segment. Find the coordinates of the other endpoint. Each midpoint is denoted by $M(x, y)$. **(Review 1.5 for 2.5)**

41. $B(5, 7)$ **42.** $C(-4, -5)$ **43.** $F(0, 9)$ **44.** $Q(-1, 14)$
$M(-1, 0)$ $M(3, -6)$ $M(6, -2)$ $M(2, 7)$

45. Given that $m\angle A = 48°$, what are the measures of a complement and a supplement of $\angle A$? **(Review 1.6)**

ANALYZING STATEMENTS Use the diagram shown at the right to determine whether the statement is *true* or *false*. **(Review 2.2)**

46. Points G, L, and J are collinear.

47. $\overline{BC} \perp \overline{FG}$

48. $\angle ECB \cong \angle ACD$

49. $\angle JHL$ and $\angle JHF$ are complementary.

50. $\overleftrightarrow{AK} \perp \overleftrightarrow{BD}$

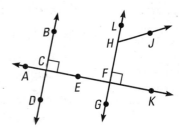

Proving Statements about Segments

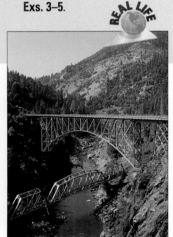

GOAL 1 PROPERTIES OF CONGRUENT SEGMENTS

A true statement that follows as a result of other true statements is called a **theorem**. All theorems must be proved. You can prove a theorem using a *two-column proof*. A **two-column proof** has numbered statements and reasons that show the logical order of an argument.

THEOREM

THEOREM 2.1 *Properties of Segment Congruence*

Segment congruence is reflexive, symmetric, and transitive. Here are some examples:

REFLEXIVE	For any segment AB, $\overline{AB} \cong \overline{AB}$.
SYMMETRIC	If $\overline{AB} \cong \overline{CD}$, then $\overline{CD} \cong \overline{AB}$.
TRANSITIVE	If $\overline{AB} \cong \overline{CD}$, and $\overline{CD} \cong \overline{EF}$, then $\overline{AB} \cong \overline{EF}$.

EXAMPLE 1 *Symmetric Property of Segment Congruence*

You can prove the Symmetric Property of Segment Congruence as follows.

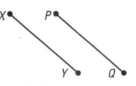

GIVEN ▶ $\overline{PQ} \cong \overline{XY}$

PROVE ▶ $\overline{XY} \cong \overline{PQ}$

Statements	Reasons
1. $\overline{PQ} \cong \overline{XY}$	1. Given
2. $PQ = XY$	2. Definition of congruent segments
3. $XY = PQ$	3. Symmetric property of equality
4. $\overline{XY} \cong \overline{PQ}$	4. Definition of congruent segments

You are asked to complete proofs for the Reflexive and Transitive Properties of Segment Congruence in Exercises 6 and 7.

· · · · · · · · · ·

A proof can be written in paragraph form, called **paragraph proof**. Here is a paragraph proof for the Symmetric Property of Segment Congruence.

Paragraph Proof You are given that $\overline{PQ} \cong \overline{XY}$. By the definition of congruent segments, $PQ = XY$. By the symmetric property of equality, $XY = PQ$. Therefore, by the definition of congruent segments, it follows that $\overline{XY} \cong \overline{PQ}$.

GOAL 2 USING CONGRUENCE OF SEGMENTS

EXAMPLE 2 *Using Congruence*

Proof

Use the diagram and the given information to complete the missing steps and reasons in the proof.

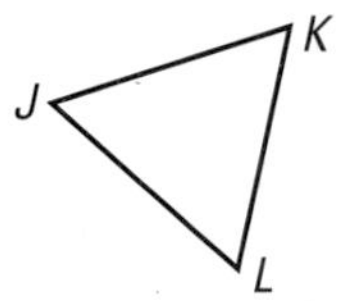

GIVEN ▶ $LK = 5$, $JK = 5$, $\overline{JK} \cong \overline{JL}$

PROVE ▶ $\overline{LK} \cong \overline{JL}$

Statements	Reasons
1. **a.**	1. Given
2. **b.**	2. Given
3. $LK = JK$	3. Transitive property of equality
4. $\overline{LK} \cong \overline{JK}$	4. **c.**
5. $\overline{JK} \cong \overline{JL}$	5. Given
6. **d.**	6. Transitive Property of Congruence

SOLUTION

a. $LK = 5$ **b.** $JK = 5$ **c.** Definition of congruent segments **d.** $\overline{LK} \cong \overline{JL}$

EXAMPLE 3 *Using Segment Relationships*

Proof

In the diagram, Q is the midpoint of $\overline{PR}$.

Show that PQ and QR are each equal to $\frac{1}{2}PR$.

SOLUTION

Decide what you know and what you need to prove. Then write the proof.

GIVEN ▶ Q is the midpoint of $\overline{PR}$.

PROVE ▶ $PQ = \frac{1}{2}PR$ and $QR = \frac{1}{2}PR$.

Statements	Reasons
1. Q is the midpoint of $\overline{PR}$.	1. Given
2. $PQ = QR$	2. Definition of midpoint
3. $PQ + QR = PR$	3. Segment Addition Postulate
4. $PQ + PQ = PR$	4. Substitution property of equality
5. $2 \cdot PQ = PR$	5. Distributive property
6. $PQ = \frac{1}{2}PR$	6. Division property of equality
7. $QR = \frac{1}{2}PR$	7. Substitution property of equality

STUDENT HELP

Study Tip
The distributive property can be used to simplify a sum, as in Step 5 of the proof. You can think of $PQ + PQ$ as follows: $1(PQ) + 1(PQ) = (1 + 1)(PQ) = 2 \cdot PQ$.

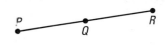

Copy a Segment

Use the following steps to construct a segment that is congruent to $\overline{AB}$.

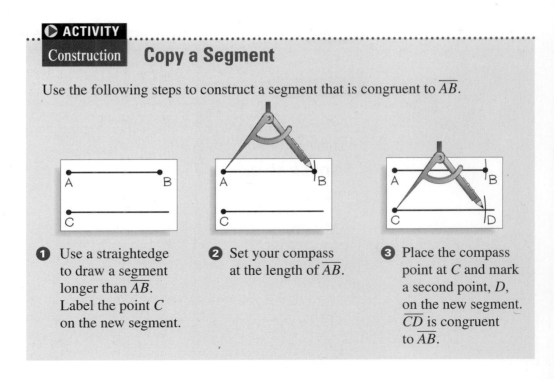

1 Use a straightedge to draw a segment longer than $\overline{AB}$. Label the point C on the new segment.

2 Set your compass at the length of $\overline{AB}$.

3 Place the compass point at C and mark a second point, D, on the new segment. $\overline{CD}$ is congruent to $\overline{AB}$.

You will practice copying a segment in Exercises 12–15. It is an important construction because copying a segment is used in many constructions throughout this course.

GUIDED PRACTICE

Vocabulary Check ✓

1. An example of the Symmetric Property of Segment Congruence is "If $\overline{AB} \cong$ ___?___, then $\overline{CD} \cong$ ___?___."

Concept Check ✓

2. ERROR ANALYSIS In the diagram below, $\overline{CB} \cong \overline{SR}$ and $\overline{CB} \cong \overline{QR}$. Explain what is wrong with Michael's argument.

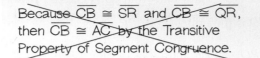

Because $\overline{CB} \cong \overline{SR}$ and $\overline{CB} \cong \overline{QR}$, then $\overline{CB} \cong \overline{AC}$ by the Transitive Property of Segment Congruence.

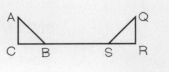

Skill Check ✓

🌐 **BRIDGES** The diagram below shows a portion of a trestle bridge, where $\overline{BF} \perp \overline{CD}$ and D is the midpoint of $\overline{BF}$.

3. Give a reason why $\overline{BD}$ and $\overline{FD}$ are congruent.

4. Are $\angle CDE$ and $\angle FDE$ complementary? Explain.

5. If $\overline{CE}$ and $\overline{BD}$ are congruent, explain why $\overline{CE}$ and $\overline{FD}$ are congruent.

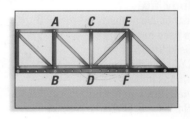

PRACTICE AND APPLICATIONS

STUDENT HELP

→ **Extra Practice**
to help you master
skills is on p. 806.

▶ **PROVING THEOREM 2.1** Copy and complete the proof for two of the
cases of the Properties of Segment Congruence Theorem.

6. Reflexive Property of Segment Congruence

    GIVEN ▶ EF is a line segment

    PROVE ▶ $\overline{EF} \cong \overline{EF}$

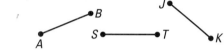

Statements	Reasons
1. $EF = EF$	1. ___?___
2. ___?___	2. Definition of congruent segments

7. Transitive Property of Segment Congruence

    GIVEN ▶ $\overline{AB} \cong \overline{JK}$, $\overline{JK} \cong \overline{ST}$

    PROVE ▶ $\overline{AB} \cong \overline{ST}$

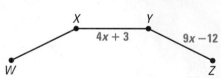

Statements	Reasons
1. $\overline{AB} \cong \overline{JK}$, $\overline{JK} \cong \overline{ST}$	1. ___?___
2. $AB = JK$, $JK = ST$	2. ___?___
3. $AB = ST$	3. ___?___
4. $\overline{AB} \cong \overline{ST}$	4. ___?___

xy **USING ALGEBRA** Solve for the variable using the given information.
Explain your steps.

8. GIVEN ▶ $\overline{AB} \cong \overline{BC}$, $\overline{CD} \cong \overline{BC}$

    A 2x + 1 B   C 4x − 11 D

9. GIVEN ▶ $PR = 46$

    P 2x + 5 Q   6x − 15 R

10. GIVEN ▶ $\overline{ST} \cong \overline{SR}$, $\overline{QR} \cong \overline{SR}$

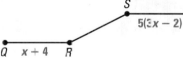

11. GIVEN ▶ $\overline{XY} \cong \overline{WX}$, $\overline{YZ} \cong \overline{WX}$

🛆 **CONSTRUCTION** In Exercises 12–15, use the segments, along with a
straightedge and compass, to construct a segment with the given length.

STUDENT HELP

→ **HOMEWORK HELP**
Example 1: Exs. 6, 7
Example 2: Exs. 16–18
Example 3: Exs. 16–18

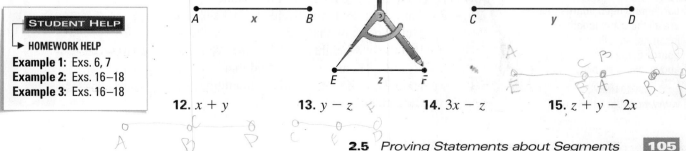

12. $x + y$ **13.** $y - z$ **14.** $3x - z$ **15.** $z + y - 2x$

16. **DEVELOPING PROOF** Write a complete proof by rearranging the reasons listed on the pieces of paper.

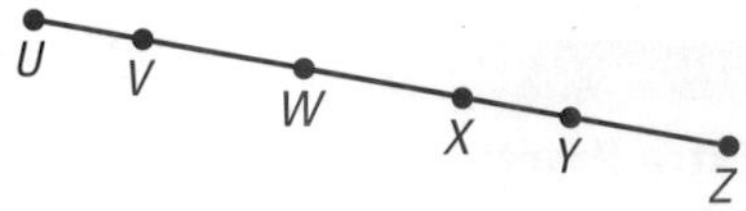

GIVEN ▶ $\overline{UV} \cong \overline{XY}$, $\overline{VW} \cong \overline{WX}$, $\overline{WX} \cong \overline{YZ}$

PROVE ▶ $\overline{UW} \cong \overline{XZ}$

Statements	Reasons
1. $\overline{UV} \cong \overline{XY}$, $\overline{VW} \cong \overline{WX}$, $\overline{WX} \cong \overline{YZ}$	Transitive Property of Segment Congruence
2. $\overline{VW} \cong \overline{YZ}$	Addition property of equality
3. $UV = XY$, $VW = YZ$	Definition of congruent segments
4. $UV + VW = XY + YZ$	Given
5. $UV + VW = UW$, $XY + YZ = XZ$	Segment Addition Postulate
6. $UW = XZ$	Definition of congruent segments
7. $\overline{UW} \cong \overline{XZ}$	Substitution property of equality

TWO-COLUMN PROOF **Write a two-column proof.**

17. **GIVEN** ▶ $XY = 8$, $XZ = 8$, $\overline{XY} \cong \overline{ZY}$

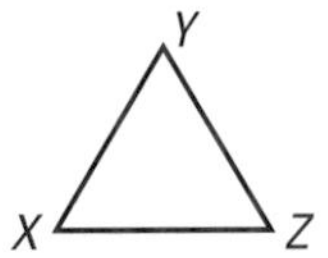

PROVE ▶ $\overline{XZ} \cong \overline{ZY}$

18. **GIVEN** ▶ $\overline{NK} \cong \overline{NL}$, $NK = 13$

PROVE ▶ $NL = 13$

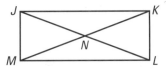

19. **CARPENTRY** You need to cut ten wood planks that are the same size. You measure and cut the first plank. You cut the second piece, using the first plank as a guide, as in the diagram below. The first plank is put aside and the second plank is used to cut a third plank. You follow this pattern for the rest of the planks. Is the last plank the same length as the first plank? Explain.

FOCUS ON CAREERS

CARPENTRY For many projects, carpenters need boards that are all the same length. For instance, equally-sized boards in the house frame above insure stability.

CAREER LINK
www.mcdougallittell.com

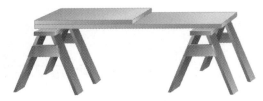

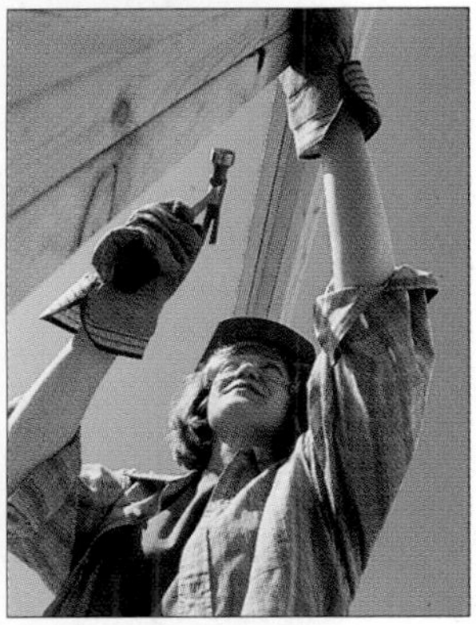

20. **OPTICAL ILLUSION** To create the illusion, a special grid was used. In the grid, corresponding row heights are the same measure. For instance, $\overline{UV}$ and $\overline{ZY}$ are congruent. You decide to make this design yourself. You draw the grid, but you need to make sure that the row heights are the same. You measure $\overline{UV}$, $\overline{UW}$, $\overline{ZY}$, and $\overline{ZX}$. You find that $\overline{UV} \cong \overline{ZY}$ and $\overline{UW} \cong \overline{ZX}$. Write an argument that allows you to conclude that $\overline{VW} \cong \overline{YX}$.

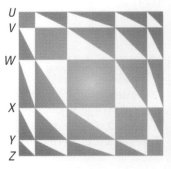

21. MULTIPLE CHOICE In $QRST$, $\overline{QT} \cong \overline{TS}$ and $\overline{RS} \cong \overline{TS}$. What is x?

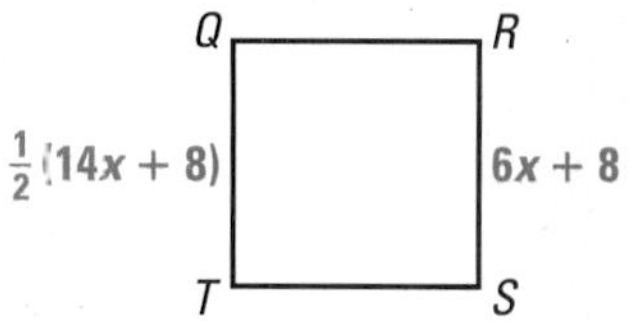

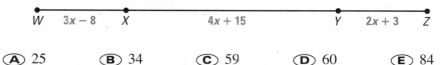

(**A**) 1   (**B**) 4   (**C**) 12

(**D**) 16   (**E**) 32

22. MULTIPLE CHOICE In the figure shown below, $\overline{WX} \cong \overline{YZ}$. What is the length of $\overline{XZ}$?

| W | 3x − 8 | X | 4x + 15 | Y | 2x + 3 | Z |

(**A**) 25   (**B**) 34   (**C**) 59   (**D**) 60   (**E**) 84

★ **Challenge**

REPRESENTING SEGMENT LENGTHS In Exercises 23–26, suppose point T is the midpoint of $\overline{RS}$ and point W is the midpoint of $\overline{RT}$. If $\overline{XY} \cong \overline{RT}$ and $\overline{TS}$ has a length of z, write the length of the segment in terms of z.

23. $\overline{RT}$ **24.** $\overline{XY}$ **25.** $\overline{RW}$ **26.** $\overline{WT}$

EXTRA CHALLENGE
www.mcdougallittell.com

27. CRITICAL THINKING Suppose M is the midpoint of $\overline{AB}$, P is the midpoint of $\overline{AM}$, and Q is the midpoint of $\overline{PM}$. If a and b are the coordinates of points A and B on a number line, find the coordinates of P and Q in terms of a and b.

MIXED REVIEW

FINDING COUNTEREXAMPLES Find a counterexample that shows the statement is false. **(Review 1.1)**

28. For every number n, $2^n > n + 1$.

29. The sum of an even number and an odd number is always even.

30. If a number is divisible by 5, then it is divisible by 10.

FINDING ANGLE MEASURES In Exercises 31–34, use the diagram to find the angle measure. **(Review 1.6 for 2.6)**

31. If $m\angle 6 = 64°$, then $m\angle 7 = $ __?__ .

32. If $m\angle 8 = 70°$, then $m\angle 6 = $ __?__ .

33. If $m\angle 9 = 115°$, then $m\angle 8 = $ __?__ .

34. If $m\angle 7 = 108°$, then $m\angle 8 = $ __?__ .

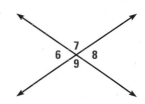

35. Write the contrapositive of the conditional statement, "If Matthew wins this wrestling match, then he will win first place." **(Review 2.1)**

36. Is the converse of a true conditional statement always true? Explain. **(Review 2.1)**

USING SYMBOLIC NOTATION Let p be "the car is in the garage" and let q be "Mark is home." Write the statement in words and symbols. **(Review 2.3)**

37. The conditional statement $p \rightarrow q$ **38.** The converse of $p \rightarrow q$

39. The inverse of $p \rightarrow q$ **40.** The contrapositive of $p \rightarrow q$

ACTIVITY 2.6

Developing Concepts

Group Activity for use with Lesson 2.6

Investigating Complementary Angles

GROUP ACTIVITY

Work with a partner.

MATERIALS

- paper
- pencils

QUESTION **If you know that two angles are complementary to the same angle, can you state that the angles are congruent?**

EXPLORING THE CONCEPT

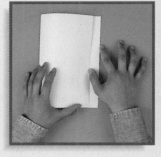

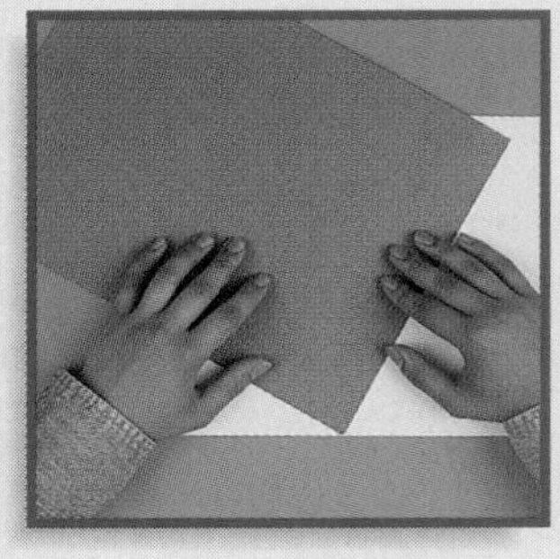

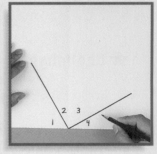

1. Fold a piece of paper in half to make a crease perpendicular to the bottom edge of the paper.
2. Open the piece of paper. Place a corner of a second piece of paper at the vertex of the right angles formed by the crease.
3. Trace the outline of the corner. Label the four angles formed by the lines and the crease.

STUDENT HELP

Look Back
For help with complementary and supplementary angles, see page 46.

DRAWING CONCLUSIONS

1. Explain how you know the following:
   a. $\angle 1$ and $\angle 2$ are complementary.
   b. $\angle 3$ and $\angle 4$ are complementary.
   c. $\angle 2$ and $\angle 3$ are complementary.
2. If $m\angle 1 + m\angle 2 = 90°$ and $m\angle 2 + m\angle 3 = 90°$, does $m\angle 1 = m\angle 3$? If $m\angle 3 + m\angle 4 = 90°$ and $m\angle 2 + m\angle 3 = 90°$, does $m\angle 2 = m\angle 4$? Explain your reasoning.
3. Repeat the steps above but change the position of the traced corner. Does $m\angle 1 = m\angle 3$? Does $m\angle 2 = m\angle 4$? Explain.

MAKE A CONJECTURE

4. Use your results to make a conjecture about two angles that are complementary to the same angle.

EXTENSION

If you know that two angles are *supplementary* to the same angle, can you state that the angles are congruent? If so, provide an argument. If not, provide a counterexample.

2.6

Proving Statements about Angles

What you should learn

GOAL 1 Use angle congruence properties.

GOAL 2 Prove properties about special pairs of angles.

Why you should learn it

▼ Properties of special pairs of angles help you determine angles in wood-working projects, such as the corners in the piece of furniture below and in the picture frame in **Ex. 30**.

GOAL 1 CONGRUENCE OF ANGLES

In Lesson 2.5, you proved segment relationships. In this lesson, you will prove statements about angles.

THEOREM

THEOREM 2.2 *Properties of Angle Congruence*

Angle congruence is reflexive, symmetric, and transitive.

Here are some examples.

REFLEXIVE	For any angle A, $\angle A \cong \angle A$.
SYMMETRIC	If $\angle A \cong \angle B$, then $\angle B \cong \angle A$.
TRANSITIVE	If $\angle A \cong \angle B$ and $\angle B \cong \angle C$, then $\angle A \cong \angle C$.

The Transitive Property of Angle Congruence is proven in Example 1. The Reflexive and Symmetric Properties are left for you to prove in Exercises 10 and 11.

EXAMPLE 1 *Transitive Property of Angle Congruence*

Prove the Transitive Property of Congruence for angles.

SOLUTION

To prove the Transitive Property of Congruence for angles, begin by drawing three congruent angles. Label the vertices as A, B, and C.

GIVEN ▶ $\angle A \cong \angle B$,
$\quad\quad\quad \angle B \cong \angle C$

PROVE ▶ $\angle A \cong \angle C$

Statements	Reasons
1. $\angle A \cong \angle B$, $\quad \angle B \cong \angle C$	1. Given
2. $m\angle A = m\angle B$	2. Definition of congruent angles
3. $m\angle B = m\angle C$	3. Definition of congruent angles
4. $m\angle A = m\angle C$	4. Transitive property of equality
5. $\angle A \cong \angle C$	5. Definition of congruent angles

EXAMPLE 2 *Using the Transitive Property*

Proof This two-column proof uses the Transitive Property.

GIVEN ▸ $m\angle 3 = 40°$, $\angle 1 \cong \angle 2$, $\angle 2 \cong \angle 3$

PROVE ▸ $m\angle 1 = 40°$

Statements	Reasons
1. $m\angle 3 = 40°$, $\angle 1 \cong \angle 2$, $\angle 2 \cong \angle 3$	1. Given
2. $\angle 1 \cong \angle 3$	2. Transitive Property of Congruence
3. $m\angle 1 = m\angle 3$	3. Definition of congruent angles
4. $m\angle 1 = 40°$	4. Substitution property of equality

THEOREM

THEOREM 2.3 *Right Angle Congruence Theorem*

All right angles are congruent.

EXAMPLE 3 *Proving Theorem 2.3*

Proof You can prove Theorem 2.3 as shown.

GIVEN ▸ $\angle 1$ and $\angle 2$ are right angles

PROVE ▸ $\angle 1 \cong \angle 2$

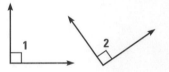

Statements	Reasons
1. $\angle 1$ and $\angle 2$ are right angles	1. Given
2. $m\angle 1 = 90°$, $m\angle 2 = 90°$	2. Definition of right angle
3. $m\angle 1 = m\angle 2$	3. Transitive property of equality
4. $\angle 1 \cong \angle 2$	4. Definition of congruent angles

▶ **ACTIVITY**

Using Technology **Investigating Supplementary Angles**

Use geometry software to draw and label two intersecting lines.

1 What do you notice about the measures of $\angle AQB$ and $\angle AQC$? $\angle AQC$ and $\angle CQD$? $\angle AQB$ and $\angle CQD$?

2 Rotate $\overleftrightarrow{BC}$ to a different position. Do the angles retain the same relationship?

3 Make a conjecture about two angles supplementary to the same angle.

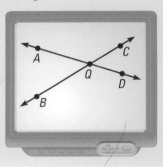

GOAL 2 **PROPERTIES OF SPECIAL PAIRS OF ANGLES**

THEOREMS

THEOREM 2.4 *Congruent Supplements Theorem*

If two angles are supplementary to
the same angle (or to congruent angles)
then they are congruent.

> If $m\angle 1 + m\angle 2 = 180°$ and
> $m\angle 2 + m\angle 3 = 180°$, then $\angle 1 \cong \angle 3$.

THEOREM 2.5 *Congruent Complements Theorem*

If two angles are complementary to the
same angle (or to congruent angles) then
the two angles are congruent.

> If $m\angle 4 + m\angle 5 = 90°$ and
> $m\angle 5 + m\angle 6 = 90°$, then $\angle 4 \cong \angle 6$.

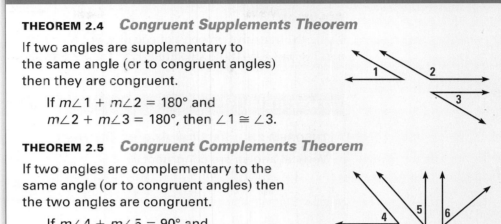

EXAMPLE 4 *Proving Theorem 2.4*

GIVEN ▶ $\angle 1$ and $\angle 2$ are supplements,
$\angle 3$ and $\angle 4$ are supplements,
$\angle 1 \cong \angle 4$

PROVE ▶ $\angle 2 \cong \angle 3$

Statements	Reasons
1. $\angle 1$ and $\angle 2$ are supplements, $\angle 3$ and $\angle 4$ are supplements, $\angle 1 \cong \angle 4$	**1.** Given
2. $m\angle 1 + m\angle 2 = 180°$ $m\angle 3 + m\angle 4 = 180°$	**2.** Definition of supplementary angles
3. $m\angle 1 + m\angle 2 = m\angle 3 + m\angle 4$	**3.** Transitive property of equality
4. $m\angle 1 = m\angle 4$	**4.** Definition of congruent angles
5. $m\angle 1 + m\angle 2 = m\angle 3 + m\angle 1$	**5.** Substitution property of equality
6. $m\angle 2 = m\angle 3$	**6.** Subtraction property of equality
7. $\angle 2 \cong \angle 3$	**7.** Definition of congruent angles

POSTULATE

POSTULATE 12 *Linear Pair Postulate*

If two angles form a linear pair,
then they are supplementary.

$m\angle 1 + m\angle 2 = 180°$

EXAMPLE 5 *Using Linear Pairs*

In the diagram, $m\angle 8 = m\angle 5$ and $m\angle 5 = 125°$.
Explain how to show $m\angle 7 = 55°$.

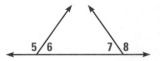

SOLUTION

Using the transitive property of equality, $m\angle 8 = 125°$. The diagram shows $m\angle 7 + m\angle 8 = 180°$. Substitute $125°$ for $m\angle 8$ to show $m\angle 7 = 55°$.

THEOREM

THEOREM 2.6 *Vertical Angles Theorem*
Vertical angles are congruent.

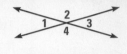

$\angle 1 \cong \angle 3, \angle 2 \cong \angle 4$

┌─ **STUDENT HELP**

▸ **Study Tip**
Remember that previously proven theorems can be used as reasons in a proof, as in **Step 3** of the proof at the right.

EXAMPLE 6 *Proving Theorem 2.6*

GIVEN ▶ $\angle 5$ and $\angle 6$ are a linear pair,
$\angle 6$ and $\angle 7$ are a linear pair

PROVE ▶ $\angle 5 \cong \angle 7$

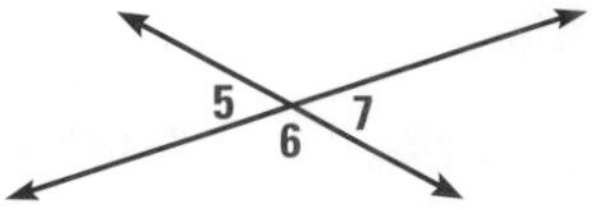

Statements	Reasons
1. $\angle 5$ and $\angle 6$ are a linear pair, $\angle 6$ and $\angle 7$ are a linear pair	1. Given
2. $\angle 5$ and $\angle 6$ are supplementary, $\angle 6$ and $\angle 7$ are supplementary	2. Linear Pair Postulate
3. $\angle 5 \cong \angle 7$	3. Congruent Supplements Theorem

GUIDED PRACTICE

Vocabulary Check ✓ **1.** "If $\angle CDE \cong$ __?__ and $\angle QRS \cong \angle XYZ$, then $\angle CDE \cong \angle XYZ$," is an example of the __?__ Property of Angle Congruence.

Concept Check ✓ **2.** To close the blades of the scissors, you close the handles. Will the angle formed by the blades be the same as the angle formed by the handles? Explain.

Skill Check ✓ **3.** By the Transitive Property of Congruence, if $\angle A \cong \angle B$ and $\angle B \cong \angle C$, then __?__ $\cong \angle C$.

In Exercises 4–9, $\angle 1$ and $\angle 3$ are a linear pair, $\angle 1$ and $\angle 4$ are a linear pair, and $\angle 1$ and $\angle 2$ are vertical angles. Is the statement true?

4. $\angle 1 \cong \angle 3$ **5.** $\angle 1 \cong \angle 2$ **6.** $\angle 1 \cong \angle 4$

7. $\angle 3 \cong \angle 2$ **8.** $\angle 3 \cong \angle 4$ **9.** $m\angle 2 + m\angle 3 = 180°$

PRACTICE AND APPLICATIONS

STUDENT HELP

▶ **Extra Practice**
to help you master
skills is on p. 806.

10. ▶ **PROVING THEOREM 2.2** Copy and complete the proof of the Symmetric Property of Congruence for angles.

GIVEN ▶ $\angle A \cong \angle B$

PROVE ▶ $\angle B \cong \angle A$

Statements	Reasons
1. $\angle A \cong \angle B$	**1.** ___?___
2. ___?___	**2.** Definition of congruent angles
3. $m\angle B = m\angle A$	**3.** ___?___
4. $\angle B \cong \angle A$	**4.** ___?___

11. ▶ **PROVING THEOREM 2.2** Write a two-column proof for the Reflexive Property of Congruence for angles.

FINDING ANGLES In Exercises 12–17, complete the statement given that $m\angle EHC = m\angle DHB = m\angle AHB = 90°$

12. If $m\angle 7 = 28°$, then $m\angle 3 = $ ___?___.

13. If $m\angle EHB = 121°$, then $m\angle 7 = $ ___?___.

14. If $m\angle 3 = 34°$, then $m\angle 5 = $ ___?___.

15. If $m\angle GHB = 158°$, then $m\angle FHC = $ ___?___.

16. If $m\angle 7 = 31°$, then $m\angle 6 = $ ___?___.

17. If $m\angle GHD = 119°$, then $m\angle 4 = $ ___?___.

18. ▶ **PROVING THEOREM 2.5** Copy and complete the proof of the Congruent Complements Theorem.

GIVEN ▶ $\angle 1$ and $\angle 2$ are complements,
$\angle 3$ and $\angle 4$ are complements,
$\angle 2 \cong \angle 4$

PROVE ▶ $\angle 1 \cong \angle 3$

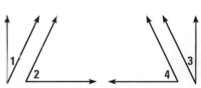

STUDENT HELP

▶ **HOMEWORK HELP**
Example 1: Exs. 10, 11
Example 2: Exs. 12–17
Example 3: Exs. 12–17
Example 4: Exs. 19–22
Example 5: Exs. 23–28
Example 6: Exs. 23–28

Statements	Reasons
1. $\angle 1$ and $\angle 2$ are complements, $\angle 3$ and $\angle 4$ are complements, $\angle 2 \cong \angle 4$	**1.** ___?___
2. ___?___ , ___?___	**2.** Def. of complementary angles
3. $m\angle 1 + m\angle 2 = m\angle 3 + m\angle 4$	**3.** Transitive property of equality
4. $m\angle 2 = m\angle 4$	**4.** ___?___
5. $m\angle 1 + m\angle 2 = m\angle 3 + m\angle 2$	**5.** ___?___
6. $m\angle 1 = m\angle 3$	**6.** ___?___
7. ___?___	**7.** Definition of congruent angles

FINDING CONGRUENT ANGLES Make a sketch using the given information. Then, state all of the pairs of congruent angles.

19. $\angle 1$ and $\angle 2$ are a linear pair. $\angle 2$ and $\angle 3$ are a linear pair. $\angle 3$ and $\angle 4$ are a linear pair.

20. $\angle XYZ$ and $\angle VYW$ are vertical angles. $\angle XYZ$ and $\angle ZYW$ are supplementary. $\angle VYW$ and $\angle XYV$ are supplementary.

21. $\angle 1$ and $\angle 3$ are complementary. $\angle 4$ and $\angle 2$ are complementary. $\angle 1$ and $\angle 2$ are vertical angles.

22. $\angle ABC$ and $\angle CBD$ are adjacent, complementary angles. $\angle CBD$ and $\angle DBF$ are adjacent, complementary angles.

▶ **WRITING PROOFS** Write a two-column proof.

23. GIVEN ▶ $m\angle 3 = 120°$, $\angle 1 \cong \angle 4$, $\angle 3 \cong \angle 4$

PROVE ▶ $m\angle 1 = 120°$

Plan for Proof First show that $\angle 1 \cong \angle 3$. Then use transitivity to show that $m\angle 1 = 120°$.

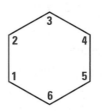

24. GIVEN ▶ $\angle 3$ and $\angle 2$ are complementary, $m\angle 1 + m\angle 2 = 90°$

PROVE ▶ $\angle 3 \cong \angle 1$

Plan for Proof First show that $\angle 1$ and $\angle 2$ are complementary. Then show that $\angle 3 \cong \angle 1$.

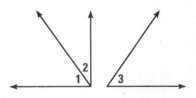

25. GIVEN ▶ $\angle QVW$ and $\angle RWV$ are supplementary

PROVE ▶ $\angle QVP \cong \angle RWV$

Plan for Proof First show that $\angle QVP$ and $\angle QVW$ are supplementary. Then show that $\angle QVP \cong \angle RWV$.

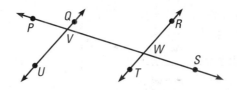

26. GIVEN ▶ $\angle 5 \cong \angle 6$

PROVE ▶ $\angle 4 \cong \angle 7$

Plan for Proof First show that $\angle 4 \cong \angle 5$ and $\angle 6 \cong \angle 7$. Then use transitivity to show that $\angle 4 \cong \angle 7$.

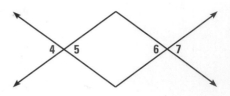

USING ALGEBRA In Exercises 27 and 28, solve for each variable. Explain your reasoning.

27.

28.

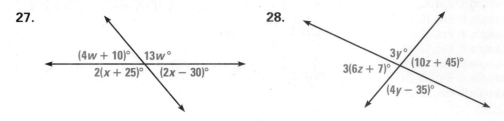

MITER BOX This box has slotted sides to guide a saw when making angled cuts.

29. 🌐 **WALL TRIM** A chair rail is a type of wall trim that is placed about three feet above the floor to protect the walls. Part of the chair rail below has been replaced because it was damaged. The edges of the replacement piece were angled for a better fit. In the diagram, ∠1 and ∠2 are supplementary, ∠3 and ∠4 are supplementary, and ∠2 and ∠3 each have measures of 50°. Is ∠1 ≅ ∠4? Explain.

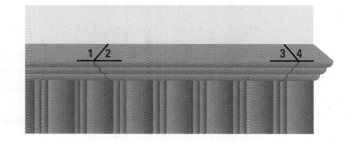

30. 🌐 **PICTURE FRAMES** Suppose you are making a picture frame, as shown at the right. The corners are all right angles, and m∠1 = m∠2 = 52°. Is ∠4 ≅ ∠3? Explain why or why not.

31. *Writing* Describe some instances of mitered, or angled, corners in the real world.

32. 🖳 **TECHNOLOGY** Use geometry software to draw two overlapping right angles with a common vertex. Observe the measures of the three angles as one right angle is rotated about the other. What theorem does this illustrate?

Test Preparation

QUANTITATIVE COMPARISON Choose the statement that is true about the diagram. In the diagram, ∠9 is a right angle and m∠3 = 42°.

(A) The quantity in column A is greater.

(B) The quantity in column B is greater.

(C) The two quantities are equal.

(D) The relationship can't be determined from the given information.

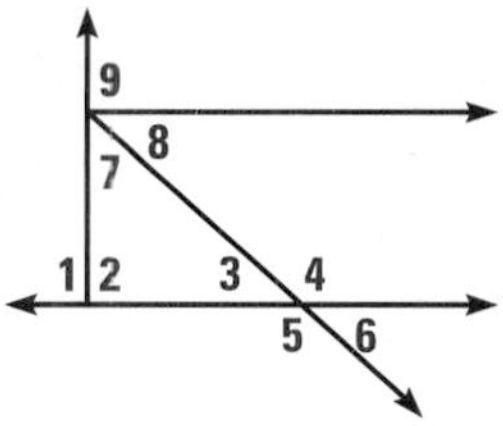

	Column A	Column B
33.	$m\angle 3 + m\angle 4$	$m\angle 1 + m\angle 2$
34.	$m\angle 3 + m\angle 6$	$m\angle 7 + m\angle 8$
35.	$m\angle 5$	$3(m\angle 3)$
36.	$m\angle 7 + m\angle 8$	$m\angle 9$

★ **Challenge**

37. ▶ **PROOF** Write a two-column proof.

GIVEN ▶ $m\angle ZYQ = 45°$,
$m\angle ZQP = 45°$

PROVE ▶ $\angle ZQR \cong \angle XYQ$

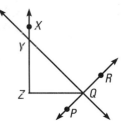

MIXED REVIEW

FINDING ANGLE MEASURES In Exercises 38–40, the measure of ∠1 and the relationship of ∠1 to ∠2 is given. Find $m\angle 2$. (Review 1.6 for 3.1)

38. $m\angle 1 = 62°$, complementary to $\angle 2$

39. $m\angle 1 = 8°$, supplementary to $\angle 2$

40. $m\angle 1 = 47°$, complementary to $\angle 2$

41. PERPENDICULAR LINES The definition of perpendicular lines states that if two lines are perpendicular, then they intersect to form a right angle. Is the converse true? Explain. (Review 2.2 for 3.1)

(xy) **USING ALGEBRA** Use the diagram and the given information to solve for the variable. (Review 2.5)

42. $\overline{AD} \cong \overline{EF}, \overline{EF} \cong \overline{CF}$

43. $\overline{AB} \cong \overline{EF}, \overline{EF} \cong \overline{BC}$

44. $\overline{DE} \cong \overline{EF}, \overline{EF} \cong \overline{JK}$

45. $\overline{JM} \cong \overline{ML}, \overline{ML} \cong \overline{KL}$

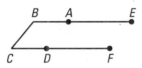

QUIZ 2

Solve the equation and state a reason for each step. (Lesson 2.4)

1. $x - 3 = 7$

2. $x + 8 = 27$

3. $2x - 5 = 13$

4. $2x + 20 = 4x - 12$

5. $3(3x - 7) = 6$

6. $-2(-2x + 4) = 16$

▶ **PROOF** In Exercises 7 and 8 write a two column proof. (Lesson 2.5)

7. GIVEN ▶ $\overline{BA} \cong \overline{BC}, \overline{BC} \cong \overline{CD},$
$\overline{AE} \cong \overline{DF}$

  PROVE ▶ $\overline{BE} \cong \overline{CF}$

8. GIVEN ▶ $\overline{EH} \cong \overline{GH}, \overline{FG} \cong \overline{GH}$

  PROVE ▶ $\overline{FG} \cong \overline{EH}$

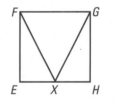

9. 🌐 **ASTRONOMY** While looking through a telescope one night, you begin looking due east. You rotate the telescope straight upward until you spot a comet. The telescope forms a 142° angle with due east, as shown. What is the angle of inclination of the telescope from due west? (Lesson 2.6)

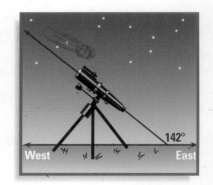

Chapter Summary

WHAT did you learn?

Recognize and analyze conditional statements, and write their inverses, converses, and contrapositives. **(2.1)**

Recognize and use definitions and biconditional statements. **(2.2)**

Use symbolic notation to represent logical statements. **(2.3)**

Use the laws of logic to write a logical argument. **(2.3)**

Use properties from algebra. **(2.4)**

Use properties of length and measure. **(2.4)**

Use the properties of segment congruence to prove statements about segments. **(2.5)**

Use the properties of angle congruence to prove properties about special pairs of angles. **(2.6)**

WHY did you learn it?

Use postulates about points, lines, and planes to analyze real-life objects, such as a research buggy. **(p. 77)**

Rewrite postulates in a form suitable for solving a particular problem, such as analyzing geographic relations. **(p. 84)**

Decide whether a logical statement is valid. **(p. 89)**

Write true statements about birds using a list of facts about birds. **(p. 90)**

Use properties from algebra to solve equations, such as an athlete's target heart rate. **(p. 97)**

Find the measure of the angle of a banked turn at the Talladega Superspeedway. **(p. 98)**

Prove statements about segments in real life, such as the segments in a trestle bridge. **(p. 104)**

Decide which angles are congruent when constructing a picture frame. **(p. 115)**

How does it fit into the BIGGER PICTURE of geometry?

In this chapter, you were introduced to the formal side of geometry. You learned that the structure of geometry consists of undefined terms, defined terms, postulates, and theorems. You were also introduced to the need for proofs, and the form of a proof. In later chapters, you will study other ways to write proofs. The goal of writing a proof will remain the same—to convince a person about the truth of a statement.

STUDY STRATEGY

How was previewing each lesson helpful?

Some of the notes you made while previewing a lesson, following the **Study Strategy** on page 70, may resemble these.

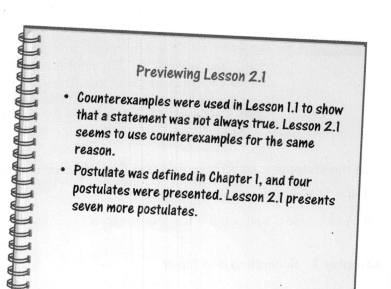

Previewing Lesson 2.1

- Counterexamples were used in Lesson 1.1 to show that a statement was not always true. Lesson 2.1 seems to use counterexamples for the same reason.

- Postulate was defined in Chapter 1, and four postulates were presented. Lesson 2.1 presents seven more postulates.

CHAPTER 2

Chapter Review

VOCABULARY

- conditional statement, p. 71
- if-then form, p. 71
- hypothesis, p. 71
- conclusion, p. 71
- converse, p. 72
- negation, p. 72
- inverse, p. 72
- contrapositive, p. 72
- equivalent statement, p. 72
- perpendicular lines, p. 79
- line perpendicular to a plane, p. 79
- biconditional statement, p. 80
- logical argument, p. 89
- Law of Detachment, p. 89
- Law of Syllogism, p. 90
- theorem, p. 102
- two-column proof, p. 102
- paragraph proof, p. 102

2.1 CONDITIONAL STATEMENTS

Examples on pp. 71–74

EXAMPLES

If-then form	If a person is 2 meters tall, then he or she is 6.56 feet tall.
Inverse	If a person is not 2 meters tall, then he or she is not 6.56 feet tall.
Converse	If a person is 6.56 feet tall, then he or she is 2 meters tall.
Contrapositive	If a person is not 6.56 feet tall, then he or she is not 2 meters tall.

Write the statement in if-then form. Determine the hypothesis and conclusion, and write the inverse, converse, and contrapositive.

1. We are dismissed early if there is a teacher's meeting.
2. I prepare dinner on Wednesday nights.

Fill in the blank. Then draw a sketch that illustrates your answer.

3. Through any three noncollinear points there exists __?__ plane.
4. A line contains at least __?__ points.

2.2 DEFINITIONS AND BICONDITIONAL STATEMENTS

Examples on pp. 79–81

EXAMPLE The statement "If a number ends in 0, then the number is divisible by 10," and its converse "If a number is divisible by 10, then the number ends in 0," are both true. This means that the statement can be written as the true biconditional statement, "A number is divisible by 10 if and only if it ends in 0."

Can the statement be written as a true biconditional statement?

5. If $x = 5$, then $x^2 = 25$.
6. A rectangle is a square if it has four congruent sides.

DEDUCTIVE REASONING

Examples on
pp. 87–90

EXAMPLES Using symbolic notation, let p be "it is summer" and let q be "school is closed."

Statement	$p \rightarrow q$	If it is summer, then school is closed.
Inverse	$\sim p \rightarrow \sim q$	If it is not summer, then school is not closed.
Converse	$q \rightarrow p$	If the school is closed, then it is summer.
Contrapositive	$\sim q \rightarrow \sim p$	If school is not closed, then it is not summer.

Write the symbolic statement in words using p and q given below.

p: $\angle A$ is a right angle. q: The measure of $\angle A$ is $90°$.

7. $q \rightarrow p$ **8.** $\sim q \rightarrow \sim p$ **9.** $\sim p$ **10.** $\sim p \rightarrow \sim q$

Use the Law of Syllogism to write the statement that follows from the pair of true statements.

11. If there is a nice breeze, then the mast is up.

If the mast is up, then we will sail to Dunkirk.

12. If Chess Club meets today, then it is Thursday.

If it is Thursday, then the garbage needs to be taken out.

REASONING WITH PROPERTIES FROM ALGEBRA

Examples on
pp. 96–98

EXAMPLE In the diagram, $m\angle 1 + m\angle 2 = 132°$ and $m\angle 2 = 105°$. The argument shows that $m\angle 1 = 27°$.

$m\angle 1 + m\angle 2 = 132°$	Given
$m\angle 2 = 105°$	Given
$m\angle 1 + 105° = 132°$	Substitution property of equality
$m\angle 1 = 27°$	Subtraction property of equality

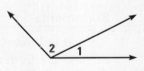

Match the statement with the property.

13. If $m\angle S = 45°$, then $m\angle S + 45° = 90°$.   **A.** Symmetric property of equality

14. If $UV = VW$, then $VW = UV$.   **B.** Multiplication property of equality

15. If $AE = EG$ and $EG = JK$, then $AE = JK$.   **C.** Addition property of equality

16. If $m\angle K = 9°$, then $3(m\angle K) = 27°$.   **D.** Transitive property of equality

Solve the equation and state a reason for each step.

17. $5(3y + 2) = 25$ **18.** $8t - 4 = 5t + 8$ **19.** $23 + 11d - 2c = 12 - 2c$

PROVING STATEMENTS ABOUT SEGMENTS

Examples on pp. 102–104

EXAMPLE A proof that shows $AC = 2 \cdot BC$ is shown below.

GIVEN ▶ $AB = BC$

PROVE ▶ $AC = 2 \cdot BC$

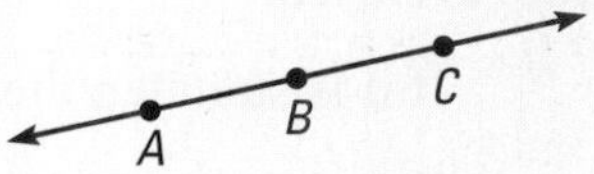

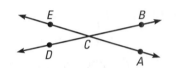

Statements	Reasons
1. $AB = BC$	1. Given
2. $AC = AB + BC$	2. Segment Addition Postulate
3. $AC = BC + BC$	3. Substitution property of equality
4. $AC = 2 \cdot BC$	4. Distributive property

20. Write a two-column proof.

GIVEN ▶ $\overline{AE} \cong \overline{BD}$, $\overline{CD} \cong \overline{CE}$

PROVE ▶ $\overline{AC} \cong \overline{BC}$

PROVING STATEMENTS ABOUT ANGLES

Examples on pp. 109–112

EXAMPLE A proof that shows $\angle 2 \cong \angle 3$ is shown below.

GIVEN ▶ $\angle 1$ and $\angle 2$ form a linear pair,
$\angle 3$ and $\angle 4$ form a linear pair,
$\angle 1 \cong \angle 4$

PROVE ▶ $\angle 2 \cong \angle 3$

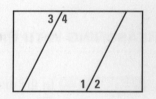

Statements	Reasons
1. $\angle 1$ and $\angle 2$ form a linear pair, $\angle 3$ and $\angle 4$ form a linear pair, $\angle 1 \cong \angle 4$	1. Given
2. $\angle 1$ and $\angle 2$ are supplementary, $\angle 3$ and $\angle 4$ are supplementary	2. Linear Pair Postulate
3. $\angle 2 \cong \angle 3$	3. Congruent Supplements Theorem

21. Write a two-column proof using the given information.

GIVEN ▶ $\angle 1$ and $\angle 2$ are complementary,
$\angle 3$ and $\angle 4$ are complementary,
$\angle 1 \cong \angle 3$

PROVE ▶ $\angle 2 \cong \angle 4$

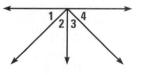

State the postulate that shows that the statement is false.

1. Plane R contains only two points A and B.

2. Plane M and plane N are two distinct planes that intersect at exactly two distinct points.

3. Any three noncollinear points define at least three distinct planes.

4. Points A and B are two distinct points in plane Q. Line $\overleftrightarrow{AB}$ does not intersect plane Q.

Find a counterexample that demonstrates that the converse of the statement is false.

5. If an angle measures 34°, then the angle is acute.

6. If the lengths of two segments are each 17 feet, then the segments are congruent.

7. If two angles measure 32° and 148°, then they are supplementary.

8. If you chose number 13, then you chose a prime number.

State what conclusions can be made if $x = 5$ and the given statement is true.

9. If $x > x - 2$, then $y = 14x$.

10. If $-x < 2x < 11$, then $x = y - 12$.

11. If $|x| > -x$, then $y = -x$.

12. If $y = 4x$, then $z = 2x + y$.

In Exercises 13–16, name the property used to make the conclusion.

13. If $13 = x$, then $x = 13$.

14. If $x = 3$, then $5x = 15$.

15. If $x = y$ and $y = 4$, then $x = 4$.

16. If $x + 3 = 17$, then $x = 14$.

17. ● **PROOF** Write a two-column proof.

    GIVEN ▶ $\overline{AX} \cong \overline{DX}$, $\overline{XB} \cong \overline{XC}$

    PROVE ▶ $\overline{AC} \cong \overline{BD}$

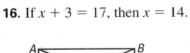

18. 🌐 **PLUMBING** A plumber is replacing a small section of a leaky pipe. To find the length of new pipe that he will need, he first measures the leaky section of the old pipe with a steel tape measure, and then uses this measure to find the same length of new pipe. What property of segment congruence does this process illustrate? Use the wording of the property to explain how it is illustrated.

19. 🌐 **PACKAGING** A tool and die company produces a part that is to be packed in triangular boxes. To maximize space and minimize cost, the boxes need to be designed to fit together in shipping cartons. If $\angle 1$ and $\angle 2$ have to be complementary, $\angle 3$ and $\angle 4$ have to be complementary, and $m\angle 2 = m\angle 3$, describe the relationship between $\angle 1$ and $\angle 4$.

Chapter Standardized Test

▶ **TEST-TAKING STRATEGY** Make sure that you are familiar with the directions before taking a standardized test. This way, you do not need to worry about the directions during the test.

1. **MULTIPLE CHOICE** What is the contrapositive of "If it is Tuesday, then Marie has soccer practice?"

   Ⓐ If it is not Tuesday, then Marie does not have soccer practice.

   Ⓑ If Marie has soccer practice, then it is Tuesday.

   Ⓒ If Marie does not have soccer practice, then it is not Tuesday.

   Ⓓ Marie has soccer practice if and only if it is Tuesday.

   Ⓔ None of the above.

2. **MULTIPLE CHOICE** Which statement about the diagram is *not* true?

   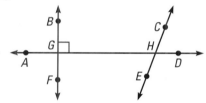

   Ⓐ $\angle GHE$ is adjacent to $\angle CHD$.

   Ⓑ $\overline{BF}$ is perpendicular to $\overline{AH}$.

   Ⓒ $\angle BGH$ and $\angle BGA$ are supplementary.

   Ⓓ $\angle GHC \cong \angle EHD$

   Ⓔ $m\angle BGH = 90°$

3. **QUANTITATIVE COMPARISON** Two quantities are described below.

Column A	Column B
The number of lines that can be drawn through two points.	The number of planes that can be drawn through three noncollinear points.

   Choose the statement that is true.

   Ⓐ The quantity in column A is greater.

   Ⓑ The quantity in column B is greater.

   Ⓒ The two quantities are equal.

   Ⓓ The relationship cannot be determined from the given information.

4. **MULTIPLE CHOICE** "If $m\angle A = 75°$, then $10° + m\angle A = 85°$" is an example of the

   Ⓐ Substitution property of equality.

   Ⓑ Addition property of equality.

   Ⓒ Symmetric property of equality.

   Ⓓ Subtraction property of equality.

   Ⓔ Distributive property.

5. **MULTIPLE CHOICE** In the diagram, $\overline{AB} \cong \overline{CD}$. Find the length of $\overline{CA}$.

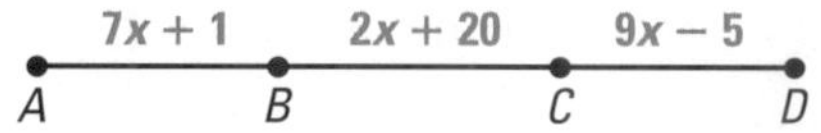

   $$\underset{A}{\bullet}\overset{7x+1}{\rule{2.5cm}{0.4pt}}\underset{B}{\bullet}\overset{2x+20}{\rule{2.5cm}{0.4pt}}\underset{C}{\bullet}\overset{9x-5}{\rule{2.5cm}{0.4pt}}\underset{D}{\bullet}$$

   Ⓐ 22   Ⓑ 26   Ⓒ 39

   Ⓓ 44   Ⓔ 48

6. **MULTIPLE CHOICE** Let p be "there is lightning" and let q be "we cannot go hiking." What is the converse of $p \rightarrow q$?

   Ⓐ If there is lightning, then we cannot go hiking.

   Ⓑ If we can go hiking, then there is no lightning.

   Ⓒ If we cannot go hiking, then there is lightning.

   Ⓓ If there is no lightning, then we can go hiking.

   Ⓔ None of the above.

7. **MULTIPLE CHOICE** In $WXYZ$, $\overline{WZ} \cong \overline{YZ}$ and $\overline{YX} \cong \overline{YZ}$. What is the value of x?

   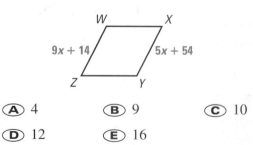

   Ⓐ 4   Ⓑ 9   Ⓒ 10

   Ⓓ 12   Ⓔ 16

8. **MULTIPLE CHOICE** Two angles $\angle PQR$ and $\angle RQS$ form a linear pair. If $m\angle PQR = 48°$, what is $m\angle RQS$?

   Ⓐ 42°   Ⓑ 48°   Ⓒ 90°

   Ⓓ 132°   Ⓔ 180°

9. MULTIPLE CHOICE Two angles, $\angle 7$ and $\angle 8$, are both complementary to $\angle 9$. If $m\angle 7 = 61°$, what is $m\angle 8$?

    A $29°$ **B** $61°$ **C** $90°$ **D** $119°$ **E** $180°$

10. MULTIPLE CHOICE In the diagram below, $\angle 1 \cong \angle 2$. Which of the following is *not* true?

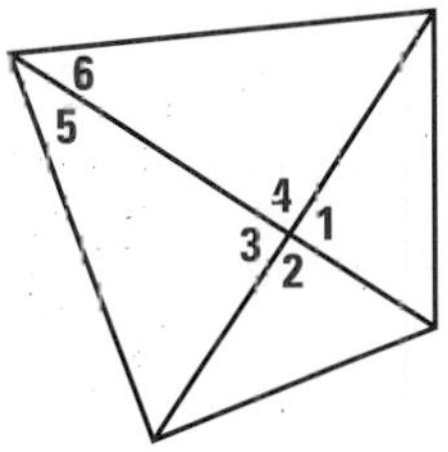

    A $\angle 1 \cong \angle 4$

    B $m\angle 1 + m\angle 2 = 180°$

    C $\angle 1 \cong \angle 3$

    D $\angle 2$ and $\angle 4$ are supplementary.

    E $m\angle 6 = m\angle 4$

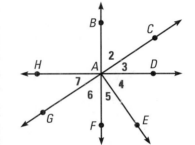

MULTI-STEP PROBLEM In Exercises 11–13, use the diagram. In the diagram, $\overleftrightarrow{BF} \perp \overleftrightarrow{HD}$ and $\overleftrightarrow{GC} \perp \overrightarrow{AE}$.

11. Complete each statement.

    a. If $m\angle 3 = 31°$, then $m\angle 5 = $ __?__ .

    b. If $m\angle 5 = 29°$, then $m\angle 4 = $ __?__ .

    c. If $m\angle CAF = 122°$, then $m\angle GAB = $ __?__ .

    d. If $m\angle 7 = 35°$, then $m\angle 3 = $ __?__ .

12. Write a two-column proof that shows $\angle BAH \cong \angle CAE$.

13. Write a paragraph proof that shows $\angle 6 \cong \angle 2$.

MULTI-STEP PROBLEM In Exercises 14–17, use the following information.

The International Space Station (ISS) is a NASA project which will involve about 45 launch missions. The space station is scheduled for completion in early 2004. The diagram shows a portion of the space station. In the diagram, $\overline{AE} \perp \overline{XC}$ and X is the midpoint of $\overline{AE}$.

14. Are $\angle DXC$ and $\angle DXE$ complementary or supplementary?

15. Determine whether there is enough information to prove each of the following. If so, write a plan for the proof.

    a. $\overline{XE} \cong \overline{XC}$

    b. $\angle AXC \cong \angle EXC$

    c. $\overline{EX} \cong \overline{AX}$

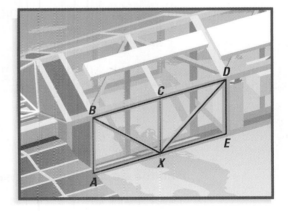

16. Tell whether the statement is *true* or *false*.

    a. $m\angle BXD + m\angle BXE = m\angle EXA$

    b. $m\angle AXD + m\angle DXE = m\angle EXA$

    c. $m\angle AXD + m\angle DXB = m\angle EXA$

17. Write a two-column proof to show that $\angle BXA$ and $\angle CXB$ are complementary.

Algebra Review

EXAMPLE 1   *Determining Whether a Point is on a Line*

Decide whether $(3, -2)$ is a solution of the equation $y = 2x - 8$.

$$-2 = 2(3) - 8 \qquad \text{Substitute 3 for } x \text{ and } -2 \text{ for } y.$$

$$-2 = -2 \qquad \text{Simplify.}$$

The statement is true, so $(3, -2)$ is a solution of the equation $y = 2x - 8$.

STUDENT HELP

▶ **Look Back**
For help with the
properties of equality,
see p. 96.

EXERCISES

Decide whether the given ordered pair is a solution of the equation.

1. $y = 6x + 4; (-2, 8)$

2. $y = -10x - 2; (1, -12)$

3. $y = -\frac{1}{4}x - 18; (-4, -17)$

4. $y = \frac{3}{2}x + 10; (4, 12)$

5. $y = \frac{5}{9}x + 34; (-9, 27)$

6. $y = \frac{2}{3}x - 6; (9, 0)$

7. $y = \frac{4}{5}x - 2; (10, -3)$

8. $y = \frac{1}{2}x + 7; (4, 7)$

9. $2x - 3y = 10; (3, 4)$

10. $9x - y = -4; (-1, -5)$

11. $y - 6 = \frac{3}{4}x; (8, 12)$

12. $y + 5 = \frac{5}{3}x; (9, 10)$

EXAMPLE 2   *Calculating Slope*

Find the slope of a line passing through $(3, -9)$ and $(2, -1)$.

$$m = \frac{y_2 - y_1}{x_2 - x_1} \qquad \text{Formula for slope}$$

$$m = \frac{-1 - (-9)}{2 - 3} = \frac{-1 + 9}{-1} \qquad \text{Substitute values and simplify.}$$

$$m = \frac{8}{-1} = -8 \qquad \text{Slope is } -8.$$

EXERCISES

Find the slope of the line that contains the points.

13. $(4, 1), (3, 6)$

14. $(-8, 0), (5, -2)$

15. $(5, 6), (9, 8)$

16. $(0, -4), (7, -3)$

17. $(-1, 7), (-3, 18)$

18. $(-6, -4), (1, 10)$

19. $(4, -10), (-2, 2)$

20. $(11, 1), (-11, 1)$

21. $(14, -5), (5, 8)$

22. $(-7, 5), (-1, -1)$

23. $(-12, 8), (-3, -6)$

24. $(-9, 13), (2, -10)$

25. $(12, 3), (0, -4)$

26. $(9, -8), (-7, 10)$

27. $(2, -5), (6, -6)$

EXAMPLE 3   *Finding the Equation of a Line*

Find an equation of the line that passes through the point (3, 4) and has a *y*-intercept of 5.

$y = mx + b$	Write the slope-intercept form.
$4 = 3m + 5$	Substitute 5 for *b*, 3 for *x*, and 4 for *y*.
$-1 = 3m$	Subtract 5 from each side.
$-\dfrac{1}{3} = m$	Divide each side by 3.

The slope is $m = -\dfrac{1}{3}$. The equation of the line is $y = -\dfrac{1}{3}x + 5$.

EXERCISES

Write the equation of the line that passes through the given point and has the given *y*-intercept.

28. $(2, 1); b = 5$ **29.** $(-5, 3); b = -12$ **30.** $(-3, 10); b = 8$

31. $(7, 0); b = 13$ **32.** $(-3, -3); b = -2$ **33.** $(-1, 4); b = -8$

34. $(-11, 8); b = -14$ **35.** $(4, -6); b = -2$ **36.** $(5, -8); b = 7$

37. $(-2, -1); b = -5$ **38.** $(2, 3); b = 2$ **39.** $(3, 0.5); b = 1.5$

EXAMPLE 4   *Finding the Equation of a Line*

Write an equation of the line that passes through the points (4, 8) and (3, 1).

Find the slope of the line.

$m = \dfrac{1 - 8}{3 - 4}$	Substitute values.
$m = \dfrac{-7}{-1} = 7$	Simplify.
$1 = 7(3) + b$	Substitute values into $y = mx + b$.
$1 = 21 + b$	Multiply.
$-20 = b$	Solve for *b*.

The equation of the line is $y = 7x - 20$.

EXERCISES

Write an equation of the line that passes through the given points.

40. $(6, -3), (1, 2)$ **41.** $(-7, 9), (-5, 3)$ **42.** $(5, -1), (4, -5)$

43. $(-2, 4), (3, -6)$ **44.** $(-3, -7), (0, 8)$ **45.** $(1, 2), (-1, -4)$

46. $(6, -2), (0, 4)$ **47.** $(-4, 3), (-3, -3)$ **48.** $(-3, 2), (-5, -2)$

49. $(10, -9), (14, -1)$ **50.** $(-1, -2), (5, 0)$ **51.** $(-6, 4), (6, -1)$

PERPENDICULAR AND PARALLEL LINES

▶ *Will the boats' paths ever cross?*

APPLICATION: Sailing

When you float in an inner tube on a windy day, you get blown in the direction of the wind. Sailboats are designed to sail against the wind.

Most sailboats can sail at an angle of 45° to the direction from which the wind is blowing, as shown below. If a sailboat heads directly into the wind, the sail flaps and is useless.

You'll learn how to analyze lines such as the paths of sailboats in Chapter 3.

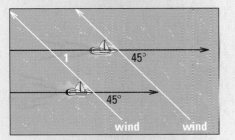

Think & Discuss

1. What do you think the measure of ∠ 1 is? Use a protractor to check your answer.

2. If the boats always sail at a 45° angle to the wind, and the wind doesn't change direction, do you think the boats' paths will ever cross?

Learn More About It

You will learn more about the paths of sailboats in Example 4 on p. 152.

 APPLICATION LINK Visit www.mcdougallittell.com for more information about sailing.

Study Guide

PREVIEW

What's the chapter about?

Chapter 3 is about **lines** and **angles**. In Chapter 3, you'll learn

- properties of parallel and perpendicular lines.
- six ways to prove that lines are parallel.
- how to write an equation of a line with given characteristics.

KEY VOCABULARY

▶ **Review**
- linear pair, p. 44
- vertical angles, p. 44
- perpendicular lines, p. 79

▶ **New**
- parallel lines, p. 129
- skew lines, p. 129
- parallel planes, p. 129

- transversal, p. 131
- alternate interior angles, p. 131
- alternate exterior angles, p. 131

- consecutive interior angles, p. 131
- flow proof, p. 136

PREPARE

Are you ready for the chapter?

SKILL REVIEW Do these exercises to review key skills that you'll apply in this chapter. See the given **reference page** if there is something you don't understand.

USING ALGEBRA **Solve each equation.** (Skills Review, p. 789 and 790)

1. $47 + x = 180$ **2.** $135 = 3x - 6$ **3.** $m = \dfrac{5 - 7}{2 - (-6)}$

4. $\dfrac{1}{2} = -5\left(\dfrac{7}{2}\right) + b$ **5.** $5x + 9 = 6x - 11$ **6.** $2(x - 1) + 15 = 90$

Use the diagram. Write the reason that supports the statement. (Review pp. 44–46)

7. $m\angle 1 = 90°$

8. $\angle 2 \cong \angle 4$

9. $\angle 2$ and $\angle 3$ are supplementary.

Write the reason that supports the statement. (Review pp. 96–98)

10. If $m\angle A = 30°$ and $m\angle B = 30°$, then $\angle A \cong \angle B$.

11. If $x + 4 = 9$, then $x = 5$.

12. $3(x + 5) = 3x + 15$

STUDY STRATEGY

Here's a study strategy!

Write Sample Questions

Write at least six questions about topics in the chapter. Focus on the concepts that you found difficult. Include both short-answer questions and more involved ones. Then answer your questions.

3.1

Lines and Angles

What you should learn

GOAL 1 Identify relationships between lines.

GOAL 2 Identify angles formed by transversals.

Why you should learn it

▼ To describe and understand **real-life** objects, such as the escalator in **Exs. 32–36**.

GOAL 1 RELATIONSHIPS BETWEEN LINES

Two lines are **parallel lines** if they are coplanar and do not intersect. Lines that do not intersect and are not coplanar are called **skew lines**. Similarly, two planes that do not intersect are called **parallel planes**.

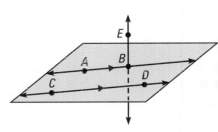

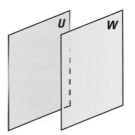

$\overleftrightarrow{AB}$ and $\overleftrightarrow{CD}$ are parallel lines.
$\overleftrightarrow{CD}$ and $\overleftrightarrow{BE}$ are skew lines.

Planes U and W are parallel planes.

To write "$\overleftrightarrow{AB}$ is parallel to $\overleftrightarrow{CD}$," you write $\overleftrightarrow{AB} \parallel \overleftrightarrow{CD}$. Triangles like those on $\overleftrightarrow{AB}$ and $\overleftrightarrow{CD}$ are used on diagrams to indicate that lines are parallel.

Segments and rays are parallel if they lie on parallel lines. For example, $\overline{AB} \parallel \overline{CD}$.

EXAMPLE 1 *Identifying Relationships in Space*

Think of each segment in the diagram as part of a line. Which of the lines appear to fit the description?

  a. parallel to $\overleftrightarrow{AB}$ and contains D

  b. perpendicular to $\overleftrightarrow{AB}$ and contains D

  c. skew to $\overleftrightarrow{AB}$ and contains D

  d. Name the plane(s) that contain D and appear to be parallel to plane ABE.

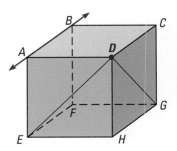

SOLUTION

  a. $\overleftrightarrow{CD}$, $\overleftrightarrow{GH}$, and $\overleftrightarrow{EF}$ are all parallel to $\overleftrightarrow{AB}$, but only $\overleftrightarrow{CD}$ passes through D and is parallel to $\overleftrightarrow{AB}$.

  b. $\overleftrightarrow{BC}$, $\overleftrightarrow{AD}$, $\overleftrightarrow{AE}$, and $\overleftrightarrow{BF}$ are all perpendicular to $\overleftrightarrow{AB}$, but only $\overleftrightarrow{AD}$ passes through D and is perpendicular to $\overleftrightarrow{AB}$.

  c. $\overleftrightarrow{DG}$, $\overleftrightarrow{DH}$, and $\overleftrightarrow{DE}$ all pass through D and are skew to $\overleftrightarrow{AB}$.

  d. Only plane DCH contains D and is parallel to plane ABE.

STUDENT HELP

▶ **Look Back**
  For help identifying perpendicular lines, see p. 79.

Notice in Example 1 that, although there are many lines through D that are skew to $\overleftrightarrow{AB}$, there is only one line through D that is parallel to $\overleftrightarrow{AB}$ and there is only one line through D that is perpendicular to $\overleftrightarrow{AB}$.

PARALLEL AND PERPENDICULAR POSTULATES

POSTULATE 13 *Parallel Postulate*

If there is a line and a point not on the line, then there is exactly one line through the point parallel to the given line.

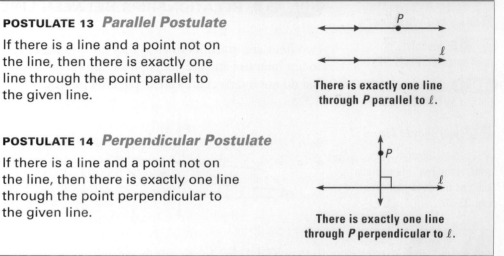

There is exactly one line through P parallel to ℓ.

POSTULATE 14 *Perpendicular Postulate*

If there is a line and a point not on the line, then there is exactly one line through the point perpendicular to the given line.

There is exactly one line through P perpendicular to ℓ.

You can use a compass and a straightedge to construct the line that passes through a given point and is perpendicular to a given line. In Lesson 6.6, you will learn why this construction works.

You will learn how to construct a parallel line in Lesson 3.5.

▶ **ACTIVITY**

Construction

A Perpendicular to a Line

Use the following steps to construct a line that passes through a given point P and is perpendicular to a given line ℓ.

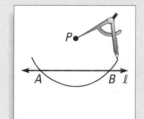 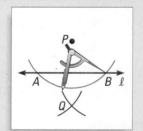 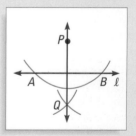

1 Place the compass point at P and draw an arc that intersects line ℓ twice. Label the intersections A and B.

2 Draw an arc with center A. Using the same radius, draw an arc with center B. Label the intersection of the arcs Q.

3 Use a straightedge to draw $\overleftrightarrow{PQ}$. $\overleftrightarrow{PQ} \perp \ell$.

GOAL 2 Identifying Angles Formed by Transversals

A **transversal** is a line that intersects two or more coplanar lines at different points. For instance, in the diagrams below, line t is a transversal. The angles formed by two lines and a transversal are given special names.

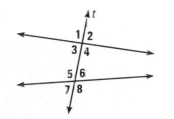

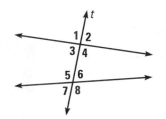

Two angles are **corresponding angles** if they occupy corresponding positions. For example, angles **1** and **5** are corresponding angles.

Two angles are **alternate exterior angles** if they lie outside the two lines on opposite sides of the transversal. Angles **1** and **8** are alternate exterior angles.

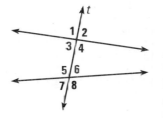

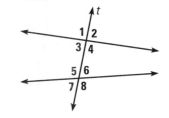

Two angles are **alternate interior angles** if they lie between the two lines on opposite sides of the transversal. Angles **3** and **6** are alternate interior angles.

Two angles are **consecutive interior angles** if they lie between the two lines on the same side of the transversal. Angles **3** and **5** are consecutive interior angles.

Consecutive interior angles are sometimes called **same side interior angles**.

EXAMPLE 2 *Identifying Angle Relationships*

STUDENT HELP

INTERNET HOMEWORK HELP
Visit our Web site www.mcdougallittell.com for extra examples.

List all pairs of angles that fit the description.

a. corresponding **b.** alternate exterior

c. alternate interior **d.** consecutive interior

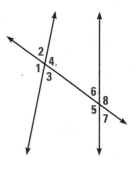

Solution

a. $\angle 1$ and $\angle 5$
$\angle 2$ and $\angle 6$
$\angle 3$ and $\angle 7$
$\angle 4$ and $\angle 8$

b. $\angle 1$ and $\angle 8$
$\angle 2$ and $\angle 7$

c. $\angle 3$ and $\angle 6$
$\angle 4$ and $\angle 5$

d. $\angle 3$ and $\angle 5$
$\angle 4$ and $\angle 6$

GUIDED PRACTICE

Vocabulary Check ✓

1. Draw two lines and a transversal. Identify a pair of alternate interior angles.

Concept Check ✓

2. How are skew lines and parallel lines alike? How are they different?

Skill Check ✓

Match the photo with the corresponding description of the chopsticks.

    A. skew   **B.** parallel   **C.** intersecting

3.

4.

5.

In Exercises 6–9, use the diagram at the right.

6. Name a pair of corresponding angles.

7. Name a pair of alternate interior angles.

8. Name a pair of alternate exterior angles.

9. Name a pair of consecutive interior angles.

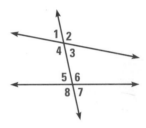

PRACTICE AND APPLICATIONS

STUDENT HELP

▶ **Extra Practice**
to help you master
skills is on p. 807.

LINE RELATIONSHIPS Think of each segment in the diagram as part of a line. Fill in the blank with *parallel*, *skew*, or *perpendicular*.

10. $\overleftrightarrow{DE}$, $\overleftrightarrow{AB}$, and $\overleftrightarrow{GC}$ are ___?___.

11. $\overleftrightarrow{DE}$ and $\overleftrightarrow{BE}$ are ___?___.

12. $\overleftrightarrow{BE}$ and $\overleftrightarrow{GC}$ are __P ?__.

13. Plane *GAD* and plane *CBE* are ___?___.

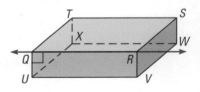

IDENTIFYING RELATIONSHIPS Think of each segment in the diagram as part of a line. There may be more than one right answer.

14. Name a line parallel to $\overleftrightarrow{QR}$.

15. Name a line perpendicular to $\overleftrightarrow{QR}$.

16. Name a line skew to $\overleftrightarrow{QR}$.

17. Name a plane parallel to plane *QRS*.

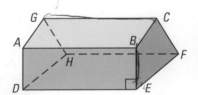

STUDENT HELP

▶ **HOMEWORK HELP**
Example 1: Exs. 10–20,
           27–36
Example 2: Exs. 21–26

APPLYING POSTULATES How many lines can be drawn that fit the description?

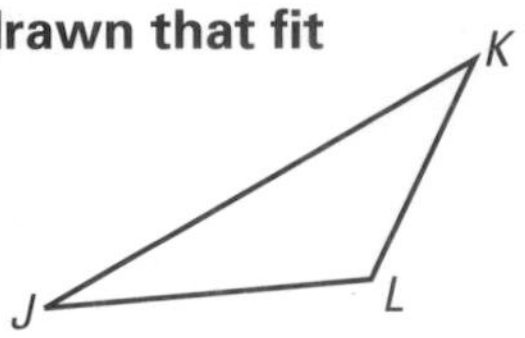

18. through *L* parallel to $\overleftrightarrow{JK}$

19. through *L* perpendicular to $\overleftrightarrow{JK}$

FOCUS ON PEOPLE

REAL LIFE **PHILIPPE PETIT** walked more than 2000 feet up an inclined cable to the Eiffel Tower. The photo above is from a performance in New York City.

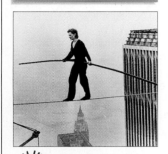

20. TIGHTROPE WALKING Philippe Petit sometimes uses a long pole to help him balance on the tightrope. Are the rope and the pole at the left *intersecting*, *perpendicular*, *parallel*, or *skew*?

ANGLE RELATIONSHIPS **Complete the statement with *corresponding, alternate interior, alternate exterior,* or *consecutive interior*.**

21. $\angle 8$ and $\angle 12$ are __?__ angles.

22. $\angle 9$ and $\angle 14$ are __?__ angles.

23. $\angle 10$ and $\angle 12$ are __?__ angles.

24. $\angle 11$ and $\angle 12$ are __?__ angles.

25. $\angle 8$ and $\angle 15$ are __?__ angles.

26. $\angle 10$ and $\angle 14$ are __?__ angles.

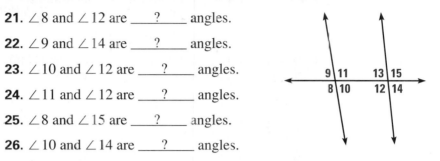

ROMAN NUMERALS **Write the Roman numeral that consists of the indicated segments. Then write the base ten value of the Roman numeral. For example, the base ten value of XII is 10 + 1 + 1 = 12.**

Roman numeral	I	V	X	L	M
Base ten value	1	5	10	50	1000

27. Three parallel segments

28. Two non-congruent perpendicular segments

29. Two congruent segments that intersect to form only one angle

30. Two intersecting segments that form vertical angles

31. Four segments, two of which are parallel

ESCALATORS **In Exercises 32–36, use the following information.**
The steps of an escalator are connected to a chain that runs around a drive wheel, which moves continuously. When a step on an up-escalator reaches the top, it flips over and goes back down to the bottom. Each step is shaped like a wedge, as shown at the right. On each step, let plane A be the plane you stand on.

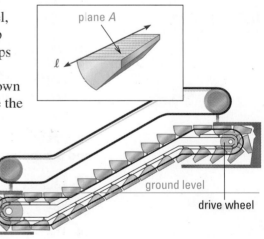

32. As each step moves around the escalator, is plane A always parallel to ground level?

33. When a person is standing on plane A, is it parallel to ground level?

34. Is line ℓ on any step always parallel to ℓ on any other step?

35. Is plane A on any step always parallel to plane A on any other step?

36. As each step moves around the escalator, how many positions are there at which plane A is perpendicular to ground level?

37. **LOGICAL REASONING** If two parallel planes are cut by a third plane, explain why the lines of intersection are parallel.

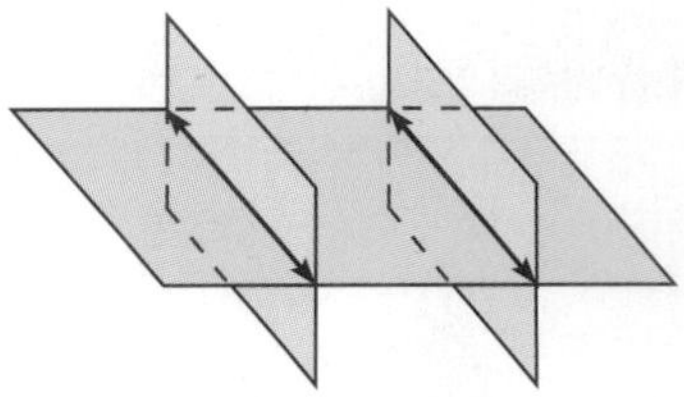

38. *Writing* What does "two lines intersect" mean?

39. **CONSTRUCTION** Draw a horizontal line ℓ and a point P above ℓ. Construct a line through P perpendicular to ℓ.

40. **CONSTRUCTION** Draw a diagonal line m and a point Q below m. Construct a line through Q perpendicular to m.

Test Preparation

41. **MULTIPLE CHOICE** In the diagram at the right, how many lines can be drawn through point P that are perpendicular to line ℓ?

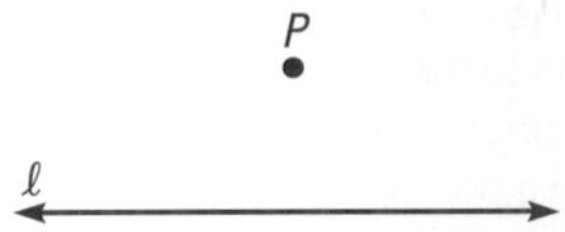

(A) 0 (B) 1 (C) 2
(D) 3 (E) More than 3

42. **MULTIPLE CHOICE** If two lines intersect, then they must be __?__.

(A) perpendicular (B) parallel (C) coplanar
(D) skew (E) None of these

★ Challenge

ANGLE RELATIONSHIPS **Complete each statement. List all possible correct answers.**

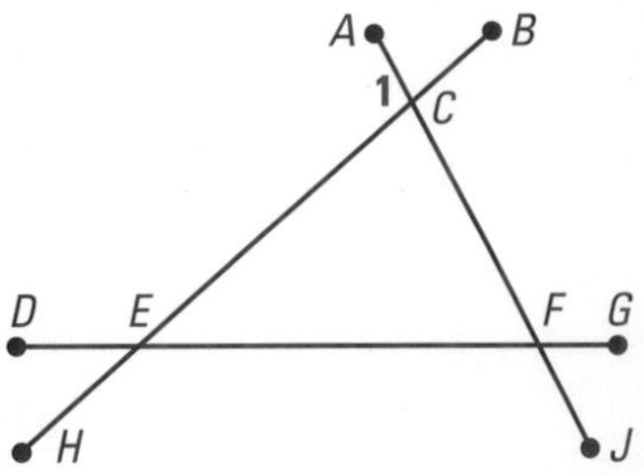

43. $\angle 1$ and __?__ are corresponding angles.

44. $\angle 1$ and __?__ are consecutive interior angles.

45. $\angle 1$ and __?__ are alternate interior angles.

46. $\angle 1$ and __?__ are alternate exterior angles.

EXTRA CHALLENGE
www.mcdougallittell.com

MIXED REVIEW

47. **ANGLE BISECTOR** The ray $\overrightarrow{BD}$ bisects $\angle ABC$, as shown at the right. Find $m\angle ABD$ and $m\angle ABC$. **(Review 1.5 for 3.2)**

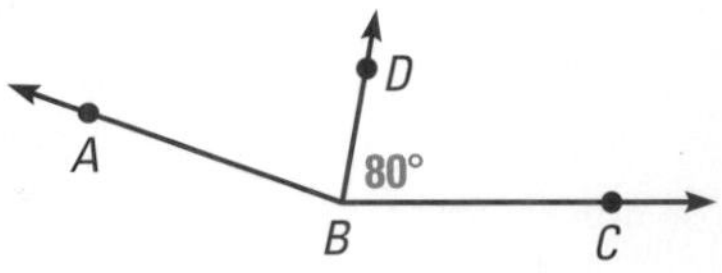

COMPLEMENTS AND SUPPLEMENTS **Find the measures of a complement and a supplement of the angle.** **(Review 1.6 for 3.2)**

48. 71° 49. 13° 50. 56°

51. 88° 52. 27° 53. 68°

54. 1° 55. 60° 56. 45°

WRITING REASONS **Solve the equation and state a reason for each step.** **(Review 2.4 for 3.2)**

57. $x + 13 = 23$ 58. $x - 8 = 17$ 59. $4x + 11 = 31$

60. $2x + 9 = 4x - 29$ 61. $2(x - 1) + 3 = 17$ 62. $5x + 7(x - 10) = -94$

ACTIVITY 3.2

Developing Concepts

GROUP ACTIVITY
Work with a partner.

MATERIALS
• slips of paper
• large piece of paper
• tape
• pencils

Forming a Flow Proof

▶ **QUESTION** How can you show the logical flow of a proof?

A *flow proof* is like a two-column proof, but the statements are connected by arrows to show how each statement comes from the ones before it.

GIVEN ▶ $\angle 1$ and $\angle 2$ are a linear pair.
$\angle 2$ and $\angle 3$ are a linear pair.

PROVE ▶ $\angle 1 \cong \angle 3$

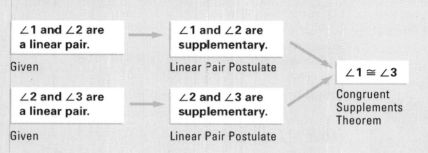

| $\angle 1$ and $\angle 2$ are a linear pair. | → | $\angle 1$ and $\angle 2$ are supplementary. |
| Given | | Linear Pair Postulate |

| $\angle 2$ and $\angle 3$ are a linear pair. | → | $\angle 2$ and $\angle 3$ are supplementary. |
| Given | | Linear Pair Postulate |

$\angle 1 \cong \angle 3$
Congruent Supplements Theorem

▶ **EXPLORING THE CONCEPT**

1. Copy the statements at the right. Then draw arrows to show the logical flow of the proof.

   GIVEN ▶ $x + y = 60$, $x = 5$

   PROVE ▶ $y = 55$

   $x + y = 60$ $5 + y = 60$

   $x = 5$ $y = 55$

2. Copy the statements below onto slips of paper. Put the slips of paper with given information on the left and put the statement you want to prove on the right. Rearrange the other statements logically to fill in the middle of the proof.

   GIVEN ▶ $\angle 5 \cong \angle 6$, $\angle 5$ and $\angle 6$ are a linear pair.

   PROVE ▶ $j \perp k$

   $\angle 5 \cong \angle 6$ $j \perp k$ $m\angle 5 = 90°$

   $m\angle 5 = m\angle 6$

   $\angle 5$ & $\angle 6$ are a linear pair. $2(m\angle 5) = 180°$

   $m\angle 5 + m\angle 6 = 180°$

   $\angle 5$ & $\angle 6$ are supplementary. $\angle 5$ is a right angle. $m\angle 5 + m\angle 5 = 180°$

3. In the flow proof at the top of the page, notice that each statement has a reason written below it. Add reasons to your flow proof from Exercise 2.

▶ **DRAWING CONCLUSIONS**

CRITICAL THINKING How are two-column proofs and flow proofs alike?

3.2

Proof and Perpendicular Lines

GOAL 1 COMPARING TYPES OF PROOFS

There is more than one way to write a proof. The two-column proof below is from Lesson 2.6. It can also be written as a paragraph proof or as a *flow* proof. A **flow proof** uses arrows to show the flow of the logical argument. Each reason in a flow proof is written below the statement it justifies.

EXAMPLE 1 *Comparing Types of Proof*

GIVEN ▶ ∠5 and ∠6 are a linear pair.
∠6 and ∠7 are a linear pair.

PROVE ▶ ∠5 ≅ ∠7

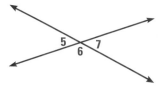

Method 1 **Two-column Proof**

Statements	Reasons
1. ∠5 and ∠6 are a linear pair. ∠6 and ∠7 are a linear pair.	**1.** Given
2. ∠5 and ∠6 are supplementary. ∠6 and ∠7 are supplementary.	**2.** Linear Pair Postulate
3. ∠5 ≅ ∠7	**3.** Congruent Supplements Theorem

Method 2 **Paragraph Proof**

Because ∠5 and ∠6 are a linear pair, the Linear Pair Postulate says that ∠5 and ∠6 are supplementary. The same reasoning shows that ∠6 and ∠7 are supplementary. Because ∠5 and ∠7 are both supplementary to ∠6, the Congruent Supplements Theorem says that ∠5 ≅ ∠7.

Method 3 **Flow Proof**

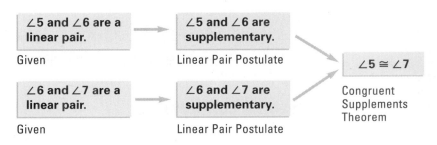

THEOREMS

THEOREM 3.1

If two lines intersect to form a linear pair of congruent angles, then the lines are perpendicular.

$g \perp h$

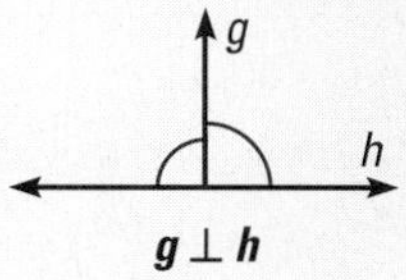

THEOREM 3.2

If two sides of two adjacent acute angles are perpendicular, then the angles are complementary.

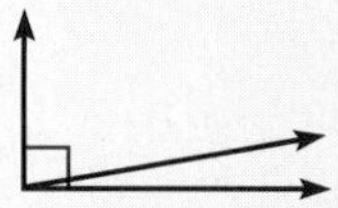

THEOREM 3.3

If two lines are perpendicular, then they intersect to form four right angles.

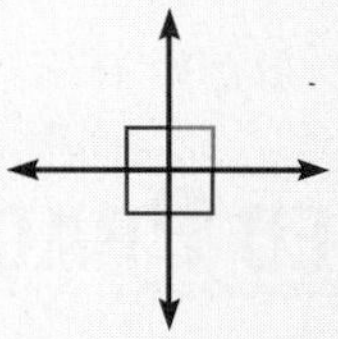

You will prove Theorem 3.2 and Theorem 3.3 in Exercises 17–19.

EXAMPLE 2 *Proof of Theorem 3.1*

Proof

Write a proof of Theorem 3.1.

SOLUTION

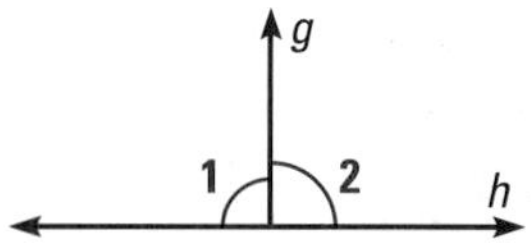

GIVEN ▸ $\angle 1 \cong \angle 2$, $\angle 1$ and $\angle 2$ are a linear pair.

PROVE ▸ $g \perp h$

Plan for Proof Use $m\angle 1 + m\angle 2 = 180°$ and $m\angle 1 = m\angle 2$ to show $m\angle 1 = 90°$.

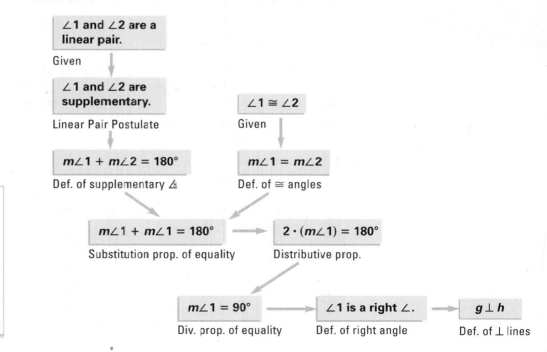

∠1 and ∠2 are a linear pair.

Given

∠1 and ∠2 are supplementary.

Linear Pair Postulate

$m\angle 1 + m\angle 2 = 180°$

Def. of supplementary ∠

∠1 ≅ ∠2

Given

$m\angle 1 = m\angle 2$

Def. of ≅ angles

$m\angle 1 + m\angle 1 = 180°$

Substitution prop. of equality

$2 \cdot (m\angle 1) = 180°$

Distributive prop.

$m\angle 1 = 90°$

Div. prop. of equality

∠1 is a right ∠.

Def. of right angle

$g \perp h$

Def. of ⊥ lines

STUDENT HELP

▸ **Study Tip**
When you write a complicated proof, it may help to write a plan first. The plan will also help others to understand your proof.

> **CONCEPT SUMMARY** **TYPES OF PROOFS**
>
> You have now studied three types of proofs.
>
> 1. **TWO-COLUMN PROOF** This is the most formal type of proof. It lists numbered statements in the left column and a reason for each statement in the right column.
>
> 2. **PARAGRAPH PROOF** This type of proof describes the logical argument with sentences. It is more conversational than a two-column proof.
>
> 3. **FLOW PROOF** This type of proof uses the same statements and reasons as a two-column proof, but the logical flow connecting the statements is indicated by arrows.

GUIDED PRACTICE

Vocabulary Check ✔

1. Define *perpendicular lines*.

Concept Check ✔

2. Which postulate or theorem guarantees that there is only one line that can be constructed perpendicular to a given line from a given point not on the line?

Skill Check ✔

Write the postulate or theorem that justifies the statement about the diagram.

3. $\angle 1 \cong \angle 2$

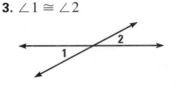

4. $j \perp k$

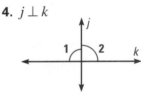

Write the postulate or theorem that justifies the statement, given that $g \perp h$.

5. $m\angle 5 + m\angle 6 = 90°$

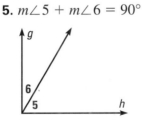

6. $\angle 3$ and $\angle 4$ are right angles.

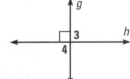

Find the value of x.

7.   **8.**   **9.**

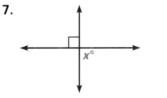 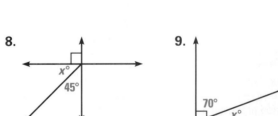

10. ERROR ANALYSIS It is given that $\angle ABC \cong \angle CBD$. A student concludes that because $\angle ABC$ and $\angle CBD$ are congruent adjacent angles, $\overleftrightarrow{AB} \perp \overleftrightarrow{CB}$. What is wrong with this reasoning? Draw a diagram to support your answer.

PRACTICE AND APPLICATIONS

USING ALGEBRA Find the value of *x*.

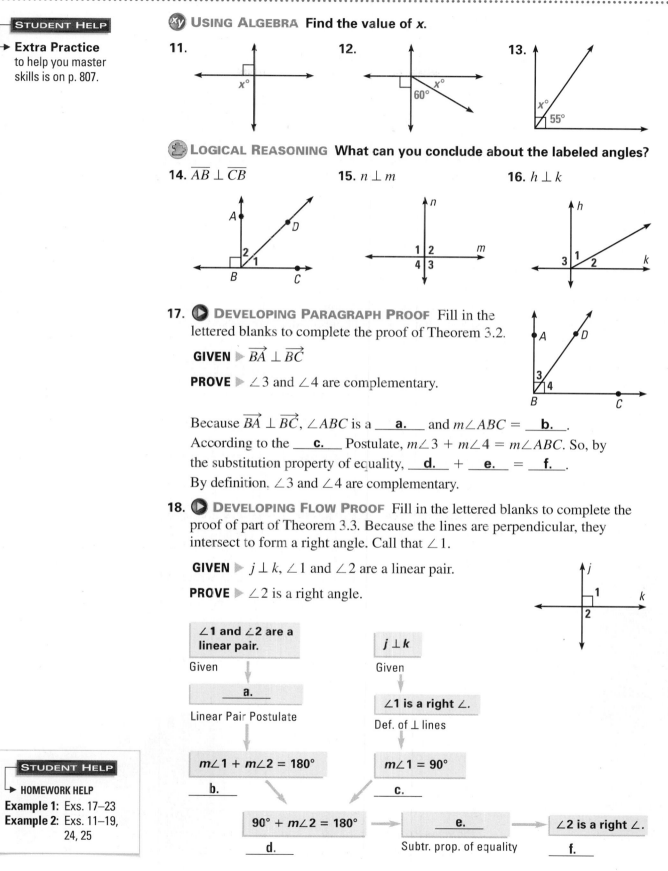

11.

12.

13.

LOGICAL REASONING What can you conclude about the labeled angles?

14. $\overline{AB} \perp \overline{CB}$

15. $n \perp m$

16. $h \perp k$

17. ▶ **DEVELOPING PARAGRAPH PROOF** Fill in the lettered blanks to complete the proof of Theorem 3.2.

GIVEN ▶ $\overrightarrow{BA} \perp \overrightarrow{BC}$

PROVE ▶ ∠3 and ∠4 are complementary.

Because $\overrightarrow{BA} \perp \overrightarrow{BC}$, ∠ABC is a ___**a.**___ and $m\angle ABC =$ ___**b.**___.
According to the ___**c.**___ Postulate, $m\angle 3 + m\angle 4 = m\angle ABC$. So, by
the substitution property of equality, ___**d.**___ + ___**e.**___ = ___**f.**___.
By definition, ∠3 and ∠4 are complementary.

18. ▶ **DEVELOPING FLOW PROOF** Fill in the lettered blanks to complete the proof of part of Theorem 3.3. Because the lines are perpendicular, they intersect to form a right angle. Call that ∠1.

GIVEN ▶ $j \perp k$, ∠1 and ∠2 are a linear pair.

PROVE ▶ ∠2 is a right angle.

| ∠1 and ∠2 are a linear pair. |
| Given |

↓

| ___**a.**___ |
| Linear Pair Postulate |

↓

| $m\angle 1 + m\angle 2 = 180°$ |
| ___**b.**___ |

| $j \perp k$ |
| Given |

↓

| ∠1 is a right ∠. |
| Def. of ⊥ lines |

↓

| $m\angle 1 = 90°$ |
| ___**c.**___ |

| $90° + m\angle 2 = 180°$ |
| ___**d.**___ |
→ | ___**e.**___ |
| Subtr. prop. of equality |
→ | ∠2 is a right ∠. |
| ___**f.**___ |

STUDENT HELP

↪ **HOMEWORK HELP**
Visit our Web site
www.mcdougallittell.com
for help with writing
proofs in Exs. 17–24.

19. ▶ **DEVELOPING TWO-COLUMN PROOF** Fill in the
blanks to complete the proof of part of Theorem 3.3.

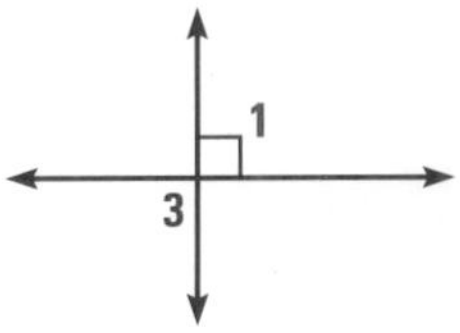

GIVEN ▶ ∠1 is a right angle.

PROVE ▶ ∠3 is a right angle.

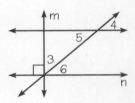

Statements	Reasons
1. ∠1 and ∠3 are vertical angles.	1. Definition of vertical angles
2. ___?___	2. Vertical Angles Theorem
3. $m\angle 1 = m\angle 3$	3. ___?___
4. ∠1 is a right angle.	4. ___?___
5. ___?___	5. Definition of right angle
6. ___?___	6. Substitution prop. of equality
7. ___?___	7. Definition of right angle

▶ **DEVELOPING PROOF** **In Exercises 20–23, use the following information.**
Dan is trying to figure out how to prove that ∠5 ≅ ∠6 below. First he wrote
everything that he knew about the diagram, as shown below in **blue**.

GIVEN **m ⊥ n, ∠3 and ∠4 are complementary.**

PROVE **∠5 ≅ ∠6**

m ⊥ n → ∠3 and ∠6 are complementary.

∠3 and ∠4 are complementary.

∠4 and ∠5 are vertical angles. → ∠4 ≅ ∠5

∠4 ≅ ∠6 → ∠5 ≅ ∠6

20. Write a justification for each statement Dan wrote in blue.

21. After writing all he knew, Dan wrote what he was supposed to prove in **red**.
He also wrote ∠4 ≅ ∠6 because he knew that if ∠4 ≅ ∠6 and ∠4 ≅ ∠5,
then ∠5 ≅ ∠6. Write a justification for this step.

22. How can you use Dan's blue statements to prove that ∠4 ≅ ∠6?

23. Copy and complete Dan's flow proof.

24. 🌐 **CIRCUIT BOARDS** The diagram
shows part of a circuit board. Write
any type of proof.

GIVEN ▶ $\overline{AB} \perp \overline{BC}, \overline{BC} \perp \overline{CD}$

PROVE ▶ ∠7 ≅ ∠8

Plan for Proof Show that ∠7 and
∠8 are both right angles.

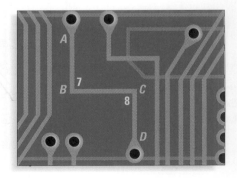

FOCUS ON
APPLICATIONS

↪ **CIRCUIT BOARDS**
The lines on circuit
boards are made of metal
and carry electricity. The
lines must not touch each
other or the electricity will
flow to the wrong place,
creating a *short circuit*.

25.  **WINDOW REPAIR** Cathy is fixing a window frame. She fit two strips of wood together to make the crosspieces. For the glass panes to fit, each angle of the crosspieces must be a right angle. Must Cathy measure all four angles to be sure they are all right angles? Explain.

26. MULTIPLE CHOICE Which of the following is true if $g \perp h$?

Ⓐ $m\angle 1 + m\angle 2 > 180°$

Ⓑ $m\angle 1 + m\angle 2 < 180°$

Ⓒ $m\angle 1 + m\angle 2 = 180°$

Ⓓ Cannot be determined

27. MULTIPLE CHOICE Which of the following must be true if $m\angle ACD = 90°$?

I. $\angle BCE$ is a right angle.

II. $\overleftrightarrow{AE} \perp \overleftrightarrow{BD}$

III. $\angle BCA$ and $\angle BCE$ are complementary.

Ⓐ I only   Ⓑ I and II only   Ⓒ III only

Ⓓ I, II, and III   Ⓔ None of these

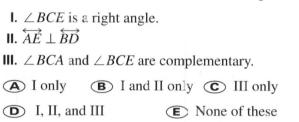

★ **Challenge**

28. 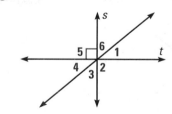 **REFLECTIONS** Ann has a full-length mirror resting against the wall of her room. Ann notices that the floor and its reflection do not form a straight angle. She concludes that the mirror is not perpendicular to the floor. Explain her reasoning.

EXTRA CHALLENGE
www.mcdougallittell.com

MIXED REVIEW

ANGLE MEASURES **Complete the statement given that $s \perp t$.** (Review 2.6 for 3.3)

29. If $m\angle 1 = 38°$, then $m\angle 4 = $ ___?___ .

30. $m\angle 2 = $ ___?___

31. If $m\angle 6 = 51°$, then $m\angle 1 = $ ___?___ .

32. If $m\angle 3 = 42°$, then $m\angle 1 = $ ___?___ .

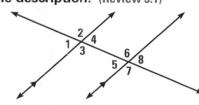

ANGLES **List all pairs of angles that fit the description.** (Review 3.1)

33. Corresponding angles

34. Alternate interior angles

35. Alternate exterior angles

36. Consecutive interior angles

▶ ACTIVITY 3.3
Using Technology

Parallel Lines and Angles

You can use geometry software to explore the properties of parallel lines.

▶ CONSTRUCT

1 Draw two points. Label them *A* and *B*. Draw $\overleftrightarrow{AB}$.

2 Draw a point not on $\overleftrightarrow{AB}$. Label it *C*.

3 Use your software's *construct parallel line* feature to construct a line through *C* parallel to $\overleftrightarrow{AB}$.

4 Draw a point on the line you constructed. Label it *D*. Move *A*, *B*, *C*, and *D* to the edges of the screen, as shown.

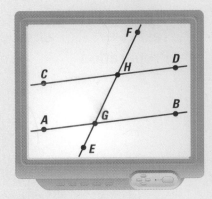

5 Draw two points outside the parallel lines. Label them *E* and *F*. Draw transversal $\overleftrightarrow{EF}$.

6 Find the intersection of $\overleftrightarrow{AB}$ and $\overleftrightarrow{EF}$. Label it *G*. Find the intersection of $\overleftrightarrow{CD}$ and $\overleftrightarrow{EF}$. Label it *H*.

▶ INVESTIGATE

1. Measure all eight angles formed by the three lines. What do you notice?

2. Drag point *E* or *F* to change the angle the transversal makes with the parallel lines. Be sure *E* and *F* stay outside the parallel lines. What do you notice?

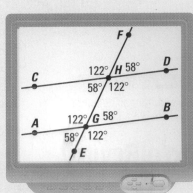

▶ MAKE A CONJECTURE

3. Make a conjecture about the measures of corresponding angles when two parallel lines are cut by a transversal.

4. Make a conjecture about the measures of alternate interior angles when two parallel lines are cut by a transversal.

EXTENSION

CRITICAL THINKING Calculate the sum of two consecutive interior angles. Make and test a conjecture about the sum.

3.3

Parallel Lines and Transversals

What you should learn

GOAL 1 Prove and use results about parallel lines and transversals.

GOAL 2 Use properties of parallel lines to solve **real-life** problems, such as estimating Earth's circumference in **Example 5**.

Why you should learn it

▼ Properties of parallel lines help you understand how rainbows are formed, as in **Ex. 30**.

GOAL 1 PROPERTIES OF PARALLEL LINES

In the activity on page 142, you may have discovered the following results.

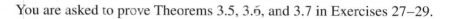

POSTULATE

POSTULATE 15 *Corresponding Angles Postulate*

If two parallel lines are cut by a transversal. then the pairs of corresponding angles are congruent.

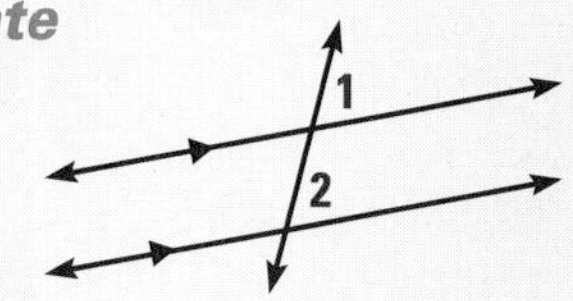

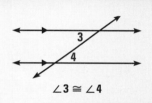

$\angle 1 \cong \angle 2$

You are asked to prove Theorems 3.5, 3.6, and 3.7 in Exercises 27–29.

THEOREMS ABOUT PARALLEL LINES

THEOREM 3.4 *Alternate Interior Angles*

If two parallel lines are cut by a transversal, then the pairs of alternate interior angles are congruent.

$\angle 3 \cong \angle 4$

THEOREM 3.5 *Consecutive Interior Angles*

If two parallel lines are cut by a transversal, then the pairs of consecutive interior angles are supplementary.

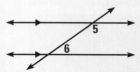

$m\angle 5 + m\angle 6 = 180°$

THEOREM 3.6 *Alternate Exterior Angles*

If two parallel lines are cut by a transversal, then the pairs of alternate exterior angles are congruent.

$\angle 7 \cong \angle 8$

THEOREM 3.7 *Perpendicular Transversal*

If a transversal is perpendicular to one of two parallel lines, then it is perpendicular to the other.

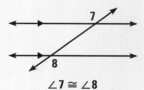

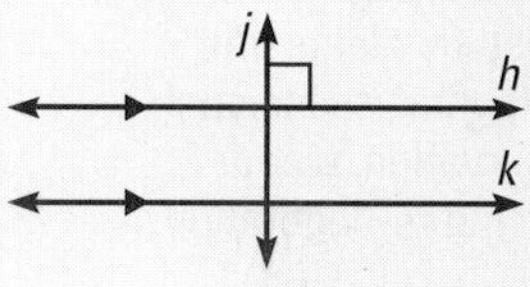

$j \perp k$

STUDENT HELP

Study Tip
When you prove a theorem, the hypotheses of the theorem becomes the GIVEN, and the conclusion is what you must PROVE.

EXAMPLE 1 *Proving the Alternate Interior Angles Theorem*

Prove the Alternate Interior Angles Theorem.

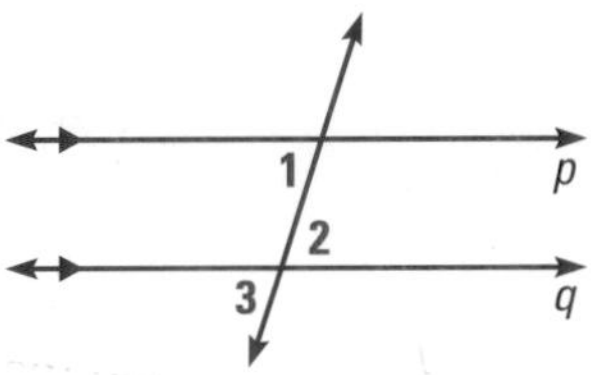

SOLUTION

GIVEN ▶ $p \parallel q$

PROVE ▶ $\angle 1 \cong \angle 2$

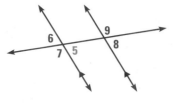

Statements	Reasons
1. $p \parallel q$	**1.** Given
2. $\angle 1 \cong \angle 3$	**2.** Corresponding Angles Postulate
3. $\angle 3 \cong \angle 2$	**3.** Vertical Angles Theorem
4. $\angle 1 \cong \angle 2$	**4.** Transitive Property of Congruence

EXAMPLE 2 *Using Properties of Parallel Lines*

Given that $m\angle 5 = 65°$, find each measure. Tell which postulate or theorem you use.

a. $m\angle 6$ **b.** $m\angle 7$

c. $m\angle 8$ **d.** $m\angle 9$

SOLUTION

a. $m\angle 6 = m\angle 5 = 65°$ — **Vertical Angles Theorem**

b. $m\angle 7 = 180° - m\angle 5 = 115°$ — **Linear Pair Postulate**

c. $m\angle 8 = m\angle 5 = 65°$ — **Corresponding Angles Postulate**

d. $m\angle 9 = m\angle 7 = 115°$ — **Alternate Exterior Angles Theorem**

FOCUS ON CAREERS

BOTANY Botanists study plants and environmental issues such as conservation, weed control, and re-vegetation.

CAREER LINK
www.mcdougallittell.com

EXAMPLE 3 *Classifying Leaves*

BOTANY Some plants are classified by the arrangement of the veins in their leaves. In the diagram of the leaf, $j \parallel k$. What is $m\angle 1$?

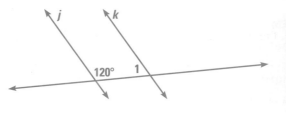

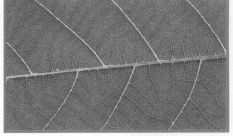

SOLUTION

$m\angle 1 + 120° = 180°$ — **Consecutive Interior Angles Theorem**

$m\angle 1 = 60°$ — **Subtract.**

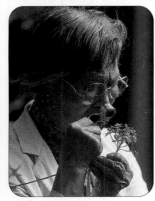

GOAL 2 **PROPERTIES OF SPECIAL PAIRS OF ANGLES**

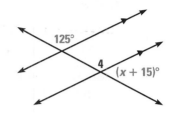

EXAMPLE 4 *Using Properties of Parallel Lines*

Use properties of parallel lines to find the value of *x*.

125°

4

$(x + 15)°$

SOLUTION

$m\angle 4 = 125°$	**Corresponding Angles Postulate**
$m\angle 4 + (x + 15)° = 180°$	**Linear Pair Postulate**
$125° + (x + 15)° = 180°$	**Substitute.**
$x = 40$	**Subtract.**

EXAMPLE 5 *Estimating Earth's Circumference*

HISTORY CONNECTION Eratosthenes was a Greek scholar. Over 2000 years ago, he estimated Earth's circumference by using the fact that the Sun's rays are parallel.

Eratosthenes chose a day when the Sun shone exactly down a vertical well in Syene at noon. On that day, he measured the angle the Sun's rays made with a vertical stick in Alexandria at noon. He discovered that

$m\angle 2 \approx \dfrac{1}{50}$ **of a circle.**

By using properties of parallel lines, he knew that $m\angle 1 = m\angle 2$. So he reasoned that

$m\angle 1 \approx \dfrac{1}{50}$ **of a circle.**

sunlight ℓ_1

$\angle 2$

shadow · stick

sunlight ℓ_2

well

1

center of Earth

Not drawn to scale

At the time, the distance from Syene to Alexandria was believed to be **575 miles**.

$\dfrac{1}{50}$ **of a circle** $\approx \dfrac{575 \text{ miles}}{\text{Earth's circumference}}$

Earth's circumference $\approx 50(575 \text{ miles})$ ⟵ **Use cross product property.**

$\approx 29{,}000$ miles

How did Eratosthenes know that $m\angle 1 = m\angle 2$?

SOLUTION

Because the Sun's rays are parallel, $\ell_1 \parallel \ell_2$. Angles 1 and 2 are alternate interior angles, so $\angle 1 \cong \angle 2$. By the definition of congruent angles, $m\angle 1 = m\angle 2$.

 **STUDENT HELP**

APPLICATION LINK
Visit our Web site
www.mcdougallittell.com
for more information
about Eratosthenes'
estimate in Example 5.

GUIDED PRACTICE

Vocabulary Check ✓

1. Sketch two parallel lines cut by a transversal. Label a pair of consecutive interior angles.

Concept Check ✓

2. In the figure at the right, $j \parallel k$. How many angle measures must be given in order to find the measure of every angle? Explain your reasoning.

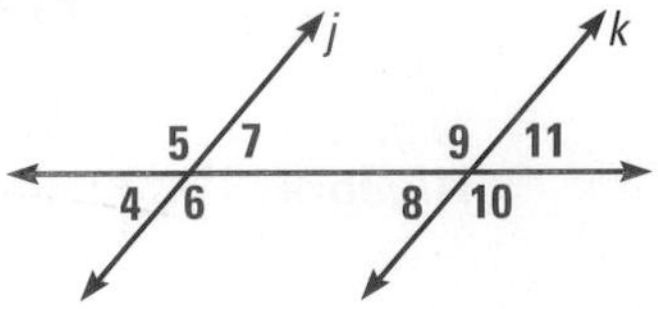

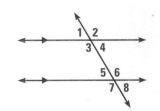

Skill Check ✓

State the postulate or theorem that justifies the statement.

3. $\angle 2 \cong \angle 7$ **4.** $\angle 4 \cong \angle 5$

5. $m\angle 3 + m\angle 5 = 180°$ **6.** $\angle 2 \cong \angle 6$

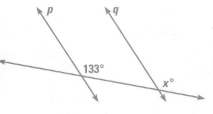

7. In the diagram of the feather below, lines p and q are parallel. What is the value of x?

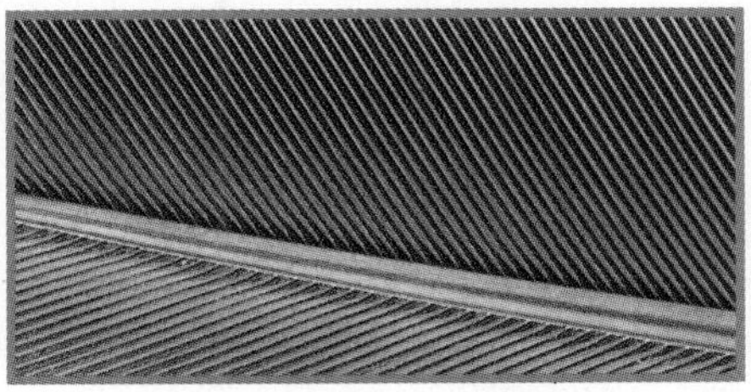

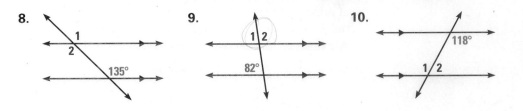

PRACTICE AND APPLICATIONS

STUDENT HELP

▶ **Extra Practice**
to help you master
skills is on p. 808.

USING PARALLEL LINES Find $m\angle 1$ and $m\angle 2$. Explain your reasoning.

8.

9.

10.

USING PARALLEL LINES Find the values of x and y. Explain your reasoning.

11.

12.

13.

STUDENT HELP

▶ **HOMEWORK HELP**
Example 1: Exs. 27–29
Example 2: Exs. 8–17
Example 3: Exs. 8–17
Example 4: Exs. 18–26
Example 5: Ex. 30

14.

15.

16.

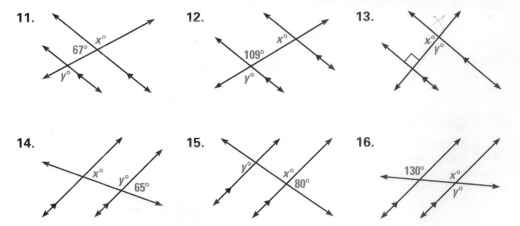

17. USING PROPERTIES OF PARALLEL LINES
Use the given information to find the measures of the other seven angles in the figure at the right.

GIVEN ▶ $j \parallel k$, $m\angle 1 = 107°$

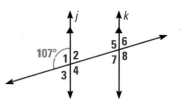

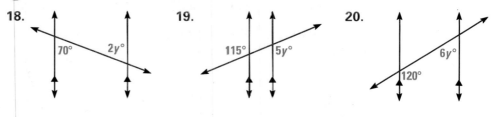

USING ALGEBRA Find the value of *y*.

18.

19.

20.

USING ALGEBRA Find the value of *x*.

21.

22.

23.

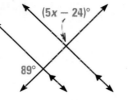

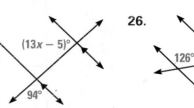

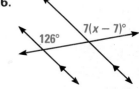

24.

25.

26.

STUDENT HELP

HOMEWORK HELP
Visit our Web site
www.mcdougallittell.com
for help with proving
theorems in Exs. 27–29.

27. ▶ **DEVELOPING PROOF** Complete the proof of the Consecutive Interior Angles Theorem.

GIVEN ▶ $p \parallel q$

PROVE ▶ $\angle 1$ and $\angle 2$ are supplementary.

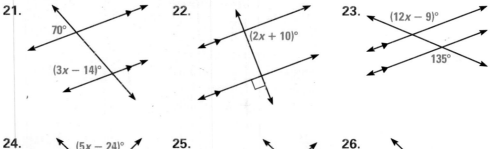

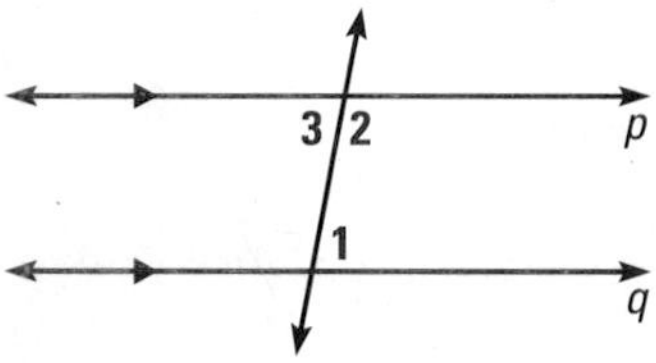

Statements	Reasons
1. ___?___	1. Given
2. $\angle 1 \cong \angle 3$	2. ___?___
3. ___?___	3. Definition of congruent angles
4. ___?___	4. Definition of linear pair
5. $m\angle 3 + m\angle 2 = 180°$	5. ___?___
6. ___?___	6. Substitution prop. of equality
7. $\angle 1$ and $\angle 2$ are supplementary.	7. ___?___

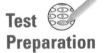

STUDENT HELP

Study Tip
When you prove a theorem you may use any previous theorem, but you may not use the one you're proving.

PROVING THEOREMS 3.6 AND 3.7 In Exercises 28 and 29, complete the proof.

28. To prove the Alternate Exterior Angles Theorem, first show that $\angle 1 \cong \angle 3$. Then show that $\angle 3 \cong \angle 2$. Finally, show that $\angle 1 \cong \angle 2$.

GIVEN ▶ $j \parallel k$

PROVE ▶ $\angle 1 \cong \angle 2$

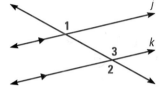

29. To prove the Perpendicular Transversal Theorem, show that $\angle 1$ is a right angle, $\angle 1 \cong \angle 2$, $\angle 2$ is a right angle, and finally that $p \perp r$.

GIVEN ▶ $p \perp q$, $q \parallel r$

PROVE ▶ $p \perp r$

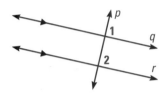

30. **FORMING RAINBOWS** When sunlight enters a drop of rain, different colors leave the drop at different angles. That's what makes a rainbow. For red light, $m\angle 2 = 42°$. What is $m\angle 1$? How do you know?

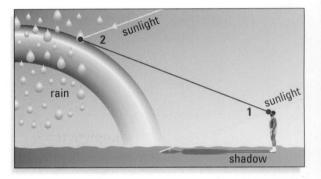

Test Preparation

31. **MULTI-STEP PROBLEM** You are designing a lunch box like the one below.

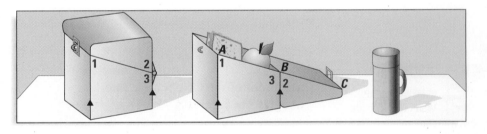

a. The measure of $\angle 1$ is 70°. What is the measure of $\angle 2$? What is the measure of $\angle 3$?

b. *Writing* Explain why $\angle ABC$ is a straight angle.

★ Challenge

32. **USING PROPERTIES OF PARALLEL LINES** Use the given information to find the measures of the other labeled angles in the figure. For each angle, tell which postulate or theorem you used.

GIVEN ▶ $\overline{PQ} \parallel \overline{RS}$,
$\overline{LM} \perp \overline{NK}$,
$m\angle 1 = 48°$

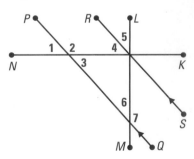

EXTRA CHALLENGE
www.mcdougallittell.com

MIXED REVIEW

ANGLE MEASURES $\angle 1$ and $\angle 2$ are supplementary. Find $m\angle 2$. (Review 1.6)

33. $m\angle 1 = 50°$ **34.** $m\angle 1 = 73°$ **35.** $m\angle 1 = 101°$

36. $m\angle 1 = 107°$ **37.** $m\angle 1 = 111°$ **38.** $m\angle 1 = 118°$

CONVERSES Write the converse of the statement. (Review 2.1 for 3.4)

39. If the measure of an angle is 19°, then the angle is acute.

40. I will go to the park if you go with me.

41. I will go fishing if I do not have to work.

FINDING ANGLES Complete the statement, given that $\overrightarrow{DE} \perp \overrightarrow{DG}$ and $\overleftrightarrow{AB} \perp \overrightarrow{DC}$. (Review 2.6)

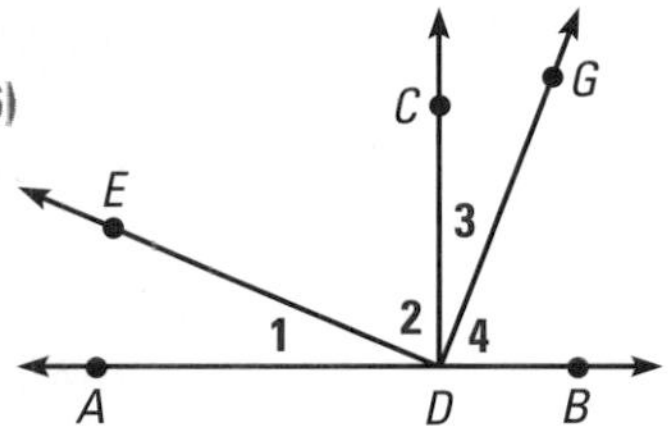

42. If $m\angle 1 = 23°$, then $m\angle 2 = $ __?__ .

43. If $m\angle 4 = 69°$, then $m\angle 3 = $ __?__ .

44. If $m\angle 2 = 70°$, then $m\angle 4 = $ __?__ .

QUIZ 1

Self-Test for Lessons 3.1–3.3

Complete the statement. (Lesson 3.1)

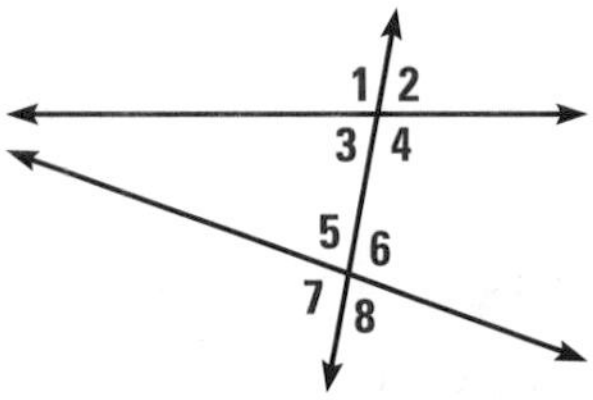

1. $\angle 2$ and __?__ are corresponding angles.

2. $\angle 3$ and __?__ are consecutive interior angles.

3. $\angle 3$ and __?__ are alternate interior angles.

4. $\angle 2$ and __?__ are alternate exterior angles.

5. ▶ **PROOF** Write a plan for a proof. (Lesson 3.2)

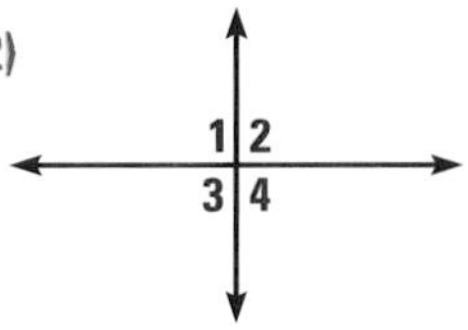

     GIVEN ▶ $\angle 1 \cong \angle 2$

     PROVE ▶ $\angle 3$ and $\angle 4$ are right angles.

Find the value of x. (Lesson 3.3)

6. $2x°$, $138°$ **7.** $151°$, $(2x + 1)°$ **8.** $81°$, $(7x + 15)°$

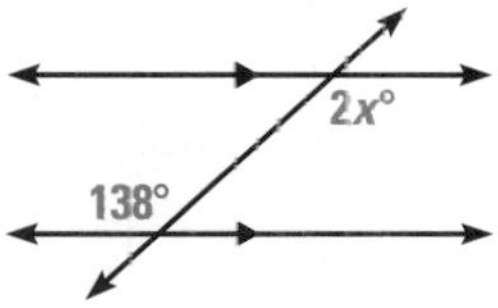

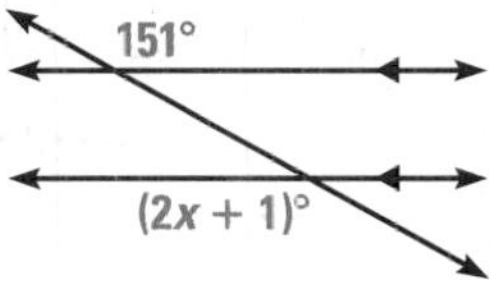

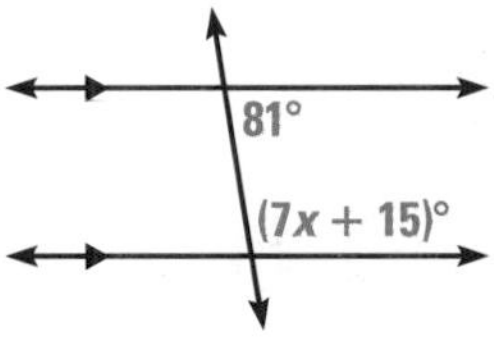

9. 🌐 **FLAG OF PUERTO RICO** Sketch the flag of Puerto Rico shown at the right. Given that $m\angle 3 = 55°$, determine the measure of $\angle 1$. Justify each step in your argument. (Lesson 3.3)

Proving Lines are Parallel

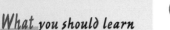

What you should learn

GOAL 1 Prove that two lines are parallel.

GOAL 2 Use properties of parallel lines to solve **real-life** problems, such as proving that prehistoric mounds are parallel in **Ex. 19.**

Why you should learn it

▼ Properties of parallel lines help you predict the paths of boats sailing into the wind, as in **Example 4.**

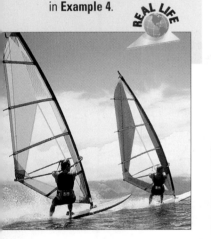

GOAL 1 PROVING LINES ARE PARALLEL

To use the theorems you learned in Lesson 3.3, you must first know that two lines are parallel. You can use the following postulate and theorems to prove that two lines are parallel.

POSTULATE

POSTULATE 16 *Corresponding Angles Converse*

If two lines are cut by a transversal so that corresponding angles are congruent, then the lines are parallel.

$j \parallel k$

The following theorems are converses of those in Lesson 3.3. Remember that the converse of a true conditional statement is not necessarily true. Thus, each of the following must be proved to be true. Theorems 3.8 and 3.9 are proved in Examples 1 and 2. You are asked to prove Theorem 3.10 in Exercise 30.

THEOREMS ABOUT TRANSVERSALS

THEOREM 3.8 *Alternate Interior Angles Converse*

If two lines are cut by a transversal so that alternate interior angles are congruent, then the lines are parallel.

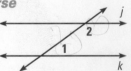

If $\angle 1 \cong \angle 3$, then $j \parallel k$.

THEOREM 3.9 *Consecutive Interior Angles Converse*

If two lines are cut by a transversal so that consecutive interior angles are supplementary, then the lines are parallel.

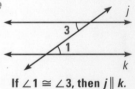

If $m\angle 1 + m\angle 2 = 180°$, then $j \parallel k$.

THEOREM 3.10 *Alternate Exterior Angles Converse*

If two lines are cut by a transversal so that alternate exterior angles are congruent, then the lines are parallel.

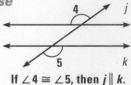

If $\angle 4 \cong \angle 5$, then $j \parallel k$.

Proof

EXAMPLE 1 **Proof of the Alternate Interior Angles Converse**

Prove the Alternate Interior Angles Converse.

SOLUTION

GIVEN ▶ $\angle 1 \cong \angle 2$

PROVE ▶ $m \parallel n$

Statements	Reasons
1. $\angle 1 \cong \angle 2$	1. Given
2. $\angle 2 \cong \angle 3$	2. Vertical Angles Theorem
3. $\angle 1 \cong \angle 3$	3. Transitive Property of Congruence
4. $m \parallel n$	4. Corresponding Angles Converse

. . . .

When you prove a theorem you may use only earlier results. For example, to prove Theorem 3.9, you may use Theorem 3.8 and Postulate 16, but you may not use Theorem 3.9 itself or Theorem 3.10.

Proof

EXAMPLE 2 **Proof of the Consecutive Interior Angles Converse**

Prove the Consecutive Interior Angles Converse.

SOLUTION

GIVEN ▶ $\angle 4$ and $\angle 5$ are supplementary.

PROVE ▶ $g \parallel h$

Paragraph Proof You are given that $\angle 4$ and $\angle 5$ are supplementary. By the Linear Pair Postulate, $\angle 5$ and $\angle 6$ are also supplementary because they form a linear pair. By the Congruent Supplements Theorem, it follows that $\angle 4 \cong \angle 6$. Therefore, by the Alternate Interior Angles Converse, g and h are parallel.

Using Algebra

EXAMPLE 3 **Applying the Consecutive Interior Angles Converse**

Find the value of x that makes $j \parallel k$.

SOLUTION

Lines j and k will be parallel if the marked angles are supplementary.

$$x° + 4x° = 180°$$
$$5x = 180$$
$$x = 36$$

▶ So, if $x = 36$, then $j \parallel k$.

GOAL 2 USING THE PARALLEL CONVERSES

STUDENT HELP

INTERNET HOMEWORK HELP
Visit our Web site www.mcdougallittell.com for extra examples.

EXAMPLE 4 *Using the Corresponding Angles Converse*

REAL LIFE **SAILING** If two boats sail at a 45° angle to the wind as shown, and the wind is constant, will their paths ever cross? Explain.

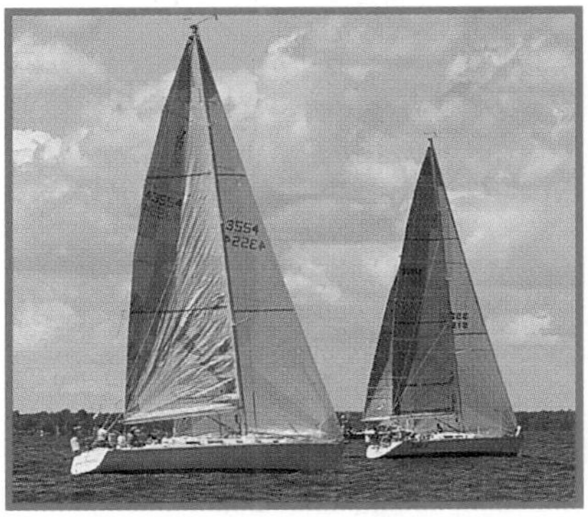

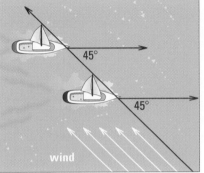

SOLUTION

Because corresponding angles are congruent, the boats' paths are parallel. Parallel lines do not intersect, so the boats' paths will not cross.

EXAMPLE 5 *Identifying Parallel Lines*

Decide which rays are parallel.

a. Is $\overrightarrow{EB}$ parallel to $\overrightarrow{HD}$?

b. Is $\overrightarrow{EA}$ parallel to $\overrightarrow{HC}$?

SOLUTION

a. Decide whether $\overrightarrow{EB} \parallel \overrightarrow{HD}$.

$m\angle BEH = 58°$

$m\angle DHG = 61°$

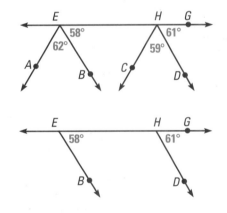

▶ $\angle BEH$ and $\angle DHG$ are corresponding angles, but they are not congruent, so $\overrightarrow{EB}$ and $\overrightarrow{HD}$ are not parallel.

b. Decide whether $\overrightarrow{EA} \parallel \overrightarrow{HC}$.

$m\angle AEH = 62° + 58°$

$= 120°$

$m\angle CHG = 59° + 61°$

$= 120°$

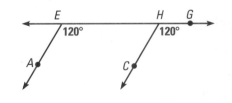

▶ $\angle AEH$ and $\angle CHG$ are congruent corresponding angles, so $\overrightarrow{EA} \parallel \overrightarrow{HC}$.

GUIDED PRACTICE

Vocabulary Check ✔

Concept Check ✔

Skill Check ✔

1. What are *parallel lines*?

2. Write the converse of Theorem 3.8. Is the converse true?

Can you prove that lines *p* and *q* are parallel? If so, describe how.

3.

4.

5.

6.

7.

8.

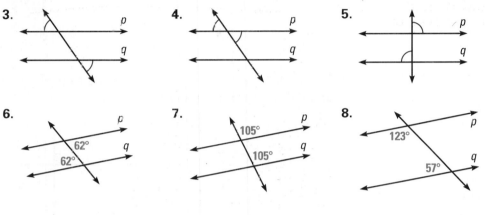

9. Find the value of *x* that makes $j \parallel k$. Which postulate or theorem about parallel lines supports your answer?

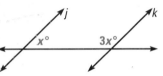

PRACTICE AND APPLICATIONS

STUDENT HELP

▶ **Extra Practice**
to help you master
skills is on p. 808.

LOGICAL REASONING **Is it possible to prove that lines *m* and *n* are parallel? If so, state the postulate or theorem you would use.**

10.

11.

12.

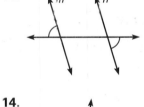

13.

14.

15.

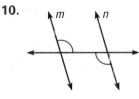 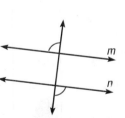 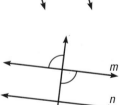

STUDENT HELP

▶ **HOMEWORK HELP**
Example 1: Exs. 28, 30
Example 2: Exs. 28, 30
Example 3: Exs. 10–18
Example 4: Exs. 19, 29,
31
Example 5: Exs. 20–27

USING ALGEBRA **Find the value of *x* that makes $r \parallel s$.**

16.

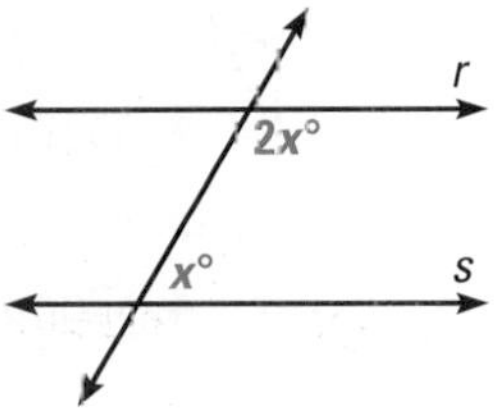

17.

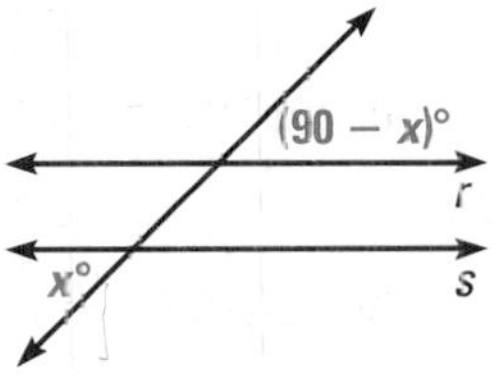

18.

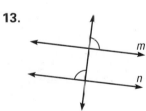 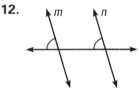

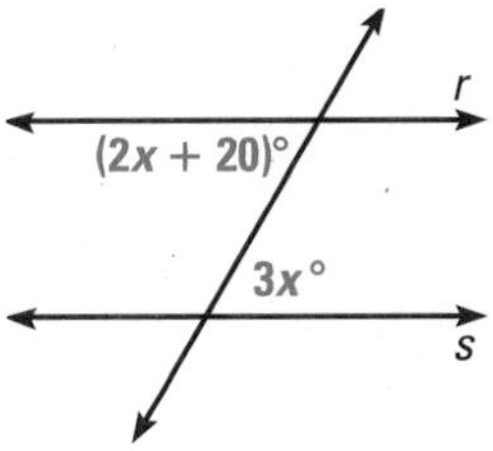

$2x°$

$x°$

$(90 - x)°$

$x°$

$(2x + 20)°$

$3x°$

FOCUS ON APPLICATIONS

REAL LIFE **THE GREAT SERPENT MOUND,** an archaeological mound near Hillsboro, Ohio, is 2 to 5 feet high, and is nearly 20 feet wide. It is over $\frac{1}{4}$ mile long.

APPLICATION LINK www.mcdougallittell.com

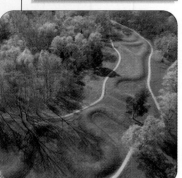

19. **ARCHAEOLOGY** A farm lane in Ohio crosses two long, straight earthen mounds that may have been built about 2000 years ago. The mounds are about 200 feet apart, and both form a 63° angle with the lane, as shown. Are the mounds parallel? How do you know?

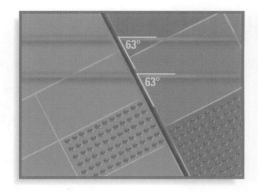

LOGICAL REASONING **Is it possible to prove that lines *a* and *b* are parallel? If so, explain how.**

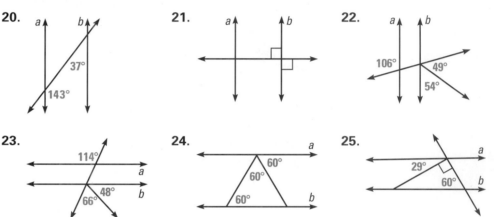

20.

21.

22.

23.

24.

25.

LOGICAL REASONING **Which lines, if any, are parallel? Explain.**

26.

27.

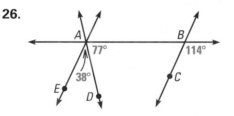

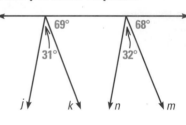

28. **PROOF** Complete the proof.

GIVEN ▶ $\angle 1$ and $\angle 2$ are supplementary.

PROVE ▶ $\ell_1 \parallel \ell_2$

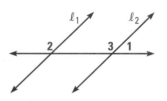

Statements	Reasons
1. $\angle 1$ and $\angle 2$ are supplementary.	**1.** ___?___
2. $\angle 1$ and $\angle 3$ are a linear pair.	**2.** Definition of linear pair
3. ___?___	**3.** Linear Pair Postulate
4. ___?___	**4.** Congruent Supplements Theorem
5. $\ell_1 \parallel \ell_2$	**5.** ___?___

29. **BUILDING STAIRS** One way to build stairs is to attach triangular blocks to an angled support, as shown at the right. If the support makes a 32° angle with the floor, what must $m\angle 1$ be so the step will be parallel to the floor? The sides of the angled support are parallel.

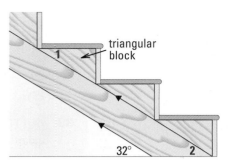

30. **PROVING THEOREM 3.10** Write a two-column proof for the Alternate Exterior Angles Converse: If two lines are cut by a transversal so that alternate exterior angles are congruent, then the lines are parallel.

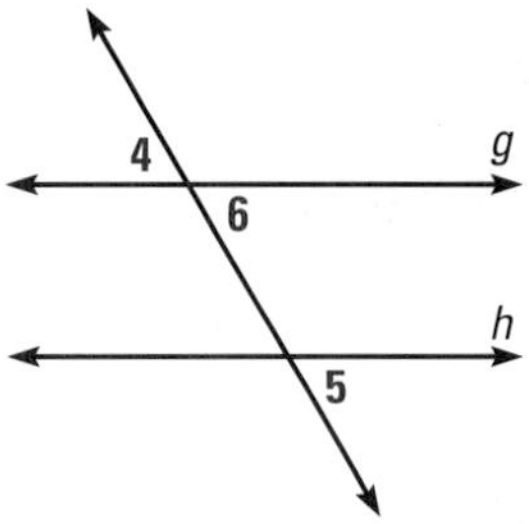

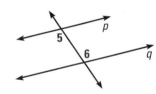

GIVEN ▶ $\angle 4 \cong \angle 5$

PROVE ▶ $g \parallel h$

Plan for Proof Show that $\angle 4$ is congruent to $\angle 6$, show that $\angle 6$ is congruent to $\angle 5$, and then use the Corresponding Angles Converse.

31. *Writing* In the diagram at the right, $m\angle 5 = 110°$ and $m\angle 6 = 110°$. Explain why $p \parallel q$.

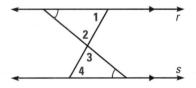

LOGICAL REASONING **Use the information given in the diagram.**

32. What can you prove about $\overline{AB}$ and $\overline{CD}$? Explain.

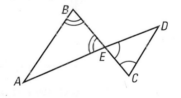

33. What can you prove about $\angle 1$, $\angle 2$, $\angle 3$, and $\angle 4$? Explain.

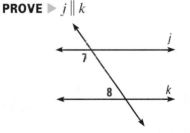

PROOF **Write a proof.**

34. **GIVEN** ▶ $m\angle 7 = 125°$, $m\angle 8 = 55°$

PROVE ▶ $j \parallel k$

35. **GIVEN** ▶ $a \parallel b$, $\angle 1 \cong \angle 2$

PROVE ▶ $c \parallel d$

STUDENT HELP

SOFTWARE HELP Visit our Web site www.mcdougallittell.com to see instructions for several software applications.

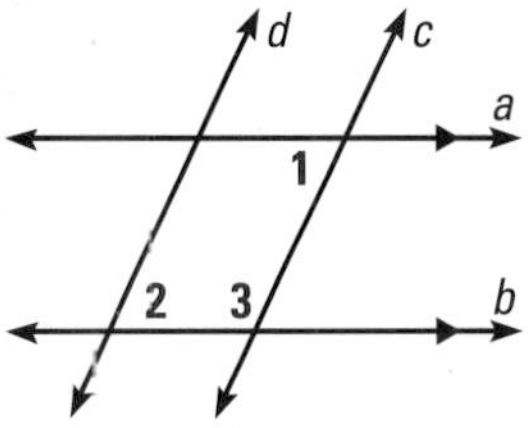

36. **TECHNOLOGY** Use geometry software to construct a line ℓ, a point P not on ℓ, and a line n through P parallel to ℓ. Construct a point Q on ℓ and construct $\overleftrightarrow{PQ}$. Choose a pair of alternate interior angles and construct their angle bisectors. Are the bisectors parallel? Make a conjecture. Write a plan for a proof of your conjecture.

Test Preparation

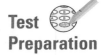

37. **MULTIPLE CHOICE** What is the converse of the following statement?

If $\angle 1 \cong \angle 2$, then $n \parallel m$.

Ⓐ $\angle 1 \cong \angle 2$ if and only if $n \parallel m$. Ⓑ If $\angle 2 \cong \angle 1$, then $m \parallel n$.

Ⓒ $\angle 1 \cong \angle 2$ if $n \parallel m$. Ⓓ $\angle 1 \cong \angle 2$ only if $n \parallel m$.

38. **MULTIPLE CHOICE** What value of x would make lines ℓ_1 and ℓ_2 parallel?

Ⓐ 13 Ⓑ 35 Ⓒ 37

Ⓓ 78 Ⓔ 102

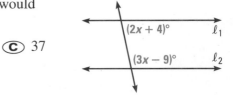

★ Challenge

39. **SNOW MAKING** To shoot the snow as far as possible, each snowmaker below is set at a 45° angle. The axles of the snowmakers are all parallel. It is possible to prove that the barrels of the snowmakers are also parallel, but the proof is difficult in 3 dimensions. To simplify the problem, think of the illustration as a flat image on a piece of paper. The axles and barrels are represented in the diagram on the right. Lines j and ℓ_2 intersect at C.

GIVEN ▶ $\ell_1 \parallel \ell_2$, $m\angle A = m\angle B = 45°$

PROVE ▶ $j \parallel k$

EXTRA CHALLENGE
www.mcdougallittell.com

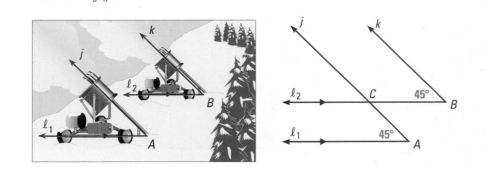

MIXED REVIEW

FINDING THE MIDPOINT **Use a ruler to draw a line segment with the given length. Then use a compass and straightedge to construct the midpoint of the line segment.** (Review 1.5 for 3.5)

40. 3 inches 41. 8 centimeters 42. 5 centimeters 43. 1 inch

44. **CONGRUENT SEGMENTS** Find the value of x if $\overline{AB} \cong \overline{AD}$ and $\overline{CD} \cong \overline{AD}$. Explain your steps. (Review 2.5)

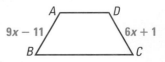

IDENTIFYING ANGLES **Use the diagram to complete the statement.** (Review 3.1)

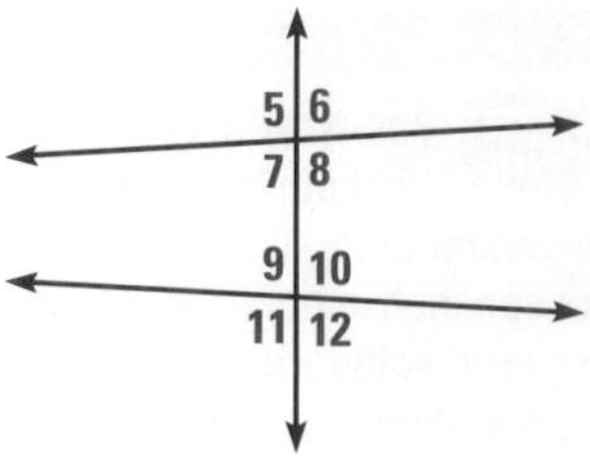

45. $\angle 12$ and ___?___ are alternate exterior angles.

46. $\angle 10$ and ___?___ are corresponding angles.

47. $\angle 10$ and ___?___ are alternate interior angles.

48. $\angle 9$ and ___?___ are consecutive interior angles.

3.5

Using Properties of Parallel Lines

What you should learn

GOAL 1 Use properties of parallel lines in **real-life** situations, such as building a CD rack in **Example 3**.

GOAL 2 Construct parallel lines using straightedge and compass.

Why you should learn it

▼ To understand how light bends when it passes through glass or water, as in **Ex. 42**.

GOAL 1 USING PARALLEL LINES IN REAL LIFE

When a team of rowers competes, each rower keeps his or her oars parallel to the adjacent rower's oars. If any two *adjacent* oars on the same side of the boat are parallel, does this imply that *any two* oars on that side are parallel? This question is examined below.

Example 1 justifies Theorem 3.11, and you will prove Theorem 3.12 in Exercise 38.

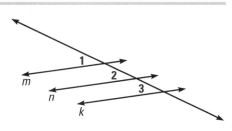

EXAMPLE 1 *Proving Two Lines are Parallel*

Lines m, n, and k represent three of the oars above. $m \parallel n$ and $n \parallel k$. Prove that $m \parallel k$.

SOLUTION

GIVEN ▶ $m \parallel n$, $n \parallel k$

PROVE ▶ $m \parallel k$

Statements	Reasons
1. $m \parallel n$	1. Given
2. $\angle 1 \cong \angle 2$	2. Corresponding Angles Postulate
3. $n \parallel k$	3. Given
4. $\angle 2 \cong \angle 3$	4. Corresponding Angles Postulate
5. $\angle 1 \cong \angle 3$	5. Transitive Property of Congruence
6. $m \parallel k$	6. Corresponding Angles Converse

THEOREMS ABOUT PARALLEL AND PERPENDICULAR LINES

THEOREM 3.11

If two lines are parallel to the same line, then they are parallel to each other.

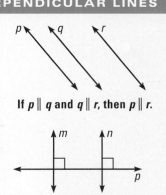

If $p \parallel q$ and $q \parallel r$, then $p \parallel r$.

THEOREM 3.12

In a plane, if two lines are perpendicular to the same line, then they are parallel to each other.

If $m \perp p$ and $n \perp p$, then $m \parallel n$.

Logical Reasoning

EXAMPLE 2 *Explaining Why Steps are Parallel*

In the diagram at the right, each step is parallel to the step immediately below it and the bottom step is parallel to the floor. Explain why the top step is parallel to the floor.

SOLUTION

You are given that $k_1 \parallel k_2$ and $k_2 \parallel k_3$. By transitivity of parallel lines, $k_1 \parallel k_3$. Since $k_1 \parallel k_3$ and $k_3 \parallel k_4$, it follows that $k_1 \parallel k_4$. So, the top step is parallel to the floor.

EXAMPLE 3 *Building a CD Rack*

You are building a CD rack. You cut the sides, bottom, and top so that each corner is composed of two 45° angles. Prove that the top and bottom front edges of the CD rack are parallel.

Proof

SOLUTION

GIVEN ▶ $m\angle 1 = 45°$, $m\angle 2 = 45°$
$m\angle 3 = 45°$, $m\angle 4 = 45°$

PROVE ▶ $\overline{BA} \parallel \overline{CD}$

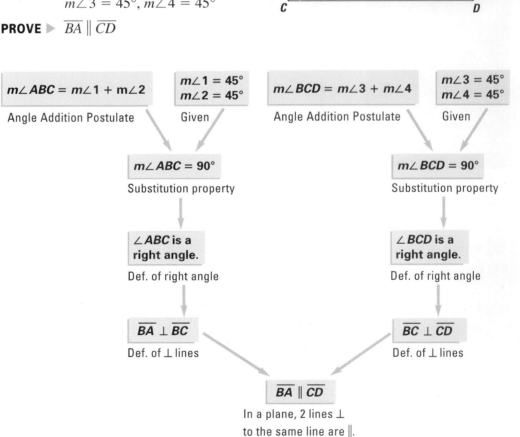

$m\angle ABC = m\angle 1 + m\angle 2$	$m\angle 1 = 45°$ $m\angle 2 = 45°$
Angle Addition Postulate	Given

$m\angle ABC = 90°$
Substitution property

$\angle ABC$ is a right angle.
Def. of right angle

$\overline{BA} \perp \overline{BC}$
Def. of $\perp$ lines

$m\angle BCD = m\angle 3 + m\angle 4$	$m\angle 3 = 45°$ $m\angle 4 = 45°$
Angle Addition Postulate	Given

$m\angle BCD = 90°$
Substitution property

$\angle BCD$ is a right angle.
Def. of right angle

$\overline{BC} \perp \overline{CD}$
Def. of $\perp$ lines

$\overline{BA} \parallel \overline{CD}$
In a plane, 2 lines $\perp$ to the same line are $\parallel$.

To construct parallel lines, you first need to know how to copy an angle.

> ▶ **ACTIVITY**
>
> Construction **Copying an Angle**

Use these steps to construct an angle that is congruent to a given ∠A.

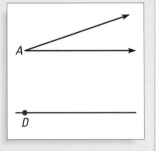 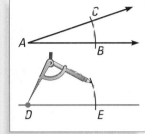 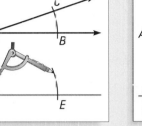 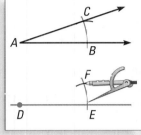 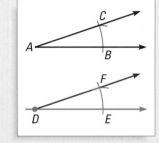

① Draw a line. Label a point on the line D.

② Draw an arc with center A. Label B and C. With the same radius, draw an arc with center D. Label E.

③ Draw an arc with radius BC and center E. Label the intersection F.

④ Draw $\overrightarrow{DF}$.
∠EDF ≅ ∠BAC.

In Chapter 4, you will learn why the *Copying an Angle* construction works. You can use the *Copying an Angle* construction to construct two congruent corresponding angles. If you do, the sides of the angles will be parallel.

> ▶ **ACTIVITY**
>
> Construction **Parallel Lines**

Use these steps to construct a line that passes through a given point P and is parallel to a given line m.

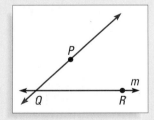 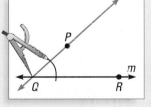 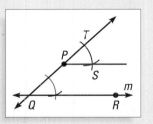 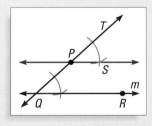

① Draw points Q and R on m. Draw $\overleftrightarrow{PQ}$.

② Draw an arc with the compass point at Q so that it crosses $\overrightarrow{QP}$ and $\overrightarrow{QR}$.

③ Copy ∠PQR on $\overleftrightarrow{QP}$ as shown. Be sure the two angles are corresponding. Label the new angle ∠TPS as shown.

④ Draw $\overleftrightarrow{PS}$. Because ∠TPS and ∠PQR are congruent corresponding angles, $\overleftrightarrow{PS} \parallel \overleftrightarrow{QR}$.

GUIDED PRACTICE

Concept Check ✓

1. Name two ways, from this lesson, to prove that two lines are parallel.

Skill Check ✓

State the theorem that you can use to prove that *r* is parallel to *s*.

2. GIVEN ▶ $r \parallel t, t \parallel s$

3. GIVEN ▶ $r \perp t, t \perp s$

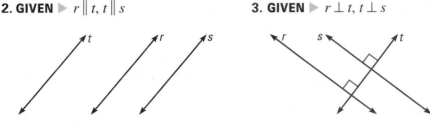

Determine which lines, if any, must be parallel. Explain your reasoning.

4.

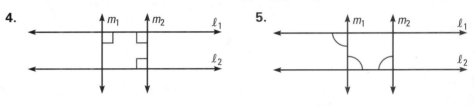

5.

6. Draw any angle $\angle A$. Then construct $\angle B$ congruent to $\angle A$.

7. Given a line ℓ and a point P not on ℓ, describe how to construct a line through P parallel to ℓ.

PRACTICE AND APPLICATIONS

STUDENT HELP

▶ **Extra Practice**
to help you master
skills is on p. 808.

🧩 **LOGICAL REASONING** **State the postulate or theorem that allows you to conclude that $j \parallel k$.**

8. GIVEN ▶ $j \parallel n, k \parallel n$ **9. GIVEN ▶** $j \perp n, k \perp n$ 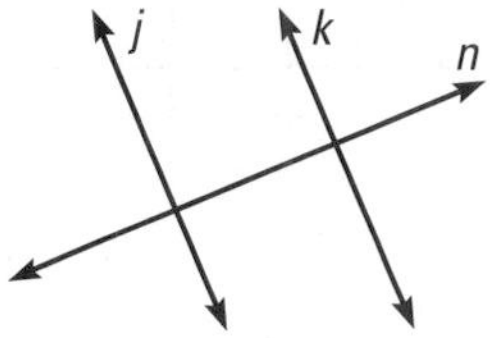   **10. GIVEN ▶** $\angle 1 \cong \angle 2$

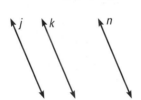

SHOWING LINES ARE PARALLEL **Explain how you would show that $k \parallel j$. State any theorems or postulates that you would use.**

11.   **12.**   **13.**

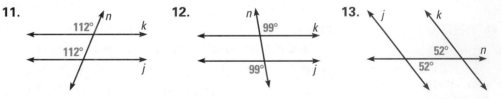

STUDENT HELP

▶ **HOMEWORK HELP**
Example 1: Exs. 8–24
Example 2: Exs. 8–24
Example 3: Exs. 8–24

14. *Writing* Make a list of all the ways you know to prove that two lines are parallel.

SHOWING LINES ARE PARALLEL **Explain how you would show that $k \parallel j$.**

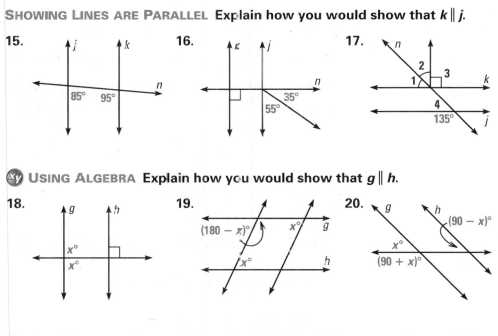

15.

16.

17.

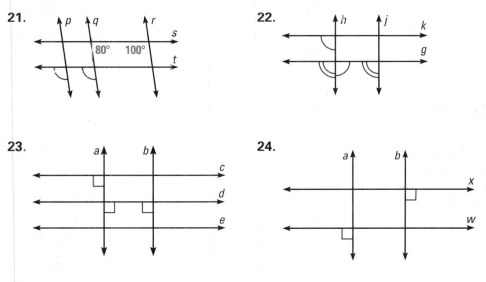

USING ALGEBRA **Explain how you would show that $g \parallel h$.**

18.

19.

20.

NAMING PARALLEL LINES **Determine which lines, if any, must be parallel. Explain your reasoning.**

21.

22.

23.

24.

CONSTRUCTIONS **Use a straightedge to draw an angle that fits the description. Then use the *Copying an Angle* construction on page 159 to copy the angle.**

25. An acute angle

26. An obtuse angle

27. **CONSTRUCTING PARALLEL LINES** Draw a horizontal line and construct a line parallel to it through a point above the line.

28. **CONSTRUCTING PARALLEL LINES** Draw a diagonal line and construct a line parallel to it through a point to the right of the line.

29. **JUSTIFYING A CONSTRUCTION** Explain why the lines in Exercise 28 are parallel. Use a postulate or theorem from Lesson 3.4 to support your answer.

STUDENT HELP

INTERNET **HOMEWORK HELP** Visit our Web site www.mcdougallittell.com for help with constructions in Exs. 25–29.

30. 🌐 **FOOTBALL FIELD** The white lines along the long edges of a football field are called *sidelines*. *Yard lines* are perpendicular to the sidelines and cross the field every five yards. Explain why you can conclude that the yard lines are parallel.

31. 🌐 **HANGING WALLPAPER** When you hang wallpaper, you use a tool called a *plumb line* to make sure one edge of the first strip of wallpaper is vertical. If the edges of each strip of wallpaper are parallel and there are no gaps between the strips, how do you know that the rest of the strips of wallpaper will be parallel to the first?

32. **ERROR ANALYSIS** It is given that $j \perp k$ and $k \perp \ell$. A student reasons that lines j and ℓ must be parallel. What is wrong with this reasoning? Sketch a counterexample to support your answer.

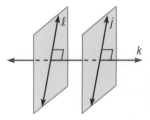

CATEGORIZING Tell whether the statement is *sometimes*, *always*, or *never* true.

33. Two lines that are parallel to the same line are parallel to each other.

34. *In a plane*, two lines that are perpendicular to the same line are parallel to each other.

35. Two *noncoplanar* lines that are perpendicular to the same line are parallel to each other.

36. Through a point not on a line you can construct a parallel line.

37. 🌐 **LATTICEWORK** You are making a lattice fence out of pieces of wood called slats. You want the top of each slat to be parallel to the bottom. At what angle should you cut ∠1?

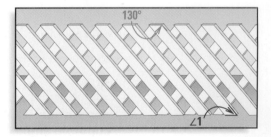

38. ▶ **PROVING THEOREM 3.12** Rearrange the statements to write a flow proof of Theorem 3.12. Remember to include a reason for each statement.

GIVEN ▶ $m \perp p$, $n \perp p$

PROVE ▶ $m \parallel n$

∠1 ≅ ∠2   n ⊥ p   ∠1 is a right ∠.

m ∥ n   m ⊥ p   ∠2 is a right ∠.

39. OPTICAL ILLUSION The radiating lines make it hard to tell if the red lines are straight. Explain how you can answer the question using only a straightedge and a protractor.

   a. Are the red lines straight?
   b. Are the red lines parallel?

40. CONSTRUCTING WITH PERPENDICULARS Draw a horizontal line ℓ and a point P not on ℓ. Construct a line m through P perpendicular to ℓ. Draw a point Q not on m or ℓ. Construct a line n through Q perpendicular to m. What postulate or theorem guarantees that the lines ℓ and n are parallel?

Test Preparation

41. MULTI-STEP PROBLEM Use the information given in the diagram at the right.

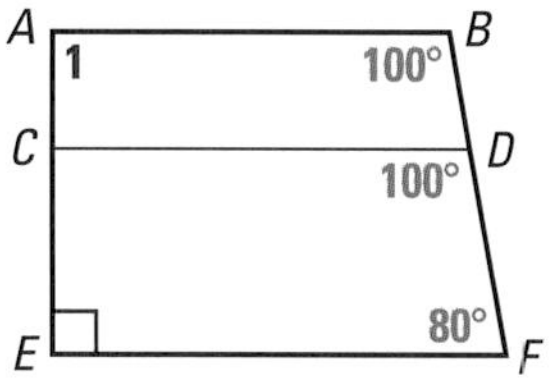

   a. Explain why $\overline{AB} \parallel \overline{CD}$.
   b. Explain why $\overline{CD} \parallel \overline{EF}$.
   c. *Writing* What is $m\angle 1$? How do you know?

★ **Challenge**

42. SCIENCE CONNECTION When light enters glass, the light bends. When it leaves glass, it bends again. If both sides of a pane of glass are parallel, light leaves the pane at the same angle at which it entered. Prove that the path of the exiting light is parallel to the path of the entering light.

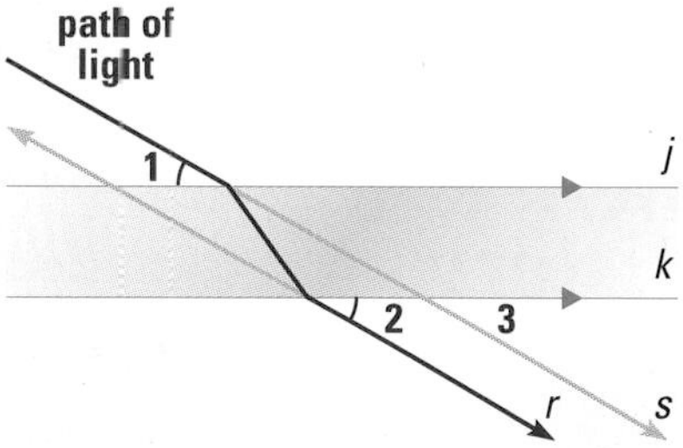

   GIVEN ▶ $\angle 1 \cong \angle 2, j \parallel k$
   PROVE ▶ $r \parallel s$

INTERNET
APPLICATION LINK
www.mcdougallittell.com

MIXED REVIEW

USING THE DISTANCE FORMULA Find the distance between the two points. **(Review 1.3 for 3.6)**

43. $A(0, -6), B(14, 0)$ **44.** $A(-3, -8), B(2, -1)$ **45.** $A(0, -7), B(6, 3)$

46. $A(-9, -5), B(-1, 11)$ **47.** $A(5, -7), B(-11, 6)$ **48.** $A(4, 4), B(-3, -3)$

FINDING COUNTEREXAMPLES Give a counterexample that demonstrates that the converse of the statement is false. **(Review 2.2)**

49. If an angle measures $42°$, then it is acute.

50. If two angles measure $150°$ and $30°$, then they are supplementary.

51. If a polygon is a rectangle, then it contains four right angles.

52. USING PROPERTIES OF PARALLEL LINES Use the given information to find the measures of the other seven angles in the figure shown at the right. **(Review 3.3)**

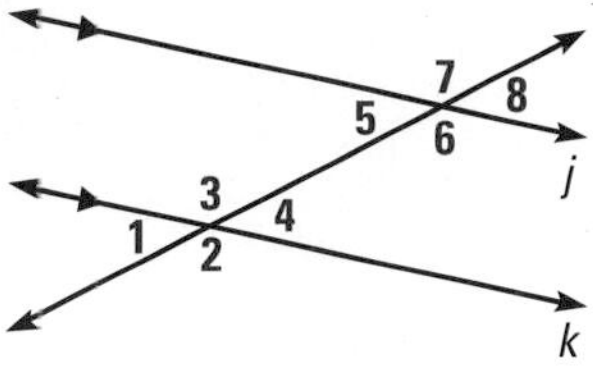

   GIVEN ▶ $j \parallel k, m\angle 1 = 33°$

1. In the diagram shown at the right, determine whether you can prove that lines *j* and *k* are parallel. If you can, state the postulate or theorem that you would use. **(Lesson 3.4)**

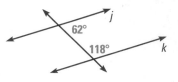

Use the given information and the diagram to determine which lines must be parallel. **(Lesson 3.5)**

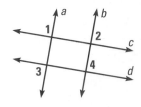

2. ∠1 and ∠2 are right angles.

3. ∠4 ≅ ∠3

4. ∠2 ≅ ∠3, ∠3 ≅ ∠4.

5. 🌐 **FIREPLACE CHIMNEY** In the illustration at the right, ∠*ABC* and ∠*DEF* are supplementary. Explain how you know that the left and right edges of the chimney are parallel. **(Lesson 3.4)**

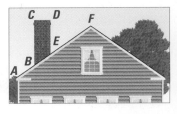

MATH & History

Measuring Earth's Circumference

APPLICATION LINK
www.mcdougallittell.com

THEN   **AROUND 230 B.C.,** the Greek scholar Eratosthenes estimated Earth's circumference. In the late 15th century, Christopher Columbus used a smaller estimate to convince the king and queen of Spain that his proposed voyage to India would take only 30 days.

NOW   **TODAY,** satellites and other tools are used to determine Earth's circumference with great accuracy.

1. The actual distance from Syene to Alexandria is about 500 miles. Use this value and the information on page 145 to estimate Earth's circumference. How close is your value to the modern day measurement in the table at the right?

Measuring Earth's Circumference	
Circumference estimated by Eratosthenes (230 B.C.)	About 29,000 mi
Circumference assumed by Columbus (about 1492)	About 17,600 mi
Modern day measurement	24,902 mi

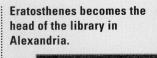

Eratosthenes becomes the head of the library in Alexandria.

235 B.C.

1492

A replica of one of the ships used by Christopher Columbus.

1999

Photograph of Earth from space.

3.6 Parallel Lines in the Coordinate Plane

What you should learn

GOAL 1 Find slopes of lines and use slope to identify parallel lines in a coordinate plane.

GOAL 2 Write equations of parallel lines in a coordinate plane.

Why you should learn it

▼ To describe steepness in **real-life**, such as the cog railway in **Example 1** and the zip line in **Ex. 46**.

GOAL 1   SLOPE OF PARALLEL LINES

In algebra, you learned that the slope of a nonvertical line is the ratio of the vertical change (the rise) to the horizontal change (the run). If the line passes through the points (x_1, y_1) and (x_2, y_2), then the slope is given by

$$\text{Slope} = \frac{\text{rise}}{\text{run}}$$

$$m = \frac{y_2 - y_1}{x_2 - x_1}.$$

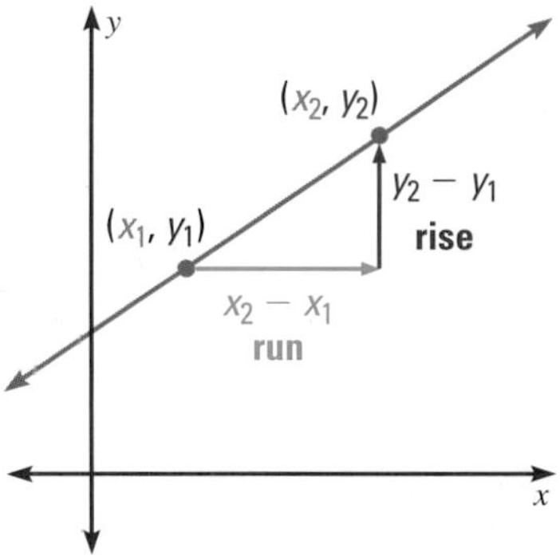

Slope is usually represented by the variable m.

EXAMPLE 1   *Finding the Slope of Train Tracks*

COG RAILWAY A cog railway goes up the side of Mount Washington, the tallest mountain in New England. At the steepest section, the train goes up about 4 feet for each 10 feet it goes forward. What is the slope of this section?

SOLUTION

$$\text{slope} = \frac{\text{rise}}{\text{run}} = \frac{4 \text{ feet}}{10 \text{ feet}} = 0.4$$

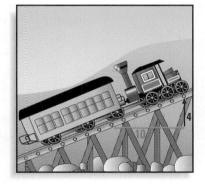

EXAMPLE 2   *Finding the Slope of a Line*

Find the slope of the line that passes through the points (0, 6) and (5, 2).

SOLUTION

Let $(x_1, y_1) = (0, 6)$ and $(x_2, y_2) = (5, 2)$.

$$m = \frac{y_2 - y_1}{x_2 - x_1}$$

$$= \frac{2 - 6}{5 - 0}$$

$$= -\frac{4}{5}$$

▶ The slope of the line is $-\frac{4}{5}$.

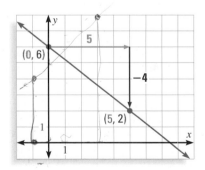

You can use the slopes of two lines to tell whether the lines are parallel.

POSTULATE

POSTULATE 17 ***Slopes of Parallel Lines***

In a coordinate plane, two nonvertical lines are parallel if and only if they have the same slope. Any two vertical lines are parallel.

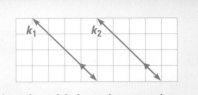

Lines k_1 and k_2 have the same slope.

STUDENT HELP

Study Tip
To find the slope in Example 3, you can either use the slope formula or you can count units on the graph.

EXAMPLE 3 *Deciding Whether Lines are Parallel*

Find the slope of each line. Is $j_1 \parallel j_2$?

SOLUTION

Line j_1 has a slope of

$$m_1 = \frac{4}{2} = 2$$

Line j_2 has a slope of

$$m_2 = \frac{2}{1} = 2$$

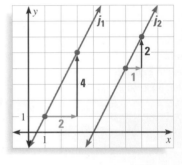

▶ Because the lines have the same slope, $j_1 \parallel j_2$.

Using Algebra

EXAMPLE 4 *Identifying Parallel Lines*

Find the slope of each line. Which lines are parallel?

SOLUTION

Find the slope of k_1. Line k_1 passes through (0, 6) and (2, 0).

$$m_1 = \frac{0 - 6}{2 - 0} = \frac{-6}{2} = -3$$

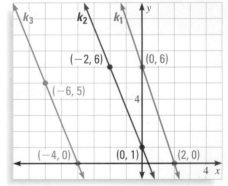

Find the slope of k_2. Line k_2 passes through (−2, 6) and (0, 1).

$$m_2 = \frac{1 - 6}{0 - (-2)} = \frac{-5}{0 + 2} = -\frac{5}{2}$$

Find the slope of k_3. Line k_3 passes through (−6, 5) and (−4, 0).

$$m_3 = \frac{0 - 5}{-4 - (-6)} = \frac{-5}{-4 + 6} = -\frac{5}{2}$$

▶ Compare the slopes. Because k_2 and k_3 have the same slope, they are parallel. Line k_1 has a different slope, so it is not parallel to either of the other lines.

GOAL 2 WRITING EQUATIONS OF PARALLEL LINES

In algebra, you learned that you can use the slope m of a nonvertical line to write an equation of the line in *slope-intercept form*.

$$\overset{\text{slope}}{y = m\overset{\downarrow}{x} + b} \; \overset{\text{y-intercept}}{\nwarrow}$$

The y-intercept is the y-coordinate of the point where the line crosses the y-axis.

Using Algebra

EXAMPLE 5 *Writing an Equation of a Line*

Write an equation of the line through the point $(2, 3)$ that has a slope of 5.

SOLUTION

Solve for b. Use $(x, y) = (2, 3)$ and $m = 5$.

$y = mx + b$	Slope-intercept form
$3 = 5(2) + b$	Substitute 2 for *x*, 3 for *y*, and 5 for *m*.
$3 = 10 + b$	Simplify.
$-7 = b$	Subtract.

▶ ***Write*** an equation. Since $m = 5$ and $b = -7$, an equation of the line is $y = 5x - 7$.

EXAMPLE 6 *Writing an Equation of a Parallel Line*

Line n_1 has the equation $y = -\frac{1}{3}x - 1$.

Line n_2 is parallel to n_1 and passes through the point $(3, 2)$. Write an equation of n_2.

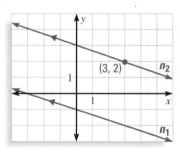

SOLUTION

Find the slope.

The slope of n_1 is $-\frac{1}{3}$. Because parallel lines have the same slope, the slope of n_2 is also $-\frac{1}{3}$.

Solve for b. Use $(x, y) = (3, 2)$ and $m = -\frac{1}{3}$.

$$y = mx + b$$
$$2 = -\frac{1}{3}(3) + b$$
$$2 = -1 + b$$
$$3 = b$$

Write an equation.

▶ Because $m = -\frac{1}{3}$ and $b = 3$, an equation of n_2 is $y = -\frac{1}{3}x + 3$.

STUDENT HELP

HOMEWORK HELP
Visit our Web site
www.mcdougallittell.com
for extra examples.

GUIDED PRACTICE

Vocabulary Check ✓   **1.** What does *intercept* mean in the expression *slope-intercept form*?

Concept Check ✓   **2.** The slope of line *j* is 2 and *j* ∥ *k*. What is the slope of line *k*?

3. What is the slope of a horizontal line? What is the slope of a vertical line?

Skill Check ✓   **Find the slope of the line that passes through the labeled points.**

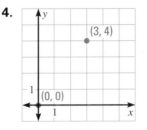

4.

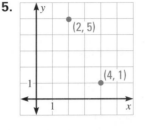

5.

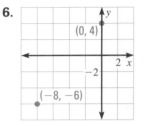

6.

Determine whether the two lines shown in the graph are parallel. If they are parallel, explain how you know.

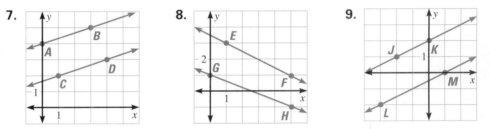

7.   **8.**   **9.**

10. Write an equation of the line that passes through the point (2, −3) and has a slope of −1.

PRACTICE AND APPLICATIONS

> **STUDENT HELP**
>
> ▶ **Extra Practice**
> to help you master
> skills is on p. 808.

CALCULATING SLOPE What is the slope of the line?

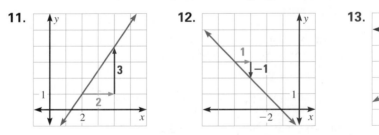

11.   **12.**   **13.**

CALCULATING SLOPE Find the slope of the line that passes through the labeled points on the graph.

> **STUDENT HELP**
>
> ▶ **HOMEWORK HELP**
> **Example 1:** Exs. 11–16,
>   23, 46, 49–52
> **Example 2:** Exs. 11–16

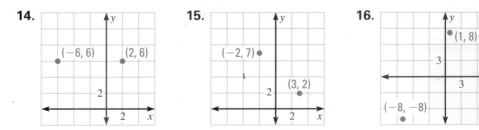

14.   **15.**   **16.**

STUDENT HELP

HOMEWORK HELP
Example 3: Exs. 17–22
Example 4: Exs. 24–26, 47, 48
Example 5: Exs. 27–41
Example 6: Exs. 42–45

IDENTIFYING PARALLELS Find the slope of each line. Are the lines parallel?

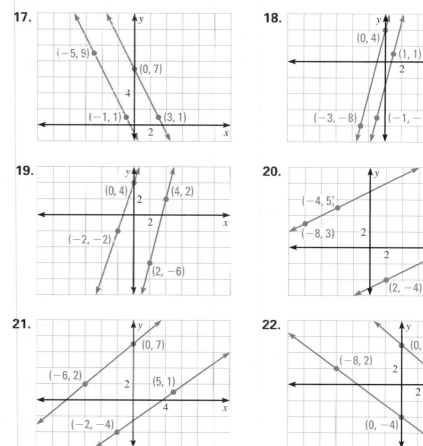

17.

18.

19.

20.

21.

22.

23. **UNDERGROUND RAILROAD** The photo at the right shows a monument in Oberlin, Ohio, that is dedicated to the Underground Railroad. The slope of each of the rails is about $-\frac{3}{5}$ and the sculpture is about 12 feet long. What is the height of the ends of the rails? Explain how you found your answer.

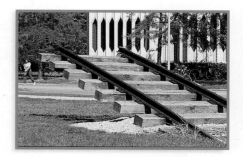

IDENTIFYING PARALLELS Find the slopes of $\overleftrightarrow{AB}$, $\overleftrightarrow{CD}$, and $\overleftrightarrow{EF}$. Which lines are parallel, if any?

24. $A(0, -6)$, $B(4, -4)$
$C(0, 2)$, $D(2, 3)$
$E(0, -4)$, $F(1, -7)$

25. $A(2, 6)$, $B(4, 7)$
$C(0, -1)$, $D(6, 2)$
$E(4, -5)$, $F(8, -2)$

26. $A(-4, 10)$, $B(-8, 7)$
$C(-5, 7)$, $D(-2, 4)$
$E(2, -3)$, $F(6, -7)$

WRITING EQUATIONS Write an equation of the line.

27. slope = 3
y-intercept = 2

28. slope = $\frac{1}{3}$
y-intercept = −4

29. slope = $-\frac{2}{9}$
y-intercept = 0

30. slope = $\frac{1}{2}$
y-intercept = 6

31. slope = 0
y-intercept = −3

32. slope = $-\frac{2}{9}$
y-intercept = $-\frac{3}{5}$

FOCUS ON PEOPLE

REAL LIFE **UNDERGROUND RAILROAD** is the name given to the network of people who helped some slaves to freedom. Harriet Tubman, a former slave, helped about 300 escape.

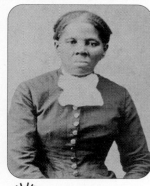

WRITING EQUATIONS Write an equation of the line that has a *y*-intercept of 3 and is parallel to the line whose equation is given.

33. $y = -6x + 2$ **34.** $y = x - 8$ **35.** $y = -\frac{4}{3}x$

WRITING EQUATIONS Write an equation of the line that passes through the given point *P* and has the given slope.

36. $P(0, -6), m = -2$ **37.** $P(-3, 9), m = -1$ **38.** $P\left(\frac{3}{2}, 4\right), m = \frac{1}{2}$

39. $P(2, -4), m = 0$ **40.** $P(-7, -5), m = \frac{3}{4}$ **41.** $P(6, 1)$, undefined slope

USING ALGEBRA Write an equation of the line that passes through point *P* and is parallel to the line with the given equation.

42. $P(-3, 6), y = -x - 5$ **43.** $P(1, -2), y = \frac{5}{4}x - 8$ **44.** $P(8, 7), y = 3$

45. **USING ALGEBRA** Write an equation of a line parallel to $y = \frac{1}{3}x - 16$.

46. **ZIP LINE** A zip line is a taut rope or cable that you can ride down on a pulley. The zip line at the right goes from a 9 foot tall tower to a 6 foot tall tower. The towers are 20 feet apart. What is the slope of the zip line?

COORDINATE GEOMETRY In Exercises 47 and 48, use the five points: *P*(0, 0), *Q*(1, 3), *R*(4, 0), *S*(8, 2), and *T*(9, 5).

47. Plot and label the points. Connect every pair of points with a segment.

48. Which segments are parallel? How can you verify this?

CIVIL ENGINEERING In Exercises 49–52, use the following information.
The slope of a road is called the road's *grade*. Grades are measured in percents. For example, if the slope of a road is $\frac{1}{20}$, the grade is 5%. A warning sign is needed before any hill that fits one of the following descriptions.

    5% grade and more than 3000 feet long
    6% grade and more than 2000 feet long
    7% grade and more than 1000 feet long
    8% grade and more than 750 feet long
    9% grade and more than 500 feet long
    ▶ Source: U.S. Department of Transportation

8%

What is the grade of the hill to the nearest percent? Is a sign needed?

49. The hill is 1400 feet long and drops 70 feet.

50. The hill is 2200 feet long and drops 140 feet.

51. The hill is 600 feet long and drops 55 feet.

52. The hill is 450 feet long and drops 40 feet.

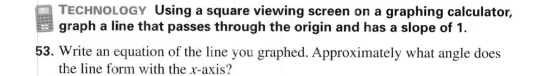 **TECHNOLOGY** **Using a square viewing screen on a graphing calculator, graph a line that passes through the origin and has a slope of 1.**

53. Write an equation of the line you graphed. Approximately what angle does the line form with the x-axis?

54. Graph a line that passes through the origin and has a slope of 2. Write an equation of the line. When you doubled the slope, did the measure of the angle formed with the x-axis double?

Test Preparation

55. MULTIPLE CHOICE If two different lines with equations $y = m_1 x + b_1$ and $y = m_2 x + b_2$ are parallel, which of the following must be true?

Ⓐ $b_1 = b_2$ and $m_1 \neq m_2$ Ⓑ $b_1 \neq b_2$ and $m_1 \neq m_2$

Ⓒ $b_1 \neq b_2$ and $m_1 = m_2$ Ⓓ $b_1 = b_2$ and $m_1 = m_2$

Ⓔ None of these

56. MULTIPLE CHOICE Which of the following is an equation of a line parallel to $y - 4 = -\frac{1}{2}x$?

Ⓐ $y = \frac{1}{2}x - 6$ Ⓑ $y = 2x + 1$ Ⓒ $y = -2x + 3$

Ⓓ $y = \frac{7}{2}x - 1$ Ⓔ $y = -\frac{1}{2}x - 8$

★ Challenge

57. ⓧⓨ **USING ALGEBRA** Find a value for k so that the line through $(4, k)$ and $(-2, -1)$ is parallel to $y = -2x + \frac{3}{2}$.

58. ⓧⓨ **USING ALGEBRA** Find a value for k so that the line through $(k, -10)$ and $(5, -6)$ is parallel to $y = -\frac{1}{4}x + 3$.

MIXED REVIEW

RECIPROCALS **Find the reciprocal of the number.** (Skills Review, p. 788)

59. 20   **60.** -3 **61.** -11 **62.** 340

63. $\frac{3}{7}$ **64.** $-\frac{13}{3}$ **65.** $-\frac{1}{2}$ **66.** 0.25

MULTIPLYING NUMBERS **Evaluate the expression.** (Skills Review, p. 785)

67. $\frac{3}{4} \cdot (-12)$ **68.** $-\frac{3}{2} \cdot \left(-\frac{8}{3}\right)$ **69.** $-10 \cdot \frac{7}{6}$ **70.** $-\frac{2}{9} \cdot (-33)$

PROVING LINES PARALLEL **Can you prove that lines m and n are parallel? If so, state the postulate or theorem you would use.** (Review 3.4)

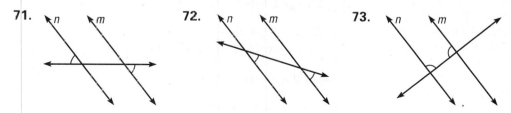

71.   **72.**   **73.**

3.7 Perpendicular Lines in the Coordinate Plane

What you should learn

GOAL 1 Use slope to identify perpendicular lines in a coordinate plane.

GOAL 2 Write equations of perpendicular lines, as applied in **Ex. 46**.

Why you should learn it

▼ Equations of perpendicular lines are used by ray tracing software to create realistic reflections, as in the illustration below and in **Example 6**.

REAL LIFE

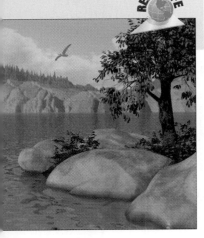

GOAL 1 SLOPE OF PERPENDICULAR LINES

In the activity below, you will trace a piece of paper to draw perpendicular lines on a coordinate grid. Points where grid lines cross are called *lattice points*.

ACTIVITY Developing Concepts

Investigating Slopes of Perpendicular Lines

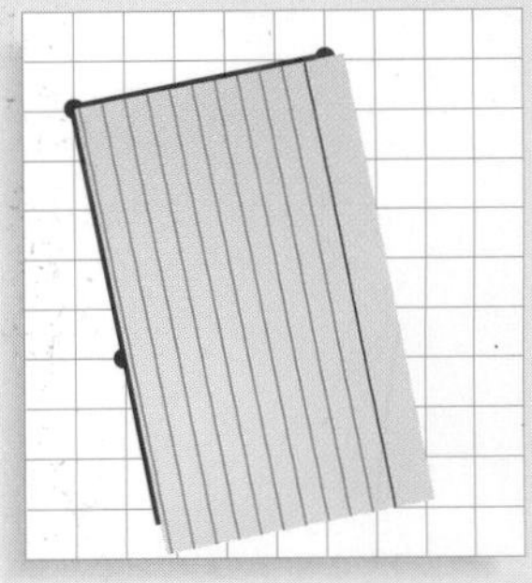

1. Put the corner of a piece of paper on a lattice point. Rotate the corner so each edge passes through another lattice point but neither edge is vertical. Trace the edges.
2. Find the slope of each line.
3. Multiply the slopes.
4. Repeat Steps 1–3 with the paper at a different angle.

In the activity, you may have discovered the following.

POSTULATE

POSTULATE 18 *Slopes of Perpendicular Lines*

In a coordinate plane, two nonvertical lines are perpendicular if and only if the product of their slopes is −1.

Vertical and horizontal lines are perpendicular.

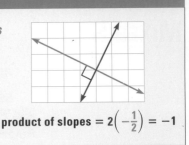

product of slopes $= 2\left(-\frac{1}{2}\right) = -1$

EXAMPLE 1 *Deciding Whether Lines are Perpendicular*

Find each slope.

$$\text{Slope of } j_1 = \frac{3-1}{0-3} = -\frac{2}{3}$$

$$\text{Slope of } j_2 = \frac{3-(-3)}{0-(-4)} = \frac{6}{4} = \frac{3}{2}$$

Multiply the slopes.

The product is $\left(-\frac{2}{3}\right)\left(\frac{3}{2}\right) = -1$, so $j_1 \perp j_2$.

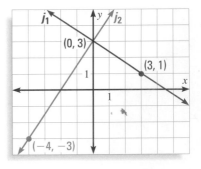

Logical Reasoning

EXAMPLE 2 *Deciding Whether Lines are Perpendicular*

Decide whether $\overleftrightarrow{AC}$ and $\overleftrightarrow{DB}$ are perpendicular.

SOLUTION

Slope of $\overleftrightarrow{AC} = \dfrac{2 - (-4)}{4 - 1} = \dfrac{6}{3} = 2$

Slope of $\overleftrightarrow{DB} = \dfrac{2 - (-1)}{-1 - 5} = \dfrac{3}{-6} = -\dfrac{1}{2}$

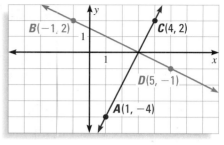

The product is $2\left(-\dfrac{1}{2}\right) = -1$, so $\overleftrightarrow{AC} \perp \overleftrightarrow{DB}$.

EXAMPLE 3 *Deciding Whether Lines are Perpendicular*

Decide whether the lines are perpendicular.

line *h*: $y = \dfrac{3}{4}x + 2$ **line *j*:** $y = -\dfrac{4}{3}x - 3$

SOLUTION

The slope of line h is $\dfrac{3}{4}$.   The slope of line j is $-\dfrac{4}{3}$.

The product is $\left(\dfrac{3}{4}\right)\left(-\dfrac{4}{3}\right) = -1$, so the lines are perpendicular.

EXAMPLE 4 *Deciding Whether Lines are Perpendicular*

Using Algebra

Decide whether the lines are perpendicular.

    line *r*: $4x + 5y = 2$ **line *s*:** $5x + 4y = 3$

SOLUTION

Rewrite each equation in slope-intercept form to find the slope.

line *r*:	line *s*:
$4x + 5y = 2$	$5x + 4y = 3$
$5y = -4x + 2$	$4y = -5x + 3$
$y = -\dfrac{4}{5}x + \dfrac{2}{5}$	$y = -\dfrac{5}{4}x + \dfrac{3}{4}$
slope $= -\dfrac{4}{5}$	slope $= -\dfrac{5}{4}$

Multiply the slopes to see if the lines are perpendicular.

$$\left(-\dfrac{4}{5}\right)\left(-\dfrac{5}{4}\right) = 1$$

▶ The product of the slopes is *not* -1. So, r and s are *not* perpendicular.

GOAL 2 WRITING EQUATIONS OF PERPENDICULAR LINES

EXAMPLE 5 *Writing the Equation of a Perpendicular Line*

Line ℓ_1 has equation $y = -2x + 1$. Find an equation of the line ℓ_2 that passes through $P(4, 0)$ and is perpendicular to ℓ_1. First you must find the slope, m_2.

$m_1 \cdot m_2 = -1$	The product of the slopes of $\perp$ lines is -1.
$-2 \cdot m_2 = -1$	The slope of ℓ_1 is -2.
$m_2 = \dfrac{1}{2}$	Divide both sides by -2.

Then use $m = \dfrac{1}{2}$ and $(x, y) = (4, 0)$ to find b.

$y = mx + b$	Slope-intercept form
$0 = \dfrac{1}{2}(4) + b$	Substitute 0 for y, $\dfrac{1}{2}$ for m, and 4 for x.
$-2 = b$	Simplify.

▶ So, an equation of ℓ_2 is $y = \dfrac{1}{2}x - 2$.

. . . .

RAY TRACING Computer illustrators use *ray tracing* to make accurate reflections. To figure out what to show in the mirror, the computer traces a ray of light as it reflects off the mirror. This calculation has many steps. One of the first steps is to find the equation of a line perpendicular to the mirror.

EXAMPLE 6 *Writing the Equation of a Perpendicular Line*

The equation $y = \dfrac{3}{2}x + 3$ represents a mirror. A ray of light hits the mirror at $(-2, 0)$. What is the equation of the line p that is perpendicular to the mirror at this point?

SOLUTION

The mirror's slope is $\dfrac{3}{2}$, so the slope of p is $-\dfrac{2}{3}$. Use $m = -\dfrac{2}{3}$ and $(x, y) = (-2, 0)$ to find b.

$$0 = -\dfrac{2}{3}(-2) + b$$

$$-\dfrac{4}{3} = b$$

▶ So, an equation for p is $y = -\dfrac{2}{3}x - \dfrac{4}{3}$.

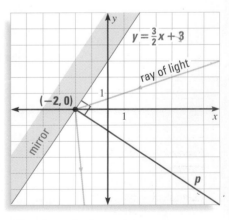

Top view of mirror

GUIDED PRACTICE

Vocabulary Check ✓
Concept Check ✓
Skill Check ✓

1. Define *slope of a line*.

2. The slope of line m is $-\frac{1}{5}$. What is the slope of a line perpendicular to m?

3. In the coordinate plane shown at the right, is $\overleftrightarrow{AC}$ perpendicular to $\overleftrightarrow{BD}$? Explain.

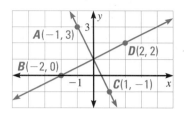

4. Decide whether the lines with the equations $y = 2x - 1$ and $y = -2x + 1$ are perpendicular.

5. Decide whether the lines with the equations $5y - x = 15$ and $y + 5x = 2$ are perpendicular.

6. The line ℓ_1 has the equation $y = 3x$. The line ℓ_2 is perpendicular to ℓ_1 and passes through the point $P(0, 0)$. Write an equation of ℓ_2.

PRACTICE AND APPLICATIONS

STUDENT HELP

▶ **Extra Practice**
to help you master
skills is on p. 808.

SLOPES OF PERPENDICULAR LINES The slopes of two lines are given. Are the lines perpendicular?

7. $m_1 = 2$, $m_2 = -\frac{1}{2}$ **8.** $m_1 = \frac{2}{3}$, $m_2 = \frac{3}{2}$ **9.** $m_1 = \frac{1}{4}$, $m_2 = -4$

10. $m_1 = \frac{5}{7}$, $m_2 = -\frac{7}{5}$ **11.** $m_1 = -\frac{1}{2}$, $m_2 = -\frac{1}{2}$ **12.** $m_1 = -1$, $m_2 = 1$

SLOPES OF PERPENDICULAR LINES Lines *j* and *n* are perpendicular. The slope of line *j* is given. What is the slope of line *n*? Check your answer.

13. 2   **14.** 5   **15.** -3 **16.** -7

17. $\frac{2}{3}$ **18.** $\frac{1}{5}$ **19.** $-\frac{1}{3}$ **20.** $-\frac{4}{3}$

IDENTIFYING PERPENDICULAR LINES Find the slope of $\overleftrightarrow{AC}$ and $\overleftrightarrow{BD}$. Decide whether $\overleftrightarrow{AC}$ is perpendicular to $\overleftrightarrow{BD}$.

21.   **22.**

23.   **24.**

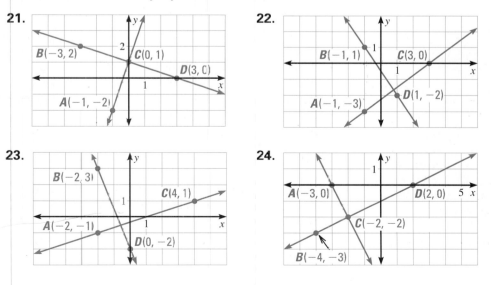

STUDENT HELP

▶ HOMEWORK HELP
Example 1: Exs. 7–20
Example 2: Exs. 21–24,
                33–37
Example 3: Exs. 25–28,
                47–50
Example 4: Exs. 29–32
Example 5: Exs. 38–41
Example 6: Exs. 42–46

USING ALGEBRA Decide whether lines k_1 and k_2 are perpendicular. Then graph the lines to check your answer.

25. line k_1: $y = 3x$

line k_2: $y = -\frac{1}{3}x - 2$

26. line k_1: $y = -\frac{4}{5}x - 2$

line k_2: $y = \frac{1}{5}x + 4$

27. line k_1: $y = -\frac{3}{4}x + 2$

line k_2: $y = \frac{4}{3}x + 5$

28. line k_1: $y = \frac{1}{3}x - 10$

line k_2: $y = 3x$

USING ALGEBRA Decide whether lines p_1 and p_2 are perpendicular.

29. line p_1: $3y - 4x = 3$

line p_2: $4y + 3x = -12$

30. line p_1: $y - 6x = 2$

line p_2: $6y - x = 12$

31. line p_1: $3y + 2x = -36$

line p_2: $4y - 3x = 16$

32. line p_1: $5y + 3x = -15$

line p_2: $3y - 5x = -33$

STUDENT HELP

INTERNET

HOMEWORK HELP
Visit our Web site
www.mcdougallittell.com
for help with Exs. 33–36.

LINE RELATIONSHIPS Find the slope of each line. Identify any parallel or perpendicular lines.

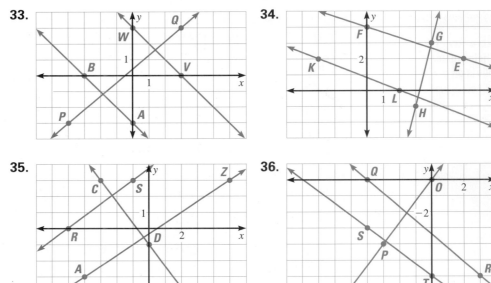

33.

34.

35.

36.

37. 🌎 **NEEDLEPOINT** To check whether two stitched lines make a right angle, you can count the squares. For example, the lines at the right are perpendicular because one goes up 8 as it goes over 4, and the other goes over 8 as it goes down 4. Why does this mean the lines are perpendicular?

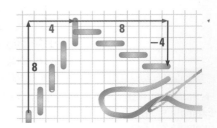

WRITING EQUATIONS Line j is perpendicular to the line with the given equation and line j passes through P. Write an equation of line j.

38. $y = \frac{1}{2}x - 1$, $P(0, 3)$

39. $y = \frac{5}{3}x + 2$, $P(5, 1)$

40. $y = -4x - 3$, $P(-2, 2)$

41. $3y + 4x = 12$, $P(-3, -4)$

FOCUS ON PEOPLE

REAL LIFE **HELAMAN FERGUSON'S** stone drill is suspended by six cables. The computer uses the lengths of the cables to calculate the coordinates of the drill tip.

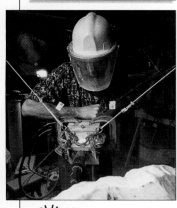

WRITING EQUATIONS The line with the given equation is perpendicular to line *j* at point *R*. Write an equation of line *j*.

42. $y = -\frac{3}{4}x + 6, R(8, 0)$

43. $y = \frac{1}{7}x - 11, R(7, -10)$

44. $y = 3x + 5, R(-3, -4)$

45. $y = -\frac{2}{5}x - 3, R(5, -5)$

46. **SCULPTURE** Helaman Ferguson designs sculptures on a computer. The computer is connected to his stone drill and tells how far he should drill at any given point. The distance from the drill tip to the desired surface of the sculpture is calculated along a line perpendicular to the sculpture.

Suppose the drill tip is at $(-1, -1)$ and the equation $y = \frac{1}{4}x + 3$ represents the surface of the sculpture. Write an equation of the line that passes through the drill tip and is perpendicular to the sculpture.

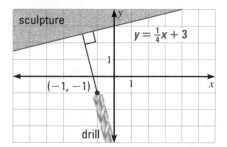

LINE RELATIONSHIPS Decide whether the lines with the given equations are *parallel, perpendicular,* or *neither*.

47. $y = -2x - 1$
$y = -2x - 3$

48. $y = -\frac{1}{2}x + 3$
$y = -\frac{1}{2}x + 5$

49. $y = -3x + 1$
$y = \frac{1}{3}x + 1$

50. $y = 4x + 10$
$y = -2x + 5$

Test Preparation

51. MULTI-STEP PROBLEM Use the diagram at the right.

a. Is $\ell_1 \parallel \ell_2$? How do you know?

b. Is $\ell_2 \perp n$? How do you know?

c. *Writing* Describe two ways to prove that $\ell_1 \perp n$.

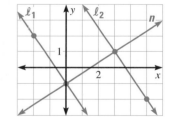

★ Challenge

DISTANCE TO A LINE In Exercises 52–54, use the following information.
The distance from a point to a line is defined to be the length of the perpendicular segment from the point to the line. In the diagram at the right, the distance d between point P and line ℓ is given by QP.

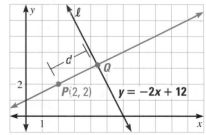

52. Find an equation of $\overleftrightarrow{QP}$.

53. Solve a system of equations to find the coordinates of point Q, the intersection of the two lines.

54. Use the Distance Formula to find QP.

EXTRA CHALLENGE
www.mcdougallittell.com

MIXED REVIEW

ANGLE MEASURES **Use the diagram to complete the statement.**
(Review 2.6 for 4.1)

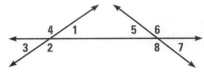

55. If $m\angle 5 = 38°$, then $m\angle 8 = $ _?_ .

56. If $m\angle 3 = 36°$, then $m\angle 4 = $ _?_ .

57. If $\angle 8 \cong \angle 4$ and $m\angle 2 = 145°$,
then $m\angle 7 = $ _?_ .

58. If $m\angle 1 = 38°$ and $\angle 3 \cong \angle 5$, then $m\angle 6 = $ _?_ .

IDENTIFYING ANGLES **Use the diagram to complete the statement.**
(Review 3.1 for 4.1)

59. $\angle 3$ and _?_ are consecutive interior angles.

60. $\angle 1$ and _?_ are alternate exterior angles.

61. $\angle 4$ and _?_ are alternate interior angles.

62. $\angle 1$ and _?_ are corresponding angles.

63. *Writing* Describe the three types of proofs you have learned so far.
(Review 3.2)

QUIZ 3   *Self-Test for Lessons 3.6 and 3.7*

Find the slope of $\overleftrightarrow{AB}$. (Lesson 3.6)

1. $A(1, 2), B(5, 8)$

2. $A(2, -3), B(-1, 5)$

Write an equation of line j_2 that passes through point P and is parallel to line j_1. (Lesson 3.6)

3. line j_1: $y = 3x - 2$
$P(0, 2)$

4. line j_1: $y = \frac{1}{2}x + 1$
$P(2, -4)$

Decide whether k_1 and k_2 are perpendicular. (Lesson 3.7)

5. line k_1: $y = 2x - 1$
line k_2: $y = -\frac{1}{2}x + 2$

6. line k_1: $y - 3x = -2$
line k_2: $3y - x = 12$

7. 🌐 **ANGLE OF REPOSE** When a
granular substance is poured into a
pile, the slope of the pile depends
only on the substance. For example,
when barley is poured into piles,
every pile has the same slope. A pile
of barley that is 5 feet tall would be
about 10 feet wide. What is the slope
of a pile of barley? (Lesson 3.6)

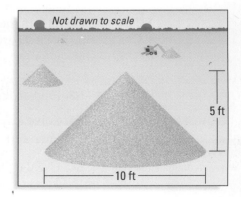

Chapter Summary

WHAT did you learn?

Identify relationships between lines. **(3.1)**

Identify angles formed by coplanar lines intersected by a transversal. **(3.1)**

Prove and use results about perpendicular lines. **(3.2)**

Write flow proofs and paragraph proofs. **(3.2)**

Prove and use results about parallel lines and transversals. **(3.3)**

Prove that lines are parallel. **(3.4)**

Use properties of parallel lines. **(3.4, 3.5)**

Use slope to decide whether lines in a coordinate plane are parallel. **(3.6)**

Write an equation of a line parallel to a given line in a coordinate plane. **(3.6)**

Use slope to decide whether lines in a coordinate plane are perpendicular. **(3.7)**

Write an equation of a line perpendicular to a given line. **(3.7)**

WHY did you learn it?

Describe lines and planes in real-life objects, such as escalators. **(p. 133)**

Lay the foundation for work with angles and proof.

Solve real-life problems, such as deciding how many angles of a window frame to measure. **(p. 141)**

Learn to write and use different types of proof.

Understand the world around you, such as how rainbows are formed. **(p. 148)**

Solve real-life problems, such as predicting paths of sailboats. **(p. 152)**

Analyze light passing through glass. **(p. 163)**

Use coordinate geometry to show that two segments are parallel. **(p. 170)**

Prepare to write coordinate proofs.

Solve real-life problems, such as deciding whether two stitched lines form a right angle. **(p. 176)**

Find the distance from a point to a line. **(p. 177)**

How does Chapter 3 fit into the BIGGER PICTURE of geometry?

In this chapter, you learned about properties of perpendicular and parallel lines. You also learned to write flow proofs and learned some important skills related to coordinate geometry. This work will prepare you to reach conclusions about triangles and other figures and to solve real-life problems in areas such as carpentry, engineering, and physics.

STUDY STRATEGY

How did your study questions help you learn?

The study questions you wrote, following the study strategy on page 128, may resemble this one.

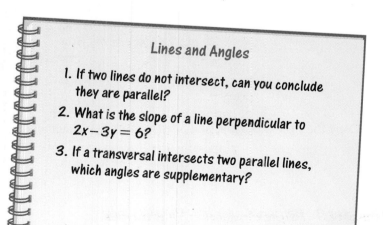

Lines and Angles

1. If two lines do not intersect, can you conclude they are parallel?

2. What is the slope of a line perpendicular to $2x - 3y = 6$?

3. If a transversal intersects two parallel lines, which angles are supplementary?

Chapter Review

- parallel lines, p. 129
- skew lines, p. 129
- parallel planes, p. 129
- transversal, p. 131
- corresponding angles, p. 131
- alternate interior angles, p. 131
- alternate exterior angles, p. 131
- consecutive interior angles, p. 131
- same side interior angles, p. 131
- flow proof, p. 136

3.1   LINES AND ANGLES

Examples on pp. 129–131

> **EXAMPLES**   In the figure, $j \parallel k$, h is a transversal, and $h \perp k$.
>
> $\angle 1$ and $\angle 5$ are corresponding angles.
>
> $\angle 3$ and $\angle 6$ are alternate interior angles.
>
> $\angle 1$ and $\angle 8$ are alternate exterior angles.
>
> $\angle 4$ and $\angle 6$ are consecutive interior angles.

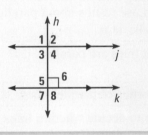

Complete the statement. Use the figure above.

1. $\angle 2$ and $\angle 7$ are ___?___ angles.

2. $\angle 4$ and $\angle 5$ are ___?___ angles.

Use the figure at the right.

3. Name a line parallel to $\overleftrightarrow{DH}$.

4. Name a line perpendicular to $\overleftrightarrow{AE}$.

5. Name a line skew to $\overleftrightarrow{FD}$.

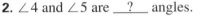
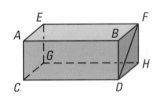

3.2   PROOF AND PERPENDICULAR LINES

Examples on pp. 136–138

> **EXAMPLE**   **GIVEN** ▶ $\angle 1$ and $\angle 2$ are complements.
>
> **PROVE** ▶ $\overrightarrow{GH} \perp \overrightarrow{GJ}$

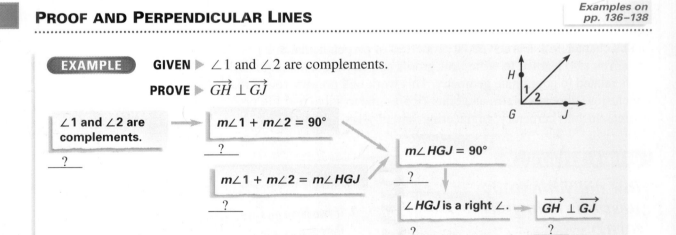

6. Copy the flow proof and add a reason for each statement.

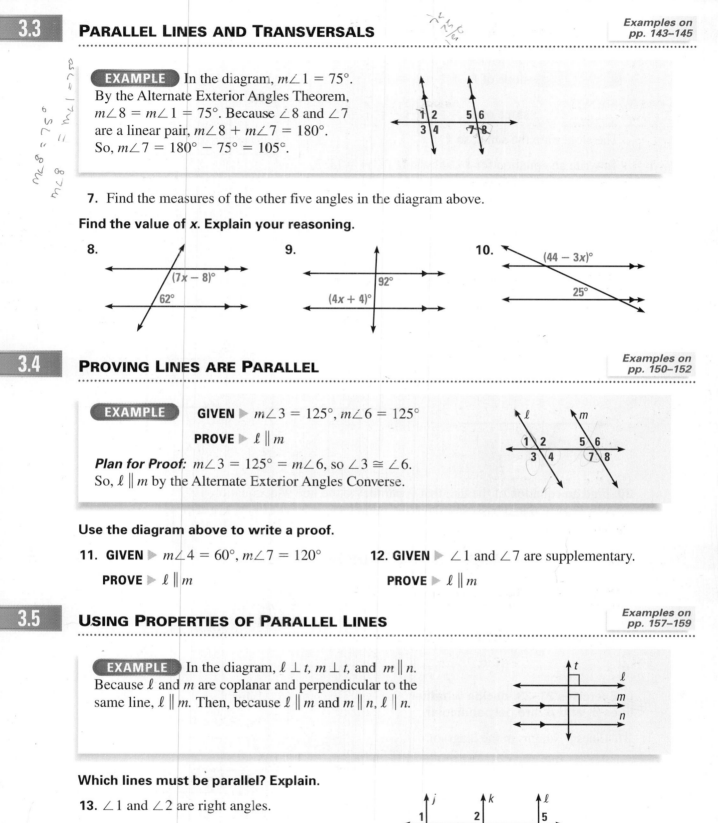

PARALLEL LINES AND TRANSVERSALS

Examples on
pp. 143–145

EXAMPLE In the diagram, $m\angle 1 = 75°$.
By the Alternate Exterior Angles Theorem,
$m\angle 8 = m\angle 1 = 75°$. Because $\angle 8$ and $\angle 7$
are a linear pair, $m\angle 8 + m\angle 7 = 180°$.
So, $m\angle 7 = 180° - 75° = 105°$.

7. Find the measures of the other five angles in the diagram above.

Find the value of *x*. Explain your reasoning.

8.

$(7x - 8)°$

$62°$

9.

$92°$

$(4x + 4)°$

10.

$(44 - 3x)°$

$25°$

PROVING LINES ARE PARALLEL

Examples on
pp. 150–152

EXAMPLE **GIVEN** ▶ $m\angle 3 = 125°, m\angle 6 = 125°$

PROVE ▶ $\ell \parallel m$

Plan for Proof: $m\angle 3 = 125° = m\angle 6$, so $\angle 3 \cong \angle 6$.
So, $\ell \parallel m$ by the Alternate Exterior Angles Converse.

Use the diagram above to write a proof.

11. GIVEN ▶ $m\angle 4 = 60°, m\angle 7 = 120°$

   PROVE ▶ $\ell \parallel m$

12. GIVEN ▶ $\angle 1$ and $\angle 7$ are supplementary.

   PROVE ▶ $\ell \parallel m$

USING PROPERTIES OF PARALLEL LINES

Examples on
pp. 157–159

EXAMPLE In the diagram, $\ell \perp t$, $m \perp t$, and $m \parallel n$.
Because ℓ and m are coplanar and perpendicular to the
same line, $\ell \parallel m$. Then, because $\ell \parallel m$ and $m \parallel n$, $\ell \parallel n$.

Which lines must be parallel? Explain.

13. $\angle 1$ and $\angle 2$ are right angles.

14. $\angle 3 \cong \angle 6$

15. $\angle 3$ and $\angle 4$ are supplements.

16. $\angle 1 \cong \angle 2$, $\angle 3 \cong \angle 5$

3.6 PARALLEL LINES IN THE COORDINATE PLANE

Examples on pp. 165–167

EXAMPLES slope of $\ell_1 = \frac{2-0}{1-0} = 2$

slope of $\ell_2 = \frac{3-(-1)}{5-3} = \frac{4}{2} = 2$

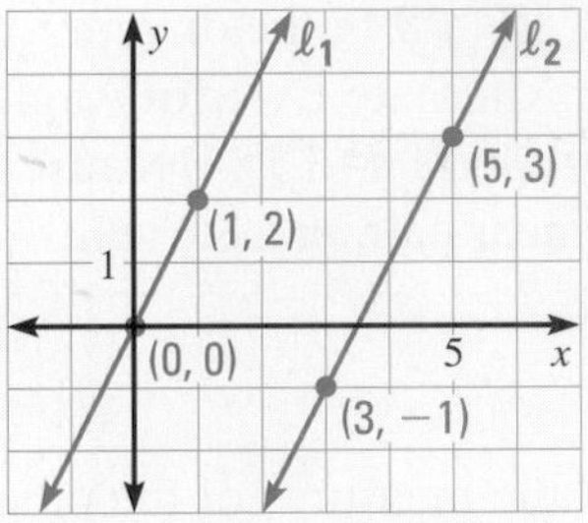

The slopes are the same, so $\ell_1 \parallel \ell_2$.

To write an equation for ℓ_2, substitute $(x, y) = (5, 3)$ and $m = 2$ into the slope-intercept form.

$y = mx + b$	**Slope-intercept form.**
$3 = (2)(5) + b$	**Substitute 5 for *x*, 3 for *y*, and 2 for *m*.**
$-7 = b$	**Solve for *b*.**

▶ So, an equation for ℓ_2 is $y = 2x - 7$.

Find the slope of each line. Are the lines parallel?

17.

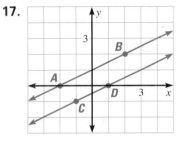

18.

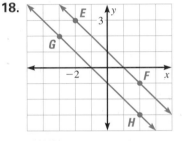

19.

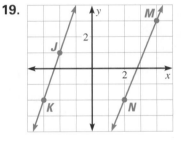

20. Find an equation of the line that is parallel to the line with equation $y = -2x + 5$ and passes through the point $(-1, -4)$.

3.7 PERPENDICULAR LINES IN THE COORDINATE PLANE

Examples on pp. 172–174

EXAMPLE The slope of line j is 3. The slope of line k is $-\frac{1}{3}$.

$3\left(-\frac{1}{3}\right) = -1$, so $j \perp k$.

In Exercises 21–23, decide whether lines p_1 and p_2 are perpendicular.

21. Lines p_1 and p_2 in the diagram.

22. p_1: $y = \frac{3}{5}x + 2$; p_2: $y = \frac{5}{3}x - 1$

23. p_1: $2y - x = 2$; p_2: $y + 2x = 4$

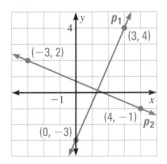

24. Line ℓ_1 has equation $y = -3x + 5$. Write an equation of line ℓ_2 which is perpendicular to ℓ_1 and passes through $(-3, 6)$.

Chapter Test

In Exercises 1–6, identify the relationship between the angles in the diagram at the right.

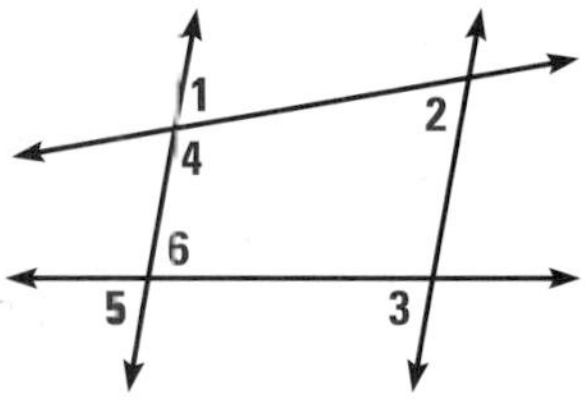

1. $\angle 1$ and $\angle 2$

2. $\angle 1$ and $\angle 4$

3. $\angle 2$ and $\angle 3$

4. $\angle 1$ and $\angle 5$

5. $\angle 4$ and $\angle 2$

6. $\angle 5$ and $\angle 6$

7. Write a flow proof.

    GIVEN ▶ $m\angle 1 = m\angle 3 = 37°$, $\overrightarrow{BA} \perp \overrightarrow{BC}$

    PROVE ▶ $m\angle 2 = 16°$

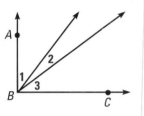
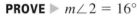

8. If $\ell \parallel m$, which angles are supplementary to $\angle 1$?

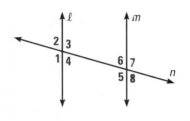

Use the given information and the diagram at the right to determine which lines must be parallel.

9. $\angle 1 \cong \angle 2$

10. $\angle 3$ and $\angle 4$ are right angles.

11. $\angle 1 \cong \angle 5$; $\angle 5$ and $\angle 7$ are supplementary.

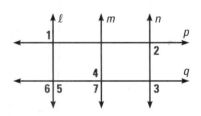

In Exercises 12 and 13, write an equation of the line described.

12. The line parallel to $y = -\frac{1}{3}x + 5$ and with a y-intercept of 1

13. The line perpendicular to $y = -2x + 4$ and that passes through the point $(-1, 2)$

14. *Writing* Describe a real-life object that has edges that are straight lines. Are any of the lines skew? If so, describe a pair.

15. A carpenter wants to cut two boards to fit snugly together. The carpenter's squares are aligned along $\overline{EF}$, as shown. Are $\overline{AB}$ and $\overline{CD}$ parallel? State the theorem that justifies your answer.

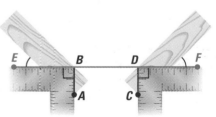

16. Use the diagram to write a proof.

    GIVEN ▶ $\angle 1 \cong \angle 2$, $\angle 3 \cong \angle 4$

    PROVE ▶ $n \parallel p$

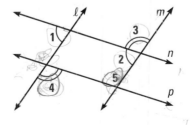

Chapter Standardized Test

TEST-TAKING STRATEGY The mathematical portion of the SAT is based on the material taught in your high school mathematics courses. One of the best ways to prepare for the SAT is to keep up with your regular studies and do your homework assignments.

1. MULTIPLE CHOICE In the diagram, how many lines can be drawn through point Q parallel to line n?

Ⓐ 0   Ⓑ 1

Ⓒ 2   Ⓓ More than 2

Ⓔ Cannot be determined

2. MULTIPLE CHOICE In the diagram, if $a \parallel b$ and $m\angle 7 = 62°$, what is $m\angle 1$?

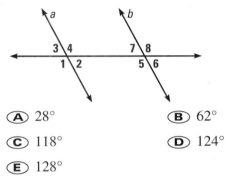

Ⓐ 28°   Ⓑ 62°

Ⓒ 118°   Ⓓ 124°

Ⓔ 128°

3. MULTIPLE CHOICE In the diagram, $j \parallel k$. Find the value of x.

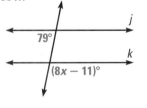

Ⓐ 11   Ⓑ 11.25

Ⓒ 14   Ⓓ 15.25

Ⓔ 23

4. MULTIPLE CHOICE Which line passes through the point $(10, -1)$ and has a slope of -2?

Ⓐ $y = -2x - 19$ Ⓑ $y = 2x - 19$

Ⓒ $y = 2x + 19$ Ⓓ $y = -2x + 19$

Ⓔ $y = -2x - 21$

5. QUANTITATIVE COMPARISON

Column A	Column B
The slope of the line through $(-2, -4)$ and $(8, 3)$	The slope of the line perpendicular to $y = \frac{10}{7}x + \frac{1}{7}$

Choose the statement that is true.

Ⓐ The quantity in column A is greater.

Ⓑ The quantity in column B is greater.

Ⓒ The two quantities are equal.

Ⓓ The relationship cannot be determined from the information given.

6. MULTIPLE CHOICE Which of the following lines is parallel to $y = -\frac{5}{7}x + 2$?

Ⓐ $y + \frac{5}{7}x = -5$ Ⓑ $y = \frac{5}{7}x + 6$

Ⓒ $y = -\frac{7}{5}x - 3$ Ⓓ $y - \frac{5}{7}x = 9$

Ⓔ $y = \frac{7}{5}x + 1$

7. MULTIPLE CHOICE A line j has equation $y = -\frac{1}{4}x - 6$. If $k \perp j$ and k passes through point $(5, -2)$, what is an equation of k?

Ⓐ $y = 4x + 22$ Ⓑ $y = \frac{1}{4}x - 22$

Ⓒ $y = -\frac{1}{4}x - 22$ Ⓓ $y = 4x - 22$

Ⓔ $y = -4x + 18$

8. MULTIPLE CHOICE Which lines are parallel?

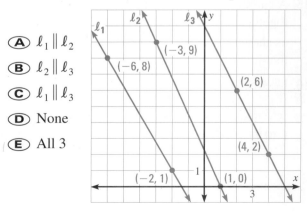

Ⓐ $\ell_1 \parallel \ell_2$

Ⓑ $\ell_2 \parallel \ell_3$

Ⓒ $\ell_1 \parallel \ell_3$

Ⓓ None

Ⓔ All 3

9. MULTIPLE CHOICE In the diagram, which two angles are alternate interior angles?

Ⓐ ∠6 and ∠3

Ⓑ ∠10 and ∠5

Ⓒ ∠12 and ∠8

Ⓓ ∠2 and ∠6

Ⓔ ∠10 and ∠11

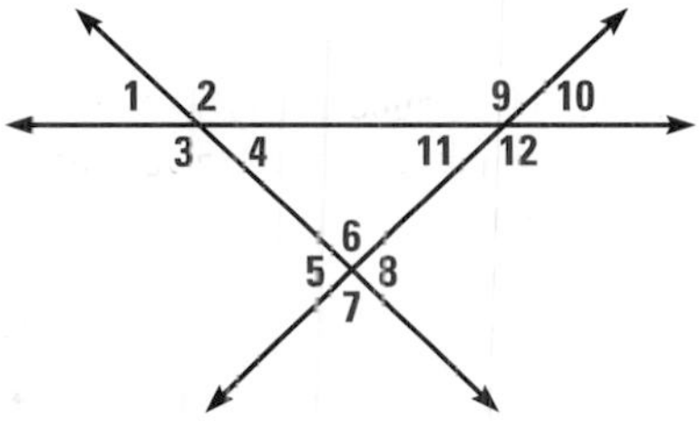

MULTI-STEP PROBLEM In Exercises 10 and 11, use the diagram at the right.

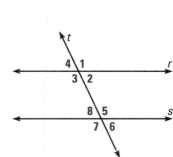

10. Suppose $r \parallel s$. Complete each statement with the word *always*, *sometimes*, or *never*.

    a. If $r \perp t$, then s is __?__ perpendicular to t.

    b. ∠3 and ∠8 are __?__ both acute angles.

    c. ∠1 and ∠6 are __?__ supplementary angles.

    d. ∠2 and ∠7 are __?__ congruent angles.

11. Given $m\angle 4 = 65°$ and $m\angle 5 = 115°$, write two different paragraph proofs to show that $r \parallel s$.

MULTI-STEP PROBLEM Line j has equation $y = 3x - 2$.

12. Write an equation for line k that is perpendicular to line j and passes through point $(1, 1)$.

13. Write an equation for a line n that is perpendicular to line k and passes through point $(4, 0)$.

14. Describe two different ways you could show that $j \parallel n$.

15. Graph lines j, k, and n in a coordinate plane.

MULTI-STEP PROBLEM In Exercises 16 and 17, use the following information.

Suppose you are constructing a wheelchair ramp. The building code requires the slope of the ramp to be no greater than $\frac{1}{12}$. The diagram at the right shows a side view of the ramp in a coordinate plane, where each unit represents one inch.

▶ Source: *Uniform Federal Accessibility Standards*

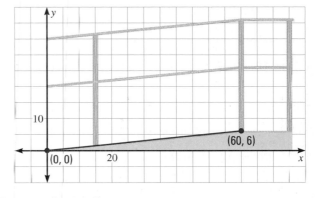

16. *Writing* Explain what is wrong with the slope of the ramp in the diagram.

17. Keeping the height of the ramp at 6 inches, how much longer must the base of the ramp be in order to meet the slope specification of $\frac{1}{12}$?

Cumulative Practice

1. Describe a pattern in the sequence 10, 12, 15, 19, 24, ... Predict the next number. **(1.1)**

In the diagram at the right, $\overleftrightarrow{AB}$, $\overleftrightarrow{AC}$, and $\overleftrightarrow{BC}$ are in plane M.

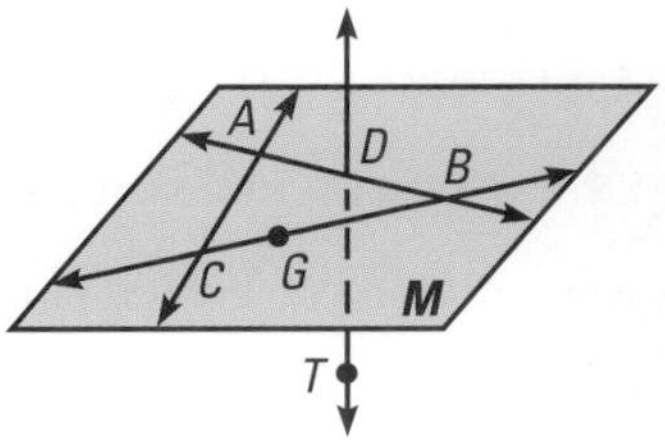

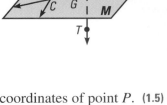

2. Name a point that is collinear with points A and D. **(1.2)**

3. Name a line skew to $\overleftrightarrow{BC}$. **(3.1)**

4. Name the ray that is opposite to $\overrightarrow{GC}$. **(1.2)**

5. How many planes contain A, B, and C? Explain. **(2.1)**

$\overline{MN}$ **has endpoints $M(7, -5)$ and $N(-3, -1)$.**

6. Find the length of $\overline{MN}$. **(1.3)**   7. If N is the midpoint of $\overline{MP}$, find the coordinates of point P. **(1.5)**

In a coordinate plane, plot the points and sketch $\angle ABC$. Classify the angle as *acute*, *right*, or *obtuse*. (1.4)

8. $A(-6, 6)$, $B(-2, 2)$, $C(4, 2)$ 9. $A(2, 1)$, $B(4, 7)$, $C(10, 5)$ 10. $A(2, 5)$, $B(2, -2)$, $C(5, 4)$

Find the values of x and y. (1.5, 1.6, 3.2)

11.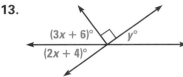

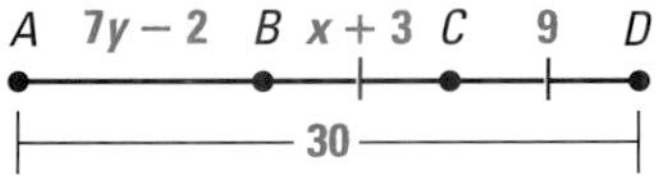

12.

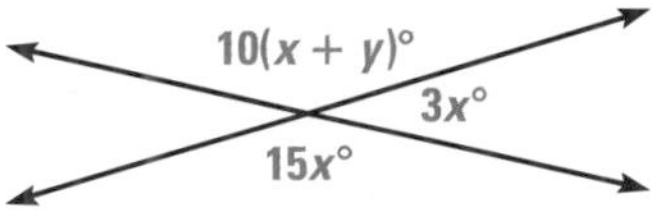

13.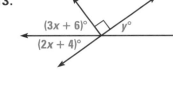

In Exercises 14 and 15, find the area of each figure. (1.7)

14. Square with a perimeter of 40 cm

15. Triangle defined by $R(0, 0)$, $S(6, 8)$, and $T(10, 0)$

16. Construct two perpendicular lines. Bisect one of the angles formed. **(1.5, 3.1)**

17. Rewrite the following statement in if-then form: *The measure of a straight angle is 180°*. Then write the inverse, converse, and contrapositive of the conditional statement. **(2.1)**

In Exercises 18–21, find a counterexample that shows the statement is false.

18. If a line intersects two other lines, then all three lines are coplanar. **(2.1)**

19. Two lines are perpendicular if they intersect. **(2.2)**

20. If $AB + BC = AC$, then B is the midpoint of $\overline{AC}$. **(2.5)**

21. If $\angle 1$ and $\angle 2$ are supplementary, then $\angle 1$ and $\angle 2$ form a linear pair. **(2.6)**

22. Solve the equation $3(s - 2) = 15$ and write a reason for each step. **(2.4)**

23. Draw a diagram of intersecting lines j and k. Label each angle with a number. Use the Linear Pair Postulate and the Vertical Angles Theorem to write true statements about the angles formed by the intersecting lines. **(2.6)**

Let p represent "$x = 0$" and let q represent "$x + x = x$."

24. Write the biconditional $p \longleftrightarrow q$ in words. Decide whether the biconditional is true. **(2.2, 2.3)**

25. If the statement $p \rightarrow q$ is true and p is true, does it follow that q is true? Explain. **(2.3)**

Use the diagram at the right.

26. Name four pairs of corresponding angles. **(3.1)**

27. If $\overleftrightarrow{AC} \parallel \overleftrightarrow{DE}$ and $m\angle 2 = 55°$, find $m\angle 6$. **(3.3)**

28. If $\overleftrightarrow{BD} \parallel \overleftrightarrow{CF}$ and $m\angle 3 = 140°$, find $m\angle 4$. **(3.3)**

29. Which lines must be parallel if $m\angle 3 + m\angle 6 = 180°$? Explain. **(3.4)**

30. ▶ **PROOF** Write a proof.

    GIVEN ▶ $\angle 6 \cong \angle 9$

    PROVE ▶ $\angle 3$ and $\angle 4$ are supplements. **(3.3, 3.4)**

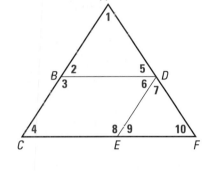

In Exercises 31–33, use $A(2, 10)$, $B(22, -5)$, $C(-1, 6)$, and $D(25, -1)$.

31. Show that $\overleftrightarrow{AD}$ is parallel to $\overleftrightarrow{BC}$. **(3.6)**

32. Use slopes to show that $\angle BAC$ is a right angle. **(3.7)**

33. Write an equation for a line through the point C and parallel to $\overleftrightarrow{AB}$. **(3.6)**

34. 🌐 **RUNNING TRACK** The inside of the running track in the diagram is formed by a rectangle and two half circles. Find the distance, to the nearest yard, around the inside of the track. Then find the area enclosed by the track. (Use $\pi \approx 3.14$.) **(1.7)**

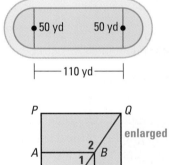

35. 🌐 **PHOTO ENLARGEMENT** A photographer took a 4-inch-by-6-inch photo and enlarged each side to 150% of the original size.

  a. Find the dimensions of the enlarged photo.

  b. Describe the relationship between $\angle 1$ and $\angle 3$. **(1.6, 3.2)**

  c. Make an accurate diagram of the original photo and the enlargement, as shown. Draw $\overline{DB}$ and $\overline{BQ}$. Make a conjecture about the relationship between $\angle 1$ and $\angle 2$. Measure the angles in your diagram to test your conjecture. **(1.1, 1.6)**

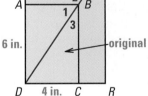

36. 🌐 **CONSTRUCTION** Two posts support a raised deck. The posts have two parallel braces, as shown.

  a. If $m\angle 1 = 35°$, find $m\angle 2$. **(3.3)**

  b. If $m\angle 3 = 40°$, what other angle has a measure of 40°? **(3.3)**

  c. Each post is perpendicular to the deck. Explain how this can be used to show that the posts are parallel to each other. **(3.5)**

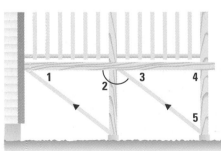

Technical Drawing

OBJECTIVE Make technical drawings of objects, including orthographic projections and isometric drawings.

Materials: ruler, graph paper, isometric dot paper, colored pencils, file folder

Technical drawings are drawings that show different viewpoints of an object. Engineers and architects create technical drawings of products and buildings before actually constructing the objects in real life.

Technical drawings may include an *orthographic projection*. This is a two-dimensional drawing of the front, top, and side views of an object. *Isometric drawings* look three-dimensional, and can be created on a grid of dots using three axes that intersect to form 120° angles.

CREATING ORTHOGRAPHIC PROJECTIONS AND ISOMETRIC DRAWINGS

Follow these steps to make a technical drawing of a set of stairs.

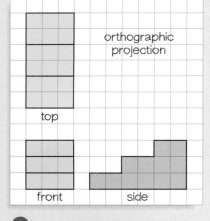

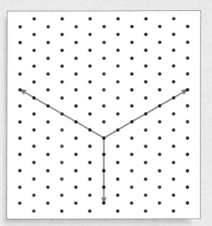

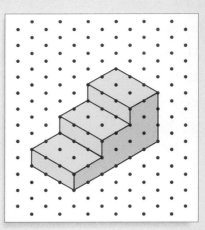

1 On graph paper, draw an orthographic projection of the stairs. Your drawing should include top, front, and side views.

2 Sketch three axes on isometric dot paper. The lines in your isometric drawing will be parallel to these three axes.

3 Copy the isometric drawing of the stairs. You can add depth by shading the top, front, and side of the stairs.

INVESTIGATION

Use your technical drawing to answer the questions below.

1. *Isometric lines* are drawn parallel to one of the isometric axes. Identify a pair of parallel isometric lines in your drawing. Mark them as parallel.

2. Identify two lines on your isometric drawing that represent perpendicular lines. Mark the right angle. What is the actual measure of the angle you marked? Explain why this angle can represent a right angle in your drawing.

3. Is there another angle in your isometric drawing that could represent a right angle between perpendicular lines? Explain why or why not.

CREATE YOUR OWN

Choose two objects at your school or home that have simple shapes. Use objects that already exist, or create your own using wooden blocks. For each object, make an orthographic projection and an isometric drawing. The measurements should be approximately proportional to the actual distances they represent.

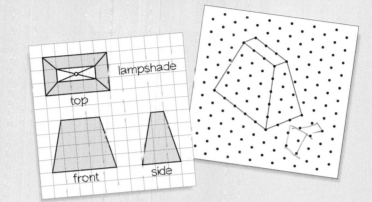

PRESENT YOUR RESULTS

Gather your drawings and present them in a file folder.

- Include your answers to the Investigation Exercises 1–3.

- Include your technical drawings of the three stairs and two other objects.

- Summarize what you have learned about technical drawing. Include an explanation of the change in appearance of parallel and perpendicular lines as you switch from an orthographic projection to an isometric drawing.

EXTENSION

Research a career that involves technical drawing. Write a job description for an open position to be advertised in the classified section of the newspaper. Include required education, skills, responsibilities, and salary. Is this a job you think you might like? Explain why or why not.

Computer-Aided Design (CAD) software allows designers to develop models and generate drawings of them.

CONGRUENT TRIANGLES

▶ *How does a cable-stayed bridge work?*

APPLICATION: Bridges

On a cable-stayed bridge, the cables attached to the sides of each tower transfer the weight of the roadway to the tower.

You can see from the diagram below that the cables balance the weight of the roadway on both sides of each tower.

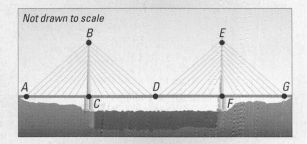

Not drawn to scale

Think & Discuss

1. In the diagram above, what type of angle does each tower of the bridge make with the roadway?

2. Use the diagram above. Find at least one pair of acute angles that appear to be congruent and one pair of obtuse angles that appear to be congruent.

Learn More About It

You will prove that triangles formed by the cables and towers of a cable-stayed bridge are congruent in Exercise 16 on p. 234.

INTERNET **APPLICATION LINK** Visit www.mcdougallittell.com for more information about bridge construction.

CHAPTER 4

Study Guide

PREVIEW

What's the chapter about?

Chapter 4 is about **congruent triangles**. Congruent triangles are triangles that are the same size and shape. In Chapter 4 you'll learn

- to prove triangles are congruent given information about their sides and angles.
- how to use congruent triangles to solve real-life problems.

KEY VOCABULARY

▶ Review
- **congruent segments, p. 19**
- **acute angle, p. 28**
- **right angle, p. 28**
- **midpoint, p. 34**
- **vertical angles, p. 44**
- **alternate interior angles, p. 131**

▶ New
- **isosceles triangle, p. 194**
- **right triangle, p. 194**
- **legs and hypotenuse of a right triangle, p. 195**
- **interior angle, p. 196**
- **exterior angle, p. 196**
- **corollary, p. 197**
- **congruent figures, p. 202**
- **corresponding sides and angles, p. 202**
- **coordinate proof, p. 243**

PREPARE

Are you ready for the chapter?

SKILL REVIEW Do these exercises to review key skills that you'll apply in this chapter. See the given **reference page** if there is something you don't understand.

STUDENT HELP

▶ Study Tip
"Student Help" boxes throughout the chapter give you study tips and tell you where to look for extra help in this book and on the Internet.

USING ALGEBRA Solve the equation. (Skills Review, pp. 789 and 790)

1. $180 = 90 + x + 60$ **2.** $6 = 2x + 2$ **3.** $2x = 4x - 6$

4. $180 = 30 + 2x$ **5.** $90 = 3x - 90$ **6.** $3x = 27 - 6x$

Use a protractor to draw an angle that has the given measure. Check your results by measuring the angle. (Review p. 27)

7. 30° **8.** 135° **9.** 72°

Use the diagram at the right. Write the theorem that supports each statement. (Review pp. 112 and 143)

10. $\angle 1 \cong \angle 2$ **11.** $\angle 3 \cong \angle 4$ **12.** $\angle 1 \cong \angle 5$

STUDY STRATEGY

Here's a study strategy!

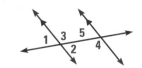

Remembering Theorems

In this chapter you will learn many theorems that you will use throughout the rest of the book.

- Keep a list of theorems in your math notebook.
- Make up a helpful name for each theorem, or draw a sketch to help you recognize it.

▷ ACTIVITY 4.1

Developing Concepts

GROUP ACTIVITY
Work in a small group.

MATERIALS
- paper
- scissors
- ruler

Investigating Angles of Triangles

▶ **QUESTION** What is the sum of the measures of the *interior angles* of a triangle? How is the measure of an *exterior angle* of a triangle related to the measures of its interior angles?

▶ **EXPLORING THE CONCEPT: INTERIOR ANGLES**

① With other students in your group, draw and cut out several different triangles.

② For each triangle, tear off the three corners and place them adjacent to each other, as shown in the diagram at the right.

③ What do you observe about the measures of the three interior angles of a triangle?

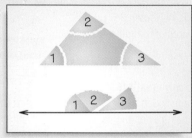

∠1, ∠2, and ∠3 are *interior angles*.

▶ **EXPLORING THE CONCEPT: EXTERIOR ANGLES**

④ With the other students in your group, draw and cut out several different triangles.

⑤ Place each triangle on a piece of paper and extend one side to form an exterior angle, as shown in the diagram at the right.

⑥ Tear off the corners that are not adjacent to the exterior angle. Use them to fill the exterior angle, as shown.

⑦ What do you observe about the measure of an exterior angle of a triangle?

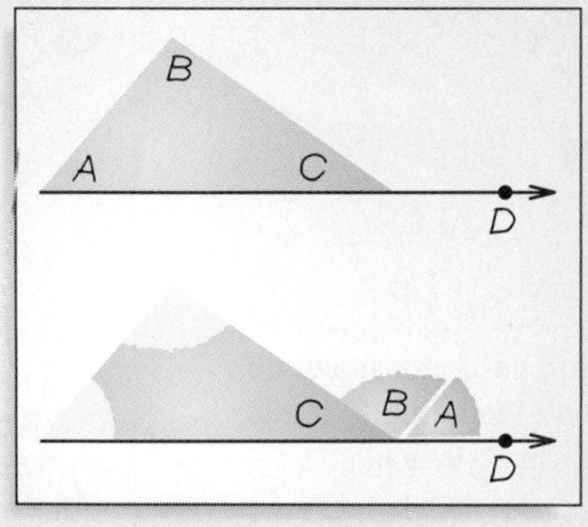

In the top figure, ∠*BCD* is an *exterior angle*.

▶ **DRAWING CONCLUSIONS**

1. Make a conjecture about the sum of the measures of the interior angles of a triangle.

2. Make a conjecture about the relationship between the measure of an exterior angle of a triangle and the measures of the nonadjacent interior angles.

3. **CRITICAL THINKING** If you know the measures of two interior angles of a triangle, how can you find the measure of the third interior angle?

4.1 Triangles and Angles

What you should learn

GOAL 1 Classify triangles by their sides and angles, as applied in **Example 2**.

GOAL 2 Find angle measures in triangles.

Why you should learn it

▼ To solve **real-life** problems, such as finding the measures of angles in a wing deflector in **Exs. 45 and 46**.

REAL LIFE

A wing deflector is used to change the velocity of the water in a stream.

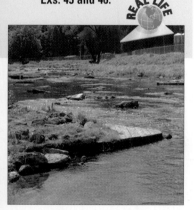

GOAL 1 CLASSIFYING TRIANGLES

A **triangle** is a figure formed by three segments joining three noncollinear points. A triangle can be classified by its sides and by its angles, as shown in the definitions below.

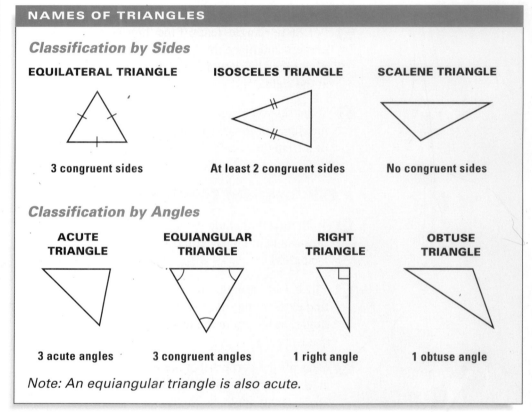

NAMES OF TRIANGLES

Classification by Sides

EQUILATERAL TRIANGLE	ISOSCELES TRIANGLE	SCALENE TRIANGLE
3 congruent sides	At least 2 congruent sides	No congruent sides

Classification by Angles

ACUTE TRIANGLE	EQUIANGULAR TRIANGLE	RIGHT TRIANGLE	OBTUSE TRIANGLE
3 acute angles	3 congruent angles	1 right angle	1 obtuse angle

Note: An equiangular triangle is also acute.

EXAMPLE 1 *Classifying Triangles*

When you classify a triangle, you need to be as specific as possible.

a. $\triangle ABC$ has three acute angles and no congruent sides. It is an acute scalene triangle. ($\triangle ABC$ is read as "triangle ABC.")

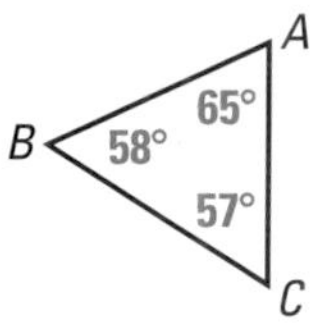

b. $\triangle DEF$ has one obtuse angle and two congruent sides. It is an obtuse isosceles triangle.

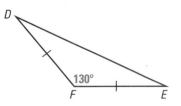

Each of the three points joining the sides of a triangle is a **vertex**. (The plural of vertex is *vertices*.) For example, in $\triangle ABC$, points A, B, and C are vertices.

In a triangle, two sides sharing a common vertex are **adjacent sides**. In $\triangle ABC$, $\overline{CA}$ and $\overline{BA}$ are adjacent sides. The third side, $\overline{BC}$, is the side *opposite* $\angle A$.

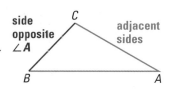

RIGHT AND ISOSCELES TRIANGLES The sides of right triangles and isosceles triangles have special names. In a right triangle, the sides that form the right angle are the **legs** of the right triangle. The side opposite the right angle is the **hypotenuse** of the triangle.

An isosceles triangle can have three congruent sides, in which case it is equilateral. When an isosceles triangle has only two congruent sides, then these two sides are the **legs** of the isosceles triangle. The third side is the **base** of the isosceles triangle.

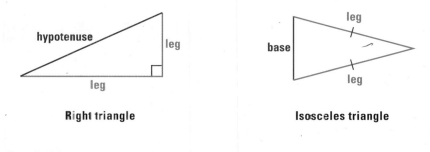

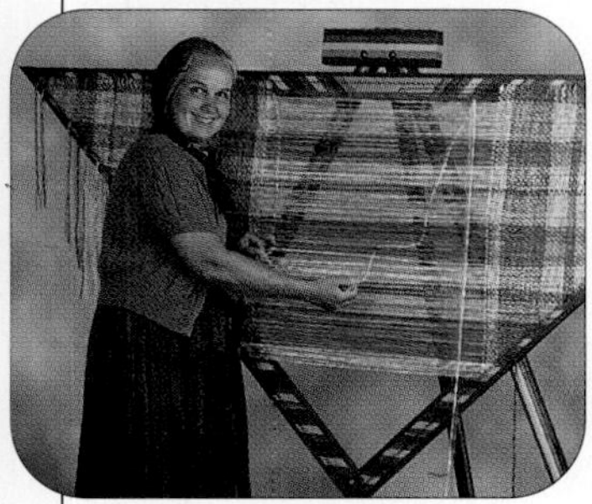

Right triangle

Isosceles triangle

EXAMPLE 2 *Identifying Parts of an Isosceles Right Triangle*

FOCUS ON APPLICATIONS

WEAVING Most looms are used to weave rectangular cloth. The loom shown in the photo is used to weave triangular pieces of cloth. A piece of cloth woven on the loom can use about 550 yards of yarn.

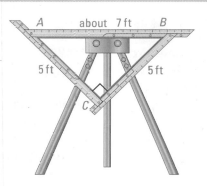

The diagram shows a triangular loom.

a. Explain why $\triangle ABC$ is an isosceles right triangle.

b. Identify the legs and the hypotenuse of $\triangle ABC$. Which side is the base of the triangle?

SOLUTION

a. In the diagram, you are given that $\angle C$ is a right angle. By definition, $\triangle ABC$ is a right triangle. Because $AC = 5$ ft and $BC = 5$ ft, $\overline{AC} \cong \overline{BC}$. By definition, $\triangle ABC$ is also an isosceles triangle.

b. Sides $\overline{AC}$ and $\overline{BC}$ are adjacent to the right angle, so they are the legs. Side $\overline{AB}$ is opposite the right angle, so it is the hypotenuse. Because $\overline{AC} \cong \overline{BC}$, side $\overline{AB}$ is also the base.

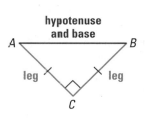

GOAL 2 USING ANGLE MEASURES OF TRIANGLES

When the sides of a triangle are extended, other angles are formed. The three original angles are the **interior angles**. The angles that are adjacent to the interior angles are the **exterior angles**. Each vertex has a *pair* of congruent exterior angles. It is common to show only *one* exterior angle at each vertex.

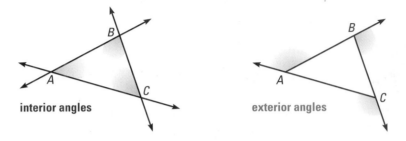

interior angles   exterior angles

In Activity 4.1 on page 193, you may have discovered the *Triangle Sum Theorem*, shown below, and the *Exterior Angle Theorem*, shown on page 197.

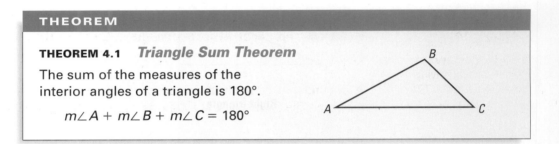

THEOREM

THEOREM 4.1 *Triangle Sum Theorem*

The sum of the measures of the interior angles of a triangle is 180°.

$$m\angle A + m\angle B + m\angle C = 180°$$

To prove some theorems, you may need to add a line, a segment, or a ray to the given diagram. Such an *auxiliary line* is used to prove the Triangle Sum Theorem.

Proof

GIVEN ▶ △ABC

PROVE ▶ $m\angle 1 + m\angle 2 + m\angle 3 = 180°$

Plan for Proof By the Parallel Postulate, you can draw an auxiliary line through point B and parallel to $\overline{AC}$. Because $\angle 4$, $\angle 2$, and $\angle 5$ form a straight angle, the sum of their measures is 180°. You also know that $\angle 1 \cong \angle 4$ and $\angle 3 \cong \angle 5$ by the Alternate Interior Angles Theorem.

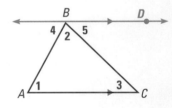

Statements	Reasons
1. Draw $\overleftrightarrow{BD}$ parallel to $\overline{AC}$.	1. Parallel Postulate
2. $m\angle 4 + m\angle 2 + m\angle 5 = 180°$	2. Angle Addition Postulate and definition of straight angle
3. $\angle 1 \cong \angle 4$ and $\angle 3 \cong \angle 5$	3. Alternate Interior Angles Theorem
4. $m\angle 1 = m\angle 4$ and $m\angle 3 = m\angle 5$	4. Definition of congruent angles
5. $m\angle 1 + m\angle 2 + m\angle 3 = 180°$	5. Substitution property of equality

---

STUDENT HELP

▶ **Study Tip**
An auxiliary line, segment, or ray used in a proof must be justified with a reason.

THEOREM

THEOREM 4.2 *Exterior Angle Theorem*

The measure of an exterior angle of a triangle is equal to the sum of the measures of the two nonadjacent interior angles.

$$m\angle 1 = m\angle A + m\angle B$$

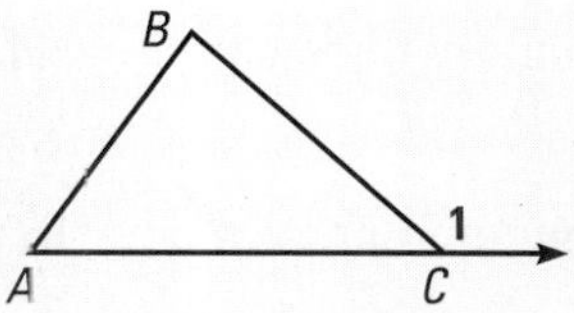

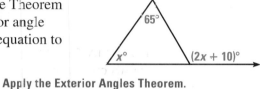

Using Algebra

EXAMPLE 3 *Finding an Angle Measure*

You can apply the Exterior Angle Theorem to find the measure of the exterior angle shown. First write and solve an equation to find the value of *x:*

$$x° + 65° = (2x + 10)°$$ **Apply the Exterior Angles Theorem.**

$$55 = x$$ **Solve for x.**

▶ So, the measure of the exterior angle is (2 · 55 + 10)°, or 120°.

· · · · · · · · · ·

A **corollary to a theorem** is a statement that can be proved easily using the theorem. The corollary below follows from the Triangle Sum Theorem.

COROLLARY

COROLLARY TO THE TRIANGLE SUM THEOREM

The acute angles of a right triangle are complementary.

$$m\angle A + m\angle B = 90°$$

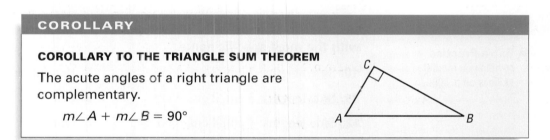

STUDENT HELP

▶ **Skills Review**
For help with solving equations, see p. 790.

EXAMPLE 4 *Finding Angle Measures*

The measure of one acute angle of a right triangle is two times the measure of the other acute angle. Find the measure of each acute angle.

SOLUTION

Make a sketch. Let $x° = m\angle A$.
Then $m\angle B = 2x°$.

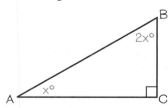

$$x° + 2x° = 90°$$ **The acute angles of a right triangle are complementary.**

$$x = 30$$ **Solve for x.**

▶ So, $m\angle A = 30°$ and $m\angle B = 2(30°) = 60°$.

GUIDED PRACTICE

Vocabulary Check ✓

1. Sketch an obtuse scalene triangle. Label its interior angles 1, 2, and 3. Then draw its exterior angles. Shade the exterior angles.

Concept Check ✓

In the figure, $\overline{PQ} \cong \overline{PS}$ and $\overline{PR} \perp \overline{QS}$. Complete the sentence.

2. $\overline{PQ}$ is the __?__ of the right triangle $\triangle PQR$.

3. In $\triangle PQR$, $\overline{PQ}$ is the side opposite angle __?__.

4. $\overline{QS}$ is the __?__ of the isosceles triangle $\triangle PQS$.

5. The legs of $\triangle PRS$ are __?__ and __?__.

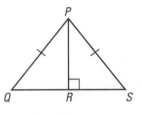

Skill Check ✓

In Exercises 6–8, classify the triangle by its angles and by its sides.

6. **7.** **8.**

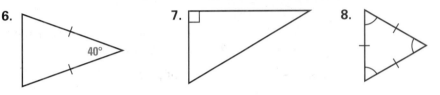

9. The measure of one interior angle of a triangle is 25°. The other interior angles are congruent. Find the measures of the other interior angles.

PRACTICE AND APPLICATIONS

STUDENT HELP

▶ **Extra Practice**
to help you master
skills is on p. 809.

MATCHING TRIANGLES In Exercises 10–15, match the triangle description with the most specific name.

10. Side lengths: 2 cm, 3 cm, 4 cm   **A.** Equilateral

11. Side lengths: 3 cm, 2 cm, 3 cm   **B.** Scalene

12. Side lengths: 4 cm, 4 cm, 4 cm   **C.** Obtuse

13. Angle measures: 60°, 60°, 60°   **D.** Equiangular

14. Angle measures: 30°, 60°, 90°   **E.** Isosceles

15. Angle measures: 20°, 145°, 15°   **F.** Right

CLASSIFYING TRIANGLES Classify the triangle by its angles and by its sides.

STUDENT HELP

▶ **HOMEWORK HELP**
Example 1: Exs. 10–26,
        34–36
Example 2: Exs. 27, 28, 45
Example 3: Exs. 31–39
Example 4: Exs. 41–44

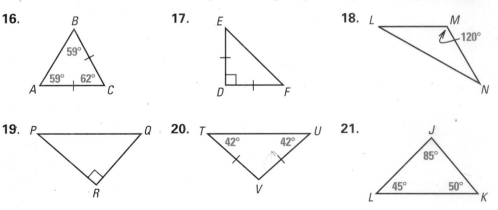

LOGICAL REASONING Complete the statement using *always, sometimes,* or *never*.

22. An isosceles triangle is ___?___ an equilateral triangle.

23. An obtuse triangle is ___?___ an isosceles triangle.

24. An interior angle of a triangle and one of its adjacent exterior angles are ___?___ supplementary.

25. The acute angles of a right triangle are ___?___ complementary.

26. A triangle ___?___ has a right angle and an obtuse angle.

IDENTIFYING PARTS OF TRIANGLES Refer to the triangles in Exercises 16–21.

27. Identify the legs and the hypotenuse of any right triangles.

28. Identify the legs and the base of any isosceles triangles. Which isosceles triangle has a base that is also the hypotenuse of a right triangle?

USING ALGEBRA Use the graph. The segment $\overline{AB}$ is a leg of an isosceles right triangle.

29. Find the coordinates of point C. Copy the graph and sketch $\triangle ABC$.

30. Find the coordinates of a point D that forms a different isosceles right triangle with leg $\overline{AB}$. Include a sketch with your answer.

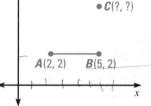

STUDENT HELP

HOMEWORK HELP
Visit our Web site
www.mcdougallittell.com
for help with Exs. 31–33.

FINDING ANGLE MEASURES Find the measure of the numbered angles.

31.   **32.**   **33.**

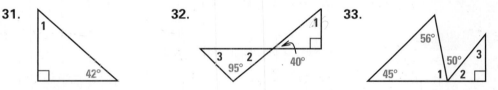

USING ALGEBRA The variable expressions represent the angle measures of a triangle. Find the measure of each angle. Then classify the triangle by its angles.

34. $m\angle A = x°$
$m\angle B = 2x°$
$m\angle C = (2x + 15)°$

35. $m\angle R = x°$
$m\angle S = 7x°$
$m\angle T = x°$

36. $m\angle W = (x - 15)°$
$m\angle Y = (2x - 165)°$
$m\angle Z = 90°$

EXTERIOR ANGLES Find the measure of the exterior angle shown.

37.   **38.**   **39.**

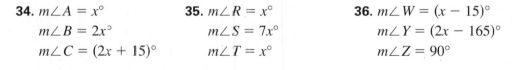

40. **TECHNOLOGY** Use geometry software to demonstrate the Triangle Sum Theorem or the Exterior Angle Theorem. Describe your procedure.

41. 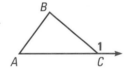 **USING ALGEBRA** In $\triangle PQR$, the measure of $\angle P$ is 36°. The measure of $\angle Q$ is five times the measure of $\angle R$. Find $m\angle Q$ and $m\angle R$.

42. **USING ALGEBRA** The measure of an exterior angle of a triangle is 120°. The interior angles that are not adjacent to this exterior angle are congruent. Find the measures of the interior angles of the triangle.

43. **BILLIARD RACK** You want to make a wooden billiard rack. The rack will be an equilateral triangle whose side length is 33.5 centimeters. You have a strip of wood that is 100 centimeters long. Do you need more wood? Explain.

44. **COAT HANGER** You are bending a wire to make a coat hanger. The length of the wire is 88 centimeters, and 20 centimeters are needed to make the hook portion of the hanger. The triangular portion of the hanger is an isosceles triangle. The length of one leg of this triangle is $\frac{3}{5}$ the length of the base. Sketch the hanger. Give the dimensions of the triangular portion.

WING DEFLECTORS **In Exercises 45 and 46, use the information about wing deflectors.**
A wing deflector is a structure built with rocks to redirect the flow of water in a stream and increase the rate of the water's flow. Its shape is a right triangle.

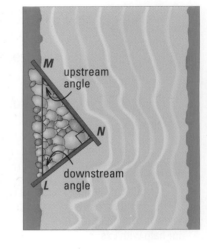

upstream angle

downstream angle

45. Identify the legs and the hypotenuse of the right triangle formed by the wing deflector.

46. It is generally recommended that the upstream angle should range from 30° to 45°. Give a range of angle measures for the downstream angle.

47. **DEVELOPING PROOF** Fill in the missing steps in the two-column proof of the Exterior Angle Theorem.

GIVEN ▶ $\angle 1$ is an exterior angle of $\triangle ABC$.

PROVE ▶ $m\angle 1 = m\angle A + m\angle B$

Statements	Reasons
1. $\angle 1$ is an exterior angle of $\triangle ABC$.	**1.** Given
2. $\angle ACB$ and $\angle 1$ are a linear pair.	**2.** Definition of exterior angle
3. $m\angle ACB + m\angle 1 = 180°$	**3.** __?__
4. __?__	**4.** Triangle Sum Theorem
5. $m\angle ACB + m\angle 1 =$ $m\angle A + m\angle B + m\angle ACB$	**5.** __?__
6. $m\angle 1 = m\angle A + m\angle B$	**6.** __?__

48. **TWO-COLUMN PROOF** Write a two-column proof of the Corollary to the Triangle Sum Theorem on page 197.

49. MULTIPLE CHOICE The lengths of the two legs of an isosceles triangle are represented by the expressions $(2x - 5)$ and $(x + 7)$. The perimeter of the triangle is 50 cm. Find the length of the base of the triangle.

   Ⓐ 11 cm   Ⓑ 19 cm   Ⓒ 12 cm   Ⓓ 26 cm   Ⓔ 32 cm

50. MULTIPLE CHOICE Which of the terms below can be used to describe a triangle with two 45° interior angles?

   Ⓐ Acute   Ⓑ Right   Ⓒ Scalene   Ⓓ Obtuse   Ⓔ Equilateral

★ **Challenge**

51. ▶ **ALTERNATIVE PROOFS** There is often more than one way to prove a theorem. In the diagram, $\overline{SP}$ is constructed parallel to $\overline{QR}$. This construction is the first step of a proof of the Triangle Sum Theorem. Use the diagram to prove the Triangle Sum Theorem.

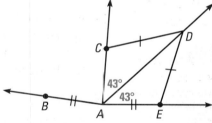

EXTRA CHALLENGE
www.mcdougallittell.com

   GIVEN ▶ $\triangle PQR$

   PROVE ▶ $m\angle 1 + m\angle 2 + m\angle 3 = 180°$

MIXED REVIEW

EVALUATING STATEMENTS Use the figure to determine whether the statement is *true* or *false*. (Review 1.5 for 4.2)

52. $\overline{AE} \cong \overline{BA}$

53. $\angle CAD \cong \angle EAD$

54. $m\angle CAD + m\angle EAB = 86°$

55. $\overline{CD} \cong \overline{AC}$

56. $\overrightarrow{AD}$ bisects $\angle CAE$.

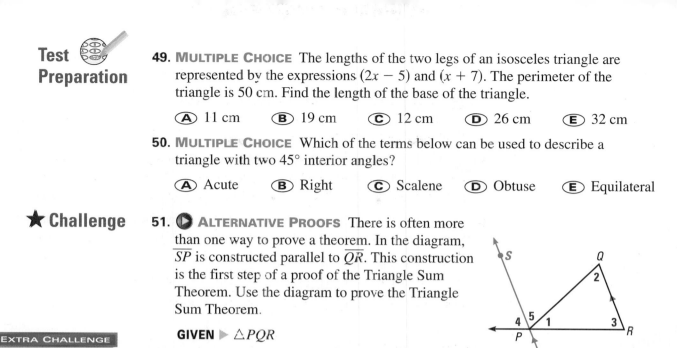

▶ **DEVELOPING PROOF** Is it possible to prove that lines *p* and *q* are parallel? If so, state the postulate or theorem you would use. (Review 3.4)

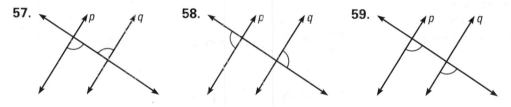

57.   **58.**   **59.**

WRITING EQUATIONS Write an equation of the line that passes through the given point *P* and has the given slope. (Review 3.6)

60. $P(0, -2), m = 0$ **61.** $P(4, 7), m = 1$ **62.** $P(-3, -5), m = -1$

63. $P(9, -1), m = \frac{2}{3}$ **64.** $P(-1, -1), m = \frac{3}{4}$ **65.** $P(-2, -3), m = -\frac{7}{2}$

66. $P(5, 2), m = 0$ **67.** $P(8, 3), m = -\frac{3}{2}$ **68.** $P(-6, -4), m = -\frac{1}{3}$

Congruence and Triangles

What you should learn

GOAL 1 Identify congruent figures and corresponding parts.

GOAL 2 Prove that two triangles are congruent.

Why you should learn it

▼ To identify and describe congruent figures in **real-life** objects, such as the sculpture described in **Example 1**.

Two Open Triangles Up Gyratory II by George Rickey

GOAL 1 **IDENTIFYING CONGRUENT FIGURES**

Two geometric figures are *congruent* if they have exactly the same size and shape. Each of the red figures is congruent to the other red figures. None of the blue figures is congruent to another blue figure.

Congruent   **Not congruent**

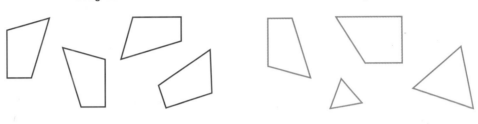

When two figures are **congruent**, there is a correspondence between their angles and sides such that **corresponding angles** are congruent and **corresponding sides** are congruent. For the triangles below, you can write $\triangle ABC \cong \triangle PQR$, which is read "triangle *ABC* is congruent to triangle *PQR*." The notation shows the congruence and the correspondence.

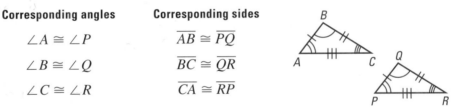

Corresponding angles	Corresponding sides
$\angle A \cong \angle P$	$\overline{AB} \cong \overline{PQ}$
$\angle B \cong \angle Q$	$\overline{BC} \cong \overline{QR}$
$\angle C \cong \angle R$	$\overline{CA} \cong \overline{RP}$

There is more than one way to write a congruence statement, but it is important to list the corresponding angles in the same order. For example, you can also write $\triangle BCA \cong \triangle QRP$.

EXAMPLE 1 *Naming Congruent Parts*

The congruent triangles represent the triangles in the photo above. Write a congruence statement. Identify all pairs of congruent corresponding parts.

STUDENT HELP

↳ **Study Tip**
Notice that single, double, and triple arcs are used to show congruent angles.

SOLUTION

The diagram indicates that $\triangle DEF \cong \triangle RST$. The congruent angles and sides are as follows.

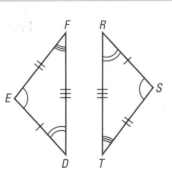

Angles: $\angle D \cong \angle R$, $\angle E \cong \angle S$, $\angle F \cong \angle T$

Sides: $\overline{DE} \cong \overline{RS}$, $\overline{EF} \cong \overline{ST}$, $\overline{FD} \cong \overline{TR}$

EXAMPLE 2 *Using Properties of Congruent Figures*

Using Algebra

In the diagram, $NPLM \cong EFGH$.

a. Find the value of x.

b. Find the value of y.

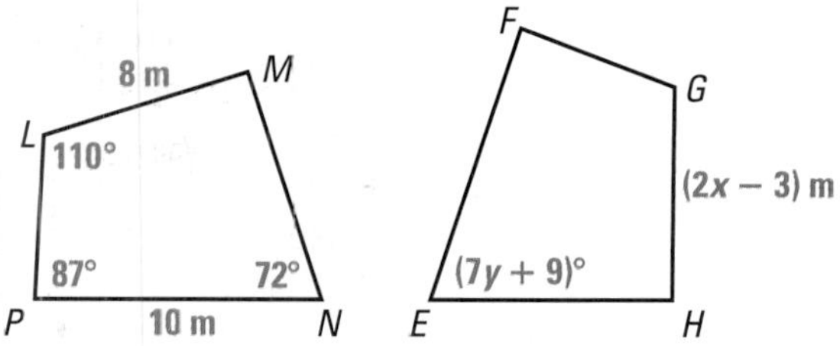

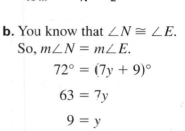

SOLUTION

a. You know that $\overline{LM} \cong \overline{GH}$.
So, $LM = GH$.

$$8 = 2x - 3$$

$$11 = 2x$$

$$5.5 = x$$

b. You know that $\angle N \cong \angle E$.
So, $m\angle N = m\angle E$.

$$72^\circ = (7y + 9)^\circ$$

$$63 = 7y$$

$$9 = y$$

The Third Angles Theorem below follows from the Triangle Sum Theorem. You are asked to prove the Third Angles Theorem in Exercise 35.

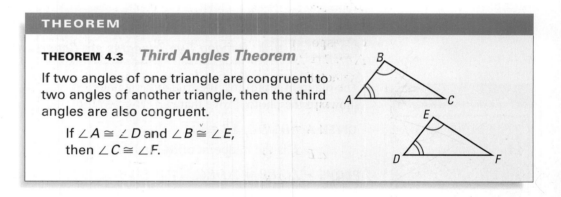

THEOREM

THEOREM 4.3 *Third Angles Theorem*

If two angles of one triangle are congruent to two angles of another triangle, then the third angles are also congruent.

If $\angle A \cong \angle D$ and $\angle B \cong \angle E$, then $\angle C \cong \angle F$.

EXAMPLE 3 *Using the Third Angles Theorem*

Find the value of x.

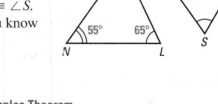

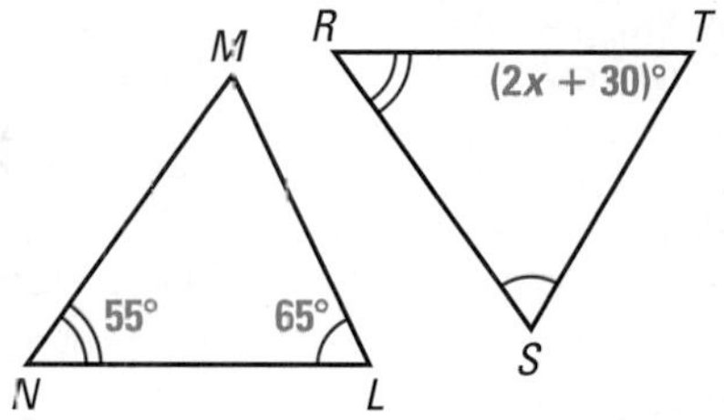

SOLUTION

In the diagram, $\angle N \cong \angle R$ and $\angle L \cong \angle S$. From the Third Angles Theorem, you know that $\angle M \cong \angle T$. So, $m\angle M = m\angle T$. From the Triangle Sum Theorem, $m\angle M = 180^\circ - 55^\circ - 65^\circ = 60^\circ$.

$m\angle M = m\angle T$	**Third Angles Theorem**
$60^\circ = (2x + 30)^\circ$	**Substitute.**
$30 = 2x$	**Subtract 30 from each side.**
$15 = x$	**Divide each side by 2.**

STUDENT HELP

HOMEWORK HELP
Visit our Web site www.mcdougallittell.com for extra examples.

EXAMPLE 4 *Determining Whether Triangles are Congruent*

Decide whether the triangles are congruent. Justify your reasoning.

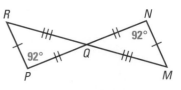

Proof

SOLUTION

Paragraph Proof From the diagram, you are given that all three pairs of corresponding sides are congruent.

$$\overline{RP} \cong \overline{MN}, \overline{PQ} \cong \overline{NQ}, \text{ and } \overline{QR} \cong \overline{QM}$$

Because $\angle P$ and $\angle N$ have the same measure, $\angle P \cong \angle N$. By the Vertical Angles Theorem, you know that $\angle PQR \cong \angle NQM$. By the Third Angles Theorem, $\angle R \cong \angle M$.

▶ So, all three pairs of corresponding sides and all three pairs of corresponding angles are congruent. By the definition of congruent triangles, $\triangle PQR \cong \triangle NQM$.

EXAMPLE 5 *Proving Two Triangles are Congruent*

The diagram represents the triangular stamps shown in the photo. Prove that $\triangle AEB \cong \triangle DEC$.

GIVEN ▶ $\overline{AB} \parallel \overline{DC}, \overline{AB} \cong \overline{DC}$,
E is the midpoint of $\overline{BC}$ and $\overline{AD}$.

PROVE ▶ $\triangle AEB \cong \triangle DEC$

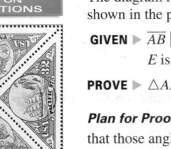

Plan for Proof Use the fact that $\angle AEB$ and $\angle DEC$ are vertical angles to show that those angles are congruent. Use the fact that $\overline{BC}$ intersects parallel segments $\overline{AB}$ and $\overline{DC}$ to identify other pairs of angles that are congruent.

SOLUTION

Statements	Reasons
1. $\overline{AB} \parallel \overline{DC}$, $\overline{AB} \cong \overline{DC}$	1. Given
2. $\angle EAB \cong \angle EDC$, $\angle ABE \cong \angle DCE$	2. Alternate Interior Angles Theorem
3. $\angle AEB \cong \angle DEC$	3. Vertical Angles Theorem
4. E is the midpoint of $\overline{AD}$, E is the midpoint of $\overline{BC}$.	4. Given
5. $\overline{AE} \cong \overline{DE}, \overline{BE} \cong \overline{CE}$	5. Definition of midpoint
6. $\triangle AEB \cong \triangle DEC$	6. Definition of congruent triangles

In this lesson, you have learned to prove that two triangles are congruent by the *definition of congruence*—that is, by showing that all pairs of corresponding angles and corresponding sides are congruent. In upcoming lessons, you will learn more efficient ways of proving that triangles are congruent. The properties below will be useful in such proofs.

THEOREM

THEOREM 4.4 *Properties of Congruent Triangles*

REFLEXIVE PROPERTY OF CONGRUENT TRIANGLES

Every triangle is congruent to itself.

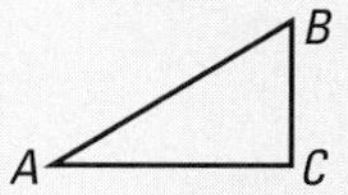

SYMMETRIC PROPERTY OF CONGRUENT TRIANGLES

If $\triangle ABC \cong \triangle DEF$, then $\triangle DEF \cong \triangle ABC$.

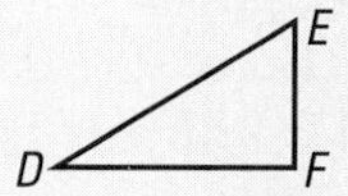

TRANSITIVE PROPERTY OF CONGRUENT TRIANGLES

If $\triangle ABC \cong \triangle DEF$ and $\triangle DEF \cong \triangle JKL$, then $\triangle ABC \cong \triangle JKL$.

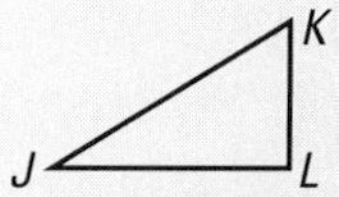

GUIDED PRACTICE

Vocabulary Check ✔

1. Copy the congruent triangles shown at the right. Then label the vertices of your triangles so that $\triangle JKL \cong \triangle RST$. Identify all pairs of congruent *corresponding angles* and *corresponding sides*.

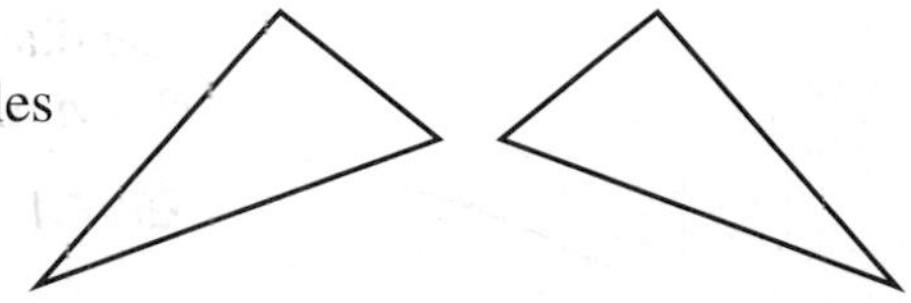

Concept Check ✔

ERROR ANALYSIS **Use the information and the diagram below.**
On an exam, a student says that $\triangle ABC \cong \triangle ADE$ because the corresponding angles of the triangles are congruent.

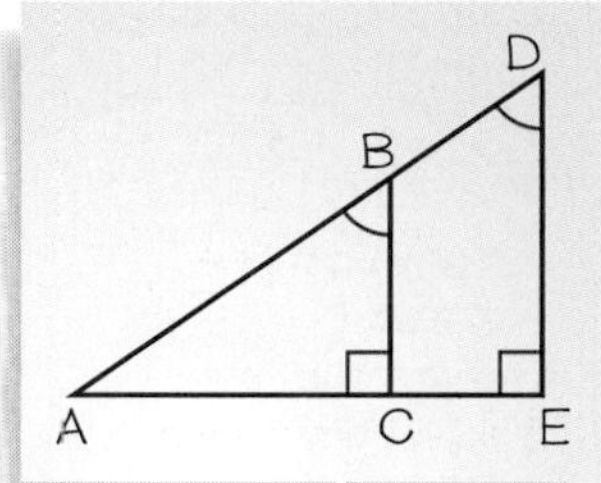

2. How does the student know that the corresponding angles are congruent?

3. Is $\triangle ABC \cong \triangle ADE$? Explain your answer.

Skill Check ✔

Use the diagram at the right, where $\triangle LMN \cong \triangle PQR$.

4. What is the measure of $\angle P$?

5. What is the measure of $\angle M$?

6. What is the measure of $\angle R$?

7. What is the measure of $\angle N$?

8. Which side is congruent to $\overline{QR}$?

9. Which side is congruent to $\overline{LN}$?

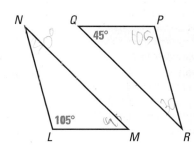

PRACTICE AND APPLICATIONS

STUDENT HELP

▶ **Extra Practice**
to help you master
skills is on p. 809.

DESCRIBING CONGRUENT TRIANGLES In the diagram, $\triangle ABC \cong \triangle TUV$.
Complete the statement.

10. $\angle A \cong \underline{\ ?\ }$

11. $\overline{VT} \cong \underline{\ ?\ }$

12. $\triangle VTU \cong \underline{\ ?\ }$

13. $BC = \underline{\ ?\ }$

14. $m\angle A = m\angle \underline{\ ?\ } = \underline{\ ?\ }°$

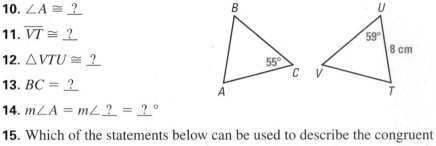

15. Which of the statements below can be used to describe the congruent
triangles in Exercises 10–14? (There may be more than one answer.)

    A. $\triangle CBA \cong \triangle TUV$ **B.** $\triangle CBA \cong \triangle VUT$

    C. $\triangle UTV \cong \triangle BAC$ **D.** $\triangle TVU \cong \triangle ACB$

NAMING CONGRUENT FIGURES Identify any figures that can be proved
congruent. Explain your reasoning. For those that can be proved
congruent, write a congruence statement.

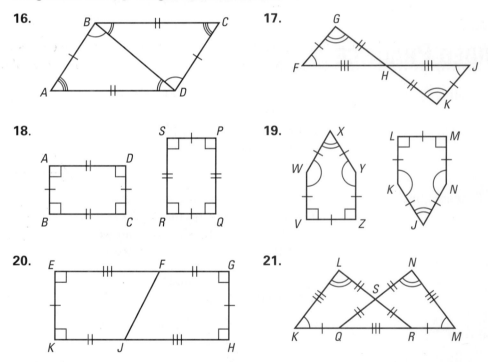

16.

17.

18.

19.

20.

21.

22. IDENTIFYING CORRESPONDING PARTS Use the triangles shown in
Exercise 17 above. Identify all pairs of congruent corresponding angles and
corresponding sides.

23. CRITICAL THINKING Use the
triangles shown at the right.
How many pairs of angles are
congruent? Are the triangles
congruent? Explain your reasoning.

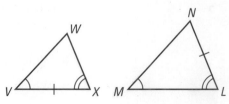

STUDENT HELP

▶ **HOMEWORK HELP**
Example 1: Exs. 10–22
Example 2: Exs. 14, 24, 25
Example 3: Exs. 26–29
Example 4: Exs. 16–21, 23
Example 5: Ex. 38

xy USING ALGEBRA Use the given information to find the indicated values.

24. Given $ABCD \cong EFGH$, find the values of x and y.

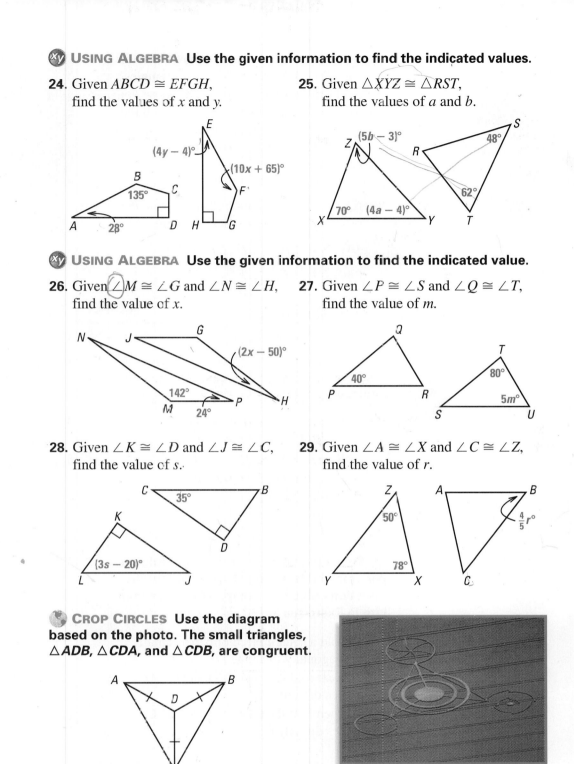

$(4y - 4)°$

$(10x + 65)°$

B $135°$ C

A $28°$ D H G

E F

25. Given $\triangle XYZ \cong \triangle RST$, find the values of a and b.

$(5b - 3)°$ Z R $48°$ S

$62°$

$70°$ $(4a - 4)°$ Y T

X

xy USING ALGEBRA Use the given information to find the indicated value.

26. Given $\angle M \cong \angle G$ and $\angle N \cong \angle H$, find the value of x.

N J G

$(2x - 50)°$

$142°$ P H

M $24°$

27. Given $\angle P \cong \angle S$ and $\angle Q \cong \angle T$, find the value of m.

Q

T $80°$

$40°$

P R $5m°$

S U

28. Given $\angle K \cong \angle D$ and $\angle J \cong \angle C$, find the value of s.

C $35°$ B

K

D

$(3s - 20)°$

L J

29. Given $\angle A \cong \angle X$ and $\angle C \cong \angle Z$, find the value of r.

Z A B

$50°$ $\frac{4}{5}r°$

$78°$

Y X C

🌐 **CROP CIRCLES** Use the diagram based on the photo. The small triangles, $\triangle ADB$, $\triangle CDA$, and $\triangle CDB$, are congruent.

A B

D

C

This pattern was made by mowing a field in England.

30. Explain why $\triangle ABC$ is equilateral.

31. The sum of the measures of $\angle ADB$, $\angle CDA$, and $\angle CDB$ is $360°$. Find $m\angle BDC$.

32. Each of the small isosceles triangles has two congruent acute angles. Find $m\angle DBC$ and $m\angle DCB$.

33. 🧩 **LOGICAL REASONING** Explain why $\triangle ABC$ is equiangular.

34.  **SCULPTURE** The sculpture shown in
the photo is made of congruent triangles
cut from transparent plastic. Suppose you
use one triangle as a pattern to cut all the
other triangles. Which property guarantees
that all the triangles are congruent to
each other?

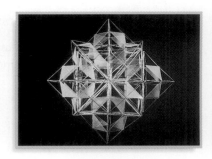

35. ▶ **DEVELOPING PROOF** Complete the
proof of the Third Angles Theorem.

GIVEN ▶ $\angle A \cong \angle D$, $\angle B \cong \angle E$

PROVE ▶ $\angle C \cong \angle F$

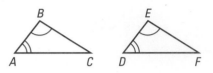

Statements	Reasons
1. $\angle A \cong \angle D$, $\angle B \cong \angle E$	**1.** ___?___
2. $m\angle\,\underline{?}\, = m\angle\,\underline{?}\,$, $m\angle\,\underline{?}\, = m\angle\,\underline{?}\,$	**2.** ___?___
3. $m\angle A + m\angle B + m\angle C = 180°$, $m\angle D + m\angle E + m\angle F = 180°$	**3.** ___?___
4. $m\angle A + m\angle B + m\angle C = m\angle D + m\angle E + m\angle F$	**4.** ___?___
5. $m\angle D + m\angle E + m\angle C = m\angle D + m\angle E + m\angle F$	**5.** ___?___
6. $m\angle C = m\angle F$	**6.** ___?___
7. ___?___	**7.** Def. of $\cong$ ⧍s.

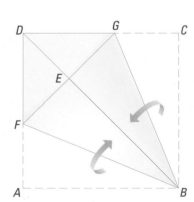

 **ORIGAMI** Origami is the art of folding
paper into interesting shapes. Follow the
directions below to create a kite. Use your
kite in Exercises 36–38.

❶ Fold a square piece of paper in half
diagonally to create $\overline{DB}$.
❷ Next fold the paper so that side $\overline{AB}$
lies directly on $\overline{DB}$.
❸ Then fold the paper so that side $\overline{CB}$
lies directly on $\overline{DB}$.

36. Is $\overline{EB}$ congruent to $\overline{AB}$? Is $\overline{EF}$ congruent to $\overline{AF}$? Explain.

37. 🔵 **LOGICAL REASONING** From folding, you know that $\overrightarrow{BF}$ bisects $\angle EBA$
and $\overrightarrow{FB}$ bisects $\angle AFE$. Given these facts and your answers to Exercise 36,
which triangles can you conclude are congruent? Explain.

38. ▶ **PROOF** Write a proof.

GIVEN ▶ $\overline{DB} \perp \overline{FG}$, E is the midpoint of $\overline{FG}$, $\overline{BF} \cong \overline{BG}$,
and $\overrightarrow{BD}$ bisects $\angle GBF$.

PROVE ▶ $\triangle FEB \cong \triangle GEB$

39. **MULTI-STEP PROBLEM** Use the diagram, in which $ABEF \cong CDEF$.

   a. Explain how you know that $\overline{BE} \cong \overline{DE}$.

   b. Explain how you know that $\angle ABE \cong \angle CDE$.

   c. Explain how you know that $\angle GBE \cong \angle GDE$.

   d. Explain how you know that $\angle GEB \cong \angle GED$.

   e. *Writing* Do you have enough information
   to prove that $\triangle BEG \cong \triangle DEG$? Explain.

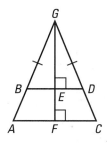

★ **Challenge**

40. **ORIGAMI REVISITED** Look back at Exercises 36–38 on page 208. Suppose
the following statements are also true about the diagram.

   $\overrightarrow{BD}$ bisects $\angle ABC$ and $\overrightarrow{DB}$ bisects $\angle ADC$.
   $\angle ABC$ and $\angle ADC$ are right angles.

EXTRA CHALLENGE
www.mcdougallittell.com

Find all of the unknown angle measures in the figure. Use a sketch to show
your answers.

MIXED REVIEW

DISTANCE FORMULA **Find the distance between each pair of points.**
(Review 1.3 for 4.3)

41. $A(3, 8)$
   $B(-1, -4)$

42. $C(3, -8)$
   $D(-13, 7)$

43. $E(-2, -6)$
   $F(3, -5)$

44. $G(0, 5)$
   $H(-5, 2)$

45. $J(0, -4)$
   $K(9, 2)$

46. $L(7, -2)$
   $M(0, 9)$

FINDING THE MIDPOINT **Find the coordinates of the midpoint of a segment**
with the given endpoints. **(Review 1.5)**

47. $N(-1, 5)$
   $P(-3, -9)$

48. $Q(5, 7)$
   $R(-1, 4)$

49. $S(-6, -2)$
   $T(8, 2)$

50. $U(0, -7)$
   $V(-6, 4)$

51. $W(12, 0)$
   $Z(8, 6)$

52. $A(-5, -7)$
   $B(0, 4)$

FINDING COMPLEMENTARY ANGLES **In Exercises 53–55, $\angle 1$ and $\angle 2$ are**
complementary. Find $m\angle 2$. **(Review 1.6)**

53. $m\angle 1 = 8°$
   $m\angle 2 = \underline{\ ?\ }$

54. $m\angle 1 = 73°$
   $m\angle 2 = \underline{\ ?\ }$

55. $m\angle 1 = 62°$
   $m\angle 2 = \underline{\ ?\ }$

IDENTIFYING PARALLELS **Find the slope of each line. Are the lines parallel?**
(Review 3.6)

56.

57.

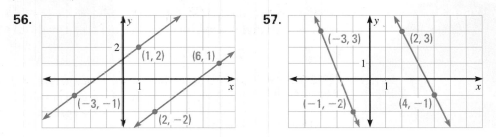

Classify the triangle by its angles and by its sides. (Lesson 4.1)

1.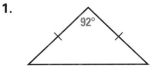

2.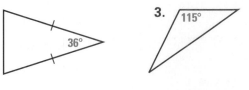

3.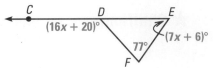

4. Find the value of *x* in the figure at the right. Then give the measure of each interior angle and the measure of the exterior angle shown. (Lesson 4.1)

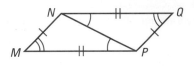

Use the diagram at the right. (Lesson 4.2)

5. Write a congruence statement. Identify all pairs of congruent corresponding parts.

6. You are given that $m\angle NMP = 46°$ and $m\angle PNQ = 27°$. Find $m\angle MNP$.

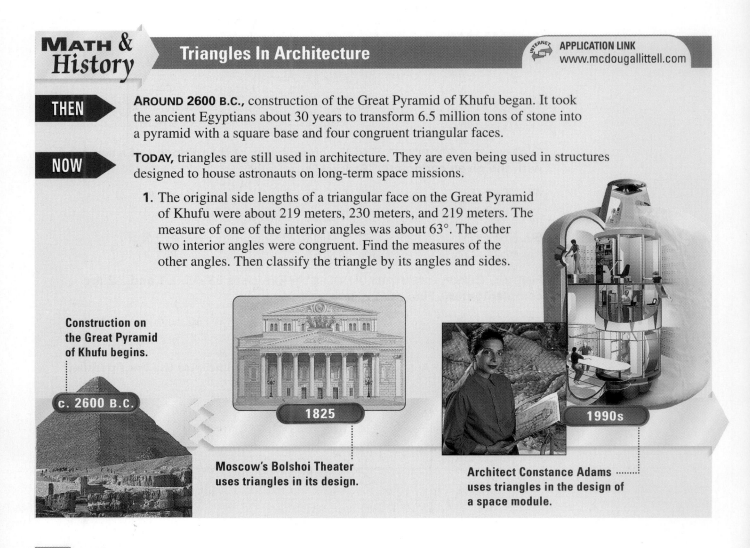

MATH & History

Triangles In Architecture

APPLICATION LINK
www.mcdougallittell.com

THEN ▶ **AROUND 2600 B.C.,** construction of the Great Pyramid of Khufu began. It took the ancient Egyptians about 30 years to transform 6.5 million tons of stone into a pyramid with a square base and four congruent triangular faces.

NOW ▶ **TODAY,** triangles are still used in architecture. They are even being used in structures designed to house astronauts on long-term space missions.

1. The original side lengths of a triangular face on the Great Pyramid of Khufu were about 219 meters, 230 meters, and 219 meters. The measure of one of the interior angles was about 63°. The other two interior angles were congruent. Find the measures of the other angles. Then classify the triangle by its angles and sides.

Construction on the Great Pyramid of Khufu begins.

c. 2600 B.C.

1825

Moscow's Bolshoi Theater uses triangles in its design.

1990s

Architect Constance Adams uses triangles in the design of a space module.

ACTIVITY 4.3
Developing Concepts

GROUP ACTIVITY
Work with a partner.

MATERIALS
- 3 pencils
- protractor
- ruler

Investigating Congruent Triangles

▶ **QUESTION** How much information do you need to know to tell whether two triangles are congruent?

▶ **EXPLORING THE CONCEPT: SSS**

1 On a piece of paper, place three pencils of different lengths so they make a triangle.

2 Mark each vertex of your triangle by pressing the pencil points to the paper.

3 Remove the pencils and draw the sides of your triangle.

4 Have your partner repeat **Steps 1–3** using the same three pencils. Try to make a triangle that is *not* congruent to the one you drew.

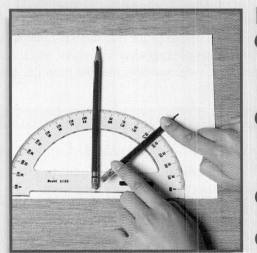

▶ **EXPLORING THE CONCEPT: SAS**

5 On a piece of paper, place two pencils so their erasers are at the center of a protractor. Arrange them to form a 45° angle.

6 Mark two vertices of a triangle by pressing the pencil points to the paper. Mark the center of the protractor as the third vertex.

7 Remove the pencils and protractor and draw the sides of your triangle.

8 Have your partner repeat **Steps 5–7** using the same two pencils. Try to make a triangle that has a 45° angle but is *not* congruent to the one you drew.

▶ **DRAWING CONCLUSIONS**

1. What do you notice about the triangles you made with three pencils? What do you notice about the triangles you made with two pencils and a 45° angle between them?

2. CRITICAL THINKING If you know that two sides of a triangle are congruent to two sides of another triangle, what other information do you need to tell whether the triangles are congruent?

Proving Triangles are Congruent: SSS and SAS

What you should learn

GOAL 1 Prove that triangles are congruent using the SSS and SAS Congruence Postulates.

GOAL 2 Use congruence postulates in **real-life** problems, such as bracing a structure in **Example 5**.

Why you should learn it

▼ Congruence postulates help you see why triangles make things stable, such as the seaplane's wing below and the objects in **Exs. 30 and 31**.

GOAL 1 SSS AND SAS CONGRUENCE POSTULATES

How much do you need to know about two triangles to prove that they are congruent? In Lesson 4.2, you learned that if all six pairs of corresponding parts (sides and angles) are congruent, then the triangles are congruent.

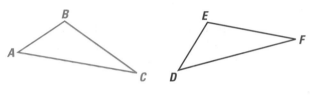

If	Sides are congruent	and	Angles are congruent	then	Triangles are congruent
	1. $\overline{AB} \cong \overline{DE}$		4. $\angle A \cong \angle D$		$\triangle ABC \cong \triangle DEF$
	2. $\overline{BC} \cong \overline{EF}$		5. $\angle B \cong \angle E$		
	3. $\overline{AC} \cong \overline{DF}$		6. $\angle C \cong \angle F$		

In this lesson and the next, you will learn that you do not need all six of the pieces of information above to prove that the triangles are congruent. For example, if all three pairs of corresponding sides are congruent, then the *SSS Congruence Postulate* guarantees that the triangles are congruent.

POSTULATE

POSTULATE 19 *Side-Side-Side (SSS) Congruence Postulate*

If three sides of one triangle are congruent to three sides of a second triangle, then the two triangles are congruent.

If   Side $\overline{MN} \cong \overline{QR}$,
        Side $\overline{NP} \cong \overline{RS}$, and
        Side $\overline{PM} \cong \overline{SQ}$,
then $\triangle MNP \cong \triangle QRS$.

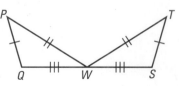

EXAMPLE 1 *Using the SSS Congruence Postulate*

Prove that $\triangle PQW \cong \triangle TSW$.

Paragraph Proof The marks on the diagram show that $\overline{PQ} \cong \overline{TS}$, $\overline{PW} \cong \overline{TW}$, and $\overline{QW} \cong \overline{SW}$.

▶ So, by the SSS Congruence Postulate, you know that $\triangle PQW \cong \triangle TSW$.

Copying a Triangle

Follow the steps below to construct a triangle that is congruent to a given △ABC.

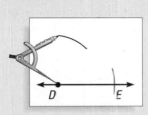

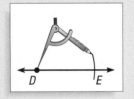

① Construct $\overline{DE}$ so that it is congruent to $\overline{AB}$. (See page 104 for the construction.)

② Open your compass to the length AC. Use this length to draw an arc with the compass point at D.

③ Draw an arc with radius BC and center E that intersects the arc from **Step 2**. Label the intersection point F.

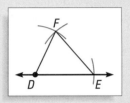

④ Draw △DEF. By the SSS Congruence Postulate, △ABC ≅ △DEF.

The SSS Congruence Postulate is a shortcut for proving two triangles are congruent without using all six pairs of corresponding parts. The postulate below is a shortcut that uses two sides and the angle that is *included* between the sides.

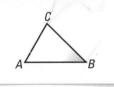
POSTULATE

POSTULATE 20 *Side-Angle-Side (SAS) Congruence Postulate*

If two sides and the included angle of one triangle are congruent to two sides and the included angle of a second triangle, then the two triangles are congruent.

If   Side $\overline{PQ} \cong \overline{WX}$,

         Angle $\angle Q \cong \angle X$, and

         Side $\overline{QS} \cong \overline{XY}$,

then   △PQS ≅ △WXY.

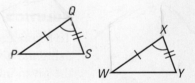

━━━━━━━━━━━━━━━━━━━━━━━━━━━━━━━━

EXAMPLE 2   *Using the SAS Congruence Postulate*

Prove that △AEB ≅ △DEC.

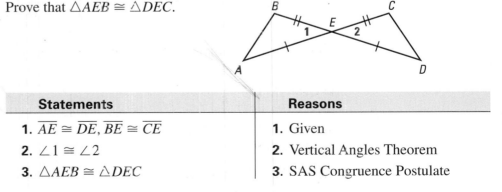

Statements	Reasons
1. $\overline{AE} \cong \overline{DE}$, $\overline{BE} \cong \overline{CE}$	**1.** Given
2. ∠1 ≅ ∠2	**2.** Vertical Angles Theorem
3. △AEB ≅ △DEC	**3.** SAS Congruence Postulate

*Logical
Reasoning*

EXAMPLE 3 *Choosing Which Congruence Postulate to Use*

Decide whether enough information is given in the diagram to prove that
$\triangle PQR \cong \triangle PSR$. If there is enough information, state the congruence postulate
you would use.

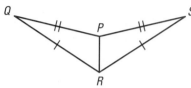

SOLUTION

Paragraph Proof The marks on the diagram show that $\overline{PQ} \cong \overline{PS}$ and
$\overline{QR} \cong \overline{SR}$. By the Reflexive Property of Congruence, $\overline{RP} \cong \overline{RP}$. Because the
sides of $\triangle PQR$ are congruent to the corresponding sides of $\triangle PSR$, you can use
the SSS Congruence Postulate to prove that the triangles are congruent.

EXAMPLE 4 *Proving Triangles Congruent*

ARCHITECTURE You are
designing the window shown
in the photo. You want to make $\triangle DRA$
congruent to $\triangle DRG$. You design the
window so that $\overline{DR} \perp \overline{AG}$ and $\overline{RA} \cong \overline{RG}$.
Can you conclude that $\triangle DRA \cong \triangle DRG$?

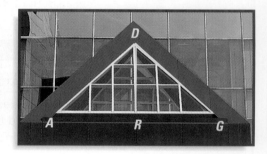

SOLUTION

Proof

To begin, copy the diagram and label it
using the given information. Then write
the given information and the statement
you need to prove.

GIVEN ▶ $\overline{DR} \perp \overline{AG}$,
$\overline{RA} \cong \overline{RG}$

PROVE ▶ $\triangle DRA \cong \triangle DRG$

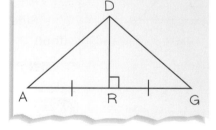

Statements	Reasons
1. $\overline{DR} \perp \overline{AG}$	1. Given
2. $\angle DRA$ and $\angle DRG$ are right angles.	2. If 2 lines are $\perp$, then they form 4 rt. ∠s.
3. $\angle DRA \cong \angle DRG$	3. Right Angle Congruence Theorem
4. $\overline{RA} \cong \overline{RG}$	4. Given
5. $\overline{DR} \cong \overline{DR}$	5. Reflexive Property of Congruence
6. $\triangle DRA \cong \triangle DRG$	6. SAS Congruence Postulate

EXAMPLE 5 **Triangular Frameworks are Rigid**

 STRUCTURAL SUPPORT To prevent a doorway from collapsing after an earthquake, you can reinforce it. Explain why the doorway with the diagonal brace is more stable, while the one without the brace can collapse.

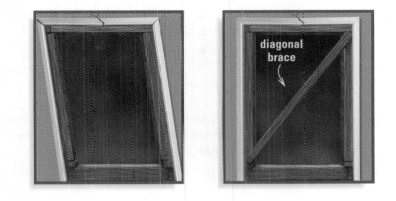

diagonal brace

SOLUTION

In the doorway with the diagonal brace, the wood forms triangles whose sides have fixed lengths. The SSS Congruence Postulate guarantees that these triangles are rigid, because a triangle with given side lengths has only one possible size and shape. The doorway without the brace is unstable because there are many possible shapes for a four-sided figure with the given side lengths.

EXAMPLE 6 **Congruent Triangles in a Coordinate Plane**

xy
Using Algebra

Use the SSS Congruence Postulate to show that $\triangle ABC \cong \triangle FGH$.

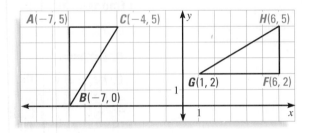

$A(-7, 5)$ $C(-4, 5)$ $H(6, 5)$
$G(1, 2)$ $F(6, 2)$
$B(-7, 0)$

SOLUTION

Because $AC = 3$ and $FH = 3$, $\overline{AC} \cong \overline{FH}$. Because $AB = 5$ and $FG = 5$, $\overline{AB} \cong \overline{FG}$. Use the Distance Formula to find the lengths BC and GH.

Look Back
For help with the Distance Formula, see page 19.

$$d = \sqrt{(x_2 - x_1)^2 + (y_2 - y_1)^2}$$

$$BC = \sqrt{(-4 - (-7))^2 + (5 - 0)^2}$$

$$= \sqrt{3^2 + 5^2}$$

$$= \sqrt{34}$$

$$d = \sqrt{(x_2 - x_1)^2 + (y_2 - y_1)^2}$$

$$GH = \sqrt{(6 - 1)^2 + (5 - 2)^2}$$

$$= \sqrt{5^2 + 3^2}$$

$$= \sqrt{34}$$

▶ Because $BC = \sqrt{34}$ and $GH = \sqrt{34}$, $\overline{BC} \cong \overline{GH}$. All three pairs of corresponding sides are congruent, so $\triangle ABC \cong \triangle FGH$ by the SSS Congruence Postulate.

GUIDED PRACTICE

Vocabulary Check ✓   1. Sketch a triangle and label its vertices. Name two sides and the included angle between the sides.

Concept Check ✓   2. **ERROR ANALYSIS** Henry believes he can use the information given in the diagram and the SAS Congruence Postulate to prove the two triangles are congruent. Explain Henry's mistake.

Skill Check ✓   **LOGICAL REASONING** Decide whether enough information is given to prove that the triangles are congruent. If there is enough information, tell which congruence postulate you would use.

3. △ABC, △DEC   4. △FGH, △JKH   5. △PQR, △SRQ

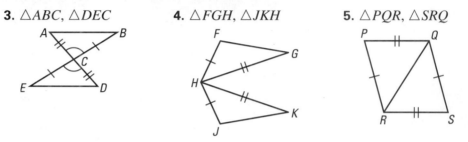

PRACTICE AND APPLICATIONS

STUDENT HELP

▶ **Extra Practice**
to help you master
skills is on p. 809.

NAMING SIDES AND INCLUDED ANGLES Use the diagram. Name the included angle between the pair of sides given.

6. $\overline{JK}$ and $\overline{KL}$ 7. $\overline{PK}$ and $\overline{LK}$

8. $\overline{LP}$ and $\overline{LK}$ 9. $\overline{JL}$ and $\overline{JK}$

10. $\overline{KL}$ and $\overline{JL}$ 11. $\overline{KP}$ and $\overline{PL}$

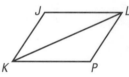

LOGICAL REASONING Decide whether enough information is given to prove that the triangles are congruent. If there is enough information, state the congruence postulate you would use.

12. △UVT, △WVT   13. △LMN, △TNM   14. △YZW, △YXW

STUDENT HELP

▶ **HOMEWORK HELP**
Example 1: Exs. 18,
         20–28
Example 2: Exs. 19–28
Example 3: Exs. 12–17
Example 4: Exs. 20–28
Example 5: Exs. 30, 31
Example 6: Exs. 33–35

15. △ACB, △ECD   16. △RST, △WVU   17. △GJH, △HLK

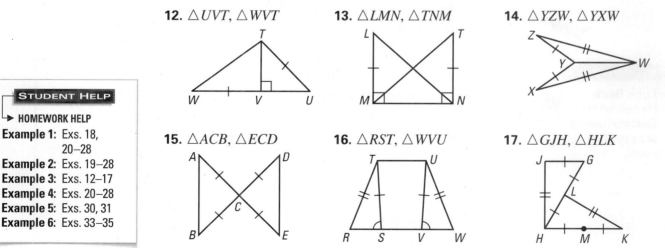

DEVELOPING PROOF In Exercises 18 and 19, use the photo of the Navajo rug. Assume that $\overline{BC} \cong \overline{DE}$ and $\overline{AC} \cong \overline{CE}$.

18. What other piece of information is needed to prove that $\triangle ABC \cong \triangle CDE$ using the SSS Congruence Postulate?

19. What other piece of information is needed to prove that $\triangle ABC \cong \triangle CDE$ using the SAS Congruence Postulate?

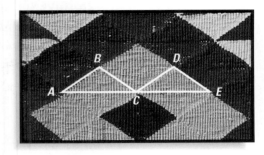

20. ▶ **DEVELOPING PROOF** Complete the proof by supplying the reasons.

GIVEN ▶ $\overline{EF} \cong \overline{GH}$,
$\overline{FG} \cong \overline{HE}$

PROVE ▶ $\triangle EFG \cong \triangle GHE$

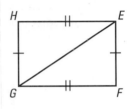

Statements	Reasons
1. $\overline{EF} \cong \overline{GH}$	1. ___?___
2. $\overline{FG} \cong \overline{HE}$	2. ___?___
3. $\overline{GE} \cong \overline{GE}$	3. ___?___
4. $\triangle EFG \cong \triangle GHE$	4. ___?___

▶ **TWO-COLUMN PROOF** Write a two-column proof.

21. GIVEN ▶ $\overline{NP} \cong \overline{QN} \cong \overline{RS} \cong \overline{TR}$,
$\overline{PQ} \cong \overline{ST}$

PROVE ▶ $\triangle NPQ \cong \triangle RST$

22. GIVEN ▶ $\overline{AB} \cong \overline{CD}$, $\overline{AB} \parallel \overline{CD}$

PROVE ▶ $\triangle ABC \cong \triangle CDA$

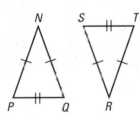

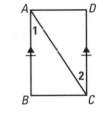

▶ **PARAGRAPH PROOF** Write a paragraph proof.

23. GIVEN ▶ $\overrightarrow{PQ}$ bisects $\angle SPT$,
$\overline{SP} \cong \overline{TP}$

PROVE ▶ $\triangle SPQ \cong \triangle TPQ$

24. GIVEN ▶ $\overline{PT} \cong \overline{RT}$, $\overline{QT} \cong \overline{ST}$

PROVE ▶ $\triangle PQT \cong \triangle RST$

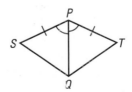

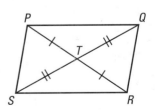

▶ **PROOF** Write a two-column proof or a paragraph proof.

25. **GIVEN** ▶ $\overline{AC} \cong \overline{BC}$,
M is the midpoint of $\overline{AB}$.
PROVE ▶ $\triangle ACM \cong \triangle BCM$

26. **GIVEN** ▶ $\overline{BC} \cong \overline{AE}$, $\overline{BD} \cong \overline{AD}$,
$\overline{DE} \cong \overline{DC}$
PROVE ▶ $\triangle ABC \cong \triangle BAE$

27. **GIVEN** ▶ $\overline{PA} \cong \overline{PB} \cong \overline{PC}$,
$\overline{AB} \cong \overline{BC}$
PROVE ▶ $\triangle PAB \cong \triangle PBC$

28. **GIVEN** ▶ $\overline{CR} \cong \overline{CS}$, $\overline{QC} \perp \overline{CR}$,
$\overline{QC} \perp \overline{CS}$
PROVE ▶ $\triangle QCR \cong \triangle QCS$

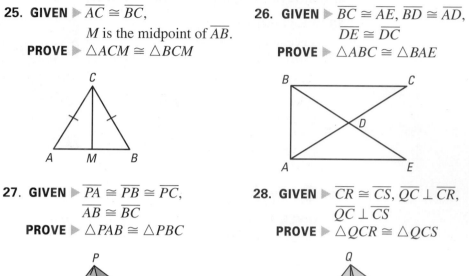

STUDENT HELP

INTERNET
SOFTWARE HELP
Visit our Web site
www.mcdougallittell.com
to see instructions for
several software
applications.

29. 🖥 **TECHNOLOGY** Use geometry software to draw a triangle. Draw a line and reflect the triangle across the line. Measure the sides and the angles of the new triangle and tell whether it is congruent to the original one.

Writing **Explain how triangles are used in the object shown to make it more stable.**

30.
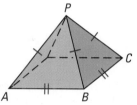

31.
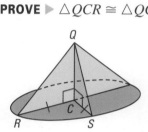

32. 📐 **CONSTRUCTION** Draw an isosceles triangle with vertices A, B, and C. Use a compass and straightedge to construct $\triangle DEF$ so that $\triangle DEF \cong \triangle ABC$.

🅧🅨 **USING ALGEBRA** Use the Distance Formula and the SSS Congruence Postulate to show that $\triangle ABC \cong \triangle DEF$.

33. **34.** **35.**

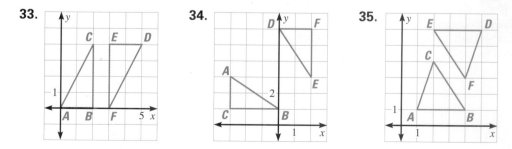

36. MULTIPLE CHOICE In $\triangle RST$ and $\triangle ABC$, $\overline{RS} \cong \overline{AB}$, $\overline{ST} \cong \overline{BC}$, and $\overline{TR} \cong \overline{CA}$. Which angle is congruent to $\angle T$?

    (A) $\angle R$ **(B)** $\angle A$ **(C)** $\angle C$ **(D)** cannot be determined

37. MULTIPLE CHOICE In equilateral $\triangle DEF$, a segment is drawn from point F to G, the midpoint of $\overline{DE}$. Which of the statements below is *not* true?

    (A) $\overline{DF} \cong \overline{EF}$ **(B)** $\overline{DG} \cong \overline{DF}$ **(C)** $\overline{DG} \cong \overline{EG}$ **(D)** $\triangle DFG \cong \triangle EFG$

★ **Challenge**

EXTRA CHALLENGE
www.mcdougallittell.com

38. CHOOSING A METHOD Describe how to show that $\triangle PMO \cong \triangle PMN$ using the SSS Congruence Postulate. Then find a way to show that the triangles are congruent using the SAS Congruence Postulate. You may not use a protractor to measure any angles. Compare the two methods. Which do you prefer? Why?

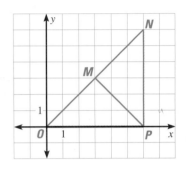

MIXED REVIEW

SCIENCE CONNECTION **Find an important angle in the photo. Copy the angle, extend its sides, and use a protractor to measure it to the nearest degree.**
(Review 1.4)

39.

40.

USING PARALLEL LINES Find $m\angle 1$ and $m\angle 2$. Explain your reasoning.
(Review 3.3 for 4.4)

41. 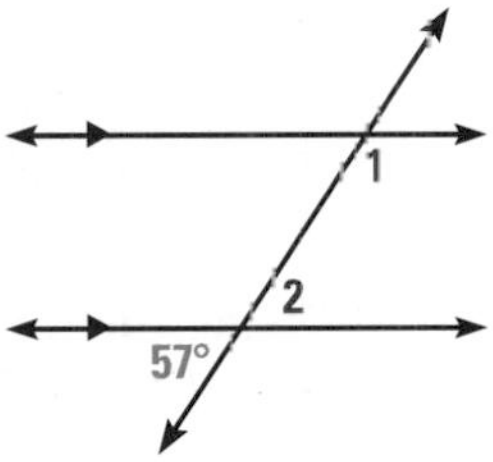
42. 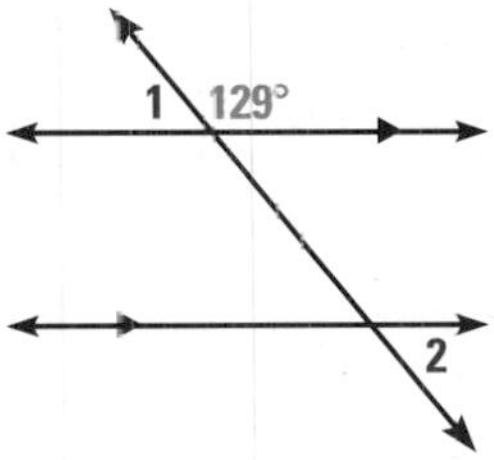
43.

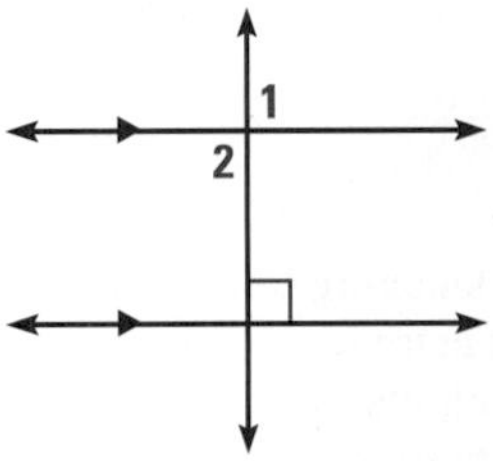

LINE RELATIONSHIPS Find the slope of each line. Identify any parallel or perpendicular lines. (Review 3.7)

44.
45.
46.

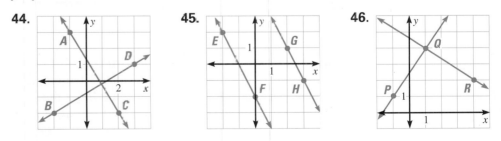

Proving Triangles are Congruent: ASA and AAS

GOAL 1 Prove that triangles are congruent using the ASA Congruence Postulate and the AAS Congruence Theorem.

GOAL 2 Use congruence postulates and theorems in **real-life** problems, such as taking measurements for a map in **Exs. 24 and 25**.

Why you should learn it

▼ To solve **real-life** problems, such as finding the location of a meteorite in **Example 3**.

Lars Lindberg Christensen is an astronomer who participated in a search for a meteorite in Greenland.

GOAL 1 USING THE ASA AND AAS CONGRUENCE METHODS

In Lesson 4.3, you studied the SSS and the SAS Congruence Postulates. Two additional ways to prove two triangles are congruent are listed below.

MORE WAYS TO PROVE TRIANGLES ARE CONGRUENT

POSTULATE 21 *Angle-Side-Angle (ASA) Congruence Postulate*

If two angles and the included side of one triangle are congruent to two angles and the included side of a second triangle, then the two triangles are congruent.

If   Angle $\angle A \cong \angle D$,

       Side $\overline{AC} \cong \overline{DF}$, and

       Angle $\angle C \cong \angle F$,

then $\triangle ABC \cong \triangle DEF$.

THEOREM 4.5 *Angle-Angle-Side (AAS) Congruence Theorem*

If two angles and a nonincluded side of one triangle are congruent to two angles and the corresponding nonincluded side of a second triangle, then the two triangles are congruent.

If   Angle $\angle A \cong \angle D$,

       Angle $\angle C \cong \angle F$, and

       Side $\overline{BC} \cong \overline{EF}$,

then $\triangle ABC \cong \triangle DEF$.

A proof of the Angle-Angle-Side (AAS) Congruence Theorem is given below.

GIVEN ▶ $\angle A \cong \angle D$, $\angle C \cong \angle F$, $\overline{BC} \cong \overline{EF}$

PROVE ▶ $\triangle ABC \cong \triangle DEF$

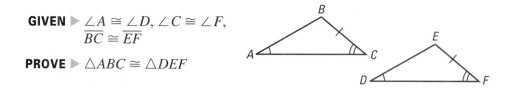

Paragraph Proof You are given that two angles of $\triangle ABC$ are congruent to two angles of $\triangle DEF$. By the Third Angles Theorem, the third angles are also congruent. That is, $\angle B \cong \angle E$. Notice that $\overline{BC}$ is the side included between $\angle B$ and $\angle C$, and $\overline{EF}$ is the side included between $\angle E$ and $\angle F$. You can apply the ASA Congruence Postulate to conclude that $\triangle ABC \cong \triangle DEF$.

EXAMPLE 1 *Developing Proof*

Logical Reasoning

Is it possible to prove that the triangles are congruent? If so, state the postulate or theorem you would use. Explain your reasoning.

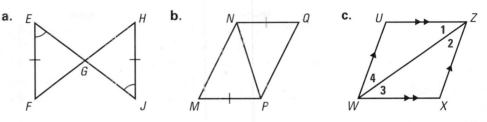

a.

b.

c.

STUDENT HELP

➤ **Study Tip**
In addition to the information that is marked on a diagram, you need to consider other pairs of angles or sides that may be congruent. For instance, look for vertical angles or a side that is shared by two triangles.

SOLUTION

a. In addition to the angles and segments that are marked, $\angle EGF \cong \angle JGH$ by the Vertical Angles Theorem. Two pairs of corresponding angles and one pair of corresponding sides are congruent. You can use the AAS Congruence Theorem to prove that $\triangle EFG \cong \triangle JHG$.

b. In addition to the congruent segments that are marked, $\overline{NP} \cong \overline{NP}$. Two pairs of corresponding sides are congruent. This is not enough information to prove that the triangles are congruent.

c. The two pairs of parallel sides can be used to show $\angle 1 \cong \angle 3$ and $\angle 2 \cong \angle 4$. Because the included side $\overline{WZ}$ is congruent to itself, $\triangle WUZ \cong \triangle ZXW$ by the ASA Congruence Postulate.

EXAMPLE 2 *Proving Triangles are Congruent*

Proof

▶ **GIVEN** ▶ $\overline{AD} \parallel \overline{EC}$, $\overline{BD} \cong \overline{BC}$

PROVE ▶ $\triangle ABD \cong \triangle EBC$

Plan for Proof Notice that $\angle ABD$ and $\angle EBC$ are congruent. You are given that $\overline{BD} \cong \overline{BC}$. Use the fact that $\overline{AD} \parallel \overline{EC}$ to identify a pair of congruent angles.

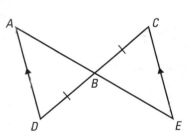

Statements	Reasons
1. $\overline{BD} \cong \overline{BC}$	**1.** Given
2. $\overline{AD} \parallel \overline{EC}$	**2.** Given
3. $\angle D \cong \angle C$	**3.** Alternate Interior Angles Theorem
4. $\angle ABD \cong \angle EBC$	**4.** Vertical Angles Theorem
5. $\triangle ABD \cong \triangle EBC$	**5.** ASA Congruence Postulate

· · · · · · · · · ·

You can often use more than one method to prove a statement. In Example 2, you can use the parallel segments to show that $\angle D \cong \angle C$ and $\angle A \cong \angle E$. Then you can use the AAS Congruence Theorem to prove that the triangles are congruent.

EXAMPLE 3 *Using Properties of Congruent Triangles*

METEORITES
When a *meteoroid* (a piece of rocky or metallic matter from space) enters Earth's atmosphere, it heats up, leaving a trail of burning gases called a *meteor*. Meteoroid fragments that reach Earth without burning up are called *meteorites*.

METEORITES On December 9, 1997, an extremely bright meteor lit up the sky above Greenland. Scientists attempted to find meteorite fragments by collecting data from eyewitnesses who had seen the meteor pass through the sky. As shown, the scientists were able to describe sightlines from observers in different towns. One sightline was from observers in Paamiut (Town *P*) and another was from observers in Narsarsuaq (Town *N*).

Assuming the sightlines were accurate, did the scientists have enough information to locate any meteorite fragments? Explain.

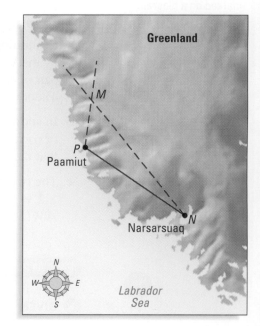

SOLUTION

Think of Town *P* and Town *N* as two vertices of a triangle. The meteorite's position *M* is the other vertex. The scientists knew $m\angle P$ and $m\angle N$. They also knew the length of the included side $\overline{PN}$.

From the ASA Congruence Postulate, the scientists could conclude that any two triangles with these measurements are congruent. In other words, there is only one triangle with the given measurements and location.

▶ Assuming the sightlines were accurate, the scientists did have enough information to locate the meteorite fragments.

· · · · · · · · · ·

ACCURACY IN MEASUREMENT The conclusion in Example 3 depends on the assumption that the sightlines were accurate. If, however, the sightlines based on that information were only approximate, then the scientists could only narrow the meteorite's location to a region near point *M*.

For instance, if the angle measures for the sightlines were off by 2° in either direction, the meteorite's location would be known to lie within a region of about 25 square miles, which is a very large area to search.

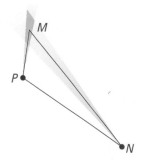

In fact, the scientists looking for the meteorite searched over 1150 square miles of rough, icy terrain without finding any meteorite fragments.

GUIDED PRACTICE

Vocabulary Check ✓

1. Name the four methods you have learned for proving triangles congruent. Only one of these is called a *theorem*. Why is it called a theorem?

Concept Check ✓

Is it possible to prove that the triangles are congruent? If so, state the postulate or theorem you would use. Explain your reasoning.

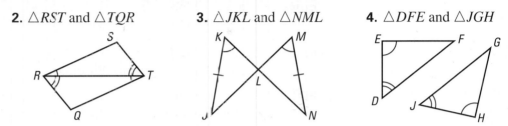

2. △RST and △TQR

3. △JKL and △NML

4. △DFE and △JGH

Skill Check ✓

State the third congruence that must be given to prove that △ABC ≅ △DEF using the indicated postulate or theorem.

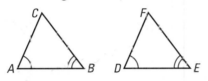

5. ASA Congruence Postulate

6. AAS Congruence Theorem

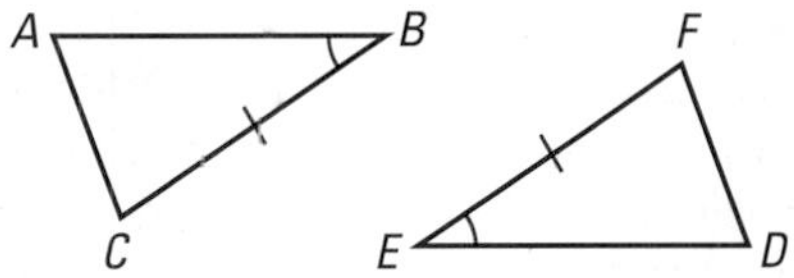

7. 🌐 **RELAY RACE** A course for a relay race is marked on the gymnasium floor. Your team starts at A, goes to B, then C, then returns to A. The other team starts at C, goes to D, then A, then returns to C. Given that $\overline{AD} \parallel \overline{BC}$ and ∠B and ∠D are right angles, explain how you know the two courses are the same length.

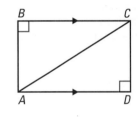

PRACTICE AND APPLICATIONS

STUDENT HELP

▸ **Extra Practice**
to help you master skills is on pp. 809 and 810.

🐢 **LOGICAL REASONING** Is it possible to prove that the triangles are congruent? If so, state the postulate or theorem you would use. Explain your reasoning.

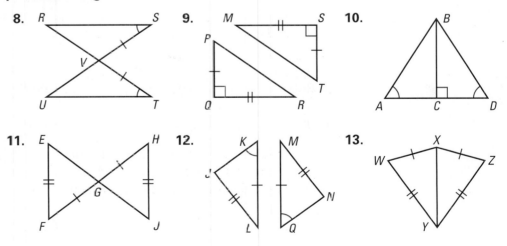

8.

9.

10.

11.

12.

13.

STUDENT HELP

▸ **HOMEWORK HELP**
Example 1: Exs. 8–13
Example 2: Exs. 14–22
Example 3: Exs. 23–25, 28

DEVELOPING PROOF State the third congruence that must be given to prove that △*PQR* ≅ △*STU* using the indicated postulate or theorem. (*Hint:* First sketch △*PQR* and △*STU*. Mark the triangles with the given information.)

14. GIVEN ▶ ∠*Q* ≅ ∠*T*, $\overline{PQ}$ ≅ $\overline{ST}$
Use the AAS Congruence Theorem.

15. GIVEN ▶ ∠*R* ≅ ∠*U*, $\overline{PR}$ ≅ $\overline{SU}$
Use the ASA Congruence Postulate.

16. GIVEN ▶ ∠*R* ≅ ∠*U*, ∠*P* ≅ ∠*S*
Use the ASA Congruence Postulate.

17. GIVEN ▶ $\overline{PR}$ ≅ $\overline{SU}$, ∠*R* ≅ ∠*U*
Use the SAS Congruence Postulate.

STUDENT HELP

→ Study Tip
When a proof involves overlapping triangles, such as the ones in Exs. 18 and 22, you may find it helpful to sketch the triangles separately.

18. ▶ **DEVELOPING PROOF** Complete the proof that △*XWV* ≅ △*ZWU*.

GIVEN ▶ $\overline{VW}$ ≅ $\overline{UW}$
∠*X* ≅ ∠*Z*

PROVE ▶ △*XWV* ≅ △*ZWU*

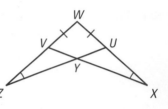

Statements	Reasons
1. $\overline{VW}$ ≅ $\overline{UW}$	1. ___?___
2. ∠*X* ≅ ∠*Z*	2. ___?___
3. ___?___	3. Reflexive Property of Congruence
4. △*XWV* ≅ △*ZWU*	4. ___?___

▶ **PROOF** Write a two-column proof or a paragraph proof.

19. GIVEN ▶ $\overline{FH}$ ∥ $\overline{LK}$, $\overline{GF}$ ≅ $\overline{GL}$
PROVE ▶ △*FGH* ≅ △*LGK*

20. GIVEN ▶ $\overline{AB}$ ⊥ $\overline{AD}$, $\overline{DE}$ ⊥ $\overline{AD}$, $\overline{BC}$ ≅ $\overline{EC}$
PROVE ▶ △*ABC* ≅ △*DEC*

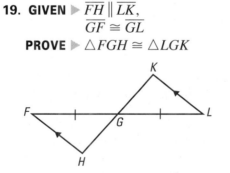

21. GIVEN ▶ $\overline{VX}$ ≅ $\overline{XY}$, $\overline{XW}$ ≅ $\overline{YZ}$, $\overline{XW}$ ∥ $\overline{YZ}$
PROVE ▶ △*VXW* ≅ △*XYZ*

22. GIVEN ▶ ∠*TQS* ≅ ∠*RSQ*, ∠*R* ≅ ∠*T*
PROVE ▶ △*TQS* ≅ △*RSQ*

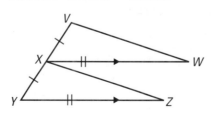

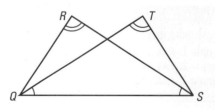

BEARINGS **Use the information about bearings in Exercises 23–25.**
In surveying and orienteering, bearings convey information about direction.
For example, the bearing W 53.1° N means 53.1° to the north of west. To find
this bearing, face west. Then turn 53.1° to the north.

23. You want to describe the boundary lines of a triangular piece of property
to a friend. You fax the note and the sketch below to your friend. Have you
provided enough information to determine the boundary lines of the
property? Explain.

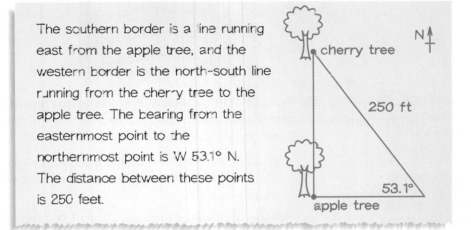

The southern border is a line running east from the apple tree, and the western border is the north-south line running from the cherry tree to the apple tree. The bearing from the easternmost point to the northernmost point is W 53.1° N. The distance between these points is 250 feet.

24. A surveyor wants to make a map of
several streets in a village. The surveyor
finds that Green Street is on an east-west
line. Plain Street is at a bearing of E 55° N
from its intersection with Green Street.
It runs 120 yards before intersecting
Ellis Avenue. Ellis Avenue runs 100 yards
between Green Street and Plain Street.

Assuming these measurements are accurate,
what additional measurements, if any, does
the surveyor need to make to draw Ellis
Avenue correctly? Explain your reasoning.

25. You are creating a map for an orienteering race. Participants start out at a
large oak tree, find a boulder that is 250 yards east of the oak tree, and then
find an elm tree that is W 50° N of the boulder and E 35° N of the oak tree.
Use this information to sketch a map. Do you have enough information to
mark the position of the elm tree? Explain.

USING ALGEBRA **Graph the equations in the same coordinate
plane. Label the vertices of the two triangles formed by the lines. Show
that the triangles are congruent.**

26. $y = 0$; $y = x$; $y = -x + 3$; $y = 3$

27. $y = 2$; $y = 6$; $x = 3$; $x = 5$; $y = 2x - 4$

FOCUS ON APPLICATIONS

ORIENTEERING
In the sport of
orienteering, participants
use a map and a compass
to navigate a course.
Along the way, they travel
to various points marked
on the map.

28. 🌐 **QUILTING** You are making a quilt block out of congruent right triangles. Before cutting out each fabric triangle, you mark a right angle and the length of each leg, as shown. What theorem or postulate guarantees that the fabric triangles are congruent?

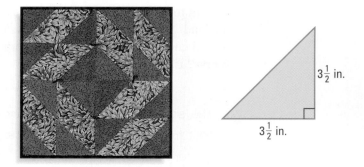

$3\frac{1}{2}$ in.

$3\frac{1}{2}$ in.

29. **MULTI-STEP PROBLEM** You can use the method described below to approximate the distance across a stream without getting wet. As shown in the diagrams, you need a cap with a visor.

• Stand on the edge of the stream and look straight across to a point on the other edge of the stream. Adjust the visor of your cap so that it is in line with that point.

• Without changing the inclination of your neck and head, turn sideways until the visor is in line with a point on your side of the stream.

• Measure the distance *BD* between your feet and that point.

a. From the description of the measuring method, what corresponding parts of the two triangles can you assume are congruent?

b. What theorem or postulate can be used to show that the two triangles are congruent?

c. ✍️ *Writing* Explain why the length of $\overline{BD}$ is also the distance across the stream.

★ Challenge

▶ **PROOF** **Use the diagram.**

30. Alicia thinks that she can prove that $\triangle MNQ \cong \triangle QPM$ based on the information in the diagram. Explain why she cannot.

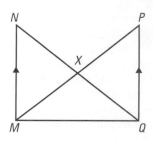

31. Suppose you are given that $\angle XMQ \cong \angle XQM$ and that $\angle N \cong \angle P$. Prove that $\triangle MNQ \cong \triangle QPM$.

MIXED REVIEW

FINDING ENDPOINTS Find the coordinates of the other endpoint of a segment with the given endpoint and midpoint *M*. (Review 1.5)

32. $B(5, 7)$, $M(-1, 0)$ **33.** $C(0, 9)$, $M(6, -2)$ **34.** $F(8, -5)$, $M(-1, -3)$

USING ANGLE BISECTORS $\overrightarrow{BD}$ is the angle bisector of $\angle ABC$. Find the two angle measures not given in the diagram. (Review 1.5 for 4.5)

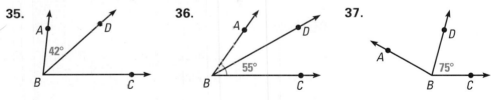

35.   **36.**   **37.**

38. 🌎 **BARN DOOR** You are making a brace for a barn door, as shown. The top and bottom pieces are parallel. To make the middle piece, you cut off the ends of a board at the same angle. What postulate or theorem guarantees that the cuts are parallel? (Review 3.4)

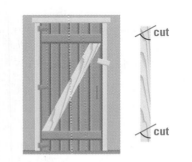

QUIZ 2

Self-Test for Lessons 4.3 and 4.4

In Exercises 1–6, decide whether it is possible to prove that the triangles are congruent. If it is possible, state the theorem or postulate you would use. Explain your reasoning. (Lessons 4.3 and 4.4)

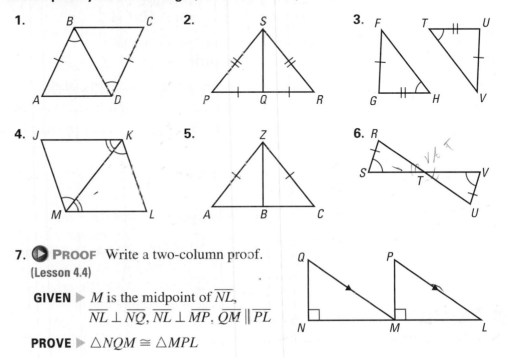

7. ▶ **PROOF** Write a two-column proof. (Lesson 4.4)

GIVEN ▶ *M* is the midpoint of $\overline{NL}$, $\overline{NL} \perp \overline{NQ}$, $\overline{NL} \perp \overline{MP}$, $\overline{QM} \parallel \overline{PL}$

PROVE ▶ $\triangle NQM \cong \triangle MPL$

ACTIVITY 4.4

Using Technology

Investigating Triangles and Congruence

You can use geometry software to show that if two sides and a nonincluded angle of one triangle are congruent to two sides and a nonincluded angle of another triangle, the triangles are not necessarily congruent.

STUDENT HELP

INTERNET SOFTWARE HELP

Visit our Web site www.mcdougallittell.com to see instructions for several different software applications.

CONSTRUCT

Follow the steps below to construct $\triangle ABG$ and $\triangle ABH$.

1. Draw a segment and label it $\overline{AB}$, as shown in the diagram.
2. Draw another point not on $\overline{AB}$. Label this point E and draw $\overleftrightarrow{AE}$.
3. Draw a circle with center at point B that intersects $\overleftrightarrow{AE}$ in two points. Label the intersection points G and H.
4. Draw $\overline{BG}$ and $\overline{BH}$.

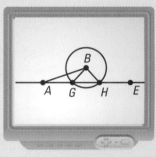

INVESTIGATE

1. Measure the lengths of $\overline{AB}$, $\overline{BH}$, $\overline{BG}$, $\overline{AG}$, and $\overline{AH}$.
2. Measure $\angle ABG$, $\angle BAG$, $\angle AGB$, $\angle ABH$, $\angle BAH$, and $\angle AHB$.
3. Name the sides of $\triangle ABG$ that are congruent to the sides of $\triangle ABH$.
4. Name the angles of $\triangle ABG$ that are congruent to the angles of $\triangle ABH$.
5. Explain why the following conjecture is false.

   If two sides and a nonincluded angle of one triangle are congruent to two sides and a nonincluded angle of the other triangle, then the triangles are congruent.

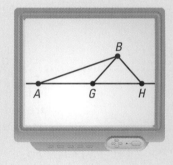

EXTENSION

CRITICAL THINKING If you know that three angles of one triangle are congruent to three angles of another triangle, can you prove that the triangles are congruent? In other words, is there an Angle-Angle-Angle Congruence Postulate or Theorem? Make a conjecture. Then test your conjecture by drawing a triangle with angle measures of 40°, 60°, and 80°. Compare your triangle with those of others in your class. Is your conjecture true or false? Explain.

Using Congruent Triangles

GOAL 1 Use congruent triangles to plan and write proofs.

GOAL 2 Use congruent triangles to prove constructions are valid.

Why you should learn it

▼ Congruent triangles are important in **real-life** problems, such as in designing and constructing bridges like the one in **Ex. 16**.

GOAL 1 PLANNING A PROOF

Knowing that all pairs of corresponding parts of congruent triangles are congruent can help you reach conclusions about congruent figures.

For instance, suppose you want to prove that $\angle PQS \cong \angle RQS$ in the diagram shown at the right. One way to do this is to show that $\triangle PQS \cong \triangle RQS$ by the SSS Congruence Postulate. Then you can use the fact that corresponding parts of congruent triangles are congruent to conclude that $\angle PQS \cong \angle RQS$.

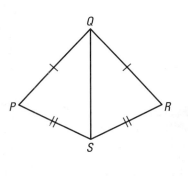

EXAMPLE 1 *Planning and Writing a Proof*

GIVEN ▶ $\overline{AB} \parallel \overline{CD}$, $\overline{BC} \parallel \overline{DA}$

PROVE ▶ $\overline{AB} \cong \overline{CD}$

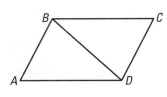

Plan for Proof Show that $\triangle ABD \cong \triangle CDB$. Then use the fact that corresponding parts of congruent triangles are congruent.

SOLUTION

First copy the diagram and mark it with the given information. Then mark any additional information that you can deduce. Because $\overline{AB}$ and $\overline{CD}$ are parallel segments intersected by a transversal, and $\overline{BC}$ and $\overline{DA}$ are parallel segments intersected by a transversal, you can deduce that two pairs of alternate interior angles are congruent.

Mark given information.   Add deduced information.

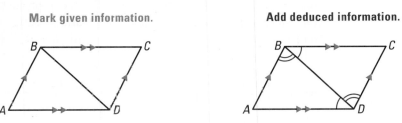

Paragraph Proof Because $\overline{AB} \parallel \overline{CD}$, it follows from the Alternate Interior Angles Theorem that $\angle ABD \cong \angle CDB$. For the same reason, $\angle ADB \cong \angle CBD$ because $\overline{BC} \parallel \overline{DA}$. By the Reflexive Property of Congruence, $\overline{BD} \cong \overline{BD}$. You can use the ASA Congruence Postulate to conclude that $\triangle ABD \cong \triangle CDB$. Finally, because corresponding parts of congruent triangles are congruent, it follows that $\overline{AB} \cong \overline{CD}$.

EXAMPLE 2 *Planning and Writing a Proof*

Proof

GIVEN ▶ *A* is the midpoint of $\overline{MT}$,
A is the midpoint of $\overline{SR}$.

PROVE ▶ $\overline{MS} \parallel \overline{TR}$

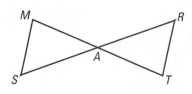

Plan for Proof Prove that $\triangle MAS \cong \triangle TAR$. Then use the fact that corresponding parts of congruent triangles are congruent to show that $\angle M \cong \angle T$. Because these angles are formed by two segments intersected by a transversal, you can conclude that $\overline{MS} \parallel \overline{TR}$.

STUDENT HELP

HOMEWORK HELP

Visit our Web site at
www.mcdougallittell.com
for extra examples.

Statements	Reasons
1. *A* is the midpoint of $\overline{MT}$, A is the midpoint of $\overline{SR}$.	**1.** Given
2. $\overline{MA} \cong \overline{TA}$, $\overline{SA} \cong \overline{RA}$	**2.** Definition of midpoint
3. $\angle MAS \cong \angle TAR$	**3.** Vertical Angles Theorem
4. $\triangle MAS \cong \triangle TAR$	**4.** SAS Congruence Postulate
5. $\angle M \cong \angle T$	**5.** Corresp. parts of $\cong$ △ are $\cong$.
6. $\overline{MS} \parallel \overline{TR}$	**6.** Alternate Interior Angles Converse

EXAMPLE 3 *Using More than One Pair of Triangles*

GIVEN ▶ $\angle 1 \cong \angle 2$
$\angle 3 \cong \angle 4$

PROVE ▶ $\triangle BCE \cong \triangle DCE$

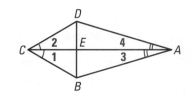

Plan for Proof The only information you have about $\triangle BCE$ and $\triangle DCE$ is that $\angle 1 \cong \angle 2$ and that $\overline{CE} \cong \overline{CE}$. Notice, however, that sides $\overline{BC}$ and $\overline{DC}$ are also sides of $\triangle ABC$ and $\triangle ADC$. If you can prove that $\triangle ABC \cong \triangle ADC$, you can use the fact that corresponding parts of congruent triangles are congruent to get a third piece of information about $\triangle BCE$ and $\triangle DCE$.

Statements	Reasons
1. $\angle 1 \cong \angle 2$ $\angle 3 \cong \angle 4$	**1.** Given
2. $\overline{AC} \cong \overline{AC}$	**2.** Reflexive Property of Congruence
3. $\triangle ABC \cong \triangle ADC$	**3.** ASA Congruence Postulate
4. $\overline{BC} \cong \overline{DC}$	**4.** Corresp. parts of $\cong$ △ are $\cong$.
5. $\overline{CE} \cong \overline{CE}$	**5.** Reflexive Property of Congruence
6. $\triangle BCE \cong \triangle DCE$	**6.** SAS Congruence Postulate

GOAL 2 **PROVING CONSTRUCTIONS ARE VALID**

STUDENT HELP

▶ **Look Back**
For help with copying an angle, see p. 159.

In Lesson 3.5, you learned how to copy an angle using a compass and a straightedge. The construction is summarized below. You can use congruent triangles to prove that this (and other) constructions are valid.

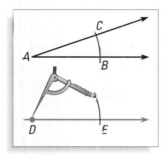 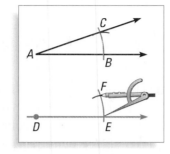 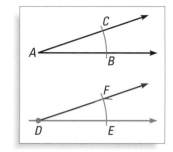

❶ To copy ∠A, first draw a ray with initial point D. Then use the same compass setting to draw an arc with center A and an arc with center D. Label points B, C, and E.

❷ Draw an arc with radius BC and center E. Label the intersection F.

❸ Draw $\overrightarrow{DF}$. ∠FDE ≅ ∠CAB

EXAMPLE 4 *Proving a Construction*

Proof

Using the construction summarized above, you can copy ∠CAB to form ∠FDE. Write a proof to verify that the construction is valid.

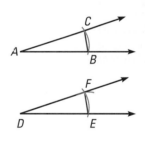

Plan for Proof Show that △CAB ≅ △FDE. Then use the fact that corresponding parts of congruent triangles are congruent to conclude that ∠CAB ≅ ∠FDE. By construction, you can assume the following statements as given.

$\overline{AB} \cong \overline{DE}$ Same compass setting is used.
$\overline{AC} \cong \overline{DF}$ Same compass setting is used.
$\overline{BC} \cong \overline{EF}$ Same compass setting is used.

SOLUTION

Statements	Reasons
1. $\overline{AB} \cong \overline{DE}$	1. Given
2. $\overline{AC} \cong \overline{DF}$	2. Given
3. $\overline{BC} \cong \overline{EF}$	3. Given
4. △CAB ≅ △FDE	4. SSS Congruence Postulate
5. ∠CAB ≅ ∠FDE	5. Corresp. parts of ≅ △ are ≅.

GUIDED PRACTICE

Concept Check ✓   **In Exercises 1–3, use the photo of the eagle ray.**

1. To prove that $\angle PQT \cong \angle RQT$, which triangles might you prove to be congruent?

2. If you know that the opposite sides of figure *PQRS* are parallel, can you prove that $\triangle PQT \cong \triangle RST$? Explain.

Skill Check ✓   3. The statements listed below are not in order. Use the photo to order them as statements in a two-column proof. Write a reason for each statement.

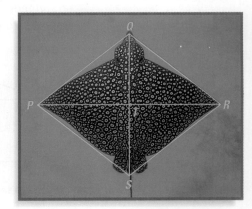

   GIVEN ▶ $\overline{QS} \perp \overline{RP}, \overline{PT} \cong \overline{RT}$

   PROVE ▶ $\overline{PS} \cong \overline{RS}$

   A. $\overline{QS} \perp \overline{RP}$ **B.** $\triangle PTS \cong \triangle RTS$ **C.** $\angle PTS \cong \angle RTS$

   D. $\overline{PS} \cong \overline{RS}$ **E.** $\overline{PT} \cong \overline{RT}$ **F.** $\overline{TS} \cong \overline{TS}$

   G. $\angle PTS$ and $\angle RTS$ are right angles.

PRACTICE AND APPLICATIONS

STUDENT HELP

▶ **Extra Practice**
to help you master
skills is on p. 810.

🌐 **STAINED GLASS WINDOW** The eight window panes in the diagram are isosceles triangles. The bases of the eight triangles are congruent.

4. Explain how you know that $\triangle NUP \cong \triangle PUQ$.

5. Explain how you know that $\triangle NUP \cong \triangle QUR$.

6. Do you have enough information to prove that all the triangles are congruent? Explain.

7. Explain how you know that $\angle UNP \cong \angle UPQ$.

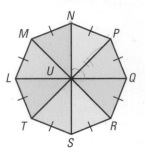

▶ **DEVELOPING PROOF** State which postulate or theorem you can use to prove that the triangles are congruent. Then explain how proving that the triangles are congruent proves the given statement.

8. **PROVE** ▶ $\overline{ML} \cong \overline{QL}$ 9. **PROVE** ▶ $\angle STV \cong \angle UVT$ 10. **PROVE** ▶ $KL = NL$

STUDENT HELP

▶ **HOMEWORK HELP**
Example 1: Exs. 4–14,
        17, 18
Example 2: Exs. 14, 17, 18
Example 3: Exs. 15, 16
Example 4: Exs. 19–21

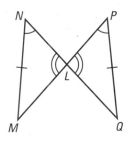

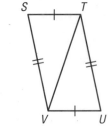

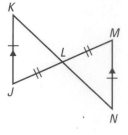

CAT'S CRADLE Use the diagram of the string game Cat's Cradle and the information given below.

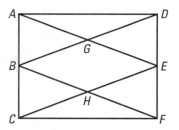

GIVEN ▶ $\triangle EDA \cong \triangle BCF$
$\triangle AGD \cong \triangle FHC$
$\triangle BFC \cong \triangle ECF$

11. PROVE ▶ $\overline{GD} \cong \overline{HC}$

12. PROVE ▶ $\angle CBH \cong \angle FEH$

13. PROVE ▶ $\overline{AE} \cong \overline{FB}$

14. ◉ **DEVELOPING PROOF** Complete the proof that $\angle BAC \cong \angle DBE$.

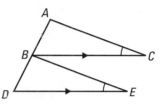

GIVEN ▶ B is the midpoint of $\overline{AD}$,
$\angle C \cong \angle E$, $\overline{BC} \parallel \overline{DE}$

PROVE ▶ $\angle BAC \cong \angle DBE$

Statements	Reasons
1. B is the midpoint of $\overline{AD}$.	1. Given
2. $\overline{AB} \cong \overline{BD}$	2. ___?___
3. $\angle C \cong \angle E$	3. Given
4. $\overline{BC} \parallel \overline{DE}$	4. Given
5. $\angle EDB \cong \angle CBA$	5. ___?___
6. ___?___	6. AAS Congruence Theorem
7. $\angle BAC \cong \angle DBE$	7. ___?___

15. ◉ **DEVELOPING PROOF** Complete the proof that $\triangle AFB \cong \triangle EFD$.

GIVEN ▶ $\angle 1 \cong \angle 2$
$\angle 3 \cong \angle 4$

PROVE ▶ $\angle AFB \cong \angle EFD$

Statements	Reasons
1. $\angle 1 \cong \angle 2$	1. ___?___
2. $\angle 3 \cong \angle 4$	2. ___?___
3. ___?___	3. Reflexive Property of Congruence
4. $\triangle AFC \cong \triangle EFC$	4. ___?___
5. $\overline{AF} \cong \overline{EF}$	5. ___?___
6. ___?___	6. Vertical Angles Theorem
7. $\triangle AFB \cong \triangle EFD$	7. ___?___

16. 🌐 **BRIDGES** The diagram represents a section of the framework of the Kap Shui Mun Bridge shown in the photo on page 229. Write a two-column proof to show that $\triangle PKJ \cong \triangle QMN$.

GIVEN ▶ L is the midpoint of $\overline{JN}$, $\overline{PJ} \cong \overline{QN}$, $\overline{PL} \cong \overline{QL}$, $\angle PKJ$ and $\angle QMN$ are right angles.

PROVE ▶ $\triangle PKJ \cong \triangle QMN$

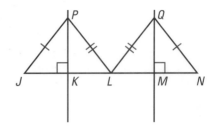

▶ **PROOF** Write a two-column proof or a paragraph proof.

17. **GIVEN** ▶ $\overline{UR} \parallel \overline{ST}$, $\angle R$ and $\angle T$ are right angles.

PROVE ▶ $\angle RSU \cong \angle TUS$

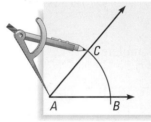

18. **GIVEN** ▶ $\overline{BD} \perp \overline{AC}$, $\overline{BD}$ bisects $\overline{AC}$.

PROVE ▶ $\angle ABD$ and $\angle BCD$ are complementary angles.

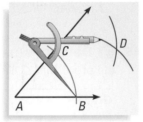

19. 📐 **PROVING A CONSTRUCTION** The diagrams below summarize the construction used to bisect $\angle A$. By construction, you can assume that $\overline{AB} \cong \overline{AC}$ and $\overline{BD} \cong \overline{CD}$. Write a proof to verify that $\overrightarrow{AD}$ bisects $\angle A$.

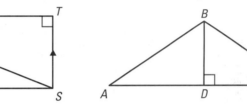

❶ First draw an arc with center A. Label the points where the arc intersects the sides of the angle points B and C.

❷ Draw an arc with center C. Using the same compass setting, draw an arc with center B. Label the intersection point D.

❸ Draw $\overrightarrow{AD}$. $\angle CAD \cong \angle BAD$

📐 **PROVING A CONSTRUCTION** Use a straightedge and a compass to perform the construction. Label the important points of your construction. Then write a flow proof to verify the results.

20. Bisect an obtuse angle.

21. Copy an obtuse angle.

22. MULTIPLE CHOICE Suppose $\overline{PQ} \parallel \overline{RS}$. You want to prove that $\overline{PR} \cong \overline{SQ}$. Which of the reasons below would *not* appear in your two-column proof?

    Ⓐ SAS Congruence Postulate

    Ⓑ Reflexive Property of Congruence

    Ⓒ AAS Congruence Theorem

    Ⓓ Right Angle Congruence Theorem

    Ⓔ Alternate Interior Angles Theorem

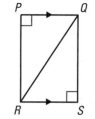

23. MULTIPLE CHOICE Which statement correctly describes the congruence of the triangles in the diagram in Exercise 22?

    Ⓐ $\triangle SRQ \cong \triangle RQP$ Ⓑ $\triangle PRQ \cong \triangle SRQ$

    Ⓒ $\triangle QRS \cong \triangle PQR$ Ⓓ $\triangle SRQ \cong \triangle PQR$

★ Challenge

24. PROVING A CONSTRUCTION Use a straightedge and a compass to bisect a segment. (For help with this construction, look back at page 34.) Then write a proof to show that the construction is valid.

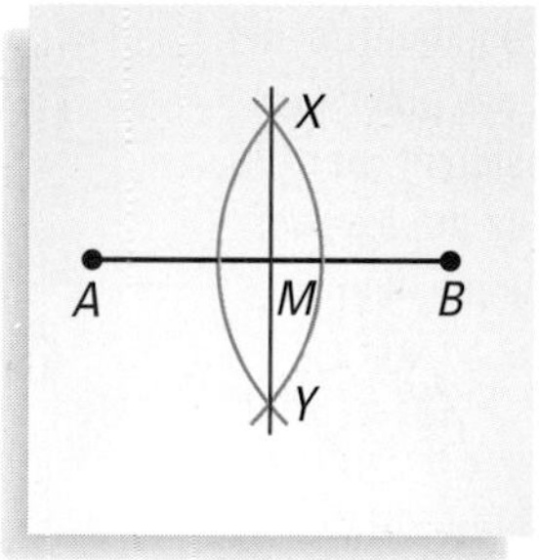

EXTRA CHALLENGE
www.mcdougallittell.com

MIXED REVIEW

FINDING PERIMETER, CIRCUMFERENCE, AND AREA Find the perimeter (or circumference) and area of the figure. (Where necessary, use $\pi \approx 3.14$.) (Review 1.7)

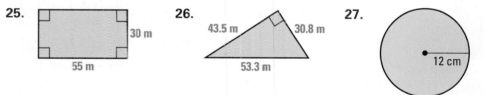

25.   30 m   55 m

26.   43.5 m   30.8 m   53.3 m

27.   12 cm

SOLVING EQUATIONS Solve the equation and state a reason for each step. (Review 2.4)

28. $x - 2 = 10$ **29.** $x + 11 = 21$ **30.** $9x + 2 = 29$

31. $8x + 13 = 3x + 38$ **32.** $3(x - 1) = 16$ **33.** $6(2x - 1) + 15 = 69$

IDENTIFYING PARTS OF TRIANGLES Classify the triangle by its angles and by its sides. Identify the legs and the hypotenuse of any right triangles. Identify the legs and the base of any isosceles triangles. (Review 4.1 for 4.6)

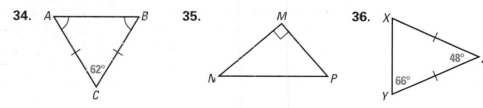

34. A B $62°$ C

35. M N P

36. X $48°$ Z $66°$ Y

4.6 Isosceles, Equilateral, and Right Triangles

What you should learn

GOAL 1 Use properties of isosceles and equilateral triangles.

GOAL 2 Use properties of right triangles.

Why you should learn it

▼ Isosceles, equilateral, and right triangles are commonly used in the design of **real-life** objects, such as the exterior structure of the building in **Exs. 29–32**.

GOAL 1 USING PROPERTIES OF ISOSCELES TRIANGLES

In Lesson 4.1, you learned that a triangle is isosceles if it has at least two congruent sides. If it has exactly two congruent sides, then they are the legs of the triangle and the noncongruent side is the base. The two angles adjacent to the base are the **base angles**. The angle opposite the base is the **vertex angle**.

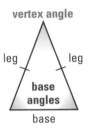

▶ **ACTIVITY**

Developing Concepts

Investigating Isosceles Triangles

1. Use a straightedge and a compass to construct an acute isosceles triangle. Then fold the triangle along a line that bisects the vertex angle, as shown.

2. Repeat the procedure for an obtuse isosceles triangle.

3. What observations can you make about the base angles of an isosceles triangle? Write your observations as a conjecture.

In the activity, you may have discovered the *Base Angles Theorem*, which is proved in Example 1. The converse of this theorem is also true. You are asked to prove the converse in Exercise 26.

THEOREMS

THEOREM 4.6 *Base Angles Theorem*

If two sides of a triangle are congruent, then the angles opposite them are congruent.

If $\overline{AB} \cong \overline{AC}$, then $\angle B \cong \angle C$.

THEOREM 4.7 *Converse of the Base Angles Theorem*

If two angles of a triangle are congruent, then the sides opposite them are congruent.

If $\angle B \cong \angle C$, then $\overline{AB} \cong \overline{AC}$.

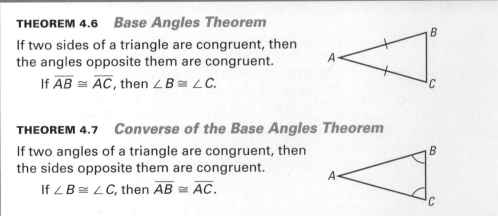

EXAMPLE 1 *Proof of the Base Angles Theorem*

Use the diagram of △*ABC* to prove
the Base Angles Theorem.

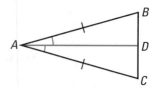

GIVEN ▶ △*ABC*, $\overline{AB} \cong \overline{AC}$

PROVE ▶ $\angle B \cong \angle C$

Paragraph Proof Draw the bisector of $\angle CAB$. By construction, $\angle CAD \cong \angle BAD$.
You are given that $\overline{AB} \cong \overline{AC}$. Also, $\overline{DA} \cong \overline{DA}$ by the Reflexive Property of
Congruence. Use the SAS Congruence Postulate to conclude that △*ADB* ≅ △*ADC*.
Because corresponding parts of congruent triangles are congruent, it follows that
$\angle B \cong \angle C$.

· · · · · · · · · ·

Recall that an *equilateral* triangle is a special type of isosceles triangle. The
corollaries below state that a triangle is equilateral if and only if it is equiangular.

COROLLARIES

COROLLARY TO THEOREM 4.6

If a triangle is equilateral, then it is equiangular.

COROLLARY TO THEOREM 4.7

If a triangle is equiangular, then it is equilateral.

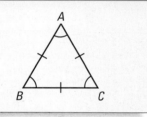

EXAMPLE 2 *Using Equilateral and Isosceles Triangles*

a. Find the value of *x*.

b. Find the value of *y*.

SOLUTION

a. Notice that *x* represents the measure of an angle of an equilateral triangle.
From the corollary above, this triangle is also equiangular.

$3x° = 180°$ **Apply the Triangle Sum Theorem.**

$x = 60$ **Solve for x.**

b. Notice that *y* represents the measure of a
base angle of an isosceles triangle. From
the Base Angles Theorem, the other base
angle has the same measure. The vertex angle
forms a linear pair with a 60° angle, so its
measure is 120°.

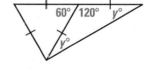

$120° + 2y° = 180°$ **Apply the Triangle Sum Theorem.**

$y = 30$ **Solve for y.**

You have learned four ways to prove that triangles are congruent.

- Side-Side-Side (SSS) Congruence Postulate (p. 212)
- Side-Angle-Side (SAS) Congruence Postulate (p. 213)
- Angle-Side-Angle (ASA) Congruence Postulate (p. 220)
- Angle-Angle-Side (AAS) Congruence Theorem (p. 220)

The Hypotenuse-Leg Congruence Theorem below can be used to prove that two *right* triangles are congruent. A proof of this theorem appears on page 837.

THEOREM

THEOREM 4.8 *Hypotenuse-Leg (HL) Congruence Theorem*

If the hypotenuse and a leg of a right triangle are congruent to the hypotenuse and a leg of a second right triangle, then the two triangles are congruent.

If $\overline{BC} \cong \overline{EF}$ and $\overline{AC} \cong \overline{DF}$, then $\triangle ABC \cong \triangle DEF$.

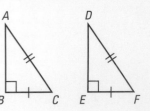

EXAMPLE 3 *Proving Right Triangles Congruent*

Proof

The television antenna is perpendicular to the plane containing the points B, C, D, and E. Each of the stays running from the top of the antenna to B, C, and D uses the same length of cable. Prove that $\triangle AEB$, $\triangle AEC$, and $\triangle AED$ are congruent.

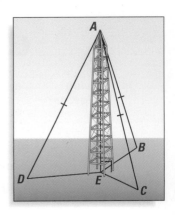

GIVEN ▶ $\overline{AE} \perp \overline{EB}, \overline{AE} \perp \overline{EC},$
$\overline{AE} \perp \overline{ED}, \overline{AB} \cong \overline{AC} \cong \overline{AD}$

PROVE ▶ $\triangle AEB \cong \triangle AEC \cong \triangle AED$

SOLUTION

Paragraph Proof You are given that $\overline{AE} \perp \overline{EB}$ and $\overline{AE} \perp \overline{EC}$, which implies that $\angle AEB$ and $\angle AEC$ are right angles. By definition, $\triangle AEB$ and $\triangle AEC$ are right triangles. You are given that the hypotenuses of these two triangles, $\overline{AB}$ and $\overline{AC}$, are congruent. Also, $\overline{AE}$ is a leg for both triangles, and $\overline{AE} \cong \overline{AE}$ by the Reflexive Property of Congruence. Thus, by the Hypotenuse-Leg Congruence Theorem, $\triangle AEB \cong \triangle AEC$.

▶ Similar reasoning can be used to prove that $\triangle AEC \cong \triangle AED$. So, by the Transitive Property of Congruent Triangles, $\triangle AEB \cong \triangle AEC \cong \triangle AED$.

STUDENT HELP

Study Tip
Before you use the HL Congruence Theorem in a proof, you need to prove that the triangles are right triangles.

GUIDED PRACTICE

Vocabulary Check ✓ 1. Describe the meaning of *equilateral* and *equiangular*.

Concept Check ✓ **Find the unknown measure(s). Tell what theorems you used.**

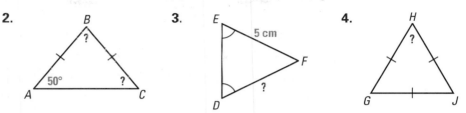

2.

3.

5 cm

4.

Skill Check ✓ **Determine whether you are given enough information to prove that the triangles are congruent. Explain your answer.**

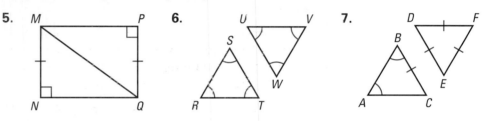

5.

6.

7.

PRACTICE AND APPLICATIONS

STUDENT HELP

▸ **Extra Practice**
to help you master
skills is on p. 810.

xy USING ALGEBRA Solve for *x* and *y*.

8.

9.

10.

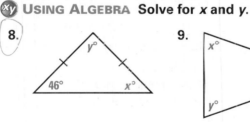

46°

y°

x°

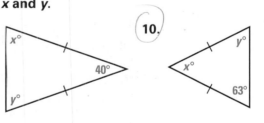

LOGICAL REASONING Decide whether enough information is given to prove that the triangles are congruent. Explain your answer.

11.

12.

13.

STUDENT HELP

▸ **HOMEWORK HELP**
Example 1: Exs. 26–28
Example 2: Exs. 8–10,
17–25
Example 3: Exs. 31, 33,
34, 39

14.

15.

16.

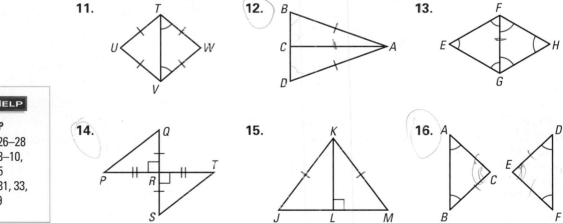

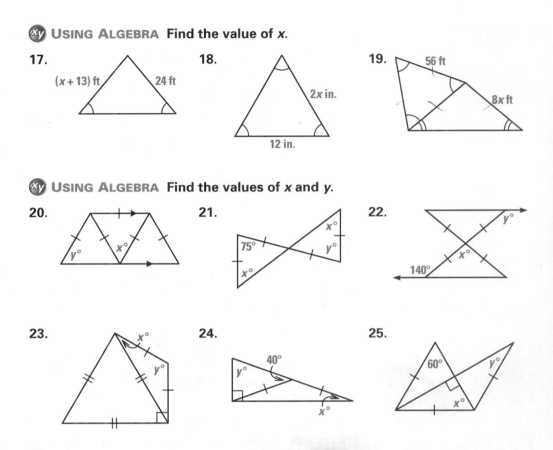

USING ALGEBRA Find the value of *x*.

17.
(*x* + 13) ft   24 ft

18.
2*x* in.

12 in.

19.
56 ft

8*x* ft

USING ALGEBRA Find the values of *x* and *y*.

20.
y°   *x*°

21.
75°   *x*°

y°

x°

22.
y°

x°

140°

23.
x°

y°

24.
40°

y°

x°

25.
60°

y°

x°

▶ **PROOF In Exercises 26–28, use the diagrams that accompany the theorems on pages 236 and 237.**

26. The Converse of the Base Angles Theorem on page 236 states, "If two angles of a triangle are congruent, then the sides opposite them are congruent." Write a proof of this theorem.

27. The Corollary to Theorem 4.6 on page 237 states, "If a triangle is equilateral, then it is equiangular." Write a proof of this corollary.

28. The Corollary to Theorem 4.7 on page 237 states, "If a triangle is equiangular, then it is equilateral." Write a proof of this corollary.

🌐 **ARCHITECTURE The diagram represents part of the exterior of the building in the photograph. In the diagram, △*ABD* and △*CBD* are congruent equilateral triangles.**

29. Explain why △*ABC* is isosceles.

30. Explain why ∠*BAE* ≅ ∠*BCE*.

31. ▶ **PROOF** Prove that △*ABE* and △*CBE* are congruent right triangles.

32. Find the measure of ∠*BAE*.

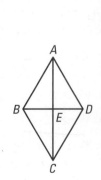

PROOF Write a two-column proof or a paragraph proof.

33. GIVEN ▶ D is the midpoint of $\overline{CE}$, $\angle BCD$ and $\angle FED$ are right angles, and $\overline{BD} \cong \overline{FD}$.

PROVE ▶ $\triangle BCD \cong \triangle FED$

34. GIVEN ▶ $\overline{VW} \parallel \overline{ZY}$, $\overline{UV} \cong \overline{XW}$, $\overline{UZ} \cong \overline{XY}$, $\overline{VW} \perp \overline{VZ}$, $\overline{VW} \perp \overline{WY}$

PROVE ▶ $\angle U \cong \angle X$

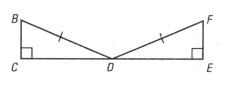
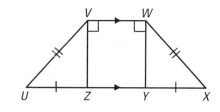

🎨 **COLOR WHEEL** Artists use a color wheel to show relationships between colors. The 12 triangles in the diagram are isosceles triangles with congruent vertex angles.

35. Complementary colors lie directly opposite each other on the color wheel. Explain how you know that the yellow triangle is congruent to the purple triangle.

36. The measure of the vertex angle of the yellow triangle is 30°. Find the measures of the base angles.

37. Trace the color wheel. Then form a triangle whose vertices are the midpoints of the bases of the red, yellow, and blue triangles. (These colors are the *primary colors*.) What type of triangle is this?

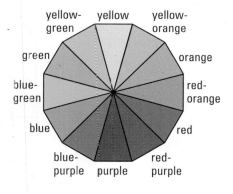

38. Form other triangles that are congruent to the triangle in Exercise 37. The colors of the vertices are called *triads*. What are the possible triads?

🌐 **PHYSICS** Use the information below.
When a light ray from an object meets a mirror, it is reflected back to your eye. For example, in the diagram, a light ray from point C is reflected at point D and travels back to point A. The *law of reflection* states that the angle of incidence $\angle CDB$ is equal to the angle of reflection $\angle ADB$.

39. GIVEN ▶ $\angle CDB \cong \angle ADB$
$\overline{DB} \perp \overline{AC}$

PROVE ▶ $\triangle ABD \cong \triangle CBD$

40. Verify that $\triangle ACD$ is isosceles.

41. Does moving away from the mirror have any effect on the amount of his or her reflection the person sees?

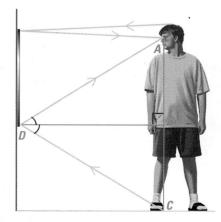

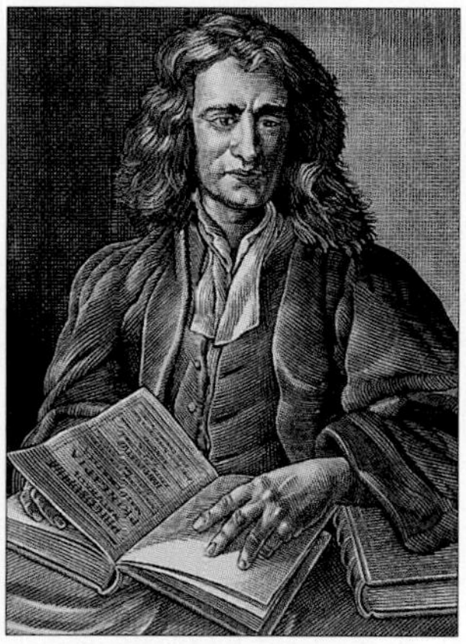

For a person to see his or her complete reflection, the mirror must be at least one half the person's height.

4.6 *Isosceles, Equilateral, and Right Triangles*

QUANTITATIVE COMPARISON In Exercises 42 and 43, refer to the figures below. Choose the statement that is true about the given values.

(A) The value in column A is greater.

(B) The value in column B is greater.

(C) The two values are equal.

(D) The relationship cannot be determined from the given information.

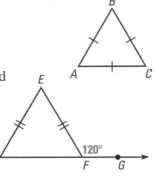

	Column A	Column B
42.	$\angle D$	$\angle EFD$
43.	$\angle B$	$\angle EFD$

★ **Challenge**

44. 🧩 **LOGICAL REASONING** A *regular hexagon* has six congruent sides and six congruent interior angles. It can be divided into six equilateral triangles. Explain how the series of diagrams below suggests a proof that when a triangle is formed by connecting every other vertex of a regular hexagon, the result is an equilateral triangle.

Regular hexagon

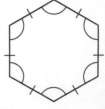

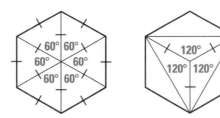

EXTRA CHALLENGE

www.mcdougallittell.com

MIXED REVIEW

CONGRUENCE Use the Distance Formula to decide whether $\overline{AB} \cong \overline{AC}$. (Review 1.3 for 4.7)

45. $A(0, -4)$
$B(5, 8)$
$C(-12, 1)$

46. $A(0, 0)$
$B(-6, -10)$
$C(6, 10)$

47. $A(1, -1)$
$B(-8, 7)$
$C(8, 7)$

FINDING THE MIDPOINT Find the coordinates of the midpoint of a segment with the given endpoints. (Review 1.5 for 4.7)

48. $C(4, 9)$, $D(10, 7)$

49. $G(0, 11)$, $H(8, -3)$

50. $L(1, 7)$, $M(-5, -5)$

51. $C(-2, 3)$, $D(5, 6)$

52. $G(0, -13)$, $H(2, -1)$

53. $L(-3, -5)$, $M(0, -20)$

WRITING EQUATIONS Line *j* is perpendicular to the line with the given equation and line *j* passes through point *P*. Write an equation of line *j*. (Review 3.7)

54. $y = -3x - 4$; $P(1, 1)$

55. $y = x - 7$; $P(0, 0)$

56. $y = -\dfrac{10}{9}x + 3$; $P(5, -12)$

57. $y = \dfrac{2}{3}x + 4$; $P(-3, 4)$

4.7

Triangles and Coordinate Proof

What you should learn

GOAL 1 Place geometric figures in a coordinate plane.

GOAL 2 Write a coordinate proof.

Why you should learn it

Sometimes a coordinate proof is the most efficient way to prove a statement.

GOAL 1 PLACING FIGURES IN A COORDINATE PLANE

So far, you have studied two-column proofs, paragraph proofs, and flow proofs. A **coordinate proof** involves placing geometric figures in a coordinate plane. Then you can use the Distance Formula and the Midpoint Formula, as well as postulates and theorems, to prove statements about the figures.

> **ACTIVITY**
> Developing
> Concepts
> ### Placing Figures in a Coordinate Plane

1. Draw a right triangle with legs of 3 units and 4 units on a piece of grid paper. Cut out the triangle.

2. Use another piece of grid paper to draw a coordinate plane.

3. Sketch different ways that the triangle can be placed on the coordinate plane. Which of the ways that you placed the triangle is best for finding the length of the hypotenuse?

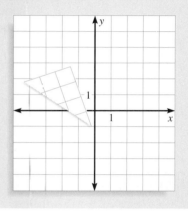

EXAMPLE 1 *Placing a Rectangle in a Coordinate Plane*

STUDENT HELP

INTERNET
HOMEWORK HELP
Visit our Web site
www.mcdougallittell.com
for extra examples.

Place a 2-unit by 6-unit rectangle in a coordinate plane.

SOLUTION

Choose a placement that makes finding distances easy. Here are two possible placements.

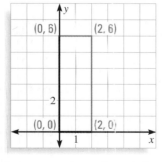

One vertex is at the origin, and three of the vertices have at least one coordinate that is 0.

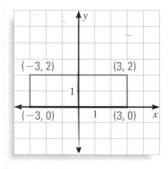

One side is centered at the origin, and the *x*-coordinates are opposites.

Once a figure has been placed in a coordinate plane, you can use the Distance Formula or the Midpoint Formula to measure distances or locate points.

Using Algebra

EXAMPLE 2   *Using the Distance Formula*

A right triangle has legs of 5 units and 12 units. Place the triangle in a coordinate plane. Label the coordinates of the vertices and find the length of the hypotenuse.

SOLUTION

One possible placement is shown. Notice that one leg is vertical and the other leg is horizontal, which assures that the legs meet at right angles. Points on the same vertical segment have the same *x*-coordinate, and points on the same horizontal segment have the same *y*-coordinate.

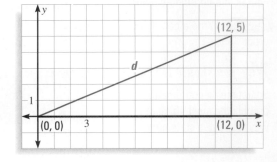

You can use the Distance Formula to find the length of the hypotenuse.

$$d = \sqrt{(x_2 - x_1)^2 + (y_2 - y_1)^2} \qquad \textbf{Distance Formula}$$

$$= \sqrt{(12 - 0)^2 + (5 - 0)^2} \qquad \textbf{Substitute.}$$

$$= \sqrt{169} \qquad \textbf{Simplify.}$$

$$= 13 \qquad \textbf{Evaluate square root.}$$

EXAMPLE 3   *Using the Midpoint Formula*

In the diagram, $\triangle MLO \cong \triangle KLO$.

Find the coordinates of point *L*.

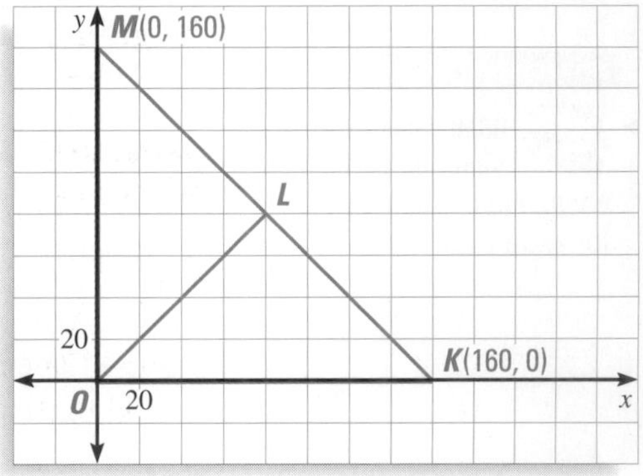

SOLUTION

Because the triangles are congruent, it follows that $\overline{ML} \cong \overline{KL}$. So, point *L* must be the midpoint of $\overline{MK}$. This means you can use the Midpoint Formula to find the coordinates of point *L*.

$$L(x, y) = \left(\frac{x_1 + x_2}{2}, \frac{y_1 + y_2}{2} \right) \qquad \textbf{Midpoint Formula}$$

$$= \left(\frac{160 + 0}{2}, \frac{0 + 160}{2} \right) \qquad \textbf{Substitute.}$$

$$= (80, 80) \qquad \textbf{Simplify.}$$

▶ The coordinates of *L* are (80, 80).

Once a figure is placed in a coordinate plane, you may be able to prove statements about the figure.

Proof

EXAMPLE 4 *Writing a Plan for a Coordinate Proof*

Write a plan to prove that $\overrightarrow{SO}$ bisects $\angle PSR$.

GIVEN ▶ Coordinates of vertices of $\triangle POS$ and $\triangle ROS$

PROVE ▶ $\overrightarrow{SO}$ bisects $\angle PSR$

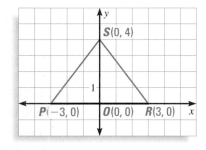

SOLUTION

Plan for Proof Use the Distance Formula to find the side lengths of $\triangle POS$ and $\triangle ROS$. Then use the SSS Congruence Postulate to show that $\triangle POS \cong \triangle ROS$. Finally, use the fact that corresponding parts of congruent triangles are congruent to conclude that $\angle PSO \cong \angle RSO$, which implies that $\overrightarrow{SO}$ bisects $\angle PSR$.

· · · · · · · · · ·

The coordinate proof in Example 4 applies to a specific triangle. When you want to prove a statement about a more general set of figures, it is helpful to use variables as coordinates.

For instance, you can use variable coordinates to duplicate the proof in Example 4. Once this is done, you can conclude that $\overrightarrow{SO}$ bisects $\angle PSR$ for *any* triangle whose coordinates fit the given pattern.

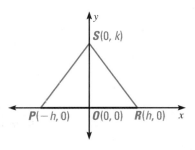

EXAMPLE 5 *Using Variables as Coordinates*

Right $\triangle OBC$ has leg lengths of h units and k units. You can find the coordinates of points B and C by considering how the triangle is placed in the coordinate plane.

Point B is h units horizontally from the origin, so its coordinates are $(h, 0)$. Point C is h units horizontally from the origin and k units vertically from the origin, so its coordinates are (h, k).

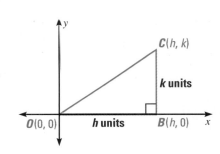

STUDENT HELP

HOMEWORK HELP
Visit our Web site
www.mcdougallittell.com
for extra examples.

You can use the Distance Formula to find the length of the hypotenuse $\overline{OC}$.

$$OC = \sqrt{(h - 0)^2 + (k - 0)^2} = \sqrt{h^2 + k^2}$$

EXAMPLE 6 *Writing a Coordinate Proof*

Proof   **GIVEN** ▸ Coordinates of figure *OTUV*

PROVE ▸ $\triangle OTU \cong \triangle UVO$

SOLUTION

▸ **COORDINATE PROOF** Segments $\overline{OV}$ and $\overline{UT}$ have the same length.

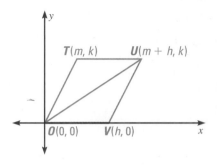

$$OV = \sqrt{(h-0)^2 + (0-0)^2} = h$$

$$UT = \sqrt{(m+h-m)^2 + (k-k)^2} = h$$

Horizontal segments $\overline{UT}$ and $\overline{OV}$ each have a slope of 0, which implies that they are parallel. Segment $\overline{OU}$ intersects $\overline{UT}$ and $\overline{OV}$ to form congruent alternate interior angles $\angle TUO$ and $\angle VOU$. Because $\overline{OU} \cong \overline{OU}$, you can apply the SAS Congruence Postulate to conclude that $\triangle OTU \cong \triangle UVO$.

GUIDED PRACTICE

Vocabulary Check ✔   **1.** Prior to this section, you have studied two-column proofs, paragraph proofs, and flow proofs. How is a *coordinate proof* different from these other types of proof? How is it the same?

Concept Check ✔   **2.** Two different ways to place the same right triangle in a coordinate plane are shown. Which placement is more convenient for finding the side lengths? Explain your thinking. Then sketch a third placement that also makes it convenient to find the side lengths.

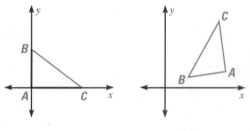

Skill Check ✔   **3.** A right triangle with legs of 7 units and 4 units has one vertex at $(0, 0)$ and another at $(0, 7)$. Give possible coordinates of the third vertex.

▸ **DEVELOPING PROOF** Describe a plan for the proof.

4. GIVEN ▸ $\overrightarrow{GJ}$ bisects $\angle OGH$.

  PROVE ▸ $\triangle GJO \cong \triangle GJH$

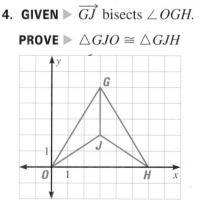

5. GIVEN ▸ Coordinates of vertices of $\triangle ABC$

  PROVE ▸ $\triangle ABC$ is isosceles.

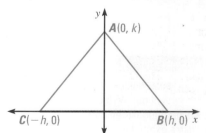

PRACTICE AND APPLICATIONS

STUDENT HELP

Extra Practice
to help you master skills is on p. 810.

PLACING FIGURES IN A COORDINATE PLANE **Place the figure in a coordinate plane. Label the vertices and give the coordinates of each vertex.**

6. A 5-unit by 8-unit rectangle with one vertex at (0, 0)

7. An 8-unit by 6-unit rectangle with one vertex at $(0, -4)$

8. A square with side length s and one vertex at $(s, 0)$

CHOOSING A GOOD PLACEMENT **Place the figure in a coordinate plane. Label the vertices and give the coordinates of each vertex. Explain the advantages of your placement.**

9. A right triangle with legs of 3 units and 8 units

10. An isosceles right triangle with legs of 20 units

11. A rectangle with length h and width k

FINDING AND USING COORDINATES **In the diagram, $\triangle ABC$ is isosceles. Its base is 60 units and its height is 50 units.**

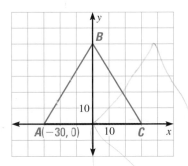

12. Give the coordinates of points B and C.

13. Find the length of a leg of $\triangle ABC$. Round your answer to the nearest hundredth.

USING THE DISTANCE FORMULA **Place the figure in a coordinate plane and find the given information.**

14. A right triangle with legs of 7 and 9 units; find the length of the hypotenuse.

15. A rectangle with length 5 units and width 4 units; find the length of a diagonal.

16. An isosceles right triangle with legs of 3 units; find the length of the hypotenuse.

17. A 3-unit by 3-unit square; find the length of a diagonal.

USING THE MIDPOINT FORMULA **Use the given information and diagram to find the coordinates of H.**

18. $\triangle FOH \cong \triangle FJH$

19. $\triangle OCH \cong \triangle HNM$

STUDENT HELP

HOMEWORK HELP
Example 1: Exs. 6–11
Example 2: Exs. 12–17
Example 3: Exs. 18, 19
Example 4: Exs. 20, 21
Example 5: Exs. 22–25
Example 6: Exs. 26, 27

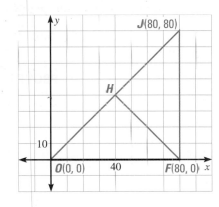

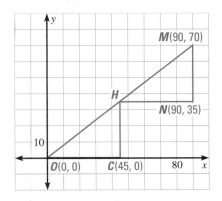

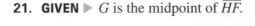 **DEVELOPING PROOF** Write a plan for a proof.

20. GIVEN ▶ $\overline{OS} \perp \overline{RT}$

PROVE ▶ $\overrightarrow{OS}$ bisects $\angle TOR$.

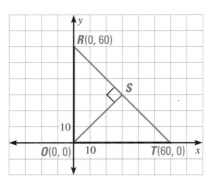

21. GIVEN ▶ G is the midpoint of $\overline{HF}$.

PROVE ▶ $\triangle GHJ \cong \triangle GFO$

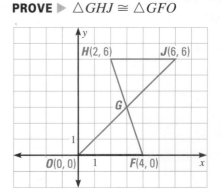

USING VARIABLES AS COORDINATES Find the coordinates of any unlabeled points. Then find the requested information.

22. Find MP.

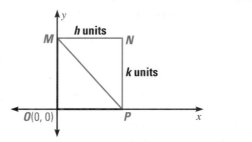

23. Find OE.

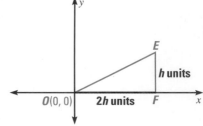

24. Find ON and MN.

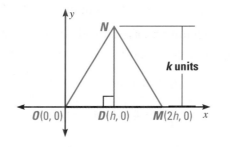

25. Find OT.

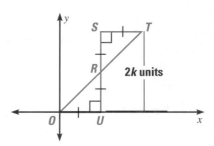

COORDINATE PROOF Write a coordinate proof.

26. GIVEN ▶ Coordinates of $\triangle NPO$ and $\triangle NMO$

PROVE ▶ $\triangle NPO \cong \triangle NMO$

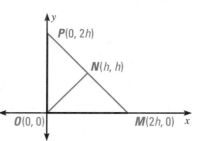

27. GIVEN ▶ Coordinates of $\triangle OBC$ and $\triangle EDC$

PROVE ▶ $\triangle OBC \cong \triangle EDC$

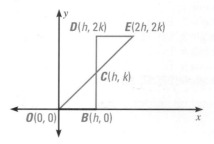

28. 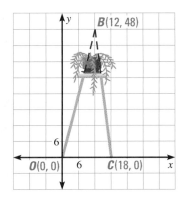 **PLANT STAND** You buy a tall, three-legged plant stand. When you place a plant on the stand, the stand appears to be unstable under the weight of the plant. The diagram at the right shows a coordinate plane superimposed on one pair of the plant stand's legs. The legs are extended to form $\triangle OBC$. Is $\triangle OBC$ an isosceles triangle? Explain why the plant stand may be unstable.

△ **TECHNOLOGY** **Use geometry software for Exercises 29–31. Follow the steps below to construct** $\triangle ABC$.

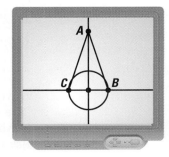

- Create a pair of axes. Construct point A on the y-axis so that the y-coordinate is positive. Construct point B on the x-axis.

- Construct a circle with a center at the origin that contains point B. Label the other point where the circle intersects the x-axis C.

- Connect points A, B, and C to form $\triangle ABC$. Find the coordinates of each vertex.

29. What type of triangle does $\triangle ABC$ appear to be? Does your answer change if you drag point A? If you drag point B?

30. Measure and compare AB and AC. What happens to these lengths as you drag point A? What happens as you drag point B?

31. Look back at the proof described in Exercise 5 on page 246. How does that proof help explain your answers to Exercises 29 and 30?

Test Preparation

32. MULTIPLE CHOICE A square with side length 4 has one vertex at $(0, 2)$. Which of the points below *could* be a vertex of the square?

(A) $(0, -2)$ (B) $(2, -2)$ (C) $(0, 0)$ (D) $(2, 2)$

33. MULTIPLE CHOICE A rectangle with side lengths $2h$ and k has one vertex at $(-h, k)$. Which of the points below *could not* be a vertex of the rectangle?

(A) $(0, k)$ (B) $(-h, 0)$ (C) (h, k) (D) $(h, 0)$

★ **Challenge**

34. ▶ **COORDINATE PROOF** Use the diagram and the given information to write a proof.

GIVEN ▶ Coordinates of $\triangle DEA$, H is the midpoint of $\overline{DA}$, G is the midpoint of $\overline{EA}$.

PROVE ▶ $\overline{DG} \cong \overline{EH}$

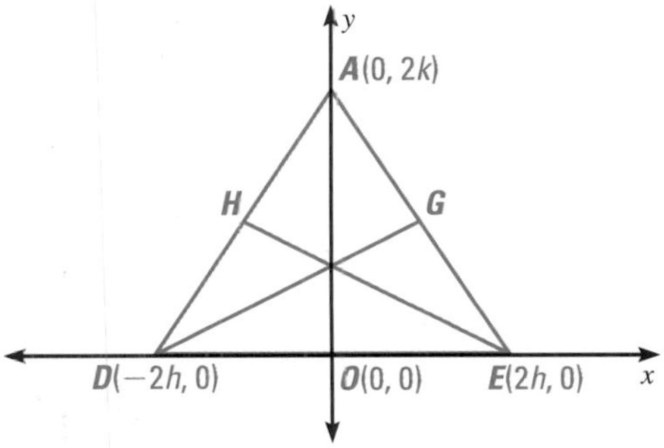

(xy) **USING ALGEBRA** In the diagram, $\overrightarrow{GR}$ bisects
∠CGF. (Review 1.5 for 5.1)

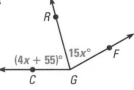

35. Find the value of x.

36. Find $m\angle CGF$.

PERPENDICULAR LINES AND SEGMENT BISECTORS Use the diagram to
determine whether the statement is *true* or *false*. (Review 1.5, 2.2 for 5.1)

37. $\overleftrightarrow{PQ}$ is perpendicular to $\overleftrightarrow{LN}$.

38. Points L, Q, and N are collinear.

39. $\overleftrightarrow{PQ}$ bisects $\overline{LN}$.

40. ∠LMQ and ∠PMN are supplementary.

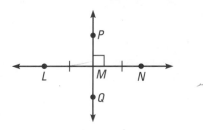

WRITING STATEMENTS Let p be "two triangles are congruent" and let q be
"the corresponding angles of the triangles are congruent." Write the
symbolic statement in words. Decide whether the statement is true.
(Review 2.3)

41. $p \rightarrow q$ **42.** $q \rightarrow p$ **43.** $\sim p \rightarrow \sim q$

QUIZ 3

Self-Test for Lessons 4.5–4.7

▶ **PROOF** Write a two-column proof or a paragraph proof.
(Lessons 4.5 and 4.6)

1. GIVEN ▶ $\overline{DF} \cong \overline{DG}$,
             $\overline{ED} \cong \overline{HD}$

      PROVE ▶ ∠EFD ≅ ∠HGD

2. GIVEN ▶ $\overline{ST} \cong \overline{UT} \cong \overline{VU}$,
             $\overline{SU} \parallel \overline{TV}$

      PROVE ▶ △STU ≅ △TUV

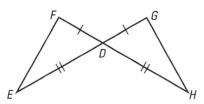

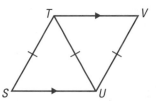

3. ▶ **COORDINATE PROOF** Write a plan
for a coordinate proof. (Lesson 4.7)

      GIVEN ▶ Coordinates of vertices of
                △OPM and △ONM

      PROVE ▶ △OPM and △ONM are
                 congruent isosceles triangles.

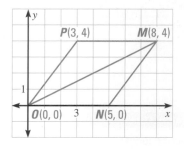

Chapter Summary

WHAT did you learn?

Classify triangles by their sides and angles. **(4.1)**

Find angle measures in triangles. **(4.1)**

Identify congruent figures and corresponding parts. **(4.2)**

Prove that triangles are congruent
- using corresponding sides and angles. **(4.2)**
- using the SSS and SAS Congruence Postulates. **(4.3)**
- using the ASA Congruence Postulate and the AAS Congruence Theorem. **(4.4)**
- using the HL Congruence Theorem. **(4.6)**
- using coordinate geometry. **(4.7)**

Use congruent triangles to plan and write proofs. **(4.5)**

Prove that constructions are valid. **(4.5)**

Use properties of isosceles, equilateral, and right triangles. **(4.6)**

WHY did you learn it?

Lay the foundation for work with triangles.

Find the angle measures in triangular objects, such as a wing deflector. **(p. 200)**

Analyze patterns, such as those made by the folds of an origami kite. **(p. 208)**

Learn to work with congruent triangles.
Explain why triangles are used in structural supports for buildings. **(p. 215)**
Understand how properties of triangles are applied in surveying. **(p. 225)**
Prove that right triangles are congruent.
Plan and write coordinate proofs.

Prove that triangular parts of the framework of a bridge are congruent. **(p. 234)**

Develop understanding of geometric constructions.

Apply a law from physics, the law of reflection. **(p. 241)**

How does Chapter 4 fit into the BIGGER PICTURE of geometry?

The ways you have learned to prove triangles are congruent will be used to prove theorems about *polygons*, as well as in other topics throughout the book. Knowing the properties of triangles will help you solve real-life problems in fields such as art, architecture, and engineering.

STUDY STRATEGY

How did you use your list of theorems?

The list of theorems you made, following the **Study Strategy** on page 192, may resemble this one.

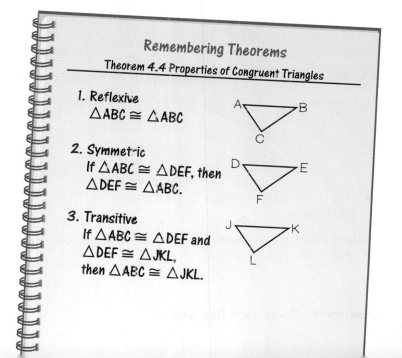

Remembering Theorems
Theorem 4.4 Properties of Congruent Triangles

1. Reflexive
   △ABC ≅ △ABC

2. Symmetric
   If △ABC ≅ △DEF, then
   △DEF ≅ △ABC.

3. Transitive
   If △ABC ≅ △DEF and
   △DEF ≅ △JKL,
   then △ABC ≅ △JKL.

Chapter Review

....

• equilateral triangle, p. 194
• isosceles triangle, p. 194
• scalene triangle, p. 194
• acute triangle, p. 194
• equiangular triangle, p. 194
• right triangle, p. 194

• obtuse triangle, p. 194
• vertex of a triangle, p. 195
• adjacent sides of a triangle, p. 195
• legs of a right triangle, p. 195
• hypotenuse, p. 195

• legs of an isosceles triangle, p. 195
• base of an isosceles triangle, p. 195
• interior angle, p. 196
• exterior angle, p. 196
• corollary, p. 197

• congruent, p. 202
• corresponding angles, p. 202
• corresponding sides, p. 202
• base angles, p. 236
• vertex angle, p. 236
• coordinate proof, p. 243

4.1   **TRIANGLES AND ANGLES**

Examples on pp. 194–197

....

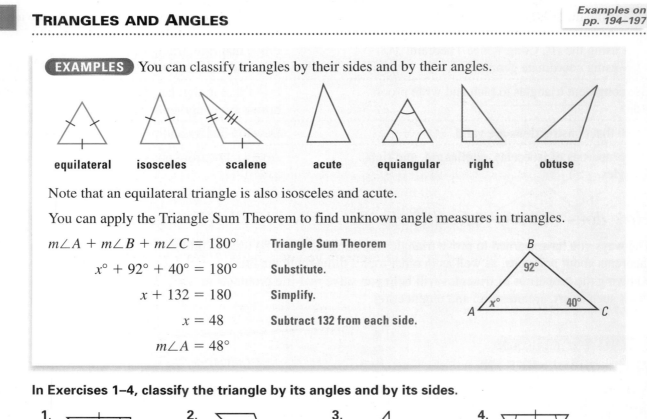

EXAMPLES You can classify triangles by their sides and by their angles.

equilateral   isosceles   scalene   acute   equiangular   right   obtuse

Note that an equilateral triangle is also isosceles and acute.

You can apply the Triangle Sum Theorem to find unknown angle measures in triangles.

$m\angle A + m\angle B + m\angle C = 180°$	Triangle Sum Theorem
$x° + 92° + 40° = 180°$	Substitute.
$x + 132 = 180$	Simplify.
$x = 48$	Subtract 132 from each side.
$m\angle A = 48°$	

In Exercises 1–4, classify the triangle by its angles and by its sides.

1.   2.   3.   4.

5. One acute angle of a right triangle measures 37°. Find the measure of the other acute angle.

6. In $\triangle MNP$, the measure of $\angle M$ is 24°. The measure of $\angle N$ is five times the measure of $\angle P$. Find $m\angle N$ and $m\angle P$.

CONGRUENCE AND TRIANGLES

Examples on pp. 202–205

EXAMPLE When two figures are congruent, their corresponding sides and corresponding angles are congruent. In the diagram, $\triangle ABC \cong \triangle XYZ$.

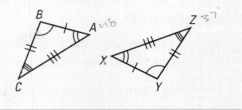

Use the diagram above of △ABC and △XYZ.

7. Identify the congruent corresponding parts of the triangles.

8. Given $m\angle A = 48°$ and $m\angle Z = 37°$, find $m\angle Y$.

PROVING TRIANGLES ARE CONGRUENT: SSS, SAS, ASA, AND AAS

Examples on pp. 212–215, 220–222

EXAMPLES You can prove triangles are congruent using congruence postulates and theorems.

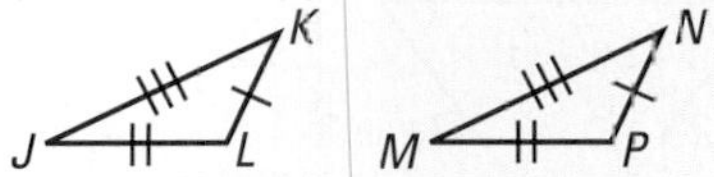

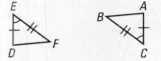

$\overline{JK} \cong \overline{MN}$, $\overline{KL} \cong \overline{NP}$, $\overline{JL} \cong \overline{MP}$, so $\triangle JKL \cong \triangle MNP$ by the SSS Congruence Postulate.

$\overline{DE} \cong \overline{AC}$, $\angle E \cong \angle C$, and $\overline{EF} \cong \overline{CB}$, so $\triangle DEF \cong \triangle ACB$ by the SAS Congruence Postulate.

Decide whether it is possible to prove that the triangles are congruent. If it is possible, tell which postulate or theorem you would use. Explain your reasoning.

9.   10.   11.

USING CONGRUENT TRIANGLES

Examples on pp. 229–231

EXAMPLE You can use congruent triangles to write proofs.

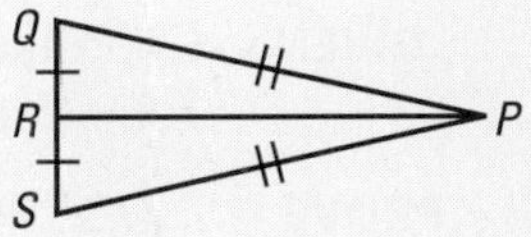

GIVEN ▶ $\overline{PQ} \cong \overline{PS}$, $\overline{RQ} \cong \overline{RS}$

PROVE ▶ $\overline{PR} \perp \overline{QS}$

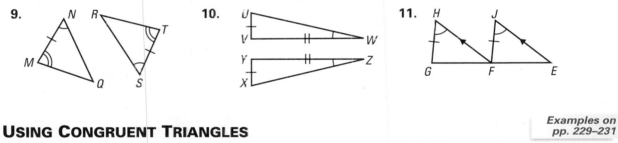

Plan for Proof Use the SSS Congruence Postulate to show that $\triangle PRQ \cong \triangle PRS$. Because corresponding parts of congruent triangles are congruent, you can conclude that $\angle PRQ \cong \angle PRS$. These angles form a linear pair, so $\overrightarrow{PR} \perp \overline{QS}$.

SURVEYING You want to determine the width of a river beside a camp. You place stakes so that $\overline{MN} \perp \overline{NP}$, $\overline{PQ} \perp \overline{NP}$, and C is the midpoint of $\overline{NP}$.

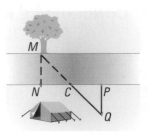

12. Are $\triangle MCN$ and $\triangle QCP$ congruent? If so, state the postulate or theorem that can be used to prove they are congruent.

13. Which segment should you measure to find the width of the river?

4.6   ISOSCELES, EQUILATERAL, AND RIGHT TRIANGLES

Examples on pp. 236–238

> **EXAMPLE** To find the value of x, notice that $\triangle ABC$ is an isosceles right triangle. By the Base Angles Theorem, $\angle B \cong \angle C$. Because $\angle B$ and $\angle C$ are complementary, their sum is $90°$. The measure of each must be $45°$. So $x = 45°$.

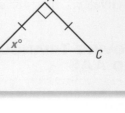

Find the value of x.

14.

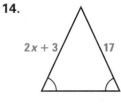

$2x + 3$ 17

15.

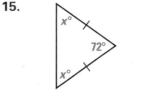

$x°$ $72°$ $x°$

16.

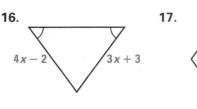

$4x - 2$ $3x + 3$

17.

$35°$ $x°$

4.7   TRIANGLES AND COORDINATE PROOF

Examples on pp. 243–246

> **EXAMPLE** You can use a coordinate proof to prove that $\triangle OPQ$ is isosceles. Use the Distance Formula to show that $\overline{OP} \cong \overline{QP}$.
>
> $$OP = \sqrt{(2-0)^2 + (3-0)^2} = \sqrt{13}$$
>
> $$QP = \sqrt{(2-4)^2 + (3-0)^2} = \sqrt{13}$$
>
> Because $\overline{OP} \cong \overline{QP}$, $\triangle OPQ$ is isosceles.

$P(2, 3)$ 1 $O(0, 0)$ $Q(4, 0)$ x y

18. Write a coordinate proof.

   GIVEN ▶ Coordinates of vertices of $\triangle OAC$ and $\triangle BCA$

   PROVE ▶ $\triangle OAC \cong \triangle BCA$

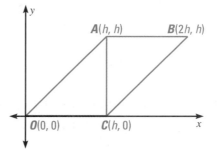

$A(h, h)$ $B(2h, h)$ $O(0, 0)$ $C(h, 0)$ x y

Chapter Test

In Exercises 1–6, identify all triangles in the figure that fit the given description.

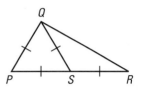

1. isosceles

2. equilateral

3. scalene

4. acute

5. obtuse

6. right

7. In $\triangle ABC$, the measure of $\angle A$ is 116°. The measure of $\angle B$ is three times the measure of $\angle C$. Find $m\angle B$ and $m\angle C$.

Decide whether it is possible to prove that the triangles are congruent. If it is possible, tell which congruence postulate or theorem you would use. Explain your reasoning.

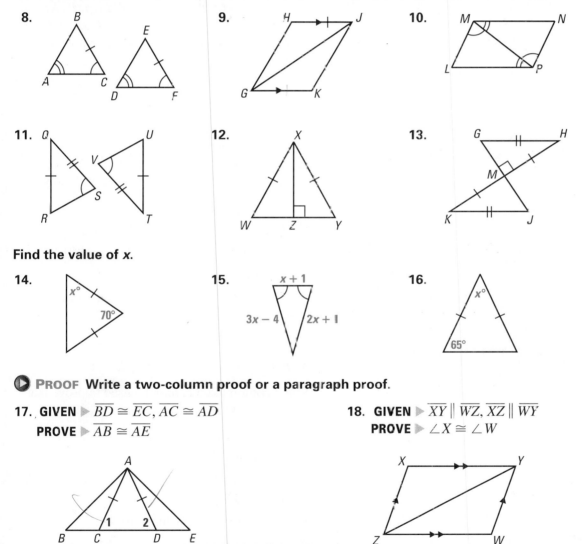

8.

9.

10.

11.

12.

13.

Find the value of x.

14.

15. $x + 1$

$3x - 4$ $2x + 1$

16.

65°

▶ PROOF **Write a two-column proof or a paragraph proof.**

17. **GIVEN** ▸ $\overline{BD} \cong \overline{EC}, \overline{AC} \cong \overline{AD}$

   PROVE ▸ $\overline{AB} \cong \overline{AE}$

18. **GIVEN** ▸ $\overline{XY} \parallel \overline{WZ}, \overline{XZ} \parallel \overline{WY}$

   PROVE ▸ $\angle X \cong \angle W$

Place the figure in a coordinate plane and find the requested information.

19. A right triangle with leg lengths of 4 units and 7 units; find the length of the hypotenuse.

20. A square with side length s and vertices at $(0, 0)$ and (s, s); find the coordinates of the midpoint of a diagonal.

▶ **TEST-TAKING STRATEGY** Avoid spending too much time on one question. Skip questions that are too difficult for you, and spend no more than a few minutes on each question.

1. **MULTIPLE CHOICE** What is the measure of ∠J?

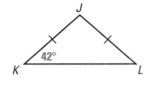

   (A) 42°
   (B) 90°
   (C) 96°
   (D) 138°
   (E) cannot be determined

2. **MULTIPLE CHOICE** What is the measure of ∠BCD?

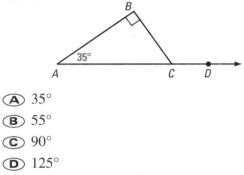

   (A) 35°
   (B) 55°
   (C) 90°
   (D) 125°
   (E) cannot be determined

3. **QUANTITATIVE COMPARISON** Four congruent equilateral triangles form the figures below.

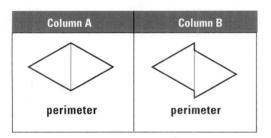

Column A	Column B
perimeter	perimeter

   Choose the statement that is true.

   (A) The perimeter in column A is greater.
   (B) The perimeter in column B is greater.
   (C) The two perimeters are equal.
   (D) The relationship cannot be determined from the given information.

4. **MULTIPLE CHOICE** Which postulate or theorem can be used to prove that △JML ≅ △LKJ?

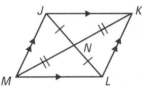

   (A) SSS
   (B) SAS
   (C) ASA
   (D) AAS
   (E) none of the above

5. **MULTIPLE CHOICE** In figure JKLM, $\overline{JM} \parallel \overline{KL}$, $\overline{JK} \parallel \overline{ML}$, and N is the midpoint of $\overline{JL}$ and $\overline{MK}$. Which statement or statements can be proved to be true?

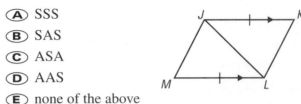

   I. △JNM ≅ △LNK   II. △JNK ≅ △LNM
   III. △JMK ≅ △JKL

   (A) I only   (B) I and II only
   (C) II and III only   (D) I, II, and III
   (E) None are true.

6. **MULTIPLE CHOICE** You are given the following information about △PQR and △XYZ.

   I. ∠P ≅ ∠X   II. ∠Q ≅ ∠Y
   III. $\overline{PQ} \cong \overline{XY}$ IV. $\overline{QR} \cong \overline{YZ}$

   Which combination *cannot* be used to prove that △PQR ≅ △XYZ?

   (A) I, II, and III
   (B) II, III, and IV
   (C) I, III, and IV
   (D) I, II, and IV
   (E) All combinations can be used.

7. **MULTIPLE CHOICE** What is the value of x?

   (A) $\frac{3}{5}$ (B) 3
   (C) 6   (D) 8
   (E) 55

8. MULTIPLE CHOICE You want to prove that $\overline{DB} \cong \overline{DF}$. As a first step, which pair of triangles would you prove congruent?

(A) $\triangle ADB$ and $\triangle GFD$

(B) $\triangle ADB$ and $\triangle EDF$

(C) $\triangle BDC$ and $\triangle FDG$

(D) $\triangle ADC$ and $\triangle EDG$

(E) $\triangle ABD$ and $\triangle EFD$

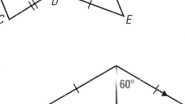

9. MULTIPLE CHOICE Use the diagram to determine which statement is true.

(A) $x = 30$ and $y = 60$

(B) $x = 60$ and $y = 60$

(C) $x = 30$ and $y = 30$

(D) $x = 60$ and $y = 30$

(E) $x = 60$ and $y = 90$

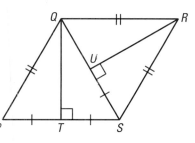

MULTI-STEP PROBLEM In Exercises 10–13, use the diagram and the information below.

GIVEN ▶ $\overline{PT} \cong \overline{ST} \cong \overline{SU}$,
$\overline{QP} \cong \overline{RQ} \cong \overline{RS}$,
$\overline{QT} \perp \overline{PS}$, $\overline{RU} \perp \overline{QS}$

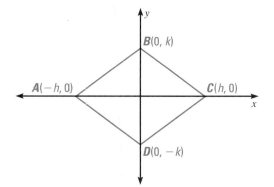

10. Show that $\triangle RUS \cong \triangle RUQ$.

11. Show that $\triangle QTP \cong \triangle QTS$.

12. Use your answers to Exercises 10 and 11 to show that $\triangle PQS \cong \triangle QRS$.

13. Classify $\triangle RQS$ and $\triangle PQS$, using the most specific names you can. Explain your answers.

MULTI-STEP PROBLEM In Exercises 14–19, use figure *ABCD*.

14. On graph paper, sketch figure $ABCD$.

15. Draw diagonal $\overline{AC}$.

16. Is $\triangle ABC \cong \triangle CDA$? Justify your answer.

17. What kind of triangles are $\triangle ABC$ and $\triangle CDA$?

18. Sketch diagonal $\overline{BD}$. What kind of triangles are $\triangle BCD$ and $\triangle DAB$?

19. *Writing* A *rhombus* is a figure with four congruent sides. Figure $ABCD$ is an example of a rhombus. Can you *always* draw a diagonal in any given rhombus so that the two triangles formed are isosceles? Explain.

PROPERTIES
OF TRIANGLES

How can a goalkeeper best defend the goal?

APPLICATION: Goalkeeping

Soccer goalkeepers use triangle relationships to help block goal attempts.

An opponent can shoot the ball from many different angles. The goalkeeper determines the best defensive position by imagining a triangle formed by the goal posts and the opponent.

Think & Discuss

Use the diagram for Exercises 1 and 2.

1. The opponent at *X* is trying to score a goal. Which position do you think is best for the goalkeeper, *A*, *B*, or *C*? Why?

2. Estimate the measure of ∠*X*, known as the *shooting angle*. How could the opponent change positions to increase the shooting angle?

Learn More About It

You will learn more about strategies of goalkeeping in Exercises 33–35 on p. 270.

APPLICATION LINK Visit www.mcdougallittell.com for more information about angles and goalkeeping.

Study Guide

What's the chapter about?

Chapter 5 is about **properties of triangles**. In Chapter 5, you'll learn how to

- use properties of special lines and segments related to triangles.
- compare side lengths and angle measures in one or more triangles.

> ### KEY VOCABULARY
>
> ▶ **Review**
> - intersect, p. 12
> - midpoint, p. 34
> - angle bisector, p. 36
> - perpendicular lines, p. 79
>
> ▶ **New**
> - perpendicular bisector, p. 264
>
> - perpendicular bisector of a triangle, p. 272
> - concurrent lines, p. 272
> - circumcenter of a triangle, p. 273
> - angle bisector of a triangle, p. 274
> - incenter of a triangle, p. 274
>
> - median of a triangle, p. 279
> - centroid of a triangle, p. 279
> - altitude of a triangle, p. 281
> - orthocenter of a triangle, p. 281
> - midsegment of a triangle, p. 287
> - indirect proof, p. 302

Are you ready for the chapter?

SKILL REVIEW Do these exercises to review key skills that you'll apply in this chapter. See the given **reference page** if there is something you don't understand.

1. Draw a segment and label it $\overline{AB}$. Construct a bisector of $\overline{AB}$. Label its midpoint M. **(Review p. 34)**

2. Draw an angle and label it $\angle P$. Construct an angle bisector of $\angle P$. **(Review p. 36)**

Use the diagram at the right.

3. Find the coordinates of the midpoint of $\overline{BC}$. **(Review p. 35)**

4. Find the length of $\overline{AB}$. **(Review p. 19)**

5. Find the slope of $\overline{BC}$. **(Review p. 165)**

6. Find the slope of a line perpendicular to $\overline{BC}$. **(Review p. 174)**

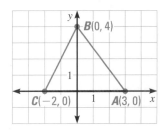

Here's a study strategy!

Check Your Memory

Without looking at your book or your notes, write a list of important vocabulary terms and skills. Then look through the chapter and your notes as you compare them with your list. Did you miss anything?

◖ ACTIVITY 5.1

Developing Concepts

Investigating Perpendicular Bisectors

GROUP ACTIVITY
Work with a partner.

MATERIALS
• paper
• pencils
• ruler
• protractor

▶ **QUESTION** What is true about any point on the perpendicular bisector of a segment?

▶ **EXPLORING THE CONCEPT**

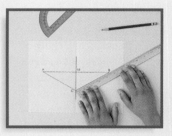

① On a piece of paper, draw $\overline{AB}$. Fold the paper so that point B lies directly on point A.

② Draw a line along the crease in the paper. Label the point where the line intersects $\overline{AB}$ as point M.

③ Label another point on the line as point C. Draw $\overline{CA}$ and $\overline{CB}$.

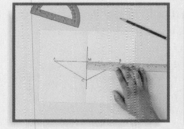
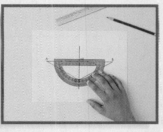
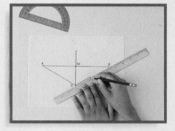

④ Measure $\overline{MA}$ and $\overline{MB}$.

⑤ Measure $\angle CMA$.

⑥ Measure $\overline{CA}$ and $\overline{CB}$.

▶ **DRAWING CONCLUSIONS**

1. $\overleftrightarrow{CM}$ is called the *perpendicular bisector* of $\overline{AB}$. Explain why.

2. Choose four other points on $\overleftrightarrow{CM}$. Label the points as D, E, F, and G.

3. Copy and complete the table by measuring the length of each segment. What do you notice?

Point *D*	Point *E*	Point *F*	Point *G*
$DA = \underline{\ ?\ }$	$EA = \underline{\ ?\ }$	$FA = \underline{\ ?\ }$	$GA = \underline{\ ?\ }$
$DB = \underline{\ ?\ }$	$EB = \underline{\ ?\ }$	$FB = \underline{\ ?\ }$	$GB = \underline{\ ?\ }$

4. **CRITICAL THINKING** What is true about any point on the perpendicular bisector of a segment?

Perpendiculars and Bisectors

GOAL 1 **USING PROPERTIES OF PERPENDICULAR BISECTORS**

In Lesson 1.5, you learned that a segment bisector intersects a segment at its midpoint. A segment, ray, line, or plane that is perpendicular to a segment at its midpoint is called a **perpendicular bisector**.

The construction below shows how to draw a line that is perpendicular to a given line or segment at a point P. You can use this method to construct a perpendicular bisector of a segment, as described below the activity.

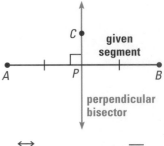

$\overleftrightarrow{CP}$ is a ⊥ bisector of $\overline{AB}$.

▶ **ACTIVITY**

Construction

Perpendicular Through a Point on a Line

Use these steps to construct a line that is perpendicular to a given line m and that passes through a given point P on m.

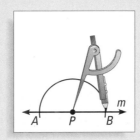

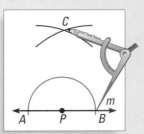

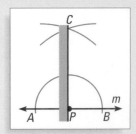

❶ Place the compass point at P. Draw an arc that intersects line m twice. Label the intersections as A and B.

❷ Use a compass setting greater than AP. Draw an arc from A. With the same setting, draw an arc from B. Label the intersection of the arcs as C.

❸ Use a straightedge to draw $\overleftrightarrow{CP}$. This line is perpendicular to line m and passes through P.

You can measure $\angle CPA$ on your construction to verify that the constructed line is perpendicular to the given line m. In the construction, $\overleftrightarrow{CP} \perp \overline{AB}$ and $PA = PB$, so $\overleftrightarrow{CP}$ is the perpendicular bisector of $\overline{AB}$.

A point is **equidistant from two points** if its distance from each point is the same. In the construction above, C is equidistant from A and B because C was drawn so that $CA = CB$.

Theorem 5.1 below states that *any* point on the perpendicular bisector $\overleftrightarrow{CP}$ in the construction is equidistant from A and B, the endpoints of the segment. The converse helps you prove that a given point lies on a perpendicular bisector.

THEOREMS

THEOREM 5.1 *Perpendicular Bisector Theorem*

If a point is on the perpendicular bisector of a segment, then it is equidistant from the endpoints of the segment.

> If $\overleftrightarrow{CP}$ is the perpendicular bisector of $\overline{AB}$, then $CA = CB$.

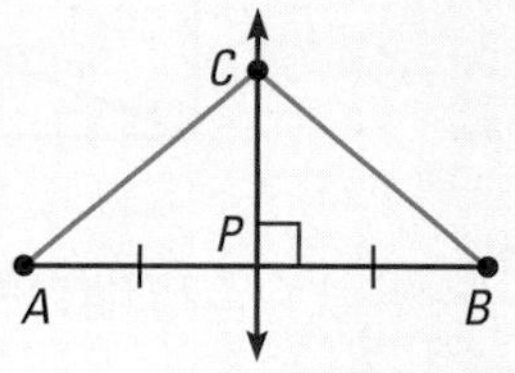

CA = CB

THEOREM 5.2 *Converse of the Perpendicular Bisector Theorem*

If a point is equidistant from the endpoints of a segment, then it is on the perpendicular bisector of the segment.

> If $DA = DB$, then D lies on the perpendicular bisector of $\overline{AB}$.

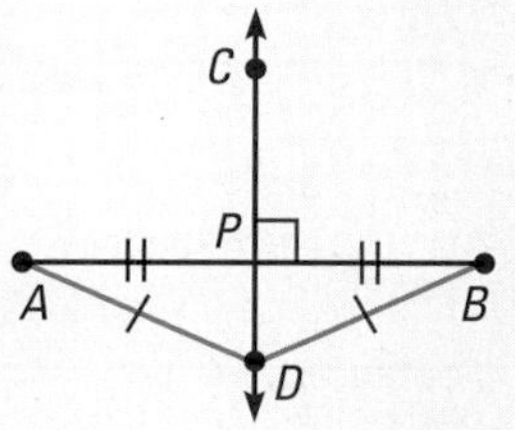

D is on $\overleftrightarrow{CP}$.

Proof

Plan for Proof of Theorem 5.1 Refer to the diagram for Theorem 5.1 above. Suppose that you are given that $\overleftrightarrow{CP}$ is the perpendicular bisector of $\overline{AB}$. Show that right triangles $\triangle APC$ and $\triangle BPC$ are congruent using the SAS Congruence Postulate. Then show that $\overline{CA} \cong \overline{CB}$.

Exercise 28 asks you to write a two-column proof of Theorem 5.1 using this plan for proof. Exercise 29 asks you to write a proof of Theorem 5.2.

EXAMPLE 1 *Using Perpendicular Bisectors*

Logical Reasoning

In the diagram shown, $\overleftrightarrow{MN}$ is the perpendicular bisector of $\overline{ST}$.

a. What segment lengths in the diagram are equal?

b. Explain why Q is on $\overleftrightarrow{MN}$.

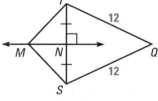

SOLUTION

a. $\overleftrightarrow{MN}$ bisects $\overline{ST}$, so $NS = NT$. Because M is on the perpendicular bisector of $\overline{ST}$, $MS = MT$ (by Theorem 5.1). The diagram shows that $QS = QT = 12$.

b. $QS = QT$, so Q is equidistant from S and T. By Theorem 5.2, Q is on the perpendicular bisector of $\overline{ST}$, which is $\overleftrightarrow{MN}$.

GOAL 2 USING PROPERTIES OF ANGLE BISECTORS

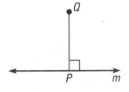

The **distance from a point to a line** is defined as the length of the perpendicular segment from the point to the line. For instance, in the diagram shown, the distance between the point *Q* and the line *m* is *QP*.

When a point is the same distance from one line as it is from another line, then the point is **equidistant from the two lines** (or rays or segments). The theorems below show that a point in the interior of an angle is equidistant from the sides of the angle if and only if the point is on the bisector of the angle.

THEOREMS

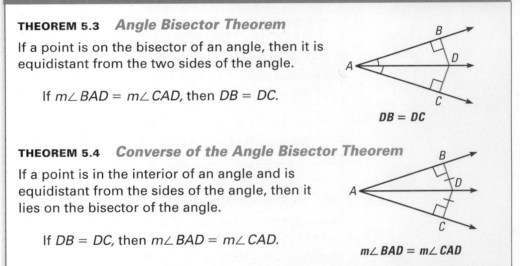

THEOREM 5.3 *Angle Bisector Theorem*

If a point is on the bisector of an angle, then it is equidistant from the two sides of the angle.

> If *m∠BAD* = *m∠CAD*, then *DB* = *DC*.

DB = DC

THEOREM 5.4 *Converse of the Angle Bisector Theorem*

If a point is in the interior of an angle and is equidistant from the sides of the angle, then it lies on the bisector of the angle.

> If *DB* = *DC*, then *m∠BAD* = *m∠CAD*.

m∠BAD = m∠CAD

A paragraph proof of Theorem 5.3 is given in Example 2. Exercise 32 asks you to write a proof of Theorem 5.4.

Proof

EXAMPLE 2 *Proof of Theorem 5.3*

GIVEN ▶ *D* is on the bisector of ∠*BAC*.
$\overline{DB} \perp \overrightarrow{AB}$, $\overline{DC} \perp \overrightarrow{AC}$

PROVE ▶ *DB* = *DC*

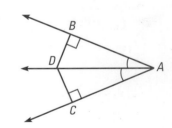

Plan for Proof Prove that △*ADB* ≅ △*ADC*.
Then conclude that $\overline{DB} \cong \overline{DC}$, so *DB* = *DC*.

SOLUTION

Paragraph Proof By the definition of an angle bisector, ∠*BAD* ≅ ∠*CAD*. Because ∠*ABD* and ∠*ACD* are right angles, ∠*ABD* ≅ ∠*ACD*. By the Reflexive Property of Congruence, $\overline{AD} \cong \overline{AD}$. Then △*ADB* ≅ △*ADC* by the AAS Congruence Theorem. Because corresponding parts of congruent triangles are congruent, $\overline{DB} \cong \overline{DC}$. By the definition of congruent segments, *DB* = *DC*.

FOCUS ON CAREERS

ENGINEERING TECHNICIAN

In manufacturing, engineering technicians prepare specifications for products such as roof trusses, and devise and run tests for quality control.

CAREER LINK
www.mcdougallittell.com

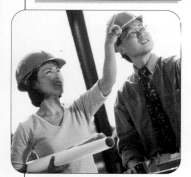

EXAMPLE 3 *Using Angle Bisectors*

ROOF TRUSSES Some roofs are built with wooden trusses that are assembled in a factory and shipped to the building site. In the diagram of the roof truss shown below, you are given that $\overrightarrow{AB}$ bisects $\angle CAD$ and that $\angle ACB$ and $\angle ADB$ are right angles. What can you say about $\overline{BC}$ and $\overline{BD}$?

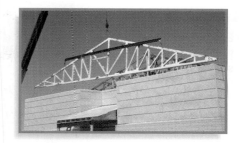

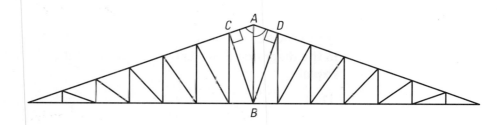

SOLUTION

Because $\overline{BC}$ and $\overline{BD}$ meet $\overline{AC}$ and $\overline{AD}$ at right angles, they are perpendicular segments to the sides of $\angle CAD$. This implies that their lengths represent the distances from the point B to $\overrightarrow{AC}$ and $\overrightarrow{AD}$. Because point B is on the bisector of $\angle CAD$, it is equidistant from the sides of the angle.

▶ So, $BC = BD$, and you can conclude that $\overline{BC} \cong \overline{BD}$.

GUIDED PRACTICE

Vocabulary Check ✓

1. If D is on the __?__ of $\overline{AB}$, then D is *equidistant* from A and B.

Concept Check ✓

2. Point G is in the interior of $\angle HJK$ and is equidistant from the sides of the angle, $\overrightarrow{JH}$ and $\overrightarrow{JK}$. What can you conclude about G? Use a sketch to support your answer.

Skill Check ✓

In the diagram, $\overleftrightarrow{CD}$ is the perpendicular bisector of $\overline{AB}$.

3. What is the relationship between $\overline{AD}$ and $\overline{BD}$?

4. What is the relationship between $\angle ADC$ and $\angle BDC$?

5. What is the relationship between $\overline{AC}$ and $\overline{BC}$? Explain your answer.

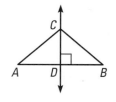

In the diagram, $\overrightarrow{PM}$ is the bisector of $\angle LPN$.

6. What is the relationship between $\angle LPM$ and $\angle NPM$?

7. How is the distance between point M and $\overrightarrow{PL}$ related to the distance between point M and $\overrightarrow{PN}$?

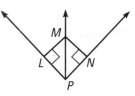

PRACTICE AND APPLICATIONS

STUDENT HELP

► **Extra Practice**
to help you master
skills is on p. 811.

🧩 **LOGICAL REASONING** Tell whether the information in the diagram allows you to conclude that C is on the perpendicular bisector of $\overline{AB}$. Explain your reasoning.

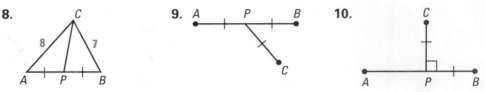

8. 9. 10.

🧩 **LOGICAL REASONING** In Exercises 11–13, tell whether the information in the diagram allows you to conclude that P is on the bisector of $\angle A$. Explain.

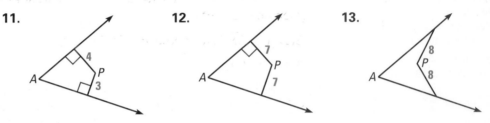

11. 12. 13.

14. 📐 **CONSTRUCTION** Draw $\overline{AB}$ with a length of 8 centimeters. Construct a perpendicular bisector and draw a point D on the bisector so that the distance between D and $\overline{AB}$ is 3 centimeters. Measure $\overline{AD}$ and $\overline{BD}$.

15. 📐 **CONSTRUCTION** Draw a large $\angle A$ with a measure of 60°. Construct the angle bisector and draw a point D on the bisector so that $AD = 3$ inches. Draw perpendicular segments from D to the sides of $\angle A$. Measure these segments to find the distance between D and the sides of $\angle A$.

USING PERPENDICULAR BISECTORS Use the diagram shown.

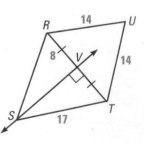

16. In the diagram, $\overleftrightarrow{SV} \perp \overline{RT}$ and $\overline{VR} \cong \overline{VT}$. Find VT.

17. In the diagram, $\overleftrightarrow{SV} \perp \overline{RT}$ and $\overline{VR} \cong \overline{VT}$. Find SR.

18. In the diagram, $\overleftrightarrow{SV}$ is the perpendicular bisector of $\overline{RT}$. Because $UR = UT = 14$, what can you conclude about point U?

STUDENT HELP

► **HOMEWORK HELP**
Example 1: Exs. 8–10, 14,
   16–18, 21–26
Example 2: Exs. 11–13,
   15, 19, 20, 21–26
Example 3: Exs. 31,
   33–35

USING ANGLE BISECTORS Use the diagram shown.

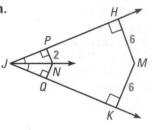

19. In the diagram, $\overrightarrow{JN}$ bisects $\angle HJK$, $\overline{NP} \perp \overrightarrow{JP}$, $\overline{NQ} \perp \overrightarrow{JQ}$, and $NP = 2$. Find NQ.

20. In the diagram, $\overrightarrow{JN}$ bisects $\angle HJK$, $\overline{MH} \perp \overrightarrow{JH}$, $\overline{MK} \perp \overrightarrow{JK}$, and $MH = MK = 6$. What can you conclude about point M?

USING BISECTOR THEOREMS In Exercises 21–26, match the angle measure or segment length described with its correct value.

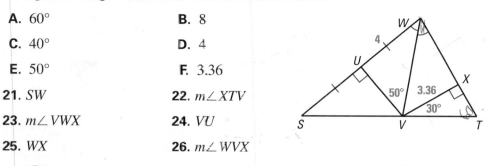

A. 60° **B.** 8

C. 40° **D.** 4

E. 50° **F.** 3.36

21. SW **22.** $m\angle XTV$

23. $m\angle VWX$ **24.** VU

25. WX **26.** $m\angle WVX$

27. **PROVING A CONSTRUCTION** Write a proof to verify that $\overleftrightarrow{CP} \perp \overline{AB}$ in the construction on page 264.

STUDENT HELP

Look Back
For help with proving that constructions are valid, see p. 231.

28. **PROVING THEOREM 5.1** Write a proof of Theorem 5.1, the Perpendicular Bisector Theorem. You may want to use the plan for proof given on page 265.

GIVEN ▶ $\overleftrightarrow{CP}$ is the perpendicular bisector of $\overline{AB}$.

PROVE ▶ C is equidistant from A and B.

29. **PROVING THEOREM 5.2** Use the diagram shown to write a two-column proof of Theorem 5.2, the Converse of the Perpendicular Bisector Theorem.

GIVEN ▶ C is equidistant from A and B.

PROVE ▶ C is on the perpendicular bisector of $\overline{AB}$.

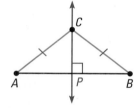

Plan for Proof Use the Perpendicular Postulate to draw $\overleftrightarrow{CP} \perp \overleftrightarrow{AB}$. Show that $\triangle APC \cong \triangle BPC$ by the HL Congruence Theorem. Then $\overline{AP} \cong \overline{BP}$, so $AP = BP$.

30. **PROOF** Use the diagram shown.

GIVEN ▶ $\overline{GJ}$ is the perpendicular bisector of $\overline{HK}$.

PROVE ▶ $\triangle GHM \cong \triangle GKM$

FOCUS ON PEOPLE

REAL LIFE **THE WRIGHT BROTHERS**
In Kitty Hawk, North Carolina, on December 17, 1903, Orville and Wilbur Wright became the first people to successfully fly an engine-driven, heavier-than-air machine.

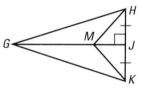

31. **EARLY AIRCRAFT** On many of the earliest airplanes, wires connected vertical posts to the edges of the wings, which were wooden frames covered with cloth. Suppose the lengths of the wires from the top of a post to the edges of the frame are the same and the distances from the bottom of the post to the ends of the two wires are the same. What does that tell you about the post and the section of frame between the ends of the wires?

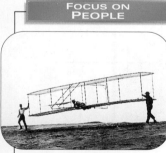

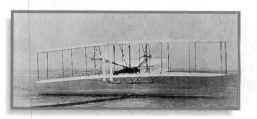

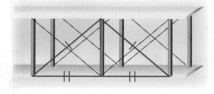

32. ▶ **DEVELOPING PROOF** Use the diagram to complete the proof of Theorem 5.4, the Converse of the Angle Bisector Theorem.

GIVEN ▶ D is in the interior of $\angle ABC$ and is equidistant from $\overrightarrow{BA}$ and $\overrightarrow{BC}$.

PROVE ▶ D lies on the angle bisector of $\angle ABC$.

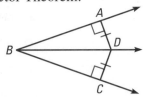

Statements	Reasons
1. D is in the interior of $\angle ABC$.	1. ___?___
2. D is ___?___ from $\overrightarrow{BA}$ and $\overrightarrow{BC}$.	2. Given
3. ___?___ = ___?___	3. Definition of equidistant
4. $\overline{DA} \perp$ ___?___ , ___?___ $\perp \overrightarrow{BC}$	4. Definition of distance from a point to a line
5. ___?___	5. If 2 lines are $\perp$, then they form 4 rt. $\angle$s.
6. ___?___	6. Definition of right triangle
7. $\overline{BD} \cong \overline{BD}$	7. ___?___
8. ___?___	8. HL Congruence Thm.
9. $\angle ABD \cong \angle CBD$	9. ___?___
10. $\overrightarrow{BD}$ bisects $\angle ABC$ and point D is on the bisector of $\angle ABC$.	10. ___?___

🌎 **ICE HOCKEY** **In Exercises 33–35, use the following information.**
In the diagram, the goalie is at point G and the puck is at point P. The goalie's job is to prevent the puck from entering the goal.

33. When the puck is at the other end of the rink, the goalie is likely to be standing on line ℓ. How is ℓ related to $\overline{AB}$?

34. As an opposing player with the puck skates toward the goal, the goalie is likely to move from line ℓ to other places on the ice. What should be the relationship between $\overrightarrow{PG}$ and $\angle APB$?

35. How does $m\angle APB$ change as the puck gets closer to the goal? Does this change make it easier or more difficult for the goalie to defend the goal? Explain.

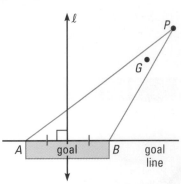

36. 🖥 **TECHNOLOGY** Use geometry software to construct $\overline{AB}$. Find the midpoint C. Draw the perpendicular bisector of $\overline{AB}$ through C. Construct a point D along the perpendicular bisector and measure $\overline{DA}$ and $\overline{DB}$. Move D along the perpendicular bisector. What theorem does this construction demonstrate?

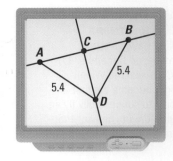

37. MULTI-STEP PROBLEM Use the map shown and the following information. A town planner is trying to decide whether a new household X should be covered by fire station A, B, or C.

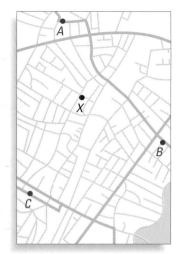

a. Trace the map and draw the segments $\overline{AB}$, $\overline{BC}$, and $\overline{CA}$.

b. Construct the perpendicular bisectors of $\overline{AB}$, $\overline{BC}$, and $\overline{CA}$. Do the perpendicular bisectors meet at a point?

c. The perpendicular bisectors divide the town into regions. Shade the region closest to fire station A red. Shade the region closest to fire station B blue. Shade the region closest to fire station C gray.

d. *Writing* In an emergency at household X, which fire station should respond? Explain your choice.

★ **Challenge**

⊕ **USING ALGEBRA** Use the graph at the right.

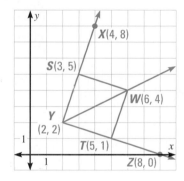

38. Use slopes to show that $\overline{WS} \perp \overrightarrow{YX}$ and that $\overline{WT} \perp \overrightarrow{YZ}$.

39. Find WS and WT.

EXTRA CHALLENGE

www.mcdougallittell.com

40. Explain how you know that $\overrightarrow{YW}$ bisects $\angle XYZ$.

MIXED REVIEW

CIRCLES **Find the missing measurement for the circle shown. Use 3.14 as an approximation for π.** (Review 1.7 for 5.2)

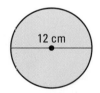

12 cm

41. radius   **42.** circumference   **43.** area

CALCULATING SLOPE **Find the slope of the line that passes through the given points.** (Review 3.6)

44. $A(-1, 5)$, $B(-2, 10)$ **45.** $C(4, -3)$, $D(-6, 5)$ **46.** $E(4, 5)$, $F(9, 5)$

47. $G(0, 8)$, $H(-7, 0)$ **48.** $J(3, 11)$, $K(-10, 12)$ **49.** $L(-3, -8)$, $M(8, -8)$

⊕ **USING ALGEBRA** **Find the value of x.** (Review 4.1)

50.

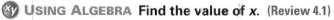

$x°$

$31°$

51. $(2x + 6)°$ $40°$

$x°$

52. $4x°$

$70°$

$(10x + 22)°$

Bisectors of a Triangle

GOAL 1 USING PERPENDICULAR BISECTORS OF A TRIANGLE

In Lesson 5.1, you studied properties of perpendicular bisectors of segments and angle bisectors. In this lesson, you will study the special cases in which the segments and angles being bisected are parts of a triangle.

A **perpendicular bisector of a triangle** is a line (or ray or segment) that is perpendicular to a side of the triangle at the midpoint of the side.

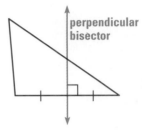

perpendicular bisector

▶ **ACTIVITY**
Developing Concepts

Perpendicular Bisectors of a Triangle

1. Cut four large acute scalene triangles out of paper. Make each one different.

2. Choose one triangle. Fold the triangle to form the perpendicular bisectors of the sides. Do the three bisectors intersect at the same point?

3. Repeat the process for the other three triangles. What do you observe? Write your observation in the form of a conjecture.

4. Choose one triangle. Label the vertices A, B, and C. Label the point of intersection of the perpendicular bisectors as P. Measure $\overline{AP}$, $\overline{BP}$, and $\overline{CP}$. What do you observe?

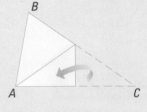

When three or more lines (or rays or segments) intersect in the same point, they are called **concurrent lines** (or rays or segments). The point of intersection of the lines is called the **point of concurrency**.

The three perpendicular bisectors of a triangle are concurrent. The point of concurrency can be *inside* the triangle, *on* the triangle, or *outside* the triangle.

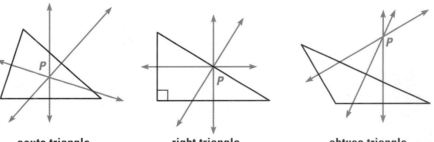

| acute triangle | right triangle | obtuse triangle |

The point of concurrency of the perpendicular bisectors of a triangle is called the **circumcenter of the triangle.** In each triangle at the bottom of page 272, the circumcenter is at *P*. The circumcenter of a triangle has a special property, as described in Theorem 5.5. You will use coordinate geometry to illustrate this theorem in Exercises 29–31. A proof appears on page 835.

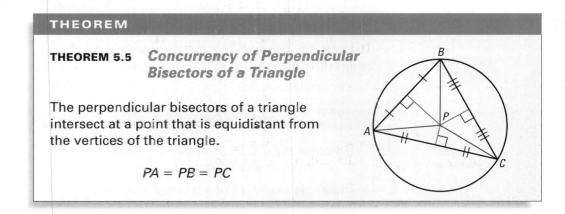

THEOREM

THEOREM 5.5 *Concurrency of Perpendicular Bisectors of a Triangle*

The perpendicular bisectors of a triangle intersect at a point that is equidistant from the vertices of the triangle.

$$PA = PB = PC$$

The diagram for Theorem 5.5 shows that the circumcenter is the center of the circle that passes through the vertices of the triangle. The circle is *circumscribed* about △*ABC*. Thus, the radius of this circle is the distance from the center to any of the vertices.

EXAMPLE 1 *Using Perpendicular Bisectors*

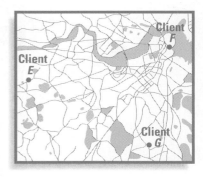

FACILITIES PLANNING A company plans to build a distribution center that is convenient to three of its major clients. The planners start by roughly locating the three clients on a sketch and finding the circumcenter of the triangle formed.

a. Explain why using the circumcenter as the location of a distribution center would be convenient for all the clients.

b. Make a sketch of the triangle formed by the clients. Locate the circumcenter of the triangle. Tell what segments are congruent.

SOLUTION

a. Because the circumcenter is equidistant from the three vertices, each client would be equally close to the distribution center.

b. Label the vertices of the triangle as *E*, *F*, and *G*. Draw the perpendicular bisectors. Label their intersection as *D*.

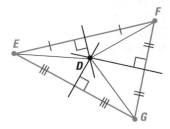

By Theorem 5.5, $DE = DF = DG$.

An **angle bisector of a triangle** is a bisector of an angle of the triangle. The three angle bisectors are concurrent. The point of concurrency of the angle bisectors is called the **incenter of the triangle**, and it always lies inside the triangle. The incenter has a special property that is described below in Theorem 5.6. Exercise 22 asks you to write a proof of this theorem.

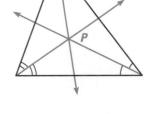

THEOREM

THEOREM 5.6 *Concurrency of Angle Bisectors of a Triangle*

The angle bisectors of a triangle intersect at a point that is equidistant from the sides of the triangle.

$$PD = PE = PF$$

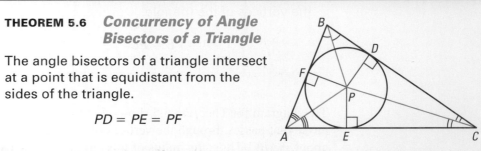

The diagram for Theorem 5.6 shows that the incenter is the center of the circle that touches each side of the triangle once. The circle is *inscribed* within $\triangle ABC$. Thus, the radius of this circle is the distance from the center to any of the sides.

Logical Reasoning

EXAMPLE 2 *Using Angle Bisectors*

The angle bisectors of $\triangle MNP$ meet at point L.

a. What segments are congruent?

b. Find LQ and LR.

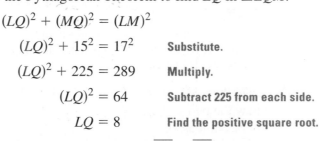

SOLUTION

a. By Theorem 5.6, the three angle bisectors of a triangle intersect at a point that is equidistant from the sides of the triangle. So, $\overline{LR} \cong \overline{LQ} \cong \overline{LS}$.

STUDENT HELP

► **Look Back**
For help with the Pythagorean Theorem, see p. 20.

b. Use the Pythagorean Theorem to find LQ in $\triangle LQM$.

$$(LQ)^2 + (MQ)^2 = (LM)^2$$
$$(LQ)^2 + 15^2 = 17^2 \qquad \text{Substitute.}$$
$$(LQ)^2 + 225 = 289 \qquad \text{Multiply.}$$
$$(LQ)^2 = 64 \qquad \text{Subtract 225 from each side.}$$
$$LQ = 8 \qquad \text{Find the positive square root.}$$

▶ So, $LQ = 8$ units. Because $\overline{LR} \cong \overline{LQ}$, $LR = 8$ units.

GUIDED PRACTICE

1. If three or more lines intersect at the same point, the lines are __?__ *Congruent*

Concept Check ✓

2. Think of something about the words *incenter* and *circumcenter* that you can use to remember which special parts of a triangle meet at each point.

Skill Check ✓

Use the diagram and the given information to find the indicated measure.

3. The perpendicular bisectors of △*ABC* meet at point *G*. Find *GC*.

4. The angle bisectors of △*XYZ* meet at point *M*. Find *MK*.

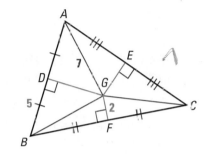

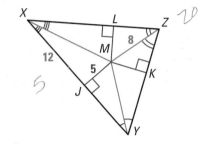

PRACTICE AND APPLICATIONS

▶ **Extra Practice**
to help you master
skills is on p. 811.

CONSTRUCTION **Draw a large example of the given type of triangle. Construct perpendicular bisectors of the sides. (See page 264.) For the type of triangle, do the bisectors intersect *inside*, *on*, or *outside* the triangle?**

5. obtuse triangle

6. acute triangle

7. right triangle

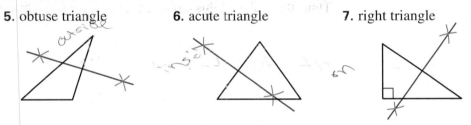

DRAWING CONCLUSIONS **Draw a large △ABC.**

8. Construct the angle bisectors of △*ABC*. Label the point where the angle bisectors meet as *D*.

9. Construct perpendicular segments from *D* to each of the sides of the triangle. Measure each segment. What do you notice? Which theorem have you just confirmed?

LOGICAL REASONING **Use the results of Exercises 5–9 to complete the statement using *always*, *sometimes*, or *never*.**

10. A perpendicular bisector of a triangle __?__ passes through the midpoint of a side of the triangle.

11. The angle bisectors of a triangle __?__ intersect at a single point.

12. The angle bisectors of a triangle __?__ meet at a point outside the triangle.

13. The circumcenter of a triangle __?__ lies outside the triangle.

▶ HOMEWORK HELP
Example 1: Exs. 5–7,
10–13, 14, 17, 20, 21
Example 2: Exs. 8, 9,
10–13, 15, 16, 22

5.2   *Bisectors of a Triangle*   **275**

BISECTORS **In each case, find the indicated measure.**

14. The perpendicular bisectors of △*RST* meet at point *D*. Find *DR*.

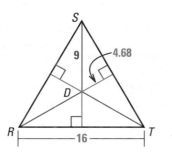

15. The angle bisectors of △*XYZ* meet at point *W*. Find *WB*.

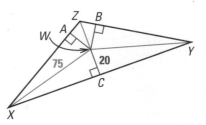

16. The angle bisectors of △*GHJ* meet at point *K*. Find *KB*.

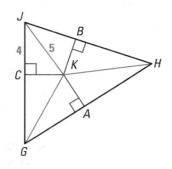

17. The perpendicular bisectors of △*MNP* meet at point *Q*. Find *QN*.

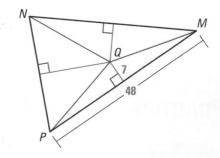

ERROR ANALYSIS **Explain why the student's conclusion is** *false*. **Then state a correct conclusion that can be deduced from the diagram.**

18.

19.

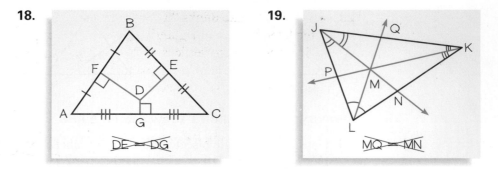

LOGICAL REASONING **In Exercises 20 and 21, use the following information and map.**

Your family is considering moving to a new home. The diagram shows the locations of where your parents work and where you go to school. The locations form a triangle.

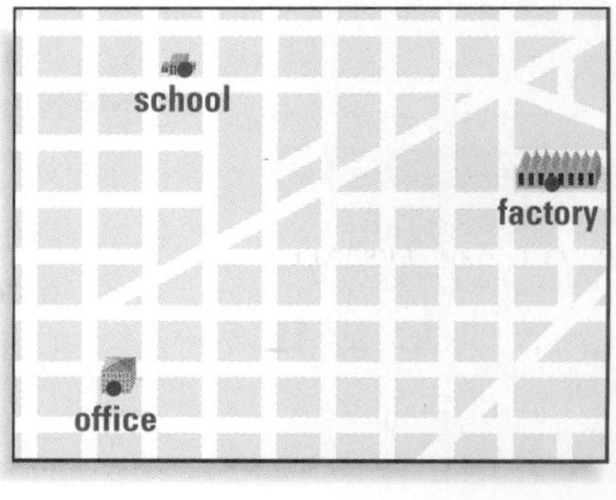

20. In the diagram, how could you find a point that is equidistant from each location? Explain your answer.

21. Make a sketch of the situation. Find the best location for the new home.

22. ▶ **DEVELOPING PROOF** Complete the proof of Theorem 5.6, the Concurrency of Angle Bisectors.

GIVEN ▶ $\triangle ABC$, the bisectors of $\angle A$, $\angle B$, and $\angle C$, $\overline{DE} \perp \overline{AB}$, $\overline{DF} \perp \overline{BC}$, $\overline{DG} \perp \overline{CA}$

PROVE ▶ The angle bisectors intersect at a point that is equidistant from $\overline{AB}$, $\overline{BC}$, and $\overline{CA}$.

Plan for Proof Show that D, the point of intersection of the bisectors of $\angle A$ and $\angle B$, also lies on the bisector of $\angle C$. Then show that D is equidistant from the sides of the triangle.

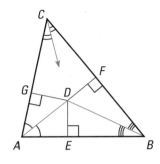

Statements	Reasons
1. $\triangle ABC$, the bisectors of $\angle A$, $\angle B$, and $\angle C$, $\overline{DE} \perp \overline{AB}$, $\overline{DF} \perp \overline{BC}$, $\overline{DG} \perp \overline{CA}$	**1.** Given
2. ___?___ $= DG$	**2.** $\overrightarrow{AD}$ bisects $\angle BAC$, so D is ___?___ from the sides of $\angle BAC$.
3. $DE = DF$	**3.** ___?___
4. $DF = DG$	**4.** ___?___
5. D is on the ___?___ of $\angle C$.	**5.** Converse of the Angle Bisector Theorem
6. ___?___	**6.** Givens and Steps ___?___

23. *Writing* Joannie thinks that the midpoint of the hypotenuse of a right triangle is equidistant from the vertices of the triangle. Explain how she could use perpendicular bisectors to verify her conjecture.

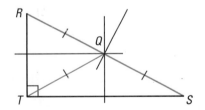

SCIENCE ▶ **CONNECTION** **In Exercises 24–26, use the following information.**
A *mycelium* fungus grows underground in all directions from a central point. Under certain conditions, mushrooms sprout up in a ring at the edge. The radius of the mushroom ring is an indication of the mycelium's age.

24. Suppose three mushrooms in a mushroom ring are located as shown. Make a large copy of the diagram and draw $\triangle ABC$. Each unit on your coordinate grid should represent 1 foot.

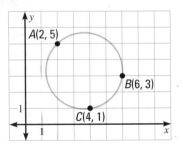

25. Draw perpendicular bisectors on your diagram to find the center of the mushroom ring. Estimate the radius of the ring.

26. Suppose the radius of the mycelium increases at a rate of about 8 inches per year. Estimate its age.

MULTIPLE CHOICE Choose the correct answer from the list given.

27. $\overline{AD}$ and $\overline{CD}$ are angle bisectors of $\triangle ABC$ and $m\angle ABC = 100°$. Find $m\angle ADC$.

Ⓐ 80°　　Ⓑ 90°　　Ⓒ 100°

Ⓓ 120°　　Ⓔ 140°

28. The perpendicular bisectors of $\triangle XYZ$ intersect at point W, $WT = 12$, and $WZ = 13$. Find XY.

Ⓐ 5　　Ⓑ 8　　Ⓒ 10

Ⓓ 12　　Ⓔ 13

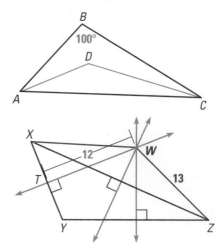

★ **Challenge**

(xy) **USING ALGEBRA** Use the graph of $\triangle ABC$ to illustrate Theorem 5.5, the Concurrency of Perpendicular Bisectors.

29. Find the midpoint of each side of $\triangle ABC$. Use the midpoints to find the equations of the perpendicular bisectors of $\triangle ABC$.

30. Using your equations from Exercise 29, find the intersection of two of the lines. Show that the point is on the third line.

31. Show that the point in Exercise 30 is equidistant from the vertices of $\triangle ABC$.

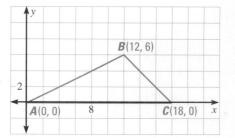

MIXED REVIEW

FINDING AREAS Find the area of the triangle described. (Review 1.7 for 5.3)

32. base = 9, height = 5

33. base = 22, height = 7

WRITING EQUATIONS The line with the given equation is perpendicular to line *j* at point *P*. Write an equation of line *j*. (Review 3.7)

34. $y = 3x - 2$, $P(1, 4)$

35. $y = -2x + 5$, $P(7, 6)$

36. $y = -\frac{2}{3}x - 1$, $P(2, 8)$

37. $y = \frac{10}{11}x + 3$, $P(-2, -9)$

🧩 **LOGICAL REASONING** Decide whether enough information is given to prove that the triangles are congruent. If there is enough information, tell which congruence postulate or theorem you would use. (Review 4.3, 4.4, and 4.6)

38.　　　　　**39.**　　　　　**40.**

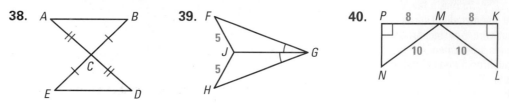

5.3

Medians and Altitudes of a Triangle

What you should learn

GOAL 1 Use properties of medians of a triangle.

GOAL 2 Use properties of altitudes of a triangle.

Why you should learn it

▼ To solve **real-life** problems, such as locating points in a triangle used to measure a person's heart fitness as in **Exs. 30–33**.

GOAL 1 USING MEDIANS OF A TRIANGLE

In Lesson 5.2, you studied two special types of segments of a triangle: perpendicular bisectors of the sides and angle bisectors. In this lesson, you will study two other special types of segments of a triangle: *medians* and *altitudes*.

A **median of a triangle** is a segment whose endpoints are a vertex of the triangle and the midpoint of the opposite side. For instance, in $\triangle ABC$ shown at the right, D is the midpoint of side $\overline{BC}$. So, $\overline{AD}$ is a median of the triangle.

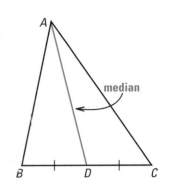

The three medians of a triangle are concurrent. The point of concurrency is called the **centroid of the triangle.** The centroid, labeled P in the diagrams below, is always inside the triangle.

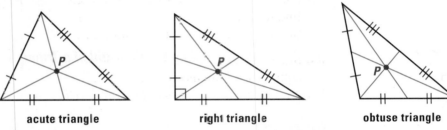

acute triangle   **right triangle**   **obtuse triangle**

The medians of a triangle have a special concurrency property, as described in Theorem 5.7. Exercises 13–16 ask you to use paper folding to demonstrate the relationships in this theorem. A proof appears on pages 836–837.

THEOREM

THEOREM 5.7   *Concurrency of Medians of a Triangle*

The medians of a triangle intersect at a point that is two thirds of the distance from each vertex to the midpoint of the opposite side.

If P is the centroid of $\triangle ABC$, then $AP = \frac{2}{3}AD$, $BP = \frac{2}{3}BF$, and $CP = \frac{2}{3}CE$.

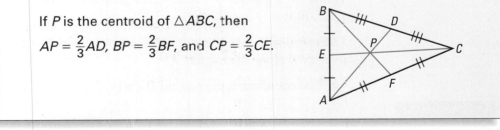

The centroid of a triangle can be used as its balancing point, as shown on the next page.

A triangular model of uniform thickness and density will balance at the centroid of the triangle. For instance, in the diagram shown at the right, the triangular model will balance if the tip of a pencil is placed at its centroid.

centroid

EXAMPLE 1 *Using the Centroid of a Triangle*

P is the centroid of $\triangle QRS$ shown below and $PT = 5$. Find RT and RP.

SOLUTION

Because P is the centroid, $RP = \frac{2}{3}RT$.

Then $PT = RT - RP = \frac{1}{3}RT$.

Substituting 5 for PT, $5 = \frac{1}{3}RT$, so $RT = 15$.

Then $RP = \frac{2}{3}RT = \frac{2}{3}(15) = 10$.

▶ So, $RP = 10$ and $RT = 15$.

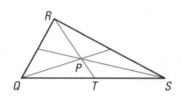

EXAMPLE 2 *Finding the Centroid of a Triangle*

Find the coordinates of the centroid of $\triangle JKL$.

SOLUTION

You know that the centroid is two thirds of the distance from each vertex to the midpoint of the opposite side.

Choose the median $\overline{KN}$. Find the coordinates of N, the midpoint of $\overline{JL}$. The coordinates of N are

$$\left(\frac{3 + 7}{2}, \frac{6 + 10}{2}\right) = \left(\frac{10}{2}, \frac{16}{2}\right) = (5, 8).$$

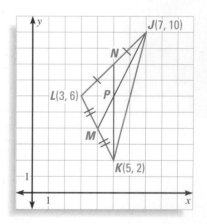

Find the distance from vertex K to midpoint N. The distance from $K(5, 2)$ to $N(5, 8)$ is $8 - 2$, or 6 units.

Determine the coordinates of the centroid, which is $\frac{2}{3} \cdot 6$, or **4 units up** from vertex K along the median $\overline{KN}$.

▶ The coordinates of centroid P are $(5, 2 + 4)$, or $(5, 6)$.

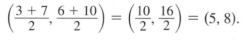

Exercises 21–23 ask you to use the Distance Formula to confirm that the distance from vertex J to the centroid P in Example 2 is two thirds of the distance from J to M, the midpoint of the opposite side.

USING ALTITUDES OF A TRIANGLE

An **altitude of a triangle** is the perpendicular segment from a vertex to the opposite side or to the line that contains the opposite side. An altitude can lie inside, on, or outside the triangle.

Every triangle has three altitudes. The lines containing the altitudes are concurrent and intersect at a point called the **orthocenter of the triangle**.

EXAMPLE 3 *Drawing Altitudes and Orthocenters*

Logical Reasoning

Where is the orthocenter located in each type of triangle?

a. Acute triangle **b.** Right triangle **c.** Obtuse triangle

SOLUTION

Draw an example of each type of triangle and locate its orthocenter.

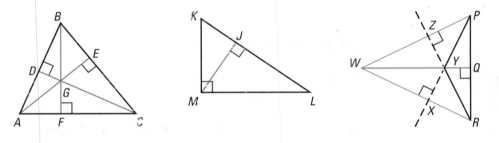

a. △*ABC* is an acute triangle. The three altitudes intersect at *G*, a point *inside* the triangle.

b. △*KLM* is a right triangle. The two legs, $\overline{LM}$ and $\overline{KM}$, are also altitudes. They intersect at the triangle's right angle. This implies that the orthocenter is *on* the triangle at *M*, the vertex of the right angle of the triangle.

c. △*YPR* is an obtuse triangle. The three lines that contain the altitudes intersect at *W*, a point that is *outside* the triangle.

THEOREM

THEOREM 5.8 *Concurrency of Altitudes of a Triangle*

The lines containing the altitudes of a triangle are concurrent.

If $\overline{AE}$, $\overline{BF}$, and $\overline{CD}$ are the altitudes of △*ABC*, then the lines $\overleftrightarrow{AE}$, $\overleftrightarrow{BF}$, and $\overleftrightarrow{CD}$ intersect at some point *H*.

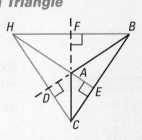

Exercises 24–26 ask you to use construction to verify Theorem 5.8. A proof appears on page 838.

GUIDED PRACTICE

Vocabulary Check ✔

1. The *centroid* of a triangle is the point where the three ___?___ intersect.

Concept Check ✔

2. In Example 3 on page 281, explain why the two legs of the right triangle in part (b) are also altitudes of the triangle.

Skill Check ✔

Use the diagram shown and the given information to decide in each case whether $\overline{EG}$ is a *perpendicular bisector*, an *angle bisector*, a *median*, or an *altitude* of $\triangle DEF$.

3. $\overline{DG} \cong \overline{FG}$

4. $\overline{EG} \perp \overline{DF}$

5. $\angle DEG \cong \angle FEG$

6. $\overline{EG} \perp \overline{DF}$ and $\overline{DG} \cong \overline{FG}$

7. $\triangle DGE \cong \triangle FGE$

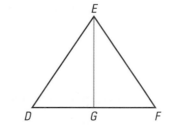

PRACTICE AND APPLICATIONS

STUDENT HELP

► **Extra Practice**
to help you master skills is on p. 811.

USING MEDIANS OF A TRIANGLE **In Exercises 8–12, use the figure below and the given information.**
P is the centroid of $\triangle DEF$, $\overline{EH} \perp \overline{DF}$, $DH = 9$, $DG = 7.5$, $EP = 8$, and $DE = FE$.

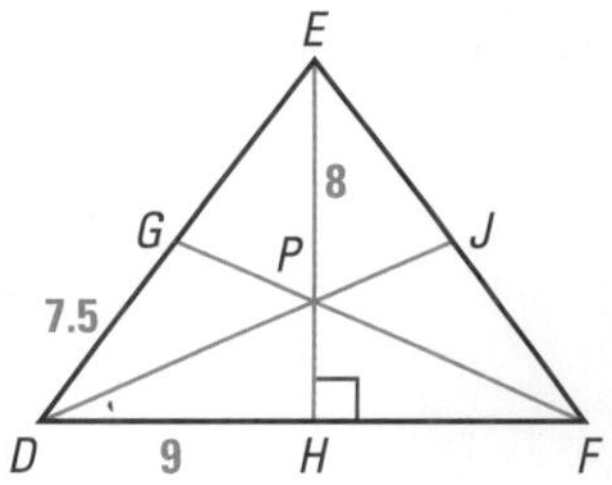

8. Find the length of $\overline{FH}$.

9. Find the length of $\overline{EH}$.

10. Find the length of $\overline{PH}$.

11. Find the perimeter of $\triangle DEF$.

12. ⬡ **LOGICAL REASONING** In the diagram of $\triangle DEF$ above, $\dfrac{EP}{EH} = \dfrac{2}{3}$.

Find $\dfrac{PH}{EH}$ and $\dfrac{PH}{EP}$.

PAPER FOLDING **Cut out a large acute, right, or obtuse triangle. Label the vertices. Follow the steps in Exercises 13–16 to verify Theorem 5.7.**

13. Fold the sides to locate the midpoint of each side. Label the midpoints.

14. Fold to form the median from each vertex to the midpoint of the opposite side.

15. Did your medians meet at about the same point? If so, label this centroid point.

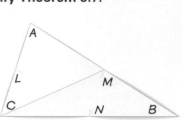

STUDENT HELP

► **HOMEWORK HELP**
Example 1: Exs. 8–11, 13–16
Example 2: Exs. 17–23
Example 3: Exs. 24–26

16. Verify that the distance from the centroid to a vertex is two thirds of the distance from that vertex to the midpoint of the opposite side.

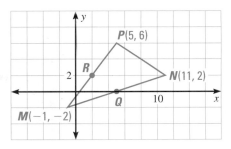

USING ALGEBRA Use the graph shown.

17. Find the coordinates of Q, the midpoint of $\overline{MN}$.

18. Find the length of the median $\overline{PQ}$.

19. Find the coordinates of the centroid. Label this point as T.

20. Find the coordinates of R, the midpoint of $\overline{MP}$. Show that the quotient $\frac{NT}{NR}$ is $\frac{2}{3}$.

USING ALGEBRA Refer back to Example 2 on page 280.

21. Find the coordinates of M, the midpoint of $\overline{KL}$.

22. Use the Distance Formula to find the lengths of $\overline{JP}$ and $\overline{JM}$.

23. Verify that $JP = \frac{2}{3}JM$.

STUDENT HELP

Look Back
To construct an altitude, use the construction of a perpendicular to a line through a point not on the line, as shown on p. 130.

CONSTRUCTION Draw and label a large scalene triangle of the given type and construct the altitudes. Verify Theorem 5.8 by showing that the lines containing the altitudes are concurrent, and label the orthocenter.

24. an acute $\triangle ABC$

25. a right $\triangle EFG$ with right angle at G

26. an obtuse $\triangle KLM$

TECHNOLOGY Use geometry software to draw a triangle. Label the vertices as *A*, *B*, and *C*.

27. Construct the altitudes of $\triangle ABC$ by drawing perpendicular lines through each side to the opposite vertex. Label them $\overline{AD}$, $\overline{BE}$, and $\overline{CF}$.

28. Find and label G and H, the intersections of $\overline{AD}$ and $\overline{BE}$ and of $\overline{BE}$ and $\overline{CF}$.

29. Prove that the altitudes are concurrent by showing that $GH = 0$.

FOCUS ON CAREERS

REAL LIFE CARDIOLOGY TECHNICIAN
Technicians use equipment like electrocardiographs to test, monitor, and evaluate heart function.

INTERNET CAREER LINK
www.mcdougallittell.com

ELECTROCARDIOGRAPH In Exercises 30–33, use the following information about electrocardiographs.
The equilateral triangle $\triangle BCD$ is used to plot electrocardiograph readings. Consider a person who has a left shoulder reading (S) of -1, a right shoulder reading (R) of 2, and a left leg reading (L) of 3.

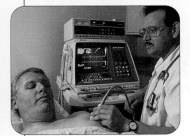

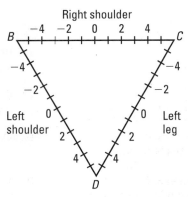

30. On a large copy of $\triangle BCD$, plot the reading to form the vertices of $\triangle SRL$. (This triangle is an *Einthoven's Triangle*, named for the inventor of the electrocardiograph.)

31. Construct the circumcenter M of $\triangle SRL$.

32. Construct the centroid P of $\triangle SRL$. Draw line r through P parallel to $\overline{BC}$.

33. Estimate the measure of the acute angle between line r and $\overline{MP}$. Cardiologists call this the angle of a person's heart.

Test Preparation

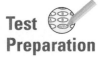

34. **MULTI-STEP PROBLEM** Recall the formula for the area of a triangle, $A = \frac{1}{2}bh$, where b is the length of the base and h is the height. The height of a triangle is the length of an altitude.

   a. Make a sketch of $\triangle ABC$. Find CD, the height of the triangle (the length of the altitude to side $\overline{AB}$).

   b. Use CD and AB to find the area of $\triangle ABC$.

   c. Draw $\overline{BE}$, the altitude to the line containing side $\overline{AC}$.

   d. Use the results of part (b) to find the length of $\overline{BE}$.

   e. *Writing* Write a formula for the length of an altitude in terms of the base and the area of the triangle. Explain.

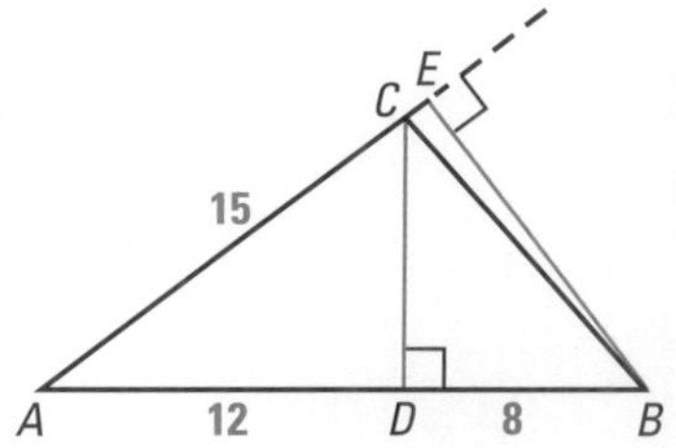

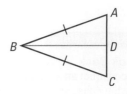

★ Challenge

SPECIAL TRIANGLES Use the diagram at the right.

35. **GIVEN** ▶ $\triangle ABC$ is isosceles.
    $\overline{BD}$ is a median to base $\overline{AC}$.

    PROVE ▶ $\overline{BD}$ is also an altitude.

36. Are the medians to the *legs* of an isosceles triangle also altitudes? Explain your reasoning.

37. Are the medians of an *equilateral* triangle also altitudes? Are they contained in the angle bisectors? Are they contained in the perpendicular bisectors?

EXTRA CHALLENGE

www.mcdougallittell.com

38. **LOGICAL REASONING** In a proof, if you are given a median of an equilateral triangle, what else can you conclude about the segment?

MIXED REVIEW

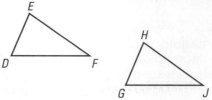

USING ALGEBRA Write an equation of the line that passes through point *P* and is parallel to the line with the given equation. (Review 3.6 for 5.4)

39. $P(1, 7), y = -x + 3$

40. $P(-3, -8), y = -2x - 3$

41. $P(4, -9), y = 3x + 5$

42. $P(4, -2), y = -\frac{1}{2}x - 1$

DEVELOPING PROOF In Exercises 43 and 44, state the third congruence that must be given to prove that $\triangle DEF \cong \triangle GHJ$ using the indicated postulate or theorem. (Review 4.4)

43. **GIVEN** ▶ $\angle D \cong \angle G$, $\overline{DF} \cong \overline{GJ}$
    AAS Congruence Theorem

44. **GIVEN** ▶ $\angle E \cong \angle H$, $\overline{EF} \cong \overline{HJ}$
    ASA Congruence Postulate

45. **USING THE DISTANCE FORMULA** Place a right triangle with legs of length 9 units and 13 units in a coordinate plane and use the Distance Formula to find the length of the hypotenuse. (Review 4.7)

Use the diagram shown and the given information. (Lesson 5.1)

$\overline{HJ}$ is the perpendicular bisector of $\overline{KL}$.

$\overrightarrow{HJ}$ bisects $\angle KHL$.

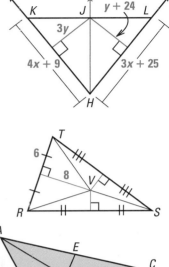

1. Find the value of x.

2. Find the value of y.

In the diagram shown, the perpendicular bisectors of $\triangle RST$ meet at V. (Lesson 5.2)

3. Find the length of $\overline{VT}$.

4. What is the length of $\overline{VS}$? Explain.

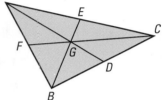

5. 🌐 **BUILDING A MOBILE** Suppose you want to attach the items in a mobile so that they hang horizontally. You would want to find the balancing point of each item. For the triangular metal plate shown, describe where the balancing point would be located. (Lesson 5.3)

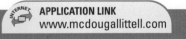

$\overline{AD}$, $\overline{BE}$, and $\overline{CF}$ are medians. $CF = 12$ in.

MATH & History

Optimization

🌐 **APPLICATION LINK**
www.mcdougallittell.com

THEN

THROUGHOUT HISTORY, people have faced problems involving minimizing resources or maximizing output, a process called optimization. The use of mathematics in solving these types of problems has increased greatly since World War II, when mathematicians found the optimal shape for naval convoys to avoid enemy fire.

NOW

TODAY, with the help of computers, optimization techniques are used in many industries, including manufacturing, economics, and architecture.

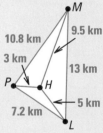

1. Your house is located at point H in the diagram. You need to do errands at the post office (P), the market (M), and the library (L). In what order should you do your errands to minimize the distance traveled?

2. Look back at Exercise 34 on page 270. Explain why the goalie's position on the angle bisector optimizes the chances of blocking a scoring shot.

1611

Johannes Kepler proposes the optimal way to stack cannonballs.

WWII naval convoy

1942

1972

This Olympic stadium roof uses a minimum of materials.

Thomas Hales proves Kepler's cannonball conjecture.

1997

Using Technology

Investigating Concurrent Lines

You can use geometry software to explore concurrent lines.

▶ **CONSTRUCT** Construct the angle bisectors of a triangle.

1 Draw any triangle *ABC*.

2 Draw the bisector $\overrightarrow{BD}$ of ∠*ABC*.
Then draw the bisector $\overrightarrow{CE}$ of ∠*BCA*.

3 Label the intersection point of the two angle bisectors as *F*.

4 Draw the ray from *A* that passes through *F*.

▶ **INVESTIGATE**

1. Measure ∠*BAF* and ∠*CAF* to show that $\overrightarrow{AF}$ is an angle bisector.

2. Explain how the results of Exercise 1 can be used to verify that the angle bisectors of a triangle are concurrent.

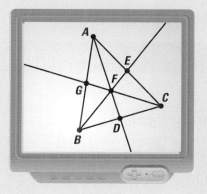

◀ **CONSTRUCT** Construct the medians of a triangle.

5 Draw any triangle *ABC*.

6 Locate the midpoint of $\overline{BC}$ and label it *D*.
Locate the midpoint of $\overline{AC}$ and label it *E*.

7 Draw the medians $\overline{AD}$ and $\overline{BE}$.

8 Label the intersection of the two medians as *F*.

9 Draw the ray from *C* that passes through *F*.
Label the intersection of $\overrightarrow{CF}$ and $\overline{AB}$ as *G*.

▶ **INVESTIGATE**

3. Measure $\overline{AG}$ and $\overline{BG}$. What do you notice? Is $\overline{CG}$ a median?

4. Explain how the results of Exercise 3 can be used to verify that the medians of a triangle are concurrent.

5. Measure $\overline{AD}$ and $\overline{AF}$. Calculate $\frac{AD}{AF}$. Is $AF = \frac{2}{3}AD$?

6. Drag point *A* to change the triangle. Does the quotient $\frac{AD}{AF}$ change?

EXTENSION

CRITICAL THINKING Find examples of triangles in which an angle bisector is contained in the same line as a median. Do the lines also contain an *altitude* and a *perpendicular bisector* of the triangle as well? Explain.

5.4

Midsegment Theorem

What you should learn

GOAL 1 Identify the midsegments of a triangle.

GOAL 2 Use properties of midsegments of a triangle.

Why you should learn it

▼ To solve **real-life** problems involving midsegments, as applied in **Exs. 32 and 35**.

The roof of the Cowles Conservatory in Minneapolis, Minnesota, shows the midsegments of a triangle.

GOAL 1 **USING MIDSEGMENTS OF A TRIANGLE**

In Lessons 5.2 and 5.3, you studied four special types of segments of a triangle: perpendicular bisectors, angle bisectors, medians, and altitudes. Another special type of segment is called a *midsegment*. A **midsegment of a triangle** is a segment that connects the midpoints of two sides of a triangle.

You can form the three midsegments of a triangle by tracing the triangle on paper, cutting it out, and folding it, as shown below.

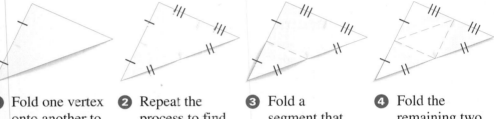

1 Fold one vertex onto another to find one midpoint.

2 Repeat the process to find the other two midpoints.

3 Fold a segment that contains two of the midpoints.

4 Fold the remaining two midsegments of the triangle.

The midsegments and sides of a triangle have a special relationship, as shown in Example 1 and Theorem 5.9 on the next page.

EXAMPLE 1 *Using Midsegments*

Show that the midsegment $\overline{MN}$ is parallel to side $\overline{JK}$ and is half as long.

SOLUTION

Use the Midpoint Formula to find the coordinates of M and N.

$$M = \left(\frac{-2+6}{2}, \frac{3+(-1)}{2}\right) = (2, 1)$$

$$N = \left(\frac{4+6}{2}, \frac{5+(-1)}{2}\right) = (5, 2)$$

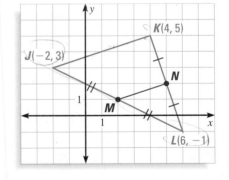

Next, find the slopes of $\overline{JK}$ and $\overline{MN}$.

$$\text{Slope of } \overline{JK} = \frac{5-3}{4-(-2)} = \frac{2}{6} = \frac{1}{3} \qquad \text{Slope of } \overline{MN} = \frac{2-1}{5-2} = \frac{1}{3}$$

▶ Because their slopes are equal, $\overline{JK}$ and $\overline{MN}$ are parallel. You can use the Distance Formula to show that $MN = \sqrt{10}$ and $JK = \sqrt{40} = 2\sqrt{10}$. So, $\overline{MN}$ is half as long as $\overline{JK}$.

THEOREM

THEOREM 5.9 *Midsegment Theorem*

The segment connecting the midpoints of two sides of a triangle is parallel to the third side and is half as long.

$$\overline{DE} \parallel \overline{AB} \text{ and } DE = \frac{1}{2}AB$$

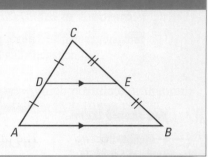

EXAMPLE 2 *Using the Midsegment Theorem*

$\overline{UW}$ and $\overline{VW}$ are midsegments of $\triangle RST$. Find UW and RT.

SOLUTION

$$UW = \frac{1}{2}(RS) = \frac{1}{2}(12) = 6$$

$$RT = 2(VW) = 2(8) = 16$$

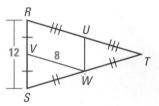

· · · · · · · · · ·

A coordinate proof of Theorem 5.9 for one midsegment of a triangle is given below. Exercises 23–25 ask for proofs about the other two midsegments. To set up a coordinate proof, remember to place the figure in a convenient location.

Proof

EXAMPLE 3 *Proving Theorem 5.9*

Write a coordinate proof of the Midsegment Theorem.

SOLUTION

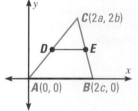

Place points A, B, and C in convenient locations in a coordinate plane, as shown. Use the Midpoint Formula to find the coordinates of the midpoints D and E.

$$D = \left(\frac{2a + 0}{2}, \frac{2b + 0}{2}\right) = (a, b) \qquad E = \left(\frac{2a + 2c}{2}, \frac{2b + 0}{2}\right) = (a + c, b)$$

Find the slope of midsegment $\overline{DE}$. Points D and E have the same y-coordinates, so the slope of $\overline{DE}$ is zero.

▶ $\overline{AB}$ also has a slope of zero, so the slopes are equal and $\overline{DE}$ and $\overline{AB}$ are parallel.

Calculate the lengths of $\overline{DE}$ and $\overline{AB}$. The segments are both horizontal, so their lengths are given by the absolute values of the differences of their x-coordinates.

$$AB = |2c - 0| = 2c \qquad\qquad DE = |a + c - a| = c$$

▶ The length of $\overline{DE}$ is half the length of $\overline{AB}$.

Suppose you are given only the three midpoints of the sides of a triangle. Is it possible to draw the original triangle? Example 4 shows one method.

Using Algebra

EXAMPLE 4 *Using Midpoints to Draw a Triangle*

The midpoints of the sides of a triangle are $L(4, 2)$, $M(2, 3)$, and $N(5, 4)$. What are the coordinates of the vertices of the triangle?

SOLUTION

Plot the midpoints in a coordinate plane.

Connect these midpoints to form the midsegments $\overline{LN}$, $\overline{MN}$, and $\overline{ML}$.

Find the slopes of the midsegments. Use the slope formula as shown.

Each midsegment contains two of the unknown triangle's midpoints and is parallel to the side that contains the third midpoint. So, you know a point on each side of the triangle and the slope of each side.

Draw the lines that contain the three sides.

▶ The lines intersect at $A(3, 5)$, $B(7, 3)$, and $C(1, 1)$, which are the vertices of the triangle.

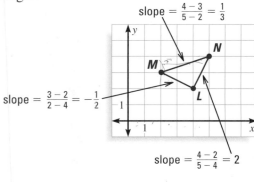
$$\text{slope} = \frac{4-3}{5-2} = \frac{1}{3}$$
$$\text{slope} = \frac{3-2}{2-4} = -\frac{1}{2}$$
$$\text{slope} = \frac{4-2}{5-4} = 2$$

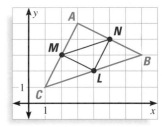

. . . .

The perimeter of the triangle formed by the three midsegments of a triangle is *half* the perimeter of the original triangle, as shown in Example 5.

EXAMPLE 5 *Perimeter of Midsegment Triangle*

ORIGAMI is an ancient method of paper folding. The pattern of folds for a number of objects, such as the flower shown, involve midsegments.

ORIGAMI $\overline{DE}$, $\overline{EF}$, and $\overline{DF}$ are midsegments in $\triangle ABC$. Find the perimeter of $\triangle DEF$.

SOLUTION The lengths of the midsegments are half the lengths of the sides of $\triangle ABC$.

$$DF = \frac{1}{2}AB = \frac{1}{2}(10) = 5$$

$$EF = \frac{1}{2}AC = \frac{1}{2}(10) = 5$$

$$ED = \frac{1}{2}BC = \frac{1}{2}(14.2) = 7.1$$

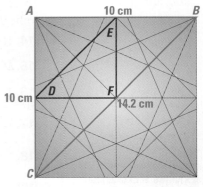

Crease pattern of origami flower

▶ The perimeter of $\triangle DEF$ is $5 + 5 + 7.1$, or 17.1. The perimeter of $\triangle ABC$ is $10 + 10 + 14.2$, or 34.2, so the perimeter of the triangle formed by the midsegments is half the perimeter of the original triangle.

GUIDED PRACTICE

Vocabulary Check ✓   **1.** In △ABC, if *M* is the midpoint of $\overline{AB}$, *N* is the midpoint of $\overline{AC}$, and *P* is the midpoint of $\overline{BC}$, then $\overline{MN}$, $\overline{NP}$, and $\overline{PN}$ are __?__ of △ABC.

Concept Check ✓   **2.** In Example 3 on page 288, why was it convenient to position one of the sides of the triangle along the *x*-axis?

Skill Check ✓   In Exercises 3–9, $\overline{GH}$, $\overline{HJ}$, and $\overline{JG}$ are midsegments of △*DEF*.

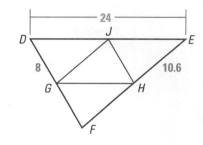

3. $\overline{JH} \parallel$ __?__   **4.** __?__ $\parallel \overline{DE}$

5. $EF =$ __?__   **6.** $GH =$ __?__

7. $DF =$ __?__   **8.** $JH =$ __?__

9. Find the perimeter of △*GHJ*.

🌐 **WALKWAYS** The triangle below shows a section of walkways on a college campus.

10. The midsegment $\overline{AB}$ represents a new walkway that is to be constructed on the campus. What are the coordinates of points *A* and *B*?

11. Each unit in the coordinate plane represents 10 yards. Use the Distance Formula to find the length of the new walkway.

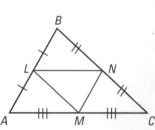

PRACTICE AND APPLICATIONS

STUDENT HELP

➤ **Extra Practice**
to help you master
skills is on p. 812.

COMPLETE THE STATEMENT In Exercises 12–19, use △*ABC*, where *L*, *M*, and *N* are midpoints of the sides.

12. $\overline{LM} \parallel$ __?__

13. $\overline{AB} \parallel$ __?__

14. If $AC = 20$, then $LN =$ __?__.

15. If $MN = 7$, then $AB =$ __?__.

16. If $NC = 9$, then $LM =$ __?__.

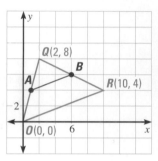

17. ⊗ᵧ **USING ALGEBRA** If $LM = 3x + 7$ and $BC = 7x + 6$, then $LM =$ __?__.

18. ⊗ᵧ **USING ALGEBRA** If $MN = x - 1$ and $AB = 6x - 18$, then $AB =$ __?__.

19. 🐾 **LOGICAL REASONING** Which angles in the diagram are congruent? Explain your reasoning.

20. 📐 **CONSTRUCTION** Use a straightedge to draw a triangle. Then use the straightedge and a compass to construct the three midsegments of the triangle.

STUDENT HELP

➤ **HOMEWORK HELP**
Example 1: Exs. 21, 22
Example 2: Exs. 12–16
Example 3: Exs. 23–25
Example 4: Exs. 26, 27
Example 5: Exs. 28, 29

USING ALGEBRA Use the diagram.

21. Find the coordinates of the endpoints of each midsegment of $\triangle ABC$.

22. Use slope and the Distance Formula to verify that the Midsegment Theorem is true for $\overline{DF}$.

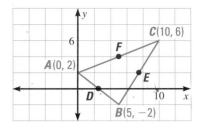

USING ALGEBRA Copy the diagram in Example 3 on page 288 to complete the proof of Theorem 5.9, the Midsegment Theorem.

23. Locate the midpoint of $\overline{AB}$ and label it F. What are the coordinates of F? Draw midsegments $\overline{DF}$ and $\overline{EF}$.

24. Use slopes to show that $\overline{DF} \parallel \overline{CB}$ and $\overline{EF} \parallel \overline{CA}$.

25. Use the Distance Formula to find DF, EF, CB, and CA. Verify that $DF = \frac{1}{2}CB$ and $EF = \frac{1}{2}CA$.

USING ALGEBRA In Exercises 26 and 27, you are given the midpoints of the sides of a triangle. Find the coordinates of the vertices of the triangle.

26. $L(1, 3)$, $M(5, 9)$, $N(4, 4)$

27. $L(7, 1)$, $M(9, 6)$, $N(5, 4)$

FINDING PERIMETER In Exercises 28 and 29, use the diagram shown.

28. Given $CD = 14$, $GF = 8$, and $GC = 5$, find the perimeter of $\triangle BCD$.

29. Given $PQ = 20$, $SU = 12$, and $QU = 9$, find the perimeter of $\triangle STU$.

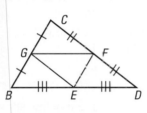

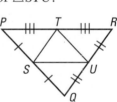

30. **TECHNOLOGY** Use geometry software to draw any $\triangle ABC$. Construct the midpoints of $\overline{AB}$, $\overline{BC}$, and $\overline{CA}$. Label them as D, E, and F. Construct the midpoints of $\overline{DE}$, $\overline{EF}$, and $\overline{FD}$. Label them as G, H, and I. What is the relationship between the perimeters of $\triangle ABC$ and $\triangle GHI$?

31. **FRACTALS** The design below, which approximates a *fractal*, is created with midsegments. Beginning with any triangle, shade the triangle formed by the three midsegments. Continue the process for each unshaded triangle. Suppose the perimeter of the original triangle is 1. What is the perimeter of the triangle that is shaded in Stage 1? What is the total perimeter of all the triangles that are shaded in Stage 2? in Stage 3?

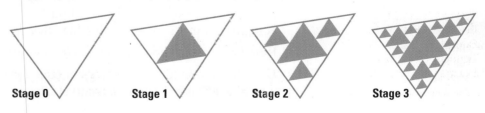

Stage 0   Stage 1   Stage 2   Stage 3

32.  **PORCH SWING** You are assembling the frame for a porch swing. The horizontal crossbars in the kit you purchased are each 30 inches long. You attach the crossbars at the midpoints of the legs. At each end of the frame, how far apart will the bottoms of the legs be when the frame is assembled? Explain.

crossbar

33. ▶ **WRITING A PROOF** Write a paragraph proof using the diagram shown and the given information.

GIVEN ▶ $\triangle ABC$ with midsegments $\overline{DE}$, $\overline{EF}$, and $\overline{FD}$

PROVE ▶ $\triangle ADE \cong \triangle DBF$

Plan for Proof Use the SAS Congruence Postulate. Show that $\overline{AD} \cong \overline{DB}$. Show that because $DE = BF = \frac{1}{2}BC$, then $\overline{DE} \cong \overline{BF}$. Use parallel lines to show that $\angle ADE \cong \angle ABC$.

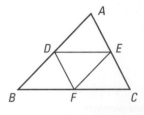

34. ▶ **WRITING A PLAN** Using the information from Exercise 33, write a plan for a proof showing how you could use the SSS Congruence Postulate to prove that $\triangle ADE \cong \triangle DBF$.

35. 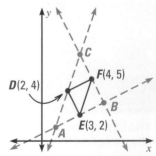 **A-FRAME HOUSE** In the A-frame house shown, the floor of the second level, labeled $\overline{PQ}$, is closer to the first floor, $\overline{RS}$, than midsegment $\overline{MN}$ is. If $\overline{RS}$ is 24 feet long, can $\overline{PQ}$ be 10 feet long? 12 feet long? 14 feet long? 24 feet long? Explain.

Test Preparation

36. MULTI-STEP PROBLEM The diagram below shows the points $D(2, 4)$, $E(3, 2)$, and $F(4, 5)$, which are midpoints of the sides of $\triangle ABC$. The directions below show how to use equations of lines to reconstruct the original $\triangle ABC$.

a. Plot D, E, and F in a coordinate plane.

b. Find the slope m_1 of one midsegment, say $\overline{DE}$.

c. The line containing side $\overline{CB}$ will have the same slope as $\overline{DE}$. Because $\overleftrightarrow{CB}$ contains $F(4, 5)$, an equation of $\overleftrightarrow{CB}$ in *point-slope form* is $y - 5 = m_1(x - 4)$. Write an equation of $\overleftrightarrow{CB}$.

d. Find the slopes m_2 and m_3 of the other two midsegments. Use these slopes to find equations of the lines containing the other two sides of $\triangle ABC$.

e. Rewrite your equations from parts (c) and (d) in *slope-intercept form*.

f. Use substitution to solve systems of equations to find the intersection of each pair of lines. Plot these points A, B, and C on your graph.

STUDENT HELP

▶ **Skills Review**
For help with writing an equation of a line, see page 795.

37. FINDING A PATTERN In △ABC, the length of $\overline{AB}$ is 24. In the triangle, a succession of midsegments are formed.

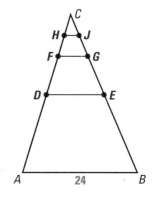

- At Stage 1, draw the midsegment of △ABC. Label it $\overline{DE}$.

- At Stage 2, draw the midsegment of △DEC. Label it $\overline{FG}$.

- At Stage 3, draw the midsegment of △FGC. Label it $\overline{HJ}$.

Copy and complete the table showing the length of the midsegment at each stage.

Stage n	0	1	2	3	4	5
Midsegment length	24	?	?	?	?	?

38. USING ALGEBRA In Exercise 37, let y represent the length of the midsegment at Stage n. Construct a scatter plot for the data given in the table. Then find a function that gives the length of the midsegment at Stage n.

MIXED REVIEW

SOLVING EQUATIONS **Solve the equation and state a reason for each step.** (Review 2.4)

39. $x - 3 = 11$

40. $3x + 13 = 46$

41. $8x - 1 = 2x + 17$

42. $5x + 12 = 9x - 4$

43. $2(4x - 1) = 14$

44. $9(3x + 10) = 27$

45. $-2(x + 1) + 3 = 23$

46. $3x + 2(x + 5) = 40$

USING ALGEBRA **Find the value of x.** (Review 4.1 for 5.5)

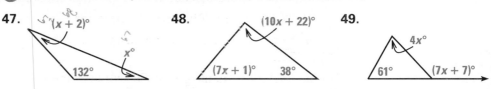

47. **48.** **49.**

ANGLE BISECTORS $\overrightarrow{AD}$, $\overrightarrow{BD}$, and $\overrightarrow{CD}$ are angle bisectors of △ABC. (Review 5.2)

50. Explain why $\angle CAD \cong \angle BAD$ and $\angle BCD \cong \angle ACD$.

51. Is point D the *circumcenter* or *incenter* of △ABC?

52. Explain why $\overline{DE} \cong \overline{DG} \cong \overline{DF}$.

53. Suppose $CD = 10$ and $EC = 8$. Find DF.

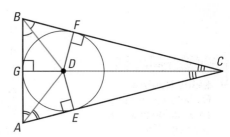

ACTIVITY 5.5

Using Technology

Side Lengths and Angle Measures

You can use geometry software to decide which sides and angles are the smallest and largest in a triangle.

STUDENT HELP

INTERNET SOFTWARE HELP

Visit our Web site www.mcdougallittell.com to see instructions for several software applications.

CONSTRUCT Construct a triangle.

1. Draw any scalene triangle. Label the vertices as A, B, and C.
2. Find the measure of each angle of the triangle.
3. Find the length of each side of the triangle.

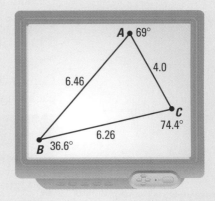

INVESTIGATE

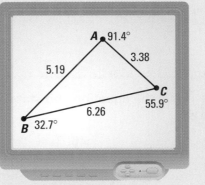

1. In $\triangle ABC$, is the longest side *adjacent to* or *opposite* the largest angle?
2. In $\triangle ABC$, is the shortest side *adjacent to* or *opposite* the smallest angle?
3. Drag point A to change the shape and size of $\triangle ABC$. Answer the questions in Exercises 1 and 2 for the new triangle.

MAKE A CONJECTURE

4. Make a conjecture about how the positions of sides of different lengths in a triangle are related to the positions of the angles of different measures.

EXTENSION

CRITICAL THINKING Use the triangle measurements from the activity above. Complete the following expressions.

$$\frac{\text{measure of smallest angle}}{\text{measure of largest angle}} = \frac{?}{?} = \underline{\quad ? \quad}$$

$$\frac{\text{length of shortest side}}{\text{length of longest side}} = \frac{?}{?} = \underline{\quad ? \quad}$$

Tell whether this statement is *true* or *false*:

"The quotient of the measures of two angles in a triangle is always the same as the quotient of the lengths of the sides opposite those angles."

5.5

Inequalities in One Triangle

What you should learn

GOAL 1 Use triangle measurements to decide which side is longest or which angle is largest, as applied in **Example 2**.

GOAL 2 Use the Triangle Inequality.

Why you should learn it

▼ To solve **real-life** problems, such as describing the motion of a crane as it clears the sediment from the mouth of a river in **Exs. 29–31**.

GOAL 1 COMPARING MEASUREMENTS OF A TRIANGLE

In Activity 5.5, you may have discovered a relationship between the positions of the longest and shortest sides of a triangle and the positions of its angles.

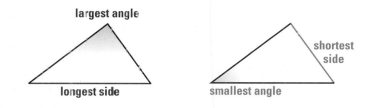

largest angle

longest side

shortest side

smallest angle

The diagrams illustrate the results stated in the theorems below.

THEOREMS

THEOREM 5.10

If one side of a triangle is longer than another side, then the angle opposite the longer side is larger than the angle opposite the shorter side.

THEOREM 5.11

If one angle of a triangle is larger than another angle, then the side opposite the larger angle is longer than the side opposite the smaller angle.

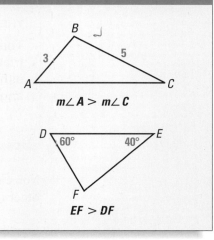

$m\angle A > m\angle C$

$EF > DF$

You can write the measurements of a triangle in order from least to greatest.

EXAMPLE 1 *Writing Measurements in Order from Least to Greatest*

Write the measurements of the triangles in order from least to greatest.

a.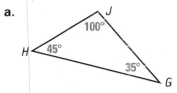

b.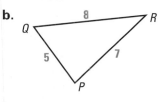

SOLUTION

a. $m\angle G < m\angle H < m\angle J$
   $JH < JG < GH$

b. $QP < PR < QR$
   $m\angle R < m\angle Q < m\angle P$

Theorem 5.11 will be proved in Lesson 5.6, using a technique called *indirect proof*. Theorem 5.10 can be proved using the diagram shown below.

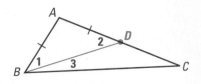

GIVEN ▶ $AC > AB$

PROVE ▶ $m\angle ABC > m\angle C$

Paragraph Proof Use the Ruler Postulate to locate a point D on $\overline{AC}$ such that $DA = BA$. Then draw the segment $\overline{BD}$. In the isosceles triangle $\triangle ABD$, $\angle 1 \cong \angle 2$. Because $m\angle ABC = m\angle 1 + m\angle 3$, it follows that $m\angle ABC > m\angle 1$. Substituting $m\angle 2$ for $m\angle 1$ produces $m\angle ABC > m\angle 2$. Because $m\angle 2 = m\angle 3 + m\angle C$, $m\angle 2 > m\angle C$. Finally, because $m\angle ABC > m\angle 2$ and $m\angle 2 > m\angle C$, you can conclude that $m\angle ABC > m\angle C$.

· · · · · · · · · ·

The proof of Theorem 5.10 above uses the fact that $\angle 2$ is an exterior angle for $\triangle BDC$, so its measure is the sum of the measures of the two nonadjacent interior angles. Then $m\angle 2$ must be greater than the measure of either nonadjacent interior angle. This result is stated below as Theorem 5.12.

THEOREM

THEOREM 5.12 *Exterior Angle Inequality*

The measure of an exterior angle of a triangle is greater than the measure of either of the two nonadjacent interior angles.

$m\angle 1 > m\angle A$ and $m\angle 1 > m\angle B$

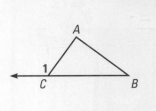

You can use Theorem 5.10 to determine possible angle measures in a chair or other real-life object.

EXAMPLE 2 *Using Theorem 5.10*

DIRECTOR'S CHAIR In the director's chair shown, $\overline{AB} \cong \overline{AC}$ and $BC > AB$. What can you conclude about the angles in $\triangle ABC$?

SOLUTION

Because $\overline{AB} \cong \overline{AC}$, $\triangle ABC$ is isosceles, so $\angle B \cong \angle C$. Therefore, $m\angle B = m\angle C$. Because $BC > AB$, $m\angle A > m\angle C$ by Theorem 5.10. By substitution, $m\angle A > m\angle B$. In addition, you can conclude that $m\angle A > 60°$, $m\angle B < 60°$, and $m\angle C < 60°$.

GOAL 2 USING THE TRIANGLE INEQUALITY

Not every group of three segments can be used to form a triangle. The lengths of the segments must fit a certain relationship.

EXAMPLE 3 *Constructing a Triangle*

Construct a triangle with the given group of side lengths, if possible.

a. 2 cm, 2 cm, 5 cm   **b.** 3 cm, 2 cm, 5 cm   **c.** 4 cm, 2 cm, 5 cm

SOLUTION

Try drawing triangles with the given side lengths. Only group (c) is possible. The sum of the first and second lengths must be greater than the third length.

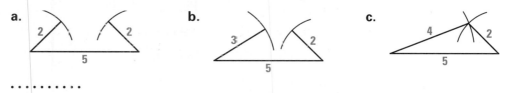

a.   **b.**   **c.**

· · · · · · · · · ·

The result of Example 3 is summarized as Theorem 5.13. Exercise 34 asks you to write a proof of this theorem.

THEOREM

THEOREM 5.13 *Triangle Inequality*

The sum of the lengths of any two sides of a triangle is greater than the length of the third side.

$AB + BC > AC$

$AC + BC > AB$

$AB + AC > BC$

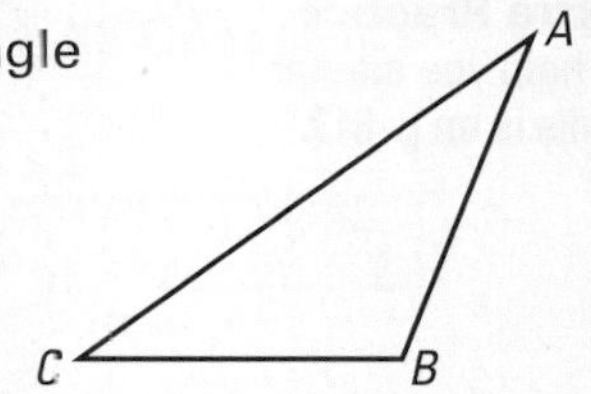

EXAMPLE 4 *Finding Possible Side Lengths*

A triangle has one side of 10 centimeters and another of 14 centimeters. Describe the possible lengths of the third side.

SOLUTION

Let x represent the length of the third side. Using the Triangle Inequality, you can write and solve inequalities.

$$x + 10 > 14 \qquad\qquad 10 + 14 > x$$

$$x > 4 \qquad\qquad\qquad 24 > x$$

▶ So, the length of the third side must be greater than 4 centimeters and less than 24 centimeters.

STUDENT HELP

↪ **Skills Review**
For help with solving inequalities, see p. 791.

GUIDED PRACTICE

Vocabulary Check ✓

1. $\triangle ABC$ has side lengths of 1 inch, $1\frac{7}{8}$ inches, and $2\frac{1}{8}$ inches and angle measures of 90°, 28°, and 62°. Which side is *opposite* each angle?

Concept Check ✓

2. Is it possible to draw a triangle with side lengths of 5 inches, 2 inches, and 8 inches? Explain why or why not.

Skill Check ✓

In Exercises 3 and 4, use the figure shown at the right.

3. Name the smallest and largest angles of $\triangle DEF$.

4. Name the shortest and longest sides of $\triangle DEF$.

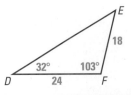

5. 🌐 **GEOGRAPHY** Suppose you know the following information about distances between cities in the Philippine Islands:

Cadiz to Masbate: 99 miles

Cadiz to Guiuan: 165 miles

Describe the range of possible distances from Guiuan to Masbate.

PRACTICE AND APPLICATIONS

STUDENT HELP

▶ **Extra Practice**
to help you master
skills is on p. 812.

COMPARING SIDE LENGTHS Name the shortest and longest sides of the triangle.

6.
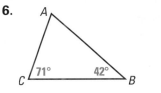

7.
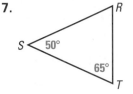

8.
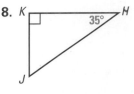

COMPARING ANGLE MEASURES Name the smallest and largest angles of the triangle.

9.
10. 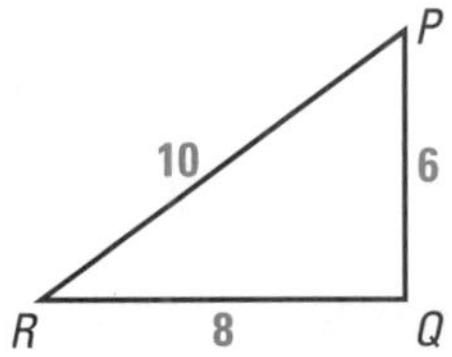
11.
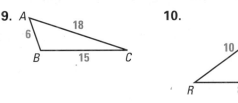

STUDENT HELP

▶ **HOMEWORK HELP**
Example 1: Exs. 6–19
Example 2: Exs. 6–19
Example 3: Exs. 20–23
Example 4: Exs. 24, 25

USING ALGEBRA Use the diagram of $\triangle RST$ with exterior angle $\angle QRT$.

12. Write an equation about the angle measures labeled in the diagram.

13. Write two inequalities about the angle measures labeled in the diagram.

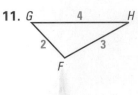

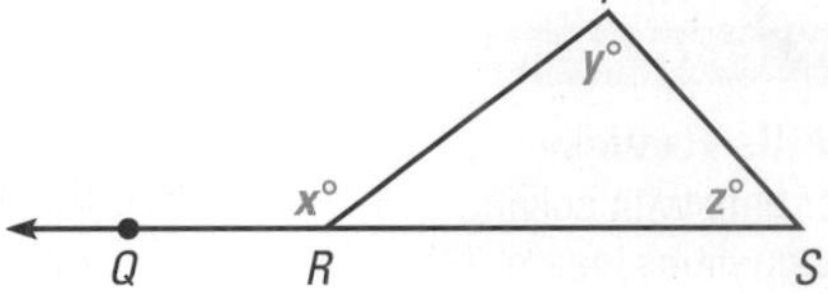

ORDERING SIDES List the sides in order from shortest to longest.

14.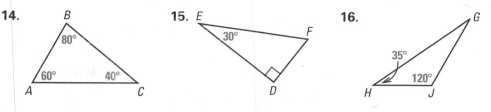

15.

16.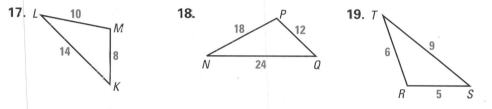

ORDERING ANGLES List the angles in order from smallest to largest.

17. L——10——M
14   8
K

18.   P
18   12
N——24——Q

19. T
6   9
R   5   S

FORMING TRIANGLES In Exercises 20–23, you are given an 18 inch piece of wire. You want to bend the wire to form a triangle so that the length of each side is a whole number.

20. Sketch four possible isosceles triangles and label each side length.

21. Sketch a possible acute scalene triangle.

22. Sketch a possible obtuse scalene triangle.

23. List three combinations of segment lengths that will not produce triangles.

(xy) USING ALGEBRA In Exercises 24 and 25, solve the inequality $AB + AC > BC$.

24.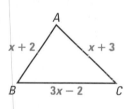

25.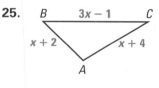

26. 🌐 **TAKING A SHORTCUT** Look at the diagram shown. Suppose you are walking south on the sidewalk of Pine Street. When you reach Pleasant Street, you cut across the empty lot to go to the corner of Oak Hill Avenue and Union Street. Explain why this route is shorter than staying on the sidewalks.

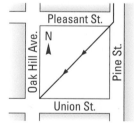

🌐 **KITCHEN TRIANGLE** In Exercises 27 and 28, use the following information.

The term "kitchen triangle" refers to the imaginary triangle formed by three kitchen appliances: the refrigerator, the sink, and the range. The distances shown are measured in feet.

27. What is wrong with the labels on the kitchen triangle?

28. Can a kitchen triangle have the following side lengths: 9 feet, 3 feet, and 5 feet? Explain why or why not.

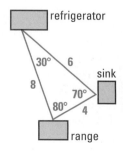

CHANNEL DREDGING In Exercises 29–31, use the figure shown and the given information.

The crane is used in dredging mouths of rivers to clear out the collected debris. By adjusting the length of the boom lines from A to B, the operator of the crane can raise and lower the boom. Suppose the mast $\overline{AC}$ is 50 feet long and the boom $\overline{BC}$ is 100 feet long.

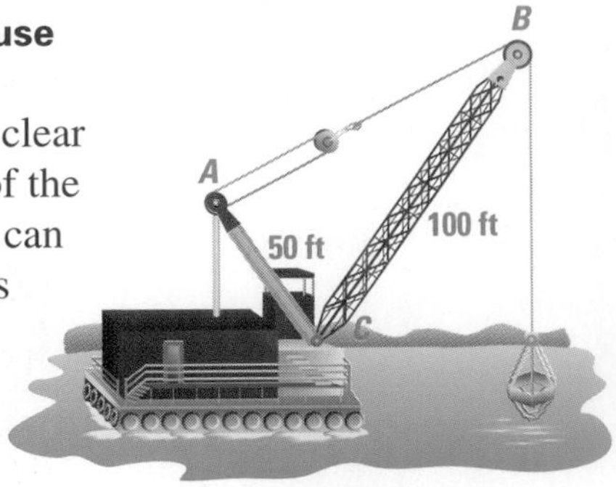

29. Is the boom *raised* or *lowered* when the boom lines are shortened?

30. AB must be less than __?__ feet.

31. As the boom and shovel are raised or lowered, is $\angle ACB$ ever larger than $\angle BAC$? Explain.

32. 🧩 **LOGICAL REASONING** In Example 4 on page 297, only two inequalities were needed to solve the problem. Write the third inequality. Why is that inequality not helpful in determining the range of values of x?

STUDENT HELP

HOMEWORK HELP
Visit our Web site
www.mcdougallittell.com
for help with proof.

33. ▶ **PROOF** Prove that a perpendicular segment is the shortest line segment from a point to a line. Prove that $\overline{MJ}$ is the shortest line segment from M to $\overleftrightarrow{JN}$.

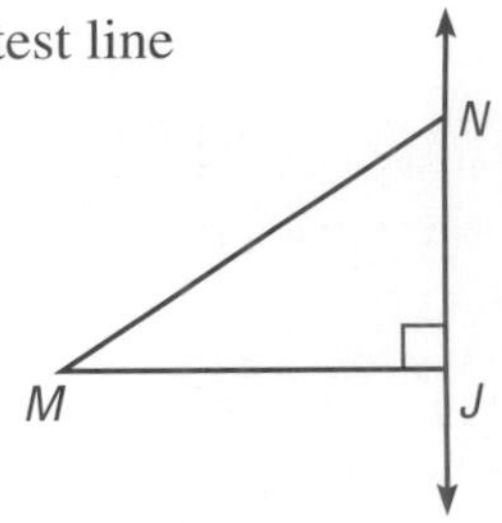

GIVEN ▶ $\overline{MJ} \perp \overleftrightarrow{JN}$

PROVE ▶ $MN > MJ$

Plan for Proof Show that $m\angle MJN > m\angle MNJ$, so $MN > MJ$.

34. ▶ **DEVELOPING PROOF** Complete the proof of Theorem 5.13, the Triangle Inequality.

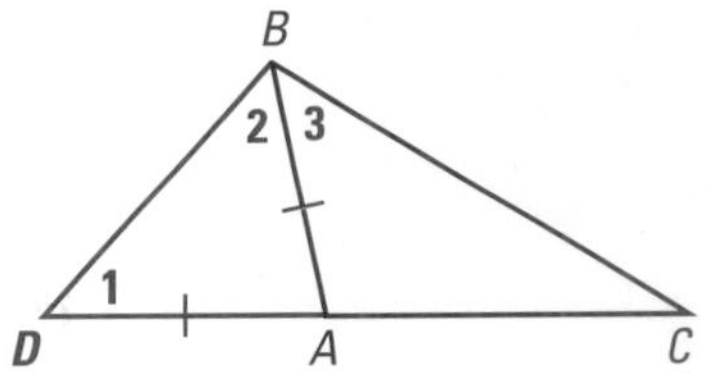

GIVEN ▶ $\triangle ABC$

PROVE ▶ (1) $AB + BC > AC$
(2) $AC + BC > AB$
(3) $AB + AC > BC$

Plan for Proof One side, say $\overline{BC}$, is longer than or is at least as long as each of the other sides. Then (1) and (2) are true. The proof for (3) is as follows.

Statements	Reasons
1. $\triangle ABC$	1. Given
2. Extend $\overline{AC}$ to D such that $\overline{AB} \cong \overline{AD}$.	2. __?__
3. $AD + AC =$ __?__	3. Segment Addition Postulate
4. $\angle 1 \cong \angle 2$	4. __?__
5. $m\angle DBC >$ __?__	5. Protractor Postulate
6. $m\angle DBC > m\angle 1$	6. __?__
7. $DC > BC$	7. __?__
8. __?__ + __?__ $> BC$	8. Substitution property of equality
9. $AB + AC >$ __?__	9. Substitution property of equality

Test Preparation

QUANTITATIVE COMPARISON In Exercises 35–37, use the diagram to choose the statement that is true about the given quantities.

  Ⓐ The quantity in column A is greater.

  Ⓑ The quantity in column B is greater.

  Ⓒ The two quantities are equal.

  Ⓓ The relationship cannot be determined from the given information.

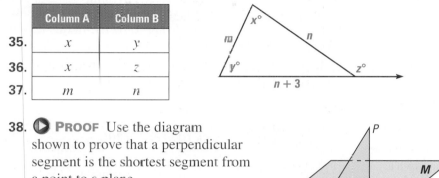

	Column A	Column B
35.	x	y
36.	x	z
37.	m	n

★ **Challenge**

38. ▶ **PROOF** Use the diagram shown to prove that a perpendicular segment is the shortest segment from a point to a plane.

  GIVEN ▶ $\overline{PC} \perp$ plane M

  PROVE ▶ $PD > PC$

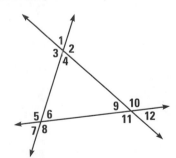

MIXED REVIEW

RECOGNIZING PROOFS In Exercises 39–41, look through your textbook to find an example of the type of proof. **(Review Chapters 2–5 for 5.6)**

39. two-column proof

40. paragraph proof

41. flow proof

ANGLE RELATIONSHIPS Complete each statement. **(Review 3.1)**

42. ∠5 and __?__ are corresponding angles. So are ∠5 and __?__ .

43. ∠12 and __?__ are vertical angles.

44. ∠6 and __?__ are alternate interior angles. So are ∠6 and __?__ .

45. ∠7 and __?__ are alternate exterior angles. So are ∠7 and __?__ .

USING ALGEBRA In Exercises 46–49, you are given the coordinates of the midpoints of the sides of a triangle. Find the coordinates of the vertices of the triangle. **(Review 5.4)**

46. $L(-2, 1), M(2, 3), N(3, -1)$ **47.** $L(-3, 5), M(-2, 2), N(-6, 0)$

48. $L(3, 6), M(9, 5), N(8, 1)$ **49.** $L(3, -2), M(0, -4), N(3, -6)$

Indirect Proof and Inequalities in Two Triangles

What you should learn

GOAL 1 Read and write an indirect proof.

GOAL 2 Use the Hinge Theorem and its converse to compare side lengths and angle measures.

Why you should learn it

▼ To solve **real-life** problems, such as deciding which of two planes is farther from an airport in **Example 4** and **Exs. 28 and 29.**

GOAL 1 USING INDIRECT PROOF

Up to now, all of the proofs in this textbook have used the Laws of Syllogism and Detachment to obtain conclusions directly. In this lesson, you will study *indirect proofs*. An **indirect proof** is a proof in which you prove that a statement is true by first assuming that its opposite is true. If this assumption leads to an impossibility, then you have proved that the original statement is true.

EXAMPLE 1 *Using Indirect Proof*

Use an indirect proof to prove that a triangle cannot have more than one obtuse angle.

SOLUTION

GIVEN ▶ $\triangle ABC$

PROVE ▶ $\triangle ABC$ does not have more than one obtuse angle.

Begin by assuming that $\triangle ABC$ *does* have more than one obtuse angle.

$m\angle A > 90°$ and $m\angle B > 90°$	Assume $\triangle ABC$ has two obtuse angles.
$m\angle A + m\angle B > 180°$	Add the two given inequalities.

You know, however, that the sum of the measures of all *three* angles is 180°.

$m\angle A + m\angle B + m\angle C = 180°$	Triangle Sum Theorem
$m\angle A + m\angle B = 180° - m\angle C$	Subtraction property of equality

So, you can substitute $180° - m\angle C$ for $m\angle A + m\angle B$ in $m\angle A + m\angle B > 180°$.

$180° - m\angle C > 180°$	Substitution property of equality
$0° > m\angle C$	Simplify.

The last statement is *not possible*; angle measures in triangles cannot be negative.

▶ So, you can conclude that the original assumption must be false. That is, $\triangle ABC$ cannot have more than one obtuse angle.

CONCEPT SUMMARY   GUIDELINES FOR WRITING AN INDIRECT PROOF

❶ Identify the statement that you want to prove is true.

❷ Begin by assuming the statement is false; assume its opposite is true.

❸ Obtain statements that logically follow from your assumption.

❹ If you obtain a contradiction, then the original statement must be true.

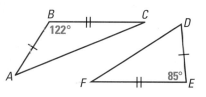

In the two triangles shown, notice that $\overline{AB} \cong \overline{DE}$ and $\overline{BC} \cong \overline{EF}$, but $m\angle B$ is greater than $m\angle E$.

It appears that the side opposite the 122° angle is longer than the side opposite the 85° angle. This relationship is guaranteed by the Hinge Theorem below.

Exercise 31 asks you to write a proof of Theorem 5.14. Theorem 5.15 can be proved using Theorem 5.14 and indirect proof, as shown in Example 2.

THEOREMS

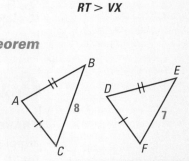

THEOREM 5.14 *Hinge Theorem*

If two sides of one triangle are congruent to two sides of another triangle, and the included angle of the first is larger than the included angle of the second, then the third side of the first is longer than the third side of the second.

RT > VX

THEOREM 5.15 *Converse of the Hinge Theorem*

If two sides of one triangle are congruent to two sides of another triangle, and the third side of the first is longer than the third side of the second, then the included angle of the first is larger than the included angle of the second.

m∠A > m∠D

EXAMPLE 2 *Indirect Proof of Theorem 5.15*

GIVEN ▶ $\overline{AB} \cong \overline{DE}$
$\overline{BC} \cong \overline{EF}$
$AC > DF$

PROVE ▶ $m\angle B > m\angle E$

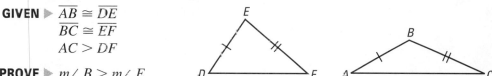

SOLUTION Begin by assuming that $m\angle B \not> m\angle E$. Then, it follows that either $m\angle B = m\angle E$ or $m\angle B < m\angle E$.

> **Case 1** If $m\angle B = m\angle E$, then $\angle B \cong \angle E$. So, $\triangle ABC \cong \triangle DEF$ by the SAS Congruence Postulate and $AC = DF$.

> **Case 2** If $m\angle B < m\angle E$, then $AC < DF$ by the Hinge Theorem.

Both conclusions contradict the given information that $AC > DF$. So the original assumption that $m\angle B \not> m\angle E$ cannot be correct. Therefore, $m\angle B > m\angle E$.

EXAMPLE 3 *Finding Possible Side Lengths and Angle Measures*

You can use the Hinge Theorem and its converse to choose possible side lengths or angle measures from a given list.

a. $\overline{AB} \cong \overline{DE}$, $\overline{BC} \cong \overline{EF}$, $AC = 12$ inches, $m\angle B = 36°$, and $m\angle E = 80°$. Which of the following is a possible length for $\overline{DF}$: 8 in., 10 in., 12 in., or 23 in.?

b. In a $\triangle RST$ and a $\triangle XYZ$, $\overline{RT} \cong \overline{XZ}$, $\overline{ST} \cong \overline{YZ}$, $RS = 3.7$ centimeters, $XY = 4.5$ centimeters, and $m\angle Z = 75°$. Which of the following is a possible measure for $\angle T$: 60°, 75°, 90°, or 105°?

SOLUTION

a. Because the included angle in $\triangle DEF$ is larger than the included angle in $\triangle ABC$, the third side $\overline{DF}$ must be longer than $\overline{AC}$. So, of the four choices, the only possible length for $\overline{DF}$ is 23 inches. A diagram of the triangles shows that this is plausible.

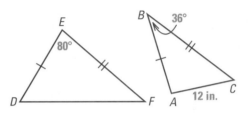

b. Because the third side in $\triangle RST$ is shorter than the third side in $\triangle XYZ$, the included angle $\angle T$ must be smaller than $\angle Z$. So, of the four choices, the only possible measure for $\angle T$ is 60°.

EXAMPLE 4 *Comparing Distances*

TRAVEL DISTANCES You and a friend are flying separate planes. You leave the airport and fly 120 miles due west. You then change direction and fly W 30° N for 70 miles. (W 30° N indicates a north-west direction that is 30° north of due west.) Your friend leaves the airport and flies 120 miles due east. She then changes direction and flies E 40° S for 70 miles. Each of you has flown 190 miles, but which plane is farther from the airport?

SOLUTION

Begin by drawing a diagram, as shown below. Your flight is represented by $\triangle PQR$ and your friend's flight is represented by $\triangle PST$.

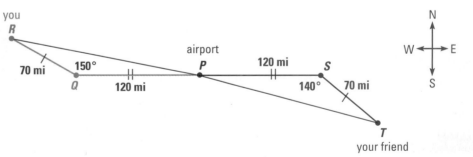

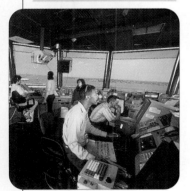

Because these two triangles have two sides that are congruent, you can apply the Hinge Theorem to conclude that $\overline{RP}$ is longer than $\overline{TP}$.

▶ So, your plane is farther from the airport than your friend's plane.

FOCUS ON CAREERS

REAL LIFE **AIR TRAFFIC CONTROLLERS** help ensure the safety of airline passengers and crews by developing air traffic flight paths that keep planes a safe distance apart.

INTERNET **CAREER LINK** www.mcdougallittell.com

GUIDED PRACTICE

Vocabulary Check ✓

1. Explain why an indirect proof might also be called a *proof by contradiction*.

Concept Check ✓

2. To use an indirect proof to show that two lines *m* and *n* are parallel, you would first make the assumption that __?__ .

Skill Check ✓

In Exercises 3–5, complete with <, >, or =.

3. $m\angle 1$ _?_ $m\angle 2$

4. KL _?_ NQ

5. DC _?_ FE

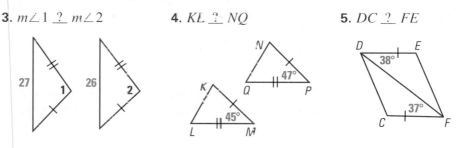

6. Suppose that in a $\triangle ABC$, you want to prove that $BC > AC$. What are the two cases you would use in an indirect proof?

PRACTICE AND APPLICATIONS

STUDENT HELP

▶ **Extra Practice**
to help you master
skills is on p. 812.

USING THE HINGE THEOREM AND ITS CONVERSE Complete with <, >, or =.

7. RS _?_ TU

8. $m\angle 1$ _?_ $m\angle 2$

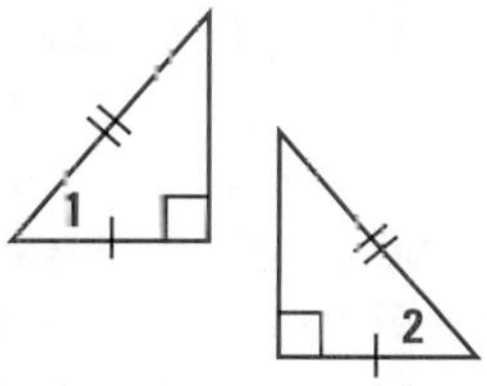

9. $m\angle 1$ _?_ $m\angle 2$

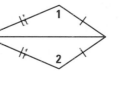

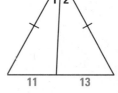

10. XY _?_ ZY

11. $m\angle 1$ _?_ $m\angle 2$

12. $m\angle 1$ _?_ $m\angle 2$

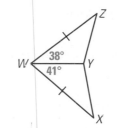

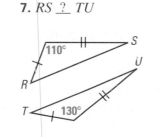

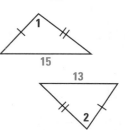

STUDENT HELP

▶ **HOMEWORK HELP**
Example 1: Exs. 21–24
Example 2: Exs. 25–27
Example 3: Exs. 7–17
Example 4: Exs. 28, 29

13. AB _?_ CB

14. UT _?_ SV

15. $m\angle 1$ _?_ $m\angle 2$

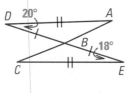

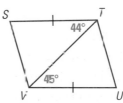

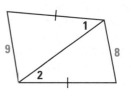

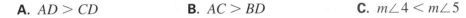

LOGICAL REASONING In Exercises 16 and 17, match the given information with conclusion A, B, or C. Explain your reasoning.

A. $AD > CD$ **B.** $AC > BD$ **C.** $m\angle 4 < m\angle 5$

16. $AC > AB$, $BD = CD$ **17.** $AB = DC$, $m\angle 3 < m\angle 5$

USING ALGEBRA Use an inequality to describe a restriction on the value of *x* as determined by the Hinge Theorem or its converse.

18.   **19.**   **20.**

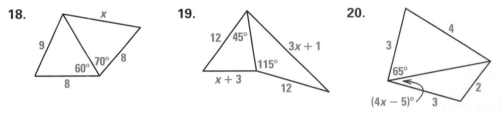

STUDENT HELP

HOMEWORK HELP
Visit our Web site
www.mcdougallittell.com
for help with negations in
Exs. 21–23.

ASSUMING THE NEGATION OF THE CONCLUSION In Exercises 21–23, write the first statement for an indirect proof of the situation.

21. If $RS + ST \neq 12$ in. and $ST = 5$ in., then $RS \neq 7$ in.

22. In $\triangle MNP$, if Q is the midpoint of $\overline{NP}$, then $\overline{MQ}$ is a median.

23. In $\triangle ABC$, if $m\angle A + m\angle B = 90°$, then $m\angle C = 90°$.

24. ▶ **DEVELOPING PROOF** Arrange statements A–D in correct order to write an indirect proof of Postulate 7 from page 73: *If two lines intersect, then their intersection is exactly one point.*

   GIVEN ▶ line *m*, line *n*

   PROVE ▶ Lines *m* and *n* intersect in exactly one point.

   A. But this contradicts Postulate 5, which states that there is exactly one line through any two points.

   B. Then there are two lines (*m* and *n*) through points *P* and *Q*.

   C. Assume that there are two points, *P* and *Q*, where *m* and *n* intersect.

   D. It is false that *m* and *n* can intersect in two points, so they must intersect in exactly one point.

25. ▶ **PROOF** Write an indirect proof of Theorem 5.11 on page 295.

   GIVEN ▶ $m\angle D > m\angle E$

   PROVE ▶ $EF > DF$

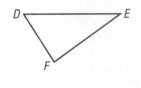

   Plan for Proof In Case 1, assume that $EF < DF$. In Case 2, assume that $EF = DF$. Show that neither case can be true, so $EF > DF$.

PROOF **Write an indirect proof in paragraph form. The diagrams, which illustrate negations of the conclusions, may help you.**

26. GIVEN ▶ $\angle 1$ and $\angle 2$ are supplementary.

PROVE ▶ $m \parallel n$

Begin by assuming that $m \nparallel n$.

27. GIVEN ▶ $\overline{RU}$ is an altitude, $\overrightarrow{RU}$ bisects $\angle SRT$.

PROVE ▶ $\triangle RST$ is isosceles.

Begin by assuming that $RS > RT$.

COMPARING DISTANCES **In Exercises 28 and 29, consider the flight paths described. Explain how to use the Hinge Theorem to determine who is farther from the airport.**

28. *Your flight:* 100 miles due west, then 50 miles N 20° W
Friend's flight: 100 miles due north, then 50 miles N 30° E

29. *Your flight:* 210 miles due south, then 80 miles S 70° W
Friend's flight: 80 miles due north, then 210 miles N 50° E

Test Preparation

30. MULTI-STEP PROBLEM Use the diagram of the tank cleaning system's expandable arm shown below.

a. As the cleaning system arm expands, $\overline{ED}$ gets longer. As ED increases, what happens to $m\angle EBD$? What happens to $m\angle DBA$?

b. Name a distance that decreases as $\overline{ED}$ gets longer.

c. *Writing* Explain how the cleaning arm illustrates the Hinge Theorem.

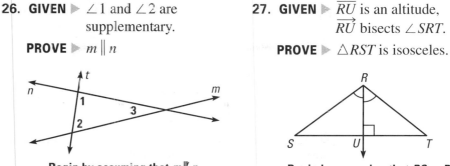

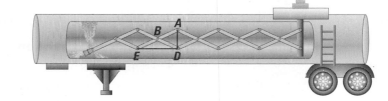

★ Challenge

31. **PROOF** Prove Theorem 5.14, the Hinge Theorem.

GIVEN ▶ $\overline{AB} \cong \overline{DE}$, $\overline{BC} \cong \overline{EF}$, $m\angle ABC > m\angle DEF$

PROVE ▶ $AC > DF$

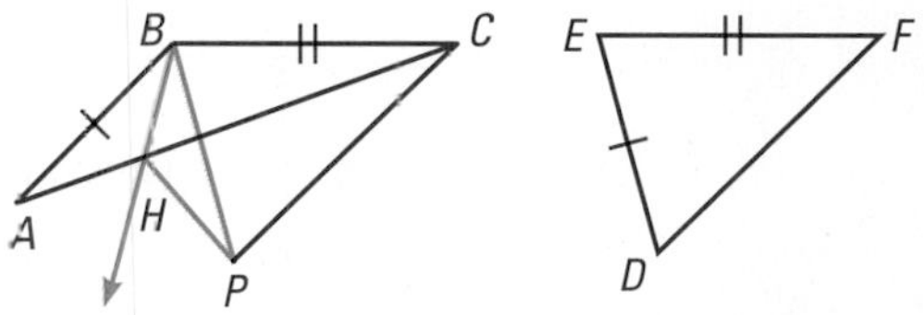

Plan for Proof

1. Locate a point P outside $\triangle ABC$ so you can construct $\triangle PBC \cong \triangle DEF$.

2. Show that $\triangle PBC \cong \triangle DEF$ by the SAS Congruence Postulate.

3. Because $m\angle ABC > m\angle DEF$, locate a point H on $\overline{AC}$ so that $\overrightarrow{BH}$ bisects $\angle PBA$.

4. Give reasons for each equality or inequality below to show that $AC > DF$.

$$AC = AH + HC = PH + HC > PC = DF$$

EXTRA CHALLENGE
www.mcdougallittell.com

MIXED REVIEW

CLASSIFYING TRIANGLES **State whether the triangle described is** *isosceles, equiangular, equilateral,* **or** *scalene.* (Review 4.1 for 6.1)

32. Side lengths:
3 cm, 5 cm, 3 cm

33. Side lengths:
5 cm, 5 cm, 5 cm

34. Side lengths:
5 cm, 6 cm, 8 cm

35. Angle measures:
30°, 30°, 120°

36. Angle measures:
60°, 60°, 60°

37. Angle measures:
65°, 50°, 65°

 USING ALGEBRA **In Exercises 38–41, use the diagram shown at the right.** (Review 4.1 for 6.1)

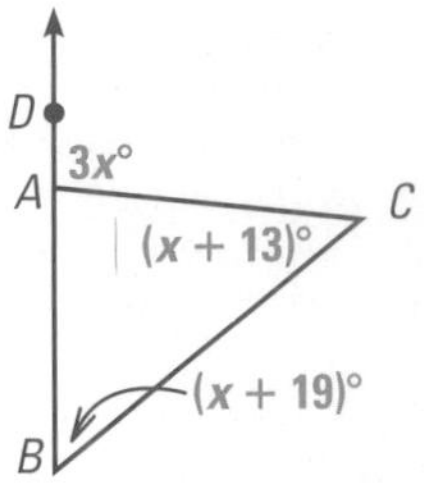

38. Find the value of *x*.

39. Find $m\angle B$.

40. Find $m\angle C$.

41. Find $m\angle BAC$.

42. DESCRIBING A SEGMENT Draw any equilateral triangle $\triangle RST$. Draw a line segment from vertex *R* to the midpoint of side $\overline{ST}$. State everything that you know about the line segment you have drawn. (Review 5.3)

QUIZ 2

Self-Test for Lessons 5.4–5.6

In Exercises 1–3, use the triangle shown at the right. The midpoints of the sides of $\triangle CDE$ are *F*, *G*, and *H*. (Lesson 5.4)

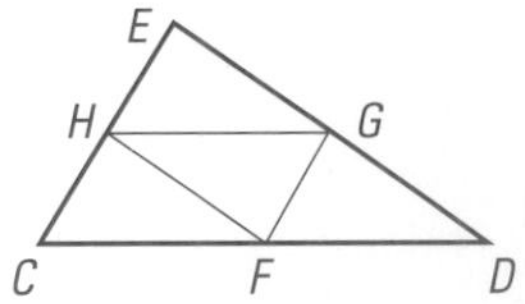

1. $\overline{FG} \parallel$ ___?___

2. If $FG = 8$, then $CE =$ ___?___.

3. If the perimeter of $\triangle CDE = 42$, then the perimeter of $\triangle GHF =$ ___?___.

In Exercises 4–6, list the sides in order from shortest to longest. (Lesson 5.5)

4.

5.

6.

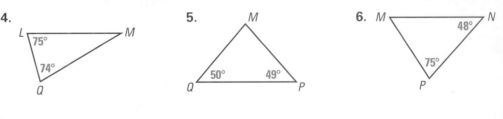

7. In $\triangle ABC$ and $\triangle DEF$ shown at the right, which is longer, $\overline{AB}$ or $\overline{DE}$? (Lesson 5.6)

8. 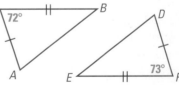 **HIKING** Two groups of hikers leave from the same base camp and head in opposite directions. The first group walks 4.5 miles due east, then changes direction and walks E 45° N for 3 miles. The second group walks 4.5 miles due west, then changes direction and walks W 20° S for 3 miles. Each group has walked 7.5 miles, but which is farther from the base camp? (Lesson 5.6)

Hikers in the Grand Canyon

Chapter Summary

WHAT did you learn?

Use properties of perpendicular bisectors and angle bisectors. **(5.1)**

Use properties of perpendicular bisectors and angle bisectors of a triangle. **(5.2)**

Use properties of medians and altitudes of a triangle. **(5.3)**

Use properties of midsegments of a triangle. **(5.4)**

Compare the lengths of the sides or the measures of the angles of a triangle. **(5.5)**

Understand and write indirect proofs. **(5.6)**

Use the Hinge Theorem and its converse to compare side lengths and angle measures of triangles. **(5.6)**

WHY did you learn it?

Decide where a hockey goalie should be positioned to defend the goal. **(p. 270)**

Find the center of a mushroom ring. **(p. 277)**

Find points in a triangle used to measure a person's heart fitness. **(p. 283)**

Determine the length of the crossbar of a swing set. **(p. 292)**

Determine how the lengths of the boom lines of a crane affect the position of the boom. **(p. 300)**

Prove theorems that cannot be easily proved directly.

Decide which of two airplanes is farther from an airport. **(p. 304)**

How does Chapter 5 fit into the BIGGER PICTURE of geometry?

In this chapter, you studied properties of special segments of triangles, which are an important building block for more complex figures that you will explore in later chapters. The special segments of a triangle have applications in many areas such as demographics (p. 280), medicine (p. 283), and room design (p. 299).

STUDY STRATEGY

Did you test your memory?

The list of important vocabulary terms and skills you made, following the **Study Strategy** on page 262, may resemble this one.

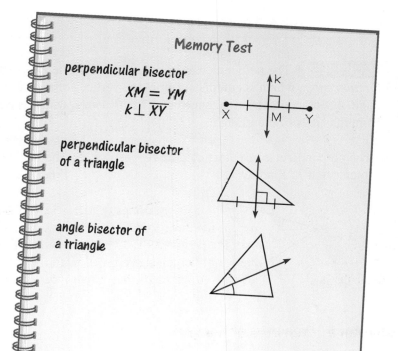

Memory Test

perpendicular bisector
$$XM = YM$$
$$k \perp \overline{XY}$$

perpendicular bisector of a triangle

angle bisector of a triangle

- perpendicular bisector, p. 264
- equidistant from two points, p. 264
- distance from a point to a line, p. 266
- equidistant from two lines, p. 266
- perpendicular bisector of a triangle, p. 272
- concurrent lines, p. 272
- point of concurrency, p. 272
- circumcenter of a triangle, p. 273
- angle bisector of a triangle, p. 274
- incenter of a triangle, p. 274
- median of a triangle, p. 279
- centroid of a triangle, p. 279
- altitude of a triangle, p. 281
- orthocenter of a triangle, p. 281
- midsegment of a triangle, p. 287
- indirect proof, p. 302

5.1 PERPENDICULARS AND BISECTORS

Examples on pp. 264–267

EXAMPLES In the figure, $\overrightarrow{AD}$ is the angle bisector of $\angle BAC$ and the perpendicular bisector of $\overline{BC}$. You know that $BE = CE$ by the definition of perpendicular bisector and that $AB = AC$ by the Perpendicular Bisector Theorem. Because $\overline{DP} \perp \overrightarrow{AP}$ and $\overline{DQ} \perp \overrightarrow{AQ}$, then DP and DQ are the distances from D to the sides of $\angle PAQ$ and you know that $DP = DQ$ by the Angle Bisector Theorem.

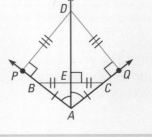

In Exercises 1–3, use the diagram.

1. If $\overrightarrow{SQ}$ is the perpendicular bisector of $\overline{RT}$, explain how you know that $\overline{RQ} \cong \overline{TQ}$ and $\overline{RS} \cong \overline{TS}$.

2. If $\overline{UR} \cong \overline{UT}$, what can you conclude about U?

3. If Q is equidistant from $\overrightarrow{SR}$ and $\overrightarrow{ST}$, what can you conclude about Q?

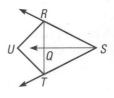

5.2 BISECTORS OF A TRIANGLE

Examples on pp. 272–274

EXAMPLES The perpendicular bisectors of a triangle intersect at the *circumcenter*, which is equidistant from the vertices of the triangle. The angle bisectors of a triangle intersect at the *incenter*, which is equidistant from the sides of the triangle.

4. The perpendicular bisectors of $\triangle RST$ intersect at K. Find KR.

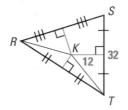

5. The angle bisectors of $\triangle XYZ$ intersect at W. Find WB.

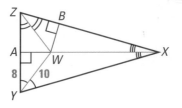

MEDIANS AND ALTITUDES OF A TRIANGLE

Examples on pp. 279–281

EXAMPLES The medians of a triangle intersect at the centroid. The lines containing the altitudes of a triangle intersect at the orthocenter.

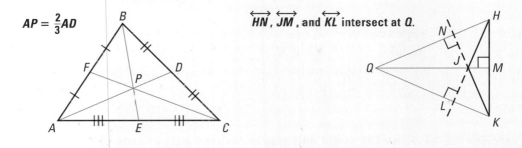

$AP = \frac{2}{3}AD$

$\overleftrightarrow{HN}$, $\overleftrightarrow{JM}$, and $\overleftrightarrow{KL}$ intersect at Q.

Name the special segments and point of concurrency of the triangle.

6.   **7.**   **8.**   **9.**

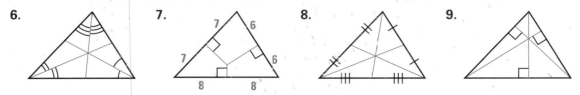

$\triangle XYZ$ has vertices $X(0, 0)$, $Y(-4, 0)$, and $Z(0, 6)$. **Find the coordinates of the indicated point.**

10. the centroid of $\triangle XYZ$

11. the orthocenter of $\triangle XYZ$

MIDSEGMENT THEOREM

Examples on pp. 287–289

EXAMPLES A midsegment of a triangle connects the midpoints of two sides of the triangle. By the Midsegment Theorem, a midsegment of a triangle is parallel to the third side and its length is half the length of the third side.

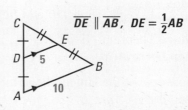

$\overline{DE} \parallel \overline{AB}$, $DE = \frac{1}{2}AB$

In Exercises 12 and 13, the midpoints of the sides of $\triangle HJK$ are $L(4, 3)$, $M(8, 3)$, and $N(6, 1)$.

12. Find the coordinates of the vertices of the triangle.

13. Show that each midsegment is parallel to a side of the triangle.

14. Find the perimeter of $\triangle BCD$.   **15.** Find the perimeter of $\triangle STU$.

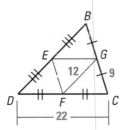   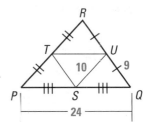

INEQUALITIES IN ONE TRIANGLE

Examples on pp. 295–297

EXAMPLES In a triangle, the side and the angle of greatest measurement are always opposite each other. In the diagram, the largest angle, $\angle MNQ$, is opposite the longest side, $\overline{MQ}$.

By the Exterior Angle Inequality,
$m\angle MQP > m\angle N$ and $m\angle MQP > m\angle M$.

By the Triangle Inequality, $MN + NQ > MQ$,
$NQ + MQ > MN$, and $MN + MQ > NQ$.

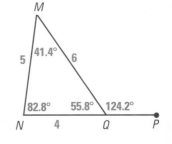

In Exercises 16–19, write the angle and side measurements in order from least to greatest.

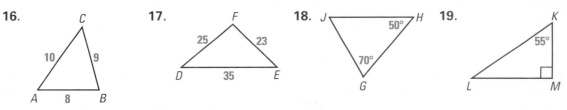

16.   **17.**   **18.**   **19.**

20. 🌐 **FENCING A GARDEN** You are enclosing a triangular garden region with a fence. You have measured two sides of the garden to be 100 feet and 200 feet. What is the maximum length of fencing you need? Explain.

INDIRECT PROOF AND INEQUALITIES IN TWO TRIANGLES

Examples on pp. 302–304

EXAMPLES $\overline{AB} \cong \overline{DE}$ and $\overline{BC} \cong \overline{EF}$

Hinge Theorem: If $m\angle E > m\angle B$,
then $DF > AC$.

Converse of the Hinge Theorem: If $DF > AC$,
then $m\angle E > m\angle B$.

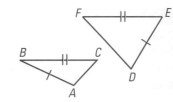

In Exercises 21–23, complete with <, >, or =.

21. $AB \underline{\ ?\ } CB$ **22.** $m\angle 1 \underline{\ ?\ } m\angle 2$ **23.** $TU \underline{\ ?\ } VS$

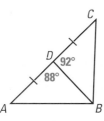   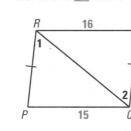   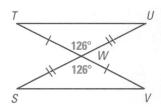

24. Write the first statement for an indirect proof of this situation: In a $\triangle MPQ$, if $\angle M \cong \angle Q$, then $\triangle MPQ$ is isosceles.

25. Write an indirect proof to show that no triangle has two right angles.

In Exercises 1–5, complete the statement with the word *always,* *sometimes,* **or** *never.*

1. If *P* is the circumcenter of △*RST*, then *PR*, *PS*, and *PT* are __?__ equal.

2. If $\overrightarrow{BD}$ bisects ∠*ABC*, then $\overline{AD}$ and $\overline{CD}$ are __?__ congruent.

3. The incenter of a triangle __?__ lies outside the triangle.

4. The length of a median of a triangle is __?__ equal to the length of a midsegment.

5. If $\overline{AM}$ is the altitude to side $\overline{BC}$ of △*ABC*, then $\overline{AM}$ is __?__ shorter than $\overline{AB}$.

In Exercises 6–10, use the diagram.

6. Find each length.

   a. *HC*   **b.** *HB*   **c.** *HE*   **d.** *BC*

7. Point *H* is the __?__ of the triangle.

8. $\overline{CG}$ is a(n) __?__ , __?__ , __?__ , and __?__ of △*ABC* .

9. *EF* = __?__ and $\overline{EF}$ ∥ __?__ by the __?__ Theorem.

10. Compare the measures of ∠*ACB* and ∠*BAC*. Justify your answer.

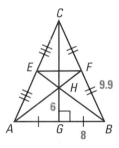

11. 🌐 **LANDSCAPE DESIGN** You are designing a circular swimming pool for a triangular lawn surrounded by apartment buildings. You want the center of the pool to be equidistant from the three sidewalks. Explain how you can locate the center of the pool.

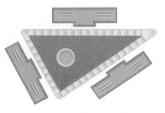

In Exercises 12–14, use the photo of the three-legged tripod.

12. As the legs of a tripod are spread apart, which theorem guarantees that the angles between each pair of legs get larger?

13. Each leg of a tripod can extend to a length of 5 feet. What is the maximum possible distance between the ends of two legs?

14. Let $\overline{OA}$, $\overline{OB}$, and $\overline{OC}$ represent the legs of a tripod. Draw and label a sketch. Suppose the legs are congruent and $m\angle AOC > m\angle BOC$. Compare the lengths of $\overline{AC}$ and $\overline{BC}$.

In Exercises 15 and 16, use the diagram at the right.

15. Write a two-column proof.

   GIVEN ▶ *AC* = *BC*

   PROVE ▶ *BE* < *AE*

16. Write an indirect proof.

   GIVEN ▶ *AD* ≠ *AB*

   PROVE ▶ *m*∠*D* ≠ *m*∠*ABC*

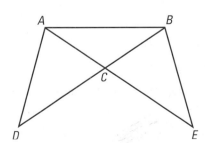

Chapter Standardized Test

🔊 **TEST-TAKING STRATEGY** If you find yourself spending too much time on one test question and getting frustrated, move on to the next question. You can revisit a difficult problem later with a fresh perspective.

1. MULTIPLE CHOICE In the diagram below, $\overleftrightarrow{PQ}$ is the perpendicular bisector of $\overline{FG}$. What are the values of x and y?

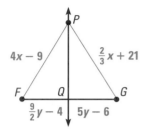

(A) $x = 9, y = 1$ (B) $x = 9, y = 4$

(C) $x = 4, y = 9$ (D) $x = \frac{1}{2}, y = 9$

(E) $x = 9, y = 6$

2. MULTIPLE CHOICE In the diagram, $\overrightarrow{ST}$ bisects $\angle RSU$. Which segments do you know are congruent?

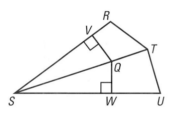

(A) $\overline{SR} \cong \overline{SU}$ (B) $\overline{VR} \cong \overline{WU}$ (C) $\overline{RT} \cong \overline{UT}$

(D) $\overline{QV} \cong \overline{QW}$ (E) $\overline{SQ} \cong \overline{QT}$

3. MULTIPLE CHOICE Which of the following statements are true about the circumcenter P of an isosceles triangle?

  I. Point P is equidistant from the sides.

  II. Point P is equidistant from the vertices.

  III. Point P is two thirds of the distance from each vertex to the midpoint of the opposite side.

(A) I only   (B) II only

(C) III only   (D) I and II

(E) none of these

4. MULTIPLE CHOICE What are the coordinates of the centroid C of a triangle whose vertices are $F(-12, 1)$, $G(-2, 1)$, and $H(-7, -11)$?

(A) $(-7, -7)$ (B) $\left(-7, -\frac{9}{2}\right)$

(C) $\left(-7, -\frac{5}{4}\right)$ (D) $\left(-7, -\frac{7}{2}\right)$

(E) $(-7, -3)$

5. MULTIPLE CHOICE Use the diagram to find the perimeter of $\triangle NPL$.

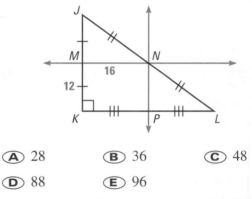

(A) 28   (B) 36   (C) 48

(D) 88   (E) 96

6. MULTIPLE CHOICE Points D, E, and F are the midpoints of the sides of $\triangle ABC$. Which of the following statements is false?

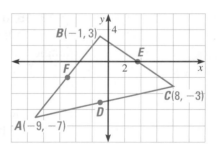

(A) The intersection of $\overline{AE}$ and $\overline{BD}$ is the orthocenter of $\triangle ABC$.

(B) $\overline{EF} \parallel \overline{CA}$

(C) $m\angle A < m\angle C$

(D) $DE = \frac{1}{2}AB$

(E) $\overline{BD}$ is a median of $\triangle ABC$.

7. MULTIPLE CHOICE A triangle has two sides that have lengths of 16 inches and 28 inches. Which of the following lengths could *not* represent the length of the third side?

  A 12 in.   **B** 26 in.   **C** 33 in.   **D** 40 in.   **E** 43 in.

8. QUANTITATIVE COMPARISON Two quantities are described below.

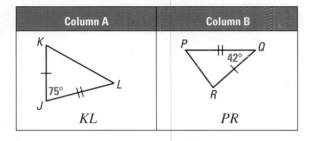

Column A	Column B
KL	PR

Choose the statement that is true.

 A The quantity in column A is greater.

 B The quantity in column B is greater.

 C The two quantities are equal.

 D The relationship cannot be determined from the given information.

MULTI-STEP PROBLEM In Exercises 9–12, use △*GHJ* at the right.

9. What is the sum of x and y?

10. Which measure is greater, $x°$ or $y°$?

11. Which of the following is true?

  A $x = 45$ **B** $x < 45$ **C** $x > 45$

12. Describe the location of the intersection point of the perpendicular bisectors of △*GHJ*.

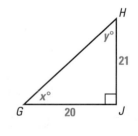

MULTI-STEP PROBLEM In Exercises 13–15, use the following information.
In 1765, a Swiss mathematician, Leonhard Euler, proved that the centroid, orthocenter, and circumcenter of a triangle are all collinear. The line containing these three points is called the *Euler Line*. Euler also proved that the centroid of a triangle is one third the distance from the circumcenter to the orthocenter.

13. Find equations of the lines that contain the medians. Use the equations to find the coordinates of the centroid of △*ABC*.

14. Find equations of the lines that contain the altitudes of △*ABC*. Use the equations to find the coordinates of the orthocenter.

15. In Exercise 30 on page 278, you found that the circumcenter of a △*ABC* with the given vertices is the point $(9, -3)$.

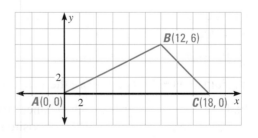

 a. Verify that the centroid and the orthocenter you found in Exercises 13 and 14 and the circumcenter above are all collinear.

 b. Verify that the distance from the circumcenter to the centroid is one third the distance from the circumcenter to the orthocenter.

Balancing Shapes

OBJECTIVE Explore the balancing points of triangles and other shapes.

Materials: cardboard, straightedge, scissors, hole punch, string, paper clip, pencil with eraser

HOW TO FIND A BALANCING POINT

1 Draw a large triangle on cardboard and cut it out. Punch holes in the triangle near the vertices.

2 Tie a weight to a string and attach the string to a paper clip. Hang your triangle from the paper clip. Mark the vertical line the string makes on the triangle.

3 Repeat Step 2 with the other holes in the triangle. The three lines should intersect near the same point. Balance the triangle by placing this point on a pencil eraser.

INVESTIGATION

1. Are the lines you drew in **Steps 2 and 3** *perpendicular bisectors*, *angle bisectors*, *medians*, or *altitudes* of the triangle?

2. Is the balancing point of the triangle the *orthocenter*, *incenter*, *circumcenter*, or *centroid*?

3. Choose one of the following special shapes: *square, rectangle, parallelogram,* or *rhombus.*

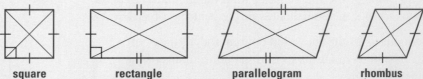

| square | rectangle | parallelogram | rhombus |

Draw and cut out a large example of the shape you have chosen. Follow the steps above to find its balancing point.

4. Make a conjecture about the location of the balancing point in relation to the *diagonals* of the shape.

5. Test your conjecture. Then explain how you tested your conjecture and describe the results of the test.

PRESENT YOUR RESULTS

Write a report to present your results.

· Include your answers to Investigation Exercises 1–5 on the previous page.

· Include your cut-out shapes or sketches of them. Mark the balancing point of each shape.

· Describe the conjectures that you made and your reasons for believing them to be true.

· What advice would you give to someone else who is going to do this project?

· Which geometric facts did this project help you to understand better?

Balancing Points
of
Triangles and Squares

by
Helen Larkin and
Tony Tabor

Mrs. Smith
Geometry
3rd Period

You may wish to display your cut-out shapes on a poster or as a mobile. Here are some hints for creating a mobile.

· Punch a small hole at the balancing point of each shape.

· Tie a knot in a string and thread the string through the hole until the string stops at the knot.

· You can hang all of your shapes from one string, or you can hang them from several strings tied to a stick.

EXTENSION

Do you think your conjecture about balancing points of certain four-sided shapes is true for *all* four-sided shapes? Cut out and test more shapes to find out. In your report, describe your investigation and the results.

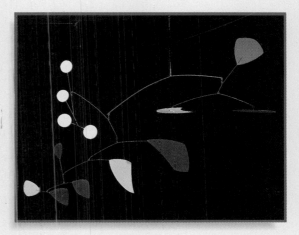

This mobile includes horizontal red and yellow plates that hang from their balancing points.

QUADRILATERALS

▶ *How are overhead shots taken for movies?*

CHAPTER
6

APPLICATION: Scissors Lift

Scissors lifts are used to lift construction workers, movie crews, and other people who need to be up high.

The platform can be raised to different heights. The design of the lift ensures that as the platform is raised or lowered, it is always parallel to the ground.

In Chapter 6, you'll learn how machines and tools like the scissors lift work.

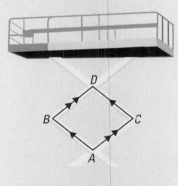

Think & Discuss

1. The lengths of $\overline{BA}$ and $\overline{BD}$ are constant. What happens to AD if $m\angle B$ increases? Explain.

2. What do you think happens to the platform of the scissors lift if $m\angle B$ increases?

Learn More About It

You will learn more about scissors lifts in Exercises 51–54 on p. 336.

 APPLICATION LINK Visit www.mcdougallittell.com for more information about scissors lifts.

319

Study Guide

PREVIEW

What's the chapter about?

Chapter 6 is about four-sided figures called **quadrilaterals** and their properties. In Chapter 6, you'll learn

- how to classify special quadrilaterals and how to use their properties.
- how to write proofs about special quadrilaterals.
- how to find areas of triangles and quadrilaterals.

KEY VOCABULARY

- polygon, p. 322
- sides and vertices of a polygon, p. 322
- convex, p. 323
- concave, p. 323
- equilateral, p. 323

- equiangular, p. 323
- regular, p. 323
- diagonal, p. 324
- parallelogram, p. 330
- rhombus, p. 347
- rectangle, p. 347

- square, p. 347
- trapezoid, p. 356
- isosceles trapezoid, p. 356
- midsegment of a trapezoid, p. 357
- kite, p. 358

PREPARE

Are you ready for the chapter?

SKILL REVIEW Do these exercises to review key skills that you'll apply in this chapter. See the given **reference page** if there is something you don't understand.

STUDENT HELP

► **Study Tip**
"Student Help" boxes throughout the chapter give you study tips and tell you where to look for extra help in this book and on the Internet.

Use the diagram at the right. Write the postulate or theorem that justifies the statement. (Review p. 143)

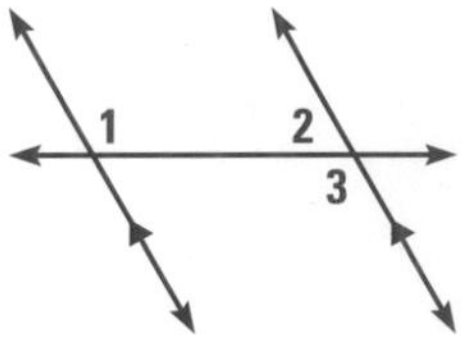

1. $\angle 1$ and $\angle 2$ are supplementary angles.

2. $\angle 1 \cong \angle 3$

Which postulate or theorem could you use to prove that $\triangle PQR \cong \triangle XYZ$?
(Review pp. 212–215, 220–222)

3. $\angle Q \cong \angle Y$, $\angle R \cong \angle Z$, $\overline{PQ} \cong \overline{XY}$ **4.** $PQ = XY$, $QR = YZ$, $PR = XZ$

5. The endpoints of $\overline{AB}$ are $A(-3, 4)$ and $B(2, -8)$. Find the length and the slope of $\overline{AB}$. Then find the coordinates of the midpoint of $\overline{AB}$. (Review pp. 19, 35, and 165)

STUDY STRATEGY

Here's a study strategy!

Form a study group

Form a study group with two or three of your friends. Each person should review a few sections of the chapter and prepare a summary of the important concepts and skills. At a group meeting, present and discuss your summaries.

▶ ACTIVITY 6.1

Developing Concepts

GROUP ACTIVITY
Work with a partner.

Classifying Shapes

▶ **QUESTION** Which shapes are polygons?

▶ **EXPLORING THE CONCEPT**

The symbols at the right are used in meteorology to represent different weather elements such as storms, precipitation, and cloud formations.

You can classify the shapes based on the tests below.

Test 1 Is the symbol made up of straight line segments only?

Test 2 Does each line segment in the symbol intersect exactly two other line segments, one at each endpoint?

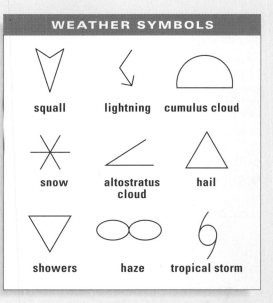

WEATHER SYMBOLS

squall   lightning   cumulus cloud

snow   altostratus cloud   hail

showers   haze   tropical storm

▶ **DRAWING CONCLUSIONS**

1. Make a list of weather symbols that pass Test 1.

2. From your list in Exercise 1, which symbols pass Test 2?

3. A shape that passes both Test 1 and Test 2 is called a *polygon*. The following symbols are used to write flow charts for computer programs. Which symbols are polygons? Explain your reasoning.

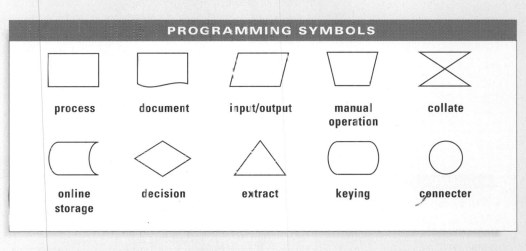

PROGRAMMING SYMBOLS

process   document   input/output   manual operation   collate

online storage   decision   extract   keying   connecter

4. **CRITICAL THINKING** What is the fewest number of sides a polygon can have? What is the greatest possible number of sides? Explain.

Polygons

What you should learn

GOAL 1 Identify, name, and describe polygons such as the building shapes in **Example 2**.

GOAL 2 Use the sum of the measures of the interior angles of a quadrilateral.

Why you should learn it

▼ To describe **real-life** objects, such as the parachute in **Exs. 21–23**.

GOAL 1 DESCRIBING POLYGONS

A **polygon** is a plane figure that meets the following conditions.

1. It is formed by three or more segments called **sides**, such that no two sides with a common endpoint are collinear.

2. Each side intersects exactly two other sides, one at each endpoint.

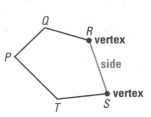

Each endpoint of a side is a **vertex** of the polygon. The plural of *vertex* is *vertices*. You can name a polygon by listing its vertices *consecutively*. For instance, *PQRST* and *QPTSR* are two correct names for the polygon above.

EXAMPLE 1 *Identifying Polygons*

State whether the figure is a polygon. If it is not, explain why.

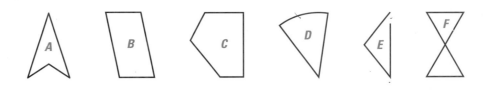

SOLUTION

Figures *A*, *B*, and *C are* polygons.

- Figure *D is not* a polygon because it has a side that is not a segment.

- Figure *E is not* a polygon because two of the sides intersect only one other side.

- Figure *F is not* a polygon because some of its sides intersect more than two other sides.

· · · · · · · · · ·

Polygons are named by the number of sides they have.

┌─ **STUDENT HELP** ─┐

▶ **Study Tip**
To name a polygon not listed in the table, use the number of sides. For example, a polygon with 14 sides is a 14-gon.

Number of sides	Type of polygon
3	Triangle
4	Quadrilateral
5	Pentagon
6	Hexagon
7	Heptagon

Number of sides	Type of polygon
8	Octagon
9	Nonagon
10	Decagon
12	Dodecagon
n	n-gon

A polygon is **convex** if no line that contains a side of the polygon contains a point in the interior of the polygon. A polygon that is not convex is called **nonconvex** or **concave**.

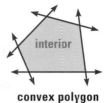
interior

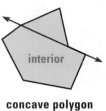
interior

convex polygon   **concave polygon**

EXAMPLE 2   *Identifying Convex and Concave Polygons*

Identify the polygon and state whether it is convex or concave.

a. 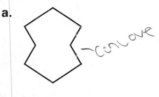 ~concave

b. ~convex

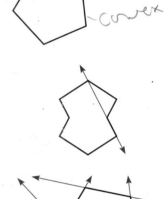

SOLUTION

a. The polygon has 8 sides, so it is an octagon. When extended, some of the sides intersect the interior, so the polygon is concave.

b. The polygon has 5 sides, so it is a pentagon. When extended, none of the sides intersect the interior, so the polygon is convex.

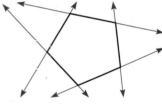

· · · · · · · · · ·

A polygon is **equilateral** if all of its sides are congruent. A polygon is **equiangular** if all of its interior angles are congruent. A polygon is **regular** if it is equilateral and equiangular.

EXAMPLE 3   *Identifying Regular Polygons*

Decide whether the polygon is regular.

~Regular   ~equilateral

a.   b.   c.

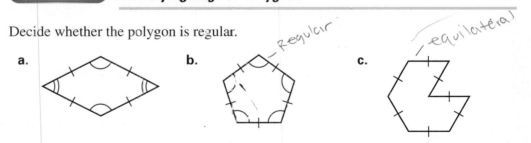

SOLUTION

a. The polygon is an equilateral quadrilateral, but not equiangular. So, it is not a regular polygon.

b. This pentagon is equilateral and equiangular. So, it is a regular polygon.

c. This heptagon is equilateral, but not equiangular. So, it is not regular.

This tile pattern in Iran contains both convex and concave polygons.

GOAL 2 INTERIOR ANGLES OF QUADRILATERALS

STUDENT HELP

Study Tip
Two vertices that are endpoints of the same side are called *consecutive vertices*. For example, *P* and *Q* are consecutive vertices.

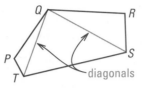

A **diagonal** of a polygon is a segment that joins two *nonconsecutive* vertices. Polygon *PQRST* has 2 diagonals from point *Q*, $\overline{QT}$ and $\overline{QS}$.

Like triangles, quadrilaterals have both *interior* and *exterior* angles. If you draw a diagonal in a quadrilateral, you divide it into two triangles, each of which has interior angles with measures that add up to 180°. So you can conclude that the sum of the measures of the interior angles of a quadrilateral is 2(180°), or 360°.

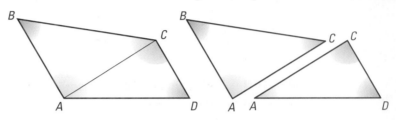

THEOREM

THEOREM 6.1 ***Interior Angles of a Quadrilateral***

The sum of the measures of the interior angles of a quadrilateral is 360°.

$m\angle 1 + m\angle 2 + m\angle 3 + m\angle 4 = 360°$

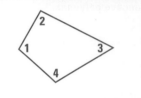

EXAMPLE 4 *Interior Angles of a Quadrilateral*

Using Algebra

Find $m\angle Q$ and $m\angle R$.

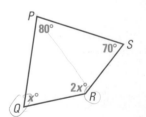

SOLUTION

Find the value of *x*. Use the sum of the measures of the interior angles to write an equation involving *x*. Then, solve the equation.

$x° + 2x° + 70° + 80° = 360°$	Sum of measures of int. ∠s of a quad. is 360°.
$3x + 150 = 360$	Combine like terms.
$3x = 210$	Subtract 150 from each side.
$x = 70$	Divide each side by 3.

Find $m\angle Q$ and $m\angle R$.

$m\angle Q = x° = 70°$

$m\angle R = 2x° = 140°$

▶ So, $m\angle Q = 70°$ and $m\angle R = 140°$.

GUIDED PRACTICE

Vocabulary Check ✓

1. What is the plural of *vertex*?

2. What do you call a polygon with 8 sides? a polygon with 15 sides?

Concept Check ✓

3. Suppose you could tie a string tightly around a convex polygon. Would the length of the string be equal to the perimeter of the polygon? What if the polygon were concave? Explain.

Skill Check ✓

Decide whether the figure is a polygon. If it is not, explain why.

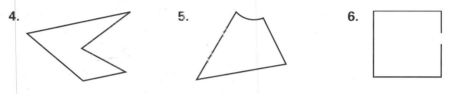

4.   5.   6.

Tell whether the polygon is best described as *equiangular*, *equilateral*, *regular*, or *none of these*.

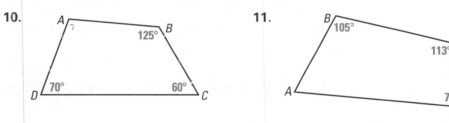

7.   8.   9.

Use the information in the diagram to find $m\angle A$.

10.   11.

PRACTICE AND APPLICATIONS

STUDENT HELP

► **Extra Practice**
to help you master
skills is on p. 813.

RECOGNIZING POLYGONS Decide whether the figure is a polygon.

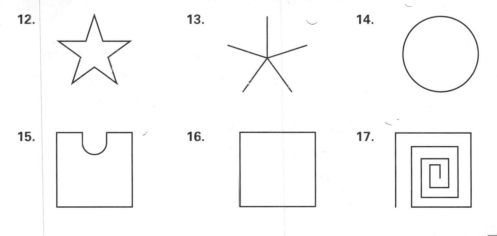

12.   13.   14.

15.   16.   17.

STUDENT HELP

HOMEWORK HELP
Example 1: Exs. 12–17, 48–51
Example 2: Exs. 18–20, 48–51
Example 3: Exs. 24–30, 48–51
Example 4: Exs. 36–46

CONVEX OR CONCAVE **Use the number of sides to tell what kind of polygon the shape is. Then state whether the polygon is *convex* or *concave*.**

18.

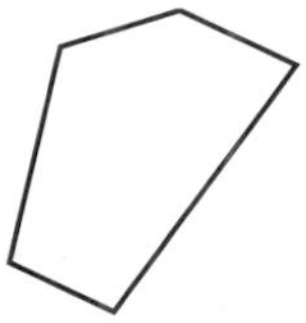

19.

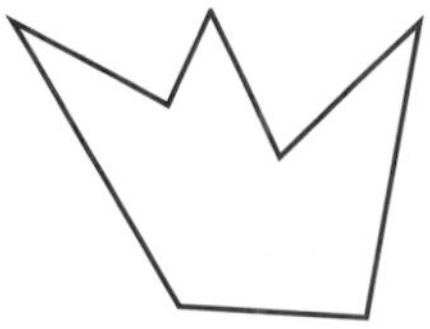

20.

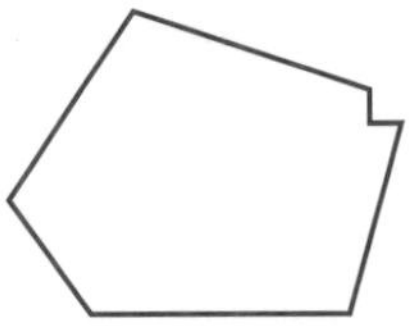

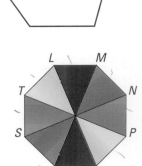

PARACHUTES **Some gym classes use parachutes that look like the polygon at the right.**

21. Is the polygon a *heptagon*, *octagon*, or *nonagon*?

22. Polygon *LMNPQRST* is one name for the polygon. State two other names.

23. Name all of the diagonals that have vertex *M* as an endpoint. Not all of the diagonals are shown.

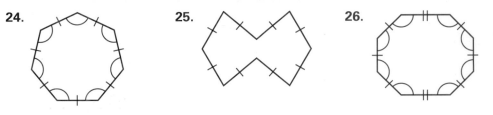

RECOGNIZING PROPERTIES **State whether the polygon is best described as *equilateral, equiangular, regular,* or *none of these*.**

24.

25.

26.

FOCUS ON APPLICATIONS

ROAD SIGNS The shape of a sign tells what it is for. For example, triangular signs like the one above are used internationally as warning signs.

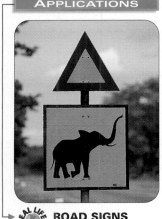

TRAFFIC SIGNS **Use the number of sides of the traffic sign to tell what kind of polygon it is. Is it *equilateral, equiangular, regular,* or *none of these*?**

27.

28.

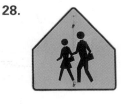

29.

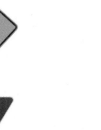

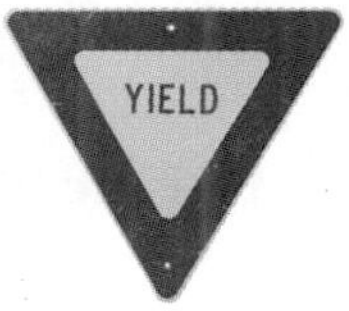

30.

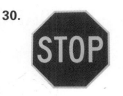

DRAWING **Draw a figure that fits the description.**

31. A convex heptagon

32. A concave nonagon

33. An equilateral hexagon that is not equiangular

34. An equiangular polygon that is not equilateral

35. **LOGICAL REASONING** Is every triangle convex? Explain your reasoning.

36. **LOGICAL REASONING** Quadrilateral *ABCD* is regular. What is the measure of $\angle ABC$? How do you know?

ANGLE MEASURES **Use the information in the diagram to find $m\angle A$.**

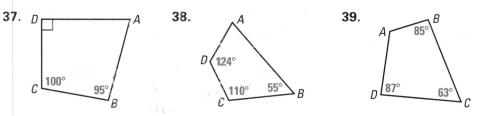

37.

D
A
C
100°
95°
B

38.

A
D
124°
110°
55°
B
C

39.

B
A
85°
D
87°
63°
C

STUDENT HELP

INTERNET **SOFTWARE HELP** Visit our Web site www.mcdougallittell.com to see instructions for several software applications.

40. **TECHNOLOGY** Use geometry software to draw a quadrilateral. Measure each interior angle and calculate the sum. What happens to the sum as you drag the vertices of the quadrilateral?

USING ALGEBRA **Use the information in the diagram to solve for x.**

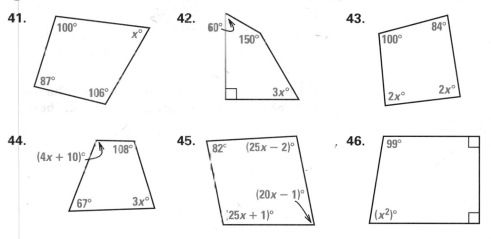

41.

100°
x°
87°
106°

42.

60°
150°
3x°

43.

84°
100°
2x°
2x°

44.

108°
(4x + 10)°
67°
3x°

45.

82°
(25x − 2)°
(20x − 1)°
(25x + 1)°

46.

99°
(x²)°

47. **LANGUAGE CONNECTION** A *decagon* has ten sides and a *decade* has ten years. The prefix *deca-* comes from Greek. It means *ten*. What does the prefix *tri-* mean? List four words that use *tri-* and explain what they mean.

PLANT SHAPES **In Exercises 48–51, use the following information.** Cross sections of seeds and fruits often resemble polygons. Next to each cross section is the polygon it resembles. Describe each polygon. Tell what kind of polygon it is, whether it is *concave* or *convex*, and whether it appears to be *equilateral*, *equiangular*, *regular*, or *none of these*. ▶ Source: The History and Folklore of N. American Wildflowers

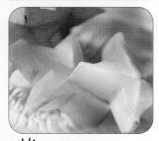

48. Virginia Snakeroot

49. Caraway

50. Fennel

51. Poison Hemlock

FOCUS ON APPLICATIONS

REAL LIFE **CARAMBOLA,** or star fruit, has a cross section shaped like a 5 pointed star. The fruit comes from an evergreen tree whose leaflets may fold at night or when the tree is shaken.

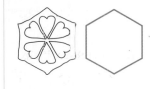

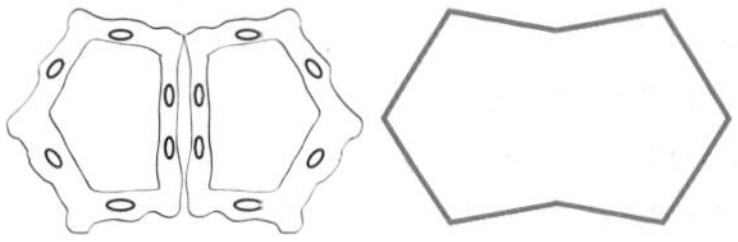

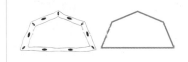

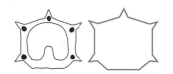

Test Preparation

52. MULTI-STEP PROBLEM Envelope manufacturers fold a specially-shaped piece of paper to make an envelope, as shown below.

a. What type of polygon is formed by the outside edges of the paper before it is folded? Is the polygon convex?

b. Tell what type of polygon is formed at each step. Which of the polygons are convex?

c. *Writing* Explain the reason for the V-shaped notches that are at the ends of the folds.

★ **Challenge**

EXTRA CHALLENGE
www.mcdougallittell.com

53. FINDING VARIABLES Find the values of *x* and *y* in the diagram at the right. Check your answer. Then copy the shape and write the measure of each angle on your diagram.

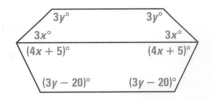

MIXED REVIEW

PARALLEL LINES In the diagram, *j* ∥ *k*. Find the value of *x*. (Review 3.3 for 6.2)

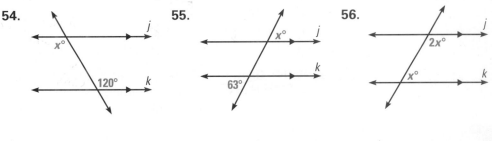

54.

55.

56.

57.

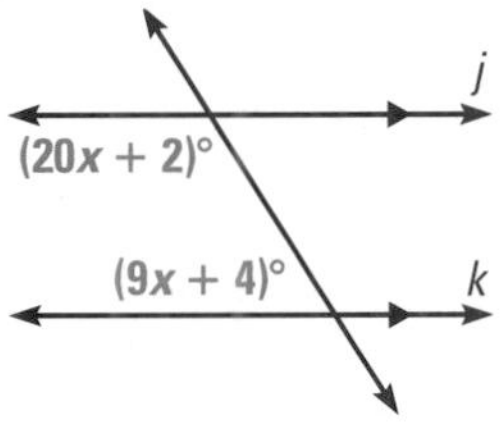

58.

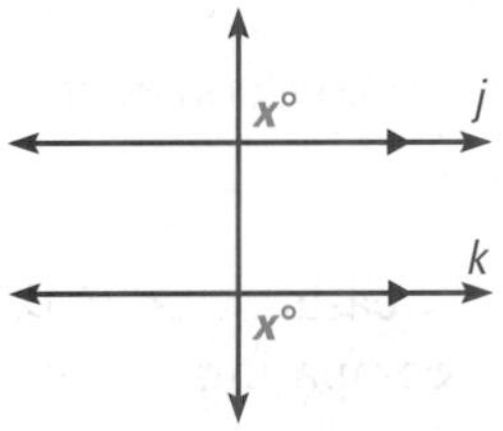

59.

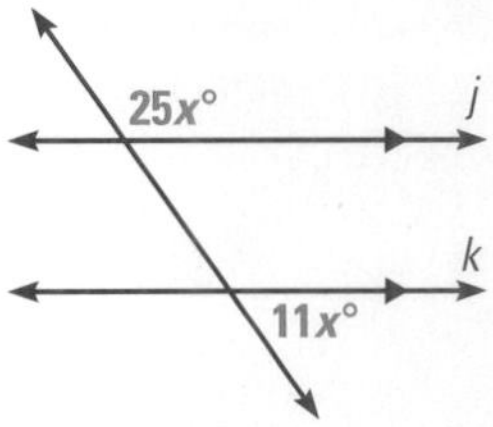

COORDINATE GEOMETRY You are given the midpoints of the sides of a triangle. Find the coordinates of the vertices of the triangle. (Review 5.4)

60. $L(-3, 7)$, $M(-5, 1)$, $N(-8, 8)$

61. $L(-4, -1)$, $M(3, 6)$, $N(-2, -8)$

62. $L(2, 4)$, $M(-1, 2)$, $N(0, 7)$

63. $L(-1, 3)$, $M(6, 7)$, $N(3, -5)$

64. ⓧⓨ **USING ALGEBRA** Use the Distance Formula to find the lengths of the diagonals of a polygon with vertices $A(0, 3)$, $B(3, 3)$, $C(4, 1)$, $D(0, -1)$, and $E(-2, 1)$. (Review 1.3)

328 **Chapter 6** *Quadrilaterals*

▶ ACTIVITY 6.2
Using Technology

Investigating Parallelograms

You can use geometry software to explore the properties of parallelograms. A parallelogram is a quadrilateral with both pairs of opposite sides parallel.

▶ **CONSTRUCT** Construct a parallelogram.

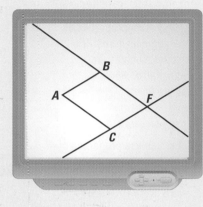

1 To construct a parallelogram, draw a segment and label it $\overline{AB}$. From point A, draw another segment. Label it $\overline{AC}$.

2 Construct a line through B parallel to $\overline{AC}$.

3 Construct a line through C parallel to $\overline{AB}$.

4 Mark the intersection of these two lines F and hide the lines.

5 Draw $\overline{BF}$ and $\overline{CF}$ to form parallelogram $ABFC$.

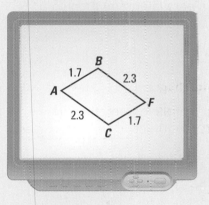

▶ **INVESTIGATE**

1. Drag points A, B, and C one at a time and notice how $ABFC$ changes. Is $ABFC$ always a parallelogram? How do you know?

2. Measure $\overline{AB}$, $\overline{BF}$, $\overline{CF}$, and $\overline{AC}$. What do you notice?

3. Drag points A, B, and C one at a time, continuing to compare the side lengths. What do you notice?

▶ **MAKE A CONJECTURE**

4. Make a conjecture about the sides of a parallelogram.

▶ **INVESTIGATE**

5. Measure $\angle A$, $\angle B$, $\angle C$, and $\angle F$. Drag points A, B, and C one at a time while comparing the angle measures. What do you notice?

▶ **MAKE A CONJECTURE**

6. Make a conjecture about opposite angles of a parallelogram.

EXTENSION

CRITICAL THINKING Draw the diagonals of parallelogram $ABFC$. Measure the distance from the intersection of the diagonals to each vertex of the parallelogram. Make and test a conjecture.

6.2

Properties of Parallelograms

What you should learn

GOAL 1 Use some properties of parallelograms.

GOAL 2 Use properties of parallelograms in **real-life** situations, such as the drafting table shown in **Example 6**.

Why you should learn it

▼ You can use properties of parallelograms to understand how a scissors lift works in **Exs. 51–54**.

GOAL 1 PROPERTIES OF PARALLELOGRAMS

In this lesson and in the rest of the chapter you will study special quadrilaterals. A **parallelogram** is a quadrilateral with both pairs of opposite sides parallel.

When you mark diagrams of quadrilaterals, use matching arrowheads to indicate which sides are parallel. For example, in the diagram at the right, $\overline{PQ} \parallel \overline{RS}$ and $\overline{QR} \parallel \overline{SP}$. The symbol $\square PQRS$ is read "parallelogram $PQRS$."

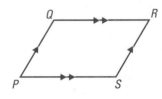

THEOREMS ABOUT PARALLELOGRAMS

THEOREM 6.2

If a quadrilateral is a parallelogram, then its **opposite sides** are congruent.

$\overline{PQ} \cong \overline{RS}$ and $\overline{SP} \cong \overline{QR}$

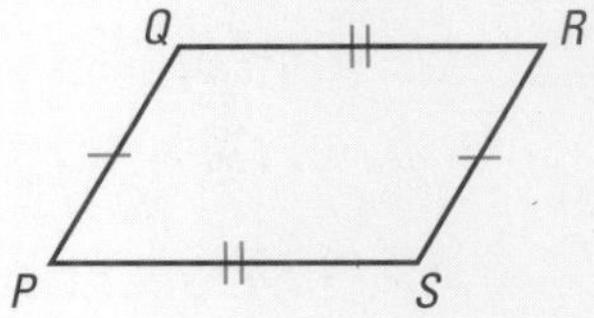

THEOREM 6.3

If a quadrilateral is a parallelogram, then its **opposite angles** are congruent.

$\angle P \cong \angle R$ and $\angle Q \cong \angle S$

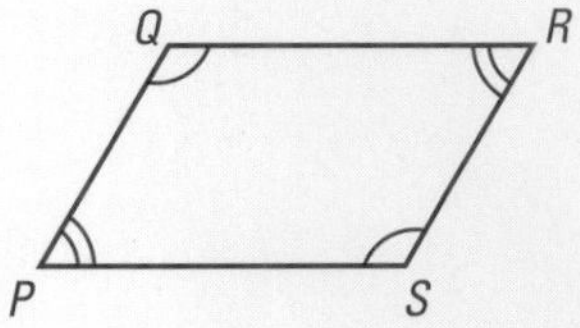

THEOREM 6.4

If a quadrilateral is a parallelogram, then its **consecutive angles** are supplementary.

$m\angle P + m\angle Q = 180°$, $m\angle Q + m\angle R = 180°$,
$m\angle R + m\angle S = 180°$, $m\angle S + m\angle P = 180°$

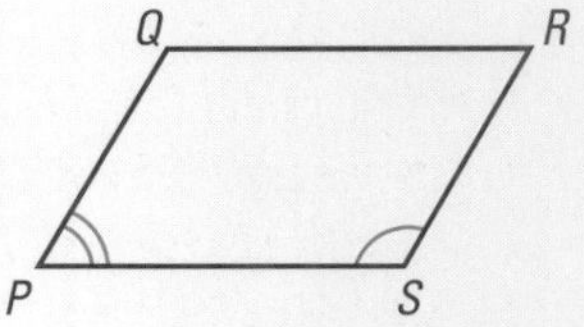

THEOREM 6.5

If a quadrilateral is a parallelogram, then its **diagonals** bisect each other.

$\overline{QM} \cong \overline{SM}$ and $\overline{PM} \cong \overline{RM}$

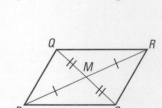

Theorem 6.2 is proved in Example 5. You are asked to prove Theorem 6.3, Theorem 6.4, and Theorem 6.5 in Exercises 38–44.

EXAMPLE 1 **Using Properties of Parallelograms**

FGHJ is a parallelogram.
Find the unknown length.
Explain your reasoning.

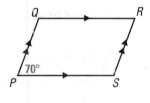

  a. *JH*

  b. *JK*

SOLUTION

  a. $JH = FG$ **Opposite sides of a ▱ are ≅.**

       $JH = 5$ **Substitute 5 for *FG*.**

  b. $JK = GK$ **Diagonals of a ▱ bisect each other.**

       $JK = 3$ **Substitute 3 for *GK*.**

EXAMPLE 2 **Using Properties of Parallelograms**

PQRS is a parallelogram.
Find the angle measure.

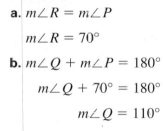

  a. $m\angle R$

  b. $m\angle Q$

SOLUTION

  a. $m\angle R = m\angle P$ **Opposite angles of a ▱ are ≅.**

       $m\angle R = 70°$ **Substitute 70° for *m∠P*.**

  b. $m\angle Q + m\angle P = 180°$ **Consecutive ⦞ of a ▱ are supplementary.**

       $m\angle Q + 70° = 180°$ **Substitute 70° for *m∠P*.**

           $m\angle Q = 110°$ **Subtract 70° from each side.**

EXAMPLE 3 **Using Algebra with Parallelograms**

PQRS is a parallelogram.
Find the value of *x*.

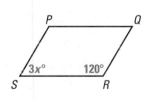

SOLUTION

           $m\angle S + m\angle R = 180°$ **Consecutive angles of a ▱ are supplementary.**

              $3x + 120 = 180$ **Substitute 3*x* for *m∠S* and 120 for *m∠R*.**

                   $3x = 60$ **Subtract 120 from each side.**

                     $x = 20$ **Divide each side by 3.**

GOAL 2 REASONING ABOUT PARALLELOGRAMS

EXAMPLE 4 *Proving Facts about Parallelograms*

GIVEN ▶ *ABCD* and *AEFG* are parallelograms.

PROVE ▶ ∠1 ≅ ∠3

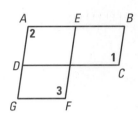

Plan Show that both angles are congruent to ∠2. Then use the Transitive Property of Congruence.

SOLUTION

Method 1 Write a two-column proof.

Statements	Reasons
1. *ABCD* is a ▱. *AEFG* is a ▱.	**1.** Given
2. ∠1 ≅ ∠2, ∠2 ≅ ∠3	**2.** Opposite angles of a ▱ are ≅.
3. ∠1 ≅ ∠3	**3.** Transitive Property of Congruence

Method 2 Write a paragraph proof.

ABCD is a parallelogram, so ∠1 ≅ ∠2 because opposite angles of a parallelogram are congruent. *AEFG* is a parallelogram, so ∠2 ≅ ∠3. By the Transitive Property of Congruence, ∠1 ≅ ∠3.

EXAMPLE 5 *Proving Theorem 6.2*

GIVEN ▶ *ABCD* is a parallelogram.

PROVE ▶ $\overline{AB} \cong \overline{CD}$, $\overline{AD} \cong \overline{CB}$

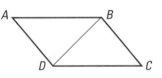

SOLUTION

Statements	Reasons
1. *ABCD* is a ▱.	**1.** Given
2. Draw $\overline{BD}$.	**2.** Through any two points there exists exactly one line.
3. $\overline{AB} \parallel \overline{CD}$, $\overline{AD} \parallel \overline{CB}$	**3.** Definition of parallelogram
4. ∠*ABD* ≅ ∠*CDB*, ∠*ADB* ≅ ∠*CBD*	**4.** Alternate Interior Angles Theorem
5. $\overline{DB} \cong \overline{DB}$	**5.** Reflexive Property of Congruence
6. △*ADB* ≅ △*CBD*	**6.** ASA Congruence Postulate
7. $\overline{AB} \cong \overline{CD}$, $\overline{AD} \cong \overline{CB}$	**7.** Corresponding parts of ≅ △ are ≅.

FOCUS ON CAREERS

REAL LIFE **FURNITURE DESIGN**

Furniture designers use geometry, trigonometry, and other skills to create designs for furniture.

INTERNET CAREER LINK
www.mcdougallittell.com

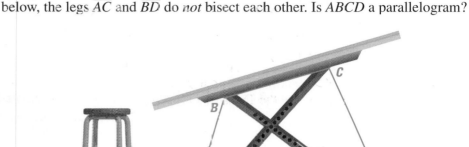

EXAMPLE 6 *Using Parallelograms in Real Life*

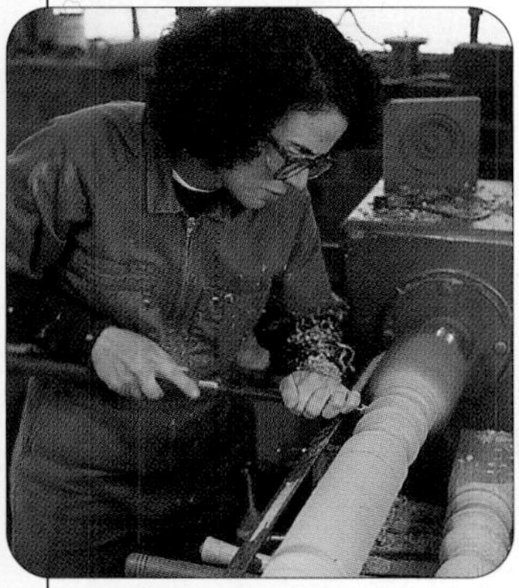

FURNITURE DESIGN A drafting table is made so that the legs can be joined in different ways to change the slope of the drawing surface. In the arrangement below, the legs $\overline{AC}$ and $\overline{BD}$ do *not* bisect each other. Is *ABCD* a parallelogram?

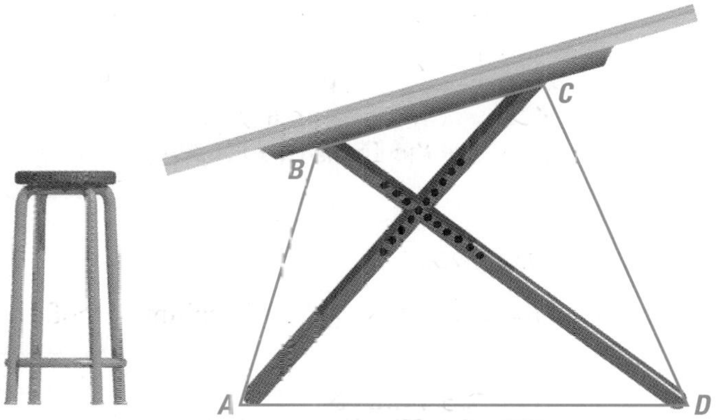

SOLUTION

No. If *ABCD* were a parallelogram, then by Theorem 6.5 $\overline{AC}$ would bisect $\overline{BD}$ and $\overline{BD}$ would bisect $\overline{AC}$.

GUIDED PRACTICE

Vocabulary Check ✓ **1.** Write a definition of *parallelogram*.

Concept Check ✓ **Decide whether the figure is a parallelogram. If it is not, explain why not.**

2.

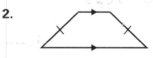

3.

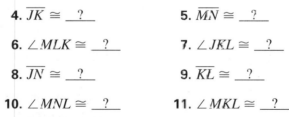

Skill Check ✓ **IDENTIFYING CONGRUENT PARTS Use the diagram of parallelogram *JKLM* at the right. Complete the statement, and give a reason for your answer.**

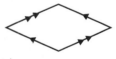

4. $\overline{JK} \cong$ __?__

5. $\overline{MN} \cong$ __?__

6. $\angle MLK \cong$ __?__

7. $\angle JKL \cong$ __?__

8. $\overline{JN} \cong$ __?__

9. $\overline{KL} \cong$ __?__

10. $\angle MNL \cong$ __?__

11. $\angle MKL \cong$ __?__

Find the measure in parallelogram *LMNQ*. Explain your reasoning.

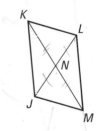

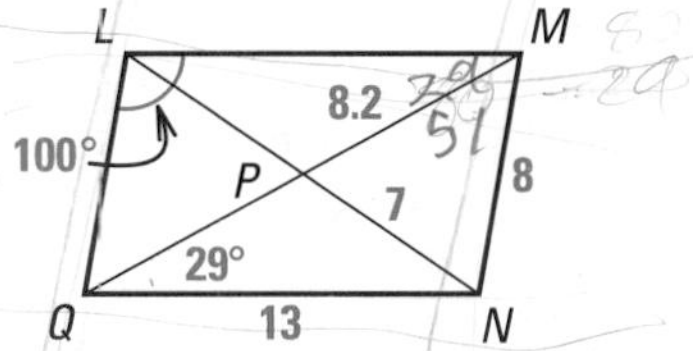

12. *LM*

13. *LP*

14. *LQ*

15. *QP*

16. $m\angle LMN$

17. $m\angle NQL$

18. $m\angle MNQ$

19. $m\angle LMQ$

PRACTICE AND APPLICATIONS

STUDENT HELP

▶ **Extra Practice**
to help you master
skills is on p. 813.

FINDING MEASURES Find the measure in
parallelogram *ABCD*. Explain your reasoning.

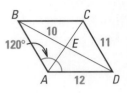

20. *DE*

21. *BA*

22. *BC*

23. $m\angle CDA$

24. $m\angle ABC$

25. $m\angle BCD$

⟨xy⟩ USING ALGEBRA Find the value of each variable in the parallelogram.

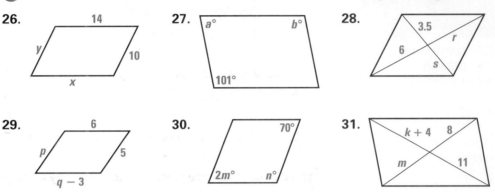

26.

27.

28.

29.

30.

31.

⟨xy⟩ USING ALGEBRA Find the value of each variable in the parallelogram.

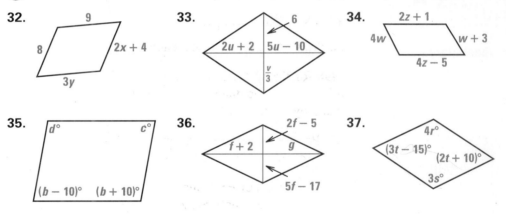

32.

33.

34.

35.

36.

37.

38. ▶ PROVING THEOREM 6.3 Copy and complete the proof of Theorem 6.3:
If a quadrilateral is a parallelogram, then its opposite angles are congruent.

GIVEN ▶ *ABCD* is a ▱.

PROVE ▶ $\angle A \cong \angle C$,
$\angle B \cong \angle D$

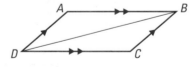

STUDENT HELP

▶ **HOMEWORK HELP**
Example 1: Exs. 20–22
Example 2: Exs. 23–25
Example 3: Exs. 26–37
Example 4: Exs. 55–58
Example 5: Exs. 38–44
Example 6: Exs. 45–54

Paragraph Proof Opposite sides of a parallelogram are congruent, so
___**a.**___ and ___**b.**___. By the Reflexive Property of Congruence, ___**c.**___.
$\triangle ABD \cong \triangle CDB$ because of the ___**d.**___ Congruence Postulate. Because
___**e.**___ parts of congruent triangles are congruent, $\angle A \cong \angle C$.

To prove that $\angle B \cong \angle D$, draw ___**f.**___ and use the same reasoning.

39. 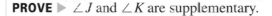 **PROVING THEOREM 6.4** Copy and complete the two-column proof of Theorem 6.4: If a quadrilateral is a parallelogram, then its consecutive angles are supplementary.

GIVEN ▶ *JKLM* is a □.

PROVE ▶ ∠*J* and ∠*K* are supplementary.

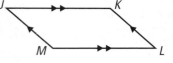

Statements	Reasons
1. ___?___	1. Given
2. $m\angle J = m\angle L$, $m\angle K = m\angle M$	2. ___?___
3. $m\angle J + m\angle L + m\angle K + m\angle M =$ ___?___	3. Sum of measures of int. ⦞ of a quad. is 360°.
4. $m\angle J + m\angle J + m\angle K + m\angle K = 360°$	4. ___?___
5. $2($ ___?___ $+$ ___?___ $) = 360°$	5. Distributive property
6. $m\angle J + m\angle K = 180°$	6. ___?___ prop. of equality
7. ∠*J* and ∠*K* are supplementary.	7. ___?___

You can use the same reasoning to prove any other pair of consecutive angles in □*JKLM* are supplementary.

▶ **DEVELOPING COORDINATE PROOF** Copy and complete the coordinate proof of Theorem 6.5.

GIVEN ▶ *PORS* is a □.

PROVE ▶ $\overline{PR}$ and $\overline{OS}$ bisect each other.

Plan for Proof Find the coordinates of the midpoints of the diagonals of □*PORS* and show that they are the same.

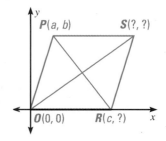

40. Point *R* is on the *x*-axis, and the length of $\overline{OR}$ is *c* units. What are the coordinates of point *R*?

41. The length of $\overline{PS}$ is also *c* units, and $\overline{PS}$ is horizontal. What are the coordinates of point *S*?

42. What are the coordinates of the midpoint of $\overline{PR}$?

43. What are the coordinates of the midpoint of $\overline{OS}$?

44. *Writing* How do you know that $\overline{PR}$ and $\overline{OS}$ bisect each other?

🌐 **BAKING** In Exercises 45 and 46, use the following information.
In a recipe for baklava, the pastry should be cut into triangles that form congruent parallelograms, as shown. Write a paragraph proof to prove the statement.

45. ∠3 is supplementary to ∠5.

46. ∠4 is supplementary to ∠5.

STAIR BALUSTERS In Exercises 47–50, use the following information.
In the diagram at the right, the slope of the handrail is equal to the slope of the stairs. The balusters (vertical posts) support the handrail.

47. Which angle in the red parallelogram is congruent to ∠1?

48. Which angles in the blue parallelogram are supplementary to ∠6?

49. Which postulate can be used to prove that ∠1 ≅ ∠5?

50. *Writing* Is the red parallelogram congruent to the blue parallelogram? Explain your reasoning.

SCISSORS LIFT Photographers can use scissors lifts for overhead shots, as shown at the left. The crossing beams of the lift form parallelograms that move together to raise and lower the platform. In Exercises 51–54, use the diagram of parallelogram *ABDC* at the right.

51. What is $m\angle B$ when $m\angle A = 120°$?

52. Suppose you decrease $m\angle A$. What happens to $m\angle B$?

53. Suppose you decrease $m\angle A$. What happens to *AD*?

54. Suppose you decrease $m\angle A$. What happens to the overall height of the scissors lift?

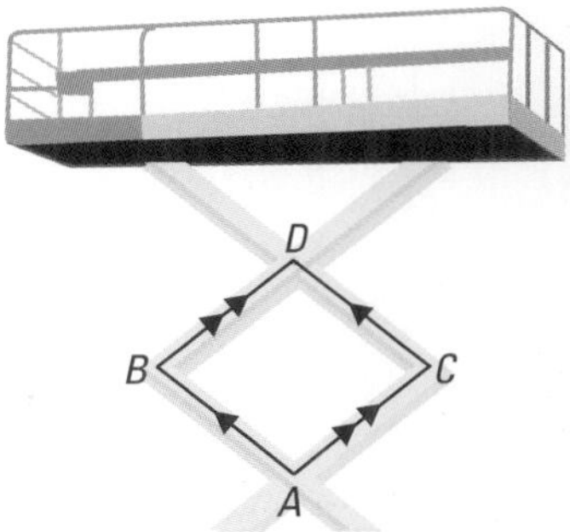

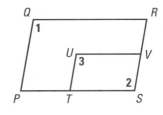

▶ **TWO-COLUMN PROOF** Write a two-column proof.

55. GIVEN ▶ *ABCD* and *CEFD* are ▱s.
   PROVE ▶ $\overline{AB} \cong \overline{FE}$

56. GIVEN ▶ *PQRS* and *TUVS* are ▱s.
   PROVE ▶ ∠1 ≅ ∠3

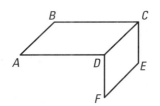

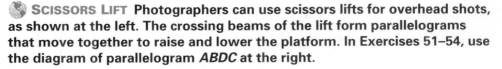

57. GIVEN ▶ *WXYZ* is a ▱.
   PROVE ▶ △*WMZ* ≅ △*YMX*

58. GIVEN ▶ *ABCD*, *EBGF*, *HJKD* are ▱s.
   PROVE ▶ ∠2 ≅ ∠3

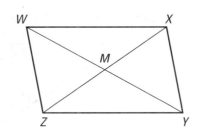

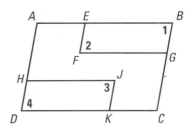

59. *Writing* In the diagram, *ABCG*, *CDEG*, and *AGEF* are parallelograms. Copy the diagram and add as many other angle measures as you can. Then describe how you know the angle measures you added are correct.

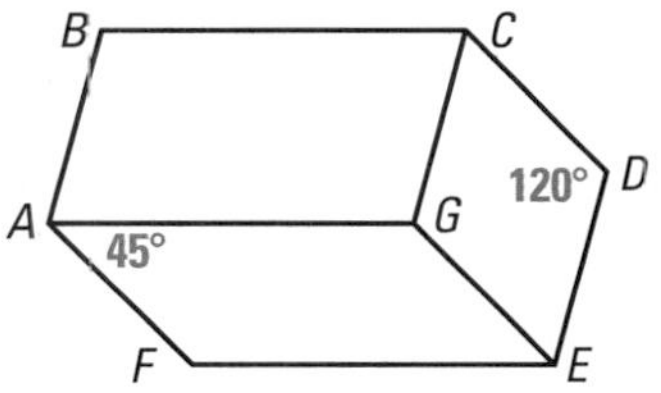

Test Preparation

60. **MULTIPLE CHOICE** In ▱*KLMN*, what is the value of *s*?

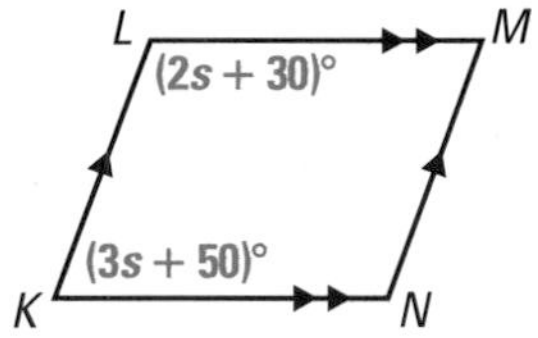

    Ⓐ 5   Ⓑ 20   Ⓒ 40

    Ⓓ 52   Ⓔ 70

61. **MULTIPLE CHOICE** In ▱*ABCD*, point *E* is the intersection of the diagonals. Which of the following is *not* necessarily true?

    Ⓐ $AB = CD$ Ⓑ $AC = BD$ Ⓒ $AE = CE$ Ⓓ $AD = BC$ Ⓔ $DE = BE$

★ **Challenge**

USING ALGEBRA **Suppose points** *A*(1, 2), *B*(3, 6), **and** *C*(6, 4) **are three vertices of a parallelogram.**

62. Give the coordinates of a point that could be the fourth vertex. Sketch the parallelogram in a coordinate plane.

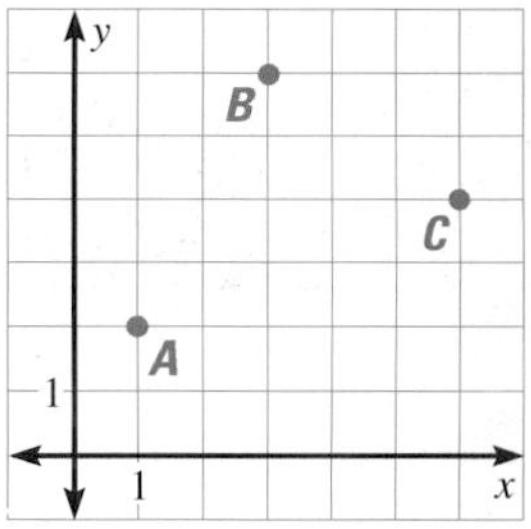

63. Explain how to check to make sure the figure you drew in Exercise 62 is a parallelogram.

64. How many different parallelograms can be formed using *A*, *B*, and *C* as vertices? Sketch each parallelogram and label the coordinates of the fourth vertex.

EXTRA CHALLENGE
www.mcdougallittell.com

MIXED REVIEW

USING ALGEBRA **Use the Distance Formula to find** *AB*. (Review 1.3 for 6.3)

65. *A*(2, 1), *B*(6, 9)   **66.** *A*(−4, 2), *B*(2, −1)   **67.** *A*(−8, −4), *B*(−1, −3)

USING ALGEBRA **Find the slope of** $\overline{AB}$. (Review 3.6 for 6.3)

68. *A*(2, 1), *B*(6, 9)   **69.** *A*(−4, 2), *B*(2, −1)   **70.** *A*(−8, −4), *B*(−1, −3)

71. 🌐 **PARKING CARS** In a parking lot, two guidelines are painted so that they are both perpendicular to the line along the curb. Are the guidelines parallel? Explain why or why not. (Review 3.5)

Name the shortest and longest sides of the triangle. Explain. (Review 5.5)

72.   **73.** 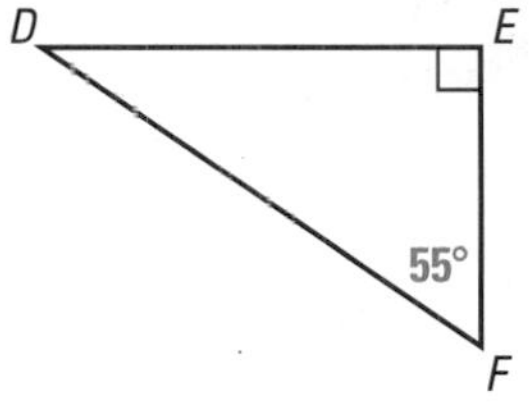   **74.**

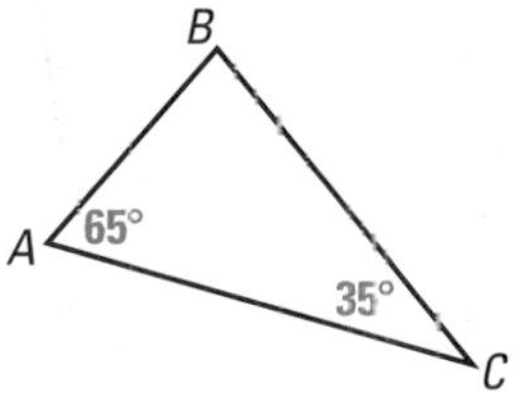

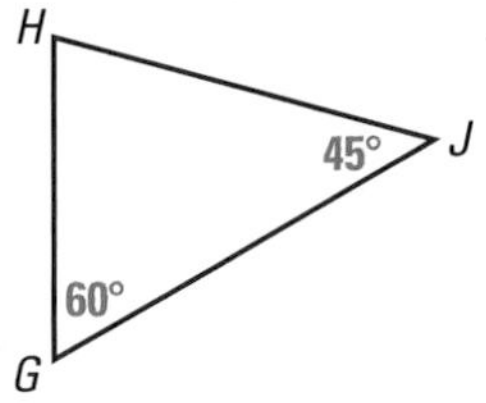

6.3

Proving Quadrilaterals are Parallelograms

What you should learn

GOAL 1 Prove that a quadrilateral is a parallelogram.

GOAL 2 Use coordinate geometry with parallelograms.

Why you should learn it

▼ To understand how **real-life** tools work, such as the bicycle derailleur in **Ex. 27**, which lets you change gears when you are biking uphill.

GOAL 1 PROVING QUADRILATERALS ARE PARALLELOGRAMS

The activity illustrates one way to prove that a quadrilateral is a parallelogram.

> ◗ **ACTIVITY**
> **Developing Concepts**
> ### Investigating Properties of Parallelograms

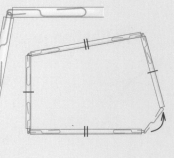

❶ Cut four straws to form two congruent pairs.

❷ Partly unbend two paperclips, link their smaller ends, and insert the larger ends into two cut straws, as shown. Join the rest of the straws to form a quadrilateral with opposite sides congruent, as shown.

❸ Change the angles of your quadrilateral. Is your quadrilateral always a parallelogram?

THEOREMS

THEOREM 6.6

If both pairs of opposite sides of a quadrilateral are congruent, then the quadrilateral is a parallelogram.

ABCD **is a parallelogram.**

THEOREM 6.7

If both pairs of opposite angles of a quadrilateral are congruent, then the quadrilateral is a parallelogram.

ABCD **is a parallelogram.**

THEOREM 6.8

If an angle of a quadrilateral is supplementary to both of its consecutive angles, then the quadrilateral is a parallelogram.

ABCD **is a parallelogram.**

THEOREM 6.9

If the diagonals of a quadrilateral bisect each other, then the quadrilateral is a parallelogram.

ABCD **is a parallelogram.**

The proof of Theorem 6.6 is given in Example 1. You will be asked to prove Theorem 6.7, Theorem 6.8, and Theorem 6.9 in Exercises 32–36.

EXAMPLE 1 *Proof of Theorem 6.6*

Prove Theorem 6.6.

GIVEN ▶ $\overline{AB} \cong \overline{CD}, \overline{AD} \cong \overline{CB}$

PROVE ▶ *ABCD* is a parallelogram.

Statements	Reasons
1. $\overline{AB} \cong \overline{CD}, \overline{AD} \cong \overline{CB}$	1. Given
2. $\overline{AC} \cong \overline{AC}$	2. Reflexive Property of Congruence
3. $\triangle ABC \cong \triangle CDA$	3. SSS Congruence Postulate
4. $\angle BAC \cong \angle DCA$, $\angle DAC \cong \angle BCA$	4. Corresponding parts of $\cong \triangle$ are $\cong$.
5. $\overline{AB} \parallel \overline{CD}, \overline{AD} \parallel \overline{CB}$	5. Alternate Interior Angles Converse
6. *ABCD* is a $\square$.	6. Definition of parallelogram

EXAMPLE 2 *Proving Quadrilaterals are Parallelograms*

As the sewing box below is opened, the trays are always parallel to each other. Why?

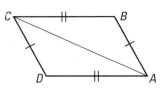

CONTAINERS
Many containers, such as tackle boxes, jewelry boxes, and tool boxes, use parallelograms in their design to ensure that the trays stay level.

FOCUS ON APPLICATIONS

SOLUTION

Each pair of hinges are opposite sides of a quadrilateral. The 2.75 inch sides of the quadrilateral are opposite and congruent. The 2 inch sides are also opposite and congruent. Because opposite sides of the quadrilateral are congruent, it is a parallelogram. By the definition of a parallelogram, opposite sides are parallel, so the trays of the sewing box are always parallel.

Theorem 6.10 gives another way to prove a quadrilateral is a parallelogram.

THEOREM

THEOREM 6.10

If one pair of opposite sides of a quadrilateral are congruent and parallel, then the quadrilateral is a parallelogram.

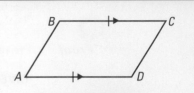

***ABCD* is a parallelogram.**

EXAMPLE 3   *Proof of Theorem 6.10*

Prove Theorem 6.10.

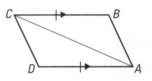

GIVEN ▸ $\overline{BC} \parallel \overline{DA}$, $\overline{BC} \cong \overline{DA}$

PROVE ▸ *ABCD* is a parallelogram.

Plan for Proof Show that $\triangle BAC \cong \triangle DCA$, so $\overline{AB} \cong \overline{CD}$. Use Theorem 6.6.

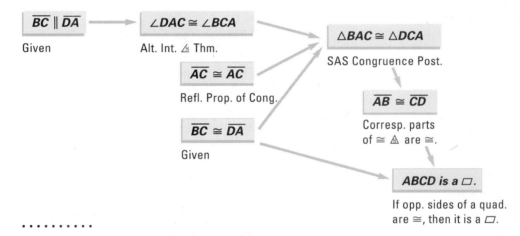

• • • • • • • • • •

You have studied several ways to prove that a quadrilateral is a parallelogram. In the box below, the first way is also the definition of a parallelogram.

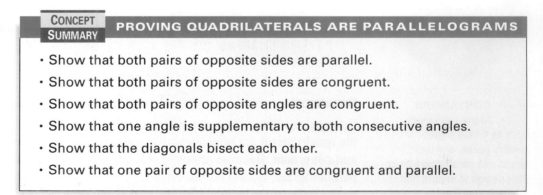

CONCEPT SUMMARY   **PROVING QUADRILATERALS ARE PARALLELOGRAMS**

• Show that both pairs of opposite sides are parallel.
• Show that both pairs of opposite sides are congruent.
• Show that both pairs of opposite angles are congruent.
• Show that one angle is supplementary to both consecutive angles.
• Show that the diagonals bisect each other.
• Show that one pair of opposite sides are congruent and parallel.

GOAL 2 **USING COORDINATE GEOMETRY**

When a figure is in the coordinate plane, you can use the Distance Formula to prove that sides are congruent and you can use the slope formula to prove that sides are parallel.

EXAMPLE 4 *Using Properties of Parallelograms*

Show that $A(2, -1)$, $B(1, 3)$, $C(6, 5)$, and $D(7, 1)$ are the vertices of a parallelogram.

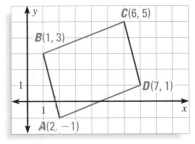

SOLUTION

There are many ways to solve this problem.

Method 1 Show that opposite sides have the same slope, so they are parallel.

$$\text{Slope of } \overline{AB} = \frac{3 - (-1)}{1 - 2} = -4$$

$$\text{Slope of } \overline{CD} = \frac{1 - 5}{7 - 6} = -4$$

$$\text{Slope of } \overline{BC} = \frac{5 - 3}{6 - 1} = \frac{2}{5}$$

$$\text{Slope of } \overline{DA} = \frac{-1 - 1}{2 - 7} = \frac{2}{5}$$

$\overline{AB}$ and $\overline{CD}$ have the same slope so they are parallel. Similarly, $\overline{BC} \parallel \overline{DA}$.

▶ Because opposite sides are parallel, *ABCD* is a parallelogram.

Method 2 Show that opposite sides have the same length.

$$AB = \sqrt{(1 - 2)^2 + [3 - (-1)]^2} = \sqrt{17}$$

$$CD = \sqrt{(7 - 6)^2 + (1 - 5)^2} = \sqrt{17}$$

$$BC = \sqrt{(6 - 1)^2 + (5 - 3)^2} = \sqrt{29}$$

$$DA = \sqrt{(2 - 7)^2 + (-1 - 1)^2} = \sqrt{29}$$

▶ $\overline{AB} \cong \overline{CD}$ and $\overline{BC} \cong \overline{DA}$. Because both pairs of opposite sides are congruent, *ABCD* is a parallelogram.

Method 3 Show that one pair of opposite sides is congruent and parallel.

Find the slopes and lengths of $\overline{AB}$ and $\overline{CD}$ as shown in Methods 1 and 2.

$$\text{Slope of } \overline{AB} = \text{Slope of } \overline{CD} = -4$$

$$AB = CD = \sqrt{17}$$

▶ $\overline{AB}$ and $\overline{CD}$ are congruent and parallel, so *ABCD* is a parallelogram.

STUDENT HELP

→ **Study Tip**
Because you don't know the measures of the angles of *ABCD*, you can *not* use Theorems 6.7 or 6.8 in Example 4.

STUDENT HELP

INTERNET
HOMEWORK HELP
Visit our Web site
www.mcdougallittell.com
for extra examples.

6.3 *Proving Quadrilaterals are Parallelograms* **341**

GUIDED PRACTICE

Concept Check ✓

1. Is a hexagon with opposite sides parallel called a parallelogram? Explain.

Skill Check ✓

Decide whether you are given enough information to determine that the quadrilateral is a parallelogram. Explain your reasoning.

2.   **3.**   **4.**

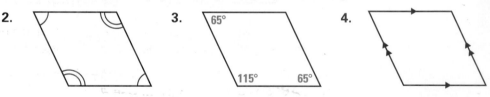

Describe how you would prove that *ABCD* is a parallelogram.

5.   **6.**   **7.**

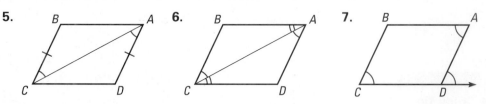

8. Describe at least three ways to show that $A(0, 0)$, $B(2, 6)$, $C(5, 7)$, and $D(3, 1)$ are the vertices of a parallelogram.

PRACTICE AND APPLICATIONS

STUDENT HELP

► **Extra Practice**
to help you master
skills is on p. 813.

LOGICAL REASONING Are you given enough information to determine whether the quadrilateral is a parallelogram? Explain.

9.   **10.**   **11.**

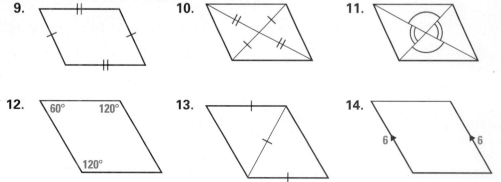

12.   **13.**   **14.**

STUDENT HELP

► **HOMEWORK HELP**
Example 1: Exs. 15, 16,
32, 33
Example 2: Exs. 21,
28, 31
Example 3: Exs. 32, 33
Example 4: Exs. 21–26,
34–36

LOGICAL REASONING Describe how to prove that *ABCD* is a parallelogram. Use the given information.

15. $\triangle ABC \cong \triangle CDA$ **16.** $\triangle AXB \cong \triangle CXD$

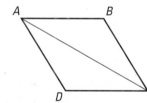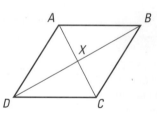

USING ALGEBRA What value of *x* will make the polygon a parallelogram?

17.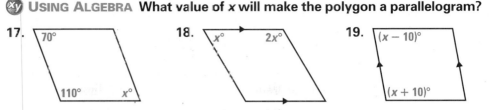

18.

19.

20. **VISUAL THINKING** Draw a quadrilateral that has one pair of congruent sides and one pair of parallel sides but that is not a parallelogram.

▶ **COORDINATE GEOMETRY** Use the given definition or theorem to prove that *ABCD* is a parallelogram. Use *A*(−1, 6), *B*(3, 5), *C*(5, −3), and *D*(1, −2).

21. Theorem 6.6   22. Theorem 6.9

23. definition of a parallelogram   24. Theorem 6.10

▶ **USING COORDINATE GEOMETRY** Prove that the points represent the vertices of a parallelogram. Use a different method for each exercise.

25. *J*(−6, 2), *K*(−1, 3), *L*(2, −3), *M*(−3, −4)

26. *P*(2, 5), *Q*(8, 4), *R*(9, −4), *S*(3, −3)

27. 🌐 **CHANGING GEARS** When you change gears on a bicycle, the *derailleur* moves the chain to the new gear. For the derailleur at the right, *AB* = 1.8 cm, *BC* = 3.6 cm, *CD* = 1.8 cm, and *DA* = 3.6 cm. Explain why $\overline{AB}$ and $\overline{CD}$ are always parallel when the derailleur moves.

28. 🌐 **COMPUTERS** Many word processors have a feature that allows a regular letter to be changed to an oblique (slanted) letter. The diagram at the right shows some regular letters and their oblique versions. Explain how you can prove that the oblique I is a parallelogram.

29. **VISUAL REASONING** Explain why the following method of drawing a parallelogram works. State a theorem to support your answer.

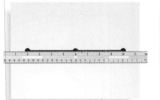

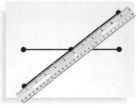

❶ Use a ruler to draw a segment and its midpoint.

❷ Draw another segment so the midpoints coincide.

❸ Connect the endpoints of the segments.

30. 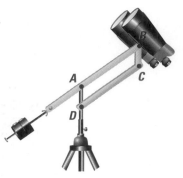 **CONSTRUCTION** There are many ways to use a compass and straightedge to construct a parallelogram. Describe a method that uses Theorem 6.6, Theorem 6.8, or Theorem 6.10. Then use your method to construct a parallelogram.

31. 🌐 **BIRD WATCHING** You are designing a binocular mount that will keep the binoculars pointed in the same direction while they are raised and lowered for different viewers. If $\overline{BC}$ is always vertical, the binoculars will always point in the same direction. How can you design the mount so $\overline{BC}$ is always vertical? Justify your answer.

▶ **PROVING THEOREMS 6.7 AND 6.8** **Write a proof of the theorem.**

32. Prove Theorem 6.7.

GIVEN ▶ $\angle R \cong \angle T$,
$\angle S \cong \angle U$

PROVE ▶ *RSTU* is a parallelogram.

Plan for Proof Show that the sum $2(m\angle S) + 2(m\angle T) = 360°$, so $\angle S$ and $\angle T$ are supplementary and $\overline{SR} \parallel \overline{UT}$.

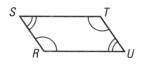

33. Prove Theorem 6.8.

GIVEN ▶ $\angle P$ is supplementary to $\angle Q$ and $\angle S$.

PROVE ▶ *PQRS* is a parallelogram.

Plan for Proof Show that opposite sides of *PQRS* are parallel.

▶ **PROVING THEOREM 6.9** **In Exercises 34–36, complete the coordinate proof of Theorem 6.9.**

GIVEN ▶ Diagonals $\overline{MP}$ and $\overline{NQ}$ bisect each other.

PROVE ▶ *MNPQ* is a parallelogram.

Plan for Proof Show that opposite sides of *MNPQ* have the same slope.

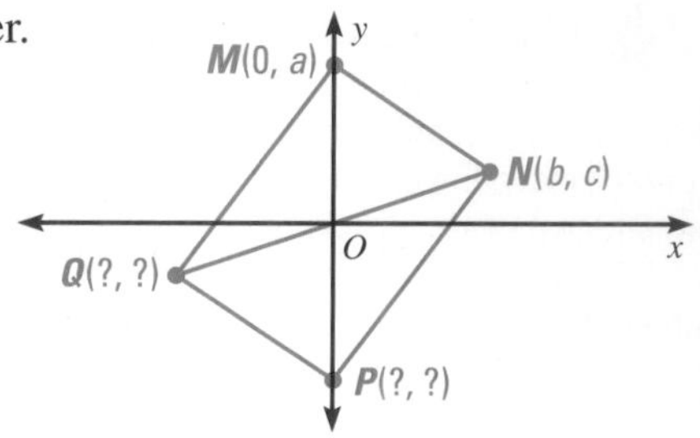

Place *MNPQ* in the coordinate plane so the diagonals intersect at the origin and $\overline{MP}$ lies on the y-axis. Let the coordinates of M be $(0, a)$ and the coordinates of N be (b, c). Copy the graph at the right.

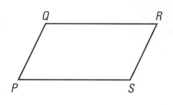

34. What are the coordinates of P? Explain your reasoning and label the coordinates on your graph.

35. What are the coordinates of Q? Explain your reasoning and label the coordinates on your graph.

36. Find the slope of each side of *MNPQ* and show that the slopes of opposite sides are equal.

STUDENT HELP

HOMEWORK HELP
Visit our Web site www.mcdougallittell.com for help with the coordinate proof in Exs. 34–36.

Test Preparation

37. MULTI-STEP PROBLEM You shoot a pool ball as shown at the right and it rolls back to where it started. The ball bounces off each wall at the same angle at which it hit the wall. Copy the diagram and add each angle measure as you know it.

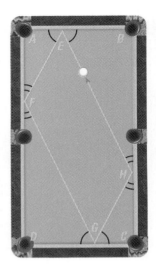

a. The ball hits the first wall at an angle of about 63°. So $m\angle AEF = m\angle BEH \approx 63°$. Explain why $m\angle AFE \approx 27°$.

b. Explain why $m\angle FGD \approx 63°$.

c. What is $m\angle GHC$? $m\angle EHB$?

d. Find the measure of each interior angle of *EFGH*. What kind of shape is *EFGH*? How do you know?

★ **Challenge**

EXTRA CHALLENGE

→ www.mcdougallittell.com

38. VISUAL THINKING *PQRS* is a parallelogram and *QTSU* is a parallelogram. Use the diagonals of the parallelograms to explain why *PTRU* is a parallelogram.

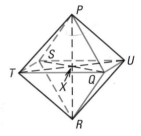

MIXED REVIEW

USING ALGEBRA **Rewrite the biconditional statement as a conditional statement and its converse.** (Review 2.2 for 6.4)

39. $x^2 + 2 = 2$ if and only if $x = 0$.

40. $4x + 7 = x + 37$ if and only if $x = 10$.

41. A quadrilateral is a parallelogram if and only if each pair of opposite sides are parallel.

WRITING BICONDITIONAL STATEMENTS **Write the pair of theorems from Lesson 5.1 as a single biconditional statement.** (Review 2.2, 5.1 for 6.4)

42. Theorems 5.1 and 5.2

43. Theorems 5.3 and 5.4

44. Write an equation of the line that is perpendicular to $y = -4x + 2$ and passes through the point $(1, -2)$. (Review 3.7)

ANGLE MEASURES **Find the value of x.** (Review 4.1)

45.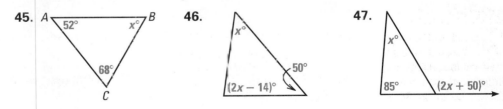

46.

47.

1. Choose the words that describe the quadrilateral at the right: *concave*, *convex*, *equilateral*, *equiangular*, and *regular*. **(Lesson 6.1)**

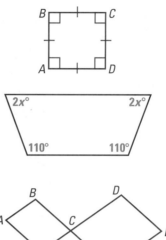

2. Find the value of *x*. Explain your reasoning. **(Lesson 6.1)**

3. Write a proof. **(Lesson 6.2)**

    GIVEN ▶ *ABCG* and *CDEF* are parallelograms.

    PROVE ▶ $\angle A \cong \angle E$

4. Describe two ways to show that $A(-4, 1)$, $B(3, 0)$, $C(5, -7)$, and $D(-2, -6)$ are the vertices of a parallelogram. **(Lesson 6.3)**

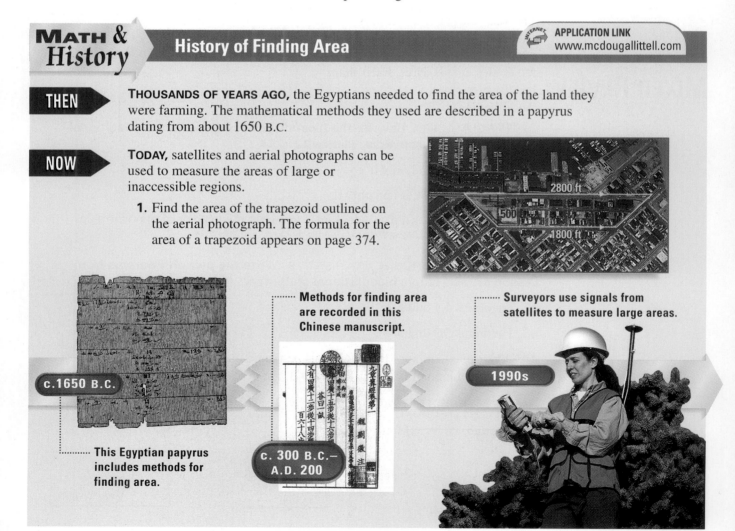

MATH & History

INTERNET APPLICATION LINK
www.mcdougallittell.com

History of Finding Area

THEN ▶ **THOUSANDS OF YEARS AGO,** the Egyptians needed to find the area of the land they were farming. The mathematical methods they used are described in a papyrus dating from about 1650 B.C.

NOW ▶ **TODAY,** satellites and aerial photographs can be used to measure the areas of large or inaccessible regions.

1. Find the area of the trapezoid outlined on the aerial photograph. The formula for the area of a trapezoid appears on page 374.

2800 ft
1500
1800 ft

Methods for finding area are recorded in this Chinese manuscript.

Surveyors use signals from satellites to measure large areas.

c.1650 B.C.

c. 300 B.C.– A.D. 200

1990s

This Egyptian papyrus includes methods for finding area.

6.4 Rhombuses, Rectangles, and Squares

GOAL 1 PROPERTIES OF SPECIAL PARALLELOGRAMS

In this lesson you will study three special types of parallelograms: *rhombuses*, *rectangles*, and *squares*.

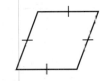

A **rhombus** is a parallelogram with four congruent sides.

A **rectangle** is a parallelogram with four right angles.

A **square** is a parallelogram with four congruent sides and four right angles.

The *Venn diagram* at the right shows the relationships among parallelograms, rhombuses, rectangles, and squares. Each shape has the properties of every group that it belongs to. For instance, a square is a rectangle, a rhombus, and a parallelogram, so it has all of the properties of each of those shapes.

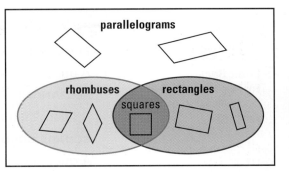

EXAMPLE 1 *Describing a Special Parallelogram*

Decide whether the statement is *always*, *sometimes*, or *never* true.

a. A rhombus is a rectangle.

b. A parallelogram is a rectangle.

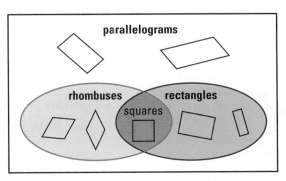

SOLUTION

a. The statement is *sometimes* true. In the Venn diagram, the regions for rhombuses and rectangles overlap. If the rhombus is a square, it is a rectangle.

b. The statement is *sometimes* true. Some parallelograms are rectangles. In the Venn diagram, you can see that some of the shapes in the parallelogram box are in the region for rectangles, but many aren't.

Logical Reasoning

EXAMPLE 2 *Using Properties of Special Parallelograms*

ABCD is a rectangle. What else do you know about *ABCD*?

SOLUTION

Because *ABCD* is a rectangle, it has four right angles by the definition. The definition also states that rectangles are parallelograms, so *ABCD* has all the properties of a parallelogram:

- Opposite sides are parallel and congruent.
- Opposite angles are congruent and consecutive angles are supplementary.
- Diagonals bisect each other.

· · · · · · · · · ·

A rectangle is defined as a *parallelogram* with four right angles. But *any quadrilateral* with four right angles is a rectangle because any quadrilateral with four right angles is a parallelogram. In Exercises 48–50 you will justify the following corollaries to the definitions of rhombus, rectangle, and square.

CEROLLARIES ABOUT SPECIAL QUADRILATERALS

RHOMBUS COROLLARY

A quadrilateral is a rhombus if and only if it has four congruent sides.

RECTANGLE COROLLARY

A quadrilateral is a rectangle if and only if it has four right angles.

SQUARE COROLLARY

A quadrilateral is a square if and only if it is a rhombus and a rectangle.

STUDENT HELP

► **Look Back**
For help with biconditional statements, see p. 80.

You can use these corollaries to prove that a quadrilateral is a rhombus, rectangle, or square without proving first that the quadrilateral is a parallelogram.

EXAMPLE 3 *Using Properties of a Rhombus*

In the diagram at the right, *PQRS* is a rhombus. What is the value of *y*?

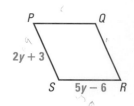

SOLUTION

All four sides of a rhombus are congruent, so $RS = PS$.

$5y - 6 = 2y + 3$	Equate lengths of congruent sides.
$5y = 2y + 9$	Add 6 to each side.
$3y = 9$	Subtract 2y from each side.
$y = 3$	Divide each side by 3.

The following theorems are about diagonals of rhombuses and rectangles. You are asked to prove Theorems 6.12 and 6.13 in Exercises 51, 52, 59, and 60.

THEOREMS

THEOREM 6.11

A parallelogram is a rhombus if and only if its diagonals are perpendicular.

ABCD is a rhombus if and only if $\overline{AC} \perp \overline{BD}$.

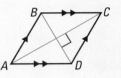

THEOREM 6.12

A parallelogram is a rhombus if and only if each diagonal bisects a pair of opposite angles.

ABCD is a rhombus if and only if
$\overline{AC}$ bisects $\angle DAB$ and $\angle BCD$ and
$\overline{BD}$ bisects $\angle ADC$ and $\angle CBA$.

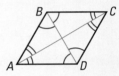

THEOREM 6.13

A parallelogram is a rectangle if and only if its diagonals are congruent.

ABCD is a rectangle if and only if $\overline{AC} \cong \overline{BD}$.

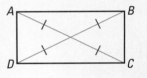

You can rewrite Theorem 6.11 as a conditional statement and its converse.

Conditional statement: If the diagonals of a parallelogram are perpendicular, then the parallelogram is a rhombus.

Converse: If a parallelogram is a rhombus, then its diagonals are perpendicular.

To prove the theorem, you must prove both statements.

EXAMPLE 4 *Proving Theorem 6.11*

Write a paragraph proof of the converse above.

GIVEN ▸ *ABCD* is a rhombus.

PROVE ▸ $\overline{AC} \perp \overline{BD}$

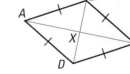

SOLUTION

Paragraph Proof *ABCD* is a rhombus, so $\overline{AB} \cong \overline{CB}$. Because *ABCD* is a parallelogram, its diagonals bisect each other so $\overline{AX} \cong \overline{CX}$ and $\overline{BX} \cong \overline{BX}$. Use the SSS Congruence Postulate to prove $\triangle AXB \cong \triangle CXB$, so $\angle AXB \cong \angle CXB$. Then, because $\overline{AC}$ and $\overline{BD}$ intersect to form congruent adjacent angles, $\overline{AC} \perp \overline{BD}$.

EXAMPLE 5 Coordinate Proof of Theorem 6.11

Proof

In Example 4, a paragraph proof was given for part of Theorem 6.11. Write a coordinate proof of the original conditional statement.

GIVEN ▶ $ABCD$ is a parallelogram, $\overline{AC} \perp \overline{BD}$.

PROVE ▶ $ABCD$ is a rhombus.

SOLUTION

Assign coordinates Because $\overline{AC} \perp \overline{BD}$, place $ABCD$ in the coordinate plane so $\overline{AC}$ and $\overline{BD}$ lie on the axes and their intersection is at the origin.

Let $(0, a)$ be the coordinates of A, and let $(b, 0)$ be the coordinates of B.

Because $ABCD$ is a parallelogram, the diagonals bisect each other and $OA = OC$. So, the coordinates of C are $(0, -a)$.

Similarly, the coordinates of D are $(-b, 0)$.

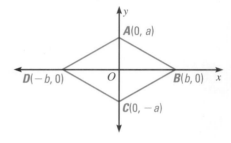

Find the lengths of the sides of $ABCD$. Use the Distance Formula.

$$AB = \sqrt{(b - 0)^2 + (0 - a)^2} = \sqrt{b^2 + a^2}$$

$$BC = \sqrt{(0 - b)^2 + (-a - 0)^2} = \sqrt{b^2 + a^2}$$

$$CD = \sqrt{(-b - 0)^2 + [0 - (-a)]^2} = \sqrt{b^2 + a^2}$$

$$DA = \sqrt{[0 - (-b)]^2 + (a - 0)^2} = \sqrt{b^2 + a^2}$$

▶ All of the side lengths are equal, so $ABCD$ is a rhombus.

FOCUS ON APPLICATIONS

CARPENTRY If a screen door is not rectangular, you can use a piece of hardware called a *turnbuckle* to shorten the longer diagonal until the door is rectangular.

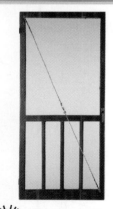

EXAMPLE 6 Checking a Rectangle

CARPENTRY You are building a rectangular frame for a theater set.

a. First, you nail four pieces of wood together, as shown at the right. What is the shape of the frame?

b. To make sure the frame is a rectangle, you measure the diagonals. One is 7 feet 4 inches and the other is 7 feet 2 inches. Is the frame a rectangle? Explain.

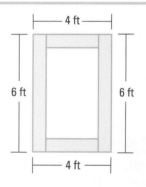

SOLUTION

a. Opposite sides are congruent, so the frame is a parallelogram.

b. The parallelogram is not a rectangle. If it were a rectangle, the diagonals would be congruent.

GUIDED PRACTICE

Vocabulary Check ✓

1. What is another name for an *equilateral quadrilateral*?

Concept Check ✓

2. Theorem 6.12 is a biconditional statement. Rewrite the theorem as a conditional statement and its converse, and tell what each statement means for parallelogram *PQRS*.

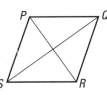

Skill Check ✓

Decide whether the statement is *sometimes*, *always*, or *never* true.

3. A rectangle is a parallelogram.

4. A parallelogram is a rhombus.

5. A rectangle is a rhombus.

6. A square is a rectangle.

Which of the following quadrilaterals have the given property?

7. All sides are congruent.

8. All angles are congruent.

9. The diagonals are congruent.

10. Opposite angles are congruent.

A. Parallelogram

B. Rectangle

C. Rhombus

D. Square

11. *MNPQ* is a rectangle. What is the value of *x*?

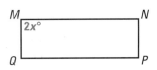

PRACTICE AND APPLICATIONS

STUDENT HELP

▶ **Extra Practice**
to help you master
skills is on p. 814.

RECTANGLE For any rectangle *ABCD*, decide whether the statement is *always*, *sometimes*, or *never* true. Draw a sketch and explain your answer.

12. $\angle A \cong \angle B$

13. $\overline{AB} \cong \overline{BC}$

14. $\overline{AC} \cong \overline{BD}$

15. $\overline{AC} \perp \overline{BD}$

PROPERTIES List each quadrilateral for which the statement is true.

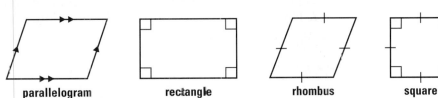

parallelogram   rectangle   rhombus   square

STUDENT HELP

▶ **HOMEWORK HELP**
Example 1: Exs. 12–15, 27–32
Example 2: Exs. 27–32, 51
Example 3: Exs. 33–43
Example 4: Exs. 44–52
Example 5: Exs. 55–60
Example 6: Exs. 61, 62

16. It is equiangular.

17. It is equiangular and equilateral.

18. The diagonals are perpendicular.

19. Opposite sides are congruent.

20. The diagonals bisect each other.

21. The diagonals bisect opposite angles.

PROPERTIES Sketch the quadrilateral and list everything you know about it.

22. parallelogram *FGHI*

23. rhombus *PQRS*

24. square *ABCD*

LOGICAL REASONING Give another name for the quadrilateral.

25. equiangular quadrilateral

26. regular quadrilateral

RHOMBUS For any rhombus *ABCD*, decide whether the statement is *always*, *sometimes*, or *never* true. Draw a sketch and explain your answer.

27. $\angle A \cong \angle C$

28. $\angle A \cong \angle B$

29. $\angle ABD \cong \angle CBD$

30. $\overline{AB} \cong \overline{BC}$

31. $\overline{AC} \cong \overline{BD}$

32. $\overline{AD} \cong \overline{CD}$

xy USING ALGEBRA Find the value of *x*.

33. *ABCD* is a square.

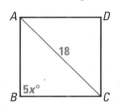

34. *EFGH* is a rhombus.

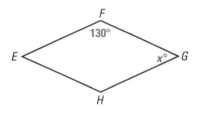
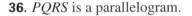

35. *KLMN* is a rectangle.

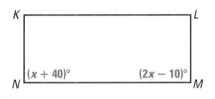

36. *PQRS* is a parallelogram.

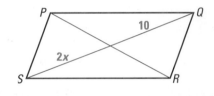

37. *TUWY* is a rhombus.

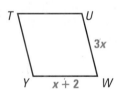

38. *CDEF* is a rectangle.

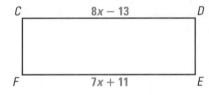

COMPLETING STATEMENTS *GHJK* is a square with diagonals intersecting at *L*. Given that *GH* = 2 and *GL* = $\sqrt{2}$, complete the statement.

39. *HK* = ___?___

40. $m\angle KLJ$ = ___?___

41. $m\angle HJG$ = ___?___

42. Perimeter of $\triangle HJK$ = ___?___

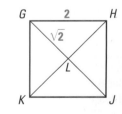

43. **xy USING ALGEBRA** *WXYZ* is a rectangle. The perimeter of $\triangle XYZ$ is 24. *XY* + *YZ* = 5*x* − 1 and *XZ* = 13 − *x*. Find *WY*.

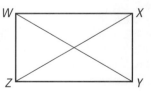

44. 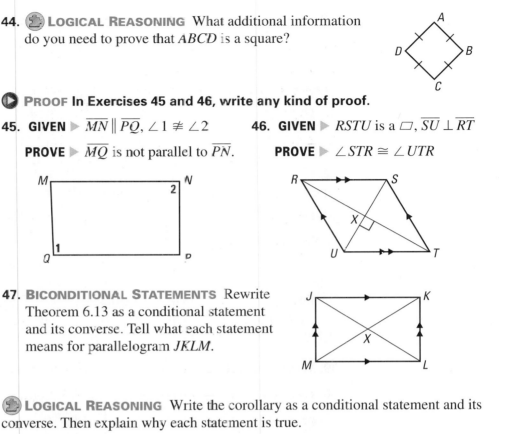 **LOGICAL REASONING** What additional information do you need to prove that *ABCD* is a square?

▶ **PROOF** In Exercises 45 and 46, write any kind of proof.

45. GIVEN ▶ $\overline{MN} \parallel \overline{PQ}$, $\angle 1 \not\cong \angle 2$

 PROVE ▶ $\overline{MQ}$ is not parallel to $\overline{PN}$.

46. GIVEN ▶ *RSTU* is a ▱, $\overline{SU} \perp \overline{RT}$

 PROVE ▶ $\angle STR \cong \angle UTR$

47. BICONDITIONAL STATEMENTS Rewrite Theorem 6.13 as a conditional statement and its converse. Tell what each statement means for parallelogram *JKLM*.

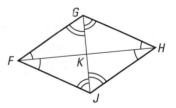

▲ **LOGICAL REASONING** Write the corollary as a conditional statement and its converse. Then explain why each statement is true.

48. Rhombus corollary   **49.** Rectangle corollary   **50.** Square corollary

▶ **PROVING THEOREM 6.12** Prove both conditional statements of Theorem 6.12.

51. GIVEN ▶ *PQRT* is a rhombus.

 PROVE ▶ $\overline{PR}$ bisects $\angle TPQ$ and $\angle QRT$. $\overline{TQ}$ bisects $\angle PTR$ and $\angle RQP$.

 Plan for Proof To prove that $\overline{PR}$ bisects $\angle TPQ$ and $\angle QRT$, first prove that $\triangle PRQ \cong \triangle PRT$.

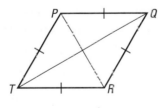

52. GIVEN ▶ *FGHJ* is a parallelogram. $\overline{FH}$ bisects $\angle JFG$ and $\angle GHJ$. $\overline{JG}$ bisects $\angle FJH$ and $\angle HGF$.

 PROVE ▶ *FGHJ* is a rhombus.

 Plan for Proof Prove $\triangle FHJ \cong \triangle FHG$ so $\overline{JH} \cong \overline{GH}$. Then use the fact that $\overline{JH} \cong \overline{FG}$ and $\overline{GH} \cong \overline{FJ}$.

△ **CONSTRUCTION** Explain how to construct the figure using a straightedge and a compass. Use a definition or theorem from this lesson to explain why your method works.

53. a rhombus that is not a square   **54.** a rectangle that is not a square

▶ **COORDINATE GEOMETRY** It is given that *PQRS* is a parallelogram. Graph □*PQRS*. Decide whether it is a *rectangle*, a *rhombus*, a *square*, or *none of the above*. Justify your answer using theorems about quadrilaterals.

55. *P*(3, 1)
   Q(3, −3)
   R(−2, −3)
   S(−2, 1)

56. *P*(5, 2)
   Q(1, 9)
   R(−3, 2)
   S(1, −5)

57. *P*(−1, 4)
   Q(−3, 2)
   R(2, −3)
   S(4, −1)

58. *P*(5, 2)
   Q(2, 5)
   R(−1, 2)
   S(2, −1)

▶ **COORDINATE PROOF OF THEOREM 6.13** In Exercises 59 and 60, you will complete a coordinate proof of one conditional statement of Theorem 6.13.

GIVEN ▶ *KMNO* is a rectangle.

PROVE ▶ $\overline{OM} \cong \overline{KN}$

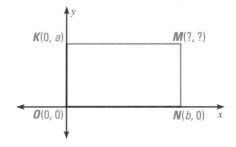

Because ∠*O* is a right angle, place *KMNO* in the coordinate plane so *O* is at the origin, $\overline{ON}$ lies on the *x*-axis and $\overline{OK}$ lies on the *y*-axis. Let the coordinates of *K* be (0, *a*) and let the coordinates of *N* be (*b*, 0).

59. What are the coordinates of *M*? Explain your reasoning.

60. Use the Distance Formula to prove that $\overline{OM} \cong \overline{KN}$.

🌐 **PORTABLE TABLE** The legs of the table shown at the right are all the same length. The cross braces are all the same length and bisect each other.

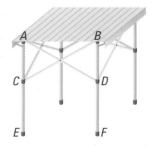

61. Show that the edge of the tabletop $\overline{AB}$ is perpendicular to legs $\overline{AE}$ and $\overline{BF}$.

62. Show that $\overline{AB}$ is parallel to $\overline{EF}$.

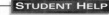
STUDENT HELP

🌐 **SOFTWARE HELP**
Visit our Web site
www.mcdougallittell.com
to see instructions for
several software
applications.

△ **TECHNOLOGY** In Exercises 63–65, use geometry software.

Draw a segment $\overline{AB}$ and a point *C* on the segment. Construct the midpoint *D* of $\overline{AB}$. Then hide $\overline{AB}$ and point *B* so only points *A*, *D*, and *C* are visible.

Construct two circles with centers *A* and *C* using the length $\overline{AD}$ as the radius of each circle. Label the points of intersection *E* and *F*. Draw $\overline{AE}$, $\overline{CE}$, $\overline{CF}$, and $\overline{AF}$.

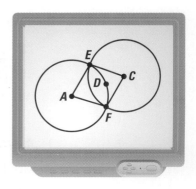

63. What kind of shape is *AECF*? How do you know? What happens to the shape as you drag *A*? drag *C*?

64. Hide the circles and point *D*, and draw diagonals $\overline{EF}$ and $\overline{AC}$. Measure ∠*EAC*, ∠*FAC*, ∠*AEF*, and ∠*CEF*. What happens to the measures as you drag *A*? drag *C*?

65. Which theorem does this construction illustrate?

66. MULTIPLE CHOICE In rectangle *ABCD*, if $AB = 7x - 3$ and $CD = 4x + 9$, then $x = \underline{\ ?\ }$.

(A) 1 (B) 2 (C) 3 (D) 4 (E) 5

67. MULTIPLE CHOICE In parallelogram *KLMN*, $KM = LN$, $m\angle KLM = 2xy$, and $m\angle LMN = 9x + 9$. Find the value of *y*.

(A) 9 (B) 5 (C) 18

(D) 10 (E) Cannot be determined.

68. *Writing* Explain why a parallelogram with one right angle is a rectangle.

★ **Challenge**

▶ COORDINATE PROOF OF THEOREM 6.13 **Complete the coordinate proof of one conditional statement of Theorem 6.13.**

GIVEN ▶ *ABCD* is a parallelogram, $\overline{AC} \cong \overline{DB}$.

PROVE ▶ *ABCD* is a rectangle.

Place *ABCD* in the coordinate plane so $\overline{DB}$ lies on the *x*-axis and the diagonals intersect at the origin. Let the coordinates of *B* be (*b*, 0) and let the *x*-coordinate of *A* be *a* as shown.

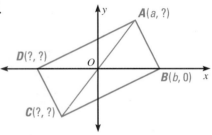

69. Explain why $OA = OB = OC = OD$.

70. Write the *y*-coordinate of *A* in terms of *a* and *b*. Explain your reasoning.

71. Write the coordinates of *C* and *D* in terms of *a* and *b*. Explain your reasoning.

EXTRA CHALLENGE
www.mcdougallittell.com

72. Find and compare the slopes of the sides to prove that *ABCD* is a rectangle.

MIXED REVIEW

USING THE SAS CONGRUENCE POSTULATE **Decide whether enough information is given to determine that** $\triangle ABC \cong \triangle DEF$. (Review 4.3)

73. $\angle A \cong \angle D, \overline{AB} \cong \overline{DE}, \overline{AC} \cong \overline{DF}$ **74.** $\overline{AB} \cong \overline{BC}, \overline{BC} \cong \overline{CA}, \angle A \cong \angle D$

75. $\angle B \cong \angle E, \overline{AC} \cong \overline{DF}, \overline{AB} \cong \overline{DE}$ **76.** $\overline{EF} \cong \overline{BC}, \overline{DF} \cong \overline{AB}, \angle A \cong \angle E$

77. $\angle C \cong \angle F, \overline{AC} \cong \overline{DF}, \overline{BC} \cong \overline{EF}$ **78.** $\angle B \cong \angle E, \overline{AB} \cong \overline{DE}, \overline{BC} \cong \overline{EF}$

CONCURRENCY PROPERTY FOR MEDIANS **Use the information given in the diagram to fill in the blanks.** (Review 5.3)

79. $AP = 1, PD = \underline{\ ?\ }$

80. $PC = 6.6, PE = \underline{\ ?\ }$

81. $PB = 6, FB = \underline{\ ?\ }$

82. $AD = 39, PD = \underline{\ ?\ }$

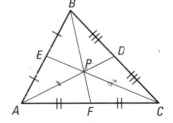

83. ▶ INDIRECT PROOF Write an indirect proof to show that there is no quadrilateral with four acute angles. (Review 6.1 for 6.5)

Trapezoids and Kites

What you should learn

GOAL 1 Use properties of trapezoids.

GOAL 2 Use properties of kites.

Why you should learn it

▼ To solve **real-life** problems, such as planning the layers of a layer cake in **Example 3**.

GOAL 1 USING PROPERTIES OF TRAPEZOIDS

A **trapezoid** is a quadrilateral with exactly one pair of parallel sides. The parallel sides are the **bases**. A trapezoid has two pairs of **base angles**. For instance, in trapezoid *ABCD*, ∠*D* and ∠*C* are one pair of base angles. The other pair is ∠*A* and ∠*B*. The nonparallel sides are the **legs** of the trapezoid.

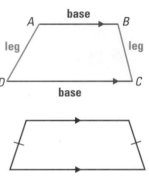

If the legs of a trapezoid are congruent, then the trapezoid is an **isosceles trapezoid**.

You are asked to prove the following theorems in the exercises.

isosceles trapezoid

THEOREMS

THEOREM 6.14

If a trapezoid is isosceles, then each pair of base angles is congruent.

∠*A* ≅ ∠*B*, ∠*C* ≅ ∠*D*

THEOREM 6.15

If a trapezoid has a pair of congruent base angles, then it is an isosceles trapezoid.

ABCD is an isosceles trapezoid.

THEOREM 6.16

A trapezoid is isosceles if and only if its diagonals are congruent.

ABCD is isosceles if and only if $\overline{AC} \cong \overline{BD}$.

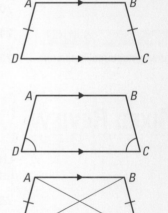

AD ≅ BC

EXAMPLE 1 *Using Properties of Isosceles Trapezoids*

PQRS is an isosceles trapezoid.
Find *m*∠*P*, *m*∠*Q*, and *m*∠*R*.

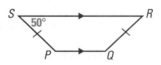

SOLUTION *PQRS* is an isosceles trapezoid, so *m*∠*R* = *m*∠*S* = 50°. Because ∠*S* and ∠*P* are consecutive interior angles formed by parallel lines, they are supplementary. So, *m*∠*P* = 180° − 50° = 130°, and *m*∠*Q* = *m*∠*P* = 130°.

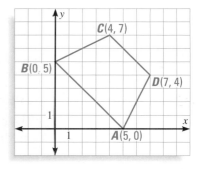

STUDENT HELP

INTERNET

HOMEWORK HELP
Visit our Web site
www.mcdougallittell.com
for extra examples.

EXAMPLE 2 *Using Properties of Trapezoids*

Show that *ABCD* is a trapezoid.

SOLUTION

Compare the slopes of opposite sides.

The slope of $\overline{AB} = \dfrac{5-0}{0-5} = \dfrac{5}{-5} = -1.$

The slope of $\overline{CD} = \dfrac{4-7}{7-4} = \dfrac{-3}{3} = -1.$

The slopes of $\overline{AB}$ and $\overline{CD}$ are equal, so $\overline{AB} \parallel \overline{CD}.$

The slope of $\overline{BC} = \dfrac{7-5}{4-0} = \dfrac{2}{4} = \dfrac{1}{2}.$

The slope of $\overline{AD} = \dfrac{4-0}{7-5} = \dfrac{4}{2} = 2.$

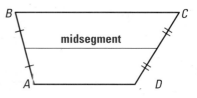

The slopes of $\overline{BC}$ and $\overline{AD}$ are not equal, so $\overline{BC}$ is not parallel to $\overline{AD}.$

▶ So, because $\overline{AB} \parallel \overline{CD}$ and $\overline{BC}$ is not parallel to $\overline{AD}$, *ABCD* is a trapezoid.

· · · · · · · · · ·

The **midsegment** of a trapezoid is the segment that connects the midpoints of its legs. Theorem 6.17 is similar to the Midsegment Theorem for triangles. You will justify part of this theorem in Exercise 42. A proof appears on page 839.

THEOREM

THEOREM 6.17 *Midsegment Theorem for Trapezoids*

The midsegment of a trapezoid is parallel to each base and its length is one half the sum of the lengths of the bases.

$$\overline{MN} \parallel \overline{AD}, \ \overline{MN} \parallel \overline{BC}, \ MN = \tfrac{1}{2}(AD + BC)$$

EXAMPLE 3 *Finding Midsegment Lengths of Trapezoids*

REAL LIFE

LAYER CAKE A baker is making a cake like the one at the right. The top layer has a diameter of 8 inches and the bottom layer has a diameter of 20 inches. How big should the middle layer be?

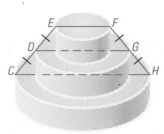

SOLUTION

Use the Midsegment Theorem for Trapezoids.

$$DG = \tfrac{1}{2}(EF + CH) = \tfrac{1}{2}(8 - 20) = 14 \text{ inches}$$

The simplest of flying kites often use the geometric kite shape.

GOAL 2 USING PROPERTIES OF KITES

A **kite** is a quadrilateral that has two pairs of consecutive congruent sides, but opposite sides are not congruent. You are asked to prove Theorem 6.18 and Theorem 6.19 in Exercises 46 and 47.

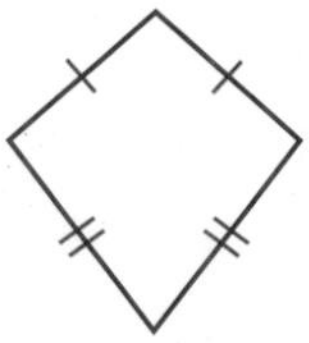

THEOREMS ABOUT KITES

THEOREM 6.18

If a quadrilateral is a kite, then its diagonals are perpendicular.

$\overline{AC} \perp \overline{BD}$

THEOREM 6.19

If a quadrilateral is a kite, then exactly one pair of opposite angles are congruent.

$\angle A \cong \angle C, \angle B \ncong \angle D$

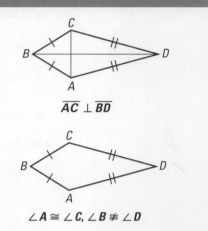

Using Algebra

EXAMPLE 4   *Using the Diagonals of a Kite*

WXYZ is a kite so the diagonals are perpendicular. You can use the Pythagorean Theorem to find the side lengths.

$$WX = \sqrt{20^2 + 12^2} \approx 23.32$$

$$XY = \sqrt{12^2 + 12^2} \approx 16.97$$

Because *WXYZ* is a kite, $WZ = WX \approx 23.32$ and $ZY = XY \approx 16.97$.

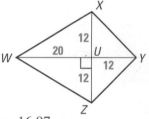

EXAMPLE 5   *Angles of a Kite*

Find $m\angle G$ and $m\angle J$ in the diagram at the right.

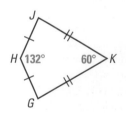

SOLUTION

GHJK is a kite, so $\angle G \cong \angle J$ and $m\angle G = m\angle J$.

$2(m\angle G) + 132° + 60° = 360°$ **Sum of measures of int. ∡ of a quad. is 360°.**

$2(m\angle G) = 168°$ **Simplify.**

$m\angle G = 84°$ **Divide each side by 2.**

▶ So, $m\angle J = m\angle G = 84°$.

GUIDED PRACTICE

Vocabulary Check ✓   1. Name the bases of trapezoid *ABCD*.

Concept Check ✓   2. Explain why a rhombus is not a kite. Use the definition of a kite.

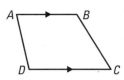

Skill Check ✓   **Decide whether the quadrilateral is a *trapezoid*, an *isosceles trapezoid*, a *kite*, or *none of these*.**

3.   4.   5.

6. How can you prove that trapezoid *ABCD* in Example 2 is isosceles?

Find the length of the midsegment.

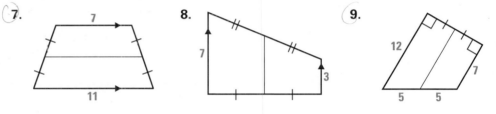

7.   8.   9.

PRACTICE AND APPLICATIONS

STUDENT HELP

▶ **Extra Practice**
to help you master
skills is on p. 814.

STUDYING A TRAPEZOID Draw a trapezoid *PQRS* with $\overline{QR} \parallel \overline{PS}$. Identify the segments or angles of *PQRS* as *bases, consecutive sides, legs, diagonals, base angles,* or *opposite angles.*

10. $\overline{QR}$ and $\overline{PS}$ 11. $\overline{PQ}$ and $\overline{RS}$ 12. $\overline{PQ}$ and $\overline{QR}$

13. $\overline{QS}$ and $\overline{PR}$ 14. $\angle Q$ and $\angle S$ 15. $\angle S$ and $\angle P$

FINDING ANGLE MEASURES Find the angle measures of *JKLM*.

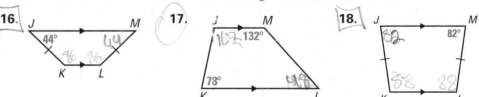

16.   17.   18.

STUDENT HELP

↳ **HOMEWORK HELP**
Example 1: Exs. 16–18
Example 2: Exs. 34, 37,
           38, 48–50
Example 3: Exs. 19–24,
           35, 39
Example 4: Exs. 28–30
Example 5: Exs. 31–33

FINDING MIDSEGMENTS Find the length of the midsegment $\overline{MN}$.

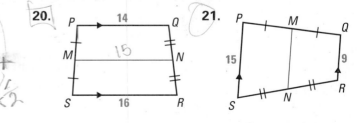

19.   20.   21.

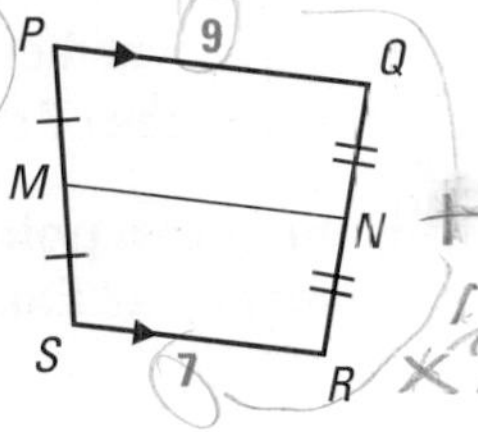

USING ALGEBRA Find the value of *x*.

22.

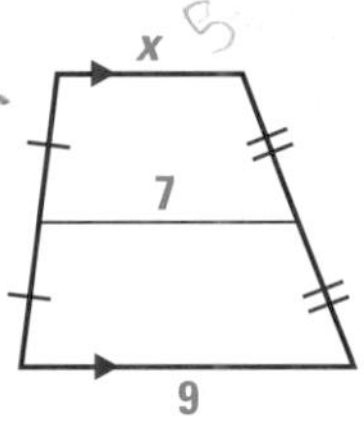

23.

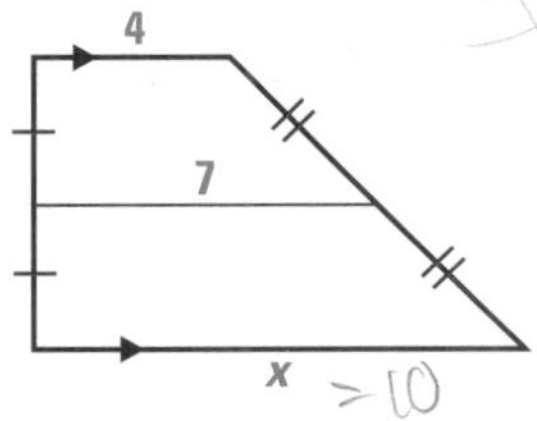

24.

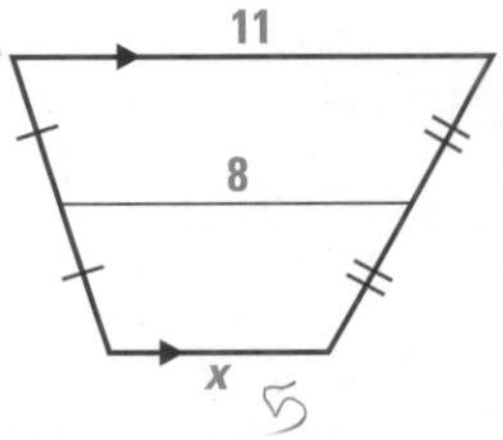

FOCUS ON APPLICATIONS

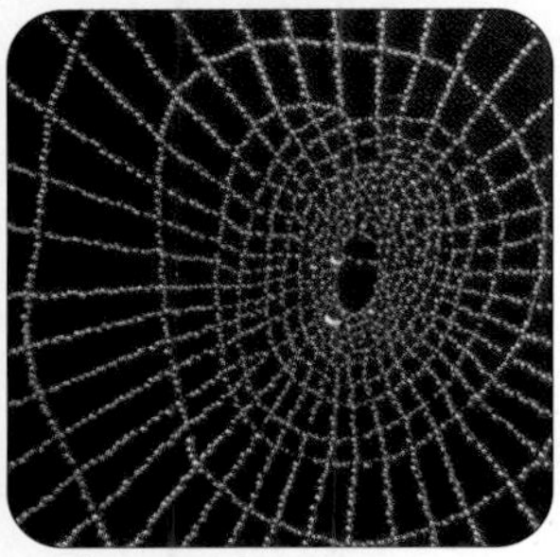

REAL LIFE **WEBS** The spider web above is called an orb web. Although it looks like concentric polygons, the spider actually followed a spiral path to spin the web.

CONCENTRIC POLYGONS **In the diagram, *ABCDEFGHJKLM* is a regular dodecagon, $\overline{AB} \parallel \overline{PQ}$, and *X* is equidistant from the vertices of the dodecagon.**

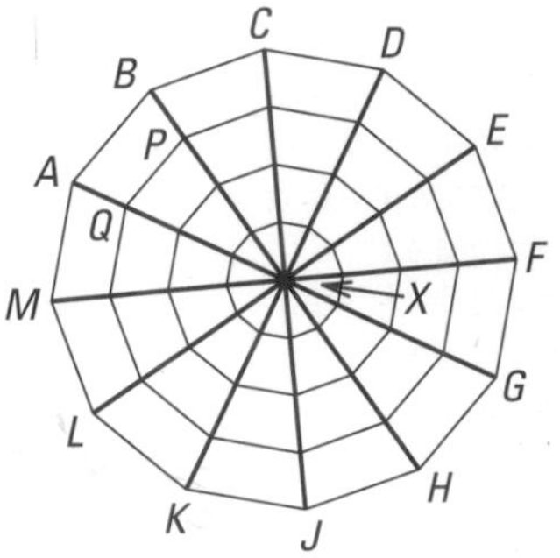

25. Are you given enough information to prove that *ABPQ* is isosceles? Explain your reasoning.

26. What is the measure of $\angle AXB$?

27. What is the measure of each interior angle of *ABPQ*?

USING ALGEBRA What are the lengths of the sides of the kite? Give your answer to the nearest hundredth.

28.

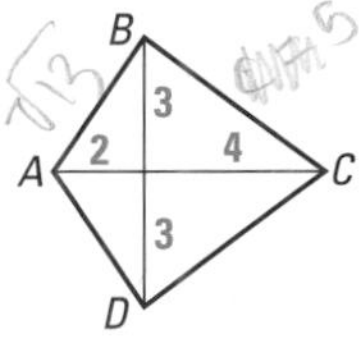

29.

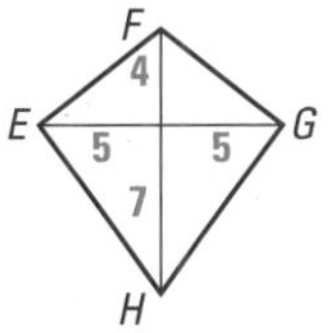

30.

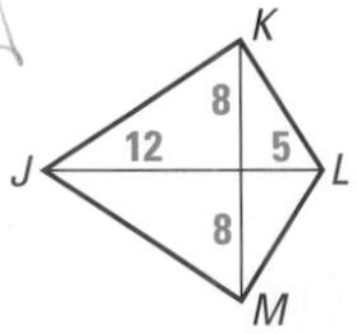

ANGLES OF KITES ***EFGH* is a kite. What is $m\angle G$?**

31.

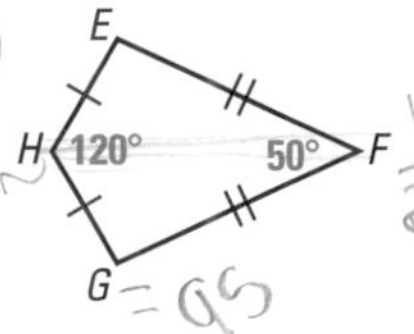

32.

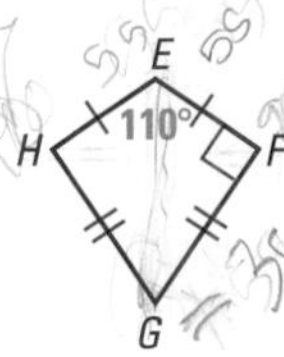

33.

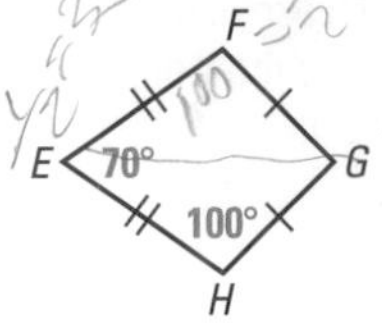

34. ERROR ANALYSIS A student says that parallelogram *ABCD* is an isosceles trapezoid because $\overline{AB} \parallel \overline{DC}$ and $\overline{AD} \cong \overline{BC}$. Explain what is wrong with this reasoning.

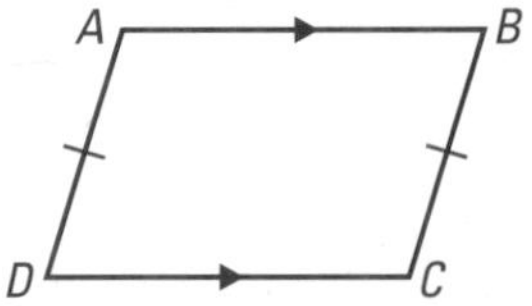

35. CRITICAL THINKING The midsegment of a trapezoid is 5 inches long. What are possible lengths of the bases?

36. COORDINATE GEOMETRY Determine whether the points $A(4, 5)$, $B(-3, 3)$, $C(-6, -13)$, and $D(6, -2)$ are the vertices of a kite. Explain your answer.

TRAPEZOIDS **Determine whether the given points represent the vertices of a trapezoid. If so, is the trapezoid isosceles? Explain your reasoning.**

37. $A(-2, 0)$, $B(0, 4)$, $C(5, 4)$, $D(8, 0)$

38. $E(1, 9)$, $F(4, 2)$, $G(5, 2)$, $H(8, 9)$

FOCUS ON CAREERS

CAKE DESIGNERS design cakes for many occasions, including weddings, birthdays, anniversaries, and graduations.

CAREER LINK
www.mcdougallittell.com

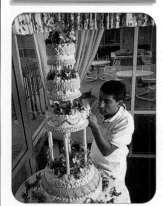

39. LAYER CAKE The top layer of the cake has a diameter of 10 inches. The bottom layer has a diameter of 22 inches. What is the diameter of the middle layer?

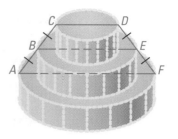

40. PROVING THEOREM 6.14 Write a proof of Theorem 6.14.

GIVEN ▶ $ABCD$ is an isosceles trapezoid.

$\overline{AB} \parallel \overline{DC}$, $\overline{AD} \cong \overline{BC}$

PROVE ▶ $\angle D \cong \angle C$, $\angle DAB \cong \angle B$

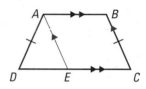

Plan for Proof To show $\angle D \cong \angle C$, first draw $\overline{AE}$ so $ABCE$ is a parallelogram. Then show $\overline{BC} \cong \overline{AE}$, so $\overline{AE} \cong \overline{AD}$ and $\angle D \cong \angle AED$. Finally, show $\angle D \cong \angle C$. To show $\angle DAB \cong \angle B$, use the consecutive interior angles theorem and substitution.

41. PROVING THEOREM 6.16 Write a proof of one conditional statement of Theorem 6.16.

GIVEN ▶ $TQRS$ is an isosceles trapezoid.

$\overline{QR} \parallel \overline{TS}$ and $\overline{QT} \cong \overline{RS}$

PROVE ▶ $\overline{TR} \cong \overline{SQ}$

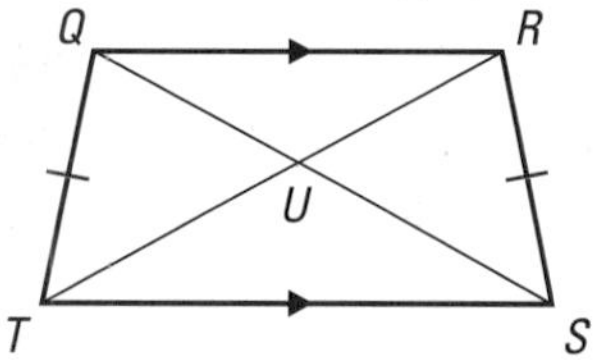

42. JUSTIFYING THEOREM 6.17 In the diagram below, $\overline{BG}$ is the midsegment of $\triangle ACD$ and $\overline{GE}$ is the midsegment of $\triangle ADF$. Explain why the midsegment of trapezoid $ACDF$ is parallel to each base and why its length is one half the sum of the lengths of the bases.

STUDENT HELP

SOFTWARE HELP
Visit our Web site www.mcdougallittell.com to see instructions for several software applications.

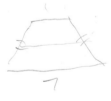

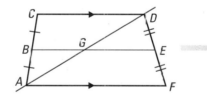

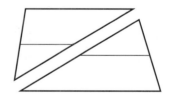

USING TECHNOLOGY In Exercises 43–45, use geometry software.

Draw points A, B, C and segments $\overline{AC}$ and $\overline{BC}$. Construct a circle with center A and radius AC. Construct a circle with center B and radius BC. Label the other intersection of the circles D. Draw $\overline{BD}$ and $\overline{AD}$.

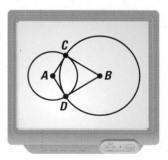

43. What kind of shape is $ACBD$? How do you know? What happens to the shape as you drag A? drag B? drag C?

44. Measure $\angle ACB$ and $\angle ADB$. What happens to the angle measures as you drag A, B, or C?

45. Which theorem does this construction illustrate?

46. ▶ **PROVING THEOREM 6.18** Write a two-column proof of Theorem 6.18.

    GIVEN ▶ $\overline{AB} \cong \overline{CB}$, $\overline{AD} \cong \overline{CD}$

    PROVE ▶ $\overline{AC} \perp \overline{BD}$

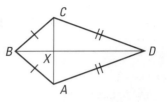

47. ▶ **PROVING THEOREM 6.19** Write a paragraph proof of Theorem 6.19.

    GIVEN ▶ $ABCD$ is a kite with $\overline{AB} \cong \overline{CB}$ and $\overline{AD} \cong \overline{CD}$.

    PROVE ▶ $\angle A \cong \angle C$, $\angle B \not\cong \angle D$

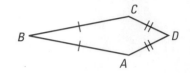

Plan for Proof First show that $\angle A \cong \angle C$. Then use an indirect argument to show $\angle B \not\cong \angle D$: If $\angle B \cong \angle D$, then $ABCD$ is a parallelogram. But opposite sides of a parallelogram are congruent. This contradicts the definition of a kite.

TRAPEZOIDS Decide whether you are given enough information to conclude that *ABCD* is an isosceles trapezoid. Explain your reasoning.

48. $\overline{AB} \parallel \overline{DC}$ **49.** $\overline{AB} \parallel \overline{DC}$ **50.** $\angle A \cong \angle B$

    $\overline{AD} \cong \overline{BC}$ $\overline{AC} \cong \overline{BD}$ $\angle D \cong \angle C$

    $\overline{AD} \cong \overline{AB}$ $\angle A \not\cong \angle C$ $\angle A \not\cong \angle C$

Test Preparation

51. MULTIPLE CHOICE In the trapezoid at the right, $NP = 15$. What is the value of x?

    (A) 2   **(B)** 3   **(C)** 4

    (D) 5   **(E)** 6

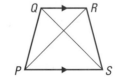

52. MULTIPLE CHOICE Which one of the following can a trapezoid have?

    (A) congruent bases

    (B) diagonals that bisect each other

    (C) exactly two congruent sides

    (D) a pair of congruent opposite angles

    (E) exactly three congruent angles

★ **Challenge**

53. ▶ **PROOF** Prove one direction of Theorem 6.16: If the diagonals of a trapezoid are congruent, then the trapezoid is isosceles.

    GIVEN ▶ $PQRS$ is a trapezoid.

            $\overline{QR} \parallel \overline{PS}$, $\overline{PR} \cong \overline{SQ}$

    PROVE ▶ $\overline{QP} \cong \overline{RS}$

EXTRA CHALLENGE

▶ www.mcdougallittell.com

Plan for Proof Draw a perpendicular segment from Q to $\overline{PS}$ and label the intersection M. Draw a perpendicular segment from R to $\overline{PS}$ and label the intersection N. Prove that $\triangle QMS \cong \triangle RNP$. Then prove that $\triangle QPS \cong \triangle RSP$.

CONDITIONAL STATEMENTS Rewrite the statement in if-then form. (Review 2.1)

54. A scalene triangle has no congruent sides.

55. A kite has perpendicular diagonals.

56. A polygon is a pentagon if it has five sides.

FINDING MEASUREMENTS Use the diagram to find the side length or angle measure. (Review 6.2 for 6.6)

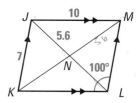

57. LN **58.** KL **59.** ML

60. JL **61.** $m\angle JML$ **62.** $m\angle MJK$

PARALLELOGRAMS Determine whether the given points represent the vertices of a parallelogram. Explain your answer. (Review 6.3 for 6.6)

63. $A(-2, 8)$, $B(5, 8)$, $C(2, 0)$, $D(-5, 0)$

64. $P(4, -3)$, $Q(9, -1)$, $R(8, -6)$, $S(3, -8)$

QUIZ 2

Self-Test for Lessons 6.4 and 6.5

1. 🌐 **POSITIONING BUTTONS** The tool at the right is used to decide where to put buttons on a shirt. The tool is stretched to fit the length of the shirt, and the pointers show where to put the buttons. Why are the pointers always evenly spaced? (*Hint:* You can prove that $\overline{HJ} \cong \overline{JK}$ if you know that $\triangle JFK \cong \triangle HEJ$.) (Lesson 6.4)

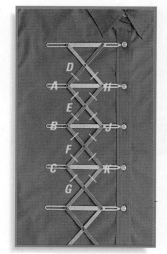

Determine whether the given points represent the vertices of a *rectangle*, **a** *rhombus*, **a** *square*, **a** *trapezoid*, **or a** *kite*. (Lessons 6.4, 6.5)

2. $P(2, 5)$, $Q(-4, 5)$, $R(2, -7)$, $S(-4, -7)$

3. $A(-3, 6)$, $B(0, 9)$, $C(3, 6)$, $D(0, -10)$

4. $J(-5, 6)$, $K(-4, -2)$, $L(4, -1)$, $M(3, 7)$

5. $P(-5, -3)$, $Q(1, -2)$, $R(6, 3)$, $S(7, 9)$

6. ▶ **PROVING THEOREM 6.15** Write a proof of Theorem 6.15.

GIVEN ▸ $ABCD$ is a trapezoid with $\overline{AB} \parallel \overline{DC}$.
        $\angle D \cong \angle C$

PROVE ▸ $\overline{AD} \cong \overline{BC}$

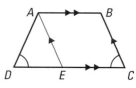

Plan for Proof Draw $\overline{AE}$ so $ABCE$ is a parallelogram. Use the Transitive Property of Congruence to show $\angle AED \cong \angle D$. Then $\overline{AD} \cong \overline{AE}$, so $\overline{AD} \cong \overline{BC}$. (Lesson 6.5)

6.6

Special Quadrilaterals

What you should learn

GOAL 1 Identify special quadrilaterals based on limited information.

GOAL 2 Prove that a quadrilateral is a special type of quadrilateral, such as a rhombus or a trapezoid.

Why you should learn it

▼ To understand and describe **real-world** shapes such as gem facets in **Exs. 42 and 43.**

GOAL 1 SUMMARIZING PROPERTIES OF QUADRILATERALS

In this chapter, you have studied the seven special types of quadrilaterals at the right. Notice that each shape has all the properties of the shapes linked above it. For instance, squares have the properties of rhombuses, rectangles, parallelograms, and quadrilaterals.

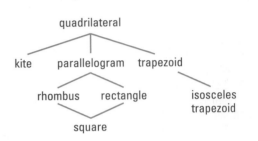

EXAMPLE 1 *Identifying Quadrilaterals*

Quadrilateral *ABCD* has at least one pair of opposite sides congruent. What kinds of quadrilaterals meet this condition?

SOLUTION

There are many possibilities.

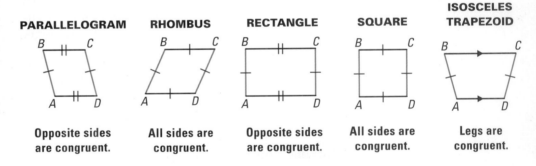

PARALLELOGRAM	RHOMBUS	RECTANGLE	SQUARE	ISOSCELES TRAPEZOID
Opposite sides are congruent.	All sides are congruent.	Opposite sides are congruent.	All sides are congruent.	Legs are congruent.

EXAMPLE 2 *Connecting Midpoints of Sides*

When you join the midpoints of the sides of any quadrilateral, what special quadrilateral is formed? Why?

SOLUTION

Let *E*, *F*, *G*, and *H* be the midpoints of the sides of any quadrilateral, *ABCD*, as shown.

If you draw $\overline{AC}$, the Midsegment Theorem for triangles says $\overline{FG} \parallel \overline{AC}$ and $\overline{EH} \parallel \overline{AC}$, so $\overline{FG} \parallel \overline{EH}$. Similar reasoning shows that $\overline{EF} \parallel \overline{HG}$.

▶ So, by definition, *EFGH* is a parallelogram.

GOAL 2 **PROOF WITH SPECIAL QUADRILATERALS**

When you want to prove that a quadrilateral has a specific shape, you can use either the definition of the shape as in Example 2, *or* you can use a theorem.

> **CONCEPT SUMMARY** | **PROVING QUADRILATERALS ARE RHOMBUSES**
>
> You have learned three ways to prove that a quadrilateral is a rhombus.
>
> 1. You can use the definition and show that the quadrilateral is a *parallelogram* that has four congruent sides. It is easier, however, to use the Rhombus Corollary and simply show that all four sides of the quadrilateral are congruent.
>
> 2. Show that the quadrilateral is a parallelogram *and* that the diagonals are perpendicular. (*Theorem 6.11*)
>
> 3. Show that the quadrilateral is a parallelogram *and* that each diagonal bisects a pair of opposite angles. (*Theorem 6.12*)

STUDENT HELP

► **Look Back**
For help with proving a quadrilateral is a parallelogram, see pp. 338–341.

EXAMPLE 3   *Proving a Quadrilateral is a Rhombus*

Show that *KLMN* is a rhombus.

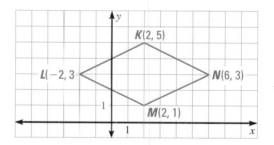

SOLUTION   You can use any of the three ways described in the concept summary above. For instance, you could show that opposite sides have the same slope and that the diagonals are perpendicular. Another way, shown below, is to prove that all four sides have the same length.

$$LM = \sqrt{[2 - (-2)]^2 + (1 - 3)^2} \qquad NK = \sqrt{(2 - 6)^2 + (5 - 3)^2}$$
$$= \sqrt{4^2 + (-2)^2} \qquad\qquad = \sqrt{(-4)^2 + 2^2}$$
$$= \sqrt{20} \qquad\qquad\qquad = \sqrt{20}$$

$$MN = \sqrt{(6 - 2)^2 + (3 - 1)^2} \qquad KL = \sqrt{(-2 - 2)^2 + (3 - 5)^2}$$
$$= \sqrt{4^2 + 2^2} \qquad\qquad = \sqrt{(-4)^2 + (-2)^2}$$
$$= \sqrt{20} \qquad\qquad\qquad = \sqrt{20}$$

▶ So, because $LM = NK = MN = KL$, *KLMN* is a rhombus.

EXAMPLE 4 *Identifying a Quadrilateral*

What type of quadrilateral is *ABCD*?
Explain your reasoning.

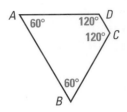

SOLUTION

$\angle A$ and $\angle D$ are supplementary, but $\angle A$ and $\angle B$ are not.
So, $\overline{AB} \parallel \overline{DC}$ but $\overline{AD}$ is not parallel to $\overline{BC}$. By definition,
ABCD is a trapezoid. Because base angles are congruent,
ABCD is an isosceles trapezoid.

EXAMPLE 5 *Identifying a Quadrilateral*

The diagonals of quadrilateral *ABCD* intersect at point *N* to produce four
congruent segments: $\overline{AN} \cong \overline{BN} \cong \overline{CN} \cong \overline{DN}$. What type of quadrilateral is
ABCD? Prove that your answer is correct.

SOLUTION

Draw a diagram:

Draw the diagonals as described. Then connect
the endpoints to draw quadrilateral *ABCD*.

Make a conjecture:

Quadrilateral *ABCD* looks like a rectangle.

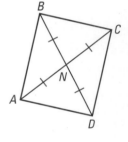

Proof

Prove your conjecture:

    GIVEN ▶ $\overline{AN} \cong \overline{BN} \cong \overline{CN} \cong \overline{DN}$

    PROVE ▶ *ABCD* is a rectangle.

Paragraph Proof Because you are given information about the diagonals, show
that *ABCD* is a parallelogram with congruent diagonals.

First prove that *ABCD* is a parallelogram.

Because $\overline{BN} \cong \overline{DN}$ and $\overline{AN} \cong \overline{CN}$, $\overline{BD}$ and $\overline{AC}$ bisect each other. Because the
diagonals of *ABCD* bisect each other, *ABCD* is a parallelogram.

Then prove that the diagonals of *ABCD* are congruent.

From the given you can write $BN = AN$ and
$DN = CN$ so, by the Addition Property of
Equality, $BN + DN = AN + CN$. By the
Segment Addition Postulate, $BD = BN + DN$
and $AC = AN + CN$ so, by substitution,
$BD = AC$.

So, $\overline{BD} \cong \overline{AC}$.

▶ *ABCD* is a parallelogram with congruent diagonals, so *ABCD* is a rectangle.

GUIDED PRACTICE

Concept Check ✓   **1.** In Example 2, explain how to prove that $\overline{EF} \parallel \overline{HG}$.

Skill Check ✓   **Copy the chart. Put an X in the box if the shape *always* has the given property.**

	Property	▱	Rectangle	Rhombus	Square	Kite	Trapezoid
2.	Both pairs of opp. sides are ‖.	?	?	?	?	?	?
3.	Exactly 1 pair of opp. sides are ‖.	?	?	?	?	?	?
4.	Diagonals are ⊥.	?	?	?	?	?	?
5.	Diagonals are ≅.	?	?	?	?	?	?
6.	Diagonals bisect each other.	?	?	?	?	?	?

7. Which quadrilaterals can you form with four sticks of the same length? You must attach the sticks at their ends and cannot bend or break any of them.

PRACTICE AND APPLICATIONS

STUDENT HELP

▶ **Extra Practice**
to help you master
skills is on p. 814.

PROPERTIES OF QUADRILATERALS Copy the chart. Put an X in the box if the shape *always* has the given property.

	Property	▱	Rectangle	Rhombus	Square	Kite	Trapezoid
8.	Both pairs of opp. sides are ≅.	?	?	?	?	?	?
9.	Exactly 1 pair of opp. sides are ≅.	?	?	?	?	?	?
10.	All sides are ≅.	?	?	?	?	?	?
11.	Both pairs of opp. ∠ are ≅.	?	?	?	?	?	?
12.	Exactly 1 pair of opp. ∠ are ≅.	?	?	?	?	?	?
13.	All ∠ are ≅.	?	?	?	?	?	?

🌐 **TENT SHAPES** What kind of special quadrilateral is the red shape?

14.

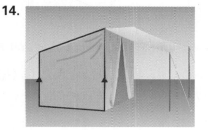

15.

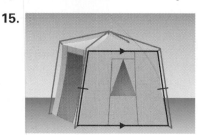

REAL LIFE Tents are designed differently for different climates. For example, winter tents are designed to shed snow. Desert tents can have flat roofs because they don't need to shed rain.

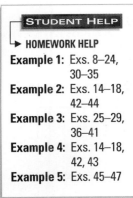

STUDENT HELP

↳ **HOMEWORK HELP**

Example 1: Exs. 8–24,
30–35

Example 2: Exs. 14–18,
42–44

Example 3: Exs. 25–29,
36–41

Example 4: Exs. 14–18,
42, 43

Example 5: Exs. 45–47

IDENTIFYING QUADRILATERALS Identify the special quadrilateral. Use the most specific name.

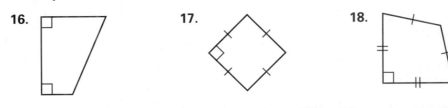

16.

17.

18.

IDENTIFYING QUADRILATERALS What kinds of quadrilaterals meet the conditions shown? *ABCD* is not drawn to scale.

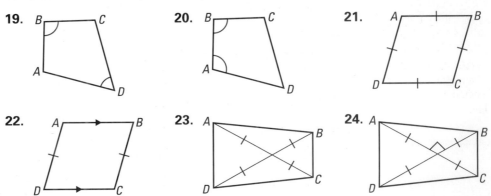

19.

20.

21.

22.

23.

24.

STUDENT HELP

↳ **Study Tip**
See the summaries for parallelograms and rhombuses on pp. 340 and 365, and the list of postulates and theorems on pp. 828–837. You can refer to your summaries as you do the rest of the exercises.

DESCRIBING METHODS OF PROOF Summarize the ways you have learned to prove that a quadrilateral is the given special type of quadrilateral.

25. kite

26. square

27. rectangle

28. trapezoid

29. isosceles trapezoid

▶ **DEVELOPING PROOF** Which two segments or angles must be congruent to enable you to prove *ABCD* is the given quadrilateral? Explain your reasoning. There may be more than one right answer.

30. isosceles trapezoid

31. parallelogram

32. rhombus

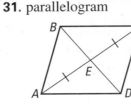

33. rectangle

34. kite

35. square

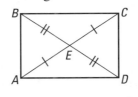

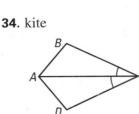

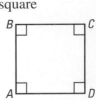

QUADRILATERALS What kind of quadrilateral is *PQRS*? Justify your answer.

36. $P(0, 0), Q(0, 2), R(5, 5), S(2, 0)$

37. $P(1, 1), Q(5, 1), R(4, 8), S(2, 8)$

38. $P(2, 1), Q(7, 1), R(7, 7), S(2, 5)$

39. $P(0, 7), Q(4, 8), R(5, 2), S(1, 1)$

40. $P(1, 7), Q(5, 9), R(8, 3), S(4, 1)$

41. $P(5, 1), Q(9, 6), R(5, 11), S(1, 6)$

FOCUS ON CAREERS

GEMOLOGISTS analyze the cut of a gem when determining its value.

CAREER LINK
www.mcdougallittell.com

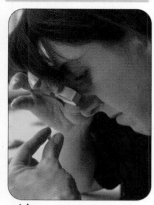

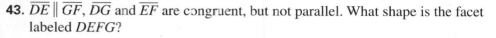

GEM CUTTING In Exercises 42 and 43, use the following information.
There are different ways of cutting gems to enhance the beauty of the jewel. One of the earliest shapes used for diamonds is called the *table cut*, as shown at the right. Each face of a cut gem is called a *facet*.

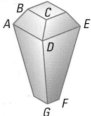

42. $\overline{BC} \parallel \overline{AD}$, $\overline{AB}$ and $\overline{DC}$ are not parallel. What shape is the facet labeled $ABCD$?

43. $\overline{DE} \parallel \overline{GF}$, $\overline{DG}$ and $\overline{EF}$ are congruent, but not parallel. What shape is the facet labeled $DEFG$?

44. **JUSTIFYING A CONSTRUCTION** Look back at the *Perpendicular to a Line* construction on page 130. Explain why this construction works.

DRAWING QUADRILATERALS Draw $\overline{AC}$ and $\overline{BD}$ as described. What special type of quadrilateral is $ABCD$? Prove that your answer is correct.

45. $\overline{AC}$ and $\overline{BD}$ bisect each other, but they are not perpendicular or congruent.

46. $\overline{AC}$ and $\overline{BD}$ bisect each other. $\overline{AC} \perp \overline{BD}$, $\overline{AC} \not\cong \overline{BD}$

47. $\overline{AC} \perp \overline{BD}$, and $\overline{AC}$ bisects $\overline{BD}$. $\overline{BD}$ does not bisect $\overline{AC}$.

48. **LOGICAL REASONING** $EFGH$, $GHJK$, and $JKLM$ are all parallelograms. If $\overline{EF}$ and $\overline{LM}$ are not collinear, what kind of quadrilateral is $EFLM$? Prove that your answer is correct.

STUDENT HELP

HOMEWORK HELP
Visit our Web site www.mcdougallittell.com for help with Exs. 45–47.

49. **PROOF** Prove that the median of a right triangle is one half the length of the hypotenuse.

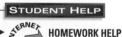

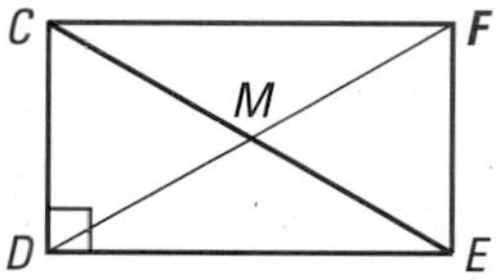

GIVEN ▶ $\angle CDE$ is a right angle. $\overline{CM} \cong \overline{EM}$

PROVE ▶ $\overline{DM} \cong \overline{CM}$

Plan for Proof First draw $\overline{CF}$ and $\overline{EF}$ so $CDEF$ is a rectangle. (How?)

50. **PROOF** Use facts about angles to prove that the quadrilateral in Example 5 is a rectangle. (*Hint:* Let $x°$ be the measure of $\angle ABN$. Find the measures of the other angles in terms of x.)

PROOF What special type of quadrilateral is $EFGH$? Prove that your answer is correct.

51. GIVEN ▶ $PQRS$ is a square. E, F, G, and H are midpoints of the sides of the square.

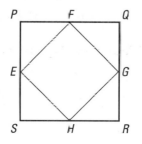

52. GIVEN ▶ $\overline{JK} \cong \overline{LM}$, E, F, G, and H are the midpoints of $\overline{JL}$, $\overline{KL}$, $\overline{KM}$, and $\overline{JM}$.

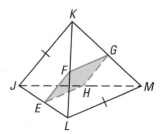

53. MULTI-STEP PROBLEM Copy the diagram. *JKLMN*
is a regular pentagon. You will identify *JPMN*.

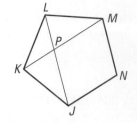

 a. What kind of triangle is △*JKL*? Use △*JKL* to
 prove that ∠*LJN* ≅ ∠*JLM*.

 b. List everything you know about the interior angles
 of *JLMN*. Use these facts to prove that $\overline{JL} \parallel \overline{NM}$.

 c. Reasoning similar to parts (a) and (b) shows that $\overline{KM} \parallel \overline{JN}$. Based on this
 and the result from part (b), what kind of shape is *JPMN*?

 d. *Writing* Is *JPMN* a rhombus? Justify your answer.

★ **Challenge**

54. ▶ **PROOF** $\overline{AC}$ and $\overline{BD}$ intersect each other at *N*. $\overline{AN} \cong \overline{BN}$ and $\overline{CN} \cong \overline{DN}$,
but $\overline{AC}$ and $\overline{BD}$ do not bisect each other. Draw $\overline{AC}$ and $\overline{BD}$, and *ABCD*.
What special type of quadrilateral is *ABCD*? Write a plan for a proof of
your answer.

MIXED REVIEW

FINDING AREA Find the area of the figure. **(Review 1.7 for 6.7)**

55.

56.

57.

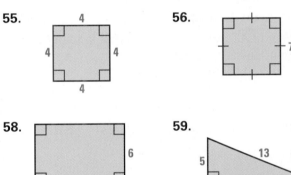

58.

59.

60.

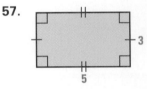

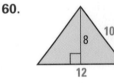

⑂ **USING ALGEBRA** In Exercises 61 and 62, use the
diagram at the right. **(Review 6.1)**

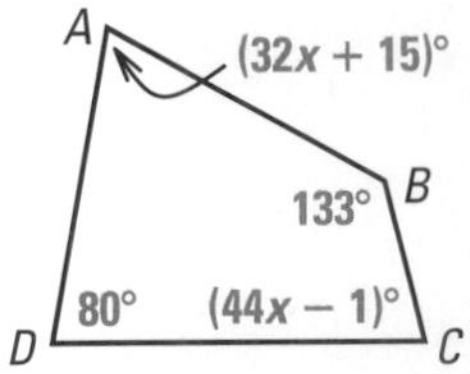

61. What is the value of *x*?

62. What is *m*∠*A*? Use your result from Exercise 61.

FINDING THE MIDSEGMENT Find the length of the midsegment of the
trapezoid. **(Review 6.5 for 6.7)**

63.

64.

65.

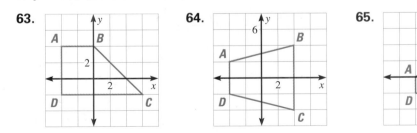

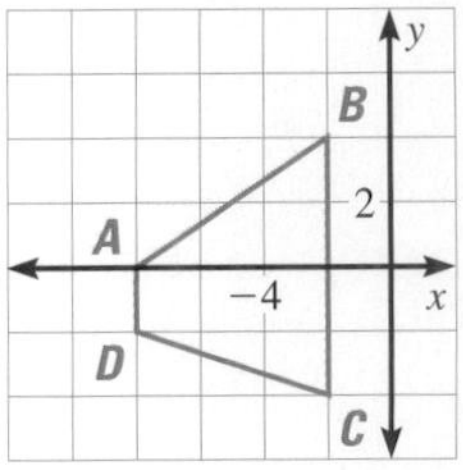

◆ ACTIVITY 6.7

Developing Concepts

Areas of Quadrilaterals

▶ **QUESTION** How are the areas of a rectangle, parallelogram, triangle, and trapezoid related to each other?

▶ **EXPLORING AREA OF A PARALLELOGRAM**

1 Use a straightedge to draw a line through one of the vertices of an index card, as shown at the right.

2 Cut off the triangle and tape it to the opposite side to form a parallelogram.

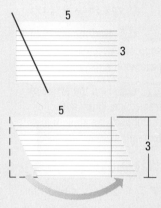

▶ **DRAWING CONCLUSIONS**

1. How does the area of the parallelogram compare to the area of the rectangular index card? How do their bases compare? their heights?

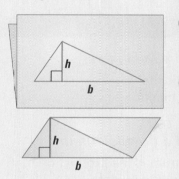

▶ **EXPLORING AREA OF A TRIANGLE**

3 On a piece of paper, use a straightedge to draw a scalene triangle. Fold the paper and cut through both thicknesses to create two congruent triangles.

4 Line up corresponding sides to form a parallelogram, as shown at the left.

▶ **DRAWING CONCLUSIONS**

2. How does the area of each triangle compare to the area of the parallelogram? How do the bases and heights compare?

▶ **EXPLORING AREA OF A TRAPEZOID**

5 On a piece of paper, draw any trapezoid. Fold and cut the paper to create two congruent trapezoids.

6 Form a parallelogram, as shown at the right.

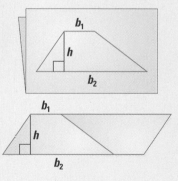

▶ **DRAWING CONCLUSIONS**

3. How does the area of each trapezoid compare to the area of the parallelogram? How do the bases and heights compare?

EXTENSION

The area A of a rectangle with base b and height h is given by the formula $A = bh$. Write formulas for the areas of a parallelogram, a triangle, and a trapezoid.

6.7 Areas of Triangles and Quadrilaterals

What you should learn

GOAL 1 Find the areas of squares, rectangles, parallelograms, and triangles.

GOAL 2 Find the areas of trapezoids, kites, and rhombuses, as applied in **Example 6**.

Why you should learn it

▼ To find areas of **real-life** surfaces, such as the roof of the covered bridge in **Exs. 48 and 49**.

GOAL 1 USING AREA FORMULAS

You can use the postulates below to prove several area theorems.

AREA POSTULATES

POSTULATE 22 *Area of a Square Postulate*

The area of a square is the square of the length of its side, or $A = s^2$.

POSTULATE 23 *Area Congruence Postulate*

If two polygons are congruent, then they have the same area.

POSTULATE 24 *Area Addition Postulate*

The area of a region is the sum of the areas of its nonoverlapping parts.

AREA THEOREMS

THEOREM 6.20 *Area of a Rectangle*

The area of a rectangle is the product of its base and height.

$A = bh$

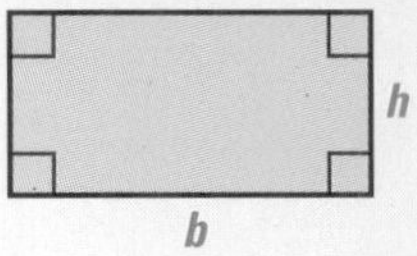

THEOREM 6.21 *Area of a Parallelogram*

The area of a parallelogram is the product of a base and its corresponding height.

$A = bh$

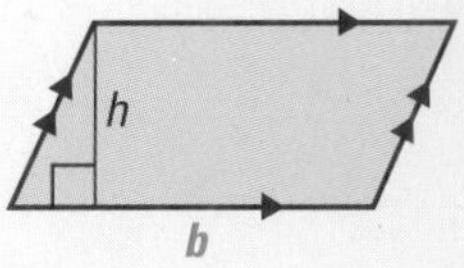

THEOREM 6.22 *Area of a Triangle*

The area of a triangle is one half the product of a base and its corresponding height.

$A = \frac{1}{2}bh$

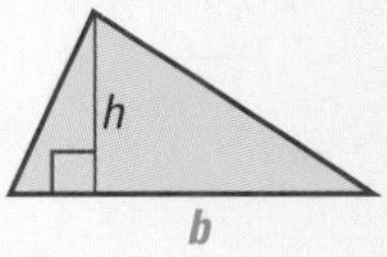

You can justify the area formulas for triangles and parallelograms as follows.

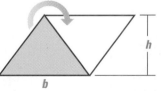

The area of a parallelogram is the area of a rectangle with the same base and height.

The area of a triangle is half the area of a parallelogram with the same base and height.

EXAMPLE 1   **Using the Area Theorems**

Find the area of $\square ABCD$.

SOLUTION

Method 1 Use $\overline{AB}$ as the base. So, $b = 16$ and $h = 9$.

Area $= bh = 16(9) = 144$ square units.

Method 2 Use $\overline{AD}$ as the base. So, $b = 12$ and $h = 12$.

Area $= bh = 12(12) = 144$ square units.

Notice that you get the same area with either base.

EXAMPLE 2   **Finding the Height of a Triangle**

Using Algebra

Rewrite the formula for the area of a triangle in terms of h. Then use your formula to find the height of a triangle that has an area of 12 and a base length of 6.

SOLUTION

Rewrite the area formula so h is alone on one side of the equation.

$A = \frac{1}{2}bh$ **Formula for the area of a triangle**

$2A = bh$ **Multiply both sides by 2.**

$\frac{2A}{b} = h$ **Divide both sides by b.**

Substitute **12** for A and **6** for b to find the height of the triangle.

$h = \frac{2A}{b} = \frac{2(12)}{6} = 4$

▶ The height of the triangle is 4.

EXAMPLE 3   **Finding the Height of a Triangle**

A triangle has an area of 52 square feet and a base of 13 feet. Are all triangles with these dimensions congruent?

SOLUTION

Using the formula from Example 2, the height is $h = \dfrac{2(52)}{13} = 8$ feet.

There are many triangles with these dimensions. Some are shown below.

STUDENT HELP

► **Study Tip**
Notice that the altitude of a triangle can be outside the triangle.

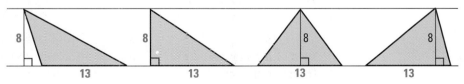

GOAL 2 AREAS OF TRAPEZOIDS, KITES, AND RHOMBUSES

THEOREMS

THEOREM 6.23 ***Area of a Trapezoid***

The area of a trapezoid is one half the product of the height and the sum of the bases.

$A = \frac{1}{2}h(b_1 + b_2)$

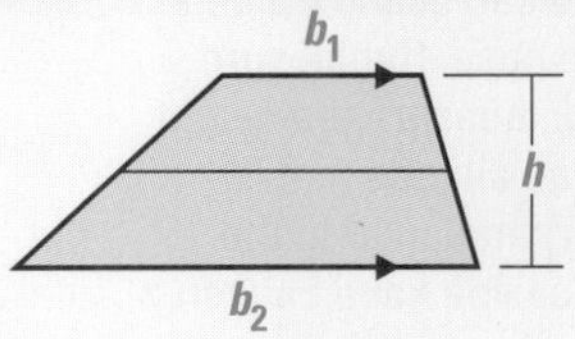

THEOREM 6.24 ***Area of a Kite***

The area of a kite is one half the product of the lengths of its diagonals.

$A = \frac{1}{2}d_1 d_2$

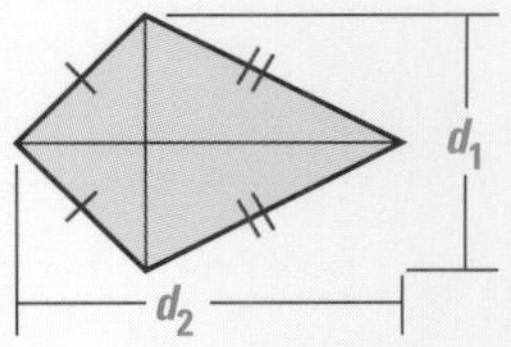

THEOREM 6.25 ***Area of a Rhombus***

The area of a rhombus is equal to one half the product of the lengths of the diagonals.

$A = \frac{1}{2}d_1 d_2$

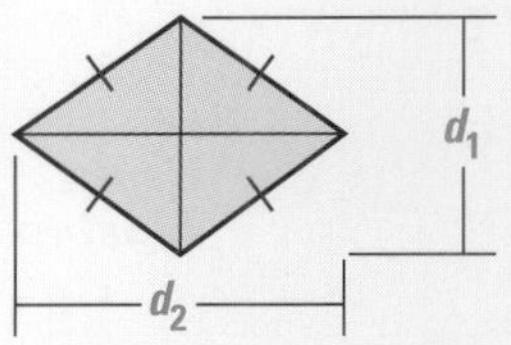

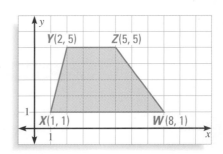

STUDENT HELP

Look Back
Remember that the length of the midsegment of a trapezoid is the average of the lengths of the bases. (p. 357)

You will justify Theorem 6.23 in Exercises 58 and 59. You may find it easier to remember the theorem this way.

Area = **Length of Midsegment** • **Height**

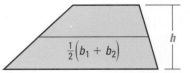

EXAMPLE 4 *Finding the Area of a Trapezoid*

Find the area of trapezoid *WXYZ*.

SOLUTION

The height of *WXYZ* is $h = 5 - 1 = 4$.

Find the lengths of the bases.

$b_1 = YZ = 5 - 2 = 3$

$b_2 = XW = 8 - 1 = 7$

Substitute 4 for h, **3** for b_1, and 7 for b_2 to find the area of the trapezoid.

$A = \frac{1}{2}h(b_1 + b_2)$	**Formula for area of a trapezoid**
$= \frac{1}{2}(4)(\mathbf{3} + 7)$	**Substitute.**
$= 20$	**Simplify.**

▶ The area of trapezoid *WXYZ* is 20 square units.

The diagram at the right justifies the formulas for the areas of kites and rhombuses.

The diagram shows that the area of a kite is half the area of the rectangle whose length and width are the lengths of the diagonals of the kite. The same is true for a rhombus.

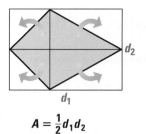

$$A = \frac{1}{2}d_1d_2$$

EXAMPLE 5   *Finding the Area of a Rhombus*

Use the information given in the diagram to find the area of rhombus *ABCD*.

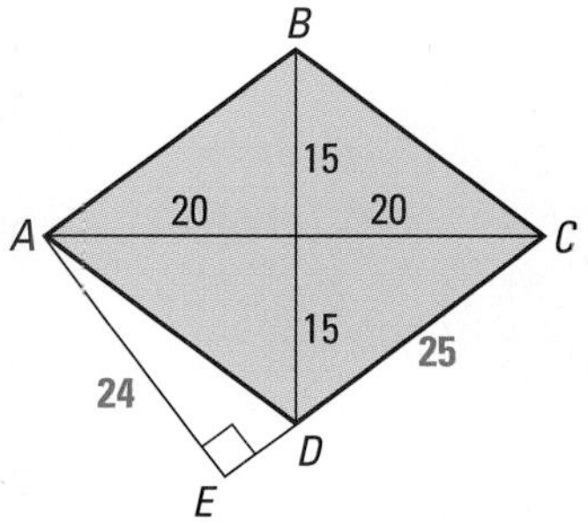

SOLUTION

Method 1 Use the formula for the area of a rhombus. $d_1 = BD = 30$ and $d_2 = AC = 40$.

$$A = \frac{1}{2}d_1d_2$$

$$= \frac{1}{2}(30)(40)$$

$$= 600 \text{ square units}$$

Method 2 Use the formula for the area of a parallelogram. $b = 25$ and $h = 24$.

$$A = bh = 25(24) = 600 \text{ square units}$$

EXAMPLE 6   *Finding Areas*

ROOF Find the area of the roof. *G*, *H*, and *K* are trapezoids and *J* is a triangle. The hidden back and left sides of the roof are the same as the front and right sides.

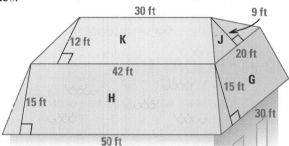

┌─ STUDENT HELP ─┐

→ Study Tip
To check that the answer is reasonable, approximate each trapezoid by a rectangle. The area of *H* should be less than 50 · 15, but more than 40 · 15.

SOLUTION

Area of $J = \frac{1}{2}(20)(9) = 90 \text{ ft}^2$ Area of $H = \frac{1}{2}(15)(42 + 50) = 690 \text{ ft}^2$

Area of $G = \frac{1}{2}(15)(20 + 30) = 375 \text{ ft}^2$ Area of $K = \frac{1}{2}(12)(30 + 42) = 432 \text{ ft}^2$

The roof has two congruent faces of each type.

Total Area $= 2(90 + 375 + 690 + 432) = 3174$

▶ The total area of the roof is 3174 square feet.

GUIDED PRACTICE

Vocabulary Check ✓ **1.** What is the *midsegment* of a trapezoid?

Concept Check ✓ **2.** If you use AB as the base to find the area of $\square ABCD$ shown at the right, what should you use as the height?

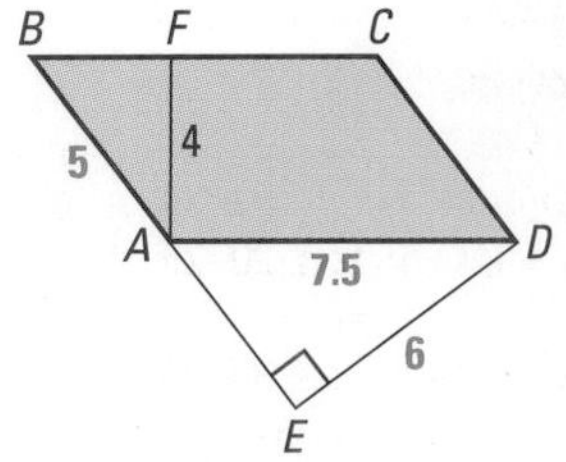

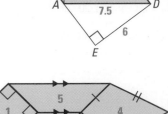

Skill Check ✓ **Match the region with a formula for its area. Use each formula exactly once.**

3. Region 1   **Ⓐ** $A = s^2$

4. Region 2   **Ⓑ** $A = \frac{1}{2}d_1 d_2$

5. Region 3   **Ⓒ** $A = \frac{1}{2}bh$

6. Region 4   **Ⓓ** $A = \frac{1}{2}h(b_1 + b_2)$

7. Region 5   **Ⓔ** $A = bh$

Find the area of the polygon.

8. 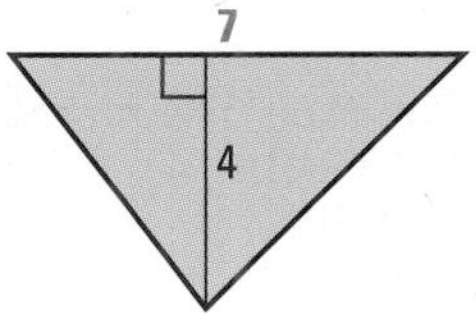 **9.** 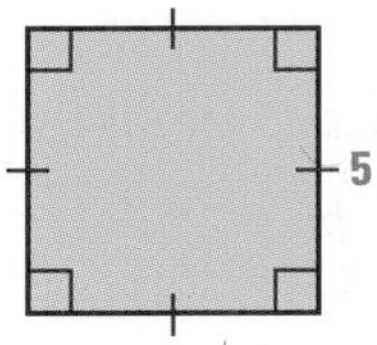 **10.**

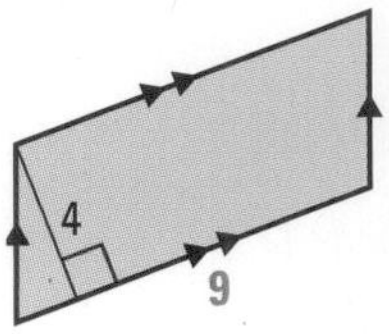

11. 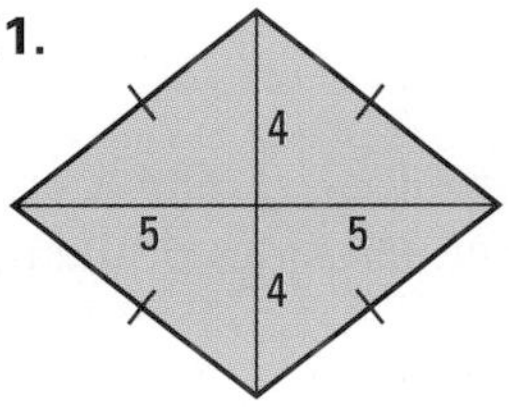 **12.** 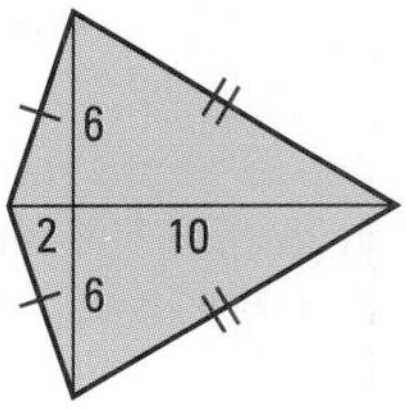 **13.**

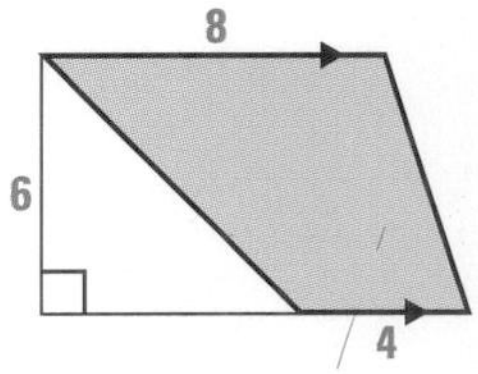

PRACTICE AND APPLICATIONS

STUDENT HELP

▶ **Extra Practice**
to help you master
skills is on p. 814.

STUDENT HELP

▶ **HOMEWORK HELP**
Example 1: Exs. 14–19,
      41–47
Example 2: Exs. 26–31

continued on p. 377

FINDING AREA **Find the area of the polygon.**

14. **15.** **16.**

17. **18.** **19.**

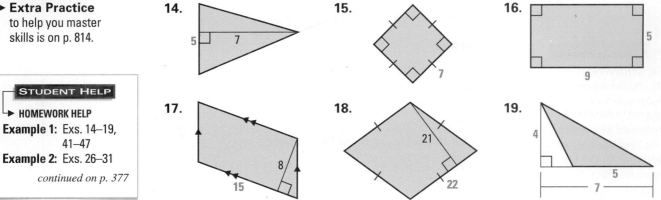

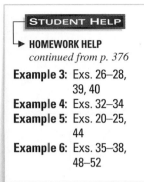

STUDENT HELP

▶ **HOMEWORK HELP**
continued from p. 376

Example 3: Exs. 26–28, 39, 40
Example 4: Exs. 32–34
Example 5: Exs. 20–25, 44
Example 6: Exs. 35–38, 48–52

FINDING AREA Find the area of the polygon.

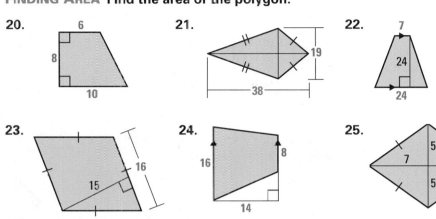

20. 6 8 10

21. 19 38

22. 7 24 24

23. 16 15

24. 16 8 14

25. 5 7 7 5

⊗ USING ALGEBRA Find the value of *x*.

26. $A = 63 \text{ cm}^2$

27. $A = 48 \text{ ft}^2$

28. $A = 48 \text{ in.}^2$

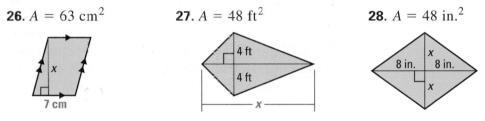

x 7 cm

4 ft 4 ft *x*

8 in. *x* 8 in. *x*

REWRITING FORMULAS Rewrite the formula for the area of the polygon in terms of the given variable. Use the formulas on pages 372 and 374.

29. triangle, b **30.** kite, d_1 **31.** trapezoid, b_1

FINDING AREA Find the area of quadrilateral *ABCD*.

32.
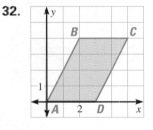

33.
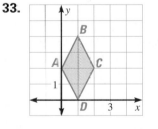

34.
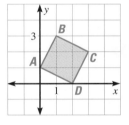

🌎 ENERGY CONSERVATION The total area of a building's windows affects the cost of heating or cooling the building. Find the area of the window.

35.
3 ft 2 ft

36.
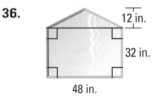
12 in. 32 in. 48 in.

37.
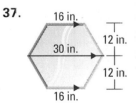
16 in. 30 in. 12 in. 12 in. 16 in.

38.
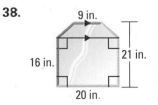
9 in. 16 in. 21 in. 20 in.

STUDENT HELP

Study Tip
Remember that two polygons are congruent if their corresponding angles and sides are congruent.

39. **LOGICAL REASONING** Are all parallelograms with an area of 24 square feet and a base of 6 feet congruent? Explain.

40. **LOGICAL REASONING** Are all rectangles with an area of 24 square feet and a base of 6 feet congruent? Explain.

USING THE PYTHAGOREAN THEOREM Find the area of the polygon.

41.

42.

43.

44. **LOGICAL REASONING** What happens to the area of a kite if you double the length of one of the diagonals? if you double the length of both diagonals?

PARADE FLOATS You are decorating a float for a parade. You estimate that, on average, a carnation will cover 3 square inches, a daisy will cover 2 square inches, and a chrysanthemum will cover 4 square inches. About how many flowers do you need to cover the shape on the float?

45. Carnations: 2 ft by 5 ft rectangle

46. Daisies: trapezoid ($b_1 = 5$ ft, $b_2 = 3$ ft, $h = 2$ ft)

47. Chrysanthemums: triangle ($b = 3$ ft, $h = 8$ ft)

BRIDGES In Exercises 48 and 49, use the following information.

The town of Elizabethton, Tennessee, restored the roof of this covered bridge with cedar shakes, a kind of rough wooden shingle. The shakes vary in width, but the average width is about 10 inches. So, on average, each shake protects a 10 inch by 10 inch square of roof.

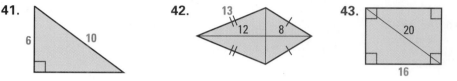

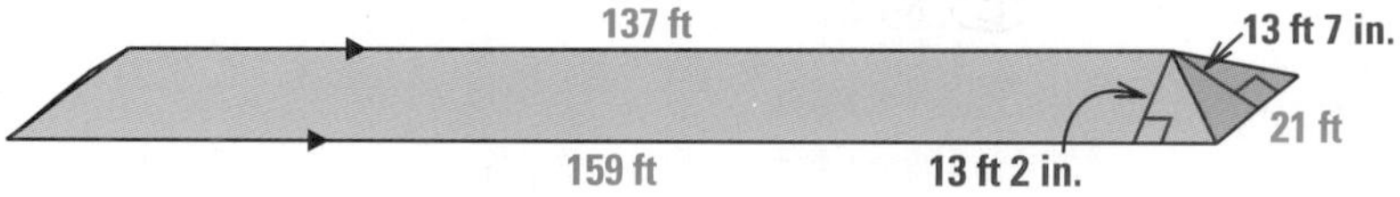

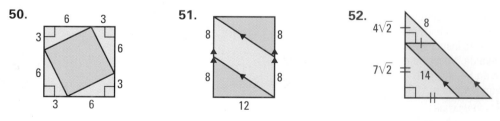

48. In the diagram of the roof, the hidden back and left sides are the same as the front and right sides. What is the total area of the roof?

49. Estimate the number of shakes needed to cover the roof.

FOCUS ON PEOPLE

MARK CANDELARIA
When Mark Candelaria restored historic buildings in Scottsdale, Arizona, he calculated the areas of the walls and floors that needed to be replaced.

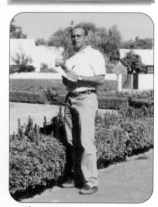

AREAS Find the areas of the blue and yellow regions.

50.

51.

52.

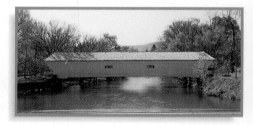

▶ **JUSTIFYING THEOREM 6.20** In Exercises 53–57, you will justify the formula for the area of a rectangle. In the diagram, *AEJH* and *JFCG* are congruent rectangles with base length *b* and height *h*.

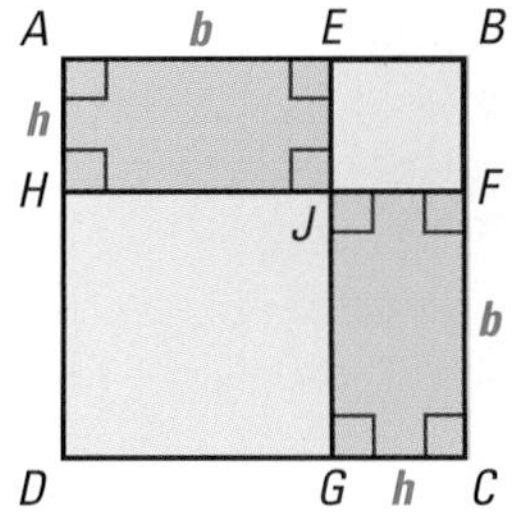

53. What kind of shape is *EBFJ*? *HJGD*? Explain.

54. What kind of shape is *ABCD*? How do you know?

55. Write an expression for the length of a side of *ABCD*. Then write an expression for the area of *ABCD*.

56. Write expressions for the areas of *EBFJ* and *HJGD*.

STUDENT HELP

▶ **Look Back**
For help with squaring binomial expressions, see p. 798.

57. Substitute your answers from Exercises 55 and 56 into the following equation.

Let A = the area of *AEJH*. Solve the equation to find an expression for A.
Area of *ABCD* = Area of *HJGD* + Area of *EBFJ* + 2(Area of *AEJH*)

▶ **JUSTIFYING THEOREM 6.23** Exercises 58 and 59 illustrate two ways to prove Theorem 6.23. Use the diagram to write a plan for a proof.

58. GIVEN ▶ *LPQK* is a trapezoid as shown. *LPQK* ≅ *PLMN*.

PROVE ▶ The area of *LPQK* is $\frac{1}{2}h(b_1 + b_2)$.

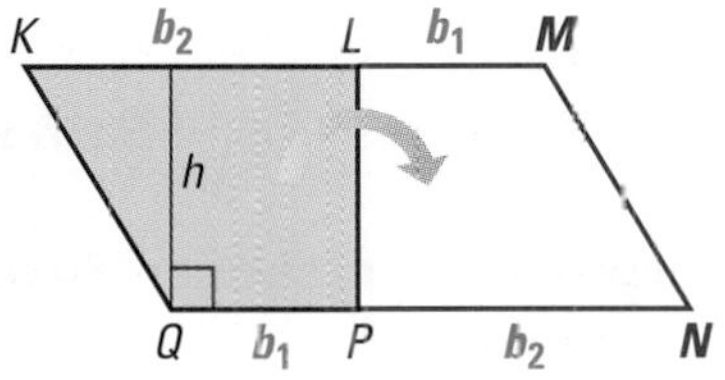

59. GIVEN ▶ *ABCD* is a trapezoid as shown. *EBCF* ≅ *GHDF*.

PROVE ▶ The area of *ABCD* is $\frac{1}{2}h(b_1 + b_2)$.

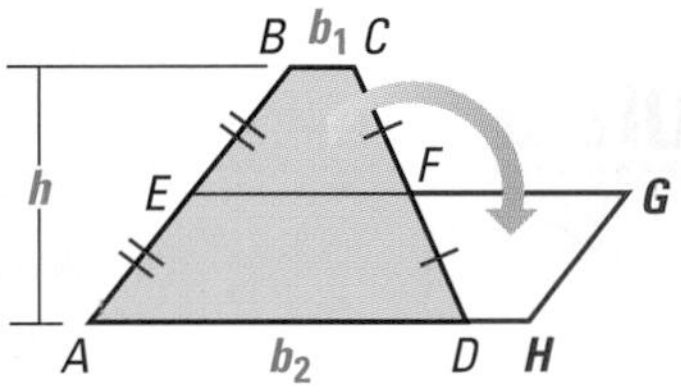

Test Preparation

60. MULTIPLE CHOICE What is the area of trapezoid *EFGH*?

Ⓐ 25 in.^{2} Ⓑ 416 in.^{2}

Ⓒ 84 in.^{2} Ⓓ 42 in.^{2}

Ⓔ 68 in.^{2}

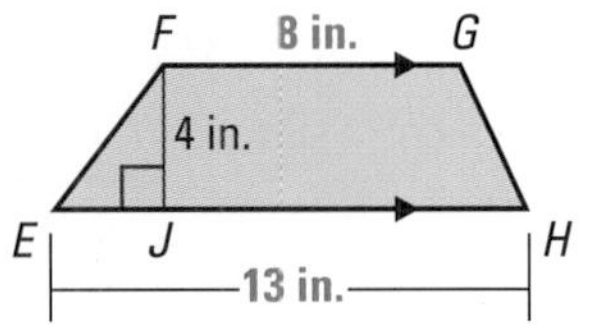

61. MULTIPLE CHOICE What is the area of parallelogram *JKLM*?

Ⓐ 12 cm^2 Ⓑ 15 cm^2

Ⓒ 18 cm^2 Ⓓ 30 cm^2

Ⓔ 40 cm^2

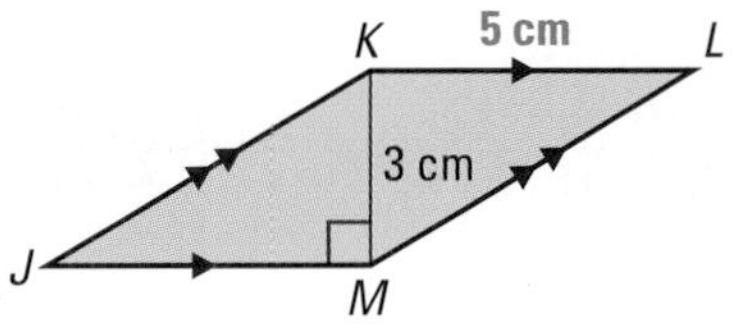

★ **Challenge**

62. *Writing* Explain why the area of *any* quadrilateral with perpendicular diagonals is $A = \frac{1}{2}d_1d_2$, where d_1 and d_2 are the lengths of the diagonals.

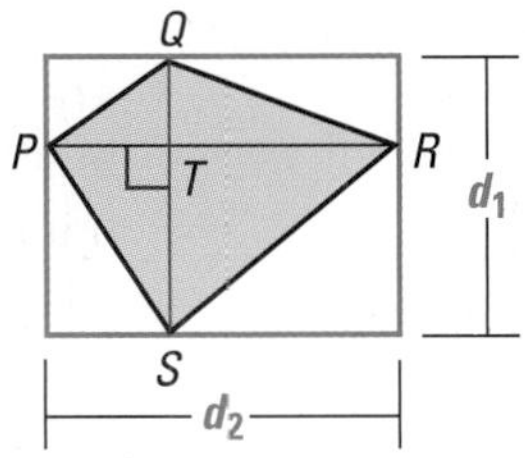

EXTRA CHALLENGE

▶ www.mcdougallittell.com

MIXED REVIEW

CLASSIFYING ANGLES State whether the angle appears to be *acute, right,* or *obtuse*. Then estimate its measure. (Review 1.4 for 7.1)

63.   64.   65.

PLACING FIGURES IN A COORDINATE PLANE Place the triangle in a coordinate plane and label the coordinates of the vertices. (Review 4.7 for 7.1)

66. A triangle has a base length of 3 units and a height of 4 units.

67. An isosceles triangle has a base length of 10 units and a height of 5 units.

USING ALGEBRA In Exercises 68–70, $\overline{AE}$, $\overline{BF}$, and $\overline{CG}$ are medians. Find the value of *x*. (Review 5.3)

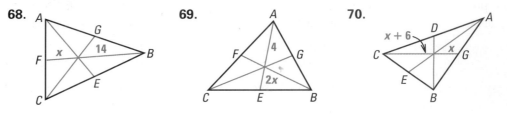

68.   69.   70.

QUIZ 3

Self-Test for Lessons 6.6 and 6.7

What special type of quadrilateral is shown? Give the most specific name, and justify your answer. (Lesson 6.6)

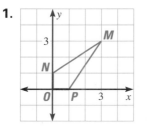

1.

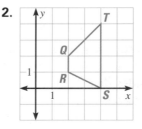

2.   3.

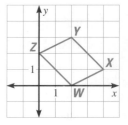

The shape has an area of 60 square inches. Find the value of *x*. (Lesson 6.7)

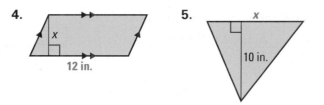

4.   5.   6.

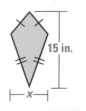

12 in.   10 in.   15 in.

7. **GOLD BULLION** Gold bullion is molded into blocks with cross sections that are isosceles trapezoids. A cross section of a 25 kilogram block has a height of 5.4 centimeters and bases of 8.3 centimeters and 11 centimeters. What is the area of the cross section? (Lesson 6.7)

Chapter Summary

WHAT did you learn?

	WHY did you learn it?
Identify, name, and describe polygons. **(6.1)**	Lay the foundation for work with polygons.
Use the sum of the measures of the interior angles of a quadrilateral. **(6.1)**	Find an unknown measure of an angle of a quadrilateral. **(p. 324)**
Use properties of parallelograms. **(6.2)**	Solve problems in areas such as furniture design. **(p. 333)**
Prove that a quadrilateral is a parallelogram. **(6.3)**	Explore real-life tools, such as a bicycle derailleur. **(p. 343)**
Use coordinate geometry with parallelograms. **(6.3)**	Use coordinates to prove theorems. **(p. 344)**
Use properties of rhombuses, rectangles, and squares, including properties of diagonals. **(6.4)**	Simplify real-life tasks, such as building a rectangular frame. **(p. 350)**
Use properties of trapezoids and kites. **(6.5)**	Reach conclusions about geometric figures and real-life objects, such as a wedding cake. **(p. 357)**
Identify special types of quadrilaterals based on limited information. **(6.6)**	Describe real-world shapes, such as tents. **(p. 367)**
Prove that a quadrilateral is a special type of quadrilateral. **(6.6)**	Use alternate methods of proof. **(p. 365)**
Find the areas of rectangles, kites, parallelograms, squares, triangles, trapezoids, and rhombuses. **(6.7)**	Find areas of real-life surfaces, such as the roof of a covered bridge. **(p. 378)**

How does Chapter 6 fit into the BIGGER PICTURE of geometry?

In this chapter, you studied properties of polygons, focusing on properties of quadrilaterals. You learned in Chapter 4 that a triangle is a rigid structure. Polygons with more than three sides do not form rigid structures. For instance, on page 336, you learned that a scissors lift can be raised and lowered because its beams form parallelograms, which are nonrigid figures. Quadrilaterals occur in many natural and manufactured structures. Understanding properties of special quadrilaterals will help you analyze real-life problems in areas such as architecture, design, and construction.

STUDY STRATEGY

How did your study group help you learn?

The notes you made, following the **Study Strategy** on page 320, may resemble this one about order of operations.

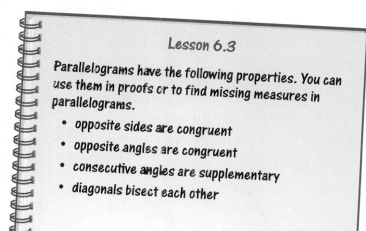

Lesson 6.3

Parallelograms have the following properties. You can use them in proofs or to find missing measures in parallelograms.

- opposite sides are congruent
- opposite angles are congruent
- consecutive angles are supplementary
- diagonals bisect each other

- polygon, p. 322
- sides of a polygon, p. 322
- vertex, vertices, p. 322
- convex, p. 323
- nonconvex, concave, p. 323
- equilateral polygon, p. 323

- equiangular polygon, p. 323
- regular polygon, p. 323
- diagonal of a polygon, p. 324
- parallelogram, p. 330
- rhombus, p. 347
- rectangle, p. 347

- square, p. 347
- trapezoid, p. 356
- bases of a trapezoid, p. 356
- base angles of a trapezoid, p. 356

- legs of a trapezoid, p. 356
- isosceles trapezoid, p. 356
- midsegment of a trapezoid, p. 357
- kite, p. 358

6.1 POLYGONS

Examples on pp. 322–324

EXAMPLES Hexagon *ABCDEF* is convex and equilateral. It is not regular because it is not both equilateral and equiangular. $\overline{AD}$ is a diagonal of *ABCDEF*. The sum of the measures of the interior angles of quadrilateral *ABCD* is 360°.

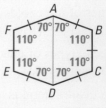

Draw a figure that fits the description.

1. a regular pentagon

2. a concave octagon

Find the value of x.

3.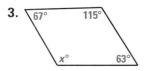

4.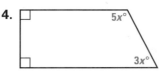

5.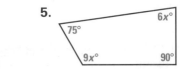

6.2 PROPERTIES OF PARALLELOGRAMS

Examples on pp. 330–333

EXAMPLES Quadrilateral *JKLM* is a parallelogram. Opposite sides are parallel and congruent. Opposite angles are congruent. Consecutive angles are supplementary. The diagonals bisect each other.

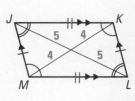

Use parallelogram *DEFG* at the right.

6. If *DH* = 9.5, find *FH* and *DF*.

7. If *m∠GDE* = 65°, find *m∠EFG* and *m∠DEF*.

8. Find the perimeter of ▱*DEFG*.

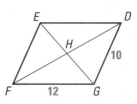

PROVING QUADRILATERALS ARE PARALLELOGRAMS

Examples on
pp. 338–341

EXAMPLES You are given that $\overline{PQ} \cong \overline{RS}$ and $\overline{PS} \cong \overline{RQ}$. Since both pairs of opposite sides are congruent, PQRS must be a parallelogram.

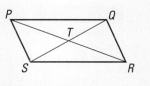

Is PQRS a parallelogram? Explain.

9. $PQ = QR$, $RS = SP$

10. $\angle SPQ \cong \angle QRS$, $\angle PQR \cong \angle RSP$

11. $\overline{PS} \cong \overline{RQ}$, $\overline{PQ} \parallel \overline{RS}$

12. $m\angle PSR + m\angle SRQ = 180°$, $\angle PSR \cong \angle RQP$

RHOMBUSES, RECTANGLES, AND SQUARES

Examples on
pp. 347–350

EXAMPLES ABCD is a rhombus since it has 4 congruent sides. The diagonals of a rhombus are perpendicular and each one bisects a pair of opposite angles.

ABCD is a rectangle since it has 4 right angles. The diagonals of a rectangle are congruent.

ABCD is a square since it has 4 congruent sides and 4 right angles.

List each special quadrilateral for which the statement is always true. Consider parallelograms, rectangles, rhombuses, and squares.

13. Diagonals are perpendicular. **14.** Opposite sides are parallel. **15.** It is equilateral.

TRAPEZOIDS AND KITES

Examples on
pp. 356–358

EXAMPLES EFGH is a trapezoid. ABCD is an isosceles trapezoid. Its base angles and diagonals are congruent. JKLM is a kite. Its diagonals are perpendicular, and one pair of opposite angles are congruent.

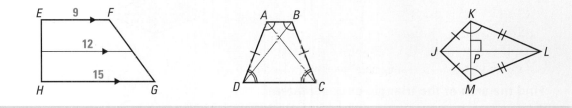

Use the diagram of isosceles trapezoid ABCD.

16. If $AB = 6$ and $CD = 16$, find the length of the midsegment.

17. If $m\angle DAB = 112°$, find the measures of the other angles of ABCD.

18. Explain how you could use congruent triangles to show that $\angle ACD \cong \angle BDC$.

SPECIAL QUADRILATERALS

Examples on pp. 364–366

EXAMPLES To prove that a quadrilateral is a rhombus, you can use any one of the following methods.

- Show that it has four congruent sides.
- Show that it is a parallelogram whose diagonals are perpendicular.
- Show that each diagonal bisects a pair of opposite angles.

What special type of quadrilateral is *PQRS*? Give the most specific name, and justify your answer.

19. $P(0, 3)$, $Q(5, 6)$, $R(2, 11)$, $S(-3, 8)$

20. $P(0, 0)$, $Q(6, 8)$, $R(8, 5)$, $S(4, -6)$

21. $P(2, -1)$, $Q(4, -5)$, $R(0, -3)$, $S(-2, 1)$

22. $P(-5, 0)$, $Q(-3, 6)$, $R(1, 6)$, $S(1, 2)$

AREAS OF TRIANGLES AND QUADRILATERALS

Examples on pp. 372–375

EXAMPLES

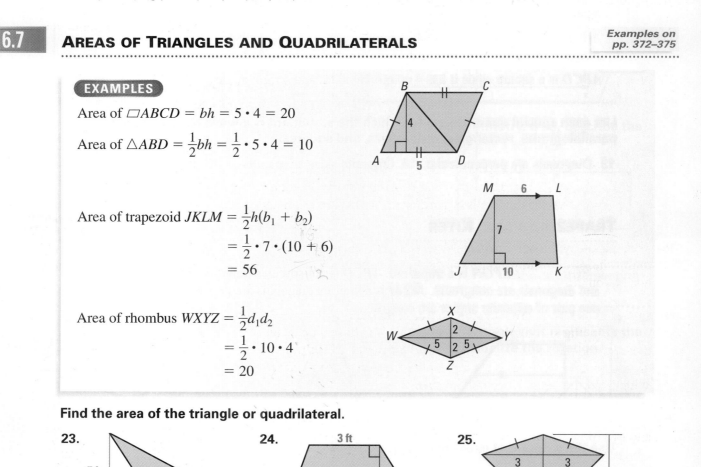

Area of $\square ABCD = bh = 5 \cdot 4 = 20$

Area of $\triangle ABD = \frac{1}{2}bh = \frac{1}{2} \cdot 5 \cdot 4 = 10$

Area of trapezoid $JKLM = \frac{1}{2}h(b_1 + b_2)$
$$= \frac{1}{2} \cdot 7 \cdot (10 + 6)$$
$$= 56$$

Area of rhombus $WXYZ = \frac{1}{2}d_1 d_2$
$$= \frac{1}{2} \cdot 10 \cdot 4$$
$$= 20$$

Find the area of the triangle or quadrilateral.

23.   7 in. $8\frac{1}{2}$ in.

24.   3 ft   3 ft   6 ft

25.   3   3   4

CHAPTER 6

Chapter Test

1. Sketch a concave pentagon.

Find the value of each variable.

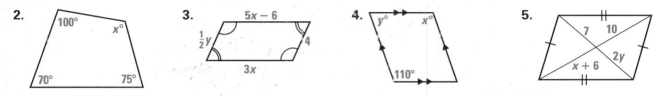

2. 100° x° 70° 75°

3. 5x − 6 ½y 4 3x

4. y° x° 110°

5. 7 10 2y x + 6

Decide if you are given enough information to prove that the quadrilateral is a parallelogram.

6. Diagonals are congruent.

7. Consecutive angles are supplementary.

8. Two pairs of consecutive angles are congruent.

9. The diagonals have the same midpoint.

Decide whether the statement is *always, sometimes,* or *never* true.

10. A rectangle is a square.

11. A parallelogram is a trapezoid.

12. A rhombus is a parallelogram.

What special type of quadrilateral is shown? Justify your answer.

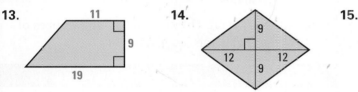

13. 11 9 19

14. 9 12 12 9

15. 24 10 24

16. 6 6 6 6

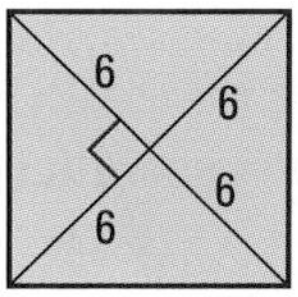

17. Refer to the coordinate diagram at the right. Use the Distance Formula to prove that *WXYZ* is a rhombus. Then explain how the diagram can be used to show that the diagonals of a rhombus bisect each other and are perpendicular.

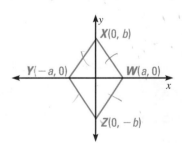

18. Sketch a kite and label it *ABCD*. Mark all congruent sides and angles of the kite. State what you know about the diagonals $\overline{AC}$ and $\overline{BD}$ and justify your answer.

19. 🌐 **PLANT STAND** You want to build a plant stand with three equally spaced circular shelves. You want the top shelf to have a diameter of 6 inches and the bottom shelf to have a diameter of 15 inches. The diagram at the right shows a vertical cross section of the plant stand. What is the diameter of the middle shelf?

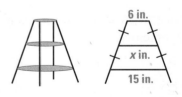

20. 🌐 **HIP ROOF** The sides of a *hip roof* form two trapezoids and two triangles, as shown. The two sides not shown are congruent to the corresponding sides that are shown. Find the total area of the sides of the roof.

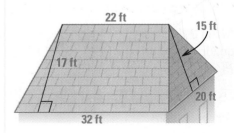

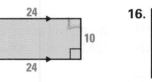

Chapter Test **385**

Chapter Standardized Test

▶ **TEST-TAKING STRATEGY** Staying physically relaxed during the SAT is very important. If you find yourself tensing up, put your pencil down and take a couple of deep breaths. This will help you stay calm.

1. MULTIPLE CHOICE In $\triangle JKL$, $\overline{JK} \cong \overline{KL} \cong \overline{JL}$. Which statements are true?

   I. $\triangle JKL$ is equilateral.

   II. $\triangle JKL$ is equiangular.

   III. $\triangle JKL$ is regular.

  Ⓐ I only   Ⓑ II only   Ⓒ III only

  Ⓓ I, II, and III   Ⓔ none of these

2. MULTIPLE CHOICE Find the value of x.

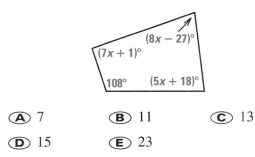

  Ⓐ 7   Ⓑ 11   Ⓒ 13

  Ⓓ 15   Ⓔ 23

3. MULTIPLE CHOICE What are the values of the variables in parallelogram $ABCD$?

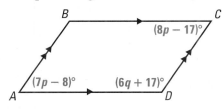

  Ⓐ $p = 8, q = 20$ Ⓑ $p = 11, q = 18$

  Ⓒ $p = 9, q = 18$ Ⓓ $p = 10, q = 18$

  Ⓔ $p = 9, q = 20$

4. MULTIPLE CHOICE The diagonals of a parallelogram must

  Ⓐ be congruent.   Ⓑ be parallel.

  Ⓒ be perpendicular.   Ⓓ bisect each other.

  Ⓔ be longer than the sides.

5. MULTIPLE CHOICE What special type of quadrilateral has the vertices $M(3, 4)$, $N(1, -6)$, $P(6, -7)$, and $Q(8, 3)$?

  Ⓐ square   Ⓑ rhombus   Ⓒ rectangle

  Ⓓ trapezoid   Ⓔ kite

6. MULTIPLE CHOICE $ABCD$ is a quadrilateral. Which information would *not* allow you to conclude that $ABCD$ is a parallelogram?

  Ⓐ $\overline{AB} \cong \overline{BC}$ and $\overline{CD} \cong \overline{AD}$

  Ⓑ $\overline{AB} \parallel \overline{CD}$ and $\overline{BC} \parallel \overline{AD}$

  Ⓒ $\angle A \cong \angle C$, $\angle B \cong \angle D$

  Ⓓ $m\angle A = 25°$, $m\angle B = 155°$, $m\angle C = 25°$

  Ⓔ $\overline{BC} \cong \overline{AD}$ and $\overline{BC} \parallel \overline{AD}$

7. MULTIPLE CHOICE What special type of quadrilateral has the vertices $R(-5, -7)$, $S(-3, -9)$, $T(-1, -7)$, and $U(-3, 11)$?

  Ⓐ parallelogram   Ⓑ kite

  Ⓒ trapezoid   Ⓓ rectangle

  Ⓔ rhombus

8. QUANTITATIVE COMPARISON The vertices of two quadrilaterals are given.

Column A	Column B
Area of $JKLM$ for $J(-5, 7)$, $K(7, 7)$, $L(6, -2)$, and $M(-2, -2)$	Area of $PQRS$ for $P(-10, 4)$, $Q(1, 4)$, $R(7, -5)$, and $S(-4, -5)$

Choose the statement that is true.

  Ⓐ The quantity in column A is greater.

  Ⓑ The quantity in column B is greater.

  Ⓒ The two quantities are equal.

  Ⓓ The relationship cannot be determined from the given information.

9. MULTIPLE CHOICE $ABCD$ is a trapezoid and $EF = 21$. Find the value of x.

  Ⓐ 18   Ⓑ 23

  Ⓒ 25   Ⓓ 30

  Ⓔ 33

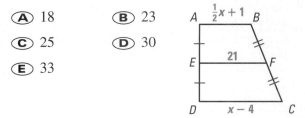

10. MULTIPLE CHOICE Find the area of a triangle with vertices $A(-3, 6)$, $B(-7, -4)$, and $C(6, -4)$.

(A) 39 square units   (B) 52 square units   (C) 60 square units

(D) 65 square units   (E) 78 square units

MULTI-STEP PROBLEM In Exercises 11–14, use the following information.
The framework of a railroad bridge is shown below. In the diagram, $\overline{GB} \parallel \overline{HC}$, $\overline{AH} \parallel \overline{BJ}$, and $\angle FBA \cong \angle DBC$.

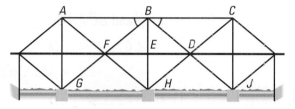

11. Are you given enough information to prove that $\overline{BE} \cong \overline{HE}$? If so, explain how.

12. If $m\angle FBA = 40°$, what are the measures of $\angle BDH$ and $\angle DHF$?

13. Are you given enough information to prove that $\triangle BEF \cong \triangle HED$? If so, write a plan for a proof.

14. Suppose you were given the additional information that $\overline{BH}$ and $\overline{FD}$ are perpendicular. What could you conclude about a special quadrilateral? Explain.

MULTI-STEP PROBLEM In Exercises 15–20, use the given information and the diagram at the right.

GIVEN ▶ $PSTU$ is a rectangle and $\overline{PQ} \cong \overline{SR}$. $\overline{YZ}$ is the midsegment of isosceles trapezoid $QRTU$.

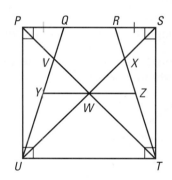

15. $QR = 3x - 10$, $UT = 2x + 3$, and $YZ = 9$. Find the value of x.

16. $PQ = 2y$, $UT = 6y + 1$, and $QR = 5$. Find the value of y.

17. $PT = 3a - 2$ and $UW = 14 - a$. Find the value of a.

18. $UY = 3b + 4$ and $TZ = 4b - 5$. Find the value of b.

19. What kind of polygon is $QRXWV$? Is it convex or concave?

20. Use the given information. Write a two-column proof that shows that $\triangle PQU \cong \triangle SRT$.

MULTI-STEP PROBLEM In Exercises 21 and 22, use the following information.

A *concrete slump test* is used to measure the water content and consistency of concrete mix. Concrete is placed in a mold for a period of time, and then the mold is removed. The distance from the top of the mold to the top of the "slumped" concrete is then evaluated. The shape of the cross section of the slump mold can be modeled by the points $A(4, 12)$, $B(8, 12)$, $C(10, 0)$, and $D(2, 0)$.

21. What special type of quadrilateral is $ABCD$? Describe two different ways that you could prove that your answer is correct.

22. What is the area of the cross section?

1. Find the decimal forms for $\frac{4}{99}$, $\frac{18}{99}$, and $\frac{35}{99}$. Use your answers to make a conjecture about the decimal form for $\frac{89}{99}$. **(1.1)**

2. Draw an obtuse angle. Then bisect it. **(1.4, 1.5)**

In Exercises 3–8, use the figure at the right, in which $\overline{QR} \parallel \overline{ST}$, $\overline{QT} \perp \overline{SU}$, $\overline{QS} \perp \overline{ST}$, and $\angle 1 \cong \angle 2$.

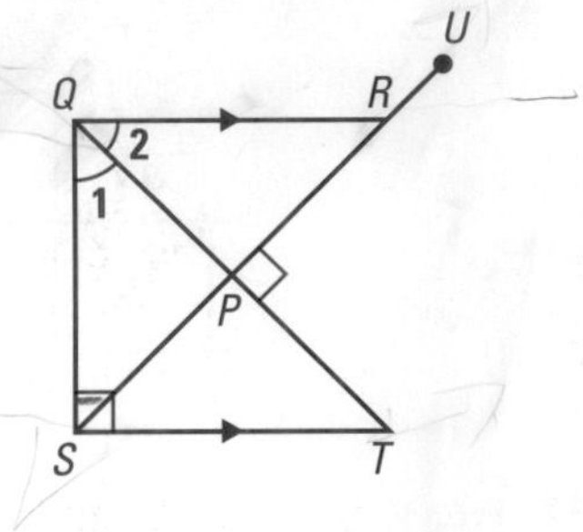

3. Find the measures of $\angle URQ$ and $\angle PTS$. **(3.3, 4.1)**

4. Name a pair of (a) vertical angles, (b) nonadjacent complementary angles, (c) congruent supplementary angles, and (d) same-side interior angles. **(1.6, 3.3, 4.1)**

5. Name two pairs of congruent triangles. Write a plan for proof to show that each pair of triangles is congruent. **(3.3, 4.4, 4.5)**

6. Use your answer to Exercise 5 to show that $RS = 2 \cdot PS$. **(2.5, 4.5)**

7. P lies on the bisector of $\angle SQR$. What can you conclude about P? Explain. **(5.1)**

8. What kind of polygon is $PRQST$? Is it *convex* or *concave*? **(6.1)**

9. The measure of an exterior angle of a triangle is $(21x + 1)°$ and the measures of the two nonadjacent interior angles are $(5x + 18)°$ and $(14x - 3)°$. Find the measures of the three interior angles of the triangle. Then classify the triangle as *acute*, *obtuse*, or *right*. **(4.1)**

Is it possible to prove that the triangles are congruent? If so, name the postulate or theorem you would use. (4.3, 4.4, 4.6)

10.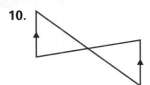

11.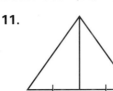

12.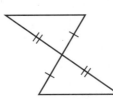

13.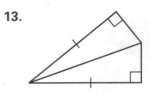

A triangle has vertices $A(11, 1)$, $B(3, 6)$, and $C(3, -4)$.

14. Find an equation of the line that is parallel to $\overleftrightarrow{AB}$ and contains point C. **(3.6)**

15. Show that the triangle is isosceles. **(4.1, 4.7)**

16. Which two angles of $\triangle ABC$ are congruent? Which theorem justifies your answer? **(4.6)**

17. Find an equation of the perpendicular bisector of $\overline{AC}$. **(3.7, 5.1)**

18. Describe the point that is equidistant from A, B, and C. **(5.2)**

19. Find the coordinates of the centroid of $\triangle ABC$. **(5.3)**

20. Find the length of the midsegment that connects sides $\overline{AB}$ and $\overline{CB}$. **(5.4)**

21. State the converse of the Linear Pair Postulate in if-then form. Decide whether the converse is *true* or *false*. If false, provide a counterexample. (2.1, 2.6)

In △XYZ, XY = 8 and YZ = 12.

22. Describe the possible lengths for $\overline{XZ}$. (5.5)

23. Complete with $<$, $>$, or $=$: $m\angle X$ __?__ $m\angle Z$. Explain your answer. (5.5)

In Exercises 24–26, the vertices A and C of square ABCD are pinched together to form quadrilateral WXYZ.

24. Explain why $m\angle D > m\angle Z$. (5.6)

25. What special kind of parallelogram is quadrilateral *WXYZ*? (6.4)

26. If $m\angle X = 25°$, find the measures of the other three angles of *WXYZ*. (6.1, 6.2)

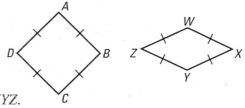

27. Determine whether $P(0, 4)$, $Q(8, 3)$, $R(9, 8)$, and $S(1, 9)$ are the vertices of a parallelogram. Explain your answer. (6.3)

28. In quadrilateral *EFGH*, $m\angle E = 90°$, $m\angle F = 90°$, and $m\angle G = 67°$. What special kind of quadrilateral must it be? Explain. (6.1, 6.5)

29. List all the types of special quadrilaterals whose diagonals are always (a) perpendicular and (b) congruent. (6.4, 6.5, 6.6)

30. A trapezoid has vertices $A(0, 0)$, $B(12, 0)$, $C(10, 6)$, and $D(5, 6)$. Find the length of its midsegment and its area. (6.5, 6.7)

BILLBOARD SUPPORTS The two 10 ft posts that support a vertical billboard form an angle of 115° with level ground, as shown.

31. How could you show that $\triangle ABC \cong \triangle DEF$? (4.4)

32. What special kind of quadrilateral must *ADEB* be? Explain. (6.6)

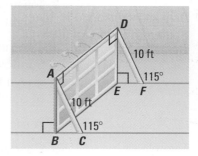

BOOKSHELF An A-frame bookshelf has two congruent supports that intersect to form an angle of 42°.

33. Find the measure of the acute angle that each shelf forms with the supports. (4.6)

34. The shelves divide each support into four congruent lengths. If the distance between the supports for the middle shelf is 30 inches, find the distance between the supports for the top shelf and at the floor. (5.4, 6.5)

35. The distance between each pair of shelves is $19\frac{1}{2}$ inches. Find the area of the region enclosed by the top shelf, the middle shelf, and the two supports. (6.7)

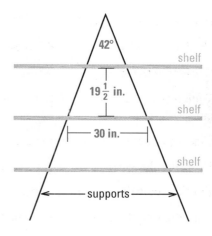

Algebra Review

EXAMPLE 1 *Writing and Simplifying Ratios*

a. Train A takes 35 minutes to travel its route. Train B, traveling the same route but making more stops, takes 47 minutes. What is the ratio of the time of Train A to Train B?

b. Jennie's height is 4 feet, 7 inches. Her younger sister's height is 25 inches. Find the ratio of Jennie's height to her sister's.

SOLUTIONS

a. 35 minutes to 47 minutes $= \dfrac{35 \text{ minutes}}{47 \text{ minutes}} = \dfrac{35}{47}$

b. Convert 4 feet, 7 inches to inches: $4(12) + 7 = 55$ inches

55 inches to 25 inches $= \dfrac{55 \text{ inches}}{25 \text{ inches}} = \dfrac{55}{25} = \dfrac{11}{5}$

EXERCISES

Write the following ratios.

1. Basmati rice needs to cook for 20 minutes, while quinoa (another grain) cooks for 25 minutes. What is the ratio of cooking times for rice to quinoa?

2. Jonathan caught 7 fish and Geogeanne caught 4. What is the ratio of fish caught of Jonathan to Geogeanne?

3. Two sunflowers' growth was measured daily. At the end of the experiment, Sunflower A had grown from 2 inches to 2 feet, 3 inches. Sunflower B had grown from 3 inches to 2 feet, 6 inches. Find the ratio of the growth in height of Sunflower A to Sunflower B.

4. A soccer team won 22 games and lost 8. What is their win-loss ratio?

5. Charlotte's essay on pigs was 824 words in length. Wilbur's essay was only 360 words long. What is the ratio of the length of Charlotte's essay to Wilbur's essay?

6. A gingham bed sheet has 220 threads per square inch while an embroidered white sheet has 180 threads per square inch. Find the ratio of threads per square inch of the gingham sheet to the white sheet.

Use the diagram at the right.

7. What is the ratio of length to width of rectangle *A*?

8. What is the ratio of the perimeter of rectangle *A* to the perimeter of rectangle *B*?

9. What is the ratio of the area of rectangle *A* to the area of rectangle *B*?

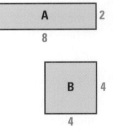

EXAMPLE 2 **Distributive Property**

Solve.

a. $4(x + 3) = 36$
$4x + 12 = 36$
$4x = 24$
$x = 6$

b. $6(x + 4) + 12 = 5(x + 3) + 7$
$6x + 24 + 12 = 5x + 15 + 7$
$6x + 36 = 5x + 22$
$x = -14$

EXERCISES

Solve.

10. $2(x + 7) = 20$

11. $8(x + 6) = 24$

12. $6(x - 2) = 24$

13. $-10(y + 8) = -40$

14. $16(3 - d) = -4$

15. $7(2 - x) = 5x$

16. $-4(x - 6) = 28$

17. $-9(5 - 3x) = 9$

18. $\frac{1}{2}(10 - 9x) = \frac{3}{2}$

19. $\frac{2}{3}(m + 4) - 8 = \frac{11}{3}$

20. $5(3a - 2) = 2(6a - 8)$

21. $3(x - 1) + 3 = 4(x - 2)$

EXAMPLE 3 **Solving Proportions**

Solve.

a. $\frac{x}{8} = \frac{3}{4}$
$4x = 8 \cdot 3$
$4x = 24$
$x = 6$

b. $\frac{6}{x + 4} = \frac{1}{9}$
$6 \cdot 9 = x + 4$
$54 = x + 4$
$50 = x$

EXERCISES

Solve.

22. $\frac{x}{20} = \frac{1}{5}$

23. $\frac{2}{q} = \frac{4}{18}$

24. $\frac{7}{100} = \frac{14}{y}$

25. $\frac{t}{27} = \frac{4}{9}$

26. $\frac{5}{6} = \frac{4}{r}$

27 $\frac{w}{6} = \frac{7}{17}$

28. $\frac{27}{5} = \frac{3}{z}$

29. $\frac{y}{50} = \frac{3}{100}$

30. $\frac{6}{19} = \frac{m}{95}$

31. $\frac{3}{8} = \frac{3}{2d}$

32. $\frac{6}{5m} = \frac{6}{25}$

33. $\frac{19}{x} = \frac{9}{5}$

34. $\frac{3w + 6}{28} = \frac{3}{4}$

35. $\frac{6}{45} = \frac{2z + 10}{15}$

36. $\frac{3a}{11} = \frac{54}{22}$

37. $\frac{-3}{8} = \frac{21}{2(y + 1)}$

38. $\frac{1}{-8} = \frac{5}{-4(x - 1)}$

39. $\frac{3}{m + 4} = \frac{9}{14}$

40. $\frac{3}{p - 6} = \frac{1}{p}$

41. $\frac{r}{3r + 1} = \frac{2}{3}$

42. $\frac{w}{4} = \frac{9}{w}$

TRANSFORMATIONS

▶ *How do architects use transformations?*

CHAPTER 7

APPLICATION: Architecture

Architects often include decorative patterns and designs in their plans for a building. These adornments add interest and give a building character.

Some designs found on buildings are created by taking an image and transforming it. For instance, an image can be slid, flipped, or turned to create a pattern.

Think & Discuss

1. What motion is used to move box *A* onto box *B*? box *C* onto box *D*?

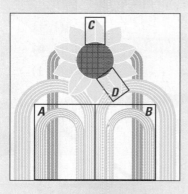

2. Describe any other uses of transformations in the design.

Learn More About It

You will identify transformations in architecture in Exercises 35–37 on p. 435.

APPLICATION LINK Visit www.mcdougallittell.com for more information about transformations and patterns in architecture.

Study Guide

PREVIEW

What's the chapter about?

Chapter 7 is about **transformations**. Transformations describe how geometric figures of the same shape are related to one another. In Chapter 7, you'll learn

- three ways to describe motion of geometric figures in the plane.
- how to use transformations in real-life situations, such as making a kaleidoscope or designing a border pattern.

KEY VOCABULARY

▶ **Review**
- Distance Formula, p. 19
- parallel lines, p. 129
- congruent figures, p. 202
- corresponding sides, p. 202
- corresponding angles, p. 202

▶ **New**
- image, p. 396
- preimage, p. 396
- transformation, p. 396
- reflection, p. 404
- rotation, p. 412

- translation, p. 421
- vector, p. 423
- glide reflection, p. 430
- frieze pattern, p. 437

PREPARE

Are you ready for the chapter?

SKILL REVIEW Do these exercises to review key skills that you'll apply in this chapter. See the given **reference page** if there is something you don't understand.

Use the Distance Formula to decide whether $\overline{AB} \cong \overline{BC}$. (Review p. 19)

1. $A(-6, 4)$
$B(1, 3)$
$C(8, 4)$

2. $A(0, 3)$
$B(3, 1)$
$C(7, 4)$

3. $A(1, 1)$
$B(4, 6)$
$C(7, 1)$

Complete the statement, given that $\triangle PQR \cong \triangle XYZ$. (Review p. 202)

4. $XZ = \underline{\ ?\ }$

5. $m\angle X = \underline{\ ?\ }$

6. $m\angle Q = \underline{\ ?\ }$

7. $m\angle Z = \underline{\ ?\ }$

8. $\overline{YZ} \cong \underline{\ ?\ }$

9. $QR = \underline{\ ?\ }$

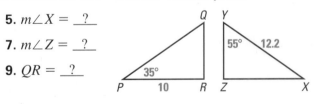

STUDENT HELP

▶ **Study Tip**
"Student Help" boxes throughout the chapter give you study tips and tell you where to look for extra help in this book and on the Internet.

STUDY
STRATEGY

Here's a study strategy!

Making Sample Exercises

Writing your own exercises can test what you have learned in this chapter. After each lesson, follow these steps:

- Write a summary of the lesson.
- Write at least three exercises that test the lesson's goals.

● ACTIVITY 7.1

Developing Concepts

Motion in the Plane

GROUP ACTIVITY
Work with a partner.

MATERIALS
• tracing paper
• pencils

▶ **QUESTION** Which types of motion in the plane maintain the congruence of a figure?

▶ **EXPLORING THE CONCEPT**

1. In the pairs of figures below, the blue figure was transformed to produce the congruent red figure. For each pair, name the corresponding sides. (For example, in part (a) $\overline{FG}$ corresponds to $\overline{KJ}$.

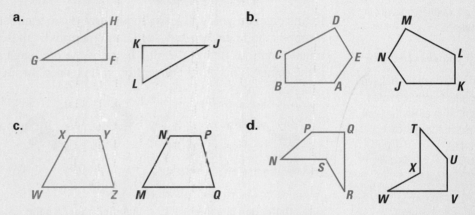

a.

b.

c.

d.

2. For each pair above, use words such as "flip," "slide," and "turn" to describe how to move from the blue figure to the red figure. Tracing paper can be used to help you.

▶ **MAKE A CONJECTURE**

3. State the types of motion that preserve the congruence of a figure when it is moved in the plane.

▶ **INVESTIGATE**

4. Describe the motion that moves *ABCD* onto *EFGH*.

5. Copy the figures at the right. Flip *EFGH* over line *m* and name the corresponding vertices of the new figure *JKLM*. Is *EFGH* congruent to *JKLM*?

6. Describe the motion that maps *ABCD* onto *JKLM*. Is *ABCD* congruent to *JKLM*?

7. Can one "flip" be used to move *ABCD* onto *JKLM*? Explain why or why not.

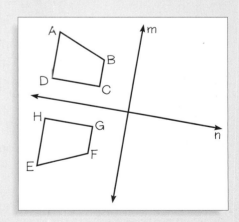

7.1

Rigid Motion in a Plane

What you should learn

GOAL 1 Identify the three basic rigid transformations.

GOAL 2 Use transformations in **real-life** situations, such as building a kayak in **Example 5**.

Why you should learn it

▼ Transformations help you when planning a stenciled design, such as on the wall below and the stencil in **Ex. 41**.

GOAL 1 **IDENTIFYING TRANSFORMATIONS**

Figures in a plane can be reflected, rotated, or translated to produce new figures. The new figure is called the **image**, and the original figure is called the **preimage**. The operation that *maps*, or moves, the preimage onto the image is called a **transformation**.

In this chapter, you will learn about three basic transformations—*reflections*, *rotations*, and *translations*—and combinations of these. For each of the three transformations below, the blue figure is the preimage and the red figure is the image. This color convention will be used throughout this book.

| Reflection in a line | Rotation about a point | Translation |

Some transformations involve labels. When you name an image, take the corresponding point of the preimage and add a prime symbol. For instance, if the preimage is *A*, then the image is *A′*, read as "*A prime*."

EXAMPLE 1 *Naming Transformations*

Use the graph of the transformation at the right.

  a. Name and describe the transformation.

  b. Name the coordinates of the vertices of the image.

  c. Is △*ABC* congruent to its image?

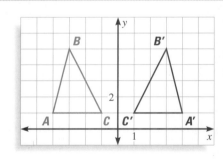

SOLUTION

  a. The transformation is a reflection in the *y*-axis. You can imagine that the image was obtained by flipping △*ABC* over the *y*-axis.

  b. The coordinates of the vertices of the image, △*A′B′C′*, are *A′*(4, 1), *B′*(3, 5), and *C′*(1, 1).

  c. Yes, △*ABC* is congruent to its image △*A′B′C′*. One way to show this would be to use the Distance Formula to find the lengths of the sides of both triangles. Then use the SSS Congruence Postulate.

An **isometry** is a transformation that preserves lengths. Isometries also preserve angle measures, parallel lines, and distances between points. Transformations that are isometries are called *rigid transformations.*

EXAMPLE 2 *Identifying Isometries*

Which of the following transformations appear to be isometries?

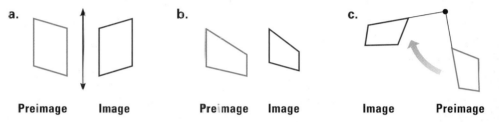

a.   b.   c.

Preimage   Image   Preimage   Image   Image   Preimage

SOLUTION

a. This transformation appears to be an isometry. The blue parallelogram is reflected in a line to produce a congruent red parallelogram.

b. This transformation is not an isometry. The image is not congruent to the preimage.

c. This transformation appears to be an isometry. The blue parallelogram is rotated about a point to produce a congruent red parallelogram.

· · · · · · · · · ·

MAPPINGS You can describe the transformation in the diagram by writing "$\triangle ABC$ is *mapped onto* $\triangle DEF$." You can also use arrow notation as follows:

$$\triangle ABC \rightarrow \triangle DEF$$

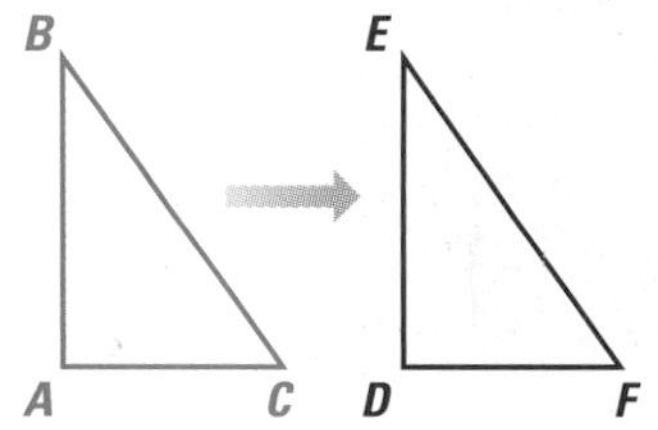

The order in which the vertices are listed specifies the correspondence. Either of the descriptions implies that $A \rightarrow D$, $B \rightarrow E$, and $C \rightarrow F$.

EXAMPLE 3 *Preserving Length and Angle Measure*

In the diagram, $\triangle PQR$ is mapped onto $\triangle XYZ$. The mapping is a rotation. Given that $\triangle PQR \rightarrow \triangle XYZ$ is an isometry, find the length of $\overline{XY}$ and the measure of $\angle Z$.

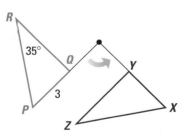

SOLUTION

The statement "$\triangle PQR$ is mapped onto $\triangle XYZ$" implies that $P \rightarrow X$, $Q \rightarrow Y$, and $R \rightarrow Z$. Because the transformation is an isometry, the two triangles are congruent.

▶ So, $XY = PQ = 3$ and $m\angle Z = m\angle R = 35°$.

FOCUS ON APPLICATIONS

CARPENTER GOTHIC The woodwork of carpenter gothic houses contains decorative patterns. Notice the translations in the patterns of the carpenter gothic house above.

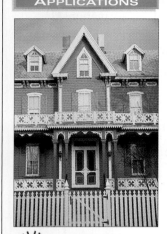

GOAL 2 USING TRANSFORMATIONS IN REAL LIFE

EXAMPLE 4 *Identifying Transformations*

CARPENTRY You are assembling pieces of wood to complete a railing for your porch. The finished railing should resemble the one below.

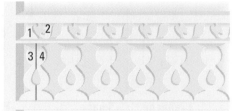

a. How are pieces 1 and 2 related? pieces 3 and 4?

b. In order to assemble the rail as shown, explain why you need to know how the pieces are related.

SOLUTION

a. Pieces 1 and 2 are related by a rotation. Pieces 3 and 4 are related by a reflection.

b. Knowing how the pieces are related helps you manipulate the pieces to create the desired pattern.

EXAMPLE 5 *Using Transformations*

BUILDING A KAYAK Many building plans for kayaks show the layout and dimensions for only half of the kayak. A plan of the top view of a kayak is shown below.

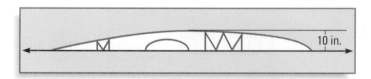

a. What type of transformation can a builder use to visualize plans for the entire body of the kayak?

b. Using the plan above, what is the maximum width of the entire kayak?

SOLUTION

a. The builder can use a reflection to visualize the entire kayak. For instance, when one half of the kayak is reflected in a line through its center, you obtain the other half of the kayak.

b. The two halves of the finished kayak are congruent, so the width of the entire kayak will be 2(10), or 20 inches.

GUIDED PRACTICE

Vocabulary Check ✓

1. An operation that maps a preimage onto an image is called a __?__.

Concept Check ✓

Complete the statement with *always*, *sometimes*, or *never*.

2. The preimage and the image of a transformation are __?__ congruent.

3. A transformation that is an isometry __?__ preserves length.

4. An isometry __?__ maps an acute triangle onto an obtuse triangle.

Skill Check ✓

Name the transformation that maps the blue pickup truck (preimage) onto the red pickup (image).

5.
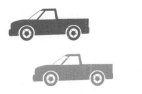

6.

7.

Use the figure shown, where figure *QRST* is mapped onto figure *VWXY*.

8. Name the preimage of $\overline{XY}$.

9. Name the image of $\overline{QR}$.

10. Name two angles that have the same measure.

11. Name a triangle that appears to be congruent to △*RST*.

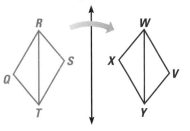

PRACTICE AND APPLICATIONS

STUDENT HELP

▶ **Extra Practice**
to help you master
skills is on p. 815.

NAMING TRANSFORMATIONS **Use the graph of the transformation below.**

12. Figure *ABCDE* → Figure __?__

13. Name and describe the transformation.

14. Name two sides with the same length.

15. Name two angles with the same measure.

16. Name the coordinates of the preimage of point *L*.

17. Show two corresponding sides have the same length, using the Distance Formula.

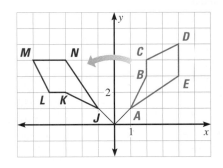

STUDENT HELP

▶ **HOMEWORK HELP**
Example 1: Exs. 12–22
Example 2: Exs. 23–25
Example 3: Exs. 26–31
Example 4: Exs. 36–39
Example 5: Ex. 41

ANALYZING STATEMENTS **Is the statement *true* or *false*?**

18. Isometries preserve angle measures and parallel lines.

19. Transformations that are *not* isometries are called rigid transformations.

20. A reflection in a line is a type of transformation.

DESCRIBING TRANSFORMATIONS Name and describe the transformation. Then name the coordinates of the vertices of the image.

21.

22.

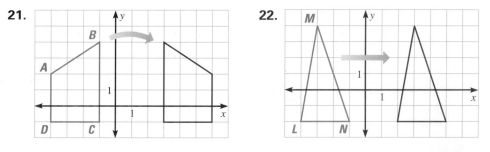

ISOMETRIES Does the transformation appear to be an isometry? Explain.

23.

24.

25.

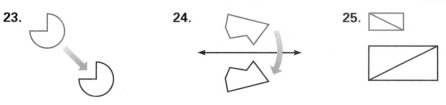

COMPLETING STATEMENTS Use the diagrams to complete the statement.

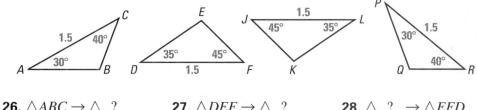

26. $\triangle ABC \to \triangle\underline{\ ?\ }$

27. $\triangle DEF \to \triangle\underline{\ ?\ }$

28. $\triangle\underline{\ ?\ } \to \triangle EFD$

29. $\triangle\underline{\ ?\ } \to \triangle ACB$

30. $\triangle LJK \to \triangle\underline{\ ?\ }$

31. $\triangle\underline{\ ?\ } \to \triangle CBA$

STUDENT HELP

INTERNET

HOMEWORK HELP
Visit our Web site
www.mcdougallittell.com
for help with Exs. 32
and 33.

SHOWING AN ISOMETRY Show that the transformation is an isometry by using the Distance Formula to compare the side lengths of the triangles.

32. $\triangle FGH \to \triangle RST$

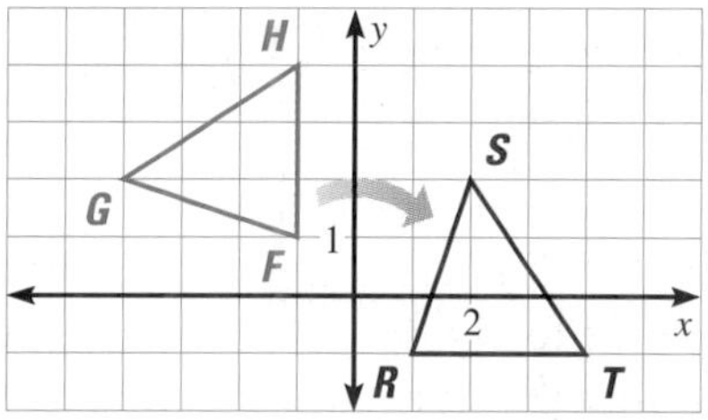

33. $\triangle ABC \to \triangle XYZ$

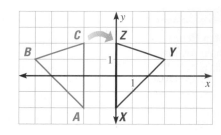

USING ALGEBRA Find the value of each variable, given that the transformation is an isometry.

34.

35.

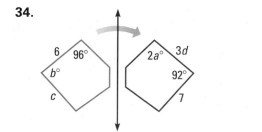

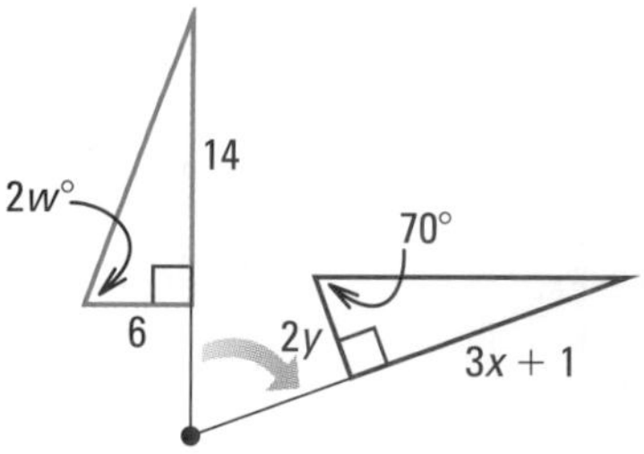

FOOTPRINTS In Exercises 36–39, name the transformation that will map footprint *A* onto the indicated footprint.

36. Footprint B

37. Footprint C

38. Footprint D

39. Footprint E

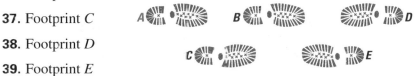

40. *Writing* Can a point or a line segment be its own preimage? Explain and illustrate your answer.

41. **STENCILING** You are stenciling the living room of your home. You want to use the stencil pattern below on the left to create the design shown. What type of transformation will you use to manipulate the stencil from A to B? from A to C? from A to D?

FOCUS ON APPLICATIONS

REAL LIFE EMBROIDERY Before machines, all stitching was done by hand. Completing samplers, such as the one above, served as practice for those learning how to stitch.

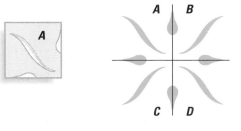

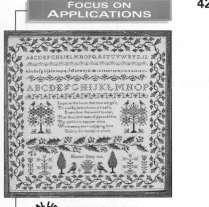

42. **MACHINE EMBROIDERY** Computerized embroidery machines are used to sew letters and designs on fabric. A computerized embroidery machine can use the same symbol to create several different letters. Which of the letters below are rigid transformations of other letters? Explain how a computerized embroidery machine can create these letters from one symbol.

a b c d e f g h i j k l m
n o p q r s t u v w x y z

43. **TILING A FLOOR** You are tiling a kitchen floor using the design shown below. You use a plan to lay the tile for the upper right corner of the floor design. Describe how you can use the plan to complete the other three corners of the floor.

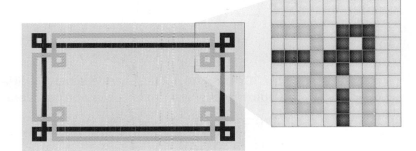

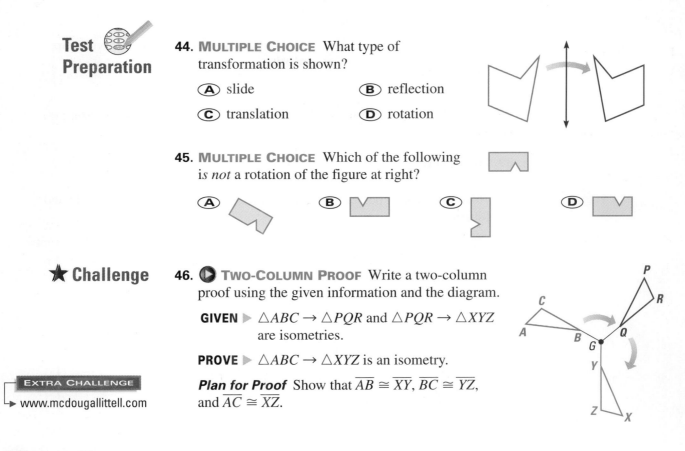

Test Preparation

44. MULTIPLE CHOICE What type of transformation is shown?

   Ⓐ slide   Ⓑ reflection

   Ⓒ translation   Ⓓ rotation

45. MULTIPLE CHOICE Which of the following is *not* a rotation of the figure at right?

   Ⓐ   Ⓑ   Ⓒ   Ⓓ

★ **Challenge**

46. ▶ **TWO-COLUMN PROOF** Write a two-column proof using the given information and the diagram.

   GIVEN ▶ $\triangle ABC \rightarrow \triangle PQR$ and $\triangle PQR \rightarrow \triangle XYZ$ are isometries.

   PROVE ▶ $\triangle ABC \rightarrow \triangle XYZ$ is an isometry.

   Plan for Proof Show that $\overline{AB} \cong \overline{XY}$, $\overline{BC} \cong \overline{YZ}$, and $\overline{AC} \cong \overline{XZ}$.

EXTRA CHALLENGE
www.mcdougallittell.com

MIXED REVIEW

USING THE DISTANCE FORMULA Find the distance between the two points. (Review 1.3 for 7.2)

47. $A(3, 10)$, $B(-2, -2)$ **48.** $C(5, -7)$, $D(-11, 6)$

49. $E(0, 8)$, $F(-8, 3)$ **50.** $G(0, -7)$, $H(6, 3)$

IDENTIFYING POLYGONS Determine whether the figure is a polygon. If it is not, explain why not. (Review 6.1 for 7.2)

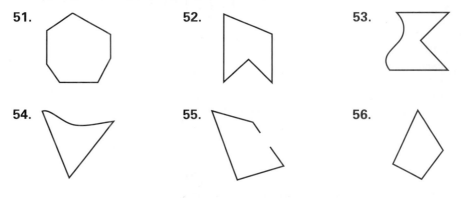

51.   **52.**   **53.**

54.   **55.**   **56.**

USING COORDINATE GEOMETRY Use two different methods to show that the points represent the vertices of a parallelogram. (Review 6.3)

57. $P(0, 4)$, $Q(7, 6)$, $R(8, -2)$, $S(1, -4)$

58. $W(1, 5)$, $X(9, 5)$, $Y(6, -1)$, $Z(-2, -1)$

▶ ACTIVITY 7.2

Developing Concepts

Reflections in the Plane

▶ **QUESTION** What is the relationship between the line of reflection and the segment connecting a point and its image?

▶ **EXPLORING THE CONCEPT**

GROUP ACTIVITY
Work with a partner.

MATERIALS
• tracing paper
• pencils
• ruler
• protractor

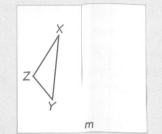

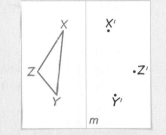

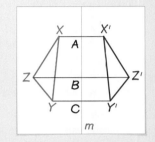

1 Fold a piece of tracing paper in half. Open the paper and label the fold line *m*. Draw a scalene triangle, △*XYZ*, on one side of line *m*.

2 Fold the tracing paper on line *m* and trace points *X*, *Y*, and *Z* on the back of the paper. Open the paper and label the reflected points *X'*, *Y'*, and *Z'*.

3 Draw △*X'Y'Z'*. Then draw $\overline{XX'}$, $\overline{ZZ'}$, and $\overline{YY'}$. Label the points where these segments intersect line *m* as *A*, *B*, and *C* respectively.

▶ **INVESTIGATE**

1. Measure and compare $\overline{XA}$ and $\overline{AX'}$, $\overline{ZB}$ and $\overline{BZ'}$, and $\overline{YC}$ and $\overline{CY'}$.

2. Measure and compare ∠*XAB*, ∠*ZBA*, and ∠*YCB*.

3. How does line *m* relate to $\overline{XX'}$, $\overline{ZZ'}$, and $\overline{YY'}$?

▶ **EXPLORING THE CONCEPT**

4 Fold a piece of tracing paper in half and label the fold line *m*. Draw $\overline{AB}$ as shown. Then draw its reflection in line *m*.

5 Draw $\overline{AA'}$ and $\overline{B'B}$. Label the points where these segments intersect line *m* as *C* and *D* as shown.

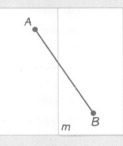

▶ **MAKE A CONJECTURE**

4. How does line *m* relate to $\overline{AA'}$ and $\overline{BB'}$? Explain your answer.

5. How does the line of reflection relate to the segment connecting a point and its image?

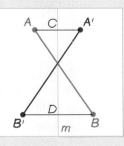

Reflections

What you should learn

GOAL 1 Identify and use reflections in a plane.

GOAL 2 Identify relationships between reflections and line symmetry.

Why you should learn it

▼ Reflections and line symmetry can help you understand how mirrors in a kaleidoscope create interesting patterns, as in **Example 5**.

GOAL 1 **USING REFLECTIONS IN A PLANE**

One type of transformation uses a line that acts like a mirror, with an image reflected in the line. This transformation is a **reflection** and the mirror line is the **line of reflection**.

A reflection in a line *m* is a transformation that maps every point *P* in the plane to a point *P′*, so that the following properties are true:

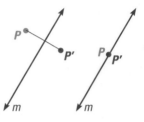

1. If *P* is not on *m*, then *m* is the perpendicular bisector of $\overline{PP'}$.

2. If *P* is on *m*, then *P = P′*.

EXAMPLE 1 *Reflections in a Coordinate Plane*

Graph the given reflection.

  a. *H*(2, 2) in the *x*-axis

  b. *G*(5, 4) in the line *y* = 4

SOLUTION

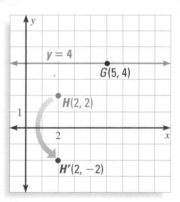

  a. Since *H* is two units above the *x*-axis, its reflection, *H′*, is two units below the *x*-axis.

  b. Start by graphing *y* = 4 and *G*. From the graph, you can see that *G* is on the line. This implies that *G = G′*.

· · · · · · · · · ·

Reflections in the coordinate axes have the following properties:

  1. If (*x*, *y*) is reflected in the *x*-axis, its image is the point (*x*, −*y*).

  2. If (*x*, *y*) is reflected in the *y*-axis, its image is the point (−*x*, *y*).

In Lesson 7.1, you learned that an isometry preserves lengths. Theorem 7.1 relates isometries and reflections.

THEOREM

THEOREM 7.1 *Reflection Theorem*

A reflection is an isometry.

Study Tip
Some theorems have more than one case, such as the Reflection Theorem. To fully prove this type of theorem, all of the cases must be proven.

To prove the Reflection Theorem, you need to show that a reflection preserves the length of a segment. Consider a segment $\overline{PQ}$ that is reflected in a line m to produce $\overline{P'Q'}$. The four cases to consider are shown below.

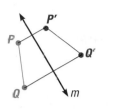

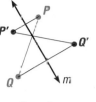

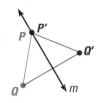

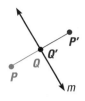

Case 1
P and Q are on the same side of m.

Case 2
P and Q are on opposite sides of m.

Case 3
One point lies on m and $\overline{PQ}$ is not perpendicular to m.

Case 4
Q lies on m and $\overline{PQ} \perp m$.

EXAMPLE 2 *Proof of Case 1 of Theorem 7.1*

Proof

GIVEN ▶ A reflection in m maps P onto P' and Q onto Q'.

PROVE ▶ $PQ = P'Q'$

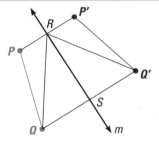

Paragraph Proof For this case, P and Q are on the same side of line m. Draw $\overline{PP'}$ and $\overline{QQ'}$, intersecting line m at R and S. Draw $\overline{RQ}$ and $\overline{RQ'}$.

By the definition of a reflection, $m \perp \overline{QQ'}$ and $\overline{QS} \cong \overline{Q'S}$. It follows that $\triangle RSQ \cong \triangle RSQ'$ using the SAS Congruence Postulate. This implies $\overline{RQ} \cong \overline{RQ'}$ and $\angle QRS \cong \angle Q'RS$. Because $\overleftrightarrow{RS}$ is a perpendicular bisector of $\overline{PP'}$, you have enough information to apply SAS to conclude that $\triangle RQP \cong \triangle RQ'P'$. Because corresponding parts of congruent triangles are congruent, $PQ = P'Q'$.

EXAMPLE 3 *Finding a Minimum Distance*

REAL LIFE

SURVEYING Two houses are located on a rural road m, as shown at the right. You want to place a telephone pole on the road at point C so that the length of the telephone cable, $AC + BC$, is a minimum. Where should you locate C?

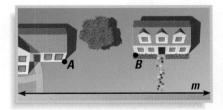

SOLUTION

Reflect A in line m to obtain A'. Then, draw $\overline{A'B}$. Label the point at which this segment intersects m as C. Because $\overline{A'B}$ represents the shortest distance between A' and B, and $AC = A'C$, you can conclude that at point C a minimum length of telephone cable is used.

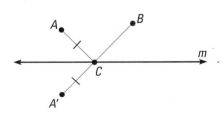

GOAL 2 REFLECTIONS AND LINE SYMMETRY

A figure in the plane has a **line of symmetry** if the figure can be mapped onto itself by a reflection in the line.

EXAMPLE 4 *Finding Lines of Symmetry*

Hexagons can have different lines of symmetry depending on their shape.

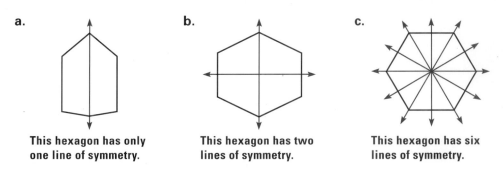

a.

This hexagon has only one line of symmetry.

b.

This hexagon has two lines of symmetry.

c.

This hexagon has six lines of symmetry.

EXAMPLE 5 *Identifying Reflections*

KALEIDOSCOPES Inside a kaleidoscope, two mirrors are placed next to each other to form a V, as shown at the right. The angle between the mirrors determines the number of lines of symmetry in the image. The formula below can be used to calculate the angle between the mirrors, A, or the number of lines of symmetry in the image, n.

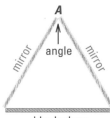

A

mirror / angle \ mirror

black glass

$$n(m\angle A) = 180°$$

Use the formula to find the angle that the mirrors must be placed for the image of a kaleidoscope to resemble the design.

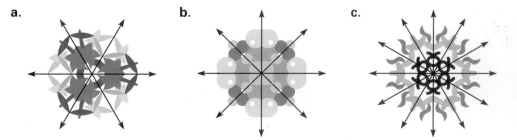

a.

b.

c.

FOCUS ON PEOPLE

KALEIDOSCOPES Sue and Bob Rioux design and make kaleidoscopes. The kaleidoscope in front of Sue is called *Sea Angel.*

APPLICATION LINK www.mcdougallittell.com

SOLUTION

a. There are 3 lines of symmetry. So, you can write $3(m\angle A) = 180°$. The solution is $m\angle A = 60°$.

b. There are 4 lines of symmetry. So, you can write $4(m\angle A) = 180°$. The solution is $m\angle A = 45°$.

c. There are 6 lines of symmetry. So, you can write $6(m\angle A) = 180°$. The solution is $m\angle A = 30°$.

GUIDED PRACTICE

Vocabulary Check ✓

Concept Check ✓

Skill Check ✓

1. Describe what a *line of symmetry* is.

2. When a point is reflected in the *x*-axis, how are the coordinates of the image related to the coordinates of the preimage?

Determine whether the blue figure maps onto the red figure by a reflection in line *m*.

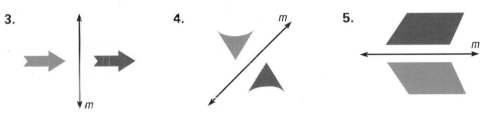

3.

4. *m*

5. *m*

Use the diagram at the right to complete the statement.

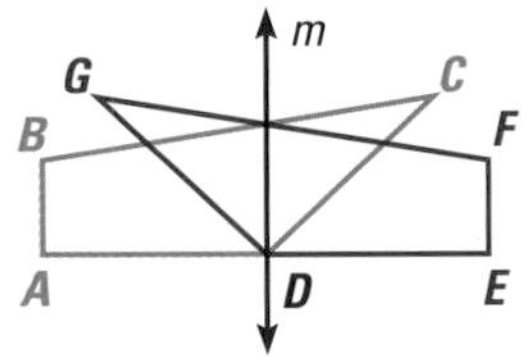

6. $\overline{AB} \rightarrow$ ___?___

7. ___?___ $\rightarrow \angle DEF$

8. $C \rightarrow$ ___?___

9. $D \rightarrow$ ___?___

10. ___?___ $\rightarrow \angle GFE$

11. ___?___ $\rightarrow \overline{DG}$

🌐 **FLOWERS** **Determine the number of lines of symmetry in the flower.**

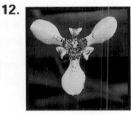

12.

13.

14.

PRACTICE AND APPLICATIONS

STUDENT HELP

↳ **Extra Practice**
to help you master
skills is on pp. 815
and 816.

DRAWING REFLECTIONS **Trace the figure and draw its reflection in line *k*.**

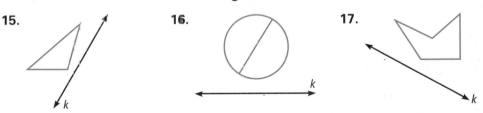

15.

16.

k

17.

k

k

STUDENT HELP

↳ **HOMEWORK HELP**
Example 1: Exs. 15–30
Example 2: Exs. 33–35
Example 3: Exs. 36–40
Example 4: Exs. 31, 32
Example 5: Exs. 44–46

ANALYZING STATEMENTS **Decide whether the conclusion is *true* or *false*. Explain your reasoning.**

18. If $N(2, 4)$ is reflected in the line $y = 2$, then N' is $(2, 0)$.

19. If $M(6, -2)$ is reflected in the line $x = 3$, then M' is $(0, -2)$.

20. If $W(-6, -3)$ is reflected in the line $y = -2$, then W' is $(-6, 1)$.

21. If $U(5, 3)$ is reflected in the line $x = 1$, then U' is $(-3, 3)$.

REFLECTIONS IN A COORDINATE PLANE **Use the diagram at the right to name the image of $\overline{AB}$ after the reflection.**

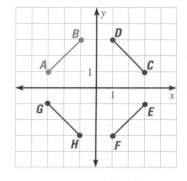

22. Reflection in the x-axis

23. Reflection in the y-axis

24. Reflection in the line $y = x$

25. Reflection in the y-axis, followed by a reflection in the x-axis.

REFLECTIONS **In Exercises 26–29, find the coordinates of the reflection without using a coordinate plane. Then check your answer by plotting the image and preimage on a coordinate plane.**

26. $S(0, 2)$ reflected in the x-axis

27. $T(3, 8)$ reflected in the x-axis

28. $Q(-3, -3)$ reflected in the y-axis

29. $R(7, -2)$ reflected in the y-axis

30. **CRITICAL THINKING** Draw a triangle on the coordinate plane and label its vertices. Then reflect the triangle in the line $y = x$. What do you notice about the coordinates of the vertices of the preimage and the image?

LINES OF SYMMETRY **Sketch the figure, if possible.**

31. An octagon with exactly two lines of symmetry

32. A quadrilateral with exactly four lines of symmetry

PARAGRAPH PROOF **In Exercises 33–35, write a paragraph proof for each case of Theorem 7.1. (Refer to the diagrams on page 405.)**

33. In Case 2, it is given that a reflection in m maps P onto P' and Q onto Q'. Also, $\overline{PQ}$ intersects m at point R.

PROVE ▶ $PQ = P'Q'$

34. In Case 3, it is given that a reflection in m maps P onto P' and Q onto Q'. Also, P lies on line m and $\overline{PQ}$ is not perpendicular to m.

PROVE ▶ $PQ = P'Q'$

35. In Case 4, it is given that a reflection in m maps P onto P' and Q onto Q'. Also, Q lies on line m and $\overline{PQ}$ is perpendicular to line m.

PROVE ▶ $PQ = P'Q'$

36. **DELIVERING PIZZA** You park your car at some point K on line n. You deliver a pizza to house H, go back to your car, and deliver a pizza to house J. Assuming that you cut across both lawns, explain how to estimate K so the distance that you travel is as small as possible.

STUDENT HELP

HOMEWORK HELP Visit our Web site www.mcdougallittell.com for help with Exs. 37–40.

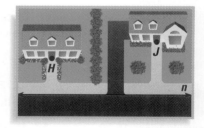

MINIMUM DISTANCE **Find point C on the x-axis so $AC + BC$ is a minimum.**

37. $A(1, 5), B(7, 1)$

38. $A(2, -2), B(11, -4)$

39. $A(-1, 4), B(6, 3)$

40. $A(-4, 6), B(3.5, 9)$

41. CHEMISTRY CONNECTION The figures
at the right show two versions of the
carvone molecule. One version is oil
of spearmint and the other is caraway.
How are the structures of these two
molecules related?

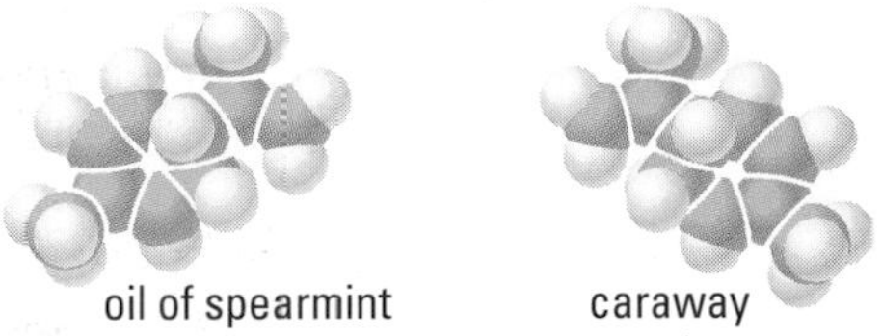

oil of spearmint   caraway

42. PAPER FOLDING Fold a piece of paper and label it as shown. Cut a scalene
triangle out of the folded paper and unfold the paper. How are triangle 2 and
triangle 3 related to triangle 1?

43. PAPER FOLDING Fold a piece of paper and label it as shown. Cut a scalene
triangle out of the folded paper and unfold the paper. How are triangles 2, 3,
and 4 related to triangle 1?

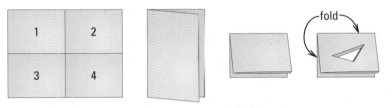

🌐 **KALEIDOSCOPES** In Exercises 44–46, calculate the angle at which the
mirrors must be placed for the image of a kaleidoscope to resemble the
given design. (Use the formula in Example 5 on page 406.)

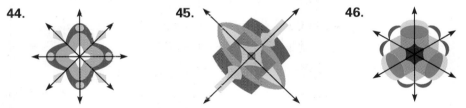

44.   **45.**   **46.**

47. 🖥️ TECHNOLOGY Use geometry software to draw a polygon reflected in
line *m*. Connect the corresponding vertices of the preimage and image.
Measure the distance between each vertex and line *m*. What do you notice
about these measures?

(xy) **USING ALGEBRA** Find the value of each variable, given that the
diagram shows a reflection in a line.

48.   **49.**

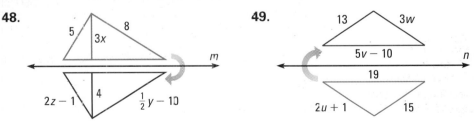

50. MULTIPLE CHOICE A piece of paper is folded in half and some cuts are made, as shown. Which figure represents the piece of paper unfolded?

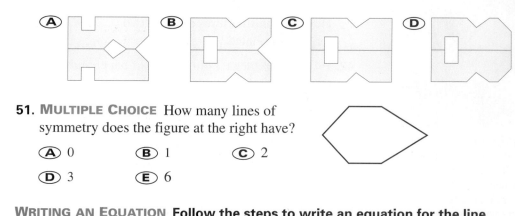

Ⓐ Ⓑ Ⓒ Ⓓ

51. MULTIPLE CHOICE How many lines of symmetry does the figure at the right have?

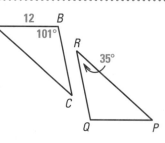

Ⓐ 0 Ⓑ 1 Ⓒ 2

Ⓓ 3 Ⓔ 6

★ **Challenge**

WRITING AN EQUATION Follow the steps to write an equation for the line of reflection.

52. Graph $R(2, 1)$ and $R'(-2, -1)$. Draw a segment connecting the two points.

53. Find the midpoint of $\overline{RR'}$ and name it Q.

54. Find the slope of $\overline{RR'}$. Then write the slope of a line perpendicular to $\overline{RR'}$.

55. Write an equation of the line that is perpendicular to $\overline{RR'}$ and passes through Q.

56. Repeat Exercises 52–55 using $R(-2, 3)$ and $R'(3, -2)$.

EXTRA CHALLENGE
www.mcdougallittell.com

MIXED REVIEW

CONGRUENT TRIANGLES Use the diagram, in which △ABC ≅ △PQR, to complete the statement. (Review 4.2 for 7.3)

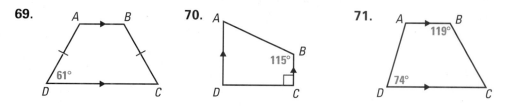

57. $\angle A \cong$ ___?___   **58.** $PQ =$ ___?___

59. $\overline{QR} \cong$ ___?___   **60.** $m\angle C =$ ___?___

61. $m\angle Q =$ ___?___   **62.** $\angle R \cong$ ___?___

FINDING SIDE LENGTHS OF A TRIANGLE Two side lengths of a triangle are given. Describe the length of the third side, *c*, with an inequality. (Review 5.5)

63. $a = 7, b = 17$ **64.** $a = 9, b = 21$ **65.** $a = 12, b = 33$

66. $a = 26, b = 6$ **67.** $a = 41.2, b = 15.5$ **68.** $a = 7.1, b = 11.9$

FINDING ANGLE MEASURES Find the angle measures of *ABCD*. (Review 6.5)

69.   **70.**   **71.**

Investigating Double Reflections

You can use geometry software to discover the type of transformation that results when a triangle is reflected twice in the plane.

▶ CONSTRUCT

1 Draw a scalene triangle similar to the one at the right. Label the vertices *A*, *B*, and *C*.

2 Draw two lines that intersect. Label the lines *k* and *m*. Make sure that the lines do not intersect the triangle.

3 Label the point of intersection of lines *k* and *m* as *P*.

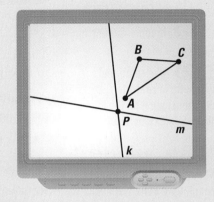

Visit our Web site www.mcdougallittell.com to see instructions for several software applications.

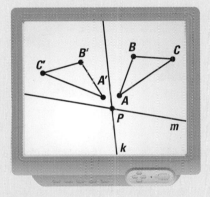

▶ INVESTIGATE

1. Reflect △*ABC* in line *k* to obtain △*A'B'C'*. Reflect △*A'B'C'* in line *m* to obtain △*A"B"C"*. How is △*ABC* related to △*A"B"C"*?

▶ MAKE A CONJECTURE

2. What other transformation maps a figure onto the same image as a reflection in two intersecting lines?

▶ INVESTIGATE

3. Draw segments connecting points *A* and *P* and points *A"* and *P*. Measure ∠*APA"*. This angle is an example of an *angle of rotation*.

4. Measure the acute angle formed by lines *k* and *m*. Compare this measure to the measure of ∠*APA"*.

5. Find the measures of ∠*BPB"* and ∠*CPC"*. What do you notice?

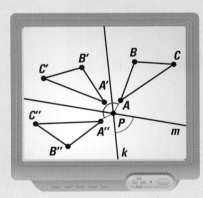

▶ MAKE A CONJECTURE

6. In the reflection of a figure in two intersecting lines, what is the relationship between the acute angle formed by the two lines and the angle of rotation?

EXTENSION

Repeat **Steps 1–3** using a different scalene triangle. Is the conjecture that you made in Exercise 6 correct?

Rotations

What you should learn

GOAL 1 Identify rotations in a plane.

GOAL 2 Use rotational symmetry in **real-life** situations, such as the logo designs in **Example 5**.

Why you should learn it

▼ Rotations and rotational symmetry can be used to create a design, as in the wheel hubs below and in **Exs. 36–38**.

GOAL 1 **USING ROTATIONS**

A **rotation** is a transformation in which a figure is turned about a fixed point. The fixed point is the **center of rotation**. Rays drawn from the center of rotation to a point and its image form an angle called the **angle of rotation**.

A rotation about a point P through x degrees ($x°$) is a transformation that maps every point Q in the plane to a point Q', so that the following properties are true:

1. If Q is not point P, then $QP = Q'P$ and $m\angle QPQ' = x°$.

2. If Q is point P, then $Q = Q'$.

Rotations can be clockwise or counterclockwise, as shown below.

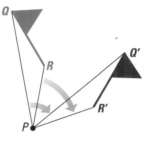

Clockwise rotation of 60°

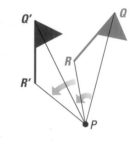

Counterclockwise rotation of 40°

THEOREM

THEOREM 7.2 *Rotation Theorem*

A rotation is an isometry.

To prove the Rotation Theorem, you need to show that a rotation preserves the length of a segment. Consider a segment $\overline{QR}$ that is rotated about a point P to produce $\overline{Q'R'}$. The three cases are shown below. The first case is proved in Example 1.

CASE 1

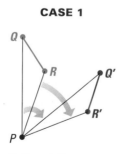

R, Q, and *P* are noncollinear.

CASE 2

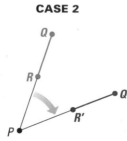

R, Q, and *P* are collinear.

CASE 3

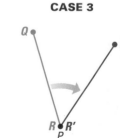

P and *R* are the same point.

Proof

EXAMPLE 1 *Proof of Theorem 7.2*

Write a paragraph proof for Case 1 of the Rotation Theorem.

GIVEN ▶ A rotation about *P* maps *Q* onto *Q'*
and *R* onto *R'*.

PROVE ▶ $\overline{QR} \cong \overline{Q'R'}$

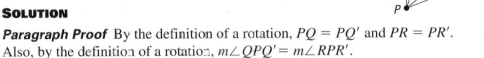

SOLUTION

Paragraph Proof By the definition of a rotation, $PQ = PQ'$ and $PR = PR'$.
Also, by the definition of a rotation, $m\angle QPQ' = m\angle RPR'$.

You can use the Angle Addition Postulate and the subtraction property of equality
to conclude that $m\angle QPR = m\angle Q'PR'$. This allows you to use the SAS
Congruence Postulate to conclude that $\triangle QPR \cong \triangle Q'PR'$. Because
corresponding parts of congruent triangles are congruent, $\overline{QR} \cong \overline{Q'R'}$.

· · · · · · · · ·

STUDENT HELP

▶ **Look Back**
For help with using a
protractor, see p. 27.

You can use a compass and a protractor to help you find the images of a polygon
after a rotation. The following construction shows you how.

▶ **ACTIVITY**
Construction

Rotating a Figure

**Use the following steps to draw the image of △ABC after a 120°
counterclockwise rotation about point P.**

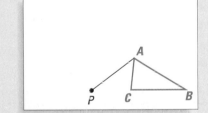

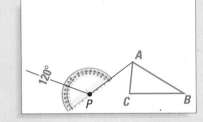

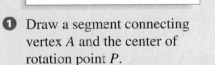

❶ Draw a segment connecting
vertex *A* and the center of
rotation point *P*.

❷ Use a protractor to measure
a 120° angle counterclockwise
and draw a ray.

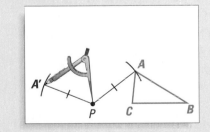

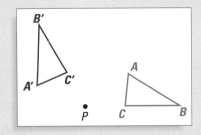

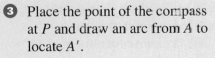

❸ Place the point of the compass
at *P* and draw an arc from *A* to
locate *A'*.

❹ Repeat **Steps 1–3** for each
vertex. Connect the vertices
to form the image.

EXAMPLE 2   *Rotations in a Coordinate Plane*

In a coordinate plane, sketch the quadrilateral whose vertices are $A(2, -2)$, $B(4, 1)$, $C(5, 1)$, and $D(5, -1)$. Then, rotate *ABCD* 90° counterclockwise about the origin and name the coordinates of the new vertices. Describe any patterns you see in the coordinates.

SOLUTION

Plot the points, as shown in blue. Use a protractor, a compass, and a straightedge to find the rotated vertices. The coordinates of the preimage and image are listed below.

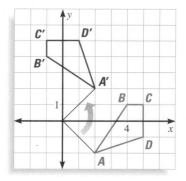

Figure *ABCD*	Figure *A'B'C'D'*
$A(2, -2)$	$A'(2, 2)$
$B(4, 1)$	$B'(-1, 4)$
$C(5, 1)$	$C'(-1, 5)$
$D(5, -1)$	$D'(1, 5)$

In the list above, the *x*-coordinate of the image is the opposite of the *y*-coordinate of the preimage. The *y*-coordinate of the image is the *x*-coordinate of the preimage.

▶ This transformation can be described as $(x, y) \rightarrow (-y, x)$.

THEOREM

THEOREM 7.3

If lines *k* and *m* intersect at point *P*, then a reflection in *k* followed by a reflection in *m* is a rotation about point *P*.

The angle of rotation is **2*x*°**, where *x*° is the measure of the acute or right angle formed by *k* and *m*.

$$m\angle BPB'' = 2x°$$

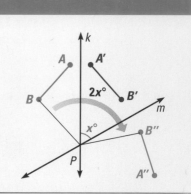

EXAMPLE 3   *Using Theorem 7.3*

In the diagram, $\triangle RST$ is reflected in line *k* to produce $\triangle R'S'T'$. This triangle is then reflected in line *m* to produce $\triangle R''S''T''$. Describe the transformation that maps $\triangle RST$ to $\triangle R''S''T''$.

SOLUTION

The acute angle between lines *k* and *m* has a measure of 60°. Applying Theorem 7.3 you can conclude that the transformation that maps $\triangle RST$ to $\triangle R''S''T''$ is a clockwise rotation of 120° about point *P*.

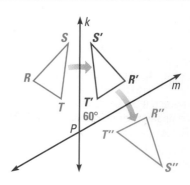

GOAL 2 **ROTATIONS AND ROTATIONAL SYMMETRY**

A figure in the plane has **rotational symmetry** if the figure can be mapped onto itself by a rotation of 180° or less. For instance, a square has rotational symmetry because it maps onto itself by a rotation of 90°.

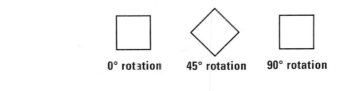

0° rotation   45° rotation   90° rotation

EXAMPLE 4 *Identifying Rotational Symmetry*

Which figures have rotational symmetry? For those that do, describe the rotations that map the figure onto itself.

a. Regular octagon   **b.** Parallelogram   **c.** Trapezoid

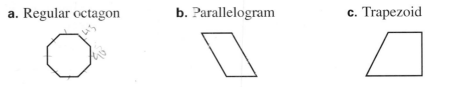

SOLUTION

a. This octagon has rotational symmetry. It can be mapped onto itself by a clockwise or counterclockwise rotation of 45°, 90°, 135°, or 180° about its center.

b. This parallelogram has rotational symmetry. It can be mapped onto itself by a clockwise or counterclockwise rotation of 180° about its center.

c. The trapezoid does not have rotational symmetry.

EXAMPLE 5 *Using Rotational Symmetry*

LOGO DESIGN A music store called Ozone is running a contest for a store logo. The winning logo will be displayed on signs throughout the store and in the store's advertisements. The only requirement is that the logo include the store's name. Two of the entries are shown below. What do you notice about them?

a.

b.

SOLUTION

a. This design has rotational symmetry about its center. It can be mapped onto itself by a clockwise or counterclockwise rotation of 180°.

b. This design also has rotational symmetry about its center. It can be mapped onto itself by a clockwise or counterclockwise rotation of 90° or 180°.

GUIDED PRACTICE

Vocabulary Check ✔

1. What is a *center of rotation*?

Concept Check ✔ Use the diagram, in which △*ABC* is mapped onto △*A′B′C′* by a rotation of 90° about the origin.

2. Is the rotation clockwise or counterclockwise?

3. Does $AB = A'B'$? Explain.

4. Does $AA' = BB'$? Explain.

5. If the rotation of △*ABC* onto △*A′B′C′* was obtained by a reflection of △*ABC* in some line *k* followed by a reflection in some line *m*, what would be the measure of the acute angle between lines *k* and *m*? Explain.

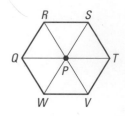

Skill Check ✔ The diagonals of the regular hexagon below form six equilateral triangles. Use the diagram to complete the sentence.

6. A clockwise rotation of 60° about *P* maps *R* onto ___?___.

7. A counterclockwise rotation of 60° about ___?___ maps *R* onto *Q*.

8. A clockwise rotation of 120° about *Q* maps *R* onto ___?___.

9. A counterclockwise rotation of 180° about *P* maps *V* onto ___?___.

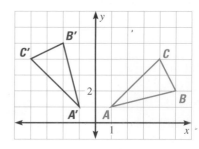

Determine whether the figure has rotational symmetry. If so, describe the rotations that map the figure onto itself.

10.   **11.**   **12.**

PRACTICE AND APPLICATIONS

STUDENT HELP

► **Extra Practice**
to help you master
skills is on p. 816.

DESCRIBING AN IMAGE State the segment or triangle that represents the image. You can use tracing paper to help you visualize the rotation.

13. 90° clockwise rotation of $\overline{AB}$ about *P*

14. 90° clockwise rotation of $\overline{KF}$ about *P*

15. 90° counterclockwise rotation of $\overline{CE}$ about *E*

16. 90° counterclockwise rotation of $\overline{FL}$ about *H*

17. 180° rotation of △*KEF* about *P*

18. 180° rotation of △*BCJ* about *P*

19. 90° clockwise rotation of △*APG* about *P*

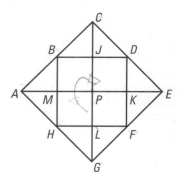

STUDENT HELP

↳ **HOMEWORK HELP**
Example 1: Exs. 13–21
Example 2: Exs. 22–29
Example 3: Exs. 30–33
Example 4: Exs. 36–38
Example 5: Exs. 39–42

▶ **PARAGRAPH PROOF** Write a paragraph proof for the case of Theorem 7.2.

20. GIVEN ▶ A rotation about F maps Q onto Q' and R onto R'.

PROVE ▶ $\overline{QR} \cong \overline{Q'R'}$

21. GIVEN ▶ A rotation about P maps Q onto Q' and R onto R'. P and R are the same point.

PROVE ▶ $\overline{QR} \cong \overline{Q'R'}$

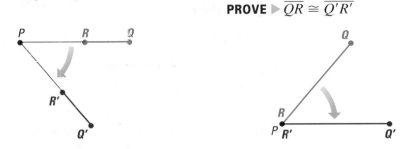

ROTATING A FIGURE Trace the polygon and point P on paper. Then, use a straightedge, compass, and protractor to rotate the polygon clockwise the given number of degrees about P.

22. 60°   **23.** 135°   **24.** 150°

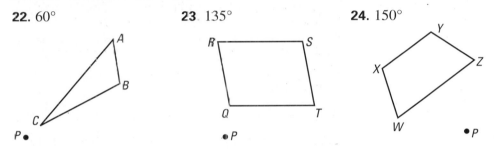

ROTATIONS IN A COORDINATE PLANE Name the coordinates of the vertices of the image after a clockwise rotation of the given number of degrees about the origin.

25. 90°   **26.** 180°   **27.** 270°

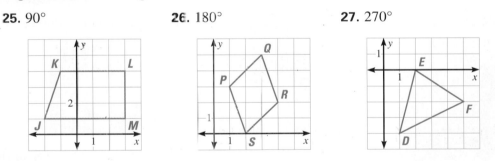

FINDING A PATTERN Use the given information to rotate the triangle. Name the vertices of the image and compare with the vertices of the preimage. Describe any patterns you see.

28. 90° clockwise about origin   **29.** 180° clockwise about origin

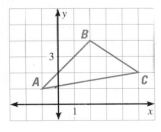
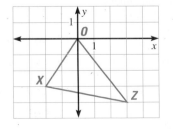

USING THEOREM 7.3 Find the angle of rotation that maps △*ABC* onto △*A″B″C″*.

30.

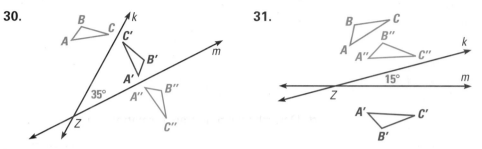

31.

LOGICAL REASONING Lines *m* and *n* intersect at point *D*. Consider a reflection of △*ABC* in line *m* followed by a reflection in line *n*.

32. What is the angle of rotation about D, when the measure of the acute angle between lines m and n is $36°$?

33. What is the measure of the acute angle between lines m and n, when the angle of rotation about D is $162°$?

USING ALGEBRA Find the value of each variable in the rotation of the polygon about point *P*.

34.

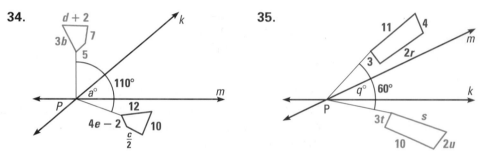

35.

FOCUS ON PEOPLE

REAL LIFE M.C. ESCHER is a Dutch graphic artist whose works include optical illusions and geometric patterns. (M.C. Escher's *"Hand with Reflecting Sphere"* © 1999 Cordon Art B.V. - Baarn - Holland. All rights reserved.)

INTERNET **APPLICATION LINK**
www.mcdougallittell.com

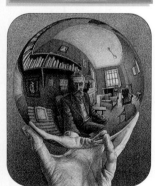

WHEEL HUBS Describe the rotational symmetry of the wheel hub.

36.

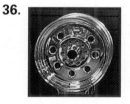

37.

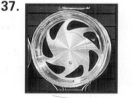

38.

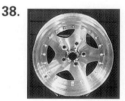

ROTATIONS IN ART In Exercises 39–42, refer to the image below by M.C. Escher. The piece is called *Development I* and was completed in 1937.

39. Does the piece have rotational symmetry? If so, describe the rotations that map the image onto itself.

40. Would your answer to Exercise 39 change if you disregard the shading of the figures? Explain your reasoning.

41. Describe the center of rotation.

42. Is it possible that this piece could be hung upside down? Explain.

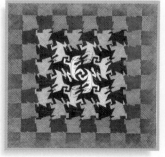

M.C. Escher's *"Development I"* © 1999 Cordon Art B.V. - Baarn - Holland. All rights reserved.

43. MULTI-STEP PROBLEM Follow the steps below.

a. Graph $\triangle RST$ whose vertices are $R(1, 1)$, $S(4, 3)$, and $T(5, 1)$.

b. Reflect $\triangle RST$ in the y-axis to obtain $\triangle R'S'T'$. Name the coordinates of the vertices of the reflection.

c. Reflect $\triangle R'S'T'$ in the line $y = -x$ to obtain $\triangle R''S''T''$. Name the coordinates of the vertices of the reflection.

d. Describe a single transformation that maps $\triangle RST$ onto $\triangle R''S''T''$.

e. *Writing* Explain how to show a 90° counterclockwise rotation of any polygon about the origin using two reflections of the figure.

★ **Challenge**

44. ▶ **PROOF** Use the diagram and the given information to write a paragraph proof for Theorem 7.3.

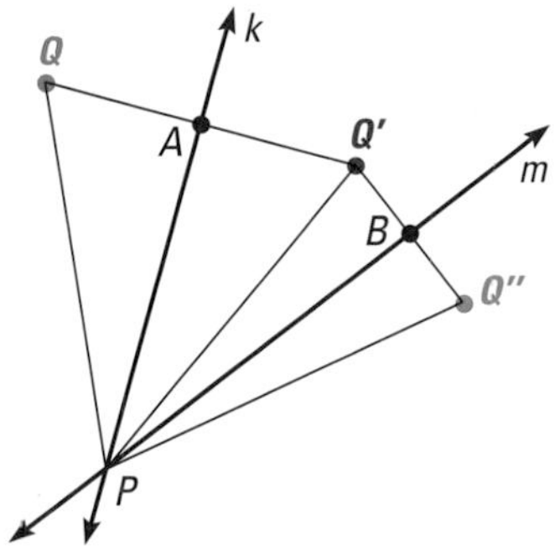

GIVEN ▶ Lines k and m intersect at point P, Q is any point not on k or m.

PROVE ▶ **a.** If you reflect point Q in k, and then reflect its image Q' in m, Q'' is the image of Q after a rotation about point P.

b. $m\angle QPQ'' = 2(m\angle APB)$.

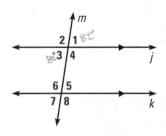

Plan for Proof First show $k \perp \overline{QQ'}$ and $\overline{QA} \cong \overline{Q'A}$. Then show $\triangle QAP \cong \triangle Q'AP$. Use a similar argument to show $\triangle Q'BP \cong \triangle Q''BP$. Use the congruent triangles and substitution to show that $\overline{QP} \cong \overline{Q''P}$. That proves part (a) by the definition of a rotation. You can use the congruent triangles to prove part (b).

EXTRA CHALLENGE
www.mcdougallittell.com

MIXED REVIEW

PARALLEL LINES Find the measure of the angle using the diagram, in which $j \parallel k$ and $m\angle 1 = 82°$. (Review 3.3 for 7.4)

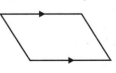

45. $m\angle 5$ **46.** $m\angle 7$

47. $m\angle 3$ **48.** $m\angle 6$

49. $m\angle 4$ **50.** $m\angle 8$

DRAWING TRIANGLES In Exercises 51–53, draw the triangle. (Review 5.2)

51. Draw a triangle whose circumcenter lies outside the triangle.

52. Draw a triangle whose circumcenter lies on the triangle.

53. Draw a triangle whose circumcenter lies inside the triangle.

54. PARALLELOGRAMS Can it be proven that the figure at the right is a parallelogram? If not, explain why not. (Review 6.2)

Use the transformation at the right. (Lesson 7.1)

1. Figure $ABCD$ → Figure __?__

2. Name and describe the transformation.

3. Is the transformation an isometry? Explain.

In Exercises 4–7, find the coordinates of the reflection without using a coordinate plane. (Lesson 7.2)

4. $L(2, 3)$ reflected in the x-axis

5. $M(-2, -4)$ reflected in the y-axis

6. $N(-4, 0)$ reflected in the x-axis

7. $P(8.2, -3)$ reflected in the y-axis

8. **KNOTS** The knot at the right is a *wall knot*, which is generally used to prevent the end of a rope from running through a pulley. Describe the rotations that map the knot onto itself and describe the center of rotation. (Lesson 7.3)

MATH & History | **History of Decorative Patterns**

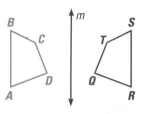

APPLICATION LINK
www.mcdougallittell.com

THEN ▸ **FOR THOUSANDS OF YEARS,** people have adorned their buildings, pottery, clothing, and jewelry with decorative patterns. Simple patterns were created by using a transformation of a shape.

NOW ▸ **TODAY,** you are likely to find computer generated patterns decorating your clothes, CD covers, sports equipment, computer desktop, and even textbooks.

1. The design at the right is based on a piece of pottery by Marsha Gomez. How many lines of symmetry does the design have?

2. Does the design have rotational symmetry? If so, describe the rotation that maps the pattern onto itself.

c. 1300 B.C.
Egyptian jewelry is decorated with patterns.

...Tiles are arranged in symmetric patterns in the Alhambra in Spain.

c. 1300

1899

Painted textile pattern called 'Bulow Birds'

...Marsha Gomez decorates pottery with symmetrical patterns.

1990s

7.4 Translations and Vectors

What you should learn

GOAL 1 Identify and use translations in the plane.

GOAL 2 Use vectors in **real-life** situations, such as navigating a sailboat in **Example 6**.

Why you should learn it

▼ You can use translations and vectors to describe the path of an aircraft, such as the hot-air balloon in **Exs. 53–55**.

REAL LIFE

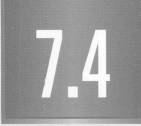

GOAL 1 USING PROPERTIES OF TRANSLATIONS

A **translation** is a transformation that maps every two points P and Q in the plane to points P' and Q', so that the following properties are true:

1. $PP' = QQ'$
2. $\overline{PP'} \parallel \overline{QQ'}$, or $\overline{PP'}$ and $\overline{QQ'}$ are collinear.

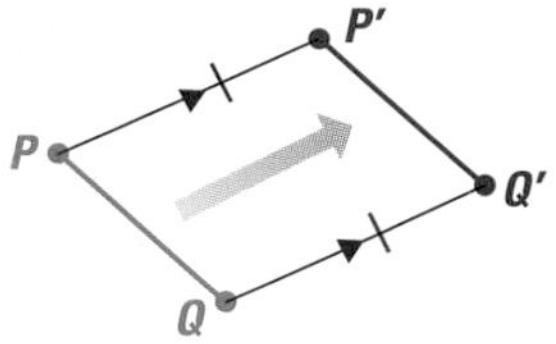

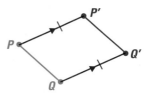

THEOREM

THEOREM 7.4 ***Translation Theorem***

A translation is an isometry.

Theorem 7.4 can be proven as follows.

GIVEN ▶ $PP' = QQ'$, $\overline{PP'} \parallel \overline{QQ'}$

PROVE ▶ $PQ = P'Q'$

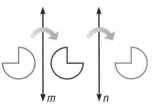

Paragraph Proof The quadrilateral $PP'Q'Q$ has a pair of opposite sides that are congruent and parallel, which implies $PP'Q'Q$ is a parallelogram. From this you can conclude $PQ = P'Q'$. (Exercise 43 asks for a coordinate proof of Theorem 7.4, which covers the case where $\overline{PQ}$ and $\overline{P'Q'}$ are collinear.)

You can find the image of a translation by gliding a figure in the plane. Another way to find the image of a translation is to complete one reflection after another in two parallel lines, as shown. The properties of this type of translation are stated below.

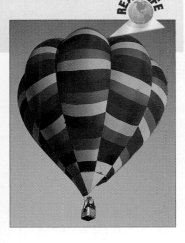

THEOREM

THEOREM 7.5

If lines k and m are parallel, then a reflection in line k followed by a reflection in line m is a translation. If P'' is the image of P, then the following is true:

1. $\overleftrightarrow{PP''}$ is perpendicular to k and m.
2. $PP'' = 2d$, where d is the distance between k and m.

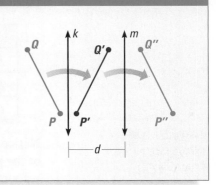

EXAMPLE 1 *Using Theorem 7.5*

In the diagram, a reflection in line k maps $\overline{GH}$ to $\overline{G'H'}$, a reflection in line m maps $\overline{G'H'}$ to $\overline{G''H''}$, $k \parallel m$, $HB = 5$, and $DH'' = 2$.

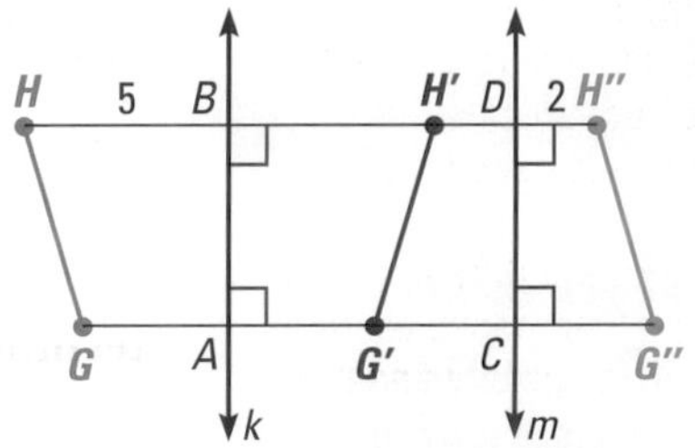

a. Name some congruent segments.

b. Does $AC = BD$? Explain.

c. What is the length of $\overline{GG''}$?

SOLUTION

a. Here are some sets of congruent segments: $\overline{GH}$, $\overline{G'H'}$, and $\overline{G''H''}$; $\overline{HB}$ and $\overline{H'B}$; $\overline{H'D}$ and $\overline{H''D}$.

b. Yes, $AC = BD$ because $\overline{AC}$ and $\overline{BD}$ are opposite sides of a rectangle.

c. Because $GG'' = HH''$, the length of $\overline{GG''}$ is $5 + 5 + 2 + 2$, or 14 units.

· · · · · · · · · ·

Translations in a coordinate plane can be described by the following coordinate notation:

$$(x, y) \rightarrow (x + a, y + b)$$

where a and b are constants. Each point shifts a units horizontally and b units vertically. For instance, in the coordinate plane at the right, the translation $(x, y) \rightarrow (x + 4, y - 2)$ shifts each point 4 units to the right and 2 units down.

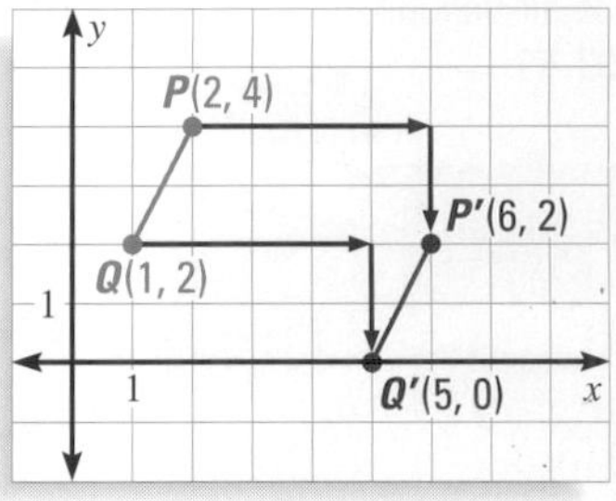

EXAMPLE 2 *Translations in a Coordinate Plane*

Sketch a triangle with vertices $A(-1, -3)$, $B(1, -1)$, and $C(-1, 0)$. Then sketch the image of the triangle after the translation $(x, y) \rightarrow (x - 3, y + 4)$.

SOLUTION

Plot the points as shown. Shift each point 3 units to the left and 4 units up to find the translated vertices. The coordinates of the vertices of the preimage and image are listed below.

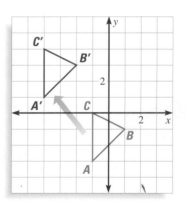

△ABC	△A'B'C'
$A(-1, -3)$	$A'(-4, 1)$
$B(1, -1)$	$B'(-2, 3)$
$C(-1, 0)$	$C'(-4, 4)$

Notice that each x-coordinate of the image is 3 units less than the x-coordinate of the preimage and each y-coordinate of the image is 4 units more than the y-coordinate of the preimage.

STUDENT HELP

Study Tip

In Lesson 7.2, you learned that the line of reflection is the perpendicular bisector of the segment connecting a point and its image. In Example 1, you can use this property to conclude that figure *ABDC* is a rectangle.

GOAL 2 TRANSLATIONS USING VECTORS

Another way to describe a translation is by using a vector. A **vector** is a quantity that has both direction and *magnitude*, or size, and is represented by an arrow drawn between two points.

The diagram shows a vector. The **initial point**, or starting point, of the vector is P and the **terminal point**, or ending point, is Q. The vector is named $\overrightarrow{PQ}$, which is read as "vector PQ." The *horizontal component* of $\overrightarrow{PQ}$ is 5 and the *vertical component* is 3.

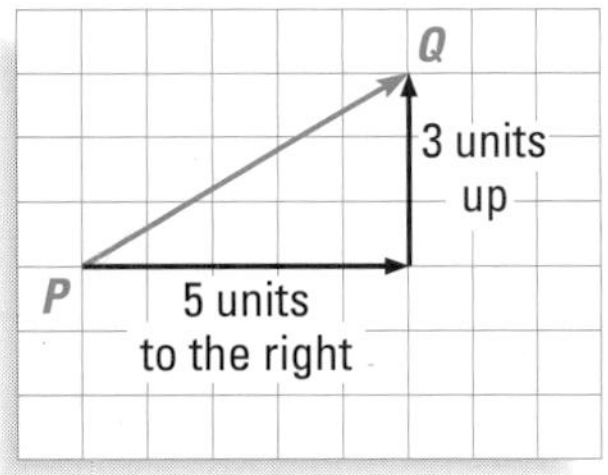

The **component form** of a vector combines the horizontal and vertical components. So, the component form of $\overrightarrow{PQ}$ is $\langle 5, 3 \rangle$.

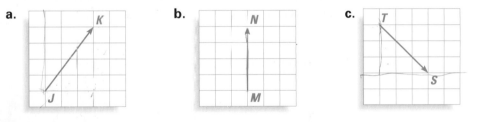

EXAMPLE 3 *Identifying Vector Components*

In the diagram, name each vector and write its component form.

a. b. c.

SOLUTION

a. The vector is $\overrightarrow{JK}$. To move from the initial point J to the terminal point K, you move 3 units to the right and 4 units up. So, the component form is $\langle 3, 4 \rangle$.

b. The vector is $\overrightarrow{MN} = \langle 0, 4 \rangle$.

c. The vector is $\overrightarrow{TS} = \langle 3, -3 \rangle$.

EXAMPLE 4 *Translation Using Vectors*

The component form of $\overrightarrow{GH}$ is $\langle 4, 2 \rangle$. Use $\overrightarrow{GH}$ to translate the triangle whose vertices are $A(3, -1)$, $B(1, 1)$, and $C(3, 5)$.

SOLUTION

First graph $\triangle ABC$. The component form of $\overrightarrow{GH}$ is $\langle 4, 2 \rangle$, so the image vertices should all be 4 units to the right and 2 units up from the preimage vertices. Label the image vertices as $A'(7, 1)$, $B'(5, 3)$, and $C'(7, 7)$. Then, using a straightedge, draw $\triangle A'B'C'$. Notice that the vectors drawn from preimage to image vertices are parallel.

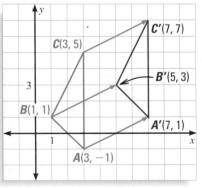

STUDENT HELP

INTERNET HOMEWORK HELP
Visit our Web site www.mcdougallittell.com for extra examples.

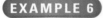

EXAMPLE 5 *Finding Vectors*

In the diagram, $QRST$ maps onto $Q'R'S'T'$ by a translation. Write the component form of the vector that can be used to describe the translation.

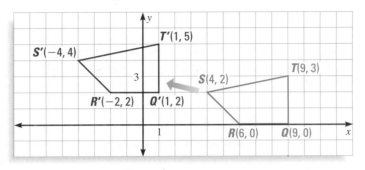

SOLUTION

Choose any vertex and its image, say R and R'. To move from R to R', you move 8 units to the left and 2 units up. The component form of the vector is $\langle -8, 2 \rangle$.

✓**CHECK** To check the solution, you can start any where on the preimage and move 8 units to the left and 2 units up. You should end on the corresponding point of the image.

EXAMPLE 6 *Using Vectors*

REAL LIFE **NAVIGATION** A boat travels a straight path between two islands, A and D. When the boat is 3 miles east and 2 miles north of its starting point it encounters a storm at point B. The storm pushes the boat off course to point C, as shown.

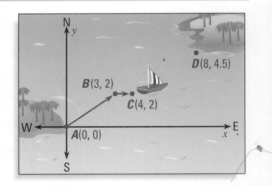

a. Write the component forms of the two vectors shown in the diagram.

b. The final destination is 8 miles east and 4.5 miles north of the starting point. Write the component form of the vector that describes the path the boat can follow to arrive at its destination.

SOLUTION

a. The component form of the vector from $A(0, 0)$ to $B(3, 2)$ is

$$\overrightarrow{AB} = \langle 3 - 0, 2 - 0 \rangle = \langle 3, 2 \rangle.$$

The component form of the vector from $B(3, 2)$ to $C(4, 2)$ is

$$\overrightarrow{BC} = \langle 4 - 3, 2 - 2 \rangle = \langle 1, 0 \rangle.$$

b. The boat needs to travel from its current position, point C, to the island, point D. To find the component form of the vector from $C(4, 2)$ to $D(8, 4.5)$, subtract the corresponding coordinates:

$$\overrightarrow{CD} = \langle 8 - 4, 4.5 - 2 \rangle = \langle 4, 2.5 \rangle.$$

GUIDED PRACTICE

Vocabulary Check ✓   **1.** A ___?___ is a quantity that has both ___?___ and magnitude.

Concept Check ✓   **2. ERROR ANALYSIS** Describe Jerome's error.

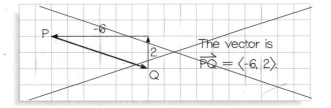

Skill Check ✓   **Use coordinate notation to describe the translation.**

3. 6 units to the right and 2 units down   **4.** 3 units up and 4 units to the right

5. 7 units to the left and 1 unit up   **6.** 8 units down and 5 units to the left

Complete the statement using the description of the translation. In the description, points (0, 2) and (8, 5) are two vertices of a pentagon.

7. If (0, 2) maps onto (0, 0), then (8, 5) maps onto (_?_ , _?_).

8. If (0, 2) maps onto (_?_ , _?_), then (8, 5) maps onto (3, 7).

9. If (0, 2) maps onto (−3, −5), then (8, 5) maps onto (_?_ , _?_).

10. If (0, 2) maps onto (_?_ , _?_), then (8, 5) maps onto (0, 0).

Draw three vectors that can be described by the given component form.

11. $\langle 3, 5 \rangle$ **12.** $\langle 0, 4 \rangle$ **13.** $\langle -6, 0 \rangle$ **14.** $\langle -5, -1 \rangle$

PRACTICE AND APPLICATIONS

STUDENT HELP

▶ **Extra Practice**
to help you master
skills is on p. 816.

DESCRIBING TRANSLATIONS Describe the translation using (a) coordinate notation and (b) a vector in component form.

15.

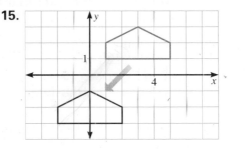

16.

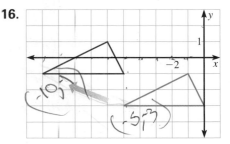

STUDENT HELP

▶ **HOMEWORK HELP**
Example 1: Exs. 20–24
Example 2: Exs. 15, 16,
25–34
Example 3: Exs. 15–19
Example 4: Exs. 39–42
Example 5: Exs. 44–47
Example 6: Exs. 53–55

IDENTIFYING VECTORS Name the vector and write its component form.

17.

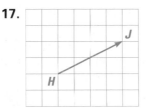

18.

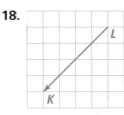

19.

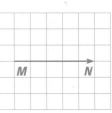

USING THEOREM 7.5 In the diagram, $k \parallel m$, $\triangle ABC$ is reflected in line k, and $\triangle A'B'C'$ is reflected in line m.

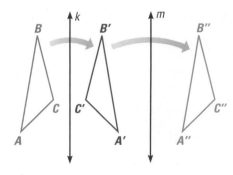

20. A translation maps $\triangle ABC$ onto which triangle?

21. Which lines are perpendicular to $\overleftrightarrow{AA''}$?

22. Name two segments parallel to $\overline{BB''}$.

23. If the distance between k and m is 1.4 inches, what is the length of $\overline{CC''}$?

24. Is the distance from B' to m the same as the distance from B'' to m? Explain.

IMAGE AND PREIMAGE Consider the translation that is defined by the coordinate notation $(x, y) \rightarrow (x + 12, y - 7)$.

25. What is the image of $(5, 3)$?　　**26.** What is the image of $(-1, -2)$?

27. What is the preimage of $(-2, 1)$?　　**28.** What is the preimage of $(0, -6)$?

29. What is the image of $(0.5, 2.5)$?　　**30.** What is the preimage of $(-5.5, -5.5)$?

DRAWING AN IMAGE Copy figure *PQRS* and draw its image after the translation.

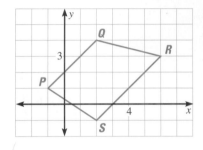

31. $(x, y) \rightarrow (x + 1, y - 4)$

32. $(x, y) \rightarrow (x - 6, y + 7)$

33. $(x, y) \rightarrow (x + 5, y - 2)$

34. $(x, y) \rightarrow (x - 1, y - 3)$

LOGICAL REASONING Use a straightedge and graph paper to help determine whether the statement is true.

35. If line p is a translation of a different line q, then p is parallel to q.

36. It is possible for a translation to map a line p onto a perpendicular line q.

37. If a translation maps $\triangle ABC$ onto $\triangle DEF$ and a translation maps $\triangle DEF$ onto $\triangle GHK$, then a translation maps $\triangle ABC$ onto $\triangle GHK$.

38. If a translation maps $\triangle ABC$ onto $\triangle DEF$, then $AD = BE = CF$.

TRANSLATING A TRIANGLE In Exercises 39–42, use a straightedge and graph paper to translate $\triangle ABC$ by the given vector.

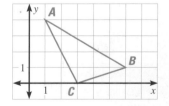

39. $\langle 2, 4 \rangle$　　　**40.** $\langle 3, -2 \rangle$

41. $\langle -1, -5 \rangle$　　　**42.** $\langle -4, 1 \rangle$

43. ▶ **PROOF** Use coordinate geometry and the Distance Formula to write a paragraph proof of Theorem 7.4.

　　GIVEN ▶ $PP' = QQ'$ and $\overline{PP'} \parallel \overline{QQ'}$

　　PROVE ▶ $PQ = P'Q'$

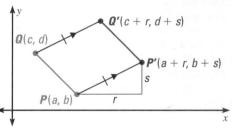

VECTORS The vertices of the image of *GHJK* after a translation are given. Choose the vector that describes the translation.

A. $\overrightarrow{PQ} = \langle 1, -3 \rangle$ **B.** $\overrightarrow{PQ} = \langle 0, 1 \rangle$

C. $\overrightarrow{PQ} = \langle -1, -3 \rangle$ **D.** $\overrightarrow{PQ} = \langle 6, -1 \rangle$

44. $G'(-6, 1), H'(-3, 2), J'(-4, -1), K'(-7, -2)$

45. $G'(1, 3), H'(4, 4), J'(3, 1), K'(0, 0)$

46. $G'(-4, 1), H'(-1, 2), J'(-2, -1), K'(-5, -2)$

47. $G'(-5, 5), H'(-2, 6), J'(-3, 3), K'(-6, 2)$

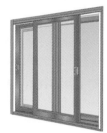

WINDOW FRAMES In Exercises 48–50, decide whether "opening the window" is a translation of the moving part.

48. Double hung **49.** Casement **50.** Sliding

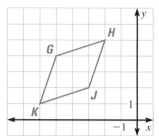

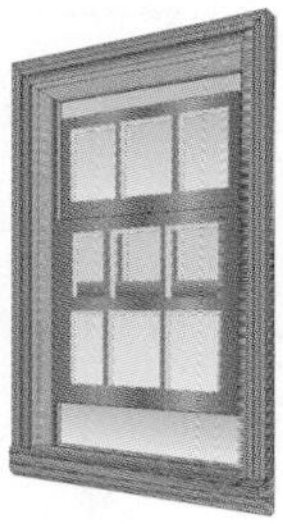

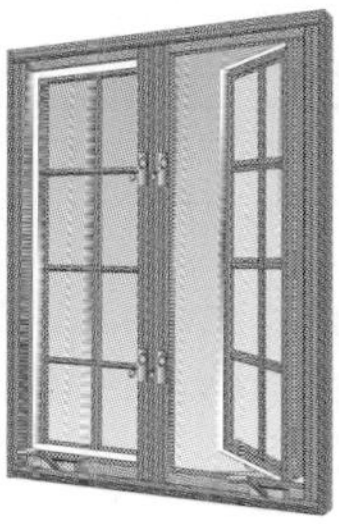

51. DATA COLLECTION Look through some newspapers and magazines to find patterns containing translations.

52. COMPUTER-AIDED DESIGN Mosaic floors can be designed on a computer. An example is shown at the right. On the computer, the design in square A is copied to cover an entire floor. The translation $(x, y) \to (x + 6, y)$ maps square A onto square B. Use coordinate notation to describe the translations that map square A onto squares C, D, E, and F.

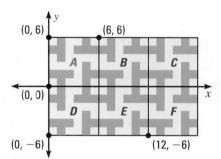

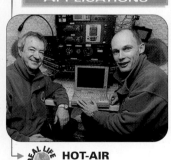

NAVIGATION A hot-air balloon is flying from town *A* to town *D*. After the balloon leaves town *A* and travels 6 miles east and 4 miles north, it runs into some heavy winds at point *B*. The balloon is blown off course as shown in the diagram.

53. Write the component forms of the two vectors in the diagram.

54. Write the component form of the vector that describes the path the balloon can take to arrive in town D.

55. Suppose the balloon was not blown off course. Write the component form of the vector that describes this journey from town A to town D.

FOCUS ON APPLICATIONS

REAL LIFE **HOT-AIR BALLOONS**

Bertrand Piccard and Brian Jones journeyed around the world in their hot-air balloon in 19 days.

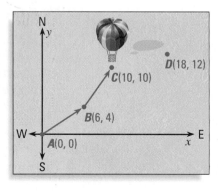

Test Preparation

QUANTITATIVE COMPARISON In Exercises 56–59, choose the statement that is true about the given quantities.

   (**A**) The quantity in column A is greater.

   (**B**) The quantity in column B is greater.

   (**C**) The two quantities are equal.

   (**D**) The relationship cannot be determined from the given information.

The translation $(x, y) \rightarrow (x + 5, y - 3)$ maps $\overline{AB}$ to $\overline{A'B'}$, and the translation $(x, y) \rightarrow (x + 5, y)$ maps $\overline{A'B'}$ to $\overline{A''B''}$.

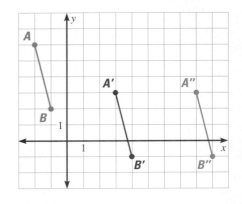

	Column A	Column B
56.	AB	$A'B'$
57.	AB	AA'
58.	BB'	$A'A''$
59.	$A'B''$	$A''B'$

★ **Challenge**

USING ALGEBRA A translation of $\overline{AB}$ is described by $\overrightarrow{PQ}$. Find the value of each variable.

60. $\overrightarrow{PQ} = \langle 4, 1 \rangle$

   $A(-1, w), A'(2x + 1, 4)$

   $B(8y - 1, 1), B'(3, 3z)$

61. $\overrightarrow{PQ} = \langle 3, -6 \rangle$

   $A(r - 1, 8), A'(3, s + 1)$

   $B(2t - 2, u), B'(5, -2u)$

MIXED REVIEW

FINDING SLOPE Find the slope of the line that passes through the given points. (Review 3.6)

62. $A(0, -2), B(-7, -8)$ **63.** $C(2, 3), D(-1, 18)$ **64.** $E(-10, 1), F(-1, 1)$

65. $G(-2, 12), H(-1, 6)$ **66.** $J(-6, 0), K(0, 10)$ **67.** $M(-3, -3), N(9, 6)$

COMPLETING THE STATEMENT In $\triangle JKL$, points Q, R, and S are midpoints of the sides. (Review 5.4)

68. If $JK = 12$, then $SR = $ ___?___ .

69. If $QR = 6$, then $JL = $ ___?___ .

70. If $RL = 6$, then $QS = $ ___?___ .

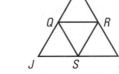

REFLECTIONS IN A COORDINATE PLANE Decide whether the statement is *true* or *false*. (Review 7.2 for 7.5)

71. If $N(3, 4)$ is reflected in the line $y = -1$, then N' is $(3, -6)$.

72. If $M(-5, 3)$ is reflected in the line $x = -2$, then M' is $(3, 1)$.

73. If $W(4, 3)$ is reflected in the line $y = 2$, then W' is $(1, 4)$.

◗ ACTIVITY 7.5

Developing Concepts

Multiple Transformations

GROUP ACTIVITY
Work with a partner.

MATERIALS
• graph paper
• ruler
• protractor
• compass

▶ **QUESTION** Does the order in which two transformations are performed affect the final image?

▶ **EXPLORING THE CONCEPT**

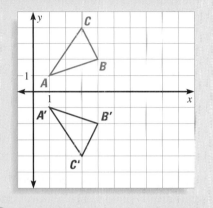

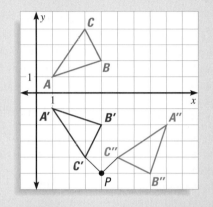

1 Draw △*ABC* with vertices *A*(1, 1), *B*(4, 2), and *C*(3, 4). Reflect △*ABC* in the *x*-axis to obtain △*A'B'C'*.

2 Rotate △*A'B'C'* 90° clockwise about *P*(4, −5) to obtain △*A"B"C"*.

▶ **INVESTIGATE**

1. Name the coordinates of △*A"B"C"*.

2. Repeat **Steps 1** and **2**, but switch the order of the transformations by performing the rotation first and the reflection second. Name the coordinates of △*A"B"C"*.

▶ **MAKE A CONJECTURE**

3. Does the order in which transformations are completed affect the final image?

▶ **INVESTIGATE**

4. Copy △*HJK*. Reflect △*HJK* in the line *x* = 6 to obtain △*H'J'K'*. Then translate △*H'J'K'* using (*x*, *y*) → (*x*, *y* − 6) to obtain △*H"J"K"*. Name the coordinates of △*H"J"K"*.

5. Repeat Exercise 4, but switch the order of the transformations. Name the coordinates of △*H"J"K"* and compare them with the coordinates of △*H"J"K"* from Exercise 4. What do you notice?

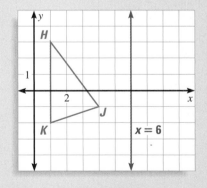

EXTENSION

CRITICAL THINKING Use the Distance Formula to show that the transformation that maps △*ABC* onto △*A"B"C"* in **Step 2** is an isometry.

7.5

Glide Reflections and Compositions

What you should learn

GOAL 1 Identify glide reflections in a plane.

GOAL 2 Represent transformations as compositions of simpler transformations.

Why you should learn it

▼ Compositions of transformations can help when creating patterns in **real life**, such as the decorative pattern below and in **Exs. 35–37.**

GOAL 1 USING GLIDE REFLECTIONS

A translation, or glide, and a reflection can be performed one after the other to produce a transformation known as a *glide reflection*. A **glide reflection** is a transformation in which every point P is mapped onto a point P'' by the following steps:

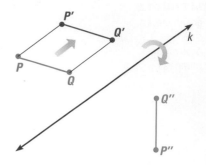

1. A translation maps P onto P'.

2. A reflection in a line k parallel to the direction of the translation maps P' onto P''.

As long as the line of reflection is parallel to the direction of the translation, it does not matter whether you glide first and then reflect, or reflect first and then glide.

EXAMPLE 1   *Finding the Image of a Glide Reflection*

Use the information below to sketch the image of $\triangle ABC$ after a glide reflection.

$A(-1, -3), B(-4, -1), C(-6, -4)$

Translation: $(x, y) \rightarrow (x + 10, y)$

Reflection: in the x-axis

SOLUTION

Begin by graphing $\triangle ABC$. Then, shift the triangle 10 units to the right to produce $\triangle A'B'C'$. Finally, reflect the triangle in the x-axis to produce $\triangle A''B''C''$.

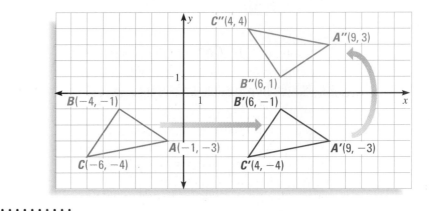

. . . .

In Example 1, try reversing the order of the transformations. Notice that the resulting image will have the same coordinates as $\triangle A''B''C''$ above. This is true because the line of reflection is parallel to the direction of the translation.

When two or more transformations are combined to produce a single transformation, the result is called a **composition** of the transformations.

THEOREM

THEOREM 7.6 *Composition Theorem*

The composition of two (or more) isometries is an isometry.

Because a glide reflection is a composition of a translation and a reflection, this theorem implies that glide reflections are isometries. In a glide reflection, the order in which the transformations are performed does not affect the final image. For other compositions of transformations, the order may affect the final image.

EXAMPLE 2 *Finding the Image of a Composition*

Sketch the image of $\overline{PQ}$ after a composition of the given rotation and reflection.

$P(2, -2)$, $Q(3, -4)$

Rotation: 90° counterclockwise about the origin

Reflection: in the y-axis

SOLUTION

Begin by graphing $\overline{PQ}$. Then rotate the segment 90° counterclockwise about the origin to produce $\overline{F'Q'}$. Finally, reflect the segment in the y-axis to produce $\overline{P''Q''}$.

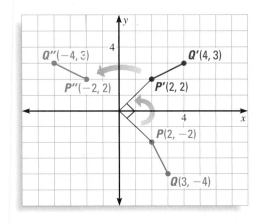

EXAMPLE 3 *Comparing Orders of Compositions*

Repeat Example 2, but switch the order of the composition by performing the reflection first and the rotation second. What do you notice?

SOLUTION

Graph $\overline{PQ}$. Then reflect the segment in the y-axis to obtain $\overline{P'Q'}$. Rotate $\overline{P'Q'}$ 90° counterclockwise about the origin to obtain $\overline{P''Q''}$. Instead of being in Quadrant II, as in Example 2, the image is in Quadrant IV.

▶ The order which the transformations are performed affects the final image.

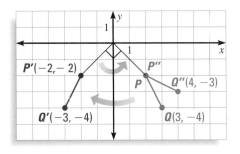

EXAMPLE 4 *Describing a Composition*

Describe the composition of
transformations in the diagram.

SOLUTION

Two transformations are shown. First,
figure *ABCD* is reflected in the line *x* = 2
to produce figure *A'B'C'D'*. Then,
figure *A'B'C'D'* is rotated 90° clockwise
about the point (2, 0) to produce
figure *A"B"C"D"*.

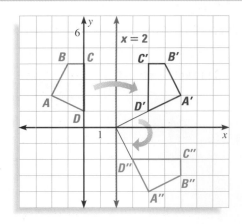

EXAMPLE 5 *Describing a Composition*

REAL LIFE **PUZZLES** The mathematical game pentominoes is a tiling game that uses
twelve different types of tiles, each composed of five squares. The tiles
are referred to by the letters they resemble. The object of the game is to pick up
and arrange the tiles to create a given shape. Use compositions of transformations
to describe how the tiles below will complete the 6 × 5 rectangle.

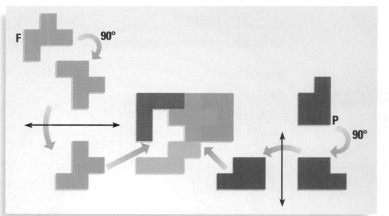

SOLUTION

To complete part of the rectangle,
rotate the F tile 90° clockwise,
reflect the tile over a horizontal
line, and translate it into place.

To complete the rest of the rectangle,
rotate the P tile 90° clockwise, reflect
the tile over a vertical line, and
translate it into place.

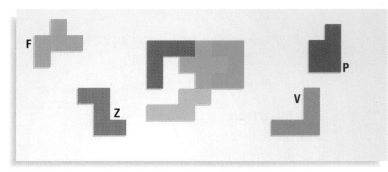

GUIDED PRACTICE

Vocabulary Check ✓

1. In a glide reflection, the direction of the __?__ must be parallel to the line of __?__.

Concept Check ✓

Complete the statement with *always*, *sometimes*, or *never*.

2. The order in which two transformations are performed __?__ affects the resulting image.

3. In a glide reflection, the order in which the two transformations are performed __?__ matters.

4. A composition of isometries is __?__ an isometry.

Skill Check ✓

In the diagram, $\overline{AB}$ is the preimage of a glide reflection.

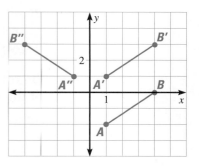

5. Which segment is a translation of $\overline{AB}$?

6. Which segment is a reflection of $\overline{A'B'}$?

7. Name the line of reflection.

8. Use coordinate notation to describe the translation.

PRACTICE AND APPLICATIONS

STUDENT HELP

▶ **Extra Practice**
to help you master skills is on p. 816.

🧩 **LOGICAL REASONING** Match the composition with the diagram, in which the blue figure is the preimage of the red figure and the red figure is the preimage of the green figure.

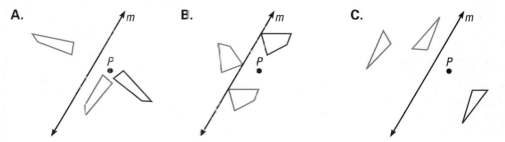

A.   **B.**   **C.**

9. Rotate about point P, then reflect in line m.

10. Reflect in line m, then rotate about point P.

11. Translate parallel to line m, then rotate about point P.

STUDENT HELP

▶ **HOMEWORK HELP**
Example 1: Exs. 9–15
Example 2: Exs. 16–19
Example 3: Exs. 20, 21
Example 4: Exs. 22–25
Example 5: Ex. 38

FINDING AN IMAGE Sketch the image of $A(-3, 5)$ after the described glide reflection.

12. **Translation:** $(x, y) \rightarrow (x, y - 4)$
    Reflection: in the y-axis

13. **Translation:** $(x, y) \rightarrow (x + 4, y + 1)$
    Reflection: in $y = -2$

14. **Translation:** $(x, y) \rightarrow (x - 6, y - 1)$
    Reflection: in $x = -1$

15. **Translation:** $(x, y) \rightarrow (x - 3, y - 3)$
    Reflection: in $y = x$

STUDENT HELP

↳ ⌁ HOMEWORK HELP
Visit our Web site
www.mcdougallittell.com
for help with Exs. 16–19.

SKETCHING COMPOSITIONS Sketch the image of △*PQR* after a composition using the given transformations in the order they appear.

16. $P(4, 2)$, $Q(7, 0)$, $R(9, 3)$
Translation: $(x, y) \rightarrow (x - 2, y + 3)$
Rotation: $90°$ clockwise about $T(0, 3)$

17. $P(4, 5)$, $Q(7, 1)$, $R(8, 8)$
Translation: $(x, y) \rightarrow (x, y - 7)$
Reflection: in the *y*-axis

18. $P(-9, -2)$, $Q(-9, -5)$, $R(-5, -4)$
Translation: $(x, y) \rightarrow (x + 14, y + 1)$
Translation: $(x, y) \rightarrow (x - 3, y + 8)$

19. $P(-7, 2)$, $Q(-6, 7)$, $R(-2, -1)$
Reflection: in the *x*-axis
Rotation: $90°$ clockwise about origin

REVERSING ORDERS Sketch the image of $\overline{FG}$ after a composition using the given transformations in the order they appear. Then, perform the transformations in reverse order. Does the order affect the final image?

20. $F(4, -4)$, $G(1, -2)$
Rotation: $90°$ clockwise about origin
Reflection: in the *y*-axis

21. $F(-1, -3)$, $G(-4, -2)$
Reflection: in the line $x = 1$
Translation: $(x, y) \rightarrow (x + 2, y + 10)$

DESCRIBING COMPOSITIONS In Exercises 22–25, describe the composition of the transformations.

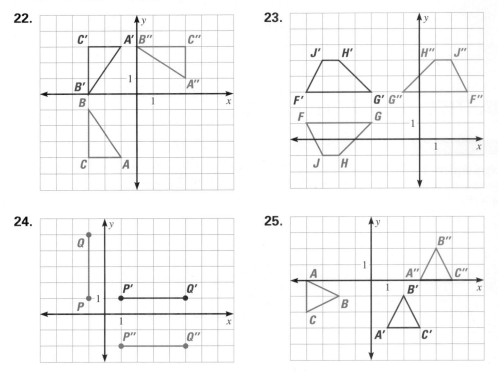

26. *Writing* Explain why a glide reflection is an isometry.

27. 🧩 **LOGICAL REASONING** Which are preserved by a glide reflection?

A. distance   **B.** angle measure   **C.** parallel lines

28. △ **TECHNOLOGY** Use geometry software to draw a polygon. Show that if you reflect the polygon and then translate it in a direction that is *not* parallel to the line of reflection, then the final image is *different* from the final image if you perform the translation first and the reflection second.

CRITICAL THINKING In Exercises 29 and 30, the first translation maps *J* to *J′* and the second maps *J′* to *J″*. Find the translation that maps *J* to *J″*.

29. Translation 1: $(x, y) \rightarrow (x + 7, y - 2)$
Translation 2: $(x, y) \rightarrow (x - 1, y + 3)$
Translation: $(x, y) \rightarrow (\underline{\ ?\ }, \underline{\ ?\ })$

30. Translation 1: $(x, y) \rightarrow (x + 9, y + 4)$
Translation 2: $(x, y) \rightarrow (x + 6, y - 4)$
Translation: $(x, y) \rightarrow (\underline{\ ?\ }, \underline{\ ?\ })$

31. 🌐 **STENCILING A BORDER** The border pattern below was made with a stencil. Describe how the border was created using one stencil four times.

🌐 **CLOTHING PATTERNS** The diagram shows the pattern pieces for a jacket arranged on some blue fabric.

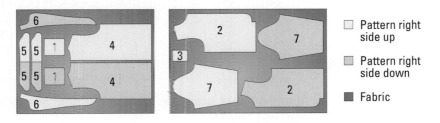

☐	Pattern right side up
☐	Pattern right side down
■	Fabric

32. Which pattern pieces are translated?

33. Which pattern pieces are reflected?

34. Which pattern pieces are glide reflected?

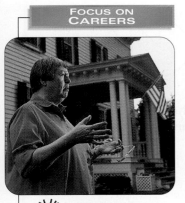
🌐 **ARCHITECTURE** In Exercises 35–37, describe the transformations that are combined to create the pattern in the architectural element.

35.

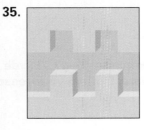

36.

37.

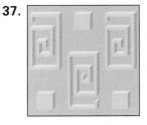

38. 🌐 **PENTOMINOES** Use compositions of transformations to describe how to pick up and arrange the tiles to complete the 6 × 10 rectangle.

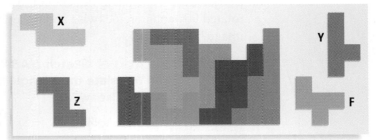

Test Preparation

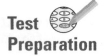

39. MULTI-STEP PROBLEM Follow the steps below.

a. On a coordinate plane, draw a point and its image after a glide reflection that uses the x-axis as the line of reflection.

b. Connect the point and its image. Make a conjecture about the midpoint of the segment.

c. Use the coordinates from part (a) to prove your conjecture.

d. CRITICAL THINKING Can you extend your conjecture to include glide reflections that do not use the x-axis as the line of reflection?

★ Challenge

40. USING ALGEBRA Solve for the variables in the glide reflection of $\triangle JKL$ described below.

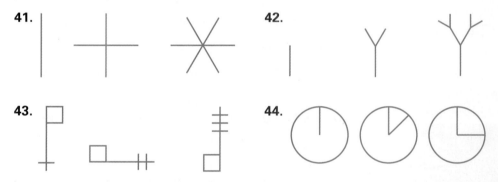

$J(-2, -1)$, $K(-4, 2a)$, $L(b-6, 6)$ → **Translate $(x, y) \to (x+3, y)$** → $J'(c+1, -1)$, $K'(5d-11, 4)$, $L'(2, 4e)$ → **Reflect in x-axis** → $J''(1, -f)$, $K''(-1, 3g+5)$, $L''(h+4, -6)$

EXTRA CHALLENGE
www.mcdougallittell.com

MIXED REVIEW

ANALYZING PATTERNS Sketch the next figure in the pattern. (Review 1.1 for 7.6)

41.

42.

43.

44.

COORDINATE GEOMETRY In Exercises 45–47, decide whether ▱*PQRS* is a *rhombus*, a *rectangle*, or a *square*. Explain your reasoning. (Review 6.4)

45. $P(1, -2)$, $Q(5, -1)$, $R(6, -5)$, $S(2, -6)$

46. $P(10, 7)$, $Q(15, 7)$, $R(15, 1)$, $S(10, 1)$

47. $P(8, -4)$, $Q(10, -7)$, $R(8, -10)$, $S(6, -7)$

48. ROTATIONS A segment has endpoints $(3, -8)$ and $(7, -1)$. If the segment is rotated 90° counterclockwise about the origin, what are the endpoints of its image? **(Review 7.3)**

STUDYING TRANSLATIONS Sketch $\triangle ABC$ with vertices $A(-9, 7)$, $B(-9, 1)$, and $C(-5, 6)$. Then translate the triangle by the given vector and name the vertices of the image. (Review 7.4)

49. $\langle 3, 2\rangle$ **50.** $\langle -1, -5\rangle$ **51.** $\langle 6, 0\rangle$

52. $\langle -4, -4\rangle$ **53.** $\langle 0, 2.5\rangle$ **54.** $\langle 1.5, -4.5\rangle$

7.6

Frieze Patterns

What you should learn

GOAL 1 Use transformations to classify frieze patterns.

GOAL 2 Use frieze patterns to design border patterns in **real life**, such as the tiling pattern in **Example 4**.

Why you should learn it

▼ You can use frieze patterns to create decorative borders for **real-life** objects, such as the pottery below and the pottery in Exs. 35–37.

GOAL 1   CLASSIFYING FRIEZE PATTERNS

A **frieze pattern** or **border pattern** is a pattern that extends to the left and right in such a way that the pattern can be mapped onto itself by a horizontal translation. In addition to being mapped onto itself by a horizontal translation, some frieze patterns can be mapped onto themselves by other transformations.

1. Translation   T

2. 180° rotation   R

3. Reflection in a horizontal line   H

4. Reflection in a vertical line   V

5. Horizontal glide reflection   G

EXAMPLE 1   *Describing Frieze Patterns*

Describe the transformations that will map each frieze pattern onto itself.

a.

b.

c.

d.

SOLUTION

a. This frieze pattern can be mapped onto itself by a horizontal translation (T).

b. This frieze pattern can be mapped onto itself by a horizontal translation (T) or by a 180° rotation (R).

c. This frieze pattern can be mapped onto itself by a horizontal translation (T) or by a horizontal glide reflection (G).

d. This frieze pattern can be mapped onto itself by a horizontal translation (T) or by a reflection in a vertical line (V).

CLASSIFICATIONS OF FRIEZE PATTERNS

T	Translation	 , , , , , ,
TR	Translation and 180° rotation	
TG	Translation and horizontal glide reflection	
TV	Translation and vertical line reflection	
THG	Translation, horizontal line reflection, and horizontal glide reflection	
TRVG	Translation, 180° rotation, vertical line reflection, and horizontal glide reflection	
TRHVG	Translation, 180° rotation, horizontal line reflection, vertical line reflection, and horizontal glide reflection	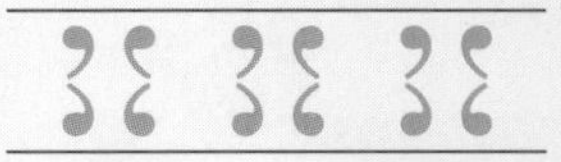

STUDENT HELP

► **Study Tip**
To help classify a frieze
pattern, you can use a
process of elimination.
This process is described
at the right and in the
tree diagram in **Ex. 53**.

To classify a frieze pattern into one of the seven categories, you first decide whether the pattern has 180° rotation. If it does, then there are three possible classifications: TR, TRVG, and TRHVG.

If the frieze pattern does not have 180° rotation, then there are four possible classifications: T, TV, TG, and THG. Decide whether the pattern has a line of reflection. By a process of elimination, you will reach the correct classification.

EXAMPLE 2 *Classifying a Frieze Pattern*

SNAKES Categorize the snakeskin pattern of the mountain adder.

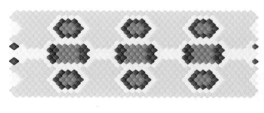

SOLUTION

This pattern is a TRHVG. The pattern can be mapped onto itself by a translation, a 180° rotation, a reflection in a horizontal line, a reflection in a vertical line, and a horizontal glide reflection.

ARCHITECTURE
Features of classical architecture from Greece and Rome are seen in "neo-classical" buildings today, such as the Supreme Court building shown.

GOAL 2 **USING FRIEZE PATTERNS IN REAL LIFE**

EXAMPLE 3 *Identifying Frieze Patterns*

ARCHITECTURE The frieze patterns of ancient Doric buildings are located between the cornice and the architrave, as shown at the right. The frieze patterns consist of alternating sections. Some sections contain a person or a symmetric design. Other sections have simple patterns of three or four vertical lines.

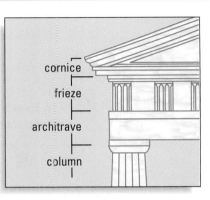

Portions of two frieze patterns are shown below. Classify the patterns.

a.
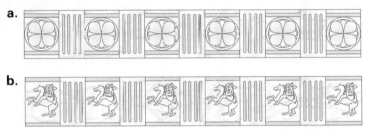

b.

SOLUTION

a. Following the diagrams on the previous page, you can see that this frieze pattern has rotational symmetry, line symmetry about a horizontal line and a vertical line, and that the pattern can be mapped onto itself by a glide reflection. So, the pattern can be classified as TRHVG.

b. The only transformation that maps this pattern onto itself is a translation. So, the pattern can be classified as T.

EXAMPLE 4 *Drawing a Frieze Pattern*

 TILING A border on a bathroom wall is created using the decorative tile at the right. The border pattern is classified as TR. Draw one such pattern.

SOLUTION

Begin by rotating the given tile 180°. Use this tile and the original tile to create a pattern that has rotational symmetry. Then translate the pattern several times to create the frieze pattern.

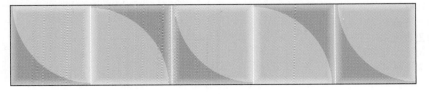

GUIDED PRACTICE

Vocabulary Check ✓

1. Describe the term *frieze pattern* in your own words.

Concept Check ✓

2. ERROR ANALYSIS Describe Lucy's error below.

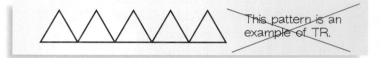

This pattern is an example of TR.

Skill Check ✓

In Exercises 3–6, describe the transformations that map the frieze pattern onto itself.

3.

4.

5.

6.

7. List the five possible transformations, along with their letter abbreviations, that can be found in a frieze pattern.

PRACTICE AND APPLICATIONS

STUDENT HELP

↳ **Extra Practice**
to help you master
skills is on p. 816.

🌐 **SWEATER PATTERN** Each row of the sweater is a frieze pattern. Match the row with its classification.

A. TRHVG   **B.** TR   **C.** TRVG   **D.** THG

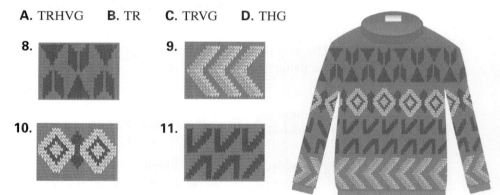

8.

9.

10.

11.

CLASSIFYING PATTERNS Name the isometries that map the frieze pattern onto itself.

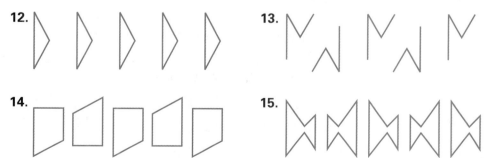

12.

13.

14.

15.

STUDENT HELP

↳ **HOMEWORK HELP**
Example 1: Exs. 8–15
Example 2: Exs. 16–23
Example 3: Exs. 32–39
Example 4: Exs. 40–43

DESCRIBING TRANSFORMATIONS Use the diagram of the frieze pattern.

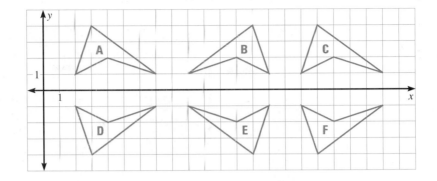

16. Is there a reflection in a vertical line? If so, describe the reflection(s).

17. Is there a reflection in a horizontal line? If so, describe the reflection(s).

18. Name and describe the transformation that maps A onto F.

19. Name and describe the transformation that maps D onto B.

20. Classify the frieze pattern.

🌐 **PET COLLARS** In Exercises 21–23, use the chart on page 438 to classify the frieze pattern on the pet collars.

21.

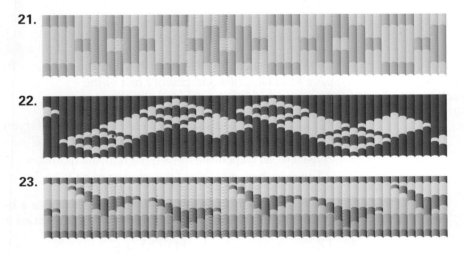

22.

23.

24. 🖳 **TECHNOLOGY** Pick one of the seven classifications of patterns and use geometry software to create a frieze pattern of that classification. Print and color your frieze pattern.

25. DATA COLLECTION Use a library, magazines, or some other reference source to find examples of frieze patterns. How many of the seven classifications of patterns can you find?

CREATING A FRIEZE PATTERN Use the design below to create a frieze pattern with the given classification.

26. TR

27. TV

28. TG

29. THG

30. TRVG

31. TRHVG

NIKKO MEMORIAL
The building shown is a memorial to Tokugawa Ieyasu (1543–1616), the founder of the Tokugawa Shogunate.

JAPANESE PATTERNS The patterns shown were used in Japan during the Tokugawa Shogunate. Classify the frieze patterns.

32.

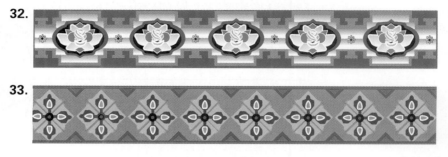

33.

34.

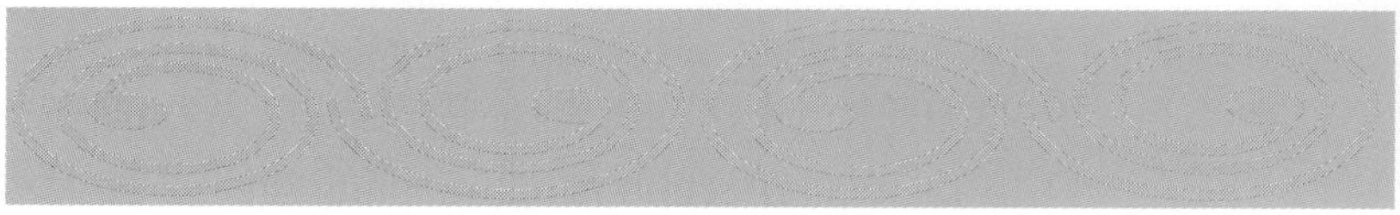

POTTERY In Exercises 35–37, use the pottery shown below. This pottery was created by the Acoma Indians. The Acoma pueblo is America's oldest continually inhabited city.

35. Identify any frieze patterns on the pottery.

36. Classify the frieze pattern(s) you found in Exercise 35.

37. Create your own frieze pattern similar to the patterns shown on the pottery.

38. Look back to the southwestern pottery on page 437. Describe and classify one of the frieze patterns on the pottery.

39. **LOGICAL REASONING** You are decorating a large circular vase and decide to place a frieze pattern around its base. You want the pattern to consist of ten repetitions of a design. If the diameter of the base is about 9.5 inches, how wide should each design be?

TILING In Exercises 40–42, use the tile to create a border pattern with the given classification. Your border should consist of one row of tiles.

40. TR   **41.** TRVG    **42.** TRHVG

43. *Writing* Explain how the design of the tiles in Exercises 40–42 is a factor in the classification of the patterns. For instance, could the tile in Exercise 40 be used to create a single row of tiles classified as THG?

CRITICAL THINKING Explain why the combination is not a category for frieze pattern classification.

44. TVG   **45.** THV   **46.** TRG

STUDENT HELP

INTERNET HOMEWORK HELP
Visit our Web site www.mcdougallittell.com for help with Exs. 47 and 48.

USING THE COORDINATE PLANE **The figure shown in the coordinate plane is part of a frieze pattern with the given classification. Copy the graph and draw the figures needed to complete the pattern.**

47. TR

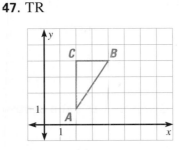

48. TRVG

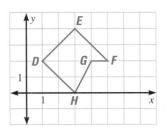

Test Preparation

MULTI-STEP PROBLEM **In Exercises 49–52, use the following information.**

In Celtic art and design, border patterns are used quite frequently, especially in jewelry. Three different designs are shown.

A.

B.

C.

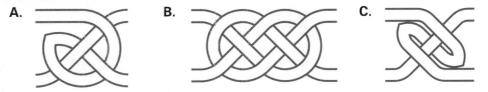

49. Use translations to create a frieze pattern of each design.

50. Classify each frieze pattern that you created.

51. Which design does not have rotational symmetry? Use rotations to create a new frieze pattern of this design.

52. *Writing* If a design has 180° rotational symmetry, it cannot be used to create a frieze pattern with classification T. Explain why not.

★ Challenge

53. **TREE DIAGRAM** The following tree diagram can help classify frieze patterns. Copy the tree diagram and fill in the missing parts.

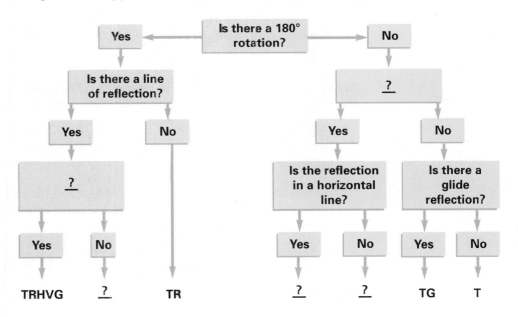

MIXED REVIEW

RATIOS Find the ratio of girls to boys in a class, given the number of boys and the total number of students. **(Skills Review for 8.1)**

54. 12 boys, 23 students

55. 8 boys, 21 students

56. 3 boys, 13 students

57. 19 boys, 35 students

58. 11 boys, 18 students

59. 10 boys, 20 students

PROPERTIES OF MEDIANS Given that *D* is the centroid of $\triangle ABC$, find the value of each variable. **(Review 5.3)**

60.

61.

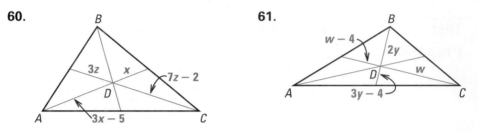

FINDING AREA Find the area of the quadrilateral. **(Review 6.7)**

62.

63.

64.

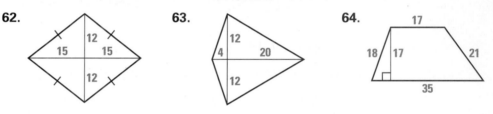

QUIZ 2

Self-Test for Lessons 7.4–7.6

Write the coordinates of the vertices *A'*, *B'*, and *C'* after $\triangle ABC$ is translated by the given vector. **(Lesson 7.4)**

1. $\langle 1, 3 \rangle$

2. $\langle -3, 4 \rangle$

3. $\langle -2, -4 \rangle$

4. $\langle 5, 2 \rangle$

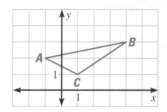

In Exercises 5 and 6, sketch the image of $\triangle PQR$ after a composition using the given transformations in the order they appear. **(Lesson 7.5)**

5. $P(5, 1)$, $Q(3, 4)$, $R(0, 1)$
Translation: $(x, y) \rightarrow (x - 2, y - 4)$
Reflection: in the *y*-axis

6. $P(7, 2)$, $Q(3, 1)$, $R(6, -1)$
Translation: $(x, y) \rightarrow (x - 4, y + 3)$
Rotation: 90° clockwise about origin

7. 🌐 **MUSICAL NOTES** Do the notes shown form a frieze pattern? If so, classify the frieze pattern. **(Lesson 7.6)**

Chapter Summary

WHAT did you learn?

Identify types of rigid transformations. **(7.1)**

Use properties of reflections. **(7.2)**

Relate reflections and line symmetry. **(7.2)**

Relate rotations and rotational symmetry. **(7.3)**

Use properties of translations. **(7.4)**

Use properties of glide reflections. **(7.5)**

Classify frieze patterns. **(7.6)**

WHY did you learn it?

Plan a stencil pattern, using one design repeated many times. **(p. 401)**

Choose the location of a telephone pole so that the length of the cable is a minimum. **(p. 405)**

Understand the construction of the mirrors in a kaleidoscope. **(p. 406)**

Use rotational symmetry to design a logo. **(p. 415)**

Use vectors to describe the path of a hot-air balloon. **(p. 427)**

Describe the transformations in patterns in architecture. **(p. 435)**

Identify the frieze patterns in pottery. **(p. 442)**

How does Chapter 7 fit into the BIGGER PICTURE of geometry?

In this chapter, you learned that the basic rigid transformations in the plane are reflections, rotations, translations, and glide reflections. Rigid transformations are closely connected to the concept of congruence. That is, two plane figures are congruent if and only if one can be mapped onto the other by exactly one rigid transformation or by a composition of rigid transformations. In the next chapter, you will study transformations that are not rigid. You will learn that some nonrigid transformations are closely connected to the concept of similarity.

STUDY STRATEGY

How did making sample exercises help you?

Some sample exercises you made, following the **Study Strategy** on p. 394, may resemble these.

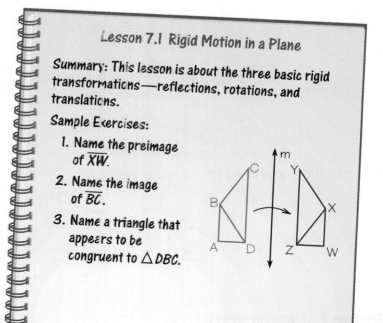

Lesson 7.1 Rigid Motion in a Plane

Summary: This lesson is about the three basic rigid transformations—reflections, rotations, and translations.

Sample Exercises:

1. Name the preimage of $\overline{XW}$.

2. Name the image of $\overline{BC}$.

3. Name a triangle that appears to be congruent to $\triangle DBC$.

Chapter Review

- image, p. 396
- preimage, p. 396
- transformation, p. 396
- isometry, p. 397
- reflection, p. 404

- line of reflection, p. 404
- line of symmetry, p. 406
- rotation, p. 412
- center of rotation, p. 412
- angle of rotation, p. 412

- rotational symmetry, p. 415
- translation, p. 421
- vector, p. 423
- initial point, p. 423
- terminal point, p. 423

- component form, p. 423
- glide reflection, p. 430
- composition, p. 431
- frieze pattern, or border pattern, p. 437

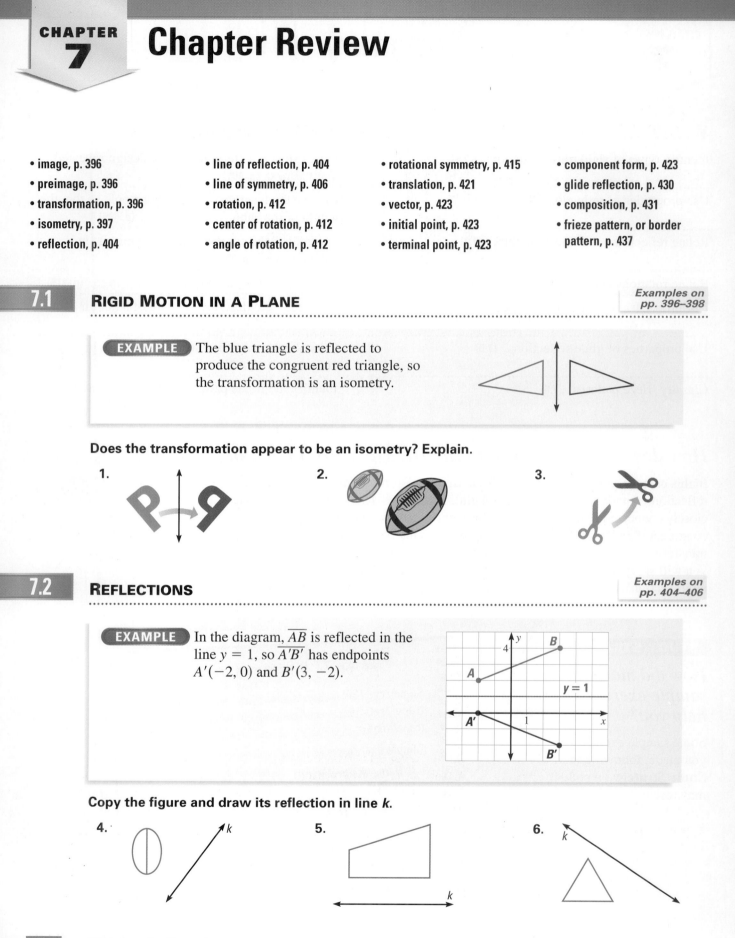

7.1 RIGID MOTION IN A PLANE

Examples on pp. 396–398

EXAMPLE The blue triangle is reflected to produce the congruent red triangle, so the transformation is an isometry.

Does the transformation appear to be an isometry? Explain.

1.

2.

3.

7.2 REFLECTIONS

Examples on pp. 404–406

EXAMPLE In the diagram, $\overline{AB}$ is reflected in the line $y = 1$, so $\overline{A'B'}$ has endpoints $A'(-2, 0)$ and $B'(3, -2)$.

$y = 1$

Copy the figure and draw its reflection in line _k_.

4.

5.

6.

ROTATIONS

Examples on
pp. 412–415

EXAMPLE In the diagram, $\triangle FGH$ is rotated 90° clockwise about the origin.

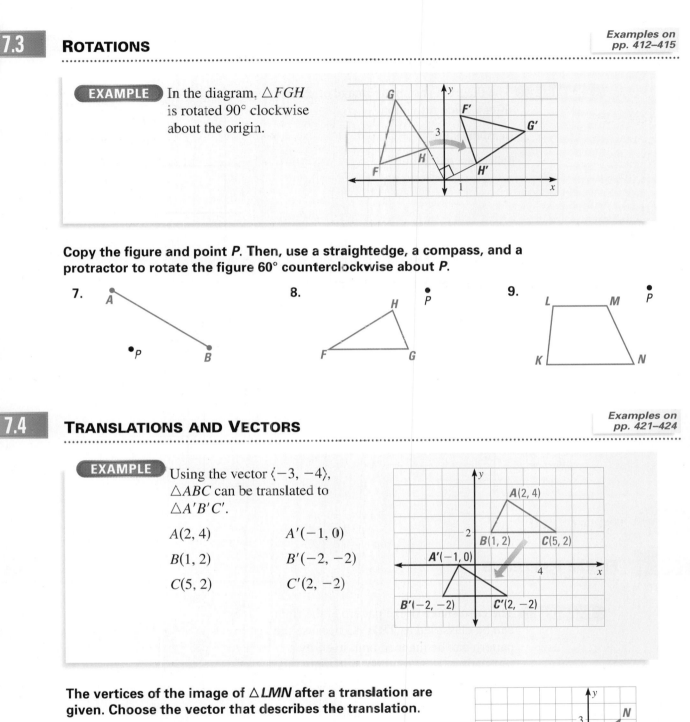

Copy the figure and point *P*. Then, use a straightedge, a compass, and a protractor to rotate the figure 60° counterclockwise about *P*.

7.

8.

9.

TRANSLATIONS AND VECTORS

Examples on
pp. 421–424

EXAMPLE Using the vector $\langle -3, -4 \rangle$, $\triangle ABC$ can be translated to $\triangle A'B'C'$.

$A(2, 4)$	$A'(-1, 0)$
$B(1, 2)$	$B'(-2, -2)$
$C(5, 2)$	$C'(2, -2)$

The vertices of the image of $\triangle LMN$ after a translation are given. Choose the vector that describes the translation.

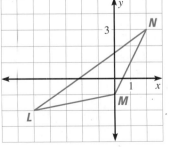

10. $L'(-1, -3), M'(4, -2), N'(6, 2)$ **A.** $\overrightarrow{PQ} = \langle 0, 3 \rangle$

11. $L'(-5, 1), M'(0, 2), N'(2, 6)$ **B.** $\overrightarrow{PQ} = \langle -2, 5 \rangle$

12. $L'(-3, 2), M'(2, 3), N'(4, 7)$ **C.** $\overrightarrow{PQ} = \langle 4, -1 \rangle$

13. $L'(-7, 3), M'(-2, 4), N'(0, 8)$ **D.** $\overrightarrow{PQ} = \langle 2, 4 \rangle$

GLIDE REFLECTIONS AND COMPOSITIONS

Examples on pp. 430–432

EXAMPLE The diagram shows the image of △*XYZ* after a glide reflection.

Translation: $(x, y) \rightarrow (x + 4, y)$

Reflection: in the line $y = 3$

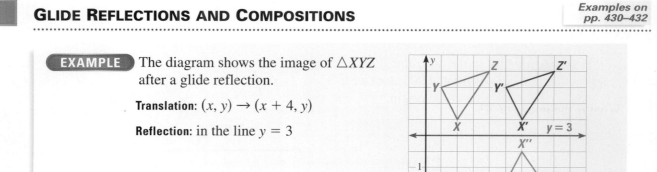

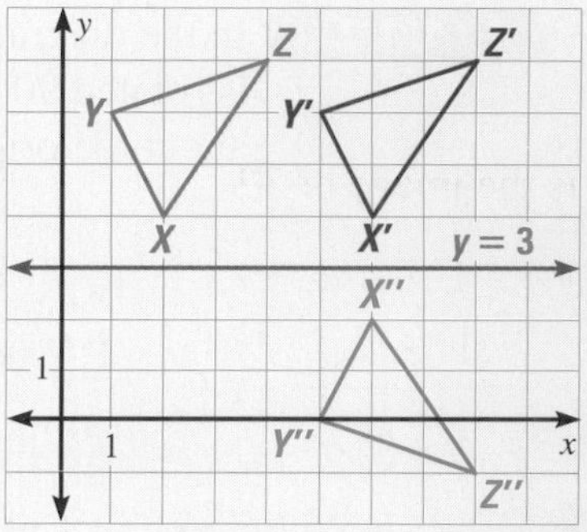

Describe the composition of the transformations.

14.

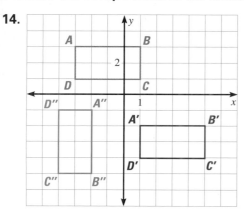

15.

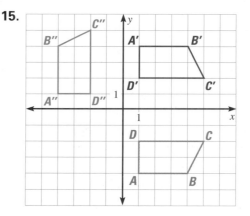

FRIEZE PATTERNS

Examples on pp. 437–439

EXAMPLE The corn snake frieze pattern at the right can be classified as TRHVG because the pattern can be mapped onto itself by a translation, 180° rotation, horizontal line reflection, vertical line reflection, and glide reflection.

Classify the snakeskin frieze pattern.

16. Rainbow boa

17. Gray-banded kingsnake

In Exercises 1–4, use the diagram.

1. Identify the transformation $\triangle RST \rightarrow \triangle XYZ$.

2. Is $\overline{RT}$ congruent to $\overline{XZ}$?

3. What is the image of T?

4. What is the preimage of Y?

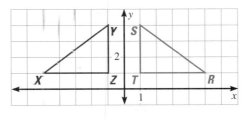

5. Sketch a polygon that has line symmetry, but not rotational symmetry.

6. Sketch a polygon that has rotational symmetry, but not line symmetry.

Use the diagram, in which lines *m* and *n* are lines of reflection.

7. Identify the transformation that maps figure T onto figure T'.

8. Identify the transformation that maps figure T onto figure T''.

9. If the measure of the acute angle between m and n is 85°, what is the angle of rotation from figure T to figure T''?

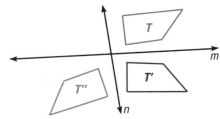

In Exercises 10–12, use the diagram, in which $k \parallel m$.

10. Identify the transformation that maps figure R onto figure R'.

11. Identify the transformation that maps figure R onto figure R''.

12. If the distance between k and m is 5 units, what is the distance between corresponding parts of figure R and figure R''?

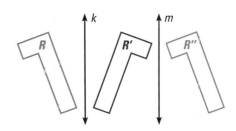

13. What type of transformation is a composition of a translation followed by a reflection in a line parallel to the translation vector?

Give an example of the described composition of transformations.

14. The order in which two transformations are performed affects the final image.

15. The order in which two transformations are performed does not affect the final image.

🌐 **FLAGS Identify any symmetry in the flag.**

16. Switzerland

17. Jamaica

18. United Kingdom

Name all of the isometries that map the frieze pattern onto itself.

19.

20.

21.

Chapter Standardized Test

● **TEST-TAKING STRATEGY** Sketch graphs or figures in your test booklet to help you solve the problems. Even though you must keep your answer sheet neat, you can make any kind of mark you want in your test booklet.

1. **MULTIPLE CHOICE** How many lines of symmetry does the polygon at the right have?

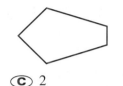

   Ⓐ 0   **Ⓑ** 1   **Ⓒ** 2

   Ⓓ 3   **Ⓔ** More than 3

2. **MULTIPLE CHOICE** The point $P(-2, -11)$ is reflected in the line $y = -1$. What are the coordinates of P'?

   Ⓐ $(-2, -11)$ **Ⓑ** $(-2, -9)$ **Ⓒ** $(-2, 10)$

   Ⓓ $(-2, 9)$ **Ⓔ** $(-2, 11)$

3. **MULTIPLE CHOICE** Suppose $\triangle ABC$ has vertices $A(-8, -2)$, $B(-5, -2)$, and $C(-8, -7)$. If $\triangle ABC$ is rotated 90° counterclockwise about the origin, what are the coordinates of the vertices of $\triangle A'B'C'$?

   Ⓐ $A'(2, -5), B'(2, -8), C'(7, -8)$

   Ⓑ $A'(2, -8), B'(2, -5), C'(8, -7)$

   Ⓒ $A'(7, -8), B'(2, -8), C'(2, -5)$

   Ⓓ $A'(-8, 2), B'(-5, 2), C'(-8, 7)$

   Ⓔ $A'(2, -8), B'(2, -5), C'(7, -8)$

4. **MULTIPLE CHOICE** The transformation below is an isometry. What are the values of the variables?

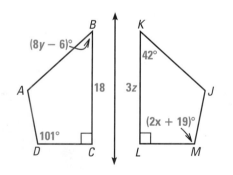

   Ⓐ $x = 41, y = 6, z = 6$

   Ⓑ $x = 40, y = 6, z = 9$

   Ⓒ $x = 50, y = 6, z = 6$

   Ⓓ $x = 6, y = 40, z = 6$

   Ⓔ $x = 41, y = 8, z = 6$

5. **MULTIPLE CHOICE** $\triangle WXY$ has vertices $W(3, 8)$, $X(7, 6)$, and $Y(5, 2)$. What are the coordinates of the vertices of $\triangle W'X'Y'$ after the translation $(x, y) \rightarrow (x - 8, y - 10)$?

   Ⓐ $W'(-5, 18), X'(-3, 12), Y'(-1, 16)$

   Ⓑ $W'(-5, -2), X'(-1, -4), Y'(-3, -8)$

   Ⓒ $W'(11, -2), X'(15, -4), Y'(13, -8)$

   Ⓓ $W'(-2, -5), X'(-1, 4), Y'(-3, -8)$

   Ⓔ $W'(11, 18), X'(15, 16), Y'(13, 12)$

6. **MULTIPLE CHOICE** Name the vector that describes the translation in the diagram.

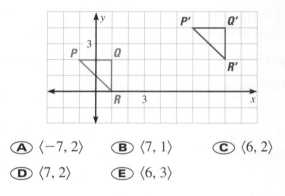

   Ⓐ $\langle -7, 2 \rangle$ **Ⓑ** $\langle 7, 1 \rangle$ **Ⓒ** $\langle 6, 2 \rangle$

   Ⓓ $\langle 7, 2 \rangle$ **Ⓔ** $\langle 6, 3 \rangle$

7. **MULTIPLE CHOICE** What two transformations were performed to obtain $\overline{A''B''}$ in the diagram?

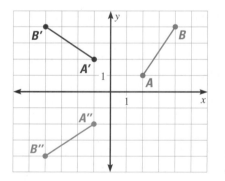

   Ⓐ A rotation and a translation

   Ⓑ A reflection and a translation

   Ⓒ A translation and a translation

   Ⓓ A rotation and a reflection

   Ⓔ A rotation and a rotation

8. MULTIPLE CHOICE What are the isometries that map the Seminole Indian frieze pattern onto itself?

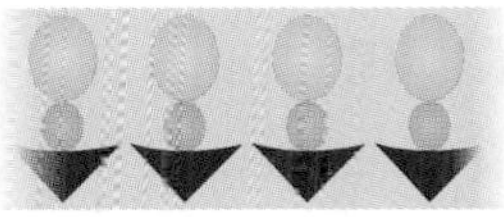

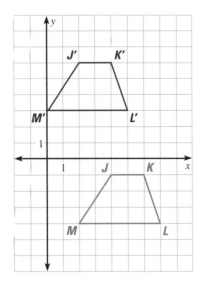

(A) translation, horizontal line reflection

(B) translation, horizontal glide reflection

(C) translation, vertical line reflection

(D) translation, 180° rotation, vertical line reflection

(E) translation, 180° rotation, horizontal glide reflection

9. MULTIPLE CHOICE Using the composition shown, what are the coordinates of the endpoints of $\overline{S''T''}$?

$S(-6, -2), T(-3, -5)$

Reflection: in $y = 1$

Rotation: 90° clockwise about the point $(-3, 2)$

(A) $S''(2, 2), T''(-1, 5)$ (B) $S''(-1, 4), T''(2, 2)$ (C) $S''(-3, 5), T''(2, 0)$

(D) $S''(-6, 4), T''(-3, 7)$ (E) $S''(-1, 5), T''(2, 2)$

MULTI-STEP PROBLEM **Use the alphabet displayed in the typeface below.**

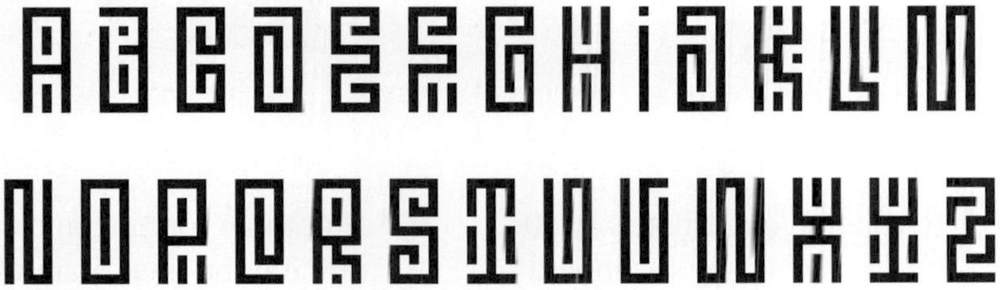

10. Which letters have a vertical line of symmetry?

11. Which letters have a horizontal line of symmetry?

12. Which letters have rotational symmetry?

MULTI-STEP PROBLEM **Use the diagram at the right.**

13. Describe the translation using (a) coordinate notation and (b) a vector in component form.

14. A translation that maps figure $J'K'L'M'$ onto figure $WXYZ$ can be described as follows: $(x, y) \rightarrow (x + 7, y - 2)$. What are the coordinates of the vertices of figure $WXYZ$?

15. A transformation that maps figure $J'K'L'M'$ onto figure $PQRS$, so that figure $PQRS$ has the following vertices: $P(6, -2), Q(6, -4), R(3, -5)$, and $S(3, 0)$. Describe the transformation.

16. Give an example of a transformation that maps figure $J'K'L'M'$ onto figure $J''K''L''M''$, so that figure $JKLM$ maps onto figure $J''K''L''M''$ by a glide reflection.

Investigating Tessellations

OBJECTIVE Create tessellations using polygons.

Materials: cardboard, scissors, protractor, colored pencils, file folder

A *tessellation*, or tiling, of a plane is a collection of tiles that fill the plane with no gaps or overlaps. The tiles in a *regular tessellation* are congruent regular polygons. The tessellation at the right is regular because it is made of congruent regular hexagons.

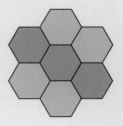

TESSELLATIONS USING ONE POLYGON

Follow these steps to make a tessellation of a quadrilateral.

1 Cut a quadrilateral that is not a rectangle from a piece of cardboard. Trace the shape on a piece of paper.

2 Rotate the quadrilateral 180° so an edge of the cardboard matches an edge of the shape on the paper. Trace the new position of the quadrilateral.

3 Continue rotating and tracing the quadrilateral to make a tessellation. Color your tessellation.

INVESTIGATION

1. Is the quadrilateral tessellation a regular tessellation? Explain.

2. Suppose the quadrilateral tessellation extends forever in all directions. Describe some transformations that map the pattern onto itself.

3. Choose any vertex on your quadrilateral tessellation and measure the angles at that vertex. What is the sum of the measures of the angles? Find the sum of the measures of the angles at a different vertex. Explain why *any* quadrilateral will tessellate.

4. There are only three possible regular tessellations. The hexagonal tessellation is shown at the top of the page. Decide what other regular polygons can be used to create regular tessellations. Explain your reasoning.

5. Draw a scalene triangle on a piece of cardboard and cut it out. Use the shape to create a tessellation. Describe any transformations that can map the tessellation onto itself.

TESSELLATIONS USING MORE THAN ONE POLYGON

In a *semiregular tessellation*, more than one kind of regular polygon is used and the same arrangement of polygons meets at any vertex of the tessellation. You can also make nonregular tessellations with more than one kind of nonregular polygon. As with any tessellation, the sum of the measures of the angles of the polygons at any vertex should be 360°. Here are some examples.

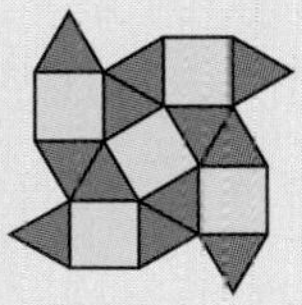

Semiregular: squares and
equilateral triangles

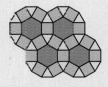

Semiregular: regular hexagons,
squares, and equilateral triangles

Nonregular: pentagons and
isosceles trapezoids

INVESTIGATION

Determine whether the shapes can be used to create a tessellation. If so, sketch the tessellation, and classify it as *semiregular* or *nonregular*.

6. Regular octagon and square

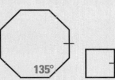

135°

7. Regular pentagon and rectangle

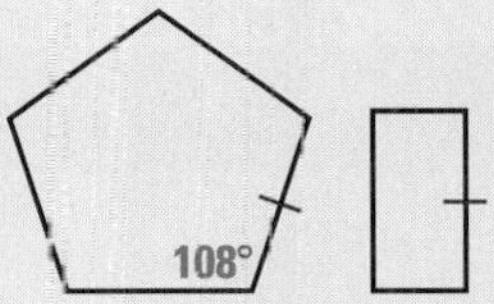

108°

8. Isosceles triangle and parallelogram

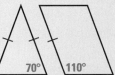

70° 110°

PRESENT YOUR RESULTS

TESSELLATIONS

Colle

Lucy Eaton

Gather your drawings of tessellations and present them in a file folder.

• Include your quadrilateral tessellation.

• Include your answers to Exercises 1–8.

• Summarize what you have learned about tessellations.

• Describe how transformations can be used to map a tessellation onto itself.

EXTENSIONS

• Create your own tessellation using polygons. The sum of the measures of the angles of the polygon at any vertex should be 360°. Color your tessellation.

• Research the Dutch graphic artist M. C. Escher and find examples of tessellations in his work.

SIMILARITY

▶ *How can you use proportions to turn a drawing into a mural?*

APPLICATION: Scale Drawing

Murals are often created by enlarging an original drawing. Different methods are used to make sure that all parts of the enlargement are in proportion to the original drawing.

One common method used in mural making is to enlarge each piece of art by the same percentage. If a drawing is enlarged to 300% of its original size, then the length and width of the enlargement will each be three times the size of the original.

Think & Discuss

1. Describe some other common methods used to enlarge a drawing.

2. Estimate how much larger Figure 2 is than Figure 1. Can you discover a way to check your estimate?

Figure 1

Figure 2

Learn More About It

You will learn another way to enlarge a drawing in Example 4 on p. 490.

 APPLICATION LINK Visit www.mcdougallittell.com for more information about scale drawings.

Study Guide

PREVIEW

What's the chapter about?

Chapter 8 is about **similar polygons**. Two polygons are similar if their corresponding angles are congruent and the lengths of corresponding sides are proportional. In Chapter 8, you'll learn

- four ways to prove triangles are similar given information about their sides and angles.
- how to use similar polygons to solve real-life problems.

KEY VOCABULARY

▶ **Review**
- angle bisector, p. 36
- slope, p. 165
- transformation, p. 396
- image, p. 396
- preimage, p. 396

▶ **New**
- ratio, p. 457
- proportion, p. 459
- means, p. 459
- extremes, p. 459
- geometric mean, p. 466

- similar polygons, p. 473
- scale factor, p. 474
- dilation, p. 506
- reduction, p. 506
- enlargement, p. 506

PREPARE

Are you ready for the chapter?

SKILL REVIEW Do these exercises to review key skills that you'll apply in this chapter. See the given **reference page** if there is something you don't understand.

STUDENT HELP

↳ **Study Tip**
"Student Help" boxes throughout the chapter give you study tips and tell you where to look for extra help in this book and on the Internet.

Find the perimeter of the figure. (Review pp. 51–54)

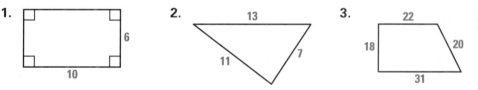

1. [rectangle] 6, 10

2. [triangle] 13, 11, 7

3. [trapezoid] 22, 18, 20, 31

Find the slope of the line that passes through the points. (Review Example 2, p. 165)

4. $A(0, 0)$ and $B(4, 2)$ **5.** $C(-1, 2)$ and $D(6, 5)$ **6.** $E(0, 3)$ and $F(-4, -8)$

STUDY
STRATEGY

Here's a study strategy!

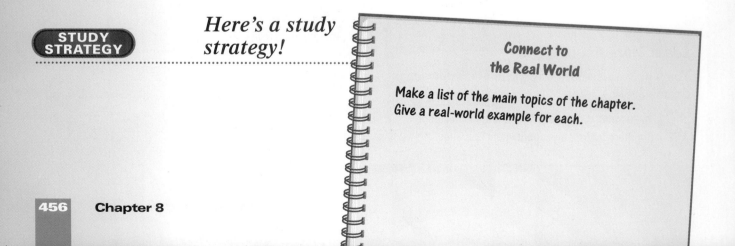

Connect to the Real World

Make a list of the main topics of the chapter. Give a real-world example for each.

Ratio and Proportion

What you should learn

GOAL 1 Find and simplify the ratio of two numbers.

GOAL 2 Use proportions to solve **real-life** problems, such as computing the width of a painting in **Example 6**.

Why you should learn it

▼ To solve **real-life** problems, such as using a scale model to determine the dimensions of a sculpture like the baseball glove below and the baseball bat in **Exs. 51–53**.

GOAL 1 COMPUTING RATIOS

If a and b are two quantities that are measured in the *same* units, then the **ratio of a to b** is $\frac{a}{b}$. The ratio of a to b can also be written as $a:b$. Because a ratio is a quotient, its denominator cannot be zero.

Ratios are usually expressed in simplified form. For instance, the ratio of $6:8$ is usually simplified as $3:4$.

EXAMPLE 1 *Simplifying Ratios*

Simplify the ratios.

a. $\dfrac{12 \text{ cm}}{4 \text{ m}}$
b. $\dfrac{6 \text{ ft}}{18 \text{ in.}}$

SOLUTION

To simplify ratios with unlike units, convert to like units so that the units divide out. Then simplify the fraction, if possible.

a. $\dfrac{12 \text{ cm}}{4 \text{ m}} = \dfrac{12 \text{ cm}}{4 \cdot \mathbf{100 \text{ cm}}} = \dfrac{12}{400} = \dfrac{3}{100}$
b. $\dfrac{6 \text{ ft}}{18 \text{ in.}} = \dfrac{6 \cdot \mathbf{12 \text{ in.}}}{18 \text{ in.}} = \dfrac{72}{18} = \dfrac{4}{1}$

▶ ACTIVITY
Developing Concepts

Investigating Ratios

1 Use a tape measure to measure the circumference of the base of your thumb, the circumference of your wrist, and the circumference of your neck. Record the results in a table.

2 Compute the ratio of your wrist measurement to your thumb measurement. Then, compute the ratio of your neck measurement to your wrist measurement.

3 Compare the two ratios.

4 Compare your ratios to those of others in the class.

5 Does it matter whether you record your measurements all in inches or all in centimeters? Explain.

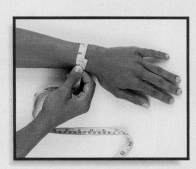

STUDENT HELP

Look Back
For help with perimeter,
see p. 51.

EXAMPLE 2   *Using Ratios*

The perimeter of rectangle *ABCD* is 60 centimeters. The
ratio of *AB*:*BC* is 3:2. Find the length and width of the
rectangle.

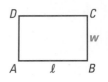

SOLUTION

Because the ratio of *AB*:*BC* is 3:2, you can represent the length *AB* as 3*x* and the
width *BC* as 2*x*.

$2\ell + 2w = P$	**Formula for perimeter of rectangle**
$2(3x) + 2(2x) = 60$	**Substitute for ℓ, w, and P.**
$6x + 4x = 60$	**Multiply.**
$10x = 60$	**Combine like terms.**
$x = 6$	**Divide each side by 10.**

▶ So, *ABCD* has a length of 18 centimeters and a width of 12 centimeters.

Using Algebra

EXAMPLE 3   *Using Extended Ratios*

The measure of the angles in △*JKL* are in the *extended
ratio* of 1:2:3. Find the measures of the angles.

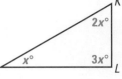

SOLUTION

Begin by sketching a triangle. Then use the extended
ratio of 1:2:3 to label the measures of the angles as $x°$, $2x°$, and $3x°$.

$x° + 2x° + 3x° = 180°$	**Triangle Sum Theorem**
$6x = 180$	**Combine like terms.**
$x = 30$	**Divide each side by 6.**

▶ So, the angle measures are 30°, 2(30°) = 60°, and 3(30°) = 90°.

**Logical
Reasoning**

EXAMPLE 4   *Using Ratios*

The ratios of the side lengths of △*DEF* to the
corresponding side lengths of △*ABC* are 2:1.
Find the unknown lengths.

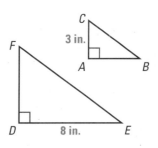

SOLUTION

• *DE* is twice *AB* and *DE* = 8, so $AB = \frac{1}{2}(8) = 4$.

• Using the Pythagorean Theorem, you can
  determine that *BC* = 5.

• *DF* is twice *AC* and *AC* = 3, so *DF* = 2(3) = 6.

• *EF* is twice *BC* and *BC* = 5, so *EF* = 2(5) = 10.

STUDENT HELP

Look Back
For help with the
Pythagorean Theorem,
see p. 20.

GOAL 2 **USING PROPORTIONS**

An equation that equates two ratios is a **proportion**. For instance, if the ratio $\frac{a}{b}$ is equal to the ratio $\frac{c}{d}$, then the following proportion can be written:

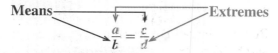

$$\frac{a}{b} = \frac{c}{d}$$

Means — Extremes

The numbers a and d are the **extremes** of the proportion. The numbers b and c are the **means** of the proportion.

PROPERTIES OF PROPORTIONS

1. **CROSS PRODUCT PROPERTY** The product of the extremes equals the product of the means.

$$\text{If } \frac{a}{b} = \frac{c}{d}, \text{ then } ad = bc.$$

2. **RECIPROCAL PROPERTY** If two ratios are equal, then their reciprocals are also equal.

$$\text{If } \frac{a}{b} = \frac{c}{d}, \text{ then } \frac{b}{a} = \frac{d}{c}.$$

STUDENT HELP

▶ **Skills Review**
For help with reciprocals, see p. 788.

To *solve the proportion* you find the value of the variable.

Using Algebra

EXAMPLE 5 *Solving Proportions*

Solve the proportions.

a. $\dfrac{4}{x} = \dfrac{5}{7}$

b. $\dfrac{3}{y+2} = \dfrac{2}{y}$

SOLUTION

a. $\dfrac{4}{x} = \dfrac{5}{7}$ Write original proportion.

$\dfrac{x}{4} = \dfrac{7}{5}$ Reciprocal property

$x = 4\left(\dfrac{7}{5}\right)$ Multiply each side by 4.

$x = \dfrac{28}{5}$ Simplify.

b. $\dfrac{3}{y+2} = \dfrac{2}{y}$ Write original proportion.

$3y = 2(y+2)$ Cross product property

$3y = 2y + 4$ Distributive property

$y = 4$ Subtract 2y from each side.

▶ The solution is 4. Check this by substituting in the original proportion.

EXAMPLE 6 **Solving a Proportion**

 PAINTING The photo shows Bev Dolittle's painting *Music in the Wind*. Her actual painting is 12 inches high. How wide is it?

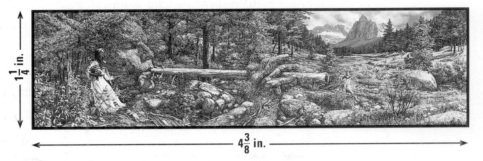

$1\frac{1}{4}$ in.

$4\frac{3}{8}$ in.

SOLUTION

You can reason that in the photograph all measurements of the artist's painting have been reduced by the same ratio. That is, the ratio of the actual width to the reduced width is equal to the ratio of the actual height to the reduced height. The photograph is $1\frac{1}{4}$ inches by $4\frac{3}{8}$ inches.

PROBLEM SOLVING STRATEGY

VERBAL MODEL

$$\frac{\boxed{\text{Width of painting}}}{\boxed{\text{Width of photo}}} = \frac{\boxed{\text{Height of painting}}}{\boxed{\text{Height of photo}}}$$

LABELS

Width of painting = x Height of painting = **12**   (inches)

Width of photo = **4.375**   Height of photo = **1.25**   (inches)

REASONING

$$\frac{x}{4.375} = \frac{12}{1.25}$$ **Substitute.**

$$x = 4.375\left(\frac{12}{1.25}\right)$$ **Multiply each side by 4.375.**

$$x = 42$$ **Use a calculator.**

▶ So, the actual painting is 42 inches wide.

EXAMPLE 7 **Solving a Proportion**

Estimate the length of the hidden flute in Bev Doolittle's actual painting.

SOLUTION

In the photo, the flute is about $1\frac{7}{8}$ inches long. Using the reasoning from above you can say that:

$$\frac{\text{Length of flute in painting}}{\text{Length of flute in photo}} = \frac{\text{Height of painting}}{\text{Height of photo}}.$$

$$\frac{f}{1.875} = \frac{12}{1.25}$$ **Substitute.**

$$f = 18$$ **Multiply each side by 1.875 and simplify.**

▶ So, the flute is about 18 inches long in the painting.

GUIDED PRACTICE

Vocabulary Check ✓   1. In the proportion $\frac{r}{s} = \frac{p}{q}$, the variables s and p are the __?__ of the proportion and r and q are the __?__ of the proportion.

Concept Check ✓   **ERROR ANALYSIS** In Exercises 2 and 3, find and correct the errors.

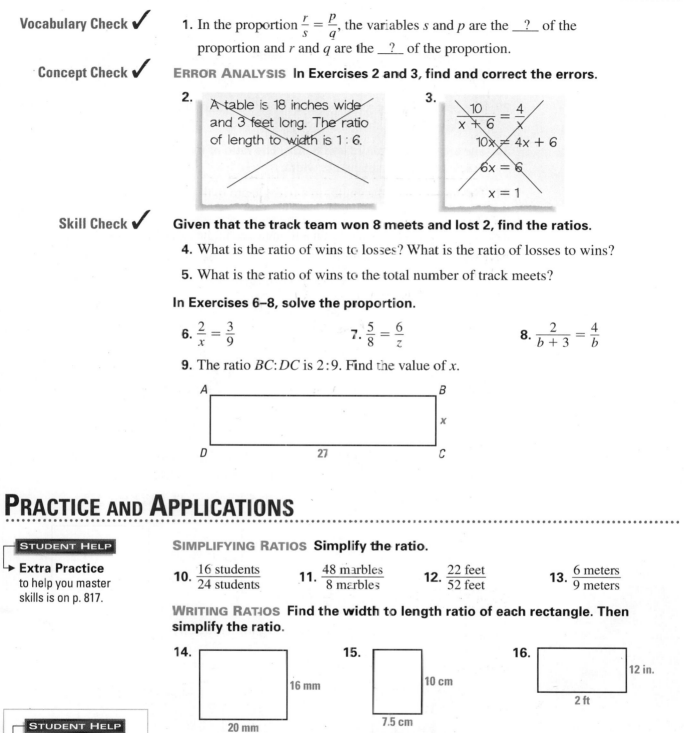

2. A table is 18 inches wide and 3 feet long. The ratio of length to width is 1 : 6.

3. $\frac{10}{x+6} = \frac{4}{x}$

$10x = 4x + 6$

$6x = 6$

$x = 1$

Skill Check ✓   **Given that the track team won 8 meets and lost 2, find the ratios.**

4. What is the ratio of wins to losses? What is the ratio of losses to wins?

5. What is the ratio of wins to the total number of track meets?

In Exercises 6–8, solve the proportion.

6. $\frac{2}{x} = \frac{3}{9}$ 7. $\frac{5}{8} = \frac{6}{z}$ 8. $\frac{2}{b+3} = \frac{4}{b}$

9. The ratio $BC : DC$ is $2 : 9$. Find the value of x.

PRACTICE AND APPLICATIONS

STUDENT HELP

▶ **Extra Practice**
to help you master
skills is on p. 817.

SIMPLIFYING RATIOS Simplify the ratio.

10. $\frac{16 \text{ students}}{24 \text{ students}}$ 11. $\frac{48 \text{ marbles}}{8 \text{ marbles}}$ 12. $\frac{22 \text{ feet}}{52 \text{ feet}}$ 13. $\frac{6 \text{ meters}}{9 \text{ meters}}$

WRITING RATIOS Find the width to length ratio of each rectangle. Then simplify the ratio.

14. 16 mm / 20 mm

15. 10 cm / 7.5 cm

16. 12 in. / 2 ft

STUDENT HELP

▶ HOMEWORK HELP
Example 1: Exs. 10–24
Example 2: Exs. 29, 30
Example 3: Exs. 31, 32
Example 4: Exs. 57, 58

continued on p. 462

CONVERTING UNITS Rewrite the fraction so that the numerator and denominator have the same units. Then simplify.

17. $\frac{3 \text{ ft}}{12 \text{ in.}}$ 18. $\frac{60 \text{ cm}}{1 \text{ m}}$ 19. $\frac{350 \text{ g}}{1 \text{ kg}}$ 20. $\frac{2 \text{ mi}}{3000 \text{ ft}}$

21. $\frac{6 \text{ yd}}{10 \text{ ft}}$ 22. $\frac{2 \text{ lb}}{20 \text{ oz}}$ 23. $\frac{400 \text{ m}}{0.5 \text{ km}}$ 24. $\frac{20 \text{ oz}}{4 \text{ lb}}$

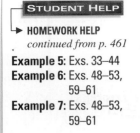

STUDENT HELP

► HOMEWORK HELP
  continued from p. 461
  Example 5: Exs. 33–44
  Example 6: Exs. 48–53,
  59–61
  Example 7: Exs. 48–53,
  59–61

FINDING RATIOS Use the number line to find the ratio of the distances.

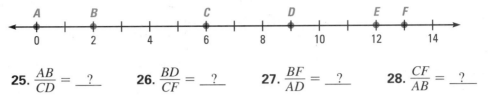

25. $\dfrac{AB}{CD} = $ ___?___   26. $\dfrac{BD}{CF} = $ ___?___   27. $\dfrac{BF}{AD} = $ ___?___   28. $\dfrac{CF}{AB} = $ ___?___

29. The perimeter of a rectangle is 84 feet. The ratio of the width to the length is 2:5. Find the length and the width.

30. The area of a rectangle is 108 cm². The ratio of the width to the length is 3:4. Find the length and the width.

31. The measures of the angles in a triangle are in the extended ratio of 1:4:7. Find the measures of the angles.

32. The measures of the angles in a triangle are in the extended ratio of 2:15:19. Find the measures of the angles.

SOLVING PROPORTIONS Solve the proportion.

33. $\dfrac{x}{4} = \dfrac{5}{7}$ 34. $\dfrac{y}{8} = \dfrac{9}{10}$ 35. $\dfrac{7}{z} = \dfrac{10}{25}$

36. $\dfrac{4}{b} = \dfrac{10}{3}$ 37. $\dfrac{30}{5} = \dfrac{14}{c}$ 38. $\dfrac{16}{3} = \dfrac{d}{6}$

39. $\dfrac{5}{x+3} = \dfrac{4}{x}$ 40. $\dfrac{4}{y-3} = \dfrac{8}{y}$ 41. $\dfrac{7}{2z+5} = \dfrac{3}{z}$

42. $\dfrac{3x-8}{6} = \dfrac{2x}{10}$ 43. $\dfrac{5y-8}{7} = \dfrac{5y}{6}$ 44. $\dfrac{4}{2z+6} = \dfrac{10}{7z-2}$

USING PROPORTIONS In Exercises 45–47, the ratio of the width to the length for each rectangle is given. Solve for the variable.

45. $AB:BC$ is 3:8.   46. $EF:FG$ is 4:5.   47. $JK:KL$ is 2:3.

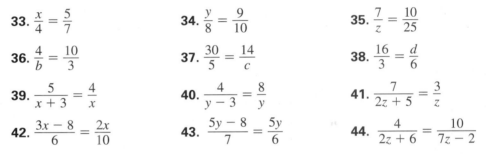

FOCUS ON
APPLICATIONS

SCIENCE CONNECTION Use the following information.

The table gives the ratios of the gravity of four different planets to the gravity of Earth. Round your answers to the nearest whole number.

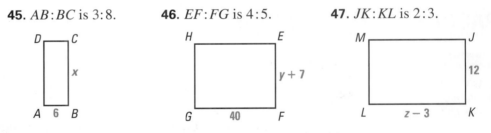

Planet	Venus	Mars	Jupiter	Pluto
Ratio of gravity	$\dfrac{9}{10}$	$\dfrac{38}{100}$	$\dfrac{236}{100}$	$\dfrac{7}{100}$

► **MOON'S GRAVITY**
Neil Armstrong's space suit weighed about 185 pounds on Earth and just over 30 pounds on the moon, due to the weaker force of gravity.

APPLICATION LINK
www.mcdougallittell.com

48. Which of the planets listed above has a gravity closest to the gravity of Earth?

49. Estimate how much a person who weighs 140 pounds on Earth would weigh on Venus, Mars, Jupiter, and Pluto.

50. If a person weighed 46 pounds on Mars, estimate how much he or she would weigh on Earth.

BASEBALL BAT SCULPTURE A huge, free-standing baseball bat sculpture stands outside a sports museum in Louisville, Kentucky. It was patterned after Babe Ruth's 35 inch bat. The sculpture is 120 feet long. Round your answers to the nearest tenth of an inch.

51. How long is the sculpture in inches?

52. The diameter of the sculpture near the base is 9 feet. Estimate the corresponding diameter of Babe Ruth's bat.

53. The diameter of the handle of the sculpture is 3.5 feet. Estimate the diameter of the handle of Babe Ruth's bat.

USING PROPORTIONS In Exercises 54–56, the ratio of two side lengths of the triangle is given. Solve for the variable.

54. $PQ:QR$ is $3:4$.

55. $SU:ST$ is $4:1$.

56. $WX:XV$ is $5:7$.

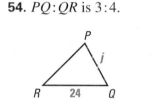

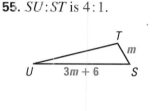

PYTHAGOREAN THEOREM The ratios of the side lengths of △*PQR* to the corresponding side lengths of △*STU* are 1:3. Find the unknown lengths.

57.

58.

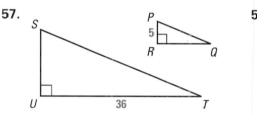

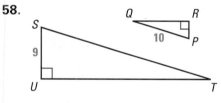

GULLIVER'S TRAVELS In Exercises 59–61, use the following information.
Gulliver's Travels was written by Jonathan Swift in 1726. In the story, Gulliver is shipwrecked and wanders ashore to the island of Lilliput. The average height of the people in Lilliput is 6 inches.

59. Gulliver is 6 feet tall. What is the ratio of his height to the average height of a Lilliputian?

60. After leaving Lilliput, Gulliver visits the island of Brobdingnag. The ratio of the average height of these natives to Gulliver's height is proportional to the ratio of Gulliver's height to the average height of a Lilliputian. What is the average height of a Brobdingnagian?

61. What is the ratio of the average height of a Brobdingnagian to the average height of a Lilliputian?

USING ALGEBRA You are given an extended ratio that compares the lengths of the sides of the triangle. Find the lengths of all unknown sides.

62. $BC:AC:AB$ is $3:4:5$.   **63.** $DE:EF:DF$ is $4:5:6$.   **64.** $GH:HR:GR$ is $5:5:6$.

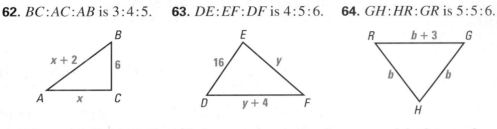

Test Preparation

65. MULTIPLE CHOICE For planting roses, a gardener uses a special mixture of soil that contains sand, peat moss, and compost in the ratio $2:5:3$. How many pounds of compost does she need to add if she uses three 10 pound bags of peat moss?

Ⓐ 12   Ⓑ 14   Ⓒ 15   Ⓓ 18   Ⓔ 20

66. MULTIPLE CHOICE If the measures of the angles of a triangle have the ratio $2:3:7$, the triangle is

Ⓐ acute.   Ⓑ right.   Ⓒ isosceles.

Ⓓ obtuse.   Ⓔ equilateral.

★ Challenge

67. FINDING SEGMENT LENGTHS Suppose the points B and C lie on $\overline{AD}$. What is the length of $\overline{AC}$ if $\dfrac{AB}{BD} = \dfrac{2}{3}$, $\dfrac{CD}{AC} = \dfrac{1}{9}$, and $BD = 24$?

MIXED REVIEW

FINDING UNKNOWN MEASURES Use the figure shown, in which $\triangle STU \cong \triangle XWV$. (Review 4.2)

68. What is the measure of $\angle X$?

69. What is the measure of $\angle V$?

70. What is the measure of $\angle T$?

71. What is the measure of $\angle U$?

72. Which side is congruent to $\overline{TU}$?

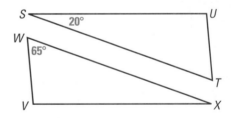

FINDING COORDINATES Find the coordinates of the endpoints of each midsegment shown in red. (Review 5.4 for 8.2)

73.   **74.**   **75.**

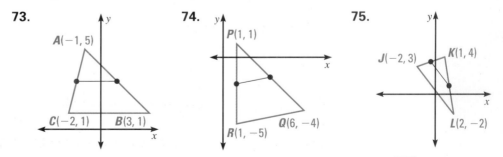

76. A line segment has endpoints $A(1, -3)$ and $B(6, -7)$. Graph $\overline{AB}$ and its image $\overline{A'B'}$ if $\overline{AB}$ is reflected in the line $x = 2$. (Review 7.2)

8.2

Problem Solving in Geometry with Proportions

What you should learn

GOAL 1 Use properties of proportions.

GOAL 2 Use proportions to solve **real-life** problems, such as using the scale of a map in **Exs. 41 and 42**.

Why you should learn it

▼ To solve **real-life** problems, such as using a scale model to calculate the dimensions of the Titanic in **Example 4**.

GOAL 1 USING PROPERTIES OF PROPORTIONS

In Lesson 8.1, you studied the reciprocal property and the cross product property. Two more properties of proportions, which are especially useful in geometry, are given below.

You can use the cross product property and the reciprocal property to help prove these properties in Exercises 36 and 37.

ADDITIONAL PROPERTIES OF PROPORTIONS

3. If $\dfrac{a}{b} = \dfrac{c}{d}$, then $\dfrac{a}{c} = \dfrac{b}{d}$.

4. If $\dfrac{a}{b} = \dfrac{c}{d}$, then $\dfrac{a+b}{b} = \dfrac{c-d}{d}$.

EXAMPLE 1   *Using Properties of Proportions*

Tell whether the statement is true.

a. If $\dfrac{p}{6} = \dfrac{r}{10}$, then $\dfrac{p}{r} = \dfrac{3}{5}$.

b. If $\dfrac{a}{3} = \dfrac{c}{4}$, then $\dfrac{a+3}{3} = \dfrac{c-3}{4}$.

SOLUTION

a. $\dfrac{p}{6} = \dfrac{r}{10}$ **Given**

$\dfrac{p}{r} = \dfrac{6}{10}$ **If $\dfrac{a}{b} = \dfrac{c}{d}$, then $\dfrac{a}{c} = \dfrac{b}{d}$.**

$\dfrac{p}{r} = \dfrac{3}{5}$ **Simplify.**

▶ The statement is true.

b. $\dfrac{a}{3} = \dfrac{c}{4}$ **Given**

$\dfrac{a+3}{3} = \dfrac{c+4}{4}$ **If $\dfrac{a}{b} = \dfrac{c}{d}$, then $\dfrac{a+b}{b} = \dfrac{c+d}{d}$.**

Because $\dfrac{c+4}{4} \neq \dfrac{c+3}{4}$, the conclusions are not equivalent.

▶ The statement is false.

Using Algebra

EXAMPLE 2 *Using Properties of Proportions*

In the diagram $\frac{AB}{BD} = \frac{AC}{CE}$. Find the length of $\overline{BD}$.

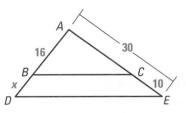

SOLUTION

$\dfrac{AB}{BD} = \dfrac{AC}{CE}$	**Given**
$\dfrac{16}{x} = \dfrac{30-10}{10}$	**Substitute.**
$\dfrac{16}{x} = \dfrac{20}{10}$	**Simplify.**
$20x = 160$	**Cross product property**
$x = 8$	**Divide each side by 20.**

▶ So, the length of $\overline{BD}$ is 8.

· · · · · · · · · ·

STUDENT HELP

HOMEWORK HELP
Visit our Web site
www.mcdougallittell.com
for extra examples.

The **geometric mean** of two positive numbers a and b is the positive number x such that $\frac{a}{x} = \frac{x}{b}$. If you solve this proportion for x, you find that $x = \sqrt{a \cdot b}$, which is a positive number.

For example, the geometric mean of 8 and 18 is **12**, because $\frac{8}{12} = \frac{12}{18}$, and also because $\sqrt{8 \cdot 18} = \sqrt{144} = 12$.

EXAMPLE 3 *Using a Geometric Mean*

PAPER SIZES International standard paper sizes are commonly used all over the world. The various sizes all have the same width-to-length ratios. Two sizes of paper are shown, called A4 and A3. The distance labeled x is the geometric mean of 210 mm and 420 mm. Find the value of x.

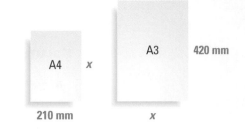

STUDENT HELP

Skills Review
For help with
simplifying square
roots, see p. 799.

SOLUTION

$\dfrac{210}{x} = \dfrac{x}{420}$	**Write proportion.**
$x^2 = 210 \cdot 420$	**Cross product property**
$x = \sqrt{210 \cdot 420}$	**Simplify.**
$x = \sqrt{210 \cdot 210 \cdot 2}$	**Factor.**
$x = 210\sqrt{2}$	**Simplify.**

▶ The geometric mean of 210 and 420 is $210\sqrt{2}$, or about 297. So, the distance labeled x in the diagram is about 297 mm.

GOAL 2 USING PROPORTIONS IN REAL LIFE

In general, when solving word problems that involve proportions, there is more than one correct way to set up the proportion.

EXAMPLE 4 *Solving a Proportion*

REAL LIFE **MODEL BUILDING** A scale model of the Titanic is 107.5 inches long and 11.25 inches wide. The Titanic itself was 882.75 feet long. How wide was it?

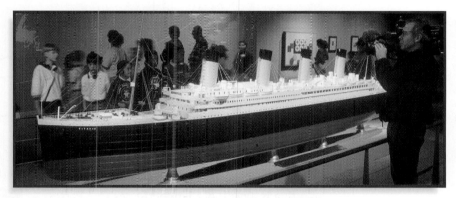

SOLUTION

One way to solve this problem is to set up a proportion that compares the measurements of the Titanic to the measurements of the scale model.

PROBLEM SOLVING STRATEGY

VERBAL MODEL

$$\frac{\text{Width of Titanic}}{\text{Width of model ship}} = \frac{\text{Length of Titanic}}{\text{Length of model ship}}$$

LABELS

Width of Titanic $= x$ (feet)

Width of model ship $= \mathbf{11.25}$ (inches)

Length of Titanic $= \mathbf{882.75}$ (feet)

Length of model ship $= \mathbf{107.5}$ (inches)

REASONING

$$\frac{x \text{ ft}}{11.25 \text{ in.}} = \frac{882.75 \text{ ft}}{107.5 \text{ in.}}$$ **Substitute.**

$$x = \frac{11.25 \cdot (882.75)}{107.5}$$ **Multiply each side by 11.25.**

$$x \approx 92.4$$ **Use a calculator.**

▶ So, the Titanic was about 92.4 feet wide.

Notice that the proportion in Example 4 contains measurements that are not in the same units. When writing a proportion with unlike units, the numerators should have the same units and the denominators should have the same units.

GUIDED PRACTICE

Vocabulary Check ✓

1. If x is the *geometric mean* of two positive numbers a and b, write a proportion that relates a, b, and x.

Concept Check ✓

2. If $\frac{x}{4} = \frac{y}{5}$, then $\frac{x+4}{4} = \frac{?}{5}$.

3. If $\frac{b}{6} = \frac{c}{2}$, then $\frac{b}{c} = \frac{?}{?}$.

Skill Check ✓

4. Decide whether the statement is *true* or *false*.

If $\frac{r}{s} = \frac{6}{15}$, then $\frac{15}{s} = \frac{6}{r}$.

5. Find the geometric mean of 3 and 12.

6. In the diagram $\frac{AB}{BC} = \frac{AD}{DE}$. Substitute the known values into the proportion and solve for DE.

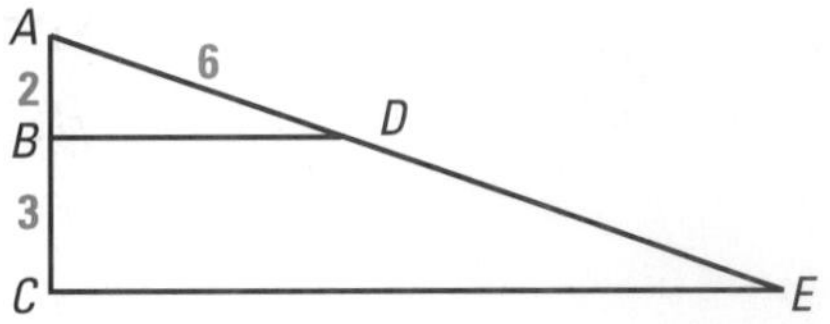

7. 🌐 **UNITED STATES FLAG** The official height-to-width ratio of the United States flag is $1 : 1.9$. If a United States flag is 6 feet high, how wide is it?

8. 🌐 **UNITED STATES FLAG** The blue portion of the United States flag is called the union. What is the ratio of the height of the union to the height of the flag?

PRACTICE AND APPLICATIONS

STUDENT HELP

▶ **Extra Practice**
to help you master
skills is on p. 817.

🧩 **LOGICAL REASONING** Complete the sentence.

9. If $\frac{2}{x} = \frac{7}{y}$, then $\frac{2}{7} = \frac{?}{?}$.

10. If $\frac{x}{6} = \frac{y}{34}$, then $\frac{x}{y} = \frac{?}{?}$.

11. If $\frac{x}{5} = \frac{y}{12}$, then $\frac{x+5}{5} = \frac{?}{?}$.

12. If $\frac{13}{7} = \frac{x}{y}$, then $\frac{20}{7} = \frac{?}{?}$.

🧩 **LOGICAL REASONING** Decide whether the statement is *true* or *false*.

13. If $\frac{7}{a} = \frac{b}{2}$, then $\frac{7+a}{a} = \frac{b+2}{2}$.

14. If $\frac{3}{4} = \frac{p}{r}$, then $\frac{4}{3} = \frac{p}{r}$.

15. If $\frac{c}{6} = \frac{d+2}{10}$, then $\frac{c}{d+2} = \frac{6}{10}$.

16. If $\frac{12+m}{12} = \frac{3+n}{n}$, then $\frac{m}{12} = \frac{3}{n}$.

GEOMETRIC MEAN Find the geometric mean of the two numbers.

17. 3 and 27

18. 4 and 16

19. 7 and 28

20. 2 and 40

21. 8 and 20

22. 5 and 15

STUDENT HELP

▶ **HOMEWORK HELP**
Example 1: Exs. 9–16
Example 2: Exs. 23–28
Example 3: Exs. 17–22,
43
Example 4: Exs. 29–32,
38–42

PROPERTIES OF PROPORTIONS Use the diagram and the given information to find the unknown length.

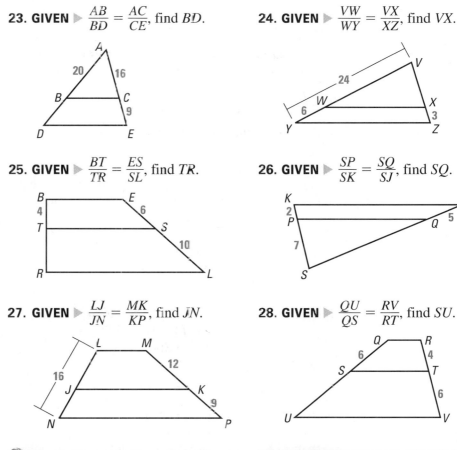

23. GIVEN $\dfrac{AB}{BD} = \dfrac{AC}{CE}$, find BD.

24. GIVEN $\dfrac{VW}{WY} = \dfrac{VX}{XZ}$, find VX.

25. GIVEN $\dfrac{BT}{TR} = \dfrac{ES}{SL}$, find TR.

26. GIVEN $\dfrac{SP}{SK} = \dfrac{SQ}{SJ}$, find SQ.

27. GIVEN $\dfrac{LJ}{JN} = \dfrac{MK}{KP}$, find JN.

28. GIVEN $\dfrac{QU}{QS} = \dfrac{RV}{RT}$, find SU.

🌐 **BLUEPRINTS** In Exercises 29 and 30, use the blueprint of the house in which $\dfrac{1}{16}$ inch = 1 foot. Use a ruler to approximate the dimension.

29. Find the approximate width of the house to the nearest 5 feet.

30. Find the approximate length of the house to the nearest 5 feet.

31. 🌐 **BATTING AVERAGE** The batting average of a baseball player is the ratio of the number of hits to the number of official at-bats. In 1998, Sammy Sosa of the Chicago Cubs had 643 official at-bats and a batting average of .308. Use the following verbal model to find the number of hits Sammy Sosa got.

$$\frac{\textit{Number of hits}}{\textit{Number of at-bats}} = \frac{\textit{Batting average}}{1.000}$$

32. 🌐 **CURRENCY EXCHANGE** Natalie has relatives in Russia. She decides to take a trip to Russia to visit them. She took 500 U.S. dollars to the bank to exchange for Russian rubles. The exchange rate on that day was 22.76 rubles per U.S. dollar. How many rubles did she get in exchange for the 500 U.S. dollars? ▶ Source: Russia Today

33. COORDINATE GEOMETRY The points $(-4, -1)$, $(1, 1)$, and $(x, 5)$ are collinear. Find the value of x by solving the proportion below.

$$\frac{1 - (-1)}{1 - (-4)} = \frac{5 - 1}{x - 1}$$

34. COORDINATE GEOMETRY The points $(2, 8)$, $(6, 18)$, and $(8, y)$ are collinear. Find the value of y by solving the proportion below.

$$\frac{18 - 8}{6 - 2} = \frac{y - 18}{8 - 6}$$

35. CRITICAL THINKING Explain why the method used in Exercises 33 and 34 is a correct way to express that three given points are collinear.

36. ▶ **PROOF** Prove property 3 of proportions (see page 465).

If $\frac{a}{b} = \frac{c}{d}$, then $\frac{a}{c} = \frac{b}{d}$.

37. ▶ **PROOF** Prove property 4 of proportions (see page 465).

If $\frac{a}{b} = \frac{c}{d}$, then $\frac{a + b}{b} = \frac{c + d}{d}$.

🌐 **RAMP DESIGN** Assume that a wheelchair ramp has a slope of $\frac{1}{12}$, which is the maximum slope recommended for a wheelchair ramp.

38. A wheelchair ramp has a 15 foot run. What is its rise?

39. A wheelchair ramp rises 2 feet. What is its run?

40. You are constructing a wheelchair ramp that must rise 3 feet. Because of space limitations, you cannot build a continuous ramp with a length greater than 21 feet. Design a ramp that solves this problem.

HISTORY ▶ **CONNECTION** Part of the Lewis and Clark Trail on which Sacagawea acted as guide is now known as the Lolo Trail. The map, which shows a portion of the trail, has a scale of 1 inch = 6.7 miles.

41. Use a ruler to estimate the distance (measured in a straight line) between Lewis and Clark Grove and Pheasant Camp. Then calculate the actual distance in miles.

42. Estimate the distance along the trail between Portable Soup Camp and Full Stomach Camp. Then calculate the actual distance in miles.

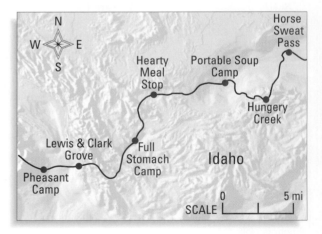

43. *Writing* Size A5 paper has a width of 148 mm and a length of 210 mm. Size A6, which is the next smaller size, shares a dimension with size A5. Use the proportional relationship stated in Example 3 and geometric mean to explain how to determine the length and width of size A6 paper.

44. MULTIPLE CHOICE There are 24 fish in an aquarium. If $\frac{1}{8}$ of the fish are tetras, and $\frac{2}{3}$ of the remaining fish are guppies, how many guppies are in the aquarium?

(A) 2   (B) 3   (C) 10   (D) 14   (E) 16

45. MULTIPLE CHOICE A basketball team had a ratio of wins to losses of $3:1$. After winning 6 games in a row, the team's ratio of wins to losses was $5:1$. How many games had the team won before it won the 6 games in a row?

(A) 3   (B) 6   (C) 9   (D) 15   (E) 24

★ Challenge

46. GOLDEN RECTANGLE A golden rectangle has its length and width in the golden ratio $\frac{1+\sqrt{5}}{2}$. If you cut a square away from a golden rectangle, the shape that remains is also a golden rectangle.

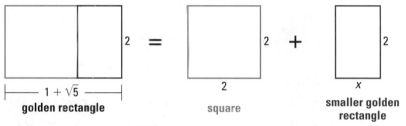

golden rectangle   square   smaller golden rectangle

a. The diagram indicates that $1 + \sqrt{5} = 2 + x$. Find x.

b. To prove that the large and small rectangles are both golden rectangles, show that $\frac{1+\sqrt{5}}{2} = \frac{2}{x}$.

c. Give a decimal approximation for the golden ratio to six decimal places.

MIXED REVIEW

FINDING AREA **Find the area of the figure described.** (Review 1.7)

47. Rectangle: width = 3 m, length = 4 m   **48.** Square: side = 3 cm

49. Triangle: base = 13 cm, height = 4 cm   **50.** Circle: diameter = 11 ft

FINDING ANGLE MEASURES **Find the angle measures.** (Review 6.5 for 8.3)

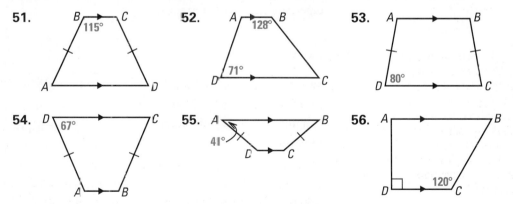

57. PENTAGON Describe any symmetry in a regular pentagon *ABCDE*. (Review 7.2, 7.3)

Making Conjectures about Similarity

▶ **QUESTION** When a figure is enlarged, what appears to be true about corresponding lengths? corresponding angles? corresponding perimeters?

▶ **EXPLORING THE CONCEPT**

1 Photo 1 is an enlargement of Photo 2. Use a ruler to find the length of $\overline{AB}$ in each photo.

2 Write the ratio of the length of $\overline{AB}$ in Photo 1 to the length of $\overline{AB}$ in Photo 2.

3 Use a protractor to find the measure of $\angle 1$ in each photo.

4 Write the ratio of $m\angle 1$ in Photo 1 to $m\angle 1$ in Photo 2.

5 Continue finding the measurements in the photos. Find the ratios of the measurements in Photo 1 to the measurements in Photo 2. Use the same units throughout the activity. Record your results in a table similar to the one shown.

Photo 1

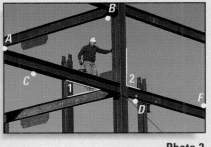

Photo 2

Measurement	Photo 1	Photo 2	Ratio
AB	4.2 cm	3.0 cm	$\frac{4.2}{3} = 1.4$
AF	?	?	?
CD	?	?	?
$m\angle 1$	?	?	?
$m\angle 2$	?	?	?
Perimeter of photo	?	?	?

▶ **DRAWING CONCLUSIONS**

1. Suppose a segment in Photo 2 has a length of 5 centimeters. Estimate the length of the corresponding segment in Photo 1.

2. Suppose an angle in Photo 1 has a measure of 35°. Estimate the measure of the corresponding angle in Photo 2.

3. Make some general conclusions about how corresponding lengths, corresponding angles, and corresponding perimeters are related when a figure is enlarged.

4. **CRITICAL THINKING** Make a conjecture about how corresponding areas are related when a figure is enlarged.

Similar Polygons

What you should learn

GOAL 1 Identify similar polygons.

GOAL 2 Use similar polygons to solve **real-life** problems, such as making an enlargement similar to an original photo in **Example 3**.

Why you should learn it

▼ To solve **real-life** problems, such as comparing television screen sizes in **Exs. 43 and 44**.

GOAL 1 **IDENTIFYING SIMILAR POLYGONS**

When there is a correspondence between two polygons such that their corresponding angles are congruent and the lengths of corresponding sides are proportional the two polygons are called **similar polygons**.

In the diagram, *ABCD* is similar to *EFGH*. The symbol ~ is used to indicate similarity. So, *ABCD* ~ *EFGH*.

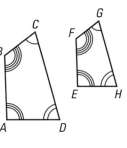

$$\frac{AB}{EF} = \frac{BC}{FG} = \frac{CD}{GH} = \frac{DA}{HE}$$

EXAMPLE 1 *Writing Similarity Statements*

Pentagons *JKLMN* and *STUVW* are similar. List all the pairs of congruent angles. Write the ratios of the corresponding sides in a statement of proportionality.

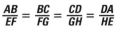

SOLUTION

Because *JKLMN* ~ *STUVW*, you can write $\angle J \cong \angle S$, $\angle K \cong \angle T$, $\angle L \cong \angle U$, $\angle M \cong \angle V$, and $\angle N \cong \angle W$.

You can write the statement of proportionality as follows:

$$\frac{JK}{ST} = \frac{KL}{TU} = \frac{LM}{UV} = \frac{MN}{VW} = \frac{NJ}{WS}.$$

EXAMPLE 2 *Comparing Similar Polygons*

Decide whether the figures are similar. If they are similar, write a similarity statement.

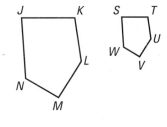

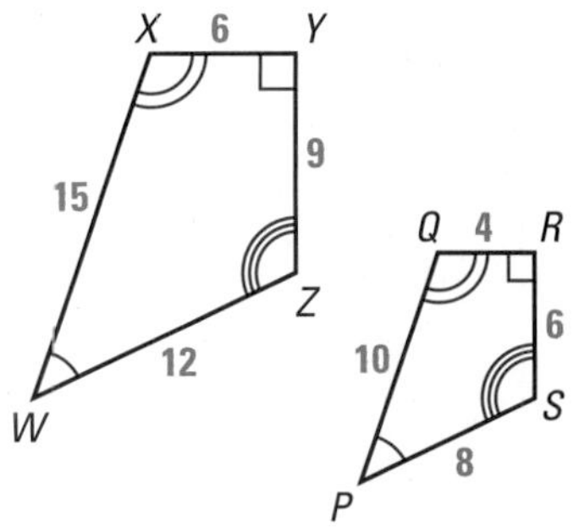

SOLUTION

As shown, the corresponding angles of *WXYZ* and *PQRS* are congruent. Also, the corresponding side lengths are proportional.

$$\frac{WX}{PQ} = \frac{15}{10} = \frac{3}{2} \qquad \frac{XY}{QR} = \frac{6}{4} = \frac{3}{2}$$

$$\frac{YZ}{RS} = \frac{9}{6} = \frac{3}{2} \qquad \frac{ZW}{SP} = \frac{12}{8} = \frac{3}{2}$$

▶ So, the two figures are similar and you can write *WXYZ* ~ *PQRS*.

STUDENT HELP

▶ **Study Tip**
When you refer to similar polygons, their corresponding vertices must be listed in the same order.

EXAMPLE 3 *Comparing Photographic Enlargements*

POSTER DESIGN You have been asked to create a poster to advertise a field trip to see the Liberty Bell. You have a 3.5 inch by 5 inch photo that you want to enlarge. You want the enlargement to be 16 inches wide. How long will it be?

SOLUTION

To find the length of the enlargement, you can compare the enlargement to the original measurements of the photo.

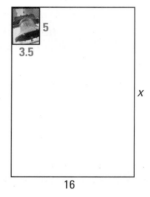

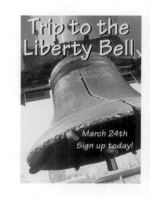

$$\frac{16 \text{ in.}}{3.5 \text{ in.}} = \frac{x \text{ in.}}{5 \text{ in.}}$$

$$x = \frac{16}{3.5} \cdot 5$$

$$x \approx 22.9 \text{ inches}$$

▶ The length of the enlargement will be about 23 inches.

· · · · · · · · · ·

If two polygons are similar, then the ratio of the lengths of two corresponding sides is called the **scale factor**. In Example 2 on the previous page, the common ratio of $\frac{3}{2}$ is the scale factor of *WXYZ* to *PQRS*.

EXAMPLE 4 *Using Similar Polygons*

The rectangular patio around a pool is similar to the pool as shown. Calculate the scale factor of the patio to the pool, and find the ratio of their perimeters.

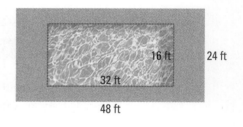

SOLUTION

Because the rectangles are similar, the scale factor of the patio to the pool is 48 ft : 32 ft, which is 3 : 2 in simplified form.

The perimeter of the patio is $2(24) + 2(48) = 144$ feet and the perimeter of the pool is $2(16) + 2(32) = 96$ feet. The ratio of the perimeters is $\frac{144}{96}$, or $\frac{3}{2}$.

· · · · · · · · · ·

Notice in Example 4 that the ratio of the perimeters is the same as the scale factor of the rectangles. This observation is generalized in the following theorem. You are asked to prove Theorem 8.1 for two similar rectangles in Exercise 45.

THEOREM 8.1

If two polygons are similar, then the ratio of their perimeters is equal to the ratios of their corresponding side lengths.

If $KLMN \sim PQRS$, then

$$\frac{KL + LM + MN + NK}{PQ + QR + RS + SP} = \frac{KL}{PQ} = \frac{LM}{QR} = \frac{MN}{RS} = \frac{NK}{SP}.$$

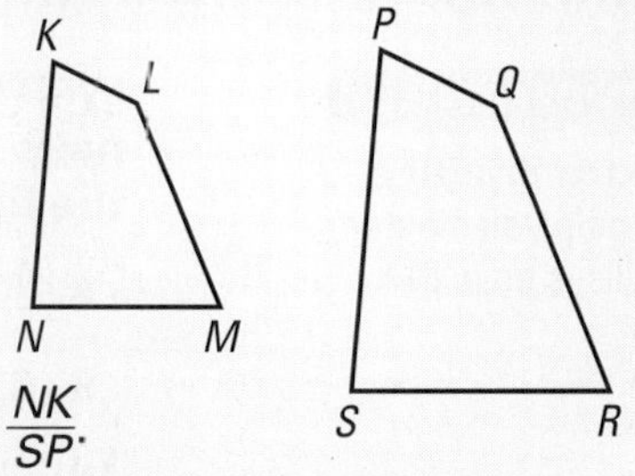

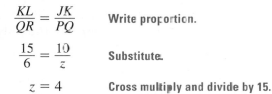

EXAMPLE 5   *Using Similar Polygons*

Using Algebra

Quadrilateral *JKLM* is similar to quadrilateral *PQRS*.

Find the value of z.

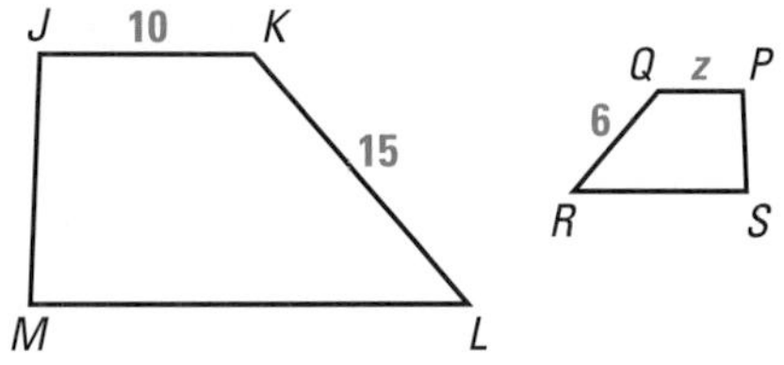

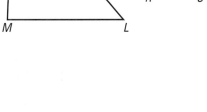

SOLUTION

Set up a proportion that contains *PQ*.

$\dfrac{KL}{QR} = \dfrac{JK}{PQ}$ Write proportion.

$\dfrac{15}{6} = \dfrac{10}{z}$ Substitute.

$z = 4$ Cross multiply and divide by 15.

GUIDED PRACTICE

Vocabulary Check ✓

1. If two polygons are similar, must they also be congruent? Explain.

Concept Check ✓

Decide whether the figures are similar. Explain your reasoning.

2.

3.

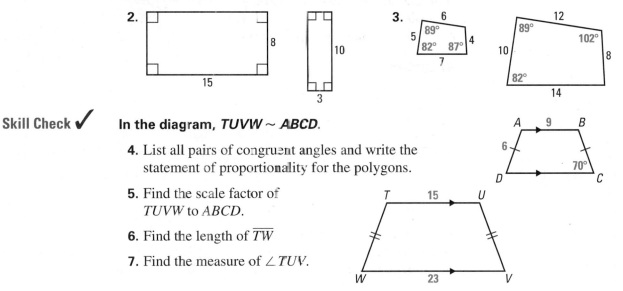

Skill Check ✓

In the diagram, *TUVW* ~ *ABCD*.

4. List all pairs of congruent angles and write the statement of proportionality for the polygons.

5. Find the scale factor of *TUVW* to *ABCD*.

6. Find the length of $\overline{TW}$

7. Find the measure of $\angle TUV$.

PRACTICE AND APPLICATIONS

STUDENT HELP

► **Extra Practice**
to help you master
skills is on p. 817.

WRITING SIMILARITY STATEMENTS Use the information given to list all pairs of congruent angles and write the statement of proportionality for the figures.

8. $\triangle DEF \sim \triangle PQR$

9. $\square JKLM \sim \square WXYZ$

10. $QRSTU \sim ABCDE$

DETERMINING SIMILARITY Decide whether the quadrilaterals are similar. Explain your reasoning.

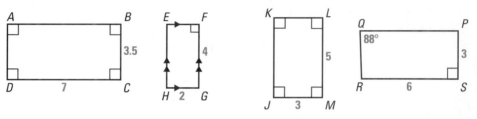

11. $ABCD$ and $FGHE$

12. $ABCD$ and $JKLM$

13. $ABCD$ and $PQRS$

14. $JKLM$ and $PQRS$

DETERMINING SIMILARITY Decide whether the polygons are similar. If so, write a similarity statement.

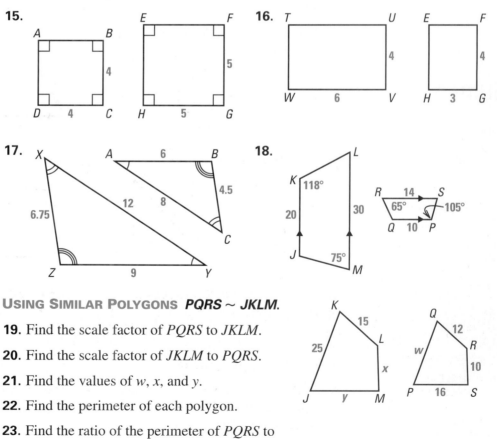

15.

16.

17.

18.

STUDENT HELP

► **HOMEWORK HELP**
Example 1: Exs. 8–10
Example 2: Exs. 11–18
Example 3: Exs. 19–30,
        43, 44
Example 4: Exs. 19–30,
        46–48
Example 5: Exs. 39–42

USING SIMILAR POLYGONS *PQRS ~ JKLM.*

19. Find the scale factor of $PQRS$ to $JKLM$.

20. Find the scale factor of $JKLM$ to $PQRS$.

21. Find the values of w, x, and y.

22. Find the perimeter of each polygon.

23. Find the ratio of the perimeter of $PQRS$ to the perimeter of $JKLM$.

USING SIMILAR POLYGONS $\square ABCD \sim \square EFGH$.

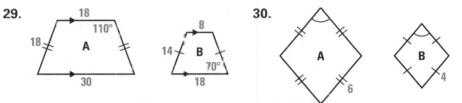

24. Find the scale factor of $\square ABCD$ to $\square EFGH$.

25. Find the length of $\overline{EH}$.

26. Find the measure of $\angle G$.

27. Find the perimeter of $\square EFGH$.

28. Find the ratio of the perimeter of $\square EFGH$ to the perimeter of $\square ABCD$.

DETERMINING SIMILARITY Decide whether the polygons are similar. If so, find the scale factor of Figure A to Figure B.

29.

30.

LOGICAL REASONING Tell whether the polygons are *always*, *sometimes*, or *never* similar.

31. Two isosceles triangles

32. Two regular polygons

33. Two isosceles trapezoids

34. Two rhombuses

35. Two squares

36. An isosceles and a scalene triangle

37. Two equilateral triangles

38. A right and an isosceles triangle

USING ALGEBRA The two polygons are similar. Find the values of x and y.

39.

40.

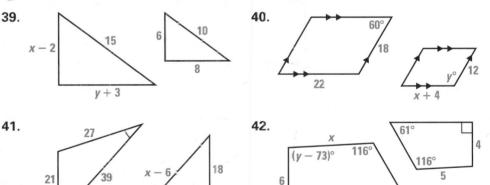

41.

42.

TV SCREENS In Exercises 43 and 44, use the following information.
Television screen sizes are based on the length of the diagonal of the screen. The *aspect ratio* refers to the length to width ratio of the screen. A standard 27 inch analog television screen has an aspect ratio of 4:3. A 27 inch digital television screen has an aspect ratio of 16:9.

43. Make a scale drawing of each television screen. Use proportions and the Pythagorean Theorem to calculate the lengths and widths of the screens in inches.

44. Are the television screens similar? Explain.

8.3 *Similar Polygons*

45. ▶ **PROOF** Prove Theorem 8.1 for two similar rectangles.

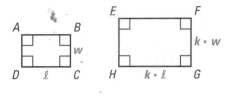

GIVEN ▶ $ABCD \sim EFGH$

PROVE ▶ $\dfrac{\text{perimeter of } ABCD}{\text{perimeter of } EFGH} = \dfrac{AB}{EF}$

46. SCALE The ratio of the perimeter of $WXYZ$ to the perimeter of $QRST$ is $7.5:2$. Find the scale factor of $QRST$ to $WXYZ$.

47. SCALE The ratio of one side of $\triangle CDE$ to the corresponding side of similar $\triangle FGH$ is $2:5$. The perimeter of $\triangle FGH$ is 28 inches. Find the perimeter of $\triangle CDE$.

48. SCALE The perimeter of $\square PQRS$ is 94 centimeters. The perimeter of $\square JKLM$ is 18.8 centimeters, and $\square JKLM \sim \square PQRS$. The lengths of the sides of $\square PQRS$ are 15 centimeters and 32 centimeters. Find the scale factor of $\square PQRS$ to $\square JKLM$, and the lengths of the sides of $\square JKLM$.

Test Preparation

49. MULTI-STEP PROBLEM Use the similar figures shown. The scale factor of Figure 1 to Figure 2 is $7:10$.

a. Copy and complete the table.

	AB	BC	CD	DE	EA
Figure 1	?	?	?	?	?
Figure 2	6.0	3.0	5.0	2.0	4.0

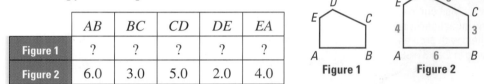

Figure 1   Figure 2

b. Graph the data in the table. Let x represent the length of a side in Figure 1 and let y represent the length of the corresponding side in Figure 2. Determine an equation that relates x and y.

c. ANALYZING DATA The equation you obtained in part (b) should be linear. What is its slope? How does its slope compare to the scale factor?

★ Challenge

🌐 **TOTAL ECLIPSE Use the following information in Exercises 50–52.**
From your perspective on Earth during a total eclipse of the sun, the moon is directly in line with the sun and blocks the sun's rays. The ratio of the radius of the moon to its distance to Earth is about the same as the ratio of the radius of the sun to its distance to Earth.

Distance between Earth and the moon: 240,000 miles

Distance between Earth and the sun: 93,000,000 miles

Radius of the sun: 432,500 miles

50. Make a sketch of Earth, the moon, and the sun during a total eclipse of the sun. Include the given distances in your sketch.

51. Your sketch should contain some similar triangles. Use the similar triangles in your sketch to explain a total eclipse of the sun.

52. Write a statement of proportionality for the similar triangles. Then use the given distances to estimate the radius of the moon.

MIXED REVIEW

FINDING SLOPE **Find the slope of the line that passes through the given points.** (Review 3.6 for 8.4)

53. $A(-1, 4)$, $B(3, 8)$ **54.** $P(0, -7)$, $Q(-6, -3)$ **55.** $J(9, 4)$, $K(2, 5)$

56. $L(-2, -3)$, $M(1, 10)$ **57.** $S(-4, 5)$, $T(2, -2)$ **58.** $Y(-1, 6)$, $Z(5, -5)$

FINDING ANGLE MEASURES **Find the value of x.** (Review 4.1 for 8.4)

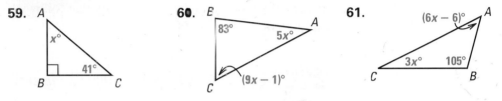

59.   **60.**   **61.**

SOLVING PROPORTIONS **Solve the proportion.** (Review 8.1)

62. $\dfrac{x}{9} = \dfrac{6}{27}$ **63.** $\dfrac{4}{y} = \dfrac{2}{19}$ **64.** $\dfrac{5}{24} = \dfrac{25}{z}$

65. $\dfrac{4}{13} = \dfrac{b}{8}$ **66.** $\dfrac{11}{x+2} = \dfrac{9}{x}$ **67.** $\dfrac{3x+7}{5} = \dfrac{4x}{6}$

QUIZ 1

Solve the proportions. (Lesson 8.1)

1. $\dfrac{p}{15} = \dfrac{2}{3}$ **2.** $\dfrac{5}{7} = \dfrac{20}{d}$ **3.** $\dfrac{4}{2x-6} = \dfrac{16}{x}$

Find the geometric mean of the two numbers. (Lesson 8.2)

4. 7 and 63   **5.** 5 and 11   **6.** 10 and 7

In Exercises 7 and 8, the two polygons are similar. Find the value of x. Then find the scale factor and the ratio of the perimeters. (Lesson 8.3)

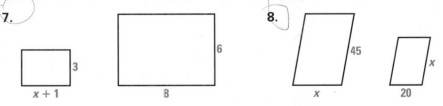

7.   **8.**

COMPARING PHOTO SIZES **Use the following information.** (Lesson 8.3)
You are ordering your school pictures. You decide to order one 8 × 10 (8 inches by 10 inches), two 5 × 7's (5 inches by 7 inches), and 24 wallets $\left(2\dfrac{1}{4}\text{ inches by }3\dfrac{1}{4}\text{ inches}\right)$.

9. Are any of these sizes similar to each other?

10. Suppose you want the wallet photos to be similar to the 8 × 10 photo. If the wallet photo were $2\dfrac{1}{2}$ inches wide, how tall would it be?

8.3 *Similar Polygons*   **479**

Similar Triangles

What you should learn

GOAL ① Identify similar triangles.

GOAL ② Use similar triangles in **real-life** problems, such as using shadows to determine the height of the Great Pyramid in **Ex. 55**.

Why you should learn it

▼ To solve **real-life** problems, such as using similar triangles to understand aerial photography in **Example 4**.

GOAL ① IDENTIFYING SIMILAR TRIANGLES

In this lesson, you will continue the study of similar polygons by looking at properties of similar triangles. The activity that follows Example 1 allows you to explore one of these properties.

EXAMPLE 1 *Writing Proportionality Statements*

In the diagram, $\triangle BTW \sim \triangle ETC$.

a. Write the statement of proportionality.

b. Find $m\angle TEC$.

c. Find ET and BE.

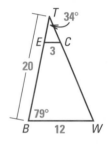

SOLUTION

a. $\dfrac{ET}{BT} = \dfrac{TC}{TW} = \dfrac{CE}{WB}$

b. $\angle B \cong \angle TEC$, so $m\angle TEC = 79°$.

c.

$\dfrac{CE}{WB} = \dfrac{ET}{BT}$ Write proportion.

$\dfrac{3}{12} = \dfrac{ET}{20}$ Substitute.

$\dfrac{3(20)}{12} = ET$ Multiply each side by 20.

$5 = ET$ Simplify.

Because $BE = BT - ET$, $BE = 20 - 5 = 15$.

▶ So, ET is 5 units and BE is 15 units.

▶ **ACTIVITY**

Developing Concepts

Investigating Similar Triangles

Use a protractor and a ruler to draw two noncongruent triangles so that each triangle has a 40° angle and a 60° angle. Check your drawing by measuring the third angle of each triangle—it should be 80°. Why? Measure the lengths of the sides of the triangles and compute the ratios of the lengths of corresponding sides. Are the triangles similar?

POSTULATE 25 *Angle-Angle (AA) Similarity Postulate*

If two angles of one triangle are
congruent to two angles of another
triangle, then the two triangles
are similar.

If $\angle JKL \cong \angle XYZ$ and $\angle KJL \cong \angle YXZ$,
then $\triangle JKL \sim \triangle XYZ$.

EXAMPLE 2 *Proving that Two Triangles are Similar*

Color variations in the tourmaline crystal shown
lie along the sides of isosceles triangles. In the
triangles each vertex angle measures 52°.
Explain why the triangles are similar.

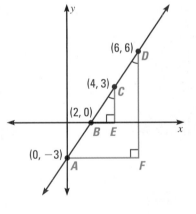

SOLUTION

Because the triangles are isosceles, you can
determine that each base angle is 64°. Using the
AA Similarity Postulate, you can conclude that
the triangles are similar.

EXAMPLE 3 *Why a Line Has Only One Slope*

Using Algebra

Use properties of similar triangles to explain
why any two points on a line can be used to
calculate the slope. Find the slope of the line
using both pairs of points shown.

SOLUTION

By the AA Similarity Postulate $\triangle BEC \sim \triangle AFD$,
so the ratios of corresponding sides
are the same. In particular, $\dfrac{CE}{DF} = \dfrac{BE}{AF}$.

By a property of proportions, $\dfrac{CE}{BE} = \dfrac{DF}{AF}$.

STUDENT HELP

▶ **Look Back**
For help with finding
slope, see p. 165.

The slope of a line is the ratio of the change in y to the corresponding change
in x. The ratios $\dfrac{CE}{BE}$ and $\dfrac{DF}{AF}$ represent the slopes of $\overline{BC}$ and $\overline{AD}$, respectively.

Because the two slopes are equal, any two points on a line can be used to
calculate its slope. You can verify this with specific values from the diagram.

$$\text{slope of } \overline{BC} = \frac{3-0}{4-2} = \frac{3}{2}$$

$$\text{slope of } \overline{AD} = \frac{6-(-3)}{6-0} = \frac{9}{6} = \frac{3}{2}$$

GOAL 2 **USING SIMILAR TRIANGLES IN REAL LIFE**

EXAMPLE 4 *Using Similar Triangles*

AERIAL PHOTOGRAPHY Low-level aerial photos can be taken using a remote-controlled camera suspended from a blimp. You want to take an aerial photo that covers a ground distance g of 50 meters. Use the proportion $\frac{f}{h} = \frac{n}{g}$ to estimate the altitude h that the blimp should fly at to take the photo. In the proportion, use $f = 8$ cm and $n = 3$ cm. These two variables are determined by the type of camera used.

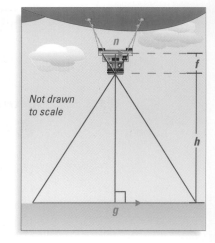

Not drawn to scale

SOLUTION

$$\frac{f}{h} = \frac{n}{g} \qquad \text{Write proportion.}$$

$$\frac{8 \text{ cm}}{h} = \frac{3 \text{ cm}}{50 \text{ m}} \qquad \text{Substitute.}$$

$$3h = 400 \qquad \text{Cross product property}$$

$$h \approx 133 \qquad \text{Divide each side by 3.}$$

▶ The blimp should fly at an altitude of about 133 meters to take a photo that covers a ground distance of 50 meters.

. . . .

In Lesson 8.3, you learned that the perimeters of similar polygons are in the same ratio as the lengths of the corresponding sides. This concept can be generalized as follows. If two polygons are similar, then the ratio of *any two corresponding lengths* (such as altitudes, medians, angle bisector segments, and diagonals) is equal to the scale factor of the similar polygons.

EXAMPLE 5 *Using Scale Factors*

Find the length of the altitude $\overline{QS}$.

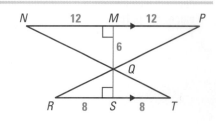

SOLUTION

Find the scale factor of $\triangle NQP$ to $\triangle TQR$.

$$\frac{NP}{TR} = \frac{12 + 12}{8 + 8} = \frac{24}{16} = \frac{3}{2}$$

Now, because the ratio of the lengths of the altitudes is equal to the scale factor, you can write the following equation.

$$\frac{QM}{QS} = \frac{3}{2}$$

▶ Substitute 6 for QM and solve for QS to show that $QS = 4$.

AERIAL PHOTOGRAPHER

An aerial photographer can take photos from a plane or using a remote-controlled blimp as discussed in Example 4.

CAREER LINK
www.mcdougallittell.com

STUDENT HELP

HOMEWORK HELP
Visit our Web site
www.mcdougallittell.com
for extra examples.

GUIDED PRACTICE

Vocabulary Check ✓

1. If $\triangle ABC \sim \triangle XYZ$, $AB = 6$, and $XY = 4$, what is the *scale factor* of the triangles?

Concept Check ✓

2. The points $A(2, 3)$, $B(-1, 6)$, $C(4, 1)$, and $D(0, 5)$ lie on a line. Which two points could be used to calculate the slope of the line? Explain.

3. Can you assume that corresponding sides and corresponding angles of any two similar triangles are congruent?

Skill Check ✓

Determine whether $\triangle CDE \sim \triangle FGH$.

4.

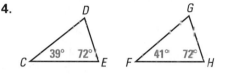

5.

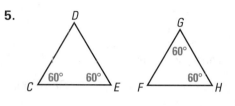

In the diagram shown $\triangle JKL \sim \triangle MNP$.

6. Find $m\angle J$, $m\angle N$, and $m\angle P$.

7. Find MP and PN.

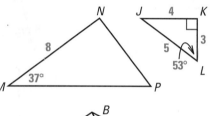

8. Given that $\angle CAB \cong \angle CBD$, how do you know that $\triangle ABC \sim \triangle BDC$? Explain your answer.

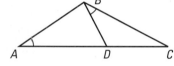

PRACTICE AND APPLICATIONS

STUDENT HELP

▶ **Extra Practice**
to help you master
skills is on p. 818.

USING SIMILARITY STATEMENTS The triangles shown are similar. List all the pairs of congruent angles and write the statement of proportionality.

9.

10.

11.

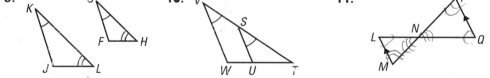

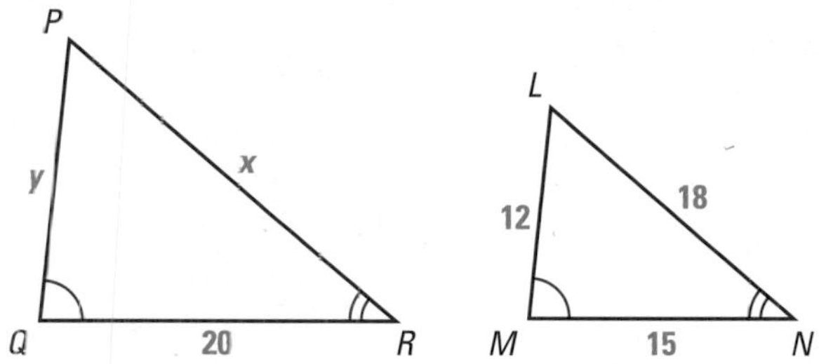

STUDENT HELP

▶ **HOMEWORK HELP**
Example 1: Exs. 9–17,
    33–38
Example 2: Exs. 18–26
Example 3: Exs. 27–32
Example 4: Exs. 39–44,
    53, 55, 56
Example 5: Exs. 45–47

🧩 **LOGICAL REASONING** Use the diagram to complete the following.

12. $\triangle PQR \sim$ ___?___

13. $\dfrac{PQ}{?} = \dfrac{QR}{?} = \dfrac{RP}{?}$

14. $\dfrac{20}{?} = \dfrac{?}{12}$

15. $\dfrac{?}{20} = \dfrac{18}{?}$

16. $y =$ ___?___

17. $x =$ ___?___

DETERMINING SIMILARITY Determine whether the triangles can be proved similar. If they are similar, write a similarity statement. If they are not similar, explain why.

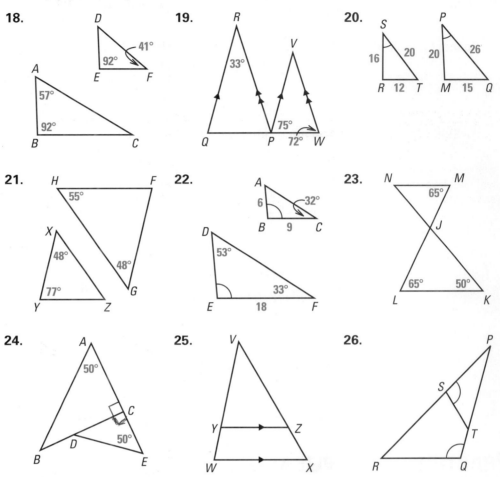

18.

19.

20.

21.

22.

23.

24.

25.

26.

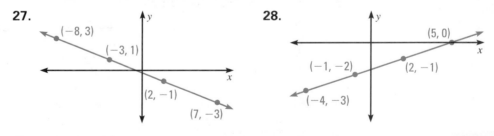

USING ALGEBRA Using the labeled points, find the slope of the line. To verify your answer, choose another pair of points and find the slope using the new points. Compare the results.

27.

28.

USING ALGEBRA Find coordinates for point *E* so that △*OBC* ~ △*ODE*.

29. $O(0, 0)$, $B(0, 3)$, $C(6, 0)$, $D(0, 5)$

30. $O(0, 0)$, $B(0, 4)$, $C(3, 0)$, $D(0, 7)$

31. $O(0, 0)$, $B(0, 1)$, $C(5, 0)$, $D(0, 6)$

32. $O(0, 0)$, $B(0, 8)$, $C(4, 0)$, $D(0, 9)$

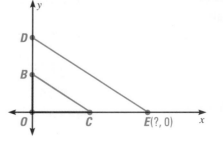

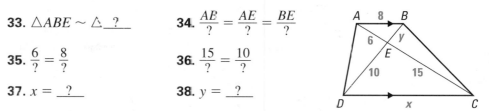

USING ALGEBRA You are given that *ABCD* is a trapezoid, *AB* = 8, *AE* = 6, *EC* = 15, and *DE* = 10.

33. $\triangle ABE \sim \triangle$ _ ? _

34. $\dfrac{AE}{?} = \dfrac{AE}{?} = \dfrac{BE}{?}$

35. $\dfrac{6}{?} = \dfrac{8}{?}$

36. $\dfrac{15}{?} = \dfrac{10}{?}$

37. $x =$ _ ? _

38. $y =$ _ ? _

STUDENT HELP

HOMEWORK HELP
Visit our Web site
www.mcdougallittell.com
for help with problem
solving in Exs. 39–44.

SIMILAR TRIANGLES The triangles are similar. Find the value of the variable.

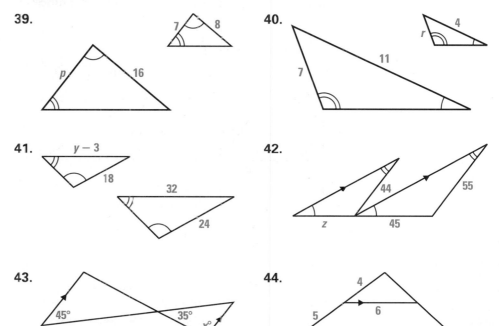

39.

40.

41.

42.

43.

44.

SIMILAR TRIANGLES The segments in blue are special segments in the similar triangles. Find the value of the variable.

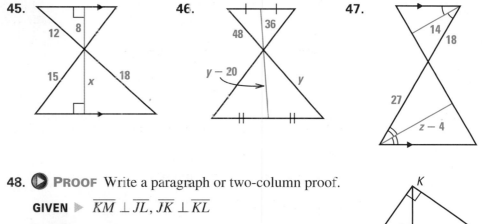

45.

46.

47.

48. ▶ **PROOF** Write a paragraph or two-column proof.

 GIVEN ▶ $\overline{KM} \perp \overline{JL}, \overline{JK} \perp \overline{KL}$

 PROVE ▶ $\triangle JKL \sim \triangle JMK$

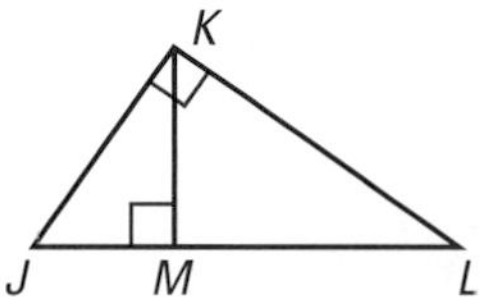

49. ▶ **PROOF** Write a paragraph proof or a two-column proof. The National Humanities Center is located in Research Triangle Park in North Carolina. Some of its windows consist of nested right triangles, as shown in the diagram. Prove that $\triangle ABE \sim \triangle CDE$.

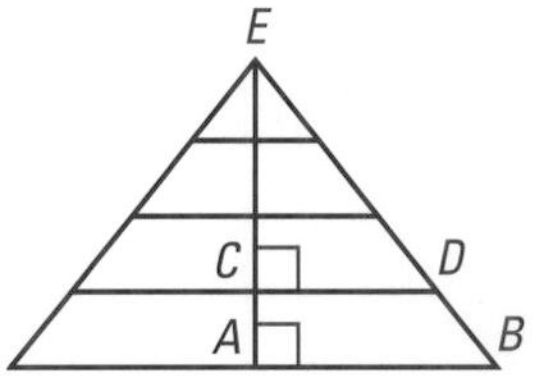

    GIVEN ▶ $\angle ECD$ is a right angle, $\angle EAB$ is a right angle.

    PROVE ▶ $\triangle ABE \sim \triangle CDE$

LOGICAL REASONING **In Exercises 50–52, decide whether the statement is *true* or *false*. Explain your reasoning.**

50. If an acute angle of a right triangle is congruent to an acute angle of another right triangle, then the triangles are similar.

51. Some equilateral triangles are not similar.

52. All isosceles triangles with a 40° vertex angle are similar.

53. 🌐 **ICE HOCKEY** A hockey player passes the puck to a teammate by bouncing the puck off the wall of the rink as shown. From physics, the angles that the path of the puck makes with the wall are congruent. How far from the wall will the pass be picked up by his teammate?

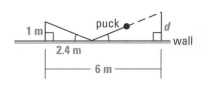

STUDENT HELP

SOFTWARE HELP
Visit our Web site www.mcdougallittell.com to see instructions for several software applications.

54. 🔺 **TECHNOLOGY** Use geometry software to verify that any two points on a line can be used to calculate the slope of the line. Draw a line k with a negative slope in a coordinate plane. Draw two right triangles of different size whose hypotenuses lie along line k and whose other sides are parallel to the x- and y-axes. Calculate the slope of each triangle by finding the ratio of the vertical side length to the horizontal side length. Are the slopes equal?

55. 🌐 **THE GREAT PYRAMID** The Greek mathematician Thales (640–546 B.C.) calculated the height of the Great Pyramid in Egypt by placing a rod at the tip of the pyramid's shadow and using similar triangles.

In the figure, $\overline{PQ} \perp \overline{QT}$, $\overline{SR} \perp \overline{QT}$, and $\overline{PR} \parallel \overline{ST}$. Write a paragraph proof to show that the height of the pyramid is 480 feet.

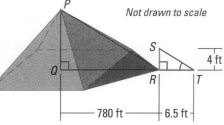

56. 🌐 **ESTIMATING HEIGHT** On a sunny day, use a rod or pole to estimate the height of your school building. Use the method that Thales used to estimate the height of the Great Pyramid in Exercise 55.

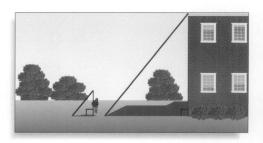

57. MULTI-STEP PROBLEM Use the following information.

Going from his own house to Raul's house, Mark drives due south one mile, due east three miles, and due south again three miles. What is the distance between the two houses as the crow flies?

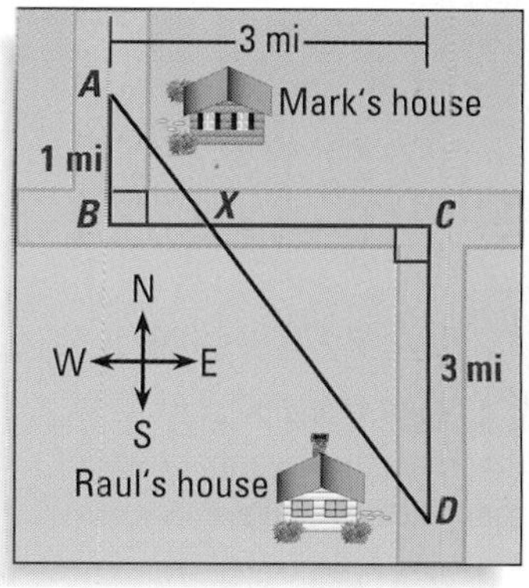

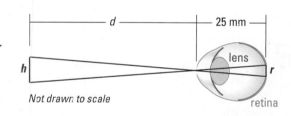

a. Explain how to prove that $\triangle ABX \sim \triangle DCX$.

b. Use corresponding side lengths of the triangles to calculate BX.

c. Use the Pythagorean Theorem to calculate AX, and then DX. Then find AD.

d. *Writing* Using the properties of rectangles, explain a way that a point E could be added to the diagram so that $\overline{AD}$ would be the hypotenuse of $\triangle AED$, and $\overline{AE}$ and $\overline{ED}$ would be its legs of known length.

★ **Challenge**

HUMAN VISION In Exercises 58–60, use the following information.

The diagram shows how similar triangles relate to human vision. An image similar to a viewed object appears on the retina. The actual height of the object h is proportional to the size of the image as it appears on the retina r. In the same manner, the distances from the object to the lens of the eye d and from the lens to the retina, 25 mm in the diagram, are also proportional.

58. Write a proportion that relates r, d, h, and 25 mm.

59. An object that is 10 meters away appears on the retina as 1 mm tall. Find the height of the object.

60. An object that is 1 meter tall appears on the retina as 1 mm tall. How far away is the object?

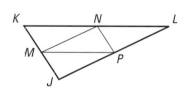

Not drawn to scale

MIXED REVIEW

61. USING THE DISTANCE FORMULA Find the distance between the points $A(-17, 12)$ and $B(14, -21)$. **(Review 1.3)**

TRIANGLE MIDSEGMENTS M, N, and P are the midpoints of the sides of $\triangle JKL$. Complete the statement. **(Review 5.4 for 8.5)**

62. $\overline{NP} \parallel$ ___?___

63. If $NP = 23$, then $KJ =$ ___?___.

64. If $KN = 16$, then $MP =$ ___?___.

65. If $JL = 24$, then $MN =$ ___?___.

PROPORTIONS Solve the proportion. **(Review 8.1)**

66. $\dfrac{x}{12} = \dfrac{3}{8}$

67. $\dfrac{3}{y} = \dfrac{12}{32}$

68. $\dfrac{17}{x} = \dfrac{11}{33}$

69. $\dfrac{34}{11} = \dfrac{x + 6}{3}$

70. $\dfrac{23}{24} = \dfrac{x}{72}$

71. $\dfrac{8}{x} = \dfrac{x}{32}$

8.5

Proving Triangles are Similar

What you should learn

GOAL 1 Use similarity theorems to prove that two triangles are similar.

GOAL 2 Use similar triangles to solve **real-life** problems, such as finding the height of a climbing wall in **Example 5**.

Why you should learn it

▼ To solve **real-life** problems, such as estimating the height of the Unisphere in **Ex. 29**.

GOAL 1 **USING SIMILARITY THEOREMS**

In this lesson, you will study two additional ways to prove that two triangles are similar: the Side-Side-Side (SSS) Similarity Theorem and the Side-Angle-Side (SAS) Similarity Theorem. The first theorem is proved in Example 1 and you are asked to prove the second theorem in Exercise 31.

THEOREMS

THEOREM 8.2 *Side-Side-Side (SSS) Similarity Theorem*

If the lengths of the corresponding sides of two triangles are proportional, then the triangles are similar.

If $\dfrac{AB}{PQ} = \dfrac{BC}{QR} = \dfrac{CA}{RP}$,

then $\triangle ABC \sim \triangle PQR$.

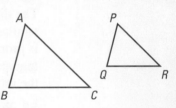

THEOREM 8.3 *Side-Angle-Side (SAS) Similarity Theorem*

If an angle of one triangle is congruent to an angle of a second triangle and the lengths of the sides including these angles are proportional, then the triangles are similar.

If $\angle X \cong \angle M$ and $\dfrac{ZX}{PM} = \dfrac{XY}{MN}$,

then $\triangle XYZ \sim \triangle MNP$.

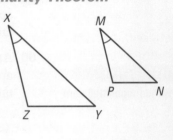

EXAMPLE 1 *Proof of Theorem 8.2*

Proof

GIVEN ▶ $\dfrac{RS}{LM} = \dfrac{ST}{MN} = \dfrac{TR}{NL}$

PROVE ▶ $\triangle RST \sim \triangle LMN$

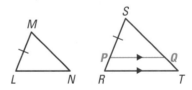

SOLUTION

Paragraph Proof Locate P on $\overline{RS}$ so that $PS = LM$. Draw $\overline{PQ}$ so that $\overline{PQ} \parallel \overline{RT}$.

Then $\triangle RST \sim \triangle PSQ$, by the AA Similarity Postulate, and $\dfrac{RS}{PS} = \dfrac{ST}{SQ} = \dfrac{TR}{QP}$.

Because $PS = LM$, you can substitute in the given proportion and find that $SQ = MN$ and $QP = NL$. By the SSS Congruence Theorem, it follows that $\triangle PSQ \cong \triangle LMN$. Finally, use the definition of congruent triangles and the AA Similarity Postulate to conclude that $\triangle RST \sim \triangle LMN$.

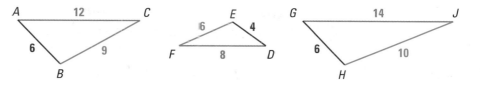

EXAMPLE 2 *Using the SSS Similarity Theorem*

Logical Reasoning

Which of the following three triangles are similar?

A ——12—— C, 6, 9, B

E 6 4, F 8 D

G ——14—— J, 6, 10, H

SOLUTION

To decide which, if any, of the triangles are similar, you need to consider the ratios of the lengths of corresponding sides.

Ratios of Side Lengths of △ABC and △DEF

$$\frac{AB}{DE} = \frac{6}{4} = \frac{3}{2},$$

Shortest sides

$$\frac{CA}{FD} = \frac{12}{8} = \frac{3}{2},$$

Longest sides

$$\frac{BC}{EF} = \frac{9}{6} = \frac{3}{2}$$

Remaining sides

▶ Because all of the ratios are equal, △ABC ~ △DEF.

Ratios of Side Lengths of △ABC and △GHJ

$$\frac{AB}{GH} = \frac{6}{6} = 1,$$

Shortest sides

$$\frac{CA}{JG} = \frac{12}{14} = \frac{6}{7},$$

Longest sides

$$\frac{BC}{HJ} = \frac{9}{10}$$

Remaining sides

▶ Because the ratios are not equal, △ABC and △GHJ are not similar.

Since △ABC is similar to △DEF and △ABC is not similar to △GHJ, △DEF is not similar to △GHJ.

STUDENT HELP

▸ **Study Tip**
Note that when using the SSS Similarity Theorem it is useful to compare the shortest sides, the longest sides, and then the remaining sides.

EXAMPLE 3 *Using the SAS Similarity Theorem*

Use the given lengths to prove that △RST ~ △PSQ.

SOLUTION

GIVEN ▶ $SP = 4$, $PR = 12$, $SQ = 5$, $QT = 15$

PROVE ▶ △RST ~ △PSQ

Paragraph Proof Use the SAS Similarity Theorem. Begin by finding the ratios of the lengths of the corresponding sides.

$$\frac{SR}{SP} = \frac{SP + PR}{SP} = \frac{4 + 12}{4} = \frac{16}{4} = 4$$

$$\frac{ST}{SQ} = \frac{SQ + QT}{SQ} = \frac{5 + 15}{5} = \frac{20}{5} = 4$$

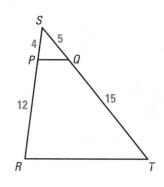

So, the lengths of sides $\overline{SR}$ and $\overline{ST}$ are proportional to the lengths of the corresponding sides of △PSQ. Because ∠S is the included angle in both triangles, use the SAS Similarity Theorem to conclude that △RST ~ △PSQ.

GOAL 2 USING SIMILAR TRIANGLES IN REAL LIFE

EXAMPLE 4 *Using a Pantograph*

SCALE DRAWING As you move the tracing pin of a *pantograph* along a figure, the pencil attached to the far end draws an enlargement. As the pantograph expands and contracts, the three brads and the tracing pin always form the vertices of a parallelogram. The ratio of PR to PT is always equal to the ratio of PQ to PS. Also, the suction cup, the tracing pin, and the pencil remain collinear.

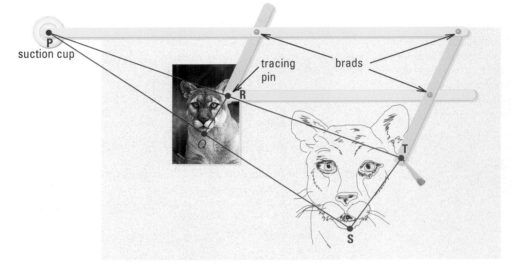

a. How can you show that $\triangle PRQ \sim \triangle PTS$?

b. In the diagram, PR is 10 inches and RT is 10 inches. The length of the cat, RQ, in the original print is 2.4 inches. Find the length TS in the enlargement.

SOLUTION

a. You know that $\frac{PR}{PT} = \frac{PQ}{PS}$. Because $\angle P \cong \angle P$, you can apply the SAS Similarity Theorem to conclude that $\triangle PRQ \sim \triangle PTS$.

b. Because the triangles are similar, you can set up a proportion to find the length of the cat in the enlarged drawing.

$\frac{PR}{PT} = \frac{RQ}{TS}$ **Write proportion.**

$\frac{10}{20} = \frac{2.4}{TS}$ **Substitute.**

$TS = 4.8$ **Solve for *TS*.**

▶ So, the length of the cat in the enlarged drawing is 4.8 inches.

. . . .

Similar triangles can be used to find distances that are difficult to measure directly. One technique is called *Thales' shadow method* (page 486), named after the Greek geometer Thales who used it to calculate the height of the Great Pyramid.

FOCUS ON APPLICATIONS

PANTOGRAPH Before photocopiers, people used pantographs to make enlargements. As the tracing pin is guided over the figure, the pencil draws an enlargement.

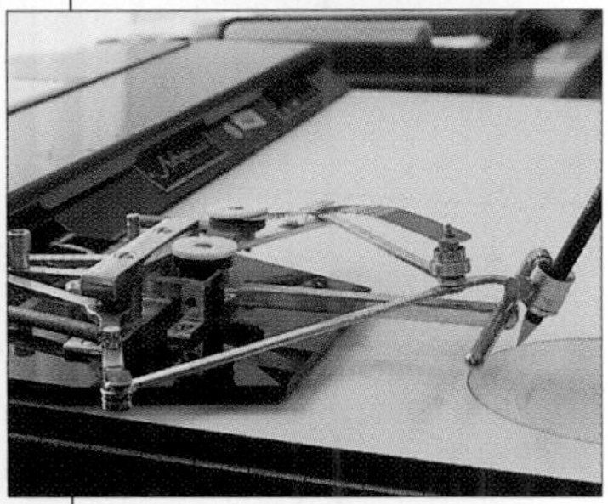

FOCUS ON APPLICATIONS

ROCK CLIMBING Interest in rock climbing appears to be growing. From 1988 to 1998, over 700 indoor rock climbing gyms opened in the United States.

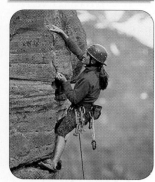

EXAMPLE 5 *Finding Distance Indirectly*

ROCK CLIMBING You are at an indoor climbing wall. To estimate the height of the wall, you place a mirror on the floor 85 feet from the base of the wall. Then you walk backward until you can see the top of the wall centered in the mirror. You are 6.5 feet from the mirror and your eyes are 5 feet above the ground. Use similar triangles to estimate the height of the wall.

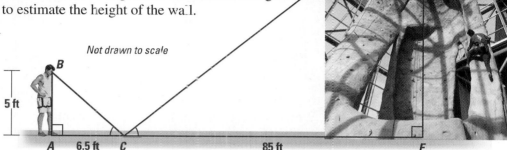

Not drawn to scale
B
5 ft
A
6.5 ft
C
85 ft
E

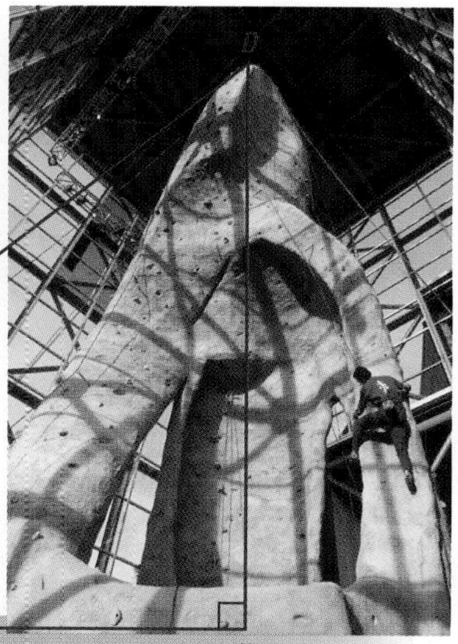

SOLUTION

Due to the reflective property of mirrors, you can reason that $\angle ACB \cong \angle ECD$. Using the fact that $\triangle ABC$ and $\triangle EDC$ are right triangles, you can apply the AA Similarity Postulate to conclude that these two triangles are similar.

$\frac{DE}{BA} = \frac{EC}{AC}$ — **Ratios of lengths of corresponding sides are equal.**

$\frac{DE}{5} = \frac{85}{6.5}$ — **Substitute.**

$65.38 \approx DE$ — **Multiply each side by 5 and simplify.**

▶ So, the height of the wall is about 65 feet.

STUDENT HELP

HOMEWORK HELP Visit our Web site www.mcdougallittell.com for extra examples.

EXAMPLE 6 *Finding Distance Indirectly*

INDIRECT MEASUREMENT To measure the width of a river, you use a surveying technique, as shown in the diagram. Use the given lengths (measured in feet) to find RQ.

P
63
Q
R
12
T
9
S

SOLUTION

By the AA Similarity Postulate, $\triangle PQR \sim \triangle STR$.

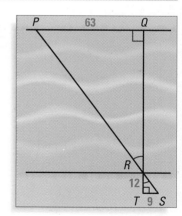

$\frac{RQ}{RT} = \frac{PQ}{ST}$ — **Write proportion.**

$\frac{RQ}{12} = \frac{63}{9}$ — **Substitute.**

$RQ = 12 \cdot 7$ — **Multiply each side by 12.**

$RQ = 84$ — **Simplify.**

▶ So, the river is 84 feet wide.

GUIDED PRACTICE

Vocabulary Check ✓
1. You want to prove that △*FHG* is similar to △*RXS* by the SSS Similarity Theorem. Complete the proportion that is needed to use this theorem.

$$\frac{FH}{?} = \frac{?}{XS} = \frac{FG}{?}$$

Concept Check ✓
Name a postulate or theorem that can be used to prove that the two triangles are similar. Then, write a similarity statement.

2.

3.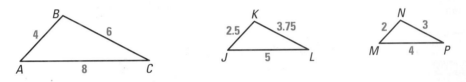

Skill Check ✓
4. Which triangles are similar to △*ABC*? Explain.

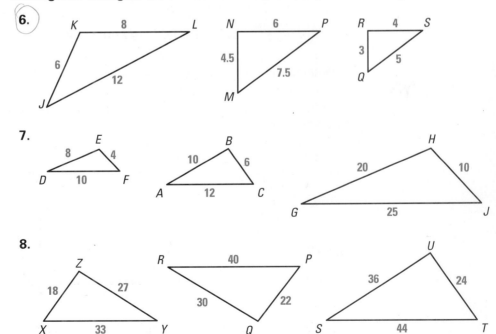

5. The side lengths of △*ABC* are 2, 5, and 6, and △*DEF* has side lengths of 12, 30, and 36. Find the ratios of the lengths of the corresponding sides of △*ABC* to △*DEF*. Are the two triangles similar? Explain.

PRACTICE AND APPLICATIONS

STUDENT HELP

▶ **Extra Practice**
to help you master
skills is on p. 818.

DETERMINING SIMILARITY In Exercises 6–8, determine which two of the three given triangles are similar. Find the scale factor for the pair.

6.

7.

STUDENT HELP

▶ **HOMEWORK HELP**
Example 1: Exs. 30, 31
Example 2: Exs. 6–18

8.

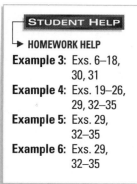

STUDENT HELP

→ HOMEWORK HELP

Example 3: Exs. 6–18, 30, 31

Example 4: Exs. 19–26, 29, 32–35

Example 5: Exs. 29, 32–35

Example 6: Exs. 29, 32–35

DETERMINING SIMILARITY Are the triangles similar? If so, state the similarity and the postulate or theorem that justifies your answer.

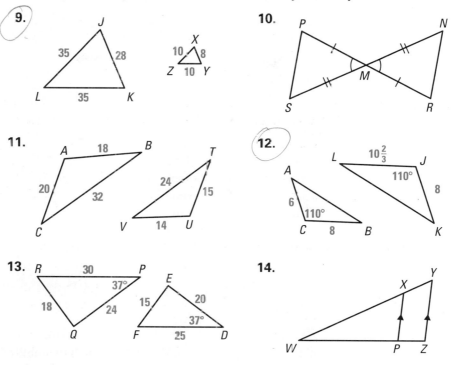

9.

10.

11.

12.

13.

14.

🐢 **LOGICAL REASONING** Draw the given triangles roughly to scale. Then, name a postulate or theorem that can be used to prove that the triangles are similar.

15. The side lengths of $\triangle PQR$ are 16, 8, and 18, and the side lengths of $\triangle XYZ$ are 9, 8, and 4.

16. In $\triangle ABC$, $m\angle A = 28°$ and $m\angle B = 62°$. In $\triangle DEF$, $m\angle D = 28°$ and $m\angle F = 90°$.

17. In $\triangle STU$, the length of $\overline{ST}$ is 18, the length of $\overline{SU}$ is 24, and $m\angle S = 65°$. The length of $\overline{JK}$ is 6, $m\angle J = 65°$, and the length of $\overline{JL}$ is 8 in $\triangle JKL$.

18. The ratio of VW to MN is 6 to 1. In $\triangle VWX$, $m\angle W = 30°$, and in $\triangle MNP$, $m\angle N = 30°$. The ratio of WX to NP is 6 to 1.

FINDING MEASURES AND LENGTHS Use the diagram shown to complete the statements.

19. $m\angle CED =$ ___?___.

20. $m\angle EDC =$ ___?___.

21. $m\angle DCE =$ ___?___.

22. $FC =$ ___?___.

23. $EC =$ ___?___.

24. $DE =$ ___?___.

25. $CB =$ ___?___.

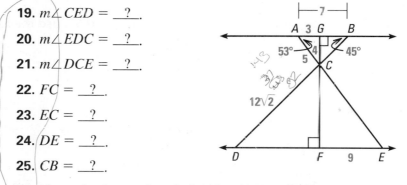

26. Name the three pairs of triangles that are similar in the figure.

DETERMINING SIMILARITY Determine whether the triangles are similar.
If they are, write a similarity statement and solve for the variable.

27.

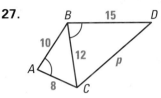

28.

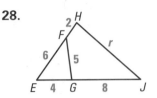

29. 🌐 **UNISPHERE** You are visiting the Unisphere at Flushing Meadow Park in New York. To estimate the height of the stainless steel model of Earth, you place a mirror on the ground and stand where you can see the top of the model in the mirror. Use the diagram shown to estimate the height of the model.

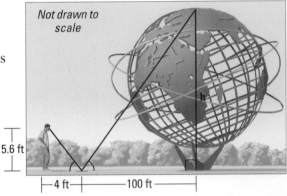

Not drawn to scale

5.6 ft

4 ft — 100 ft

30. ▶ **PARAGRAPH PROOF** Two isosceles triangles are similar if the vertex angle of one triangle is congruent to the vertex angle of the other triangle. Write a paragraph proof of this statement and include a labeled figure.

31. ▶ **PARAGRAPH PROOF** Write a paragraph proof of Theorem 8.3.

GIVEN ▶ $\angle A \cong \angle D, \dfrac{AB}{DE} = \dfrac{AC}{DF}$

PROVE ▶ $\triangle ABC \sim \triangle DEF$

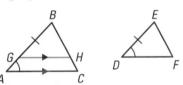

FINDING DISTANCES INDIRECTLY Find the distance labeled *x*.

32.

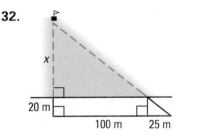

33.

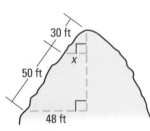

🌐 **FLAGPOLE HEIGHT** In Exercises 34 and 35, use the following information.
Julia uses the shadow of the flagpole to estimate its height. She stands so that the tip of her shadow coincides with the tip of the flagpole's shadow as shown. Julia is 5 feet tall. The distance from the flagpole to Julia is 28 feet and the distance between the tip of the shadows and Julia is 7 feet.

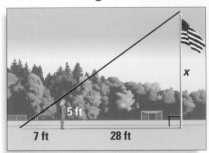

34. Calculate the height of the flagpole.

35. Explain why Julia's shadow method works.

Test Preparation

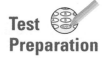

QUANTITATIVE COMPARISON In Exercises 36 and 37, use the diagram, in which $\triangle ABC \sim \triangle XYZ$, and the ratio $AB:XY$ is 2:5. Choose the statement that is true about the given quantities.

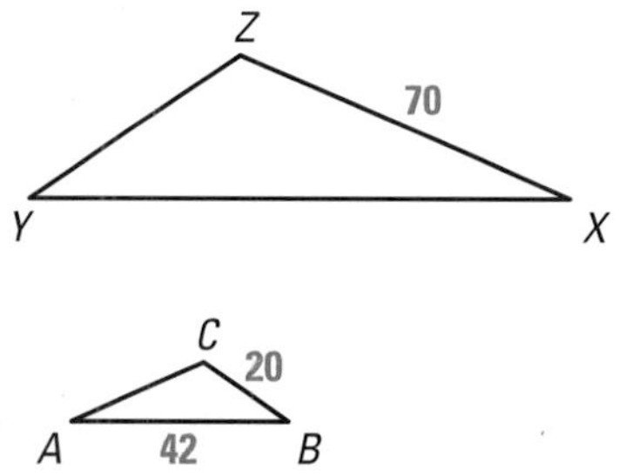

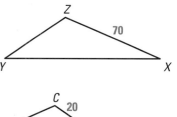

Ⓐ The quantity in column A is greater.

Ⓑ The quantity in column B is greater.

Ⓒ The two quantities are equal.

Ⓓ The relationship cannot be determined from the given information.

	Column A	Column B
36.	The perimeter of $\triangle ABC$	The length XY
37.	The distance $XY + BC$	The distance $XZ + YZ$

★ Challenge

EXTRA CHALLENGE

www.mcdougallittell.com

38. **DESIGNING THE LOOP** A portion of an amusement park ride called the Loop is shown. Find the length of $\overline{EF}$. (*Hint:* Use similar triangles.)

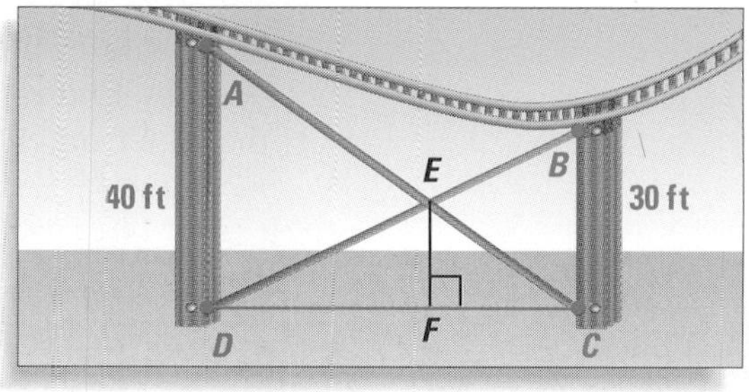

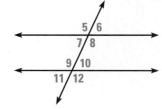

MIXED REVIEW

ANALYZING ANGLE BISECTORS $\overrightarrow{BD}$ is the angle bisector of $\angle ABC$. Find any angle measures not given in the diagram. (Review 1.5 for 8.6)

39.

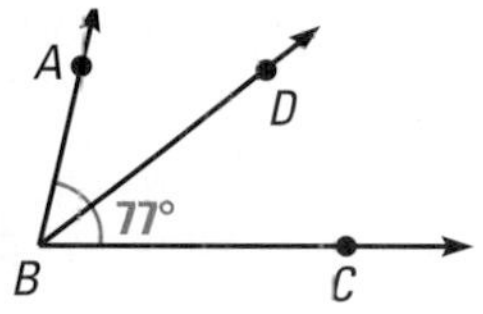

40.

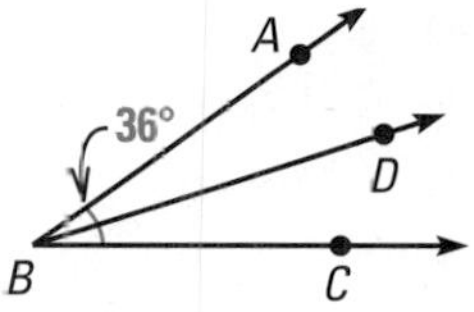

41.

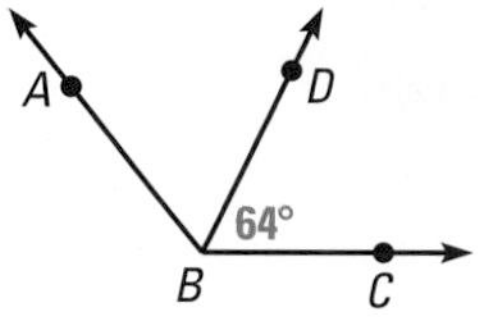

RECOGNIZING ANGLES Use the diagram shown to complete the statement. (Review 3.1 for 8.6)

42. $\angle 5$ and __?__ are alternate exterior angles.

43. $\angle 8$ and __?__ are consecutive interior angles.

44. $\angle 10$ and __?__ are alternate interior angles.

45. $\angle 9$ and __?__ are corresponding angles.

FINDING COORDINATES Find the coordinates of the image after the reflection without using a coordinate plane. (Review 7.2)

46. $T(0, 5)$ reflected in the x-axis

47. $P(-2, 7)$ reflected in the y-axis

48. $B(-3, -10)$ reflected in the y-axis

49. $C(-5, -1)$ reflected in the x-axis

Determine whether you can show that the triangles are similar. State any angle measures that are not given. (Lesson 8.4)

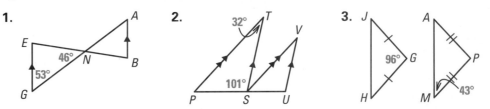

1.

2.

3.

In Exercises 4–6, you are given the ratios of the lengths of the sides of △DEF. If △ABC has sides of lengths 3, 6, and 7 units, are the triangles similar? (Lesson 8.5)

4. $4:7:8$

5. $6:12:14$

6. $1:2:\dfrac{7}{3}$

7. 🌐 **DISTANCE ACROSS WATER**
Use the known distances in the diagram to find the distance across the lake from *A* to *B*. (Lesson 8.5)

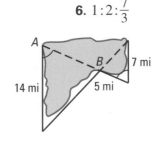

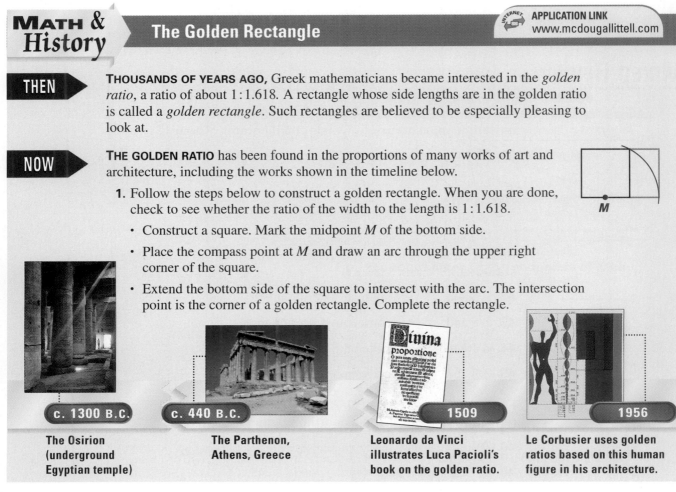

**MATH &
History**

The Golden Rectangle

🌐 INTERNET
APPLICATION LINK
www.mcdougallittell.com

THEN

THOUSANDS OF YEARS AGO, Greek mathematicians became interested in the *golden ratio*, a ratio of about 1:1.618. A rectangle whose side lengths are in the golden ratio is called a *golden rectangle*. Such rectangles are believed to be especially pleasing to look at.

NOW

THE GOLDEN RATIO has been found in the proportions of many works of art and architecture, including the works shown in the timeline below.

1. Follow the steps below to construct a golden rectangle. When you are done, check to see whether the ratio of the width to the length is 1:1.618.

 • Construct a square. Mark the midpoint *M* of the bottom side.

 • Place the compass point at *M* and draw an arc through the upper right corner of the square.

 • Extend the bottom side of the square to intersect with the arc. The intersection point is the corner of a golden rectangle. Complete the rectangle.

M

c. 1300 B.C.

**The Osirion
(underground
Egyptian temple)**

c. 440 B.C.

**The Parthenon,
Athens, Greece**

1509

**Leonardo da Vinci
illustrates Luca Pacioli's
book on the golden ratio.**

1956

**Le Corbusier uses golden
ratios based on this human
figure in his architecture.**

▶ **ACTIVITY 8.6**

Using Technology

Investigating Proportional Segments

You can use geometry software to compare segment lengths in triangles.

▶ **CONSTRUCT** Construct a line parallel to a triangle's third side.

1 Draw a triangle. Label the vertices A, B, and C.

2 Draw a point on $\overline{AB}$. Label the point D.

3 Draw a line through D that is parallel to $\overline{AC}$. Label the intersection of the line and $\overline{BC}$ as point E.

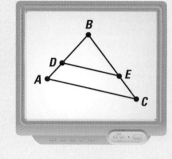

▶ **INVESTIGATE**

1. Measure $\overline{BD}$, $\overline{DA}$, $\overline{BE}$, and $\overline{EC}$. Calculate the ratios $\frac{BD}{DA}$ and $\frac{BE}{EC}$.

2. Drag $\overline{DE}$ to different locations and compare the ratios from Exercise 1.

3. Drag one or more of the triangle's vertices to change its shape. Continue to compare the ratios as the shape changes.

▶ **MAKE A CONJECTURE**

4. Make a conjecture about the ratios of segment lengths of a triangle's sides when the triangle is cut by a line parallel to the triangle's third side.

▶ **CONSTRUCT** Construct an angle bisector of a triangle.

4 Draw a triangle. Label the vertices P, Q, and R.

5 Draw the angle bisector of $\angle QPR$. Label the intersection of the angle bisector and $\overline{QR}$ as point B.

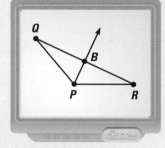

▶ **INVESTIGATE**

5. Measure $\overline{BR}$, $\overline{RP}$, $\overline{BQ}$, and $\overline{QP}$. Calculate the ratios $\frac{BR}{BQ}$ and $\frac{RP}{QP}$.

6. Drag one or more of the triangle's vertices to change its shape. Continue to compare the ratios as the shape changes.

▶ **MAKE A CONJECTURE**

7. Make a conjecture about how the ratio of two side lengths of a triangle relates to the ratio of the segment lengths of the third side formed by an angle bisector.

EXTENSION

CRITICAL THINKING Are the two triangles formed by the angle bisector similar? Explain your reasoning.

Proportions and Similar Triangles

What you should learn

GOAL 1 Use proportionality theorems to calculate segment lengths.

GOAL 2 To solve **real-life** problems, such as determining the dimensions of a piece of land in **Exs. 29 and 30**.

Why you should learn it

▼ Model **real-life** situations using proportionality theorems, as in the construction problem in **Example 5**.

GOAL 1 USING PROPORTIONALITY THEOREMS

In this lesson, you will study four proportionality theorems. Similar triangles are used to prove each theorem. You are asked to prove the theorems in Exercises 31–33 and 38.

THEOREMS

THEOREM 8.4 *Triangle Proportionality Theorem*

If a line parallel to one side of a triangle intersects the other two sides, then it divides the two sides proportionally.

If $\overline{TU} \parallel \overline{QS}$, then $\dfrac{RT}{TQ} = \dfrac{RU}{US}$.

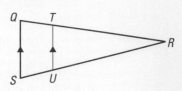

THEOREM 8.5 *Converse of the Triangle Proportionality Theorem*

If a line divides two sides of a triangle proportionally, then it is parallel to the third side.

If $\dfrac{RT}{TQ} = \dfrac{RU}{US}$, then $\overline{TU} \parallel \overline{QS}$.

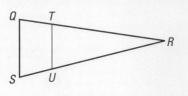

EXAMPLE 1 *Finding the Length of a Segment*

In the diagram $\overline{AB} \parallel \overline{ED}$, $BD = 8$, $DC = 4$, and $AE = 12$. What is the length of $\overline{EC}$?

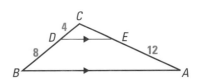

SOLUTION

$$\frac{DC}{BD} = \frac{EC}{AE}$$ **Triangle Proportionality Theorem**

$$\frac{4}{8} = \frac{EC}{12}$$ **Substitute.**

$$\frac{4(12)}{8} = EC$$ **Multiply each side by 12.**

$$6 = EC$$ **Simplify.**

▶ So, the length of $\overline{EC}$ is 6.

EXAMPLE 2 *Determining Parallels*

Given the diagram, determine whether $\overline{MN} \parallel \overline{GH}$.

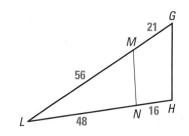

SOLUTION

Begin by finding and simplifying the ratios
of the two sides divided by $\overline{MN}$

$$\frac{LM}{MG} = \frac{56}{21} = \frac{8}{3} \qquad\qquad \frac{LN}{NH} = \frac{48}{16} = \frac{3}{1}$$

Because $\frac{8}{3} \neq \frac{3}{1}$, $\overline{MN}$ is not parallel to $\overline{GH}$.

THEOREMS

THEOREM 8.6

If three parallel lines intersect two
transversals, then they divide the
transversals proportionally.

If $r \parallel s$ and $s \parallel t$, and ℓ and m

intersect r, s, and t, then $\frac{UW}{WY} = \frac{VX}{XZ}$.

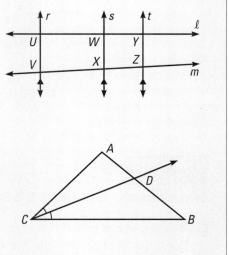

THEOREM 8.7

If a ray bisects an angle of a triangle, then
it divides the opposite side into segments
whose lengths are proportional to the
lengths of the other two sides.

If $\overrightarrow{CD}$ bisects $\angle ACB$, then $\frac{AD}{DB} = \frac{CA}{CB}$.

EXAMPLE 3 *Using Proportionality Theorems*

In the diagram, $\angle 1 \cong \angle 2 \cong \angle 3$, and $PQ = 9$,
$QR = 15$, and $ST = 11$. What is the length of $\overline{TU}$?

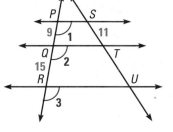

SOLUTION

Because corresponding angles are congruent the lines
are parallel and you can use Theorem 8.6.

$$\frac{PQ}{QR} = \frac{ST}{TU} \qquad \text{Parallel lines divide}$$
transversals proportionally.

$$\frac{9}{15} = \frac{11}{TU} \qquad \text{Substitute.}$$

$$9 \cdot TU = 15 \cdot 11 \qquad \text{Cross product property}$$

$$TU = \frac{15(11)}{9} = \frac{55}{3} \qquad \text{Divide each side by 9 and simplify.}$$

▶ So, the length of $\overline{TU}$ is $\frac{55}{3}$ or $18\frac{1}{3}$.

EXAMPLE 4 *Using Proportionality Theorems*

Using Algebra

In the diagram, $\angle CAD \cong \angle DAB$. Use the given side lengths to find the length of $\overline{DC}$.

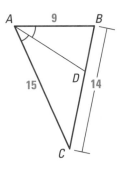

SOLUTION

Since $\overrightarrow{AD}$ is an angle bisector of $\angle CAB$, you can apply Theorem 8.7.

Let $x = DC$. Then, $BD = 14 - x$.

$$\frac{AB}{AC} = \frac{BD}{DC}$$ **Apply Theorem 8.7.**

$$\frac{9}{15} = \frac{14 - x}{x}$$ **Substitute.**

$$9 \cdot x = 15(14 - x)$$ **Cross product property**

$$9x = 210 - 15x$$ **Distributive property**

$$24x = 210$$ **Add 15x to each side.**

$$x = 8.75$$ **Divide each side by 24.**

▶ So, the length of $\overline{DC}$ is 8.75 units.

◐ ACTIVITY

Construction

Dividing a Segment into Equal Parts (4 shown)

❶ Draw a line segment that is about 3 inches long. Label the endpoints A and B. Choose any point C not on $\overleftrightarrow{AB}$. Draw $\overrightarrow{AC}$.

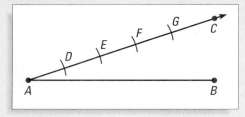

❷ Using any length, place the compass point at A and make an arc intersecting $\overrightarrow{AC}$ at D.

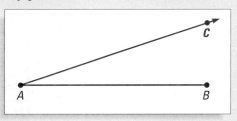

❸ Using the same compass setting, make additional arcs on $\overrightarrow{AC}$. Label the points E, F, and G so that $AD = DE = EF = FG$.

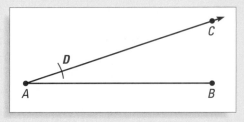

❹ Draw $\overline{GB}$. Construct a line parallel to $\overline{GB}$ through D. Continue constructing parallel lines and label the points as shown. Explain why $AJ = JK = KL = LB$.

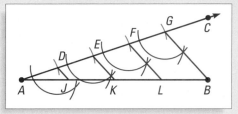

500   **Chapter 8** *Similarity*

GOAL 2 USING PROPORTIONALITY THEOREMS IN REAL LIFE

EXAMPLE 5 *Finding the Length of a Segment*

REAL LIFE **BUILDING CONSTRUCTION** You are insulating your attic, as shown. The vertical 2 × 4 studs are evenly spaced. Explain why the diagonal cuts at the tops of the strips of insulation should have the same lengths.

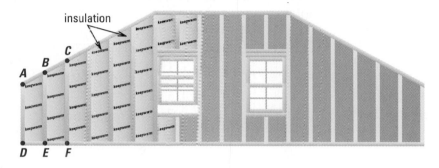

SOLUTION

Because the studs $\overline{AD}$, $\overline{BE}$, and $\overline{CF}$ are each vertical, you know that they are parallel to each other. Using Theorem 8.6, you can conclude that $\frac{DE}{EF} = \frac{AB}{BC}$. Because the studs are evenly spaced, you know that $DE = EF$. So, you can conclude that $AB = BC$, which means that the diagonal cuts at the tops of the strips have the same lengths.

EXAMPLE 6 *Finding Segment Lengths*

In the diagram $\overline{KL} \parallel \overline{MN}$. Find the values of the variables.

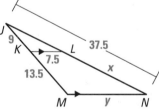

SOLUTION

To find the value of x, you can set up a proportion.

$\frac{9}{13.5} = \frac{37.5 - x}{x}$ **Write proportion.**

$13.5(37.5 - x) = 9x$ **Cross product property**

$506.25 - 13.5x = 9x$ **Distributive property**

$506.25 = 22.5x$ **Add 13.5*x* to each side.**

$22.5 = x$ **Divide each side by 22.5.**

Since $\overline{KL} \parallel \overline{MN}$, $\triangle JKL \sim \triangle JMN$ and $\frac{JK}{JM} = \frac{KL}{MN}$.

$\frac{9}{13.5 + 9} = \frac{7.5}{y}$ **Write proportion.**

$9y = 7.5(22.5)$ **Cross product property**

$y = 18.75$ **Divide each side by 9.**

GUIDED PRACTICE

Vocabulary Check ✓

1. Complete the following: If a line divides two sides of a triangle proportionally, then it is __?__ to the third side. This theorem is known as the __?__.

Concept Check ✓

2. In $\triangle ABC$, $\overrightarrow{AR}$ bisects $\angle CAB$. Write the proportionality statement for the triangle that is based on Theorem 8.7.

Determine whether the statement is _true_ or _false_. Explain your reasoning.

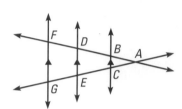

3. $\dfrac{FE}{ED} = \dfrac{FG}{GH}$

4. $\dfrac{FE}{FD} = \dfrac{FG}{FH}$

5. $\dfrac{EG}{DH} = \dfrac{EF}{DF}$

6. $\dfrac{ED}{FE} = \dfrac{EG}{DH}$

Skill Check ✓

Use the figure to complete the proportion.

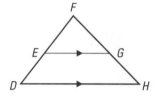

7. $\dfrac{BD}{BF} = \dfrac{?}{CG}$

8. $\dfrac{AE}{CE} = \dfrac{?}{BD}$

9. $\dfrac{?}{GA} = \dfrac{FD}{FA}$

10. $\dfrac{GA}{?} = \dfrac{FA}{DA}$

PRACTICE AND APPLICATIONS

STUDENT HELP

▶ **Extra Practice**
to help you master skills is on p. 818.

🧩 **LOGICAL REASONING** Determine whether the given information implies that $\overline{QS} \parallel \overline{PT}$. Explain.

11.

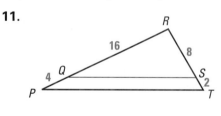

12.

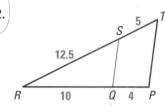

13.

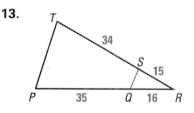

14.

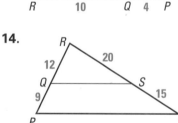

STUDENT HELP

▶ **HOMEWORK HELP**
Example 1: Exs. 21–28
Example 2: Exs. 11–20
Example 3: Exs. 21–28
Example 4: Exs. 21–28
Example 5: Exs. 29, 30, 36, 37
Example 6: Exs. 34–37

🧩 **LOGICAL REASONING** Use the diagram shown to decide if you are given enough information to conclude that $\overline{LP} \parallel \overline{MQ}$. If so, state the reason.

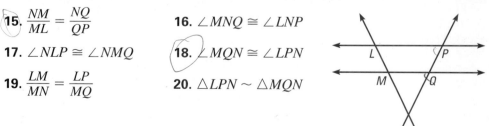

15. $\dfrac{NM}{ML} = \dfrac{NQ}{QP}$

16. $\angle MNQ \cong \angle LNP$

17. $\angle NLP \cong \angle NMQ$

18. $\angle MQN \cong \angle LPN$

19. $\dfrac{LM}{MN} = \dfrac{LP}{MQ}$

20. $\triangle LPN \sim \triangle MQN$

USING PROPORTIONALITY THEOREMS Find the value of the variable.

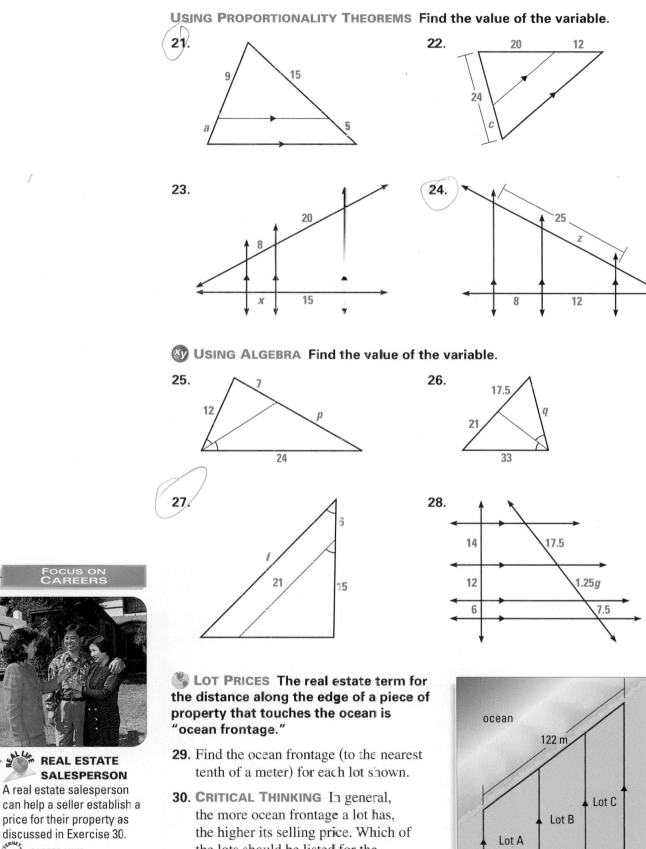

21.

9   15

a   5

22.

20   12

24

c

23.

20

8

x   15

24.

25

z

8   12

USING ALGEBRA Find the value of the variable.

25.

7

12   p

24

26.

17.5

21   q

33

27.

5

f

21   15

28.

14   17.5

12   1.25g

6   7.5

LOT PRICES The real estate term for
the distance along the edge of a piece of
property that touches the ocean is
"ocean frontage."

29. Find the ocean frontage (to the nearest
tenth of a meter) for each lot shown.

30. **CRITICAL THINKING** In general,
the more ocean frontage a lot has,
the higher its selling price. Which of
the lots should be listed for the
highest price?

ocean

122 m

Lot C

Lot B

Lot A

38 m   32 m   27 m

Coastline Drive

STUDENT HELP

INTERNET **HOMEWORK HELP** Visit our Web site www.mcdougallittell.com for help with proofs in Exs. 31–33.

31. **TWO-COLUMN PROOF** Use the diagram shown to write a two-column proof of Theorem 8.4.

GIVEN ▶ $\overline{DE} \parallel \overline{AC}$

PROVE ▶ $\frac{DA}{BD} = \frac{EC}{BE}$

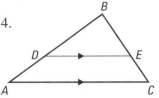

32. **PARAGRAPH PROOF** Use the diagram with the auxiliary line drawn to write a paragraph proof of Theorem 8.6.

GIVEN ▶ $k_1 \parallel k_2$, $k_2 \parallel k_3$

PROVE ▶ $\frac{CB}{BA} = \frac{DE}{EF}$

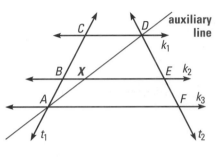

33. **PARAGRAPH PROOF** Use the diagram with the auxiliary lines drawn to write a paragraph proof of Theorem 8.7.

GIVEN ▶ $\angle YXW \cong \angle WXZ$

PROVE ▶ $\frac{YW}{WZ} = \frac{XY}{XZ}$

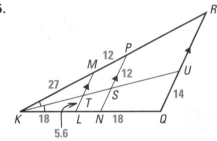

FINDING SEGMENT LENGTHS **Use the diagram to determine the lengths of the missing segments.**

34.

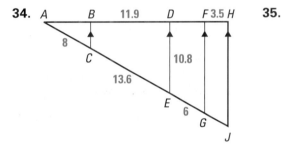

35.

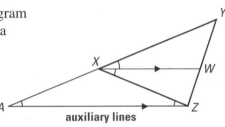

NEW YORK CITY **Use the following information and the map of New York City.** On Fifth Avenue, the distance between E 33rd Street and E 24th Street is about 2600 feet. The distance between those same streets on Broadway is about 2800 feet. All numbered streets are parallel.

36. On Fifth Avenue, the distance between E 24th Street and E 29th Street is about 1300 feet. What is the distance between these two streets on Broadway?

37. On Broadway, the distance between E 33rd Street and E 30th Street is about 1120 feet. What is the distance between these two streets on Fifth Avenue?

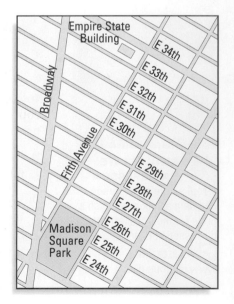

38. *Writing* Use the diagram given for the proof of Theorem 8.4 from Exercise 31 to explain how you can prove the Triangle Proportionality Converse, Theorem 8.5.

39. **MULTI-STEP PROBLEM** Use the diagram shown.

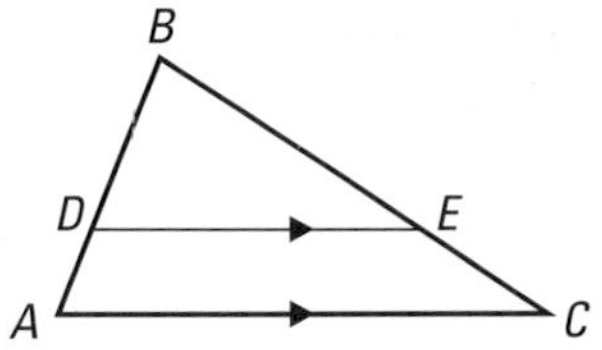

   a. If $DB = 6$, $AD = 2$, and $CB = 20$, find EB.

   b. Use the diagram to state three correct proportions.

   c. If $DB = 4$, $AB = 10$, and $CB = 20$, find CE.

   d. *Writing* Explain how you know that $\triangle ABC$ is similar to $\triangle DBE$.

★ **Challenge**

40. **CONSTRUCTION** Perform the following construction.

   GIVEN ▶ Segments with lengths x, y, and z

   CONSTRUCT ▶ A segment of length p, such that $\frac{x}{y} = \frac{z}{p}$.

   (*Hint:* This construction is like the construction on page 500.)

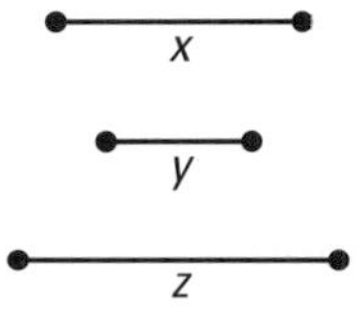

MIXED REVIEW

USING THE DISTANCE FORMULA **Find the distance between the two points.** (Review 1.3)

41. $A(10, 5)$
$B(-6, -4)$

42. $A(7, -3)$
$B(-9, 4)$

43. $A(-1, -9)$
$B(6, -2)$

44. $A(0, 11)$
$B(-5, 2)$

45. $A(0, -10)$
$B(4, 7)$

46. $A(8, -5)$
$B(0, 4)$

USING THE DISTANCE FORMULA **Place the figure in a coordinate plane and find the requested information.** (Review 4.7)

47. Draw a right triangle with legs of 12 units and 9 units. Find the length of the hypotenuse.

48. Draw a rectangle with length 16 units and width 12 units. Find the length of a diagonal.

49. Draw an isosceles right triangle with legs of 6 units. Find the length of the hypotenuse.

50. Draw an isosceles triangle with base of 16 units and height of 6 units. Find the length of the legs.

TRANSFORMATIONS **Name the type of transformation.** (Review 7.1– 7.3, 7.5 for 8.7)

51.   **52.**   **53.**

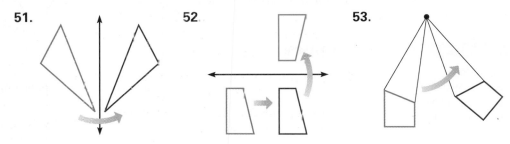

8.7

Dilations

What you should learn

GOAL 1 Identify dilations.

GOAL 2 Use properties of dilations to create a **real-life** perspective drawing in **Ex. 34**.

Why you should learn it

▼ To solve **real-life** problems, such as estimating the height of the shadow of a shadow puppet in **Example 3**.

GOAL 1 IDENTIFYING DILATIONS

In Chapter 7, you studied rigid transformations, in which the image and preimage of a figure are *congruent*. In this lesson, you will study a type of nonrigid transformation called a *dilation*, in which the image and preimage of a figure are *similar*.

A **dilation** with center C and scale factor k is a transformation that maps every point P in the plane to a point P' so that the following properties are true.

1. If P is not the center point C, then the image point P' lies on $\overrightarrow{CP}$. The scale factor k is a positive number such that $k = \dfrac{CP'}{CP}$, and $k \neq 1$.

2. If P is the center point C, then $P = P'$.

The dilation is a **reduction** if $0 < k < 1$ and it is an **enlargement** if $k > 1$.

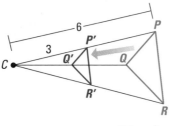 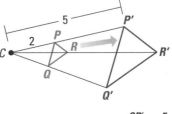

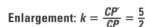

Reduction: $k = \dfrac{CP'}{CP} = \dfrac{3}{6} = \dfrac{1}{2}$ **Enlargement:** $k = \dfrac{CP'}{CP} = \dfrac{5}{2}$

Because $\triangle PQR \sim \triangle P'Q'R'$, $\dfrac{P'Q'}{PQ}$ is equal to the scale factor of the dilation.

EXAMPLE 1 *Identifying Dilations*

Identify the dilation and find its scale factor.

a.   b.

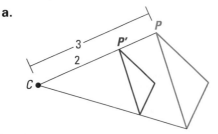 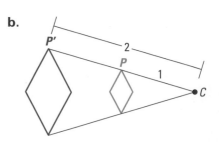

STUDENT HELP

► **Look Back**
For help with the blue to red color scheme used in transformations, see p. 396.

SOLUTION

a. Because $\dfrac{CP'}{CP} = \dfrac{2}{3}$, the scale factor is $k = \dfrac{2}{3}$. This is a reduction.

b. Because $\dfrac{CP'}{CP} = \dfrac{2}{1}$, the scale factor is $k = 2$. This is an enlargement.

In a coordinate plane, dilations whose centers are the origin have the property that the image of $P(x, y)$ is $P'(kx, ky)$.

EXAMPLE 2 *Dilation in a Coordinate Plane*

Draw a dilation of rectangle $ABCD$ with $A(2, 2)$, $B(6, 2)$, $C(6, 4)$, and $D(2, 4)$. Use the origin as the center and use a scale factor of $\frac{1}{2}$. How does the perimeter of the preimage compare to the perimeter of the image?

SOLUTION

Because the center of the dilation is the origin, you can find the image of each vertex by multiplying its coordinates by the scale factor.

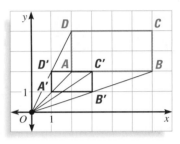

$$A(2, 2) \rightarrow A'(1, 1)$$

$$B(6, 2) \rightarrow B'(3, 1)$$

$$C(6, 4) \rightarrow C'(3, 2)$$

$$D(2, 4) \rightarrow D'(1, 2)$$

From the graph, you can see that the preimage has a perimeter of 12 and the image has a perimeter of 6. A preimage and its image after a dilation are similar figures. Therefore, the ratio of the perimeters of a preimage and its image is equal to the scale factor of the dilation.

▶ **ACTIVITY**

Construction **Drawing a Dilation**

Use the following steps to construct a dilation ($k = 2$) of a triangle using a straightedge and a compass.

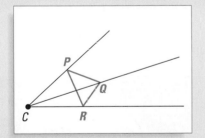 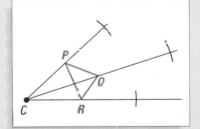 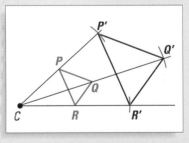

❶ Draw $\triangle PQR$ and choose the center of the dilation C. Use a straightedge to draw lines from C through the vertices of the triangle.

❷ Use the compass to locate F' on $\overrightarrow{CP}$ so that $CP' = 2(CP)$. Locate Q' and R' in the same way.

❸ Connect the points P', Q', and R'.

In the construction above, notice that $\triangle PQR \sim \triangle P'Q'R'$. You can prove this by using the SAS and SSS Similarity Theorems.

GOAL 2 USING DILATIONS IN REAL LIFE

EXAMPLE 3 *Finding the Scale Factor*

FOCUS ON APPLICATIONS

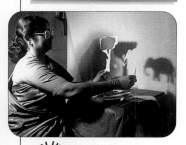

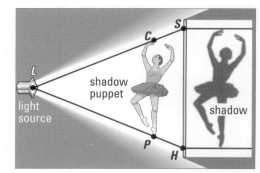

REAL LIFE SHADOW PUPPETS
Some experienced shadowmaster puppeteers can manipulate over 20 carved leather puppets at the same time.

SHADOW PUPPETS Shadow puppets have been used in many countries for hundreds of years. A flat figure is held between a light and a screen. The audience on the other side of the screen sees the puppet's shadow. The shadow is a dilation, or enlargement, of the shadow puppet. When looking at a cross sectional view, $\triangle LCP \sim \triangle LSH$.

The shadow puppet shown is 12 inches tall (CP in the diagram). Find the height of the shadow, SH, for each distance from the screen. In each case, by what percent is the shadow larger than the puppet?

a. $LC = LP = 59$ in.; $LS = LH = 74$ in.

b. $LC = LP = 66$ in.; $LS = LH = 74$ in.

SOLUTION

a. $\frac{59}{74} = \frac{12}{SH}$ $\qquad$ $\frac{LC}{LS} = \frac{CP}{SH}$

$59(SH) = 888$

$SH \approx 15$ inches

To find the percent of size increase, use the scale factor of the dilation.

scale factor $= \frac{SH}{CP}$

$\frac{15}{12} = 1.25$

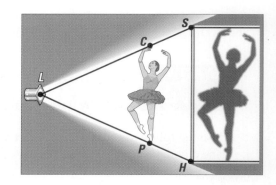

▶ So, the shadow is 25% larger than the puppet.

b. $\frac{66}{74} = \frac{12}{SH}$

$66(SH) = 888$

$SH \approx 13.45$ inches

Use the scale factor again to find the percent of size increase.

scale factor $= \frac{SH}{CP}$

$\frac{13.45}{12} \approx 1.12$

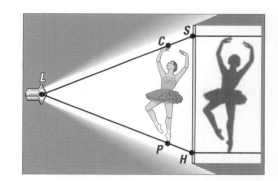

▶ So, the shadow is about 12% larger than the puppet.

Notice that as the puppet moves closer to the screen, the shadow height decreases.

GUIDED PRACTICE

Vocabulary Check ✓

1. In a *dilation* every image is __?__ to its preimage.

Concept Check ✓

2. **ERROR ANALYSIS** Katie found the scale factor of the dilation shown to be $\frac{1}{2}$. What did Katie do wrong?

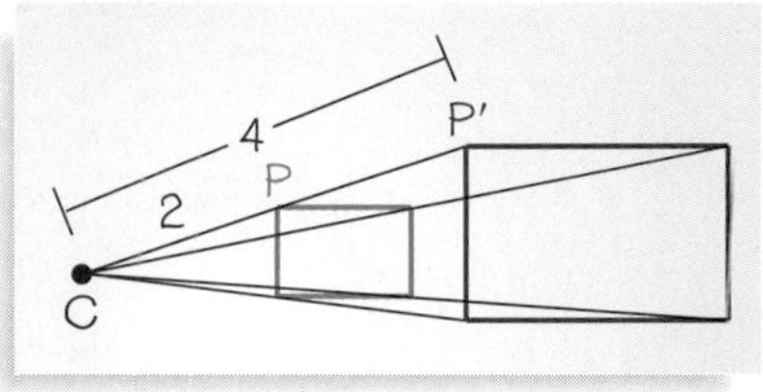

3. Is the dilation shown a reduction or an enlargement? How do you know?

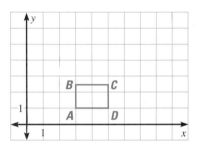

Skill Check ✓

$\triangle PQR$ **is mapped onto** $\triangle P'Q'R'$ **by a dilation with center** *C*. **Complete the statement.**

4. $\triangle PQR$ is (similar, congruent) to $\triangle P'Q'R'$.

5. If $\frac{CP'}{CP} = \frac{4}{3}$, then $\triangle P'Q'R'$ is (larger, smaller) than $\triangle PQR$, and the dilation is (a reduction, an enlargement).

Use the following information to draw a dilation of rectangle *ABCD*.

6. Draw a dilation of rectangle *ABCD* on a coordinate plane, with $A(3, 1)$, $B(3, 2.5)$, $C(5, 2.5)$, and $D(5, 1)$. Use the origin as the center and use a scale factor of 2.

7. Is $ABCD \sim A'B'C'D'$? Explain your answer.

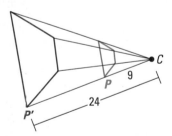

PRACTICE AND APPLICATIONS

STUDENT HELP

▶ **Extra Practice**
to help you master skills is on p. 818.

IDENTIFYING DILATIONS Identify the dilation and find its scale factor.

8.

9.

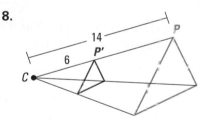

FINDING SCALE FACTORS Identify the dilation, and find its scale factor. Then, find the values of the variables.

10.

11.

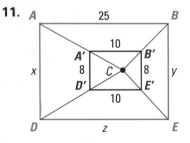

STUDENT HELP

→ **HOMEWORK HELP**
Example 1: Exs. 8–11, 20–23
Example 2: Exs. 12–15
Example 3: Exs. 24–26, 33

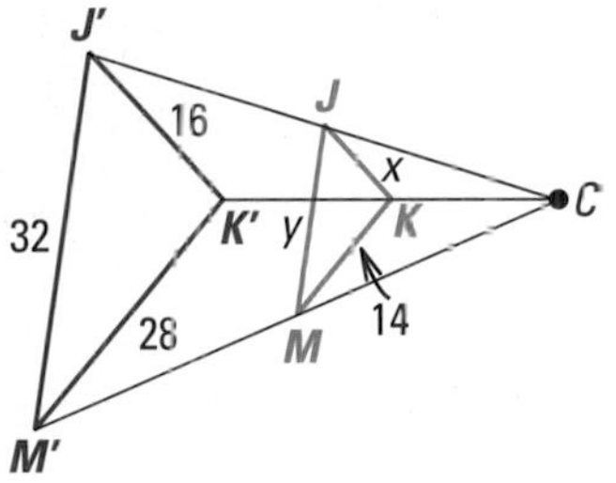

DILATIONS IN A COORDINATE PLANE Use the origin as the center of the dilation and the given scale factor to find the coordinates of the vertices of the image of the polygon.

12. $k = \frac{1}{2}$

13. $k = 2$

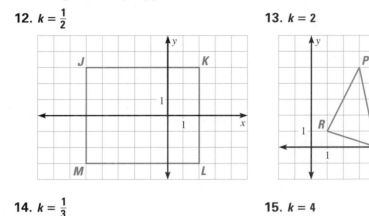

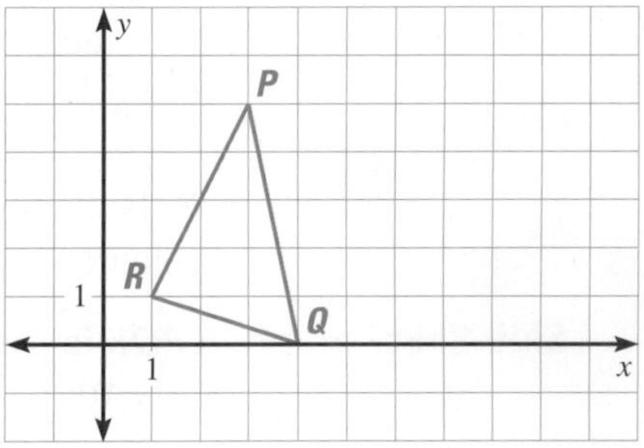

14. $k = \frac{1}{3}$

15. $k = 4$

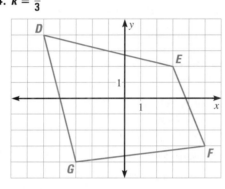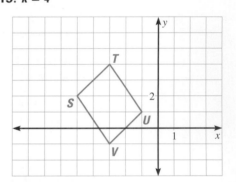

16. COMPARING RATIOS Use the triangle shown. Let P and Q be the midpoints of the sides $\overline{EG}$ and $\overline{FG}$, respectively. Find the scale factor and the center of the dilation that enlarges $\triangle PQG$ to $\triangle EFG$. Find the ratio of EF to PQ. How does this ratio compare to the scale factor?

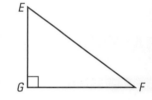

CONSTRUCTION Copy $\triangle DEF$ and points G and H as shown. Then, use a straightedge and a compass to construct the dilation.

17. $k = 3$; Center: G

18. $k = \frac{1}{2}$; Center: H

19. $k = 2$; Center: E

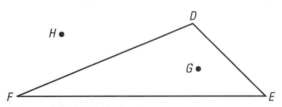

SIMILAR TRIANGLES The red triangle is the image of the blue triangle after a dilation. Find the values of the variables. Then find the ratio of their perimeters.

20.

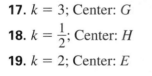

21.

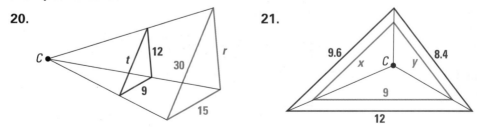

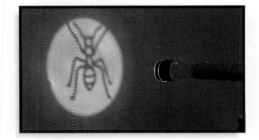

STUDENT HELP

HOMEWORK HELP
Visit our Web site
www.mcdougallittell.com
for help with problem
solving in Exs. 22 and 23.

IDENTIFYING DILATIONS $\triangle ABC$ is mapped onto $\triangle A'B'C'$ by a dilation. Use the given information to sketch the dilation, identify it as a reduction or an enlargement, and find the scale factor. Then find the missing lengths.

22. In $\triangle ABC$, $AB = 6$, $BC = 9$, and $AC = 12$. In $\triangle A'B'C'$, $A'B' = 2$. Find the lengths of $\overline{B'C'}$ and $\overline{A'C'}$.

23. In $\triangle ABC$, $AB = 5$ and $BC = 7$. In $\triangle A'B'C'$, $A'B' = 20$ and $A'C' = 36$. Find the lengths of $\overline{AC}$ and $\overline{B'C'}$

🌐 **FLASHLIGHT IMAGE** **In Exercises 24–26, use the following information.**
You are projecting images onto a wall with a flashlight. The lamp of the flashlight is 8.3 centimeters away from the wall. The preimage is imprinted onto a clear cap that fits over the end of the flashlight. This cap has a diameter of 3 centimeters. The preimage has a height of 2 centimeters, and the lamp of the flashlight is located 2.7 centimeters from the preimage.

24. Sketch a diagram of the dilation.

25. Find the diameter of the circle of light projected onto the wall from the flashlight.

26. Find the height of the image projected onto the wall.

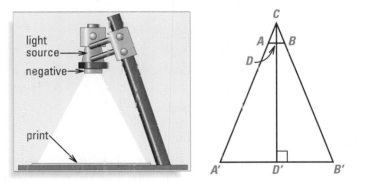

🌐 **ENLARGEMENTS** **In Exercises 27 and 28, use the following information.**
By adjusting the distance between the negative and the enlarged print in the photographic enlarger shown you can make prints of different sizes.
In the diagram shown, you want the enlarged print to be 7 inches wide ($A'B'$). The negative is 1 inch wide (AB), and the distance between the light source and the negative is 1.25 inches (CD).

27. What is the scale factor of the enlargement?

28. What is the distance between the light source and the enlarged print?

🌐 **DIMENSIONS OF PHOTOS** **Use the diagram from Exercise 27 to determine the missing information.**

	CD	CD'	AB	A'B'
29.	1.2 in.	7.2 in.	0.8 in.	?
30.	?	14 cm	2 cm	12 cm
31.	2 in.	10 in.	?	8.5 in.

32. LOGICAL REASONING Draw any triangle, and label it $\triangle PQR$. Using a scale factor of 2, draw the image of $\triangle PQR$ after a dilation with a center outside the triangle, with a center inside the triangle, and with a center on the triangle. Explain the relationship between the three images created.

33. *Writing* Use the information about shadow puppet theaters from Example 3, page 508. Explain how you could use a shadow puppet theater to help another student understand the terms *image*, *preimage*, *center of dilation*, and *dilation*. Draw a diagram and label the terms on the diagram.

34. PERSPECTIVE DRAWING Create a perspective drawing by following the given steps.

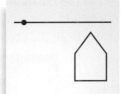 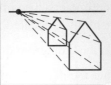 

① Draw a horizontal line across the paper, and choose a point on this line to be the center of the dilation, also called the *vanishing point*. Next, draw a polygon.

② Draw rays from the vanishing point to all vertices of the polygon. Draw a reduction of the polygon by locating image points on the rays.

③ Connect the preimage to the image by darkening the segments between them. Erase all hidden lines.

Test Preparation

35. MULTIPLE CHOICE Identify the dilation shown as an enlargement or reduction and find its scale factor.

Ⓐ enlargement; $k = 2$

Ⓑ enlargement; $k = \frac{1}{3}$

Ⓒ reduction; $k = \frac{1}{3}$

Ⓓ reduction; $k = \frac{1}{2}$

Ⓔ reduction; $k = 3$

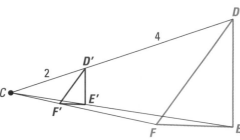

36. MULTIPLE CHOICE In the diagram shown, the center of the dilation of $\square JKLM$ is point C. The length of a side of $\square J'K'L'M'$ is what percent of the length of the corresponding side of $\square JKLM$?

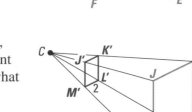

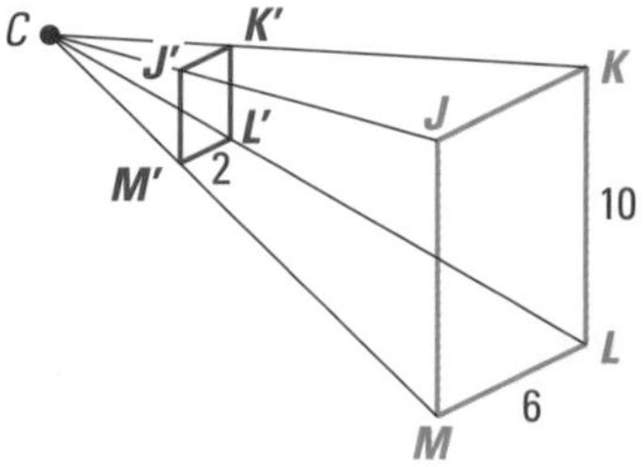

Ⓐ 3% Ⓑ 12% Ⓒ 20%

Ⓓ $33\frac{1}{3}$% Ⓔ 300%

★ Challenge

37. CREATING NEW IMAGES A polygon is reduced by a dilation with center C and scale factor $\frac{1}{k}$. The image is then enlarged by a dilation with center C and scale factor k. Describe the size and shape of this new image.

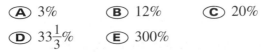

MIXED REVIEW

USING THE PYTHAGOREAN THEOREM Refer to the triangle shown to find the length of the missing side by using the Pythagorean Theorem.
(Review 1.3 for 9.1)

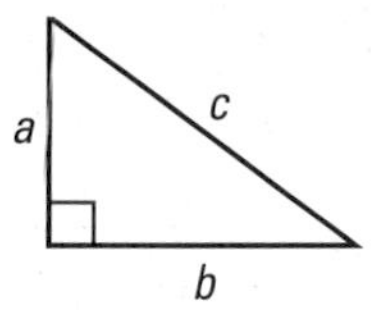

38. $a = 5, b = 12$　　　　**39.** $a = 8, c = 2\sqrt{65}$

40. $b = 2, c = 5\sqrt{5}$　　　　**41.** $b = 1, c = \sqrt{50}$

42. Find the geometric mean of 11 and 44. **(Review 8.2 for 9.1)**

DETERMINING SIMILARITY Determine whether the triangles can be proved similar or not. Explain your reasoning. **(Review 8.4 and 8.5)**

43.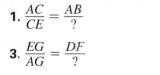　　　　**44.**

QUIZ 3　　　　　　　　　　　　　　　　　　*Self-Test for Lessons 8.6 and 8.7*

Use the figure to complete the proportion.
(Lesson 8.6)

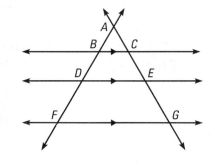

1. $\dfrac{AC}{CE} = \dfrac{AB}{?}$　　　　　　**2.** $\dfrac{BD}{BF} = \dfrac{?}{CG}$

3. $\dfrac{EG}{AG} = \dfrac{DF}{?}$　　　　　　**4.** $\dfrac{GA}{EA} = \dfrac{?}{DA}$

In Exercises 5 and 6, identify the dilation and find its scale factor. **(Lesson 8.7)**

5.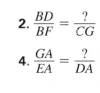　　　　　　**6.**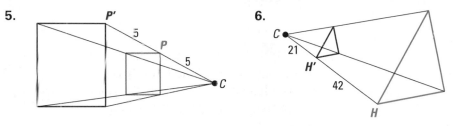

7. $\triangle JKL$ is mapped onto $\triangle J'K'L'$ by a dilation, with center C. If $\dfrac{CJ'}{CJ} = \dfrac{5}{6}$, then the dilation is (a reduction, an enlargement) and $\triangle JKL$ is (larger, smaller) than $\triangle J'K'L'$. **(Lesson 8.7)**

8. 🌐 **ENLARGING PHOTOS** An 8 inch by 10 inch photo is enlarged to produce an 18 inch by $22\frac{1}{2}$ inch photo. What is the scale factor? **(Lesson 8.7)**

▶ ACTIVITY 8.7

Using Technology

Exploring Dilations

You can use geometry software to explore properties of dilations.

▶ CONSTRUCT

1 Draw a pentagon and label it *ABCDE*.

2 Draw a point outside the polygon. Label it *P*.

3 Dilate the polygon using a scale factor of $\frac{1}{2}$ and center *P*. Label the image *A'B'C'D'E'*.

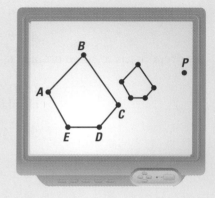

▶ INVESTIGATE

1. Measure *AP* and *A'P* and calculate the ratio $\frac{AP}{A'P}$. What do you notice?

2. Measure *AB* and *A'B'* and calculate the ratio $\frac{AB}{A'B'}$. What do you notice?

3. Drag point *P* to several locations outside *ABCDE*. Do the ratios you found in Exercises 1 and 2 change?

4. Drag point *P* to several locations inside *ABCDE*. What do you notice about the position of *A'B'C'D'E'*?

5. Determine the areas of *ABCDE* and *A'B'C'D'E'*. Calculate the ratio of the area of *ABCDE* to the area of *A'B'C'D'E'*.

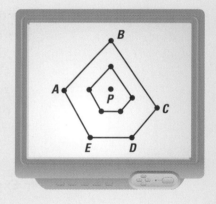

▶ CONJECTURE

6. Make a conjecture about how the area of a polygon and the area of its image after a dilation are related to the scale factor of the dilation. Test your conjecture using a different polygon and scale factor.

EXTENSION

CRITICAL THINKING Suppose a polygon is dilated with scale factor *x* and then the image is dilated with scale factor *y*. What scale factor could you use to dilate the original polygon to the final polygon? Explain.

Chapter Summary

WHAT did you learn?

Write and simplify the ratio of two numbers. **(8.1)**

Use proportions to solve problems. **(8.1)**

Understand properties of proportions. **(8.2)**

Identify similar polygons and use properties of similar polygons. **(8.3)**

Prove that two triangles are similar using the definition of similar triangles and the AA Similarity Postulate. **(8.4)**

Prove that two triangles are similar using the SSS Similarity Theorem and the SAS Similarity Theorem. **(8.5)**

Use proportionality theorems to solve problems. **(8.6)**

Identify and draw dilations and use properties of dilations. **(8.7)**

WHY did you learn it?

Find the ratio of the track team's wins to losses. **(p. 461)**

Use measurements of a baseball bat sculpture to find the dimensions of Babe Ruth's bat. **(p. 463)**

Determine the width of the actual Titanic ship from the dimensions of a scale model. **(p. 467)**

Determine whether two television screens are similar. **(p. 477)**

Use similar triangles to determine the altitude of an aerial photography blimp. **(p. 482)**

Use similar triangles to estimate the height of the Unisphere. **(p. 494)**

Explain why the diagonal cuts on insulation strips have the same length. **(p. 501)**

Understand how the shadows in a shadow puppet show change size. **(p. 508)**

How does Chapter 8 fit into the BIGGER PICTURE of geometry?

In this chapter, you learned that if two polygons are similar, then the lengths of their corresponding sides are proportional. You also studied several connections among real-life situations, geometry, and algebra. For instance, solving a problem that involves similar polygons (geometry) often requires the use of a proportion (algebra). In later chapters, remember that the measures of corresponding angles of similar polygons are equal, but the lengths of corresponding sides of similar polygons are proportional.

STUDY STRATEGY

How did you use your list of real-world examples?

The list of the main topics of the chapter with corresponding real-world examples that you made following the **Study Strategy** on page 456, may resemble this one.

> **Real-World Examples**
>
> Lesson 8.1
>
> Topic writing ratios: to find the ratio of wins to losses of the track team.
>
> Topic solving proportions: to estimate the weight of a person on Mars.

VOCABULARY

- ratio, p. 457
- proportion, p. 459
- extremes, p. 459
- means, p. 459
- geometric mean, p. 466
- similar polygons, p. 473
- scale factor, p. 474
- dilation, p. 506
- reduction, p. 506
- enlargement, p. 506

8.1   **RATIO AND PROPORTION**

Examples on pp. 457–460

EXAMPLE   You can solve a proportion by finding the value of the variable.

$$\frac{x}{12} = \frac{x+6}{30}$$ **Write original proportion.**

$$30x = 12(x+6)$$ **Cross product property**

$$30x = 12x + 72$$ **Distributive property**

$$18x = 72$$ **Subtract 12x from each side.**

$$x = 4$$ **Divide each side by 18.**

Solve the proportion.

1. $\dfrac{3}{x} = \dfrac{2}{7}$

2. $\dfrac{a+1}{5} = \dfrac{2a}{9}$

3. $\dfrac{2}{x+1} = \dfrac{4}{x+6}$

4. $\dfrac{d-4}{d} = \dfrac{3}{7}$

8.2   **PROBLEM SOLVING IN GEOMETRY WITH PROPORTIONS**

Examples on pp. 465–467

EXAMPLE   In 1997, the ratio of the population of South Carolina to the population of Wyoming was $47:6$. The population of South Carolina was about 3,760,000. You can find the population of Wyoming by solving a proportion.

$$\frac{47}{6} = \frac{3,760,000}{x}$$

$$47x = 22,560,000$$

$$x = 480,000 \quad \text{The population of Wyoming was about 480,000.}$$

5. You buy a 13 inch scale model of the sculpture *The Dancer* by Edgar Degas. The ratio of the height of the scale model to the height of the sculpture is $1:3$. Find the height of the sculpture.

6. The ratio of the birth weight to the adult weight of a male black bear is $3:1000$. The average birth weight is 12 ounces. Find the average adult weight in pounds.

SIMILAR POLYGONS

Examples on
pp. 473–475

EXAMPLE The two parallelograms shown are similar because their corresponding angles are congruent and the lengths of their corresponding sides are proportional.

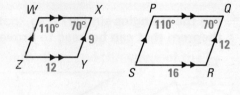

$$\frac{WX}{PQ} = \frac{ZY}{SR} = \frac{XY}{QR} = \frac{WZ}{PS} = \frac{3}{4}$$

$m\angle P = m\angle R = m\angle W = m\angle Y = 110°$

$m\angle Q = m\angle S = m\angle X = m\angle Z = 70°$

The scale factor of $\square WXYZ$ to $\square PQRS$ is $\frac{3}{4}$.

In Exercises 7–9, $\square DEFG \sim \square HJKL$.

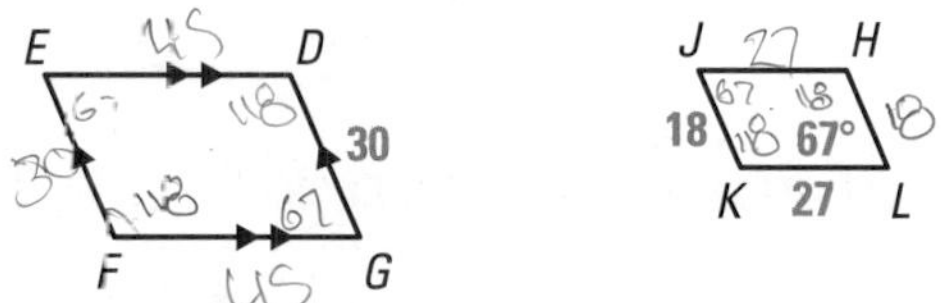

7. Find the scale factor of $\square DEFG$ to $\square HJKL$.

8. Find the length of $\overline{DE}$ and the measure of $\angle F$.

9. Find the ratio of the perimeter of $\square HJKL$ to the perimeter of $\square DEFG$.

SIMILAR TRIANGLES

Examples on
pp. 480–482

EXAMPLE Because two angles of $\triangle ABC$ are congruent to two angles of $\triangle DEF$, $\triangle ABC \sim \triangle DEF$ by the Angle-Angle (AA) Similarity Postulate.

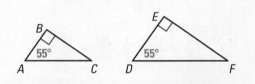

Determine whether the triangles can be proved similar or not. Explain why or why not. If they are similar, write a similarity statement.

10.

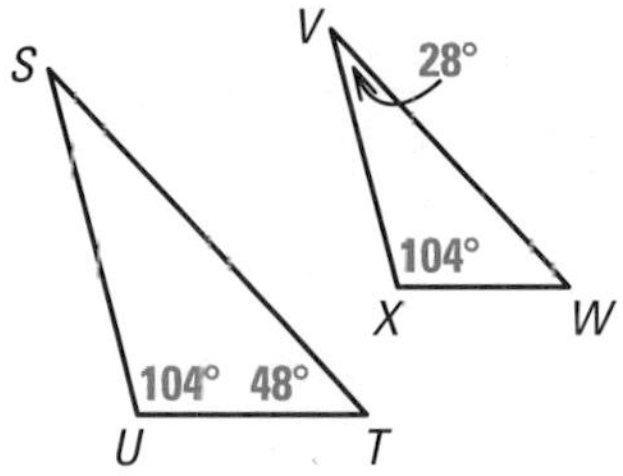

11.

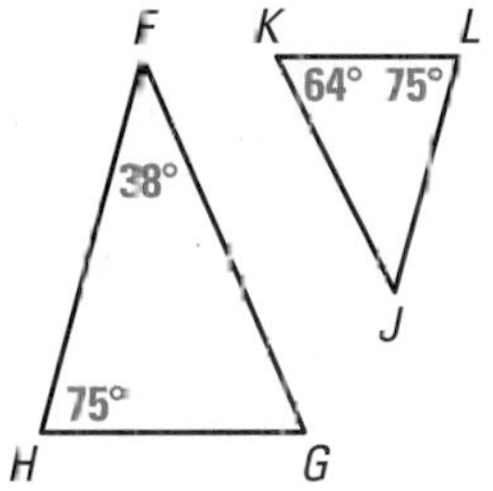

12.

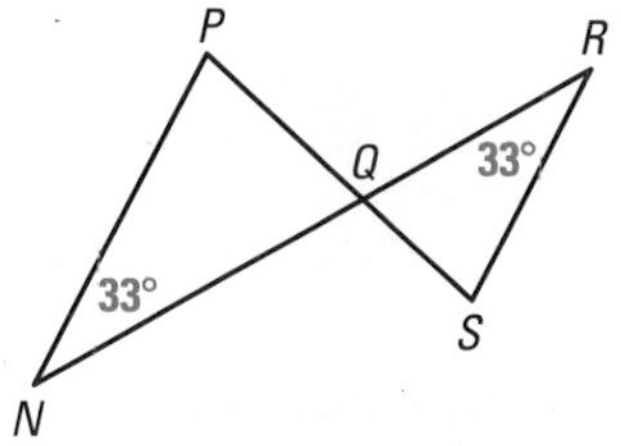

PROVING TRIANGLES ARE SIMILAR

Examples on
pp. 488–491

EXAMPLES Three sides of $\triangle JKL$ are proportional to three sides of $\triangle MNP$, so $\triangle JKL \sim \triangle MNP$ by the Side-Side-Side (SSS) Similarity Theorem.

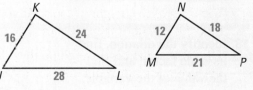

Two sides of $\triangle XYZ$ are proportional to two sides of $\triangle WXY$, and the included angles are congruent. By the Side-Angle-Side (SAS) Similarity Theorem, $\triangle XYZ \sim \triangle WXY$.

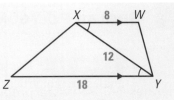

Are the triangles similar? If so, state the similarity and a postulate or theorem that can be used to prove that the triangles are similar.

13.

14.

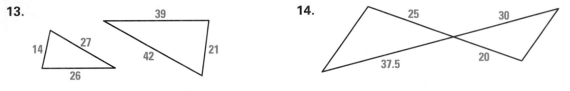

8.6 PROPORTIONS AND SIMILAR TRIANGLES

Examples on pp. 498–501

EXAMPLES You can use proportionality theorems to compare proportional lengths.

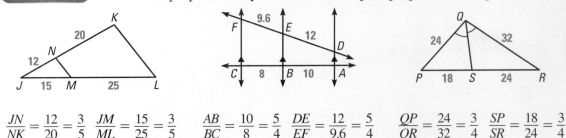

$$\frac{JN}{NK} = \frac{12}{20} = \frac{3}{5} \quad \frac{JM}{ML} = \frac{15}{25} = \frac{3}{5} \qquad \frac{AB}{BC} = \frac{10}{8} = \frac{5}{4} \quad \frac{DE}{EF} = \frac{12}{9.6} = \frac{5}{4} \qquad \frac{QP}{QR} = \frac{24}{32} = \frac{3}{4} \quad \frac{SP}{SR} = \frac{18}{24} = \frac{3}{4}$$

Find the value of the variable.

15.

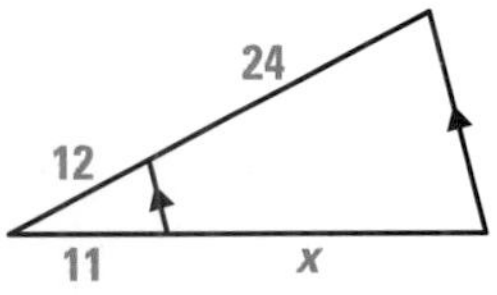

16.

17.

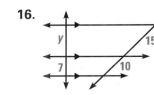
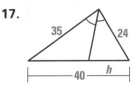

8.7 DILATIONS

Examples on pp. 506–508

EXAMPLE The blue triangle is mapped onto the red triangle by a dilation with center C. The scale factor is $\frac{1}{5}$, so the dilation is a reduction.

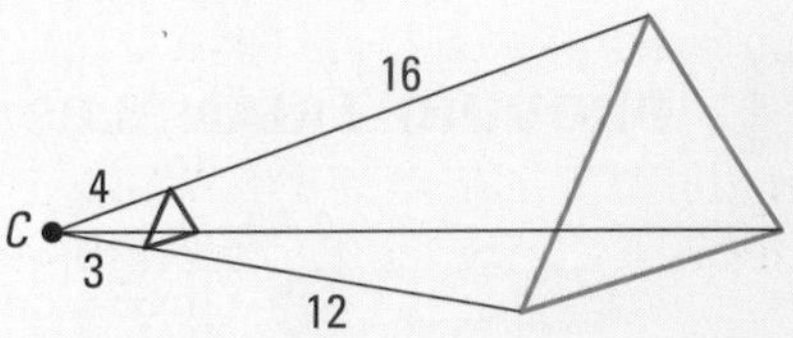

18. Identify the dilation, find its scale factor, and find the value of the variable.

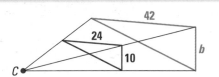

In Exercises 1–3, solve the proportion.

1. $\dfrac{x}{3} = \dfrac{12}{9}$

2. $\dfrac{18}{y} = \dfrac{15}{20}$

3. $\dfrac{11}{110} = \dfrac{z}{10}$

Complete the sentence.

4. If $\dfrac{5}{2} = \dfrac{a}{b}$, then $\dfrac{5}{a} = \dfrac{?}{b}$.

5. If $\dfrac{8}{x} = \dfrac{3}{y}$, then $\dfrac{8-x}{x} = \dfrac{?}{y}$.

In Exercises 6–8, use the figure shown.

6. Find the length of $\overline{EF}$.

7. Find the length of $\overline{FG}$.

8. Is quadrilateral $FECB$ similar to quadrilateral $GFBA$? If so, what is the scale factor?

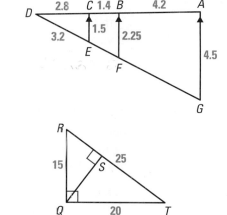

In Exercises 9–12, use the figure shown.

9. Prove that $\triangle RSQ \sim \triangle RQT$.

10. What is the scale factor of $\triangle RSQ$ to $\triangle RQT$?

11. Is $\triangle RSQ$ similar to $\triangle QST$? Explain.

12. Find the length of $\overline{QS}$.

In Exercises 13–15, use the figure shown to decide if you are given enough information to conclude that $\overline{JK} \parallel \overline{LM}$. If so, state the reason.

13. $\dfrac{LJ}{JH} = \dfrac{MK}{KH}$

14. $\angle HJK \cong \angle HLM$

15. $\dfrac{LH}{JH} = \dfrac{MH}{KH}$

16. The triangle $\triangle RST$ is mapped onto $\triangle R'S'T'$ by a dilation with $RS = 24$, $ST = 12$, $RT = 20$, and $R'S' = 6$. Find the scale factor k, and side lengths $S'T'$ and $R'T'$.

17. Two sides of a triangle have lengths of 14 inches and 18 inches. The measure of the angle included by the sides is 45°. Two sides of a second triangle have lengths of 7 inches and 8 inches. The measure of the angle included by the sides is 45°. Are the two triangles similar? Explain.

18. You shine a flashlight on a book that is 9 inches tall and 6 inches wide. It makes a shadow on the wall that is 3 feet tall and 2 feet wide. What is the scale factor of the book to its shadow?

Chapter Standardized Test

● **TEST-TAKING STRATEGY** When checking your work, try to use a method other than the one you originally used to get your answer. If you use the same method, you may make the same mistake twice.

1. **MULTIPLE CHOICE** If $\frac{a}{b} = \frac{m}{n}$, then which of the following is *not* necessarily true?

  (A) $\frac{a}{m} = \frac{b}{n}$ (B) $\frac{a}{n} = \frac{b}{m}$

  (C) $an = bm$ (D) $\frac{b}{a} = \frac{n}{m}$

  (E) $\frac{a+b}{b} = \frac{m+n}{n}$

2. **MULTIPLE CHOICE** Simplify $\frac{20\text{ft}}{5\text{ yd}}$.

  (A) $\frac{1}{4}$ (B) $\frac{3}{4}$ (C) $\frac{5}{4}$

  (D) $\frac{4}{3}$ (E) $\frac{4}{1}$

3. **MULTIPLE CHOICE** The perimeter of a parallelogram is 54. The ratio of the lengths of the sides is $2:7$. What are the lengths of the sides?

  (A) 4 and 14   (B) 8 and 28

  (C) 6 and 21   (D) 24 and 30

  (E) 12 and 42

4. **MULTIPLE CHOICE** Which of the following pairs of numbers has a geometric mean of 64?

  (A) 4 and 6   (B) 16 and 256

  (C) 32 and 96   (D) 2 and 32

  (E) 2 and 1024

5. **MULTIPLE CHOICE** The two polygons shown are similar. What are the values of x and y?

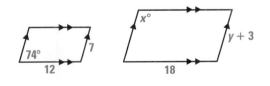

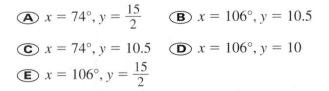

  (A) $x = 74°, y = \frac{15}{2}$ (B) $x = 106°, y = 10.5$

  (C) $x = 74°, y = 10.5$ (D) $x = 106°, y = 10$

  (E) $x = 106°, y = \frac{15}{2}$

6. **MULTIPLE CHOICE** The triangles shown are similar. Which of the following is *not* a correct statement?

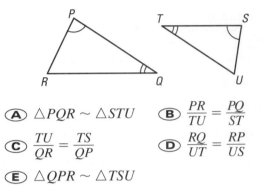

  (A) $\triangle PQR \sim \triangle STU$ (B) $\frac{PR}{TU} = \frac{PQ}{ST}$

  (C) $\frac{TU}{QR} = \frac{TS}{QP}$ (D) $\frac{RQ}{UT} = \frac{RP}{US}$

  (E) $\triangle QPR \sim \triangle TSU$

7. **MULTIPLE CHOICE** You use a pantograph to enlarge a drawing of a car that is 4 inches long. You want your enlargement to be 12 inches long. What is the scale factor of the enlargement to the drawing?

  (A) 3 to 1   (B) 4 to 1   (C) 1 to 3

  (D) 1 to 4   (E) 1 to 2

8. **MULTIPLE CHOICE** What is the perimeter of $\triangle ABC$?

  (A) 90   (B) 97

  (C) 98   (D) 100

  (E) 105

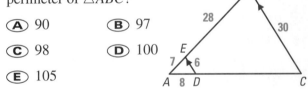

9. **MULTIPLE CHOICE** What is JN?

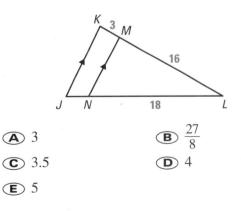

  (A) 3   (B) $\frac{27}{8}$

  (C) 3.5   (D) 4

  (E) 5

10. MULTIPLE CHOICE What is *CD*?

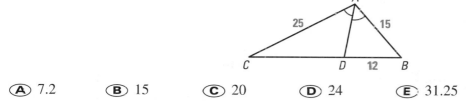

(A) 7.2   (B) 15   (C) 20   (D) 24   (E) 31.25

QUANTITATIVE COMPARISON In Exercises 11 and 12, use the dilation shown to choose the statement that is true about the given quantities.

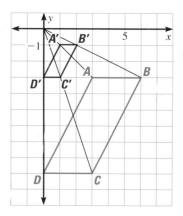

(A) The quantity in column A is greater.

(B) The quantity in column B is greater

(C) The two quantities are equal.

(D) The relationship cannot be determined from the given information.

	Column A	Column B
11.	The perimeter of the preimage	The perimeter of the image
12.	The scale factor of the dilation	$\frac{1}{2}$

MULTI-STEP PROBLEM In Exercises 13–17, use the table, which shows the color popularity survey results for sport/compact cars manufactured during the 1997 model year in North America.

Color	Percent
white	14%
black	13%
bright red	9%
silver	6%
purple	3%
medium red	8%
dark green	20%
light brown	13%
bright blue	3%
dark blue	5%
other	6%

13. Find the ratio of the number of medium red cars to the number of dark green cars.

14. Find the ratio of the number of purple cars to the number of bright red cars.

15. Suppose that in 1997 a manufacturer produced cars in colors that approximate the percents given in the table. If the manufacturer produced 12,560 sport/compact cars in 1997, how many would be dark blue?

16. Suppose a car dealer is ordering 800 sport/compact cars. How many light brown cars should he order?

17. *Writing* Explain why you do not need to know the total number of cars manufactured to find the ratios in Exercises 13 and 14.

MULTI-STEP PROBLEM In Exercises 18–21, use the diagram shown, where *ABCD* ~ *EFGD*.

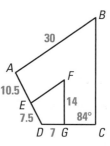

18. a. *ED* = ___?___   **b.** *BC* = ___?___

    c. *EF* = ___?___   **d.** $m\angle DGF$ = ___?___

19. Find the scale factor of *ABCD* to *EFGD*.

20. What is the perimeter of *ABCD*? and *EFGD*?

21. Find the ratio of the perimeter of *ABCD* to the perimeter of *EFGD*.

CHAPTER
8

Algebra Review

EXAMPLE 1 *Simplifying Radicals*

Simplify the expression $\sqrt{20}$.

$$\sqrt{20} = \sqrt{4} \cdot \sqrt{5} \qquad \text{Use product property.}$$
$$= 2\sqrt{5} \qquad \text{Simplify.}$$

EXERCISES

Simplify the expression.

1. $\sqrt{121}$ **2.** $\sqrt{52}$ **3.** $\sqrt{45}$

4. $\sqrt{72}$ **5.** $\sqrt{40}$ **6.** $\sqrt{27}$

7. $\sqrt{80}$ **8.** $\sqrt{50}$ **9.** $\sqrt{243}$

10. $\sqrt{288}$ **11.** $\sqrt{320}$ **12.** $\sqrt{225}$

EXAMPLE 2 *Simplifying Radical Expressions*

Simplify the radical expression.

a. $5\sqrt{3} - \sqrt{3} - \sqrt{2}$ **b.** $(2\sqrt{2})(5\sqrt{3})$ **c.** $(5\sqrt{7})^2$

$\quad = 4\sqrt{3} - \sqrt{2}$ $= 2 \cdot 5 \cdot \sqrt{2} \cdot \sqrt{3}$ $= 5^2\sqrt{7^2}$

                                         $= 10\sqrt{6}$ $= 25 \cdot 7$

                                                                       $= 175$

EXERCISES

Simplify the radical expression.

13. $\sqrt{75} + \sqrt{3}$ **14.** $\sqrt{50} - \sqrt{18}$ **15.** $\sqrt{64} - \sqrt{28}$

16. $\sqrt{44} + 2\sqrt{11}$ **17.** $\sqrt{125} - \sqrt{80}$ **18.** $\sqrt{242} + \sqrt{200}$

19. $-\sqrt{147} - \sqrt{243}$ **20.** $\sqrt{28} + \sqrt{63}$ **21.** $\sqrt{20} + \sqrt{45} - \sqrt{5}$

22. $(\sqrt{13})(\sqrt{26})$ **23.** $(3\sqrt{14})(\sqrt{35})$ **24.** $(\sqrt{363})(\sqrt{300})$

25. $(6\sqrt{2})(2\sqrt{2})$ **26.** $(\sqrt{18})(\sqrt{72})$ **27.** $(\sqrt{21})(\sqrt{24})$

28. $(\sqrt{32})(\sqrt{2})$ **29.** $(\sqrt{98})(\sqrt{128})$ **30.** $(5\sqrt{4})(2\sqrt{4})$

31. $(6\sqrt{5})^2$ **32.** $(4\sqrt{2})^2$ **33.** $(8\sqrt{3})^2$

34. $(2\sqrt{3})^2$ **35.** $(5\sqrt{5})^2$ **36.** $(10\sqrt{11})^2$

EXAMPLE 3 *Simplifying Quotients with Radicals*

Simplify the quotient $\dfrac{6}{\sqrt{5}}$.

$$\dfrac{6}{\sqrt{5}} = \dfrac{6}{\sqrt{5}} \cdot \dfrac{\sqrt{5}}{\sqrt{5}}$$ Multiply numerator and denominator by $\sqrt{5}$, to eliminate a radical in the denominator.

$$= \dfrac{6\sqrt{5}}{\sqrt{5}\,\sqrt{5}}$$

$$= \dfrac{6\sqrt{5}}{5}$$

EXERCISES

Simplify the quotient.

37. $\dfrac{4}{\sqrt{3}}$ **38.** $\dfrac{5}{\sqrt{7}}$ **39.** $\dfrac{2\sqrt{3}}{\sqrt{6}}$ **40.** $\dfrac{2\sqrt{3}}{\sqrt{5}}$

41. $\dfrac{\sqrt{18}}{3\sqrt{2}}$ **42.** $\dfrac{4}{\sqrt{8}}$ **43.** $\dfrac{16}{\sqrt{24}}$ **44.** $\dfrac{\sqrt{5}}{\sqrt{10}}$

45. $\dfrac{4}{\sqrt{12}}$ **46.** $\dfrac{3\sqrt{5}}{\sqrt{20}}$ **47.** $\dfrac{9}{\sqrt{52}}$ **48.** $\dfrac{\sqrt{12}}{\sqrt{24}}$

49. $\dfrac{\sqrt{18}}{\sqrt{10}}$ **50.** $\dfrac{\sqrt{32}}{\sqrt{5}}$ **51.** $\dfrac{\sqrt{27}}{\sqrt{45}}$ **52.** $\dfrac{\sqrt{50}}{\sqrt{75}}$

EXAMPLE 4 *Solving Quadratic Equations*

Solve.

$$x^2 - 5 = 16$$

$$x^2 = 21$$ Add 5 to each side.

$$x = \pm\sqrt{21}$$ Find square roots.

EXERCISES

Solve.

53. $x^2 = 9$ **54.** $x^2 = 625$ **55.** $x^2 = 289$

56. $x^2 + 3 = 13$ **57.** $x^2 - 4 = 12$ **58.** $x^2 - 7 = 6$

59. $7x^2 = 252$ **60.** $3x^2 = 192$ **61.** $6x^2 = 294$

62. $4x^2 + 5 = 45$ **63.** $2x^2 + 5 = 23$ **64.** $9x^2 + 7 = 52$

65. $11x^2 + 4 = 48$ **66.** $6x^2 - 3 = 9$ **67.** $10x^2 - 16 = -6$

68. $5x^2 - 6 = 29$ **69.** $8x^2 - 12 = 36$ **70.** $5x^2 - 61 = 64$

71. $x^2 + 3^2 = 5^2$ **72.** $7^2 + x^2 = 25^2$ **73.** $5^2 + 12^2 = x^2$

RIGHT TRIANGLES AND TRIGONOMETRY

► *How do builders find the dimensions of a skywalk support beam?*

APPLICATION: Support Beam

*W*hen constructing a skywalk for a skyscraper, builders often use mathematics to measure some lengths indirectly.

One method for indirect measurement involves using relationships in a right triangle.

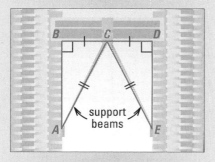

support beams

Think & Discuss

Use the diagram of a skywalk connecting two buildings for Exercises 1 and 2.

1. Given the information in the diagram, how do you know that the skyscrapers are parallel to each other?

2. How do you know that the two right triangles created by the skywalk, beams, and buildings are congruent?

Learn More About It

You will see how the Pythagorean Theorem is used to find the length of a skywalk support beam in Example 4 on p. 537.

APPLICATION LINK Visit www.mcdougallittell.com for more information about skyscrapers.

Study Guide

PREVIEW

What's the chapter about?

Chapter 9 is about **right triangles** and a related branch of mathematics called **trigonometry**. In Chapter 9, you'll learn

- about properties related to general right triangles, similar right triangles, and special right triangles.

- about some applications of right triangles, including *trigonometry*, or triangle measurement, and vectors.

KEY VOCABULARY

▶ **Review**
- converse, p. 72
- right triangle, p. 194
- altitude, p. 281
- proportion, p. 459
- geometric mean, p. 466

- similar polygons, p. 473
▶ **New**
- Pythagorean triple, p. 536
- special right triangles, p. 551
- trigonometric ratio, p. 558

- angle of elevation, p. 561
- solve a right triangle, p. 567
- magnitude of a vector, p. 573
- direction of a vector, p. 574
- sum of two vectors, p. 575

PREPARE

Are you ready for the chapter?

SKILL REVIEW Do these exercises to review key skills that you'll apply in this chapter. See the given **reference page** if there is something you don't understand.

Exercises 1 and 2 refer to △*JKL* **with** $m\angle J = 30°$ **and** $m\angle K = 60°$.

1. Find $m\angle L$. Classify △*JKL* as *acute*, *right*, or *obtuse*. **(Review pp. 194–197)**

2. Sketch △*JKL*. Label its legs, hypotenuse, and altitudes. **(Review pp. 195, 281)**

3. Draw a vector in a coordinate plane whose component form is $\langle 5, -2 \rangle$. **(Review p. 423)**

4. Solve the proportion: $\dfrac{x+3}{5} = \dfrac{x}{3}$. **(Review p. 459)**

5. Refer to △*JKL* in Exercises 1 and 2 above. Sketch a triangle, △*ABC*, that is similar to △*JKL*. Explain how you know the triangles are similar. **(Review p. 481)**

STUDY STRATEGY

Here's a study strategy!

What Do You Know?

Make a list of what you already know about right triangles and trigonometry. Make another list of what you expect to learn about these topics. After studying Chapter 9, review these lists as you review the chapter to see what you have learned.

9.1

Similar Right Triangles

What you should learn

GOAL 1 Solve problems involving similar right triangles formed by the altitude drawn to the hypotenuse of a right triangle.

GOAL 2 Use a geometric mean to solve problems, such as estimating a climbing distance in **Ex. 32**.

Why you should learn it

▼ You can use right triangles and a geometric mean to help you estimate distances, such as finding the approximate height of a monorail track in **Example 3**.

GOAL 1 PROPORTIONS IN RIGHT TRIANGLES

In Lesson 8.4, you learned that two triangles are similar if two of their corresponding angles are congruent. For example, $\triangle PQR \sim \triangle STU$. Recall that the corresponding side lengths of similar triangles are in proportion.

In the activity, you will see how a right triangle can be divided into two similar right triangles.

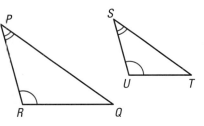

> ● **ACTIVITY**
> **Developing Concepts**
> **Investigating Similar Right Triangles**
>
> ❶ Cut an index card along one of its diagonals.
>
> ❷ On one of the right triangles, draw an altitude from the right angle to the hypotenuse. Cut along the altitude to form two right triangles.
>
> ❸ You should now have three right triangles. Compare the triangles. What special property do they share? Explain.

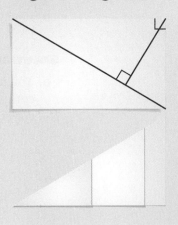

In the activity, you may have discovered the following theorem. A plan for proving the theorem appears on page 528, and you are asked to prove it in Exercise 34 on page 533.

THEOREM

THEOREM 9.1

If the altitude is drawn to the hypotenuse of a right triangle, then the two triangles formed are similar to the original triangle and to each other.

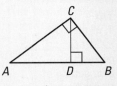

$\triangle CBD \sim \triangle ABC$, $\triangle ACD \sim \triangle ABC$, and $\triangle CBD \sim \triangle ACD$

A plan for proving Theorem 9.1 is shown below.

GIVEN ▶ $\triangle ABC$ is a right triangle; altitude $\overline{CD}$ is drawn to hypotenuse $\overline{AB}$.

PROVE ▶ $\triangle CBD \sim \triangle ABC$, $\triangle ACD \sim \triangle ABC$, and $\triangle CBD \sim \triangle ACD$.

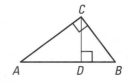

Plan for Proof First prove that $\triangle CBD \sim \triangle ABC$. Each triangle has a right angle, and each includes $\angle B$. The triangles are similar by the AA Similarity Postulate. You can use similar reasoning to show that $\triangle ACD \sim \triangle ABC$. To show that $\triangle CBD \sim \triangle ACD$, begin by showing that $\angle ACD \cong \angle B$ because they are both complementary to $\angle DCB$. Then you can use the AA Similarity Postulate.

EXAMPLE 1 **Finding the Height of a Roof**

ROOF HEIGHT A roof has a cross section that is a right triangle. The diagram shows the approximate dimensions of this cross section.

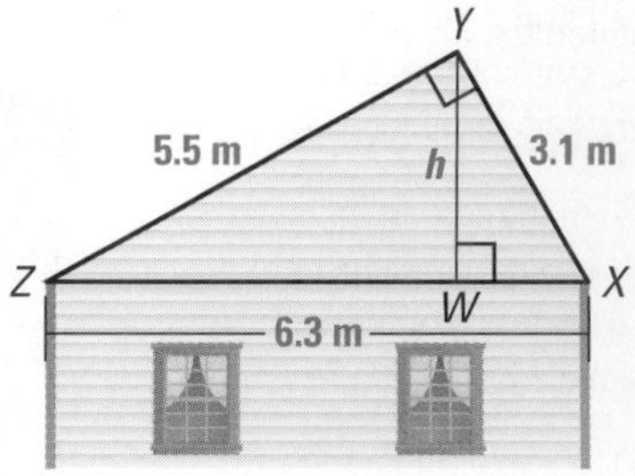

a. Identify the similar triangles.

b. Find the height h of the roof.

SOLUTION

a. You may find it helpful to sketch the three similar right triangles so that the corresponding angles and sides have the same orientation. Mark the congruent angles. Notice that some sides appear in more than one triangle. For instance, $\overline{XY}$ is the hypotenuse in $\triangle XYW$ and the shorter leg in $\triangle XZY$.

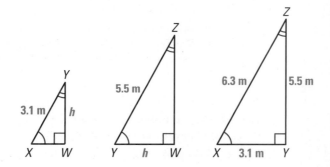

▶ $\triangle XYW \sim \triangle YZW \sim \triangle XZY$

b. Use the fact that $\triangle XYW \sim \triangle XZY$ to write a proportion.

$$\frac{YW}{ZY} = \frac{XY}{XZ} \qquad \text{Corresponding side lengths are in proportion.}$$

$$\frac{h}{5.5} = \frac{3.1}{6.3} \qquad \text{Substitute.}$$

$$6.3h = 5.5(3.1) \qquad \text{Cross product property}$$

$$h \approx 2.7 \qquad \text{Solve for } h.$$

▶ The height of the roof is about 2.7 meters.

STUDENT HELP

▶ **Study Tip**
In Example 1, all the side lengths of $\triangle XZY$ are given. This makes it a good choice for setting up a proportion to find an unknown side length of $\triangle XYW$.

In right $\triangle ABC$, altitude $\overline{CD}$ is drawn to the hypotenuse, forming two smaller right triangles that are similar to $\triangle ABC$. From Theorem 9.1, you know that $\triangle CBD \sim \triangle ACD \sim \triangle ABC$.

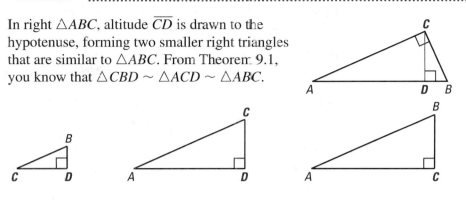

STUDENT HELP

► Look Back
The geometric mean of two numbers *a* and *b* is the positive number *x* such that $\frac{a}{x} = \frac{x}{b}$. For more help with finding a geometric mean, see p. 466.

Notice that $\overline{CD}$ is the longer leg of $\triangle CBD$ and the shorter leg of $\triangle ACD$. When you write a proportion comparing the leg lengths of $\triangle CBD$ and $\triangle ACD$, you can see that CD is the *geometric mean* of BD and AD.

$$\begin{array}{ll} \text{shorter leg of } \triangle CBD & \\ \text{shorter leg of } \triangle ACD & \end{array} \quad \frac{BD}{CD} = \frac{CD}{AD} \quad \begin{array}{ll} \text{longer leg of } \triangle CBD \\ \text{longer leg of } \triangle ACD \end{array}$$

Sides $\overline{CB}$ and $\overline{AC}$ also appear in more than one triangle. Their side lengths are also geometric means, as shown by the proportions below:

$$\begin{array}{ll} \text{hypotenuse of } \triangle ABC & \\ \text{hypotenuse of } \triangle CBD & \end{array} \quad \frac{AB}{CB} = \frac{CB}{DB} \quad \begin{array}{ll} \text{shorter leg of } \triangle ABC \\ \text{shorter leg of } \triangle CBD \end{array}$$

$$\begin{array}{ll} \text{hypotenuse of } \triangle ABC & \\ \text{hypotenuse of } \triangle ACD & \end{array} \quad \frac{AB}{AC} = \frac{AC}{AD} \quad \begin{array}{ll} \text{longer leg of } \triangle ABC \\ \text{longer leg of } \triangle ACD \end{array}$$

These results are expressed in the theorems below. You are asked to prove the theorems in Exercises 35 and 36.

GEOMETRIC MEAN THEOREMS

THEOREM 9.2

In a right triangle, the altitude from the right angle to the hypotenuse divides the hypotenuse into two segments.

The length of the altitude is the geometric mean of the lengths of the two segments.

$$\frac{BD}{CD} = \frac{CD}{AD}$$

THEOREM 9.3

In a right triangle, the altitude from the right angle to the hypotenuse divides the hypotenuse into two segments.

The length of each leg of the right triangle is the geometric mean of the lengths of the hypotenuse and the segment of the hypotenuse that is adjacent to the leg.

$$\frac{AB}{CB} = \frac{CB}{DB}$$

$$\frac{AB}{AC} = \frac{AC}{AD}$$

EXAMPLE 2 **Using a Geometric Mean**

Find the value of each variable.

a.
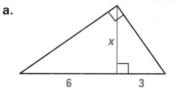

b.
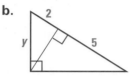

SOLUTION

a. Apply Theorem 9.2.

$$\frac{6}{x} = \frac{x}{3}$$

$$18 = x^2$$

$$\sqrt{18} = x$$

$$\sqrt{9} \cdot \sqrt{2} = x$$

$$3\sqrt{2} = x$$

b. Apply Theorem 9.3.

$$\frac{5+2}{y} = \frac{y}{2}$$

$$\frac{7}{y} = \frac{y}{2}$$

$$14 = y^2$$

$$\sqrt{14} = y$$

EXAMPLE 3 **Using Indirect Measurement**

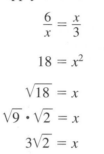
MONORAIL TRACK To estimate the height of a monorail track, your friend holds a cardboard square at eye level. Your friend lines up the top edge of the square with the track and the bottom edge with the ground. You measure the distance from the ground to your friend's eye and the distance from your friend to the track.

In the diagram, $XY = h - 5.75$ is the difference between the track height h and your friend's eye level. Use Theorem 9.2 to write a proportion involving XY. Then you can solve for h.

$$\frac{XY}{WY} = \frac{WY}{ZY} \qquad \text{Geometric Mean Theorem 9.2}$$

$$\frac{h - 5.75}{16} = \frac{16}{5.75} \qquad \text{Substitute.}$$

$$5.75(h - 5.75) = 16^2 \qquad \text{Cross product property}$$

$$5.75h - 33.0625 = 256 \qquad \text{Distributive property}$$

$$5.75h = 289.0625 \qquad \text{Add 33.0625 to each side.}$$

$$h \approx 50 \qquad \text{Divide each side by 5.75.}$$

▸ The height of the track is about 50 feet.

GUIDED PRACTICE

Vocabulary Check ✓

In Exercises 1–3, use the diagram at the right.

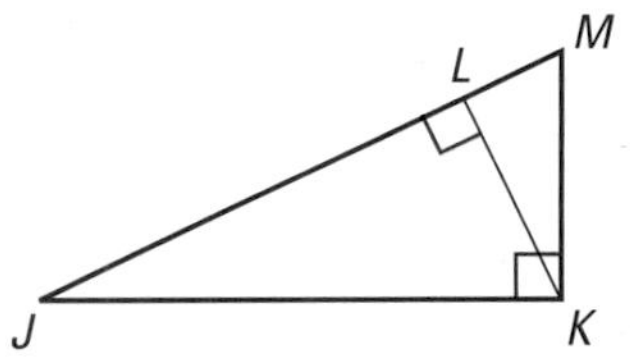

1. In the diagram, KL is the ___?___ of ML and JL.

Concept Check ✓

2. Complete the following statement:
   $\triangle JKL \sim \triangle$ ___?___ $\sim \triangle$ ___?___ .

3. Which segment's length is the geometric mean of ML and MJ?

Skill Check ✓

In Exercises 4–9, use the diagram above. Complete the proportion.

4. $\dfrac{KM}{KL} = \dfrac{?}{JK}$

5. $\dfrac{JM}{?} = \dfrac{JK}{JL}$

6. $\dfrac{?}{LK} = \dfrac{LK}{LM}$

7. $\dfrac{JM}{?} = \dfrac{KM}{LM}$

8. $\dfrac{LK}{LM} = \dfrac{JK}{?}$

9. $\dfrac{?}{JK} = \dfrac{MK}{MJ}$

10. Use the diagram at the right. Find DC. Then find DF. Round decimals to the nearest tenth.

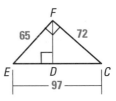

PRACTICE AND APPLICATIONS

STUDENT HELP

▶ **Extra Practice**
to help you master
skills is on p. 819.

SIMILAR TRIANGLES Use the diagram.

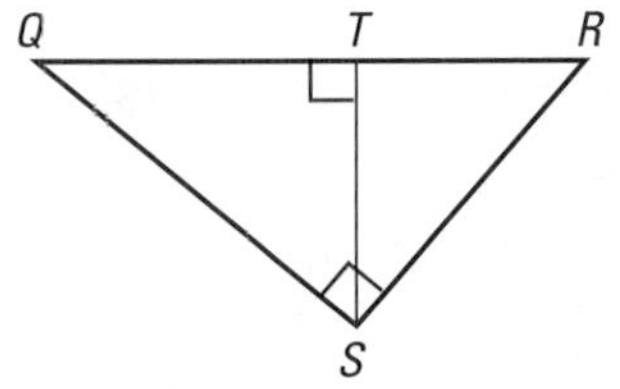

11. Sketch the three similar triangles in the diagram. Label the vertices.

12. Write similarity statements for the three triangles.

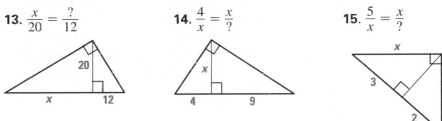

USING PROPORTIONS Complete and solve the proportion.

13. $\dfrac{x}{20} = \dfrac{?}{12}$

14. $\dfrac{4}{x} = \dfrac{x}{?}$

15. $\dfrac{5}{x} = \dfrac{x}{?}$

COMPLETING PROPORTIONS Write similarity statements for the three similar triangles in the diagram. Then complete the proportion.

STUDENT HELP

▶ **HOMEWORK HELP**
Example 1: Exs. 11–31
Example 2: Exs. 11–31
Example 3: Ex. 32

16. $\dfrac{XW}{ZW} = \dfrac{?}{YW}$

17. $\dfrac{QT}{SQ} = \dfrac{SQ}{?}$

18. $\dfrac{?}{EG} = \dfrac{EG}{EF}$

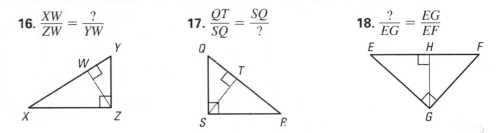

FINDING LENGTHS Write similarity statements for three triangles in the diagram. Then find the given length. Round decimals to the nearest tenth.

19. Find *DB*.

20. Find *HF*.

21. Find *JK*.

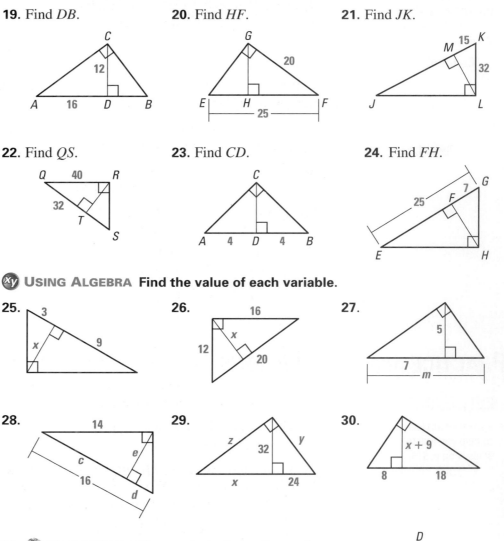

22. Find *QS*.

23. Find *CD*.

24. Find *FH*.

(xy) **USING ALGEBRA** Find the value of each variable.

25.

26.

27.

STUDENT HELP

↓ INTERNET **HOMEWORK HELP**
Visit our Web site
www.mcdougallittell.com
for help with Exs. 28–30.

28.

29.

30.

31. 🌐 **KITE DESIGN** You are designing a diamond-shaped kite. You know that *AD* = 44.8 centimeters, *DC* = 72 centimeters, and *AC* = 84.8 centimeters. You want to use a straight crossbar $\overline{BD}$. About how long should it be? Explain.

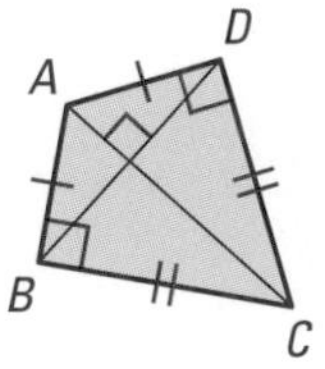

32. 🌐 **ROCK CLIMBING** You and a friend want to know how much rope you need to climb a large rock. To estimate the height of the rock, you use the method from Example 3 on page 530. As shown at the right, your friend uses a square to line up the top and the bottom of the rock. You measure the vertical distance from the ground to your friend's eye and the distance from your friend to the rock. Estimate the height of the rock.

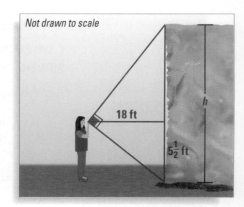

Not drawn to scale

18 ft

h

$5\frac{1}{2}$ ft

33. FINDING AREA Write similarity statements for the three similar right triangles in the diagram. Then find the area of each triangle. Explain how you got your answers.

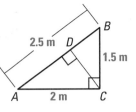

2.5 m *D*
B
1.5 m
A 2 m *C*

> ▶ **PROVING THEOREMS 9.1, 9.2, AND 9.3** In Exercises 34–36, use the diagram at the right.

34. Use the diagram to prove Theorem 9.1 on page 527. (*Hint:* Look back at the plan for proof on page 528.)

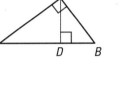

C
A *D* *B*

    GIVEN ▶ $\triangle ABC$ is a right triangle; altitude $\overline{CD}$ is drawn to hypotenuse $\overline{AB}$.

    PROVE ▶ $\triangle CBD \sim \triangle ABC$, $\triangle ACD \sim \triangle ABC$, and $\triangle CBD \sim \triangle ACD$.

35. Use the diagram to prove Theorem 9.2 on page 529.

    GIVEN ▶ $\triangle ABC$ is a right triangle; altitude $\overline{CD}$ is drawn to hypotenuse $\overline{AB}$.

    PROVE ▶ $\dfrac{BD}{CD} = \dfrac{CD}{AD}$

36. Use the diagram to prove Theorem 9.3 on page 529.

    GIVEN ▶ $\triangle ABC$ is a right triangle; altitude $\overline{CD}$ is drawn to hypotenuse $\overline{AB}$.

    PROVE ▶ $\dfrac{AB}{BC} = \dfrac{BC}{BD}$ and $\dfrac{AB}{AC} = \dfrac{AC}{AD}$

⊿ **USING TECHNOLOGY** In Exercises 37–40, use geometry software. You will demonstrate that Theorem 9.2 is true only for a *right* triangle. Follow the steps below to construct a triangle.

    ① Draw a triangle and label its vertices *A*, *B*, and *C*. The triangle should *not* be a right triangle.

    ② Draw altitude $\overline{CD}$ from point *C* to side $\overline{AB}$.

    ③ Measure $\angle C$. Then measure $\overline{AD}$, $\overline{CD}$, and $\overline{BD}$.

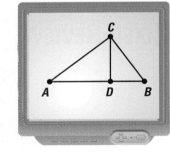

37. Calculate the values of the ratios $\dfrac{BD}{CD}$ and $\dfrac{CD}{AD}$. What does Theorem 9.2 say about the values of these ratios?

38. Drag point *C* until $m\angle C = 90°$. What happens to the values of the ratios $\dfrac{BD}{CD}$ and $\dfrac{CD}{AD}$?

39. Explain how your answers to Exercises 37 and 38 support the conclusion that Theorem 9.2 is true only for a right triangle.

40. Use the triangle you constructed to show that Theorem 9.3 is true only for a right triangle. Describe your procedure.

41. MULTIPLE CHOICE Use the diagram at the right. Decide which proportions are true.

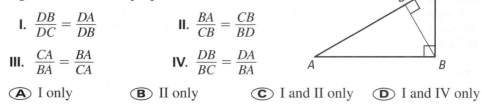

I. $\dfrac{DB}{DC} = \dfrac{DA}{DB}$ 　　　　 II. $\dfrac{BA}{CB} = \dfrac{CB}{BD}$

III. $\dfrac{CA}{BA} = \dfrac{BA}{CA}$ 　　　　 IV. $\dfrac{DB}{BC} = \dfrac{DA}{BA}$

A I only 　　 **B** II only 　　 **C** I and II only 　　 **D** I and IV only

42. MULTIPLE CHOICE In the diagram above, $AC = 24$ and $BC = 12$. Find AD. If necessary, round to the nearest hundredth.

A 6 　　　　 **B** 16.97 　　　　 **C** 18 　　　　 **D** 20.78

★ **Challenge**

43. *Writing* Two methods for indirectly measuring the height of a building are shown below. For each method, describe what distances need to be measured directly. Explain how to find the height of the building using these measurements. Describe one advantage and one disadvantage of each method. Copy and label the diagrams as part of your explanations.

Method 1 Use the method described in Example 3 on page 530.

Method 2 Use the method described in Exercises 55 and 56 on page 486.

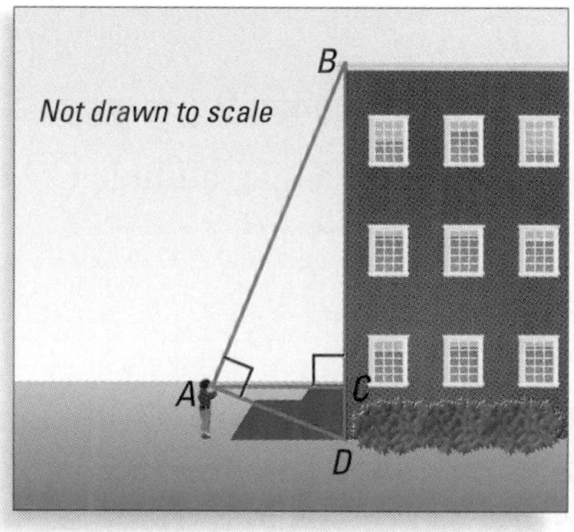

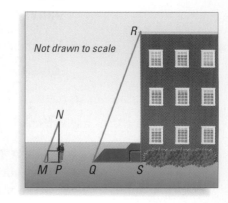

MIXED REVIEW

SOLVING EQUATIONS Solve the equation. (Skills Review, p. 800, for 9.2)

44. $n^2 = 169$ 　　　　 **45.** $14 + x^2 = 78$ 　　　　 **46.** $d^2 + 18 = 99$

LOGICAL REASONING Write the converse of the statement. Decide whether the converse is *true* or *false*. (Review 2.1)

47. If a triangle is obtuse, then one of its angles is greater than $90°$.

48. If two triangles are congruent, then their corresponding angles are congruent.

FINDING AREA Find the area of the figure. (Review 1.7, 6.7 for 9.2)

49. 6 in. 12 in. 　　　　 **50.** 4.5 cm 7 cm 　　　　 **51.** 12 m 5 m 13 m

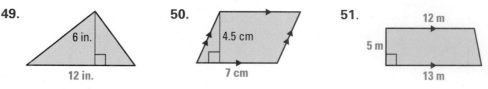

9.2

The Pythagorean Theorem

What you should learn

GOAL 1 Prove the Pythagorean Theorem.

GOAL 2 Use the Pythagorean Theorem to solve **real-life** problems, such as determining how far a ladder will reach in **Ex. 32**.

Why you should learn it

▼ To measure **real-life** lengths indirectly, such as the length of the support beam of a skywalk in **Example 4**.

GOAL 1 PROVING THE PYTHAGOREAN THEOREM

In this lesson, you will study one of the most famous theorems in mathematics—the *Pythagorean Theorem*. The relationship it describes has been known for thousands of years.

THEOREM

THEOREM 9.4 *Pythagorean Theorem*

In a right triangle, the square of the length of the hypotenuse is equal to the sum of the squares of the lengths of the legs.

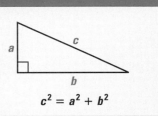

$$c^2 = a^2 + b^2$$

PROVING THE PYTHAGOREAN THEOREM There are many different proofs of the Pythagorean Theorem. One is shown below. Other proofs are found in Exercises 37 and 38 on page 540, and in the *Math and History* feature on page 557.

GIVEN ▶ In $\triangle ABC$, $\angle BCA$ is a right angle.

PROVE ▶ $a^2 + b^2 = c^2$

Plan for Proof Draw altitude $\overline{CD}$ to the hypotenuse. Then apply Geometric Mean Theorem 9.3, which states that when the altitude is drawn to the hypotenuse of a right triangle, each leg of the right triangle is the geometric mean of the hypotenuse and the segment of the hypotenuse that is adjacent to that leg.

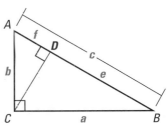

Proof

Statements	Reasons
1. Draw a perpendicular from C to $\overline{AB}$.	1. Perpendicular Postulate
2. $\dfrac{c}{a} = \dfrac{a}{e}$ and $\dfrac{c}{b} = \dfrac{b}{f}$	2. Geometric Mean Theorem 9.3
3. $ce = a^2$ and $cf = b^2$	3. Cross product property
4. $ce + cf = a^2 + b^2$	4. Addition property of equality
5. $c(e + f) = a^2 + b^2$	5. Distributive property
6. $e + f = c$	6. Segment Addition Postulate
7. $c^2 = a^2 + b^2$	7. Substitution property of equality

GOAL 2 **USING THE PYTHAGOREAN THEOREM**

A **Pythagorean triple** is a set of three positive integers a, b, and c that satisfy the equation $c^2 = a^2 + b^2$. For example, the integers 3, 4, and 5 form a Pythagorean triple because $5^2 = 3^2 + 4^2$.

EXAMPLE 1 *Finding the Length of a Hypotenuse*

Find the length of the hypotenuse of the right triangle. Tell whether the side lengths form a Pythagorean triple.

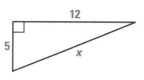

SOLUTION

$(\text{hypotenuse})^2 = (\text{leg})^2 + (\text{leg})^2$	**Pythagorean Theorem**
$x^2 = 5^2 + 12^2$	**Substitute.**
$x^2 = 25 + 144$	**Multiply.**
$x^2 = 169$	**Add.**
$x = 13$	**Find the positive square root.**

▶ Because the side lengths 5, 12, and 13 are integers, they form a Pythagorean triple.

· · · · · · · · · ·

Many right triangles have side lengths that do not form a Pythagorean triple, as shown in Example 2.

EXAMPLE 2 *Finding the Length of a Leg*

Find the length of the leg of the right triangle.

SOLUTION

$(\text{hypotenuse})^2 = (\text{leg})^2 + (\text{leg})^2$	**Pythagorean Theorem**
$14^2 = 7^2 + x^2$	**Substitute.**
$196 = 49 + x^2$	**Multiply.**
$147 = x^2$	**Subtract 49 from each side.**
$\sqrt{147} = x$	**Find the positive square root.**
$\sqrt{49} \cdot \sqrt{3} = x$	**Use product property.**
$7\sqrt{3} = x$	**Simplify the radical.**

STUDENT HELP

► **Skills Review**
For help with simplifying radicals, see p. 799.

· · · · · · · · · ·

In Example 2, the side length was written as a radical in simplest form. In real-life problems, it is often more convenient to use a calculator to write a decimal approximation of the side length. For instance, in Example 2, $x = 7 \cdot \sqrt{3} \approx 12.1$.

EXAMPLE 3 *Finding the Area of a Triangle*

STUDENT HELP

↳ **Look Back**
For help with finding the area of a triangle, see p. 51.

Find the area of the triangle to the nearest tenth of a meter.

SOLUTION

You are given that the base of the triangle is 10 meters, but you do not know the height h.

Because the triangle is isosceles, it can be divided into two congruent right triangles with the given dimensions. Use the Pythagorean Theorem to find the value of h.

$$7^2 = 5^2 + h^2 \qquad \text{Pythagorean Theorem}$$

$$49 = 25 + h^2 \qquad \text{Multiply.}$$

$$24 = h^2 \qquad \text{Subtract 25 from both sides.}$$

$$\sqrt{24} = h \qquad \text{Find the positive square root.}$$

Now find the area of the original triangle.

$$\text{Area} = \frac{1}{2}bh$$

$$= \frac{1}{2}(10)\left(\sqrt{24}\right)$$

$$\approx 24.5 \text{ m}^2$$

▶ The area of the triangle is about 24.5 m².

EXAMPLE 4 *Indirect Measurement*

FOCUS ON PEOPLE

CESAR PELLI is an architect who designed the twin skyscrapers shown on page 535. These 1483 foot buildings tower over the city of Kuala Lumpur, Malaysia.

SUPPORT BEAM The skyscrapers shown on page 535 are connected by a skywalk with support beams. You can use the Pythagorean Theorem to find the approximate length of each support beam.

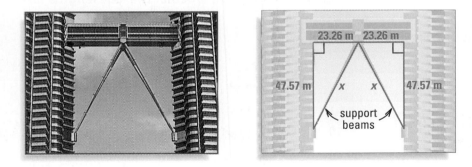

Each support beam forms the hypotenuse of a right triangle. The right triangles are congruent, so the support beams are the same length.

$$x^2 = (23.26)^2 + (47.57)^2 \qquad \text{Pythagorean Theorem}$$

$$x = \sqrt{(23.26)^2 + (47.57)^2} \qquad \text{Find the positive square root.}$$

$$x \approx 52.95 \qquad \text{Use a calculator to approximate.}$$

▶ The length of each support beam is about 52.95 meters.

GUIDED PRACTICE

Vocabulary Check ✔

Concept Check ✔

1. State the Pythagorean Theorem in your own words.

2. Which equations are true for $\triangle PQR$?

A. $r^2 = p^2 + q^2$

B. $q^2 = p^2 + r^2$

C. $p^2 = r^2 - q^2$

D. $r^2 = (p + q)^2$

E. $p^2 = q^2 + r^2$

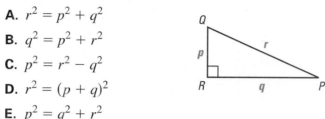

Skill Check ✔

Find the unknown side length. Tell whether the side lengths form a Pythagorean triple.

3.

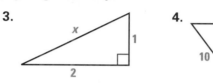

4.

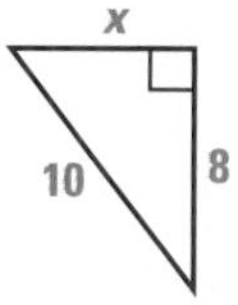

5.

6. 🌐 **ANEMOMETER** An anemometer (an uh MAHM ih tur) is a device used to measure windspeed. The anemometer shown is attached to the top of a pole. Support wires are attached to the pole 5 feet above the ground. Each support wire is 6 feet long. How far from the base of the pole is each wire attached to the ground?

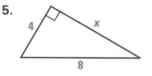

PRACTICE AND APPLICATIONS

STUDENT HELP

▶ **Extra Practice**
to help you master
skills is on p. 819.

FINDING SIDE LENGTHS Find the unknown side length. Simplify answers that are radicals. Tell whether the side lengths form a Pythagorean triple.

7.

8.

9.

10.

11.

12.

STUDENT HELP

▶ **HOMEWORK HELP**
Example 1: Exs. 7–24
Example 2: Exs. 7–24
Example 3: Exs. 25–30
Example 4: Exs. 31–36

13.

14.

15.

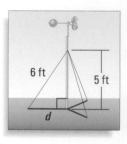

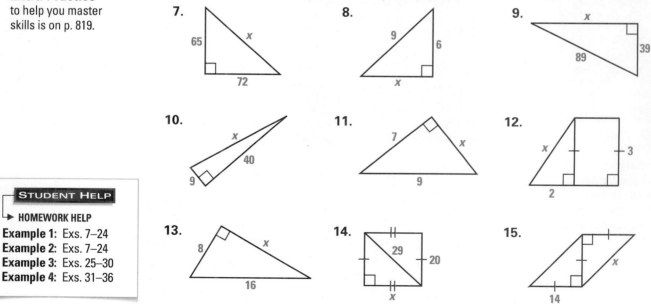

538   **Chapter 9** *Right Triangles and Trigonometry*

FINDING LENGTHS Find the value of *x*. Simplify answers that are radicals.

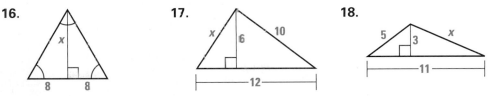

16.

17.

18.

PYTHAGOREAN TRIPLES The variables *r* and *s* represent the lengths of the legs of a right triangle, and *t* represents the length of the hypotenuse. The values of *r, s,* and *t* form a Pythagorean triple. Find the unknown value.

19. $r = 12, s = 16$

20. $r = 9, s = 12$

21. $r = 18, t = 30$

22. $s = 20, t = 101$

23. $r = 35, t = 37$

24. $t = 757, s = 595$

━━ STUDENT HELP

▸ **Look Back**
For help with finding areas of quadrilaterals, see pp. 372–375.

FINDING AREA Find the area of the figure. Round decimal answers to the nearest tenth.

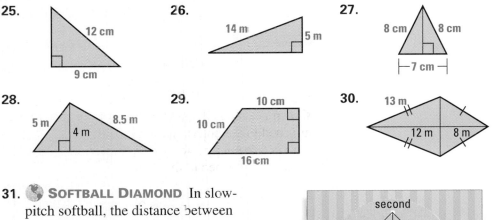

25.

12 cm

9 cm

26.

14 m

5 m

27.

8 cm   8 cm

├─7 cm─┤

28.

5 m   8.5 m

4 m

29.

10 cm

10 cm

16 cm

30.

13 m

12 m   8 m

31. 🌐 **SOFTBALL DIAMOND** In slow-pitch softball, the distance between consecutive bases is 65 feet. The pitcher's plate is located on a line between second base and home plate, 50 feet from home plate. How far is the pitcher's plate from second base? Justify your answer.

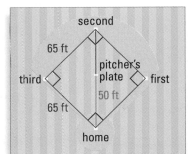

second

65 ft

third   pitcher's plate   first

65 ft   50 ft

home

32. 🌐 **SAFETY** The distance of the base of a ladder from the wall it leans against should be at least $\frac{1}{4}$ of the ladder's total length. Suppose a 10 foot ladder is placed according to these guidelines. Give the minimum distance of the base of the ladder from the wall. How far up the wall will the ladder reach? Explain. Include a sketch with your explanation.

33. 🌐 **ART GALLERY** You want to hang a painting 3 feet from a hook near the ceiling of an art gallery, as shown. In addition to the length of wire needed for hanging, you need 16 inches of wire to secure the wire to the back of the painting. Find the total length of wire needed to hang the painting.

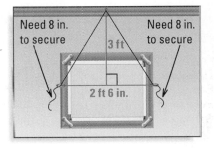

Need 8 in. to secure   Need 8 in. to secure

3 ft

2 ft 6 in.

FOCUS ON CAREERS

MECHANICAL ENGINEERS use science, mathematics, and engineering principles in their work. They evaluate, install, operate, and maintain mechanical products and systems, such as the Trans-Alaska pipeline.

CAREER LINK
www.mcdougallittell.com

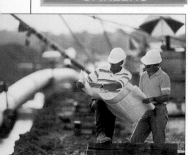

34. **TRANS-ALASKA PIPELINE** Metal expands and contracts with changes in temperature. The Trans-Alaska pipeline was built to accommodate expansion and contraction. Suppose that it had not been built this way. Consider a 600 foot section of pipe that expands 2 inches and buckles, as shown below. Estimate the height *h* of the buckle.

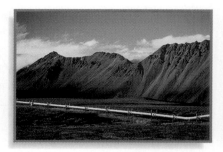

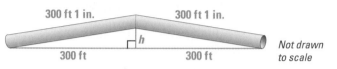

300 ft 1 in.
300 ft 1 in.
h
300 ft
300 ft
Not drawn to scale

WRAPPING A BOX **In Exercises 35 and 36, two methods are used to wrap ribbon around a rectangular box with the dimensions shown below. The amount of ribbon needed does not include a knot or bow.**

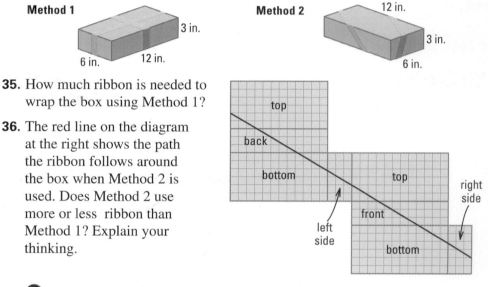

Method 1
3 in.
6 in.
12 in.
Method 2
12 in.
3 in.
6 in.

35. How much ribbon is needed to wrap the box using Method 1?

36. The red line on the diagram at the right shows the path the ribbon follows around the box when Method 2 is used. Does Method 2 use more or less ribbon than Method 1? Explain your thinking.

top
back
bottom
top
front
bottom
left side
right side

STUDENT HELP

HOMEWORK HELP
Visit our Web site www.mcdougallittell.com for help with the proofs in Exs. 37 and 38.

37. **PROVING THE PYTHAGOREAN THEOREM** Explain how the diagram at the right can be used to prove the Pythagorean Theorem algebraically. (*Hint:* Write two different expressions that represent the area of the large square. Then set them equal to each other.)

a
b
a
b
a
b
b
a
c
c
c
c

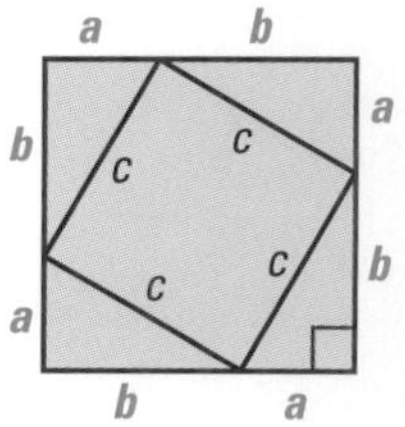

38. **GARFIELD'S PROOF** James Abram Garfield, the twentieth president of the United States, discovered a proof of the Pythagorean Theorem in 1876. His proof involved the fact that a trapezoid can be formed from two congruent right triangles and an isosceles right triangle.

Use the diagram to write a paragraph proof showing that $a^2 + b^2 = c^2$. (*Hint:* Write two different expressions that represent the area of the trapezoid. Then set them equal to each other.)

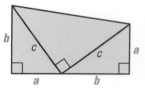

b
c
c
a
a
b

Test Preparation

39. MULTI-STEP PROBLEM To find the length of a diagonal of a rectangular box, you can use the Pythagorean Theorem twice. Use the theorem once with right $\triangle ABC$ to find the length of the diagonal of the base.

$$AB = \sqrt{(AC)^2 + (BC)^2}$$

Then use the theorem with right $\triangle ABD$ to find the length of the diagonal of the box.

$$BD = \sqrt{(AB)^2 + (AD)^2}$$

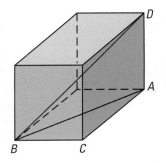

a. Is it possible to carry a 9 foot piece of lumber in an enclosed rectangular trailer that is 4 feet by 8 feet by 4 feet?

b. Is it possible to store a 20 foot long pipe in a rectangular room that is 10 feet by 12 feet by 8 feet? Explain.

c. *Writing* Write a formula for finding the diagonal d of a rectangular box with length ℓ, width w, and height h. Explain your reasoning.

★ **Challenge**

PERIMETER OF A RHOMBUS The diagonals of a rhombus have lengths a and b. Use this information in Exercises 40 and 41.

40. Prove that the perimeter of the rhombus is $2\sqrt{a^2 + b^2}$.

41. The perimeter of a rhombus is 80 centimeters. The lengths of its diagonals are in the ratio 3:4. Find the length of each diagonal.

MIXED REVIEW

USING RADICALS Evaluate the expression. (Algebra Review, p. 522, for 9.3)

42. $\left(\sqrt{6}\right)^2$ **43.** $\left(\sqrt{9}\right)^2$ **44.** $\left(\sqrt{14}\right)^2$ **45.** $\left(2\sqrt{2}\right)^2$

46. $\left(4\sqrt{13}\right)^2$ **47.** $-\left(5\sqrt{49}\right)^2$ **48.** $4\left(\sqrt{9}\right)^2$ **49.** $\left(-7\sqrt{3}\right)^2$

LOGICAL REASONING Determine whether the true statement can be combined with its converse to form a true biconditional statement. (Review 2.2)

50. If a quadrilateral is a square, then it has four congruent sides.

51. If a quadrilateral is a kite, then it has two pairs of congruent sides.

52. For all real numbers x, if $x \geq 1$, then $x^2 \geq 1$.

53. For all real numbers x, if $x > 1$, then $\frac{1}{x} < 1$.

54. If one interior angle of a triangle is obtuse, then the sum of the other two interior angles is less than 90°.

USING ALGEBRA Prove that the points represent the vertices of a parallelogram. (Review 6.3)

55. $P(4, 3)$, $Q(6, -8)$, $R(10, -3)$, $S(8, 8)$

56. $P(5, 0)$, $Q(2, 9)$, $R(-6, 6)$, $S(-3, -3)$

Investigating Sides and Angles of Triangles

You can use geometry software to explore how the angle measures of a triangle are related to its side lengths.

► CONSTRUCT

1 Construct a triangle. Label the vertices A, B, and C.

2 Measure $\overline{AC}$, $\overline{BC}$, and $\overline{AB}$.

3 Calculate the value of $(AC)^2 + (BC)^2$. Calculate the value of $(AB)^2$.

4 Measure $\angle C$.

2.11 cm C 98.07°
A 2.59 cm
3.56 cm
B

$(AC)^2 + (BC)^2 = 11.16$
$(AB)^2 = 12.67$

► INVESTIGATE

1. Make a table like the one shown. Record the side lengths, the value of $(AC)^2 + (BC)^2$, the value of $(AB)^2$, and the measure of $\angle C$. Round decimals to the nearest hundredth.

	AC	BC	AB	$(AC)^2 + (BC)^2$	$(AB)^2$	$m\angle C$
Triangle 1	2.11 cm	2.59 cm	3.56 cm	11.16 cm	12.67 cm	98.07°
Triangle 2	?	?	?	?	?	?
Triangle 3	?	?	?	?	?	?
Triangle 4	?	?	?	?	?	?
Triangle 5	?	?	?	?	?	?
Triangle 6	?	?	?	?	?	?

2. Drag point C to change the measure of $\angle C$ and the shape of $\triangle ABC$. Find and record the values in the table.

3. Repeat Step 2 for several more triangles. In your table, be sure to include some triangles for which $\angle C$ is an acute angle, some for which $\angle C$ is a right angle, and some for which $\angle C$ is an obtuse angle.

► CONJECTURE

4. Use the data in the table to look for a pattern. Make a conjecture about how the value of $(AC)^2 + (BC)^2$ compares with the value of $(AB)^2$ when the measure of $\angle C$ is less than 90°, equal to 90°, and greater than 90°.

9.3

The Converse of the Pythagorean Theorem

What you should learn

GOAL 1 Use the Converse of the Pythagorean Theorem to solve problems.

GOAL 2 Use side lengths to classify triangles by their angle measures.

Why you should learn it

▼ To determine whether **real-life** angles are right angles, such as the four angles formed by the foundation of a building in **Example 3**.

GOAL 1 USING THE CONVERSE

In Lesson 9.2, you learned that if a triangle is a right triangle, then the square of the length of the hypotenuse is equal to the sum of the squares of the lengths of the legs. The Converse of the Pythagorean Theorem is also true, as stated below. Exercise 43 asks you to prove the Converse of the Pythagorean Theorem.

THEOREM

THEOREM 9.5 *Converse of the Pythagorean Theorem*

If the square of the length of the longest side of a triangle is equal to the sum of the squares of the lengths of the other two sides, then the triangle is a right triangle.

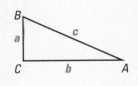

If $c^2 = a^2 + b^2$, then $\triangle ABC$ is a right triangle.

You can use the Converse of the Pythagorean Theorem to verify that a given triangle is a right triangle, as shown in Example 1.

EXAMPLE 1 *Verifying Right Triangles*

The triangles below appear to be right triangles. Tell whether they are right triangles.

a.
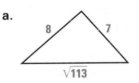

b.
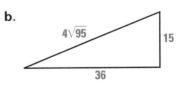

SOLUTION

Let c represent the length of the longest side of the triangle. Check to see whether the side lengths satisfy the equation $c^2 = a^2 + b^2$.

a. $(\sqrt{113})^2 \stackrel{?}{=} 7^2 + 8^2$

$113 \stackrel{?}{=} 49 + 64$

$113 = 113$ ✓

The triangle is a right triangle.

b. $(4\sqrt{95})^2 \stackrel{?}{=} 15^2 + 36^2$

$4^2 \cdot (\sqrt{95})^2 \stackrel{?}{=} 15^2 + 36^2$

$16 \cdot 95 \stackrel{?}{=} 225 + 1296$

$1520 \neq 1521$

The triangle is not a right triangle.

GOAL 2 CLASSIFYING TRIANGLES

Sometimes it is hard to tell from looking whether a triangle is obtuse or acute. The theorems below can help you tell.

THEOREMS

THEOREM 9.6

If the square of the length of the longest side of a triangle is less than the sum of the squares of the lengths of the other two sides, then the triangle is acute.

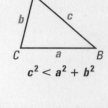

If $c^2 < a^2 + b^2$, then $\triangle ABC$ is acute.

$$c^2 < a^2 + b^2$$

THEOREM 9.7

If the square of the length of the longest side of a triangle is greater than the sum of the squares of the lengths of the other two sides, then the triangle is obtuse.

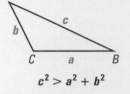

If $c^2 > a^2 + b^2$, then $\triangle ABC$ is obtuse.

$$c^2 > a^2 + b^2$$

EXAMPLE 2 *Classifying Triangles*

Decide whether the set of numbers can represent the side lengths of a triangle. If they can, classify the triangle as *right*, *acute*, or *obtuse*.

a. 38, 77, 86 **b.** 10.5, 36.5, 37.5

SOLUTION

STUDENT HELP

▶ **Look Back**
For help with the Triangle Inequality, see p. 297.

You can use the Triangle Inequality to confirm that each set of numbers can represent the side lengths of a triangle.

Compare the square of the length of the longest side with the sum of the squares of the lengths of the two shorter sides.

a. $c^2 \; \underline{?} \; a^2 + b^2$ **Compare c^2 with $a^2 + b^2$.**

$86^2 \; \underline{?} \; 38^2 + 77^2$ **Substitute.**

$7396 \; \underline{?} \; 1444 + 5929$ **Multiply.**

$7396 > 7373$ **c^2 is greater than $a^2 + b^2$.**

▶ Because $c^2 > a^2 + b^2$, the triangle is obtuse.

b. $c^2 \; \underline{?} \; a^2 + b^2$ **Compare c^2 with $a^2 + b^2$.**

$37.5^2 \; \underline{?} \; 10.5^2 + 36.5^2$ **Substitute.**

$1406.25 \; \underline{?} \; 110.25 + 1332.25$ **Multiply.**

$1406.25 < 1442.5$ **c^2 is less than $a^2 + b^2$.**

▶ Because $c^2 < a^2 + b^2$, the triangle is acute.

EXAMPLE 3 *Building a Foundation*

CONSTRUCTION You use four stakes and string to mark the foundation of a house. You want to make sure the foundation is rectangular.

a. A friend measures the four sides to be 30 feet, 30 feet, 72 feet, and 72 feet. He says these measurements prove the foundation is rectangular. Is he correct?

b. You measure one of the diagonals to be 78 feet. Explain how you can use this measurement to tell whether the foundation will be rectangular.

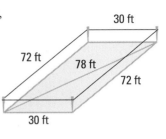

SOLUTION

a. Your friend is not correct. The foundation could be a nonrectangular parallelogram, as shown at the right.

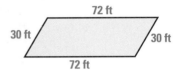

b. The diagonal divides the foundation into two triangles. Compare the square of the length of the longest side with the sum of the squares of the shorter sides of one of these triangles. Because $30^2 + 72^2 = 78^2$, you can conclude that both the triangles are right triangles.

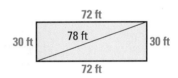

▸ The foundation is a parallelogram with two right angles, which implies that it is rectangular.

GUIDED PRACTICE

Vocabulary Check ✔ **1.** State the Converse of the Pythagorean Theorem in your own words.

Concept Check ✔ **2.** Use the triangle shown at the right. Find values for c so that the triangle is acute, right, and obtuse.

Skill Check ✔ **In Exercises 3–6, match the side lengths with the appropriate description.**

3. 2, 10, 11   **A.** right triangle

4. 13, 5, 7   **B.** acute triangle

5. 5, 11, 6   **C.** obtuse triangle

6. 6, 8, 10   **D.** not a triangle

7. 🌐 KITE DESIGN You are making the diamond-shaped kite shown at the right. You measure the crossbars to determine whether they are perpendicular. Are they? Explain.

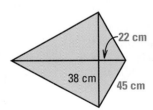

PRACTICE AND APPLICATIONS

STUDENT HELP

► **Extra Practice**
to help you master
skills is on pp. 819
and 820.

VERIFYING RIGHT TRIANGLES Tell whether the triangle is a right triangle.

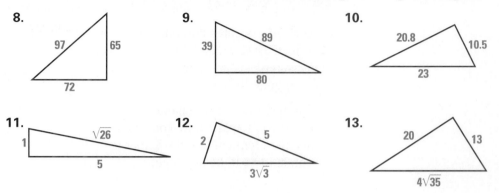

8. 97 65 72

9. 39 89 80

10. 20.8 10.5 23

11. 1 $\sqrt{26}$ 5

12. 2 5 $3\sqrt{3}$

13. 20 13 $4\sqrt{35}$

CLASSIFYING TRIANGLES Decide whether the numbers can represent the side lengths of a triangle. If they can, classify the triangle as *right*, *acute*, or *obtuse*.

14. 20, 99, 101   **15.** 21, 28, 35   **16.** 26, 10, 17

17. 2, 10, 12   **18.** 4, $\sqrt{67}$, 9   **19.** $\sqrt{13}$, 6, 7

20. 16, 30, 34   **21.** 10, 11, 14   **22.** 4, 5, 5

23. 17, 144, 145   **24.** 10, 49, 50   **25.** $\sqrt{5}$, 5, 5.5

CLASSIFYING QUADRILATERALS Classify the quadrilateral. Explain how you can prove that the quadrilateral is that type.

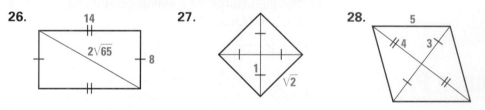

26. 14 $2\sqrt{65}$ 8

27. 1 $\sqrt{2}$

28. 5 4 3

CHOOSING A METHOD In Exercises 29–31, you will use two different methods for determining whether △*ABC* is a right triangle.

29. *Method 1* Find the slope of $\overline{AC}$ and the slope of $\overline{BC}$. What do the slopes tell you about ∠*ACB*? Is △*ABC* a right triangle? How do you know?

30. *Method 2* Use the Distance Formula and the Converse of the Pythagorean Theorem to determine whether △*ABC* is a right triangle.

31. Which method would you use to determine whether a given triangle is right, acute, or obtuse? Explain.

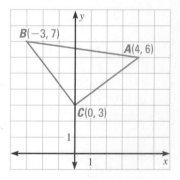

$B(-3, 7)$ $A(4, 6)$ $C(0, 3)$

STUDENT HELP

► **HOMEWORK HELP**
Example 1: Exs. 8–13, 30
Example 2: Exs. 14–28,
        31–35
Example 3: Exs. 39, 40

⟨xy⟩ USING ALGEBRA Graph points *P*, *Q*, and *R*. Connect the points to form △*PQR*. Decide whether △*PQR* is *right*, *acute*, or *obtuse*.

32. $P(-3, 4)$, $Q(5, 0)$, $R(-6, -2)$ **33.** $P(-1, 2)$, $Q(4, 1)$, $R(0, -1)$

PROOF Write a proof.

34. GIVEN ▶ $AB = 3$, $BC = 2$, $AC = 4$

PROVE ▶ $\angle 1$ is acute.

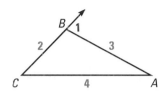

35. GIVEN ▶ $AB = 4$, $BC = 2$, $AC = \sqrt{10}$

PROVE ▶ $\angle 1$ is acute.

STUDENT HELP

HOMEWORK HELP Visit our Web site www.mcdougallittell.com for help with Ex. 36.

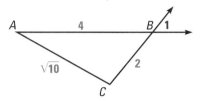

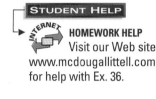

36. **PROOF** Prove that if a, b, and c are a Pythagorean triple, then ka, kb, and kc (where $k > 0$) represent the side lengths of a right triangle.

37. PYTHAGOREAN TRIPLES Use the results of Exercise 36 and the Pythagorean triple 5, 12, 13. Which sets of numbers can represent the side lengths of a right triangle?

A. 50, 120, 130 **B.** 20, 48, 56 **C.** $1\frac{1}{4}$, 3, $3\frac{1}{4}$ **D.** 1, 2.4, 2.6

38. **TECHNOLOGY** Use geometry software to construct each of the following figures: a nonspecial quadrilateral, a parallelogram, a rhombus, a square, and a rectangle. Label the sides of each figure a, b, c, and d. Measure each side. Then draw the diagonals of each figure and label them e and f. Measure each diagonal. For which figures does the following statement appear to be true?

$$a^2 + b^2 + c^2 + d^2 = e^2 + f^2$$

FOCUS ON APPLICATIONS

BABYLONIAN TABLET
This photograph shows part of a Babylonian clay tablet made around 350 B.C. The tablet contains a table of numbers written in cuneiform characters.

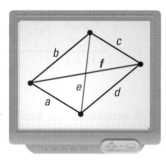

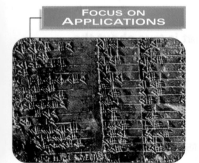

39. HISTORY CONNECTION The Babylonian tablet shown at the left contains several sets of triangle side lengths, suggesting that the Babylonians may have been aware of the relationships among the side lengths of right triangles. The side lengths in the table at the right show several sets of numbers from the tablet. Verify that each set of side lengths forms a Pythagorean triple.

a	b	c
120	119	169
4,800	4,601	6,649
13,500	12,709	18,541

40. **AIR TRAVEL** You take off in a jet from Cincinnati, Ohio, and fly 403 miles due east to Washington, D.C. You then fly 714 miles to Tallahassee, Florida. Finally, you fly 599 miles back to Cincinnati. Is Cincinnati directly north of Tallahassee? If not, how would you describe its location relative to Tallahassee?

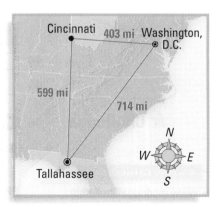

ACTIVITY 9.4

Developing Concepts

Investigating Special Right Triangles

GROUP ACTIVITY
Work in a group of three students.

MATERIALS
• paper
• pencil
• ruler
• compass

▶ **QUESTION** A triangle with angle measures of 45°, 45°, and 90°, or 30°, 60°, and 90° is called a *special right triangle*. How are the side lengths of a 45°-45°-90° triangle or a 30°-60°-90° triangle related?

▶ **EXPLORING THE CONCEPT: 45°-45°-90° TRIANGLE**

1. Construct an isosceles right triangle. The length of a leg of the triangle should be 3, 4, or 5 centimeters. Each person in your group should choose a different length.

2. Use the Pythagorean Theorem to find the length of the hypotenuse. Write the length in simplest radical form.

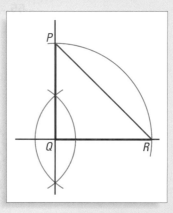

▶ **CONJECTURE**

3. Compare your results with those of the other students in your group. What pattern do you observe? Make a conjecture about the relationships among the side lengths of an isosceles right triangle.

▶ **EXPLORING THE CONCEPT: 30°-60°-90° TRIANGLE**

4. Construct an equilateral triangle with side lengths of 4, 6, or 8 centimeters. Each person in your group should choose a different length.

5. Next construct the altitude from one of the vertices. The equilateral triangle is now divided into two congruent right triangles whose angle measures are 30°-60°-90°.

6. Find the side lengths of one of the right triangles. Write each length in simplest radical form.

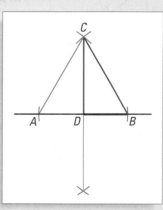

▶ **CONJECTURE**

7. Find each of the following ratios:

 • the length of the hypotenuse to the length of the shorter leg

 • the length of the longer leg to the length of the shorter leg

Compare your ratios with those of the other students in your group. What patterns do you observe? Make a conjecture about the ratios of the side lengths of a 30°-60°-90° triangle.

9.4

Special Right Triangles

What you should learn

GOAL 1 Find the side lengths of special right triangles.

GOAL 2 Use special right triangles to solve **real-life** problems, such as finding the side lengths of the triangles in the spiral quilt design in **Exs. 31–34**.

Why you should learn it

▼ To use special right triangles to solve **real-life** problems, such as finding the height of a tipping platform in **Example 4**.

GOAL 1 SIDE LENGTHS OF SPECIAL RIGHT TRIANGLES

Right triangles whose angle measures are 45°–45°–90° or 30°–60°–90° are called **special right triangles**. In the Activity on page 550, you may have noticed certain relationships among the side lengths of each of these special right triangles. The theorems below describe these relationships. Exercises 35 and 36 ask you to prove the theorems.

THEOREMS ABOUT SPECIAL RIGHT TRIANGLES

THEOREM 9.8 *45°-45°-90° Triangle Theorem*

In a 45°-45°-90° triangle, the hypotenuse is $\sqrt{2}$ times as long as each leg.

Hypotenuse = $\sqrt{2}$ · leg

THEOREM 9.9 *30°-60°-90° Triangle Theorem*

In a 30°-60°-90° triangle, the hypotenuse is twice as long as the shorter leg, and the longer leg is $\sqrt{3}$ times as long as the shorter leg.

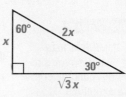

Hypotenuse = 2 · shorter leg
Longer leg = $\sqrt{3}$ · shorter leg

EXAMPLE 1 *Finding the Hypotenuse in a 45°-45°-90° Triangle*

Find the value of x.

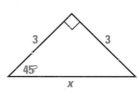

SOLUTION

By the Triangle Sum Theorem, the measure of the third angle is 45°. The triangle is a 45°-45°-90° right triangle, so the length x of the hypotenuse is $\sqrt{2}$ times the length of a leg.

$$\text{Hypotenuse} = \sqrt{2} \cdot \text{leg} \qquad \text{45°-45°-90° Triangle Theorem}$$

$$x = \sqrt{2} \cdot 3 \qquad \text{Substitute.}$$

$$x = 3\sqrt{2} \qquad \text{Simplify.}$$

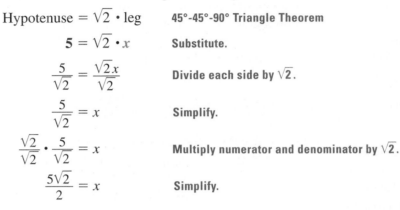

EXAMPLE 2 *Finding a Leg in a 45°-45°-90° Triangle*

Find the value of x.

SOLUTION

Because the triangle is an isosceles right triangle, its base angles are congruent. The triangle is a 45°-45°-90° right triangle, so the length of the hypotenuse is $\sqrt{2}$ times the length x of a leg.

$$\text{Hypotenuse} = \sqrt{2} \cdot \text{leg} \qquad \text{45°-45°-90° Triangle Theorem}$$

$$5 = \sqrt{2} \cdot x \qquad \text{Substitute.}$$

$$\frac{5}{\sqrt{2}} = \frac{\sqrt{2}\,x}{\sqrt{2}} \qquad \text{Divide each side by } \sqrt{2}.$$

$$\frac{5}{\sqrt{2}} = x \qquad \text{Simplify.}$$

$$\frac{\sqrt{2}}{\sqrt{2}} \cdot \frac{5}{\sqrt{2}} = x \qquad \text{Multiply numerator and denominator by } \sqrt{2}.$$

$$\frac{5\sqrt{2}}{2} = x \qquad \text{Simplify.}$$

EXAMPLE 3 *Side Lengths in a 30°-60°-90° Triangle*

STUDENT HELP

HOMEWORK HELP
Visit our Web site
www.mcdougallittell.com
for extra examples.

Find the values of s and t.

SOLUTION

Because the triangle is a 30°-60°-90° triangle, the longer leg is $\sqrt{3}$ times the length s of the shorter leg.

$$\text{Longer leg} = \sqrt{3} \cdot \text{shorter leg} \qquad \text{30°-60°-90° Triangle Theorem}$$

$$5 = \sqrt{3} \cdot s \qquad \text{Substitute.}$$

$$\frac{5}{\sqrt{3}} = \frac{\sqrt{3} \cdot s}{\sqrt{3}} \qquad \text{Divide each side by } \sqrt{3}.$$

$$\frac{5}{\sqrt{3}} = s \qquad \text{Simplify.}$$

$$\frac{\sqrt{3}}{\sqrt{3}} \cdot \frac{5}{\sqrt{3}} = s \qquad \text{Multiply numerator and denominator by } \sqrt{3}.$$

$$\frac{5\sqrt{3}}{3} = s \qquad \text{Simplify.}$$

The length t of the hypotenuse is twice the length s of the shorter leg.

$$\text{Hypotenuse} = 2 \cdot \text{shorter leg} \qquad \text{30°-60°-90° Triangle Theorem}$$

$$t = 2 \cdot \frac{5\sqrt{3}}{3} \qquad \text{Substitute.}$$

$$t = \frac{10\sqrt{3}}{3} \qquad \text{Simplify.}$$

GOAL 2 **USING SPECIAL RIGHT TRIANGLES IN REAL LIFE**

EXAMPLE 4 *Finding the Height of a Ramp*

TIPPING PLATFORM A tipping platform is a ramp used to unload trucks, as shown on page 551. How high is the end of an 80 foot ramp when it is tipped by a 30° angle? by a 45° angle?

SOLUTION

When the angle of elevation is 30°, the height h of the ramp is the length of the shorter leg of a 30°-60°-90° triangle. The length of the hypotenuse is 80 feet.

$80 = 2h$ **30°-60°-90° Triangle Theorem**

$40 = h$ **Divide each side by 2.**

When the angle of elevation is 45°, the height of the ramp is the length of a leg of a 45°-45°-90° triangle. The length of the hypotenuse is 80 feet.

$80 = \sqrt{2} \cdot h$ **45°-45°-90° Triangle Theorem**

$\dfrac{80}{\sqrt{2}} = h$ **Divide each side by $\sqrt{2}$.**

$56.6 \approx h$ **Use a calculator to approximate.**

▶ When the angle of elevation is 30°, the ramp height is 40 feet. When the angle of elevation is 45°, the ramp height is about 56 feet 7 inches.

EXAMPLE 5 *Finding the Area of a Sign*

ROAD SIGN The road sign is shaped like an equilateral triangle. Estimate the area of the sign by finding the area of the equilateral triangle.

SOLUTION

First find the height h of the triangle by dividing it into two 30°-60°-90° triangles. The length of the longer leg of one of these triangles is h. The length of the shorter leg is 18 inches.

$h = \sqrt{3} \cdot 18 = 18\sqrt{3}$ **30°-60°-90° Triangle Theorem**

Use $h = 18\sqrt{3}$ to find the area of the equilateral triangle.

$\text{Area} = \dfrac{1}{2}bh = \dfrac{1}{2}(36)\left(18\sqrt{3}\right) \approx 561.18$

▶ The area of the sign is about 561 square inches.

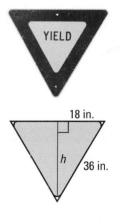

GUIDED PRACTICE

Vocabulary Check ✓ **1.** What is meant by the term *special right triangles*?

Concept Check ✓ **2.** CRITICAL THINKING Explain why any two 30°-60°-90° triangles are similar.

Use the diagram to tell whether the equation is *true* or *false*.

3. $t = 7\sqrt{3}$ **4.** $t = \sqrt{3}h$ **5.** $h = 2t$

6. $h = 14$ **7.** $7 = \dfrac{h}{2}$ **8.** $7 = \dfrac{t}{\sqrt{3}}$

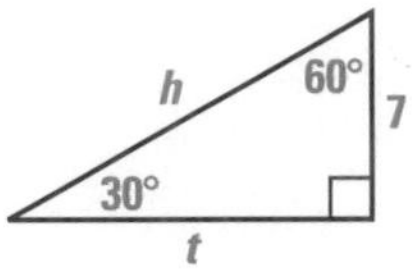

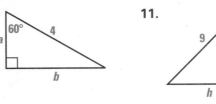

Skill Check ✓ Find the value of each variable. Write answers in simplest radical form.

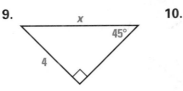

9.   **10.**   **11.**

PRACTICE AND APPLICATIONS

STUDENT HELP

► **Extra Practice**
to help you master
skills is on p. 820.

(xy) USING ALGEBRA Find the value of each variable.
Write answers in simplest radical form.

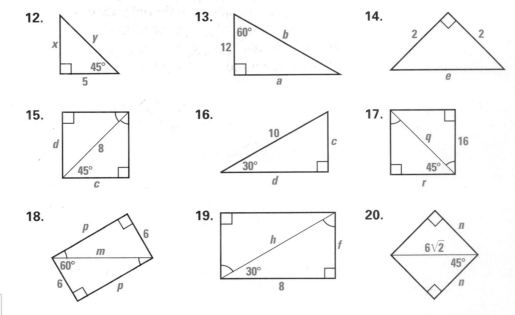

12.   **13.**   **14.**

15.   **16.**   **17.**

18.   **19.**   **20.**

STUDENT HELP

► **HOMEWORK HELP**
Example 1: Exs. 12–23
Example 2: Exs. 12–23
Example 3: Exs. 12–23
Example 4: Exs. 28–29,
         34
Example 5: Exs. 24–27

FINDING LENGTHS Sketch the figure that is described. Find the requested length. Round decimals to the nearest tenth.

21. The side length of an equilateral triangle is 5 centimeters. Find the length of an altitude of the triangle.

22. The perimeter of a square is 36 inches. Find the length of a diagonal.

23. The diagonal of a square is 26 inches. Find the length of a side.

FINDING AREA Find the area of the figure. Round decimal answers to the nearest tenth.

24.

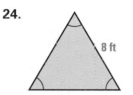

8 ft

25.

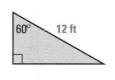

60°   12 ft

26.

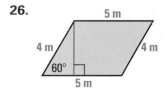

5 m

4 m   4 m

60°

5 m

27. 🌐 **AREA OF A WINDOW** A hexagonal window consists of six congruent panes of glass. Each pane is an equilateral triangle. Find the area of the entire window.

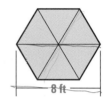

8 ft

🌐 **JEWELRY** Estimate the length *x* of each earring.

28.

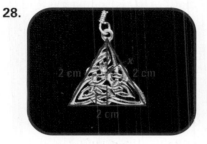

2 cm   *x*   2 cm

2 cm

29.

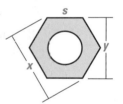

1.4 cm   *x*

1.4 cm   1.4 cm

30. 🌐 **TOOLS** Find the values of *x* and *y* for the hexagonal nut shown at the right when *s* = 2 centimeters. (*Hint:* In Exercise 27 above, you saw that a regular hexagon can be divided into six equilateral triangles.)

s

y

x

🧩 **LOGICAL REASONING** The quilt design in the photo is based on the pattern in the diagram below. Use the diagram in Exercises 31–34.

Wheel of Theodorus

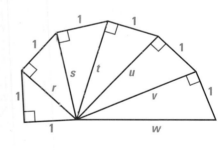

1   1

1   1

s   *t*   *u*

r   *v*

1   1

1   *w*

31. Find the values of *r*, *s*, *t*, *u*, *v*, and *w*. Explain the procedure you used to find the values.

32. Which of the triangles, if any, is a 45°-45°-90° triangle?

33. Which of the triangles, if any, is a 30°-60°-90° triangle?

34. ⓧ⁄ᵧ **USING ALGEBRA** Suppose there are *n* triangles in the spiral. Write an expression for the hypotenuse of the *n*th triangle.

35. ▶ **PARAGRAPH PROOF** Write a paragraph proof of Theorem 9.8 on page 551.

 GIVEN ▶ △*DEF* is a 45°-45°-90° triangle.

 PROVE ▶ The hypotenuse is √2 times as long as each leg.

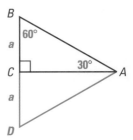

36. ▶ **PARAGRAPH PROOF** Write a paragraph proof of Theorem 9.9 on page 551.

 GIVEN ▶ △*ABC* is a 30°-60°-90° triangle.

 PROVE ▶ The hypotenuse is twice as long as the shorter leg and the longer leg is √3 times as long as the shorter leg.

 Plan for Proof Construct △*ADC* congruent to △*ABC*. Then prove that △*ABD* is equilateral. Express the lengths *AB* and *AC* in terms of *a*.

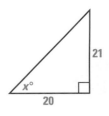

37. MULTIPLE CHOICE Which of the statements below is true about the diagram at the right?

 Ⓐ $x < 45$ Ⓑ $x = 45$

 Ⓒ $x > 45$ Ⓓ $x \le 45$

 Ⓔ Not enough information is given to determine the value of *x*.

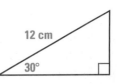

38. MULTIPLE CHOICE Find the perimeter of the triangle shown at the right to the nearest tenth of a centimeter.

 Ⓐ 28.4 cm Ⓑ 30 cm

 Ⓒ 31.2 cm Ⓓ 41.6 cm

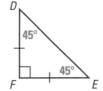

★ **Challenge**

VISUAL THINKING **In Exercises 39–41, use the diagram below. Each triangle in the diagram is a 45°-45°-90° triangle. At Stage 0, the legs of the triangle are each 1 unit long.**

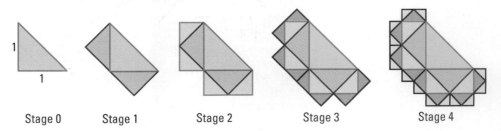

Stage 0   Stage 1   Stage 2   Stage 3   Stage 4

39. Find the exact lengths of the legs of the triangles that are added at each stage. Leave radicals in the denominators of fractions.

40. Describe the pattern of the lengths in Exercise 39.

41. Find the length of a leg of a triangle added in Stage 8. Explain how you found your answer.

42. FINDING A SIDE LENGTH A triangle has one side of 9 inches and another of 14 inches. Describe the possible lengths of the third side. (Review 5.5)

FINDING REFLECTIONS Find the coordinates of the reflection without using a coordinate plane. (Review 7.2)

43. $Q(-1, -2)$ reflected in the x-axis   **44.** $P(8, 3)$ reflected in the y-axis

45. $A(4, -5)$ reflected in the y-axis   **46.** $B(0, 10)$ reflected in the x-axis

▶ **DEVELOPING PROOF** Name a postulate or theorem that can be used to prove that the two triangles are similar. (Review 8.5 for 9.5)

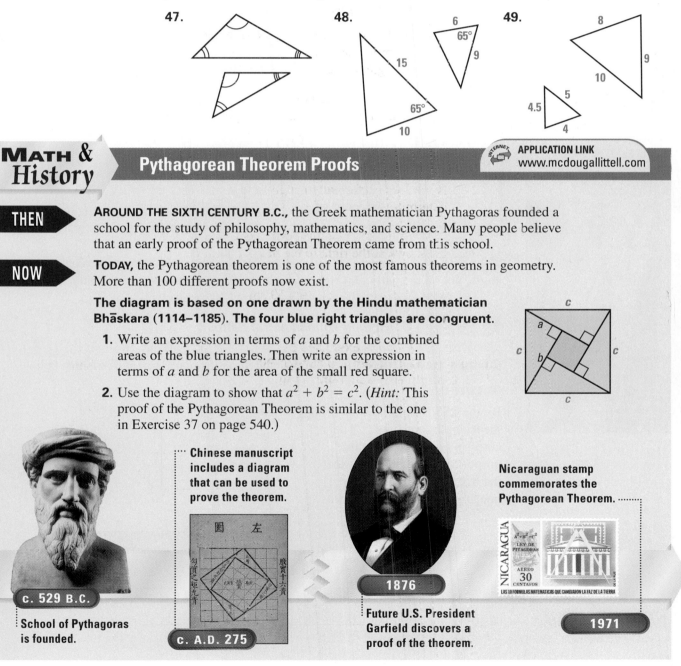

47.

48.   6   65°   9   15   65°   10

49.   8   9   10   5   4.5   4

Pythagorean Theorem Proofs

APPLICATION LINK
www.mcdougallittell.com

THEN   **AROUND THE SIXTH CENTURY B.C.,** the Greek mathematician Pythagoras founded a school for the study of philosophy, mathematics, and science. Many people believe that an early proof of the Pythagorean Theorem came from this school.

NOW   **TODAY,** the Pythagorean theorem is one of the most famous theorems in geometry. More than 100 different proofs now exist.

The diagram is based on one drawn by the Hindu mathematician Bhāskara (1114–1185). The four blue right triangles are congruent.

1. Write an expression in terms of a and b for the combined areas of the blue triangles. Then write an expression in terms of a and b for the area of the small red square.

2. Use the diagram to show that $a^2 + b^2 = c^2$. (*Hint:* This proof of the Pythagorean Theorem is similar to the one in Exercise 37 on page 540.)

c. 529 B.C.

School of Pythagoras is founded.

Chinese manuscript includes a diagram that can be used to prove the theorem.

圖   左

c. A.D. 275

1876

Future U.S. President Garfield discovers a proof of the theorem.

Nicaraguan stamp commemorates the Pythagorean Theorem.

NICARAGUA   LEY DE PITAGORAS   AEREO 30 CENTAVOS   LAS 10 FORMULAS MATEMATICAS QUE CAMBIARON LA FAZ DE LA TIERRA

1971

9.5

Trigonometric Ratios

What you should learn

GOAL 1 Find the sine, the cosine, and the tangent of an acute angle.

GOAL 2 Use trigonometric ratios to solve **real-life** problems, such as estimating the height of a tree in **Example 6**.

Why you should learn it

▼ To solve **real-life** problems, such as in finding the height of a water slide in **Ex. 37**.

A **trigonometric ratio** is a ratio of the lengths of two sides of a right triangle. The word *trigonometry* is derived from the ancient Greek language and means measurement of triangles. The three basic trigonometric ratios are **sine, cosine,** and **tangent,** which are abbreviated as *sin*, *cos*, and *tan*, respectively.

TRIGONOMETRIC RATIOS

Let △*ABC* be a right triangle. The sine, the cosine, and the tangent of the acute angle ∠*A* are defined as follows.

$$\sin A = \frac{\text{side opposite } \angle A}{\text{hypotenuse}} = \frac{a}{c}$$

$$\cos A = \frac{\text{side adjacent to } \angle A}{\text{hypotenuse}} = \frac{b}{c}$$

$$\tan A = \frac{\text{side opposite } \angle A}{\text{side adjacent to } \angle A} = \frac{a}{b}$$

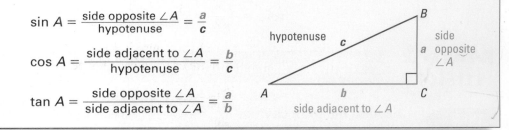

The value of a trigonometric ratio depends only on the measure of the acute angle, not on the particular right triangle that is used to compute the value.

EXAMPLE 1 *Finding Trigonometric Ratios*

Compare the sine, the cosine, and the tangent ratios for ∠*A* in each triangle below.

SOLUTION

By the SSS Similarity Theorem, the triangles are similar. Their corresponding sides are in proportion, which implies that the trigonometric ratios for ∠*A* in each triangle are the same.

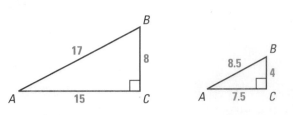

		Large triangle	Small triangle
$\sin A =$	$\dfrac{\text{opposite}}{\text{hypotenuse}}$	$\dfrac{8}{17} \approx 0.4706$	$\dfrac{4}{8.5} \approx 0.4706$
$\cos A =$	$\dfrac{\text{adjacent}}{\text{hypotenuse}}$	$\dfrac{15}{17} \approx 0.8824$	$\dfrac{7.5}{8.5} \approx 0.8824$
$\tan A =$	$\dfrac{\text{opposite}}{\text{adjacent}}$	$\dfrac{8}{15} \approx 0.5333$	$\dfrac{4}{7.5} \approx 0.5333$

Trigonometric ratios are frequently expressed as decimal approximations.

STUDENT HELP

INTERNET
HOMEWORK HELP
Visit our Web site
www.mcdougallittell.com
for extra examples.

EXAMPLE 2 *Finding Trigonometric Ratios*

Find the sine, the cosine, and the tangent
of the indicated angle.

   a. $\angle S$ **b.** $\angle R$

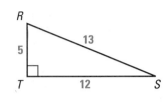

SOLUTION

a. The length of the hypotenuse is 13. For $\angle S$, the length of the opposite side
is 5, and the length of the adjacent side is 12.

$$\sin S = \frac{\text{opp.}}{\text{hyp.}} = \frac{5}{13} \approx 0.3846$$

$$\cos S = \frac{\text{adj.}}{\text{hyp.}} = \frac{12}{13} \approx 0.9231$$

$$\tan S = \frac{\text{opp.}}{\text{adj.}} = \frac{5}{12} \approx 0.4167$$

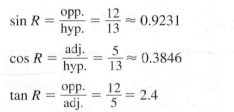

b. The length of the hypotenuse is 13. For $\angle R$, the length of the opposite side
is 12, and the length of the adjacent side is 5.

$$\sin R = \frac{\text{opp.}}{\text{hyp.}} = \frac{12}{13} \approx 0.9231$$

$$\cos R = \frac{\text{adj.}}{\text{hyp.}} = \frac{5}{13} \approx 0.3846$$

$$\tan R = \frac{\text{opp.}}{\text{adj.}} = \frac{12}{5} = 2.4$$

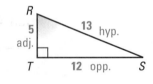

· · · · · · · · · ·

You can find trigonometric ratios for 30°, 45°, and 60° by applying what you
know about special right triangles.

EXAMPLE 3 *Trigonometric Ratios for 45°*

Find the sine, the cosine, and the tangent of 45°.

SOLUTION

Begin by sketching a 45°-45°-90° triangle. Because all such
triangles are similar, you can make calculations simple by
choosing 1 as the length of each leg. From Theorem 9.8 on
page 551, it follows that the length of the hypotenuse is $\sqrt{2}$.

STUDENT HELP

▶ **Study Tip**
The expression sin 45°
means the sine of an
angle whose measure
is 45°.

$$\sin 45° = \frac{\text{opp.}}{\text{hyp.}} = \frac{1}{\sqrt{2}} = \frac{\sqrt{2}}{2} \approx 0.7071$$

$$\cos 45° = \frac{\text{adj.}}{\text{hyp.}} = \frac{1}{\sqrt{2}} = \frac{\sqrt{2}}{2} \approx 0.7071$$

$$\tan 45° = \frac{\text{opp.}}{\text{adj.}} = \frac{1}{1} = 1$$

EXAMPLE 4 *Trigonometric Ratios for 30°*

Find the sine, the cosine, and the tangent of 30°.

SOLUTION

Begin by sketching a 30°-60°-90° triangle. To make the calculations simple, you can choose 1 as the length of the shorter leg. From Theorem 9.9 on page 551, it follows that the length of the longer leg is $\sqrt{3}$ and the length of the hypotenuse is 2.

$$\sin 30° = \frac{\text{opp.}}{\text{hyp.}} = \frac{1}{2} = 0.5$$

$$\cos 30° = \frac{\text{adj.}}{\text{hyp.}} = \frac{\sqrt{3}}{2} \approx 0.8660$$

$$\tan 30° = \frac{\text{opp.}}{\text{adj.}} = \frac{1}{\sqrt{3}} = \frac{\sqrt{3}}{3} \approx 0.5774$$

EXAMPLE 5 *Using a Calculator*

You can use a calculator to approximate the sine, the cosine, and the tangent of 74°. Make sure your calculator is in *degree mode.* The table shows some sample keystroke sequences accepted by most calculators.

Sample keystroke sequences	Sample calculator display	Rounded approximation
74 SIN or SIN 74 ENTER	0.961261695	0.9613
74 COS or COS 74 ENTER	0.275637355	0.2756
74 TAN or TAN 74 ENTER	3.487414444	3.4874

· · · · · · · · ·

STUDENT HELP

▶ **Trig Table**
For a table of trigonometric ratios, see p. 845.

If you look back at Examples 1–5, you will notice that the sine or the cosine of an acute angle is always less than 1. The reason is that these trigonometric ratios involve the ratio of a leg of a right triangle to the hypotenuse. The length of a leg of a right triangle is always less than the length of its hypotenuse, so the ratio of these lengths is always less than one.

Because the tangent of an acute angle involves the ratio of one leg to another leg, the tangent of an angle can be less than 1, equal to 1, or greater than 1.

TRIGONOMETRIC IDENTITIES A trigonometric identity is an equation involving trigonometric ratios that is true for all acute angles. You are asked to prove the following identities in Exercises 47 and 52:

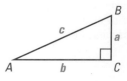

$$(\sin A)^2 + (\cos A)^2 = 1$$

$$\tan A = \frac{\sin A}{\cos A}$$

GOAL 2 USING TRIGONOMETRIC RATIOS IN REAL LIFE

Suppose you stand and look up at a point in the distance, such as the top of the tree in Example 6. The angle that your line of sight makes with a line drawn horizontally is called the **angle of elevation**.

EXAMPLE 6 *Indirect Measurement*

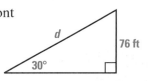
FORESTRY You are measuring the height of a Sitka spruce tree in Alaska. You stand 45 feet from the base of the tree. You measure the angle of elevation from a point on the ground to the top of the tree to be 59°. To estimate the height of the tree, you can write a trigonometric ratio that involves the height h and the known length of 45 feet.

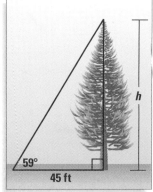

$$\tan 59° = \frac{\text{opposite}}{\text{adjacent}} \qquad \text{Write ratio.}$$

$$\tan 59° = \frac{h}{45} \qquad \text{Substitute.}$$

$$45 \tan 59° = h \qquad \text{Multiply each side by 45.}$$

$$45(1.6643) \approx h \qquad \text{Use a calculator or table to find tan 59°.}$$

$$74.9 \approx h \qquad \text{Simplify.}$$

▶ The tree is about 75 feet tall.

EXAMPLE 7 *Estimating a Distance*

ESCALATORS The escalator at the Wilshire/Vermont Metro Rail Station in Los Angeles rises 76 feet at a 30° angle. To find the distance d a person travels on the escalator stairs, you can write a trigonometric ratio that involves the hypotenuse and the known leg length of 76 feet.

$$\sin 30° = \frac{\text{opposite}}{\text{hypotenuse}} \qquad \text{Write ratio for sine of 30°.}$$

$$\sin 30° = \frac{76}{d} \qquad \text{Substitute.}$$

$$d \sin 30° = 76 \qquad \text{Multiply each side by } d.$$

$$d = \frac{76}{\sin 30°} \qquad \text{Divide each side by sin 30°.}$$

$$d = \frac{76}{0.5} \qquad \text{Substitute 0.5 for sin 30°.}$$

$$d = 152 \qquad \text{Simplify.}$$

▶ A person travels 152 feet on the escalator stairs.

GUIDED PRACTICE

Vocabulary Check ✓

In Exercises 1 and 2, use the diagram at the right.

1. Use the diagram to explain what is meant by the *sine*, the *cosine*, and the *tangent* of ∠A.

Concept Check ✓

2. **ERROR ANALYSIS** A student says that sin *D* > sin *A* because the side lengths of △*DEF* are greater than the side lengths of △*ABC*. Explain why the student is incorrect.

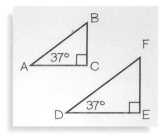

Skill Check ✓

In Exercises 3–8, use the diagram shown at the right to find the trigonometric ratio.

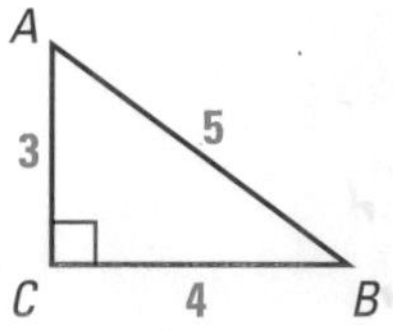

3. sin *A*   4. cos *A*

5. tan *A*   6. sin *B*

7. cos *B*   8. tan *B*

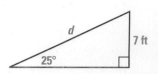

9. **ESCALATORS** One early escalator built in 1896 rose at an angle of 25°. As shown in the diagram at the right, the vertical lift was 7 feet. Estimate the distance *d* a person traveled on this escalator.

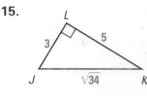

PRACTICE AND APPLICATIONS

STUDENT HELP

▶ **Extra Practice**
to help you master
skills is on p. 820.

FINDING TRIGONOMETRIC RATIOS Find the sine, the cosine, and the tangent of the acute angles of the triangle. Express each value as a decimal rounded to four places.

10.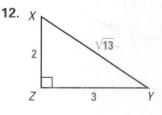

11.

12.

13.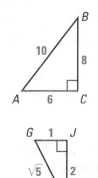

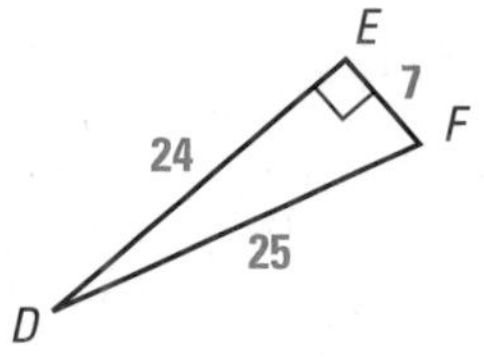

14.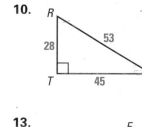

15.

STUDENT HELP

▶ HOMEWORK HELP
Example 1: Exs. 10–15,
          28–36
Example 2: Exs. 10–15,
          28–36
Example 3: Exs. 34–36
Example 4: Exs. 34–36
Example 5: Exs. 16–27
Example 6: Exs. 37–42
Example 7: Exs. 37–42

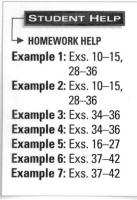

CALCULATOR Use a calculator to approximate the given value to four decimal places.

16. sin 48°   17. cos 13°   18. tan 81°   19. sin 27°

20. cos 70°   21. tan 2°   22. sin 78°   23. cos 36°

24. tan 23°   25. cos 63°   26. sin 56°   27. tan 66°

USING TRIGONOMETRIC RATIOS Find the value of each variable. Round decimals to the nearest tenth.

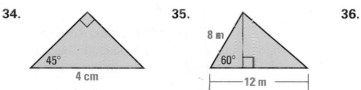

28.

29.

30.

31.

32.

33.

FINDING AREA Find the area of the triangle. Round decimals to the nearest tenth.

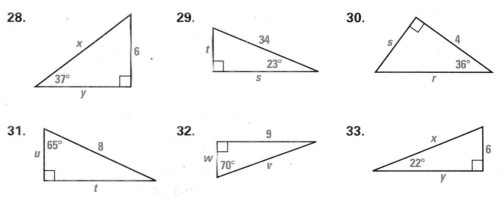

34.

35.

36.

WATER SLIDE
Even though riders on a water slide may travel at only 20 miles per hour, the curves on the slide can make riders feel as though they are traveling much faster.

37. 🌐 **WATER SLIDE** The angle of elevation from the base to the top of a waterslide is about 13°. The slide extends horizontally about 58.2 meters. Estimate the height h of the slide.

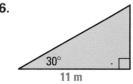

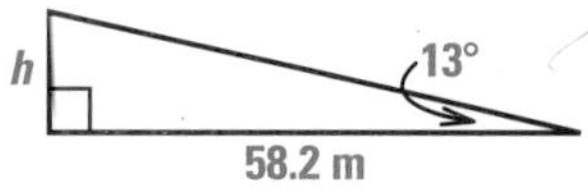

38. 🌐 **SURVEYING** To find the distance d from a house on shore to a house on an island, a surveyor measures from the house on shore to point B, as shown in the diagram. An instrument called a *transit* is used to find the measure of $\angle B$. Estimate the distance d.

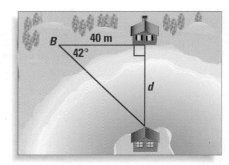

39. 🌐 **SKI SLOPE** Suppose you stand at the top of a ski slope and look down at the bottom. The angle that your line of sight makes with a line drawn horizontally is called the *angle of depression*, as shown below. The *vertical drop* is the difference in the elevations of the top and the bottom of the slope. Find the vertical drop x of the slope in the diagram. Then estimate the distance d a person skiing would travel on this slope.

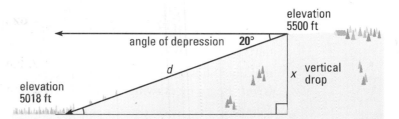

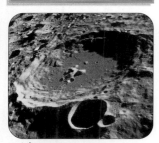

LUNAR CRATERS
Because the moon
has no atmosphere to
protect it from being hit by
meteorites, its surface is
pitted with craters. There is
no wind, so a crater can
remain undisturbed for
millions of years—unless
another meteorite crashes
into it.

40. SCIENCE CONNECTION Scientists can
measure the depths of craters on the
moon by looking at photos of shadows.
The length of the shadow cast by the
edge of a crater is about 500 meters.
The sun's angle of elevation is 55°.
Estimate the depth d of the crater.

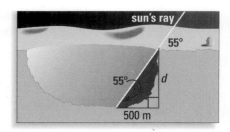

41. 🌐 **LUGGAGE DESIGN** Some luggage
pieces have wheels and a handle so that
the luggage can be pulled along the ground.
Suppose a person's hand is about 30 inches
from the floor. About how long should the
handle be on the suitcase shown so that
it can roll at a comfortable angle of 45°
with the floor?

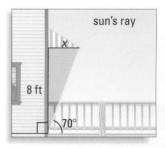

42. 🌐 **BUYING AN AWNING** Your family room
has a sliding-glass door with a southern exposure.
You want to buy an awning for the door that will
be just long enough to keep the sun out when it
is at its highest point in the sky. The angle of
elevation of the sun at this point is 70°, and the
height of the door is 8 feet. About how far should
the overhang extend?

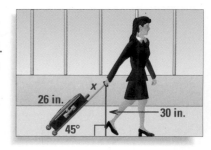

CRITICAL THINKING In Exercises 43 and 44, use the diagram.

43. Write expressions for the sine, the cosine, and the tangent
of each acute angle in the triangle.

44. *Writing* Use your results from Exercise 43 to explain
how the tangent of one acute angle of a right triangle
is related to the tangent of the other acute angle. How
are the sine and the cosine of one acute angle of a right
triangle related to the sine and the cosine of the other
acute angle?

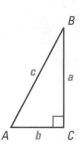

45. 📐 **TECHNOLOGY** Use geometry software to construct a right triangle.
Use your triangle to explore and answer the questions below. Explain
your procedure.

- For what angle measure is the tangent of an acute angle equal to 1?
- For what angle measures is the tangent of an acute angle greater than 1?
- For what angle measures is the tangent of an acute angle less than 1?

46. ERROR ANALYSIS To find the length of $\overline{BC}$
in the diagram at the right, a student writes
$\tan 55° = \dfrac{18}{BC}$. What mistake is the student
making? Show how the student can find BC.
(*Hint:* Begin by drawing an altitude from
B to $\overline{AC}$.)

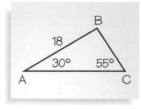

47. ▶ **PROOF** Use the diagram of △*ABC*. Complete the proof of the trigonometric identity below.

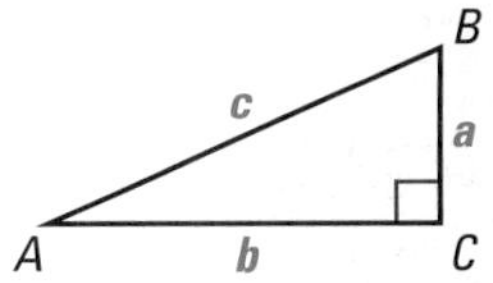

$$(\sin A)^2 + (\cos A)^2 = 1$$

GIVEN ▶ $\sin A = \dfrac{a}{c},\ \cos A = \dfrac{b}{c}$

PROVE ▶ $(\sin A)^2 + (\cos A)^2 = 1$

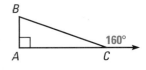

Statements	Reasons
1. $\sin A = \dfrac{a}{c},\ \cos A = \dfrac{b}{c}$	**1.** ___?___
2. $a^2 + b^2 = c^2$	**2.** ___?___
3. $\dfrac{a^2}{c^2} + \dfrac{b^2}{c^2} = 1$	**3.** ___?___
4. $\left(\dfrac{a}{c}\right)^2 + \left(\dfrac{b}{c}\right)^2 = 1$	**4.** A property of exponents
5. $(\sin A)^2 + (\cos A)^2 = 1$	**5.** ___?___

DEMONSTRATING A FORMULA Show that $(\sin A)^2 + (\cos A)^2 = 1$ for the given angle measure.

48. $m\angle A = 30°$ **49.** $m\angle A = 45°$ **50.** $m\angle A = 60°$ **51.** $m\angle A = 13°$

52. ▶ **PROOF** Use the diagram in Exercise 47. Write a two-column proof of the following trigonometric identity: $\tan A = \dfrac{\sin A}{\cos A}$.

Test Preparation

53. MULTIPLE CHOICE Use the diagram at the right. Find *CD*.

  Ⓐ 8 cos 25°   Ⓑ 8 sin 25°   Ⓒ 8 tan 25°

  Ⓓ $\dfrac{8}{\sin 25°}$ Ⓔ $\dfrac{8}{\cos 25°}$

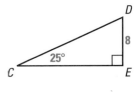

54. MULTIPLE CHOICE Use the diagram at the right. Which expression is *not* equivalent to *AC*?

  Ⓐ *BC* sin 70°   Ⓑ *BC* cos 20°   Ⓒ $\dfrac{BC}{\tan 20°}$

  Ⓓ $\dfrac{BA}{\tan 20°}$ Ⓔ *BA* tan 70°

★ Challenge

55. ● **PARADE** You are at a parade looking up at a large balloon floating directly above the street. You are 60 feet from a point on the street directly beneath the balloon. To see the top of the balloon, you look up at an angle of 53°. To see the bottom of the balloon, you look up at an angle of 29°.

Estimate the height *h* of the balloon to the nearest foot.

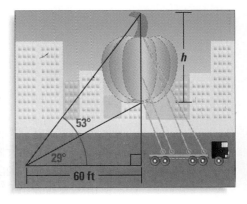

56. SKETCHING A DILATION △*PQR* is mapped onto △*P'Q'R'* by a dilation. In △*PQR*, *PQ* = 3, *QR* = 5, and *PR* = 4. In △*P'Q'R'*, *P'Q'* = 6. Sketch the dilation, identify it as a reduction or an enlargement, and find the scale factor. Then find the length of *Q'R'* and *P'R'*. (Review 8.7)

57. FINDING LENGTHS Write similarity statements for the three similar triangles in the diagram. Then find *QP* and *NP*. Round decimals to the nearest tenth. (Review 9.1)

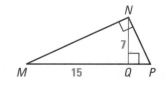

PYTHAGOREAN THEOREM **Find the unknown side length. Simplify answers that are radicals. Tell whether the side lengths form a Pythagorean triple.** (Review 9.2 for 9.6)

58.   **59.**   **60.**

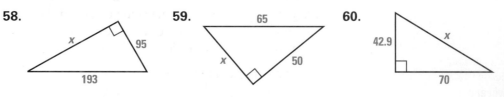

QUIZ 2

Sketch the figure that is described. Then find the requested information. Round decimals to the nearest tenth. (Lesson 9.4)

1. The side length of an equilateral triangle is 4 meters. Find the length of an altitude of the triangle.

2. The perimeter of a square is 16 inches. Find the length of a diagonal.

3. The side length of an equilateral triangle is 3 inches. Find the area of the triangle.

Find the value of each variable. Round decimals to the nearest tenth. (Lesson 9.5)

4.   **5.**   **6.**

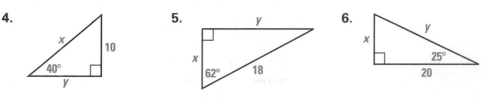

7. 🎈 **HOT-AIR BALLOON** The ground crew for a hot-air balloon can see the balloon in the sky at an angle of elevation of 11°. The pilot radios to the crew that the hot-air balloon is 950 feet above the ground. Estimate the horizontal distance *d* of the hot-air balloon from the ground crew. (Lesson 9.5)

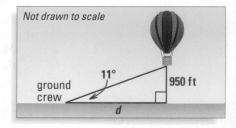

Not drawn to scale

9.6

Solving Right Triangles

What you should learn

GOAL 1 Solve a right triangle.

GOAL 2 Use right triangles to solve **real-life** problems, such as finding the glide angle and altitude of a space shuttle in **Example 3**.

Why you should learn it

▼ To solve **real-life** problems such as determining the correct dimensions of a wheel-chair ramp in **Exs. 39–41**.

GOAL 1 SOLVING A RIGHT TRIANGLE

Every right triangle has one right angle, two acute angles, one hypotenuse, and two legs. To **solve a right triangle** means to determine the measures of all six parts. You can solve a right triangle if you know either of the following:

• Two side lengths
• One side length and one acute angle measure

As you learned in Lesson 9.5, you can use the side lengths of a right triangle to find trigonometric ratios for the acute angles of the triangle. As you will see in this lesson, once you know the sine, the cosine, or the tangent of an acute angle, you can use a calculator to find the measure of the angle.

In general, for an acute angle A:

if $\sin A = x$, then $\sin^{-1} x = m\angle A$. ◄—— **The expression $\sin^{-1} x$ is read as "the inverse sine of x."**

if $\cos A = y$, then $\cos^{-1} y = m\angle A$.

if $\tan A = z$, then $\tan^{-1} z = m\angle A$.

▶ **ACTIVITY**

Developing Concepts

Finding Angles in Right Triangles

1 Carefully draw right $\triangle ABC$ with side lengths of 3 centimeters, 4 centimeters, and 5 centimeters, as shown.

2 Use trigonometric ratios to find the sine, the cosine, and the tangent of $\angle A$. Express the ratios in decimal form.

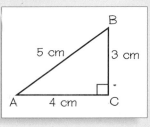

3 In Step 2, you found that $\sin A = \frac{3}{5} = 0.6$. You can use a calculator to find $\sin^{-1} 0.6$. Most calculators use one of the keystroke sequences below.

$\sin^{-1}$ $\sin^{-1}$

| 2nd | SIN | 0.6 | ENTER | or   0.6 | 2nd | SIN |

Make sure your calculator is in degree mode. Then use each of the trigonometric ratios you found in Step 2 to approximate the measure of $\angle A$ to the nearest tenth of a degree.

4 Use a protractor to measure $\angle A$. How does the measured value compare with your calculated values?

EXAMPLE 1 *Solving a Right Triangle*

Solve the right triangle. Round decimals
to the nearest tenth.

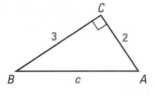

SOLUTION

Begin by using the Pythagorean Theorem to find the length of the hypotenuse.

$(\text{hypotenuse})^2 = (\text{leg})^2 + (\text{leg})^2$	**Pythagorean Theorem**
$c^2 = 3^2 + 2^2$	**Substitute.**
$c^2 = 13$	**Simplify.**
$c = \sqrt{13}$	**Find the positive square root.**
$c \approx 3.6$	**Use a calculator to approximate.**

Then use a calculator to find the measure of $\angle B$:

(2 ÷ 3) 2nd TAN $\approx 33.7°$

Finally, because $\angle A$ and $\angle B$ are complements, you can write

$$m\angle A = 90° - m\angle B \approx 90° - 33.7° = 56.3°.$$

▶ The side lengths of the triangle are 2, 3, and $\sqrt{13}$, or about 3.6. The triangle has
one right angle and two acute angles whose measures are about 33.7° and 56.3°.

EXAMPLE 2 *Solving a Right Triangle*

Solve the right triangle. Round decimals
to the nearest tenth.

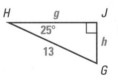

SOLUTION

Use trigonometric ratios to find the values of g and h.

$\sin H = \dfrac{\text{opp.}}{\text{hyp.}}$	$\cos H = \dfrac{\text{adj.}}{\text{hyp.}}$
$\sin 25° = \dfrac{h}{13}$	$\cos 25° = \dfrac{g}{13}$
$13 \sin 25° = h$	$13 \cos 25° = g$
$13(0.4226) \approx h$	$13(0.9063) \approx g$
$5.5 \approx h$	$11.8 \approx g$

Because $\angle H$ and $\angle G$ are complements, you can write

$$m\angle G = 90° - m\angle H = 90° - 25° = 65°.$$

▶ The side lengths of the triangle are about 5.5, 11.8, and 13. The triangle has
one right angle and two acute angles whose measures are 65° and 25°.

STUDENT HELP

▶ Study Tip
There are other ways to
find the side lengths in
Examples 1 and 2. For
instance, in Example 2,
you can use a trigono-
metric ratio to find one
side length, and then
use the Pythagorean
Theorem to find the other
side length.

EXAMPLE 3 *Solving a Right Triangle*

SPACE SHUTTLE During its approach to
Earth, the space shuttle's glide angle changes.

a. When the shuttle's altitude is about
15.7 miles, its horizontal distance to
the runway is about 59 miles. What
is its glide angle? Round your answer
to the nearest tenth.

b. When the space shuttle is 5 miles from
the runway, its glide angle is about 19°.
Find the shuttle's altitude at this point in
its descent. Round your answer to the
nearest tenth.

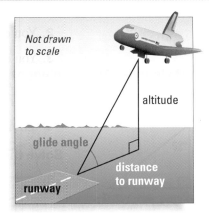
Not drawn to scale

altitude

glide angle

distance to runway

runway

ASTRONAUT
  Some astronauts are
pilots who are qualified to fly
the space shuttle. Some
shuttle astronauts are
mission specialists whose
responsibilities include
conducting scientific
experiments in space. All
astronauts need to have a
strong background in
science and mathematics.

CAREER LINK
www.mcdougallittell.com

SOLUTION

a. Sketch a right triangle to model the situation.
Let $x°$ = the measure of the shuttle's glide angle.
You can use the tangent ratio and a calculator to
find the approximate value of x.

$x°$
59 mi
15.7 mi

$$\tan x° = \frac{\text{opp.}}{\text{adj.}}$$

$$\tan x° = \frac{15.7}{59}$$ **Substitute.**

$$x = \boxed{(} \ 15.7 \ \boxed{\div} \ 59 \ \boxed{)} \ \boxed{\text{2nd}} \ \boxed{\text{TAN}}$$ **Use a calculator to find** $\tan^{-1}\left(\frac{15.7}{59}\right)$.

$$x \approx 14.9$$

▶ When the space shuttle's altitude is about 15.7 miles, the glide angle is
about 14.9°.

b. Sketch a right triangle to model the situation.
Let h = the altitude of the shuttle. You can
use the tangent ratio and a calculator to find
the approximate value of h.

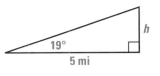
19°
5 mi
h

$$\tan 19° = \frac{\text{opp.}}{\text{adj.}}$$

$$\tan 19° = \frac{h}{5}$$ **Substitute.**

$$0.3443 \approx \frac{h}{5}$$ **Use a calculator.**

$$1.7 \approx h$$ **Multiply each side by 5.**

▶ The shuttle's altitude is about 1.7 miles.

STUDENT HELP

HOMEWORK HELP
  Visit our Web site
www.mcdougallittell.com
for extra examples.

near your home or school. Find the ramp angle. Does the ramp meet the
specifications described above? Explain.

GUIDED PRACTICE

Vocabulary Check ✓   **1.** Explain what is meant by *solving* a right triangle.

Concept Check ✓   **Tell whether the statement is *true* or *false*.**

CHAPTER 9

Chapter Standardized Test

▶ **TEST-TAKING STRATEGY** When checking your work, try to use a method other than the one you originally used to get your answer. If you use the same method, you may make the same mistake twice.

1. MULTIPLE CHOICE Use the diagram to find the value of *x*.

(A) 6   (B) 7

(C) 9   (D) 10

(E) 11

In Questions 2 and 3, use the diagram below.

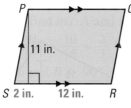

2. MULTIPLE CHOICE Find the area of □*PQRS*.

(A) 132 in.^{2} (B) 143 in.^{2} (C) 154 in.^{2}

(D) 156 in.^{2} (E) 166 in.^{2}

3. MULTIPLE CHOICE Find the perimeter of □*PQRS* rounded to the nearest tenth.

(A) 44.4 in.   (B) 46.4 in.   (C) 50 in.

(D) 50.4 in.   (E) 52.4 in.

4. MULTIPLE CHOICE Let the numbers represent the lengths of the sides of a triangle. Which of the triangles are right triangles?

I. 11, 14, $\sqrt{317}$ **II.** 7, 26, $5\sqrt{30}$

III. 18, $2\sqrt{19}$, 20   **IV.** 9, 25, 27

(A) I, II, and III only   (B) I and III only

(C) III only   (D) IV only

(E) none

5. MULTIPLE CHOICE Which set of numbers can represent the side lengths of an obtuse triangle?

(A) 71, 70, 68   (B) 30, 40, 50

(C) 41, 39, 2   (D) 25, 25, 40

(E) 17, 17, $17\sqrt{2}$

6. MULTIPLE CHOICE The length of a diagonal of a square is 16 inches. What is its perimeter?

(A) $8\sqrt{2}$ in.   (B) $16\sqrt{2}$ in.   (C) $30\sqrt{2}$ in.

(D) $32\sqrt{2}$ in.   (E) $48\sqrt{2}$ in.

7. MULTIPLE CHOICE Use the diagram below to find the values of *x* and *y*. The values are rounded to the nearest tenth.

(A) *x* = 8.7, *y* = 18.8

(B) *x* = 18.8, *y* = 20.1

(C) *x* = 14.4, *y* = 19.2

(D) *x* = 12.6, *y* = 18.5

(E) *x* = 18.8, *y* = 20.5

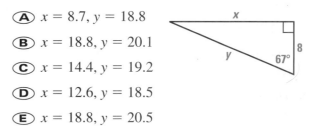

8. MULTIPLE CHOICE The base of an isosceles triangle is 18 centimeters long. The altitude to the base is 12 centimeters long. What is the approximate measure of a base angle of the triangle?

(A) 53.1°   (B) 36.9°   (C) 38.7°

(D) 33.7°   (E) 56.3°

9. MULTIPLE CHOICE In the diagram below, what is the measure of ∠*A* to the nearest tenth of a degree?

(A) 31.6°

(B) 38.0°

(C) 38.7°

(D) 51.3°

(E) 52.0°

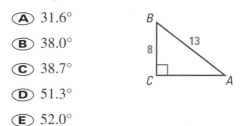

10. MULTIPLE CHOICE Let $\vec{v} = \langle -2, y \rangle$ and $\vec{w} = \langle x, 4 \rangle$. If $\vec{v} + \vec{w} = \langle 6, 11 \rangle$, what are the values of *x* and *y*?

(A) *x* = 8, *y* = 8   (B) *x* = 8, *y* = 7

(C) *x* = 7, *y* = 8   (D) *x* = −8, *y* = 7

(E) *x* = 4, *y* = 7

11. **MULTIPLE CHOICE** Points $A(-8, 3)$ and $B(1, -9)$ are the initial and the terminal points of $\overrightarrow{AB}$. Find the magnitude of $\overrightarrow{AB}$.

(A) $\langle 9, -12 \rangle$ (B) $\langle -9, 12 \rangle$ (C) 225   (D) 15   (E) $\langle -7, -6 \rangle$

MULTI-STEP PROBLEM **In Exercises 12–14, use the diagram at the right.**

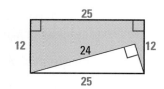

12. Find the perimeter of the right triangle.

13. Find the measures of the acute angles of the right triangle.

14. Find the area of the shaded region.

MULTI-STEP PROBLEM **In Exercises 15–18, use the diagram at the right. Round decimals to the nearest tenth.**

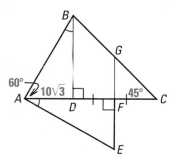

15. Find each of the following segment lengths: BD, BC, FG, GC, DC, and AF.

16. Find $m\angle ABC$, $m\angle FEA$, and $m\angle BGF$.

17. Find the approximate lengths of $\overline{FE}$ and $\overline{AE}$.

18. Find the area of $\triangle ABC$.

MULTI-STEP PROBLEM **In Exercises 19–22, use the information and the diagram.**

You can use a device like the one shown to measure the sun's angle of elevation, $\angle A$, above the horizon. The variable b represents the length of the shadow cast by a vertical marker on a ruler.

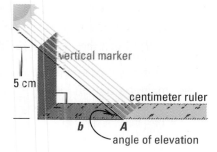

19. Find the shadow length b for each of the angle measures below.

   a. $m\angle A = 30°$

   b. $m\angle A = 40°$

   c. $m\angle A = 50°$

   d. $m\angle A = 60°$

   e. $m\angle A = 70°$

20. Based on your answers to Exercise 19, what happens to the value of b as the sun rises in the sky?

21. At a certain hour, the shadow length b is 5.25 centimeters. Estimate the sun's angle of elevation.

22. The amount of Earth's atmosphere that sunlight passes through depends on the position of the sun in the sky. This amount is measured in "air masses." When the sun is not directly overhead, the number of air masses its rays pass through is approximately $\dfrac{1}{\sin A}$. What happens to the value of this expression as the sun approaches the horizon?

1. If three points all lie in two different planes, can the points be the vertices of a triangle? Explain why or why not. **(2.1)**

In Exercises 2–4, use *always*, *sometimes*, or *never* to complete the statement.

2. Lines m, n, and t are three different coplanar lines. If $m \perp t$ and $n \perp t$, then line m and line n are __?__ parallel. **(3.1, 3.5)**

3. The numbers 8, 14, and 23 can __?__ represent the lengths of the sides of a triangle. **(5.5)**

4. A rhombus is __?__ a parallelogram. **(6.6)**

5. ▶ **PROOF** Prove that the median to the base of an isosceles triangle bisects the vertex angle. **(4.6, 5.3)**

   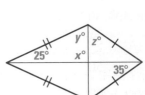

   GIVEN ▶ In $\triangle ABC$, $\overline{AB} \cong \overline{CB}$; $\overline{BD}$ is a median to $\overline{AC}$.

   PROVE ▶ $\overline{BD}$ bisects $\angle ABC$.

6. In quadrilateral $ABCD$, $m\angle A = 37°$, $m\angle B = 143°$, and $m\angle C = 37°$. Prove that quadrilateral $ABCD$ is a parallelogram. **(6.1, 6.3)**

7. Does the design at the right have rotational symmetry? If so, describe the rotations that map the image onto itself. **(7.3)**

Find the value of each variable. **(3.2, 3.3, 6.5)**

8.

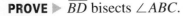

$26°$

$(x + 10)°$

$4y°$

9.

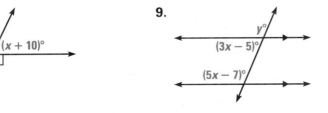

$y°$

$(3x - 5)°$

$(5x - 7)°$

10.

$y°$ $z°$

$25°$ $x°$

$35°$

In Exercises 11–15, use $\triangle ABC$ with vertices $A(1, -2)$, $B(-3, -5)$, and $C(-5, 6)$.

11. Find an equation of the perpendicular bisector of $\overline{AC}$. **(5.1)**

12. Classify $\triangle ABC$ by its sides and by its angles. **(4.1, 9.3)**

13. Find the coordinates of the vertices of the image of $\triangle ABC$ after a reflection in the y-axis. **(7.2)**

14. Find the coordinates of the vertices of the image of $\triangle ABC$ after a rotation of $90°$ counterclockwise about the origin. **(7.3)**

15. Find the coordinates of the image of $\triangle ABC$ after the translation $(x, y) \rightarrow (x - 4, y - 4)$ and then a reflection in the x-axis. **(7.5)**

Solve the proportion. **(8.1)**

16. $\dfrac{12}{x} = \dfrac{5}{2}$

17. $\dfrac{3}{7} = \dfrac{x}{8}$

18. $\dfrac{7}{9} = \dfrac{y}{y + 3}$

19. Rectangle $ABCD$ has coordinates $A(0, 4)$, $B(8, 4)$, $C(8, -2)$, and $D(0, -2)$. Points P and Q are the midpoints of $\overline{AB}$ and $\overline{DC}$, respectively. Is rectangle $ABCD$ similar to rectangle $APQD$? Explain your answer. **(8.3)**

20. Show that the midsegment of a triangle forms one side of a triangle that is similar to the original triangle. **(5.4, 8.4)**

21. Is a triangle with sides of lengths 6, 8, and 12 similar to a triangle with sides of lengths 9, 12, and 18? Explain your answer. **(8.5)**

22. The side lengths of a triangle are 7 centimeters, 8 centimeters, and 9 centimeters. A ray bisects the largest angle, dividing the side opposite the angle into two segments. Find the lengths of these segments. **(8.6)**

23. A segment has endpoints at $A(6, -4)$ and $B(12, 9)$. Find the images of the segment under two dilations, one with scale factor $\dfrac{1}{3}$ and center $(0, 0)$, and the other with scale factor $\dfrac{1}{2}$ and center $(0, 0)$. Then tell whether the two image segments are parallel. **(8.7)**

In Exercises 24–26, use the diagram at the right.

24. If $XP = 2$ and $PY = 6$, find ZP and XZ. **(9.1)**

25. Find XY if $ZY = 2\sqrt{3}$ and $PY = 3$. **(9.1)**

26. Find XY if $XZ = 10$ and $ZY = 24$. **(9.2)**

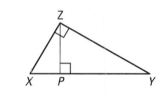

27. Is a triangle with side lengths 12, 15, and 19 *acute*, *right*, or *obtuse*? **(9.3)**

28. A square and an equilateral triangle have sides that are 8 feet long. Find the ratio of the length of a diagonal of the square to the height of the triangle. **(9.4)**

29. The lengths of the legs of a right triangle are 8 and 15. Find the sine, the cosine, and the tangent of the smaller acute angle of the triangle. Express each value as a fraction. **(9.5)**

30. In right $\triangle RST$, $m\angle R = 57°$. The length of the hypotenuse, $\overline{RS}$, is 20 inches. Solve the right triangle. Round decimals to the nearest tenth. **(9.6)**

31. Add the vectors $\vec{u} = \langle 5, 7 \rangle$ and $\vec{v} = \langle -3, 9 \rangle$. Draw the sum vector $\vec{u} + \vec{v}$ in a coordinate plane. Find its magnitude and its direction relative to east. **(9.7)**

32. JEWELRY DESIGN A jewelry designer has a triangular piece of flat silver. The designer wants to cut out the largest possible circle from the piece of silver. Explain how to find the center and the radius of that circle. **(5.2)**

33. CAR TRIP On the first four days of an automobile trip, a family drove 376 miles on 16 gallons of gasoline. At that rate, how many gallons of gas will they need for the next 470 miles of their trip? **(8.1)**

34. PHOTOGRAPHY A 3 inch by 5 inch photograph is enlarged so its perimeter is 36 inches. What are the dimensions of the enlargement? **(8.3)**

35. AIRPLANES Two jets leave an airport at the same time. One jet flies west, averaging 510 miles per hour. The other jet flies north, averaging 560 miles per hour. To the nearest tenth of a mile, how far apart are the jets after 15 minutes? **(9.2)**

Investigating Fractals

OBJECTIVE Learn how fractals are formed and explore the properties of fractals.

Materials: ruler, protractor, graphing calculator, graph paper

A *fractal* is a mathematical object that has the property of *self-similarity*: a part of the shape resembles the whole shape.

Many fractals are formed by a repetitive process called *iteration*. The stages that lead to a simple fractal called a *Koch curve* are shown below.

STAGES OF A KOCH CURVE

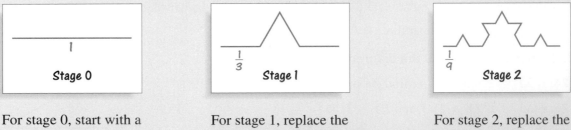

For stage 0, start with a segment of length 1.

For stage 1, replace the middle third of the segment in stage 0 with two congruent segments of length $\frac{1}{3}$.

For stage 2, replace the middle third of every segment of stage 1 with two congruent segments of length $\frac{1}{9}$.

For later stages, replace the middle third of every segment of the previous stage with two congruent segments of the appropriate length. The fractal is the shape that would result if you could continue this process infinitely many times.

INVESTIGATION

Copy the table below. Then answer the exercises.

Stage, n	0	1	2	3	4
Length, L	1	?	?	?	?

1. Use the diagrams above to fill in the lengths for stages 1 and 2.

2. Look for a pattern in the lengths at stages 0, 1, and 2. Use the pattern to predict the lengths of the Koch curve at stages 3 and 4.

3. Predict what happens to the length if you repeat this iteration many times. Explain your reasoning.

4. The length L of the fractal can be written as a function of stage n using this formula: $L = \left(\frac{4}{3}\right)^n$. Use a graphing calculator to sketch a graph of this function. Does the graph support your answer to Exercise 3? Explain.

STAGES OF A KOCH SNOWFLAKE

If you join three Koch curves, you can create a closed shape known as a *Koch snowflake*.

5. Sketch stage 0, stage 1, and stage 2 of the Koch snowflake.

6. Make a table like the one on the previous page to find the perimeter of the Koch snowflake at stage 3 and stage 4.

7. Write a formula for the perimeter P of the Koch snowflake at stage n.

PRESENT YOUR RESULTS

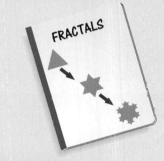

Write a report or make a poster of your results.

- Include your drawing of the stages of the Koch snowflake fractal.

- Include the tables you made and the answers to Exercises 1–7.

- Describe what you learned about fractals.

EXTENSIONS

- Research the Sierpinski Triangle or the Cantor Set. Sketch the first four stages of these fractals.

- Create a fractal of your own. Start with a geometric shape and perform some alteration or transformation. Show the first three stages of your fractal.

- Suppose a Koch snowflake has an area of 1 at stage 0. Find the area of the snowflake at stage 1 and stage 2.

- Research the Mandelbrot Set and find some images of it. Many Web sites on the Internet feature images of this fractal.

The Mandelbrot Set reveals dramatic images as you zoom in to see details.

CIRCLES

► *From how far away can you see fireworks?*

APPLICATION: *Fireworks*

If you watch fireworks as you sail out to sea on a clear night, the fireworks will gradually disappear over the horizon.

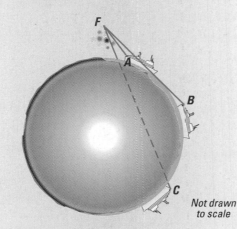

Not drawn to scale

Think & Discuss

1. As you sail away, at which point do the fireworks disappear over the horizon?

2. Imagine that the surface of the water is perfectly smooth. How many points of intersection do $\overline{FB}$ and the circle have when the fireworks disappear?

3. The diagram is not drawn to scale. How would the diagram be different if it were to scale?

Learn More About It

You will learn more about fireworks in Exercise 35 on p. 625.

INTERNET **APPLICATION LINK** Visit www.mcdougallittell.com for more information about fireworks.

Study Guide

PREVIEW

What's the chapter about?

Chapter 10 is about **circles** and their properties. In Chapter 10, you'll learn

- how to use arcs, angles, and segments in circles to solve real-life problems.
- how to use the graph of an equation of a circle to model real-life situations.

KEY VOCABULARY

- circle, p. 595
- secant, p. 595
- tangent, p. 595
- point of tangency, p. 597
- central angle, p. 603

- arc, p. 603
- measure of an arc, p. 603
- inscribed angle, p. 613
- intercepted arc, p. 613
- inscribed polygon, p. 615

- circumscribed circle, p. 615
- standard equation of a circle, p. 636
- locus, p. 642

PREPARE

Are you ready for the chapter?

SKILL REVIEW Do these exercises to review key skills that you'll apply in this chapter. See the given **reference page** if there is something you don't understand.

Solve the equation or system of equations. (Skills Review pp. 789, 790, 796, 798, 800, 801)

1. $(x + 4)^2 = x^2 + 6^2$

2. $132 = \frac{1}{2}[(360 - x) - x]$

3. $15(y + 15) = 24^2$

4. $2z^2 + 7 = 19$

5. $8^2 = x(x + 12)$

6. $x + y = 18$
$3x + 4y = 64$

7. In $\triangle JKL$, $JK = 8$, $KL = 9$, and $\angle K$ is a right angle. Solve the right triangle. Round decimals to the nearest tenth. **(Review Example 1, p. 568)**

8. Use $A(-3, 0)$ and $B(9, -9)$. Find (a) AB, (b) the coordinates of the midpoint of $\overline{AB}$, (c) an equation for $\overleftrightarrow{AB}$, and (d) the image of $\overline{AB}$ after the translation $(x, y) \rightarrow (x - 4, y)$. **(Review pp. 19, 35, 165–167, 422)**

STUDY STRATEGY

Here's a study strategy!

Answer Your Questions

Use a red pen to write a large question mark next to any part of a homework question you don't understand. Be sure to get your questions answered by the teacher or another student. Then write a check mark through the question mark when you are able to complete an exercise with which you had difficulty.

10.1

Tangents to Circles

What you should learn

GOAL 1 Identify segments and lines related to circles.

GOAL 2 Use properties of a tangent to a circle.

Why you should learn it

▼ You can use properties of tangents of circles to find **real-life** distances, such as the radius of the silo in **Example 5**.

GOAL 1 COMMUNICATING ABOUT CIRCLES

A **circle** is the set of all points in a plane that are equidistant from a given point, called the **center** of the circle. A circle with center P is called "circle P", or $\odot P$.

The distance from the center to a point on the circle is the **radius** of the circle. Two circles are **congruent** if they have the same radius.

The distance across the circle, through its center, is the **diameter** of the circle. The diameter is twice the radius.

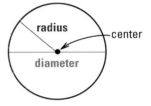

The terms *radius* and *diameter* describe segments as well as measures. A **radius** is a segment whose endpoints are the center of the circle and a point on the circle. $\overline{QP}$, $\overline{QR}$, and $\overline{QS}$ are radii of $\odot Q$ below. All radii of a circle are congruent.

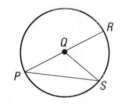

A **chord** is a segment whose endpoints are points on the circle. $\overline{PS}$ and $\overline{PR}$ are chords.

A **diameter** is a chord that passes through the center of the circle. $\overline{PR}$ is a diameter.

A **secant** is a line that intersects a circle in two points. Line j is a secant.

A **tangent** is a line in the plane of a circle that intersects the circle in exactly one point. Line k is a tangent.

EXAMPLE 1 *Identifying Special Segments and Lines*

Tell whether the line or segment is best described as a *chord*, a *secant*, a *tangent*, a *diameter*, or a *radius* of $\odot C$.

a. $\overline{AD}$ **b.** $\overline{CD}$

c. $\overleftrightarrow{EG}$ **d.** $\overline{HB}$

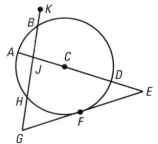

SOLUTION

a. $\overline{AD}$ is a diameter because it contains the center C.

b. $\overline{CD}$ is a radius because C is the center and D is a point on the circle.

c. $\overleftrightarrow{EG}$ is a tangent because it intersects the circle in one point.

d. $\overline{HB}$ is a chord because its endpoints are on the circle.

In a plane, two circles can intersect in two points, one point, or no points. Coplanar circles that intersect in one point are called **tangent circles**. Coplanar circles that have a common center are called **concentric**.

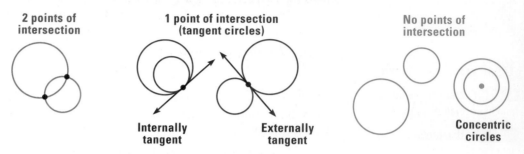

2 points of intersection

1 point of intersection (tangent circles)

Internally tangent   Externally tangent

No points of intersection

Concentric circles

A line or segment that is tangent to two coplanar circles is called a **common tangent**. A *common internal tangent* intersects the segment that joins the centers of the two circles. A *common external tangent* does not intersect the segment that joins the centers of the two circles.

EXAMPLE 2   *Identifying Common Tangents*

Tell whether the **common tangents** are *internal* or *external*.

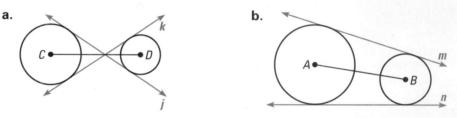

a.

b.

SOLUTION

 a. The lines *j* and *k* intersect $\overline{CD}$, so they are common internal tangents.

 b. The lines *m* and *n* do not intersect $\overline{AB}$, so they are common external tangents.

· · · · · · · · · ·

In a plane, the **interior of a circle** consists of the points that are inside the circle. The **exterior of a circle** consists of the points that are outside the circle.

EXAMPLE 3   *Circles in Coordinate Geometry*

Give the center and the radius of each circle. Describe the intersection of the two circles and describe all common tangents.

SOLUTION

The center of ⊙*A* is *A*(4, 4) and its radius is 4. The center of ⊙*B* is *B*(5, 4) and its radius is 3. The two circles have only one point of intersection. It is the point (8, 4). The vertical line $x = 8$ is the only common tangent of the two circles.

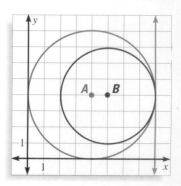

The point at which a tangent line intersects the circle to which it is tangent is the **point of tangency.** You will justify the following theorems in the exercises.

THEOREMS

THEOREM 10.1

If a line is tangent to a circle, then it is perpendicular to the radius drawn to the point of tangency.

If ℓ is tangent to $\odot Q$ at P, then $\ell \perp \overline{QP}$.

THEOREM 10.2

In a plane, if a line is perpendicular to a radius of a circle at its endpoint on the circle, then the line is tangent to the circle.

If $\ell \perp \overline{QP}$ at P, then ℓ is tangent to $\odot Q$.

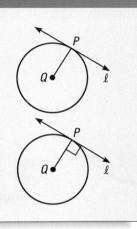

STUDENT HELP

↳ **Study Tip**
A secant can look like a tangent if it intersects the circle in two points that are close together.

EXAMPLE 4 *Verifying a Tangent to a Circle*

You can use the Converse of the Pythagorean Theorem to tell whether $\overleftrightarrow{EF}$ is tangent to $\odot D$.

Because $11^2 + 60^2 = 61^2$, $\triangle DEF$ is a right triangle and $\overline{DE}$ is perpendicular to $\overline{EF}$. So, by Theorem 10.2, $\overleftrightarrow{EF}$ is tangent to $\odot D$.

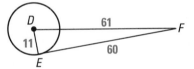

EXAMPLE 5 *Finding the Radius of a Circle*

You are standing at C, 8 feet from a grain silo. The distance from you to a point of tangency on the tank is 16 feet. What is the radius of the silo?

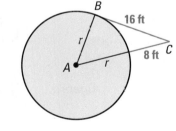

SOLUTION

Tangent $\overleftrightarrow{BC}$ is perpendicular to radius $\overline{AB}$ at B, so $\triangle ABC$ is a right triangle. So, you can use the Pythagorean Theorem.

$$(r + 8)^2 = r^2 + 16^2 \qquad \text{Pythagorean Theorem}$$
$$r^2 + 16r + 64 = r^2 + 256 \qquad \text{Square of binomial}$$
$$16r + 64 = 256 \qquad \text{Subtract } r^2 \text{ from each side.}$$
$$16r = 192 \qquad \text{Subtract 64 from each side.}$$
$$r = 12 \qquad \text{Divide.}$$

STUDENT HELP

↳ **Skills Review**
For help squaring a binomial, see p. 798.

▶ The radius of the silo is 12 feet.

From a point in a circle's exterior, you can draw exactly two different tangents to the circle. The following theorem tells you that the segments joining the external point to the two points of tangency are congruent.

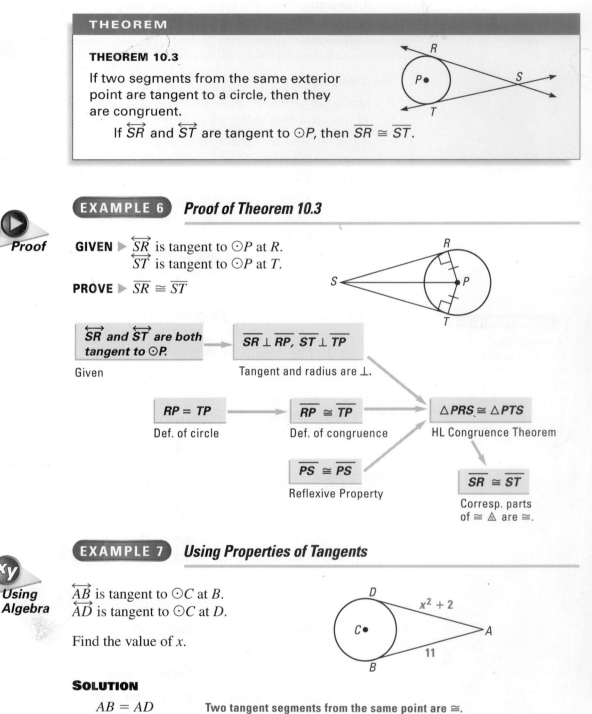

THEOREM

THEOREM 10.3

If two segments from the same exterior point are tangent to a circle, then they are congruent.

If $\overleftrightarrow{SR}$ and $\overleftrightarrow{ST}$ are tangent to $\odot P$, then $\overline{SR} \cong \overline{ST}$.

EXAMPLE 6   *Proof of Theorem 10.3*

Proof

GIVEN ▶ $\overleftrightarrow{SR}$ is tangent to $\odot P$ at R.
$\overleftrightarrow{ST}$ is tangent to $\odot P$ at T.

PROVE ▶ $\overline{SR} \cong \overline{ST}$

$\overleftrightarrow{SR}$ and $\overleftrightarrow{ST}$ are both tangent to $\odot P$.
Given

→ | $\overline{SR} \perp \overline{RP}, \overline{ST} \perp \overline{TP}$ |
|---|
| Tangent and radius are $\perp$. |

$RP = TP$
Def. of circle

→ | $\overline{RP} \cong \overline{TP}$ |
|---|
| Def. of congruence |

→ | $\triangle PRS \cong \triangle PTS$ |
|---|
| HL Congruence Theorem |

$\overline{PS} \cong \overline{PS}$
Reflexive Property

$\overline{SR} \cong \overline{ST}$
Corresp. parts of $\cong \triangle$ are $\cong$.

EXAMPLE 7   *Using Properties of Tangents*

Using Algebra

$\overleftrightarrow{AB}$ is tangent to $\odot C$ at B.
$\overleftrightarrow{AD}$ is tangent to $\odot C$ at D.

Find the value of x.

SOLUTION

$AB = AD$	Two tangent segments from the same point are $\cong$.
$11 = x^2 + 2$	Substitute.
$9 = x^2$	Subtract 2 from each side.
$\pm 3 = x$	Find the square roots of 9.

▶ The value of x is 3 or -3.

GUIDED PRACTICE

Vocabulary Check ✓

1. Sketch a circle. Then sketch and label a *radius*, a *diameter*, and a *chord*.

2. How are chords and secants of circles alike? How are they different?

Concept Check ✓

3. $\overleftrightarrow{XY}$ is tangent to $\odot C$ at point P. What is $m\angle CPX$? Explain.

4. The diameter of a circle is 13 cm. What is the radius of the circle?

Skill Check ✓

5. In the diagram at the right, $AB = BD = 5$ and $AD = 7$. Is $\overleftrightarrow{BD}$ tangent to $\odot C$? Explain.

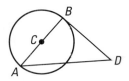

$\overrightarrow{AB}$ **is tangent to** $\odot C$ **at** A **and** $\overleftrightarrow{DB}$ **is tangent to** $\odot C$ **at** D. **Find the value of** x.

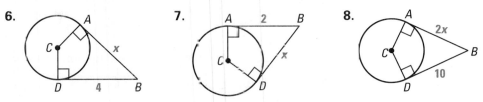

6.   7.   8.

PRACTICE AND APPLICATIONS

STUDENT HELP

▶ **Extra Practice**
to help you master
skills is on p. 821.

FINDING RADII **The diameter of a circle is given. Find the radius.**

9. $d = 15$ cm   10. $d = 6.7$ in.   11. $d = 3$ ft   12. $d = 8$ cm

FINDING DIAMETERS **The radius of** $\odot C$ **is given. Find the diameter of** $\odot C$.

13. $r = 26$ in.   14. $r = 62$ ft   15. $r = 8.7$ in.   16. $r = 4.4$ cm

17. **CONGRUENT CIRCLES** Which two circles below are congruent? Explain your reasoning.

MATCHING TERMS **Match the notation with the term that best describes it.**

18. $\overline{AB}$ A. Center

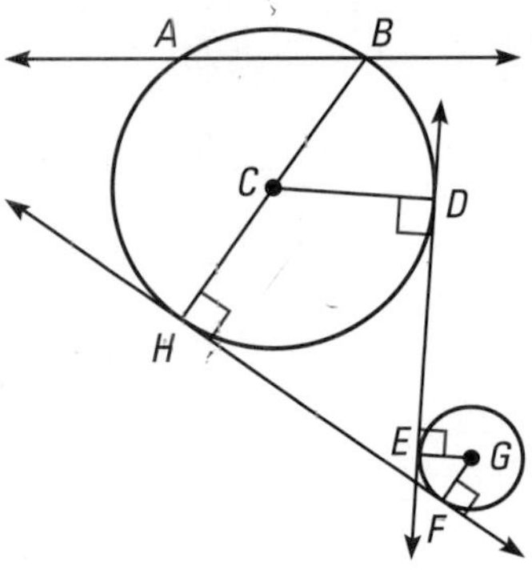

STUDENT HELP

▶ **HOMEWORK HELP**
Example 1: Exs. 18–25,
          42–45
Example 2: Exs. 26–31
Example 3: Exs. 32–35
Example 4: Exs. 36–39
Example 5: Exs. 40, 41
Example 6: Exs. 49–53
Example 7: Exs. 46–48

19. H B. Chord

20. $\overleftrightarrow{HF}$ C. Diameter

21. $\overline{CH}$ D. Radius

22. C E. Point of tangency

23. $\overline{HB}$ F. Common external tangent

24. $\overleftrightarrow{AB}$ G. Common internal tangent

25. $\overleftrightarrow{DE}$ H. Secant

IDENTIFYING TANGENTS **Tell whether the common tangent(s) are *internal* or *external*.**

26.

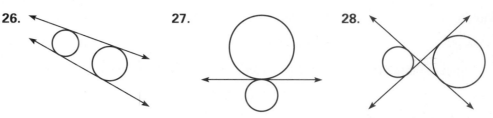

27.

28.

DRAWING TANGENTS **Copy the diagram. Tell how many common tangents the circles have. Then sketch the tangents.**

29.

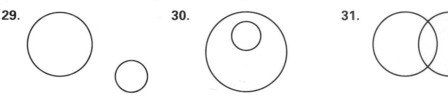

30.

31.

COORDINATE GEOMETRY **Use the diagram at the right.**

32. What are the center and radius of $\odot A$?

33. What are the center and radius of $\odot B$?

34. Describe the intersection of the two circles.

35. Describe all the common tangents of the two circles.

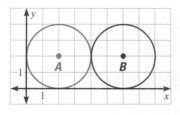

DETERMINING TANGENCY **Tell whether $\overleftrightarrow{AB}$ is tangent to $\odot C$. Explain your reasoning.**

36.

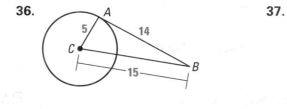

37.

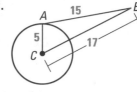

38.

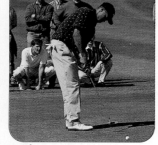

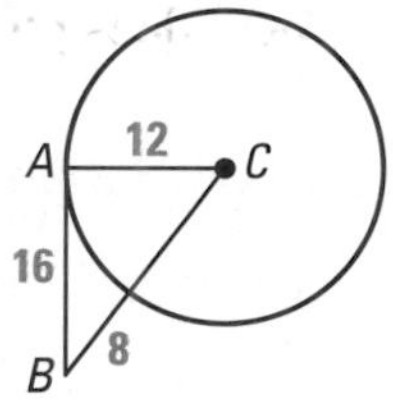

39.

FOCUS ON PEOPLE

TIGER WOODS At age 15 Tiger Woods became the youngest golfer ever to win the U.S. Junior Amateur Championship, and at age 21 he became the youngest Masters champion ever.

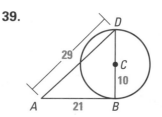

GOLF **In Exercises 40 and 41, use the following information.**
A green on a golf course is in the shape of a circle. A golf ball is 8 feet from the edge of the green and 28 feet from a point of tangency on the green, as shown at the right. Assume that the green is flat.

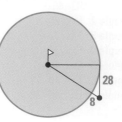

40. What is the radius of the green?

41. How far is the golf ball from the cup at the center?

Mexcaltitlán Island, Mexico

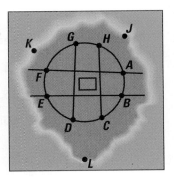

🌐 **MEXCALTITLÁN** The diagram shows the layout of the streets on Mexcaltitlán Island.

42. Name two secants.

43. Name two chords.

44. Is the diameter of the circle greater than *HC*? Explain.

45. If △*LJK* were drawn, one of its sides would be tangent to the circle. Which side is it?

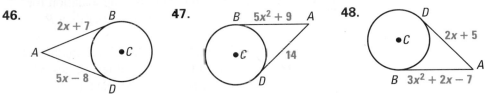

USING ALGEBRA $\overleftrightarrow{AB}$ and $\overleftrightarrow{AD}$ are tangent to ⊙*C*. Find the value of *x*.

46.

$2x + 7$
$5x - 8$

47.

$5x^2 + 9$
14

48.

$2x + 5$
$3x^2 + 2x - 7$

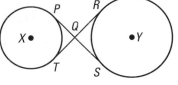

49. ▶ **PROOF** Write a proof.

GIVEN ▶ $\overleftrightarrow{PS}$ is tangent to ⊙*X* at *P*.
$\overleftrightarrow{PS}$ is tangent to ⊙*Y* at *S*.
$\overleftrightarrow{RT}$ is tangent to ⊙*X* at *T*.
$\overleftrightarrow{RT}$ is tangent to ⊙*Y* at *R*.

PROVE ▶ $\overline{PS} \cong \overline{RT}$

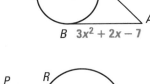

▶ **PROVING THEOREM 10.1** In Exercises 50–52, you will use an indirect argument to prove Theorem 10.1.

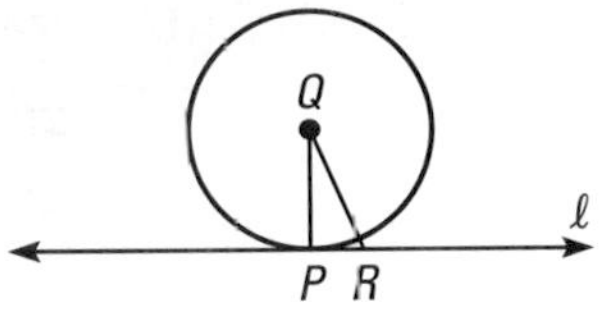

GIVEN ▶ ℓ is tangent to ⊙*Q* at *P*.

PROVE ▶ ℓ ⊥ $\overline{QP}$

50. Assume ℓ and $\overline{QP}$ are not perpendicular. Then the perpendicular segment from *Q* to ℓ intersects ℓ at some other point *R*. Because ℓ is a tangent, *R* cannot be in the interior of ⊙*Q*. So, how does *QR* compare to *QP*? Write an inequality.

51. $\overline{QR}$ is the perpendicular segment from *Q* to ℓ, so $\overline{QR}$ is the shortest segment from *Q* to ℓ. Write another inequality comparing *QR* to *QP*.

52. Use your results from Exercises 50 and 51 to complete the indirect proof of Theorem 10.1.

53. ▶ **PROVING THEOREM 10.2** Write an indirect proof of Theorem 10.2. (*Hint:* The proof is like the one in Exercises 50–52.)

GIVEN ▶ ℓ is in the plane of ⊙*Q*.
ℓ ⊥ radius $\overline{QP}$ at *P*.

PROVE ▶ ℓ is tangent to ⊙*Q*.

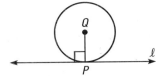

LOGICAL REASONING In ⊙*C*, radii $\overline{CA}$ and $\overline{CB}$ are perpendicular. $\overleftrightarrow{BD}$ and $\overleftrightarrow{AD}$ are tangent to ⊙*C*.

54. Sketch ⊙*C*, $\overline{CA}$, $\overline{CB}$, $\overline{BD}$, and $\overline{AD}$.

55. What type of quadrilateral is *CADB*? Explain.

Test Preparation

56. MULTI-STEP PROBLEM In the diagram, line *j* is tangent to ⊙*C* at *P*.

   a. What is the slope of radius $\overline{CP}$?

   b. What is the slope of *j*? Explain.

   c. Write an equation for *j*.

   d. *Writing* Explain how to find an equation for a line tangent to ⊙*C* at a point other than *P*.

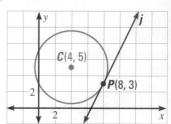

★ **Challenge**

57. CIRCLES OF APOLLONIUS The Greek mathematician Apollonius (c. 200 B.C.) proved that for any three circles with no common points or common interiors, there are eight ways to draw a circle that is tangent to the given three circles. The red, blue, and green circles are given. Two ways to draw a circle that is tangent to the given three circles are shown below. Sketch the other six ways.

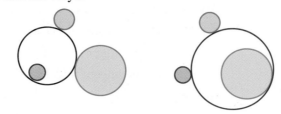

EXTRA CHALLENGE
www.mcdougallittell.com

MIXED REVIEW

58. TRIANGLE INEQUALITIES The lengths of two sides of a triangle are 4 and 10. Use an inequality to describe the length of the third side. **(Review 5.5)**

PARALLELOGRAMS Show that the vertices represent the vertices of a parallelogram. Use a different method for each proof. **(Review 6.3)**

59. *P*(5, 0), *Q*(2, 9), *R*(−6, 6), *S*(−3, −3)

60. *P*(4, 3), *Q*(6, −8), *R*(10, −3), *S*(8, 8)

SOLVING PROPORTIONS Solve the proportion. **(Review 8.1)**

61. $\dfrac{x}{11} = \dfrac{3}{5}$ **62.** $\dfrac{x}{6} = \dfrac{9}{2}$ **63.** $\dfrac{x}{7} = \dfrac{12}{3}$ **64.** $\dfrac{33}{x} = \dfrac{18}{42}$

65. $\dfrac{10}{3} = \dfrac{8}{x}$ **66.** $\dfrac{3}{x+2} = \dfrac{4}{x}$ **67.** $\dfrac{2}{x-3} = \dfrac{3}{x}$ **68.** $\dfrac{5}{x-1} = \dfrac{9}{2x}$

SOLVING TRIANGLES Solve the right triangle. Round decimals to the nearest tenth. **(Review 9.6)**

69.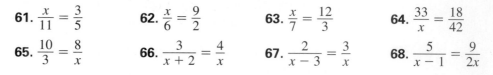

70.

71.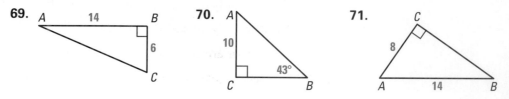

10.2

Arcs and Chords

What you should learn

GOAL 1 Use properties of arcs of circles, as applied in **Exs. 49–51**.

GOAL 2 Use properties of chords of circles, as applied in **Ex. 52**.

Why you should learn it

▼ To find the centers of **real-life** arcs, such as the arc of an ax swing in **Example 6**.

GOAL 1 USING ARCS OF CIRCLES

In a plane, an angle whose vertex is the center of a circle is a **central angle** of the circle.

If the measure of a central angle, ∠APB, is less than 180°, then A and B and the points of ⊙P in the interior of ∠APB form a **minor arc** of the circle. The points A and B and the points of ⊙P in the *exterior* of ∠APB form a **major arc** of the circle. If the endpoints of an arc are the endpoints of a diameter, then the arc is a **semicircle**.

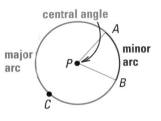

NAMING ARCS Arcs are named by their endpoints. For example, the minor arc associated with ∠APB above is $\widehat{AB}$. Major arcs and semicircles are named by their endpoints and by a point on the arc. For example, the major arc associated with ∠APB above is $\widehat{ACB}$. $\widehat{EGF}$ below is a semicircle.

MEASURING ARCS The **measure of a minor arc** is defined to be the measure of its central angle. For instance, $m\widehat{GF} = m\angle GHF = 60°$. "$m\widehat{GF}$" is read "the measure of arc *GF*." You can write the measure of an arc next to the arc. The measure of a semicircle is 180°.

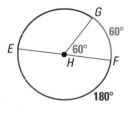

The **measure of a major arc** is defined as the difference between 360° and the measure of its associated minor arc. For example, $m\widehat{GEF} = 360 - 60° = 300°$. The measure of a whole circle is 360°.

EXAMPLE 1 Finding Measures of Arcs

Find the measure of each arc of ⊙R.

  a. $\widehat{MN}$

  b. $\widehat{MPN}$

  c. $\widehat{PMN}$

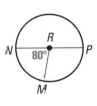

SOLUTION

  a. $\widehat{MN}$ is a minor arc, so $m\widehat{MN} = m\angle MRN = 80°$

  b. $\widehat{MPN}$ is a major arc, so $m\widehat{MPN} = 360° - 80° = 280°$

  c. $\widehat{PMN}$ is a semicircle, so $m\widehat{PMN} = 180°$

Two arcs of the same circle are *adjacent* if they intersect at exactly one point. You can add the measures of adjacent arcs.

POSTULATE

POSTULATE 26 *Arc Addition Postulate*

The measure of an arc formed by two adjacent arcs is the sum of the measures of the two arcs.

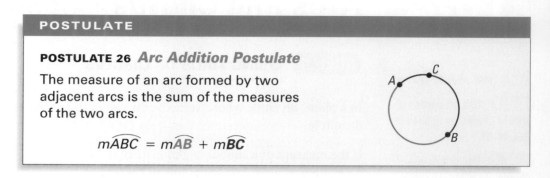

$$m\overset{\frown}{ABC} = m\overset{\frown}{AB} + m\overset{\frown}{BC}$$

EXAMPLE 2 *Finding Measures of Arcs*

Find the measure of each arc.

    a. $\overset{\frown}{GE}$ **b.** $\overset{\frown}{GEF}$ **c.** $\overset{\frown}{GF}$

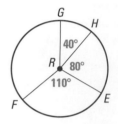

SOLUTION

    a. $m\overset{\frown}{GE} = m\overset{\frown}{GH} + m\overset{\frown}{HE} = 40° + 80° = 120°$

    b. $m\overset{\frown}{GEF} = m\overset{\frown}{GE} + m\overset{\frown}{EF} = 120° + 110° = 230°$

    c. $m\overset{\frown}{GF} = 360° - m\overset{\frown}{GEF} = 360° - 230° = 130°$

· · · · · · · · · ·

Two arcs of the same circle or of congruent circles are **congruent arcs** if they have the same measure. So, two minor arcs of the same circle or of congruent circles are congruent if their central angles are congruent.

Logical Reasoning

EXAMPLE 3 *Identifying Congruent Arcs*

Find the measures of the blue arcs. Are the arcs congruent?

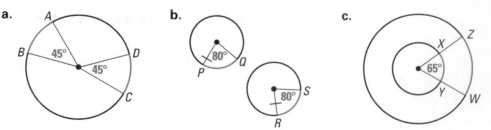

    a.   **b.**   **c.**

SOLUTION

    a. $\overset{\frown}{AB}$ and $\overset{\frown}{DC}$ are in the same circle and $m\overset{\frown}{AB} = m\overset{\frown}{DC} = 45°$. So, $\overset{\frown}{AB} \cong \overset{\frown}{DC}$.

    b. $\overset{\frown}{PQ}$ and $\overset{\frown}{RS}$ are in congruent circles and $m\overset{\frown}{PQ} = m\overset{\frown}{RS} = 80°$. So, $\overset{\frown}{PQ} \cong \overset{\frown}{RS}$.

    c. $m\overset{\frown}{XY} = m\overset{\frown}{ZW} = 65°$, but $\overset{\frown}{XY}$ and $\overset{\frown}{ZW}$ are not arcs of the same circle or of congruent circles, so $\overset{\frown}{XY}$ and $\overset{\frown}{ZW}$ are *not* congruent.

GOAL 2 **USING CHORDS OF CIRCLES**

A point *Y* is called the *midpoint* of $\overset{\frown}{XYZ}$ if $\overset{\frown}{XY} \cong \overset{\frown}{YZ}$. Any line, segment, or ray that contains *Y* *bisects* $\overset{\frown}{XYZ}$. You will prove Theorems 10.4–10.6 in the exercises.

THEOREMS ABOUT CHORDS OF CIRCLES

THEOREM 10.4

In the same circle, or in congruent circles, two minor arcs are congruent if and only if their corresponding chords are congruent.

$\overset{\frown}{AB} \cong \overset{\frown}{BC}$ if and only if $\overline{AB} \cong \overline{BC}$.

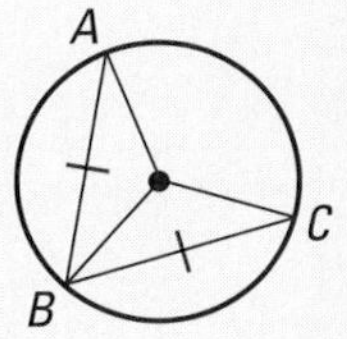

THEOREM 10.5

If a diameter of a circle is perpendicular to a chord, then the diameter bisects the chord and its arc.

$\overline{DE} \cong \overline{EF}$, $\overset{\frown}{DG} \cong \overset{\frown}{GF}$

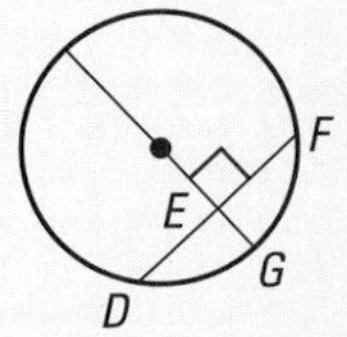

THEOREM 10.6

If one chord is a perpendicular bisector of another chord, then the first chord is a diameter.

$\overline{JK}$ is a diameter of the circle.

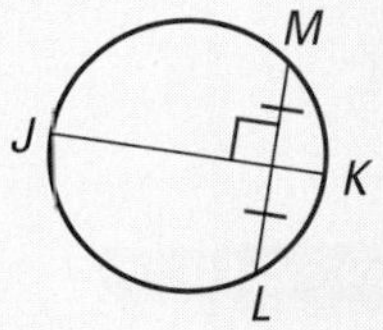

 Using Algebra

EXAMPLE 4 *Using Theorem 10.4*

You can use Theorem 10.4 to find $m\overset{\frown}{AD}$.

Because $\overline{AD} \cong \overline{DC}$, $\overset{\frown}{AD} \cong \overset{\frown}{DC}$. So, $m\overset{\frown}{AD} = m\overset{\frown}{DC}$.

$2x = x + 40$ Substitute.

$x = 40$ Subtract *x* from each side.

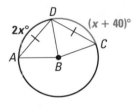

EXAMPLE 5 *Finding the Center of a Circle*

Theorem 10.6 can be used to locate a circle's center, as shown below.

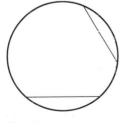 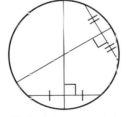 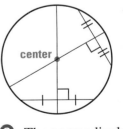

1 Draw any two chords that are not parallel to each other.

2 Draw the perpendicular bisector of each chord. These are diameters.

3 The perpendicular bisectors intersect at the circle's center.

EXAMPLE 6 *Using Properties of Chords*

 MASONRY HAMMER A masonry hammer has a hammer on one end and a curved pick on the other. The pick works best if you swing it along a circular curve that matches the shape of the pick. Find the center of the circular swing.

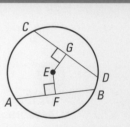

SOLUTION

Draw a segment $\overline{AB}$, from the top of the masonry hammer to the end of the pick. Find the midpoint *C*, and draw a perpendicular bisector $\overline{CD}$. Find the intersection of $\overline{CD}$ with the line formed by the handle.

▶ So, the center of the swing lies at *E*.

· · · · · · · · · ·

You are asked to prove Theorem 10.7 in Exercises 61 and 62.

STUDENT HELP

▸ **Look Back**
Remember that the distance from a point to a line is the length of the perpendicular segment from the point to the line. (p. 266)

THEOREM

THEOREM 10.7

In the same circle, or in congruent circles, two chords are congruent if and only if they are equidistant from the center.

$$\overline{AB} \cong \overline{CD} \text{ if and only if } \overline{EF} \cong \overline{EG}.$$

EXAMPLE 7 *Using Theorem 10.7*

$AB = 8$, $DE = 8$, and $CD = 5$. Find *CF*.

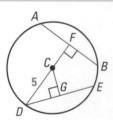

SOLUTION

Because $\overline{AB}$ and $\overline{DE}$ are congruent chords, they are equidistant from the center. So, $\overline{CF} \cong \overline{CG}$. To find *CG*, first find *DG*.

$\overline{CG} \perp \overline{DE}$, so $\overline{CG}$ bisects $\overline{DE}$. Because $DE = 8$, $DG = \frac{8}{2} = 4$.

Then use *DG* to find *CG*.

$DG = 4$ and $CD = 5$, so $\triangle CGD$ is a 3-4-5 right triangle. So, $CG = 3$.

Finally, use *CG* to find *CF*.

▶ Because $\overline{CF} \cong \overline{CG}$, $CF = CG = 3$.

GUIDED PRACTICE

Vocabulary Check ✓

1. The measure of an arc is 170°. Is the arc a *major arc*, a *minor arc*, or a *semicircle*?

Concept Check ✓

2. In the figure at the right, what is $m\widehat{KL}$? What is $m\widehat{MN}$? Are $\widehat{KL}$ and $\widehat{MN}$ congruent? Explain.

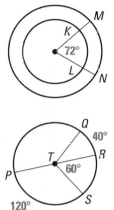

Skill Check ✓

Find the measure in ⊙*T*.

3. $m\widehat{RS}$

4. $m\widehat{RPS}$

5. $m\widehat{PQR}$

6. $m\widehat{QS}$

7. $m\widehat{QSP}$

8. $m\angle QTR$

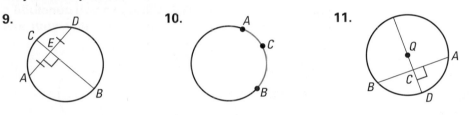

What can you conclude about the diagram? State a postulate or theorem that justifies your answer.

9.

10.

11.

PRACTICE AND APPLICATIONS

STUDENT HELP

▸ **Extra Practice**
to help you master
skills is on p. 821.

UNDERSTANDING THE CONCEPT Determine whether the arc is a *minor arc*, a *major arc*, or a *semicircle* of ⊙*R*.

12. $\widehat{PQ}$

13. $\widehat{SU}$

14. $\widehat{PQT}$

15. $\widehat{QT}$

16. $\widehat{TUQ}$

17. $\widehat{TUP}$

18. $\widehat{QUT}$

19. $\widehat{PUQ}$

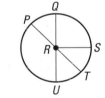

MEASURING ARCS AND CENTRAL ANGLES $\overline{KN}$ and $\overline{JL}$ are diameters. Copy the diagram. Find the indicated measure.

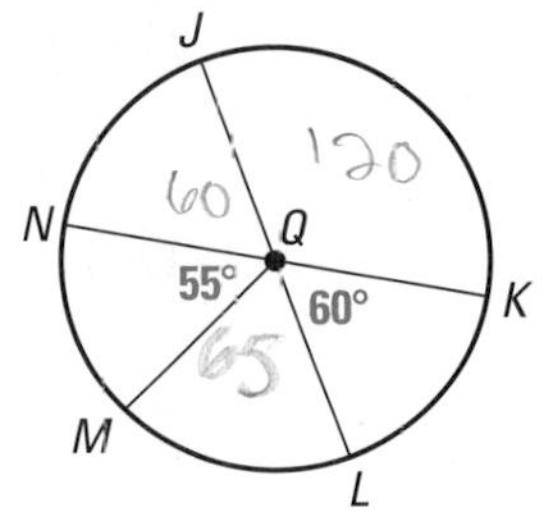

STUDENT HELP

▸ **HOMEWORK HELP**
Example 1: Exs. 12–29
Example 2: Exs. 30–34,
49, 50
Example 3: Ex. 35

continued on p. 608

20. $m\widehat{KL}$

21. $m\widehat{MN}$

22. $m\widehat{LNK}$

23. $m\widehat{MKN}$

24. $m\widehat{NJK}$

25. $m\widehat{JML}$

26. $m\angle JQN$

27. $m\angle MQL$

28. $m\widehat{JN}$

29. $m\widehat{ML}$

30. $m\widehat{JM}$

31. $m\widehat{LN}$

FINDING ARC MEASURES Find the measure of the red arc.

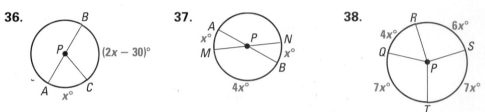

32.

33.

34.

35. Name two pairs of congruent arcs in Exercises 32–34. Explain your reasoning.

xy **USING ALGEBRA** Use ⊙*P* to find the value of *x*. Then find the measure of the red arc.

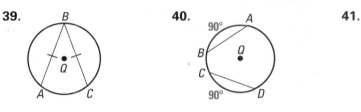
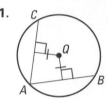

36.

37.

38.

🧩 **LOGICAL REASONING** What can you conclude about the diagram? State a postulate or theorem that justifies your answer.

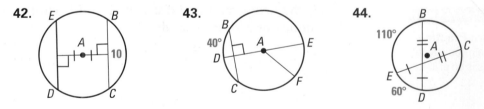

39.

40.

41.

MEASURING ARCS AND CHORDS Find the measure of the red arc or chord in ⊙*A*. Explain your reasoning.

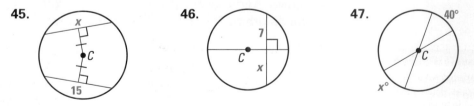

42.

43.

44.

MEASURING ARCS AND CHORDS Find the value of *x* in ⊙*C*. Explain your reasoning.

45.

46.

47.

48. **SKETCHING** Draw a circle with two noncongruent chords. Is the shorter chord's midpoint farther from the center or closer to the center than the longer chord's midpoint?

TIME ZONE WHEEL In Exercises 49–51, use the following information.

The time zone wheel shown at the right consists of two concentric circular pieces of cardboard fastened at the center so the smaller wheel can rotate. To find the time in Tashkent when it is 4 P.M. in San Francisco, you rotate the small wheel until 4 P.M. and San Francisco line up as shown. Then look at Tashkent to see that it is 6 A.M. there. The arcs between cities are congruent.

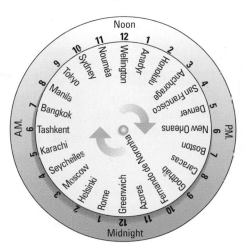

49. What is the arc measure for each time zone on the wheel?

50. What is the measure of the minor arc from the Tokyo zone to the Anchorage zone?

51. If two cities differ by 180° on the wheel, then it is 3:00 P.M. in one city if and only if it is _?_ in the other city.

52. **AVALANCHE RESCUE BEACON** An avalanche rescue beacon is a small device carried by backcountry skiers that gives off a signal that can be picked up only within a circle of a certain radius. During a practice drill, a ski patrol uses steps similar to the following to locate a beacon buried in the snow. Write a paragraph explaining why this procedure works. ▶ Source: The Mountaineers

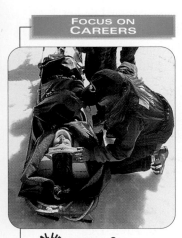
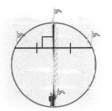

1 Walk until the signal disappears, turn around, and pace the distance in a straight line until the signal disappears again.

2 Pace back to the halfway point, and walk away from the line at a 90° angle until the signal disappears.

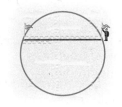

3 Turn around and pace the distance in a straight line until the signal disappears again.

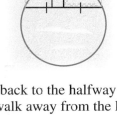

hidden beacon →

4 Pace back to the halfway point. You will be at or near the center of the circle. The beacon is underneath you.

53. **LOGICAL REASONING** Explain why two minor arcs of the same circle or of congruent circles are congruent if and only if their central angles are congruent.

54. **CONSTRUCTION** Trace a circular object like a cup or can. Then use a compass and straightedge to find the center of the circle. Explain your steps.

55. **CONSTRUCTION** Construct a large circle with two congruent chords. Are the chords the same distance from the center? How can you tell?

STUDENT HELP

HOMEWORK HELP
Visit our Web site www.mcdougallittell.com for help with Exs. 56–62.

PROVING THEOREM 10.4 In Exercises 56 and 57, you will prove Theorem 10.4 for the case in which the two chords are in the same circle. Write a plan for a proof.

56. **GIVEN** ▶ $\overline{AB}$ and $\overline{DC}$ are in $\odot P$.
$\overline{AB} \cong \overline{DC}$

PROVE ▶ $\widehat{AB} \cong \widehat{DC}$

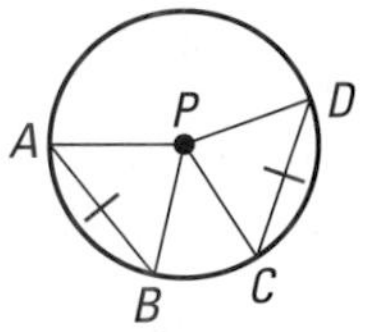

57. **GIVEN** ▶ $\overline{AB}$ and $\overline{DC}$ are in $\odot P$.
$\widehat{AB} \cong \widehat{DC}$

PROVE ▶ $\overline{AB} \cong \overline{DC}$

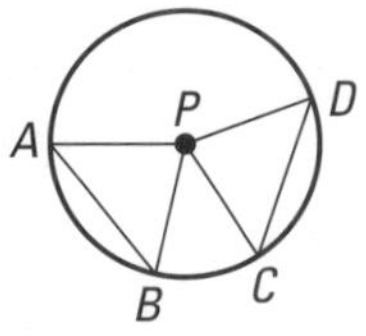

58. **JUSTIFYING THEOREM 10.4** Explain how the proofs in Exercises 56 and 57 would be different if $\overline{AB}$ and $\overline{DC}$ were in congruent circles rather than the same circle.

PROVING THEOREMS 10.5 AND 10.6 Write a proof.

59. **GIVEN** ▶ $\overline{EF}$ is a diameter of $\odot L$.
$\overline{EF} \perp \overline{GH}$

PROVE ▶ $\overline{GJ} \cong \overline{JH}$, $\widehat{GE} \cong \widehat{EH}$

Plan for Proof Draw $\overline{LG}$ and $\overline{LH}$. Use congruent triangles to show $\overline{GJ} \cong \overline{JH}$ and $\angle GLE \cong \angle HLE$. Then show $\widehat{GE} \cong \widehat{EH}$.

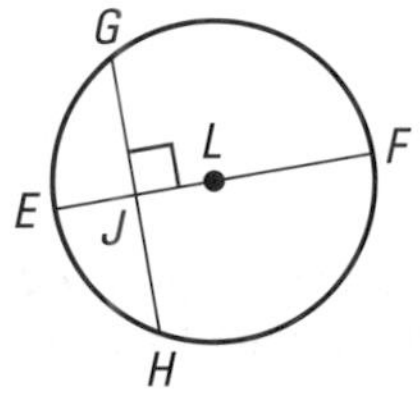

60. **GIVEN** ▶ $\overline{EF}$ is the $\perp$ bisector of $\overline{GH}$.

PROVE ▶ $\overline{EF}$ is a diameter of $\odot L$.

Plan for Proof Use indirect reasoning. Assume center L is not on $\overline{EF}$. Prove that $\triangle GLJ \cong \triangle HLJ$, so $\overline{JL} \perp \overline{GH}$. Then use the Perpendicular Postulate.

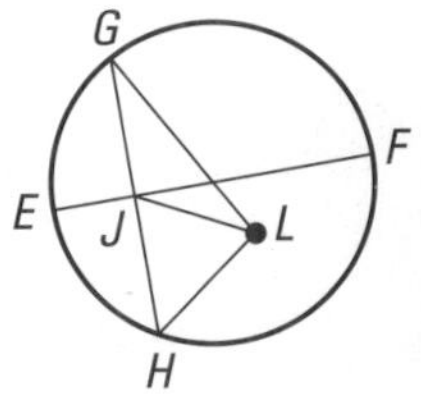

PROVING THEOREM 10.7 Write a proof.

61. **GIVEN** ▶ $\overline{PE} \perp \overline{AB}$, $\overline{PF} \perp \overline{DC}$,
$\overline{PE} \cong \overline{PF}$

PROVE ▶ $\overline{AB} \cong \overline{DC}$

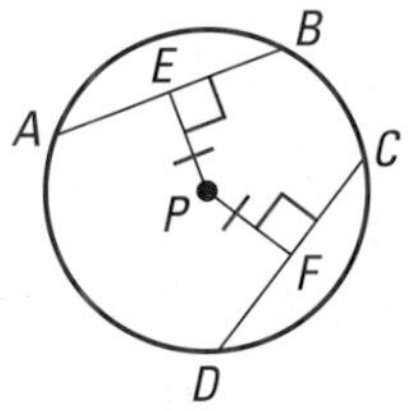

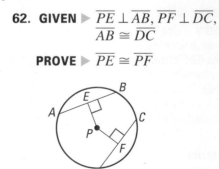

62. **GIVEN** ▶ $\overline{PE} \perp \overline{AB}$, $\overline{PF} \perp \overline{DC}$,
$\overline{AB} \cong \overline{DC}$

PROVE ▶ $\overline{PE} \cong \overline{PF}$

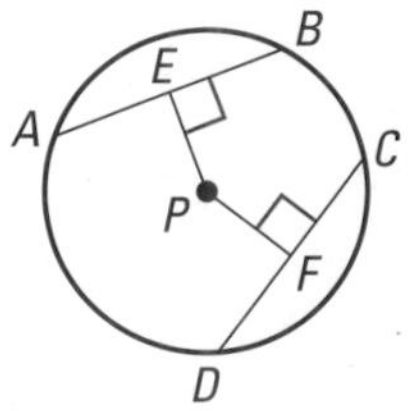

POLAR COORDINATES In Exercises 63–67, use the following information.

A *polar coordinate system* locates a point in a plane by its distance from the origin O and by the measure of a central angle. For instance, the point $A(2, 30°)$ at the right is 2 units from the origin and $m\angle XOA = 30°$. Similarly, the point $B(4, 120°)$ is 4 units from the origin and $m\angle XOB = 120°$.

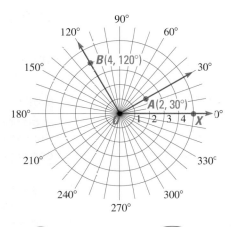

63. Use polar graph paper or a protractor and a ruler to graph points A and B. Also graph $C(4, 210°)$, $D(4, 330°)$, and $E(2, 150°)$.

64. Find $m\overset{\frown}{AE}$.   **65.** Find $m\overset{\frown}{BC}$.   **66.** Find $m\overset{\frown}{BD}$.   **67.** Find $m\overset{\frown}{BCD}$.

Test Preparation

68. MULTI-STEP PROBLEM You want to find the radius of a circular object. First you trace the object on a piece of paper.

  a. Explain how to use two chords that are not parallel to each other to find the radius of the circle.

  b. Explain how to use two tangent lines that are not parallel to each other to find the radius of the circle.

  c. *Writing* Would the methods in parts (a) and (b) work better for small objects or for large objects? Explain your reasoning.

★ **Challenge**

69. The plane at the right intersects the sphere in a circle that has a diameter of 12. If the diameter of the sphere is 18, what is the value of x? Give your answer in simplified radical form.

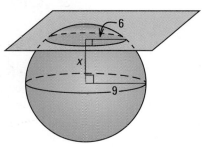

MIXED REVIEW

INTERIOR OF AN ANGLE Plot the points in a coordinate plane and sketch $\angle ABC$. Write the coordinates of a point that lies in the interior and a point that lies in the exterior of $\angle ABC$. (Review 1.4 for 10.3)

70. $A(4, 2)$, $B(0, 2)$, $C(3, 0)$ **71.** $A(-2, 3)$, $B(0, 0)$, $C(4, -1)$

72. $A(-2, -3)$, $B(0, -1)$, $C(2, -3)$ **73.** $A(-3, 2)$, $B(0, 0)$, $C(3, 2)$

COORDINATE GEOMETRY The coordinates of the vertices of parallelogram *PQRS* are given. Decide whether □*PQRS* is best described as a *rhombus*, a *rectangle*, or a *square*. Explain your reasoning. (Review 6.4 for 10.3)

74. $P(-2, 1)$, $Q(-1, 4)$, $R(0, 1)$, $S(-1, -2)$

75. $P(-1, 2)$, $Q(2, 5)$, $R(5, 2)$, $S(2, -1)$

GEOMETRIC MEAN Find the geometric mean of the numbers. (Review 8.2)

76. 9, 16   **77.** 8, 32   **78.** 4, 49   **79.** 9, 36

ACTIVITY 10.3

Developing Concepts

Investigating Inscribed Angles

GROUP ACTIVITY
Work with a partner.

MATERIALS
- paper
- pencil
- compass
- straightedge
- protractor

QUESTION **An angle in a circle is an *inscribed angle* if its vertex is on the circle and its sides contain chords of the circle. How is the measure of an inscribed angle related to the measure of the corresponding central angle?**

EXPLORING THE CONCEPT

Follow the steps to construct an inscribed angle.

1. Construct a circle. Label its center P.
2. Use a straightedge to construct a central angle. Label it $\angle RPS$.
3. Locate three points on $\odot P$ in the exterior of $\angle RPS$ and label them T, U, and V. Use a straightedge to draw the inscribed angles $\angle RTS$, $\angle RUS$, and $\angle RVS$.

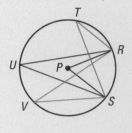

INVESTIGATE

1. Use a protractor to measure $\angle RPS$, $\angle RTS$, $\angle RUS$, and $\angle RVS$. Make a table similar to the one below. Record the angle measures for Circle 1 in the table.

	$m\angle RPS$	$m\angle RTS$	$m\angle RUS$	$m\angle RVS$
Circle 1	?	?	?	?
Circle 2	?	?	?	?
Circle 3	?	?	?	?

2. Repeat Steps 1 through 3 using different central angles. Record the measures in your table.

MAKE A CONJECTURE

3. Use the results in your table to make a conjecture about how the measure of an inscribed angle is related to the measure of the corresponding central angle.

EXTENSION

CRITICAL THINKING The star divides the circle into congruent arcs. Use the conjecture you made in Exercise 3 to find the measures of the angles that form the points of the star. Explain your reasoning. Then use a protractor to measure the angles to verify your conjecture.

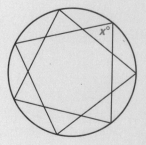

10.3

Inscribed Angles

What you should learn

GOAL 1 Use inscribed angles to solve problems.

GOAL 2 Use properties of inscribed polygons.

Why you should learn it

▼ To solve **real-life** problems, such as finding the different seats in a theater that will give you the same viewing angle, as in **Example 4**.

GOAL 1 USING INSCRIBED ANGLES

An **inscribed angle** is an angle whose vertex is on a circle and whose sides contain chords of the circle. The arc that lies in the interior of an inscribed angle and has endpoints on the angle is called the **intercepted arc** of the angle.

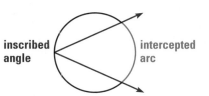

inscribed angle   intercepted arc

THEOREM

THEOREM 10.8 *Measure of an Inscribed Angle*

If an angle is inscribed in a circle, then its measure is half the measure of its intercepted arc.

$$m\angle ADB = \frac{1}{2}m\widehat{AB}$$

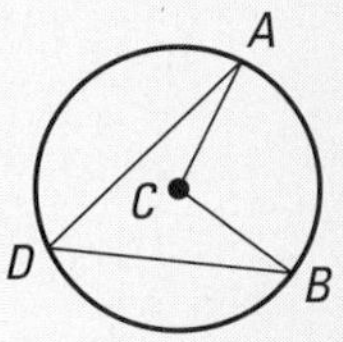

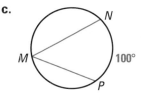

EXAMPLE 1 *Finding Measures of Arcs and Inscribed Angles*

Find the measure of the blue arc or angle.

a.   **b.**   **c.**

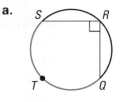 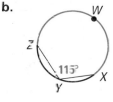 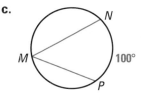

SOLUTION

a. $m\widehat{QTS} = 2m\angle QRS = 2(90°) = 180°$

b. $m\widehat{ZWX} = 2m\angle ZYX = 2(115°) = 230°$

c. $m\angle NMP = \frac{1}{2}m\widehat{NP} = \frac{1}{2}(100°) = 50°$

EXAMPLE 2 *Comparing Measures of Inscribed Angles*

Find $m\angle ACB$, $m\angle ADB$, and $m\angle AEB$.

SOLUTION

The measure of each angle is half the measure of $\widehat{AB}$. $m\widehat{AB} = 60°$, so the measure of each angle is 30°.

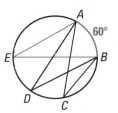

Example 2 suggests the following theorem. You are asked to prove Theorem 10.8 and Theorem 10.9 in Exercises 35–38.

> **THEOREM**
>
> **THEOREM 10.9**
>
> If two inscribed angles of a circle intercept the same arc, then the angles are congruent.
>
>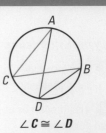
>
> $\angle C \cong \angle D$

EXAMPLE 3 *Finding the Measure of an Angle*

It is given that $m\angle E = 75°$. What is $m\angle F$?

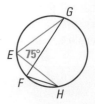

SOLUTION

$\angle E$ and $\angle F$ both intercept $\overparen{GH}$, so $\angle E \cong \angle F$.

▶ So, $m\angle F = m\angle E = 75°$.

EXAMPLE 4 *Using the Measure of an Inscribed Angle*

THEATER DESIGN When you go to the movies, you want to be close to the movie screen, but you don't want to have to move your eyes too much to see the edges of the picture. If E and G are the ends of the screen and you are at F, $m\angle EFG$ is called your *viewing angle*.

You decide that the middle of the sixth row has the best viewing angle. If someone is sitting there, where else can you sit to have the same viewing angle?

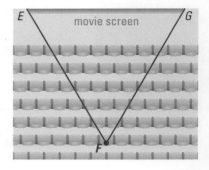

SOLUTION

Draw the circle that is determined by the endpoints of the screen and the sixth row center seat. Any other location on the circle will have the same viewing angle.

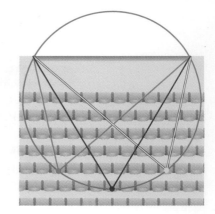

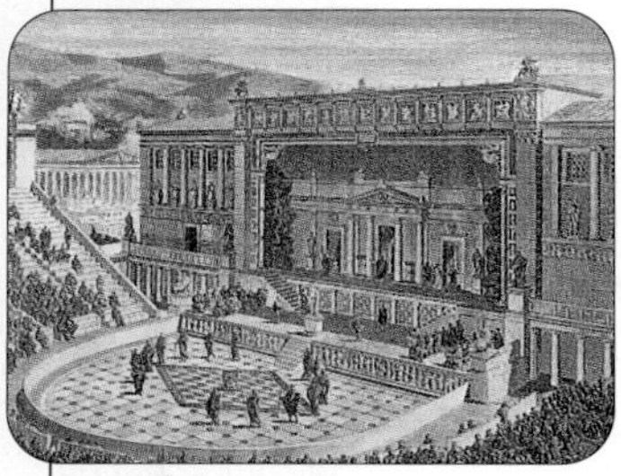

GOAL 2 USING PROPERTIES OF INSCRIBED POLYGONS

If all of the vertices of a polygon lie on a circle, the polygon is **inscribed** in the circle and the circle is **circumscribed** about the polygon. The polygon is an *inscribed polygon* and the circle is a *circumscribed circle*. You are asked to justify Theorem 10.10 and part of Theorem 10.11 in Exercises 39 and 40. A complete proof of Theorem 10.11 appears on page 840.

THEOREMS ABOUT INSCRIBED POLYGONS

THEOREM 10.10

If a right triangle is inscribed in a circle, then the hypotenuse is a diameter of the circle. Conversely, if one side of an inscribed triangle is a diameter of the circle, then the triangle is a right triangle and the angle opposite the diameter is the right angle.

∠ B is a right angle if and only if $\overline{AC}$ is a diameter of the circle.

THEOREM 10.11

A quadrilateral can be inscribed in a circle if and only if its opposite angles are supplementary.

D, E, F, and *G* lie on some circle, ⊙*C*, if and only if
$m\angle D + m\angle F = 180°$ and $m\angle E + m\angle G = 180°$.

EXAMPLE 5 *Using Theorems 10.10 and 10.11*

Find the value of each variable.

a.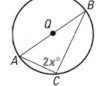

b.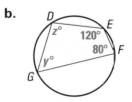

SOLUTION

a. $\overline{AB}$ is a diameter. So, ∠ *C* is a right angle and $m\angle C = 90°$.

$$2x° = 90°$$

$$x = 45$$

b. *DEFG* is inscribed in a circle, so opposite angles are supplementary.

$$m\angle D + m\angle F = 180° \qquad\qquad m\angle E + m\angle G = 180°$$

$$z + 80 = 180 \qquad\qquad\qquad 120 + y = 180$$

$$z = 100 \qquad\qquad\qquad\qquad y = 60$$

STUDENT HELP

▶ **Skills Review**
For help with solving systems of equations, see p. 796.

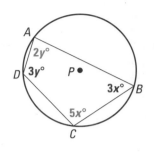

EXAMPLE 6   *Using an Inscribed Quadrilateral*

In the diagram, *ABCD* is inscribed in ⊙*P*. Find the measure of each angle.

SOLUTION

ABCD is inscribed in a circle, so opposite angles are supplementary.

$$3x + 3y = 180 \qquad 5x + 2y = 180$$

To solve this system of linear equations, you can solve the first equation for *y* to get $y = 60 - x$. Substitute this expression into the second equation.

$5x + 2y = 180$	Write second equation.
$5x + 2(60 - x) = 180$	Substitute $60 - x$ for *y*.
$5x + 120 - 2x = 180$	Distributive property
$3x = 60$	Subtract 120 from each side.
$x = 20$	Divide each side by 3.
$y = 60 - 20 = 40$	Substitute and solve for *y*.

▶ $x = 20$ and $y = 40$, so $m\angle A = 80°$, $m\angle B = 60°$, $m\angle C = 100°$, and $m\angle D = 120°$.

GUIDED PRACTICE

Vocabulary Check ✔   **1.** Draw a circle and an inscribed angle, $\angle ABC$. Name the intercepted arc of $\angle ABC$. Label additional points on your sketch if you need to.

Concept Check ✔   **2.** Determine whether the quadrilateral can be inscribed in a circle. Explain your reasoning.

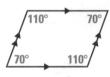

Skill Check ✔   **Find the measure of the blue arc.**

3. 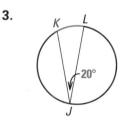   **4.** 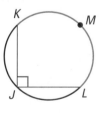   **5.**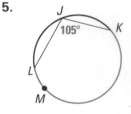

Find the value of each variable.

6.   **7.**   **8.**

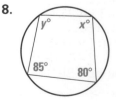

PRACTICE AND APPLICATIONS

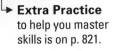

Extra Practice
to help you master
skills is on p. 821.

ARC AND ANGLE MEASURES Find the measure of the blue arc or angle.

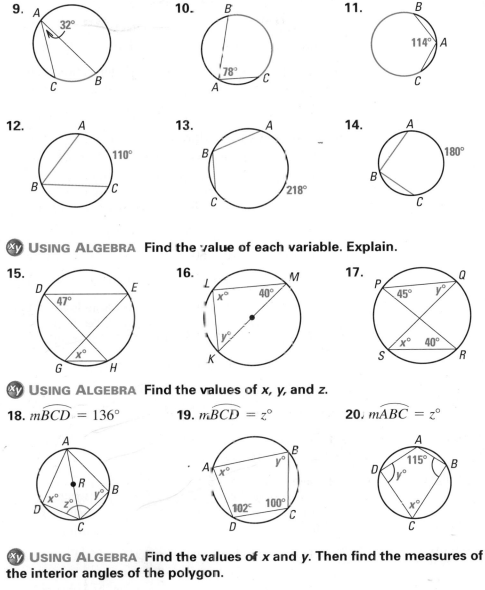

9.

10.

11.

12.

13.

14.

xy USING ALGEBRA Find the value of each variable. Explain.

15.

16.

17.

xy USING ALGEBRA Find the values of x, y, and z.

18. $m\widehat{BCD} = 136°$

19. $m\widehat{BCD} = z°$

20. $m\widehat{ABC} = z°$

xy USING ALGEBRA Find the values of x and y. Then find the measures of the interior angles of the polygon.

21.

22.

23.

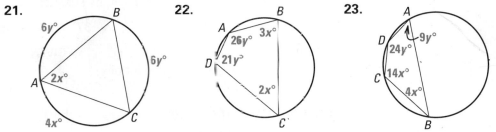

🧩 **LOGICAL REASONING** Can the quadrilateral always be inscribed in a circle? Explain your reasoning.

24. square

25. rectangle

26. parallelogram

27. kite

28. rhombus

29. isosceles trapezoid

STUDENT HELP

HOMEWORK HELP
Example 1: Exs. 9–14,
19–21
Example 2: Exs. 15, 17
Example 3: Exs. 15, 17
Example 4: Exs. 15, 17
Example 5: Exs. 15–20,
24–29, 31–34
Example 6: Exs. 21–23

30. 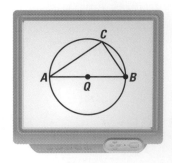 CONSTRUCTION Construct a $\odot C$ and a point A on $\odot C$. Construct the tangent to $\odot C$ at A. Explain why your construction works.

CONSTRUCTION **In Exercises 31–33, you will construct a tangent to a circle from a point outside the circle.**

31. Construct a $\odot C$ and a point outside the circle, A. Draw $\overline{AC}$ and construct its midpoint M. Construct $\odot M$ with radius MC. What kind of chord is $\overline{AC}$?

32. $\odot C$ and $\odot M$ have two points of intersection. Label one of the points B. Draw $\overline{AB}$ and $\overline{CB}$. What is $m\angle CBA$? How do you know?

33. Which segment is tangent to $\odot C$ from A? Explain.

34. USING TECHNOLOGY Use geometry software to construct $\odot Q$, diameter $\overline{AB}$, and point C on $\odot Q$. Construct $\overline{AC}$ and $\overline{CB}$. Measure the angles of $\triangle ABC$. Drag point C along $\odot Q$. Record and explain your observations.

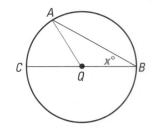

▶ PROVING THEOREM 10.8 **If an angle is inscribed in $\odot Q$, the center Q can be on a side of the angle, in the interior of the angle, or in the exterior of the angle. To prove Theorem 10.8, you must prove each of these cases.**

35. Fill in the blanks to complete the proof.

GIVEN ▶ $\angle ABC$ is inscribed in $\odot Q$.
Point Q lies on $\overline{BC}$.

PROVE ▶ $m\angle ABC = \frac{1}{2}m\widehat{AC}$

Paragraph Proof Let $m\angle ABC = x°$. Because $\overline{QA}$ and $\overline{QB}$ are both radii of $\odot Q$, $\overline{QA} \cong$ __?__ and $\triangle AQB$ is __?__. Because $\angle A$ and $\angle B$ are __?__ of an isosceles triangle, __?__. So, by substitution, $m\angle A = x°$.

By the __?__ Theorem, $m\angle AQC = m\angle A + m\angle B =$ __?__. So, by the definition of the measure of a minor arc, $m\widehat{AC} =$ __?__. Divide each side by __?__ to show that $x° =$ __?__. Then, by substitution, $m\angle ABC =$ __?__.

36. Write a plan for a proof.

GIVEN ▶ $\angle ABC$ is inscribed in $\odot Q$.
Point Q is in the interior of $\angle ABC$.

PROVE ▶ $m\angle ABC = \frac{1}{2}m\widehat{AC}$

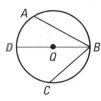

37. Write a plan for a proof.

GIVEN ▶ $\angle ABC$ is inscribed in $\odot Q$.
Point Q is in the exterior of $\angle ABC$.

PROVE ▶ $m\angle ABC = \frac{1}{2}m\widehat{AC}$

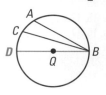

38. ▶ **PROVING THEOREM 10.9** Write a proof of Theorem 10.9. First draw a diagram and write GIVEN and PROVE statements.

39. ▶ **PROVING THEOREM 10.10** Theorem 10.10 is written as a conditional statement and its converse. Write a plan for a proof of each statement.

40. ▶ **PROVING THEOREM 10.11** Draw a diagram and write a proof of part of Theorem 10.11.

    GIVEN ▶ *DEFG* is inscribed in a circle.

    PROVE ▶ $m\angle D + m\angle F = 180°$, $m\angle E + m\angle G = 180°$

41. 🌐 **CARPENTER'S SQUARE** A carpenter's square is an L-shaped tool used to draw right angles. Suppose you are making a copy of a wooden plate. You trace the plate on a piece of wood. How could you use a carpenter's square to find the center of the circle?

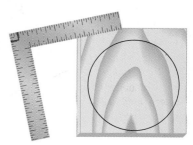

Test Preparation

42. **MULTIPLE CHOICE** In the diagram at the right, if $\angle ACB$ is a central angle and $m\angle ACB = 80°$, what is $m\angle ADB$?

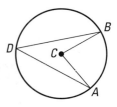

    Ⓐ 20   Ⓑ 40   Ⓒ 80

    Ⓓ 100   Ⓔ 160

43. **MULTIPLE CHOICE** In the diagram at the right, what is the value of x?

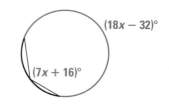

    Ⓐ $\dfrac{48}{11}$ Ⓑ 12   Ⓒ 16

    Ⓓ 18   Ⓔ 24

★ **Challenge**

🌐 **CUTTING BOARD** **In Exercises 44–47, use the following information.**
You are making a circular cutting board. To begin, you glue eight 1 inch by 2 inch boards together, as shown at the right. Then you draw and cut a circle with an 8 inch diameter from the boards.

44. $\overline{FH}$ is a diameter of the circular cutting board. What kind of triangle is $\triangle FGH$?

45. How is *GJ* related to *FJ* and *JH*? State a theorem to justify your answer.

46. Find *FJ*, *JH*, and *JG*. What is the length of the seam of the cutting board that is labeled $\overline{GK}$?

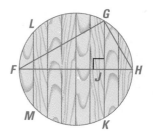

47. Find the length of $\overline{LM}$.

EXTRA CHALLENGE

www.mcdougallittell.com

WRITING EQUATIONS Write an equation in slope-intercept form of the line that passes through the given point and has the given slope. (Review 3.6)

48. $(-2, -6)$, $m = -1$ **49.** $(5, 1)$, $m = 2$ **50.** $(3, 3)$, $m = 0$

51. $(0, 7)$, $m = \dfrac{4}{3}$ **52.** $(-8, 4)$, $m = -\dfrac{1}{2}$ **53.** $(-5, -12)$, $m = -\dfrac{4}{5}$

SKETCHING IMAGES Sketch the image of $\triangle PQR$ after a composition using the given transformations in the order in which they appear. $\triangle PQR$ has vertices $P(-5, 4)$, $Q(-2, 1)$, and $R(-1, 3)$. (Review 7.5)

54. translation: $(x, y) \rightarrow (x + 6, y)$
reflection: in the x-axis

55. translation: $(x, y) \rightarrow (x + 8, y + 1)$
reflection: in the line $y = 1$

56. reflection: in the line $x = 3$
translation: $(x, y) \rightarrow (x - 1, y - 7)$

57. reflection: in the y-axis
rotation: $90°$ clockwise about
the origin

58. What is the length of an altitude of an equilateral triangle whose sides have lengths of $26\sqrt{2}$? (Review 9.4)

FINDING TRIGONOMETRIC RATIOS $\triangle ABC$ is a right triangle in which $AB = 4\sqrt{3}$, $BC = 4$, and $AC = 8$. (Review 9.5 for 10.4)

59. $\sin A = \underline{\ ?\ }$ **60.** $\cos A = \underline{\ ?\ }$

61. $\sin C = \underline{\ ?\ }$ **62.** $\tan C = \underline{\ ?\ }$

QUIZ 1

Self-Test for Lessons 10.1–10.3

$\overleftrightarrow{AB}$ is tangent to $\odot C$ at A and $\overleftrightarrow{DB}$ is tangent to $\odot C$ at D. Find the value of x. Write the postulate or theorem that justifies your answer. (Lesson 10.1)

1.
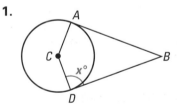

2.
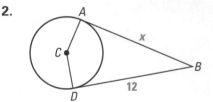

Find the measure of the arc of $\odot Q$. (Lesson 10.2)

3. $\overarc{AB}$ **4.** $\overarc{BC}$

5. $\overarc{ABD}$ **6.** $\overarc{BCA}$

7. $\overarc{ADC}$ **8.** $\overarc{CD}$

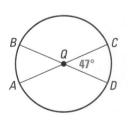

9. If an angle that has a measure of $42.6°$ is inscribed in a circle, what is the measure of its intercepted arc? (Lesson 10.3)

10.4

Other Angle Relationships in Circles

What you should learn

GOAL 1 Use angles formed by tangents and chords to solve problems in geometry.

GOAL 2 Use angles formed by lines that intersect a circle to solve problems.

Why you should learn it

▼ To solve **real-life** problems, such as finding from how far away you can see fireworks, as in **Ex. 35**.

GOAL 1   USING TANGENTS AND CHORDS

You know that the measure of an angle inscribed in a circle is half the measure of its intercepted arc. This is true even if one side of the angle is tangent to the circle. You will be asked to prove Theorem 10.12 in Exercises 37–39.

THEOREM

THEOREM 10.12

If a tangent and a chord intersect at a point on a circle, then the measure of each angle formed is one half the measure of its intercepted arc.

$$m\angle 1 = \tfrac{1}{2}m\overset{\frown}{AB} \qquad\qquad m\angle 2 = \tfrac{1}{2}m\overset{\frown}{BCA}$$

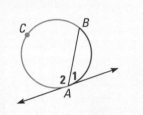

EXAMPLE 1   Finding Angle and Arc Measures

Line m is tangent to the circle. Find the measure of the red angle or arc.

a.

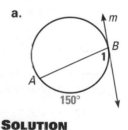

b.

SOLUTION

a. $m\angle 1 = \tfrac{1}{2}(150°) = 75°$

b. $m\overset{\frown}{RSP} = 2(130°) = 260°$

EXAMPLE 2   Finding an Angle Measure

In the diagram below, $\overleftrightarrow{BC}$ is tangent to the circle. Find $m\angle CBD$.

SOLUTION

$$m\angle CBD = \tfrac{1}{2}m\overset{\frown}{DAB}$$

$$5x = \tfrac{1}{2}(9x + 20)$$

$$10x = 9x + 20$$

$$x = 20$$

▶ $m\angle CBD = 5(20°) = 100°$

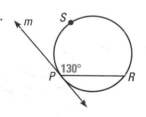

GOAL 2   LINES INTERSECTING INSIDE OR OUTSIDE A CIRCLE

If two lines intersect a circle, there are three places where the lines can intersect.

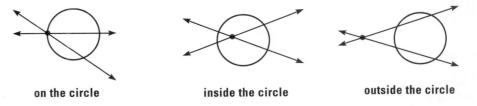

on the circle   **inside the circle**   **outside the circle**

You know how to find angle and arc measures when lines intersect *on* the circle. You can use Theorems 10.13 and 10.14 to find measures when the lines intersect *inside* or *outside* the circle. You will prove these theorems in Exercises 40 and 41.

THEOREMS

THEOREM 10.13

If two chords intersect in the *interior* of a circle, then the measure of each angle is one half the *sum* of the measures of the arcs intercepted by the angle and its vertical angle.

$$m\angle 1 = \tfrac{1}{2}(m\widehat{CD} + m\widehat{AB}), \ m\angle 2 = \tfrac{1}{2}(m\widehat{BC} + m\widehat{AD})$$

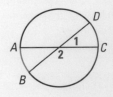

THEOREM 10.14

If a tangent and a secant, two tangents, or two secants intersect in the *exterior* of a circle, then the measure of the angle formed is one half the *difference* of the measures of the intercepted arcs.

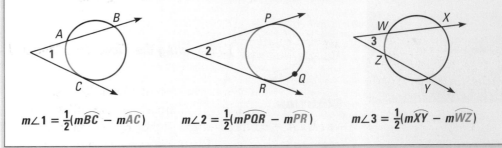

$$m\angle 1 = \tfrac{1}{2}(m\widehat{BC} - m\widehat{AC}) \qquad m\angle 2 = \tfrac{1}{2}(m\widehat{PQR} - m\widehat{PR}) \qquad m\angle 3 = \tfrac{1}{2}(m\widehat{XY} - m\widehat{WZ})$$

EXAMPLE 3   *Finding the Measure of an Angle Formed by Two Chords*

Find the value of x.

SOLUTION

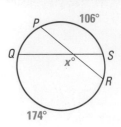

$$x° = \tfrac{1}{2}(m\widehat{PS} + m\widehat{RQ}) \qquad \text{Apply Theorem 10.13.}$$

$$x° = \tfrac{1}{2}(106° + 174°) \qquad \text{Substitute.}$$

$$x = 140 \qquad\qquad \text{Simplify.}$$

STUDENT HELP

INTERNET

HOMEWORK HELP
Visit our Web site
www.mcdougallittell.com
for extra examples.

EXAMPLE 4   *Using Theorem 10.14*

Find the value of *x*.

a.

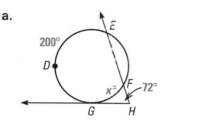

b.

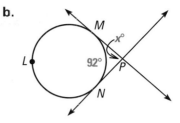

SOLUTION

a. $m\angle GHF = \frac{1}{2}(m\widehat{EDG} - m\widehat{GF})$ **Apply Theorem 10.14.**

$\quad\quad 72° = \frac{1}{2}(200° - x°)$ **Substitute.**

$\quad\quad 144 = 200 - x$ **Multiply each side by 2.**

$\quad\quad x = 56$ **Solve for *x*.**

b. Because $\widehat{MN}$ and $\widehat{MLN}$ make a whole circle, $m\widehat{MLN} = 360° - 92° = 268°$.

$\quad x = \frac{1}{2}(m\widehat{MLN} - m\widehat{MN})$ **Apply Theorem 10.14.**

$\quad\quad = \frac{1}{2}(268 - 92)$ **Substitute.**

$\quad\quad = \frac{1}{2}(176)$ **Subtract.**

$\quad\quad = 88$ **Multiply.**

EXAMPLE 5   *Describing the View from Mount Rainier*

REAL LIFE

VIEWS You are on top of Mount Rainier on a clear day. You are about 2.73 miles above sea level. Find the measure of the arc $\widehat{CD}$ that represents the part of Earth that you can see.

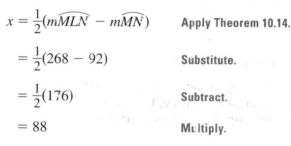

Not drawn to scale

Mount Rainier, Washington

SOLUTION

$\overrightarrow{BC}$ and $\overrightarrow{BD}$ are tangent to Earth. You can solve right $\triangle BCA$ to see that $m\angle CBA \approx 87.9°$. So, $m\angle CBD \approx 175.8°$. Let $m\widehat{CD} = x°$.

$\quad 175.8 \approx \frac{1}{2}[(360 - x) - x]$ **Apply Theorem 10.14.**

$\quad 175.8 \approx \frac{1}{2}(360 - 2x)$ **Simplify.**

$\quad 175.8 \approx 180 - x$ **Distributive property**

$\quad\quad x \approx 4.2$ **Solve for *x*.**

▶ From the peak, you can see an arc of about 4°.

STUDENT HELP

▶ **Look Back**
For help with solving a right triangle, see pp. 567–569.

10.4 *Other Angle Relationships in Circles*   **623**

GUIDED PRACTICE

Concept Check ✓   **1.** If a chord of a circle intersects a tangent to the circle at the point of tangency, what is the relationship between the angles formed and the intercepted arcs?

Skill Check ✓   **Find the indicated measure or value.**

2. $m\widehat{STU}$

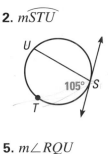

3. $m\angle 1$

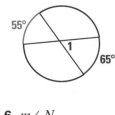

4. $m\angle DBR$

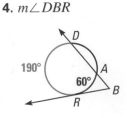

5. $m\angle RQU$

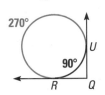

6. $m\angle N$

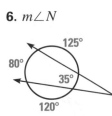

7. $m\angle 1$

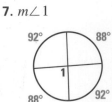

PRACTICE AND APPLICATIONS

STUDENT HELP

▶ **Extra Practice**
to help you master
skills is on p. 822.

FINDING MEASURES **Find the indicated measure.**

8. $m\angle 1$

9. $m\widehat{GHJ}$

10. $m\angle 2$

11. $m\widehat{DE}$

12. $m\widehat{ABC}$

13. $m\angle 3$

USING ALGEBRA **Find the value of x.**

STUDENT HELP

▶ **HOMEWORK HELP**
Example 1: Exs. 8–13
Example 2: Exs. 14–16
Example 3: Exs. 17–25
Example 4: Exs. 26–28
Example 5: Ex. 35

14. $m\widehat{AB} = x°$

15. $m\widehat{PQ} = (5x + 17)°$

16. $m\widehat{HJK} = (10x + 50)°$

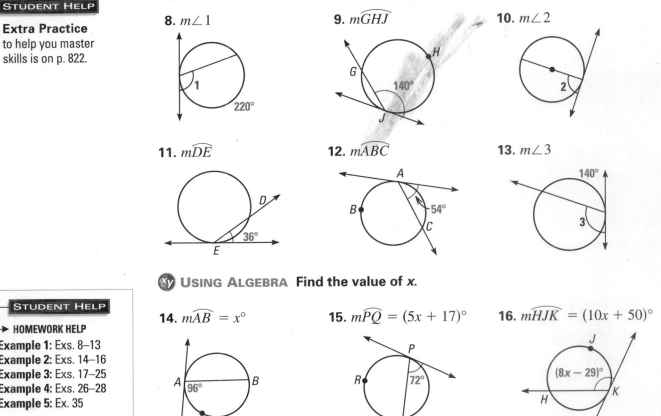

FINDING ANGLE MEASURES Find $m\angle 1$.

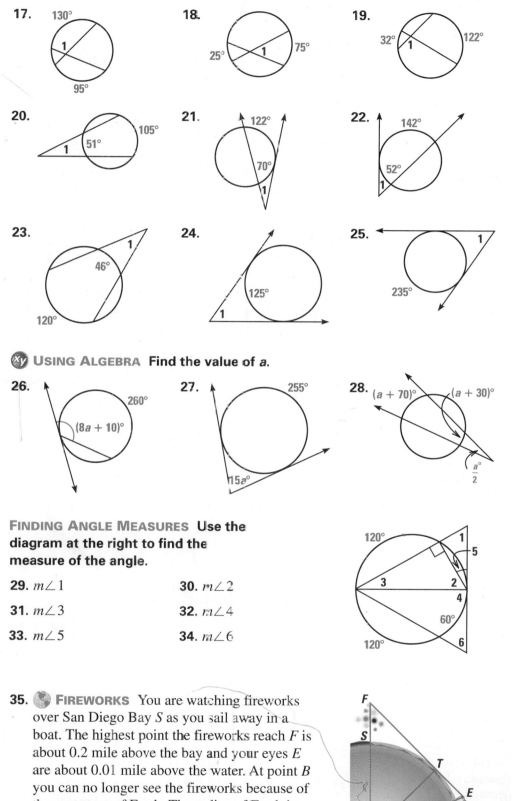

17.

130°
1
95°

18.

25°
1
75°

19.

32°
1
122°

20.

51°
1
105°

21.

122°
70°
1

22.

142°
52°
1

23.

1
46°
120°

24.

125°
1

25.

1
235°

USING ALGEBRA Find the value of a.

26.

260°
(8a + 10)°

27.

255°
15a°

28.

(a + 70)°
(a + 30)°
a°/2

FINDING ANGLE MEASURES Use the diagram at the right to find the measure of the angle.

120°
1
5
3
2
4
60°
120°
6

29. $m\angle 1$

30. $m\angle 2$

31. $m\angle 3$

32. $m\angle 4$

33. $m\angle 5$

34. $m\angle 6$

STUDENT HELP

INTERNET APPLICATION LINK
Visit our Web site www.mcdougallittell.com.

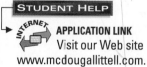

35. **FIREWORKS** You are watching fireworks over San Diego Bay S as you sail away in a boat. The highest point the fireworks reach F is about 0.2 mile above the bay and your eyes E are about 0.01 mile above the water. At point B you can no longer see the fireworks because of the curvature of Earth. The radius of Earth is about 4000 miles and $\overline{FE}$ is tangent to Earth at T. Find $m\widehat{SB}$. Give your answer to the nearest tenth of a degree.

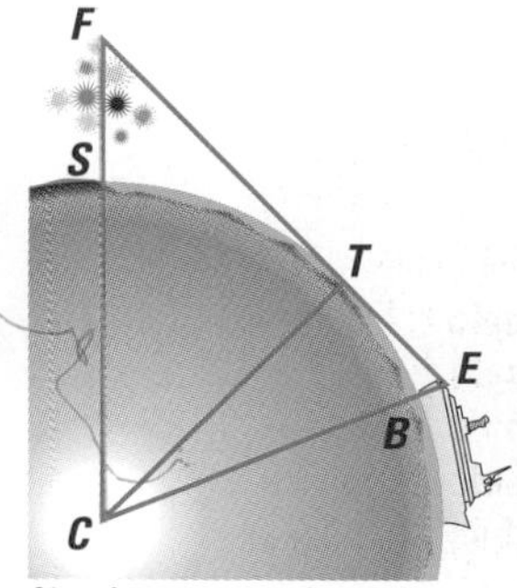

F
S
T
E
B
C

Not drawn to scale

STUDENT HELP

INTERNET SOFTWARE HELP Visit our Web site www.mcdougallittell.com to see instructions for several software applications.

36. **TECHNOLOGY** Use geometry software to construct and label circle O, $\overline{AB}$ which is tangent to $\odot O$ at point A, and any point C on $\odot O$. Then construct secant $\overline{AC}$. Measure $\angle BAC$ and $\widehat{AC}$. Compare the measures of $\angle BAC$ and its intercepted arc as you drag point C on the circle. What do you notice? What theorem from this lesson have you illustrated?

PROVING THEOREM 10.12 **The proof of Theorem 10.12 can be split into three cases, as shown in the diagrams.**

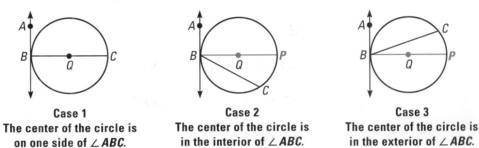

Case 1
The center of the circle is on one side of $\angle ABC$.

Case 2
The center of the circle is in the interior of $\angle ABC$.

Case 3
The center of the circle is in the exterior of $\angle ABC$.

37. In Case 1, what type of chord is $\overline{BC}$? What is the measure of $\angle ABC$? What theorem earlier in this chapter supports your conclusion?

38. Write a plan for a proof of Case 2 of Theorem 10.12. (*Hint:* Use the auxiliary line and the Angle Addition Postulate.)

39. Describe how the proof of Case 3 of Theorem 10.12 is different from the proof of Case 2.

40. **PROVING THEOREM 10.13** Fill in the blanks to complete the proof of Theorem 10.13.

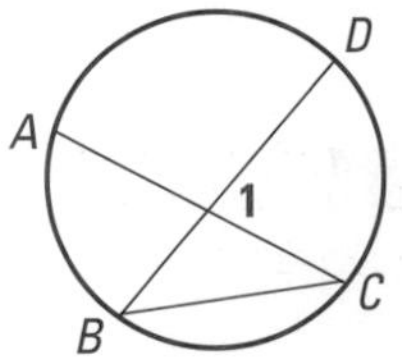

GIVEN ▶ Chords $\overline{AC}$ and $\overline{BD}$ intersect.

PROVE ▶ $m\angle 1 = \frac{1}{2}(m\widehat{DC} + m\widehat{AB})$

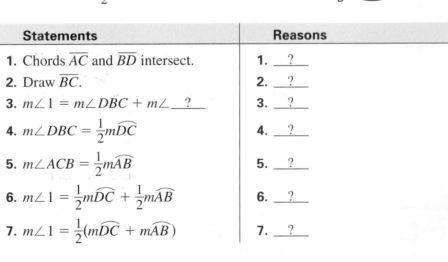

Statements	Reasons
1. Chords $\overline{AC}$ and $\overline{BD}$ intersect.	**1.** ?
2. Draw $\overline{BC}$.	**2.** ?
3. $m\angle 1 = m\angle DBC + m\angle$?	**3.** ?
4. $m\angle DBC = \frac{1}{2}m\widehat{DC}$	**4.** ?
5. $m\angle ACB = \frac{1}{2}m\widehat{AB}$	**5.** ?
6. $m\angle 1 = \frac{1}{2}m\widehat{DC} + \frac{1}{2}m\widehat{AB}$	**6.** ?
7. $m\angle 1 = \frac{1}{2}(m\widehat{DC} + m\widehat{AB})$	**7.** ?

41. **JUSTIFYING THEOREM 10.14** Look back at the diagrams for Theorem 10.14 on page 622. Copy the diagram for the case of a tangent and a secant and draw $\overline{BC}$. Explain how to use the Exterior Angle Theorem in the proof of this case. Then copy the diagrams for the other two cases, draw appropriate auxiliary segments, and write plans for the proofs of the cases.

42. MULTIPLE CHOICE The diagram at the right is not drawn to scale. $\overline{AB}$ is any chord of the circle. The line is tangent to the circle at point A. Which of the following must be true?

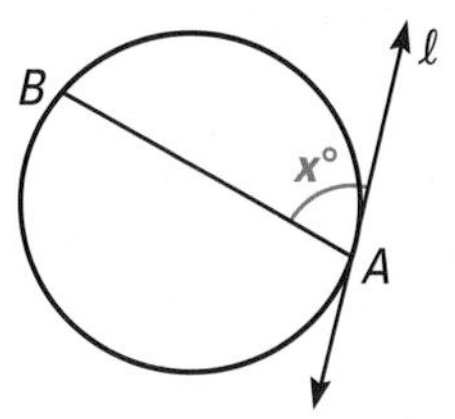

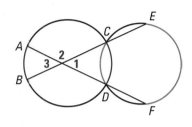

Ⓐ $x < 90°$ Ⓑ $x \leq 90°$ Ⓒ $x = 90°$

Ⓓ $x > 90°$ Ⓔ Cannot be determined from given information

43. MULTIPLE CHOICE In the figure at the right, which relationship is *not* true?

Ⓐ $m\angle 1 = \frac{1}{2}(m\widehat{CD} - m\widehat{AB})$

Ⓑ $m\angle 1 = \frac{1}{2}(m\widehat{EF} - m\widehat{CD})$

Ⓒ $m\angle 2 = \frac{1}{2}(m\widehat{BD} - m\widehat{AC})$

Ⓓ $m\angle 3 = \frac{1}{2}(m\widehat{EF} - m\widehat{CD})$

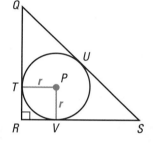

★ Challenge

44. ▶ PROOF Use the plan to write a paragraph proof.

GIVEN ▶ $\angle R$ is a right angle. Circle P is inscribed in $\triangle QRS$. T, U, and V are points of tangency.

PROVE ▶ $r = \frac{1}{2}(QR + RS - QS)$

Plan for Proof Prove that $TPVR$ is a square. Then show that $\overline{QT} \cong \overline{QU}$ and $\overline{SU} \cong \overline{SV}$. Finally, use the Segment Addition Postulate and substitution.

45. FINDING A RADIUS Use the result from Exercise 44 to find the radius of an inscribed circle of a right triangle with side lengths of 3, 4, and 5.

MIXED REVIEW

USING SIMILAR TRIANGLES Use the diagram at the right and the given information. (Review 9.1)

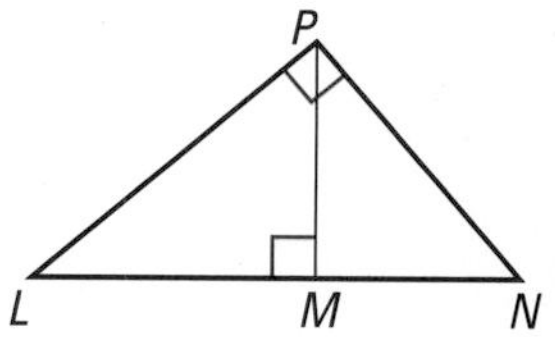

46. $MN = 9$, $PM = 12$, $LP = \underline{\ ?\ }$

47. $LM = 4$, $LN = 9$, $LP = \underline{\ ?\ }$

48. FINDING A RADIUS You are 10 feet from a circular storage tank. You are 22 feet from a point of tangency on the tank. Find the tank's radius. (Review 10.1)

⟨xy⟩ USING ALGEBRA $\overline{AB}$ and $\overline{AD}$ are tangent to $\odot L$. Find the value of x. (Review 10.1)

49.   **50.**   **51.**

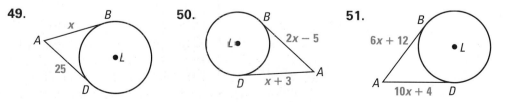

▶ **ACTIVITY 10.5**

Using Technology

Investigating Segment Lengths

You can use geometry software to explore the lengths of segments in a circle.

▶ **CONSTRUCT** Follow the steps to construct a circle and two intersecting lines.

1 Draw a circle.

2 On the circle, draw and label points *A*, *B*, *C*, and *D*.

3 Draw lines $\overleftrightarrow{AB}$ and $\overleftrightarrow{CD}$.

4 Draw the point of intersection of $\overleftrightarrow{AB}$ and $\overleftrightarrow{CD}$. Label it point *E*.

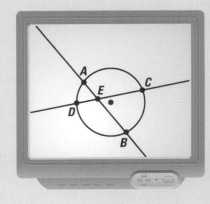

▶ **INVESTIGATE**

1. Drag points *A*, *B*, *C*, and *D*. Can you rearrange the points so that point *E* is outside the circle? on the circle? inside the circle?

2. Draw $\overline{EA}$, $\overline{EC}$, $\overline{EB}$, and $\overline{ED}$. Hide $\overleftrightarrow{AB}$ and $\overleftrightarrow{CD}$.

3. Rearrange the points *A*, *B*, *C*, and *D* so that point *E* is inside the circle. Measure $\overline{EA}$, $\overline{EC}$, $\overline{EB}$, and $\overline{ED}$. Calculate $EA \cdot EB$ and $EC \cdot ED$. What do you notice?

4. Drag points *A*, *B*, *C*, and *D*, keeping point *E* inside the circle. What do you notice about $EA \cdot EB$ and $EC \cdot ED$?

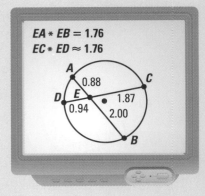

▶ **CONJECTURE**

5. Make a conjecture about the lengths of the segments of intersecting chords.

▶ **INVESTIGATE**

6. Drag points *A*, *B*, *C*, and *D* so that point *E* is outside the circle. What do you notice about $EA \cdot EB$ and $EC \cdot ED$?

▶ **CONJECTURE**

7. Make a conjecture about the lengths of the segments of secants from a point outside a circle to the circle.

EXTENSION

CRITICAL THINKING Move point *A* until it is in the same place as point *B*. What kind of line is $\overleftrightarrow{EA}$? What is the relationship between *EA*, *EC*, and *ED*? Make and test a conjecture.

10.5

Segment Lengths in Circles

What you should learn

GOAL 1 Find the lengths of segments of chords.

GOAL 2 Find the lengths of segments of tangents and secants.

Why you should learn it

▼ To find **real-life** measures, such as the radius of an aquarium tank in **Example 3**.

GOAL 1 FINDING LENGTHS OF SEGMENTS OF CHORDS

When two chords intersect in the interior of a circle, each chord is divided into two segments which are called *segments of a chord*. The following theorem gives a relationship between the lengths of the four segments that are formed.

THEOREM

THEOREM 10.15

If two chords intersect in the interior of a circle, then the product of the lengths of the segments of one chord is equal to the product of the lengths of the segments of the other chord.

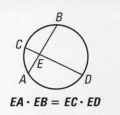

$$EA \cdot EB = EC \cdot ED$$

You can use similar triangles to prove Theorem 10.15.

GIVEN ▶ $\overline{AB}$, $\overline{CD}$ are chords that intersect at E.

PROVE ▶ $EA \cdot EB = EC \cdot ED$

Paragraph Proof Draw $\overline{DB}$ and $\overline{AC}$. Because $\angle C$ and $\angle B$ intercept the same arc, $\angle C \cong \angle B$. Likewise, $\angle A \cong \angle D$. By the AA Similarity Postulate, $\triangle AEC \sim \triangle DEB$. So, the lengths of corresponding sides are proportional.

$$\frac{EA}{ED} = \frac{EC}{EB} \qquad \text{The lengths of the sides are proportional.}$$

$$EA \cdot EB = EC \cdot ED \qquad \text{Cross Product Property}$$

EXAMPLE 1 *Finding Segment Lengths*

Chords $\overline{ST}$ and $\overline{PQ}$ intersect inside the circle. Find the value of x.

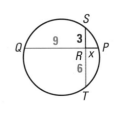

SOLUTION

$$RQ \cdot RP = RS \cdot RT \qquad \text{Use Theorem 10.15.}$$

$$9 \cdot x = 3 \cdot 6 \qquad \text{Substitute.}$$

$$9x = 18 \qquad \text{Simplify.}$$

$$x = 2 \qquad \text{Divide each side by 9.}$$

GOAL 2 USING SEGMENTS OF TANGENTS AND SECANTS

In the figure shown below, $\overline{PS}$ is called a **tangent segment** because it is tangent to the circle at an endpoint. Similarly, $\overline{PR}$ is a **secant segment** and $\overline{PQ}$ is the **external segment** of $\overline{PR}$.

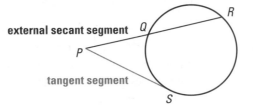

external secant segment

tangent segment

You are asked to prove the following theorems in Exercises 31 and 32.

THEOREMS

THEOREM 10.16

If two secant segments share the same endpoint outside a circle, then the product of the length of one secant segment and the length of its external segment equals the product of the length of the other secant segment and the length of its external segment.

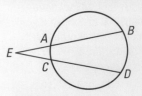

$EA \cdot EB = EC \cdot ED$

THEOREM 10.17

If a secant segment and a tangent segment share an endpoint outside a circle, then the product of the length of the secant segment and the length of its external segment equals the square of the length of the tangent segment.

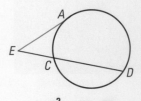

$(EA)^2 = EC \cdot ED$

EXAMPLE 2 *Finding Segment Lengths*

Using Algebra

Find the value of x.

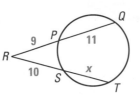

SOLUTION

$$RP \cdot RQ = RS \cdot RT \qquad \text{Use Theorem 10.16.}$$

$$9 \cdot (11 + 9) = 10 \cdot (x + 10) \qquad \text{Substitute.}$$

$$180 = 10x + 100 \qquad \text{Simplify.}$$

$$80 = 10x \qquad \text{Subtract 100 from each side.}$$

$$8 = x \qquad \text{Divide each side by 10.}$$

FOCUS ON APPLICATIONS

AQUARIUM TANK The Caribbean Coral Reef Tank at the New England Aquarium is a circular tank 24 feet deep. The 200,000 gallon tank contains an elaborate coral reef and many exotic fishes.

APPLICATION LINK
www.mcdougallittell.com

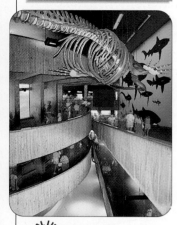

In Lesson 10.1, you learned how to use the Pythagorean Theorem to estimate the radius of a grain silo. Example 3 shows you another way to estimate the radius of a circular object.

EXAMPLE 3 *Estimating the Radius of a Circle*

AQUARIUM TANK You are standing at point C, about 8 feet from a circular aquarium tank. The distance from you to a point of tangency on the tank is about 20 feet. Estimate the radius of the tank.

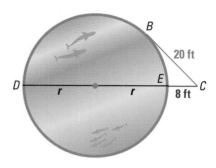

SOLUTION

You can use Theorem 10.17 to find the radius.

$(CB)^2 = CE \cdot CD$	Use Theorem 10.17.
$20^2 \approx 8 \cdot (2r + 8)$	Substitute.
$400 \approx 16r + 64$	Simplify.
$336 \approx 16r$	Subtract 64 from each side.
$21 \approx r$	Divide each side by 16.

▶ So, the radius of the tank is about 21 feet.

EXAMPLE 4 *Finding Segment Lengths*

Using Algebra

Use the figure at the right to find the value of x.

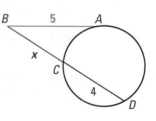

SOLUTION

$(BA)^2 = BC \cdot BD$	Use Theorem 10.17.
$5^2 = x \cdot (x + 4)$	Substitute.
$25 = x^2 + 4x$	Simplify.
$0 = x^2 + 4x - 25$	Write in standard form.
$x = \frac{-4 \pm \sqrt{4^2 - 4(1)(-25)}}{2}$	Use Quadratic Formula.
$x = -2 \pm \sqrt{29}$	Simplify.

Use the positive solution, because lengths cannot be negative.

▶ So, $x = -2 + \sqrt{29} \approx 3.39$.

GUIDED PRACTICE

Vocabulary Check ✓

1. Sketch a circle with a secant segment. Label each endpoint and point of intersection. Then name the external segment.

Concept Check ✓

2. How are the lengths of the segments in the figure at the right related to each other?

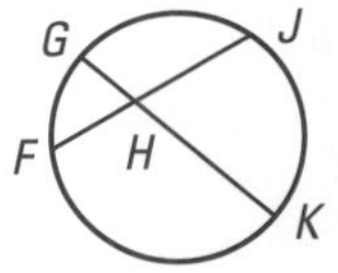

Skill Check ✓

Fill in the blanks. Then find the value of _x_.

3. $x \cdot \underline{?} = 10 \cdot \underline{?}$

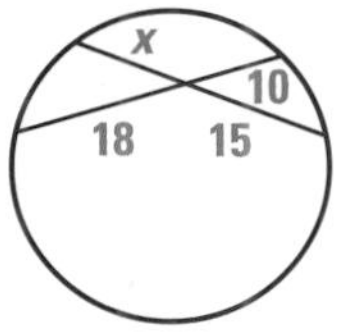

4. $\underline{?} \cdot x = \underline{?} \cdot 40$

5. $6 \cdot \underline{?} = 8 \cdot \underline{?}$

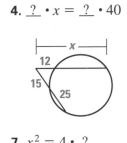
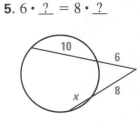

6. $4^2 = 2 \cdot (\underline{?} + x)$

7. $x^2 = 4 \cdot \underline{?}$

8. $x \cdot \underline{?} = \underline{?}$

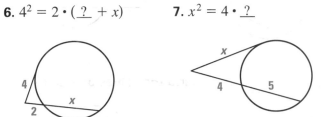

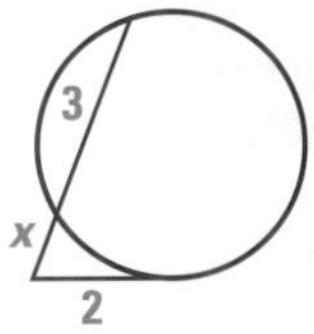

9. 🌐 **ZOO HABITAT** A zoo has a large circular aviary, a habitat for birds. You are standing about 40 feet from the aviary. The distance from you to a point of tangency on the aviary is about 60 feet. Describe how to estimate the radius of the aviary.

PRACTICE AND APPLICATIONS

STUDENT HELP

▶ **Extra Practice**
to help you master
skills is on p. 822.

FINDING SEGMENT LENGTHS **Fill in the blanks. Then find the value of _x_.**

10. $x \cdot \underline{?} = 12 \cdot \underline{?}$

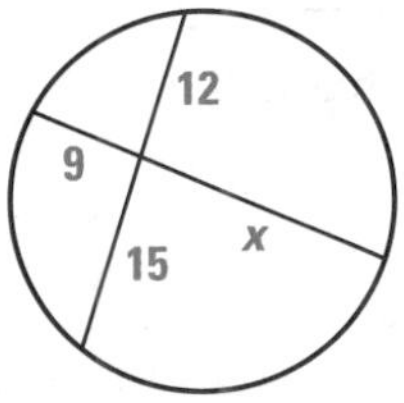

11. $x \cdot \underline{?} = \underline{?} \cdot 50$

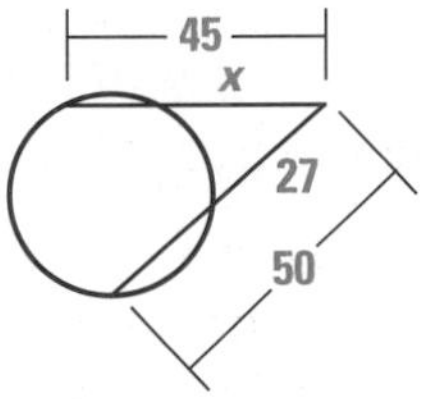

12. $x^2 = 9 \cdot \underline{?}$

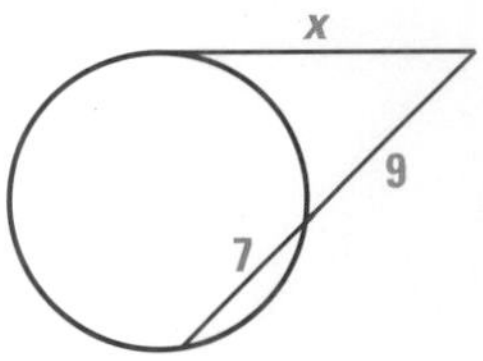

STUDENT HELP

▶ **HOMEWORK HELP**
Example 1: Exs. 10,
      14–17, 26–29
Example 2: Exs. 11, 13,
      18, 19, 24, 25

FINDING SEGMENT LENGTHS **Find the value of _x_.**

13.

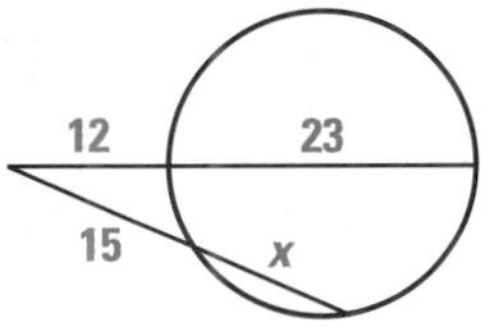

14.

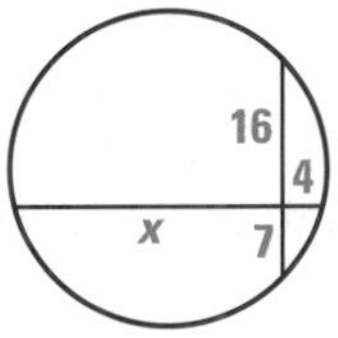

15.

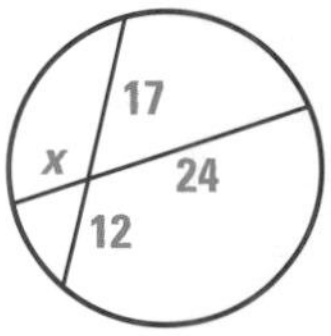

FINDING SEGMENT LENGTHS Find the value of *x*.

16.
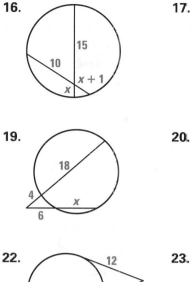

17.
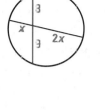

18.
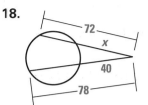

STUDENT HELP

▶ **HOMEWORK HELP**
Visit our Web site
www.mcdougallittell.com
for help with using the
Quadratic Formula in
Exs. 21–27.

19.

20.
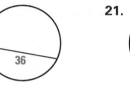

21.
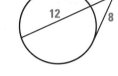

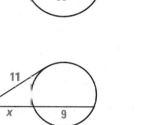

22.

23.

24.
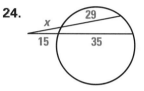

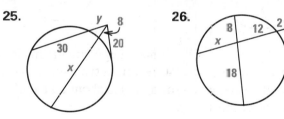

USING ALGEBRA Find the values of *x* and *y*.

25.

26.

27.

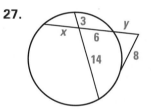

28. 🌐 **DESIGNING A LOGO** Suppose you are
designing an animated logo for a television
commercial. You want sparkles to leave
point *C* and move to the circle along the
segments shown. You want each of the
sparkles to reach the circle at the same time.
To calculate the speed for each sparkle, you
need to know the distance from point *C* to
the circle along each segment. What is the
distance from *C* to *N*?

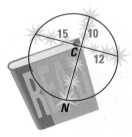

29. 🌐 **BUILDING STAIRS** You are
making curved stairs for students
to stand on for photographs at a
homecoming dance. The diagram
shows a top view of the stairs.
What is the radius of the circle
shown? Explain how you can use
Theorem 10.15 to find the answer.

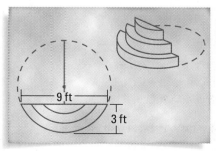

FOCUS ON APPLICATIONS

REAL LIFE **GPS** Some cars have navigation systems that use GPS to tell you where you are and how to get where you want to go.

INTERNET **APPLICATION LINK**
www.mcdougallittell.com

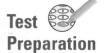

30. **GLOBAL POSITIONING SYSTEM** Satellites in the Global Positioning System (GPS) orbit 12,500 miles above Earth. GPS signals can't travel through Earth, so a satellite at point B can transmit signals only to points on $\overset{\frown}{AC}$. How far must the satellite be able to transmit to reach points A and C? Find BA and BC. The diameter of Earth is about 8000 miles. Give your answer to the nearest thousand miles.

Not drawn to scale

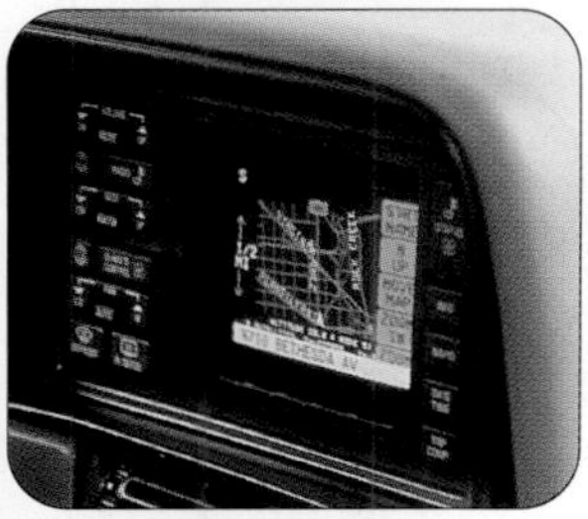

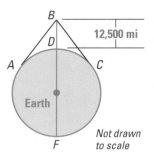

31. **PROVING THEOREM 10.16** Use the plan to write a paragraph proof.

GIVEN ▶ $\overline{EB}$ and $\overline{ED}$ are secant segments.

PROVE ▶ $EA \cdot EB = EC \cdot ED$

Plan for Proof Draw $\overline{AD}$ and $\overline{BC}$, and show that $\triangle BCE$ and $\triangle DAE$ are similar. Use the fact that corresponding sides of similar triangles are proportional.

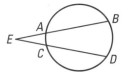

32. **PROVING THEOREM 10.17** Use the plan to write a paragraph proof.

GIVEN ▶ $\overline{EA}$ is a tangent segment and $\overline{ED}$ is a secant segment.

PROVE ▶ $(EA)^2 = EC \cdot ED$

Plan for Proof Draw $\overline{AD}$ and $\overline{AC}$. Use the fact that corresponding sides of similar triangles are proportional.

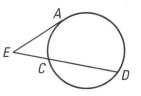

Test Preparation

MULTI-STEP PROBLEM In Exercises 33–35, use the following information.

A person is standing at point A on a beach and looking 2 miles down the beach to point B, as shown at the right. The beach is very flat but, because of Earth's curvature, the ground between A and B is x mi higher than $\overline{AB}$.

Not drawn to scale

33. Find the value of x.

34. Convert your answer to inches. Round to the nearest inch.

35. *Writing* Why do you think people historically thought that Earth was flat?

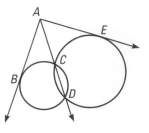

★ Challenge

In the diagram at the right, $\overrightarrow{AB}$ and $\overrightarrow{AE}$ are tangents.

36. Write an equation that shows how AB is related to AC and AD.

37. Write an equation that shows how AE is related to AC and AD.

38. How is AB related to AE? Explain.

39. Make a conjecture about tangents to intersecting circles. Then test your conjecture by looking for a counterexample.

EXTRA CHALLENGE
www.mcdougallittell.com

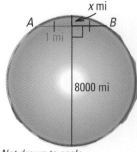

FINDING DISTANCE AND MIDPOINT Find *AB* to the nearest hundredth. Then find the coordinates of the midpoint of $\overline{AB}$. (Review 1.3, 1.5 for 10.6)

40. $A(2, 5), B(-3, 3)$

41. $A(6, -4), B(0, 4)$

42. $A(-8, -6), B(1, 9)$

43. $A(-1, -5), B(-10, 7)$

44. $A(0, -11), B(8, 2)$

45. $A(5, -2), B(-9, -2)$

WRITING EQUATIONS Write an equation of a line perpendicular to the given line at the given point. (Review 3.7 for 10.6)

46. $y = -2x - 5, (-2, -1)$

47. $y = \frac{2}{3}x + 4, (6, 8)$

48. $y = -x + 9, (0, 9)$

49. $y = 3x - 10, (2, -4)$

50. $y = \frac{1}{5}x + 1, (-10, -1)$

51. $y = -\frac{7}{3}x - 5, (-6, 9)$

DRAWING TRANSLATIONS Quadrilateral *ABCD* has vertices $A(-6, 8)$, $B(-1, 4)$, $C(-2, 2)$, and $D(-7, 3)$. Draw its image after the translation. (Review 7.4 for 10.6)

52. $(x, y) \rightarrow (x + 7, y)$ **53.** $(x, y) \rightarrow (x - 2, y + 3)$ **54.** $(x, y) \rightarrow \left(x, y - \frac{11}{2}\right)$

QUIZ 2

Self-Test for Lessons 10.4 and 10.5

Find the value of *x*. (Lesson 10.4)

1.
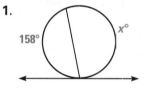

2.

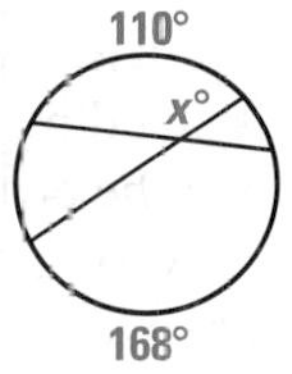

3.
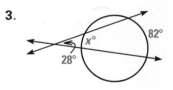

Find the value of *x*. (Lesson 10.5)

4.
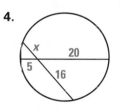

5.
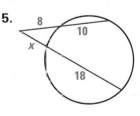

6.
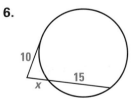

7. 🌐 **SWIMMING POOL** You are standing 20 feet from the circular wall of an above ground swimming pool and 49 feet from a point of tangency. Describe two different methods you could use to find the radius of the pool. What is the radius? (Lesson 10.5)

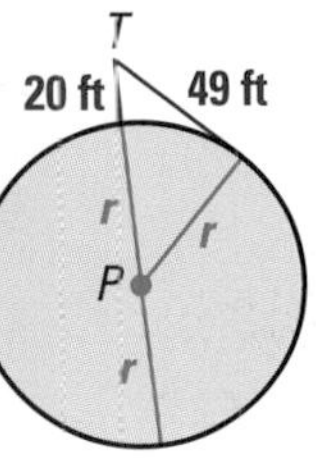

10.6

Equations of Circles

What you should learn

GOAL 1 Write the equation of a circle.

GOAL 2 Use the equation of a circle and its graph to solve problems.

Why you should learn it

▼ To solve **real-life** problems, such as determining cellular phone coverage, as in **Exs. 41 and 42.**

GOAL 1 FINDING EQUATIONS OF CIRCLES

You can write an equation of a circle in a coordinate plane if you know its radius and the coordinates of its center. Suppose the radius of a circle is r and the center is (h, k). Let (x, y) be any point on the circle. The distance between (x, y) and (h, k) is r, so you can use the Distance Formula.

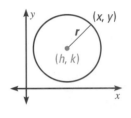

$$\sqrt{(x - h)^2 + (y - k)^2} = r$$

Square both sides to find the **standard equation of a circle** with radius r and center (h, k).

> **Standard equation of a circle:** $(x - h)^2 + (y - k)^2 = r^2$

If the center is the origin, then the standard equation is $x^2 + y^2 = r^2$.

EXAMPLE 1 *Writing a Standard Equation of a Circle*

Write the standard equation of the circle with center $(-4, 0)$ and radius **7.1**.

SOLUTION

$$(x - h)^2 + (y - k)^2 = r^2 \qquad \text{Standard equation of a circle}$$
$$[x - (-4)]^2 + (y - 0)^2 = 7.1^2 \qquad \text{Substitute.}$$
$$(x + 4)^2 + y^2 = 50.41 \qquad \text{Simplify.}$$

EXAMPLE 2 *Writing a Standard Equation of a Circle*

The point $(1, 2)$ is on a circle whose center is $(5, -1)$. Write the standard equation of the circle.

SOLUTION

Find the radius. The radius is the distance from the point $(1, 2)$ to the center $(5, -1)$.

$$r = \sqrt{(5 - 1)^2 + (-1 - 2)^2} \qquad \text{Use the Distance Formula.}$$
$$r = \sqrt{4^2 + (-3)^2} \qquad \text{Simplify.}$$
$$r = 5 \qquad \text{Simplify.}$$

Substitute $(h, k) = (5, -1)$ and $r = 5$ into the standard equation of a circle.

$$(x - 5)^2 + (y - (-1))^2 = 5^2 \qquad \text{Standard equation of a circle}$$
$$(x - 5)^2 + (y + 1)^2 = 25 \qquad \text{Simplify.}$$

GOAL 2 GRAPHING CIRCLES

If you know the equation of a circle, you can graph the circle by identifying its center and radius.

EXAMPLE 3 *Graphing a Circle*

The equation of a circle is $(x + 2)^2 + (y - 3)^2 = 9$. Graph the circle.

Rewrite the equation to find the center and radius:

$$(x + 2)^2 + (y - 3)^2 = 9$$
$$[x - (-2)]^2 + (y - 3)^2 = 3^2$$

The center is $(-2, 3)$ and the radius is **3**. To graph the circle, place the point of a compass at $(-2, 3)$, set the radius at 3 units, and swing the compass to draw a full circle.

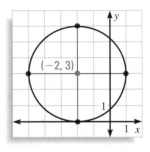

EXAMPLE 4 *Applying Graphs of Circles*

THEATER LIGHTING A bank of lights is arranged over a stage. Each light illuminates a circular area on the stage. A coordinate plane is used to arrange the lights, using the corner of the stage as the origin. The equation $(x - 13)^2 + (y - 4)^2 = 16$ represents one of the disks of light.

a. Graph the disk of light.

b. Three actors are located as follows: Henry is at $(11, 4)$, Jolene is at $(8, 5)$, and Martin is at $(15, 5)$. Which actors are in the disk of light?

SOLUTION

a. Rewrite the equation to find the center and radius:

$$(x - 13)^2 + (y - 4)^2 = 16$$
$$(x - 13)^2 + (y - 4)^2 = 4^2$$

The center is $(13, 4)$ and the radius is **4**. The circle is shown below.

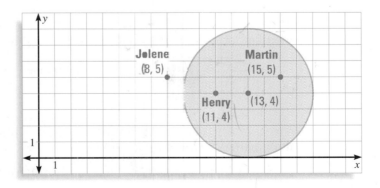

b. The graph shows that Henry and Martin are both in the disk of light.

GUIDED PRACTICE

Vocabulary Check ✔   **1.** The standard form of an equation of a circle is ___?___ .

Concept Check ✔   **2.** Describe how to graph the circle $(x - 3)^2 + (y - 4)^2 = 9$.

Skill Check ✔   **Give the coordinates of the center and the radius. Write an equation of the circle in standard form.**

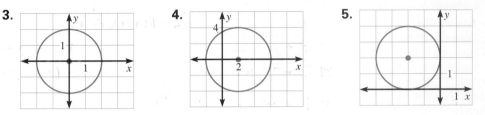

3.   **4.**   **5.**

6. $P(-1, 3)$ is on a circle whose center is $C(0, 0)$. Write an equation of $\odot C$.

PRACTICE AND APPLICATIONS

STUDENT HELP

▶ **Extra Practice**
to help you master
skills is on p. 822.

USING STANDARD EQUATIONS   **Give the center and radius of the circle.**

7. $(x - 4)^2 + (y - 3)^2 = 16$ **8.** $(x - 5)^2 + (y - 1)^2 = 25$

9. $x^2 + y^2 = 4$ **10.** $(x + 2)^2 + (y - 3)^2 = 36$

11. $(x + 5)^2 + (y + 3)^2 = 1$ **12.** $\left(x - \frac{1}{2}\right)^2 + \left(y + \frac{3}{4}\right)^2 = \frac{1}{4}$

USING GRAPHS   **Give the coordinates of the center, the radius, and the equation of the circle.**

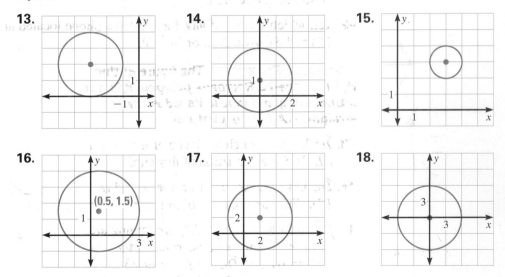

13.   **14.**   **15.**

16.   **17.**   **18.**

(0.5, 1.5)

STUDENT HELP

▶ **HOMEWORK HELP**
Example 1: Exs. 13–22
Example 2: Exs. 23–26
Example 3: Exs. 27–40
Example 4: Exs. 33–42

WRITING EQUATIONS   **Write the standard equation of the circle with the given center and radius.**

19. center $(0, 0)$, radius 1   **20.** center $(4, 0)$, radius 4

21. center $(3, -2)$, radius 2   **22.** center $(-1, -3)$, radius 6

WRITING EQUATIONS Use the given information to write the standard equation of the circle.

23. The center is $(0, 0)$, a point on the circle is $(0, 3)$.

24. The center is $(1, 2)$, a point on the circle is $(4, 6)$.

25. The center is $(3, 2)$, a point on the circle is $(5, 2)$.

26. The center is $(-5, 3)$ and the diameter is 8.

$(x-h)^2+(y-k)^2=r^2$
center: (h,k)

GRAPHING CIRCLES Graph the equation.

27. $x^2 + y^2 = 25$
$(x+0)^2$

28. $x^2 + (y - 4)^2 = 1$

29. $(x + 3)^2 + y^2 = 9$

30. $(x - 3)^2 + (y - 4)^2 = 16$

31. $(x + 5)^2 + (y - 1)^2 = 49$

32. $\left(x - \frac{1}{2}\right)^2 + \left(y + \frac{1}{2}\right)^2 = \frac{1}{4}$

USING GRAPHS The equation of a circle is $(x - 2)^2 + (y + 3)^2 = 4$. Tell whether each point is *on* the circle, in the *interior* of the circle, or in the *exterior* of the circle.

33. $(0, 0)$

34. $(2, -4)$

35. $(0, -3)$

36. $(3, -1)$

37. $(1, -4)$

38. $(2, -5)$

39. $(2, 0)$

40. $(2.5, -3)$

🌐 **CELL PHONES** In Exercises 41 and 42, use the following information.
A cellular phone network uses towers to transmit calls. Each tower transmits to a circular area. On a grid of a city, the coordinates of the location and the radius each tower covers are as follows (integers represent miles): Tower A is at $(0, 0)$ and covers a 3 mile radius, Tower B is at $(5, 3)$ and covers a 2.5 mile radius, and Tower C is at $(2, 5)$ and covers a 2 mile radius.

41. Write the equations that represent the transmission boundaries of the towers. Graph each equation.

42. Tell which towers, if any, transmit to a phone located at $J(1, 1)$, $K(4, 2)$, $L(3.5, 4.5)$, $M(2, 2.8)$, or $N(1, 6)$.

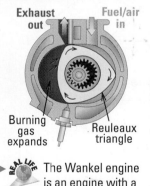
REULEAUX POLYGONS The figure at the right is called a *Reuleaux polygon*. It is not a true polygon because its sides are not straight. $\triangle ABC$ is equilateral.

43. $\overparen{JD}$ lies on a circle with center A and radius AD. Write an equation of this circle.

44. $\overparen{DE}$ lies on a circle with center B and radius BD. Write an equation of this circle.

45. 📐 **CONSTRUCTION** The remaining arcs of the polygon are constructed in the same way as $\overparen{JD}$ and $\overparen{DE}$ in Exercises 43 and 44. Construct a Reuleaux polygon on a piece of cardboard.

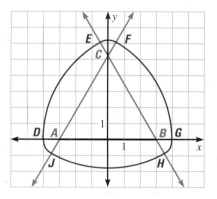

46. Cut out the Reauleaux polygon from Exercise 45. Roll it on its edge like a wheel and measure its height when it is in different orientations. Explain why a Reuleaux polygon is said to have constant width.

47. TRANSLATIONS Sketch the circle whose equation is $x^2 + y^2 = 16$. Then sketch the image of the circle after the translation $(x, y) \rightarrow (x - 2, y - 4)$. What is the equation of the image?

48. WRITING AN EQUATION A circle has a center (p, q) and is tangent to the x-axis. Write the standard equation of the circle.

Test Preparation

49. MULTIPLE CHOICE What is the standard form of the equation of a circle with center $(-3, 1)$ and radius 2?

   Ⓐ $(x - 3)^2 + (y - 1)^2 = 2$ **Ⓑ** $(x + 3)^2 + (y - 1)^2 = 2$

   Ⓒ $(x - 3)^2 + (y - 1)^2 = 4$ **Ⓓ** $(x + 3)^2 + (y - 1)^2 = 4$

50. MULTIPLE CHOICE The center of a circle is $(-3, 0)$ and its radius is 5. Which point does *not* lie on the circle?

   Ⓐ $(2, 0)$ **Ⓑ** $(0, 4)$ **Ⓒ** $(-3, 0)$ **Ⓓ** $(-3, -5)$ **Ⓔ** $(-8, 0)$

★ **Challenge**

51. CRITICAL THINKING ⊙A and ⊙B are externally tangent. Suppose you know the equation of ⊙A, the coordinates of the single point of intersection of ⊙A and ⊙B, and the radius of ⊙B. Do you know enough to find the equation of ⊙B? Explain.

xy USING ALGEBRA Find the missing coordinate of the center of the circle with the given characteristics.

EXTRA CHALLENGE
www.mcdougallittell.com

52. The center is $(1, b)$, the radius is 3, and a point on the circle is $(-2, 0)$.

53. The center is $(-3, b)$, the radius is 5, and a point on the circle is $(2, -2)$.

MIXED REVIEW

IDENTIFYING QUADRILATERALS What kind(s) of quadrilateral could *ABCD* be? *ABCD* is not drawn to scale. (Review 6.6)

54.   **55.**   **56.**

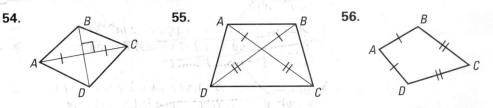

VECTORS Write the component form of vector $\overrightarrow{PQ}$. Use the component form to find the magnitude of $\overrightarrow{PQ}$ to the nearest tenth. (Review 9.7)

57. $P = (0, 0)$, $Q = (-6, 7)$ **58.** $P = (3, -4)$, $Q = (-11, 2)$

59. $P = (-6, -6)$, $Q = (9, -5)$ **60.** $P = (5, 6)$, $Q = (-3, 7)$

ANGLE BISECTORS Does *P* lie on the bisector of $\angle A$? Explain your reasoning. (Review 5.1)

61.   **62.**

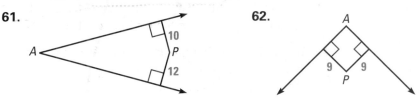

ACTIVITY 10.7

Using Technology

Investigating Points Equidistant from a Point and a Line

Point *P* and line *k* lie in a plane. Which points in the plane are equidistant from *P* and *k*? You can use geometry software to find out.

▶ **CONSTRUCT** Follow the steps to construct a line *k*, a point *P* not on *k*, and two points that are equidistant from *P* and *k*.

1 Draw a line *k* and a point *P* not on *k*. Near the corner of the screen, draw a segment and label it $\overline{AB}$.

2 Construct a line perpendicular to *k*. Label the intersection *C*. Construct a circle with center *C* and radius *AB*. The circle intersects the line perpendicular to *k* in two points. Choose the point that is on the same side of *k* as *P* and label it *D*. Construct a line through *D* parallel to *k*. Label this line *m*. Hide $\overleftrightarrow{CD}$, $\odot C$, *C*, and *D*.

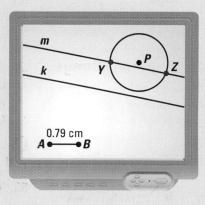

3 Construct a circle with center *P* and radius *AB*.

4 Draw the intersection points of circle *P* and line *m*. Label the points *Y* and *Z*.

▶ **INVESTIGATE**

1. Is *Y* equidistant from *P* and *k*? How do you know? Is *Z* equidistant from *P* and *k*? How do you know?

2. Drag point *B*. What happens to *m*? What happens to circle *P*? Do *Y* and *Z* remain equidistant from *P* and *k*?

3. Use the *Trace* feature to trace *Y* and *Z* as you slowly drag *B*. What shape is formed? You should recognize it from your algebra class.

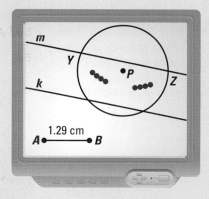

▶ **CONJECTURE**

4. Make a conjecture about the points in a plane that are equidistant from a line and a point in the plane.

EXTENSION

CRITICAL THINKING Use the *Coordinate* feature of the geometry software to find the coordinates of some points that are equidistant from the line $y = -\frac{1}{4}$ and the point $\left(0, \frac{1}{4}\right)$. Make and test a conjecture.

10.7

Locus

What you should learn

GOAL 1 Draw the locus of points that satisfy a given condition.

GOAL 2 Draw the locus of points that satisfy two or more conditions.

Why you should learn it

▼ To use **real-life** constraints, such as using seismograph readings to find an epicenter in **Example 4** and **Ex. 29**.

In ancient China, a seismometer like this one could measure the direction to an epicenter.

GOAL 1 DRAWING A LOCUS SATISFYING ONE CONDITION

A **locus** in a plane is the set of all points in a plane that satisfy a given condition or a set of given conditions. The word *locus* is derived from the Latin word for "location." The plural of locus is *loci*, pronounced "low-sigh."

A locus is often described as the path of an object moving in a plane. For instance, the reason that many clock faces are circular is that the locus of the end of a clock's minute hand is a circle.

EXAMPLE 1 *Finding a Locus*

Draw point *C* on a piece of paper. Draw and describe the locus of all points on the paper that are 3 inches from *C*.

SOLUTION

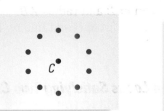

1 Draw point *C*. Locate several points 3 inches from *C*.

2 Recognize a pattern: the points lie on a circle.

3 Draw the circle.

▶ The locus of points on the paper that are 3 inches from *C* is a circle with center *C* and a radius of 3 inches.

CONCEPT SUMMARY	FINDING A LOCUS

To find the locus of points that satisfy a given condition, use the following steps.

1 Draw any figures that are given in the statement of the problem.

2 Locate several points that satisfy the given condition.

3 Continue drawing points until you can recognize the pattern.

4 Draw the locus and describe it in words.

GOAL 2 LOCI SATISFYING TWO OR MORE CONDITIONS

To find the locus of points that satisfy two or more conditions, first find the locus of points that satisfy each condition alone. Then find the intersection of these loci.

Logical Reasoning

EXAMPLE 2 *Drawing a Locus Satisfying Two Conditions*

Points *A* and *B* lie in a plane. What is the locus of points in the plane that are equidistant from points *A* and *B* and are a distance of *AB* from *B*?

SOLUTION

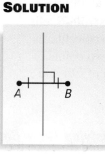

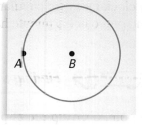

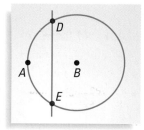

The locus of all points that are equidistant from *A* and *B* is the perpendicular bisector of $\overline{AB}$.

The locus of all points that are a distance of *AB* from *B* is the circle with center *B* and radius *AB*.

These loci intersect at *D* and *E*. So *D* and *E* are the locus of points that satisfy both conditions.

EXAMPLE 3 *Drawing a Locus Satisfying Two Conditions*

Point *P* is in the interior of ∠*ABC*. What is the locus of points in the interior of ∠*ABC* that are equidistant from both sides of ∠*ABC* and 2 inches from *P*? How does the location of *P* within ∠*ABC* affect the locus?

SOLUTION

The locus of points equidistant from both sides of ∠*ABC* is the angle bisector. The locus of points 2 inches from *P* is a circle. The intersection of the angle bisector and the circle depends on the location of *P*. The locus can be 2 points, 1 point, or 0 points.

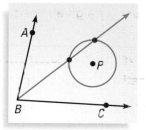

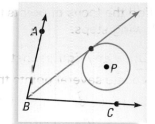

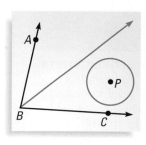

The locus is 2 points.

The locus is 1 point.

The locus is 0 points.

EARTHQUAKES The *epicenter* of an earthquake is the point on Earth's surface that is directly above the earthquake's origin. A seismograph can measure the distance to the epicenter, but not the direction to the epicenter. To locate the epicenter, readings from three seismographs in different locations are needed.

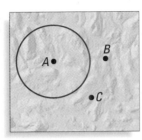

The reading from seismograph *A* tells you that the epicenter is somewhere on a circle centered at *A*.

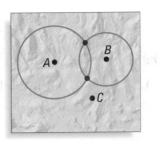

The reading from *B* tells you that the epicenter is one of the two points of intersection of ⊙*A* and ⊙*B*.

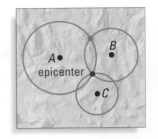

The reading from *C* tells you which of the two points of intersection is the epicenter.

EXAMPLE 4 *Finding a Locus Satisfying Three Conditions*

LOCATING AN EPICENTER You are given readings from three seismographs.

- At *A*(−5, 5), the epicenter is 4 miles away.
- At *B*(−4, −3.5), the epicenter is 5 miles away.
- At *C*(1, 1.5), the epicenter is 7 miles away.

Where is the epicenter?

SOLUTION

Each seismograph gives you a locus that is a circle.

Circle *A* has center (−5, 5) and radius 4.

Circle *B* has center (−4, −3.5) and radius 5.

Circle *C* has center (1, 1.5) and radius 7.

Draw the three circles in a coordinate plane. The point of intersection of the three circles is the epicenter.

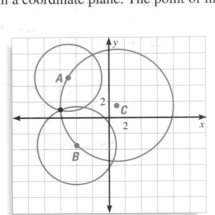

▶ The epicenter is at about (−6, 1).

GUIDED PRACTICE

Vocabulary Check ✓

1. The radius of ⊙C is 3 inches. The locus of points in the plane that are more than 3 inches from C is the ___?___ of ⊙C.

Concept Check ✓

2. Draw two points A and B on a piece of paper. Draw and describe the locus of points on the paper that are equidistant from A and B.

Skill Check ✓

Match the object with the locus of point P.

A. Arc **B.** Circle **C.** Parabola **D.** Line segment

3.   4.   5.   6.

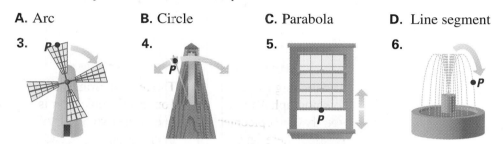

7. What is the locus of points in the coordinate plane that are equidistant from A(0, 0) and B(6, 0) and 5 units from A? Make a sketch.

8. Points C and D are in a plane. What is the locus of points in the plane that are 3 units from C and 5 units from D?

PRACTICE AND APPLICATIONS

STUDENT HELP

▶ **Extra Practice**
to help you master
skills is on p. 822.

🧩 **LOGICAL REASONING Draw the figure. Then sketch and describe the locus of points on the paper that satisfy the given condition.**

9. Point P, the locus of points that are 1 inch from P

10. Line k, the locus of points that are 1 inch from k

11. Point C, the locus of points that are no more than 1 inch from C

12. Line j, the locus of points that are at least 1 inch from j

🧩 **LOGICAL REASONING Copy the figure. Then sketch and describe the locus of points on the paper that satisfy the given condition(s).**

13. equidistant from j and k

14. in the interior of ∠A and equidistant from both sides of ∠A

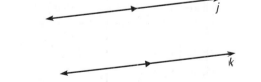

STUDENT HELP

▶ **HOMEWORK HELP**
Example 1: Exs. 9–23
Example 2: Exs. 14, 24,
      25
Example 3: Exs. 26, 27,
      31
Example 4: Exs. 19–25,
      28–30

15. midpoint of a radius of ⊙C

16. equidistant from r and s

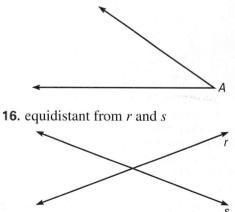

CRITICAL THINKING Draw $\overline{AB}$. Then sketch and describe the locus of points on the paper that satisfy the given condition.

17. the locus of points P such that $\angle PAB$ is $30°$

18. the locus of points Q such that $\triangle QAB$ is an isosceles triangle with base $\overline{AB}$

USING ALGEBRA Use the graph at the right to write equation(s) for the locus of points in the coordinate plane that satisfy the given condition.

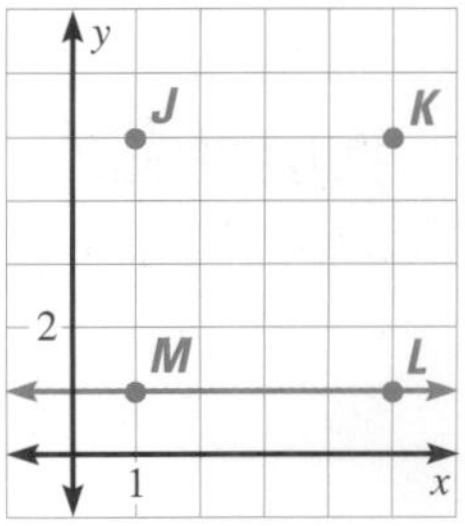

19. equidistant from J and K

20. equidistant from J and M

21. equidistant from M and K

22. 3 units from K

23. 3 units from $\overleftrightarrow{ML}$

COORDINATE GEOMETRY Copy the graph. Then sketch and describe the locus of points in the plane that satisfy the given conditions. Explain your reasoning.

24. equidistant from A and B and less than 4 units from the origin

25. equidistant from C and D and 1 unit from line k

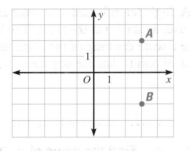

LOGICAL REASONING Sketch and describe the locus. How do the positions of the given points affect the locus?

26. Point R and line k are in a plane. What is the locus of points in the plane that are 1 unit from k and 2 units from R?

27. Noncollinear points P, Q, and R are in a plane. What is the locus of points in the plane that are equidistant from P and Q and 4 units from R?

EARTHQUAKES In Exercises 28–30, use the following information.
You are given seismograph readings from three locations.

- At $A(-5, 6)$, the epicenter is 13 miles away.
- At $B(6, 2)$, the epicenter is 10 miles away.
- At $O(0, 0)$, the epicenter is 6 miles away.

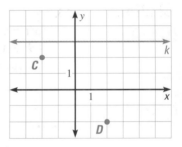

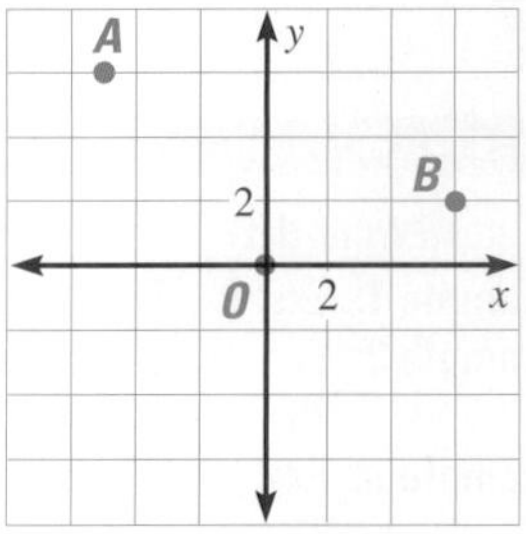

28. For each seismograph, graph the locus of all possible locations for the epicenter.

29. Where is the epicenter?

30. People could feel the earthquake up to 14 miles away. If your friend lives at $(-3, 20)$, could your friend feel the earthquake? Explain your reasoning.

FOCUS ON APPLICATIONS

REAL LIFE **SAN ANDREAS FAULT** In 1857, an earthquake on this fault made a river run upstream and flung the water out of a lake, stranding fish miles away.

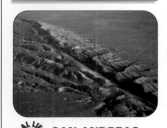

31. 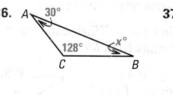 **TECHNOLOGY** Using geometry software, construct and label a line k and a point P not on k. Construct the locus of points that are 2 units from P. Construct the locus of points that are 2 units from k. What is the locus of points that are 2 units from P and 2 units from k? Drag P and k to determine how the location of P and k affects the locus.

32. CRITICAL THINKING Given points A and B, describe the locus of points P such that $\triangle APB$ is a right triangle.

33. MULTIPLE CHOICE What is the locus of points in the coordinate plane that are 3 units from the origin?

    Ⓐ The line $x = 3$ Ⓑ The line $y = 3$ Ⓒ The circle $x^2 + y^2 = 3$

    Ⓓ The circle $x^2 + y^2 = 9$ Ⓔ None of the above

34. MULTIPLE CHOICE Circles C and D are externally tangent. The radius of circle C is 6 centimeters and the radius of circle D is 9 centimeters. What is the locus of all points that are a distance of CD from point C?

    Ⓐ Circle with center C and a radius of 3 centimeters

    Ⓑ Circle with center D and a radius of 3 centimeters

    Ⓒ Circle with center C and a radius of 15 centimeters

    Ⓓ Circle with center D and a radius of 15 centimeters

★ **Challenge**

35. 🌐 **DOG LEASH** A dog's leash is tied to a stake at the corner of its doghouse, as shown at the right. The leash is 9 feet long. Make a scale drawing of the doghouse and sketch the locus of points that the dog can reach.

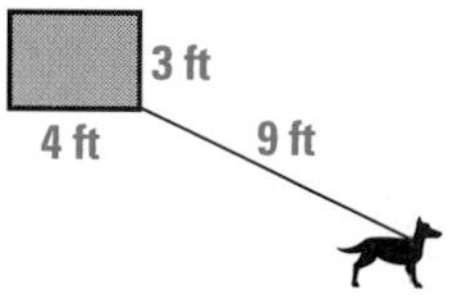

3 ft
4 ft   9 ft

MIXED REVIEW

FINDING ANGLE MEASURES Find the value of x. (Review 4.1, 4.6, 6.1 for 11.1)

36.

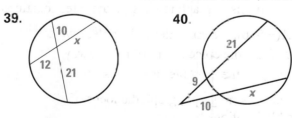

A   30°
128°
C   B $x°$

37.

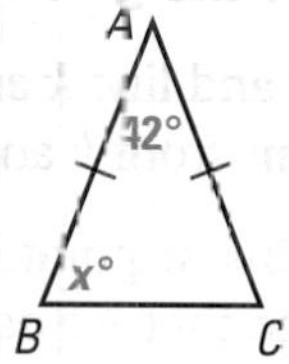

A
42°
$x°$
B   C

38.

106° 96°
$x°$ 88°

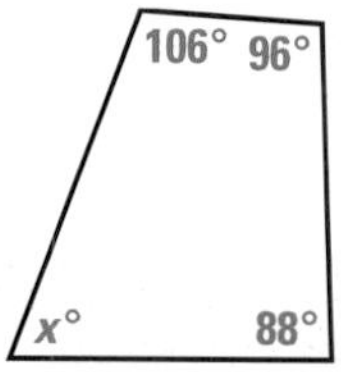

FINDING LENGTHS Find the value of x. (Review 10.5)

39.

10
x
12
21

40.

21
9
x
10

41.

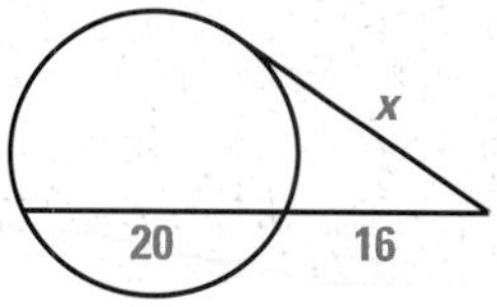

20   16
x

DRAWING GRAPHS Graph the equation. (Review 10.6)

42. $x^2 + y^2 = 81$ **43.** $(x + 6)^2 + (y - 4)^2 = 9$

44. $x^2 + (y - 7)^2 = 100$ **45.** $(x - 4)^2 + (y - 5)^2 = 1$

Graph the equation. (Lesson 10.6)

1. $x^2 + y^2 = 100$

2. $(x + 3)^2 + (y + 3)^2 = 49$

3. $(x - 1)^2 + y^2 = 36$

4. $(x + 4)^2 + (y - 7)^2 = 25$

5. The point $(-3, -9)$ is on a circle whose center is $(2, -2)$. What is the standard equation of the circle? (Lesson 10.6)

6. Draw point P on a piece of paper. Draw and describe the locus of points on the paper that are more than 6 units and less than 9 units from P. (Lesson 10.7)

7. Draw the locus of all points in a plane that are 4 centimeters from a ray $\overrightarrow{AB}$. (Lesson 10.7)

8. SOCCER In a soccer game, play begins with a kick-off. All players not involved in the kick-off must stay at least 10 yards from the ball. The ball is in the center of the field. Sketch a 50 yard by 100 yard soccer field with a ball in the center. Then draw and describe the locus of points at which the players not involved in the kick-off can stand. (Lesson 10.7)

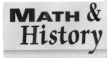

History of Timekeeping

INTERNET APPLICATION LINK
www.mcdougallittell.com

THEN

SCHOLARS BELIEVE THAT the practice of dividing a circle into 360 equal parts has its origins in ancient Babylon. Around 1000 B.C., the Babylonians divided the day (one rotation of Earth) into 12 equal time units. Each unit was divided into 30 smaller units. So one of Earth's rotations was divided into $12 \times 30 = 360$ equal parts.

1. Before the introduction of accurate clocks, other civilizations divided the time between sunrise and sunset into 12 equal "temporary hours." These hours varied in length, depending on the time of year.

The table at the right shows the times of sunrise and sunset in New York City. To the nearest minute, find the length of a temporary hour on June 21 and the length of a temporary hour on December 21.

New York City		
Date	**Sunrise**	**Sunset**
June 21	4:25 A.M.	7:30 P.M.
Dec. 21	7:16 A.M.	4:31 P.M.

NOW

TODAY, a day is divided into 24 hours. Atomic clocks are used to give the correct time with an accuracy of better than one second in six million years.

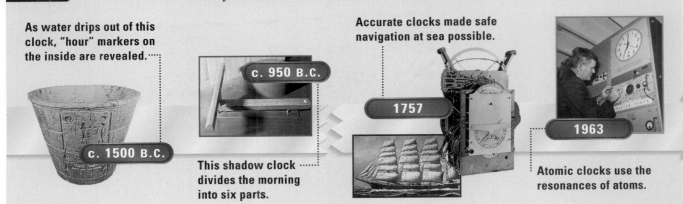

As water drips out of this clock, "hour" markers on the inside are revealed.

c. 1500 B.C.

c. 950 B.C.

This shadow clock divides the morning into six parts.

Accurate clocks made safe navigation at sea possible.

1757

1963

Atomic clocks use the resonances of atoms.

Chapter Summary

WHAT did you learn?

Identify segments and lines related to circles.
(10.1)

Use properties of tangents of circles. (10.1)

Use properties of arcs and chords of circles.
(10.2)

Use properties of inscribed angles and inscribed
polygons of circles. (10.3)

Use angles formed by tangents, chords, and
secants. (10.4)

Find the lengths of segments of tangents, chords,
and lines that intersect a circle. (10.5)

Find and graph the equation of a circle. (10.6)

Draw loci in a plane that satisfy one or more
conditions. (10.7)

WHY did you learn it?

Lay the foundation for work with circles.

Find real-life distances, such as the radius of a silo.
(p. 597)

Solve real-life problems such as analyzing a
procedure used to locate an avalanche rescue
beacon. (p. 609)

Reach conclusions about angles in real-life objects,
such as your viewing angle at the movies. (p. 614)

Estimate distances, such as the maximum distance
at which fireworks can be seen. (p. 625)

Find real-life distances, such as the distance a
satellite transmits a signal. (p. 634)

Solve real-life problems, such as determining
cellular phone coverage. (p. 639)

Make conclusions based on real-life constraints,
such as using seismograph readings to locate the
epicenter of an earthquake. (p. 644)

How does Chapter 10 fit into the BIGGER PICTURE of geometry?

In this chapter, you learned that circles have many connections with other
geometric figures. For instance, you learned that a quadrilateral can be inscribed
in a circle if and only if its opposite angles are supplementary. Circles also occur
in natural settings, such as the ripples in a pond, and in manufactured structures,
such as a cross section of a storage tank. The properties of circles that you
studied in this chapter will help you solve problems related to mathematics and
the real world.

STUDY STRATEGY

Did you answer your questions?

Your record of questions about
difficult exercises, following the
study strategy on page 594, may
resemble this one.

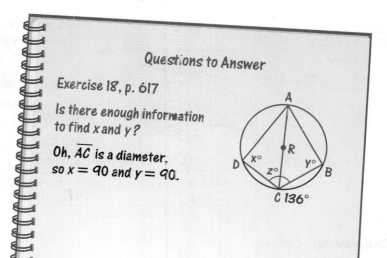

Questions to Answer

Exercise 18, p. 617

Is there enough information
to find x and y?

Oh, $\overline{AC}$ is a diameter,
so $x = 90$ and $y = 90$.

Chapter Review

- circle, p. 595
- center of circle, p. 595
- radius of circle, p. 595
- congruent circles, p. 595
- diameter of circle, p. 595
- chord, secant, tangent, p. 595
- tangent circles, p. 596

- concentric circles, p. 596
- common tangent, p. 596
- interior of a circle, p. 596
- exterior of a circle, p. 596
- point of tangency, p. 597
- central angle, p. 603
- minor arc and its measure, p. 603

- major arc and its measure, p. 603
- semicircle, p. 603
- congruent arcs, p. 604
- inscribed angle, p. 613
- intercepted arc, p. 613
- inscribed polygon, p. 615
- circumscribed circle, p. 615

- tangent segment, p. 630
- secant segment, p. 630
- external segment, p. 630
- standard equation of a circle, p. 636
- locus, p. 642

10.1 TANGENTS TO CIRCLES

Examples on pp. 595–598

EXAMPLES In $\odot R$, R is the center. $\overline{RJ}$ is a radius, and $\overline{JL}$ is a diameter. $\overline{MP}$ is a chord, and $\overleftrightarrow{MP}$ is a secant. $\overleftrightarrow{KS}$ is a tangent and so it is perpendicular to the radius $\overline{RS}$. $\overline{KS} \cong \overline{KP}$ because they are two tangents from the same exterior point.

Name a point, segment, line, or circle that represents the phrase.

1. Diameter of $\odot P$
2. Point of tangency of $\odot Q$
3. Chord of $\odot P$
4. Center of larger circle
5. Radius of $\odot Q$
6. Common tangent
7. Secant
8. Point of tangency of $\odot P$ and $\odot Q$
9. Is $\angle PBC$ a right angle? Explain.
10. Show that $\triangle SCD$ is isosceles.

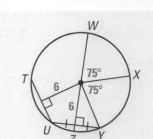

10.2 ARCS AND CHORDS

Examples on pp. 603–606

EXAMPLES $\widehat{WX}$ and $\widehat{XY}$ are congruent minor arcs with measure 75°.

$\widehat{WYX}$ is a major arc, and $m\widehat{WYX} = 360° - 75° = 285°$. Chords $\overline{TU}$ and $\overline{UY}$ are congruent because they are equidistant from the center of the circle. $\overline{TU} \cong \overline{UY}$ because $\overline{TU} \cong \overline{UY}$. Chord $\overline{WZ}$ is a perpendicular bisector of chord $\overline{UY}$, so $\overline{WZ}$ is a diameter.

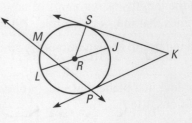

Use ⊙Q in the diagram to find the measure of the indicated arc. $\overline{AD}$ is a diameter, and $m\widehat{CE} = 121°$.

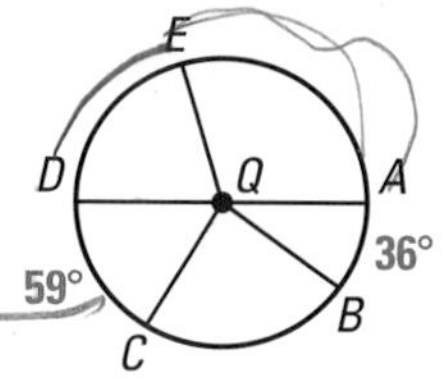

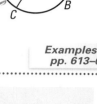

11. $\widehat{DE}$ 12. $\widehat{AE}$ 13. $\widehat{AEC}$

14. $\widehat{BC}$ 15. $\widehat{BDC}$ 16. $\widehat{BDA}$

10.3   INSCRIBED ANGLES

Examples on pp. 613–616

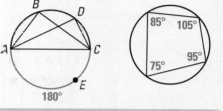

EXAMPLES $\angle ABC$ and $\angle ADC$ are congruent inscribed angles, each with measure $\frac{1}{2} \cdot m\widehat{AEC} = 90°$. Because $\triangle ADC$ is an inscribed right triangle, $\overline{AC}$ is a diameter. The quadrilateral can be inscribed in a circle because its opposite angles are supplementary.

Kite *ABCD* is inscribed in ⊙*P*. Decide whether the statement is *true* or *false*. Explain your reasoning.

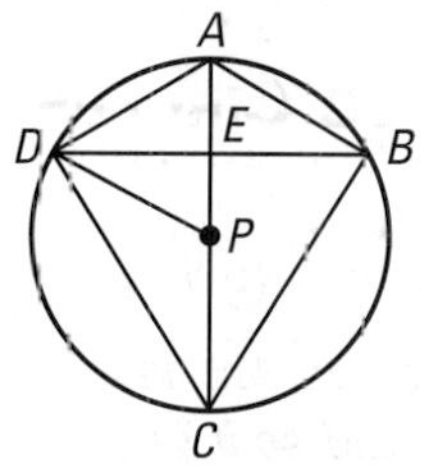

17. $\angle ABC$ and $\angle ADC$ are right angles.

18. $m\angle ACD = \frac{1}{2} \cdot m\angle AED$

19. $m\angle DAB + m\angle BCD = 180°$

10.4   OTHER ANGLE RELATIONSHIPS IN CIRCLES

Examples on pp. 621–623

EXAMPLES

$m\angle ABD = \frac{1}{2} \cdot 120°$ $m\angle CED = \frac{1}{2}(30° + 40°)$ $m\angle CED = \frac{1}{2}(100° - 20°)$

$= 60°$ $= 35°$ $= 40°$

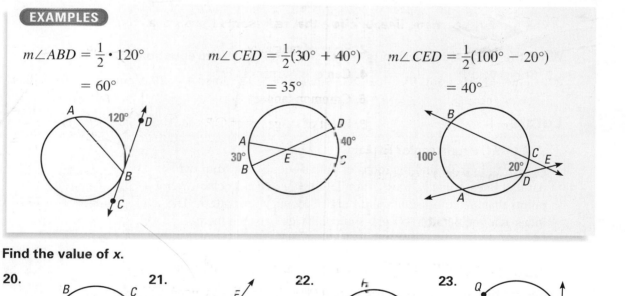

Find the value of *x*.

20.   21.   22.   23.

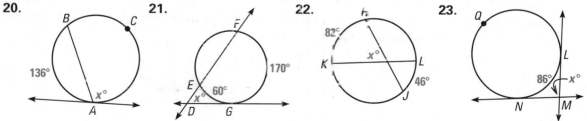

SEGMENT LENGTHS IN CIRCLES

Examples on
pp. 629–631

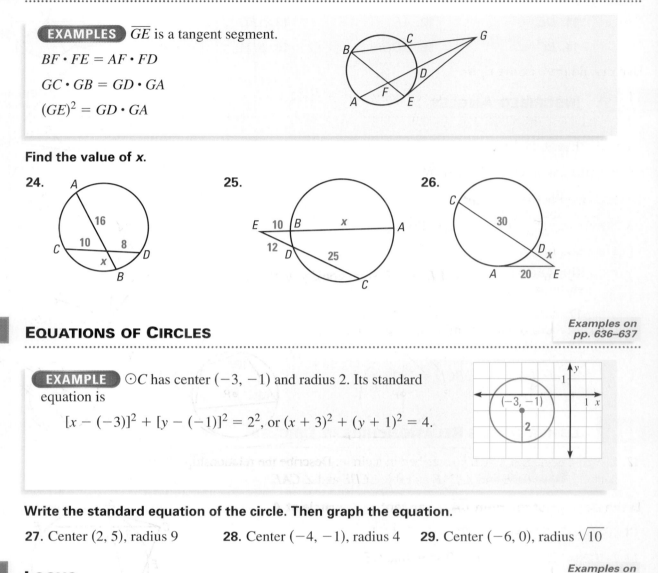

EXAMPLES $\overline{GE}$ is a tangent segment.

$BF \cdot FE = AF \cdot FD$

$GC \cdot GB = GD \cdot GA$

$(GE)^2 = GD \cdot GA$

Find the value of *x*.

24. **25.** **26.**

EQUATIONS OF CIRCLES

Examples on
pp. 636–637

EXAMPLE $\odot C$ has center $(-3, -1)$ and radius 2. Its standard equation is

$$[x - (-3)]^2 + [y - (-1)]^2 = 2^2, \text{ or } (x + 3)^2 + (y + 1)^2 = 4.$$

Write the standard equation of the circle. Then graph the equation.

27. Center $(2, 5)$, radius 9 **28.** Center $(-4, -1)$, radius 4 **29.** Center $(-6, 0)$, radius $\sqrt{10}$

LOCUS

Examples on
pp. 642–644

EXAMPLE To find the locus of points equidistant from two parallel lines, *r* and *s*, draw 2 parallel lines, *r* and *s*. Locate several points that are equidistant from *r* and *s*. Identify the pattern. The locus is a line parallel to *r* and *s* and halfway between them.

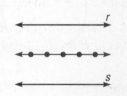

Draw the figure. Then sketch and describe the locus of points on the paper that satisfy the given condition(s).

30. $\triangle RST$, the locus of points that are equidistant from *R* and *S*

31. Line ℓ, the locus of points that are no more than 4 inches from ℓ

32. $\overline{AB}$ with length 4 cm, the locus of points 3 cm from *A* and 4 cm from *B*

Chapter Test

Use the diagram at the right.

1. Which theorems allow you to conclude that $\overline{JK} \cong \overline{MK}$?

2. Find the lengths of $\overline{JK}$, $\overline{MP}$, and $\overline{PK}$.

3. Show that $\overparen{JL} \cong \overparen{LM}$.

4. Find the measures of $\overparen{JM}$ and $\overparen{JN}$.

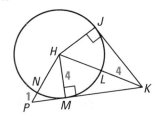

Use the diagram at the right.

5. Show that $\overparen{AF} \cong \overparen{AB}$ and $\overline{FH} \cong \overline{BH}$.

6. Show that $\overparen{FE} \cong \overparen{BC}$.

7. Suppose you were given that $PH = PG$. What could you conclude?

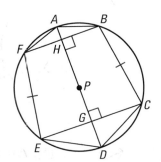

Find the measure of each numbered angle in $\odot P$.

8.

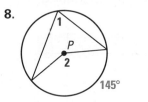

9.

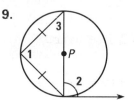

10.

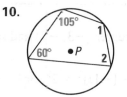

11.

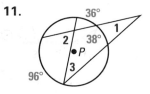

12. Sketch a pentagon $ABCDE$ inscribed in a circle. Describe the relationship between (a) $\angle CDE$ and $\angle CAE$ and (b) $\angle CBE$ and $\angle CAE$.

In the diagram at the right $\overline{CA}$ is tangent to the circle at A.

13. If $AG = 2$, $GD = 9$, and $BG = 3$, find GF.

14. If $CF = 12$, $CB = 3$, and $CD = 9$, find CE.

15. If $BF = 9$ and $CB = 3$, find CA.

16. Graph the circle with equation $(x - 4)^2 + (y + 6)^2 = 64$.

17. Sketch and describe the locus of points in the coordinate plane that are equidistant from $(0, 3)$ and $(3, 0)$ and 4 units from the point $(4, 0)$.

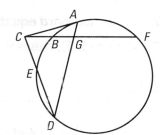

18. 🌐 **ROCK CIRCLE** This circle of rock is in the Ténéré desert in the African country of Niger. The circle is about 60 feet in diameter. About a mile away to the north, south, east, and west, stone arrows point away from the circle. It's not known who created the circle or why. Suppose the center of the circle is at $(30, 30)$ on a grid measured in units of feet. Write an equation for the circle.

19. 🌐 **DOG RUN** A dog on a leash is able to move freely along a cable that is attached to the ground. The leash allows the dog to move anywhere within 3.5 feet from any point on the 10-foot straight cable. Draw and describe the locus of points that the dog can reach.

▶ **TEST-TAKING STRATEGY** Read each test question carefully. Always look for shortcuts that will allow you to work through a problem more quickly.

1. MULTIPLE CHOICE How many common tangents do the circles at the right have?

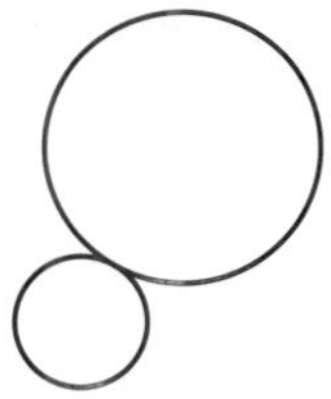

Ⓐ 0   Ⓑ 1

Ⓒ 2   Ⓓ 3

Ⓔ 4

2. MULTIPLE CHOICE Suppose $\overline{AB}$ is a diameter of $\odot O$, line r is tangent to $\odot O$ at A, and line s is tangent to $\odot O$ at B. Which statements are true?

I. r bisects $\overline{AB}$.   **II.** $OA = 2 \cdot AB$

III. $r \parallel s$

Ⓐ I only   Ⓑ II only   Ⓒ III only

Ⓓ I and II   Ⓔ II and III

3. MULTIPLE CHOICE Use the diagram to find the value of x.

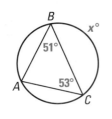

Ⓐ 38   Ⓑ 106

Ⓒ 114   Ⓓ 76

Ⓔ 152

4. MULTIPLE CHOICE Find the length of a chord that is 21 cm from the center of a circle with radius 29 cm.

Ⓐ 20 cm   Ⓑ 40 cm   Ⓒ 42 cm

Ⓓ 8 cm   Ⓔ 16 cm

5. MULTIPLE CHOICE If $m\angle A = 42°$, find the value of y in the diagram.

Ⓐ 42   Ⓑ 138

Ⓒ 318   Ⓓ 222

Ⓔ cannot be determined

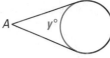

QUANTITATIVE COMPARISON In Exercises 6 and 7, use the diagram to choose the statement that is true. $\overleftrightarrow{KF}$ is tangent to the circle.

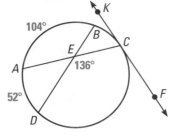

Ⓐ The quantity in column A is greater.

Ⓑ The quantity in column B is greater.

Ⓒ The two quantities are equal.

Ⓓ The relationship cannot be determined from the given information.

	Column A	Column B
6.	$m\widehat{DC}$	168°
7.	$m\widehat{ABC}$	$m\angle FCA$

8. MULTIPLE CHOICE A diameter of a circle has endpoints $(-4, 8)$ and $(6, 2)$. What is an equation of the circle?

Ⓐ $(x - 1)^2 + (y - 5)^2 = 34$

Ⓑ $(x + 1)^2 + (y + 5)^2 = 34$

Ⓒ $(x - 6)^2 + (y - 2)^2 = 136$

Ⓓ $(x - 1)^2 + (y - 5)^2 = 136$

Ⓔ $(x + 1)^2 + (y - 5)^2 = 34$

9. MULTIPLE CHOICE Describe the locus of all points in the coordinate plane that are equidistant from points $(-3, 1)$ and $(1, 9)$ and 2 units from the line $x = -7$.

Ⓐ $(-5, 7)$

Ⓑ The line $y = -5$

Ⓒ $(-5, 8)$ and $(-9, 10)$

Ⓓ $(-5, 7)$ and $(-9, 9)$

Ⓔ $(-7, 8)$

MULTI-STEP PROBLEM Quadrilateral *EFGH* is inscribed in a circle.
$m\angle E = x^2 + 15$, $m\angle F = 27x$, and $m\angle G = 6x^2 - 10$.

10. Find the value of x.

11. Find the measure of each angle of the quadrilateral.

12. If $m\overparen{GH} = 30°$, find the measures of $\overparen{EF}$, $\overparen{FG}$, and $\overparen{EH}$.

MULTI-STEP PROBLEM The points *A*(0, 0), *B*(3, 0), and *C*(0, 4) lie on ⊙*P*.

13. Explain why $\overline{BC}$ is a diameter of ⊙*P*.

14. Find the coordinates of point *P* and the radius of ⊙*P*.

15. Write an equation of ⊙*P*.

16. What is the locus of points in the coordinate plane that are equidistant from *A*, *B*, and *C*?

MULTI-STEP PROBLEM In Exercises 17–20, use the diagram at the right.
$\overrightarrow{CJ}$ is tangent to ⊙*E* at *C* and $\overline{KH}$ is tangent to ⊙*E* at *H*.

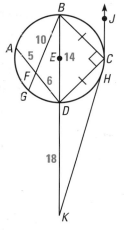

17. Find the length of the segment, the measure of the arc, or the measure of the angle. Round your answer to two decimal places, if necessary.

   a. *GF*   b. *KH*   c. $m\overparen{BGD}$

   d. $m\overparen{BC}$ e. $m\angle CDB$ f. $m\angle BCJ$

18. Name two congruent arcs. Justify your answer.

19. If $m\angle BFD = 120°$, find $m\overparen{AG}$.

20. If $m\angle K = 16°$, find the measures of $\overparen{BH}$ and $\overparen{HD}$.

MULTI-STEP PROBLEM Sketch and describe the locus.

21. The locus of points that are equidistant from *A* and *B*.

22. The locus of points that are 2 inches or less from $\overleftrightarrow{AB}$.

23. The locus of points that are equidistant from *A* and *B* and are 2 inches or less from $\overleftrightarrow{AB}$.

MULTI-STEP PROBLEM In Exercises 24–26, use the diagram. Television cameras are positioned at *A*, *B*, and *Q*. The stage is an arc of ⊙*Q*.

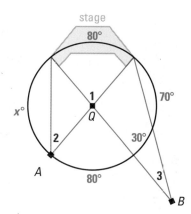

24. Find the value of x.

25. Find the measures of $\angle 1$, $\angle 2$, and $\angle 3$.

26. *Writing* Suppose you are operating the camera located at point *B*. If you want a 20° angle of the stage, should you move closer to the stage or farther away? Explain.

MULTI-STEP PROBLEM You are visiting a museum that has a circular yurt on display. You are not allowed to enter the yurt. To estimate its radius, you stand 5 feet from the yurt and measure 10 feet to a point of tangency.

27. Sketch a diagram to model the problem.

28. Find the radius and diameter of the yurt. Explain your method.

Algebra Review

EXAMPLE 1   *Solving Literal Equations*

Given the formula for the surface area of a right cylinder, solve for h.
$S = 2\pi r^2 + 2\pi rh$

$$S = 2\pi r(r + h) \qquad \text{or} \qquad S - 2\pi r^2 = 2\pi rh$$

$$\frac{S}{2\pi r} = r + h \qquad\qquad\qquad \frac{(S - 2\pi r^2)}{2\pi r} = h$$

$$\frac{S}{2\pi r} - r = h$$

EXERCISES

Solve the literal equation for the indicated variable. Assume variables are positive.

1. $A = \ell w$; w **2.** $V = \frac{4}{3}\pi r^3$; r **3.** $A = \frac{1}{2}bh$; h **4.** $A = \frac{1}{2}h(b_1 + b_2)$; b_1

5. $A = \pi r^2$; r **6.** $C = 2\pi r$; r **7.** $V = s^3$; s **8.** $P = 2\ell + 2w$; ℓ

9. $V = \ell wh$; h **10.** $V = \pi r^2 h$; h **11.** $S = 6s^2$; s **12.** $a^2 + b^2 = c^2$; b

EXAMPLE 2   *Algebraic Expressions*

a. Write an expression for seven less than a number.
$x - 7$

b. Write an equation for three less than six times a number is five times the same number plus 5, then solve.
$6x - 3 = 5x + 5$
$x - 3 = 5$
$x = 8$

EXERCISES

Write the expression or equation. Solve the equations.

13. Five plus a number

14. A number squared increased by the square root of 2

15. Twice a number decreased by fourteen

16. Six less than three times a number

17. A number plus two decreased by nine times the number

18. Half of a number plus three times the number

19. The product of five and a number decreased by seven equals thirteen.

20. Sixteen less than twice a number is 10.

21. Twice a number increased by the product of the number and fourteen results in forty-eight.

22. Half of a number is three times the sum of the number and five.

EXAMPLE 3 **Percent Problems**

a. What number is 12% of 75?
$$x = 0.12(75)$$
$$x = 9$$

b. 6 is what percent of 40?
$$6 = 40p$$
$$0.15 = p$$
$$p = 15\%$$

EXERCISES

Solve.

23. What number is 30% of 120?

24. What distance is 15% of 340 miles?

25. What number is 71% of 200?

26. How much money is 50% of $25?

27. 34 is what percent of 136?

28. 11 dogs is what percent of 50 dogs?

29. 200 is what percent of 50?

30. 8 weeks is what percent of a year?

31. 3 is 30% of what number?

32. 16 meters is 64% of what distance?

33. If sales tax is 8%, how much tax is charged on a $25.95 purchase?

34. 15 out of 18 players on a team came to a tournament. What percent of the players were absent?

EXAMPLE 4 **Simplifying Rational Expressions**

Simplify.

a. $\dfrac{8x^2 + 12x}{4x^2 + 16x}$

$\dfrac{4x(2x + 3)}{4x(x + 4)}$

$\dfrac{2x + 3}{x + 4}$

b. $\dfrac{y^2 - 9}{y^2 + 6y + 9}$

$\dfrac{(y + 3)(y - 3)}{(y + 3)(y + 3)}$

$\dfrac{y - 3}{y + 3}$

EXERCISES

Simplify.

35. $\dfrac{5x}{10x^2}$

36. $\dfrac{16a^3}{8a}$

37. $\dfrac{(5x^2 + x)}{(5x + 1)}$

38. $\dfrac{9w^3 + 27w}{3w^3 + 9w}$

39. $\dfrac{5a + 10}{5a - 40}$

40. $\dfrac{5x^2 + 15x}{30x^2 - 5x}$

41. $\dfrac{14d^2 - 2d}{6d^2 + 8d}$

42. $\dfrac{2y - 12}{24 - 2y}$

43. $\dfrac{36s^2 - 4s}{4s^2 - 12s}$

44. $\dfrac{-5h + 1}{h + 1}$

45. $\dfrac{t^2 - 1}{t^2 + 2t + 1}$

46. $\dfrac{m^2 - 4m + 4}{m^2 - 4}$

AREA OF POLYGONS AND CIRCLES

▶  *Where do hexagons occur in nature?*

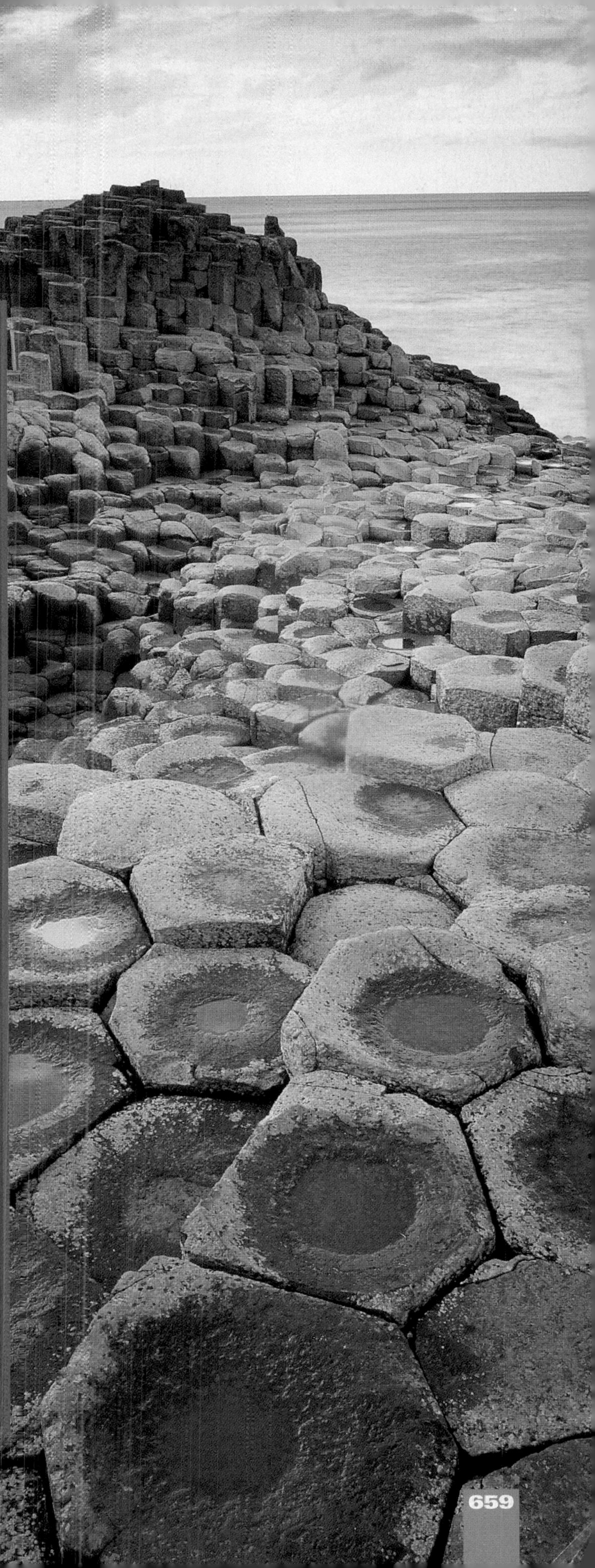

CHAPTER 11

APPLICATION: Area of Columns

Basaltic columns are geological formations that result from rapidly cooling lava.

Most basaltic columns are hexagonal, or six sided. The Giant's Causeway in Ireland, pictured here, features hexagonal columns ranging in size from 15 to 20 inches across and up to 82 feet high.

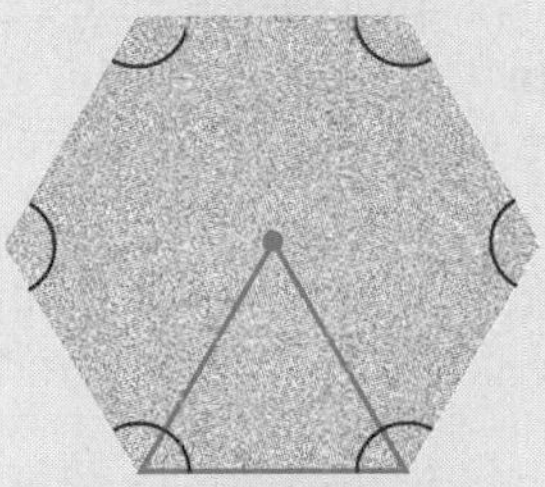

Think & Discuss

1. A regular hexagon, like the one above, can be divided into equilateral triangles by drawing segments to connect the center to each vertex. How many equilateral triangles make up the hexagon?
2. Find the sum of the angles in a hexagon by adding together the base angles of the equilateral triangles.

Learn More About It

You will learn more about the shape of the top of a basaltic column in Exercise 34 on p. 673.

INTERNET **APPLICATION LINK** Visit www.mcdougallittell.com for more information about basaltic columns.

Study Guide

PREVIEW

What's the chapter about?

Chapter 11 is about **areas of polygons and circles**. In Chapter 11, you'll learn

- how to find angle measures and areas of polygons.

- how to compare perimeters and areas of similar figures.

- how to find the circumference and area of a circle and to find other measures related to circles.

KEY VOCABULARY

▶ **Review**
- polygon, p. 322
- *n*-gon, p. 322
- convex polygon, p. 323
- regular polygon, p. 323
- similar polygons, p. 473
- trigonometric ratio, p. 558

- circle, p. 595
- center of a circle, p. 595
- radius of a circle, p. 595
- measure of an arc, p. 603
▶ **New**
- apothem of a polygon, p. 670

- central angle of a regular polygon, p. 671
- circumference, p. 683
- arc length, p. 683
- sector of a circle, p. 692
- probability, p. 699
- geometric probability, p. 699

PREPARE

Are you ready for the chapter?

SKILL REVIEW Do these exercises to review key skills that you'll apply in this chapter. See the given **reference page** if there is something you don't understand.

1. Find the area of a triangle with height 8 in. and base 12 in. **(Review p. 51)**

2. In $\triangle ABC$, $m\angle A = 57°$ and $m\angle C = 79°$. Find the measure of $\angle B$ and the measure of an exterior angle at each vertex. **(Review pp. 196–197)**

3. If $\triangle DEF \sim \triangle XYZ$, $DF = 8$, and $XZ = 12$, find each ratio.

    a. $\dfrac{XY}{DE}$ **b.** $\dfrac{\text{Perimeter of } \triangle DEF}{\text{Perimeter of } \triangle XYZ}$ **(Review pp. 475, 480)**

4. A right triangle has sides of length 20, 21, and 29. Find the measures of the acute angles of the triangle to the nearest tenth. **(Review pp. 567–568)**

STUDY
STRATEGY

Here's a study strategy!

A *concept map* is a diagram that highlights the connections between ideas. Drawing a concept map for a chapter can help you focus on the important ideas and on how they are related.

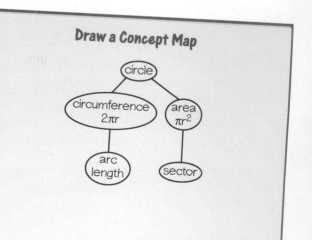

Draw a Concept Map

Angle Measures in Polygons

GOAL 1 **MEASURES OF INTERIOR AND EXTERIOR ANGLES**

You have already learned that the name of a polygon depends on the number of sides in the polygon: triangle, quadrilateral, pentagon, hexagon, and so forth. The sum of the measures of the interior angles of a polygon also depends on the number of sides.

In Lesson 6.1, you found the sum of the measures of the interior angles of a quadrilateral by dividing the quadrilateral into two triangles. You can use this triangle method to find the sum of the measures of the interior angles of any convex polygon with n sides, called an n-gon.

▶ **ACTIVITY**
Developing Concepts

Investigating the Sum of Polygon Angle Measures

Draw examples of 3-sided, 4-sided, 5-sided, and 6-sided convex polygons. In each polygon, draw all the diagonals from one vertex. Notice that this divides each polygon into triangular regions.

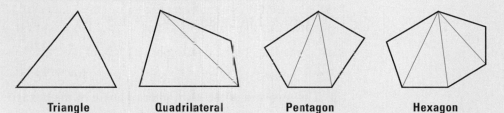

| Triangle | Quadrilateral | Pentagon | Hexagon |

Complete the table below. What is the pattern in the sum of the measures of the interior angles of any convex n-gon?

Polygon	Number of sides	Number of triangles	Sum of measures of interior angles
Triangle	3	1	$1 \cdot 180° = 180°$
Quadrilateral	?	?	$2 \cdot 180° = 360°$
Pentagon	?	?	?
Hexagon	?	?	?
⋮	⋮	⋮	⋮
n-gon	n	?	?

STUDENT HELP

Look Back
For help with *regular* polygons, see p. 323.

You may have found in the activity that the sum of the measures of the interior angles of a convex *n*-gon is $(n - 2) \cdot 180°$. This relationship can be used to find the measure of each interior angle in a *regular n*-gon, because the angles are all congruent. Exercises 43 and 44 ask you to write proofs of the following results.

THEOREMS ABOUT INTERIOR ANGLES

THEOREM 11.1 *Polygon Interior Angles Theorem*

The sum of the measures of the interior angles of a convex *n*-gon is $(n - 2) \cdot 180°$.

COROLLARY TO THEOREM 11.1

The measure of each interior angle of a regular *n*-gon is
$$\frac{1}{n} \cdot (n - 2) \cdot 180°, \text{ or } \frac{(n - 2) \cdot 180°}{n}.$$

Using Algebra

EXAMPLE 1 *Finding Measures of Interior Angles of Polygons*

Find the value of *x* in the diagram shown.

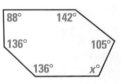

SOLUTION

The sum of the measures of the interior angles of any hexagon is $(6 - 2) \cdot 180° = 4 \cdot 180° = 720°$.

Add the measures of the interior angles of the hexagon.

$$136° + 136° + 88° + 142° + 105° + x° = 720° \qquad \text{The sum is 720°.}$$
$$607 + x = 720 \qquad \text{Simplify.}$$
$$x = 113 \qquad \text{Subtract 607 from each side.}$$

▶ The measure of the sixth interior angle of the hexagon is 113°.

EXAMPLE 2 *Finding the Number of Sides of a Polygon*

The measure of each interior angle of a regular polygon is 140°. How many sides does the polygon have?

SOLUTION

$$\frac{1}{n} \cdot (n - 2) \cdot 180° = 140° \qquad \text{Corollary to Theorem 11.1}$$
$$(n - 2) \cdot 180 = 140n \qquad \text{Multiply each side by } n.$$
$$180n - 360 = 140n \qquad \text{Distributive property}$$
$$40n = 360 \qquad \text{Addition and subtraction properties of equality}$$
$$n = 9 \qquad \text{Divide each side by 40.}$$

▶ The polygon has 9 sides. It is a regular nonagon.

STUDENT HELP

HOMEWORK HELP
Visit our Web site
www.mcdougallittell.com
for extra examples.

The diagrams below show that the sum of the measures of the *exterior* angles of any convex polygon is 360°. You can also find the measure of each exterior angle of a *regular* polygon. Exercises 45 and 46 ask for proofs of these results.

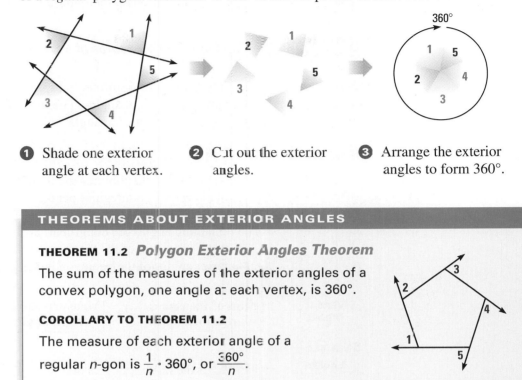

① Shade one exterior angle at each vertex.

② Cut out the exterior angles.

③ Arrange the exterior angles to form 360°.

THEOREMS ABOUT EXTERIOR ANGLES

THEOREM 11.2 *Polygon Exterior Angles Theorem*

The sum of the measures of the exterior angles of a convex polygon, one angle at each vertex, is 360°.

COROLLARY TO THEOREM 11.2

The measure of each exterior angle of a regular n-gon is $\frac{1}{n} \cdot 360°$, or $\frac{360°}{n}$.

EXAMPLE 3 *Finding the Measure of an Exterior Angle*

Using Algebra

Find the value of x in each diagram.

a.

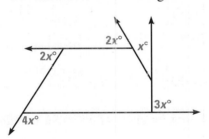

b.

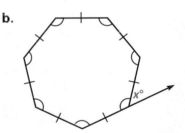

SOLUTION

a. $2x° + x° + 3x° + 4x° + 2x° = 360°$ **Use Theorem 11.2.**

$\qquad\qquad\qquad\quad 12x = 360$ **Combine like terms.**

$\qquad\qquad\qquad\quad\ \ x = 30$ **Divide each side by 12.**

b. $x° = \frac{1}{7} \cdot 360°$ **Use $n = 7$ in the Corollary to Theorem 11.2.**

$\quad\ \approx 51.4$ **Use a calculator.**

▶ The measure of each exterior angle of a regular heptagon is about 51.4°.

GOAL 2 USING ANGLE MEASURES IN REAL LIFE

You can use Theorems 11.1 and 11.2 and their corollaries to find angle measures.

EXAMPLE 4 *Finding Angle Measures of a Polygon*

SOFTBALL A home plate marker for a softball field is a pentagon. Three of the interior angles of the pentagon are right angles. The remaining two interior angles are congruent. What is the measure of each angle?

SOLUTION

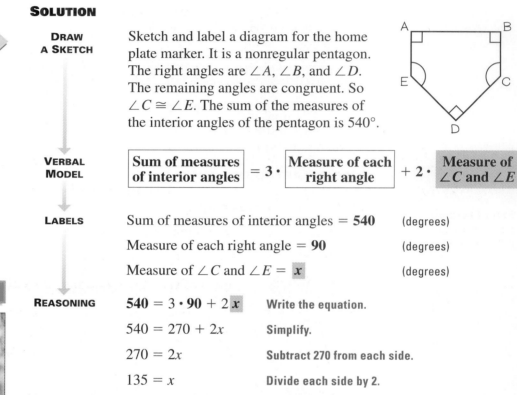

PROBLEM SOLVING STRATEGY

DRAW A SKETCH Sketch and label a diagram for the home plate marker. It is a nonregular pentagon. The right angles are $\angle A$, $\angle B$, and $\angle D$. The remaining angles are congruent. So $\angle C \cong \angle E$. The sum of the measures of the interior angles of the pentagon is 540°.

VERBAL MODEL

| Sum of measures of interior angles | = 3 · | Measure of each right angle | + 2 · | Measure of $\angle C$ and $\angle E$ |

LABELS

Sum of measures of interior angles = **540**   (degrees)

Measure of each right angle = **90**   (degrees)

Measure of $\angle C$ and $\angle E$ = **x**   (degrees)

REASONING

$540 = 3 \cdot 90 + 2x$ Write the equation.

$540 = 270 + 2x$ Simplify.

$270 = 2x$ Subtract 270 from each side.

$135 = x$ Divide each side by 2.

▶ So, the measure of each of the two congruent angles is 135°.

EXAMPLE 5 *Using Angle Measures of a Regular Polygon*

SPORTS EQUIPMENT If you were designing the home plate marker for some new type of ball game, would it be possible to make a home plate marker that is a regular polygon with each interior angle having a measure of (**a**) 135°? (**b**) 145°?

SOLUTION

a. Solve the equation $\frac{1}{n} \cdot (n - 2) \cdot 180° = 135°$ for n. You get $n = 8$.

▶ Yes, it would be possible. A polygon can have 8 sides.

b. Solve the equation $\frac{1}{n} \cdot (n - 2) \cdot 180° = 145°$ for n. You get $n \approx 10.3$.

▶ No, it would not be possible. A polygon cannot have 10.3 sides.

FOCUS ON PEOPLE

JOAN JOYCE set a number of softball pitching records from 1956–1975. She delivered 40 pitches to slugger Ted Williams during an exhibition game in 1962. Williams only connected twice, for one foul ball and one base hit.

GUIDED PRACTICE

Vocabulary Check ✓   1. Name an *interior angle* and an *exterior angle* of the polygon shown at the right.

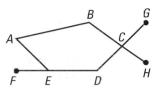

Concept Check ✓   2. How many exterior angles are there in an *n*-gon? Are they all considered when using the Polygon Exterior Angles Theorem? Explain.

Skill Check ✓   **Find the value of *x*.**

3.   4. 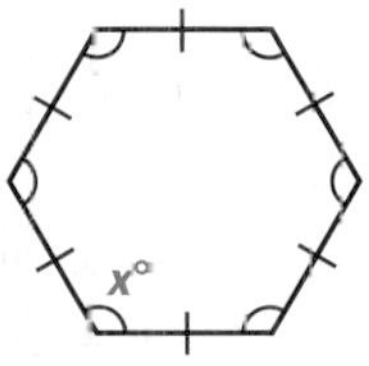   5.

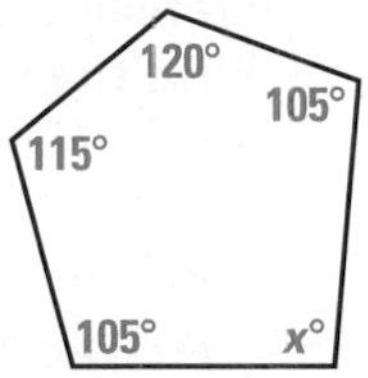

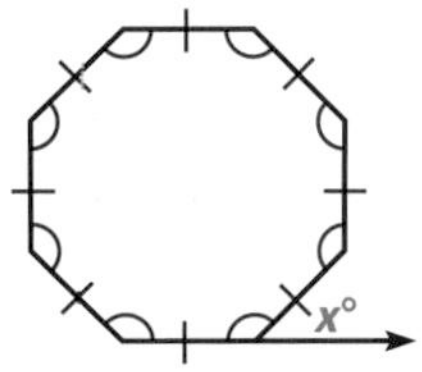

PRACTICE AND APPLICATIONS

STUDENT HELP

▶ **Extra Practice**
to help you master skills is on p. 823.

SUMS OF ANGLE MEASURES Find the sum of the measures of the interior angles of the convex polygon.

6. 10-gon   **7.** 12-gon   **8.** 15-gon   **9.** 18-gon

10. 20-gon   **11.** 30-gon   **12.** 40-gon   **13.** 100-gon

ANGLE MEASURES In Exercises 14–19, find the value of *x*.

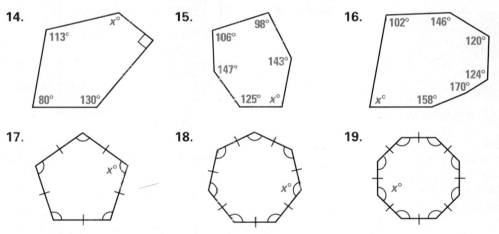

STUDENT HELP

▶ **HOMEWORK HELP**
Example 1: Exs. 6–16, 20, 21
Example 2: Exs. 17–19, 22–28
Example 3: Exs. 29–38
Example 4: Exs. 39, 40, 49, 50
Example 5: Exs. 51–54

20. A convex quadrilateral has interior angles that measure 80°, 110°, and 80°. What is the measure of the fourth interior angle?

21. A convex pentagon has interior angles that measure 60°, 80°, 120°, and 140°. What is the measure of the fifth interior angle?

DETERMINING NUMBER OF SIDES In Exercises 22–25, you are given the measure of each interior angle of a regular *n*-gon. Find the value of *n*.

22. 144°   **23.** 120°   **24.** 140°   **25.** 157.5°

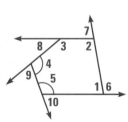

CONSTRUCTION **Use a compass, protractor, and ruler to check the results of Example 2 on page 662.**

26. Draw a large angle that measures 140°. Mark congruent lengths on the sides of the angle.

27. From the end of one of the congruent lengths in Exercise 26, draw the second side of another angle that measures 140°. Mark another congruent length along this new side.

28. Continue to draw angles that measure 140° until a polygon is formed. Verify that the polygon is regular and has 9 sides.

DETERMINING ANGLE MEASURES **In Exercises 29–32, you are given the number of sides of a regular polygon. Find the measure of each exterior angle.**

29. 12 **30.** 11 **31.** 21 **32.** 15

DETERMINING NUMBER OF SIDES **In Exercises 33–36, you are given the measure of each exterior angle of a regular *n*-gon. Find the value of *n*.**

33. 60° **34.** 20° **35.** 72° **36.** 10°

37. A convex hexagon has exterior angles that measure 48°, 52°, 55°, 62°, and 68°. What is the measure of the exterior angle of the sixth vertex?

38. What is the measure of each exterior angle of a regular decagon?

FOCUS ON APPLICATIONS

STAINED GLASS is tinted glass that has been cut into shapes and arranged to form a picture or design. The pieces of glass are held in place by strips of lead.

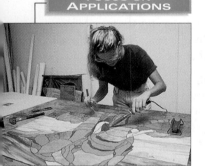

STAINED GLASS WINDOWS **In Exercises 39 and 40, the purple and green pieces of glass are in the shape of regular polygons. Find the measure of each interior angle of the red and yellow pieces of glass.**

39.

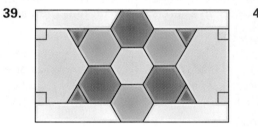

40.

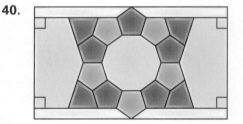

41. FINDING MEASURES OF ANGLES In the diagram at the right, $m\angle 2 = 100°$, $m\angle 8 = 40°$, $m\angle 4 = m\angle 5 = 110°$. Find the measures of the other labeled angles and explain your reasoning.

42. *Writing* Explain why the sum of the measures of the interior angles of any two *n*-gons with the same number of sides (two octagons, for example) is the same. Do the *n*-gons need to be regular? Do they need to be similar?

43. **PROOF** Use *ABCDE* to write a paragraph proof to prove Theorem 11.1 for pentagons.

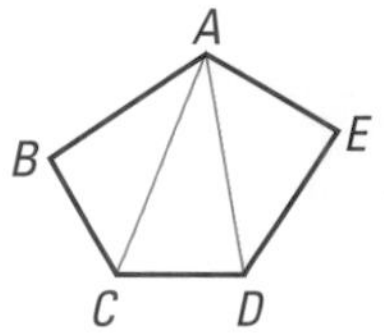

44. **PROOF** Use a paragraph proof to prove the Corollary to Theorem 11.1.

45. ▶ **PROOF** Use this plan to write a paragraph proof of Theorem 11.2.
Plan for Proof In a convex n-gon, the sum of the measures of an interior angle and an adjacent exterior angle at any vertex is 180°. Multiply by n to get the sum of all such sums at each vertex. Then subtract the sum of the interior angles derived by using Theorem 11.1.

46. ▶ **PROOF** Use a paragraph proof to prove the Corollary to Theorem 11.2.

△ **TECHNOLOGY** In Exercises 47 and 48, use geometry software to construct a polygon. At each vertex, extend one of the sides of the polygon to form an exterior angle.

47. Measure each exterior angle and verify that the sum of the measures is 360°.

48. Move any vertex to change the shape of your polygon. What happens to the measures of the exterior angles? What happens to their sum?

49. 🌐 **HOUSES** Pentagon *ABCDE* is an outline of the front of a house. Find the measure of each angle.

50. 🌐 **TENTS** Heptagon *PQRSTUV* is an outline of a camping tent. Find the unknown angle measures.

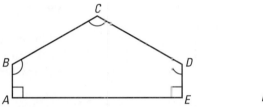

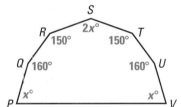

POSSIBLE POLYGONS Would it be possible for a regular polygon to have interior angles with the angle measure described? Explain.

51. 150°   **52.** 90°   **53.** 72°   **54.** 18°

🆇🆈 **USING ALGEBRA** In Exercises 55 and 56, you are given a function and its graph. In each function, n is the number of sides of a polygon and $f(n)$ is measured in degrees. How does the function relate to polygons? What happens to the value of $f(n)$ as n gets larger and larger?

55. $f(n) = \dfrac{180n - 360}{n}$

56. $f(n) = \dfrac{360}{n}$

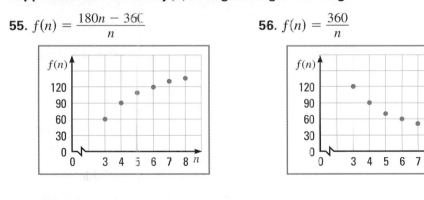

57. 🪙 **LOGICAL REASONING** You are shown part of a convex n-gon. The pattern of congruent angles continues around the polygon. Use the Polygon Exterior Angles Theorem to find the value of n.

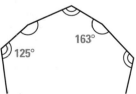

QUANTITATIVE COMPARISON In Exercises 58–61, choose the statement that is true about the given quantities.

Ⓐ The quantity in column A is greater.

Ⓑ The quantity in column B is greater.

Ⓒ The two quantities are equal.

Ⓓ The relationship cannot be determined from the given information.

	Column A	Column B
58.	The sum of the interior angle measures of a decagon	The sum of the interior angle measures of a 15-gon
59.	The sum of the exterior angle measures of an octagon	$8(45°)$
60.	$m\angle 1$ 118° 135° 91° 156° 146° 1	$m\angle 2$ 72° 70° 111° 2
61.	Number of sides of a polygon with an exterior angle measuring 72°	Number of sides of a polygon with an exterior angle measuring 144°

★ **Challenge**

62. Polygon *STUVWXYZ* is a regular octagon. Suppose sides $\overline{ST}$ and $\overline{UV}$ are extended to meet at a point *R*. Find the measure of $\angle TRU$.

MIXED REVIEW

FINDING AREA **Find the area of the triangle described.** (Review 1.7 for 11.2)

63. base: 11 inches; height: 5 inches   **64.** base: 43 meters; height: 11 meters

65. vertices: $A(2, 0)$, $B(7, 0)$, $C(5, 15)$ **66.** vertices: $D(-3, 3)$, $E(3, 3)$, $F(-7, 11)$

VERIFYING RIGHT TRIANGLES **Tell whether the triangle is a right triangle.** (Review 9.3)

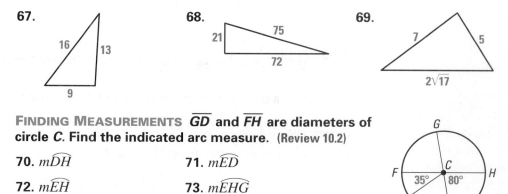

67. (16, 13, 9)   **68.** (21, 75, 72)   **69.** (7, 5, $2\sqrt{17}$)

FINDING MEASUREMENTS $\overline{GD}$ and $\overline{FH}$ are diameters of circle *C*. **Find the indicated arc measure.** (Review 10.2)

70. $m\widehat{DH}$ **71.** $m\widehat{ED}$

72. $m\widehat{EH}$ **73.** $m\widehat{EHG}$

What you should learn

GOAL 1 Find the area of an equilateral triangle.

GOAL 2 Find the area of a regular polygon, such as the area of a dodecagon in **Example 4**.

Why you should learn it

▼ To solve **real-life** problems, such as finding the area of a hexagonal mirror on the Hobby-Eberly Telescope in **Exs. 45 and 46**.

GOAL 1 FINDING THE AREA OF AN EQUILATERAL TRIANGLE

The area of *any* triangle with base length b and height h is given by $A = \frac{1}{2}bh$. The following formula for equilateral triangles, however, uses only the side length.

THEOREM

THEOREM 11.3 *Area of an Equilateral Triangle*

The area of an equilateral triangle is one fourth the square of the length of the side times $\sqrt{3}$.

$$A = \frac{1}{4}\sqrt{3}\,s^2$$

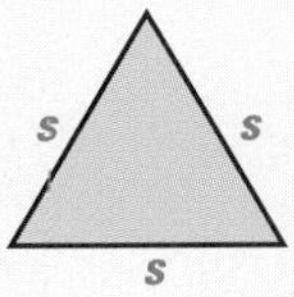

EXAMPLE 1 *Proof of Theorem 11.3*

Prove Theorem 11.3. Refer to the figure below.

SOLUTION

GIVEN ▶ $\triangle ABC$ is equilateral.

PROVE ▶ Area of $\triangle ABC$ is $A = \frac{1}{4}\sqrt{3}\,s^2$.

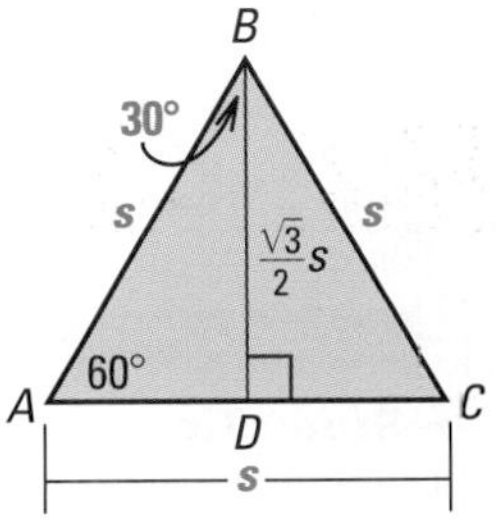

Paragraph Proof Draw the altitude from B to side $\overline{AC}$. Then $\triangle ABD$ is a 30°-60°-90° triangle. From Lesson 9.4, the length of $\overline{BD}$, the side opposite the 60° angle in $\triangle ABD$, is $\frac{\sqrt{3}}{2}s$. Using the formula for the area of a triangle,

$$A = \frac{1}{2}bh = \frac{1}{2}(s)\left(\frac{\sqrt{3}}{2}s\right) = \frac{1}{4}\sqrt{3}\,s^2.$$

EXAMPLE 2 *Finding the Area of an Equilateral Triangle*

Find the area of an equilateral triangle with 8 inch sides.

STUDENT HELP

→ **Study Tip**
Be careful with radical signs. Notice in Example 1 that $\sqrt{3}s^2$ and $\sqrt{3s^2}$ do not mean the same thing.

SOLUTION

Use $s = 8$ in the formula from Theorem 11.3.

$$A = \frac{1}{4}\sqrt{3}\,s^2 = \frac{1}{4}\sqrt{3}\,(8^2) = \frac{1}{4}\sqrt{3}\,(64) = \frac{1}{4}(64)\sqrt{3} = 16\sqrt{3} \text{ square inches}$$

▶ Using a calculator, the area is about 27.7 square inches.

GOAL 2 FINDING THE AREA OF A REGULAR POLYGON

You can use equilateral triangles to find the area of a regular hexagon.

Investigating the Area of a Regular Hexagon

Use a protractor and ruler to draw a regular hexagon. Cut out your hexagon. Fold and draw the three lines through opposite vertices. The point where these lines intersect is the *center* of the hexagon.

1 How many triangles are formed? What kind of triangles are they?

2 Measure a side of the hexagon. Find the area of one of the triangles. What is the area of the entire hexagon? Explain your reasoning.

Think of the hexagon in the activity above, or another regular polygon, as inscribed in a circle.

The **center of the polygon** and **radius of the polygon** are the center and radius of its circumscribed circle, respectively.

The distance from the center to any side of the polygon is called the **apothem of the polygon.** The apothem is the height of a triangle between the center and two consecutive vertices of the polygon.

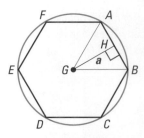

Hexagon *ABCDEF* with center *G*, radius *GA*, and apothem *GH*

STUDENT HELP

► Study Tip
In a regular polygon, the length of each side is the same. If this length is s and there are n sides, then the perimeter P of the polygon is $n \cdot s$, or $P = ns$.

As in the activity, you can find the area of any regular n-gon by dividing the polygon into congruent triangles.

A = area of one triangle · number of triangles

$= \left(\frac{1}{2} \cdot \text{apothem} \cdot \text{side length } s \right) \cdot \text{number of sides}$

$= \frac{1}{2} \cdot \text{apothem} \cdot \text{number of sides} \cdot \text{side length } s$

$= \frac{1}{2} \cdot \text{apothem} \cdot \text{perimeter of polygon}$

The number of congruent triangles formed will be the same as the number of sides of the polygon.

This approach can be used to find the area of any regular polygon.

THEOREM

THEOREM 11.4 *Area of a Regular Polygon*
The area of a regular n-gon with side length s is half the product of the apothem a and the perimeter P, so $A = \frac{1}{2}aP$, or $A = \frac{1}{2}a \cdot ns$.

A **central angle of a regular polygon** is an angle whose vertex is the center and whose sides contain two consecutive vertices of the polygon. You can divide 360° by the number of sides to find the measure of each central angle of the polygon.

EXAMPLE 3 **Finding the Area of a Regular Polygon**

A regular pentagon is inscribed in a circle with radius 1 unit. Find the area of the pentagon.

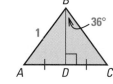

SOLUTION

To apply the formula for the area of a regular pentagon, you must find its apothem and perimeter.

The measure of central $\angle ABC$ is $\frac{1}{5} \cdot 360°$, or $72°$.

STUDENT HELP

Look Back
For help with trigonometric ratios, see p. 558.

In isosceles triangle $\triangle ABC$, the altitude to base $\overline{AC}$ also bisects $\angle ABC$ and side $\overline{AC}$. The measure of $\angle DBC$, then, is $36°$. In right triangle $\triangle BDC$, you can use trigonometric ratios to find the lengths of the legs.

$$\cos 36° = \frac{BD}{BC} \qquad\qquad \sin 36° = \frac{DC}{BC}$$

$$= \frac{BD}{1} \qquad\qquad\qquad = \frac{DC}{1}$$

$$= BD \qquad\qquad\qquad\quad = DC$$

▶ So, the pentagon has an apothem of $a = BD = \cos 36°$ and a perimeter of $P = 5(AC) = 5(2 \cdot DC) = 10 \sin 36°$. The area of the pentagon is

$$A = \frac{1}{2}aP = \frac{1}{2}(\cos 36°)(10 \sin 36°) \approx 2.38 \text{ square units.}$$

EXAMPLE 4 **Finding the Area of a Regular Dodecagon**

FOCUS ON APPLICATIONS

PENDULUMS The enclosure on the floor underneath the Foucault Pendulum at the Houston Museum of Natural Sciences in Houston, Texas, is a regular dodecagon with a side length of about 4.3 feet and a radius of about 8.3 feet. What is the floor area of the enclosure?

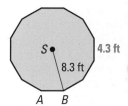

SOLUTION

A dodecagon has 12 sides. So, the perimeter of the enclosure is

$$P \approx 12(4.3) = 51.6 \text{ feet.}$$

In $\triangle SBT$, $BT = \frac{1}{2}(BA) = \frac{1}{2}(4.3) = 2.15$ feet. Use the Pythagorean Theorem to find the apothem ST.

$$a = \sqrt{8.3^2 - 2.15^2} \approx 8 \text{ feet}$$

▶ So, the floor area of the enclosure is

$$A = \frac{1}{2}aP \approx \frac{1}{2}(8)(51.6) = 206.4 \text{ square feet.}$$

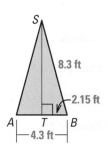

FOUCAULT PENDULUMS
swing continuously in a straight line. Watching the pendulum, though, you may think its path shifts. Instead, it is Earth and you that are turning. The floor under this pendulum in Texas rotates fully about every 48 hours.

APPLICATION LINK
www.mcdougallittell.com

GUIDED PRACTICE

Vocabulary Check ✔

In Exercises 1–4, use the diagram shown.

1. Identify the *center* of polygon *ABCDE*.

2. Identify the *radius* of the polygon.

3. Identify a *central angle* of the polygon.

4. Identify a segment whose length is the *apothem*.

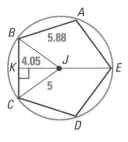

Concept Check ✔

5. In a regular polygon, how do you find the measure of each central angle?

Skill Check ✔

6. What is the area of an equilateral triangle with 3 inch sides?

🌐 **STOP SIGN The stop sign shown is a regular octagon. Its perimeter is about 80 inches and its height is about 24 inches.**

7. What is the measure of each central angle?

8. Find the apothem, radius, and area of the stop sign.

PRACTICE AND APPLICATIONS

STUDENT HELP

▶ **Extra Practice** to help you master skills is on p. 823.

FINDING AREA Find the area of the triangle.

9.

10.

11.

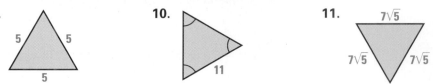

MEASURES OF CENTRAL ANGLES Find the measure of a central angle of a regular polygon with the given number of sides.

12. 9 sides   **13.** 12 sides   **14.** 15 sides   **15.** 180 sides

FINDING AREA Find the area of the inscribed regular polygon shown.

16.

17.

18.

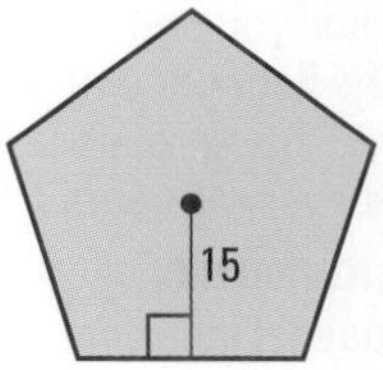

STUDENT HELP

▶ **HOMEWORK HELP**
Example 1: Exs. 9–11, 17, 19, 25, 33
Example 2: Exs. 9–11, 17, 19, 25, 33
Example 3: Exs. 12–24, 26, 34
Example 4: Exs. 34, 45–49

PERIMETER AND AREA Find the perimeter and area of the regular polygon.

19.

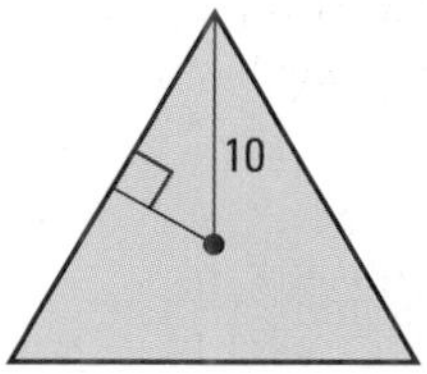

20.

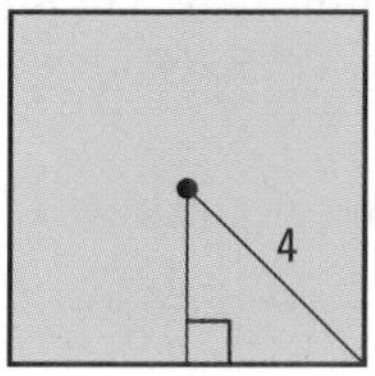

21.

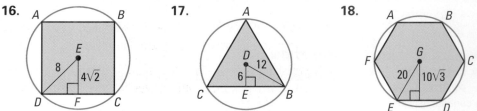

PERIMETER AND AREA In Exercises 22–24, find the perimeter and area of the regular polygon.

22.

23.

24.

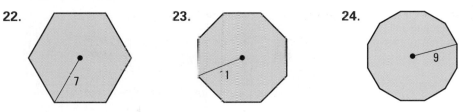

25. AREA Find the area of an equilateral triangle that has a height of 15 inches.

26. AREA Find the area of a regular dodecagon (or 12-gon) that has 4 inch sides.

LOGICAL REASONING Decide whether the statement is *true* or *false*. Explain your choice.

27. The area of a regular polygon of fixed radius r increases as the number of sides increases.

28. The apothem of a regular polygon is always less than the radius.

29. The radius of a regular polygon is always less than the side length.

AREA In Exercises 30–32, find the area of the regular polygon. The area of the portion shaded in red is given. Round answers to the nearest tenth.

30. Area = $16\sqrt{3}$ **31.** Area = $4 \tan 67.5°$ **32.** Area = $\tan 54°$

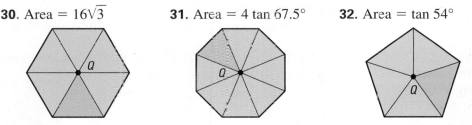

33. USING THE AREA FORMULAS Show that the area of a regular hexagon is six times the area of an equilateral triangle with the same side length.

$\left(\textit{Hint}: \text{Show that for a hexagon with side lengths } s, \frac{1}{2}aP = 6 \cdot \left(\frac{1}{4}\sqrt{3}s^2\right).\right)$

34. BASALTIC COLUMNS Suppose the top of one of the columns along the Giant's Causeway (see p. 659) is in the shape of a regular hexagon with a diameter of 18 inches. What is its apothem?

CONSTRUCTION In Exercises 35–39, use a straightedge and a compass to construct a regular hexagon and an equilateral triangle.

35. Draw $\overline{AB}$ with a length of 1 inch. Open the compass to 1 inch and draw a circle with that radius.

36. Using the same compass setting, mark off equal parts along the circle.

37. Connect the six points where the compass marks and circle intersect to draw a regular hexagon.

38. What is the area of the hexagon?

39. *Writing* Explain how you could use this construction to construct an equilateral triangle.

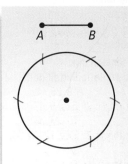

STUDENT HELP

HOMEWORK HELP
Visit our Web site www.mcdougallittell for help with construction in Exs. 40–44.

CONSTRUCTION In Exercises 40–44, use a straightedge and a compass to construct a regular pentagon as shown in the diagrams below.

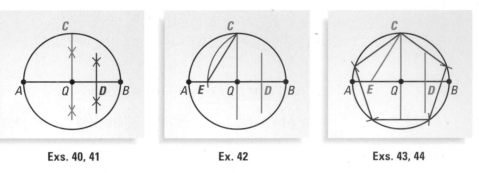

Exs. 40, 41

Ex. 42

Exs. 43, 44

40. Draw a circle with center Q. Draw a diameter $\overline{AB}$. Construct the perpendicular bisector of $\overline{AB}$ and label its intersection with the circle as point C.

41. Construct point D, the midpoint of $\overline{QB}$.

42. Place the compass point at D. Open the compass to the length DC and draw an arc from C so it intersects $\overline{AB}$ at a point, E. Draw $\overline{CE}$.

43. Open the compass to the length CE. Starting at C, mark off equal parts along the circle.

44. Connect the five points where the compass marks and circle intersect to draw a regular pentagon. What is the area of your pentagon?

FOCUS ON CAREERS

ASTRONOMERS use physics and mathematics to study the universe, including the sun, moon, planets, stars, and galaxies.

CAREER LINK
www.mcdougallittell.com

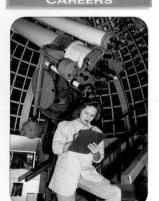

TELESCOPES In Exercises 45 and 46, use the following information.
The Hobby-Eberly Telescope in Fort Davis, Texas, is the largest optical telescope in North America. The primary mirror for the telescope consists of 91 smaller mirrors forming a hexagon shape. Each of the smaller mirror parts is itself a hexagon with side length 0.5 meter.

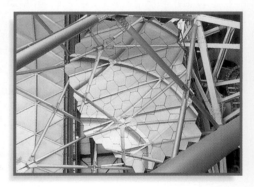

45. What is the apothem of one of the smaller mirrors?

46. Find the perimeter and area of one of the smaller mirrors.

TILING In Exercises 47–49, use the following information.
You are tiling a bathroom floor with tiles that are regular hexagons, as shown. Each tile has 6 inch sides. You want to choose different colors so that no two adjacent tiles are the same color.

47. What is the minimum number of colors that you can use?

48. What is the area of each tile?

49. The floor that you are tiling is rectangular. Its width is 6 feet and its length is 8 feet. At least how many tiles of each color will you need?

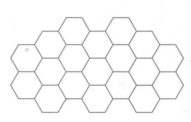

QUANTITATIVE COMPARISON In Exercises 50–52, choose the statement that is true about the given quantities.

(A) The quantity in column A is greater.

(B) The quantity in column B is greater.

(C) The two quantities are equal.

(D) The relationship cannot be determined from the given information.

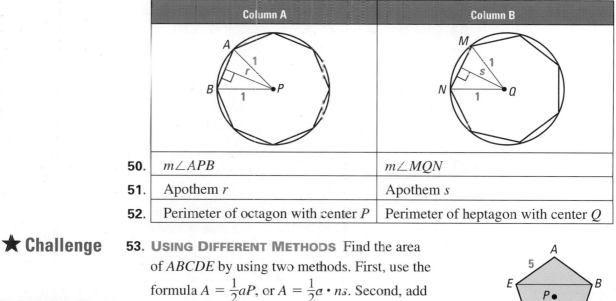

	Column A	Column B
50.	$m\angle APB$	$m\angle MQN$
51.	Apothem r	Apothem s
52.	Perimeter of octagon with center P	Perimeter of heptagon with center Q

★ **Challenge**

EXTRA CHALLENGE
www.mcdougallittell.com

53. USING DIFFERENT METHODS Find the area of $ABCDE$ by using two methods. First, use the formula $A = \frac{1}{2}aP$, or $A = \frac{1}{2}a \cdot ns$. Second, add the areas of the smaller polygons. Check that both methods yield the same area.

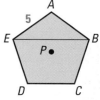

MIXED REVIEW

SOLVING PROPORTIONS Solve the proportion. (Review 8.1 for 11.3)

54. $\dfrac{x}{6} = \dfrac{11}{12}$ **55.** $\dfrac{20}{4} = \dfrac{15}{z}$ **56.** $\dfrac{12}{x+7} = \dfrac{13}{x}$ **57.** $\dfrac{x+6}{9} = \dfrac{x}{11}$

USING SIMILAR POLYGONS In the diagram shown, $\triangle ABC \sim \triangle DEF$. Use the figures to determine whether the statement is true. (Review 8.3 for 11.3)

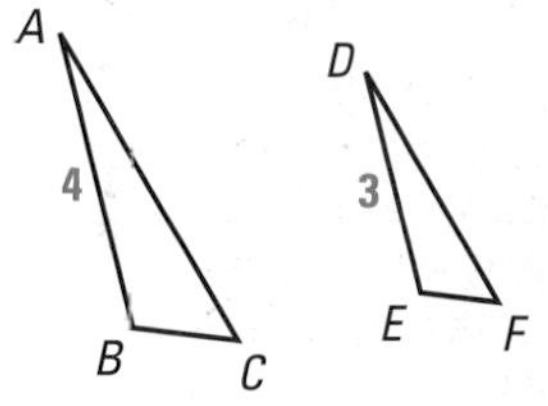

58. $\dfrac{AC}{BC} = \dfrac{DF}{EF}$ **59.** $\dfrac{DF}{AC} = \dfrac{EF + DE + DF}{BC + AB + AC}$

60. $\angle B \cong \angle E$ **61.** $\overline{BC} \cong \overline{EF}$

FINDING SEGMENT LENGTHS Find the value of *x*. (Review 10.5)

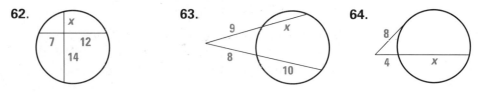

62.   **63.**   **64.**

▶ ACTIVITY 11.3

Developing Concepts

GROUP ACTIVITY
Work with a partner.

MATERIALS
• graph paper
• pencil
• ruler

Area Relationships in Similar Figures

▶ **QUESTION** How does the ratio of the areas of any two similar polygons compare to the scale factor?

▶ **EXPLORING THE CONCEPT**

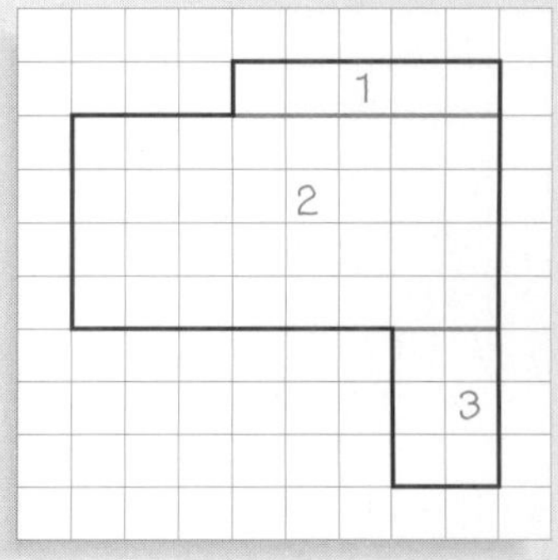

① On a piece of graph paper draw a polygon. Use grid lines as sides of the polygon. An example is shown.

② Divide your polygon into several rectangles. Calculate the area of each rectangle. Create a table like the one shown below to record the area of each rectangle.

③ Add the areas of the rectangles to find the total area of the polygon. Record your results.

Original polygon	Area	Similar polygon	Area
Rectangle 1	?	Rectangle 1	?
Rectangle 2	?	Rectangle 2	?
Rectangle 3	?	Rectangle 3	?
⋮	⋮	⋮	⋮
Total	?	Total	?

④ On another piece of graph paper draw a polygon that is similar to your original polygon. The ratio of the side lengths of the second polygon to the first polygon should be 2 : 1.

⑤ Repeat **Steps 2** and **3** to find the area of the similar polygon.

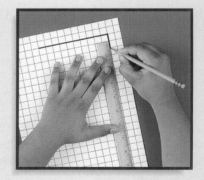

▶ **DRAWING CONCLUSIONS**

1. Use a ratio to compare the area of the similar polygon to the area of the original polygon.

2. Make a conjecture about the relationship between the scale factor of two similar polygons and the ratio of their areas.

EXTENSION

CRITICAL THINKING Compare and discuss your conjecture with your partner. Work together to create a new pair of similar polygons to test the conjecture.

11.3

Perimeters and Areas of Similar Figures

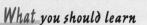

What you should learn

GOAL 1 Compare perimeters and areas of similar figures.

GOAL 2 Use perimeters and areas of similar figures to solve **real-life** problems, as applied in **Example 2**.

Why you should learn it

▼ To solve **real-life** problems, such as finding the area of the walkway around a polygonal pool in **Exs. 25–27**.

Frank Lloyd Wright included this triangular pool and walkway in his design of *Taliesin West* in Scottsdale, Arizona.

► **Study Tip**
The ratio "*a* to *b*," for example, can be written using a fraction bar $\left(\frac{a}{b}\right)$ or a colon (*a*:*b*).

GOAL 1 **COMPARING PERIMETER AND AREA**

For any polygon, the *perimeter of the polygon* is the sum of the lengths of its sides and the *area of the polygon* is the number of square units contained in its interior.

In Lesson 8.3, you learned that if two polygons are *similar*, then the ratio of their perimeters is the same as the ratio of the lengths of their corresponding sides. In Activity 11.3 on page 676, you may have discovered that the ratio of the areas of two similar polygons is *not* this same ratio, as shown in Theorem 11.5. Exercise 22 asks you to write a proof of this theorem for rectangles.

THEOREM

THEOREM 11.5 *Areas of Similar Polygons*

If two polygons are similar with the lengths of corresponding sides in the ratio of $a:b$, then the ratio of their areas is $a^2:b^2$.

$$\frac{\text{Side length of Quad. I}}{\text{Side length of Quad. II}} = \frac{a}{b}$$

$$\frac{\text{Area of Quad. I}}{\text{Area of Quad. II}} = \frac{a^2}{b^2}$$

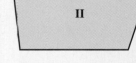
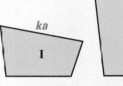

Quad. I ~ Quad. II

EXAMPLE 1 *Finding Ratios of Similar Polygons*

Pentagons *ABCDE* and *LMNPQ* are similar.

a. Find the ratio (red to blue) of the perimeters of the pentagons.

b. Find the ratio (red to blue) of the areas of the pentagons.

SOLUTION

The ratio of the lengths of corresponding sides in the pentagons is $\frac{5}{10} = \frac{1}{2}$, or $1:2$.

a. The ratio of the perimeters is also $1:2$. So, the perimeter of pentagon *ABCDE* is half the perimeter of pentagon *LMNPQ*.

b. Using Theorem 11.5, the ratio of the areas is $1^2:2^2$, or $1:4$. So, the area of pentagon *ABCDE* is one fourth the area of pentagon *LMNPQ*.

GOAL 2 **USING PERIMETER AND AREA IN REAL LIFE**

EXAMPLE 2 *Using Areas of Similar Figures*

REAL LIFE **COMPARING COSTS** You are buying photographic paper to print a photo in different sizes. An 8 inch by 10 inch sheet of the paper costs $.42. What is a reasonable cost for a 16 inch by 20 inch sheet?

SOLUTION

Because the ratio of the lengths of the sides of the two rectangular pieces of paper is $1:2$, the ratio of the areas of the pieces of paper is $1^2:2^2$, or $1:4$. Because the cost of the paper should be a function of its area, the larger piece of paper should cost about four times as much, or $1.68.

EXAMPLE 3 *Finding Perimeters and Areas of Similar Polygons*

FOCUS ON APPLICATIONS

REAL LIFE **CHICAGO BOARD OF TRADE**

Commodities such as grains, coffee, and financial securities are exchanged at this marketplace. Associated traders stand on the descending steps in the same "pie-slice" section of an octagonal pit. The different levels allow buyers and sellers to see each other as orders are yelled out.

INTERNET **APPLICATION LINK**
www.mcdougallittell.com

OCTAGONAL FLOORS A trading pit at the Chicago Board of Trade is in the shape of a series of regular octagons. One octagon has a side length of about 14.25 feet and an area of about 980.4 square feet. Find the area of a smaller octagon that has a perimeter of about 76 feet.

SOLUTION

All regular octagons are similar because all corresponding angles are congruent and the corresponding side lengths are proportional.

Draw and label a sketch.

Find the ratio of the side lengths of the two octagons, which is the same as the ratio of their perimeters.

$$\frac{\text{perimeter of } ABCDEFGH}{\text{perimeter of } JKLMNPQR} = \frac{a}{b} \approx \frac{76}{8(14.25)} = \frac{76}{114} = \frac{2}{3}$$

Calculate the area of the smaller octagon. Let A represent the area of the smaller octagon. The ratio of the areas of the smaller octagon to the larger is $a^2:b^2 = 2^2:3^2$, or $4:9$.

$\dfrac{A}{980.4} = \dfrac{4}{9}$	**Write proportion.**
$9A = 980.4 \cdot 4$	**Cross product property**
$A = \dfrac{3921.6}{9}$	**Divide each side by 9.**
$A \approx 435.7$	**Use a calculator.**

▶ The area of the smaller octagon is about 435.7 square feet.

GUIDED PRACTICE

Vocabulary Check ✓

1. If two polygons are *similar* with the lengths of corresponding sides in the ratio of $a:b$, then the ratio of their perimeters is ___?___ and the ratio of their areas is ___?___.

Concept Check ✓

Tell whether the statement is *true* or *false*. Explain.

2. Any two regular polygons with the same number of sides are similar.

3. Doubling the side length of a square doubles the area.

Skill Check ✓

In Exercises 4 and 5, the red and blue figures are similar. Find the ratio (red to blue) of their perimeters and of their areas.

4.

5.

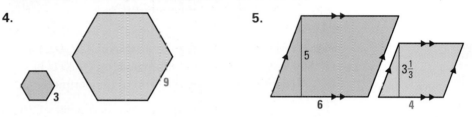

6. 🌐 **PHOTOGRAPHY** Use the information from Example 2 on page 678 to find a reasonable cost for a sheet of 4 inch by 5 inch photographic paper.

PRACTICE AND APPLICATIONS

STUDENT HELP

▶ **Extra Practice**
to help you master
skills is on p. 823.

FINDING RATIOS In Exercises 7–10, the polygons are similar. Find the ratio (red to blue) of their perimeters and of their areas.

7.

16   8

8.

5   7

9.

2.5   3

10.

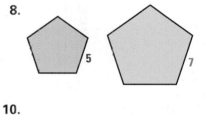

12.5   5   7.5   3

🪙 **LOGICAL REASONING In Exercises 11–13, complete the statement using *always*, *sometimes*, or *never*.**

11. Two similar hexagons ___?___ have the same perimeter.

12. Two rectangles with the same area are ___?___ similar.

13. Two regular pentagons are ___?___ similar.

STUDENT HELP

↳ **HOMEWORK HELP**
Example 1: Exs. 7–10,
          14–18
Example 2: Exs. 23, 24
Example 3: Exs. 25–28

14. **HEXAGONS** The ratio of the lengths of corresponding sides of two similar hexagons is $2:5$. What is the ratio of their areas?

15. **OCTAGONS** A regular octagon has an area of 49 m². Find the scale factor of this octagon to a similar octagon that has an area of 100 m².

11.3 *Perimeters and Areas of Similar Figures* **679**

16. RIGHT TRIANGLES △ABC is a right triangle whose hypotenuse $\overline{AC}$ is 8 inches long. Given that the area of △ABC is 13.9 square inches, find the area of similar triangle △DEF whose hypotenuse $\overline{DF}$ is 20 inches long.

17. FINDING AREA Explain why △CDE is similar to △ABE. Find the area of △CDE.

18. FINDING AREA Explain why □JBKL ~ □ABCD. The area of □JBKL is 15.3 square inches. Find the area of □ABCD.

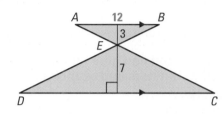

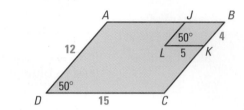

19. SCALE FACTOR Regular pentagon *ABCDE* has a side length of $6\sqrt{5}$ centimeters. Regular pentagon *QRSTU* has a perimeter of 40 centimeters. Find the ratio of the perimeters of *ABCDE* to *QRSTU*.

20. SCALE FACTOR A square has a perimeter of 36 centimeters. A smaller square has a side length of 4 centimeters. What is the ratio of the areas of the larger square to the smaller one?

21. SCALE FACTOR A regular nonagon has an area of 90 square feet. A similar nonagon has an area of 25 square feet. What is the ratio of the perimeters of the first nonagon to the second?

22. ▶ **PROOF** Prove Theorem 11.5 for rectangles.

🌐 **RUG COSTS Suppose you want to be sure that a large rug is priced fairly. The price of a small rug (29 inches by 47 inches) is $79 and the price of the large rug (4 feet 10 inches by 7 feet 10 inches) is $299.**

23. What are the areas of the two rugs? What is the ratio of the areas?

24. Compare the rug costs. Do you think the large rug is a good buy? Explain.

🌐 **TRIANGULAR POOL In Exercises 25–27, use the following information. The pool at *Taliesin West* (see page 677) is a right triangle with legs of length 40 feet and 41 feet.**

25. Find the area of the triangular pool, △DEF.

26. The walkway bordering the pool is 40 inches wide, so the scale factor of the similar triangles is about 1.3 : 1. Find *AB*.

27. Find the area of △ABC. What is the area of the walkway?

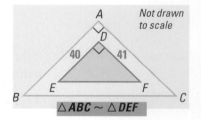

28. 🌐 **FORT JEFFERSON** The outer wall of Fort Jefferson, which was originally constructed in the mid-1800s, is in the shape of a hexagon with an area of about 466,170 square feet. The length of one side is about 477 feet. The inner courtyard is a similar hexagon with an area of about 446,400 square feet. Calculate the length of a corresponding side in the inner courtyard to the nearest foot.

STUDENT HELP

HOMEWORK HELP Visit our Web site www.mcdougallittell.com for help with scale factors in Exs. 19–21.

FOCUS ON APPLICATIONS

FORT JEFFERSON is in the Dry Tortugas National Park 70 miles west of Key West, Florida. The fort has been used as a prison, a navy base, a seaplane port, and an observation post.

29. MULTI-STEP PROBLEM Use the following information about similar triangles △ABC and △DEF.

The scale factor of △ABC to △DEF is 15:2.

The area of △ABC is 25x.   The area of △DEF is x − 5.

The perimeter of △ABC is 8 + y.   The perimeter of △DEF is 3y − 19.

a. Use the scale factor to find the ratio of the area of △ABC to the area of △DEF.

b. Write and solve a proportion to find the value of x.

c. Use the scale factor to find the ratio of the perimeter of △ABC to the perimeter of △DEF.

d. Write and solve a proportion to find the value of y.

e. *Writing* Explain how you could find the value of z if AB = 22.5 and the length of the corresponding side $\overline{DE}$ is 13z − 10.

★ **Challenge**

Use the figure shown at the right. PQRS is a parallelogram.

30. Name three pairs of similar triangles and explain how you know that they are similar.

31. The ratio of the area of △PVQ to the area of △RVT is 9:25, and the length RV is 10. Find PV.

32. If VT is 15, find VQ, VU, and UT.

33. Find the ratio of the areas of each pair of similar triangles that you found in Exercise 30.

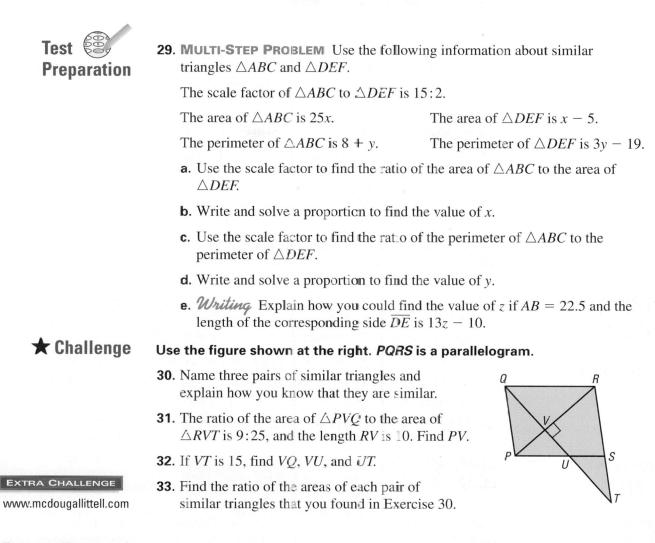

MIXED REVIEW

FINDING MEASURES In Exercises 34–37, use the diagram shown at the right. (Review 10.2 for 11.4)

34. Find $m\widehat{AD}$.   **35.** Find $m\angle AEC$.

36. Find $m\widehat{AC}$.   **37.** Find $m\widehat{ABC}$.

38. USING AN INSCRIBED QUADRILATERAL In the diagram shown at the right, quadrilateral RSTU is inscribed in circle P. Find the values of x and y, and use them to find the measures of the angles of RSTU. (Review 10.3)

FINDING ANGLE MEASURES Find the measure of ∠1. (Review 10.4 for 11.4)

39.   **40.**   **41.**

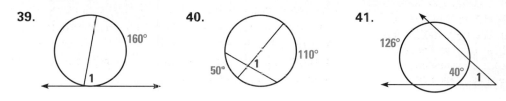

1. Find the sum of the measures of the interior angles of a convex 20-gon.
   (**Lesson 11.1**)

2. What is the measure of each exterior angle of a regular 25-gon? (**Lesson 11.1**)

3. Find the area of an equilateral triangle with a side length of 17 inches.
   (**Lesson 11.2**)

4. Find the area of a regular nonagon with an apothem of 9 centimeters.
   (**Lesson 11.2**)

In Exercises 5 and 6, the polygons are similar. Find the ratio (red to blue) of their perimeters and of their areas. (**Lesson 11.3**)

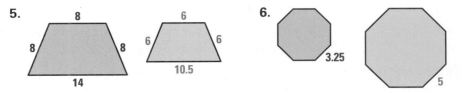

5.

6.

7. 🌐 **CARPET** You just carpeted a 9 foot by 12 foot room for $480. The carpet is priced by the square foot. About how much would you expect to pay for the same carpet in another room that is 21 feet by 28 feet? (**Lesson 11.3**)

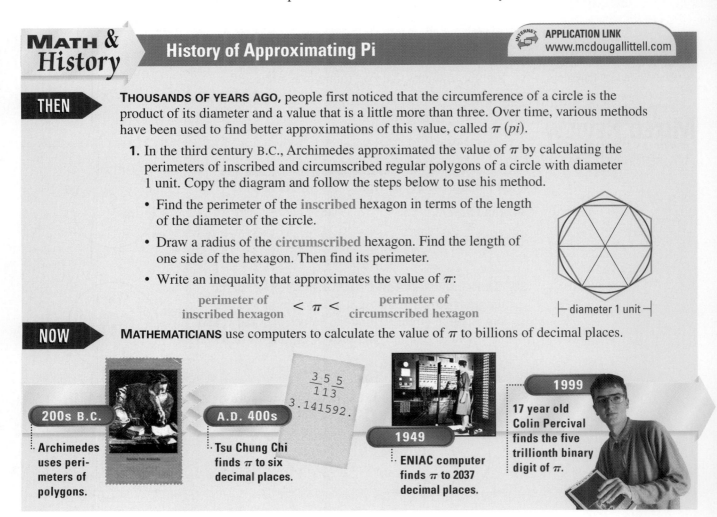

MATH & History

History of Approximating Pi

🔄 **APPLICATION LINK**
www.mcdougallittell.com

THEN

THOUSANDS OF YEARS AGO, people first noticed that the circumference of a circle is the product of its diameter and a value that is a little more than three. Over time, various methods have been used to find better approximations of this value, called π (*pi*).

1. In the third century B.C., Archimedes approximated the value of π by calculating the perimeters of inscribed and circumscribed regular polygons of a circle with diameter 1 unit. Copy the diagram and follow the steps below to use his method.

   • Find the perimeter of the **inscribed** hexagon in terms of the length of the diameter of the circle.

   • Draw a radius of the **circumscribed** hexagon. Find the length of one side of the hexagon. Then find its perimeter.

   • Write an inequality that approximates the value of π:

     perimeter of inscribed hexagon $< \pi <$ perimeter of circumscribed hexagon

   ⊢ diameter 1 unit ⊣

NOW

MATHEMATICIANS use computers to calculate the value of π to billions of decimal places.

200s B.C.
Archimedes uses perimeters of polygons.

A.D. 400s
Tsu Chung Chi finds π to six decimal places.

$\frac{355}{113}$
3.141592.

1949
ENIAC computer finds π to 2037 decimal places.

1999
17 year old Colin Percival finds the five trillionth binary digit of π.

11.4

Circumference and Arc Length

What you should learn

GOAL 1 Find the circumference of a circle and the length of a circular arc.

GOAL 2 Use circumference and arc length to solve **real-life** problems such as finding the distance around a track in **Example 5**.

Why you should learn it

▼ To solve **real-life** problems, such as finding the number of revolutions a tire needs to make to travel a given distance in **Example 4** and **Exs. 39–41**.

GOAL 1 FINDING CIRCUMFERENCE AND ARC LENGTH

The **circumference** of a circle is the distance around the circle. For all circles, the ratio of the circumference to the diameter is the same. This ratio is known as π, or *pi*.

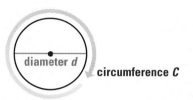

THEOREM

THEOREM 11.6 *Circumference of a Circle*

The circumference C of a circle is $C = \pi d$ or $C = 2\pi r$, where d is the diameter of the circle and r is the radius of the circle.

EXAMPLE 1 *Using Circumference*

Find (**a**) the circumference of a circle with radius 6 centimeters and (**b**) the radius of a circle with circumference 31 meters. Round decimal answers to two decimal places.

SOLUTION

a. $C = 2\pi r$

$= 2 \cdot \pi \cdot 6$

$= 12\pi$ **Use a calculator.**

≈ 37.70

▶ So, the circumference is about 37.70 centimeters.

b. $C = 2\pi r$

$31 = 2\pi r$

$\dfrac{31}{2\pi} = r$ **Use a calculator.**

$4.93 \approx r$

▶ So, the radius is about 4.93 meters.

· · · · · · · · · ·

An **arc length** is a portion of the circumference of a circle. You can use the measure of the arc (in degrees) to find its length (in linear units).

COROLLARY

ARC LENGTH COROLLARY

In a circle, the ratio of the length of a given arc to the circumference is equal to the ratio of the measure of the arc to 360°.

$$\frac{\text{Arc length of } \widehat{AB}}{2\pi r} = \frac{m\widehat{AB}}{360°}, \text{ or Arc length of } \widehat{AB} = \frac{m\widehat{AB}}{360°} \cdot 2\pi r$$

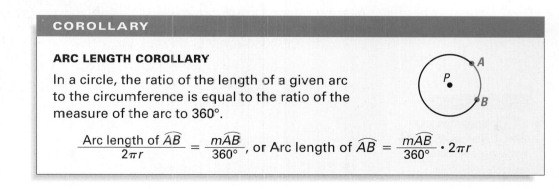

The length of a **semicircle** is one half the circumference, and the length of a **90° arc** is one quarter of the circumference.

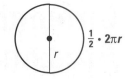 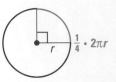

EXAMPLE 2 *Finding Arc Lengths*

STUDENT HELP

▶ **Study Tip**
Throughout this chapter, you should use the π key on a calculator, then round decimal answers to two decimal places unless instructed otherwise.

Find the length of each arc.

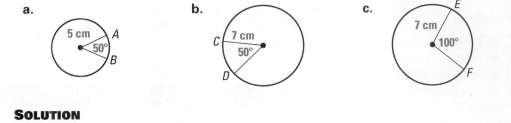

a.   b.   c.

SOLUTION

    a. Arc length of $\overset{\frown}{AB} = \dfrac{50°}{360°} \cdot 2\pi(5) \approx 4.36$ centimeters

    b. Arc length of $\overset{\frown}{CD} = \dfrac{50°}{360°} \cdot 2\pi(7) \approx 6.11$ centimeters

    c. Arc length of $\overset{\frown}{EF} = \dfrac{100°}{360°} \cdot 2\pi(7) \approx 12.22$ centimeters

· · · · · · · · ·

In parts (a) and (b) in Example 2, note that the arcs have the same measure, but different lengths because the circumferences of the circles are not equal.

EXAMPLE 3 *Using Arc Lengths*

Find the indicated measure.

     a. Circumference   **b.** $m\overset{\frown}{XY}$

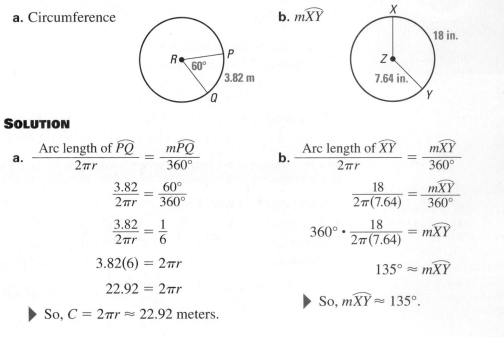

SOLUTION

STUDENT HELP

HOMEWORK HELP
Visit our Web site
www.mcdougallittell.com
for extra examples.

  a. $\dfrac{\text{Arc length of } \overset{\frown}{PQ}}{2\pi r} = \dfrac{m\overset{\frown}{PQ}}{360°}$ b. $\dfrac{\text{Arc length of } \overset{\frown}{XY}}{2\pi r} = \dfrac{m\overset{\frown}{XY}}{360°}$

$$\dfrac{3.82}{2\pi r} = \dfrac{60°}{360°} \qquad\qquad \dfrac{18}{2\pi(7.64)} = \dfrac{m\overset{\frown}{XY}}{360°}$$

$$\dfrac{3.82}{2\pi r} = \dfrac{1}{6} \qquad\qquad 360° \cdot \dfrac{18}{2\pi(7.64)} = m\overset{\frown}{XY}$$

$$3.82(6) = 2\pi r \qquad\qquad\qquad 135° \approx m\overset{\frown}{XY}$$

$$22.92 = 2\pi r$$

     ▶ So, $C = 2\pi r \approx 22.92$ meters.   ▶ So, $m\overset{\frown}{XY} \approx 135°$.

GOAL 2 CIRCUMFERENCE CIRCUMFERENCES

EXAMPLE 4 *Comparing Circumferences*

TIRE REVOLUTIONS Tires from two different automobiles are shown below. How many revolutions does each tire make while traveling 100 feet? Round decimal answers to one decimal place.

SOLUTION

Tire A has a diameter of $14 + 2(5.1)$, or 24.2 inches. Its circumference is $\pi(24.2)$, or about 76.03 inches.

Tire B has a diameter of $15 + 2(5.25)$, or 25.5 inches. Its circumference is $\pi(25.5)$, or about 80.11 inches.

Divide the distance traveled by the tire circumference to find the number of revolutions made. First convert 100 feet to 1200 inches.

Tire A: $\dfrac{100 \text{ ft}}{76.03 \text{ in.}} = \dfrac{1200 \text{ in.}}{76.03 \text{ in.}}$ $\approx$ 15.8 revolutions

Tire B: $\dfrac{100 \text{ ft}}{80.11 \text{ in.}} = \dfrac{1200 \text{ in.}}{80.11 \text{ in.}}$ $\approx$ 15.0 revolutions

FOCUS ON PEOPLE

 JACOB HEILVEIL was born in Korea and now lives in the United States. He was the top American finisher in the 10,000 meter race at the 1996 Paralympics held in Atlanta, Georgia.

EXAMPLE 5 *Finding Arc Length*

TRACK The track shown has six lanes. Each lane is 1.25 meters wide. There is a 180° arc at each end of the track. The radii for the arcs in the first two lanes are given.

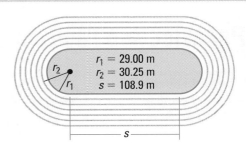

a. Find the distance around Lane 1.

b. Find the distance around Lane 2.

SOLUTION

The track is made up of two semicircles and two straight sections with length s. To find the total distance around each lane, find the sum of the lengths of each part. Round decimal answers to one decimal place.

a. Distance $= 2s + 2\pi r_1$
$= 2(108.9) + 2\pi(29.00)$
≈ 400.0 meters

b. Distance $= 2s + 2\pi r_2$
$= 2(108.9) + 2\pi(30.25)$
≈ 407.9 meters

GUIDED PRACTICE

Vocabulary Check ✔   **1.** What is the difference between *arc measure* and *arc length*?

Concept Check ✔   **2.** In the diagram, $\overline{BD}$ is a diameter and $\angle 1 \cong \angle 2$. Explain why $\widehat{AB}$ and $\widehat{CD}$ have the same length.

Skill Check ✔   **In Exercises 3–8, match the measure with its value.**

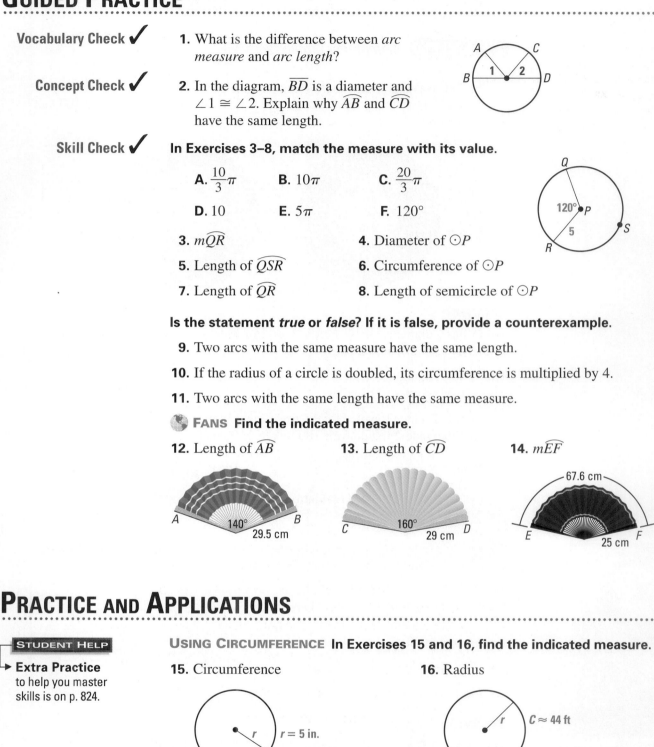

A. $\dfrac{10}{3}\pi$ **B.** 10π **C.** $\dfrac{20}{3}\pi$

D. 10 **E.** 5π **F.** $120°$

3. $m\widehat{QR}$ **4.** Diameter of $\odot P$

5. Length of $\widehat{QSR}$ **6.** Circumference of $\odot P$

7. Length of $\widehat{QR}$ **8.** Length of semicircle of $\odot P$

Is the statement *true* or *false*? If it is false, provide a counterexample.

9. Two arcs with the same measure have the same length.

10. If the radius of a circle is doubled, its circumference is multiplied by 4.

11. Two arcs with the same length have the same measure.

🌐 **FANS Find the indicated measure.**

12. Length of $\widehat{AB}$ **13.** Length of $\widehat{CD}$ **14.** $m\widehat{EF}$

PRACTICE AND APPLICATIONS

STUDENT HELP

▶ **Extra Practice**
to help you master
skills is on p. 824.

USING CIRCUMFERENCE In Exercises 15 and 16, find the indicated measure.

15. Circumference   **16.** Radius

$r = 5$ in.

$C \approx 44$ ft

17. Find the circumference of a circle with diameter 8 meters.

18. Find the circumference of a circle with radius 15 inches. (Leave your answer in terms of π.)

19. Find the radius of a circle with circumference 32 yards.

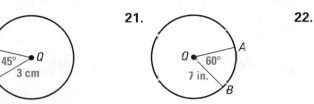

FINDING ARC LENGTHS In Exercises 20–22, find the length of $\overset{\frown}{AB}$.

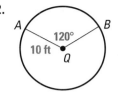

STUDENT HELP

→ **HOMEWORK HELP**
Example 1: Exs. 15–19
Example 2: Exs. 20–23
Example 3: Exs. 24–29
Example 4: Exs. 39–41
Example 5: Exs. 42–46

20.

21.

22.

23. FINDING VALUES Complete the table.

Radius	?	3	0.6	3.5	?	$3\sqrt{3}$
$m\overset{\frown}{AB}$	45°	30°	?	192°	90°	?
Length of $\overset{\frown}{AB}$	3π	?	0.4π	?	2.55π	3.09π

FINDING MEASURES Find the indicated measure.

24. Length of $\overset{\frown}{XY}$

25. Circumference

26. Radius

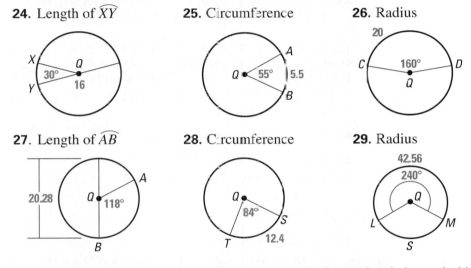

27. Length of $\overset{\frown}{AB}$

28. Circumference

29. Radius

CALCULATING PERIMETERS In Exercises 30–32, the region is bounded by circular arcs and line segments. Find the perimeter of the region.

30.

31.

32.

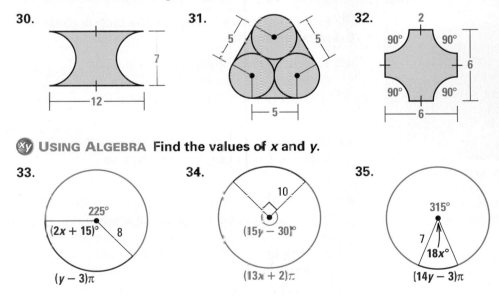

🅧🅨 **USING ALGEBRA** Find the values of *x* and *y*.

33.

34.

35.

$\overset{xy}{}$ **USING ALGEBRA** Find the circumference of the circle whose equation is given. (Leave your answer in terms of π.)

36. $x^2 + y^2 = 9$　　　　　**37.** $x^2 + y^2 = 28$　　　　　**38.** $(x + 1)^2 + (y - 5)^2 = 4$

🌐 **AUTOMOBILE TIRES** **In Exercises 39–41, use the table below. The table gives the rim diameters and sidewall widths of three automobile tires.**

	Rim diameter	Sidewall width
Tire A	15 in.	4.60 in.
Tire B	16 in.	4.43 in.
Tire C	17 in.	4.33 in.

39. Find the diameter of each automobile tire.

40. How many revolutions does each tire make while traveling 500 feet?

41. A student determines that the circumference of a tire with a rim diameter of 15 inches and a sidewall width of 5.5 inches is 64.40 inches. Explain the error.

🌐 **GO-CART TRACK** **Use the diagram of the go-cart track for Exercises 42 and 43. Turns 1, 2, 4, 5, 6, 8, and 9 all have a radius of 3 meters. Turns 3 and 7 each have a radius of 2.25 meters.**

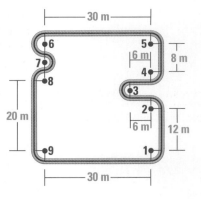

42. Calculate the length of the track.

43. How many laps do you need to make to travel 1609 meters (about 1 mile)?

44. 🌐 **MOUNT RAINIER** In Example 5 on page 623 of Lesson 10.4, you calculated the measure of the arc of Earth's surface seen from the top of Mount Rainier. Use that information to calculate the distance in miles that can be seen looking in one direction from the top of Mount Rainier.

🌐 **BICYCLES** **Use the diagram of a bicycle chain for a fixed gear bicycle in Exercises 45 and 46.**

45. The chain travels along the front and rear sprockets. The circumference of each sprocket is given. About how long is the chain?

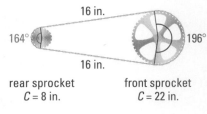

rear sprocket
$C = 8$ in.

front sprocket
$C = 22$ in.

46. On a chain, the teeth are spaced in $\frac{1}{2}$ inch intervals. How many teeth are there on this chain?

47. 🌐 **ENCLOSING A GARDEN** Suppose you have planted a circular garden adjacent to one of the corners of your garage, as shown at the right. If you want to fence in your garden, how much fencing do you need?

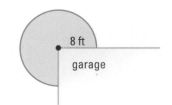

8 ft

garage

48. MULTIPLE CHOICE In the diagram shown, $\overline{YZ}$ and $\overline{WX}$ each measure 8 units and are diameters of $\odot T$. If $\overset{\frown}{YX}$ measures $120°$, what is the length of $\overset{\frown}{XZ}$?

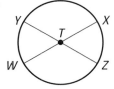

Ⓐ $\frac{2}{3}\pi$ Ⓑ $\frac{4}{3}\pi$ Ⓒ $\frac{8}{3}\pi$

Ⓓ 4π Ⓔ 8π

49. MULTIPLE CHOICE In the diagram shown, the ratio of the length of $\overset{\frown}{PQ}$ to the length of $\overset{\frown}{RS}$ is 2 to 1. What is the ratio of x to y?

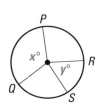

Ⓐ 4 to 1   Ⓑ 2 to 1   Ⓒ 1 to 1

Ⓓ 1 to 2   Ⓔ 1 to 4

★ **Challenge**

CALCULATING ARC LENGTHS Suppose $\overline{AB}$ is divided into four congruent segments and semicircles with radius r are drawn.

50. What is the sum of the four arc lengths if the radius of each arc is r?

51. Imagine that $\overline{AB}$ is divided into n congruent segments and that semicircles are drawn. What would the sum of the arc lengths be for 8 segments? 16 segments? n segments? Does the number of segments matter?

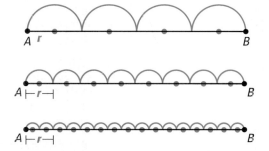

EXTRA CHALLENGE
www.mcdougallittell.com

MIXED REVIEW

FINDING AREA In Exercises 52–55, the radius of a circle is given. Use the formula $A = \pi r^2$ to calculate the area of the circle. (Review 1.7 for 11.5)

52. $r = 9$ ft   **53.** $r = 3.3$ in.   **54.** $r = \frac{27}{5}$ cm   **55.** $r = 4\sqrt{11}$ m

56. ⓧⓨ **USING ALGEBRA** Line n_1 has the equation $y = \frac{2}{3}x + 8$. Line n_2 is parallel to n_1 and passes through the point $(9, -2)$. Write an equation for n_2. (Review 3.6)

USING PROPORTIONALITY THEOREMS In Exercises 57 and 58, find the value of the variable. (Review 8.6)

57.

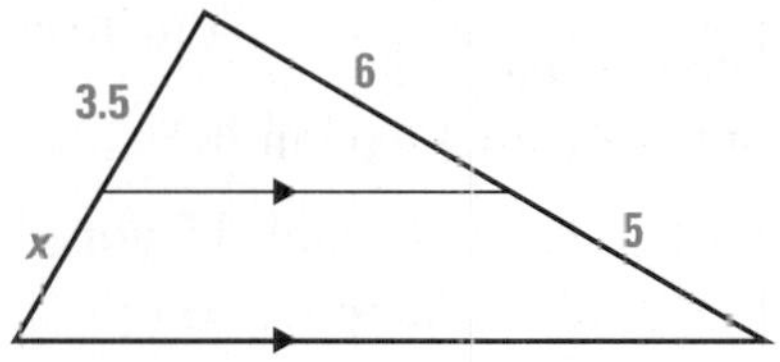

58.

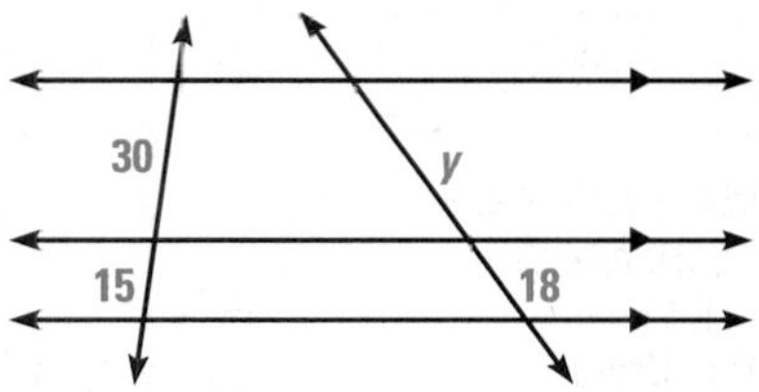

CALCULATING ARC MEASURES You are given the measure of an inscribed angle of a circle. Find the measure of its intercepted arc. (Review 10.3)

59. $48°$ **60.** $88°$ **61.** $129°$ **62.** $15.5°$

Using Technology

Perimeters of Regular Polygons

You can use a spreadsheet to explore the perimeters of regular polygons that are inscribed in a circle with radius 1 unit.

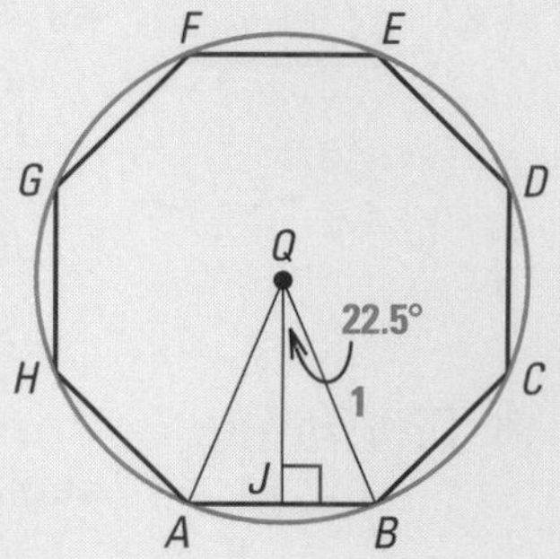

The regular octagon shown at the right is inscribed in a circle with radius 1 unit.

The measure of the interior angle $\angle AQB$ is $\frac{1}{8} \cdot 360°$ or $45°$, so the measure of $\angle JQB$ is $22.5°$.

You can find the length of $\overline{JB}$ using a sine ratio.

$$\sin 22.5° = \frac{JB}{QB} = \frac{JB}{1} = JB$$

The length of each side of the octagon is $s = AB = 2(JB) = 2 \cdot \sin 22.5°$. The perimeter of the octagon is $P = 8s = 8(2 \cdot \sin 22.5°) = 16 \cdot \sin 22.5°$.

This procedure used for an octagon can be generalized to conclude that the perimeter of a regular n-gon inscribed in a circle of radius 1 is

$$P = 2n \sin \frac{180°}{n}.$$

▶ **CONSTRUCT** Use a spreadsheet to construct a table.

① Use a spreadsheet to make a table with two columns. The first column is for the number of sides, n, of the regular polygon. In cell A3, start with a value of 3. In cell A4 use the formula =A3+1.

Polygon Perimeter		
	A	B
1	Number of sides	Perimeter
2	n	2*n*sin(180/n)
3	3	=2*A3*sin(pi()/A3)
4	=A3+1	=2*A4*sin(pi()/A4)

② The second column is for the perimeter of the regular polygon. In cell B3 use the formula =2*A3*sin(180/A3). If your spreadsheet uses radian measure, you may need to use "pi()" instead of "180" so that the formula is =2*A3*sin(pi()/A3).

③ Use the Fill Down feature to create more rows. You may need to select Row 4 and drag down to highlight rows before using the Fill Down command.

▶ **INVESTIGATE**

1. Describe how the perimeter changes as n increases.

2. Explain why the perimeter of a regular hexagon is 6.

3. Find the perimeter of a regular 12-gon, 15-gon, 18-gon, and 24-gon.

EXTENSION

Critical Thinking Modify your spreadsheet so that the number of sides increases by 100 instead of 1. (Use =A3+100 in cell A4.) Does the perimeter of the polygon approach 2π, the circumference of the circle with radius 1 unit?

Areas of Circles and Sectors

What you should learn

GOAL 1 Find the area of a circle and a sector of a circle.

GOAL 2 Use areas of circles and sectors to solve **real-life** problems, such as finding the area of a boomerang in **Example 6**.

Why you should learn it

▼ To solve **real-life** problems, such as finding the area of portions of tree trunks that are used to build Viking ships in **Exs. 38 and 39**.

GOAL 1 **AREAS OF CIRCLES AND SECTORS**

The diagrams below show regular polygons inscribed in circles with radius r. Exercise 42 on page 697 demonstrates that as the number of sides increases, the area of the polygon approaches the value πr^2.

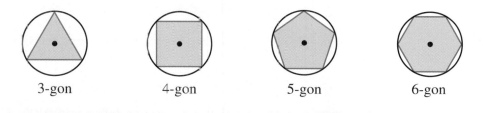

3-gon   4-gon   5-gon   6-gon

THEOREM

THEOREM 11.7 *Area of a Circle*

The area of a circle is π times the square of the radius, or $A = \pi r^2$.

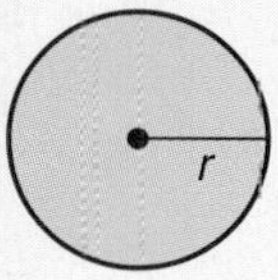

EXAMPLE 1 *Using the Area of a Circle*

a. Find the area of $\odot P$.

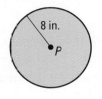

8 in.

P

b. Find the diameter of $\odot Z$.

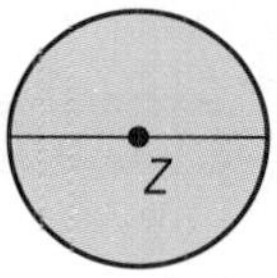

Z

Area of $\odot Z$ = 96 cm²

SOLUTION

a. Use $r = 8$ in the area formula.

$$A = \pi r^2$$
$$= \pi \cdot 8^2$$
$$= 64\pi$$
$$\approx 201.06$$

▶ So, the area is 64π, or about 201.06, square inches.

b. The diameter is twice the radius.

$$A = \pi r^2$$
$$96 = \pi r^2$$
$$\frac{96}{\pi} = r^2$$
$$30.56 \approx r^2$$
$$5.53 \approx r \qquad \text{Find the square roots.}$$

▶ The diameter of the circle is about 2(5.53), or about 11.06, centimeters.

A **sector of a circle** is the region bounded by two radii of the circle and their intercepted arc. In the diagram, sector APB is bounded by $\overline{AP}$, $\overline{BP}$, and $\widehat{AB}$. The following theorem gives a method for finding the area of a sector.

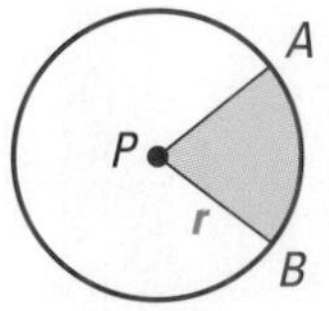

THEOREM

THEOREM 11.8 ***Area of a Sector***

The ratio of the area A of a sector of a circle to the area of the circle is equal to the ratio of the measure of the intercepted arc to 360°.

$$\frac{A}{\pi r^2} = \frac{m\widehat{AB}}{360^\circ}, \text{ or } A = \frac{m\widehat{AB}}{360^\circ} \cdot \pi r^2$$

EXAMPLE 2 *Finding the Area of a Sector*

Find the area of the sector shown at the right.

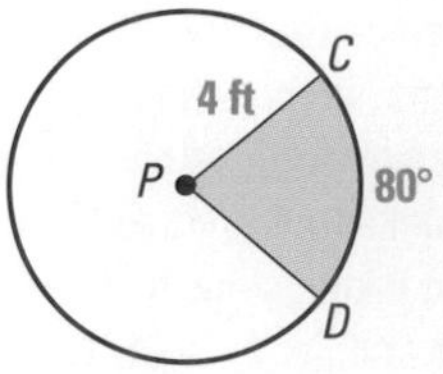

SOLUTION

Sector CPD intercepts an arc whose measure is 80°. The radius is 4 feet.

$A = \frac{m\widehat{CD}}{360^\circ} \cdot \pi r^2$ **Write the formula for the area of a sector.**

$= \frac{80^\circ}{360^\circ} \cdot \pi \cdot 4^2$ **Substitute known values.**

≈ 11.17 **Use a calculator.**

▶ So, the area of the sector is about 11.17 square feet.

EXAMPLE 3 *Finding the Area of a Sector*

A and B are two points on a $\odot P$ with radius 9 inches and $m\angle APB = 60^\circ$. Find the areas of the sectors formed by $\angle APB$.

SOLUTION

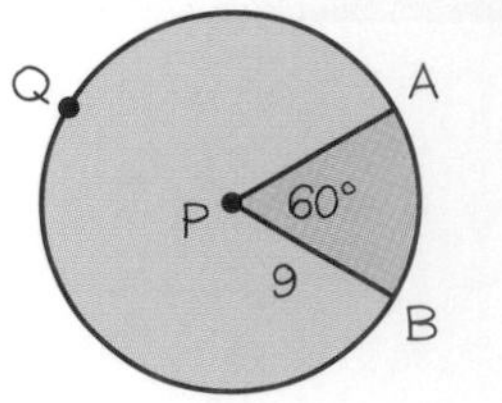

Draw a diagram of $\odot P$ and $\angle APB$. Shade the sectors.

Label a point Q on the major arc.

Find the measures of the minor and major arcs.

Because $m\angle APB = 60^\circ$, $m\widehat{AB} = 60^\circ$ and $m\widehat{AQB} = 360^\circ - 60^\circ = 300^\circ$.

Use the formula for the area of a sector.

Area of small sector $= \frac{60^\circ}{360^\circ} \cdot \pi \cdot 9^2 = \frac{1}{6} \cdot \pi \cdot 81 \approx 42.41$ square inches

Area of larger sector $= \frac{300^\circ}{360^\circ} \cdot \pi \cdot 9^2 = \frac{5}{6} \cdot \pi \cdot 81 \approx 212.06$ square inches

STUDENT HELP

INTERNET

HOMEWORK HELP
Visit our Web site www.mcdougallittell.com for extra examples.

You may need to divide a figure into different regions to find its area. The regions may be polygons, circles, or sectors. To find the area of the entire figure, add or subtract the areas of the separate regions as appropriate.

EXAMPLE 4 *Finding the Area of a Region*

Find the area of the shaded region shown at the right.

SOLUTION

The diagram shows a regular hexagon inscribed in a circle with radius 5 meters. The shaded region is the part of the circle that is outside of the hexagon.

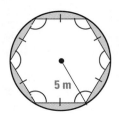

5 m

Area of shaded region	=	Area of circle	−	Area of hexagon

$$= \quad \pi r^2 \quad - \quad \frac{1}{2}aP$$

$$= \pi \cdot 5^2 - \frac{1}{2} \cdot \left(\frac{5}{2}\sqrt{3}\right) \cdot (6 \cdot 5)$$

The apothem of a hexagon is $\frac{1}{2}\cdot$ side length $\cdot\sqrt{3}$.

$$= 25\pi - \frac{75}{2}\sqrt{3}$$

▶ So, the area of the shaded region is $25\pi - \frac{75}{2}\sqrt{3}$, or about 13.59 square meters.

EXAMPLE 5 *Finding the Area of a Region*

WOODWORKING You are cutting the front face of a clock out of wood, as shown in the diagram. What is the area of the front of the case?

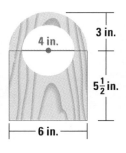

3 in.

4 in.

$5\frac{1}{2}$ in.

6 in.

SOLUTION

The front of the case is formed by a rectangle and a sector, with a circle removed. Note that the intercepted arc of the sector is a semicircle.

Area	=	Area of rectangle	+	Area of sector	−	Area of circle

$$= \quad 6 \cdot \frac{11}{2} \quad + \quad \frac{180°}{360°} \cdot \pi \cdot 3^2 \quad - \quad \pi \cdot \left(\frac{1}{2} \cdot 4\right)^2$$

$$= 33 + \frac{1}{2} \cdot \pi \cdot 9 - \pi \cdot (2)^2$$

$$= 33 + \frac{9}{2}\pi - 4\pi$$

$$\approx 34.57$$

▶ The area of the front of the case is about 34.57 square inches.

Complicated shapes may involve a number of regions. In Example 6, the curved region is a portion of a ring whose edges are formed by concentric circles. Notice that the area of a portion of the ring is the difference of the areas of two sectors.

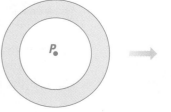

EXAMPLE 6 *Finding the Area of a Boomerang*

BOOMERANGS Find the area of the boomerang shown. The dimensions are given in inches. Give your answer in terms of π and to two decimal places.

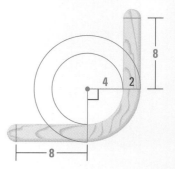

SOLUTION

Separate the boomerang into different regions. The regions are two semicircles (at the ends), two rectangles, and a portion of a ring. Find the area of each region and add these areas together.

PROBLEM
SOLVING
STRATEGY

DRAW AND LABEL A SKETCH Draw and label a sketch of each region in the boomerang.

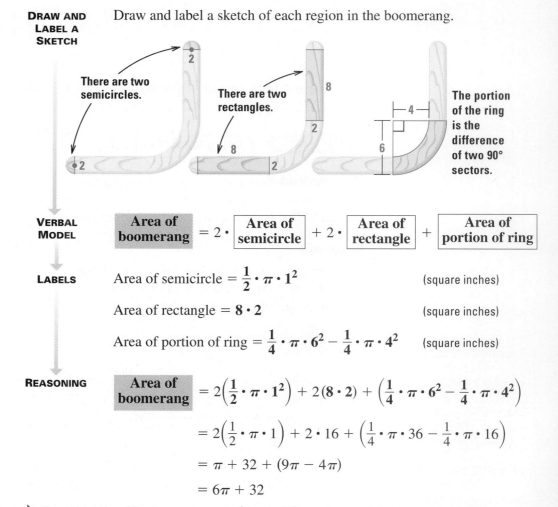

There are two semicircles.

There are two rectangles.

The portion of the ring is the difference of two 90° sectors.

VERBAL MODEL

$$\boxed{\text{Area of boomerang}} = 2 \cdot \boxed{\text{Area of semicircle}} + 2 \cdot \boxed{\text{Area of rectangle}} + \boxed{\text{Area of portion of ring}}$$

LABELS

Area of semicircle $= \dfrac{1}{2} \cdot \pi \cdot 1^2$ (square inches)

Area of rectangle $= 8 \cdot 2$ (square inches)

Area of portion of ring $= \dfrac{1}{4} \cdot \pi \cdot 6^2 - \dfrac{1}{4} \cdot \pi \cdot 4^2$ (square inches)

REASONING

$$\boxed{\text{Area of boomerang}} = 2\left(\dfrac{1}{2} \cdot \pi \cdot 1^2\right) + 2(8 \cdot 2) + \left(\dfrac{1}{4} \cdot \pi \cdot 6^2 - \dfrac{1}{4} \cdot \pi \cdot 4^2\right)$$

$$= 2\left(\dfrac{1}{2} \cdot \pi \cdot 1\right) + 2 \cdot 16 + \left(\dfrac{1}{4} \cdot \pi \cdot 36 - \dfrac{1}{4} \cdot \pi \cdot 16\right)$$

$$= \pi + 32 + (9\pi - 4\pi)$$

$$= 6\pi + 32$$

▶ So, the area of the boomerang is $(6\pi + 32)$, or about 50.85 square inches.

GUIDED PRACTICE

Vocabulary Check ✓

1. Describe the boundaries of a *sector of a circle*.

Concept Check ✓

2. In Example 5 on page 693, explain why the expression $\pi \cdot \left(\frac{1}{2} \cdot 4\right)^2$ represents the area of the circle cut from the wood.

Skill Check ✓

In Exercises 3–8, find the area of the shaded region.

3.

4.

5.

6.

7.

8.

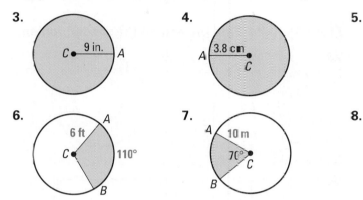

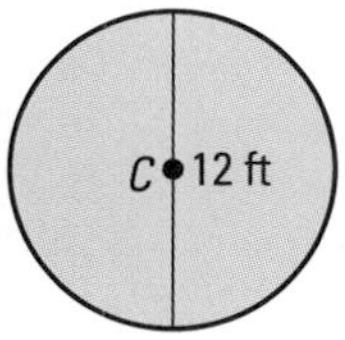

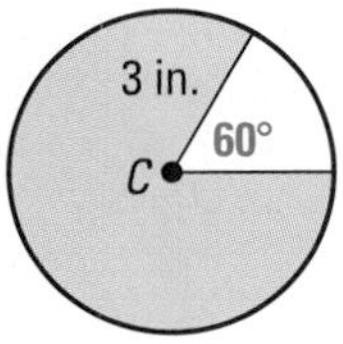

9. **PIECES OF PIZZA** Suppose the pizza shown is divided into 8 equal pieces. The diameter of the pizza is 16 inches. What is the area of one piece of pizza?

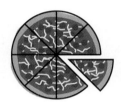

PRACTICE AND APPLICATIONS

STUDENT HELP

Extra Practice to help you master skills is on p. 824.

FINDING AREA In Exercises 10–18, find the area of the shaded region.

10.

11.

12.

13.

14.

15.

16.

17.

18.

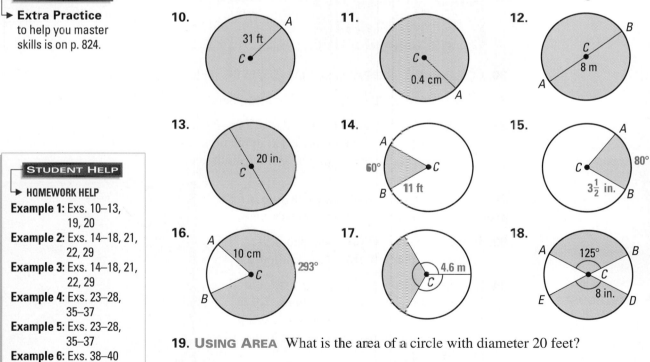

STUDENT HELP

HOMEWORK HELP
Example 1: Exs. 10–13, 19, 20
Example 2: Exs. 14–18, 21, 22, 29
Example 3: Exs. 14–18, 21, 22, 29
Example 4: Exs. 23–28, 35–37
Example 5: Exs. 23–28, 35–37
Example 6: Exs. 38–40

19. **USING AREA** What is the area of a circle with diameter 20 feet?

20. **USING AREA** What is the radius of a circle with area 50 square meters?

USING AREA Find the indicated measure. The area given next to the diagram refers to the shaded region only.

21. Find the radius of $\odot C$.

A
C
40° Area = 59 in.²
B

22. Find the diameter of $\odot G$.

72°
G
Area = 277 m²

FINDING AREA Find the area of the shaded region.

23.

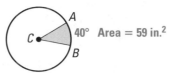

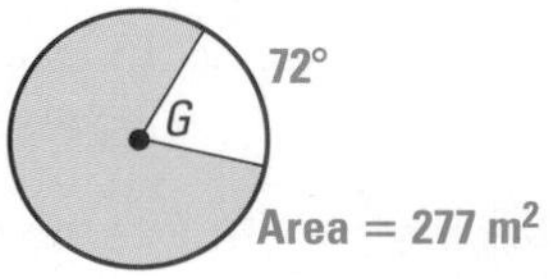

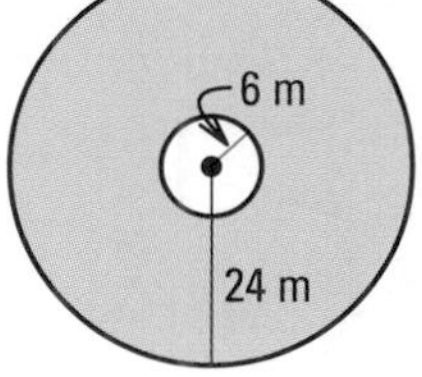

6 m
24 m

24.

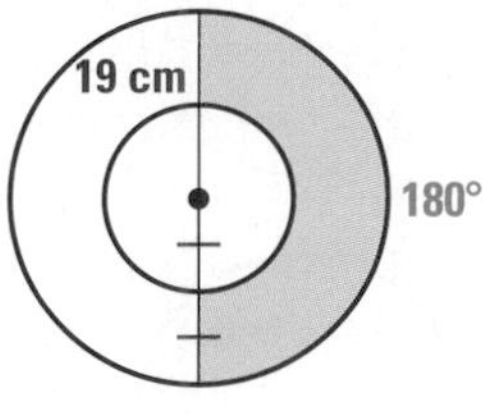

19 cm
180°

25.

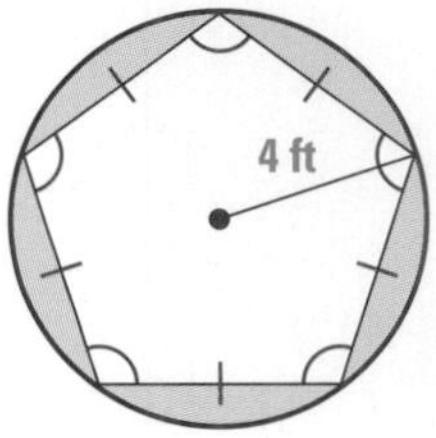

4 ft

26.

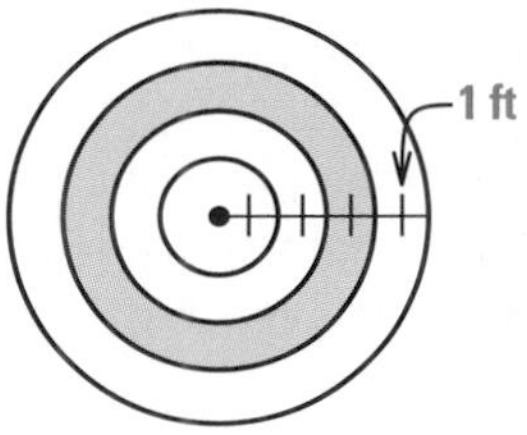

1 ft

27.

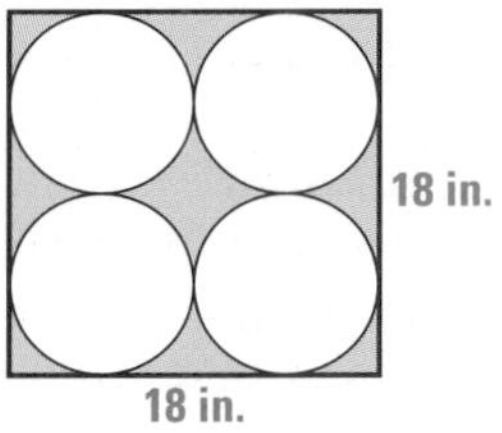

18 in.
18 in.

28.

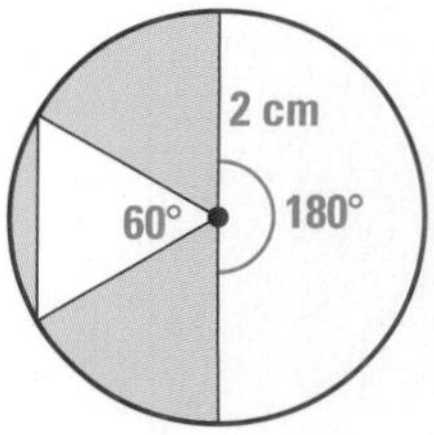

2 cm
60°
180°

FINDING A PATTERN In Exercises 29–32, consider an arc of a circle with a radius of 3 inches.

29. Copy and complete the table. Round your answers to the nearest tenth.

Measure of arc, x	30°	60°	90°	120°	150°	180°
Area of corresponding sector, y	?	?	?	?	?	?

30. USING ALGEBRA Graph the data in the table.

31. USING ALGEBRA Is the relationship between x and y linear? Explain.

32. LOGICAL REASONING If Exercises 29–31 were repeated using a circle with a 5 inch radius, would the areas in the table change? Would your answer to Exercise 31 change? Explain your reasoning.

FOCUS ON APPLICATIONS

REAL LIFE **LIGHTHOUSES** use special lenses that increase the intensity of the light projected. Some lenses are 8 feet high and 6 feet in diameter.

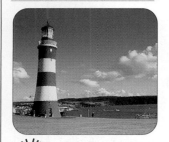

LIGHTHOUSES The diagram shows a projected beam of light from a lighthouse.

28 mi
245°
lighthouse
18 mi

33. What is the area of water that can be covered by the light from the lighthouse?

34. Suppose a boat traveling along a straight line is illuminated by the lighthouse for approximately 28 miles of its route. What is the closest distance between the lighthouse and the boat?

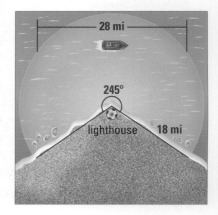

USING AREA In Exercises 35–37, find the area of the shaded region in the circle formed by a chord and its intercepted arc. (*Hint:* Find the difference between the areas of a sector and a triangle.)

35.

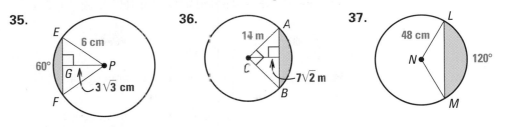

E
6 cm
60°
P
G
3√3 cm
F

36.

14 m
A
C
7√2 m
B

37.

L
48 cm
N
120°
M

**VIKING
LONGSHIPS**
The planks in the hull of a longship were cut in a radial pattern from a single green log, providing uniform resiliency and strength.

APPLICATION LINK
www.mcdougallittell.com

🌐 **VIKING LONGSHIPS** Use the information below for Exercises 38 and 39.

When Vikings constructed *longships*, they cut hull-hugging frames from curved trees. Straight trees provided angled knees, which were used to brace the frames.

38. Find the area of a cross-section of the frame piece shown in red.

39. *Writing* The angled knee piece shown in blue has a cross section whose shape results from subtracting a sector from a kite. What measurements would you need to know to find its area?

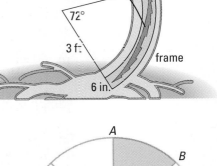

angled knee

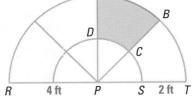

72°
3 ft
frame
6 in.

40. 🌐 **WINDOW DESIGN** The window shown is in the shape of a semicircle with radius 4 feet. The distance from *S* to *T* is 2 feet, and the measure of $\overarc{AB}$ is 45°. Find the area of the glass in the region *ABCD*.

A
B
D
C
R   4 ft   P   S 2 ft T

41. 🧩 **LOGICAL REASONING** Suppose a circle has a radius of 4.5 inches. If you double the radius of the circle, does the area of the circle double as well? What happens to the circle's circumference? Explain.

42. 🖥 **TECHNOLOGY** The area of a regular *n*-gon inscribed in a circle with radius 1 unit can be written as

$$A = \frac{1}{2}\left(\cos\left(\frac{180°}{n}\right)\right)\left(2n \cdot \sin\left(\frac{180°}{n}\right)\right).$$

Use a spreadsheet to make a table. The first column is for the number of sides *n* and the second column is for the area of the *n*-gon. Fill in your table up to a 16-gon. What do you notice as *n* gets larger and larger?

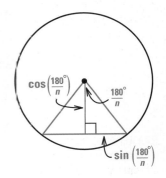

$\cos\left(\frac{180°}{n}\right)$
$\frac{180°}{n}$
$\sin\left(\frac{180°}{n}\right)$

⊙**Q** and ⊙**P** are tangent. Use the diagram for Exercises 43 and 44.

43. MULTIPLE CHOICE If ⊙Q is cut away, what is the remaining area of ⊙P?

(**A**) 6π (**B**) 9π (**C**) 27π

(**D**) 60π (**E**) 180π

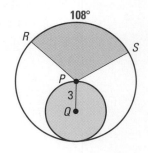

44. MULTIPLE CHOICE What is the area of the region shaded in red?

(**A**) 0.3 (**B**) 1.8π (**C**) 6π

(**D**) 10.8π (**E**) 108π

★ **Challenge**

45. FINDING AREA Find the area between the three congruent tangent circles. The radius of each circle is 6 centimeters. (*Hint:* △*ABC* is equilateral.)

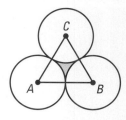

MIXED REVIEW

SIMPLIFYING RATIOS In Exercises 46–49, simplify the ratio. (Review 8.1 for 11.6)

46. $\dfrac{8 \text{ cats}}{20 \text{ cats}}$ **47.** $\dfrac{6 \text{ teachers}}{32 \text{ teachers}}$ **48.** $\dfrac{12 \text{ inches}}{63 \text{ inches}}$ **49.** $\dfrac{52 \text{ weeks}}{143 \text{ weeks}}$

50. The length of the diagonal of a square is 30. What is the length of each side? (Review 9.4)

FINDING MEASURES Use the diagram to find the indicated measure. Round decimals to the nearest tenth. (Review 9.6)

51. *BD*   **52.** *DC*

53. $m\angle DBC$ **54.** *BC*

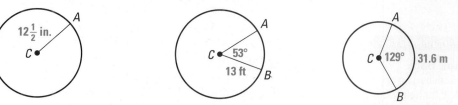

WRITING EQUATIONS Write the standard equation of the circle with the given center and radius. (Review 10.6)

55. center $(-2, -7)$, radius 6   **56.** center $(0, -9)$, radius 10

57. center $(-4, 5)$, radius 3.2   **58.** center $(8, 2)$, radius $\sqrt{11}$

FINDING MEASURES Find the indicated measure. (Review 11.4)

59. Circumference   **60.** Length of $\overarc{AB}$ **61.** Radius

11.6

Geometric Probability

What you should learn

GOAL ① Find a geometric probability.

GOAL ② Use geometric probability to solve **real-life** problems, as applied in **Example 2**.

Why you should learn it

▼ Geometric probability is one model for calculating **real-life** probabilities, such as the probability that a bus will be waiting outside a hotel in **Ex. 28**.

GOAL 1 FINDING A GEOMETRIC PROBABILITY

A **probability** is a number from 0 to 1 that represents the chance that an event will occur. Assuming that all outcomes are equally likely, an event with a probability of 0 *cannot* occur. An event with a probability of 1 is *certain* to occur, and an event with a probability of 0.5 is just as likely to occur as not.

In an earlier course, you may have evaluated probabilities by counting the number of favorable outcomes and dividing that number by the total number of possible outcomes. In this lesson, you will use a related process in which the division involves geometric measures such as length or area. This process is called **geometric probability**.

GEOMETRIC PROBABILITY

PROBABILITY AND LENGTH

Let $\overline{AB}$ be a segment that contains the segment $\overline{CD}$. If a point K on $\overline{AB}$ is chosen at random, then the probability that it is on $\overline{CD}$ is as follows:

$$P(\text{Point } K \text{ is on } \overline{CD}) = \frac{\text{Length of } \overline{CD}}{\text{Length of } \overline{AB}}$$

PROBABILITY AND AREA

Let J be a region that contains region M. If a point K in J is chosen at random, then the probability that it is in region M is as follows:

$$P(\text{Point } K \text{ is in region } M) = \frac{\text{Area of } M}{\text{Area of } J}$$

EXAMPLE 1 *Finding a Geometric Probability*

Find the probability that a point chosen at random on $\overline{RS}$ is on $\overline{TU}$.

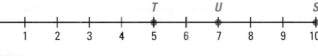

SOLUTION

$$P(\text{Point is on } \overline{TU}) = \frac{\text{Length of } \overline{TU}}{\text{Length of } \overline{RS}} = \frac{2}{10} = \frac{1}{5}$$

▶ The probability can be written as $\frac{1}{5}$, 0.2, or 20%.

STUDENT HELP

↳ **Study Tip**
When applying a formula for geometric probability, it is important that every point on the segment or in the region is equally likely to be chosen.

EXAMPLE 2 *Using Areas to Find a Geometric Probability*

DART BOARD A dart is tossed and hits the dart board shown. The dart is equally likely to land on any point on the dart board. Find the probability that the dart lands in the red region.

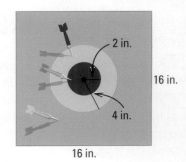

SOLUTION

Find the ratio of the area of the red region to the area of the dart board.

$P(\text{Dart lands in red region}) = \dfrac{\text{Area of red region}}{\text{Area of dart board}}$

$$= \dfrac{\pi(2^2)}{16^2}$$

$$= \dfrac{4\pi}{256}$$

$$\approx 0.05$$

▶ The probability that the dart lands in the red region is about 0.05, or 5%.

EXAMPLE 3 *Using a Segment to Find a Geometric Probability*

TRANSPORTATION You are visiting San Francisco and are taking a trolley ride to a store on Market Street. You are supposed to meet a friend at the store at 3:00 P.M. The trolleys run every 10 minutes and the trip to the store is 8 minutes. You arrive at the trolley stop at 2:48 P.M. What is the probability that you will arrive at the store by 3:00 P.M.?

Logical Reasoning

SOLUTION

To begin, find the greatest amount of time you can afford to wait for the trolley and still get to the store by 3:00 P.M.

Because the ride takes 8 minutes, you need to catch the trolley no later than 8 minutes before 3:00 P.M., or in other words by 2:52 P.M.

So, you can afford to wait 4 minutes (2:52 − 2:48 = 4 min). You can use a line segment to model the probability that the trolley will come within 4 minutes.

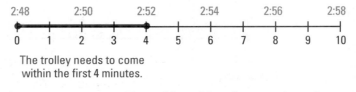

The trolley needs to come within the first 4 minutes.

STUDENT HELP

HOMEWORK HELP
Visit our Web site
www.mcdougallittell.com
for extra examples.

$P(\text{Get to store by 3:00}) = \dfrac{\text{Favorable waiting time}}{\text{Maximum waiting time}} = \dfrac{4}{10} = \dfrac{2}{5}$

▶ The probability is $\dfrac{2}{5}$, or 40%.

EXAMPLE 4 *Finding a Geometric Probability*

JOB LOCATION You work for a temporary employment agency. You live on the west side of town and prefer to work there. The work assignments are spread evenly throughout the rectangular region shown. Find the probability that an assignment chosen at random for you is on the west side of town.

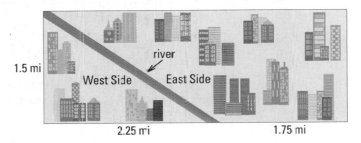

SOLUTION

The west side of town is approximately triangular. Its area is $\frac{1}{2} \cdot 2.25 \cdot 1.5$, or about 1.69 square miles. The area of the rectangular region is $1.5 \cdot 4$, or 6 square miles. So, the probability that the assignment is on the west side of town is

$$P(\text{Assignment is on west side}) = \frac{\text{Area of west side}}{\text{Area of rectangular region}} \approx \frac{1.69}{6} \approx 0.28.$$

▶ So, the probability that the work assignment is on the west side is about 28%.

GUIDED PRACTICE

Vocabulary Check ✓

1. Explain how a *geometric probability* is different from a *probability* found by dividing the number of favorable outcomes by the total number of possible outcomes.

Concept Check ✓

Determine whether you would use the *length method* or *area method* to find the geometric probability. Explain your reasoning.

2. The probability that an outcome lies in a triangular region

3. The probability that an outcome occurs within a certain time period

Skill Check ✓

In Exercises 4–7, *K* is chosen at random on $\overline{AF}$. Find the probability that *K* is on the indicated segment.

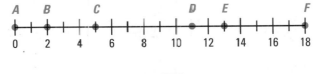

4. $\overline{AB}$ 5. $\overline{BD}$ 6. $\overline{BF}$

7. Explain the relationship between your answers to Exercises 4 and 6.

8. Find the probability that a point chosen at random in the trapezoid shown lies in either of the shaded regions.

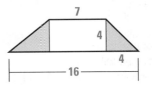

Practice and Applications

Student Help

Extra Practice to help you master skills is on p. 824.

Probability on a Segment **In Exercises 9–12, find the probability that a point *A*, selected randomly on $\overline{GN}$, is on the given segment.**

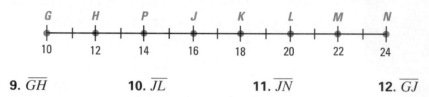

9. $\overline{GH}$ **10.** $\overline{JL}$ **11.** $\overline{JN}$ **12.** $\overline{GJ}$

Probability on a Segment **In Exercises 13–16, find the probability that a point *K*, selected randomly on $\overline{PU}$, is on the given segment.**

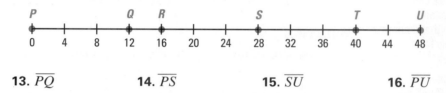

13. $\overline{PQ}$ **14.** $\overline{PS}$ **15.** $\overline{SU}$ **16.** $\overline{PU}$

Finding a Geometric Probability **Find the probability that a randomly chosen point in the figure lies in the shaded region.**

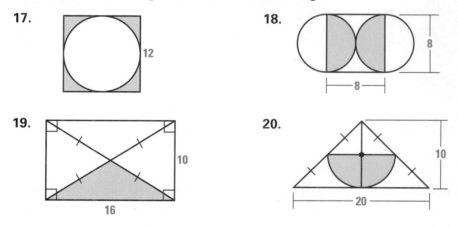

17.

18.

19.

20.

Targets **A regular hexagonal shaped target with sides of length 14 centimeters has a circular bull's eye with a diameter of 3 centimeters. In Exercises 21–23, darts are thrown and hit the target at random.**

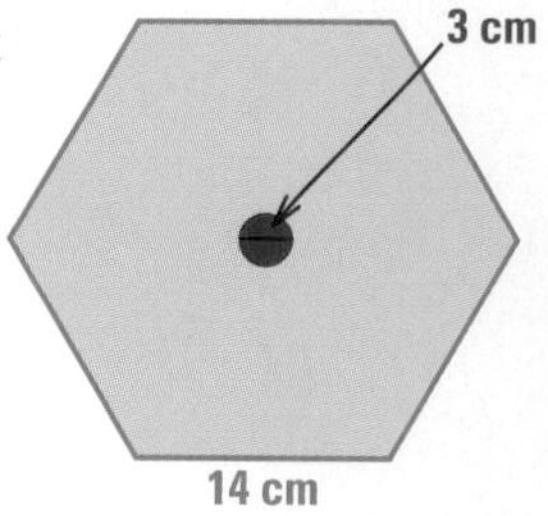

21. What is the probability that a dart that hits the target will hit the bull's eye?

22. Estimate how many times a dart will hit the bull's eye if 100 darts hit the target.

23. Find the probability that a dart will hit the bull's eye if the bull's eye's radius is doubled.

24. **Logical Reasoning** The midpoint of $\overline{JK}$ is M. What is the probability that a randomly selected point on $\overline{JK}$ is closer to M than to J or to K?

25. **Logical Reasoning** A circle with radius $\sqrt{2}$ units is circumscribed about a square with side length 2 units. Find the probability that a randomly chosen point will be inside the circle but outside the square.

Student Help

Homework Help
Example 1: Exs. 9–16
Example 2: Exs. 17–23, 29–34
Example 3: Exs. 26–28
Example 4: Exs. 40–42

26. 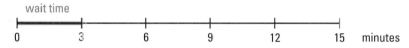 **FIRE ALARM** Suppose that your school day begins at 7:30 A.M. and ends at 3:00 P.M. You eat lunch at 11:00 A.M. If there is a fire drill at a random time during the day, what is the probability that it begins before lunch?

27. **PHONE CALL** You are expecting a call from a friend anytime between 6:00 P.M. and 7:00 P.M. Unexpectedly, you have to run an errand for a relative and are gone from 5:45 P.M. until 6:10 P.M. What is the probability that you missed your friend's call?

28. **TRANSPORTATION** Buses arrive at a resort hotel every 15 minutes. They wait for three minutes while passengers get on and get off, and then the buses depart. What is the probability that there is a bus waiting when a hotel guest walks out of the door at a randomly chosen time?

wait time

| 0 | 3 | 6 | 9 | 12 | 15 | minutes |

SHIP SALVAGE In Exercises 29 and 30, use the following information.
A ship is known to have sunk off the coast, between an island and the mainland as shown. A salvage vessel anchors at a random spot in this rectangular region for divers to search for the ship.

29. Find the approximate area of the rectangular region where the ship sank.

30. The divers search 500 feet in all directions from a point on the ocean floor directly below the salvage vessel. Estimate the probability that the divers will find the sunken ship on the first try.

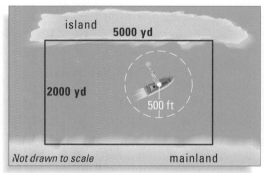

island **5000 yd**

2000 yd

500 ft

Not drawn to scale   mainland

ARCHERY In Exercises 31–35, use the following information.
Imagine that an arrow hitting the target shown is equally likely to hit any point on the target. The 10-point circle has a 4.8 inch diameter and each of the other rings is 2.4 inches wide. Find the probability that the arrow hits the region described.

31. The 10-point region

32. The yellow region

33. The white region

34. The 5-point region

35. **CRITICAL THINKING** Does the geometric probability model hold true when an expert archer shoots an arrow? Explain your reasoning.

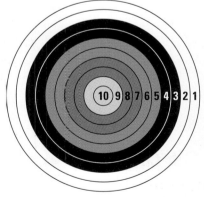

10 9 8 7 6 5 4 3 2 1

36. **USING ALGEBRA** If $0 < y < 1$ and $0 < x < 1$, find the probability that $y < x$. Begin by sketching the graph, and then use the *area method* to find the probability.

USING ALGEBRA Find the value of *x* so that the probability of the spinner landing on a blue sector is the value given.

37. $\frac{1}{3}$ **38.** $\frac{1}{4}$ **39.** $\frac{1}{6}$

BALLOON RACE In Exercises 40–42, use the following information.
In a "Hare and Hounds" balloon race, one balloon (the hare) leaves the ground first. About ten minutes later, the other balloons (the hounds) leave. The hare then lands and marks a square region as the target. The hounds each try to drop a marker in the target zone.

40. Suppose that a hound's marker dropped onto a rectangular field that is 200 feet by 250 feet is equally likely to land anywhere in the field. The target region is a 15 foot square that lies in the field. What is the probability that the marker lands in the target region?

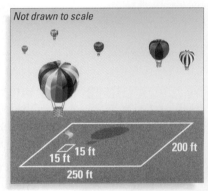

41. If the area of the target region is doubled, how does the probability change?

42. If each side of the target region is doubled, how does the probability change?

Test Preparation

43. MULTI-STEP PROBLEM Use the following information.
You organize a fund-raiser at your school. You fill a large glass jar that has a 25 centimeter diameter with water. You place a dish that has a 5 centimeter diameter at the bottom of the jar. A person donates a coin by dropping it in the jar. If the coin lands in the dish, the person wins a small prize.

a. Calculate the probability that a coin dropped, with an equally likely chance of landing anywhere at the bottom of the jar, lands in the dish.

b. Use the probability in part (a) to estimate the average number of coins needed to win a prize.

c. From past experience, you expect about 250 people to donate 5 coins each. How many prizes should you buy?

d. *Writing* Suppose that instead of the dish, a circle with a diameter of 5 centimeters is painted on the bottom of the jar, and any coin touching the circle wins a prize. Will the probability change? Explain.

★ Challenge

44. USING ALGEBRA Graph the lines $y = x$ and $y = 3$ in a coordinate plane. A point is chosen randomly from within the boundaries $0 < y < 4$ and $0 < x < 4$. Find the probability that the coordinates of the point are a solution of this system of inequalities:

$$y < 3$$
$$y > x$$

MIXED REVIEW

DETERMINING TANGENCY Tell whether $\overleftrightarrow{AB}$ is tangent to $\odot C$. Explain your reasoning. (Review 10.1)

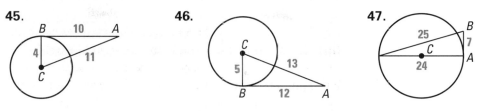

45.

46.

47.

DESCRIBING LINES In Exercises 48–51, graph the line with the circle $(x-2)^2+(y+4)^2=16$. Is the line a *tangent* or a *secant*? (Review 10.6)

48. $x=-y$

49. $y=0$

50. $x=6$

51. $y=x-1$

52. **LOCUS** Find the locus of all points in the coordinate plane that are equidistant from points $(3, 2)$ and $(1, 2)$ and within $\sqrt{2}$ units of the point $(1, -1)$. (Review 10.7)

QUIZ 2

Self-Test for Lessons 11.4–11.6

Find the indicated measure. (Lesson 11.4)

1. Circumference

2. Length of $\widehat{AB}$

3. Radius

In Exercises 4–6, find the area of the shaded region. (Lesson 11.5)

4.

5.

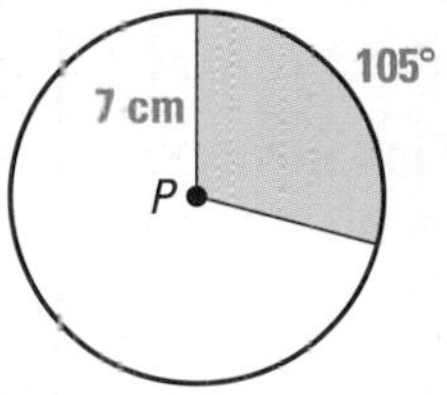

6.

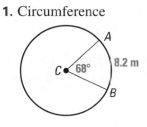

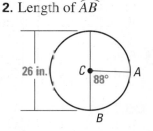

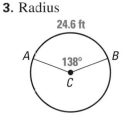

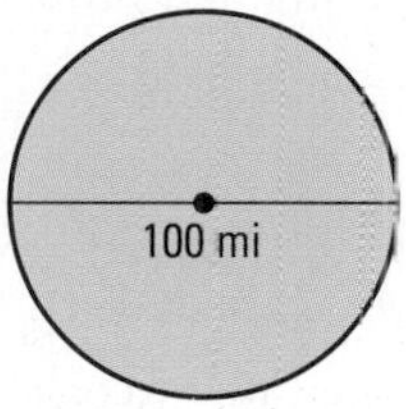

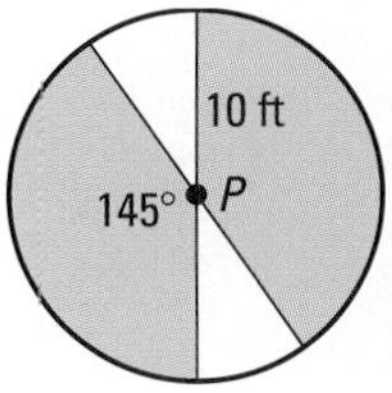

7. **TARGETS** A square target with 20 cm sides includes a triangular region with equal side lengths of 5 cm. A dart is thrown and hits the target at random. Find the probability that the dart hits the triangle. (Lesson 11.6)

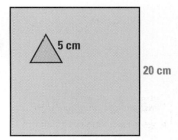

Investigating Experimental Probability

In Lesson 11.6 you found the *theoretical probability* of a dart landing in a region on a dart board. You can also find the *experimental probability* of this event using a graphing calculator simulation.

STUDENT HELP

INTERNET KEYSTROKE HELP

Visit our Web site www.mcdougallittell.com to see keystrokes for several models of calculators.

INVESTIGATE

1. Calculate the theoretical probability that a randomly thrown dart that lands on the dart board shown below will land in the region shaded red.

2. To find the experimental probability, you can physically throw a dart many times and record the results. You can also use a graphing calculator program that simulates throwing a dart as many times as you like. You can simulate this experiment on a TI-82 or TI-83 graphing calculator using the following program.

```
PROGRAM: DARTS
:ClrHome
:Input "HOW MANY THROWS?",N
:0 → H
:For (I, 1, N)
:rand → X
:rand → Y
:If (X² + Y²) < 0.25
:H + 1 → H
:End
:Disp "NUMBER OF HITS",H
```

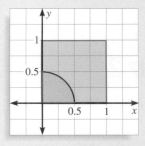

3. Enter and run the program to simulate 40 throws. Determine the proportion of darts thrown that landed in the region shaded red.

CONJECTURE

1. Explain why "If $(X^2 + Y^2) < 0.25$" is in the program.

2. Compare the theoretical and experimental probabilities you found in **Steps 1**, **2**, and **3**.

3. Find the experimental probability for the entire class by combining the number of throws and the number of hits and determining the proportion of dart throws that landed in the region shaded red.

4. How does the number of trials affect the relationship between the theoretical and experimental probabilities?

EXTENSION

CRITICAL THINKING The results of a calculator simulation tend to be more reliable than those of a human-generated simulation. Explain why a calculator simulation would be easier and more accurate than a human-generated one.

Chapter Summary

WHAT did you learn?

Find the measures of the interior and exterior angles of polygons. **(11.1)**

Find the areas of equilateral triangles and other regular polygons. **(11.2)**

Compare perimeters and areas of similar figures. **(11.3)**

Find the circumference of a circle and the length of an arc of a circle. **(11.4)**

Find the areas of circles and sectors. **(11.5)**

Find a geometric probability. **(11.6)**

WHY did you learn it?

Find the measures of angles in real-world objects, such as a home plate marker. **(p. 664)**

Solve problems by finding real-life areas, such as the area of a hexagonal mirror in a telescope. **(p. 674)**

Solve real-life problems, such as estimating a reasonable cost for photographic paper. **(p. 678)**

Find real-life distances, such as the distance around a track. **(p. 685)**

Find areas of real-life regions containing circles or parts of circles, such as the area of the front of a case for a clock. **(p. 693)**

Estimate the likelihood that an event will occur, such as the likelihood that divers will find a sunken ship on their first dive. **(p. 703)**

How does Chapter 11 fit into the BIGGER PICTURE of geometry?

The word *geometry* is derived from Greek words meaning "land measurement." The ability to measure angles, arc lengths, perimeters, circumferences, and areas allows you to calculate measurements required to solve problems in the real world. Keep in mind that a region that lies in a plane has two types of measures. The perimeter or circumference of a region is a *one*-dimensional measure that uses units such as centimeters or feet. The area of a region is a *two*-dimensional measure that uses units such as square centimeters or square feet. In the next chapter, you will study a *three*-dimensional measure called *volume*.

STUDY STRATEGY

Did your concept map help you organize your work?

The concept map you made, following the **Study Strategy** on page 660, may include these ideas.

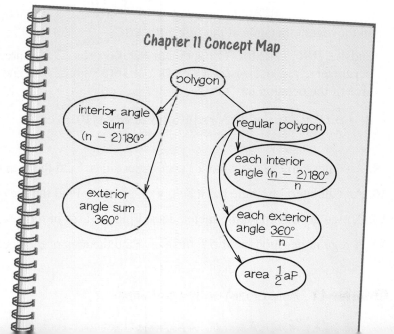

Chapter 11 Concept Map

Chapter Review

• center of a polygon, p. 670
• radius of a polygon, p. 670
• apothem of a polygon, p. 670

• central angle of a regular polygon, p. 671
• circumference, p. 683

• arc length, p. 683
• sector of a circle, p. 692

• probability, p. 699
• geometric probability, p. 699

11.1   **ANGLE MEASURES IN POLYGONS**

Examples on
pp. 661–664

> **EXAMPLES** If a regular polygon has 15 sides, then the sum of the measures of its interior angles is $(15 - 2) \cdot 180° = 2340°$. The measure of each interior angle is $\frac{1}{15} \cdot 2340° = 156°$. The measure of each exterior angle is $\frac{1}{15} \cdot 360° = 24°$.

In Exercises 1–4, you are given the number of sides of a regular polygon. Find the measure of each interior angle and each exterior angle.

1. 9   **2.** 13   **3.** 16   **4.** 24

In Exercises 5–8, you are given the measure of each interior angle of a regular *n*-gon. Find the value of *n*.

5. 172°   **6.** 135°   **7.** 150°   **8.** 170°

11.2   **AREAS OF REGULAR POLYGONS**

Examples on
pp. 669–671

> **EXAMPLES** The area of an equilateral triangle with sides of length 14 inches is
>
> $$A = \frac{1}{4}\sqrt{3}\,(14^2) = \frac{1}{4}\sqrt{3}\,(196) = 49\sqrt{3} \approx 84.9 \text{ in.}^2$$
>
> In the regular octagon at the right, $m\angle ABC = \frac{1}{8} \cdot 360° = 45°$ and $m\angle DBC = 22.5°$. The apothem BD is $6 \cdot \cos 22.5°$. The perimeter of the octagon is $8 \cdot 2 \cdot DC$, or $16(6 \cdot \sin 22.5°)$. The area of the octagon is
>
> $$A = \frac{1}{2}aP = \frac{1}{2}(6\cos 22.5°) \cdot 16(6\sin 22.5°) \approx 101.8 \text{ cm}^2.$$

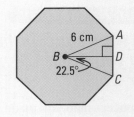

9. An equilateral triangle has 12 centimeter sides. Find the area of the triangle.

10. An equilateral triangle has a height of 6 inches. Find the area of the triangle.

11. A regular hexagon has 5 meter sides. Find the area of the hexagon.

12. A regular decagon has 1.5 foot sides. Find the area of the decagon.

PERIMETERS AND AREAS OF SIMILAR FIGURES

Examples on pp. 677–678

EXAMPLE The two pentagons at the right are similar. Their corresponding sides are in the ratio $2:3$, so the ratio of their areas is $2^2:3^2 = 4:9$.

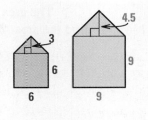

$$\frac{\text{Area (smaller)}}{\text{Area (larger)}} = \frac{6 \cdot 6 + \frac{1}{2}(3 \cdot 6)}{9 \cdot 9 + \frac{1}{2}(4.5 \cdot 9)} = \frac{45}{101.25} = \frac{4}{9}$$

Complete the statement using *always*, *sometimes*, or *never*.

13. If the ratio of the perimeters of two rectangles is $3:5$, then the ratio of their areas is __?__ $9:25$.

14. Two parallelograms are __?__ similar.

15. Two regular dodecagons with perimeters in the ratio 4 to 7 __?__ have areas in the ratio 16 to 49.

In the diagram at the right, $\triangle ADG$, $\triangle BDF$, and $\triangle CDE$ are similar.

16. Find the ratio of the perimeters and of the areas of $\triangle CDE$ and $\triangle BDF$.

17. Find the ratio of the perimeters and of the areas of $\triangle ADG$ and $\triangle BDF$.

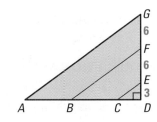

CIRCUMFERENCE AND ARC LENGTH

Examples on pp. 683–685

EXAMPLES The circumference of the circle at the right is $C = 2\pi(9) = 18\pi$.

The length of $\overset{\frown}{AB} = \frac{m\overset{\frown}{AB}}{360°} \cdot 2\pi r = \frac{60°}{360°} \cdot 18\pi = 3\pi$.

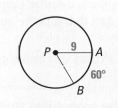

In Exercises 18–20, find the circumference of $\odot P$ and the length of $\overset{\frown}{AB}$.

18.   **19.**   **20.**

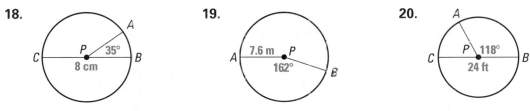

21. Find the radius of a circle with circumference 12 inches.

22. Find the diameter of a circle with circumference 15π meters.

AREAS OF CIRCLES AND SECTORS

Examples on pp. 691–694

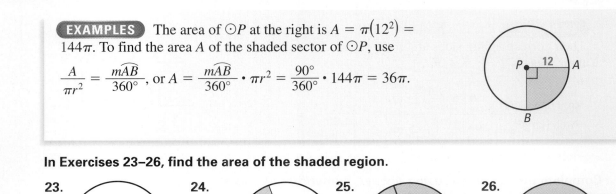

EXAMPLES The area of $\odot P$ at the right is $A = \pi(12^2) = 144\pi$. To find the area A of the shaded sector of $\odot P$, use

$$\frac{A}{\pi r^2} = \frac{m\widehat{AB}}{360°}, \text{ or } A = \frac{m\widehat{AB}}{360°} \cdot \pi r^2 = \frac{90°}{360°} \cdot 144\pi = 36\pi.$$

In Exercises 23–26, find the area of the shaded region.

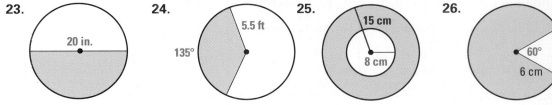

23.

20 in.

24.

135°

5.5 ft

25.

15 cm

8 cm

26.

60°

6 cm

27. What is the area of a circle with diameter 28 feet?

28. What is the radius of a circle with area 40 square inches?

GEOMETRIC PROBABILITY

Examples on pp. 699–701

EXAMPLES The probability that a randomly chosen point on $\overline{AB}$ is on $\overline{CD}$ is

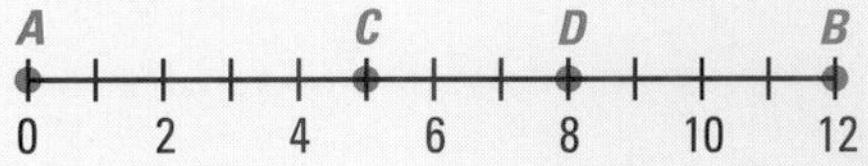

A ——————————— C ——— D ——————— B
0   2   4   6   8   10   12

$$P(\text{Point is on } \overline{CD}) = \frac{\text{Length of } \overline{CD}}{\text{Length of } \overline{AB}} = \frac{3}{12} = \frac{1}{4}.$$

Suppose a circular target has radius 12 inches and its bull's eye has radius 2 inches. If a dart that hits the target hits it at a random point, then

$$P(\text{Dart hits bull's eye}) = \frac{\text{Area of bull's eye}}{\text{Area of target}} = \frac{4\pi}{144\pi} = \frac{1}{36}.$$

Find the probability that a point A, selected randomly on $\overline{JN}$, is on the given segment.

J   K   L   M   N
0   8   16   24   32   40

29. $\overline{LM}$ **30.** $\overline{JL}$ **31.** $\overline{KM}$

Find the probability that a randomly chosen point in the figure lies in the shaded region.

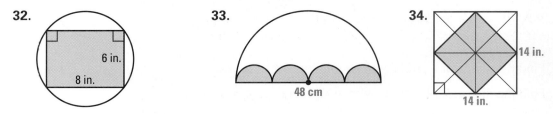

32.

6 in.

8 in.

33.

48 cm

34.

14 in.

14 in.

Chapter Test

In Exercises 1 and 2, use the figure at the right.

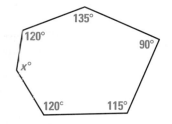

1. What is the value of x?

2. Find the sum of the measures of the exterior angles, one at each vertex.

3. What is the measure of each interior angle of a regular 30-gon?

4. What is the measure of each exterior angle of a regular 27-gon?

In Exercises 5−8, find the area of the regular polygon to two decimal places.

5. An equilateral triangle with perimeter 30 feet

6. A regular pentagon with apothem 8 inches

7. A regular hexagon with 9 centimeter sides

8. A regular nonagon (9-gon) with radius 1 meter

Rhombus *ABCD* has sides of length 8 centimeters. *EFGH* is a similar rhombus with sides of length 6 centimeters.

9. Find the ratio of the perimeters of *ABCD* to *EFGH*. Then find the ratio of their areas.

10. The area of *ABCD* is 56 square centimeters. Find the area of *EFGH*.

Use the diagram of ⊙*R*.

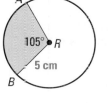

11. Find the circumference and the area of ⊙*R*.

12. Find the length of $\widehat{AB}$.

13. Find the area of the sector *ARB*.

Find the area of the shaded region.

14.

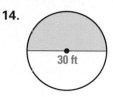

15.

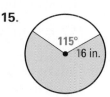

16.

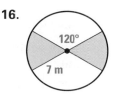

In Exercises 17 and 18, a point is chosen randomly in the 20 inch by 20 inch square at the right.

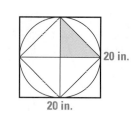

17. Find the probability that the point is inside the circle.

18. Find the probability that the point is in the shaded area.

19. 🌐 **WATER-SKIER** A boat that is pulling a water-skier drives in a circle that has a radius of 80 feet. The skier is moving outside the path of the boat in a circle that has a radius of 110 feet. Find the distance traveled by the boat when it has completed a full circle. How much farther has the skier traveled?

20. 🌐 **WAITING TIME** You are expecting friends to come by your house any time between 6:00 P.M. and 8:00 P.M. Meanwhile, a problem at work has delayed you. If you get home at 6:20 P.M., what is the probability that your friends are already there?

Chapter Standardized Test

🔻 **TEST-TAKING STRATEGY** Do not panic if you run out of time before answering all of the questions. You can still receive a high test score without answering every question.

1. MULTIPLE CHOICE A regular polygon has an interior angle with a measure of 160°. How many sides does the polygon have?

(A) 14   (B) 16   (C) 18

(D) 20   (E) 22

2. MULTIPLE CHOICE What is the value of *x*?

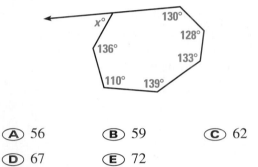

(A) 56   (B) 59   (C) 62

(D) 67   (E) 72

QUANTITATIVE COMPARISON In Exercises 3–5, use the two regular polygons shown to choose the statement that is true.

(A) The quantity in column A is greater.

(B) The quantity in column B is greater.

(C) The two quantities are equal.

(D) The relationship cannot be determined from the given information.

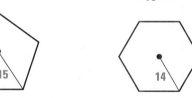

Polygon A   Polygon B

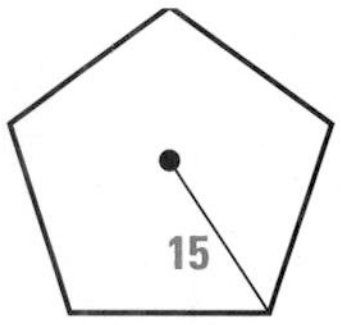

	Column A	Column B
3.	Apothem of polygon A	Apothem of polygon B
4.	Perimeter of polygon A	Perimeter of polygon B
5.	Area of polygon A	Area of polygon B

6. MULTIPLE CHOICE A regular octagon has sides of length 12 cm. Another regular octagon has sides of length 18 cm. Find the ratio of the area of the smaller octagon to the area of the larger octagon.

(A) 4:9   (B) 2:3   (C) 12:18

(D) 18:12   (E) 9:4

In Exercises 7 and 8, use the diagram below.

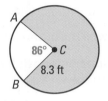

7. MULTIPLE CHOICE What is the length of $\overarc{AB}$?

(A) about 12.10 ft   (B) about 12.46 ft

(C) about 13.56 ft   (D) about 14.81 ft

(E) about 21.64 ft

8. MULTIPLE CHOICE What is the area of the shaded region?

(A) about 51.70 ft²   (B) about 84.50 ft²

(C) about 160.27 ft²   (D) about 162.72 ft²

(E) about 164.72 ft²

9. MULTIPLE CHOICE What is the area of the shaded region in the diagram below?

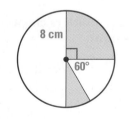

(A) about 33.51 cm²   (B) about 50.27 cm²

(C) about 67.02 cm²   (D) about 83.78 cm²

(E) about 100.53 cm²

10. MULTIPLE CHOICE ⊙*P* and ⊙*Q* are tangent. If a point is chosen at random in ⊙*P*, what is the probability that the chosen point lies in the shaded region?

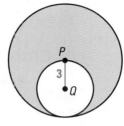

   (**A**) 25%   (**B**) 50%   (**C**) 75%

   (**D**) $133\frac{1}{3}$%   (**E**) 200%

11. MULTIPLE CHOICE Suppose that in a one-hour television program, 24 minutes are used for advertising. If you start watching the program at a random time during the show, what is the probability that you tune in during a commercial?

   (**A**) 0.4   (**B**) 0.6   (**C**) about 0.67

   (**D**) 0.24   (**E**) cannot be determined

MULTI-STEP PROBLEM In the diagram at the right, the polygon is a regular octagon inscribed in a circle.

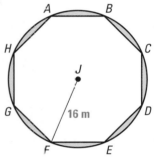

12. Find the circumference and the area of ⊙*J*.

13. What is the measure of each interior angle of the octagon?

14. What is the measure of each exterior angle?

15. Find the perimeter and the area of the octagon.

16. Find the length of $\overset{\frown}{AB}$.

17. *Writing* Describe two different methods you could use to find the area of the shaded region. Does each method yield the same result? Which method do you prefer? Explain your answer by comparing the methods.

MULTI-STEP PROBLEM In Exercises 18–22, use the following information.
Suppose you are at a carnival playing a game in which you throw darts and hit the dart board shown at the right. A dart is equally likely to hit any point on the dart board. The red regions are congruent trapezoids.

18. Find the radius, the circumference, and the area of the green circular region.

19. What is the probability that a dart lands in the green circular region?

20. What is the probability that a dart lands in the blue rectangular region?

21. Suppose you win a prize if your dart hits a red, green, or blue region. If you throw a dart that hits the board, what is the probability that you win a prize?

22. Suppose you win a prize if your dart hits a red, green, or blue region. If you throw a dart that hits the board, what is the probability that you do not win a prize?

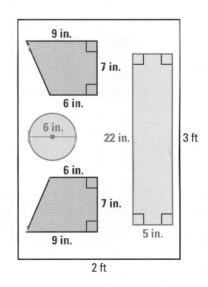

Geometry on a Sphere

OBJECTIVE Explore lines and triangles on a sphere, and compare geometry on a sphere to Euclidean geometry.

Materials: round balloon and markers (or ball and rubber bands), protractor

A DIFFERENT UNDERSTANDING OF PLANE AND LINE

In Euclidean geometry, you can think of a plane as a flat surface that extends forever, and you can think of a line that lies in a plane as a set of points that extends forever in two directions.

Geometry on a sphere is different: a *plane* is a spherical surface and a *line* is a special kind of circle on that surface.

   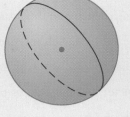

a **plane** in the
geometry of a sphere

a **line** in the
geometry of a sphere

A *line* on a sphere can be defined as a *great circle*, that is, a circle on the sphere whose center is the center of the sphere. Circles on the sphere that do not have the same center as the sphere are not considered lines.

If you imagine Earth as a sphere, then the equator is an example of a great circle. Circles of longitude, which pass through the north and south poles, are also great circles.

INVESTIGATION

Use an inflated balloon as a sphere and use a marker to draw lines, or use a large ball and fit rubber bands around it to represent lines.

1. Draw one line on a sphere. If a point lies on the line, does the point that is opposite it on the sphere also lie on the line?

2. Draw another line on a sphere. Do your two lines intersect?

3. Is it possible to draw two lines on the sphere that do not intersect?

4. In Euclidean geometry, the Parallel Postulate states that given a line and a point not on the line, there is exactly one line through the point parallel to the given line. Does the Parallel Postulate apply to geometry on a sphere? Explain.

5. Is it possible to draw two lines on a sphere that intersect to form right angles?

TRIANGLES ON A SPHERE

If you draw three lines on a sphere, you can divide the sphere into eight 3-sided regions, which can be considered *triangles* in the geometry of a sphere.

INVESTIGATION

6. Draw three lines on a sphere. Find a triangular region enclosed by three lines. Measure the angles of the triangle with a protractor.

7. What is the sum of the angles of the triangle you drew on the sphere?

8. Draw three lines on a sphere so that the triangular region formed is equiangular. What are the measures of the angles?

9. Is it possible to draw a 60°-60°-60° triangle on a sphere? a 90°-90°-90° triangle? a 120°-120°-120° triangle?

10. What is the range of values for the sum of the angles of a triangle on a sphere?

PRESENT YOUR RESULTS

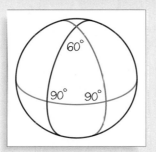

Make a bulletin board display of your results.

- Include a description of how *plane* and *line* are viewed differently in Euclidean geometry and the geometry of a sphere.

- Include drawings or balloons with markings of lines that intersect on a sphere.

- Summarize your results about the angles of triangles on a sphere.

EXTENSION

These mathematicians investigated non-Euclidean geometries, such as elliptic geometry and hyperbolic geometry. Research and write a report about one of them. How did the mathematician's work challenge the Parallel Postulate?

- Carl Friedrich Gauss (1777–1855)
- Nikolay Lobachevsky (1792–1856)
- János Bolyai (1802–1860)
- G. F. Bernhard Riemann (1826–1866)
- Felix Klein (1849–1925)
- David Hilbert (1862–1943)

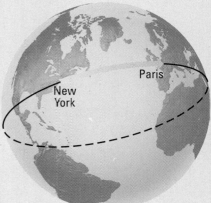

Pilots save time and fuel by using great circle routes to travel between cities on the globe.

SURFACE AREA
AND VOLUME

▶ How are geometric solids used in planetarium design?

APPLICATION: Spherical Buildings

Planetariums create space shows by projecting images of the moon, stars, and planets onto the interior surface of a dome, or *hemisphere*. The planetarium in these architectural drawings is shaped like a ball, or *sphere*.

When constructing the dome of a planetarium, the builders need to estimate the amount of material needed to cover the interior surface of the dome. The diagram below shows the radius *r* of the dome of a planetarium.

Think & Discuss

1. Use the formula $2\pi r^2$ to find the amount of material needed to cover the interior of a hemisphere with a radius of 40 feet.

2. Describe any other buildings that are shaped like spheres or hemispheres.

Learn More About It

You will investigate spherical buildings in Exercises 38–40 on p. 764.

INTERNET APPLICATION LINK Visit www.mcdougallittell.com for more information about spheres in architecture.

Study Guide

PREVIEW

What's the chapter about?

Chapter 12 is about **surface area and volume of solids**. Surface area and volume are the measurements used to describe three-dimensional geometric figures. In Chapter 12, you'll learn

- how to calculate the surface area and volume of various solids.

- how to use surface area and volume in real-life situations, such as finding the amount of wax needed to make a candle.

KEY VOCABULARY		
▶ **Review**	• scale factor, p. 474	• cylinder, p. 730
• equilateral triangle, p. 194	• locus, p. 642	• pyramid, p. 735
• polygon, p. 322	▶ **New**	• circular cone, p. 737
• convex, p. 323	• polyhedron, p. 719	• sphere, p. 759
• nonconvex, p. 323	• Platonic solids, p. 721	• similar solids, p. 766
• ratio, p. 457	• prism, p. 728	

PREPARE

Are you ready for the chapter?

SKILL REVIEW Do these exercises to review key skills that you'll apply in this chapter. See the given **reference page** if there is something you don't understand.

Find the scale factor of the similar polygons. (Review p. 474)

1.

26

13

2.
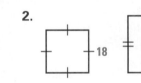
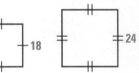
18   24

Calculate the area of the regular polygon. (Review pp. 669–671)

3.
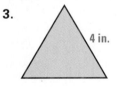
4 in.

4.
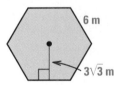
6 m

$3\sqrt{3}$ m

5.
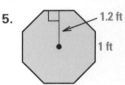
1.2 ft

1 ft

STUDENT HELP

▶ **Study Tip**
"Student Help" boxes throughout the chapter give you study tips and tell you where to look for extra help in this book and on the Internet.

STUDY STRATEGY

Here's a study strategy!

Generalizing Formulas

When faced with having to remember many formulas, try to find an underlying concept that links some or all of the formulas together. Then, you only have to remember the concept instead of all the formulas.

Exploring Solids

What you should learn

GOAL 1 Use properties of polyhedra.

GOAL 2 Use Euler's Theorem in **real-life** situations, such as analyzing the molecular structure of salt in **Example 5**.

Why you should learn it

▼ You can use properties of polyhedra to classify various crystals, as in **Exs. 39–41**.

GOAL 1 USING PROPERTIES OF POLYHEDRA

A **polyhedron** is a solid that is bounded by polygons, called **faces**, that enclose a single region of space. An **edge** of a polyhedron is a line segment formed by the intersection of two faces. A **vertex** of a polyhedron is a point where three or more edges meet. The plural of polyhedron is *polyhedra*, or *polyhedrons*.

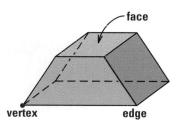

face

vertex   edge

EXAMPLE 1 *Identifying Polyhedra*

Decide whether the solid is a polyhedron. If so, count the number of faces, vertices, and edges of the polyhedron.

a.

b.
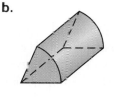

c.
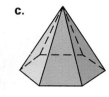

SOLUTION

a. This is a polyhedron. It has 5 faces, 6 vertices, and 9 edges.

b. This is not a polyhedron. Some of its faces are not polygons.

c. This is a polyhedron. It has 7 faces, 7 vertices, and 12 edges.

CONCEPT SUMMARY   **TYPES OF SOLIDS**

Of the five solids below, the prism and pyramid are polyhedra. The cone, cylinder, and sphere are not polyhedra.

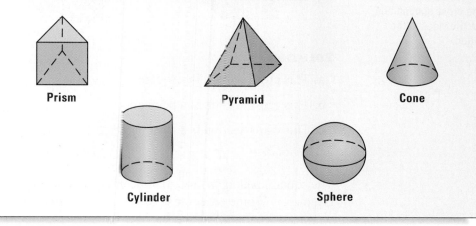

Prism   Pyramid   Cone

Cylinder   Sphere

A polyhedron is **regular** if all of its faces are congruent regular polygons. A polyhedron is **convex** if any two points on its surface can be connected by a segment that lies entirely inside or on the polyhedron. If this segment goes outside the polyhedron, then the polyhedron is *nonconvex*, or *concave*.

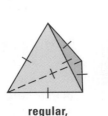

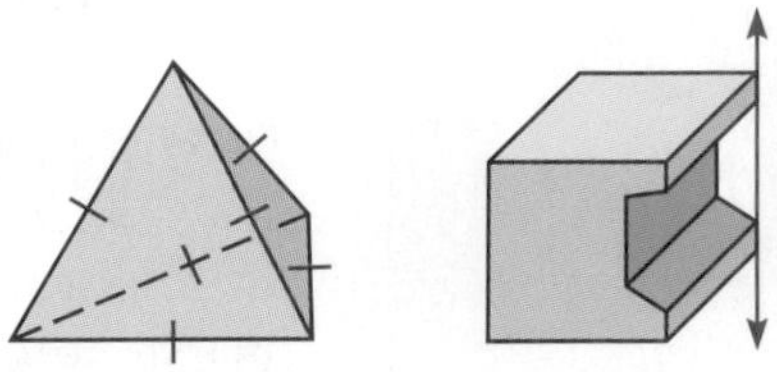

regular, convex

nonregular, nonconvex

EXAMPLE 2 *Classifying Polyhedra*

Is the octahedron convex? Is it regular?

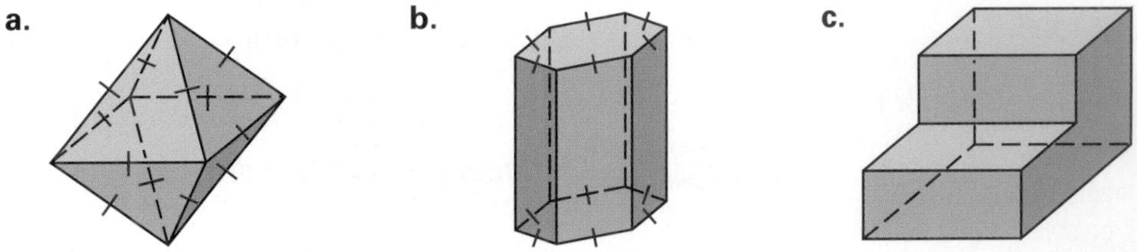

a.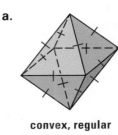

convex, regular

b.

convex, nonregular

c.

nonconvex, nonregular

. . . .

Imagine a plane slicing through a solid. The intersection of the plane and the solid is called a **cross section**. For instance, the diagram shows that the intersection of a plane and a sphere is a circle.

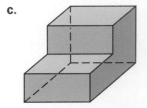

sphere

plane

cross section

EXAMPLE 3 *Describing Cross Sections*

Describe the shape formed by the intersection of the plane and the cube.

a.

b.

c.

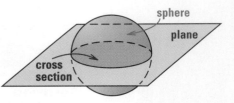

SOLUTION

　a. This cross section is a square.

　b. This cross section is a pentagon.

　c. This cross section is a triangle.

. . . .

The square, pentagon, and triangle cross sections of a cube are described in Example 3. Some other cross sections are the rectangle, trapezoid, and hexagon.

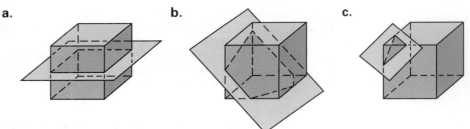

GOAL 2 USING EULER'S THEOREM

> **STUDENT HELP**
>
> **Study Tip**
> Notice that four of the Platonic solids end in "hedron." *Hedron* is Greek for "side" or "face." A cube is sometimes called a *hexahedron*.

There are five regular polyhedra, called *Platonic solids*, after the Greek mathematician and philosopher Plato The **Platonic solids** are a regular **tetrahedron** (4 faces), a cube (6 faces), a regular **octahedron** (8 faces), a regular **dodecahedron** (12 faces), and a regular **icosahedron** (20 faces).

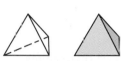

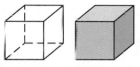

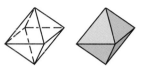

Regular tetrahedron
4 faces, 4 vertices, 6 edges

Cube
6 faces, 8 vertices, 12 edges

Regular octahedron
8 faces, 6 vertices, 12 edges

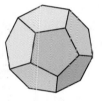

Regular dodecahedron
12 faces, 20 vertices, 30 edges

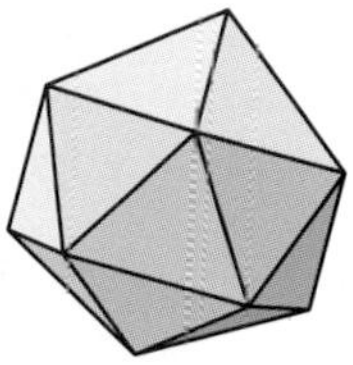

Regular icosahedron
20 faces, 12 vertices, 30 edges

Notice that the sum of the number of faces and vertices is two more than the number of edges in the solids above. This result was proved by the Swiss mathematician Leonhard Euler (1707–1783).

> **THEOREM**
>
> **THEOREM 12.1** ***Euler's Theorem***
>
> The number of faces (F), vertices (V), and edges (E) of a polyhedron are related by the formula $F + V = E + 2$.

EXAMPLE 4 *Using Euler's Theorem*

The solid has 14 faces; 8 triangles and 6 octagons. How many vertices does the solid have?

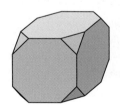

SOLUTION

On their own, 8 triangles and 6 octagons have $8(3) + 6(8)$, or 72 edges. In the solid, each side is shared by exactly two polygons. So, the number of edges is one half of 72, or 36. Use Euler's Theorem to find the number of vertices.

$F + V = E + 2$	**Write Euler's Theorem.**
$14 + V = 36 + 2$	**Substitute.**
$V = 24$	**Solve for V.**

▶ The solid has 24 vertices.

EXAMPLE 5 *Finding the Number of Edges*

 CHEMISTRY In molecules of sodium chloride, commonly known as table salt, chloride atoms are arranged like the vertices of regular octahedrons. In the crystal structure, the molecules share edges. How many sodium chloride molecules share the edges of one sodium chloride molecule?

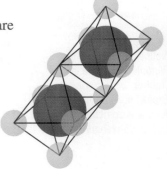

SOLUTION

To find the number of molecules that share edges with a given molecule, you need to know the number of edges of the molecule.

You know that the molecules are shaped like regular octahedrons. So, they each have 8 faces and 6 vertices. You can use Euler's Theorem to find the number of edges, as shown below.

$$F + V = E + 2 \qquad \text{Write Euler's Theorem.}$$

$$8 + 6 = E + 2 \qquad \text{Substitute.}$$

$$12 = E \qquad \text{Simplify.}$$

▶ So, 12 other molecules share the edges of the given molecule.

EXAMPLE 6 *Finding the Number of Vertices*

SPORTS A soccer ball resembles a polyhedron with 32 faces; 20 are regular hexagons and 12 are regular pentagons. How many vertices does this polyhedron have?

SOLUTION

Each of the 20 hexagons has 6 sides and each of the 12 pentagons has 5 sides. Each edge of the soccer ball is shared by two polygons. Thus, the total number of edges is as follows:

$$E = \frac{1}{2}(6 \cdot 20 + 5 \cdot 12) \qquad \text{Expression for number of edges}$$

$$= \frac{1}{2}(180) \qquad \text{Simplify inside parentheses.}$$

$$= 90 \qquad \text{Multiply.}$$

Knowing the number of edges, 90, and the number of faces, 32, you can apply Euler's Theorem to determine the number of vertices.

$$F + V = E + 2 \qquad \text{Write Euler's Theorem.}$$

$$32 + V = 90 + 2 \qquad \text{Substitute.}$$

$$V = 60 \qquad \text{Simplify.}$$

▶ So, the polyhedron has 60 vertices.

GUIDED PRACTICE

Vocabulary Check ✓

1. Define *polyhedron* in your own words.

Concept Check ✓

2. Is a regular octahedron convex? Are all the Platonic solids convex? Explain.

Skill Check ✓

Decide whether the solid is a polyhedron. Explain.

3.   **4.**   **5.**

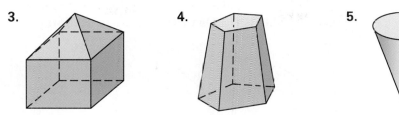

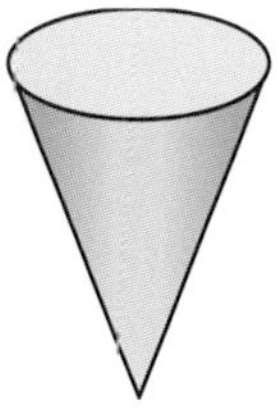

Use Euler's Theorem to find the unknown number.

6. Faces: __?__
Vertices: 6
Edges: 12

7. Faces: 5
Vertices: __?__
Edges: 9

8. Faces: __?__
Vertices: 10
Edges: 15

9. Faces: 20
Vertices: 12
Edges: __?__

PRACTICE AND APPLICATIONS

STUDENT HELP

▶ **Extra Practice**
to help you master
skills is on p. 825.

IDENTIFYING POLYHEDRA **Tell whether the solid is a polyhedron. Explain your reasoning.**

10.   **11.**   **12.**

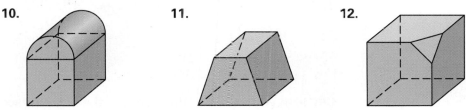

ANALYZING SOLIDS **Count the number of faces, vertices, and edges of the polyhedron.**

13.   **14.**   **15.**

STUDENT HELP

▶ **HOMEWORK HELP**
Example 1: Exs. 10–15
Example 2: Exs. 16–24
Example 3: Exs. 25–35
Example 4: Exs. 36–52
Example 5: Ex. 53
Example 6: Exs. 47–52

ANALYZING POLYHEDRA **Decide whether the polyhedron is regular and/or convex. Explain.**

16.   **17.**   **18.**

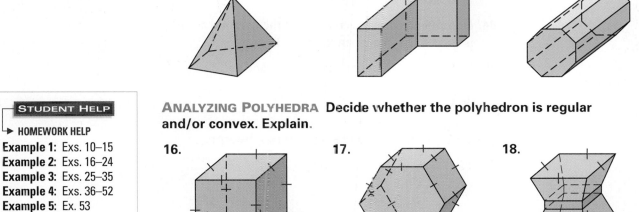

LOGICAL REASONING Determine whether the statement is *true* or *false*. **Explain your reasoning.**

19. Every convex polyhedron is regular.　　**20.** A polyhedron can have exactly 3 faces.

21. A cube is a regular polyhedron.　　**22.** A polyhedron can have exactly 4 faces.

23. A cone is a regular polyhedron.　　**24.** A polyhedron can have exactly 5 faces.

CROSS SECTIONS Describe the cross section.

25.

26.

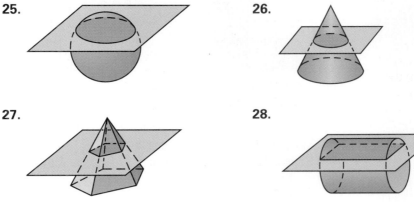

27.

28.

COOKING Describe the shape that is formed by the cut made in the food shown.

29. Carrot　　**30.** Cheese　　**31.** Cake

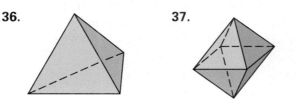

CRITICAL THINKING In the diagram, the bottom face of the pyramid is a square.

32. Name the cross section shown.

33. Can a plane intersect the pyramid at a point? If so, sketch the intersection.

34. Describe the cross section when the pyramid is sliced by a plane parallel to its bottom face.

35. Is it possible to have an isosceles trapezoid as a cross section of this pyramid? If so, draw the cross section.

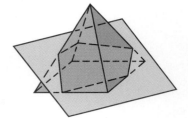

POLYHEDRONS Name the regular polyhedron.

36.　　　　**37.**　　　　**38.**

FOCUS ON CAREERS

MINERALOGY
By studying the arrangement of atoms in a crystal, mineralogists are able to determine the chemical and physical properties of the crystal.

CAREER LINK
www.mcdougallittell.com

STUDENT HELP

HOMEWORK HELP
Visit our Web site www.mcdougallittell.com for help with problem solving in Exs. 47–52.

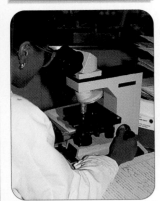

CRYSTALS In Exercises 39–41, name the Platonic solid that the crystal resembles.

39. Cobaltite

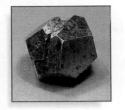

40. Fluorite

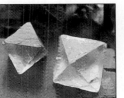

41. Pyrite

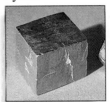

42. VISUAL THINKING Sketch a cube and describe the figure that results from connecting the centers of adjoining faces.

EULER'S THEOREM In Exercises 43–45, find the number of faces, edges, and vertices of the polyhedron and use them to verify Euler's Theorem.

43.

44.

45.

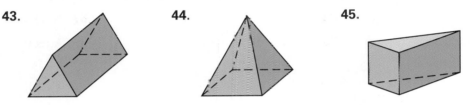

46. MAKING A TABLE Make a table of the number of faces, vertices, and edges for the Platonic solids. Use it to show Euler's Theorem is true for each solid.

USING EULER'S THEOREM In Exercises 47–52, calculate the number of vertices of the solid using the given information.

47. 20 faces; all triangles

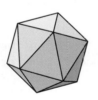

48. 14 faces; 8 triangles and 6 squares

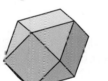

49. 14 faces; 8 hexagons and 6 squares

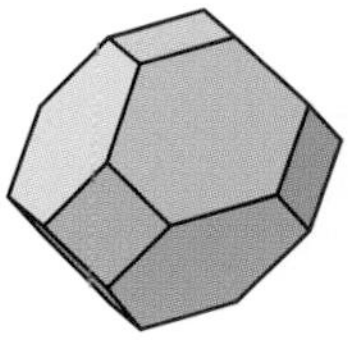

50. 26 faces; 18 squares and 8 triangles

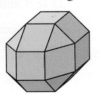

51. 8 faces; 4 hexagons and 4 triangles

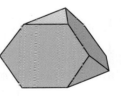

52. 12 faces; all pentagons

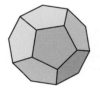

53. SCIENCE CONNECTION In molecules of cesium chloride, chloride atoms are arranged like the vertices of cubes. In its crystal structure, the molecules share faces to form an array of cubes. How many cesium chloride molecules share the faces of a given cesium chloride molecule?

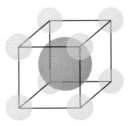

54. MULTIPLE CHOICE A polyhedron has 18 edges and 12 vertices. How many faces does it have?

 Ⓐ 4   Ⓑ 6   Ⓒ 8   Ⓓ 10   Ⓔ 12

55. MULTIPLE CHOICE In the diagram, Q and S are the midpoints of two edges of the cube. What is the length of $\overline{QS}$, if each edge of the cube has length h?

 Ⓐ $\dfrac{h}{2}$ Ⓑ $\dfrac{h}{\sqrt{2}}$ Ⓒ $\dfrac{2h}{\sqrt{2}}$

 Ⓓ $\sqrt{2}h$ Ⓔ $2h$

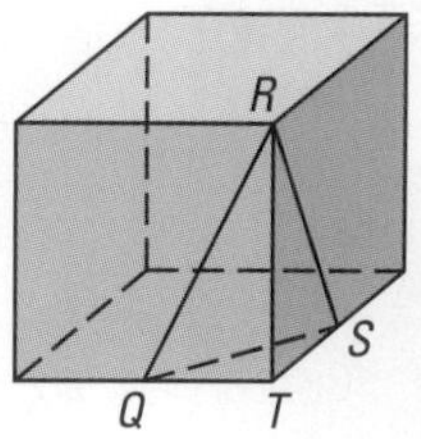

★ **Challenge**

SKETCHING CROSS SECTIONS Sketch the intersection of a cube and a plane so that the given shape is formed.

EXTRA CHALLENGE
www.mcdougallittell.com

56. An equilateral triangle   **57.** A regular hexagon

58. An isosceles trapezoid   **59.** A rectangle

MIXED REVIEW

FINDING AREA OF QUADRILATERALS Find the area of the figure. (Review 6.7 for 12.2)

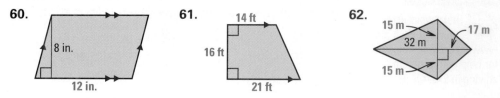

60. 8 in.   12 in.

61. 14 ft   16 ft   21 ft

62. 15 m   17 m   32 m   15 m

FINDING AREA OF REGULAR POLYGONS Find the area of the regular polygon described. Round your answer to two decimal places. (Review 11.2 for 12.2)

63. An equilateral triangle with a perimeter of 48 meters and an apothem of 4.6 meters.

64. A regular octagon with a perimeter of 28 feet and an apothem of 4.22 feet.

65. An equilateral triangle whose sides measure 8 centimeters.

66. A regular hexagon whose sides measure 4 feet.

67. A regular dodecagon whose sides measure 16 inches.

FINDING AREA Find the area of the shaded region. Round your answer to two decimal places. (Review 11.5)

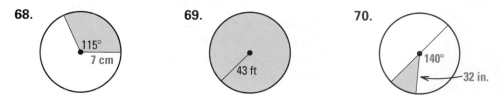

68. 115°   7 cm

69. 43 ft

70. 140°   32 in.

● ACTIVITY 12.2

Developing Concepts

GROUP ACTIVITY
Work with a partner.

MATERIALS
• graph paper
• pencil
• scissors

Investigating Surface Area

▶ **QUESTION** A *net* is a pattern that can be folded to form a polyhedron. How can a net be used to find the surface area of a polyhedron?

▶ **EXPLORING THE CONCEPT**

① Copy the net below on graph paper. Be sure to label the sections of the net.

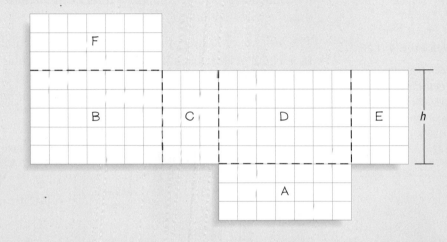

② Cut out the net and fold it along the dotted lines to form a polyhedron. Describe the polyhedron. Is it regular? Is it convex?

▶ **INVESTIGATE**

1. The *surface area* of a polyhedron is the sum of the areas of its faces. Find the surface area of the polyhedron you just made. (Each square on the graph paper measures 1 unit by 1 unit.)

2. Lay the net flat again and find the following measures.

   A: the area of rectangle *A*

   P: the perimeter of rectangle *A*

   h: the height of rectangles *B*, *C*, *D*, and *E*

3. Using the values from Exercise 2, find $2A + Ph$. Compare this value to the surface area you found in Exercise 1. What do you notice?

▶ **MAKE A CONJECTURE**

4. Make a conjecture about how to find the surface area of a rectangular solid.

EXTENSION

CRITICAL THINKING Use graph paper to draw the net of another rectangular solid. Fold the net to make sure that it forms a rectangular solid. Use your conjecture from Exercise 4 to calculate the surface area of the solid.

Surface Area of Prisms and Cylinders

What you should learn

GOAL 1 Find the surface area of a prism.

GOAL 2 Find the surface area of a cylinder.

Why you should learn it

▼ You can find the surface area of **real-life** objects, such as the cylinder records used on phonographs during the late 1800s. See **Ex. 43**.

GOAL 1 **FINDING THE SURFACE AREA OF A PRISM**

A **prism** is a polyhedron with two congruent faces, called **bases**, that lie in parallel planes. The other faces, called **lateral faces**, are parallelograms formed by connecting the corresponding vertices of the bases. The segments connecting these vertices are *lateral edges*.

The *altitude* or *height* of a prism is the perpendicular distance between its bases. In a **right prism**, each lateral edge is perpendicular to both bases. Prisms that have lateral edges that are not perpendicular to the bases are **oblique prisms**. The length of the oblique lateral edges is the *slant height* of the prism.

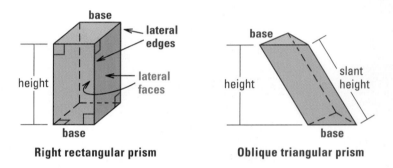

Right rectangular prism   Oblique triangular prism

Prisms are classified by the shapes of their bases. For example, the figures above show one rectangular prism and one triangular prism. The **surface area** of a polyhedron is the sum of the areas of its faces. The **lateral area** of a polyhedron is the sum of the areas of its lateral faces.

EXAMPLE 1 *Finding the Surface Area of a Prism*

Find the surface area of a right rectangular prism with a height of 8 inches, a length of 3 inches, and a width of 5 inches.

SOLUTION

Begin by sketching the prism, as shown. The prism has 6 faces, two of each of the following:

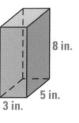

STUDENT HELP

↳ Study Tip
When sketching prisms, first draw the two bases. Then connect the corresponding vertices of the bases.

Faces	Dimensions	Area of faces
Left and right	8 in. by 5 in.	40 in.^{2}
Front and back	8 in. by 3 in.	24 in.^{2}
Top and bottom	3 in. by 5 in.	15 in.^{2}

▶ The surface area of the prism is $S = 2(40) + 2(24) + 2(15) = 158$ in.^{2}

Imagine that you cut some edges of a right hexagonal prism and unfolded it. The two-dimensional representation of all of the faces is called a **net**.

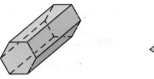  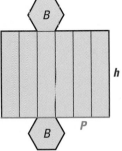

In the net of the prism, notice that the lateral area (the sum of the areas of the lateral faces) is equal to the perimeter of the base multiplied by the height.

THEOREM

THEOREM 12.2 *Surface Area of a Right Prism*

The surface area S of a right prism can be found using the formula $S = 2B + Ph$, where B is the area of a base, P is the perimeter of a base, and h is the height.

EXAMPLE 2 *Using Theorem 12.2*

Find the surface area of the right prism.

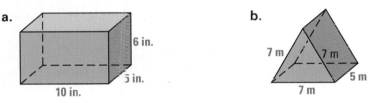

a.

6 in.
5 in.
10 in.

b.

7 m   7 m
7 m
5 m

STUDENT HELP

↳ **Study Tip**
The prism in part (a) has three pairs of parallel, congruent faces. Any pair can be called bases, whereas the prism in part (b) has only one pair of parallel, congruent faces that can be bases.

SOLUTION

a. Each base measures 5 inches by 10 inches with an area of

$$B = 5(10) = 50 \text{ in.}^2$$

The perimeter of the base is $P = 30$ in. and the height is $h = 6$ in.

▶ So, the surface area is

$$S = 2B + Ph = 2(50) + 30(6) = 280 \text{ in.}^2$$

b. Each base is an equilateral triangle with a side length, s, of 7 meters. Using the formula for the area of an equilateral triangle, the area of each base is

$$B = \tfrac{1}{4}\sqrt{3}\,(s^2) = \tfrac{1}{4}\sqrt{3}\,(7^2) = \tfrac{49}{4}\sqrt{3} \text{ m}^2.$$

7 m   7 m
7 m

STUDENT HELP

↳ **Look Back**
For help with finding the area of an equilateral triangle, see p. 669.

The perimeter of each base is $P = 21$ m and the height is $h = 5$ m.

▶ So, the surface area is

$$S = 2B + Ph = 2\!\left(\tfrac{49}{4}\sqrt{3}\right) + 21(5) \approx 147 \text{ m}^2.$$

GOAL 2 FINDING THE SURFACE AREA OF A CYLINDER

A **cylinder** is a solid with congruent circular bases that lie in parallel planes. The *altitude*, or *height*, of a cylinder is the perpendicular distance between its bases. The radius of the base is also called the *radius* of the cylinder. A cylinder is called a **right cylinder** if the segment joining the centers of the bases is perpendicular to the bases.

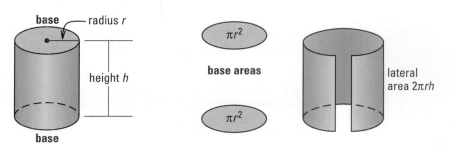

The **lateral area of a cylinder** is the area of its curved surface. The lateral area is equal to the product of the circumference and the height, which is $2\pi rh$. The entire **surface area of a cylinder** is equal to the sum of the lateral area and the areas of the two bases.

THEOREM

THEOREM 12.3 *Surface Area of a Right Cylinder*

The surface area S of a right cylinder is

$$S = 2B + Ch = 2\pi r^2 + 2\pi rh,$$

where B is the area of a base, C is the circumference of a base, r is the radius of a base, and h is the height.

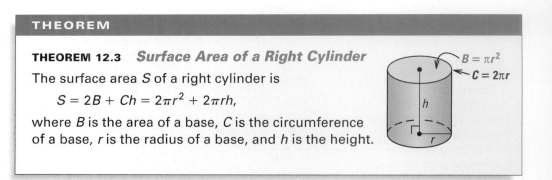

EXAMPLE 3 *Finding the Surface Area of a Cylinder*

Find the surface area of the right cylinder.

SOLUTION

Each base has a radius of 3 feet, and the cylinder has a height of 4 feet.

$S = 2\pi r^2 + 2\pi rh$ Formula for surface area of cylinder

$\quad = 2\pi(3^2) + 2\pi(3)(4)$ Substitute.

$\quad = 18\pi + 24\pi$ Simplify.

$\quad = 42\pi$ Add.

$\quad \approx 131.95$ Use a calculator.

▶ The surface area is about 132 square feet.

Using
Algebra

EXAMPLE 4 *Finding the Height of a Cylinder*

Find the height of a cylinder which has a radius of 6.5 centimeters and a surface area of 592.19 square centimeters.

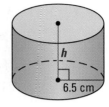

SOLUTION

Use the formula for the surface area of a cylinder and solve for the height h.

$S = 2\pi r^2 + 2\pi rh$	Formula for surface area
$592.19 = 2\pi(6.5)^2 + 2\pi(6.5)h$	Substitute 6.5 for r.
$592.19 = 34.5\pi + 13\pi h$	Simplify.
$592.19 - 84.5\pi = 13\pi h$	Subtract 84.5π from each side.
$326.73 \approx 13\pi h$	Simplify.
$8 \approx h$	Divide each side by 13π.

▶ The height is about 8 centimeters.

GUIDED PRACTICE

Vocabulary Check ✓ **1.** Describe the differences between a prism and a cylinder. Describe their similarities.

Concept Check ✓ **2.** Sketch a triangular prism. Then sketch a net of the triangular prism. Describe how to find its lateral area and surface area.

Skill Check ✓ **Give the mathematical name of the solid.**

3. Soup can

4. Door stop

5. Shoe box

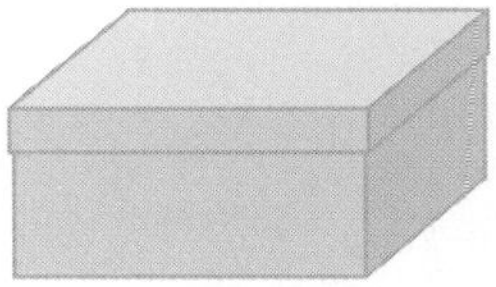

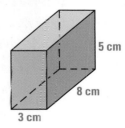

Use the diagram to find the measurement of the right rectangular prism.

6. Perimeter of a base

7. Length of a lateral edge

8. Lateral area of the prism

9. Area of a base

10. Surface area of the prism

Make a sketch of the described solid.

11. Right rectangular prism with a 3.4 foot square base and a height of 5.9 feet

12. Right cylinder with a diameter of 14 meters and a height of 22 meters

PRACTICE AND APPLICATIONS

STUDENT HELP

→ **Extra Practice**
to help you master
skills is on p. 825.

STUDYING PRISMS Use the diagram at the right.

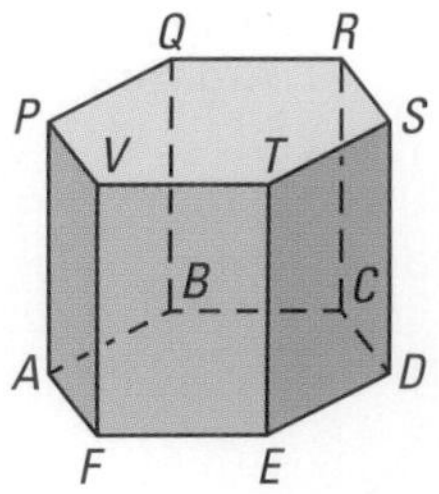

13. Give the mathematical name of the solid.

14. How many lateral faces does the solid have?

15. What kind of figure is each lateral face?

16. Name four lateral edges.

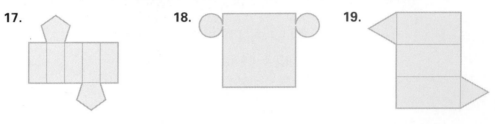

ANALYZING NETS Name the solid that can be folded from the net.

17.

18.

19.

SURFACE AREA OF A PRISM Find the surface area of the right prism.
Round your result to two decimal places.

20.

10 in.

11 in.

9 in.

21.

7 m

9 m

2 m

22.

6 ft

14 ft

23.

6 m

7.2 m

4 m

24.

2.9 cm

6.4 cm

2 cm

25.

6.1 in.

2 in.

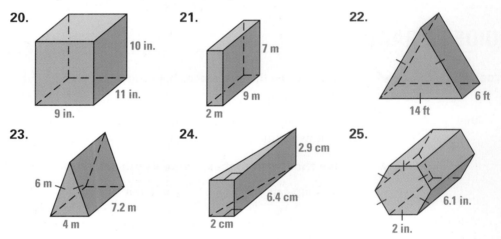

SURFACE AREA OF A CYLINDER Find the surface area of the right cylinder.
Round the result to two decimal places.

26.

11 ft

6 ft

27.

8 cm

8 cm

28.

6.2 in.

10 in.

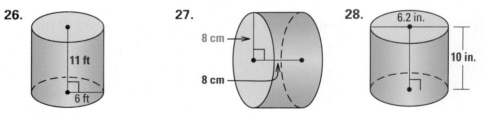

STUDENT HELP

→ **HOMEWORK HELP**
Example 1: Exs. 13–16,
　　　　　　20–25
Example 2: Exs. 20–25,
　　　　　　29–31, 35–37
Example 3: Exs. 26–28
Example 4: Exs. 32–34

VISUAL THINKING Sketch the described solid and find its surface area.

29. Right rectangular prism with a height of 10 feet, length of 3 feet, and
width of 6 feet

30. Right regular hexagonal prism with all edges measuring 12 millimeters

31. Right cylinder with a diameter of 2.4 inches and a height of 6.1 inches

USING ALGEBRA Solve for the variable given the surface area *S* of the right prism or right cylinder. Round the result to two decimal places.

32. $S = 298$ ft^2

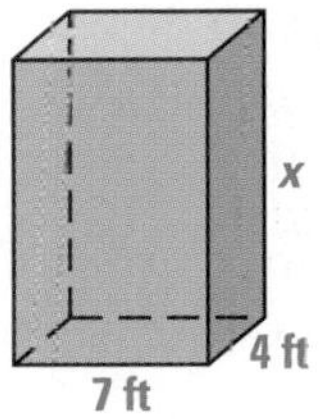

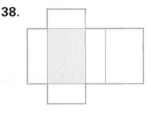

33. $S = 870$ m^2

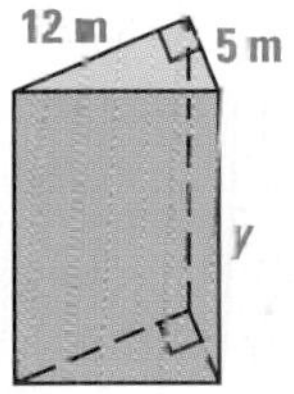

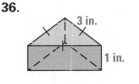

34. $S = 1202$ in.^{2}

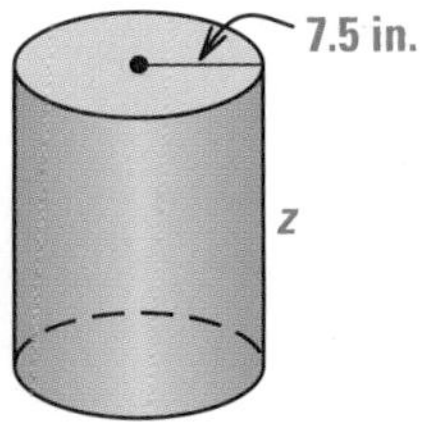

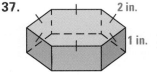

LOGICAL REASONING Find the surface area of the right prism when the height is 1 inch, and then when the height is 2 inches. When the height doubles, does the surface area double?

35.

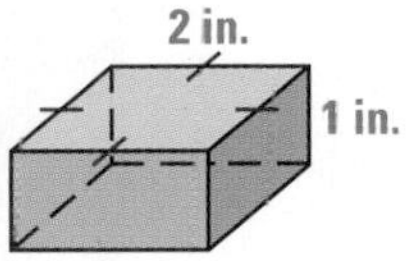

2 in.

1 in.

36.

3 in.

1 in.

37.

2 in.

1 in.

PACKAGING In Exercises 38–40, sketch the box that results after the net has been folded. Use the shaded face as a base.

38.

39.

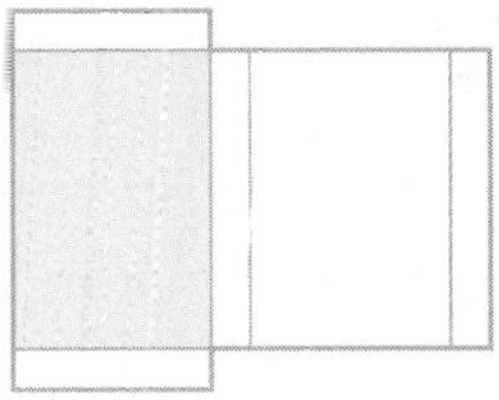

40.

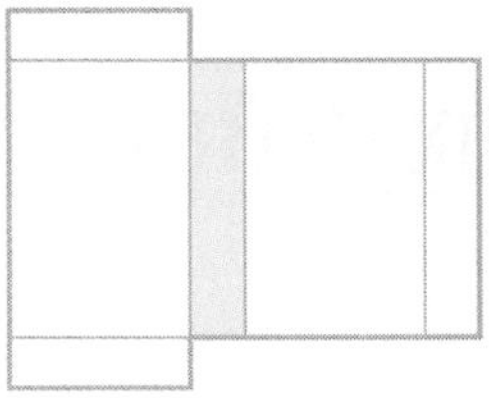

41. CRITICAL THINKING If you were to unfold a cardboard box, the cardboard would not match the net of the original solid. What sort of differences would there be? Why do these differences exist?

42. **ARCHITECTURE** Each tower of the World Trade Center in New York City is 414 meters high. The bases are squares with sides that are 64 meters. What is the surface area of each tower (including both bases)?

43. **WAX CYLINDER RECORDS** The first versions of phonograph records were hollow wax cylinders. Grooves were cut into the lateral surface of the cylinder, and the cylinder was rotated on a phonograph to reproduce the sound. In the late 1800's, a standard sized cylinder was about 2 inches in diameter and 4 inches long. Find the exterior lateral area of the cylinder described.

44. **CAKE DESIGN** Two layers of a cake are right regular hexagonal prisms as shown in the diagram. Each layer is 3 inches high. Calculate the area of the cake that will be frosted. If one can of frosting will cover 130 square inches of cake, how many cans do you need? (*Hint:* The bottom of each layer will not be frosted and the entire top of the bottom layer will be frosted.)

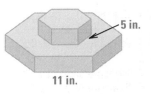

5 in.

11 in.

MULTI-STEP PROBLEM Use the following information.
A canned goods company manufactures cylindrical
cans resembling the one at the right.

1.5 in.

4 in.

45. Find the surface area of the can.

46. Find the surface area of a can whose radius and
height are twice that of the can shown.

47. *Writing* Use the formula for the surface area of a right cylinder to explain
why the answer in Exercise 46 is not twice the answer in Exercise 45.

★ **Challenge**

FINDING SURFACE AREA Find the surface area of the solid. Remember to
include both lateral areas. Round the result to two decimal places.

48.
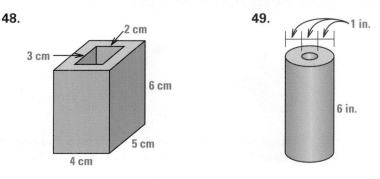
2 cm

3 cm

6 cm

5 cm

4 cm

49.
1 in.

6 in.

MIXED REVIEW

EVALUATING TRIANGLES Solve the right triangle. Round your answers to
two decimal places. (Review 9.6)

50.
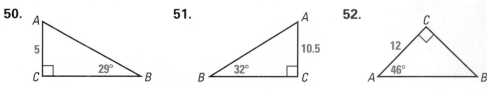
A

5

C   29°   B

51.
A

10.5

B   32°   C

52.
C

12

A   46°   B

FINDING AREA Find the area of the regular polygon or circle. Round the
result to two decimal places. (Review 11.2, 11.5 for 12.3)

53.
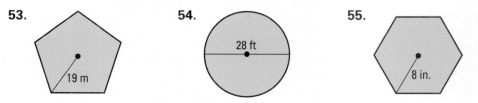
19 m

54.
28 ft

55.
8 in.

FINDING PROBABILITY Find the probability that a point chosen at random
on $\overline{PW}$ is on the given segment. (Review 11.6)

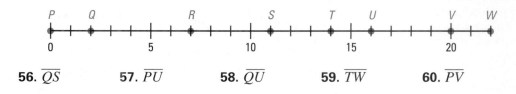

P   Q   R   S   T   U   V   W

0   5   10   15   20

56. $\overline{QS}$ **57.** $\overline{PU}$ **58.** $\overline{QU}$ **59.** $\overline{TW}$ **60.** $\overline{PV}$

12.3

Surface Area of Pyramids and Cones

What you should learn

GOAL 1 Find the surface area of a pyramid.

GOAL 2 Find the surface area of a cone.

Why you should learn it

▼ To find the surface area of solids in **real life**, such as the Pyramid Arena in Memphis, Tennessee, shown below and in **Example 1**.

GOAL 1 FINDING THE SURFACE AREA OF A PYRAMID

A **pyramid** is a polyhedron in which the *base* is a polygon and the *lateral faces* are triangles with a common *vertex*. The intersection of two lateral faces is a *lateral edge*. The intersection of the base and a lateral face is a *base edge*. The *altitude*, or *height*, of the pyramid is the perpendicular distance between the base and the vertex.

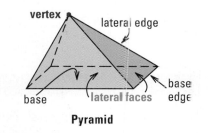

Pyramid

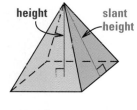

Regular pyramid

A **regular pyramid** has a regular polygon for a base and its height meets the base at its center. The *slant height* of a regular pyramid is the altitude of any lateral face. A nonregular pyramid does not have a slant height.

EXAMPLE 1 Finding the Area of a Lateral Face

ARCHITECTURE The lateral faces of the Pyramid Arena in Memphis, Tennessee, are covered with steel panels. Use the diagram of the arena at the right to find the area of each lateral face of this regular pyramid.

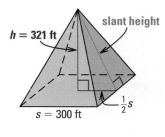

SOLUTION

To find the slant height of the pyramid, use the Pythagorean Theorem.

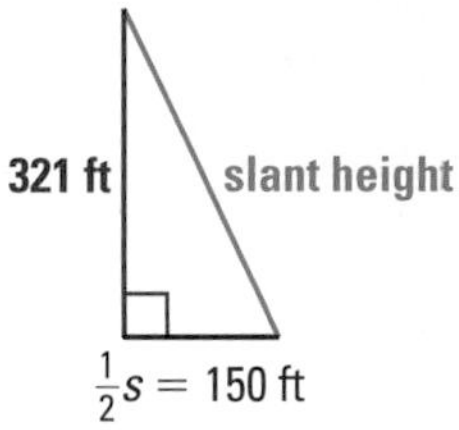

$$(\text{Slant height})^2 = h^2 + \left(\frac{1}{2}s\right)^2 \qquad \textbf{Write formula.}$$

$$(\text{Slant height})^2 = 321^2 + 150^2 \qquad \textbf{Substitute.}$$

$$(\text{Slant height})^2 = 125{,}541 \qquad \textbf{Simplify.}$$

$$\text{Slant height} = \sqrt{125{,}541} \qquad \textbf{Take the positive square root.}$$

$$\text{Slant height} \approx 354.32 \qquad \textbf{Use a calculator.}$$

▶ So, the area of each lateral face is $\frac{1}{2}$(base of lateral face)(slant height), or about $\frac{1}{2}$(300)(354.32), which is about 53,148 square feet.

STUDENT HELP

▶ **Study Tip**

A *regular pyramid* is considered a regular polyhedron only if *all* its faces, including the base, are congruent. So, the only pyramid that is a regular polyhedron is the regular triangular pyramid, or *tetrahedron*. See page 721.

STUDENT HELP

Study Tip
When sketching the net of a pyramid, first sketch the base. Then sketch the lateral faces.

A regular hexagonal pyramid and its net are shown at the right. Let b represent the length of a base edge, and let ℓ represent the slant height of the pyramid.

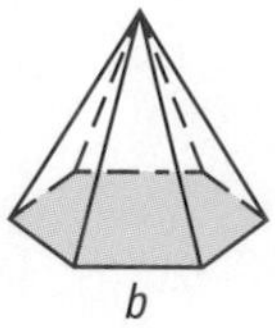

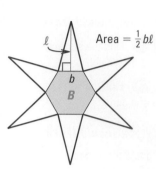

The area of each lateral face is $\frac{1}{2}b\ell$ and the perimeter of the base is $P = 6b$. So, the surface area is as follows:

$S = (\text{Area of base}) + 6(\text{Area of lateral face})$

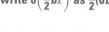

$S = B + 6\left(\frac{1}{2}b\ell\right)$ **Substitute.**

$S = B + \frac{1}{2}(6b)\ell$ **Rewrite $6\left(\frac{1}{2}b\ell\right)$ as $\frac{1}{2}(6b)\ell$.**

$S = B + \frac{1}{2}P\ell$ **Substitute P for $6b$.**

THEOREM

THEOREM 12.4 ***Surface Area of a Regular Pyramid***

The surface area S of a regular pyramid is $S = B + \frac{1}{2}P\ell$, where B is the area of the base, P is the perimeter of the base, and ℓ is the slant height.

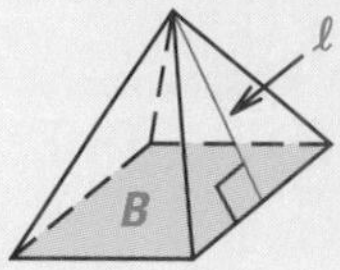

EXAMPLE 2 *Finding the Surface Area of a Pyramid*

To find the surface area of the regular pyramid shown, start by finding the area of the base.

STUDENT HELP

Look Back
For help with finding the area of regular polygons see pp. 669–671.

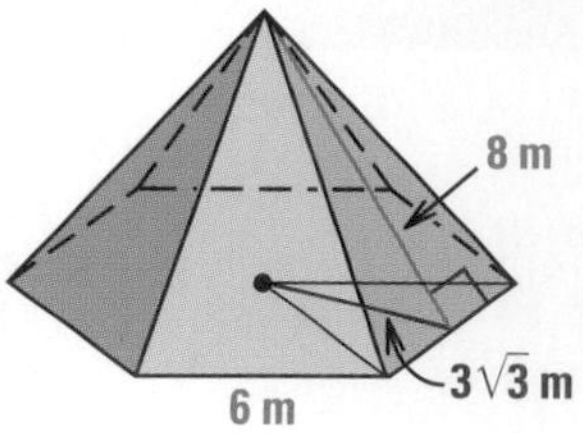

Use the formula for the area of a regular polygon, $\frac{1}{2}$(apothem)(perimeter). A diagram of the base is shown at the right. After substituting, the area of the base is $\frac{1}{2}(3\sqrt{3})(6 \cdot 6)$, or $54\sqrt{3}$ square meters.

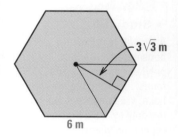

Now you can find the surface area, using $54\sqrt{3}$ for the area of the base, B.

$S = B + \frac{1}{2}P\ell$ **Write formula.**

$= 54\sqrt{3} + \frac{1}{2}(36)(8)$ **Substitute.**

$= 54\sqrt{3} + 144$ **Simplify.**

≈ 237.5 **Use a calculator.**

▶ So, the surface area is about 237.5 square meters.

A **circular cone,** or **cone,** has a circular *base* and a *vertex* that is not in the same plane as the base. The *altitude,* or *height,* is the perpendicular distance between the vertex and the base. In a **right cone,** the height meets the base at its center and the *slant height* is the distance between the vertex and a point on the base edge.

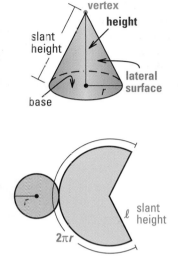

The **lateral surface** of a cone consists of all segments that connect the vertex with points on the base edge. When you cut along the slant height and lie the cone flat, you get the net shown at the right. In the net, the circular base has an area of πr^2 and the lateral surface is the sector of a circle. You can find the area of this sector by using a proportion, as shown below.

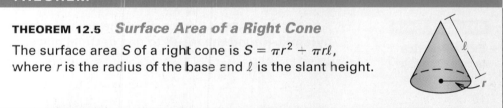

$$\frac{\text{Area of sector}}{\text{Area of circle}} = \frac{\text{Arc length}}{\text{Circumference of circle}} \qquad \text{Set up proportion.}$$

$$\frac{\text{Area of sector}}{\pi \ell^2} = \frac{2\pi r}{2\pi \ell} \qquad \text{Substitute.}$$

$$\text{Area of sector} = \pi \ell^2 \cdot \frac{2\pi r}{2\pi \ell} \qquad \text{Multiply each side by } \pi \ell^2.$$

$$\text{Area of sector} = \pi r \ell \qquad \text{Simplify.}$$

The surface area of a cone is the sum of the base area and the lateral area, $\pi r \ell$.

THEOREM

THEOREM 12.5 *Surface Area of a Right Cone*

The surface area S of a right cone is $S = \pi r^2 + \pi r \ell$, where r is the radius of the base and ℓ is the slant height.

EXAMPLE 3 *Finding the Surface Area of a Right Cone*

To find the surface area of the right cone shown, use the formula for the surface area.

$$S = \pi r^2 + \pi r \ell \qquad \text{Write formula.}$$

$$= \pi 4^2 + \pi(4)(6) \qquad \text{Substitute.}$$

$$= 16\pi + 24\pi \qquad \text{Simplify.}$$

$$= 40\pi \qquad \text{Simplify.}$$

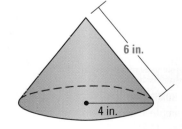

▶ The surface area is 40π square inches, or about 125.7 square inches.

GUIDED PRACTICE

Vocabulary Check ✓

1. Describe the differences between pyramids and cones. Describe their similarities.

Concept Check ✓

2. Can a pyramid have rectangles for lateral faces? Explain.

Skill Check ✓

Match the expression with the correct measurement.

3. Area of base

A. $4\sqrt{2}$ cm^2

4. Height

B. $\sqrt{2}$ cm

5. Slant height

C. 4 cm^2

6. Lateral area

D. $\left(4 + 4\sqrt{2}\right)$ cm^2

7. Surface area

E. 1 cm

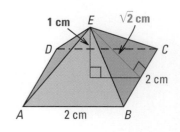

In Exercises 8–11, sketch a right cone with _r_ = 3 ft and _h_ = 7 ft.

8. Find the area of the base.

9. Find the slant height.

10. Find the lateral area.

11. Find the surface area.

Find the surface area of the regular pyramid described.

12. The base area is 9 square meters, the perimeter of the base is 12 meters, and the slant height is 2.5 meters.

13. The base area is $25\sqrt{3}$ square inches, the perimeter of the base is 30 inches, and the slant height is 12 inches.

PRACTICE AND APPLICATIONS

STUDENT HELP

▶ **Extra Practice**
to help you master
skills is on p. 825.

AREA OF A LATERAL FACE Find the area of a lateral face of the regular pyramid. Round the result to one decimal place.

14.   15.   16.

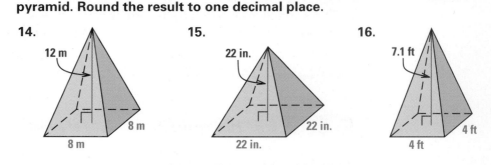

SURFACE AREA OF A PYRAMID Find the surface area of the regular pyramid.

STUDENT HELP

▶ **HOMEWORK HELP**
Example 1: Exs. 14–16
Example 2: Exs. 17–19
Example 3: Exs. 20–25

17.   18.   19.

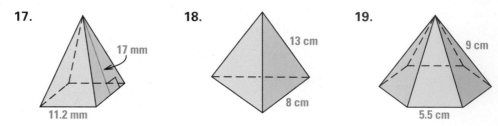

FINDING SLANT HEIGHT Find the slant height of the right cone.

20.   **21.**   **22.**

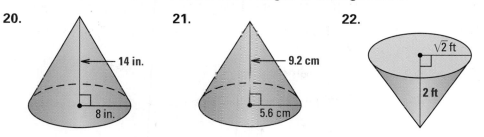

SURFACE AREA OF A CONE Find the surface area of the right cone. Leave your answers in terms of π.

23.   **24.** 5.9 mm   **25.**

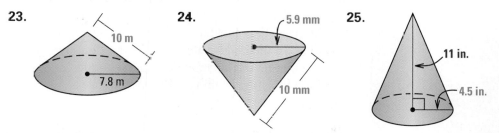

USING NETS Name the figure that is represented by the net. Then find its surface area. Round the result to one decimal place.

26.   **27.**

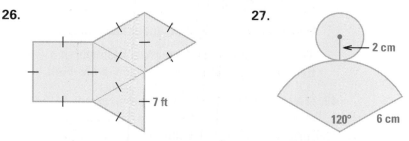

VISUAL THINKING Sketch the described solid and find its surface area. Round the result to one decimal place.

28. A regular pyramid has a triangular base with a base edge of 8 centimeters, a height of 12 centimeters, and a slant height of 12.2 centimeters.

29. A regular pyramid has a hexagonal base with a base edge of 3 meters, a height of 5.8 meters, and a slant height of 6.2 meters.

30. A right cone has a diameter of 11 feet and a slant height of 7.2 feet.

31. A right cone has a radius of 9 inches and a height of 12 inches.

STUDENT HELP

INTERNET

HOMEWORK HELP
Visit our Web site
www.mcdougallittell.com
for help with Exs. 32–34.

COMPOSITE SOLIDS Find the surface area of the solid. The pyramids are regular and the prisms, cylinders, and cones are right. Round the result to one decimal place.

32.   **33.**   **34.**

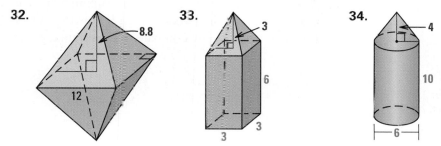

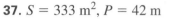

USING ALGEBRA In Exercises 35–37, find the missing measurements of the solid. The pyramids are regular and the cones are right.

35. $P = 72$ cm

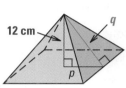

36. $S = 75.4$ in.²

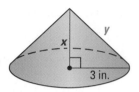

37. $S = 333$ m², $P = 42$ m

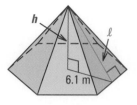

FOCUS ON APPLICATIONS

LAMPSHADES
Many stained-glass lampshades are shaped like cones or pyramids. These shapes help direct the light down.

38. **LAMPSHADES** Some stained-glass lampshades are made out of decorative pieces of glass. Estimate the amount of glass needed to make the lampshade shown at the right by calculating the lateral area of the pyramid formed by the framing. The pyramid has a square base.

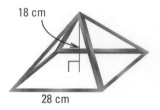

18 cm
28 cm

39. **PYRAMIDS** The three pyramids of Giza, Egypt, were built as regular square pyramids. The pyramid in the middle of the photo is Chephren's Pyramid and when it was built its base edge was $707\frac{3}{4}$ feet, and it had a height of 471 feet. Find the surface area of Chephren's Pyramid, including its base, when it was built.

40. **DATA COLLECTION** Find the dimensions of Chephren's Pyramid today and calculate its surface area. Compare this surface area with the surface area you found in Exercise 39.

41. **SQUIRREL BARRIER** Some bird feeders have a metal cone that prevents squirrels from reaching the bird seed, as shown. You are planning to manufacture this metal cone. The slant height of the cone is 12 inches and the radius is 8 inches. Approximate the amount of sheet metal you need.

42. **CRITICAL THINKING** A regular hexagonal pyramid with a base edge of 9 feet and a height of 12 feet is inscribed in a right cone. Find the lateral area of the cone.

43. **PAPER CUP** To make a paper drinking cup, start with a circular piece of paper that has a 3 inch radius, then follow the steps below. How does the surface area of the cup compare to the original paper circle? Find $m\angle ABC$.

QUANTITATIVE COMPARISON **Choose the statement that is true about the given quantities.**

(A) The quantity in column A is greater.

(B) The quantity in column B is greater.

(C) The two quantities are equal.

(D) The relationship cannot be determined from the given information.

	Column A	Column B
	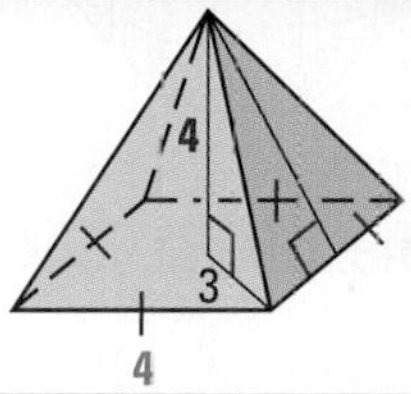 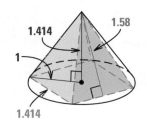	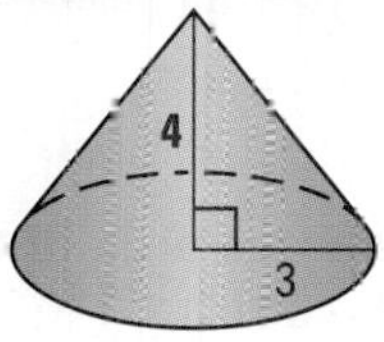
44.	Area of base	Area of base
45.	Lateral edge length	Slant height
46.	Lateral area	Lateral area

★ **Challenge**

INSCRIBED PYRAMIDS **Each of three regular pyramids are inscribed in a right cone whose radius is 1 unit and height is $\sqrt{2}$ units. The dimensions of each pyramid are listed in the table and the square pyramid is shown.**

Base	Base edge	Slant height
Square	1.414	1.58
Hexagon	1	1.65
Octagon	0.765	1.68

47. Find the surface area of the cone.

48. Find the surface area of each of the three pyramids.

49. What happens to the surface area as the number of sides of the base increases? If the number of sides continues to increase, what number will the surface area approach?

EXTRA CHALLENGE

www.mcdougallittell.com

MIXED REVIEW

FINDING AREA **In Exercises 50–52, find the area of the regular polygon. Round your result to two decimal places.** (Review 11.2 for 12.4)

50. **51.** **52.**

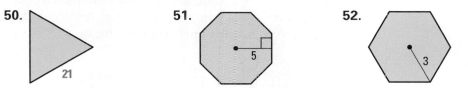

53. **AREA OF A SEMICIRCLE** A semicircle has an area of 190 square inches. Find the approximate length of the radius. (Review 11.5 for 12.4)

State whether the polyhedron is regular and/or convex. Then calculate the number of vertices of the solid using the given information. (Lesson 12.1)

1. 4 faces;
all triangles

2. 8 faces; 4 triangles
and 4 trapezoids

3. 8 faces; 2 hexagons
and 6 rectangles

Find the surface area of the solid. Round your result to two decimal places.
(Lesson 12.2 and 12.3)

4.

14 ft
7 ft

5.

9 m
10 m

6.

9 mm
16 mm

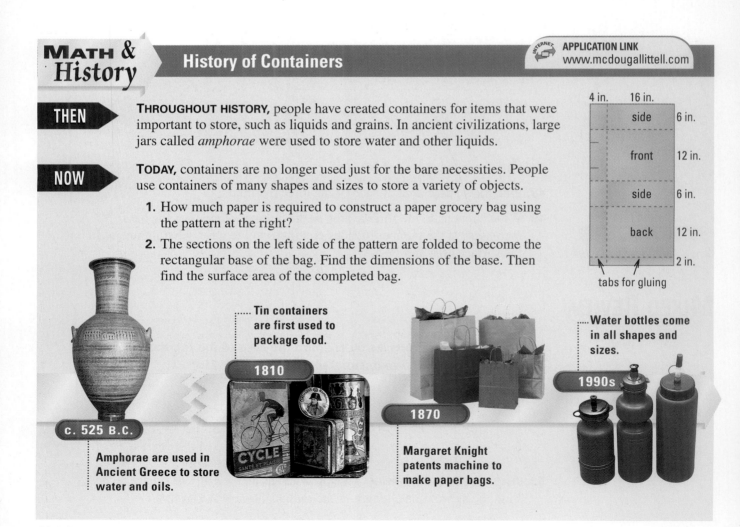

MATH & History

History of Containers

APPLICATION LINK
www.mcdougallittell.com

THEN

THROUGHOUT HISTORY, people have created containers for items that were important to store, such as liquids and grains. In ancient civilizations, large jars called *amphorae* were used to store water and other liquids.

NOW

TODAY, containers are no longer used just for the bare necessities. People use containers of many shapes and sizes to store a variety of objects.

1. How much paper is required to construct a paper grocery bag using the pattern at the right?

2. The sections on the left side of the pattern are folded to become the rectangular base of the bag. Find the dimensions of the base. Then find the surface area of the completed bag.

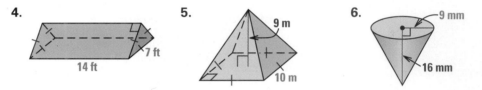

4 in.   16 in.
side   6 in.
front   12 in.
side   6 in.
back   12 in.
2 in.
tabs for gluing

..... **Tin containers
are first used to
package food.**

1810

CYCLE

**Water bottles come
in all shapes and
sizes.**

1990s

c. 525 B.C.

**Amphorae are used in
Ancient Greece to store
water and oils.**

1870

**Margaret Knight
patents machine to
make paper bags.**

Volume of Prisms and Cylinders

What you should learn

GOAL 1 Use volume postulates.

GOAL 2 Find the volume of prisms and cylinders in **real life**, such as the concrete block in **Example 4**.

Why you should learn it

▼ Learning to find the volumes of prisms and cylinders is important in **real life**, such as in finding the volume of a fish tank in **Exs. 7–9, and 46**.

GOAL 1 EXPLORING VOLUME

The **volume of a solid** is the number of cubic units contained in its interior. Volume is measured in cubic units, such as cubic meters (m^3).

VOLUME POSTULATES

POSTULATE 27 *Volume of a Cube*

The volume of a cube is the cube of the length of its side, or $V = s^3$.

POSTULATE 28 *Volume Congruence Postulate*

If two polyhedra are congruent, then they have the same volume.

POSTULATE 29 *Volume Addition Postulate*

The volume of a solid is the sum of the volumes of all its nonoverlapping parts.

EXAMPLE 1 *Finding the Volume of a Rectangular Prism*

The box shown is 5 units long, 3 units wide, and 4 units high. How many unit cubes will fit in the box? What is the volume of the box?

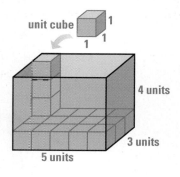

SOLUTION

The base of the box is 5 units by 3 units. This means 5 • 3, or 15 unit cubes, will cover the base.

Three more layers of 15 cubes each can be placed on top of the lower layer to fill the box. Because the box contains 4 layers with 15 cubes in each layer, the box contains a total of 4 • 15, or 60 unit cubes.

▶ Because the box is completely filled by the 60 cubes and each cube has a volume of 1 cubic unit, it follows that the volume of the box is 60 • 1, or 60 cubic units.

. . . .

In Example 1, the area of the base, 15 square units, multiplied by the height, 4 units, yields the volume of the box, 60 cubic units. So, the volume of the prism can be found by multiplying the area of the base by the height. This method can also be used to find the volume of a cylinder.

GOAL 2 **FINDING VOLUMES OF PRISMS AND CYLINDERS**

> **THEOREM**
>
> **THEOREM 12.6** *Cavalieri's Principle*
>
> If two solids have the same height and the same cross-sectional area at every level, then they have the same volume.

Theorem 12.6 is named after mathematician Bonaventura Cavalieri (1598–1647). To see how it can be applied, consider the solids below. All three have cross sections with equal areas, B, and all three have equal heights, h. By Cavalieri's Principle, it follows that each solid has the same volume.

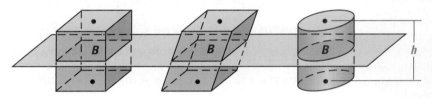

> **VOLUME THEOREMS**
>
> **THEOREM 12.7** *Volume of a Prism*
>
> The volume V of a prism is $V = Bh$, where B is the area of a base and h is the height.
>
> **THEOREM 12.8** *Volume of a Cylinder*
>
> The volume V of a cylinder is $V = Bh = \pi r^2 h$, where B is the area of a base, h is the height, and r is the radius of a base.

EXAMPLE 2 *Finding Volumes*

Find the volume of the right prism and the right cylinder.

a.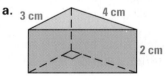

b.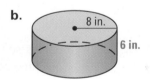

SOLUTION

a. The area B of the base is $\frac{1}{2}(3)(4)$, or 6 cm². Use $h = 2$ to find the volume.

$$V = Bh = 6(2) = 12 \text{ cm}^3$$

b. The area B of the base is $\pi \cdot 8^2$, or 64π in.² Use $h = 6$ to find the volume.

$$V = Bh = 64\pi(6) = 384\pi \approx 1206.37 \text{ in.}^3$$

EXAMPLE 3   *Using Volumes*

Using Algebra

Use the measurements given to solve for *x*.

a. Cube, $V = 100$ ft^3

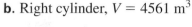
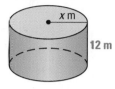

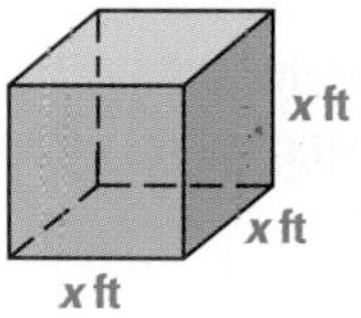

b. Right cylinder, $V = 4561$ m^3

x ft
x ft
x ft

x m
12 m

SOLUTION

a. A side length of the cube is *x* feet.

$$V = s^3 \qquad \text{Formula for volume of cube}$$
$$100 = x^3 \qquad \text{Substitute.}$$
$$4.64 \approx x \qquad \text{Take the cube root.}$$

▶ So, the height, width, and length of the cube are about 4.64 feet.

b. The area of the base is πx^2 square meters.

$$V = Bh \qquad \text{Formula for volume of cylinder}$$
$$4561 = \pi x^2(12) \qquad \text{Substitute.}$$
$$4561 = 12\pi x^2 \qquad \text{Rewrite.}$$
$$\frac{4561}{12\pi} = x^2 \qquad \text{Divide each side by 12}\pi.$$
$$11 \approx x \qquad \text{Find the positive square root.}$$

▶ So, the radius of the cylinder is about 11 meters.

STUDENT HELP

KEYSTROKE HELP

If your calculator does not have a cube root key, you can raise a number to the $\frac{1}{3}$ to find its cube root. For example, the cube root of 8 can be found as follows:

`8` `^` `(` `1`
`÷` `3` `)`

EXAMPLE 4   *Using Volumes in Real Life*

CONSTRUCTION Concrete weighs 145 pounds per cubic foot. To find the weight of the concrete block shown, you need to find its volume. The area of the base can be found as follows:

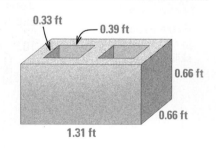

0.33 ft
0.39 ft
0.66 ft
0.66 ft
1.31 ft

$$B = \boxed{\begin{array}{c}\textbf{Area of large}\\\textbf{rectangle}\end{array}} - 2 \cdot \boxed{\begin{array}{c}\textbf{Area of small}\\\textbf{rectangle}\end{array}}$$
$$= (1.31)(0.66) - 2(0.33)(0.39)$$
$$\approx 0.61 \text{ ft}^2$$

Using the formula for the volume of a prism, the volume is

$$V = Bh \approx 0.61(0.66) \approx 0.40 \text{ ft}^3$$

▶ To find the weight of the block, multiply the pounds per cubic foot, 145 lb/ft^3, by the number of cubic feet, 0.40 ft^3.

$$\text{Weight} = \frac{145 \text{ lb}}{1 \text{ ft}^3} \cdot 0.4 \text{ ft}^3 \approx 58 \text{ lb}$$

FOCUS ON APPLICATIONS

CONSTRUCTION The Ennis-Brown House, shown above, was designed by Frank Lloyd Wright. It was built using concrete blocks.

GUIDED PRACTICE

Vocabulary Check ✓

1. Surface area is measured in __?__ and volume is measured in __?__.

Concept Check ✓

2. Each stack of memo papers shown contains 500 sheets of paper. Explain why the stacks have the same volume. Then calculate the volume, given that each sheet of paper is 3 inches by 3 inches by 0.01 inches.

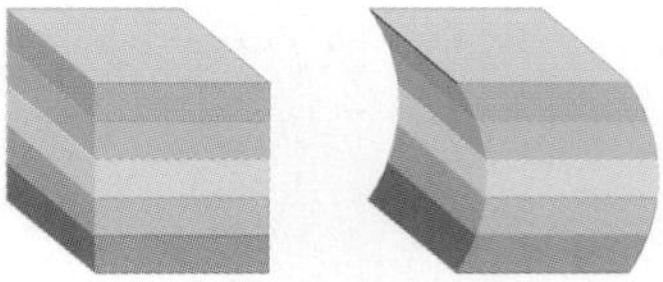

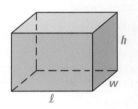

Skill Check ✓

Use the diagram to complete the table.

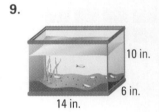

	ℓ	w	h	Volume
3.	17	3	5	?
4.	?	8	10	160
5.	4.8	6.1	?	161.04
6.	$6t$	?	$3t$	$54t^3$

h
w
ℓ

FISH TANKS **Find the volume of the tank.**

7.
6 in.
15 in.

8.
10 in.
8 in.
10 in.

9.
10 in.
6 in.
14 in.

PRACTICE AND APPLICATIONS

STUDENT HELP

Extra Practice to help you master skills is on p. 826.

USING UNIT CUBES **Find the number of unit cubes that will fit in the box. Explain your reasoning.**

10.
3
4
10

11.
4
5
5

12.
6
3
2

STUDENT HELP

HOMEWORK HELP
Example 1: Exs. 10–12
Example 2: Exs. 13–27
Example 3: Exs. 28–33
Example 4: Exs. 34–37

VOLUME OF A PRISM **Find the volume of the right prism.**

13.
8 in.
8 in.
8 in.

14.
12 cm
5 cm
4 cm

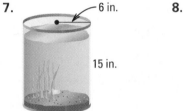

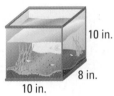

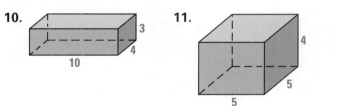

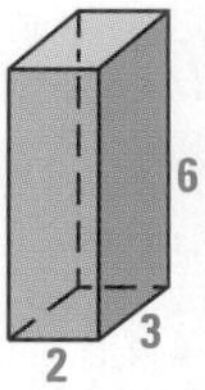

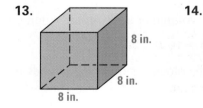

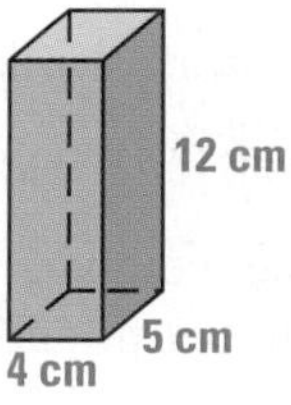

15.
10 in.
3.5 in.

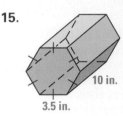

VOLUME OF A CYLINDER Find the volume of the right cylinder. Round the result to two decimal places.

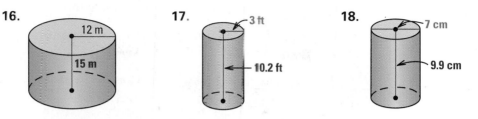

16.

17.

18.

VISUAL THINKING Make a sketch of the solid and find its volume. Round the result to two decimal places.

19. A prism has a square base with 4 meter sides and a height of 15 meters.

20. A pentagonal prism has a base area of 24 square feet and a height of 3 feet.

21. A prism has a height of 11.2 centimeters and an equilateral triangle for a base, where each base edge measures 8 centimeters.

22. A cylinder has a radius of 4 meters and a height of 8 meters.

23. A cylinder has a radius of 21.4 feet and a height of 33.7 feet.

24. A cylinder has a diameter of 15 inches and a height of 26 inches.

STUDENT HELP

HOMEWORK HELP
Visit our Web site
www.mcdougallittell.com
for help with Exs. 25–27.

VOLUMES OF OBLIQUE SOLIDS Use Cavalieri's Principle to find the volume of the oblique prism or cylinder.

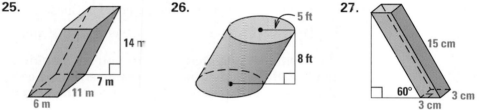

25.

26.

27.

(xy) **USING ALGEBRA** Solve for the variable using the given measurements. The prisms and the cylinders are right.

28. Volume = 560 ft³

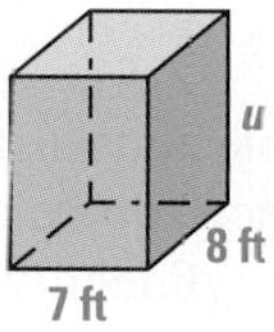

29. Volume = 2700 yd³

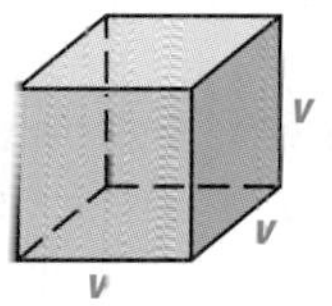

30. Volume = 80 cm³

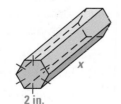

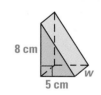

31. Volume = 72.66 in.³

32. Volume = 3000 ft³

33. Volume = 1696.5 m³

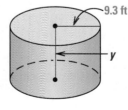

34. 🌐 **CONCRETE BLOCK** In Example 4 on page 745, find the volume of the entire block and subtract the volume of the two rectangular prisms. How does your answer compare with the volume found in Example 4?

FINDING VOLUME Find the volume of the entire solid. The prisms and cylinders are right.

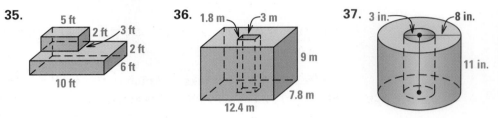

35. 5 ft 2 ft 3 ft 2 ft 6 ft 10 ft

36. 1.8 m 3 m 9 m 7.8 m 12.4 m

37. 3 in. 8 in. 11 in.

🌐 **CONCRETE** In Exercises 38–40, determine the number of yards of concrete you need for the given project. To builders, a "yard" of concrete means a cubic yard. (A cubic yard is equal to $(36 \text{ in.})^3$, or $46,656 \text{ in.}^3$.)

38. A driveway that is 30 feet long, 18 feet wide, and 4 inches thick

39. A tennis court that is 100 feet long, 50 feet wide, and 6 inches thick

40. A circular patio that has a radius of 24 feet and is 8 inches thick

41. 🧩 **LOGICAL REASONING** Take two sheets of paper that measure $8\frac{1}{2}$ inches by 11 inches and form two cylinders; one with the height as $8\frac{1}{2}$ inches and one with the height as 11 inches. Do the cylinders have the same volume? Explain.

🌐 **CANDLES** In Exercises 42–44, you are melting a block of wax to make candles. How many candles of the given shape can be made using a block that measures 10 cm by 9 cm by 20 cm? The prisms and cylinder are right.

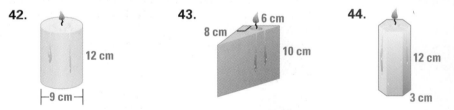

42. 12 cm 9 cm

43. 6 cm 8 cm 10 cm

44. 12 cm 3 cm

45. 🌐 **CANNED GOODS** Find the volume and surface area of a prism with a height of 4 inches and a 3 inch by 3 inch square base. Compare the results with the volume and surface area of a cylinder with a height of 5.1 inches and a diameter of 3 inches. Use your results to explain why canned goods are usually packed in cylindrical containers.

🌐 **AQUARIUM TANK** The Caribbean Coral Reef Tank at the New England Aquarium is a cylindrical tank that is 23 feet deep and 40 feet in diameter, as shown.

46. How many gallons of water are needed to fill the tank? (One gallon of water equals 0.1337 cubic foot.)

47. Determine the weight of the water in the tank. (One gallon of salt water weighs about 8.56 pounds.)

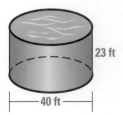

23 ft 40 ft

48. MULTIPLE CHOICE If the volume of the rectangular prism at the right is 1, what does x equal?

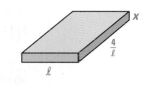

(A) $\frac{1}{4}$ (B) $\frac{\ell}{4}$ (C) ℓ

(D) 4 (E) 4ℓ

49. MULTIPLE CHOICE What is the volume of a cylinder with a radius of 6 and a height of 10?

(A) 60π (B) 90π (C) 120π (D) 180π (E) 360π

★ **Challenge**

50. Suppose that a 3 inch by 5 inch index card is rotated around a horizontal line and a vertical line to produce two different solids, as shown. Which solid has a greater volume? Explain your reasoning.

MIXED REVIEW

USING RATIOS Find the measures of the angles in the triangle whose angles are in the given extended ratio. **(Review 8.1)**

51. $2:5:5$ **52.** $1:2:3$ **53.** $3:4:5$

FINDING AREA In Exercises 54–56, find the area of the figure. Round your result to two decimal places. **(Review 11.2, 11.5 for 12.5)**

54.

10.12 ft

55.

7 m

56.

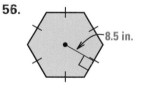

8.5 in.

57. SURFACE AREA OF A PRISM A right rectangular prism has a height of 13 inches, a length of 1 foot, and a width of 3 inches. Sketch the prism and find its surface area. **(Review 12.2)**

SURFACE AREA Find the surface area of the solid. The cone is right and the pyramids are regular. **(Review 12.3)**

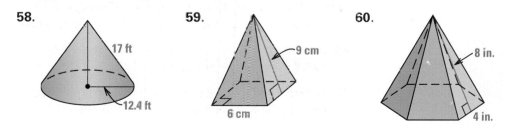

58.

17 ft

12.4 ft

59.

9 cm

6 cm

60.

8 in.

4 in.

▶ ACTIVITY 12.4

Using Technology

Minimizing Surface Area

A spreadsheet can be used to find the minimum surface area of a solid with a given volume.

▶ EXPLORING THE CONCEPT

A canned goods manufacturer needs to design a cylindrical container with a volume of 72 cm^3. To use the least amount of material, the dimensions of the container must be chosen so the surface area is a minimum. Find the dimensions.

The dimensions you must find are the radius and the height for the given volume. You can vary the radius and find the resulting height and surface area. A spreadsheet is helpful in organizing the data.

▶ USE A SPREADSHEET

1 Make a table with four columns. The first column is for the given volume. Cell A2 stores the volume V. In cell A3, use the formula $=$A2.

2 The second column is for the radius. Cell B2 stores the starting value for the radius r. In cell B3, use the formula $=$B2$+0.05$ to increase the radius in increments of 0.05 centimeter.

3 The third column is for the height. In cell C2, use the formula $=$A2/(PI()*B2^2). Your spreadsheet might use a different expression for π.

4 The fourth column is for the surface area. In cell D2, use the formula $=$2*PI()*B2^2+2*PI()*B2*C2.

	A	B	C	D
1	Volume V	Radius r	Height $h = \dfrac{V}{\pi r^2}$	Surface area $SA = 2\pi r^2 + 2\pi rh$
2	V	r	$=$ A2/(PI()*B2^2)	$=$ 2*PI()*B2^2 + 2*PI()*B2*C2
3	$=$ A2	$=$ B2 + 0.05	$=$ A3/(PI()*B3^2)	$=$ 2*PI()*B3^2 + 2*PI()*B3*C3

5 Fill in Cells C3 and D3 as shown above. Then use the Fill Down feature to create more rows. Replace the V in cell A2 with 72 and replace the r in cell B2 with 2. Your spreadsheet should resemble the one below.

	A	B	C	D
1	Volume V	Radius r	Height $h = \dfrac{V}{\pi r^2}$	Surface area $SA = 2\pi r^2 + 2\pi rh$
2	72	2.00	5.73	97.14
3	72	2.05	5.45	96.60
4	72	2.10	5.20	96.32

▶ MAKE A CONJECTURE

1. From the data in your spreadsheet, which dimensions yield a minimum surface area for the given volume? Explain how you know.

● ACTIVITY 12.5

Developing Concepts

Investigating Volume

▶ **QUESTION** How is the volume of a pyramid related to the volume of a prism with the same base and height?

▶ **EXPLORING THE CONCEPT**

① Use a ruler to draw the two nets shown below on poster board.

$\left(\text{Use } 1\frac{7}{16} \text{ inches to approximate } \sqrt{2} \text{ inches.}\right)$

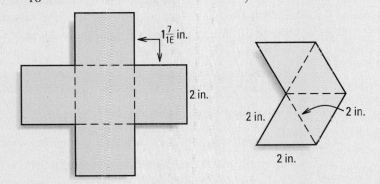

② Cut out the nets. Fold along the dotted lines to form an open prism and an open pyramid, as shown below. Tape each solid to hold it in place, making sure that the edges do not overlap.

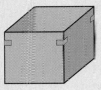

▶ **INVESTIGATE**

1. Compare the area of the base of the pyramid to the area of the base of the prism. Fitting the pyramid inside the prism will help. What do you notice?

2. Compare the heights of the solids. What do you notice?

▶ **MAKE A CONJECTURE**

3. Compare the volumes of the solids visually. Which solid has a greater volume? About how many times greater is the volume?

4. Fill the pyramid with unpopped popcorn, uncooked rice, or dried beans and pour it into the prism. Repeat this as many times as needed to fill the prism. How many times did you fill the pyramid? What does this tell you about the volume of the solids?

EXTENSION

CRITICAL THINKING Use your results to write a formula for the volume of a pyramid that uses the formula for the volume of a prism.

GROUP ACTIVITY
Work with a partner.

MATERIALS
• poster board
• ruler
• scissors
• tape
• unpopped popcorn, uncooked rice, or dried beans

12.5
Volume of Pyramids and Cones

What you should learn

GOAL 1 Find the volume of pyramids and cones.

GOAL 2 Find the volume of pyramids and cones in **real life**, such as the nautical prism in **Example 4**.

Why you should learn it

▼ Learning to find volumes of pyramids and cones is important in **real life**, such as in finding the volume of a volcano shown below and in **Ex. 34**.

Mount St. Helens

GOAL 1 FINDING VOLUMES OF PYRAMIDS AND CONES

In Lesson 12.4, you learned that the volume of a prism is equal to Bh, where B is the area of the base and h is the height. From the figure at the right, it is clear that the volume of the pyramid with the same base area B and the same height h must be less than the volume of the prism. The volume of the pyramid is one third the volume of the prism.

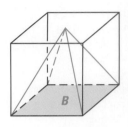

THEOREMS

THEOREM 12.9 *Volume of a Pyramid*

The volume V of a pyramid is $V = \frac{1}{3}Bh$, where B is the area of the base and h is the height.

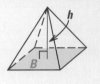

THEOREM 12.10 *Volume of a Cone*

The volume V of a cone is $V = \frac{1}{3}Bh = \frac{1}{3}\pi r^2 h$, where B is the area of the base, h is the height, and r is the radius of the base.

EXAMPLE 1 *Finding the Volume of a Pyramid*

Find the volume of the pyramid with the regular base.

SOLUTION

The base can be divided into six equilateral triangles. Using the formula for the area of an equilateral triangle, $\frac{1}{4}\sqrt{3} \cdot s^2$, the area of the base B can be found as follows:

$$6 \cdot \frac{1}{4}\sqrt{3} \cdot s^2 = 6 \cdot \frac{1}{4}\sqrt{3} \cdot 3^2 = \frac{27}{2}\sqrt{3} \text{ cm}^2.$$

Use Theorem 12.9 to find the volume of the pyramid.

$V = \frac{1}{3}Bh$ **Formula for volume of pyramid**

$= \frac{1}{3}\left(\frac{27}{2}\sqrt{3}\right)(4)$ **Substitute.**

$= 18\sqrt{3}$ **Simplify.**

▶ So, the volume of the pyramid is $18\sqrt{3}$, or about 31.2 cubic centimeters.

STUDENT HELP

Study Tip
The formulas given in Theorems 12.9 and 12.10 apply to all pyramids and cones, whether right or oblique. This follows from Cavalieri's Principle, stated in Lesson 12.4.

EXAMPLE 2 *Finding the Volume of a Cone*

Find the volume of each cone.

a. Right circular cone

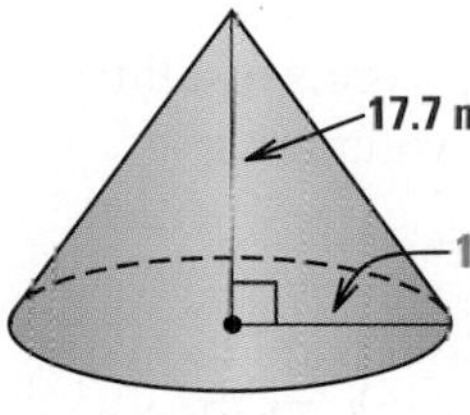

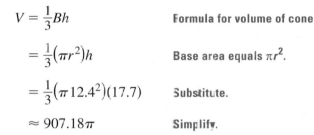

b. Oblique circular cone

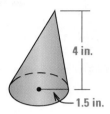

SOLUTION

a. Use the formula for the volume of a cone.

$V = \frac{1}{3}Bh$	Formula for volume of cone
$= \frac{1}{3}(\pi r^2)h$	Base area equals πr^2.
$= \frac{1}{3}(\pi 12.4^2)(17.7)$	Substitute.
$\approx 907.18\pi$	Simplify.

▶ So, the volume of the cone is about 907.18π, or 2850 cubic millimeters.

b. Use the formula for the volume of a cone.

$V = \frac{1}{3}Bh$	Formula for volume of cone
$= \frac{1}{3}(\pi r^2)h$	Base area equals πr^2.
$= \frac{1}{3}(\pi 1.5^2)(4)$	Substitute.
$= 3\pi$	Simplify.

▶ So, the volume of the cone is 3π, or about 9.42 cubic inches.

EXAMPLE 3 *Using the Volume of a Cone*

Use the given measurements to solve for x.

Volume = 2614 ft^3

SOLUTION

$V = \frac{1}{3}\pi r^2 h$	Formula for volume
$2614 = \frac{1}{3}(\pi x^2)(13)$	Substitute.
$7842 = 13\pi x^2$	Multiply each side by 3.
$192 \approx x^2$	Divide each side by 13π.
$13.86 \approx x$	Find positive square root.

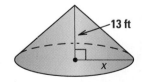

▶ So, the radius of the cone is about 13.86 feet.

STUDENT HELP

Study Tip
To eliminate the fraction in an equation, you can multiply each side by the reciprocal of the fraction. This was done in Example 3.

EXAMPLE 4 *Finding the Volume of a Solid*

NAUTICAL PRISMS A nautical prism is a solid piece of glass, as shown. Find its volume.

3.25 in.

3 in.

1.5 in.

3 in.

SOLUTION

To find the volume of the entire solid, add the volumes of the prism and the pyramid. The bases of the prism and the pyramid are regular hexagons made up of six equilateral triangles. To find the area of each base, B, multiply the area of one of the equilateral triangles by 6, or $6\left(\frac{\sqrt{3}}{4}s^2\right)$, where s is the base edge.

$$\begin{aligned}\textbf{Volume of prism} &= 6\left(\frac{\sqrt{3}}{4}s^2\right)h && \text{Formula for volume of prism}\\[1mm] &= 6\left(\frac{\sqrt{3}}{4}(3.25)^2\right)(1.5) && \text{Substitute.}\\[1mm] &\approx 41.16 && \text{Use a calculator.}\\[1mm] \textbf{Volume of pyramid} &= \frac{1}{3}\cdot 6\left(\frac{\sqrt{3}}{4}s^2\right)h && \text{Formula for volume of pyramid}\\[1mm] &= \frac{1}{3}\cdot 6\left(\frac{\sqrt{3}}{4}\cdot 3^2\right)(3) && \text{Substitute.}\\[1mm] &\approx 23.38 && \text{Use a calculator.}\end{aligned}$$

▶ The volume of the nautical prism is **41.16** + **23.38** or 64.54 cubic inches.

NAUTICAL PRISMS Before electricity, nautical prisms were placed in the decks of sailing ships. By placing the hexagonal face flush with the deck, the prisms would draw light to the lower regions of the ship.

EXAMPLE 5 *Using the Volume of a Cone*

AUTOMOBILES If oil is being poured into the funnel at a rate of 147 milliliters per second and flows out of the funnel at a rate of 42 milliliters per second, estimate the time it will take for the funnel to overflow. $\left(1 \text{ mL} = 1 \text{ cm}^3\right)$

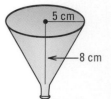

5 cm

8 cm

SOLUTION

First, find the approximate volume of the funnel.

$$V = \frac{1}{3}\pi r^2 h = \frac{1}{3}\pi(5^2)(8) \approx 209 \text{ cm}^3 = 209 \text{ mL}$$

The rate of accumulation of oil in the funnel is $147 - 42 = 105$ mL/s. To find the time it will take for the oil to fill the funnel, divide the volume of the funnel by the rate of accumulation of oil in the funnel as follows:

$$209 \text{ mL} \div \frac{105 \text{ mL}}{1 \text{ s}} = 209 \text{ mL} \times \frac{1 \text{ s}}{105 \text{ mL}} \approx 2 \text{ s}$$

▶ The funnel will overflow after about 2 seconds.

GUIDED PRACTICE

Vocabulary Check ✓

1. The volume of a cone with radius r and height h is $\frac{1}{3}$ the volume of a ___?___ with radius r and height h.

Concept Check ✓

Do the two solids have the same volume? Explain your answer.

2. 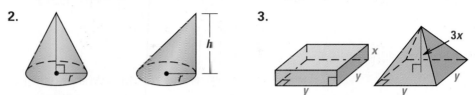   3.

Skill Check ✓

In Exercises 4–6, find (a) the area of the base of the solid and (b) the volume of the solid.

4.   5.   6.

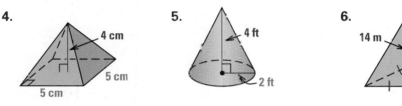

7. **CRITICAL THINKING** You are given the radius and the slant height of a right cone. Explain how you can find the height of the cone.

PRACTICE AND APPLICATIONS

STUDENT HELP

▶ **Extra Practice**
to help you master
skills is on p. 826.

FINDING BASE AREAS **Find the area of the base of the solid.**

8.   9. 12.2 ft   10. Regular base

VOLUME OF A PYRAMID **Find the volume of the pyramid. Each pyramid has a regular polygon for a base.**

11.   12.   13.

14.   15.   16.

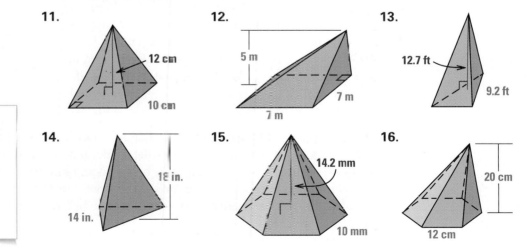

STUDENT HELP

▶ **HOMEWORK HELP**
Example 1: Exs. 11–16
Example 2: Exs. 17–19
Example 3: Exs. 20–22
Example 4: Exs. 23–28
Example 5: Ex. 29

VOLUME OF A CONE Find the volume of the cone. Round your result to two decimal places.

17.

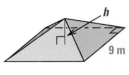

6 ft

3 ft

18.

11.5 cm

15.2 cm

19.

13 in.

7 in.

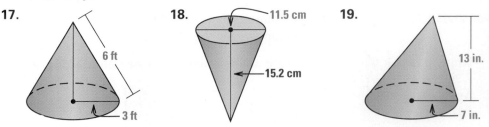

USING ALGEBRA Solve for the variable using the given information.

20. Volume = 270 m³

21. Volume = 100π in.³

22. Volume = $5\sqrt{3}$ cm³

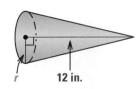

h

9 m

r

12 in.

h

$2\sqrt{3}$ cm

STUDENT HELP

HOMEWORK HELP
Visit our Web site
www.mcdougallittell.com
for help with Exs. 23–25.

COMPOSITE SOLIDS Find the volume of the solid. The prisms, pyramids, and cones are right. Round the result to two decimal places.

23.

6 ft

6 ft

6 ft

6 ft

24.

2.3 cm

2.3 cm

3.3 cm

25.

5.1 m

5.1 m

5.1 m

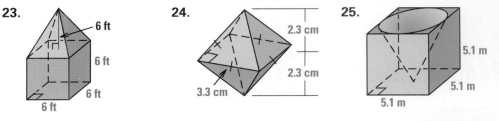

AUTOMATIC FEEDER In Exercises 26 and 27, use the diagram of the automatic pet feeder. $\left(1 \text{ cup} = 14.4 \text{ in.}^3\right)$

26. Calculate the amount of food that can be placed in the feeder.

27. If a cat eats half of a cup of food, twice per day, will the feeder hold enough food for three days?

2.5 in.

7.5 in.

4 in.

28. **ANCIENT CONSTRUCTION** Early civilizations in the Andes Mountains in Peru used cone-shaped adobe bricks to build homes. Find the volume of an adobe brick with a diameter of 8.3 centimeters and a slant height of 10.1 centimeters. Then calculate the amount of space 27 of these bricks would occupy in a mud mortar wall.

29. **SCIENCE CONNECTION** During a chemistry lab, you use a funnel to pour a solvent into a flask. The radius of the funnel is 5 centimeters and its height is 10 centimeters. If the solvent is being poured into the funnel at a rate of 80 milliliters per second and the solvent flows out of the funnel at a rate of 65 milliliters per second, how long will it be before the funnel overflows? $\left(1 \text{ mL} = 1 \text{ cm}^3\right)$

USING NETS In Exercises 30–32, use the net to sketch the solid. Then find the volume of the solid. Round the result to two decimal places.

30.

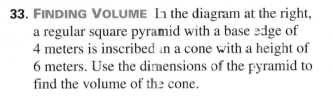

5 ft

31.

10 cm

6 cm

32.

4 m

16 m

33. FINDING VOLUME In the diagram at the right, a regular square pyramid with a base edge of 4 meters is inscribed in a cone with a height of 6 meters. Use the dimensions of the pyramid to find the volume of the cone.

6 m

4 m

r

34. 🌐 **VOLCANOES** Before 1980, Mount St. Helens was cone shaped with a height of about 1.83 miles and a base radius of about 3 miles. In 1980, Mount St. Helens erupted. The tip of the cone was destroyed, as shown, reducing the volume by 0.043 cubic mile. The cone-shaped tip that was destroyed had a radius of about 0.4 mile. How tall is the volcano today? (*Hint:* Find the height of the destroyed cone-shaped tip.)

Test Preparation

MULTI-STEP PROBLEM Use the diagram of the hourglass below.

35. Find the volume of the cone-shaped pile of sand.

36. The sand falls through the opening at a rate of one cubic inch per minute. Is the hourglass a true "hour"-glass? Explain. (1 hr = 60 min)

37. *Writing* The sand in the hourglass falls into a conical shape with a one-to-one ratio between the radius and the height. Without doing the calculations, explain how to find the radius and height of the pile of sand that has accumulated after 30 minutes.

3.9 in.

3.9 in.

★ **Challenge**

FRUSTUMS A *frustum* of a cone is the part of the cone that lies between the base and a plane parallel to the base, as shown. Use the information below to complete Exercises 38 and 39.

One method for calculating the volume of a frustum is to add the areas of the two bases to their geometric mean, then multiply the result by $\frac{1}{3}$ the height.

2 ft

9 ft

6 ft

STUDENT HELP

▶ **Look Back**
For help with finding geometric means, see p. 466.

38. Use the measurements in the diagram to calculate the volume of the frustum.

39. Write a formula for the volume of a frustum that has bases with radii r_1 and r_2 and a height h.

MIXED REVIEW

FINDING ANGLE MEASURES **Find the measure of each interior and exterior angle of a regular polygon with the given number of sides.** (Review 11.1)

40. 9   **41.** 10   **42.** 19

43. 22   **44.** 25   **45.** 30

FINDING THE AREA OF A CIRCLE **Find the area of the described circle.**
(Review 11.5 for 12.6)

46. The diameter of the circle is 25 inches.

47. The radius of the circle is 16.3 centimeters.

48. The circumference of the circle is 48π feet.

49. The length of a 36° arc of the circle is 2π meters.

USING EULER'S THEOREM **Calculate the number of vertices of the solid using the given information.** (Review 12.1)

50. 32 faces; 12 octagons and 20 triangles   **51.** 14 faces; 6 squares and 8 hexagons

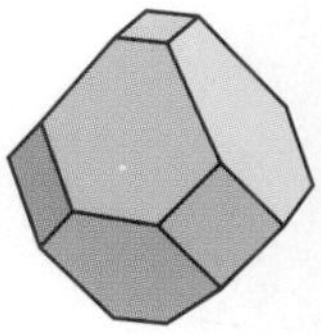

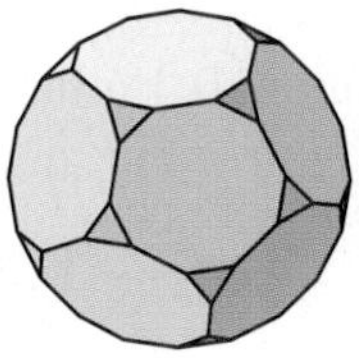

QUIZ 2

Self-Test for Lessons 12.4 and 12.5

In Exercises 1–6, find the volume of the solid. (Lessons 12.4 and 12.5)

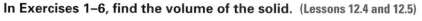

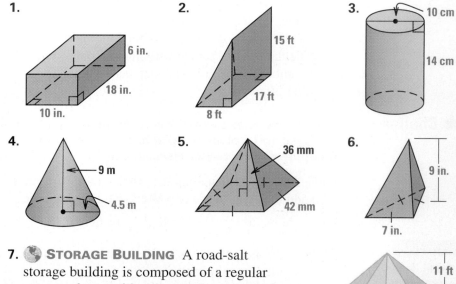

1.

6 in.

18 in.

10 in.

2.

15 ft

17 ft

8 ft

3.

10 cm

14 cm

4.

9 m

4.5 m

5.

36 mm

42 mm

6.

9 in.

7 in.

7. 🌎 **STORAGE BUILDING** A road-salt storage building is composed of a regular octagonal pyramid and a regular octagonal prism as shown. Find the volume of salt that the building can hold. (Lesson 12.5)

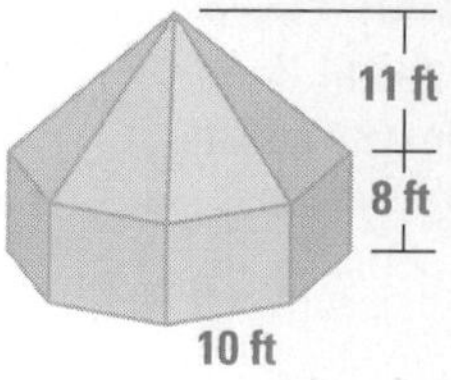

11 ft

8 ft

10 ft

12.6

Surface Area and Volume of Spheres

What you should learn

GOAL 1 Find the surface area of a sphere.

GOAL 2 Find the volume of a sphere in **real life**, such as the ball bearing in **Example 4**.

Why you should learn it

▼ You can find the surface area and volume of **real-life** spherical objects, such as the planets and moons in **Exs. 18 and 19**.

Saturn

GOAL 1 FINDING THE SURFACE AREA OF A SPHERE

In Lesson 10.7, a circle was described as the locus of points in a plane that are a given distance from a point. A **sphere** is the locus of points in *space* that are a given distance from a point. The point is called the **center of the sphere**. A **radius of a sphere** is a segment from the center to a point on the sphere.

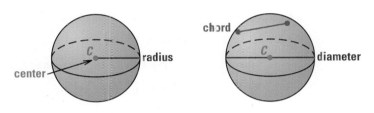

A **chord of a sphere** is a segment whose endpoints are on the sphere. A **diameter** is a chord that contains the center. As with circles, the terms radius and diameter also represent distances, and the diameter is twice the radius.

THEOREM

THEOREM 12.11 *Surface Area of a Sphere*

The surface area S of a sphere with radius r is $S = 4\pi r^2$.

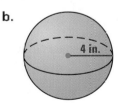

EXAMPLE 1 *Finding the Surface Area of a Sphere*

Find the surface area. When the radius doubles, does the surface area double?

a.

2 in.

b.

4 in.

SOLUTION

a. $S = 4\pi r^2 = 4\pi(2)^2 = 16\pi$ in.^{2}

b. $S = 4\pi r^2 = 4\pi(4)^2 = 64\pi$ in.^{2}

The surface area of the sphere in part (b) is four times greater than the surface area of the sphere in part (a) because $16\pi \cdot 4 = 64\pi$.

▶ So, when the radius of a sphere doubles, the surface area does *not* double.

If a plane intersects a sphere, the intersection is either a single point or a circle. If the plane contains the center of the sphere, then the intersection is a **great circle** of the sphere. Every great circle of a sphere separates a sphere into two congruent halves called **hemispheres**.

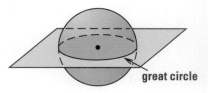

great circle

EXAMPLE 2 *Using a Great Circle*

The circumference of a great circle of a sphere is 13.8π feet. What is the surface area of the sphere?

13.8 π ft

SOLUTION

Begin by finding the radius of the sphere.

$$C = 2\pi r \qquad \text{Formula for circumference of circle}$$

$$13.8\pi = 2\pi r \qquad \text{Substitute 13.8π for } C.$$

$$6.9 = r \qquad \text{Divide each side by 2π.}$$

Using a radius of 6.9 feet, the surface area is

$$S = 4\pi r^2 = 4\pi(6.9)^2 = 190.44\pi \text{ ft}^2.$$

▶ So, the surface area of the sphere is $190.44\,\pi$, or about 598 ft².

EXAMPLE 3 *Finding the Surface Area of a Sphere*

BASEBALL A baseball and its leather covering are shown. The baseball has a radius of about 1.45 inches.

a. Estimate the amount of leather used to cover the baseball.

b. The surface of a baseball is sewn from two congruent shapes, each of which resembles two joined circles. How does this relate to the formula for the surface area of a sphere?

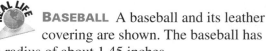

r = 1.45 in.

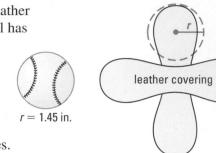

leather covering

SOLUTION

a. Because the radius r is about 1.45 inches, the surface area is as follows:

$$S = 4\pi r^2 \qquad \text{Formula for surface area of sphere}$$

$$\approx 4\pi(1.45)^2 \qquad \text{Substitute 1.45 for } r.$$

$$\approx 26.4 \text{ in.}^2 \qquad \text{Use a calculator.}$$

b. Because the covering has two pieces, each resembling two joined circles, then the entire covering consists of four circles with radius r. The area of a circle of radius r is $A = \pi r^2$. So, the area of the covering can be approximated by $4\pi r^2$. This is the same as the formula for the surface area of a sphere.

GOAL 2   FINDING THE VOLUME OF A SPHERE

Imagine that the interior of a sphere with radius r is approximated by n pyramids, each with a base area of B and a height of r, as shown. The volume of each pyramid is $\frac{1}{3}Br$ and the sum of the base areas is nB. The surface area of the sphere is approximately equal to nB, or $4\pi r^2$. So, you can approximate the volume V of the sphere as follows.

$$V \approx n\frac{1}{3}Br \qquad \text{Each pyramid has a volume of } \tfrac{1}{3}Br.$$

$$= \frac{1}{3}(nB)r \qquad \text{Regroup factors.}$$

$$\approx \frac{1}{3}\left(4\pi r^2\right)r \qquad \text{Substitute } 4\pi r^2 \text{ for } nB.$$

$$= \frac{4}{3}\pi r^3 \qquad \text{Simplify.}$$

Area = B

THEOREM

THEOREM 12.12   *Volume of a Sphere*

The volume V of a sphere with radius r is $V = \dfrac{4}{3}\pi r^3$.

EXAMPLE 4   *Finding the Volume of a Sphere*

BALL BEARINGS To make a steel ball bearing, a cylindrical *slug* is heated and pressed into a spherical shape with the same volume. Find the radius of the ball bearing below.

slug

SOLUTION

To find the volume of the slug, use the formula for the volume of a cylinder.

$$V = \pi r^2 h = \pi\left(1^2\right)(2) = 2\pi \text{ cm}^3$$

To find the radius of the ball bearing, use the formula for the volume of a sphere and solve for r.

ball bearing

$$V = \frac{4}{3}\pi r^3 \qquad \text{Formula for volume of sphere}$$

$$2\pi = \frac{4}{3}\pi r^3 \qquad \text{Substitute } 2\pi \text{ for } V.$$

$$6\pi = 4\pi r^3 \qquad \text{Multiply each side by 3.}$$

$$1.5 = r^3 \qquad \text{Divide each side by } 4\pi.$$

$$1.14 \approx r \qquad \text{Use a calculator to take the cube root.}$$

▶ So, the radius of the ball bearing is about 1.14 centimeters.

GUIDED PRACTICE

Vocabulary Check ✓

1. The locus of points in space that are __?__ from a __?__ is called a sphere.

Concept Check ✓

2. **ERROR ANALYSIS** Melanie is asked to find the volume of a sphere with a diameter of 10 millimeters. Explain her error(s).

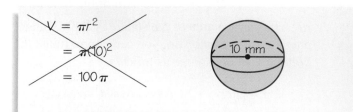

Skill Check ✓

In Exercises 3–8, use the diagram of the sphere, whose center is *P*.

3. Name a chord of the sphere.

4. Name a segment that is a radius of the sphere.

5. Name a segment that is a diameter of the sphere.

6. Find the circumference of the great circle that contains *Q* and *S*.

7. Find the surface area of the sphere.

8. Find the volume of the sphere.

9. 🌐 **CHEMISTRY** A helium atom is approximately spherical with a radius of about 0.5×10^{-8} centimeter. What is the volume of a helium atom?

PRACTICE AND APPLICATIONS

STUDENT HELP

▶ **Extra Practice**
to help you master
skills is on p. 826.

FINDING SURFACE AREA **Find the surface area of the sphere. Round your result to two decimal places.**

10.

11.

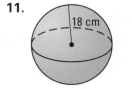

12.

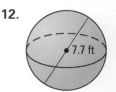

USING A GREAT CIRCLE **In Exercises 13–16, use the sphere below. The center of the sphere is *C* and its circumference is 7.4π inches.**

13. What is half of the sphere called?

14. Find the radius of the sphere.

15. Find the diameter of the sphere.

16. Find the surface area of half of the sphere.

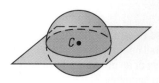

STUDENT HELP

▶ **HOMEWORK HELP**
Example 1: Exs. 10–12
Example 2: Exs. 13–16
Example 3: Ex. 17
Example 4: Exs. 20–22,
    41–43

17. 🌐 **SPORTS** The diameter of a softball is 3.8 inches. Estimate the amount of leather used to cover the softball.

18. 🌎 **PLANETS** The circumference of Earth at the equator (great circle of Earth) is 24,903 miles. The diameter of the moon is 2155 miles. Find the surface area of Earth and of the moon to the nearest hundred. How does the surface area of the moon compare to the surface area of Earth?

19. **DATA COLLECTION** Research to find the diameters of Neptune and its two moons, Triton and Nereid. Use the diameters to find the surface area of each.

FINDING VOLUME Find the volume of the sphere. Round your result to two decimal places.

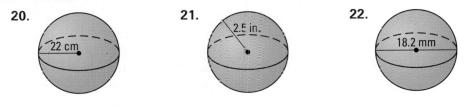

20.

22 cm

21.

2.5 in.

22.

18.2 mm

USING A TABLE Copy and complete the table below. Leave your answers in terms of π.

	Radius of sphere	Circumference of great circle	Surface area of sphere	Volume of sphere
23.	7 mm	?	?	?
24.	?	?	144π in.^{2}	?
25.	?	10π cm	?	?
26.	?	?	?	$\dfrac{4000\pi}{3}$ m^3

COMPOSITE SOLIDS Find (a) the surface area of the solid and (b) the volume of the solid. The cylinders and cones are right. Round your results to two decimal places.

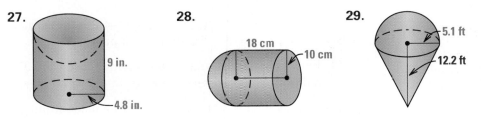

27.

9 in.

4.8 in.

28.

18 cm

10 cm

29.

5.1 ft

12.2 ft

△ **TECHNOLOGY** In Exercises 30–33, consider five spheres whose radii are 1 meter, 2 meters, 3 meters, 4 meters, and 5 meters.

30. Find the volume and surface area of each sphere. Leave your results in terms of π.

31. Use your answers to Exercise 30 to find the ratio of the volume to the surface area, $\dfrac{V}{S}$, for each sphere.

32. Use a graphing calculator to plot the graph of $\dfrac{V}{S}$ as a function of the radius. What do you notice?

33. *Writing* If the radius of a sphere triples, does its surface area triple? Explain your reasoning.

34. VISUAL THINKING A sphere with radius r is inscribed in a cylinder with height $2r$. Make a sketch and find the volume of the cylinder in terms of r.

STUDENT HELP

HOMEWORK HELP
Visit our Web site
www.mcdougallittell.com
for help with Exs. 35
and 36.

USING ALGEBRA **In Exercises 35 and 36, solve for the variable. Then find the area of the intersection of the sphere and the plane.**

35.

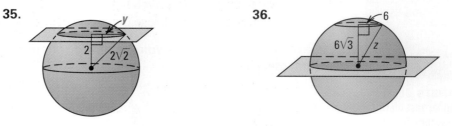

36.

37. CRITICAL THINKING Sketch the intersection of a sphere and a plane that does not pass through the center of the sphere. If you know the circumference of the circle formed by the intersection, can you find the surface area of the sphere? Explain.

SPHERES IN ARCHITECTURE **The spherical building below has a diameter of 165 feet.**

38. Find the surface area of a sphere with a diameter of 165 feet. Looking at the surface of the building, do you think its surface area is the same? Explain.

39. The surface of the building consists of 1000 (nonregular) triangular pyramids. If the lateral area of each pyramid is about 267.3 square feet, estimate the actual surface area of the building.

40. Estimate the volume of the building using the formula for the volume of a sphere.

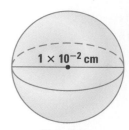

BALL BEARINGS **In Exercises 41–43, refer to the description of how ball bearings are made in Example 4 on page 761.**

41. Find the radius of a steel ball bearing made from a cylindrical slug with a radius of 3 centimeters and a height of 6 centimeters.

42. Find the radius of a steel ball bearing made from a cylindrical slug with a radius of 2.57 centimeters and a height of 4.8 centimeters.

43. If a steel ball bearing has a radius of 5 centimeters, and the radius of the cylindrical slug it was made from was 4 centimeters, then what was the height of the cylindrical slug?

44. **COMPOSITION OF ICE CREAM** In making ice cream, a mix of solids, sugar, and water is frozen. Air bubbles are whipped into the mix as it freezes. The air bubbles are about 1×10^{-2} centimeter in diameter. If one quart, 946.34 cubic centimeters, of ice cream has about 1.446×10^{9} air bubbles, what percent of the ice cream is air? (*Hint:* Start by finding the volume of one air bubble.)

Air bubble

MULTI-STEP PROBLEM Use the solids below.

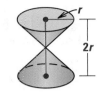

45. Write an expression for the volume of the sphere in terms of *r*.

46. Write an expression for the volume of the cylinder in terms of *r*.

47. Write an expression for the volume of the solid composed of two cones in terms of *r*.

48. Compare the volumes of the cylinder and the cones to the volume of the sphere. What do you notice?

★ **Challenge**

EXTRA CHALLENGE
www.mcdougallittell.com

49. A cone is inscribed in a sphere with a radius of 5 centimeters, as shown. The distance from the center of the sphere to the center of the base of the cone is *x*. Write an expression for the volume of the cone in terms of *x*. (*Hint:* Use the radius of the sphere as part of the height of the cone.)

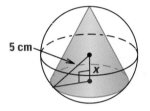

MIXED REVIEW

CLASSIFYING PATTERNS Name the isometries that map the frieze pattern onto itself. (Review 7.6)

50.

51.

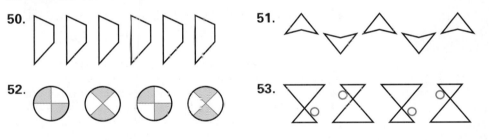

52.

53.

FINDING AREA In Exercises 54–56, determine whether △*ABC* is similar to △*EDC*. If so, then find the area of △*ABC*. (Review 8.4, 11.3 for 12.7)

54.

55.

56.

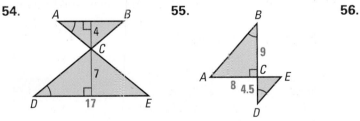

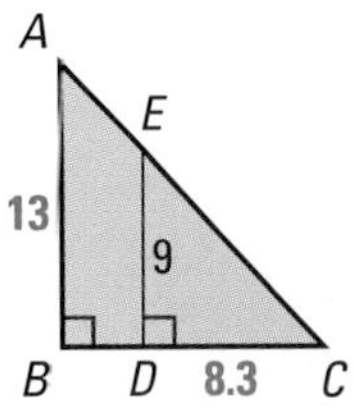

57. MEASURING CIRCLES The tire at the right has an outside diameter of 26.5 inches. How many revolutions does the tire make when traveling 100 feet? (Review 11.4)

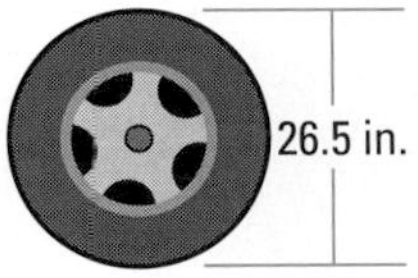

26.5 in.

12.7

Similar Solids

What you should learn

GOAL 1 Find and use the scale factor of similar solids.

GOAL 2 Use similar solids to solve **real-life** problems, such as finding the lift power of the weather balloon in **Example 4**.

Why you should learn it

▼ You can use similar solids when building a model, such as the model planes below and the model car in Exs. 25–27.

GOAL 1 COMPARING SIMILAR SOLIDS

Two solids with equal ratios of corresponding *linear* measures, such as heights or radii, are called **similar solids**. This common ratio is called the *scale factor* of one solid to the other solid. Any two cubes are similar; so are any two spheres. Here are other examples of similar and nonsimilar solids.

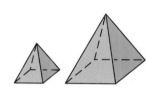 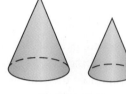 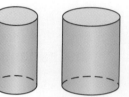

Similar pyramids   **Similar cones**   **Nonsimilar cylinders**

EXAMPLE 1 *Identifying Similar Solids*

Decide whether the two solids are similar. If so, compare the surface areas and volumes of the solids.

a.
b.

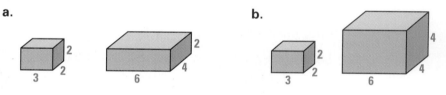

SOLUTION

a. The solids are not similar because the ratios of corresponding linear measures are not equal, as shown.

$$\text{lengths: } \frac{3}{6} = \frac{1}{2} \qquad \text{widths: } \frac{2}{4} = \frac{1}{2} \qquad \text{heights: } \frac{2}{2} = \frac{1}{1}$$

b. The solids are similar because the ratios of corresponding linear measures are equal, as shown. The solids have a scale factor of $1:2$.

$$\text{lengths: } \frac{3}{6} = \frac{1}{2} \qquad \text{widths: } \frac{2}{4} = \frac{1}{2} \qquad \text{heights: } \frac{2}{4} = \frac{1}{2}$$

The surface area and volume of the solids are as follows:

Prism	Surface area	Volume
Smaller	$S = 2B + Ph = 2(6) + 10(2) = \mathbf{32}$	$V = Bh = 6(2) = \mathbf{12}$
Larger	$S = 2B + Ph = 2(24) + 20(4) = \mathbf{128}$	$V = Bh = 24(4) = \mathbf{96}$

▶ The ratio of side lengths is $1:2$, the ratio of surface areas is $\mathbf{32:128}$, or $1:4$, and the ratio of volumes is $\mathbf{12:96}$, or $1:8$.

THEOREM 12.13 *Similar Solids Theorem*

If two similar solids have a scale factor of $a:b$, then corresponding areas have a ratio of $a^2:b^2$, and corresponding volumes have a ratio of $a^3:b^3$.

The term *areas* in the theorem above can refer to any pair of corresponding areas in the similar solids, such as lateral areas, base areas, and surface areas.

EXAMPLE 2 *Using the Scale Factor of Similar Solids*

The prisms are similar with a scale factor of $1:3$. Find the surface area and volume of prism G given that the surface area of prism F is 24 square feet and the volume of prism F is 7 cubic feet.

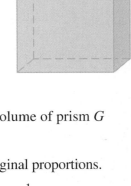

STUDENT HELP

▶ **Look Back**
For help with solving a proportion with an unknown, see p. 459.

SOLUTION

Begin by using Theorem 12.13 to set up two proportions.

$$\frac{\text{Surface area of } F}{\text{Surface area of } G} = \frac{a^2}{b^2}$$

$$\frac{24}{\text{Surface area of } G} = \frac{1^2}{3^2}$$

$$\text{Surface area of } G = 216$$

$$\frac{\text{Volume of } F}{\text{Volume of } G} = \frac{a^3}{b^3}$$

$$\frac{7}{\text{Volume of } G} = \frac{1^3}{3^3}$$

$$\text{Volume of } G = 189$$

▶ So, the surface area of prism G is 216 square feet and the volume of prism G is 189 cubic feet.

✓**CHECK** Check your answers by substituting back into the original proportions.

$$\frac{\text{Surface area of } F}{\text{Surface area of } G} = \frac{24}{216} = \frac{1}{9} \qquad \frac{\text{Volume of } F}{\text{Volume of } G} = \frac{7}{189} = \frac{1}{27}$$

EXAMPLE 3 *Finding the Scale Factor of Similar Solids*

To find the scale factor of the two cubes, find the ratio of the two volumes.

$$\frac{a^3}{b^3} = \frac{512}{1728} \qquad \text{Write ratio of volumes.}$$

$$\frac{a}{b} = \frac{8}{12} \qquad \text{Use a calculator to take the cube root.}$$

$$= \frac{2}{3} \qquad \text{Simplify.}$$

$V = 512 \text{ m}^3$

$V = 1728 \text{ m}^3$

▶ So, the two cubes have a scale factor of $2:3$.

METEOROLOGY
Meteorologists rely on data collected from weather balloons and radar to make predictions about the weather.

CAREER LINK
www.mcdougallittell.com

EXAMPLE 4 *Using Volumes of Similar Solids*

METEOROLOGY The lift power of a weather balloon is the amount of weight the balloon can lift. Find the missing measures in the table below, given that the ratio of the lift powers is equal to the ratio of the volumes of the balloons.

Diameter	Volume	Lift power
8 ft	_?_ ft³	17 lb
16 ft	_?_ ft³	_?_ lb

SOLUTION

Find the volume of the smaller balloon, whose radius is 4 feet.

smaller balloon $\qquad V = \frac{4}{3}\pi r^3 = \frac{4}{3}\pi(4)^3 \approx 85.3\pi \text{ ft}^3$

The scale factor of the two balloons is $\frac{8}{16}$, or $1:2$. So, the ratio of the volumes is $1^3:2^3$, or $1:8$. To find the volume of the larger balloon, multiply the volume of the smaller balloon by 8.

larger balloon $\qquad V \approx 8(85.3\pi) \approx 682.4\pi \text{ ft}^3$

The ratio of the lift powers is $1:8$. To find the lift power of the larger balloon, multiply the lift power of the smaller balloon by 8, as follows: $8(17) = 136$ lb.

Diameter	Volume	Lift power
8 ft	85.3π ft³	17 lb
16 ft	682.4π ft³	136 lb

EXAMPLE 5 *Comparing Similar Solids*

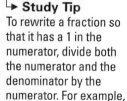

SWIMMING POOLS Two swimming pools are similar with a scale factor of $3:4$. The amount of a chlorine mixture to be added is proportional to the volume of water in the pool. If two cups of the chlorine mixture are needed for the smaller pool, how much of the chlorine mixture is needed for the larger pool?

SOLUTION

Using the scale factor, the ratio of the volume of the smaller pool to the volume of the larger pool is as follows:

$$\frac{a^3}{b^3} = \frac{3^3}{4^3} = \frac{27}{64} \approx \frac{1}{2.4}$$

The ratio of the volumes of the mixtures is $1:2.4$. The amount of the chlorine mixture for the larger pool can be found by multiplying the amount of the chlorine mixture for the smaller pool by 2.4 as follows: $2(2.4) = 4.8$ c.

▶ So, the larger pool needs 4.8 cups of the chlorine mixture.

STUDENT HELP

▶ **Study Tip**
To rewrite a fraction so that it has a 1 in the numerator, divide both the numerator and the denominator by the numerator. For example,
$\frac{27}{64} = \frac{27 \div 27}{64 \div 27} \approx \frac{1}{2.4}$.

GUIDED PRACTICE

Vocabulary Check ✓　**1.** If two solids are similar with a scale factor of $p:q$, then corresponding areas have a ratio of ___?___, and corresponding volumes have a ratio of ___?___.

Concept Check ✓　**Determine whether the pair of solids are similar. Explain your reasoning.**

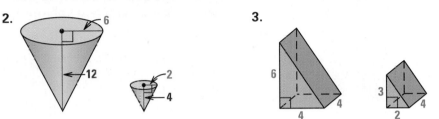

2.

3.

Skill Check ✓　**In Exercises 4–6, match the right prism with a similar right prism.**

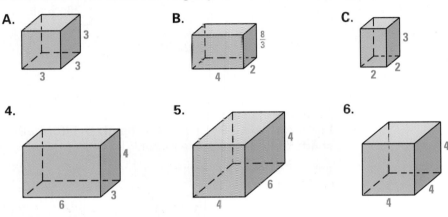

A.

B.

C.

4.

5.

6.

7. Two cubes have volumes of 216 cubic inches and 1331 cubic inches. Find their scale factor.

8. Two spheres have a scale factor of $1:3$. The smaller sphere has a surface area of 36π square meters. Find the surface area of the larger sphere.

PRACTICE AND APPLICATIONS

STUDENT HELP

▶ **Extra Practice**
to help you master
skills is on p. 826.

IDENTIFYING SIMILAR SOLIDS **Decide whether the solids are similar.**

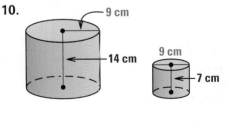

9.

10.

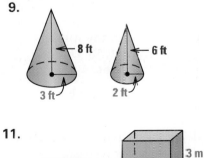

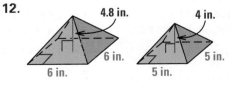

11.

12.

STUDENT HELP

▸ **HOMEWORK HELP**
Example 1: Exs. 9–16
Example 2: Exs. 17–20
Example 3: Exs. 21–24
Example 5: Ex. 34

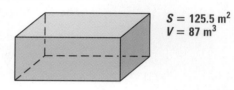 **LOGICAL REASONING** Complete the statement using *always,
sometimes,* or *never.*

13. Two cubes are ___?___ similar.   **14.** Two cylinders are ___?___ similar.

15. A solid is ___?___ similar to itself.   **16.** A pyramid is ___?___ similar to a cone.

USING SCALE FACTOR The solid is similar to a larger solid with the given
scale factor. Find the surface area *S* and volume *V* of the larger solid.

17. Scale factor 1 : 2

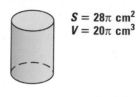

$S = 28\pi$ cm^2
$V = 20\pi$ cm^3

18. Scale factor 1 : 3

$S = 125.5$ m^2
$V = 87$ m^3

19. Scale factor 1 : 4

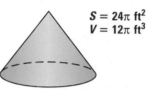

$S = 24\pi$ ft^2
$V = 12\pi$ ft^3

20. Scale factor 2 : 5

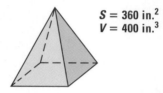

$S = 360$ in.^{2}
$V = 400$ in.^{3}

FINDING SCALE FACTOR Use the given information about the two similar
solids to find their scale factor.

21.

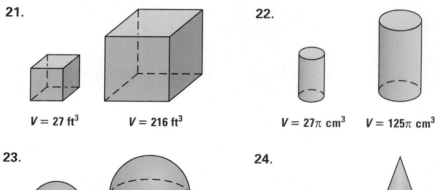

$V = 27$ ft^3 $V = 216$ ft^3

22.

$V = 27\pi$ cm^3 $V = 125\pi$ cm^3

23.

$V = 36\pi$ m^3 $V = 121.5\pi$ m^3

24.

$S = 24\pi$ in.^{2} $S = 384\pi$ in.^{2}

🌐 **MODEL CAR** The scale factor of the model
car at the right to the actual car is 1 : 16. Use the
scale factor to complete the exercises.

25. The model has a height of 5.5 inches. What is
the height of the actual car?

26. Each tire of the model has a surface area of 12.9 square inches. What is the
surface area of each tire of the actual car?

27. The model's engine has a volume of 2 cubic inches. Find the volume of the
actual car's engine.

CRITICAL THINKING Decide whether the statement is true. Explain your reasoning.

28. If sphere A has a radius of x and sphere B has a radius of y, then the corresponding volumes have a ratio of $x^3 : y^3$.

29. If cube A has an edge length of x and cube B has an edge length of y, then the corresponding surface areas have a ratio of $x^2 : y^2$.

 **ARCHITECTURE** In Exercises 30–33, you are building a scale model of the Civil Rights Institute shown at the left.

30. You decide that 0.125 inch in your model will correspond to 12 inches of the actual building. What is your scale factor?

31. The dome of the building is a hemisphere with a diameter of $50\frac{2}{3}$ feet. Find the surface area of the hemisphere.

32. Use your results from Exercises 30 and 31 to find the surface area of the dome of your model. $\left(1 \text{ ft}^2 = 144 \text{ in.}^2\right)$

33. Use your results from Exercises 30 and 31 to find the volume of the actual dome. What is the volume of your model's dome?

34. **MAKING JUICE** Two similar cylindrical juice containers have a scale factor of $2:3$. To make juice in the smaller container, you use $\frac{1}{2}$ cup of concentrated juice and fill the rest with water. Find the amount of concentrated juice needed to make juice in the larger container. (*Hint:* Start by finding the ratio of the volumes of the containers.)

35. **MULTIPLE CHOICE** The dimensions of the right rectangular prism shown are doubled. How many times larger is the volume of the new prism?

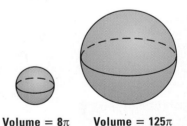

    Ⓐ $\frac{1}{4}$ Ⓑ $\frac{1}{2}$ Ⓒ 2   Ⓓ 4   Ⓔ 8

36. **MULTIPLE CHOICE** What is the ratio of the surface areas of the spheres shown?

    Ⓐ $\frac{\sqrt{2}}{\sqrt{5}}$ Ⓑ $\frac{2}{5}$ Ⓒ $\frac{\sqrt{8}}{\sqrt{125}}$

    Ⓓ $\frac{4}{25}$ Ⓔ $\frac{8}{125}$

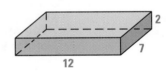

Volume = 8π Volume = 125π

37. **SPORTS** Twelve basketballs, each with a diameter of 9.55 inches, fill a crate. Estimate the number of volleyballs it would take to fill the crate. The diameter of a volleyball is 8.27 inches. Explain why your answer is an estimate and not an exact number.

38. **CRITICAL THINKING** Two similar cylinders have surface areas of 96π square feet and 150π square feet. The height of each cylinder is equal to its diameter. Find the dimensions of one cylinder and use their scale factor to find the dimensions of the other cylinder.

Test Preparation

★ Challenge

EXTRA CHALLENGE
www.mcdougallittell.com

MIXED REVIEW

TRANSFORMATIONS **Use the diagram of the isometry to complete the statement.** (Review 7.1)

39. $\overline{BC} \rightarrow$?

40. $\overline{AB} \rightarrow$?

41. ? $\rightarrow \overline{KJ}$

42. $\angle BCA \rightarrow$?

43. ? $\rightarrow \angle LJK$

44. $\triangle ABC \rightarrow$?

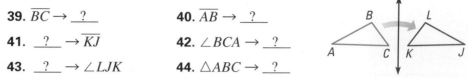

FINDING SURFACE AREA **In Exercises 45–47, find the surface area of the solid.** (Review 12.2, 12.3, and 12.6)

45.

46.

47.

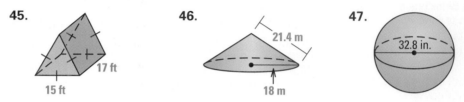

45. 17 ft, 15 ft

46. 21.4 m, 18 m

47. 32.8 in.

48. The volume of a cylinder is about 14,476.46 cubic meters. If the cylinder has a height of 32 meters, what is its diameter? (Review 12.4)

49. The volume of a cone is about 40,447.07 cubic inches. If the cone has a radius of 22.8 inches, what is its height? (Review 12.5)

QUIZ 3

Self-Test for Lessons 12.6 and 12.7

You are given the diameter *d* of a sphere. Find the surface area and volume of the sphere. Round your result to two decimal places. (Lesson 12.6)

1. $d = 20$ cm

2. $d = 3.76$ in.

3. $d = 10.8$ ft

4. $d = 30\sqrt{5}$ m

In Exercises 5 and 6, you are given two similar solids. Find the missing measurement. Then calculate the surface area and volume of each solid. (Lesson 12.7)

5.

6.

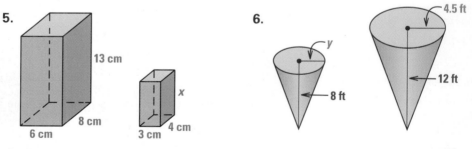

5. 13 cm, 8 cm, 6 cm, x, 4 cm, 3 cm

6. 4.5 ft, y, 12 ft, 8 ft

7. 🌐 **WORLD'S FAIR** The Trylon and Perisphere were the symbols of the New York World's Fair in 1939–40. The Perisphere, shown at the left, was a spherical structure with a diameter of 200 feet. Find the surface area and volume of the Perisphere. (Lesson 12.6)

8. 🌐 **SCALE MODEL** The scale factor of a model of the Perisphere to the actual Perisphere is 1 : 20. Use the information in Exercise 7 and the scale factor to find the radius, surface area, and volume of the model. (Lesson 12.7)

WHAT did you learn?

Use properties of polyhedra. (12.1)

Find the surface area of prisms and cylinders. (12.2)

Find the surface area of pyramids and cones. (12.3)

Find the volume of prisms and cylinders. (12.4)

Find the volume of pyramids and cones. (12.5)

Find the surface area and volume of a sphere. (12.6)

Find the surface area and volume of similar solids. (12.7)

WHY did you learn it?

Classify crystals by their shape. (p. 725)

Determine the surface area of a wax cylinder record. (p. 733)

Find the area of each lateral face of a pyramid, such as the Pyramid Arena in Tennessee. (p. 735)

Find the volume of a fish tank, such as the tank at the New England Aquarium. (p. 748)

Find the volume of a volcano, such as Mount St. Helens. (p. 757)

Find the surface area of a planet, such as Earth. (p. 763)

Use the scale factor of a model car to determine dimensions on the actual car. (p. 770)

How does Chapter 12 fit into the BIGGER PICTURE of geometry?

Solids can be assigned three types of measure. For instance, the height and radius of a cylinder are one-dimensional measures. The surface area of a cylinder is a two-dimensional measure, and the volume of a cylinder is a three-dimensional measure. Assigning measures to plane regions and to solids is one of the primary goals of geometry. In fact, the word geometry means "Earth measure."

STUDY STRATEGY

How did generalizing formulas help you?

The list of similar concepts you made, following the **Study Strategy** on p. 718, may resemble this one.

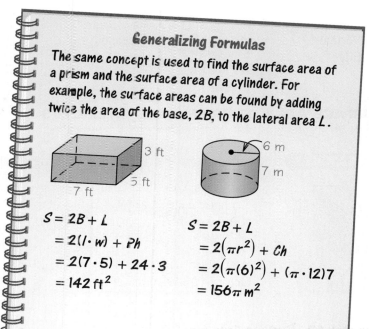

Generalizing Formulas

The same concept is used to find the surface area of a prism and the surface area of a cylinder. For example, the surface areas can be found by adding twice the area of the base, 2B, to the lateral area L.

$S = 2B + L$
$= 2(l \cdot w) + Ph$
$= 2(7 \cdot 5) + 24 \cdot 3$
$= 142 \text{ ft}^2$

$S = 2B + L$
$= 2(\pi r^2) + Ch$
$= 2(\pi(6)^2) + (\pi \cdot 12)7$
$= 156\pi \text{ m}^2$

Chapter Review

- polyhedron, p. 719
- face, p. 719
- edge, p. 719
- vertex, p. 719
- regular polyhedron, p. 720
- convex, p. 720
- cross section, p. 720
- Platonic solids, p. 721
- tetrahedron, p. 721
- octahedron, p. 721
- dodecahedron, p. 721

- icosahedron, p. 721
- prism, p. 728
- bases, p. 728
- lateral faces, p. 728
- right prism, p. 728
- oblique prism, p. 728
- surface area of a polyhedron, p. 728
- lateral area of a polyhedron, p. 728
- net, p. 729

- cylinder, p. 730
- right cylinder, p. 730
- lateral area of a cylinder, p. 730
- surface area of a cylinder, p. 730
- pyramid, p. 735
- regular pyramid, p. 735
- circular cone, p. 737
- lateral surface of a cone, p. 737

- right cone, p. 737
- volume of a solid, p. 743
- sphere, p. 759
- center of a sphere, p. 759
- radius of a sphere, p. 759
- chord of a sphere, p. 759
- diameter of a sphere, p. 759
- great circle, p. 760
- hemisphere, p. 760
- similar solids, p. 766

12.1 EXPLORING SOLIDS

Examples on pp. 719–722

EXAMPLE The solid at the right has 6 faces and 10 edges. The number of vertices can be found using Euler's Theorem.

$$F + V = E + 2$$
$$6 + V = 10 + 2$$
$$V = 6$$

Use Euler's Theorem to find the unknown number.

1. Faces: 32
   Vertices: __?__
   Edges: 90

2. Faces: __?__
   Vertices: 6
   Edges: 10

3. Faces: 5
   Vertices: 5
   Edges: __?__

12.2 SURFACE AREA OF PRISMS AND CYLINDERS

Examples on pp. 728–731

EXAMPLES The surface area of a right prism and a right cylinder are shown.

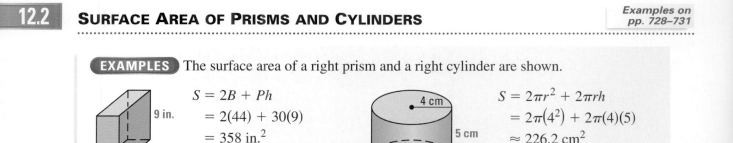

$$S = 2B + Ph$$
$$= 2(44) + 30(9)$$
$$= 358 \text{ in.}^2$$

9 in.

11 in.

4 in.

4 cm

5 cm

$$S = 2\pi r^2 + 2\pi rh$$
$$= 2\pi(4^2) + 2\pi(4)(5)$$
$$\approx 226.2 \text{ cm}^2$$

Find the surface area of the right prism or right cylinder. Round your result to two decimal places.

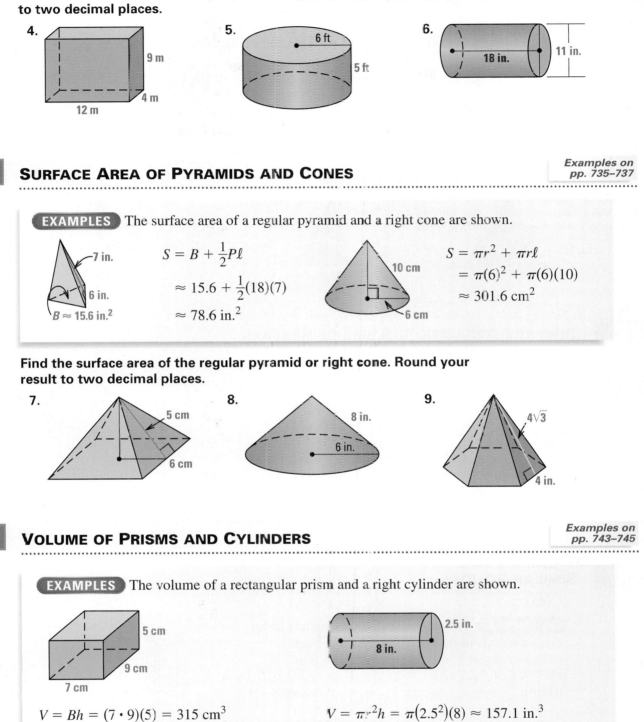

4.

9 m

4 m

12 m

5.

6 ft

5 ft

6.

18 in.

11 in.

Examples on
pp. 735–737

12.3 SURFACE AREA OF PYRAMIDS AND CONES

EXAMPLES The surface area of a regular pyramid and a right cone are shown.

7 in.

6 in.

$B \approx 15.6$ in.^{2}

$$S = B + \frac{1}{2}P\ell$$

$$\approx 15.6 + \frac{1}{2}(18)(7)$$

$$\approx 78.6 \text{ in.}^2$$

10 cm

6 cm

$$S = \pi r^2 + \pi r \ell$$

$$= \pi(6)^2 + \pi(6)(10)$$

$$\approx 301.6 \text{ cm}^2$$

Find the surface area of the regular pyramid or right cone. Round your result to two decimal places.

7.

5 cm

6 cm

8.

8 in.

6 in.

9.

$4\sqrt{3}$

4 in.

Examples on
pp. 743–745

12.4 VOLUME OF PRISMS AND CYLINDERS

EXAMPLES The volume of a rectangular prism and a right cylinder are shown.

5 cm

9 cm

7 cm

2.5 in.

8 in.

$$V = Bh = (7 \cdot 9)(5) = 315 \text{ cm}^3$$

$$V = \pi r^2 h = \pi(2.5^2)(8) \approx 157.1 \text{ in.}^3$$

Find the volume of the described solid.

10. A side of a cube measures 8 centimeters.

11. A right prism has a height of 37.2 meters and regular hexagonal bases, each with a base edge of 21 meters.

12. A right cylinder has a radius of 3.5 inches and a height of 8 inches.

VOLUME OF PYRAMIDS AND CONES

Examples on
pp. 752–754

EXAMPLES The volume of a right pyramid and a right cone are shown.

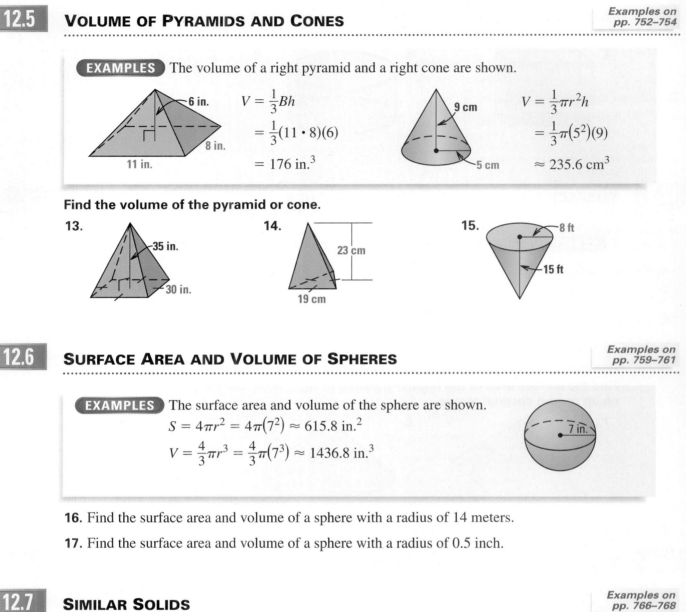

$$V = \frac{1}{3}Bh$$
$$= \frac{1}{3}(11 \cdot 8)(6)$$
$$= 176 \text{ in.}^3$$

$$V = \frac{1}{3}\pi r^2 h$$
$$= \frac{1}{3}\pi(5^2)(9)$$
$$\approx 235.6 \text{ cm}^3$$

Find the volume of the pyramid or cone.

13.

35 in.

30 in.

14.

23 cm

19 cm

15.

8 ft

15 ft

SURFACE AREA AND VOLUME OF SPHERES

Examples on
pp. 759–761

EXAMPLES The surface area and volume of the sphere are shown.

$$S = 4\pi r^2 = 4\pi(7^2) \approx 615.8 \text{ in.}^2$$
$$V = \frac{4}{3}\pi r^3 = \frac{4}{3}\pi(7^3) \approx 1436.8 \text{ in.}^3$$

7 in.

16. Find the surface area and volume of a sphere with a radius of 14 meters.

17. Find the surface area and volume of a sphere with a radius of 0.5 inch.

SIMILAR SOLIDS

Examples on
pp. 766–768

EXAMPLES The ratios of the corresponding linear measurements of the two right prisms are equal, so the solids are similar with a scale factor of 3:4.

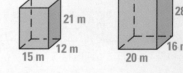

21 m

12 m

15 m

28 m

16 m

20 m

lengths: $\frac{15}{20} = \frac{3}{4}$ **widths:** $\frac{12}{16} = \frac{3}{4}$ **heights:** $\frac{21}{28} = \frac{3}{4}$

Decide whether the solids are similar. If so, find their scale factor.

18.

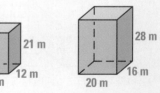

12 cm

6 cm

40 cm

20 cm

19.

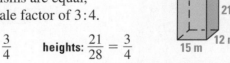

16 ft

8 ft

4 ft

5 ft

12 ft

15 ft

Chapter Test

Determine the number of faces, vertices, and edges of the solids.

1.
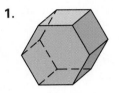

2.
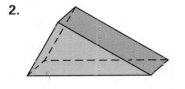

3.
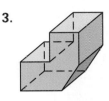

 **USING ALGEBRA** Sketch the solid described and find its missing
measurement. (*B* is the base area, *P* is the base perimeter, *h* is the height,
S is the surface area, *r* is the radius, and ℓ is the slant height.)

4. Right rectangular prism: $B = 44$ m², $P = 30$ m, $h = 7$ m, $S = $ __?__

5. Right cylinder: $r = 8.6$ in., $h = $ __?__ , $S = 784\pi$ in.²

6. Regular pyramid: $B = 100$ ft², $P = 40$ ft, $\ell = $ __?__ , $S = 340$ ft²

7. Right cone: $r = 12$ yd, $\ell = 17$ yd, $S = $ __?__

8. Sphere: $r = 34$ cm, $S = $ __?__

In Exercises 9–11, find the volume of the right solid.

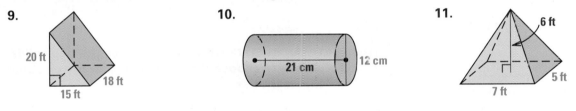

9.   20 ft   18 ft   15 ft

10.   21 cm   12 cm

11.   6 ft   5 ft   7 ft

12. Draw a net for each solid in Exercises 9–11. Label the dimensions of the net.

13. The scale factor of two spheres is 1 : 5. The radius of the
smaller sphere is 3 centimeters. What is the volume of
the larger sphere?

14. Describe the possible intersections of a plane and a sphere.

15. What is the scale factor of the two cylinders at the right?

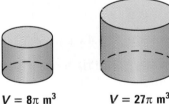

$V = 8\pi$ m³ $V = 27\pi$ m³

16. 🌐 **CANNED GOODS** Find the volume and surface area of a prism with a
height of 6 inches and a 4 inch by 4 inch square base. Compare the results
with the volume and surface area of a cylinder with a height of 7.64 inches
and a diameter of 4 inches.

🌐 **SILOS** Suppose you are building a silo. The shape of your silo is a
right prism with a regular 15-gon for a base, as shown. The height of
your silo is 59 feet.

17. What is the area of the floor of your silo?

18. Find the lateral area and volume of your silo.

$9\frac{2}{5}$ ft   4 ft

19. What are the lateral area and volume of a larger silo
that is in a 1 : 1.25 ratio with yours?

Chapter Standardized Test

● **TEST-TAKING STRATEGY** It is important to remember that your SAT score will not solely determine your acceptance into a college or university. Do not put added pressure on yourself to do well. If you are not satisfied with your SAT score, remember that you can take it again.

1. MULTIPLE CHOICE Which of the figures shown below are *not* convex?

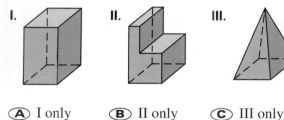

I.　　　　II.　　　　III.

- Ⓐ I only
- Ⓑ II only
- Ⓒ III only
- Ⓓ I and III
- Ⓔ I, II, and III

2. MULTIPLE CHOICE A right rectangular prism has a width of 6.8 meters and a length of 28 meters. If the surface area of the prism is 2608 square meters, what is its height?

- Ⓐ 20 m
- Ⓑ 22.5 m
- Ⓒ 24.8 m
- Ⓓ 30 m
- Ⓔ 32 m

3. MULTIPLE CHOICE What is the lateral area of the right cylinder below?

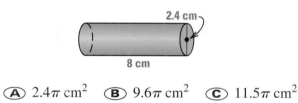

2.4 cm

8 cm

- Ⓐ 2.4π cm^2
- Ⓑ 9.6π cm^2
- Ⓒ 11.5π cm^2
- Ⓓ 19.2π cm^2
- Ⓔ 38.4π cm^2

4. MULTIPLE CHOICE The right triangular prism below has a volume of 1650 cubic meters. What is the value of x?

- Ⓐ 8 m
- Ⓑ 8.5 m
- Ⓒ 10 m
- Ⓓ 12 m
- Ⓔ 12.5 m

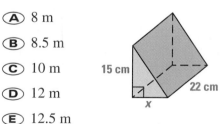

15 cm

22 cm

x

5. MULTIPLE CHOICE What is the radius of a sphere whose volume is 972π cubic yards?

- Ⓐ 6 yd
- Ⓑ 9 yd
- Ⓒ 12 yd
- Ⓓ 14 yd
- Ⓔ 18 yd

6. MULTIPLE CHOICE What is the volume of the solid shown below?

- Ⓐ 34.75 ft^3
- Ⓑ 36 ft^3
- Ⓒ 38.58 ft^3
- Ⓓ 40.79 ft^3
- Ⓔ 42.22 ft^3

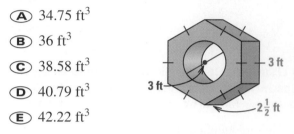

3 ft

3 ft

$2\frac{1}{2}$ ft

7. MULTIPLE CHOICE What is the ratio of the volumes of the right cones shown below?

- Ⓐ 2:5
- Ⓑ 1:3
- Ⓒ 3:20
- Ⓓ 1:9
- Ⓔ 1:27

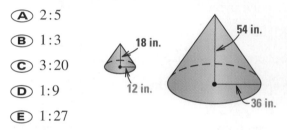

54 in.

18 in.

12 in.

36 in.

QUANTITATIVE COMPARISON Use the two solids shown to choose the statement that is true about the quantities.

- Ⓐ The quantity in column A is greater.
- Ⓑ The quantity in column B is greater.
- Ⓒ The two quantities are equal.
- Ⓓ The relationship cannot be determined from the given information.

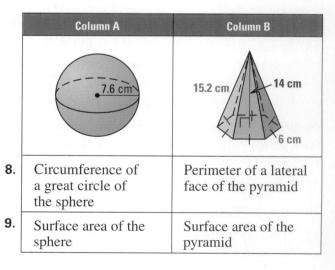

7.6 cm

15.2 cm

14 cm

6 cm

	Column A	Column B
8.	Circumference of a great circle of the sphere	Perimeter of a lateral face of the pyramid
9.	Surface area of the sphere	Surface area of the pyramid

10. MULTIPLE CHOICE The side lengths of a cube are doubled. How many times larger is the surface area of the new cube?

Ⓐ 2 times   Ⓑ 3 times   Ⓒ 4 times   Ⓓ 8 times   Ⓔ 16 times

11. MULTIPLE CHOICE The scale factor of two cylinders is $1:4$. The radius of a base of the smaller cylinder is 4 feet and its height is 5 feet. What is the volume of the larger cylinder?

Ⓐ 320π ft^3 Ⓑ 1280π ft^3 Ⓒ 2560π ft^3 Ⓓ 5120π ft^3 Ⓔ 6480π ft^3

MULTI-STEP PROBLEM Use the diagram of the storage building shown.

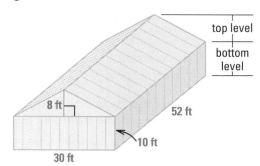

12. You decide to cover the roof with 8 foot by 4 foot plywood sheets. Estimate the number of sheets of plywood you need. Explain how you calculated your answer.

13. Find the volume of the entire storage building.

14. What is the surface area of the top level of the building? Include the floor separating the top level from the bottom level.

MULTI-STEP PROBLEM Terry plans to use 12 sliced peaches for a peach cobbler. The cylindrical soufflé dish she will bake it in has a diameter of 18 centimeters and a height of 9 centimeters.

15. What is the volume of Terry's soufflé dish?

16. The 12 sliced peaches fill a bowl with a diameter of 20 centimeters. Given that the bowl is a hemisphere, how can you determine whether the peaches will fit in the soufflé dish?

17. How many peaches should she use to make two single servings in custard cups that have diameters of 7 centimeters and heights of 3.5 centimeters?

18. *Writing* Mark says that to reduce the volume of a dessert by half, a baking dish with dimensions that are half the dimensions of the original dish must be used. Is Mark correct? Explain.

MULTI-STEP PROBLEM Use the similar cylindrical weights shown.

19. What is the scale factor of the smaller cylinder to the larger cylinder?

20. What is the height of the larger cylindrical weight?

21. Find the surface area of the smaller cylinder. Use the scale factor from Exercise 19 to find the surface area of the larger cylinder.

22. Find the volume of the smaller cylinder. Use the scale factor from Exercise 19 to find the volume of the larger cylinder.

23. A third cylindrical weight is larger than the two shown. This third weight is similar to the larger weight with a scale factor of $1:3$. Use your results from Exercises 21 and 22 to find the surface area and volume of the third weight.

1. Two lines intersect to form vertical angles with measures of $(4x - 2)°$ and $6(x - 3)°$. Find the measures of the four angles formed at the intersection of the two lines. **(2.6)**

2. Sketch two parallel lines intersected by a transversal. Then sketch the bisectors of two consecutive interior angles. What kind of triangle is formed by the transversal and the two bisectors? Explain your answer. **(3.3, 4.1)**

3. Write a coordinate proof to show that in a right triangle, the length of the median to the hypotenuse is half the length of the hypotenuse. Use $\triangle RST$, which is right with vertices $R(0, 0)$, $S(2h, 0)$, and $T(0, 2k)$. **(4.7, 5.3)**

Decide whether the triangle is *acute, right,* or *obtuse*. Name the largest and the smallest angles of the triangle. (5.5, 9.3)

4. $\triangle ABC$, $AB = 12$, $BC = 8$, and $AC = 15$

5. $\triangle XYZ$, $XY = 10$, $YZ = 8$, and $XZ = 6$

▶ **TWO-COLUMN PROOF** Write a two-column proof. **(3.3, 6.2)**

6. **GIVEN** ▶ $j \parallel k$, $m\angle 1 = 73°$

   PROVE ▶ $m\angle 2 = 107°$

7. **GIVEN** ▶ $ABDE$ and $CDEF$ are $\square$s.

   PROVE ▶ $\angle 4$ and $\angle 6$ are supplementary.

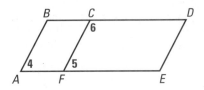

In Exercises 8 and 9, use *always, sometimes,* or *never* to complete the statement.

8. The sides of a rhombus are __?__ congruent. **(6.4)**

9. A trapezoid __?__ has rotational symmetry. **(6.5, 7.3)**

10. A segment has endpoints $X(-3, 3)$ and $Y(-5, 8)$. The segment is reflected in the x-axis and then in the y-axis. Sketch the image of the segment after the two reflections. Describe a single transformation that would map $\overline{XY}$ to the final image. **(7.2, 7.3, 7.5)**

In Exercises 11–13, use the diagram.

11. Show that $\triangle ABC \sim \triangle ADE$. **(8.4)**

12. Find the value of x. **(8.6)**

13. Find the ratio of the perimeter of $\triangle ABC$ to the perimeter of $\triangle ADE$. Then find the ratio of their areas. **(11.3)**

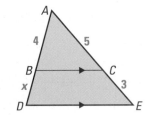

A right triangle has legs of lengths 7 and 24.

14. Find the lengths of the hypotenuse and the altitude to the hypotenuse. **(9.1, 9.2)**

15. Find the measures of the acute angles of the triangle. **(9.6)**

In ⊙*Q*, $\overline{EF} \perp \overline{DB}$, *m*∠*AQB* = 50°, and *m*∠*F* = 40°. **Find the measure of the angle or the arc.** (10.2, 10.3, 10.4)

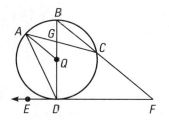

16. $\overset{\frown}{AD}$

17. ∠*ADB*

18. ∠*ACB*

19. ∠*EDB*

20. ∠*EDA*

21. $\overset{\frown}{DC}$

22. $\overset{\frown}{BC}$

23. $\overset{\frown}{ABD}$

24. ∠*BGC*

Suppose *A* is in the exterior of ⊙*P*, and $\overline{AB}$ and $\overline{AC}$ are tangent to ⊙*P*.

25. What can you conclude about ∠*BAC* and ∠*BPC*? Explain. (10.1)

26. What special kind of quadrilateral is *BACP*? Explain. (6.5, 10.1)

In Exercises 27–29, use the diagram at the right. (10.5)

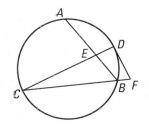

27. Find *AE* if *EB* = 6, *CE* = 18, and *ED* = 4.

28. Find *BC* if *DF* = 6 and *FB* = 4.

29. Find *CE* if *AE* = 10, *EB* = 7, and *ED* = 3.5.

In Exercises 30 and 31, the endpoints of a diameter of a circle are (−2, 1) and (6, −5).

30. Write the standard equation of the circle. (10.6)

31. Find the circumference of the circle. Use $\pi \approx 3.14$. (11.4)

In Exercises 32 and 33, describe the locus of points in a plane. (10.7)

32. Points that are equidistant from the vertices of a regular hexagon.

33. Points that are equidistant from two perpendicular lines, *j* and *k*.

34. What is the sum of the measures of the interior angles of a convex polygon with 25 sides? (11.1)

35. Find the area of a regular octagon whose perimeter is 240 centimeters. (11.2)

36. A quarter circle and a diagonal are drawn inside a square, shown at the right. Find the probability that a randomly chosen point in the interior of the square lies in the shaded region. (11.6)

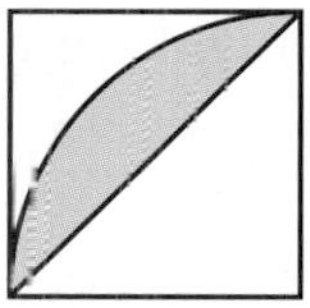

Ex. 36

37. Find the volume of a cone that is 7 feet in diameter and 6 feet high. (12.5)

38. Two right rectangular prisms are similar. The dimensions of the smaller prism are 4 inches, 5 inches, and 5 inches, and the volume of the larger prism is 1562.5 cubic inches. What is the scale factor of the two prisms? (12.4, 12.7)

39. 🌐 **TABLE** A square table has hinged leaves that can be raised to enlarge the table. When all four leaves are up, the table top is a circle. If the area of the square table is 16 square feet, what is the area of the round table? (9.4, 11.5)

40. 🌐 **HONEYCOMB** A cell of a honeycomb is a right regular hexagonal prism with base edges of 0.25 inch and a height of 0.75 inch. Find the lateral area of one cell. (12.2)

41. 🌐 **TABLE TENNIS** The diameter of a table tennis ball is 1.5 inches. Find its surface area to the nearest tenth. (12.6)

Contents
of Student Resources

Skills Review Handbook

PROBLEM SOLVING

One of your primary goals in mathematics should be to become a good problem solver. It will help to approach every problem with an organized plan.

STEP 1 UNDERSTAND THE PROBLEM.
Read the problem carefully. Decide what information you are given and what you need to find. Check whether some of the information given is unnecessary, or whether you need additional information to solve the problem. Supply missing facts, if possible.

STEP 2 MAKE A PLAN TO SOLVE THE PROBLEM.
Choose a strategy. (You can get ideas from the list on page 784.) Choose the correct operations. Decide if you will use a tool such as a calculator, a graph, or a spreadsheet.

STEP 3 CARRY OUT THE PLAN TO SOLVE THE PROBLEM.
Use the strategy and any tools you have chosen. Estimate before you calculate, if possible. Do any necessary calculations. Answer the question that the problem asks.

STEP 4 CHECK TO SEE IF YOUR ANSWER IS REASONABLE.
Reread the problem. See if your answer agrees with the given information and with your estimate if you calculated one.

EXAMPLE In how many ways can two students be chosen to receive an award from a list of ten nominees?

SOLUTION

1 You are given the number of nominated students and the number of students to be chosen. You need to determine how many ways there are to do this.

2 Some strategies to consider are the following: make an organized list, look for a pattern, and solve a simpler problem.

3 Consider the problem when fewer students are nominated. Look for a pattern.

Number of students	2: A, B	3: A, B, C	4: A, B, C, D	5: A, B, C, D, E
Number of ways to choose 2 students	1	3: AB; AC; BC	6: AB; AC; AD; BC; BD; CD	10: AB; AC; AD; AE; BC; BD; BE; CD; CE; DE
Pattern	1	1 + 2	1 + 2 + 3	1 + 2 + 3 + 4

Continue the pattern to find the number of ways to choose 2 out of 10 students.

▶ There are $1 + 2 + 3 + 4 + 5 + 6 + 7 + 8 + 9 = 45$ ways to choose two students from a list of ten to receive an award.

4 You can check your solution by using an organized list.

Step 2 of the problem-solving plan on the previous page asks you to select a strategy. When you solve a problem, you may want to consider these strategies.

PROBLEM SOLVING STRATEGIES

- **Guess, check, and revise.** Use when you do not seem to have enough information.

- **Draw a diagram or a graph.** Use when words describe a visual representation.

- **Make a table or an organized list.** Use when you have data or choices to organize.

- **Use an equation or a formula.** Use when you know a relationship between quantities.

- **Use a proportion.** Use when you know that two ratios are equal.

- **Look for a pattern.** Use when you can examine several cases.

- **Break the problem into simpler parts.** Use when you have a multi-step problem.

- **Solve a simpler problem.** Use when smaller numbers make the problem easier to understand.

- **Work backwards.** Use when you are looking for a fact leading to a known result.

- **Act out the situation.** Use when visualizing the problem is helpful.

PRACTICE

Solve, if possible.

1. During the month of May, Rosa made deposits of $128.50 and $165.19 into her checking account. She wrote checks for $55.12, $25, and $83.98. If her account balance at the end of May was $327.05, what was her balance at the beginning of May?

2. You make 20 silk flower arrangements and plan to sell them at a craft show. Each flower arrangement costs $12 in materials, and your booth at the craft show costs $30. If you sell the arrangements for $24 each, how many must you sell to make at least $100 profit?

3. A store sells sweatshirts in small, medium, large, and extra large. A customer can choose a long sleeve sweatshirt or sweatshirt with a hood There are four choices of colors: white, blue, gray, and black. How many different kinds of sweatshirts are available at the store?

4. If 4.26 lb of chicken costs $6.77, what would 3.75 lb of chicken cost?

5. Roger bought some 33¢ stamps and some 20¢ stamps, and spent $4.50. How many of each type of stamp did he buy?

6. Anita, Betty, Carla, and Dominique are competing in a race. In how many different orders can the four athletes cross the finish line?

7. Stan and Margaret Wu are planning to paint their living room walls. The living room is 18 ft long and 12 ft wide, and the walls are 10 ft high. If a can of paint costs $8.75, what will it cost to paint the living room walls?

POSITIVE AND NEGATIVE NUMBERS

You can use a number line to find the sum of two numbers. Add a positive number by moving to the right. Add a negative number by moving to the left.

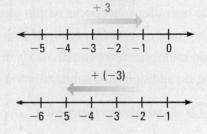

EXAMPLES

a. To find the sum $-4 + 3$, start at -4. Go 3 units to the right. End at -1. So, $-4 + 3 = -1$.

b. To find the sum $-2 + (-3)$, start at -2. Go 3 units to the left. End at -5. So, $-2 + (-3) = -5$.

To subtract a number, add its opposite.

EXAMPLES

a. $7 - 9 = 7 + (-9) = -2$

b. $2.1 - (-5.5) = 2.1 + 5.5 = 7.6$

When you multiply or divide numbers, use these rules.

- The product or quotient of two numbers with the same sign is positive.
- The product or quotient of two numbers with opposite signs is negative.

EXAMPLES

a. $-2(4) = -8$

b. $-\frac{1}{2}\left(-\frac{2}{3}\right) = \frac{1 \cdot 2}{2 \cdot 3} = \frac{1}{3}$

c. $18 \div (-9) = -2$

d. $\frac{-3.5}{-7} = 0.5$

PRACTICE

Add, subtract, multiply, or divide.

1. $0 + (-3.3)$

2. $-7 + (-2)$

3. $5.2 + (-2.5)$

4. $\frac{1}{2} + \left(-\frac{1}{2}\right)$

5. $-\frac{1}{3} + \left(-\frac{3}{4}\right)$

6. $-75 + 48$

7. $-1 - (-1)$

8. $\frac{1}{2} - \left(-\frac{1}{2}\right)$

9. $8 - 9$

10. $8 - (-9)$

11. $-4.8 - 3.2$

12. $24 - 67$

13. $(-3)(-3)$

14. $-8 \cdot 9$

15. $7 \cdot 0 \cdot (-12)$

16. $(-4)(-4)(-4)$

17. $6\left(-\frac{1}{6}\right)$

18. $-\frac{1}{4} \cdot 20$

19. $0.65(-0.24)$

20. $-120(-46)$

21. $-33 \div 11$

22. $0 \div (-1)$

23. $45 \div (-5)$

24. $\frac{-108}{8}$

25. $7.2 \div (-2.5)$

26. $\frac{-128}{-16}$

27. $-\frac{1}{3} \div (-10)$

28. $-\frac{7}{12} \div \frac{2}{3}$

RECIPROCALS

The product of a nonzero number and its **reciprocal** is 1.

The reciprocal of a is $\frac{1}{a}$, and the reciprocal of $\frac{a}{b}$ is $\frac{b}{a}$. Zero has no reciprocal.

EXAMPLES $-\frac{3}{7}$ and $-\frac{7}{3}$ are reciprocals because $-\frac{3}{7}\left(-\frac{7}{3}\right) = 1$.

6 and $\frac{1}{6}$ are reciprocals because $6 \cdot \frac{1}{6} = 1$.

PRACTICE

Find the reciprocal of the number.

1. 12   **2.** -99 **3.** $\frac{1}{4}$ **4.** $-\frac{5}{2}$ **5.** $-\frac{1}{10}$

6. 1   **7.** $\frac{6}{13}$ **8.** -1 **9.** 0.2   **10.** -0.75

RATIOS

If a and b are two quantities measured in the *same* units, then the **ratio of a to b** is $\frac{a}{b}$, usually written in simplest form. The ratio of a to b can also be written as $a : b$. Because a ratio is a quotient, its denominator cannot be zero.

EXAMPLE $\dfrac{9 \text{ inches}}{2 \text{ feet}} = \dfrac{9 \text{ inches}}{2 \cdot 12 \text{ inches}} = \dfrac{9}{24} = \dfrac{3}{8}$

Notice that to simplify a ratio with different units, you rewrite the ratio so that the numerator and denominator have the same units. Then simplify if possible.

EXAMPLE Suppose there are 18 boys in a class of 30 students. To find the ratio of girls to boys, compute the number of girls, $30 - 18 = 12$. Then $\dfrac{\text{girls}}{\text{boys}} = \dfrac{12}{18} = \dfrac{2}{3}$.

PRACTICE

Simplify the ratio.

1. $\dfrac{48 \text{ miles}}{120 \text{ miles}}$ **2.** $\dfrac{72 \text{ cm}}{1.5 \text{ m}}$ **3.** $\dfrac{9 \text{ yards}}{15 \text{ feet}}$ **4.** $\dfrac{12 \text{ ounces}}{2 \text{ pounds}}$

5. $\dfrac{3 \text{ ft}}{36 \text{ in.}}$ **6.** $\dfrac{980 \text{ g}}{2 \text{ kg}}$ **7.** $\dfrac{40 \text{ km}}{500 \text{ m}}$ **8.** $\dfrac{5 \text{ mi}}{6200 \text{ ft}}$

Find the ratio of girls to boys in a class, given the number of boys and the total number of students.

9. 15 boys, 28 students   **10.** 12 boys, 27 students   **11.** 12 boys, 20 students

SOLVING LINEAR EQUATIONS (SINGLE-STEP)

The equations $\frac{1}{2}x = 4$ and $3t - 1 = 4t$ are examples of **linear** equations.

When the variable in a single-variable equation is replaced by a number and the resulting statement is true, the number is a **solution** of the equation. You can *solve an equation* by writing an *equivalent* equation that has the variable alone on one side. One way to do this is to add or subtract the same number *from each side* of the equation.

EXAMPLES Solve the equation.

    a. $x + 6 = -2$

    b. $y - 7 = 3$

SOLUTION   **a.** $x + 6 = -2$

        $x + 6 - 6 = -2 - 6$ **Subtract 6 from each side.**

               $x = -8$ **Simplify.**

  b. $y - 7 = 3$

    $y - 7 + 7 = 3 + 7$ **Add 7 to each side.**

           $y = 10$ **Simplify.**

Another way to solve a linear equation is to multiply or divide each side by the same nonzero number. Notice the use of reciprocals in the example below.

EXAMPLE Solve the equation $8 = \frac{4}{3}a$.

SOLUTION $8 = \frac{4}{3}a$

        $\frac{3}{4} \cdot 8 = \frac{3}{4} \cdot \frac{4}{3}a$ **Multiply each side by the reciprocal.**

           $6 = a$ **Simplify.**

Check your solution by substituting it in the original equation.

PRACTICE

Solve the equation.

1. $x + 12 = 25$

2. $k - 6 = 0$

3. $-36 = -9s$

4. $\frac{1}{5}n = 5$

5. $-32h = 4$

6. $4.6 + z = 3.6$

7. $-\frac{3}{4}d = 24$

8. $0.02v = 8$

9. $w - 5 = -13$

10. $4z = 132$

11. $-6 = c + 4$

12. $-\frac{4}{7}p = -8$

13. $\frac{2}{3}y = 7$

14. $37 = r - (-9)$

15. $\frac{1}{2}x = -40$

16. $-m = 5$

17. $\frac{n}{3} = 6$

18. $330 = -15f$

19. $y + 7 = -16$

20. $-4.2z = 42$

21. $t - \frac{1}{8} = \frac{5}{8}$

22. $\frac{9}{2}x = -1$

23. $120 = -120b$

24. $0 = 6.4k$

SOLVING LINEAR EQUATIONS (MULTI-STEP)

Solving a linear equation may require several steps. You may need to simplify one or both sides of the equation, use the distributive property, or collect variable terms on one side of the equation.

EXAMPLES Solve the equation.

a. $\frac{1}{5}x + 7 = 3$
b. $5 - 2(r + 6) = 1$

SOLUTION **a.** $\frac{1}{5}x + 7 = 3$
b. $5 - 2(r + 6) = 1$

$\frac{1}{5}x + 7 - 7 = 3 - 7$ Subtract 7 from each side. $5 - 2r - 12 = 1$ Distributive property

$\frac{1}{5}x = -4$ Simplify. $-2r - 7 = 1$ Simplify.

$5 \cdot \frac{1}{5}x = 5(-4)$ Multiply by the reciprocal. $-2r - 7 + 7 = 1 + 7$ Add 7 to each side.

$x = -20$ Simplify. $-2r = 8$ Simplify.

CHECK $\frac{-2r}{-2} = \frac{8}{-2}$ Divide each side by -2.

$\frac{1}{5}(-20) + 7 = 3$ ✔ $r = -4$ Simplify.

PRACTICE

Solve the equation.

1. $3y - 4 = 20$

2. $\frac{c}{7} + 2 = 1$

3. $6 - \frac{3a}{2} = -6$

4. $3r - (2r + 1) = 21$

5. $5(z + 3) = 12$

6. $44 = 5g - 8 - g$

7. $75 + 7x = 2x$

8. $14r + 81 = -r$

9. $3n - 1 = 5n - 9$

10. $12r - 5 = 7r$

11. $4 - 6p = 2p - 3$

12. $7(b - 3) = 8b + 2$

13. $60c - 54(c - 2) = 0$

14. $22d - (6 + 2d) = 4$

15. $s - (-4s + 2) = 13$

16. $-\frac{1}{2}(16 - 2h) = 11$

17. $1 + j = 2(2j + 1)$

18. $4x + 2(x - 3) = 0$

19. $\frac{1}{4}y + 27 = 41$

20. $\frac{3 + m}{2} = 5$

21. $\frac{x + (-2)}{2} = -6$

22. $\frac{8 + x}{2} = 10$

23. $2 \cdot 3.14 \cdot r = 157$

24. $\frac{1}{2} \cdot 9 \cdot h = 94.5$

25. $12 \cdot b \cdot 13 = 338$

26. $4(t - 7) + 6 = 30$

27. $7y - 84 = 2y + 61$

28. $85 = \frac{1}{2}(226 - x)$

29. $104 = \frac{1}{2}[(360 - x) - x]$

30. $18(x + 18) = 21^2$

31. $18^2 = 15(x + 15)$

32. $12 - 23c = 7(9 - c)$

33. $2.7(z - 7) + 6 = 2.1(3z + 1)$

34. $7(4h + 1) - 2(2h - 3) = -23$ **35.** $4(5n + 7) - 3n = 3(4n - 9)$ **36.** $4.7(2f - 0.5) = -6(1.6f - 8.3f)$

SOLVING INEQUALITIES

You can solve a linear inequality in one variable in much the same way you solve a linear equation in one variable.

EXAMPLES Solve the inequality.

a.
$$x + 18 > 24$$
$$x + 18 - 18 > 24 - 18$$
$$x > 6$$

b. $x + (2x - 5) > x + 3$

$3x - 5 > x + 3$	Simplify.
$3x - 5 + 5 > x + 3 + 5$	Add 5 to each side.
$3x > x + 8$	Simplify.
$-x + 3x > -x + x + 8$	Add $-x$ to each side.
$2x > 8$	Combine like terms.
$\frac{2x}{2} > \frac{8}{2}$	Divide each side by 2.
$x > 4$	Simplify.

A **solution of an inequality** is a number that produces a true statement when it is substituted for the variable in the inequality.

EXAMPLE Decide whether 3 is a solution of the inequality $3x - 8 < 10$.

SOLUTION

$3(3) - 8 < 10$	Substitute.
$1 < 10$	Simplify.

So, 3 is a solution of the inequality.

PRACTICE

Solve the inequality.

1. $24 + 32 > x$

2. $16 + x > 21$

3. $x + 7.8 > 15.1$

4. $x < 125 + 175$

5. $x + \frac{7}{2} < \frac{11}{2}$

6. $55 < 5 + x$

7. $x + 3x > 2x + 6$

8. $(x + 4) + (x + 6) > 3x - 1$

9. $(2x - 1) + (x + 3) > 18 - x$

Check whether the given number is a solution of the inequality.

10. $m + 12 > 30$; 16

11. $n - 3 < 6$; 2

12. $5 + 2p > 10$; 3

13. $3r - 4 < 0$; 0.5

14. $10s - 2 > 40$; 4

15. $6t - 2 < 4t$; 3

16. $7u + 7 < 38$; 5

17. $8(w - 3) > 95$; 15

18. $6.2x - 3.7 < -14$; -2.2

19. Name three solutions of the inequality $(2x - 3) + (x + 5) > x + 8$. Is 3 a solution? Explain.

PLOTTING POINTS

A **coordinate plane** is formed by a horizontal **x-axis** and a vertical **y-axis** that intersect at the **origin,** forming right angles. Each point in a coordinate plane corresponds to an **ordered pair** of real numbers. Point $W(3, -2)$, shown on the graph, has an **x-coordinate** of 3 and a **y-coordinate** of -2.

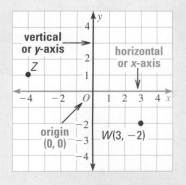

EXAMPLE Use the graph to name the coordinates of point Z.

SOLUTION

The x-coordinate of Z is -4 and the y-coordinate is 1.

So, the ordered pair corresponding to Z is $(-4, 1)$.

EXAMPLES Plot each point in a coordinate plane.

a. $P(-5, 2)$ **b.** $Q(3, 0)$

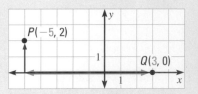

SOLUTION **a.** To plot the point $P(-5, 2)$, start at the origin.
Move 5 units to the left and 2 units up.

b. To plot the point $Q(3, 0)$, start at the origin.
Move 3 units to the right and 0 units up.

PRACTICE

Give the coordinates of each of the following points.

1. A   **2.** B

3. C   **4.** D

5. E   **6.** F

7. G   **8.** H

9. J   **10.** K

11. M   **12.** N

Plot each point in a coordinate plane.

13. $A(4, 6)$ **14.** $B(-3, 2)$ **15.** $C(2, -3)$ **16.** $D(0, -1)$

17. $E(-6, -7)$ **18.** $F(5, 5)$ **19.** $G(1, 0)$ **20.** $H\left(\frac{5}{2}, \frac{5}{2}\right)$

21. $J(0, 2.5)$ **22.** $K\left(\frac{5}{2}, -\frac{9}{2}\right)$ **23.** $L(-3, -2)$ **24.** $M(-2, 3)$

25. $N(-4, 6)$ **26.** $P\left(4, -\frac{3}{2}\right)$ **27.** $Q(-5, 0)$ **28.** $R\left(-\frac{9}{2}, -3\right)$

LINEAR EQUATIONS AND THEIR GRAPHS

A **solution** of an equation in two variables x and y is an ordered pair (x, y) that makes the equation true. Equations like $2x + 3y = -6$, $y = 5x - 1$, and $y = 3$ are **linear equations**. Their graphs are lines.

EXAMPLE Graph the equation $y - 4x = 2$.

SOLUTION You can use a table of values to graph the equation $y - 4x = 2$. Rewrite the equation in *function form* by solving for y: $y - 4x = 2$, so $y = 4x + 2$. Choose a few values of x. Substitute to find the corresponding y-value.

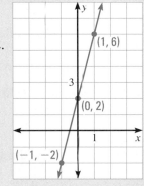

x	$y = 4x + 2$	(x, y)
-1	$y = 4(-1) + 2 = -2$	$(-1, -2)$
0	$y = 4 \cdot 0 + 2 = 2$	$(0, 2)$
1	$y = 4 \cdot 1 + 2 = 6$	$(1, 6)$

Plot the points in the table. Draw a line through the points.

EXAMPLE Graph the equation $3x - 4y = 12$.

SOLUTION You can quickly draw a graph of an equation such as $3x - 4y = 12$ by using the *intercepts*. The **x-intercept** is the x-coordinate of a point where the graph crosses the x-axis. The **y-intercept** is the y-coordinate of a point where the graph crosses the y-axis.

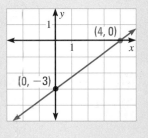

Substitute 0 for x: $3 \cdot 0 - 4y = 12$; $y = -3$, and so the y-intercept is -3.

Substitute 0 for y: $3x - 4 \cdot 0 = 12$; $x = 4$, and so the x-intercept is 4.

Now you can graph the equation $3x - 4y = 12$ by plotting the points $(4, 0)$ and $(0, -3)$ and then drawing a line through the points.

PRACTICE

Use a table of values to graph the equation.

1. $y = -2x + 3$ **2.** $y = 3x - 5$ **3.** $y = \frac{1}{3}x - 2$ **4.** $y = 2.5 + 1.5x$

5. $y = -\frac{3}{4}x$ **6.** $4x + y = -8$ **7.** $x - 3y = 6$ **8.** $y = \frac{3}{2}(x + 1)$

Use the x-intercept and the y-intercept to graph the equation. Label the points where the line crosses the coordinate axes.

9. $x + 5y = -10$ **10.** $-5x + 6y = 30$ **11.** $3x - 3y = -48$ **12.** $y = -(2x - 1)$

13. $y = 4x + 1$ **14.** $y = -x - 2$ **15** $y = 5 - \frac{1}{2}x$ **16.** $y = 0.75x + 1.25$

SLOPE-INTERCEPT FORM

Another way to draw the graph of a linear equation is to use the slope and the y-intercept. Recall that the slope of a nonvertical line is $m = \dfrac{\text{rise}}{\text{run}} = \dfrac{\text{change in } y}{\text{change in } x}$.

The linear equation $y = mx + b$ is written in **slope-intercept form**. The slope of the line is m and the y-intercept is b.

EXAMPLE Graph the equation $\frac{1}{2}x + 2y = 4$.

SOLUTION To graph the equation $\frac{1}{2}x + 2y = 4$, write the equation in slope-intercept form:

$$2y = -\frac{1}{2}x + 4; \; y = -\frac{1}{4}x + 2.$$

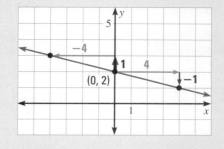

The slope m is $-\frac{1}{4}$, and the y-intercept b is 2.

Plot the point $(0, 2)$.

Draw a *slope triangle* to locate a second point on the line:

$$m = -\frac{1}{4} = \frac{\text{rise}}{\text{run}}.$$

Draw a line through the two points.

EXAMPLES Graph $x = 3$ and $y = -1$.

SOLUTION

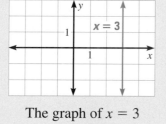

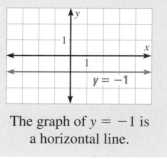

The graph of $x = 3$ is a vertical line.

The graph of $y = -1$ is a horizontal line.

PRACTICE

Use the slope and the y-intercept to graph the equation.

1. $y = \frac{1}{2}x + 4$
2. $y = \frac{1}{2}x - 4$
3. $y = -\frac{1}{2}x - 4$
4. $y = -\frac{1}{2}x + 4$

5. $x - y - 3 = 0$
6. $2x + 3y = -9$
7. $3x - y = 0$
8. $x + 2y = 5$

9. $-4x = 8$
10. $0.25y = 3$
11. $-y - 3x = 4$
12. $2x = 6 - 3y$

13. Graph the equation $x = -2$. Explain why the graph has no slope and no y-intercept.

14. Graph the equation $y = 3$. Find the slope of the graph. Name three different ordered pairs that are solutions of the graph.

WRITING LINEAR EQUATIONS

The slope of a nonvertical line is $m = \dfrac{\text{rise}}{\text{run}} = \dfrac{\text{change in } y}{\text{change in } x}$.

Given the slope and the y-intercept of a line, the slope and a point on a line, or two points on a line, you can use the slope-intercept form to write an equation of the line.

EXAMPLE Write an equation of a line that has a slope of $\frac{1}{2}$ and passes through the point $(-4, -3)$.

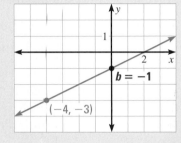

SOLUTION
$$y = mx + b \qquad \text{Write slope formula.}$$
$$-3 = \frac{1}{2}(-4) + b \qquad \text{Substitute.}$$
$$-1 = b \qquad \text{Simplify.}$$

▶ So, $m = \frac{1}{2}$ and $b = -1$, and an equation of the line is $y = \frac{1}{2}x - 1$.

EXAMPLE Write an equation of a line that passes through the points $(4, 0)$ and $(-5, 3)$.

SOLUTION First find the slope of the line.

$$m = \frac{y_2 - y_1}{x_2 - x_1} = \frac{3 - 0}{-5 - 4} = -\frac{1}{3}$$

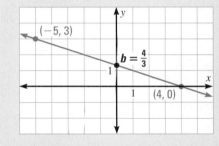

Then substitute the slope and the coordinates of either point into the slope-intercept formula to find the y-intercept. Let $m = -\frac{1}{3}, x = 4,$ and $y = 0$.

$$0 = -\frac{1}{3} \cdot 4 + b \qquad \text{Substitute.}$$
$$b = \frac{4}{3} \qquad \text{Simplify.}$$

▶ An equation of the line is $y = -\frac{1}{3}x + \frac{4}{3}$.

PRACTICE

Write an equation in slope-intercept form of the line that passes through the given point and has the given slope.

1. $(0, -4), m = 1$ **2.** $(0, 8), m = -3$ **3.** $(0, -0.75), m = 2.5$ **4.** $(0, 1.6), m = 0$

5. $(0, 0), m = 0.7$ **6.** $(0, -24), m = 50$ **7.** $(1, -5), m = 2$ **8.** $(3, 0), m = -4$

9. $(-6, -6), m = 12$ **10.** $(-9, 7), m = -1$ **11.** $(3, -11), m = 0$ **12.** $(0.5, -1.5), m = 2$

Write an equation in slope-intercept form of the line that passes through the given points.

13. $(1, 3), (7, 4)$ **14.** $(0, -3), (-5, 0)$ **15.** $(-6, -7), (-5, 1)$ **16.** $(4, 2), (7, -4)$

17. $(2, 0), (-6, -5)$ **18.** $(11, -1), (-1, -7)$ **19.** $(-5, 4), (2, -3)$ **20.** $(4, -9), (8, -9)$

21. $(1.4, 2.7), (3.9, 1.1)$ **22.** $(0, 11), (16, 87)$ **23.** $(0.5, 2), (-1.25, 0.5)$ **24.** $(58, 20), (80, 108)$

SOLVING SYSTEMS OF EQUATIONS

EXAMPLE Use substitution to solve the linear system: $3x + 2y = 16$ **Equation 1**

$x + 3y = 10$ **Equation 2**

SOLUTION

Solve for x in Equation 2 since it is easy to isolate x: $x = 10 - 3y$.

Substitute $10 - 3y$ for x in Equation 1: $3(10 - 3y) + 2y = 16$.

Solve for y to get $y = 2$. Then $x = 10 - 3y = 10 - 3 \cdot 2 = 4$.

The solution is $(4, 2)$. One way to check this solution is to substitute 4 for x and 2 for y in each of the original equations. Another way is to graph the original equations in the same coordinate plane to see if the graphs intersect at the point $(4, 2)$.

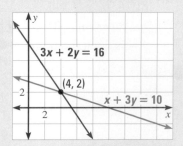

EXAMPLE Use linear combinations to solve the linear system.

$$4x - 3y = -5$$
$$7x + 2y = -16$$

SOLUTION The goal is to obtain coefficients that are opposites for one of the variables.

$4x - 3y = -5$ **Multiply by 2.** ➡ $8x - 6y = -10$

$7x + 2y = -16$ **Multiply by 3.** ➡ $\underline{21x + 6y = -48}$

$29x = -58$ **Add the equations.**

$x = -2$ **Solve for x.**

Substitute -2 for x: $4(-2) - 3y = -5$. Solve to get $y = -1$.

▶ The solution is $(-2, -1)$. Check this in the original equations.

PRACTICE

Use substitution to solve the system of linear equations.

1. $2x - 3y = -16$
$y = 5x + 1$

2. $3x + y = -6$
$x = 0.5y - 3$

3. $7x - y = 0$
$x - y = 12$

4. $x + y = 8$
$2x + 5y = 3$

5. $9x + 4y = 3$
$x + 8y = 6$

6. $3x + 5y = -8$
$4x - y = -3$

7. $x - 0.5y = 6$
$0.5x + 0.2y = 8$

8. $3x + y = 6$
$5(x + y) = 22$

Use linear combinations to solve the system of linear equations.

9. $4x - 5y = 18$
$3x + 10y = -3$

10. $7x + y = 8.5$
$-4x - 3y = 0$

11. $3x - 2y = -6$
$7x - 6y = 12$

12. $8x + 7y = 56$
$7x + 3y = 45$

13. $5x + 9y = -6$
$2x - 6y = 6$

14. $8x + y = -8$
$-2x - 3y = 35$

15. $8x - 4y = 15$
$7x + 9y = 25$

16. $13x - 5y = 10$
$3x - 2y = 14$

PROPERTIES OF EXPONENTS

An expression like 5^3 is called a **power**. The **exponent** 3 represents the number of times the **base** 5 is used as a factor: $5^3 = 5 \cdot 5 \cdot 5$ (3 factors of 5). To simplify expressions involving exponents, you often use properties of exponents. Let a and b be numbers and let m and n be integers.

- **Product of powers property:** $a^m \cdot a^n = a^{m+n}$

  Example: $4^2 \cdot 4^5 = 4^{2+5} = 4^7$

- **Power of a power property:** $\left(a^m\right)^n = a^{m \cdot n}$

  Example: $\left(x^4\right)^3 = x^{4 \cdot 3} = x^{12}$

- **Power of a product property:** $(a \cdot b)^m = a^m \cdot b^m$

  Example: $(-3k)^4 = (-3)^4 \cdot k^4 = 81\,k^4$

- If $a \neq 0$, then $a^0 = 1$.

  Example: $5^0 = 1$

- If $a \neq 0$, then $a^{-n} = \dfrac{1}{a^n}$.

  Example: $x^{-5} = \dfrac{1}{x^5}$

- **Quotient of powers property:** If $a \neq 0$, then $\dfrac{a^m}{a^n} = a^{m-n}$.

  Example: $\dfrac{7^6}{7} = 7^{6-1} = 7^5 = 16{,}807$

- **Power of a quotient property:** If $b \neq 0$, then $\left(\dfrac{a}{b}\right)^m = \dfrac{a^m}{b^m}$.

  Example: $\left(\dfrac{z}{3}\right)^4 = \dfrac{z^4}{3^4} = \dfrac{z^4}{81}$

EXAMPLES Simplify the expression.

    a. $\left(-3xy^2\right)^3 \cdot y$ **b.** $\dfrac{1}{r^7} \cdot r^4$ **c.** $\dfrac{1}{x^6} \cdot \left(\dfrac{x}{2}\right)^6$

SOLUTION

a. $\left(-3xy^2\right)^3 \cdot y = (-3)^3 \cdot x^3 \cdot \left(y^2\right)^3 \cdot y^1 = -27x^3 \cdot y^{6+1} = -27x^3 y^7$

b. $\dfrac{1}{r^7} \cdot r^4 = \dfrac{r^4}{r^7} = r^{4-7} = r^{-3} = \dfrac{1}{r^3}$

c. $\dfrac{1}{x^6} \cdot \left(\dfrac{x}{2}\right)^6 = \dfrac{1}{x^6} \cdot \dfrac{x^6}{2^6} = \dfrac{x^6}{64x^6} = \dfrac{1}{64}$

PRACTICE

Simplify the expression. The simplified expression should have no negative exponents.

1. $\left(-\dfrac{2}{3}\right)^3$ **2.** $x^3 \cdot x \cdot x^3$ **3.** $\left(\dfrac{1}{2}ab\right)^5$ **4.** $2n^4 \cdot (3n)^2$

5. $(rst)^0$ **6.** $\left(8^{-1}\right)^{-3}$ **7.** $4x^{-3} \cdot y^{-6}$ **8.** $c \cdot c^{-9}$

9. $4^3 \cdot 4^6$ **10.** $(3 \cdot a^2 \cdot 6)^2$ **11.** $\left(\dfrac{5}{m}\right)^2$ **12.** $\dfrac{(-3)^5}{-3^5}$

13. $(2b)^3 \cdot b$ **14.** $\left(5x \cdot x^3\right)^4$ **15.** $\left(\dfrac{x^4}{x^3}\right)^2$ **16.** $c^6 \cdot \dfrac{1}{c^9}$

17. $\dfrac{1}{a^{-4}}$ **18.** $\dfrac{2x^0}{8y^{-7}}$ **19.** $\left(2a^{-2}bc^3\right)^{-1}$ **20.** $\left(\dfrac{r}{3s}\right)^{-3}$

21. $\left(5ab^3\right)^2 \cdot (-7b^2c)$ **22.** $w^5 \cdot \left(\dfrac{7}{w^4}\right)^2$ **23.** $4y^3z \cdot \left(\dfrac{y}{2z}\right)^{-3}$ **24.** $\left(3c^{-4}d^5\right)^{-2} \cdot 12cd^{-4}$

MULTIPLYING BINOMIALS

To multiply binomials, use the distributive property. Each term in the first binomial is multiplied by each term in the second binomial. The **FOIL** method can help you remember the pattern of the distributive property. **FOIL** stands for **F** irst, **O** uter, **I** nner, and **L** ast, which is the order in which you multiply terms.

EXAMPLE
$(x + 1)(2x - 4) = x(2x) + x(-4) + 1(2x) + 1(-4)$ Multiply using FOIL.

$= 2x^2 - 4x + 2x - 4$ Simplify.

$= 2x^2 - 2x - 4$ Add like terms.

PRACTICE

Simplify.

1. $(x + 1)(x + 1)$ **2.** $(4b + 1)(2 + b)$ **3.** $(3c + 3)(c - 1)$

4. $(t + 3)(2t - 3)$ **5.** $(a + 5)(4a - 7)$ **6.** $(5d + 3)(d - 2)$

7. $(2f - 4)(2f + 4)$ **8.** $(1 - 2g)(g + 3)$ **9.** $(6h + 3)(h + 1)$

SQUARING BINOMIALS

One way to square a binomial is to use a pattern for the square of a binomial.

Patterns for the Square of a Binomial: $(a + b)^2 = a^2 + 2ab + b^2$

$(a - b)^2 = a^2 - 2ab + b^2$

EXAMPLES $(k + 9)^2 = k^2 + 2(k)(9) + 9^2$ $(x - 4)^2 = x^2 - 2(x)(4) + 4^2$

$= k^2 + 18k + 81$ $= x^2 - 8x + 16$

If you have trouble remembering the patterns, you can always use the distributive property to find the square of a binomial.

EXAMPLE $(r + 3)^2 = (r + 3)(r + 3)$

$= r(r + 3) + 3(r + 3)$ Distributive property

$= r^2 + 3r + 3r + 9$ Distributive property

$= r^2 + 6r + 9$ Combine like terms.

PRACTICE

Find the product by squaring the binomial.

1. $(x + 2)^2$ **2.** $(x - 1)^2$ **3.** $(x + 8)^2$ **4.** $(10 + x)^2$

5. $(n - 5)^2$ **6.** $(x - 0.5)^2$ **7.** $(15 - x)^2$ **8.** $(y + 12)^2$

RADICAL EXPRESSIONS

If $a^2 = b$, then b is a **square root** of a. Every positive number has two square roots: a positive square root and a negative square root. For example:

$4^2 = 16$ and $(-4)^2 = 16$, so the square roots of 16 are 4 and -4. We write:

$$\sqrt{16} = 4 \text{ and } -\sqrt{16} = -4.$$

Zero has just one square root: $\sqrt{0} = 0$.

EXAMPLES $11^2 = 121$, so $-\sqrt{121} = -11$ $\left(\frac{1}{5}\right)^2 = \frac{1}{25}$, so $\sqrt{\frac{1}{25}} = \frac{1}{5}$

$\sqrt{-4}$ is undefined, because the square of every real number is either positive or zero.

$\sqrt{5 + 4} = \sqrt{9} = 3$. Begin by simplifying an expression under the square root symbol.

When you simplify a radical expression, you will often use the following properties of radicals.

If a and b are positive numbers, then $\sqrt{ab} = \sqrt{a} \cdot \sqrt{b}$ and $\sqrt{\frac{a}{b}} = \frac{\sqrt{a}}{\sqrt{b}}$.

EXAMPLES   Simplify the expression.

  a. $\sqrt{56}$ **b.** $\sqrt{6} \cdot \sqrt{15}$ **c.** $\frac{\sqrt{150}}{\sqrt{2}}$ **d.** $\frac{5}{\sqrt{8}}$

SOLUTION

  a. $\sqrt{56} = \sqrt{4} \cdot \sqrt{14} = 2\sqrt{14}$

  b. $\sqrt{6} \cdot \sqrt{15} = \sqrt{6 \cdot 15} = \sqrt{90} = \sqrt{9 \cdot 10} = \sqrt{9} \cdot \sqrt{10} = 3\sqrt{10}$

  c. $\frac{\sqrt{150}}{\sqrt{2}} = \sqrt{\frac{150}{2}} = \sqrt{75} = \sqrt{25 \cdot 3} = \sqrt{25} \cdot \sqrt{3} = 5\sqrt{3}$

  d. $\frac{5}{\sqrt{8}} = \frac{5}{2\sqrt{2}} = \frac{5}{2\sqrt{2}} \cdot \frac{\sqrt{2}}{\sqrt{2}} = \frac{5\sqrt{2}}{4}$ **Do not leave a square root in a denominator.**

PRACTICE

Find all square roots of the number or write *no square roots*. Check the results by squaring each root.

  1. 64 **2.** -36 **3.** $\frac{49}{81}$ **4.** $\frac{7}{100}$ **5.** 0.09

Simplify the expression. Give the exact value in simplified form.

  6. $\sqrt{36 + 64}$ **7.** $\sqrt{4 + 9}$ **8.** $\sqrt{16 + 16}$ **9.** $\sqrt{(-1)^2 + 7^2}$

Simplify the expression. Give the exact value in simplified form.

  10. $-\sqrt{0}$ **11.** $-\sqrt{196}$ **12.** $\sqrt{54}$ **13.** $\sqrt{60}$

  14. $\sqrt{7} \cdot \sqrt{3}$ **15.** $\sqrt{12} \cdot \sqrt{6}$ **16.** $\sqrt{10} \cdot \sqrt{15}$ **17.** $\sqrt{120} \cdot 105$

  18. $\frac{\sqrt{147}}{\sqrt{3}}$ **19.** $\frac{\sqrt{20}}{\sqrt{500}}$ **20.** $\frac{\sqrt{48}}{\sqrt{6}}$ **21.** $\frac{\sqrt{6}}{\sqrt{96}}$

  22. $\frac{4}{\sqrt{3}}$ **23.** $\frac{6}{\sqrt{2}}$ **24.** $\frac{5}{\sqrt{20}}$ **25.** $\frac{4}{\sqrt{27}}$

SOLVING $AX^2 + C = 0$

A **quadratic equation** is an equation that can be written in the **standard form** $ax^2 + bx + c = 0$ where $a \neq 0$.

When $b = 0$, the quadratic equation has the form $ax^2 + c = 0$. In this case, you can solve for x. Solving $ax^2 + c = 0$ for x^2 you get $x^2 = \frac{-c}{a}$ and the following rules apply.

- If $\frac{-c}{a} > 0$, then $x^2 = \frac{-c}{a}$ has two solutions, $x = \sqrt{\frac{-c}{a}}$ and $x = -\sqrt{\frac{-c}{a}}$.

- If $\frac{-c}{a} = 0$, then $x^2 = \frac{-c}{a}$ has one solution, $x = 0$.

- If $\frac{-c}{a} < 0$, $x^2 = \frac{-c}{a}$ has no real solution.

EXAMPLES Solve the equation.

    a. $3x^2 - 1 = 23$ **b.** $12 - x^2 = 13$ **c.** $4 + 2n^2 = 4$

SOLUTION

a. $3x^2 - 1 = 23$	**b.** $12 - x^2 = 13$	**c.** $4 + 2n^2 = 4$
$3x^2 = 24$	$-x^2 = 1$	$2n^2 = 0$
$x^2 = 8$	$x^2 = -1$	$n^2 = 0$
$x = \pm\sqrt{8}$	no real solution	$n = 0$
$x = \pm 2\sqrt{2}$		

EXAMPLE Solve $(x + 2)^2 = x^2 + 9$.

SOLUTION
$$(x + 2)^2 = x^2 + 9$$
$$x^2 + 4x + 4 = x^2 + 9 \qquad \text{See page 798 for help with squaring a binomial.}$$
$$4x = 5 \qquad \text{The given equation simplifies to a linear equation.}$$
$$x = 1.25 \qquad \text{Simplify.}$$

PRACTICE

Solve the equation or write *no solution*. Round solutions to the nearest hundredth.

1. $x^2 = 625$ **2.** $x^2 = -9$ **3.** $x^2 + 6 = 11$

4. $4x^2 = 0$ **5.** $-8 + 3r^2 = 4$ **6.** $\frac{1}{2}k^2 + 3 = 245$

7. $7a^2 + 25 = -6$ **8.** $4x^2 - 2 = 1$ **9.** $(x + 5)^2 = x^2 + 49$

10. $x^2 + 81 = (x + 6)^2$ **11.** $(x + 1)^2 = 27 + x^2$ **12.** $(x + 4)^2 = (x - 4)^2 + 96$

SOLVING $AX^2 + BX + C = 0$

You can solve any quadratic equation by using the **quadratic formula.**
This formula, which you used in Algebra, states that the solutions of the
quadratic equation $ax^2 + bx + c = 0$ are

$$x = \frac{-b \pm \sqrt{b^2 - 4ac}}{2a} \text{ when } a \neq 0 \text{ and } b^2 - 4ac \geq 0.$$

EXAMPLE Solve $x^2 - 4x - 12 = 0$ by using the quadratic formula.

SOLUTION Substitute $a = 1$, $b = -4$, and $c = -12$ in the quadradic formula.

$$x = \frac{-b \pm \sqrt{b^2 - 4ac}}{2a} = \frac{4 \pm \sqrt{(-4)^2 - 4(1)(-12)}}{2 \cdot 1} = \frac{4 \pm \sqrt{64}}{2}$$

▶ The solutions are $\frac{4 + 8}{2} = 6$ and $\frac{4 - 8}{2} = -2$.

Check your solutions by substituting each solution into the original equation.

$6^2 - 4(6) - 12 = 0$ $(-2)^2 - 4(-2) - 12 = 0$

$36 - 24 - 12 = 0$ ✓ $4 + 8 - 12 = 0$ ✓

EXAMPLE Solve $2x^2 + 6x = 1$ by using the quadratic formula.

SOLUTION

Begin by writing the equation in *standard form*: $2x^2 + 6x - 1 = 0$.

Substitute $a = 2$, $b = 6$, and $c = -1$ in the quadratic formula

$$x = \frac{-b \pm \sqrt{b^2 - 4ac}}{2a} = \frac{-6 \pm \sqrt{6^2 - 4 \cdot 2(-1)}}{2 \cdot 2} = \frac{-6 \pm \sqrt{44}}{4} = \frac{-6 \pm 2\sqrt{11}}{4} = \frac{-3 \pm \sqrt{11}}{2}$$

▶ The solutions are $\frac{-3 + \sqrt{11}}{2} \approx 0.16$ and $\frac{-3 - \sqrt{11}}{2} \approx -3.16$.

PRACTICE

**Use the quadratic formula to solve each equation. Round solutions to the
nearest hundredth.**

1. $x^2 + 5x + 4 = 0$ **2.** $x^2 - x - 6 = 0$ **3.** $x^2 + 6x = 0$

4. $a^2 + 8 = 6a$ **5.** $z^2 = 9z - 1$ **6.** $-25 = x^2 + 10x$

7. $2x^2 + 4x + 1 = 0$ **8.** $4c^2 = 4c - 1$ **9.** $-8m + 3m^2 = -1$

10. $3x^2 + 6x + 2 = 0$ **11.** $5y^2 = 1 - 5y$ **12.** $4x^2 - 3x = 7$

13. Solve the quadratic equation $x^2 - 3x + 2 = 0$. Then graph the function
$y = x^2 - 3x + 2$ in a coordinate plane. Describe the relationship between
the solutions of the quadratic equation and the x-intercepts of the graph.

SOLVING FORMULAS

A **formula** is an algebraic equation that relates two or more real-life quantities. You can solve a formula for one of the variables by rewriting the formula so that the required variable is isolated on one side of the equation.

EXAMPLE The formula for the perimeter of the figure shown is $P = 2r + \pi r$. Solve the formula for r.

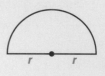

SOLUTION $P = 2r + \pi r$

$P = (2 + \pi)r$ **Distributive property**

$\dfrac{P}{2 + \pi} = r$ **Divide each side by $(2 + \pi)$.**

EXAMPLE Rewrite the equation $2x + 3y = -6$ so that y is a function of x.

SOLUTION $2x + 3y = -6$

$3y = -2x - 6$

$y = \dfrac{-2x - 6}{3}$ or $y = -\dfrac{2}{3}x - 2$

PRACTICE

Solve the formula for the indicated variable.

1. Area of a parallelogram: $A = bh$. Solve for b.

2. Volume of a pyramid: $V = \frac{1}{3}Bh$. Solve for h.

3. Perimeter of a triangle: $P = a + b + c$. Solve for b.

4. Circumference of a circle: $C = 2\pi r$. Solve for r.

5. Perimeter of a parallelogram: $P = 2(a + b)$. Solve for a.

6. Sum of the measures of the interior angles of a convex polygon with n sides: $S = (n - 2)180$. Solve for n.

7. Surface area of a rectangular solid: $S = 2\ell w + 2\ell h + 2wh$. Solve for ℓ.

8. Surface area of a right cylinder: $S = 2\pi r^2 + 2\pi rh$. Solve for h.

9. Surface area of a right cone: $S = \pi r^2 + \pi r\ell$. Solve for ℓ.

10. Area of a trapezoid: $A = \frac{1}{2}hb_1 + \frac{1}{2}hb_2$. Solve for h.

Rewrite the equation so that y is a function of x.

11. $3x + y = 9$ **12.** $5x - y = 0$ **13.** $2y + 6 = 3 - x$ **14.** $\frac{1}{2}x + 4y = -8$

15. $6x - 7y = 42$ **16.** $1.5x + 0.2y = 3$ **17.** $ax + by = c$ **18.** $ax^2 - by = c$

Extra Practice

CHAPTER 1

Describe a pattern in the sequence of numbers. Predict the next number. (Lesson 1.1)

1. 16, 8, 4, 2, 1, . . .

2. 1, 2, 4, 7, 11, . . .

3. 1, 5, 25, 125, . . .

4. 7, 2, 2, 8, 2, 2, 9, 2, 2, . . .

5. 32, 48, 72, 108, . . .

6. 2, −6, 18, −54, . . .

7. Complete the conjecture based on the pattern you observe in the specific cases. (Lesson 1.1)

Conjecture: Any negative number cubed is __?__.

$$-1^3 = -1 \qquad\qquad -7^3 = -343$$
$$-3^3 = -27 \qquad\qquad -9^3 = -729$$
$$-5^3 = -125 \qquad\qquad -11^3 = -1331$$

8. Show that $n^{n+1} > (n+1)^n$ for the values $n = 3, 4,$ and 5. Then show that the values $n = 1$ and $n = 2$ are counterexamples to the conjecture that $n^{n+1} > (n+1)^n$. (Lesson 1.1)

Sketch the points, lines, segments, planes, and rays. (Lesson 1.2)

9. Draw four collinear points A, B, C, and D.

10. Draw two opposite rays $\overrightarrow{MN}$ and $\overrightarrow{MP}$.

11. Draw a plane that contains two intersecting lines.

12. Draw three points E, F, and G that are coplanar, but are not collinear.

13. Draw two points, R and S. Then sketch $\overrightarrow{RS}$. Add a point T on the ray so that S is between R and T.

In the diagram of the collinear points, $AE = 24$, C is the midpoint of $\overline{AE}$, $AB = 8$, and $DE = 5$. Find each length. (Lesson 1.3)

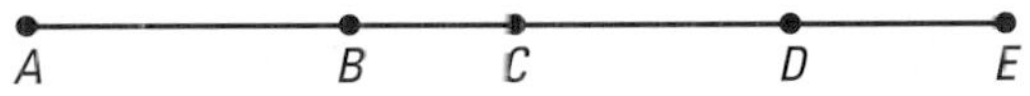

14. BC

15. AD

16. BD

17. AC

18. CD

19. BE

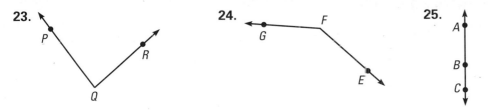

Use the Distance Formula to decide whether $\overline{HM} \cong \overline{ML}$. (Lesson 1.3)

20. $H(-1, 3)$
$M(1, 7)$
$L(3, 3)$

21. $H(3, -1)$
$M(8, 2)$
$L(3, 5)$

22. $H(-5, 2)$
$M(-4, 6)$
$L(-6, 2)$

Name the vertex and sides of the angle, then write two names for the angle. (Lesson 1.4)

23.

24.

25.

Use the Angle Addition Postulate to find the measure of the unknown angle. (Lesson 1.4)

26. $m\angle STR = $ _?_

27. $m\angle HJK = $ _?_

28. $m\angle DEF = $ _?_

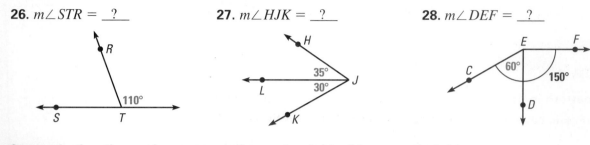

State whether the angle appears to be *acute*, *right*, *obtuse*, or *straight*.
Then estimate its measure. (Lesson 1.4)

29.

30.

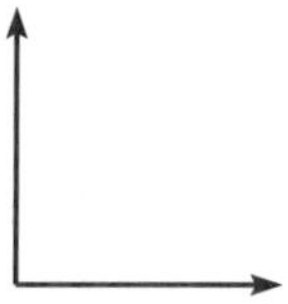

31.

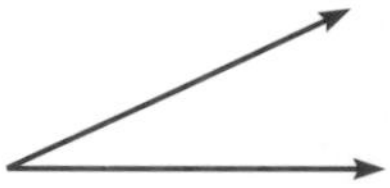

Find the coordinates of the midpoint of a segment with the given endpoints. (Lesson 1.5)

32. $P(-4, 2)$
$Q(8, -4)$

33. $P(-1, 3.5)$
$Q(7, -5.5)$

34. $P(-12, 4)$
$Q(-3, -6)$

$\overrightarrow{XY}$ **is the angle bisector of** $\angle UXB$. **Find** $m\angle UXY$. (Lesson 1.5)

35.

36.

37.

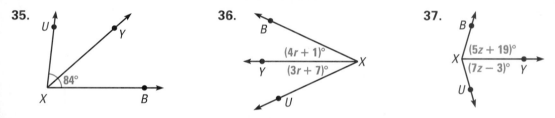

Find the measure of each angle. (Lesson 1.6)

38. Two vertical angles are complementary. Find the measure of each angle.

39. The measure of one angle of a linear pair is 3 times the measure of the other angle. Find the measures of the two angles.

40. The supplement of an angle is 130°. Find the complement of the angle.

Find the perimeter (or circumference) and area of the figure.
(Where necessary, use $\pi \approx 3.14$.) (Lesson 1.7)

41.

42.

43.

44.

45.

46.

47.

48.

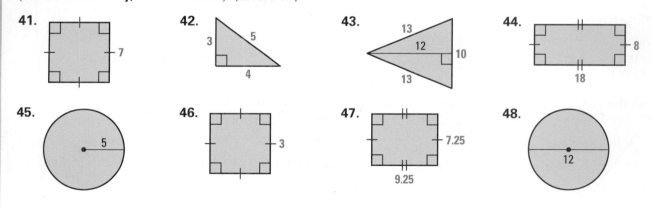

CHAPTER 2

Rewrite the conditional statement in if-then form. (Lesson 2.1)

1. It must be true if you read it in a newspaper.

2. An apple a day keeps the doctor away.

3. The square of an odd number is odd.

Write the inverse, converse, and contrapositive of the conditional statement. (Lesson 2.1)

4. If $x = 12$, then $x^2 = 144$.

5. If you are indoors, then you are not caught in a rainstorm.

6. If four points are collinear, then they are coplanar.

7. If two angles are vertical angles, then they are congruent.

Write the converse of the true statement. Decide whether the converse is _true_ or _false_. If false, provide a counterexample. (Lesson 2.1)

8. If two angles form a linear pair, then they are supplementary.

9. If $2x - 5 = 7$, then $x = 6$.

Rewrite the biconditional statement as a conditional statement and its converse. (Lesson 2.2)

10. Two segments have the same length if and only if they are congruent.

11. Two angles are right angles if and only if they are supplementary.

12. $x = 10$ if and only if $x^2 = 100$.

Determine whether the statement can be combined with its converse to form a true biconditional statement. (Lesson 2.2)

13. If $\angle ABC$ is a right angle, then $\overline{AB} \perp \overline{BC}$.

14. If $\angle 1$ and $\angle 2$ are adjacent, supplementary angles, then $\angle 1$ and $\angle 2$ form a linear pair.

15. If two angles are vertical angles, then they are congruent.

Using _p, q, r,_ and _s_ below, write the symbolic statement in words. (Lesson 2.3)

_p_: We go shopping.
_q_: We need a shopping list.

_r_: We stop at the bank.
_s_: We see our friends.

16. $p \rightarrow q$
17. $\sim r \rightarrow \sim s$
18. $r \rightarrow s$

19. $p \leftrightarrow q$
20. $\sim p \rightarrow \sim s$
21. $p \leftrightarrow r$

Given that the statement is of the form _p_ → _q_, write _p_ and _q_. Then write the inverse and the contrapositive of _p_ → _q_ both symbolically and in words. (Lesson 2.3)

22. If it is hot, May will go to the beach.

23. If the hockey team wins the game tonight, they will play in the championship.

24. If John misses the bus, then he will be late for school.

Use the property to complete the statement. (**Lesson 2.4**)

25. Reflexive property of equality: $AB =$ ___?___ .

26. Symmetric property of equality: If $ED = DF$, then ___?___ .

27. Transitive property of equality: If $AB = AC$ and $AC = DF$, then ___?___ .

28. Division property of equality: If $2x = 3y$, then $\dfrac{2x}{z} =$ ___?___ .

29. Subtraction property of equality: If $x = 6$, then $x - 4 =$ ___?___ .

Copy and complete the proof using the diagram and the given information. (**Lesson 2.5**)

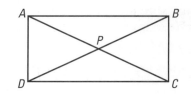

30. GIVEN ▶ $\overline{PD} \cong \overline{PC}$,
      P is the midpoint of $\overline{AC}$ and $\overline{BD}$

PROVE ▶ $\overline{AP} \cong \overline{BP}$

Statements	Reasons
1. P is the midpoint of $\overline{AC}$ and $\overline{BD}$.	**1.** ___?___
2. $AP = PC$	**2.** ___?___
3. $BP = PD$	**3.** ___?___
4. ___?___	**4.** Given
5. $PD = PC$	**5.** ___?___
6. ___?___	**6.** Transitive property of equality
7. $\overline{AP} \cong \overline{BP}$	**7.** Definition of congruent segments

In Exercises 31–32, use the diagram to complete the statement. (**Lesson 2.6**)

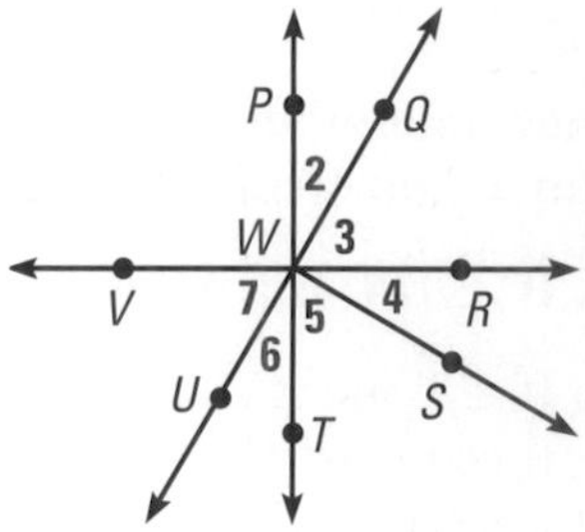

31. $\angle 2$ and ___?___ are vertical angles.

32. $\angle QWR$ is supplementary to ___?___ .

33. In the diagram, suppose that $\angle 3$ and $\angle 4$ are complementary and that $\angle 4$ and $\angle 5$ are complementary. Prove that $\angle 3 \cong \angle 5$. (**Lesson 2.6**)

Solve for each variable. (**Lesson 2.6**)

34.   **35.**   **36.**

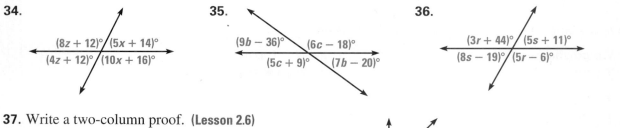

$(8z + 12)°$ $(5x + 14)°$ $(9b - 36)°$ $(6c - 18)°$ $(3r + 44)°$ $(5s + 11)°$
$(4z + 12)°$ $(10x + 16)°$ $(5c + 9)°$ $(7b - 20)°$ $(8s - 19)°$ $(5r - 6)°$

37. Write a two-column proof. (**Lesson 2.6**)

    GIVEN ▶ $\angle 1$ and $\angle 4$ are complementary,
                  $\angle DBE$ is a right angle.

    PROVE ▶ $\angle 2$ and $\angle 3$ are complementary.

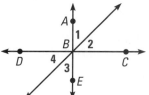

CHAPTER 3

Think of each segment in the diagram as part of a line. Fill in the blank with *parallel*, *skew*, or *perpendicular*. (Lesson 3.1)

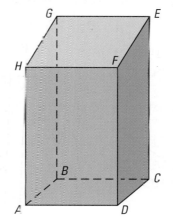

1. $\overleftrightarrow{HA}$ and $\overleftrightarrow{EC}$ are ___?___ .

2. $\overleftrightarrow{FD}$ and $\overleftrightarrow{AD}$ are ___?___ .

3. $\overleftrightarrow{AD}$ and $\overleftrightarrow{GB}$ are ___?___ .

Think of each segment in the diagram as part of a line. There may be more than one right answer. (Lesson 3.1)

4. Name a line parallel to $\overleftrightarrow{AD}$.

5. Name a line perpendicular to $\overleftrightarrow{GB}$.

6. Name a line skew to $\overleftrightarrow{EC}$.

7. Name a plane parallel to GBC.

Complete the statement with *corresponding*, *alternate interior*, *alternate exterior*, or *consecutive interior*. (Lesson 3.1)

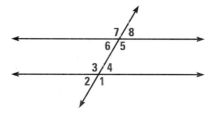

8. $\angle 3$ and $\angle 7$ are ___?___ angles.

9. $\angle 4$ and $\angle 6$ are ___?___ angles.

10. $\angle 8$ and $\angle 2$ are ___?___ angles.

11. $\angle 4$ and $\angle 5$ are ___?___ angles.

12. $\angle 5$ and $\angle 1$ are ___?___ angles.

13. Fill in the blanks to complete the proof. (Lesson 3.2)

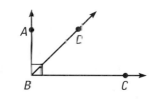

GIVEN ▸ $\overline{AB} \perp \overline{BC}$,
$\overrightarrow{BD}$ bisects $\angle ABC$

PROVE ▸ $m\angle ABD = 45°$

Statements	Reasons
1. $\overline{AB} \perp \overline{BC}$	1. ___?___
2. ___?___	2. Definition of perpendicular lines
3. $m\angle ABC = 90°$	3. ___?___
4. $\overrightarrow{BD}$ bisects $\angle ABC$	4. ___?___
5. $m\angle ABD = m\angle DBC$	5. ___?___
6. $m\angle ABD + m\angle DBC = 90°$	6. ___?___
7. $m\angle ABD + $ ___?___ $= 90°$	7. Substitution property of equality
8. $2(m\angle ABD) = 90°$	8. ___?___
9. $m\angle ABD = 45°$	9. ___?___

Find the values of x and y. Explain your reasoning. (Lesson 3.3)

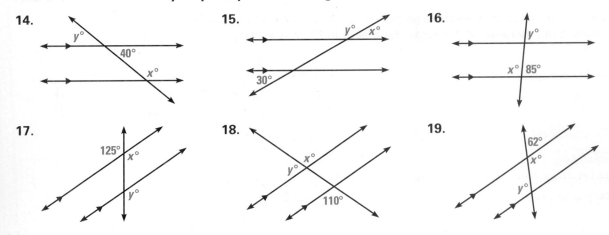

14.

$40°$

$y°$

$x°$

15.

$y°$ $x°$

$30°$

16.

$y°$

$x°$ $85°$

17.

$125°$ $x°$

$y°$

18.

$x°$

$y°$

$110°$

19.

$62°$

$x°$

$y°$

Which lines, if any, are parallel? Explain. (Lesson 3.4)

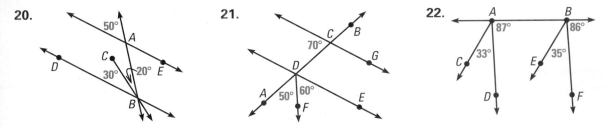

20.

$50°$

A

C

D

$30°$ $20°$ E

B

21.

C B

$70°$

D

G

A $50°$ $60°$

F E

22.

A B

$87°$ $86°$

C $33°$ E $35°$

D F

Explain how you would show that $a \parallel b$. State any theorems or postulates that you would use. (Lesson 3.5)

23.

$60°$

$60°$

24.

$130°$

$50°$

25.

$70°$ $70°$

Find the slopes of $\overleftrightarrow{AB}$, $\overleftrightarrow{CD}$, and $\overleftrightarrow{EF}$. Which lines are parallel, if any?
(Lesson 3.6)

26. $A(3, 7)$, $B(1, 5)$
$C(4, 1)$, $D(9, 6)$
$E(2, 5)$, $F(-8, -5)$

27. $A(-4, 1)$, $B(3, 1)$
$C(-2, -1)$, $D(4, -3)$
$E(-10, 3)$, $F(4, -8)$

28. $A(-3, 2)$, $B(-3, 5)$
$C(7, -1)$, $D(7, 7)$
$E(4, -11)$, $F(4, -6)$

Write an equation of the line that passes through point P and is parallel to the line with the given equation. (Lesson 3.6)

29. $P(-4, -5)$, $y = 6x - 7$

30. $P(2, -3)$, $y = -\frac{1}{2}x + 4$

31. $P(-9, 8)$, $x = -12$

Decide whether lines p_1 and p_2 are perpendicular. (Lesson 3.7)

32. line p_1: $-7y + 3x = 6$
line p_2: $-9y - 21x = 3$

33. line p_1: $3y + 12x = 15$
line p_2: $8y - 2x = 9$

34. line p_1: $16y - 2x = 11$
line p_2: $-12x - 2y = 6$

Line j is perpendicular to the line with the given equation and line j passes through P. Write an equation of line j. (Lesson 3.7)

35. $y = -2x + 1$, $P(4, -1)$

36. $2x + 5y = 20$, $P(4, 10)$

37. $y = \frac{1}{2}x + 6$, $P(-2, -7)$

CHAPTER 4

In Exercises 1–4, the variable expressions represent the angle measures of a triangle. Find the measure of each angle. Then classify the triangle by its angles. (Lesson 4.1)

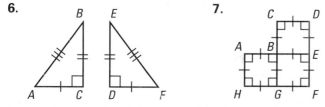

1. $m\angle E = x°$
$m\angle F = 3x°$
$m\angle G = 5x°$

2. $m\angle H = 60°$
$m\angle K = x°$
$m\angle L = x°$

3. $m\angle P = x°$
$m\angle Q = (2x + 10)°$
$m\angle R = (x + 10)°$

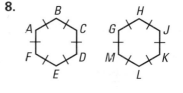

4. $m\angle S = (2x)°$
$m\angle T = (2x - 4)°$
$m\angle U = (2x - 2)°$

5. The measure of an exterior angle of a right triangle is 135°. Find the measures of the interior angles of the triangle. (Lesson 4.1)

Identify any figures that can be proved congruent. For those that can be proved congruent, write a congruence statement. (Lesson 4.2)

6.

7.

8.

9. Use the triangles in Exercise 6 above. Identify all pairs of congruent corresponding angles and corresponding sides. (Lesson 4.2)

Use the given information to find the value of *x*. (Lesson 4.2)

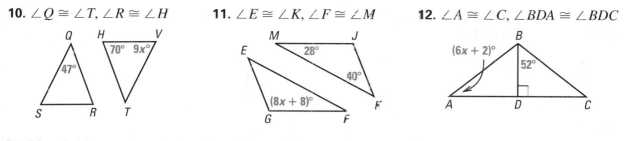

10. $\angle Q \cong \angle T, \angle R \cong \angle H$

11. $\angle E \cong \angle K, \angle F \cong \angle M$

12. $\angle A \cong \angle C, \angle BDA \cong \angle BDC$

Decide whether enough information is given to prove that the triangles are congruent. If there is enough information, state the congruence postulate you would use. (Lesson 4.3)

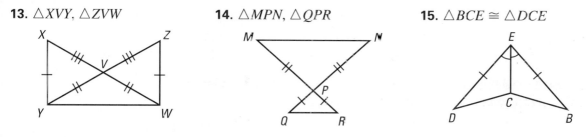

13. $\triangle XVY, \triangle ZVW$

14. $\triangle MPN, \triangle QPR$

15. $\triangle BCE \cong \triangle DCE$

16. Use the diagram in Exercise 13. Prove that $\triangle XYW \cong \triangle ZWY$.

Is it possible to prove that the triangles are congruent? If so, state the congruence postulate or theorem you would use. (Lesson 4.4)

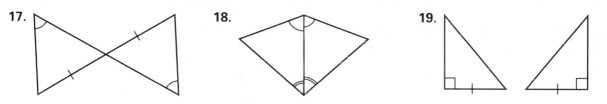

17.

18.

19.

Write a two-column proof or a paragraph proof. (Lesson 4.4)

20. GIVEN ▶ $\overline{AD} \parallel \overline{BC}$,
$\overline{AC}$ bisects $\overline{BD}$

   PROVE ▶ $\triangle AED \cong \triangle CEB$

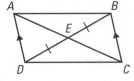

State which postulate or theorem you can use to prove that the triangles are congruent. Then explain how proving that the triangles are congruent proves the given statement. (Lesson 4.5)

21. PROVE ▶ $\overline{AB} \cong \overline{CD}$ **22. PROVE** ▶ $\angle GEF \cong \angle GHJ$ 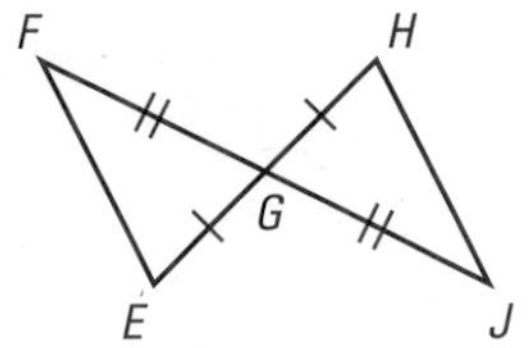   **23. PROVE** ▶ $\angle RQT \cong \angle RST$

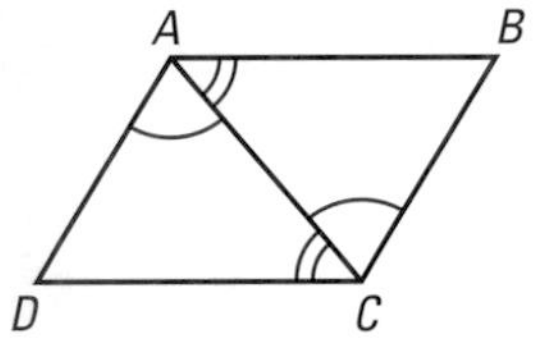

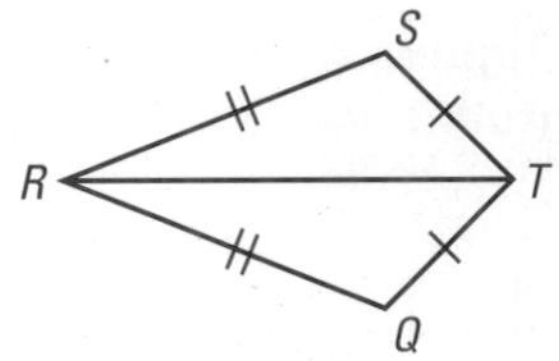

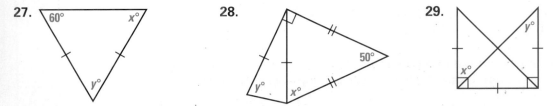

Use the diagram and the information given below. (Lesson 4.5)

   GIVEN ▶ $\triangle CBD \cong \triangle BAF$
   $\triangle BAF \cong \triangle FBD$
   $\triangle FBD \cong \triangle DFE$

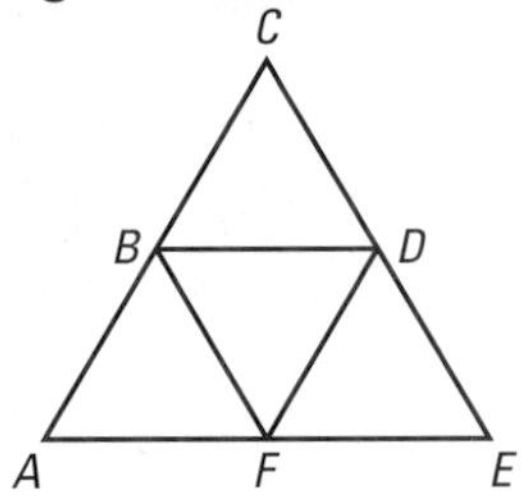

24. PROVE ▶ $\angle AFB \cong \angle BDF$

25. PROVE ▶ $\overline{BC} \cong \overline{AB}$

26. PROVE ▶ $\overline{FD} \cong \overline{DE}$

Find the values of x and y. (Lesson 4.6)

27.   **28.**   **29.**

Place the figure in a coordinate plane. Label the vertices and give the coordinates of each vertex. (Lesson 4.7)

30. A 4 unit by 3 unit rectangle with one vertex at $(-5, 2)$

31. A square with side length 6 and one vertex at $(3, -4)$

In the diagram, $\triangle EFG$ is a right triangle. Its base is 80 units and its height is 60 units. (Lesson 4.7)

32. Give the coordinates of points F and G.

33. Find the length of the hypotenuse of $\triangle EFG$.

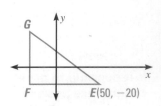

Place the figure in a coordinate plane and find the given information. (Lesson 4.7)

34. A rectangle with length 6 units and width 3 units; find the length of a diagonal of the rectangle.

35. An isosceles right triangle with legs of 7 units; find the length of the hypotenuse.

CHAPTER 5

Use the diagram shown. (Lesson 5.1)

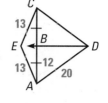

1. In the diagram, $\overrightarrow{DB} \perp \overline{AC}$ and $\overline{BA} \cong \overline{BC}$. Find BC.

2. In the diagram, $\overrightarrow{DB} \perp \overline{AC}$ and $\overline{BA} \cong \overline{BC}$. Find DC.

3. In the diagram, $\overrightarrow{DB}$ is the perpendicular bisector of $\overline{AC}$.
   Because $EA = EC = 13$, what can you conclude about the point E?

Use the diagram shown. (Lesson 5.1)

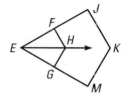

4. In the diagram, $m\angle FEH = m\angle GEH = 30°$, $m\angle HGE = m\angle HFE = 90°$,
   and $HF = 5$. Find HG.

5. In the diagram, $\overrightarrow{EH}$ bisects $\angle JEM$, $m\angle EJK = m\angle EMK = 90°$ and
   $JK = MK = 10$. What can you conclude about point K?

In each case, find the indicated measure. (Lesson 5.2)

6. The perpendicular bisectors of
   $\triangle ABC$ meet at point D. Find AC.

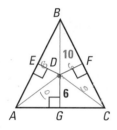

7. The perpendicular bisectors of
   $\triangle EFG$ meet at point H. Find HJ.

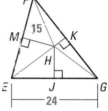

8. The angle bisectors of $\triangle RST$
   meet at point Q. Find WS.

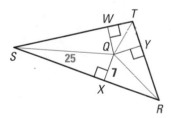

9. The angle bisectors of $\triangle AEC$
   meet at point G. Find GF.

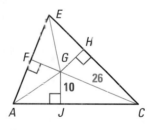

Use the figure below and the given information. (Lesson 5.3)
T is the centroid of $\triangle ABC$, $BT = 14$, $XC = 24$, and $TZ = 8.5$.

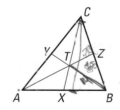

10. Find the length of $\overline{BY}$.

11. Find the length of $\overline{TX}$.

12. Find the length of $\overline{AT}$.

Draw and label a large triangle of the given type and construct altitudes.
Verify Theorem 5.8 by showing that the lines containing the altitudes are
concurrent and label the orthocenter. (Lesson 5.3)

13. an isosceles $\triangle MNP$

14. an equilateral $\triangle DEF$

15. a right isosceles $\triangle STR$

Use △ABC, where X, Y, and Z are midpoints of the sides. (Lesson 5.4)

16. $\overline{CB} \parallel$ __?__ .

17. $\overline{XY} \parallel$ __?__ .

18. If $AB = 8$, then $YZ =$ __?__ .

19. If $AC = 10$, then $XY =$ __?__ .

20. If $XZ = 6$, then $BC =$ __?__ .

21. If $YZ = 4x - 11$ and $AB = 3x + 3$, then $YZ =$ __?__ .

22. If $AZ = 4x - 5$ and $XY = 2x + 1$, then $AC =$ __?__ .

Name the shortest and longest sides of the triangle. (Lesson 5.5)

23. **24.** **25.**

Name the smallest and largest angles of the triangle. (Lesson 5.5)

26. **27.** **28.**

Complete with >, <, or =. (Lesson 5.6)

29. AC __?__ DF

30. QS __?__ TU

31. $m\angle 1$ __?__ $m\angle 2$

32. MN __?__ PR

33. $m\angle 1$ __?__ $m\angle 2$

34. $m\angle 1$ __?__ $m\angle 2$

35. JK __?__ ST

36. XY __?__ WV

37. $m\angle 1$ __?__ $m\angle 2$

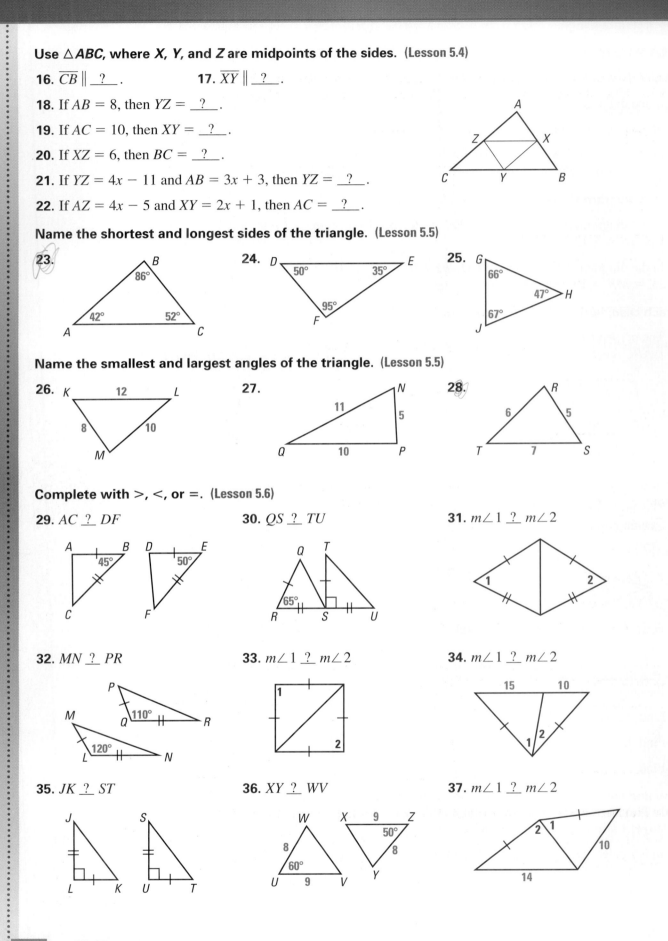

Decide whether the figure is a polygon. If it is, use the number of sides to tell what kind of polygon the shape is. Then state whether the polygon is *convex* or *concave*. (Lesson 6.1)

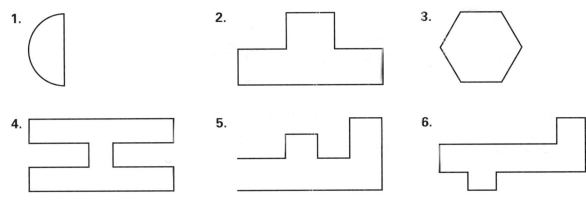

1.

2.

3.

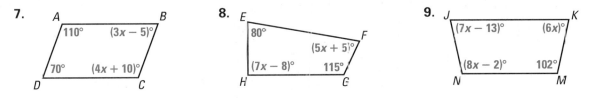

4.

5.

6.

Use the information in the diagram to solve for *x*. (Lesson 6.1)

7.

A ____ *B*
110°   (3x − 5)°
70°   (4x + 10)°
D ____ *C*

8.

E
80°
(5x + 5)°   *F*
(7x − 8)°   115°
H ____ *G*

9.

J ____ *K*
(7x − 13)°   (6x)°
(8x − 2)°   102°
N ____ *M*

Use the diagram of parallelogram *VWXY* at the right. Complete each statement, and give a reason for your answer. (Lesson 6.2)

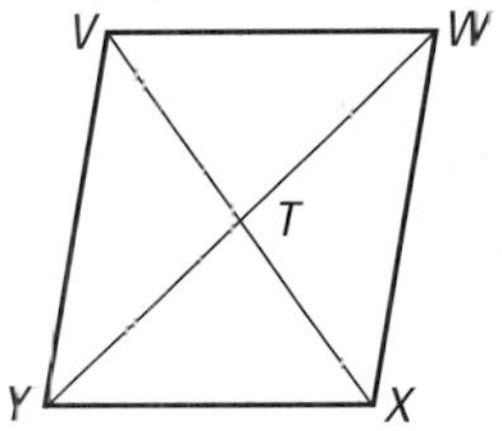

10. $\overline{VW} \cong$ __?__

11. $\angle VWX \cong$ __?__

12. $\overline{XW} \cong$ __?__

13. $\overline{VT} \cong$ __?__

14. $\angle XYW \cong$ __?__

15. $\overline{WX} \parallel$ __?__

16. $\angle VYX$ is supplementary to __?__ and __?__ .

17. Point *T* is the midpoint of __?__ and __?__ .

Are you given enough information to determine whether the quadrilateral is a parallelogram? Explain. (Lesson 6.3)

18.

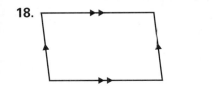

19.

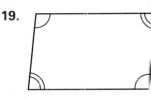

20.

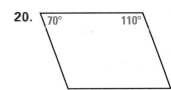

70°   110°

Prove that the points represent the vertices of a parallelogram. (Lesson 6.3)

21. $A(2, 4)$, $B(4, -3)$, $C(9, -6)$, $D(7, 1)$

22. $E(-7, -1)$, $F(-1, -2)$, $G(-4, -9)$, $H(-10, -8)$

23. $R(-5, 5)$, $S(6, 4)$, $T(2, -5)$, $U(-9, -4)$

24. $M(-7, -3)$, $N(6, 10)$, $P(8, 4)$, $Q(-5, -9)$

List each quadrilateral for which the statement is true. (Lesson 6.4)

25. Adjacent angles are supplementary.

26. Adjacent angles are congruent.

27. Adjacent sides are perpendicular.

28. Diagonals are congruent.

29. Adjacent sides are congruent.

30. Opposite sides are parallel.

It is given that *PQRS* is a parallelogram. Graph ▱*PQRS*. Decide whether it is a *rectangle*, a *rhombus*, a *square*, or *none of the above*. Justify your answer using theorems about quadrilaterals. (Lesson 6.4)

31. *P*(6, 7), *Q*(−2, 1), *R*(6, −5), *S*(14, 1)

32. *P*(−6, 5), *Q*(4, 11), *R*(7, 7), *S*(−3, 1)

33. *P*(−2, 7), *Q*(4, 7), *R*(4, 1), *S*(−2, 1)

34. *P*(−7, −2), *Q*(−2, −2), *R*(−2, −7), *S*(−7, −7)

Find the missing angle measures. (Lesson 6.5)

35.
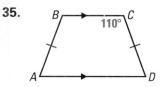

36.
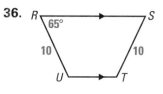

37.
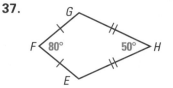

Find the value of *x*. (Lesson 6.5)

38.
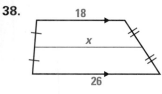

39.
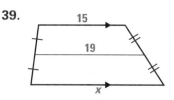

40.
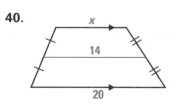

What are the lengths of the sides of the kite? (Lesson 6.5)

41.
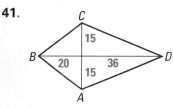

42.
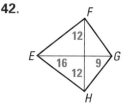

43.
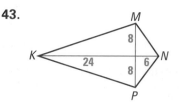

What kind of quadrilateral could *EFGH* be? *EFGH* is not drawn to scale. (Lesson 6.6)

44.
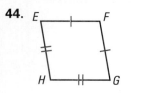

45.
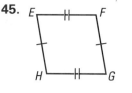

46.
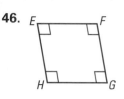

Find the area of the polygon. (Lesson 6.7)

47.
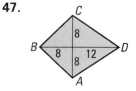

48.
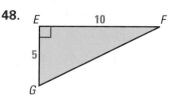

49.
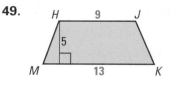

CHAPTER 7

Use the graph of the transformation below. (Lesson 7.1)

1. Name the image of Q.

2. Name and describe the transformation.

3. Name two sides with the same length.

4. Name two angles with the same measure.

5. Name the coordinates of the preimage of point Y.

6. Show two corresponding sides have the same length, using the Distance Formula.

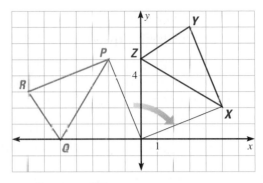

Name and describe the transformation. Then name the coordinates of the vertices of the image. (Lesson 7.1)

7.

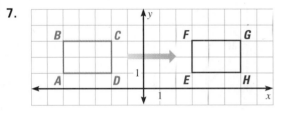

8.

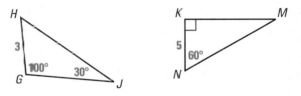

Use the diagrams to complete the statement. (Lesson 7.1)

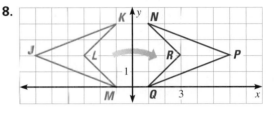

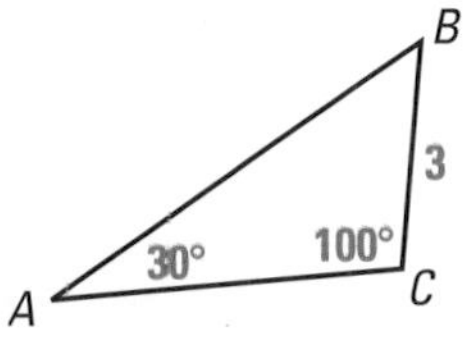

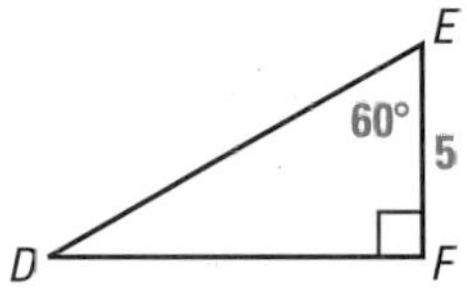

9. $\triangle CBA \rightarrow$ ___?___   **10.** $\triangle DEF \rightarrow$ ___?___   **11.** ___?___ $\rightarrow \triangle KNM$

Use the diagram at the right to name the image of $\triangle ABC$ after the reflection. If the reflection does not appear in the diagram, write *not shown*. (Lesson 7.2)

12. Reflection in the x-axis

13. Reflection in the y-axis

14. Reflection in the line $y = x$

15. Reflection in the x-axis, followed by a reflection in the y-axis

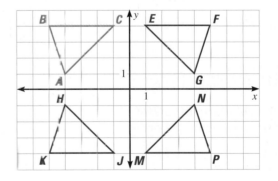

Find the coordinates of the reflection without using a coordinate plane. Then check your answer by plotting the image and preimage on a coordinate plane.
(Lesson 7.2)

16. $M(5, 2)$ reflected in the x-axis

17. $N(-2, 4)$ reflected in the y-axis

18. $P(1, -8)$ reflected in the y-axis

19. $Q(1, 12)$ reflected in the x-axis

Find point *C* on the *x*-axis so *AC* + *BC* is a minimum. (Lesson 7.2)

20. $A(1, 2), B(12, 5)$ **21.** $A(3, 7), B(11, 7)$ **22.** $A(-2, 7), B(-9, 5)$

Name the coordinates of the vertices of the image after a clockwise rotation of the given number of degrees about the origin. (Lesson 7.3)

23. 90° **24.** 270° **25.** 180°

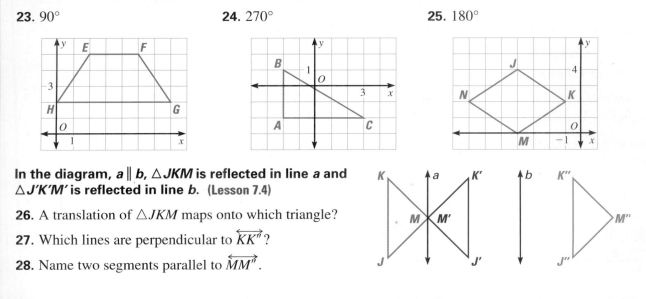

In the diagram, $a \parallel b$, $\triangle JKM$ is reflected in line a and $\triangle J'K'M'$ is reflected in line b. (Lesson 7.4)

26. A translation of $\triangle JKM$ maps onto which triangle?

27. Which lines are perpendicular to $\overleftrightarrow{KK''}$?

28. Name two segments parallel to $\overleftrightarrow{MM''}$.

Copy figure *RSTV* and draw its image after the translation. Then describe the translation using a vector in component form. (Lesson 7.4)

29. $(x, y) \rightarrow (x - 3, y + 5)$

30. $(x, y) \rightarrow (x + 1, y - 4)$

31. $(x, y) \rightarrow (x - 7, y + 7)$

32. $(x, y) \rightarrow (x + 2, y - 6)$

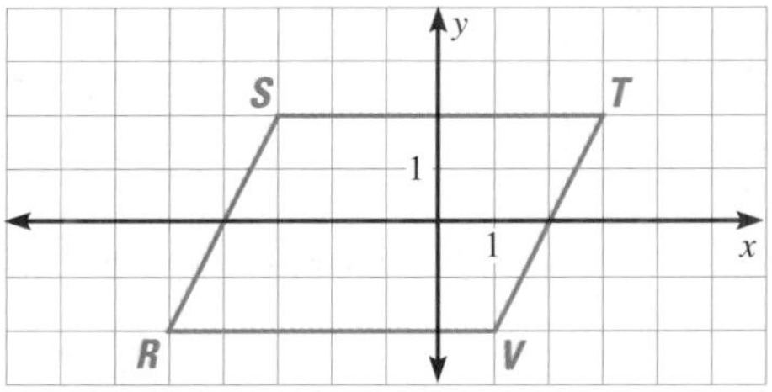

Sketch the image of $A(-6, -2)$ after the described glide reflection. (Lesson 7.5)

33. Translation: $(x, y) \rightarrow (x + 1, y + 3)$
Reflection: in the *x*-axis

34. Translation: $(x, y) \rightarrow (x + 4, y - 3)$
Reflection: in $x = -4$

Sketch the image of $\triangle GHK$ after a composition using the given transformations in the order they appear. (Lesson 7.5)

35. $G(5, 3), H(-2, 6), K(-1, -4)$

Translation: $(x, y) \rightarrow (x - 7, y)$
Reflection: in the *x*-axis

36. $G(2, 1), H(0, -6), K(-5, -4)$

Translation: $(x, y) \rightarrow (x + 8, y)$
Reflection: in the *x*-axis

Describe each frieze pattern according to the following seven categories: T, TR, TG, TV, THG, TRVG, and TRHVG. (Lesson 7.6)

37.

38.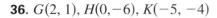

CHAPTER 8

Rewrite the fraction so that the numerator and denominator have the same units. Then simplify. (Lesson 8.1)

1. $\dfrac{5 \text{ m}}{250 \text{ cm}}$

2. $\dfrac{15 \text{ ft}}{4 \text{ yd}}$

3. $\dfrac{15 \text{ in.}}{2 \text{ ft}}$

4. $\dfrac{10 \text{ km}}{900 \text{ m}}$

Use ratios to solve the following problems. (Lesson 8.1)

5. The measures of the angles in a quadrilateral are in the extended ratio of $3:4:5:6$. Find the measures of the angles.

6. The perimeter of isosceles triangle ABC is 35 cm. The extended ratio of $AB:BC:AC$ is $x:3x:3x$. Find the lengths of the three sides.

Solve the proportion. (Lesson 8.1)

7. $\dfrac{a}{21} = \dfrac{1}{3}$

8. $\dfrac{-5}{b} = \dfrac{20}{8}$

9. $\dfrac{-2}{6} = \dfrac{c}{-9}$

10. $\dfrac{7}{d+5} = \dfrac{28}{8}$

11. $\dfrac{2}{-9} = \dfrac{f-3}{9}$

12. $\dfrac{11}{1} = \dfrac{g+6}{g-4}$

Complete the sentence. (Lesson 8.2)

13. If $\dfrac{x}{10} = \dfrac{30}{y}$, then $\dfrac{x}{30} = \dfrac{?}{?}$.

14. If $\dfrac{9}{4} = \dfrac{x}{y}$, then $\dfrac{13}{4} = \dfrac{?}{?}$.

15. If $\dfrac{9}{x} = \dfrac{12}{y}$, then $\dfrac{3}{4} = \dfrac{?}{?}$.

16. If $\dfrac{z}{12} = \dfrac{y}{8}$, then $\dfrac{z+12}{12} = \dfrac{?}{?}$.

Find the geometric mean of the two numbers. (Lesson 8.2)

17. 4 and 9

18. 1 and 4

19. 2.5 and 10

20. 9 and 16

21. 256 and 4

22. 100 and 10,000

Use the diagram and the given information to find the unknown length.
(Lesson 8.2)

23. GIVEN ▶ $\dfrac{PS}{SR} = \dfrac{PT}{TQ}$, find SR.

24. GIVEN ▶ $\dfrac{CE}{EG} = \dfrac{DF}{FH}$, find CE.

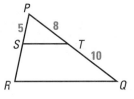

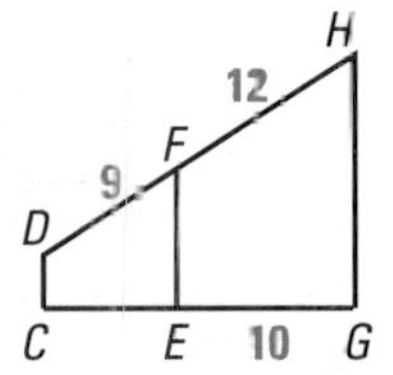

In the diagram, *PQRS* ~ *TVWX*. (Lesson 8.3)

25. Find the scale factor of *PQRS* to *TVWX*.

26. Find the scale factor of *TVWX* to *PQRS*.

27. Find the values of u, y, and z.

28. Find the perimeter of each polygon.

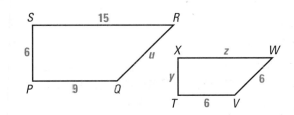

Determine whether the triangles can be proved similar. If they are similar, write a similarity statement. If they are not similar, explain why. (Lesson 8.4)

29.
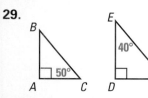

30.
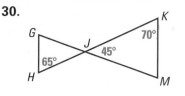

31.
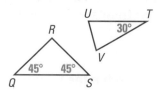

Find coordinates for point Z so that △OWX ~ △OYZ. (Lesson 8.4)

32. $O(0, 0)$, $W(4, 0)$, $X(0, 3)$, $Y(12, 0)$

33. $O(0, 0)$, $W(2, 0)$, $X(0, 5)$, $Y(5, 0)$

34. $O(0, 0)$, $W(-4, 0)$, $X(0, 2)$, $Y(-6, 0)$

35. $O(0, 0)$, $W(-1, 0)$, $X(0, -4)$, $Y(-3, 0)$

Are the triangles similar? If so, state the similarity and the postulate or theorem that justifies your answer. (Lesson 8.5)

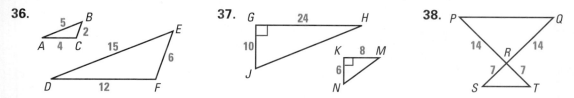

36.   **37.**   **38.**

Determine whether the triangles are similar. If they are, write a similarity statement and solve for the variable. (Lesson 8.5)

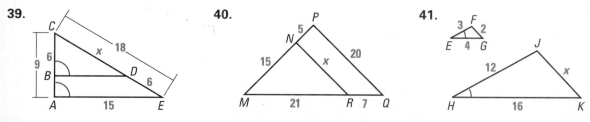

39.   **40.**   **41.**

Determine whether the given information implies that $\overline{QS} \parallel \overline{PT}$. Explain. (Lesson 8.6)

42.
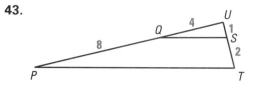

43.
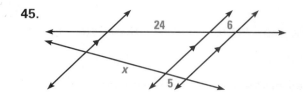

Find the value of the variable. (Lesson 8.6)

44.
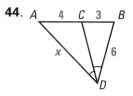

45.
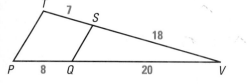

Use the origin as the center of the dilation and the given scale factor to find the coordinates of the vertices of the image of the polygon. (Lesson 8.7)

46. $A(-2, 3)$, $B(-1, 5)$, $C(3, 3)$, $D(2, -4)$, $k = 2$

47. $A(2, 0)$, $B(5, 3)$, $C(4, 5)$, $D(1, 3)$, $k = 5$

48. $A(3, -6)$, $B(6, -6)$, $C(6, 9)$, $D(-3, 9)$, $k = \frac{1}{3}$

49. $A(4, -4)$, $B(6, 4)$, $C(2, 8)$, $D(-8, -4)$, $k = \frac{1}{4}$

CHAPTER 9

Write similarity statements for the three similar triangles in the diagram. Then complete the proportion. (Lesson 9.1)

1. $\dfrac{AD}{AC} = \dfrac{?}{AB}$

2. $\dfrac{?}{EH} = \dfrac{EH}{GH}$

3. $\dfrac{JM}{KJ} = \dfrac{KJ}{?}$

Find the value of the variable. (Lesson 9.1)

4.

5.

6.

Find the unknown side length. Simplify answers that are radicals. Tell whether the side lengths form a Pythagorean triple. (Lesson 9.2)

7.

8.

9.

The variables _r_ and _s_ represent the lengths of the legs of a right triangle, and _t_ represents the length of the hypotenuse. The values of _r_, _s_, and _t_ form a Pythagorean Triple. Find the unknown value. (Lesson 9.2)

10. $r = 7, t = 25$

11. $r = 5, s = 12$

12. $s = 25, t = 65$

13. $r = 49, s = 168$

14. $s = 198, t = 202$

15. $r = 21, t = 35$

Find the area of the figure. Round decimal answers to the nearest tenth. (Lesson 9.2)

16.

17.

18.

Tell whether the triangle is a right triangle. (Lesson 9.3)

19.

20.

21.

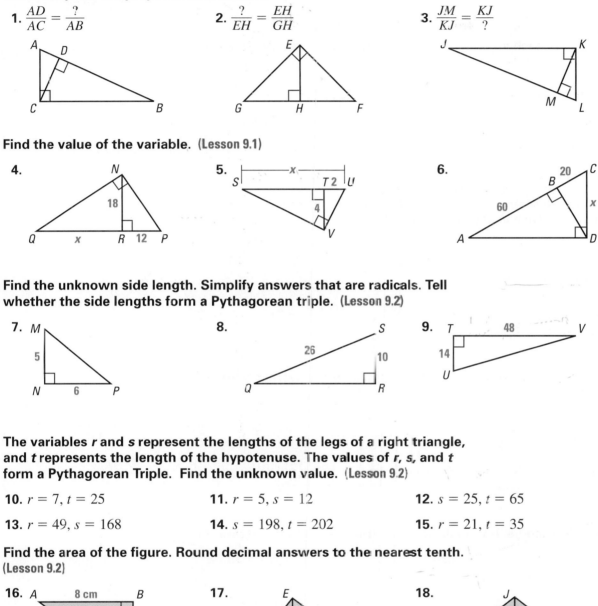

Decide whether the numbers can represent the side lengths of a triangle. If they can, classify the triangle as *right*, *acute*, or *obtuse*. (Lesson 9.3)

22. 17, 18, 19

23. 15, 36, 39

24. 3, 5, 8

25. 7, 9, 12

26. 100, 300, 500

27. $\sqrt{91}$, 12, 20

Find the value of each variable. Write answers in simplest radical form. (Lesson 9.4)

28.

29.

30.

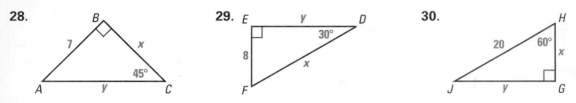

Find the sine, the cosine, and the tangent of the acute angles of the triangle. Express each value as a decimal rounded to four places. (Lesson 9.5)

31.

32.

33.

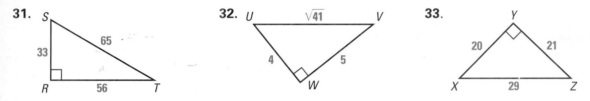

Find the value of each variable. Round decimals to the nearest tenth. (Lesson 9.5)

34.

35.

36.

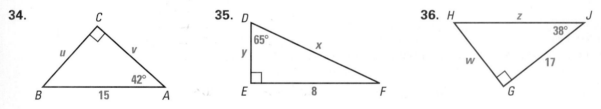

Solve the right triangle. Round decimals to the nearest tenth. (Lesson 9.6)

37.

38.

39.

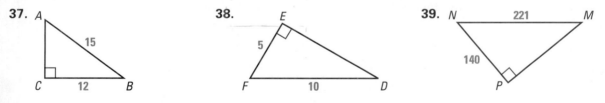

Draw vector $\overrightarrow{PQ}$ in a coordinate plane. Write the component form of the vector and find its magnitude. Round your answer to the nearest tenth. (Lesson 9.7)

40. $P(2, 3)$, $Q(5, 7)$

41. $P(-1, -5)$, $Q(3, 6)$

42. $P(-4, 3)$, $Q(2, -8)$

Let $\vec{a} = \langle 3, 5 \rangle$, $\vec{b} = \langle -7, 2 \rangle$, $\vec{c} = \langle 1, -6 \rangle$, and $\vec{d} = \langle 2, 9 \rangle$. Find the given sum. (Lesson 9.7)

43. $\vec{a} + \vec{b}$

44. $\vec{a} + \vec{c}$

45. $\vec{c} + \vec{d}$

46. $\vec{b} + \vec{c}$

CHAPTER 10

Match the notation with the term that best describes it. (Lesson 10.1)

1. $\overline{EF}$ **A.** Secant
2. G **B.** Chord
3. $\overleftrightarrow{HJ}$ **C.** Radius
4. $\overline{BF}$ **D.** Diameter
5. A **E.** Point of tangency
6. $\overleftrightarrow{KF}$ **F.** Common external tangent
7. $\overleftrightarrow{CD}$ **G.** Common internal tangent
8. $\overline{GK}$ **H.** Center

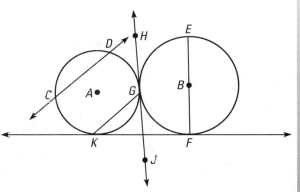

Tell whether the common tangent(s) are *internal* or *external*. (Lesson 10.1)

9.   10.   11.

Use the diagram at the right. (Lesson 10.1)

12. What are the center and radius of $\odot C$?

13. What are the center and radius of $\odot D$?

14. Describe the intersection of the two circles.

15. Describe all the common tangents of the two circles.

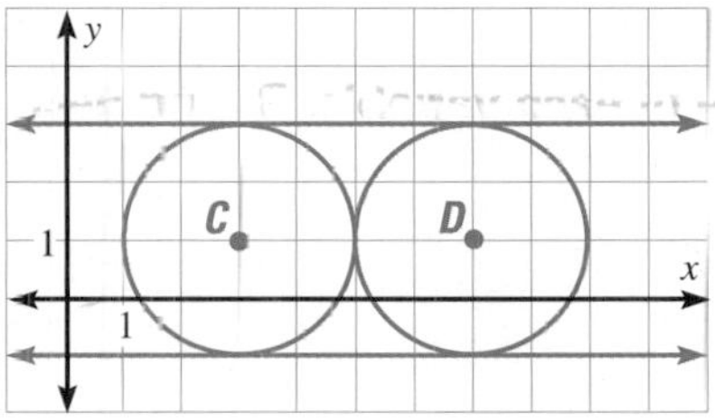

$\overline{AD}$ **and** $\overline{BE}$ **are diameters. Copy the diagram. Find the indicated measure.**
(Lesson 10.2)

16. $m\widehat{AB}$ 17. $m\widehat{DC}$
18. $m\widehat{AC}$ 19. $m\widehat{ED}$
20. $m\angle CQE$ 21. $m\angle AQE$
22. $m\widehat{BC}$ 23. $m\widehat{BDC}$

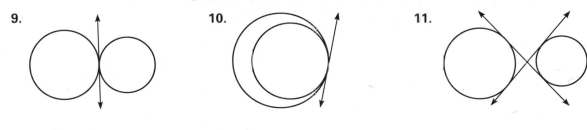

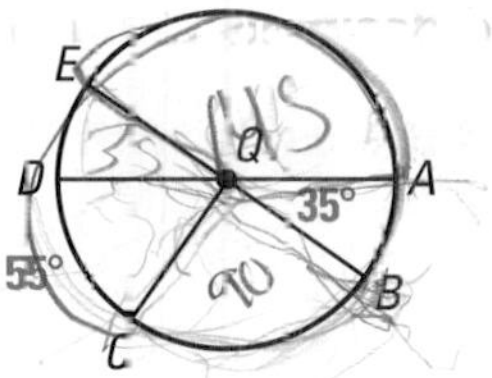

Find the value of each variable. (Lesson 10.3)

24.   25.   26.

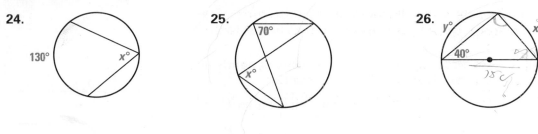

Find the value of x. (Lesson 10.4)

27.
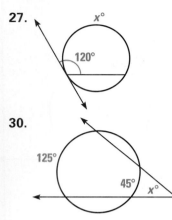
$x°$
$120°$

28.
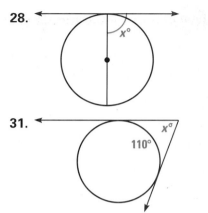
$x°$

29.
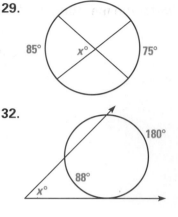
$85°$ $x°$ $75°$

30.
$125°$
$45°$
$x°$

31.
$110°$
$x°$

32.
$180°$
$88°$
$x°$

Find the value of x. (Lesson 10.5)

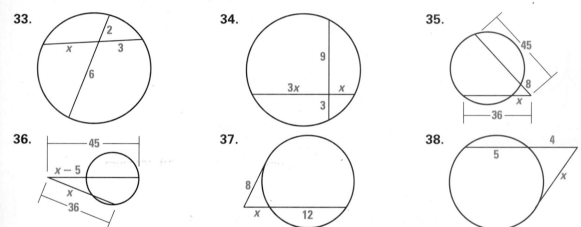

33.
2
x 3
6

34.
9
$3x$ x
3

35.
45
8
x
36

36.
45
$x - 5$
x
36

37.
8
x 12

38.
4
5
x

Give the center and radius of the circle. (Lesson 10.6)

39. $(x - 12)^2 + (y + 3)^2 = 49$ **40.** $(x + 15)^2 + y^2 = 20$

41. $(x + 3.8)^2 + (y - 4.9)^2 = 0.81$ **42.** $(x - 1)^2 + (y + 7)^2 = 1$

Write the standard equation of the circle with the given center and radius. (Lesson 10.6)

43. center $(5, 8)$, radius 6   **44.** center $(-2, 7)$, radius 10

Use the given information to write the standard equation of the circle. (Lesson 10.6)

45. The center is $(2, 2)$; a point on the circle is $(2, 0)$.

46. The center is $(0, 1)$; a point on the circle is $(-3, 1)$.

Use the graph at the right to write equation(s) for the locus of points in the coordinate plane that satisfy the given condition. (Lesson 10.7)

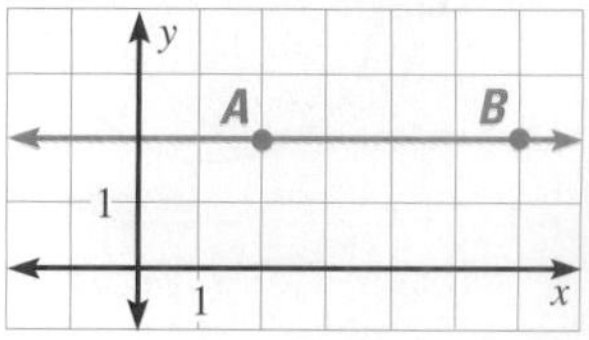

47. equidistant from A and B **48.** 5 units from A

49. 4 units from $\overleftrightarrow{AB}$ **50.** 6 units from B

CHAPTER 11

Find the sum of the measures of the interior angles of the convex polygon.
(Lesson 11.1)

1. 36-gon   **2.** 45-gon   **3.** 60-gon   **4.** 90-gon

Find the value of x. (Lesson 11.1)

5.

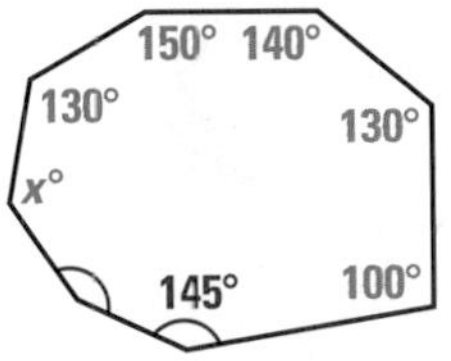

6.

7.

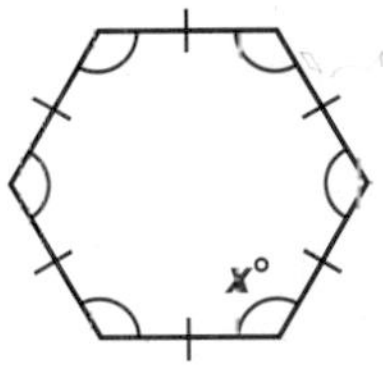

You are given the number of sides of a regular polygon. Find the measure of each exterior angle. (Lesson 11.1)

8. 180   **9.** 24   **10.** 48   **11.** 36

You are given the measure of each exterior angle of a regular n-gon. Find the value of n. (Lesson 11.1)

12. $40°$ **13.** $18°$ **14.** $45°$ **15.** $90°$

Find the measure of a central angle of a regular polygon with the given number of sides. (Lesson 11.2)

16. 10 sides   **17.** 18 sides   **18.** 25 sides   **19.** 90 sides

Find the perimeter and area of the regular polygon. (Lesson 11.2)

20.

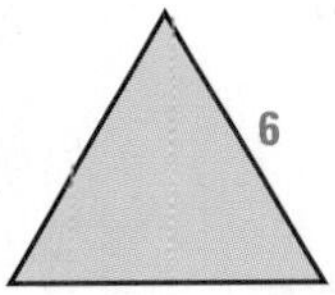

21.

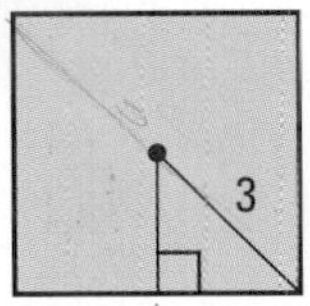

22.

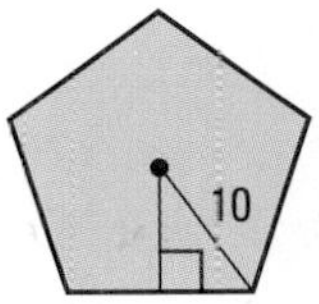

23.

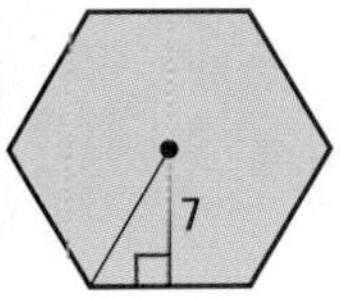

24.

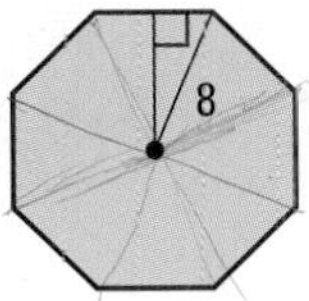

25.

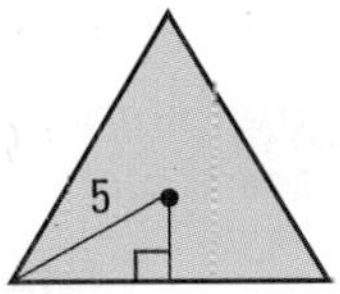

In Exercises 26–28, the polygons are similar. Find the ratio (red to blue) of their perimeters and of their areas. (Lesson 11.3)

26.

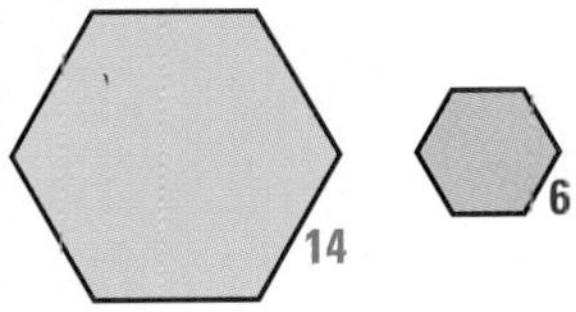

27.

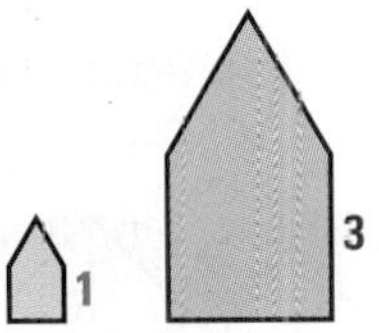

28.

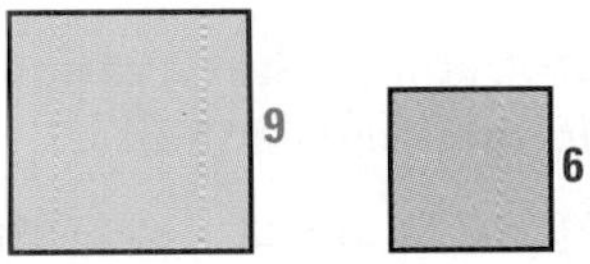

29. The ratio of the perimeters of two similar hexagons is $5:8$. The area of the larger hexagon is 320 square inches. What is the area of the smaller hexagon? **(Lesson 11.3)**

Find the indicated measure. (Lesson 11.4)

30. Circumference

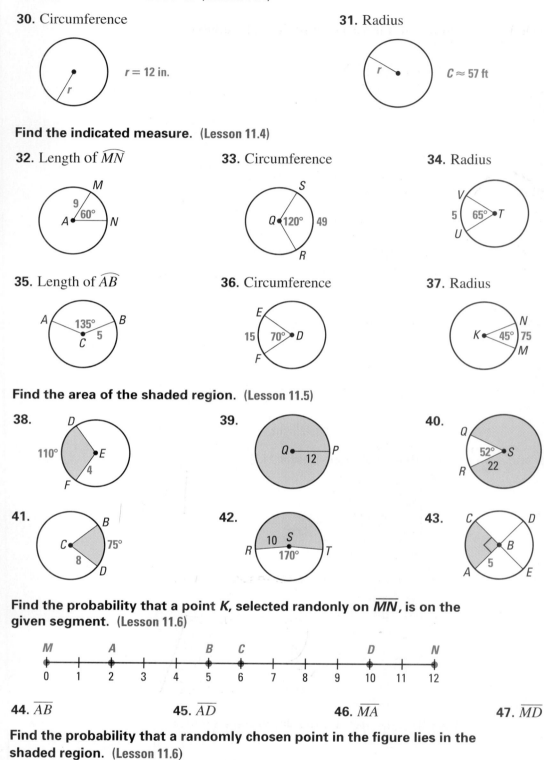

$r = 12$ in.

31. Radius

$C \approx 57$ ft

Find the indicated measure. (Lesson 11.4)

32. Length of $\widehat{MN}$

33. Circumference

34. Radius

35. Length of $\widehat{AB}$

36. Circumference

37. Radius

Find the area of the shaded region. (Lesson 11.5)

38.

39.

40.

41.

42.

43.

Find the probability that a point K**, selected randonly on** $\overline{MN}$**, is on the given segment.** (Lesson 11.6)

44. $\overline{AB}$

45. $\overline{AD}$

46. $\overline{MA}$

47. $\overline{MD}$

Find the probability that a randomly chosen point in the figure lies in the shaded region. (Lesson 11.6)

48.

49.

CHAPTER 12

Tell whether the solid is a polyhedron. If it is, decide whether it is regular and/or convex. Explain. (Lesson 12.1)

1.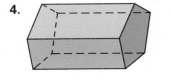

2.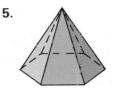

3.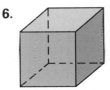

Count the number of faces, vertices, and edges of the polyhedron. Verify your results using Euler's Theorem. (Lesson 12.1)

4. **5.** **6.**

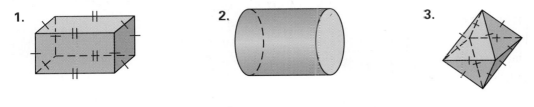

Describe the cross section. (Lesson 12.1)

7. **8.**

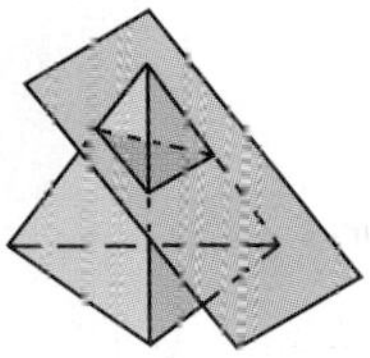

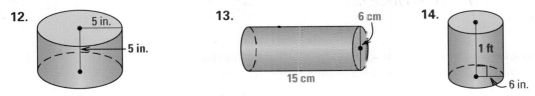

Find the surface area of the right prism. (Lesson 12.2)

9. **10.** 8 cm **11.**

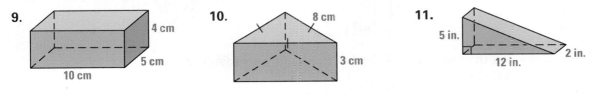

4 cm
5 cm
10 cm

3 cm

5 in.
12 in.
2 in.

Find the surface area of the right cylinder. Round the result to two decimal places. (Lesson 12.2)

12. 5 in. **13.** 6 cm **14.**

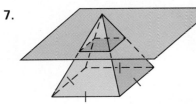

5 in.

15 cm

1 ft
6 in.

Find the surface area of the solid. The pyramids are regular and the cone is right. (Lesson 12.3)

15. 6 in. **16.** Area = 93.5 cm² **17.**

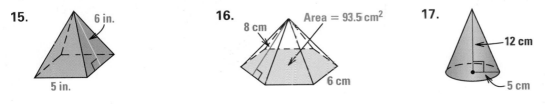

5 in.

8 cm
6 cm

12 cm
5 cm

Find the volume of the solid. (Lesson 12.4)

18. Right rectangular prism

19. Right cylinder

20. Oblique square prism

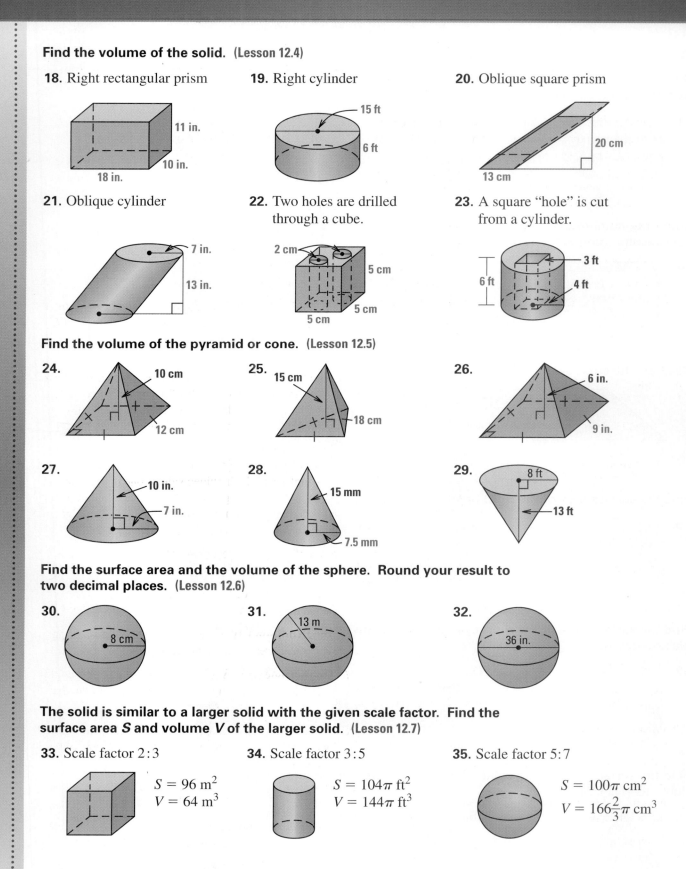

21. Oblique cylinder

22. Two holes are drilled through a cube.

23. A square "hole" is cut from a cylinder.

Find the volume of the pyramid or cone. (Lesson 12.5)

24.

25.

26.

27.

28.

29.

Find the surface area and the volume of the sphere. Round your result to two decimal places. (Lesson 12.6)

30.

31.

32.

The solid is similar to a larger solid with the given scale factor. Find the surface area S and volume V of the larger solid. (Lesson 12.7)

33. Scale factor $2:3$

$S = 96 \text{ m}^2$
$V = 64 \text{ m}^3$

34. Scale factor $3:5$

$S = 104\pi \text{ ft}^2$
$V = 144\pi \text{ ft}^3$

35. Scale factor $5:7$

$S = 100\pi \text{ cm}^2$
$V = 166\frac{2}{3}\pi \text{ cm}^3$

Postulates

1 **Ruler Postulate** The points on a line can be matched one to one with the real numbers. The real number that corresponds to a point is the coordinate of the point. The distance between points A and B, written as AB, is the absolute value of the difference between the coordinates of A and B. **(p. 17)**

2 **Segment Addition Postulate** If B is between A and C, then $AB + BC = AC$. If $AB + BC = AC$, then B is between A and C. **(p. 18)**

3 **Protractor Postulate** Consider a point A on one side of $\overleftrightarrow{OB}$. The rays of the form $\overrightarrow{OA}$ can be matched one to one with the real numbers from 0 to 180. The measure of $\angle AOB$ is equal to the absolute value of the difference between the real numbers for $\overrightarrow{OA}$ and $\overrightarrow{OB}$. **(p. 27)**

4 **Angle Addition Postulate** If P is in the interior of $\angle RST$, then $m\angle RSP + m\angle PST = m\angle RST$. **(p. 27)**

5 Through any two points there exists exactly one line. **(p. 73)**

6 A line contains at least two points. **(p. 73)**

7 If two lines intersect, then their intersection is exactly one point. **(p. 73)**

8 Through any three noncollinear points there exists exactly one plane. **(p. 73)**

9 A plane contains at least three noncollinear points. **(p. 73)**

10 If two points lie in a plane, then the line containing them lies in the plane. **(p. 73)**

11 If two planes intersect, then their intersection is a line. **(p. 73)**

12 **Linear Pair Postulate** If two angles form a linear pair, then they are supplementary. **(p. 111)**

13 **Parallel Postulate** If there is a line and a point not on the line, then there is exactly one line through the point parallel to the given line. **(p. 130)**

14 **Perpendicular Postulate** If there is a line and a point not on the line, then there is exactly one line through the point perpendicular to the given line. **(p. 130)**

15 **Corresponding Angles Postulate** If two parallel lines are cut by a transversal, then the pairs of corresponding angles are congruent. **(p. 143)**

16 **Corresponding Angles Converse** If two lines are cut by a transversal so that corresponding angles are congruent, then the lines are parallel. **(p. 150)**

17 **Slopes of Parallel Lines** In a coordinate plane, two nonvertical lines are parallel if and only if they have the same slope. Any two vertical lines are parallel. **(p. 166)**

18 **Slopes of Perpendicular Lines** In a coordinate plane, two nonvertical lines are perpendicular if and only if the product of their slopes is -1. Vertical and horizontal lines are perpendicular. **(p. 172)**

19 **Side-Side-Side (SSS) Congruence Postulate** If three sides of one triangle are congruent to three sides of a second triangle, then the two triangles are congruent. **(p. 212)**

20 **Side-Angle-Side (SAS) Congruence Postulate** If two sides and the included angle of one triangle are congruent to two sides and the included angle of a second triangle, then the two triangles are congruent. **(p. 213)**

21 **Angle-Side-Angle (ASA) Congruence Postulate** If two angles and the included side of one triangle are congruent to two angles and the included side of a second triangle, then the two triangles are congruent. **(p. 220)**

22 **Area of a Square Postulate** The area of a square is the square of the length of its side, or $A = s^2$. **(p. 372)**

23 **Area Congruence Postulate** If two polygons are congruent, then they have the same area. **(p. 372)**

24 **Area Addition Postulate** The area of a region is the sum of the areas of its nonoverlapping parts. **(p. 372)**

25 **Angle-Angle (AA) Similarity Postulate** If two angles of one triangle are congruent to two angles of another triangle, then the two triangles are similar. **(p. 481)**

26 **Arc Addition Postulate** The measure of an arc formed by two adjacent arcs is the sum of the measures of the two arcs. **(p. 604)**

27 **Volume of a Cube** The volume of a cube is the cube of the length of its side, or $V = s^3$. **(p. 743)**

28 **Volume Congruence Postulate** If two polyhedra are congruent, then they have the same volume. **(p. 743)**

29 **Volume Addition Postulate** The volume of a solid is the sum of the volumes of all its nonoverlapping parts. **(p. 743)**

Theorems

2.1 Properties of Segment Congruence Segment congruence is reflexive, symmetric, and transitive.

Reflexive: For any segment AB, $\overline{AB} \cong \overline{AB}$.

Symmetric: If $\overline{AB} \cong \overline{CD}$, then $\overline{CD} \cong \overline{AB}$.

Transitive: If $\overline{AB} \cong \overline{CD}$ and $\overline{CD} \cong \overline{EF}$, then $\overline{AB} \cong \overline{EF}$. **(p. 102)**

2.2 Properties of Angle Congruence Angle congruence is reflexive, symmetric, and transitive.

Reflexive: For any angle A, $\angle A \cong \angle A$.

Symmetric: If $\angle A \cong \angle B$, then $\angle B \cong \angle A$.

Transitive: If $\angle A \cong \angle B$ and $\angle B \cong \angle C$, then $\angle A \cong \angle C$. **(p. 109)**

2.3 Right Angle Congruence Theorem All right angles are congruent. **(p. 110)**

2.4 Congruent Supplements Theorem If two angles are supplementary to the same angle (or to congruent angles) then they are congruent. **(p. 111)**

2.5 Congruent Complements Theorem If two angles are complementary to the same angle (or to congruent angles) then the two angles are congruent. **(p. 111)**

2.6 Vertical Angles Theorem Vertical angles are congruent. **(p. 112)**

3.1 If two lines intersect to form a linear pair of congruent angles, then the lines are perpendicular. **(p. 137)**

3.2 If two sides of two adjacent acute angles are perpendicular, then the angles are complementary. **(p. 137)**

3.3 If two lines are perpendicular, then they intersect to form four right angles. **(p. 137)**

3.4 Alternate Interior Angles If two parallel lines are cut by a transversal, then the pairs of alternate interior angles are congruent. **(p. 143)**

3.5 Consecutive Interior Angles If two parallel lines are cut by a transversal, then the pairs of consecutive interior angles are supplementary. **(p. 143)**

3.6 Alternate Exterior Angles If two parallel lines are cut by a transversal, then the pairs of alternate exterior angles are congruent. **(p. 143)**

3.7 Perpendicular Transversal If a transversal is perpendicular to one of two parallel lines, then it is perpendicular to the other. **(p. 143)**

3.8 Alternate Interior Angles Converse If two lines are cut by a transversal so that alternate interior angles are congruent, then the lines are parallel. **(p. 150)**

3.9 Consecutive Interior Angles Converse If two lines are cut by a transversal so that consecutive interior angles are supplementary, then the lines are parallel. **(p. 150)**

3.10 Alternate Exterior Angles Converse If two lines are cut by a transversal so that alternate exterior angles are congruent, then the lines are parallel. **(p. 150)**

3.11 If two lines are parallel to the same line, then they are parallel to each other. **(p. 157)**

3.12 In a plane, if two lines are perpendicular to the same line, then they are parallel to each other. **(p. 157)**

4.1 Triangle Sum Theorem The sum of the measures of the interior angles of a triangle is 180°. **(p. 196)**

Corollary The acute angles of a right triangle are complementary. **(p. 197)**

4.2 Exterior Angle Theorem The measure of an exterior angle of a triangle is equal to the sum of the measures of the two nonadjacent interior angles. **(p. 197)**

4.3 Third Angles Theorem If two angles of one triangle are congruent to two angles of another triangle, then the third angles are also congruent. **(p. 203)**

4.4 Reflexive Property of Congruent Triangles Every triangle is congruent to itself.

Symmetric Property of Congruent Triangles If $\triangle ABC \cong \triangle DEF$, then $\triangle DEF \cong \triangle ABC$.

Transitive Property of Congruent Triangles If $\triangle ABC \cong \triangle DEF$ and $\triangle DEF \cong \triangle JKL$, then $\triangle ABC \cong \triangle JKL$. **(p. 205)**

4.5 Angle-Angle-Side (AAS) Congruence Theorem If two angles and a nonincluded side of one triangle are congruent to two angles and the corresponding nonincluded side of a second triangle, then the two triangles are congruent. **(p. 220)**

4.6 Base Angles Theorem If two sides of a triangle are congruent, then the angles opposite them are congruent. (**p. 236**)

Corollary If a triangle is equilateral, then it is equiangular. (**p. 237**)

4.7 Converse of the Base Angles Theorem If two angles of a triangle are congruent, then the sides opposite them are congruent. (**p. 236**)

Corollary If a triangle is equiangular, then it is equilateral. (**p. 237**)

4.8 Hypotenuse-Leg (HL) Congruence Theorem If the hypotenuse and a leg of a right triangle are congruent to the hypotenuse and a leg of a second right triangle, then the two triangles are congruent. (**p. 238**)

5.1 Perpendicular Bisector Theorem If a point is on a perpendicular bisector of a segment, then it is equidistant from the endpoints of the segment. (**p. 265**)

5.2 Converse of the Perpendicular Bisector Theorem If a point is equidistant from the endpoints of a segment, then it is on the perpendicular bisector of the segment. (**p. 265**)

5.3 Angle Bisector Theorem If a point is on the bisector of an angle, then it is equidistant from the two sides of the angle. (**p. 266**)

5.4 Converse of the Angle Bisector Theorem If a point is in the interior of an angle and is equidistant from the sides of the angle, then it lies on the bisector of the angle. (**p. 266**)

5.5 Concurrency of Perpendicular Bisectors of a Triangle The perpendicular bisectors of a triangle intersect at a point that is equidistant from the vertices of the triangle. (**p. 273**)

5.6 Concurrency of Angle Bisectors of a Triangle The angle bisectors of a triangle intersect at a point that is equidistant from the sides of the triangle. (**p. 274**)

5.7 Concurrency of Medians of a Triangle The medians of a triangle intersect at a point that is two thirds of the distance from each vertex to the midpoint of the opposite side. (**p. 279**)

5.8 Concurrency of Altitudes of a Triangle The lines containing the altitudes of a triangle are concurrent. (**p. 281**)

5.9 Midsegment Theorem The segment connecting the midpoints of two sides of a triangle is parallel to the third side and is half as long. (**p. 288**)

5.10 If one side of a triangle is longer than another side, then the angle opposite the longer side is larger than the angle opposite the shorter side. (**p. 295**)

5.11 If one angle of a triangle is larger than another angle, then the side opposite the larger angle is longer than the side opposite the smaller angle. (**p. 295**)

5.12 Exterior Angle Inequality The measure of an exterior angle of a triangle is greater than the measure of either of the two nonadjacent interior angles. (**p. 296**)

5.13 Triangle Inequality The sum of the lengths of any two sides of a triangle is greater than the length of the third side. (**p. 297**)

5.14 Hinge Theorem If two sides of one triangle are congruent to two sides of another triangle, and the included angle of the first is larger than the included angle of the second, then the third side of the first is longer than the third side of the second. (**p. 303**)

5.15 Converse of the Hinge Theorem If two sides of one triangle are congruent to two sides of another triangle, and the third side of the first is longer than the third side of the second, then the included angle of the first is larger than the included angle of the second. (**p. 303**)

6.1 Interior Angles of a Quadrilateral The sum of the measures of the interior angles of a quadrilateral is 360°. (**p. 324**)

6.2 If a quadrilateral is a parallelogram, then its opposite sides are congruent. (**p. 330**)

6.3 If a quadrilateral is a parallelogram, then its opposite angles are congruent. (**p. 330**)

6.4 If a quadrilateral is a parallelogram, then its consecutive angles are supplementary. (**p. 330**)

6.5 If a quadrilateral is a parallelogram, then its diagonals bisect each other. (**p. 330**)

6.6 If both pairs of opposite sides of a quadrilateral are congruent, then the quadrilateral is a parallelogram. (**p. 338**)

6.7 If both pairs of opposite angles of a quadrilateral are congruent, then the quadrilateral is a parallelogram. (**p. 338**)

6.8 If an angle of a quadrilateral is supplementary to both of its consecutive angles, then the quadrilateral is a parallelogram. (**p. 338**)

6.9 If the diagonals of a quadrilateral bisect each other, then the quadrilateral is a parallelogram. (**p. 338**)

6.10 If one pair of opposite sides of a quadrilateral are congruent and parallel, then the quadrilateral is a parallelogram. **(p. 340)**

    Rhombus Corollary A quadrilateral is a rhombus if and only if it has four congruent sides. **(p. 348)**

    Rectangle Corollary A quadrilateral is a rectangle if and only if it has four right angles. **(p. 348)**

    Square Corollary A quadrilateral is a square if and only if it is a rhombus and a rectangle. **(p. 348)**

6.11 A parallelogram is a rhombus if and only if its diagonals are perpendicular. **(p. 349)**

6.12 A parallelogram is a rhombus if and only if each diagonal bisects a pair of opposite angles. **(p. 349)**

6.13 A parallelogram is a rectangle if and only if its diagonals are congruent. **(p. 349)**

6.14 If a trapezoid is isosceles, then each pair of base angles is congruent. **(p. 356)**

6.15 If a trapezoid has a pair of congruent base angles, then it is an isosceles trapezoid. **(p. 356)**

6.16 A trapezoid is isosceles if and only if its diagonals are congruent. **(p. 356)**

6.17 **Midsegment Theorem for Trapezoids** The midsegment of a trapezoid is parallel to each base and its length is one half the sum of the lengths of the bases. **(p. 357)**

6.18 If a quadrilateral is a kite, then its diagonals are perpendicular. **(p. 358)**

6.19 If a quadrilateral is a kite, then exactly one pair of opposite angles are congruent. **(p. 358)**

6.20 **Area of a Rectangle** The area of a rectangle is the product of its base and height. $A = bh$ **(p. 372)**

6.21 **Area of a Parallelogram** The area of a parallelogram is the product of a base and its corresponding height. $A = bh$ **(p. 372)**

6.22 **Area of a Triangle** The area of a triangle is one half the product of a base and its corresponding height.
$A = \frac{1}{2}bh$ **(p. 372)**

6.23 **Area of a Trapezoid** The area of a trapezoid is one half the product of the height and the sum of the bases.
$A = \frac{1}{2}h(b_1 + b_2)$ **(p. 374)**

6.24 **Area of a Kite** The area of a kite is one half the product of the lengths of its diagonals. $A = \frac{1}{2}d_1d_2$ **(p. 374)**

6.25 **Area of a Rhombus** The area of a rhombus is equal to one half the product of the lengths of the diagonals. $A = \frac{1}{2}d_1d_2$ **(p. 374)**

7.1 **Reflection Theorem** A reflection is an isometry. **(p. 404)**

7.2 **Rotation Theorem** A rotation is an isometry. **(p. 412)**

7.3 If lines k and m intersect at point P, then a reflection in k followed by a reflection in m is a rotation about point P. The angle of rotation is $2x°$, where $x°$ is the measure of the acute or right angle formed by k and m. **(p. 414)**

7.4 **Translation Theorem** A translation is an isometry. **(p. 421)**

7.5 If lines k and m are parallel, then a reflection in line k followed by a reflection in line m is a translation. If P'' is the image of P, then the following is true: (1) $\overleftrightarrow{PP''}$ is perpendicular to k and m. (2) $PP'' = 2d$, where d is the distance between k and m. **(p. 421)**

7.6 **Composition Theorem** The composition of two (or more) isometries is an isometry. **(p. 431)**

8.1 If two polygons are similar, then the ratio of their perimeters is equal to the ratios of their corresponding side lengths. **(p. 475)**

8.2 **Side-Side-Side (SSS) Similarity Theorem** If the lengths of the corresponding sides of two triangles are proportional, then the triangles are similar. **(p. 488)**

8.3 **Side-Angle-Side (SAS) Similarity Theorem** If an angle of one triangle is congruent to an angle of a second triangle and the lengths of the sides including these angles are proportional, then the triangles are similar. **(p. 488)**

8.4 **Triangle Proportionality Theorem** If a line parallel to one side of a triangle intersects the other two sides, then it divides the two sides proportionally. **(p. 498)**

8.5 **Converse of the Triangle Proportionality Theorem** If a line divides two sides of a triangle proportionally, then it is parallel to the third side. **(p. 498)**

8.6 If three parallel lines intersect two transversals, then they divide the transversals proportionally. **(p. 499)**

8.7 If a ray bisects an angle of a triangle, then it divides the opposite side into segments whose lengths are proportional to the lengths of the other two sides. **(p. 499)**

9.1 If an altitude is drawn to the hypotenuse of a right triangle, then the two triangles formed are similar to the original triangle and to each other. **(p. 527)**

9.2 In a right triangle, the altitude from the right angle to the hypotenuse divides the hypotenuse into two segments. The length of the altitude is the geometric mean of the lengths of the two segments. **(p. 529)**

9.3 In a right triangle, the altitude from the right angle to the hypotenuse divides the hypotenuse into two segments. Each leg of the right triangle is the geometric mean of the hypotenuse and the segment of the hypotenuse that is adjacent to the leg. **(p. 529)**

9.4 **Pythagorean Theorem** In a right triangle, the square of the length of the hypotenuse is equal to the sum of the squares of the lengths of the legs. **(p. 535)**

9.5 **Converse of the Pythagorean Theorem** If the square of the length of the longest side of a triangle is equal to the sum of the squares of the lengths of the other two sides, then the triangle is a right triangle. **(p. 543)**

9.6 If the square of the length of the longest side of a triangle is less than the sum of the squares of the lengths of the other two sides, then the triangle is acute. **(p. 544)**

9.7 If the square of the length of the longest side of a triangle is greater than the sum of the squares of the length of the other two sides, then the triangle is obtuse. **(p. 544)**

9.8 **45°-45°-90° Triangle Theorem** In a 45°-45°-90° triangle, the hypotenuse is $\sqrt{2}$ times as long as each leg. **(p. 551)**

9.9 **30°-60°-90° Triangle Theorem** In a 30°-60°-90° triangle, the hypotenuse is twice as long as the shorter leg, and the longer leg is $\sqrt{3}$ times as long as the shorter leg. **(p. 551)**

10.1 If a line is tangent to a circle, then it is perpendicular to the radius drawn to the point of tangency. **(p. 597)**

10.2 In a plane, if a line is perpendicular to a radius of a circle at its endpoint on the circle, then the line is tangent to the circle. **(p. 597)**

10.3 If two segments from the same exterior point are tangent to a circle, then they are congruent. **(p. 598)**

10.4 In the same circle, or in congruent circles, two minor arcs are congruent if and only if their corresponding chords are congruent. **(p. 605)**

10.5 If a diameter of a circle is perpendicular to a chord, then the diameter bisects the chord and its arc. **(p. 605)**

10.6 If one chord is a perpendicular bisector of another chord, then the first chord is a diameter. **(p. 605)**

10.7 In the same circle or in congruent circles, two chords are congruent if and only if they are equidistant from the center. **(p. 606)**

10.8 If an angle is inscribed in a circle, then its measure is half the measure of its intercepted arc. **(p. 613)**

10.9 If two inscribed angles of a circle intercept the same arc, then the angles are congruent. **(p. 614)**

10.10 If a right triangle is inscribed in a circle, then the hypotenuse is a diameter of the circle. Conversely, if one side of an inscribed triangle is a diameter of the circle, then the triangle is a right triangle and the angle opposite the diameter is the right angle. **(p. 615)**

10.11 A quadrilateral can be inscribed in a circle if and only if its opposite angles are supplementary. **(p. 615)**

10.12 If a tangent and a chord intersect at a point on a circle, then the measure of each angle formed is one half the measure of its intercepted arc. **(p. 621)**

10.13 If two chords intersect in the interior of a circle, then the measure of each angle is one half the sum of the measures of the arcs intercepted by the angle and its vertical angle. **(p. 622)**

10.14 If a tangent and a secant, two tangents, or two secants intersect in the exterior of a circle, then the measure of the angle formed is one half the difference of the measures of the intercepted arcs. **(p. 622)**

10.15 If two chords intersect in the interior of a circle, then the product of the lengths of the segments of one chord is equal to the product of the lengths of the segments of the other chord. **(p. 629)**

10.16 If two secant segments share the same endpoint outside a circle, then the product of the length of one secant segment and the length of its external segment equals the product of the length of the other secant segment and the length of its external segment. **(p. 630)**

10.17 If a secant segment and a tangent segment share an endpoint outside a circle, then the product of the length of the secant segment and the length of its external segment equals the square of the length of the tangent segment. **(p. 630)**

11.1 Polygon Interior Angles Theorem The sum of the measures of the interior angles of a convex n-gon is $(n - 2) \cdot 180°$. **(p. 662)**

Corollary The measure of each interior angle of a regular n-gon is $\frac{1}{n} \cdot (n - 2) \cdot 180°$, or $\frac{(n - 2) \cdot 180°}{n}$. **(p. 662)**

11.2 Polygon Exterior Angles Theorem The sum of the measures of the exterior angles of a convex polygon, one angle at each vertex, is $360°$. **(p. 663)**

Corollary The measure of each exterior angle of a regular n-gon is $\frac{1}{n} \cdot 360°$, or $\frac{360°}{n}$. **(p. 663)**

11.3 Area of an Equilateral Triangle The area of an equilateral triangle is one fourth the square of the length of the side times $\sqrt{3}$. $A = \frac{1}{4}\sqrt{3}\,s^2$ **(p. 669)**

11.4 Area of a Regular Polygon The area of a regular n-gon with side length s is half the product of the apothem a and the perimeter P, so $A = \frac{1}{2}aP$, or $A = \frac{1}{2}a \cdot ns$. **(p. 670)**

11.5 Areas of Similar Polygons If two polygons are similar with the lengths of corresponding sides in the ratio of $a:b$, then the ratio of their areas is $a^2:b^2$. **(p. 677)**

11.6 Circumference of a Circle The circumference C of a circle is $C = \pi d$ or $C = 2\pi r$, where d is the diameter of the circle and r is the radius of the circle. **(p. 683)**

Arc Length Corollary In a circle, the ratio of the length of a given arc to the circumference is equal to the ratio of the measure of the arc to $360°$.

$$\frac{\text{Arc length of } \overset{\frown}{AB}}{2\pi r} = \frac{m\overset{\frown}{AB}}{360°}, \text{ or}$$

$$\text{Arc length of } \overset{\frown}{AB} = \frac{m\overset{\frown}{AB}}{360°} \cdot 2\pi r \text{ (p. 683)}$$

11.7 Area of a Circle The area of a circle is π times the square of the radius, or $A = \pi r^2$. **(p. 691)**

11.8 Area of a Sector The ratio of the area A of a sector of a circle to the area of the circle is equal to the ratio of the measure of the intercepted arc to $360°$.

$$\frac{A}{\pi r^2} = \frac{m\overset{\frown}{AB}}{360°}, \text{ or } A = \frac{m\overset{\frown}{AB}}{360°} \cdot \pi r^2 \text{ (p. 692)}$$

12.1 Euler's Theorem The number of faces (F), vertices (V), and edges (E) of a polyhedron are related by the formula $F + V = E + 2$. **(p. 721)**

12.2 Surface Area of a Right Prism The surface area S of a right prism can be found using the formula $S = 2B + Ph$, where B is the area of a base, P is the perimeter of a base, and h is the height. **(p. 729)**

12.3 Surface Area of a Right Cylinder The surface area S of a right cylinder is $S = 2B + Ch = 2\pi r^2 + 2\pi rh$, where B is the area of a base, C is the circumference of a base, r is the radius of a base, and h is the height. **(p. 730)**

12.4 Surface Area of a Regular Pyramid The surface area S of a regular pyramid is $S = B + \frac{1}{2}P\ell$, where B is the area of a base, P is the perimeter of the base, and ℓ is the slant height. **(p. 736)**

12.5 Surface Area of a Right Cone The surface area S of a right cone is $S = \pi r^2 + \pi r\ell$, where r is the radius of the base and ℓ is the slant height. **(p. 737)**

12.6 Cavalieri's Principle If two solids have the same height and the same cross-sectional area at every level, then they have the same volume. **(p. 744)**

12.7 Volume of a Prism The volume V of a prism is $V = Bh$, where B is the area of a base and h is the height. **(p. 744)**

12.8 Volume of a Cylinder The volume V of a cylinder is $V = Bh = \pi r^2 h$, where B is the area of a base, h is the height, and r is the radius of a base. **(p. 744)**

12.9 Volume of a Pyramid The volume V of a pyramid is $V = \frac{1}{3}Bh$, where B is the area of the base and h is the height. **(p. 752)**

12.10 Volume of a Cone The volume V of a cone is $V = \frac{1}{3}Bh = \frac{1}{3}\pi r^2 h$, where B is the area of the base, h is the height, and r is the radius of the base. **(p. 752)**

12.11 Surface Area of a Sphere The surface area S of a sphere with radius r is $S = 4\pi r^2$. **(p. 759)**

12.12 Volume of a Sphere The volume V of a sphere with radius r is $V = \frac{4}{3}\pi r^3$. **(p. 761)**

12.13 Similar Solids Theorem If two similar solids have a scale factor of $a:b$, then corresponding areas have a ratio of $a^2:b^2$, and corresponding volumes have a ratio of $a^3:b^3$. **(p. 767)**

Additional Proofs

PROOF OF THEOREM 4.8
HYPOTENUSE-LEG (HL) CONGRUENCE THEOREM

THEOREM 4.8
page 238

If the hypotenuse and a leg of a right triangle are congruent to the hypotenuse and a leg of a second right triangle, then the two triangles are congruent.

GIVEN ▶ In $\triangle ABC$, $\angle C$ is a right angle.
In $\triangle DEF$, $\angle F$ is a right angle.
$\overline{AB} \cong \overline{DE}$, $\overline{BC} \cong \overline{EF}$

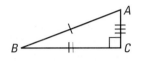

PROVE ▶ $\triangle ABC \cong \triangle DEF$

Plan for Proof Construct $\triangle GEF$ with $\overline{GF} \cong \overline{AC}$, as shown. Prove that $\triangle ABC \cong \triangle GEF$. Then use the fact that corresponding parts of congruent triangles are congruent to show that $\triangle GEF \cong \triangle DEF$. By the transitive property of congruence, you can show that $\triangle ABC \cong \triangle DEF$.

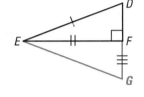

Statements	Reasons
1. $\angle C$ is a right angle. $\angle DFE$ is a right angle.	1. Given
2. $\overline{EF} \perp \overline{DG}$	2. Definition of perpendicular lines
3. $\angle EFG$ is a right angle.	3. If 2 lines are $\perp$, then they form 4 rt. $\angle$s.
4. $\angle C \cong \angle EFG$	4. Right Angles Congruence Theorem
5. $\overline{BC} \cong \overline{EF}$	5. Given
6. $\overline{AC} \cong \overline{GF}$	6. Given by construction
7. $\triangle ABC \cong \triangle GEF$	7. SAS Congruence Postulate
8. $\overline{GE} \cong \overline{AB}$	8. Corresp. parts of $\cong$ $\triangle$ are $\cong$.
9. $\overline{AB} \cong \overline{DE}$	9. Given
10. $\overline{GE} \cong \overline{DE}$	10. Transitive Property of Congruence
11. $\angle D \cong \angle G$	11. If 2 sides of a $\triangle$ are $\cong$, then the $\angle$s opposite them are $\cong$.
12. $\angle GFE \cong \angle DFE$	12. Right Angles Congruence Theorem
13. $\triangle GEF \cong \triangle DEF$	13. AAS Congruence Theorem
14. $\triangle ABC \cong \triangle DEF$	14. Transitive Prop. of $\cong$ $\triangle$

ANOTHER PROOF OF THEOREM 4.8
HYPOTENUSE-LEG (HL) CONGRUENCE THEOREM

GIVEN ▶ $\triangle ABC$ and $\triangle DEF$ are right triangles; $c = f$, $b = e$

PROVE ▶ $\triangle ABC \cong \triangle DEF$

Plan for Proof Use the Pythagorean Theorem to show that $a = d$. Then use the SSS Congruence Postulate.

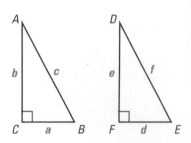

Statements	Reasons
1. $\triangle ABC$ and $\triangle DEF$ are right triangles.	**1.** Given
2. $c = f$, $b = e$	**2.** Given
3. $c^2 = f^2$, $b^2 = e^2$	**3.** A property of squares
4. $a^2 + b^2 = c^2$; $d^2 + e^2 = f^2$	**4.** Pythagorean Theorem
5. $a^2 + b^2 = d^2 + e^2$	**5.** Substitution property of equality
6. $a^2 + e^2 = d^2 + e^2$	**6.** Substitution property of equality
7. $a^2 = d^2$	**7.** Subtraction property of equality
8. $a = d$	**8.** A property of square roots
9. $\triangle ABC \cong \triangle DEF$	**9.** SSS Congruence Postulate

▶ Study Tip
This second proof of the HL Theorem uses the Pythagorean Theorem, which is introduced in Chapter 1 and further developed in Chapter 9.

PROOF OF THEOREM 5.5
CONCURRENCY OF PERPENDICULAR BISECTORS OF A TRIANGLE

THEOREM 5.5
page 273

The perpendicular bisectors of a triangle intersect at a point that is equidistant from the vertices of the triangle.

GIVEN ▶ $\triangle ABC$; the $\perp$ bisectors of $\overline{AB}$, $\overline{BC}$, and $\overline{AC}$

PROVE ▶ The $\perp$ bisectors intersect in a point; that point is equidistant from A, B, and C.

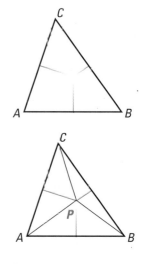

Plan for Proof Show that P, the point of intersection of the perpendicular bisectors of $\overline{BC}$ and $\overline{AC}$, also lies on the perpendicular bisector of $\overline{AB}$. Then show that P is equidistant from the vertices of the triangle, A, B, and C.

Statements	Reasons
1. The perpendicular bisectors of $\overline{BC}$ and $\overline{AC}$ intersect at some point P.	1. ABC is a triangle, so its sides $\overline{BC}$ and $\overline{AC}$ cannot be parallel; therefore, segments perpendicular to those sides cannot be parallel. So, the perpendicular bisectors must intersect in some point. Call it P.
2. Draw $\overline{PA}$, $\overline{PB}$, and $\overline{PC}$.	2. Through any two points there is exactly one line.
3. $PA = PC$, $PC = PB$	3. If a point is on the perpendicular bisector of a segment, then it is equidistant from the endpoints of the segment. (Theorem 5.1)
4. $PA = PB$	4. Substitution property of equality
5. P is on the perpendicular bisector of $\overline{AB}$.	5. If a point is equidistant from the endpoints of a segment, then it is on the perpendicular bisector of the segment. (Theorem 5.2)
6. $PA = PB = PC$, so P is equidistant from the vertices of the triangle.	6. Steps 3 and 4 and definition of equidistant

PROOF OF THEOREM 5.7
CONCURRENCY OF MEDIANS OF A TRIANGLE

··

GIVEN ▶ △OBC; medians $\overline{OM}$, $\overline{BN}$, and $\overline{CQ}$

PROVE ▶ The medians intersect in a point P; that point is two thirds of the distance from vertices O, B, and C to midpoints M, N, and Q.

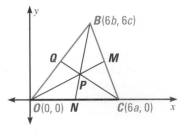

Plan for Proof The medians $\overline{OM}$ and $\overline{BN}$ intersect at some point P. Show that point P lies on $\overleftrightarrow{CQ}$. Then show that

$$OP = \frac{2}{3}OM, \quad BP = \frac{2}{3}BN, \text{ and } CP = \frac{2}{3}CQ.$$

❶ Find the equations of the medians $\overline{OM}$, $\overline{BN}$, and $\overline{CQ}$.

By the *Midpoint Formula*,

the coordinates of M are $\left(\dfrac{6b + 6a}{2}, \dfrac{6c + 0}{2}\right) = (3b + 3a, 3c)$;

the coordinates of N are $\left(\dfrac{0 + 6a}{2}, \dfrac{0 + 0}{2}\right) = (3a, 0)$;

the coordinates of Q are $\left(\dfrac{6b + 0}{2}, \dfrac{6c + 0}{2}\right) = (3b, 3c)$.

By the *slope formula*,

slope of $\overline{OM} = \dfrac{3c - 0}{(3b + 3a) - 0} = \dfrac{3c}{3b + 3a} = \dfrac{c}{b + a}$;

slope of $\overline{BN} = \dfrac{6c - 0}{6b - 3a} = \dfrac{6c}{6b - 3a} = \dfrac{2c}{2b - a}$;

slope of $\overline{CQ} = \dfrac{0 - 3c}{6a - 3b} = \dfrac{-3c}{6a - 3b} = \dfrac{-c}{2a - b} = \dfrac{c}{b - 2a}$.

Using the *point-slope form of an equation of a line*,

the equation of $\overleftrightarrow{OM}$ is $y - 0 = \dfrac{c}{b + a}(x - 0)$, or $y = \dfrac{c}{b + a}x$;

the equation of $\overleftrightarrow{BN}$ is $y - 0 = \dfrac{2c}{2b - a}(x - 3a)$, or $y = \dfrac{2c}{2b - a}(x - 3a)$;

the equation of $\overleftrightarrow{CQ}$ is $y - 0 = \dfrac{c}{b - 2a}(x - 6a)$, or $y = \dfrac{c}{b - 2a}(x - 6a)$.

❷ Find the coordinates of the point P where two medians (say, $\overline{OM}$ and $\overline{BN}$) intersect. Using the substitution method, set the values of y in the equations of $\overleftrightarrow{OM}$ and $\overleftrightarrow{BN}$ equal to each other:

$$\frac{c}{b + a}x = \frac{2c}{2b - a}(x - 3a)$$

$$cx(2b - a) = 2c(x - 3a)(b + a)$$

$$2cxb - cxa = 2cxb + 2cxa - 6cab - 6ca^2$$

$$-3cxa = -6cab - 6ca^2$$

$$x = 2b + 2a$$

Substituting to find y, $y = \dfrac{c}{b + a}x = \dfrac{c}{b + a}(2b + 2a) = 2c$.

So, the coordinates of P are $(2b + 2a, 2c)$.

❸ Show that P is on $\overleftrightarrow{CQ}$.

Substituting the x coordinate for P into the equation of $\overleftrightarrow{CQ}$,

$y = \dfrac{c}{b-2a}([2b+2a]-6a) = \dfrac{c}{b-2a}(2b-4a) = 2c$. So, $P(2b+2a, 2c)$

is on $\overleftrightarrow{CQ}$ and the three medians intersect at the same point.

❹ Find the distances OM, OP, BN, BP, CQ, and CP.
Use the *Distance Formula.*

$$OM = \sqrt{((3b+3a)-0)^2 + (3c-0)^2} = \sqrt{(3(b+a))^2 + (3c)^2} =$$
$$\sqrt{9((b+a)^2 + c^2)} = 3\sqrt{(b+a)^2 + c^2}$$

$$OP = \sqrt{((2b+2a)-0)^2 + (2c-0)^2} = \sqrt{(2(b+a))^2 + (2c)^2} =$$
$$\sqrt{4((b+a)^2 + c^2)} = 2\sqrt{(b+a)^2 + c^2}$$

$$BN = \sqrt{(3a-6b)^2 - (0-6c)^2} = \sqrt{(3a-6b)^2 + (-6c)^2} =$$
$$\sqrt{(3(a-2b))^2 + (3(-2c))^2} = \sqrt{9(a-2b)^2 + 9(4c^2)} =$$
$$\sqrt{9((a-2b)^2 + 4c^2)} = 3\sqrt{(a-2b)^2 + 4c^2}$$

$$BP = \sqrt{((2b+2a)-6b)^2 + (2c-6c)^2} = \sqrt{(2a-4b)^2 + (-4c)^2} =$$
$$\sqrt{(2(a-2b))^2 + (2(-2c))^2} = \sqrt{4(a-2b)^2 + 4(4c^2)} =$$
$$\sqrt{4((a-2b)^2 + 4c^2)} = 2\sqrt{(a-2b)^2 + 4c^2}$$

$$CQ = \sqrt{(6a-3b)^2 + (0-3c)^2} = \sqrt{(3(2a-b))^2 + (-3c)^2} =$$
$$\sqrt{9((2a-b)^2 + c^2)} = 3\sqrt{(2a-b)^2 + c^2}$$

$$CP = \sqrt{(6a-(2b+2a))^2 + (0-2c)^2} = \sqrt{(4a-2b)^2 + (-2c)^2} =$$
$$\sqrt{(2(2a-b))^2 + 4c^2} = \sqrt{4((2a-b)^2 + c^2)} = 2\sqrt{(2a-b)^2 + c^2}$$

❺ Multiply OM, BN, and CQ by $\dfrac{2}{3}$.

$$\tfrac{2}{3}OM = \tfrac{2}{3}(3\sqrt{(b+a)^2 - c^2})$$
$$= 2\sqrt{(b+a)^2 + c^2}$$

$$\tfrac{2}{3}BN = \tfrac{2}{3}(3\sqrt{(a-2b)^2 + 4c^2})$$
$$= 2\sqrt{(a-2b)^2 + 4c^2}$$

$$\tfrac{2}{3}CQ = \tfrac{2}{3}(3\sqrt{(2a-b)^2 + c^2})$$
$$= 2\sqrt{(2a-b)^2 + c^2}$$

Thus, $OP = \dfrac{2}{3}OM$, $BP = \dfrac{2}{3}BN$, and $CP = \dfrac{2}{3}CQ$.

PROOF OF THEOREM 5.8
CONCURRENCY OF ALTITUDES OF A TRIANGLE

THEOREM 5.8
page 281

The lines containing the altitudes of a triangle are concurrent.

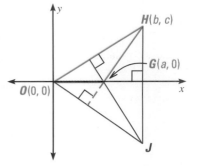

STUDENT HELP

▶ **Study Tip**
Choose a general triangle, with one vertex at the origin and one side along an axis. In the proof shown, the triangle is obtuse.

GIVEN ▶ $\triangle OGH$

PROVE ▶ The altitudes to the sides of $\triangle OGH$ all intersect at J.

Plan for Proof Find the equations of the lines containing the altitudes of $\triangle OGH$. Find the intersection point of two of these lines. Show that the intersection point is also on the line containing the third altitude.

❶ ***Find*** the slopes of the lines containing the sides $\overline{OH}$, $\overline{GH}$, and $\overline{OG}$.

$$\text{slope of } \overleftrightarrow{OH} = \frac{c}{b} \qquad \text{slope of } \overleftrightarrow{GH} = \frac{c}{b-a} \qquad \text{slope of } \overleftrightarrow{OG} = 0$$

❷ ***Use*** the *Slopes of Perpendicular Lines Postulate* to find the slopes of the lines containing the altitudes.

$$\text{slope of line containing altitude to } \overline{OH} = \frac{-b}{c}$$

$$\text{slope of line containing altitude to } \overline{GH} = \frac{-(b-a)}{c} = \frac{a-b}{c}$$

The line containing the altitude to $\overline{OG}$ has an undefined slope.

❸ ***Use*** the *point-slope form of an equation of a line* to write equations for the lines containing the altitudes.
An equation of the line containing the altitude to $\overline{OH}$ is

$$y - 0 = \frac{-b}{c}(x - a), \text{ or } y = \frac{-b}{c}x + \frac{ab}{c}.$$

An equation of the line containing the altitude to $\overline{GH}$ is

$$y - 0 = \frac{a-b}{c}(x - 0), \text{ or } y = \frac{a-b}{c}x.$$

An equation of the vertical line containing the altitude to $\overline{OG}$ is $x = b$.

❹ ***Find*** the coordinates of the point J where the lines containing two of the altitudes intersect. Using substitution, set the values of y in two of the above equations equal to each other, then solve for x:

$$\frac{-b}{c}x + \frac{ab}{c} = \frac{a-b}{c}x$$

$$\frac{ab}{c} = \frac{a-b}{c}x + \frac{b}{c}x$$

$$\frac{ab}{c} = \frac{a}{c}x$$

$$x = b$$

Next, substitute to find y: $y = \frac{-b}{c}x + \frac{ab}{c} = \frac{-b}{c}(b) + \frac{ab}{c} = \frac{ab - b^2}{c}$.

So, the coordinates of J are $\left(b, \dfrac{ab - b^2}{c}\right)$.

❺ ***Show*** that J is on the line that contains the altitude to side $\overline{OG}$. J is on the vertical line with equation $x = b$ because its x-coordinate is b. Thus, the lines containing the altitudes of $\triangle OGH$ are concurrent.

PROOF OF THEOREM 6.17
MIDSEGMENT THEOREM FOR TRAPEZOIDS

THEOREM 6.17
page 357

The midsegment of a trapezoid is parallel to each base and its length is one half the sum of the lengths of the bases.

GIVEN ▸ Trapezoid $ABCD$ with midsegment $\overline{MN}$

PROVE ▸ $\overline{MN} \parallel \overline{AD}$, $\overline{MN} \parallel \overline{BC}$,

$MN = \frac{1}{2}(AD + BC)$

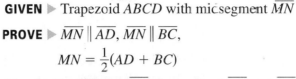

Plan for Proof Draw $\overline{BN}$, then extend $\overline{BN}$ and $\overline{AD}$ so that they intersect at point G. Then prove that $\triangle BNC \cong \triangle GND$, and use the fact that $\overline{MN}$ is a midsegment of $\triangle BAG$ to prove $MN = \frac{1}{2}(AD + BC)$.

Statements	Reasons
1. $ABCD$ is a trapezoid with midsegment $\overline{MN}$.	1. Given
2. Draw $\overline{BN}$, then extend $\overline{BN}$ and $\overline{AD}$ so that they intersect at point G.	2. Through any two points there is exactly one line.
3. N is the midpoint of $\overline{CD}$.	3. Definition of midsegment of a trapezoid
4. $\overline{CN} \cong \overline{ND}$	4. Definition of midpoint
5. $\overline{AD} \parallel \overline{BC}$	5. Definition of trapezoid
6. $\angle BCN \cong \angle GDN$	6. Alternate Interior $\angle$s Theorem
7. $\angle BNC \cong \angle GND$	7. Vertical angles are congruent.
8. $\triangle BNC \cong \triangle GND$	8. ASA Congruence Postulate
9. $\overline{BN} \cong \overline{GN}$	9. Corresp. parts of $\cong$ $\triangle$s are $\cong$.
10. N is the midpoint of $\overline{BG}$.	10. Definition of midpoint
11. $\overline{MN}$ is the midsegment of $\triangle BGA$.	11. Definition of midsegment of a $\triangle$
12. $\overline{MN} \parallel \overline{AG}$ (so $\overline{MN} \parallel \overline{AD}$)	12. Midsegment of a $\triangle$ Theorem
13. $\overline{MN} \parallel \overline{BC}$	13. Two lines $\parallel$ to the same line are $\parallel$.
14. $MN = \frac{1}{2}AG$	14. Midsegment of a $\triangle$ Theorem
15. $AG = AD + DG$	15. Segment Addition Postulate
16. $\overline{DG} \cong \overline{BC}$	16. Corresp. parts of $\cong$ $\triangle$s are $\cong$.
17. $DG = BC$	17. Definition of congruent segments
18. $AG = AD + BC$	18. Substitution property of equality
19. $MN = \frac{1}{2}(AD + BC)$	19. Substitution property of equality

PROOF OF THEOREM 10.11
A THEOREM ABOUT INSCRIBED QUADRILATERALS

❶ Prove that if a quadrilateral is inscribed in a circle, then its opposite angles are supplementary.

THEOREM 10.11
page 615

A quadrilateral can be inscribed in a circle if and only if its opposite angles are supplementary.

GIVEN ▶ $DEFG$ is inscribed in $\odot C$.

PROVE ▶ $\angle D$ and $\angle F$ are supplementary,
$\angle E$ and $\angle G$ are supplementary.

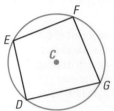

Paragraph Proof Arcs $\overset{\frown}{EFG}$ and $\overset{\frown}{GDE}$ together make a circle, so $m\overset{\frown}{EFG} + m\overset{\frown}{GDE} = 360°$ by the Arc Addition Postulate. $\angle D$ is inscribed in $\overset{\frown}{EFG}$ and $\angle F$ is inscribed in $\overset{\frown}{GDE}$, so the angle measures are half the arc measures. Using the Substitution and Distributive properties, the sum of the measures of the opposite angles is

$$m\angle D + m\angle F = \tfrac{1}{2}m\overset{\frown}{EFG} + \tfrac{1}{2}m\overset{\frown}{GDE} = \tfrac{1}{2}(m\overset{\frown}{EFG} + m\overset{\frown}{GDE}) = \tfrac{1}{2}(360°) = 180°.$$

So, $\angle D$ and $\angle F$ are supplementary by definition. Similarly, $\angle E$ and $\angle G$ are inscribed in $\overset{\frown}{FGD}$ and $\overset{\frown}{DEF}$ and $m\angle E + m\angle G = 180°$. Then $\angle E$ and $\angle G$ are supplementary by definition.

❷ Prove that if the opposite angles of a quadrilateral are supplementary, then the quadrilateral can be inscribed in a circle.

GIVEN ▶ $\angle E$ and $\angle G$ are supplementary
(or $\angle D$ and $\angle F$ are supplementary).

PROVE ▶ $DEFG$ is inscribed in $\odot C$.

Plan for Proof Draw the circle that passes through D, E, and F. Use an *indirect proof* to show that the circle also passes through G. Begin by assuming that G does not lie on $\odot C$.

Case 1 G *lies inside* $\odot C$. Let H be the intersection of $\overrightarrow{DG}$ and $\odot C$. Then $DEFH$ is inscribed in $\odot C$ and $\angle E$ is supplementary to $\angle DHF$ (by proof above). Then $\angle DGF \cong \angle DHF$ by the given information and the Congruent Supplements Theorem. This implies that $\overline{FG} \parallel \overline{FH}$, which is a contradiction.

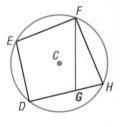

Case 2 G *lies outside* $\odot C$. Let H be the intersection of $\overrightarrow{DG}$ and $\odot C$. Then $DEFH$ is inscribed in $\odot C$ and $\angle E$ is supplementary to $\angle DHF$ (by proof above). Then $\angle DGF \cong \angle DHF$ by the given information and the Congruent Supplements Theorem. This implies that $\overline{FG} \parallel \overline{FH}$, which is a contradiction.

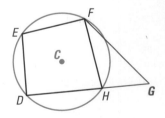

Because the original assumption leads to a contradiction in both cases, G lies on $\odot C$ and $DEFG$ is inscribed in $\odot C$.

Table of Symbols

Symbol		Page
$\sqrt{a}$	square root of a	2
$-a$	opposite of a	2
$\ldots$	and so on	3
$\cdot$	multiplication, times	6
(x, y)	ordered pair	8
$\overleftrightarrow{AB}$	line AB	10
$\overline{AB}$	segment AB	11
$\overrightarrow{AB}$	ray AB	11
AB	the length of AB	17
$|x|$	absolute value of x	17
x_1	x sub 1	19
$=$	is equal to	19
$\cong$	is congruent to	19
$\angle ABC$	angle ABC	26
$m\angle A$	measure of angle A	26
$\circ$	degree(s)	26
π	pi; irrational number ≈ 3.14	51
$\approx$	is approximately equal to	52
$\neq$	not equal to	72
$\perp$	is perpendicular to	79
$\rightarrow$	implies	87
$\leftrightarrow$	if and only if	87
$\sim p$	negation of statement p	88
$\parallel$	is parallel to	129
m	slope	165

Symbol		Page
$\triangle ABC$	triangle ABC	194
$\triangle$	triangles	230
$\angle$	angles	270
$<$	is less than	295
$>$	is greater than	296
$\square ABCD$	parallelogram $ABCD$	330
$\ncong$	not congruent to	353
A'	A prime	396
A''	A double prime	411
$\overrightarrow{AB}$	vector AB	423
$\langle a, b \rangle$	component form of a vector	423
$\frac{a}{b}, a{:}b$	ratio of a to b	457
$\sim$	is similar to	473
$\overset{?}{=}$	is this statement true?	543
$\sin$	sine	558
$\cos$	cosine	558
$\tan$	tangent	558
$\sin^{-1}$	inverse sine	567
$\cos^{-1}$	inverse cosine	567
$\tan^{-1}$	inverse tangent	567
$\left|\overrightarrow{AB}\right|$	magnitude of a vector	573
$\odot P$	circle P	595
$m\overset{\frown}{AB}$	measure of minor arc AB	603
$m\overset{\frown}{ABC}$	measure of major arc ABC	603
n-gon	polygon with n sides	661

Formulas

Angles

Sum of the measures of the interior angles of a triangle: $180°$

Sum of the measures of the interior angles of a convex n-gon: $(n - 2) \cdot 180°$

Measure of each interior angle of a regular n-gon:
$\frac{1}{n}(n - 2) \cdot 180°$

Exterior angle of a triangle:
$m\angle 1 = m\angle A + m\angle B$

Sum of the measure of the exterior angles of a convex polygon: $360°$

Measure of each exterior angle of a regular n-gon:
$\frac{1}{n} \cdot 360°$

Right Triangles

Pythagorean Theorem:
$a^2 + b^2 = c^2$

Trigonometric ratios:
$\sin A = \frac{a}{c} \quad \cos A = \frac{b}{c} \quad \tan A = \frac{a}{b}$

45°-45°-90° triangle

Ratio of sides
$1 : 1 : \sqrt{2}$

30°-60°-90° triangle

Ratio of sides
$1 : \sqrt{3} : 2$

$\triangle ABC \sim \triangle ACD \sim \triangle CBD$

$\frac{BD}{CD} = \frac{CD}{AD}, \frac{AB}{CB} = \frac{CB}{DB}, \frac{AB}{AC} = \frac{AC}{AD}$

$CD = \sqrt{AD \cdot DB}$

Circles

Angle and segments formed by two chords:
$m\angle 1 = \frac{1}{2}(m\widehat{CD} + m\widehat{AB})$
$EA \cdot EC = EB \cdot ED$

Angle and segments formed by a tangent and a secant:
$m\angle 2 = \frac{1}{2}(m\widehat{BC} - m\widehat{AB})$
$EA \cdot EC = (EB)^2$

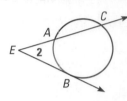

Angle and segments formed by two tangents:
$m\angle 3 = \frac{1}{2}(m\widehat{AQB} - m\widehat{AB})$
$EA = EB$

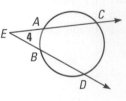

Angle and segments formed by two secants:
$m\angle 4 = \frac{1}{2}(m\widehat{CD} - m\widehat{AB})$
$EA \cdot EC = EB \cdot ED$

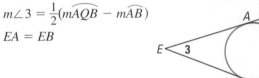

Coordinate Geometry

Given: Points $A(x_1, y_1)$ and $B(x_2, y_2)$
$AB = \sqrt{(x_2 - x_1)^2 + (y_2 - y_1)^2}$

Midpoint of $\overline{AB} = \left(\frac{x_1 + x_2}{2}, \frac{y_1 + y_2}{2}\right)$

Slope of $\overleftrightarrow{AB} = \frac{\text{rise}}{\text{run}} = \frac{y_2 - y_1}{x_2 - x_1}$

Slope-intercept form of a linear equation with slope m and y-intercept b: $y = mx + b$

Standard equation of a circle with center (h, k) and radius r: $(x - h)^2 + (y - k)^2 = r^2$

Vectors

$\vec{u} = \langle a_1, b_1 \rangle$, $\vec{v} = \langle a_2, b_2 \rangle$

$\vec{u} + \vec{v} = \langle a_1 + a_2, b_1 + b_2 \rangle$

Perimeter

P = perimeter, C = circumference,
s = side, ℓ = length, w = width,
$a, b, c,$ = lengths of the sides of a triangle,
r = radius

Square: $P = 4s$

Rectangle: $P = 2\ell + 2w$

Triangle: $P = a + b + c$

Circle: $C = 2\pi r$

Arc length of $\widehat{AB} = \dfrac{m\widehat{AB}}{360°} \cdot 2\pi r$

Area

A = area, s = side, b = base, h = height,
ℓ = length, w = width, d = diagonal,
a = apothem, P = perimeter, r = radius

Square: $A = s^2$

Rectangle: $A = \ell w$

Parallelogram: $A = bh$

Triangle: $A = \frac{1}{2}bh$

Trapezoid: $A = \frac{1}{2}h(b_1 + b_2)$

Quadrilateral with
$\perp$ diagonals: $A = \frac{1}{2}d_1 d_2$

Equilateral triangle: $A = \frac{1}{4}\sqrt{3}\,s^2$

Regular polygon: $A = \frac{1}{2}aP$

Circle: $A = \pi r^2$

Area of a sector: $A = \dfrac{m\widehat{AB}}{360°} \cdot \pi r^2$

Surface Area

B = area of the base, P = perimeter,
h = height, r = radius, ℓ = slant height

Right prism: $S = 2B + Ph$

Right cylinder: $S = 2\pi r^2 + 2\pi rh$

Regular pyramid: $S = B + \frac{1}{2}P\ell$

Right cone: $S = \pi r^2 + \pi r\ell$

Sphere $S = 4\pi r^2$

Volume

V = volume, B = area of a base,
h = height, r = radius, s = side

Cube: $V = s^3$

Pyramid: $V = \frac{1}{3}Bh$

Cone: $V = \frac{1}{3}\pi r^2 h$

Cylinder: $V = \pi r^2 h$

Prism: $V = Bh$

Sphere: $V = \frac{4}{3}\pi r^3$

Miscellaneous

Geometric mean of a and b: $\sqrt{a \cdot b}$

Euler's Theorem for Polyhedra, F = faces,
V = vertices, E = edges: $F + V = E + 2$

Given similar solids with corresponding sides
of lengths a and b

Ratio of areas $= a^2 : b^2$

Ratio of volumes $= a^3 : b^3$

Table of
Squares and Square Roots

No.	Square	Sq. Root	No.	Square	Sq. Root	No.	Square	Sq. Root
1	1	1.000	51	2,601	7.141	101	10,201	10.050
2	4	1.414	52	2,704	7.211	102	10,404	10.100
3	9	1.732	53	2,809	7.280	103	10,609	10.149
4	16	2.000	54	2,916	7.348	104	10,816	10.198
5	25	2.236	55	3,025	7.416	105	11,025	10.247
6	36	2.449	56	3,136	7.483	106	11,236	10.296
7	49	2.646	57	3,249	7.550	107	11,449	10.344
8	64	2.828	58	3,364	7.616	108	11,664	10.392
9	81	3.000	59	3,481	7.681	109	11,881	10.440
10	100	3.162	60	3,600	7.746	110	12,100	10.488
11	121	3.317	61	3,721	7.810	111	12,321	10.536
12	144	3.464	62	3,844	7.874	112	12,544	10.583
13	169	3.606	63	3,969	7.937	113	12,769	10.630
14	196	3.742	64	4,096	8.000	114	12,996	10.677
15	225	3.873	65	4,225	8.062	115	13,225	10.724
16	256	4.000	66	4,356	8.124	116	13,456	10.770
17	289	4.123	67	4,489	8.185	117	13,689	10.817
18	324	4.243	68	4,624	8.246	118	13,924	10.863
19	361	4.359	69	4,761	8.307	119	14,161	10.909
20	400	4.472	70	4,900	8.367	120	14,400	10.954
21	441	4.583	71	5,041	8.426	121	14,641	11.000
22	484	4.690	72	5,184	8.485	122	14,884	11.045
23	529	4.796	73	5,329	8.544	123	15,129	11.091
24	576	4.899	74	5,476	8.602	124	15,376	11.136
25	625	5.000	75	5,625	8.660	125	15,625	11.180
26	676	5.099	76	5,776	8.718	126	15,876	11.225
27	729	5.196	77	5,929	8.775	127	16,129	11.269
28	784	5.292	78	6,084	8.832	128	16,384	11.314
29	841	5.385	79	6,241	8.888	129	16,641	11.358
30	900	5.477	80	6,400	8.944	130	16,900	11.402
31	961	5.568	81	6,561	9.000	131	17,161	11.446
32	1,024	5.657	82	6,724	9.055	132	17,424	11.489
33	1,089	5.745	83	6,889	9.110	133	17,689	11.533
34	1,156	5.831	84	7,056	9.165	134	17,956	11.576
35	1,225	5.916	85	7,225	9.220	135	18,225	11.619
36	1,296	6.000	86	7,396	9.274	136	18,496	11.662
37	1,369	6.083	87	7,569	9.327	137	18,769	11.705
38	1,444	6.164	88	7,744	9.381	138	19,044	11.747
39	1,521	6.245	89	7,921	9.434	139	19,321	11.790
40	1,600	6.325	90	8,100	9.487	140	19,600	11.832
41	1,681	6.403	91	8,281	9.539	141	19,881	11.874
42	1,764	6.481	92	8,464	9.592	142	20,164	11.916
43	1,849	6.557	93	8,649	9.644	143	20,449	11.958
44	1,936	6.633	94	8,836	9.695	144	20,736	12.000
45	2,025	6.708	95	9,025	9.747	145	21,025	12.042
46	2,116	6.782	96	9,216	9.798	146	21,316	12.083
47	2,209	6.856	97	9,409	9.849	147	21,609	12.124
48	2,304	6.928	98	9,604	9.899	148	21,904	12.166
49	2,401	7.000	99	9,801	9.950	149	22,201	12.207
50	2,500	7.071	100	10,000	10.000	150	22,500	12.247

Table of Trigonometric Ratios

Angle	Sine	Cosine	Tangent
1°	.0175	.9998	.0175
2°	.0349	.9994	.0349
3°	.0523	.9986	.0524
4°	.0698	.9976	.0699
5°	.0872	.9962	.0875
6°	.1045	.9945	.1051
7°	.1219	.9925	.1228
8°	.1392	.9903	.1405
9°	.1564	.9877	.1584
10°	.1736	.9848	.1763
11°	.1908	.9816	.1944
12°	.2079	.9781	.2126
13°	.2250	.9744	.2309
14°	.2419	.9703	.2493
15°	.2588	.9659	.2679
16°	.2756	.9613	.2867
17°	.2924	.9563	.3057
18°	.3090	.9511	.3249
19°	.3256	.9455	.3443
20°	.3420	.9397	.3640
21°	.3584	.9336	.3839
22°	.3746	.9272	.4040
23°	.3907	.9205	.4245
24°	.4067	.9135	.4452
25°	.4226	.9063	.4663
26°	.4384	.8988	.4877
27°	.4540	.8910	.5095
28°	.4695	.8829	.5317
29°	.4848	.8746	.5543
30°	.5000	.8660	.5774
31°	.5150	.8572	.6009
32°	.5299	.8480	.6249
33°	.5446	.8387	.6494
34°	.5592	.8290	.6745
35°	.5736	.8192	.7002
36°	.5878	.8090	.7265
37°	.6018	.7986	.7536
38°	.6157	.7880	.7813
39°	.6293	.7771	.8098
40°	.6428	.7660	.8391
41°	.6561	.7547	.8693
42°	.6691	.7431	.9004
43°	.6820	.7314	.9325
44°	.6947	.7193	.9657
45°	.7071	.7071	1.0000

Angle	Sine	Cosine	Tangent
46°	.7193	.6947	1.0355
47°	.7314	.6820	1.0724
48°	.7431	.6691	1.1106
49°	.7547	.6561	1.1504
50°	.7660	.6428	1.1918
51°	.7771	.6293	1.2349
52°	.7880	.6157	1.2799
53°	.7986	.6018	1.3270
54°	.8090	.5878	1.3764
55°	.8192	.5736	1.4281
56°	.8290	.5592	1.4826
57°	.8387	.5446	1.5399
58°	.8480	.5299	1.6003
59°	.8572	.5150	1.6643
60°	.8660	.5000	1.7321
61°	.8746	.4848	1.8040
62°	.8829	.4695	1.8807
63°	.8910	.4540	1.9626
64°	.8988	.4384	2.0503
65°	.9063	.4226	2.1445
66°	.9135	.4067	2.2460
67°	.9205	.3907	2.3559
68°	.9272	.3746	2.4751
69°	.9336	.3584	2.6051
70°	.9397	.3420	2.7475
71°	.9455	.3256	2.9042
72°	.9511	.3090	3.0777
73°	.9563	.2924	3.2709
74°	.9613	.2756	3.4874
75°	.9659	.2588	3.7321
76°	.9703	.2419	4.0108
77°	.9744	.2250	4.3315
78°	.9781	.2079	4.7046
79°	.9816	.1908	5.1446
80°	.9848	.1736	5.6713
81°	.9877	.1564	6.3138
82°	.9903	.1392	7.1154
83°	.9925	.1219	8.1443
84°	.9945	.1045	9.5144
85°	.9962	.0872	11.4301
86°	.9976	.0698	14.3007
87°	.9986	.0523	19.0811
88°	.9994	.0349	28.6363
89°	.9998	.0175	57.2900

Glossary

acute angle (p. 28) An angle with measure between 0° and 90°.

acute triangle (p. 194) A triangle with three acute angles.

adjacent angles (p. 28) Two angles with a common vertex and side but no common interior points.

adjacent sides of a triangle (p. 195) Two sides of a triangle with a common vertex.

alternate exterior angles (p. 131) Two angles that are formed by two lines and a transversal and that lie outside the two lines on opposite sides of the transversal. See angles 1 and 8.

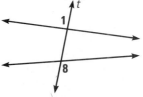

alternate interior angles (p. 131) Two angles that are formed by two lines and a transversal and that lie between the two lines on opposite sides of the transversal. See angles 3 and 6.

altitude of a triangle (p. 281) The perpendicular segment from a vertex of a triangle to the opposite side or to the line that contains the opposite side.

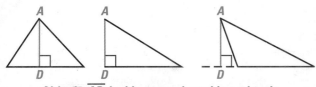

Altitude $\overline{AD}$, inside, on, and outside a triangle

angle (p. 26) Consists of two different rays that have the same initial point. The rays are the *sides* of the angle, and the initial point is the *vertex* of the angle. The angle symbol is ∠.

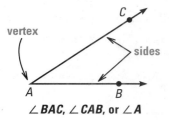

∠*BAC*, ∠*CAB*, or ∠*A*

angle bisector (p. 36) A ray that divides an angle into two adjacent angles that are congruent.

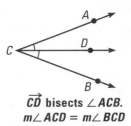

$\overrightarrow{CD}$ bisects ∠*ACB*.
$m∠ACD = m∠BCD$

angle bisector of a triangle (p. 274) A bisector of an angle of the triangle.

angle of elevation (p. 561) When you stand and look up at a point in the distance, the angle that your line of sight makes with a line drawn horizontally.

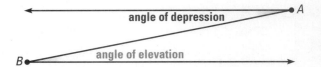

angle of rotation (p. 412) The angle formed when rays are drawn from the center of rotation to a point and its image. *See also* rotation.

apothem of a polygon (p. 670) The distance from the center of a polygon to any side of the polygon.

arc length (p. 683) A portion of the circumference of a circle.

axioms (p. 17) *See* postulates.

base of an isosceles triangle (p. 195) The noncongruent side of an isosceles triangle that has only two congruent sides.

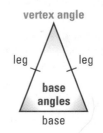

bases of a prism (p. 728) *See* prism.

bases of a trapezoid (p. 356) *See* trapezoid.

base angles of an isosceles triangle (p. 236) The two angles that contain the base of an isosceles triangle. *See also* base of an isosceles triangle.

base angles of a trapezoid (p. 356) Two pairs of angles whose common side is the base of a trapezoid.

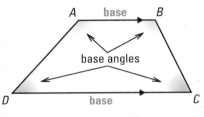

∠ *A* and ∠ *B* are a pair of base angles.
∠ *C* and ∠ *D* are another pair.

between (p. 18) When three points lie on a line, you can say that one of them is *between* the other two.

Point *B* is between points *A* and *C*.

biconditional statement (pp. 80, 87) A statement that contains the phrase "if and only if." The symbol for "if and only if" is ⟷.

bisect (pp. 34, 36) To divide into two congruent parts.

border pattern (p. 437) *See* frieze pattern.

C

center of a circle (p. 595) *See* circle.

center of a polygon (p. 670) The center of its circumscribed circle.

center of a sphere (p. 759) *See* sphere.

center of rotation (p. 412) *See* rotation.

central angle of a circle (p. 603) An angle whose vertex is the center of a circle.

∠ *PCQ* is a central angle.

central angle of a regular polygon (p. 671) An angle whose vertex is the center of the polygon and whose sides contain two consecutive vertices of the polygon.

centroid of a triangle (p. 279) The point of concurrency of the medians of a triangle.

chord of a circle (p. 595) A segment whose endpoints are points on the circle.

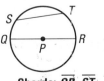

Chords: $\overline{QR}$, $\overline{ST}$

chord of a sphere (p. 759) A segment whose endpoints are on the sphere.

circle (p. 595) The set of all points in a plane that are equidistant from a given point, called the *center* of the circle.

Circle with center *P*, or ⊙*P*

circular cone (p. 737) A solid with a circular *base* and a *vertex* that is not in the same plane as the base. The *lateral surface* consists of all segments that connect the vertex with points on the edge of the base. The *altitude*, or *height*, is the perpendicular distance between the vertex and the plane that contains the base.

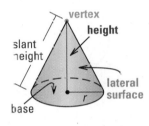

circumcenter of a triangle (p. 273) The point of concurrency of the perpendicular bisectors of a triangle.

circumference (p. 683) The distance around a circle.

circumscribed circle (p. 615) A circle with an inscribed polygon. *See also* inscribed polygon.

collinear points (p. 10) Points that lie on the same line.

common tangent (p. 596) A line or segment that is tangent to two circles. A common internal tangent intersects the segment that joins the centers of the two circles. A common external tangent does not intersect the segment that joins the centers of the two circles.

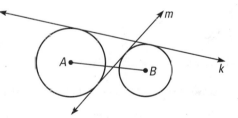

Line *m* is a common internal tangent.
Line *k* is a common external tangent.

compass (p. 34) A construction tool used to draw arcs.

complement (p. 46) The sum of the measures of an angle and its *complement* is 90°.

complementary angles (p. 46) Two angles whose measures have the sum 90°.

component form (p. 423) The form of a vector that combines the horizontal and vertical components of the vector.

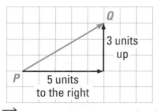

$\overrightarrow{PQ}$ with component form ⟨5, 3⟩

composition of transformations (p. 431) The result when two or more transformations are combined to produce a single transformation. An example is a glide reflection.

concave polygon (p. 323) *See* convex polygon.

concentric circles (p. 596) Circles that have a common center.

conclusion (p. 71) The "then" part of a conditional statement.

concurrent lines (p. 272) Three or more lines that intersect in the same point.

conditional statement (p. 71) A type of logical statement that has two parts, a hypothesis and a conclusion.

cone (p. 737) *See* circular cone.

congruent angles (p. 26) Angles that have the same measure.

congruent arcs (p. 604) Two arcs of the same circle or of congruent circles that have the same measure.

congruent circles (p. 595) Two circles that have the same radius.

congruent figures (p. 202) Two geometric figures that have exactly the same size and shape. When two figures are congruent, all pairs of corresponding angles and corresponding sides are congruent. The symbol for "is congruent to" is ≅.

congruent segments (p. 19) Segments that have the same length.

conjecture (p. 4) An unproven statement that is based on observations.

consecutive interior angles (p. 131) Two angles that are formed by two lines and a transversal and that lie between the two lines on the same side of the transversal. Also called *same side interior angles*. See angles 3 and 5.

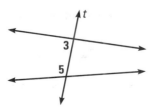

construct (p. 34) To draw using a limited set of tools, usually a compass and a straightedge.

construction (p. 34) A geometric drawing that uses a limited set of tools, usually a compass and a straightedge.

contrapositive (p. 72) The statement formed when you negate the hypothesis and conclusion of the converse of a conditional statement.

converse (p. 72) The statement formed by switching the hypothesis and conclusion of a conditional statement.

convex polygon (p. 323) A polygon such that no line containing a side of the polygon contains a point in the interior of the polygon. A polygon that is not convex is *nonconvex*, or *concave*.

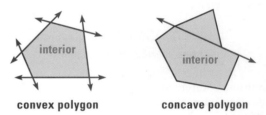

convex polygon   concave polygon

convex polyhedron (p. 720) A polyhedron such that any two points on its surface can be connected by a line segment that lies entirely inside or on the polyhedron. If this line goes outside the polyhedron, then the polyhedron is *nonconvex*, or *concave*.

coordinate (p. 17) The real number that corresponds to a point on a line.

coordinate proof (p. 243) A type of proof that involves placing geometric figures in a coordinate plane.

coplanar points (p. 10) Points that lie on the same plane.

corollary (p. 197) A statement that can be proved easily using a theorem or a definition.

corresponding angles (p. 131) Two angles that are formed by two lines and a transversal and occupy corresponding positions. See angles 1 and 5.

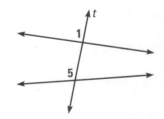

corresponding angles of congruent figures (p. 202) When two figures are congruent, the angles that are in corresponding positions and are congruent.

corresponding sides of congruent figures (p. 202) When two figures are congruent, the sides that are in corresponding positions and are congruent.

cosine (p. 558) A trigonometric ratio, abbreviated as *cos*. For right triangle *ABC*, the cosine of the acute angle *A* is

$$\cos A = \frac{\text{side adjacent to } \angle A}{\text{hypotenuse}}$$
$$= \frac{b}{c}$$

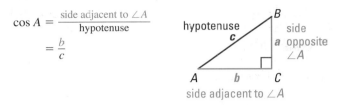

counterexample (p. 4) An example that shows a conjecture is false.

cross section (p. 720) The intersection of a plane and a solid.

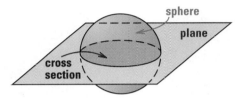

cylinder (p. 730) A solid with congruent circular bases that lie in parallel planes. The *altitude*, or *height*, of a cylinder is the perpendicular distance between its bases. The radius of the base is also called the *radius* of the cylinder.

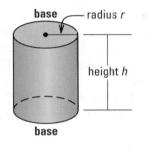

D

definition (p. 10) Uses known words to describe a new word.

diagonal of a polygon (p. 324) A segment that joins two nonconsecutive vertices of a polygon.

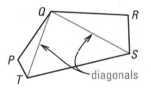

diameter of a circle (p. 595) A chord that passes through the center of the circle. The distance across a circle, through its center.

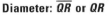

Diameter: $\overline{QR}$ or QR

diameter of a sphere (p. 759) A chord that contains the center of the sphere. The length of a chord that contains the center of the sphere.

dilation (p. 506) A type of transformation, with center *C* and scale factor *k*, that maps every point *P* in the plane to a point *P′* so that the following two properties are true. (1) If *P* is not the center point *C*, then the image point *P′* lies on $\overrightarrow{CP}$. The scale factor *k* is a positive number such that $CP' = k(CP)$, and $k \neq 1$. (2) If *P* is the center point *C*, then $P = P'$.

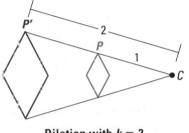

Dilation with $k = 2$

direction of a vector (p. 574) Determined by the angle that the vector makes with a horizontal line.

distance between two points on a line (p. 17) The absolute value of the difference between the coordinates of the points. The distance between *A* and *B* is written as *AB*, which is also called the *length* of $\overline{AB}$.

$$AB = |x_2 - x_1|$$

Distance Formula (p. 19) If $A(x_1, y_1)$ and $B(x_2, y_2)$ are points in a coordinate plane, then the distance between *A* and *B* is

$$AB = \sqrt{(x_2 - x_1)^2 + (y_2 - y_1)^2}.$$

distance from a point to a line (p. 266) The length of the perpendicular segment from the point to the line.

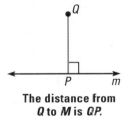

The distance from
Q to M is QP.

dodecahedron (p. 721) A polyhedron with twelve faces.

E

edge (p. 719) A line segment formed by the intersection of two faces of a polyhedron. *See also* polyhedron.

endpoints (p. 11) *See* line segment.

enlargement (p. 506) A dilation with $k > 1$.

equal vectors (p. 574) Two vectors that have the same magnitude and direction.

equiangular polygon (p. 323) A polygon with all of its interior angles congruent.

equiangular triangle (p. 194) A triangle with three congruent angles.

equidistant from two lines (p. 266) The same distance from one line as from another line.

equidistant from two points (p. 264) The same distance from one point as from another point.

equilateral polygon (p. 323) A polygon with all of its sides congruent.

equilateral triangle (p. 194) A triangle with three congruent sides.

equivalent statements (p. 72) Two statements that are both true or both false.

exterior of an angle (p. 27) All points not on the angle or in its interior. *See also* interior of an angle.

exterior of a circle (p. 596) All points of the plane that are outside a circle.

exterior angles of a triangle (p. 196) When the sides of a triangle are extended, the angles that are adjacent to the interior angles.

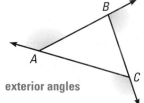

exterior angles

external segment (p. 630) The part of a secant segment that is not inside the circle.

extremes of a proportion (p. 459) The first and last terms of a proportion. The extremes of $\frac{a}{b} = \frac{c}{d}$ are a and d.

F

face (p. 719) *See* polyhedron.

flow proof (pp. 135, 136) A type of proof that uses arrows to show the flow of a logical argument. Statements are connected by arrows to show how each statement comes from the ones before it, and each reason is written below the statement it justifies.

frieze pattern (p. 437) A pattern that extends to the left and right in such a way that the pattern can be mapped onto itself by a horizontal translation. Also called *border pattern*.

G

geometric mean (p. 466) For two positive numbers a and b, the positive number x such that $\frac{a}{x} = \frac{x}{b}$, or $x = \sqrt{a \cdot b}$.

geometric probability (p. 699) A probability that involves a geometric measure such as length or area.

glide reflection (p. 430) A transformation in which every point P is mapped onto a point P'' by the following two steps. (1) A translation maps P onto P'. (2) A reflection in a line k parallel to the direction of the translation maps P' onto P''.

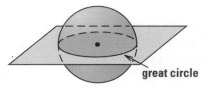

great circle (p. 760) The intersection of a sphere and a plane that contains the center of the sphere.

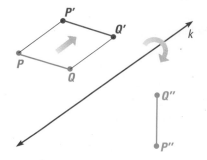

great circle

H

hemisphere (p. 760) Half of a sphere, formed when a great circle separates a sphere into two congruent halves.

hypotenuse (p. 195) In a right triangle, the side opposite the right angle. *See also* legs of a right triangle.

hypothesis (p. 71) The "if" part of a conditional statement.

I

icosahedron (p. 721) A polyhedron with twenty faces.

if-then form (p. 71) The form of a conditional statement that uses the words "if" and "then." The "if" part contains the hypothesis and the "then" part contains the conclusion.

image (p. 396) The new figure that results from the transformation of a figure in a plane. *See also* preimage.

incenter of a triangle (p. 274) The point of concurrency of the angle bisectors of a triangle.

indirect proof (p. 302) A proof in which you prove that a statement is true by first assuming that its opposite is true. If this assumption leads to an impossibility, then you have proved that the original statement is true.

inductive reasoning (p. 4) A process that includes looking for patterns and making conjectures.

initial point of a ray (p. 11) *See* ray.

initial point of a vector (p. 423) The starting point of a vector. *See also* vector.

inscribed angle (p. 613) An angle whose vertex is on a circle and whose sides contain chords of the circle.

inscribed polygon (p. 615) A polygon whose vertices all lie on a circle.

intercepted arc (p. 613) The arc that lies in the interior of an inscribed angle and has endpoints on the angle. *See also* inscribed angle.

interior of a circle (p. 596) All points of the plane that are inside a circle.

interior of an angle (p. 27) All points between the points that lie on each side of the angle.

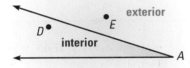

interior angles of a triangle (p. 196) When the sides of a triangle are extended, the three original angles of the triangle.

intersect (p. 12) To have one or more points in common.

intersection (p. 12) The set of points that two or more geometric figures have in common.

inverse (p. 72) The statement formed when you negate the hypothesis and conclusion of a conditional statement.

isometry (p. 397) A transformation that preserves lengths. Also called *rigid transformation*.

isosceles trapezoid (p. 356) A trapezoid with congruent legs.

isosceles triangle (p. 194) A triangle with at least two congruent sides.

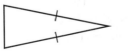

K ....

kite (p. 353) A quadrilateral that has two pairs of consecutive congruent sides, but in which opposite sides are not congruent.

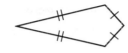

L ....

lateral area of a cylinder (p. 730) The area of the curved surface of a cylinder.

lateral area of a polyhedron (p. 728) The sum of the areas of the lateral faces of a polyhedron.

lateral faces of a prism (p. 728) *See* prism.

lateral surface of a cone (p. 737) *See* circular cone.

Law of Detachment (p. 89) If $p \rightarrow q$ is a true conditional statement and p is true, then q is true.

Law of Syllogism (pp. 89, 90) If $p \rightarrow q$ and $q \rightarrow r$ are true conditional statements, then $p \rightarrow r$ is true.

legs of an isosceles triangle (p. 195) The two congruent sides of an isosceles triangle that has only two congruent sides. *See also* base of an isosceles triangle.

legs of a right triangle (p. 195) In a right triangle, the sides that form the right angle.

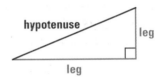

legs of a trapezoid (p. 356) *See* trapezoid.

length of a segment (p. 17) The distance between the endpoints of a segment. *See also* distance between two points on a line.

line (pp. 10, 11) A line extends in one dimension. It is usually represented by a straight line with two arrowheads to indicate that the line extends without end in two directions. In this book, lines are always straight lines. *See also* undefined term.

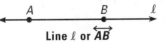

Line ℓ or $\overleftrightarrow{AB}$

linear pair (p. 44) Two adjacent angles whose noncommon sides are opposite rays.

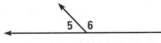

$\angle 5$ and $\angle 6$ are a linear pair.

line of reflection (p. 404) *See* reflection.

line of symmetry (p. 406) A line that a figure in the plane has if the figure can be mapped onto itself by a reflection in the line.

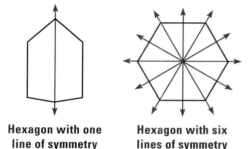

Hexagon with one line of symmetry   **Hexagon with six lines of symmetry**

line perpendicular to a plane (p. 79) A line that intersects the plane in a point and is perpendicular to every line in the plane that intersects it.

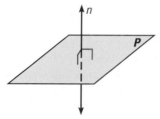

line segment (p. 11) Part of a line that consists of two points, called *endpoints*, and all points on the line that are between the endpoints. Also called *segment*.

$\overline{AB}$ **with endpoints A and B**

locus (p. 642) The set of all points that satisfy a given condition or a set of given conditions. Plural is *loci*.

logical argument (p. 89) An argument based on deductive reasoning, which uses facts, definitions, and accepted properties in a logical order.

M

magnitude of a vector (p. 573) The distance from the initial point to the terminal point of a vector. The magnitude of $\overrightarrow{AB}$ is the distance from A to B and is written $\left| \overrightarrow{AB} \right|$.

major arc (p. 603) Part of a circle that measures between 180° and 360°. *See also* minor arc.

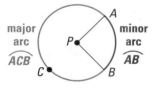

means of a proportion (p. 459) The middle terms of a proportion. The means of $\frac{a}{b} = \frac{c}{d}$ are b and c.

measure of an angle (p. 27) Consider a point A on one side of $\overleftrightarrow{OB}$. The rays of the form $\overrightarrow{OA}$ can be matched one to one with the real numbers from 0 to 180. The measure of $\angle AOB$ is equal to the absolute value of the difference between the real numbers for $\overrightarrow{OA}$ and $\overrightarrow{OB}$.

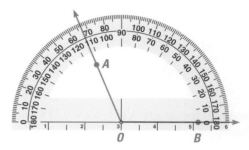

measure of a major arc (p. 603) The difference between 360° and the measure of its associated minor arc.

measure of a minor arc (p. 603) The measure of its central angle.

median of a triangle (p. 279) A segment whose endpoints are a vertex of the triangle and the midpoint of the opposite side.

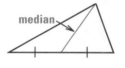

midpoint (p. 34) The point that divides, or bisects, a segment into two congruent segments.

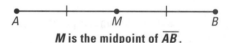

M is the midpoint of $\overline{AB}$.

Midpoint Formula (p. 35) If $A(x_1, y_1)$ and $B(x_2, y_2)$ are points in a coordinate plane, then the midpoint of $\overline{AB}$ has coordinates $\left(\dfrac{x_1 + x_2}{2}, \dfrac{y_1 + y_2}{2} \right)$.

midsegment of a trapezoid (p. 357) A segment that connects the midpoints of the legs of a trapezoid.

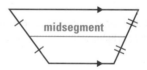

midsegment of a triangle (p. 287) A segment that connects the midpoints of two sides of a triangle.

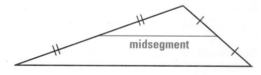

minor arc (p. 603) Part of a circle that measures less than 180°. *See also* major arc.

N

negation (pp. 72, 88) The negative of a statement. The negation symbol is ~.

net (p. 729) A two-dimensional representation of all the faces of a polyhedron.

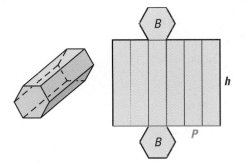

nonconvex polygon (p. 323) *See* convex polygon.

O

oblique prism (p. 728) A prism whose lateral edges are not perpendicular to the bases. The length of the oblique lateral edges is the *slant height* of the prism.

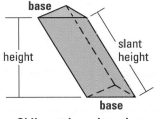

Oblique triangular prism

obtuse angle (p. 28) An angle with measure between 90° and 180°.

obtuse triangle (p. 194) A triangle with one obtuse angle.

octahedron (p. 721) A polyhedron with eight faces.

opposite rays (p. 11) If *C* is between *A* and *B*, then $\overrightarrow{CA}$ and $\overrightarrow{CB}$ are opposite rays.

orthocenter of a triangle (p. 281) The point of concurrency of the lines containing the altitudes of a triangle.

P

paragraph proof (p. 102) A type of proof written in paragraph form.

parallel lines (p. 129) Two lines that are coplanar and do not intersect. The symbol for "is parallel to" is ∥.

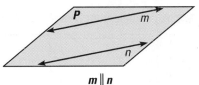

m ∥ n

parallelogram (p. 330) A quadrilateral with both pairs of opposite sides parallel. The parallelogram symbol is ▱.

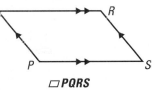

▱PQRS

parallel planes (p. 129) Two planes that do not intersect.

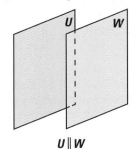

U ∥ W

parallel vectors (p. 574) Two vectors that have the same or opposite directions.

perpendicular bisector (p. 264) A segment, ray, line, or plane that is perpendicular to a segment at its midpoint.

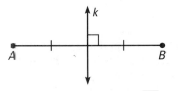

Line *k* is a ⊥ bisector of $\overline{AB}$.

perpendicular bisector of a triangle (p. 272) A line, ray, or segment that is perpendicular to a side of a triangle at the midpoint of the side.

perpendicular lines (p. 79) Two lines that intersect to form a right angle. The symbol for "is perpendicular to" is ⊥.

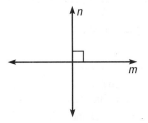

plane (p. 10) A plane extends in two dimensions. It is usually represented by a shape that looks like a tabletop or wall. You must imagine that the plane extends without end, even though the drawing of a plane appears to have edges. *See also* undefined term.

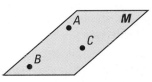

Plane *M* or plane *ABC*

Platonic solids (p. 721) Five regular polyhedra, named after the Greek mathematician and philosopher Plato, including a regular tetrahedron, a cube, a regular octahedron, a regular dodecahedron, and a regular icosahedron.

point (p. 10) A point has no dimension. It is usually represented by a small dot. *See also* undefined term.

A.

point of concurrency (p. 272) The point of intersection of concurrent lines.

point of tangency (p. 597) *See* tangent line.

polygon (p. 322) A plane figure that meets the following two conditions. (1) It is formed by three or more segments called sides, such that no two sides with a common endpoint are collinear. (2) Each side intersects exactly two other sides, one at each endpoint. *See also* vertex of a polygon.

polyhedron (p. 719) A solid that is bounded by polygons, called *faces*, that enclose a single region of space. Plural is *polyhedra*, or *polyhedrons*.

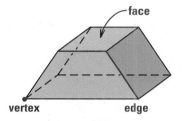

postulates (p. 17) Rules that are accepted without proof. Also called *axioms*.

preimage (p. 396) The original figure in the transformation of a figure in a plane. *See also* image.

prism (p. 728) A polyhedron with two congruent faces, called *bases*, that lie in parallel planes. The other faces, called *lateral faces*, are parallelograms formed by connecting the corresponding vertices of the bases. The segments connecting the vertices are *lateral edges*. The *altitude*, or *height*, of a prism is the perpendicular distance between its bases.

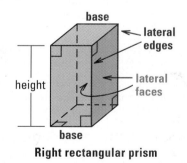

Right rectangular prism

probability (p. 699) A ratio from 0 to 1 that represents the likelihood an event will occur.

proportion (p. 459) An equation that equates two ratios.
Example: $\frac{a}{b} = \frac{c}{d}$

pyramid (p. 735) A polyhedron in which the base is a polygon and the *lateral faces* are triangles with a common *vertex*. The intersection of two lateral faces is a *lateral edge*. The intersection of the base and a lateral face is a *base edge*. The *altitude*, or *height*, is the perpendicular distance between the base and the vertex.

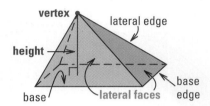

Pythagorean triple (p. 536) A set of three positive integers a, b, and c that satisfy the equation $c^2 = a^2 + b^2$.

R.

radius of a circle (p. 595) The distance from the center of a circle to a point on the circle. A segment whose endpoints are the center of the circle and a point on the circle. Plural is *radii*.

Radius: *PQ* or $\overline{PQ}$

radius of a polygon (p. 670) The radius of its circumscribed circle.

radius of a sphere (p. 759) A segment from the center of a sphere to a point on the sphere. The length of a segment from the center of a sphere to a point on the sphere.

ratio of *a* to *b* (p. 457) The quotient $\frac{a}{b}$ if a and b are two quantities that are measured in the same units. Can also be written as $a:b$.

ray (p. 11) Part of a line that consists of a point, called an *initial point*, and all points on the line that extend in one direction.

$\overrightarrow{AB}$ with initial point *A*

rectangle (p. 347) A parallelogram with four right angles.

reduction (p. 506) A dilation with $0 < k < 1$.

reflection (p. 404) A type of transformation that uses a line that acts like a mirror, called the *line of reflection*, with an image reflected in the line.

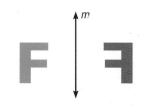

Line *m* is a line of reflection.

regular polygon (p. 323) A polygon that is equilateral and equiangular.

regular polyhedron (p. 720) A polyhedron whose faces are all congruent regular polygons.

regular pyramid (p. 735) A pyramid such that the base is a regular polygon and the segment from the vertex to the center of the base is perpendicular to the base. In a regular pyramid, the lateral faces all have the same slant height.

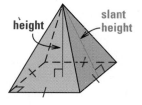

rhombus (p. 347) A parallelogram with four congruent sides.

right angle (p. 28) An angle with measure equal to 90°.

right cone (p. 737) A cone with a vertex that lies directly above the center of the base. The *slant height* of a right cone is the distance between the vertex and a point on the edge of the base. *See also* circular cone.

right cylinder (p. 730) A cylinder such that the segment joining the centers of the bases is perpendicular to the bases.

right prism (p. 728) A prism whose lateral edges are perpendicular to both bases. *See also* prism.

right triangle (p. 194) A triangle with one right angle.

rotation (p. 412) A type of transformation in which a figure is turned about a fixed point, called the *center of rotation*.

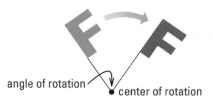

angle of rotation — center of rotation

rotational symmetry (p. 415) A figure in the plane has *rotational symmetry* if the figure can be mapped onto itself by a rotation of 180° or less.

same side interior angles (p. 131) *See* consecutive interior angles.

scale factor (p. 474) The ratio of the lengths of two corresponding sides of two similar polygons.

scalene triangle (p. 194) A triangle with no congruent sides.

secant line (p. 595) A line that intersects a circle in two points.

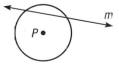

Line *m* is a secant.

secant segment (p. 630) A segment that intersects a circle in two points, with one point as an endpoint of the segment.

sector of a circle (p. 692) The region bounded by two radii of a circle and their intercepted arc.

Sector *APB*

segment (p. 11) *See* line segment.

segment bisector (p. 34) A segment, ray, line, or plane that intersects a segment at its midpoint.

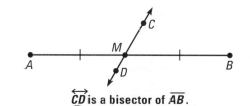

$\overleftrightarrow{CD}$ **is a bisector of** $\overline{AB}$.

semicircle (p. 603) An arc whose endpoints are the endpoints of a diameter of the circle.

side opposite a vertex of a triangle (p. 195) A side of a triangle that does not contain the given vertex.

sides of an angle (p. 26) *See* angle.

similar polygons (p. 473) Two polygons such that their corresponding angles are congruent and the lengths of corresponding sides are proportional. The symbol for "is similar to" is $\sim$.

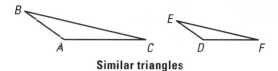

Similar triangles

similar solids (p. 766) Two solids with equal ratios of corresponding linear measures, such as heights or radii.

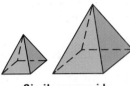

Similar pyramids

sine (p. 558) A trigonometric ratio, abbreviated as *sin*. For right triangle *ABC*, the sine of the acute angle *A* is

$$\sin A = \frac{\text{side opposite } \angle A}{\text{hypotenuse}}$$
$$= \frac{a}{c}$$

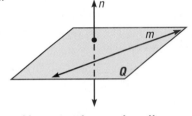

skew lines (p. 129) Two lines that do not intersect and are not coplanar.

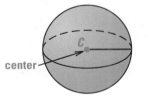

Lines *m* and *n* are skew lines.

solve a right triangle (p. 567) Determine the measurements of all sides and angles of a right triangle.

special right triangles (pp. 550, 551) Right triangles whose angle measures are 45°-45°-90° or 30°-60°-90°.

sphere (p. 759) The locus of points in space that are a given distance from a point, called the *center* of the sphere.

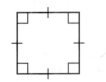

center

square (p. 347) A parallelogram with four congruent sides and four right angles.

standard equation of a circle (p. 636) A circle with radius *r* and center (h, k) has this standard equation:

$$(x - h)^2 + (y - k)^2 = r^2.$$

straight angle (p. 28) An angle with measure equal to 180°.

straightedge (p. 34) A construction tool used to draw segments. A ruler without marks.

sum of two vectors (p. 575) The sum of $\vec{u} = \langle a_1, b_1 \rangle$ and $\vec{v} = \langle a_2, b_2 \rangle$ is $\vec{u} + \vec{v} = \langle a_1 + a_2, b_1 + b_2 \rangle$.

supplement (p. 46) The sum of the measures of an angle and its supplement is 180°.

supplementary angles (p. 46) Two angles whose measures have the sum 180°.

surface area of a cylinder (p. 730) The sum of the lateral area of the cylinder and the areas of the two bases.

surface area of a polyhedron (p. 728) The sum of the areas of its faces.

T

tangent (p. 558) A trigonometric ratio, abbreviated as *tan*. For right triangle *ABC*, the tangent of the acute angle *A* is

$$\tan A = \frac{\text{side opposite } \angle A}{\text{side adjacent to } \angle A}$$
$$= \frac{a}{b}$$

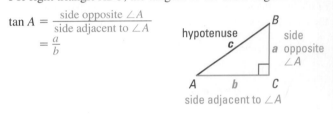

tangent circles (p. 596) Circles that intersect in one point.

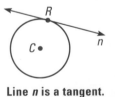

Internally tangent   Externally tangent

tangent line (p. 595) A line that intersects a circle in exactly one point, called the *point of tangency*.

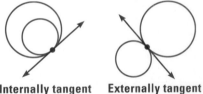

**Line *n* is a tangent.
R is the point of tangency.**

tangent segment (p. 630) A segment that is tangent to a circle at an endpoint.

terminal point of a vector (p. 423) The ending point of a vector. *See also* vector.

tetrahedron (p. 721) A polyhedron with four faces.

theorem (p. 102) A true statement that follows as a result of other true statements.

transformation (p. 396) The operation that maps, or moves, a preimage onto an image. Three basic transformations are reflections, rotations, and translations.

translation (p. 421) A type of transformation that maps every two points P and Q in the plane to points P' and Q', so that the following two properties are true. (1) $PP' = QQ'$. (2) $\overline{PP'} \parallel \overline{QQ'}$ or $\overline{PP'}$ and $\overline{QQ'}$ are collinear.

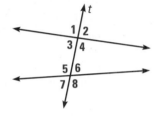

transversal (p. 131) A line that intersects two or more coplanar lines at different points.

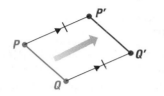

Line t is a transversal.

trapezoid (p. 356) A quadrilateral with exactly one pair of parallel sides, called *bases*. The nonparallel sides are *legs*.

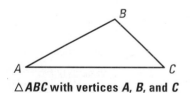

triangle (p. 194) A figure formed by three segments joining three noncollinear points, called *vertices*. The triangle symbol is $\triangle$.

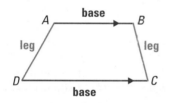

$\triangle ABC$ with vertices A, B, and C

trigonometric ratio (p. 558) A ratio of the lengths of two sides of a right triangle. *See also* sine, cosine, *and* tangent.

two-column proof (p. 102) A type of proof written as numbered statements and reasons that show the logical order of an argument.

U

undefined term (p. 10) A word, such as *point*, *line*, or *plane*, that is not formally defined, although there is general agreement about what the word means.

V

vector (p. 423) A quantity that has both direction and magnitude, and is represented by an arrow drawn between two points.

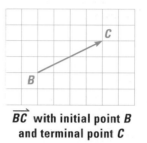

$\overrightarrow{BC}$ with initial point B and terminal point C

vertex of an angle (p. 26) *See* angle.

vertex of a polygon (p. 322) Each endpoint of a side of a polygon. Plural is *vertices*.

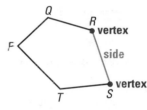

vertex of a polyhedron (p. 719) A point where three or more edges of a polyhedron meet. *See also* polyhedron.

vertex of a triangle (p. 195) Each of the three points joining the sides of a triangle. Plural is *vertices*. *See also* triangle.

vertex angle of an isosceles triangle (p. 236) The angle opposite the base of an isosceles triangle. *See also* base of an isosceles triangle.

vertical angles (p. 44) Two angles whose sides form two pairs of opposite rays.

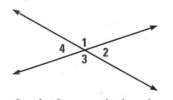

$\angle 1$ and $\angle 3$ are vertical angles.
$\angle 2$ and $\angle 4$ are vertical angles.

volume of a solid (p. 743) The number of cubic units contained in the interior of a solid.

Index

544, 548, 550–556
vertex of, 26
vertical, 44–45, 47–50, 62, 112
viewing, 614
Angle-side-angle (ASA)
    congruence, 220–227
postulate, 220
Apollonius, 602
Apothem, 670
Applications, *See also* Connections;
    Math and History;
    Multicultural connections
advertising, 77
amusement park rides, 495, 579
animals, 93, 647, 653, 740, 756
aquariums, 571, 748
archaeology, 154, 442
architecture, 210, 214, 240, 393,
    398, 435, 439, 442, 555, 564,
    733, 764, 771
art, 208, 209, 241, 289, 378, 401,
    406, 409, 418, 435, 440, 441,
    442, 455, 460, 474, 496, 539,
    740
astronomy, 116, 222, 478, 763
automobiles, 639, 688, 754
auto racing, 98, 100
aviation, 1, 32, 269, 547, 575,
    589
ball bearings, 761, 764
baseball/softball, 40, 49, 463, 469,
    539, 664, 760, 762
bearings, 1, 32, 225
bicycles and bicycling, 57, 343,
    688
biology, 8, 83, 360, 516
botany, 144, 277, 327, 390, 407
business, 273, 503
calendars, 5
chemistry, 8, 409, 722, 762
communication, 639
computers, 174, 427
construction, 54, 55, 56, 58, 106,
    115, 121, 141, 155, 158, 162,
    164, 187, 191, 200, 227, 232,
    234, 267, 292, 300, 336, 350,
    377, 378, 385, 387, 398, 401,
    427, 439, 470, 501, 525, 545,
    555, 571, 619, 633, 666, 674,
    678, 697, 745, 748, 756, 777
consumer economics, 678, 679,
    680, 682
containers, 339, 540, 742, 748
crop circles, 207

currency exchange, 469
design, 37, 54, 299, 313, 406, 415,
    427, 470, 474, 495, 532, 545,
    564, 589, 614, 633, 666, 697,
    733, 740, 772
earth science, 57, 478, 623, 644,
    646, 688, 757
electronics, 140
employment, 100, 408, 701
engineering, 170
entertainment, 133, 477, 508, 563,
    637
escalators, 561, 562
fireworks, 593, 625
fitness, 97
food and food preparation, 335,
    357, 361, 390, 695, 724, 733,
    764, 771
football, 162
fractals, 291
furniture, 781
games, 31, 40, 95, 432, 435, 577,
    700, 702, 703, 704, 705, 781
geography, 31
geology, 481, 659, 725
golf, 600
hiking, 308, 571
history, 25, 145, 169, 486, 547,
    697, 756
horticulture, 50, 57, 72
hot-air balloon, 566
ice hockey, 270, 486
jewelry, 555, 539
knots, 420
language arts, 77
manufacturing, 156, 521
map reading, 13, 20, 23, 290, 299,
    504, 547, 601
mechanics, 170
medicine, 283
miniature golf, 25
music, 84, 444, 733
navigation, 424, 427, 574, 577,
    634, 696
needlepoint, 176
optical illusion, 106, 163
orienteering, 225
packaging, 121, 733, 777
paper sizes, 466
parades, 565
pendulums, 671
photography, 187, 511, 513, 589,
    678, 679
physics, 178, 241

planetariums, 717
polar coordinates, 611
population, 280, 516
quilting, 226
railroads, 22, 165
road signs, 326, 672
robotics, 69, 77, 93
rock climbing, 491, 532
rowing, 157
safety, 539
sailing, 127, 152, 754
scale drawing/scale model, 455,
    467, 469, 490, 516, 770
science, 148, 174
scissors lift, 319, 336
sculpture, 177, 208
sewing, 363, 401, 435
ships, 697, 703, 754
skiing, 563, 609
skydiving, 578
soccer, 53, 261, 390, 648, 722
social studies, 149
space science, 123, 462, 569
structural support, 215, 354, 389,
    537, 538
structures, 49, 56, 92, 133, 169,
    200, 249, 344, 367, 385, 387,
    486, 494, 525, 540, 553, 571,
    631, 632, 635, 673, 680, 696,
    722, 740, 758, 768, 781
surveying, 225, 254, 298, 405, 563
telescopes, 674
temperature, 99
time, 700, 703, 711
time zones, 609
tools, 606, 619
toys, 57, 694
track and field, 187, 223, 685
transportation, 530, 700, 703
travel, 304, 547, 589, 685
United States flag, 468
vision, 27, 487
water skiing, 711
weather, 84, 768
weaving, 195
woodworking, 693
Approximation *See* Estimation;
    Prediction
Arc addition postulate, 604
Archimedes, 682
Arc length corollary, 683
Arc(s)
adjacent, 604
of a circle, 603–611, 650

congruent, 604, 605
intercepted, 613
length of, 683–689, 709
major, 603
measures of, 603–611, 621–627
midpoint of, 605
minor, 603
naming, 603
semicircle, 603, 684

Area, *See also* Formulas; Lateral area; Surface area
of a circle, 51, 52, 55, 56, 57, 62, 691–698, 710
formulas, 51
history of finding, 346
of an irregular figure, 54–57, 693–698
of a kite, 374–380, 384
lateral, 735
of a parallelogram, 371–373, 375–380, 384
perimeter and, 677–681
probability and, 699–706, 710
of a quadrilateral, 371–380
of a rectangle, 51, 53, 55–57
of a regular polygon, 669–675, 708
of a rhombus, 374–380
of a sector, 692–698, 710
of similar figures, 676–682, 709
of a square, 51, 54–57, 372, 376–379
of a trapezoid, 371, 374–380, 384
of a triangle, 51, 52, 54, 57, 371–373, 376, 378, 380, 537, 539, 669

Area addition postulate, 372
Area of a circle theorem, 691
Area congruence postulate, 372
Area of an equilateral triangle theorem, 669
Area of a kite theorem, 374
Area of a parallelogram theorem, 372
Area of a rectangle theorem, 372
Area of a regular polygon theorem, 670
Area of a rhombus theorem, 374
Area of a sector theorem, 692
Area of a square postulate, 372
Areas of similar polygons theorem, 677
Area of a trapezoid theorem, 374, 379
Area of a triangle theorem, 372

Argument, logical, 89–94
Armstrong, Neil, 462
Aspect ratio, 477
Assessment, *See also* Projects; Reviews
Chapter Standardized Test, 64–65, 122–123, 184–185, 256–257, 314–315, 386–387, 450–451, 520–521, 586–587, 654–655, 712–713, 778–779
Chapter Test, 63, 121, 183, 255, 313, 385, 449, 519, 585, 653, 711, 777
Quiz, 25, 42, 58, 95, 116, 149, 164, 178, 210, 227, 250, 285, 308, 346, 363, 380, 420, 444, 479, 496, 513, 549, 566, 580, 620, 635, 648, 682, 705, 742, 758, 772
Auxiliary line, 196
Axiom, definition of, 17, *See also* Postulate(s)

B

Balancing point, 316–317
Base angles
of an isosceles triangle, 236
of a trapezoid, 356
Base angles theorem, 236–237
converse of, 236, 240
corollary to, 237, 240
Base edge, of a pyramid, 735
Base(s)
of a cone, 737
of a cylinder, 730
of an exponential expression, 797
of a prism, 728
of a pyramid, 735
of a trapezoid, 356
of a triangle, 195, 236
Bearing(s), 32, 225
definition, 1
Between, 11, 18, 67
Bhaskara, 557
Biconditional statement, 80–85, 118
symbolic notation and, 87–94
Binomial(s)
multiplying, 798
squaring, 798
Bisector
angle, 33, 36–41, 62, 266–270, 310
construction, 36, 234, 286

of a triangle, 274–278, 286, 310, 499
perpendicular, 263–265, 268–271, 310
of a chord, 605
construction, 264
of a triangle, 272–273, 275–278, 310
segment, 33–35, 38–41, 62
Bolyai, János, 715
Border pattern, 437–443
Brisson, Harriet, 208

C

Calatrava, Santiago, 49
Calculator, *See also* Geometry Software Activities; Graphing calculator; Student Help
for approximating pi, 684
for approximating trigonometric ratios, 560
exercises, 7, 562, 570
finding angles of right triangles with, 567, 568
finding cube root with, 745
finding the direction of a vector, 574
Careers
advertising copywriter, 77
aerial photographer, 482
air traffic controller, 304
architect, 733
architectural historian, 435
architectural renderer, 512
astronaut, 569
astronomer, 220, 674
botanist, 144
cake designer, 361
cardiology technician, 283
carpenter, 106
chemist, 409
civil engineer, 170
construction manager, 234
emergency medical technician (EMT), 609
employment counselor, 701
engineering technician, 267
forester, 561
furniture designer, 333
gemologist, 369
geoscientist, 644
graphic artist, 174
hydrologist, 200
laboratory technologist, 8

Detachment, Law of, 89, 92–94
Diagonal(s)
  of a kite, 358, 362
  of a parallelogram, 330, 338
    vector sums and, 575
  of a polygon, 324, 661
  of special parallelograms, 349
Diameter
  of a circle, 595
  of a sphere, 759
Dilation, 506–514, 518
  in a coordinate plane, 507, 509,
    510
  percent increase, 508
  properties of, 506, 514
Dimensions
  effect of changing on area and
    perimeter, 676–682, 709
  effect of changing on volume,
    766–772
Direction, of a vector, 574, 576–579,
  584
Discrete mathematics, *See also*
    Algorithm; Logical reasoning
  inductive reasoning, 4–9
  Platonic solids, 721–723, 725
  probability, 699–704, 706, 710
  tiling, 452–453
  tree diagram, 443
Distance
  between two points, 17–24, 61
  equidistance, 264–266
  Euclidean geometry and, 66–67
  from a point to a line, 266
  minimum, 405, 408
  taxicab geometry and, 66–67
  three-dimensional, 24
Distance formula, 19–24, 61,
    244–247, 258, 284, 426
  centroid of a triangle and, 280
  equation of a circle and, 636
  magnitude of a vector and, 573
  midsegments and, 287
  perimeter and, 52
  three-dimensional, 24
Distributive property, 96–97, 391,
  787
  for finding the square of a
    binomial, 798
  multiplying binomials with, 798
**Division, of positive and negative
  numbers,** 785
Division property of equality,
  96–97, 99–101

Dodecacon, 322
Dodecahedron, 721
Dolittle, Beverly, 460
Drawing diagrams, *See also*
    Construction; Geometry
    software
  examples, 11, 12, 28, 54, 74, 197,
    243–244, 281, 297, 304, 366,
    405, 422, 423, 430, 431, 439,
    458, 528, 605, 642, 652, 692,
    728
  exercises, 8, 14, 15, 16, 39, 42, 47,
    57, 75, 76, 276, 283, 284, 299,
    308, 326, 343, 407, 408, 426,
    441–443, 446, 447, 511, 539,
    548, 566, 571, 578, 579, 599,
    600, 602, 608, 611, 632, 634,
    635, 655, 725, 726, 777
  graphing circles, 637–640
  investigations, 43, 243, 403, 411,
    429, 527, 567, 661, 676
  isometric drawing, 188–189
  locus, 642–648, 652
  orthographic projection, 188–189
  perspective drawing, 15, 512
  problem-solving strategy, 54, 664,
    694
  scale drawing, 490
  solids, 720, 728
  technical drawing, 188–189
  to solve logic puzzles, 86
Drawing program *See* Geometry
    software

E

Edge(s)
  Euler's Theorem and, 721–723,
    725, 774
  lateral, 728, 735
  of a polyhedron, 719
  of a prism, 728
  of a pyramid, 735
Einthoven's Triangle, 283
Elevation, angle of, 553, 561, 563,
  564, 566
Elliot, William, 100
Endpoint(s)
  of a line segment, 11
  of a ray, 11
Enlargement, 506–514
Enrichment *See* Challenge;
    Extension
Equality, properties of, 96–97
Equal vectors, 574

Equation(s), *See also* Formulas
  absolute value, 259
  of a circle, 636–640, 652
    standard, 636, 652
  equivalent, 789
  in function form, 793
  of a line, 125, 167, 795
  linear, 789–790
    slope-intercept form of, 167, 794
    systems of, 796
    writing, 125, 167, 795
  literal, 656
  of parallel lines, 167–171
  of perpendicular lines, 174,
    176–177
  quadratic, 523, 800–801
  with variables on both sides, 258
Equiangular polygon, 323
Equiangular triangle, 194, 237, 252
Equidistance, 264–266
Equilateral polygon, 323
Equilateral triangle, 194, 252
  area of, 669
  properties of, 237, 239–242, 254,
    284
Equivalent statements, 72
Eratosthenes, 145, 164
Error analysis, 82, 104, 138, 162,
    205, 216, 276, 360, 425, 440,
    461, 509, 562, 564, 762
Escher, M.C., 418
Estimation
  angle measure, 31, 261
  using area, 378
  using the distance formula, 20, 22
  of Earth's circumference, 145, 164
  using geometric probability,
    700–704
  using indirect measurement, 491,
    494, 530, 532
  of minimum distance, 408
  using properties of parallel lines,
    145
  using proportion, 460, 462, 463,
    470, 472
  using the Pythagorean Theorem,
    540
  using right triangles, 553
  using the segment addition
    postulate, 18
  using segments of secants and
    tangents, 631, 632
  using similar triangles, 486
  using surface area, 760, 762–764

M

nonrigid, 506–514
order and, 429, 430–431
reflection, 395–411, 446
rigid, 396–402, 446
rotation, 395–402, 412–419, 447
translation, 395–402, 421–429, 447
in space, 398, 409, 427, 432, 435, 749

Transitive property
of angle congruence, 109–115
of congruent triangles, 205
of segment congruence, 102, 105
used in algebra, 96–97
used in geometry, 98

Translation, 395–402, 421–429, 447
compositions and, 429–436
coordinate notation for, 422
in the coordinate plane, 422–428
frieze patterns and, 437–443
theorems about, 421, 426
using vectors, 423–428, 447

Translation theorem, 421

Transversal(s), 131–134, 181
perpendicular, 143, 148
proportionality and, 499–505
theorems about, 150, 499

Trapezoid
area of, 371, 374–379, 384
isosceles, 356–357, 359–363
midsegment of, 357, 359–362
properties of, 356–357, 359–363, 383
theorems about, 356, 357, 361, 362, 363

Tree diagram, 364, 443

Triangle inequality, 295–301

Triangle inequality theorem, 297, 300

Triangle proportionality converse, 498

Triangle proportionality theorem, 498, 504

Triangle(s), *See also* Right triangle
acute, 194, 252
altitudes of, 281–284, 311
right, 527–534
angle bisectors of, 274–278, 310
construction, 286
angles of, 193–201, 295–301
area of, 51, 52, 54, 55–57, 371–373, 376, 378, 384, 537, 539, 669
balancing point of, 316–317

centroid of, 279–280, 282–283, 311
circumcenter of, 273
classifying, 194–195, 198–199, 252, 544, 545, 546
comparing measurements of, 295–301
congruent, 202–235, 238–241, 253–254
coordinate proof and, 243–250, 254
definition of, 194
equiangular, 194, 237, 252
equilateral, 194, 237, 239–242, 252, 254, 284
area of, 669, 708
exterior angles of, 193, 196–201, 296, 312
interior angles of, 193, 196–201
legs of, 195
medians of, 279–280, 282–284, 311
construction, 286
midsegments of, 287–293
in non-Euclidean geometry, 715
obtuse, 194, 252
orthocenters of, 281–284, 311
perimeter of, 51, 52, 55–57
perpendicular bisectors of, 272–273, 275–278, 310
properties of isosceles, equilateral, and right, 236–242
proportionality and, 497–505
scalene, 194, 252
similar, 480–505, 517–518
right, 527–534
slope, 794
sum of the measures of the angles of, 193
theorems about, 196–197, 203, 205, 220, 236, 295, 296, 297, 372, 498–499, 504, 544, 548
vertices of, 195

Triangle sum theorem, 196, 201
corollary to, 197, 200

Trigonometric functions, *See* Trigonometric ratio(s)

Trigonometric identity, 560

Trigonometric ratio(s), 558–572, 583–584
angle of elevation and, 553, 561, 563, 564, 566
for 45°- 45°- 90° right triangles, 559

for indirect measurement, 561–566
for solving right triangles, 567–572
for 30°- 60°- 90° right triangles, 560
vectors and, 574, 577–579

Trigonometry, 558

Tubman, Harriet, 169

Two-column proof, 102–107, 109–115, 136, 138, 140

U

Undefined terms, 10

Unit analysis, 53

Unit cube, 743

Unproven conjecture, 5

Using algebra
examples, 19, 35, 37, 45, 46, 80, 96, 145, 151, 166, 167, 173, 197, 203, 215, 237, 244, 289, 324, 331, 358, 373, 458, 459, 466, 475, 481, 500, 598, 605, 615, 630, 631, 662, 663, 745
exercises, 8, 22, 30, 32, 39, 40, 48, 49, 50, 58, 77, 83, 92, 105, 114, 116, 139, 147, 153, 161, 170, 171, 176, 199, 200, 201, 207, 218, 225, 239, 240, 250, 271, 278, 283, 284, 290, 291, 293, 298, 299, 301, 306, 308, 327, 328, 334, 337, 343, 345, 352, 360, 370, 377, 380, 400, 409, 418, 428, 436, 464, 477, 484, 485, 503, 532, 541, 546, 549, 554, 555, 580, 601, 608, 617, 624, 625, 627, 633, 640, 646, 667, 687, 688, 689, 696, 703, 704, 733, 740, 747, 756, 764, 777

V

Vanishing point, in perspective drawing, 15, 512

Variable expression, 786

Variable(s)
on both sides of an equation, 258
as coordinates, 245, 248

Vector components, 423

Vector(s)
adding, 575, 576, 578, 579, 584
component form of, 423
direction of, 574, 576–579, 584
equal, 574
initial point of, 423
magnitude of, 573, 576–579, 584

Credits

Bob Daemmrich/The Image Works (br);   **421** D. Long/Visuals Unlimited;   **427** Alain Morvan/Liaison Agency;   **430** Angelo Cavalli/Superstock;   **435** Paula Lerner/Woodfin Camp & Associates;   **437** The Newark Museum/Art Resource, NY;   **438** Michael Fogden/DRK Photo;   **439** Superstock;   **442** Timothy Hursley/Superstock (tl);   Christie's Images (mr);   **454** Cathlyn Melloan/Tony Stone Images;   **455** Cathlyn Melloan/Tony Stone Images;   **457** Louisville Slugger Museum (l) RMIP/Richard Haynes (r);   **460** Bev Doolittle/The Greenwich Workshop;   **462** NASA;   **463** Louisville Slugger Museum (t);   Stock Montage/Superstock (b);   **465** UPI/CORBIS-Bettmann;   **467** CORBIS/Tod Gipstein;   **468** PhotoDisc, Inc.;   **469** Matthew Stockman/Allsport;   **470** Courtesy of the U.S. Mint;   **472** Greig Cranna/Stock Boston;   **473** Dana White/PhotoEdit;   **474** Joseph Nettis/Tony Stone Images;   **477** Michael Newman/PhotoEdit;   **478** Joel Simon/Tony Stone Images;   **480** Custom Aerial Photography, Inc.;   **481** Manfred Kage/Peter Arnold, Inc.;   **482** CORBIS/Chuck O'Rear;   **486** Ron Jautz;   **488** Superstock;   **490** Tom & Pat Leeson/DRK Photo (t);   David Liebman (br);   **491** CORBIS/Doug Berry (l);   CORBIS/David Samuel Robbins (r);   **496** CORBIS/Robert Holmes (bl);   CRD/CORBIS (ml);   Page from Luca Pacioli's book, *Divine Proportion* illustrated by Leonardo da Vinci, 1494 (mr);   ©2001 Artists Rights Society (ARS), New York/ADAGP, Paris/FLC (r);   **498** Bob Daemmrich/Stock Boston/PNI;   **503** Michael Newman/PhotoEdit;   **506** Vinay Parelkar/Dinodia Picture Agency;   **508** Vinay Parelkar/Dinodia Picture Agency;   **511** RMIP/Richard Haynes;   **512** Bob Daemmrich/Tony Stone Images;   **524** Robert & Linda Mitchell;   **525** Robert & Linda Mitchell;   **527** Jacksonville Transportation Authority;   **530** Jacksonville Transportation Authority;   **535** Bill Lai/The Image Works;   **537** Hank Morgan/Cesar Pelli & Associates, Inc.;   **540** Keith Wood/Tony Stone Images (tl);   Superstock (tr);   **543** Tony Freeman/PhotoEdit;   **547** Rare Book & Manuscript Library/Columbia University, Cunieform, Plimpton 322;   **551** Ken Frick;   **553** PhotoDisc, Inc.;   **555** Diana Venters, "Wheel of Theodorus" (b);   **557** CORBIS/Gianni Dagli Orti (l);   The British Library (ml);   CORBIS/Bettmann (mr);   Nicaraguan Postal Authority (r);   **558** Jeff Greenberg/PhotoEdit;   **561** Kathy Adams Clark/KAC Productions;   **563** Bob Shaw/The Stock Market;   **564** CORBIS;   **567** Mark Gibson;   **569** CORBIS/AFP;   **571** Jose Carrillo/PhotoEdit (l);   CORBIS/Joe Sohm/ChromoSohm;   **573** Photri/Tom Sanders/The Stock Market;   **574** The Stock Shop;   **577** Bob Daemmrich;   **578** Agency Vandystadt/Allsport;   **579** ChromoSohm/Sohm/PNI/Picture Quest;   **592** CORBIS/Michael S. Yamashita;   **593** Mark & Audrey Gibson/Stock Connection/PNI;   **595** Mark Gibson;   **600** John Taylor/FPG International;   **601** George Gerster/Photo Researchers, Inc.;   **603** John Terence Turner/FPG International;   **609** Mark Gibson;   **613** Mark Gibson;   **614** The Granger Collection;   **621** Tony Stone Images;   **623** David Hiser/Tony Stone Images;   **629** CORBIS/Jeffrey L. Rotman;   **631** Mark Gibson/The Stock Market;   **634** M. Reinstein/The Image Works;   **636** Bob Daemmrich;   **642** The Granger Collection (tr);   The Natural History Museum, London (ml);   **644** Andrew Rafkind/Tony Stone Images;   **646** CORBIS/Craig Aurness;   **648** The Granger Collection (l);   Ancient Art & Architecture (ml);   Brown Brothers (3rd from left);   CORBIS (4th from left);   CORBIS (r);   **653** George Steinmetz;   **658** Paul Wakefield/Tony Stone Images;   **659** Tom Till/DRK Photo;   **661** R. Von Briel/PhotoEdit;   **664** UPI/CORBIS-Bettmann;   **666** Tony Freeman/PhotoEdit;   **669** Bob Daemmrich;   **671** Houston Museum of Natural Sciences;   **672** Philip & Karen Smith/Tony Stone Images;   **674** Tony Freeman/PhotoEdit (l);   Bob Daemmrich (r);   **676** RMIP/Richard Haynes;   **677** Don & Pat Valenti/Tony Stone Images;   **678** Steve Leonard/Tony Stone Images (l);   Art Wolfe/Tony Stone Images (r);   **680** Connie Toops;   **682** CORBIS-Bettmann (mr);   John Denniston/Province (r);   **683** Mark Gibson;   **685** Todd Warshaw/Allsport (bl);   **688** Greg Probst/Tony Stone Images;   **691** CORBIS/Ted Spiegel;   **694** RMIP/Richard Haynes;   **696** Hugh Sitton/Tony Stone Images;   **697** Catherine Gehm;   **699** Don Smetzer/Tony Stone Images;   **701** Bill Lai/Index Stock Imagery;

703 CORBIS/Stephen Frink;   **716** Polshek Partnership/Dbox/American Museum of Natural History;   **717** Polshek Partnership/Dbox/American Museum of Natural History;   **719** Pierre Belzeaux/Rapho/Liaison Agency;   **722** Mark Gibson (l);   Mike Wilson/FPG International (r);   **725** Phil Borden/PhotoEdit (l);   Harvard University Mineralogical and Geological Museum (2nd from left);   Charles D. Winters/Photo Researchers, Inc (3rd from left);   Jerome Wycoff/Visuals Unlimited (r);   **728** Gary Buss/FPG International;   **733** Jeff Greenberg/Leo de Wys, Inc. (l);   Brown Brothers (br)   **735** C. Ron Chapple/FPG International;   **740** Cooper-Hewitt Museum, Smithsonian Institution/Art Resource, NY (l);   Fergus O'Brien/FPG International (r);   **742** Australian Picture Library/E.T. Archive (l);   Van Den Broucke/Photo News/ Liaison Agency (ml);   C Squared Studios/PhotoDisc, Inc. (mr);   Tom Pantages (r);   **743** Telegraph Colour Library/FPG International;   **745** Tim Street-Porter/Ennis-Brown House;   **752** Carmona Photography/FPG International;   **754** ©Mystic Seaport, Mystic, Connecticut;   **757** G. Brad Lewis/Liaison Agency (l);   Harvey Lloyd/FPG International (r);   **759** NASA/FPG International;   **761** Courtesy of Rollerblade, Inc.;   **763** NASA/FPG International;   **764** James Blank/FPG International;   **766** Jeffrey Sylvester/FPG International;   **768** Jean Higgins/Unicorn Stock Photo;   **770** CORBIS;   **771** Mark E. Gibson;   **772** CORBIS.

Illustration

Steve Cowden **40, 241, 261, 491, 494**
Laurie O'Keefe **27**
Doug Stevens **69, 77, 98, 123, 508**
School Division, Houghton Mifflin Company **133, 170**

Selected Answers

CHAPTER 1

SKILL REVIEW (p. 2) **1.** 8 **2.** −8 **3.** 8 **4.** 8 **5.** −9 **6.** −5
7. −1 **8.** 1 **9.** 20 **10.** 29 **11.** 2 **12.** 25 **13.** 6.32 **14.** 7.07
15. 18.03 **16.** 4.24

1.1 PRACTICE (pp. 6–9)

3. 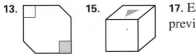 **5.** Each number is 3 times the previous number; 162.

7. Each number is $\frac{1}{4}$ the previous number; 1.

9. Each number is 0.5 greater than the previous number; 9.0.

11. 3 times the middle integer

13. **15.** **17.** Each number is half the previous number; 0.625.

19. Each number is 5 less than the previous number; −15.
21. Numbers after the first are found by adding consecutive whole numbers; 21. **23.** Numbers after the first are found by adding a zero after the decimal point of the previous number; 1.00001. **25.** 28 blocks **27.** The distance is 4 times the figure number. **29.** even **31.** $n^2 - 1$
33. 121; 12,321; 1,234,321; 123,454,321; the square of the n-digit number consisting of all 1's is the number obtained by writing the digits from 1 to n in increasing order, then the digits from $n − 1$ to 1 in decreasing order. This pattern does not continue forever. **35–39.** *Sample answers are given.*
35. $2 + (−5) = −3$, which is not greater than 2.
37. $(−4)(−5) = 20$ **39.** Let $m = −1$; $\frac{−1 + 1}{−1} = 0$.

41. *Sample answer:* 3

43.
$$C_5F_{12} \qquad C_6F_{14}$$

45. The y-coordinate is $\frac{1}{2}$ more than the opposite of the x-coordinate; $−2\frac{1}{2}$.

1.1 MIXED REVIEW (p. 9)

53–59 odd:
(−3, 8)
(−2, −6)
(3, −8)
(1, −10)

61. 25 **63.** −49
65. 169 **67.** 125
69. 40,000.4 **71.** +3

1.2 PRACTICE (pp. 13–16)

3. false **5.** false **7.** true **9.** false
11. true **13.** true **15.** false **17.** K **19.** M **21.** L **23.** J
25. N, P, and R; N, Q, and R; P, Q, and R **27.** A, W, and X; A, W, and Z; A, X, and Y; A, Y, and Z; W, X, and Y; W, X, and Z; W, Y, and Z; X, Y, and Z **29.** G **31.** H **33.** E **35.** H
37. K, N, Q, and R **39.** M, N, P, and Q **41.** L, M, P, and S
43. M, N, R, and S **45.** on the same side of C as point D
47. A, B, and C are collinear and C is between A and B.
49–51. Sample figures are given.

49. **51.**
A B C

53. the intersection of a line and a plane **55.** B **57.** H
59. $\overleftrightarrow{DH}$

61–67. Sample figures are given.
61. **63.**
65. **67.**

69. $\overleftrightarrow{CE}$, $\overleftrightarrow{DF}$
70–72.
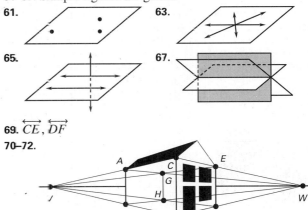

1.2 MIXED REVIEW (p. 16)

77. Each number is 6 times the previous number; 1296. **79.** Numbers after the first are found by adding an 8 immediately before the decimal point of the previous number and a 1 immediately after the decimal point; 88,888.11111. **81.** −2 **83.** 13 **85.** 5 **87.** 11 **89.** 11 **91.** 13 **93.** 8.60 **95.** 4.24

1.3 PRACTICE (pp. 21–24)

5. $5\sqrt{5}$ **7.** $\sqrt{61}$ **9.** 5
11. $\overline{JK}$ and $\overline{KL}$ are not congruent; $JK = \sqrt{137}$, $KL = 2\sqrt{34}$.
13–17. Answers may vary slightly. **13.** 3 cm **15.** 2.4 cm
17. 1.8 cm **19.** D E F ; $DE + EF = DF$
21. N M P ; $NM + MP = NP$ **23.** 3 **25.** 3
27. 6 **29.** 9 **31.** 4; 20, 3, 23 **33.** 1; $2\frac{1}{2}$, $4\frac{1}{2}$; 7
35. $DE = \sqrt{85}$, $EF = 6\sqrt{2}$, $DF = 5$ **37.** $AC = 3\sqrt{5}$, $BC = 3\sqrt{5}$, $CD = 2\sqrt{10}$; $\overline{AC}$ and $\overline{BC}$ have the same length.
39. $LN = 3\sqrt{13}$, $MN = \sqrt{109}$, $PN = 3\sqrt{10}$; no two segments have the same length. **41.** $\overline{PQ} \cong \overline{QR}$; $PQ = QR = \sqrt{170}$

43. $\overline{PQ} \cong \overline{QR}$; $PQ = QR = 2\sqrt{85}$ **45.** about 896 ft
47. *Sample answer:* about 63 mi   **49–51.** Answers are rounded to the nearest whole unit.   **49.** 5481 units
51. 8079 units   **53.** 115 yards, 80 yards, 65 yards

1.3 MIXED REVIEW (p. 24)
61. 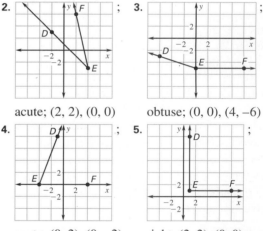   **63.** false   **65.** true   **67.** true   **69.** $\overrightarrow{NM}$, $\overrightarrow{NQ}$
71. $\overrightarrow{NM}$ and $\overrightarrow{NQ}$

QUIZ 1 (p. 25)   **1.** 8   **2.** 6

3. ⬤━━━⬤   **4.** ⤢   **5.**

6.   **7.** ; $TB = 5$ ft, $BC = 5$ ft

1.4 PRACTICE (pp. 29–32)   **9.** E, $\overrightarrow{ED}$, $\overrightarrow{EF}$; about $35°$
11. J, $\overrightarrow{JH}$, $\overrightarrow{JK}$; about $75°$ **13.** straight   **15.** obtuse
17. X, $\overrightarrow{XF}$, $\overrightarrow{XT}$ **19.** Q, $\overrightarrow{QR}$, $\overrightarrow{QS}$ **21.** $\angle C$, $\angle BCD$, $\angle DCB$
23. $55°$ **25.** $140°$ **27.** $180°$
29–33.   **29.** $50°$ **31.** $180°$ **33.** $130°$
35. acute; about $40°$
37. obtuse; about $150°$

39.

41–43. Coordinates of sample points are given.
41.   ; **43.**   ;
right; $(4, -3)$, $(0, 0)$ obtuse; $(-3, 3)$, $(0, 0)$
45–49. Estimates may vary.   **45.** about $150°$ **47.** about $140°$
49. about $135°$ **51.** 12 points   **53.** 40 points

1.4 MIXED REVIEW (p. 32)   **61.** 3   **63.** -12 **65.** -27 **67.** 15
69. -5 **71.** false   **73.** false   **75.** $\sqrt{89}$ **77.** $\sqrt{221}$ **79.** $3\sqrt{2}$

1.5 PRACTICE (pp. 38–41)   **5.** $(5, -7)$ **7.** $(3, 8)$ **9.** $(-2, -6)$
11. $m\angle RQS = 40°$, $m\angle PQR = 80°$ **13.** $m\angle PQS = 52°$,
$m\angle PQR = 104°$ **17.** $(-4, 3)$ **19.** $\left(4, 6\frac{1}{2}\right)$ **21.** $(-3, 3)$
23. $(-0.625, 3.5)$ **25.** $(-4, -4)$ **27.** $(1, 10)$ **29.** $(14, -21)$
31. $\overline{AC}$ and $\overline{BC}$, $\angle A$ and $\angle B$ **33.** $\overline{XW}$ and $\overline{XY}$, $\angle ZXW$ and $\angle ZXY$ **37.** $m\angle PQS = 22°$, $m\angle PQR = 44°$

39. $m\angle RQS = 80°$, $m\angle PQR = 160°$ **41.** $m\angle RQS = 45°$,
$m\angle PQR = 90°$ **43.** No; yes; the angle bisector of an angle of a triangle passes through the midpoint of the opposite side if the two sides of the triangle contained in the angle are congruent.   **45.** 19   **47.** 8   **49.** 42   **51.** 54
53. $65°, 65°, 25°, 25°$ **55.** *Sample answer:* $\overline{AB}$ and $\overline{AL}$, $\overline{AC}$ and $\overline{AK}$, $\overline{AN}$ and $\overline{AM}$, $\overline{AE}$ and $\overline{AI}$, $\overline{NE}$ and $\overline{MI}$, $\overline{ND}$ and $\overline{MJ}$, $\angle BAC$, $\angle CAN$, $\angle NAG$, $\angle GAM$, $\angle MAK$, and $\angle KAL$; $\angle DNE$, $\angle ENF$, $\angle HMI$, and $\angle JMI$
57. Yes; $x_1 + \frac{1}{2}(x_2 - x_1) = x_1 + \frac{1}{2}x_2 - \frac{1}{2}x_1 = \frac{1}{2}x_1 + \frac{1}{2}x_2 = \frac{x_1 + x_2}{2}$. Similarly, $y_1 + \frac{1}{2}(y_2 - y_1) = \frac{y_1 + y_2}{2}$.

1.5 MIXED REVIEW (p. 42)
61.   **63.** $\sqrt{233}$ **65.** $2\sqrt{130}$ **67.** $\sqrt{97}$
69. $20°$ **71.** $115°$

QUIZ 2 (p. 42)   **1.** If Q is in the interior of $\angle PSR$, then $m\angle PSQ + m\angle QSR = m\angle PSR$.   **2–5.** Coordinates of sample points are given.
2.   ; **3.**   ;
acute; $(2, 2)$, $(0, 0)$ obtuse; $(0, 0)$, $(4, -6)$
4.   ; **5.**   ;
acute; $(0, 2)$, $(0, -2)$ right; $(2, 2)$, $(0, 0)$
6. $21°, 42°$

1.6 PRACTICE (pp. 47–50)   **5.** $20°$ **7.** $40°$ **9.** yes   **11.** yes
13. no   **15.** always   **17.** always   **19.** never   **21.** $80°$
23. $123°$ **25.** $167°$ **27.** $154°$ **29.** 23   **31.** $x = 29$, $y = 50$
33. $x = 48$, $y = 31$ **35.** $x = 8$, $y = 12$ **37.** supplementary
39. complementary   **41.** $88°; 80°; 65°; 57°; 50°; 41°; 35°; 28°; 14°; 4°$ **43.** $m\angle A = 22.5°$; $m\angle B = 67.5°$
45. $m\angle A = 73°$, $m\angle B = 17°$ **47.** $m\angle A = 89°$, $m\angle B = 1°$
49. $m\angle A = 129°$, $m\angle B = 51°$ **51.** $m\angle A = 157°$, $m\angle B = 23°$
53. $122°, 156°$ **55.** $135°, 45°$

1.6 MIXED REVIEW (p. 50)   **61.** 8   **63.** $-10\sqrt{2}$, $10\sqrt{2}$
65. -10, 10   **67.** C **69.** A **71.** $(-4, 6)$ **73.** $(-7, 1)$
75. $(2.6, 7)$

1.7 PRACTICE (pp. 55–57)   **3.** 36 square units
5. 28.3 square units   **7.** 25.1 in.^{2} **9.** 32 units, 60 square units
11. 16 units, 12 square units   **13.** 48 units, 84 square units
15. 54 units, 126 square units   **17.** 60 units, 225 square units

19. $10 + 5\sqrt{2}$ units, 12.5 square units **21.** 15 cm^2 **23.** 64 ft^2
25. 36 m^2 **27.** 6 square units **29.** 12.6 square units

31.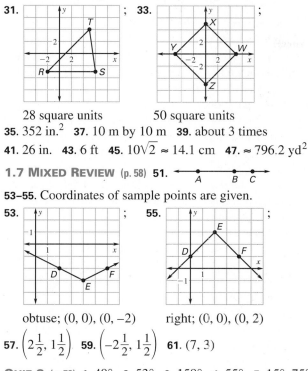

28 square units   50 square units

35. 352 in.^{2} **37.** 10 m by 10 m **39.** about 3 times
41. 26 in. **43.** 6 ft **45.** $10\sqrt{2} \approx 14.1$ cm **47.** ≈ 796.2 yd^2

1.7 MIXED REVIEW (p. 58) **51.**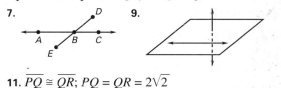

53–55. Coordinates of sample points are given.

53.
obtuse; (0, 0), (0, −2)   right; (0, 0), (0, 2)

57. $\left(2\frac{1}{2}, 1\frac{1}{2}\right)$ **59.** $\left(-2\frac{1}{2}, 1\frac{1}{2}\right)$ **61.** (7, 3)

QUIZ 3 (p. 58) **1.** 49° **2.** 53° **3.** 158° **4.** 55° **5.** 15°, 75°
6. 1017.4 m^2, 113.0 m **7.** 71.5 in.^{2} **8.** 46 cm^2, 29.2 cm
9. 40 square units **10.** at least 21 rolls

CHAPTER 1 REVIEW (pp. 60–62) **1.** Each number is 7 more than the previous number. **3.** Each number is 3 times the previous number. **5.** If 1 is added to the product of four consecutive positive integers, n through $n + 3$, the sum is equal to the square of $[n(n + 3) + 1]$.

7.   **9.**

11. $\overline{PQ} \cong \overline{QR}$; $PQ = QR = 2\sqrt{2}$
13. $\overline{PQ}$ and $\overline{QR}$ are not congruent; $PQ = \sqrt{13}$, $QR = \sqrt{10}$.
15. obtuse;   **17.** 105° **19.** 70°
150°   **21.** (1, 2)
A

23. $m\angle RQS = 50°$, $m\angle PQR = 100°$ **25.** $m\angle RQS = 46°$, $m\angle PQR = 92°$ **27.** sometimes **29.** sometimes
31. 56.52 in., 254.34 in.^{2} **33.** 56 ft

CHAPTER 2

SKILL REVIEW (p. 70)
1. D **2.** B **3.** F **4.** E **5.** 142° **6.** 142° **7.** 38°

2.1 PRACTICE (pp. 75–77) **3.** hypothesis: the dew point equals the air temperature; conclusion: it will rain **5.** If an angle is a right angle, then its measure is 90°. **7.** false
9. If an object weighs 2000 pounds, then it weighs one ton.

11. If three points lie on the same line, then the points are collinear. **13.** If a fish is a hagfish, then it lives in salt water. **15.** False; let $x = -3$. The hypothesis is true because $(-3)^4 = 81$. However, the conclusion is false, so the conditional statement is false. **17.** True **19.** If $\angle 2$ is acute, then $\angle 2$ measures 38°. **21.** If I go to the movies, then it is raining. **23.** if-then form: If three noncollinear points are distinct, then there is exactly one plane that they lie in; inverse: If three noncollinear points are not distinct, then it is not true that there is exactly one plane that they lie in; converse: If exactly one plane contains three noncollinear points, then the three points are distinct; contrapositive: If it is not true that there is exactly one plane that contains three noncollinear points, then the three points are not distinct. **25.** one **27.** a line
29. Postulate 5: Through any two points there exists exactly one line. **31.** Postulate 8: Through any three noncollinear points there exists exactly one plane.
33. Postulate 11: If two planes intersect, then their intersection is a line. **35.** Postulate 6: A line contains at least two points. **37.** Postulate 8: Through any three noncollinear points there exists exactly one plane.
41. Yes; points A and B could lie on the line intersecting two planes. **43.** Yes; the plane that runs from the front of the room to the back of the room through points A and B contains both points and a point on the front wall.
45. inverse: If $x \neq 4$, then $6x - 6 \neq x + 14$; converse: If $6x - 6 = x + 14$, then $x = 4$; contrapositive: If $6x - 6 \neq x + 14$, then $x \neq 4$. **47.** if-then form: If one feels the impulse to soar, then one can never consent to creep. **a.** hypothesis: one feels the impulse to soar; conclusion: one can never consent to creep **b.** If one does not feel the impulse to soar, then one can consent to creep. **49.** if-then form: If a man is early to bed and early to rise, then the man will be healthy, wealthy, and wise. **a.** hypothesis: a man is early to bed and early to rise; conclusion: the man is healthy, wealthy, and wise **b.** If a man is not early to bed and early to rise, then the man is not healthy, wealthy, and wise.
51. inverse: If you do not want a great selection of used cars, then do not come and see Bargain Bob's Used Cars; converse: If you come and see Bargain Bob's Used Cars, then you want a great selection of used cars; contrapositive: If you do not come and see Bargain Bob's Used Cars, then you do not want a great selection of used cars.

MIXED REVIEW (p. 78) **61.** obtuse **63.** right
65. (1, −2) **67.** (−1.5, 1.5) **69.** (6, −1) **71.** 113.04 m^2; 37.68 m **73.** 1501.5625 mm^2; 155 mm

2.2 PRACTICE (pp. 82–85) **3.** No; for a statement to be a biconditional statement it must contain the phrase "if and only if." **5.** yes **7.** conditional statement: If you scored a touchdown, then the football crossed the goal line; converse: If the football crossed the goal line, then you scored a touchdown. **9.** False; the points do not lie on the same line.

11. True; $\angle DBA$ and $\angle EBC$ each are supplementary to right angle $\angle DBC$, so each measures $90°$. **13.** false **15.** false **17.** false **19.** true **21.** conditional statement: If a ray bisects an angle, then it divides the angle into two congruent angles; converse: If an angle is divided into two congruent angles, then it is bisected by a ray. **23.** conditional statement: If a point is a midpoint of a segment, then it divides the segment into two congruent segments; converse: If a point divides a segment into two congruent segments, then the point is the midpoint of the segment. **25.** Two angles measuring $30°$ and $60°$ are complementary, but they do not measure $42°$ and $48°$. **27.** A rectangle with width 2 cm and length 3 cm has four sides, but it is not a square. **29.** False; PQ and PS are equal if they are both 5 cm. **31.** true **33.** if-then form: If two circles have the same diameter, then they have the same circumference; converse: If two circles have the same circumference, then they have the same diameter; true; biconditional statement: Two circles have the same circumference if and only if they have the same diameter. **35.** if-then form: If an animal is a leopard, then it has spots; converse: If an animal has spots, then it is a leopard; false; counterexample: A giraffe has spots, but it is not a leopard. **37.** if-then form: If a leopard has pale gray fur, then it is a snow leopard; converse: If a leopard is a snow leopard, then it has pale gray fur; true; biconditional statement: A leopard is a snow leopard if and only if it has pale gray fur. **39.** No; v can be any number if $9v - 4v = 2v + 3v$. **41.** Yes; $x^3 - 27 = 0$ if and only if $x = 3$. **43.** No; z can be any number if $7 + 18z = 5z + 7 + 13z$. **47.** quadrupled **49.** The statements from Exercises 47 and 48 can both be written as true biconditionals. The sides of the square are doubled if and only if the area is quadrupled, and the sides of a square are doubled if and only if the perimeter is doubled, are both true. **51.** true **53.** False; winds are classified as 9 on the Beaufort scale if the winds measure 41–47 knots.

2.2 MIXED REVIEW (p. 85) **59.** $3°$; $93°$ **61.** $76°$; $166°$ **63.** 36 ft^2; 30 ft **65.** 200.96 in.^{2}; 50.24 in. **67.** If a rectangle is a square, then the sides of the rectangle are all congruent.

2.3 PRACTICE (pp. 91–94) **3.** converse **5.** If you like this movie, then you enjoy scary movies. **7.** Yes; if f is true, then by the Law of Detachment, g is true. If g is true, then by the Law of Detachment, h is true. Therefore, if f is true, then h is true. **9.** Points X, Y, and Z do not lie on the same line. **11.** If points X, Y, and Z are not collinear, then points X, Y, and Z do not lie on the same line. **13.** If points X, Y, and Z do not lie on the same line, then points X, Y, and Z are not collinear. **15.** p: Alberto finds a summer job; q: Alberto will buy a car; inverse: $\sim p \rightarrow \sim q$, If Alberto does not find a summer job, then he will not buy a car; contrapositive: $\sim q \rightarrow \sim p$, If Alberto does not buy a car, then he did not find a summer job.

17. p: the car is running; q: the key is in the ignition; inverse: $\sim p \rightarrow \sim q$, If the car is not running, then the key is not in the ignition; contrapositive: $\sim q \rightarrow \sim p$, If the key is not in the ignition, then the car is not running. **19.** p: Gina walks to the store; q: Gina buys a newspaper; inverse: $\sim p \rightarrow \sim q$, If Gina does not walk to the store, then she will not buy a newspaper; contrapositive: $\sim q \rightarrow \sim p$, If Gina does not buy a newspaper, then she did not walk to the store. **21.** inductive reasoning; Inductive reasoning depends on previous examples and patterns to form a conjecture. Dana came to her conclusion based on previous examples. **23.** valid; p: the sum of the measures of $\angle A$ and $\angle C$ is $90°$. q: $\angle A$ and $\angle C$ are complementary. $p \rightarrow q$ is true and p is true, so q is true. **25.** valid; It can be concluded that $\angle B$ is acute, since the measure of $\angle B$ is between the measures of $\angle A$ and $\angle C$. **27.** It can be concluded that $y \leq 3$. Since the hypothesis is true, $2 \times 3 + 3 < 4 \times 3 < 5 \times 3$, the conclusion is true, $y \leq x$. **29.** No conclusions can be made because the hypothesis is not true for the given value of x. **31.** If the stereo is on, then the neighbors will complain. **33.** may not **35.** may have **37.** $\angle 1$ and $\angle 2$ are supplementary angles; therefore, their measures add up to $180°$. **39.** $\angle 4$ and $\angle 3$ are vertical angles; therefore, their measures are equal. **41.** $\angle 5$ and $\angle 6$ are supplementary angles; therefore, their measures add up to $180°$.

45. True; the mall is open; therefore, Angela and Diego went shopping and, therefore, Diego bought a pretzel. **47.** False; the mall is open; therefore, Angela and Diego went shopping and, therefore, Angela bought a pizza. We cannot conclude that she also bought a pretzel. **49.** D, B, A, E, C; the robot extinguishes the fire.

2.3 MIXED REVIEW (p. 94) **57.** *Sample answer: F* **59.** *Sample answer: B* **61.** $41°$ **63.** $3f + 4g + 7$

QUIZ 1 (p. 95) **1.** The statement is already in if-then form; converse: If tomorrow is June 5, then today is June 4. Both the statement and its converse are true, so they can be combined to form a biconditional statement: Today is June 4 if and only if tomorrow is June 5. **2.** if-then form: If a time period is a century, then it is a period of 100 years; converse: If a time period is 100 years, then it is a century. Both the statement and its converse are true so they can be combined to form a biconditional statement: A time period is a century if and only if it is a period of 100 years. **3.** if-then form: If two circles have the same diameter, then they are congruent; converse: If two circles are congruent, then they have the same diameter. Both the statement and its converse are true, so they can be combined to form a biconditional statement: Two circles are congruent if and only if they have the same diameter. **4.** Yes; John backs the car out; therefore, he drives into the fence. **5.** Yes; John backs the car out; therefore, he drives into the fence and, therefore, his father is angry.

2.4 PRACTICE (pp. 99–101) **5.** A **7.** E

9. $W = 1.42T - 38.5$ (Given)

$W + 38.5 = 1.42T$ (Addition property of equality)

$\dfrac{W + 38.5}{1.42} = T$ (Division property of equality)

If $W = -24.3°F$, then $T = 10°F$.

11. $BC = EF$ **13.** $PQ = RS$

15. Distributive property; Subtraction property of equality; Subtraction property of equality

17. $q + 9 = 13$ (Given)

$q = 4$ (Subtraction prop. of equality)

19. $7s + 20 = 4s - 13$ (Given)

$3s + 20 = -13$ (Subtraction prop. of equality)

$3s = -33$ (Subtraction prop. of equality)

$s = -11$ (Division prop. of equality)

21. $-2(-w + 3) = 15$ (Given)

$2w - 6 = 15$ (Distributive prop.)

$2w = 21$ (Addition prop. of equality)

$w = 10.5$ (Division prop. of equality)

23. $3(4v - 1) - 8v = 17$ (Given)

$12v - 3 - 8v = 17$ (Distributive prop.)

$4v - 3 = 17$ (Simplify.)

$4v = 20$ (Addition prop. of equality)

$v = 5$ (Division prop. of equality)

25. Given; Given; Transitive property of equality; Definition of right angles; Definition of perpendicular lines

27. B lies between A and C (Given)

$AB + BC = AC$ (Segment Addition Post.)

$AB = 3$, $BC = 8$ (Given)

$3 + 8 = AC$ (Substitution prop. of equality)

$AC = 11$ (Simplify.)

29. $c(r + 1) = n$ (Given)

$cr + c = n$ (Distributive prop.)

$cr = n - c$ (Subtraction prop. of equality)

$r = \dfrac{n - c}{c}$ (Division prop. of equality)

31. To find Donald's old wage, solve the formula $c(r + 1) = n$ for c.

$c(r + 1) = n$ (Given)

$c = \dfrac{n}{r + 1}$ (Division prop. of equality)

$c = \dfrac{12.72}{0.06 + 1}$ (Substitution prop. of equality)

$c = \$12.00$ (Simplify.)

2.4 MIXED REVIEW (p. 101) **35.** 9.90 **37.** 10.20 **39.** 8.60
41. $(-7, -7)$ **43.** $(12, -13)$ **45.** $42°; 132°$ **47.** false
49. false

2.5 PRACTICE (pp. 104–107) **3.** By the definition of midpoint, Point D is halfway between B and F. Therefore, $\overline{BD} \cong \overline{FD}$. **5.** By the Transitive Property of Segment Congruence, if $\overline{CE} \cong \overline{BD}$ and $\overline{BD} \cong \overline{FD}$, then $\overline{CE} \cong \overline{FD}$.
7. Given; Definition of congruent segments; Transitive property of equality; Definition of congruent segments

9. $PR = 46$ (Given)

$PQ + QR = PR$ (Segment Addition Post.)

$2x + 5 - 6x - 15 = 46$ (Substitution prop. of equality)

$8x - 10 = 46$ (Simplify.)

$8x = 56$ (Addition prop. of equality)

$x = 7$ (Division prop. of equality)

11. $\overline{XY} \cong \overline{WX}$, $\overline{YZ} \cong \overline{WX}$ (Given)

$\overline{XY} \cong \overline{YZ}$ (Transitive Prop. of Segment Cong.)

$XY = YZ$ (Definition of congruent segments)

$4x + 3 = 9x - 12$ (Substitution prop. of equality)

$-5x + 3 = -12$ (Subtraction prop. of equality)

$-5x = -15$ (Subtraction prop. of equality)

$x = 3$ (Division prop. of equality)

17. $XY = 8$, $XZ = 8$ (Given)

$XY = XZ$ (Transitive prop. of equality)

$\overline{XY} \cong \overline{XZ}$ (Definition of congruent segments)

$\overline{XY} \cong \overline{ZY}$ (Given)

$\overline{XZ} \cong \overline{ZY}$ (Transitive Prop. of Segment Cong.)

19. yes; by the Transitive Property of Segment Congruence

2.5 MIXED REVIEW (p. 107) **29.** *Sample answer:* $2 + 3 = 5$
31. $116°$ **33.** $65°$ **35.** If Matthew does not win first place, then Matthew did not win the wrestling match. **37.** $p \rightarrow q$; If the car is in the garage, then Mark is home. **39.** $\sim p \rightarrow \sim q$; If the car is not in the garage, then Mark is not home.

2.6 PRACTICE (pp. 112–115) **3.** $\angle A$ **5.** yes **7.** no **9.** yes
11. A is an angle. (Given)

$m\angle A = m\angle A$ (Reflexive prop. of equality)

$\angle A \cong \angle A$ (Definition of congruent angles)

13. $31°$ **15.** $158°$ **17.** $61°$ **19.** $\angle 1 \cong \angle 3$, $\angle 2 \cong \angle 4$
21. $\angle 1 \cong \angle 2$, $\angle 3 \cong \angle 4$
23. $m\angle 3 = 120°$, $\angle 1 \cong \angle 4$, $\angle 3 \cong \angle 4$ (Given)

$\angle 1 \cong \angle 3$ (Transitive Prop. of Angle Cong.)

$m\angle 1 = m\angle 3$ (Definition of congruent angles)

$m\angle 1 = 120°$ (Substitution prop. of equality)

25. $\angle QVW$ and $\angle RWV$ are supplementary. (Given)

$\angle QVW$ and $\angle QVP$ are a linear pair. (Definition of linear pair)

$\angle QVP$ and $\angle QVW$ are supplementary. (Linear Pair Post.)

$\angle QVP \cong \angle RWV$ (Congruent Supplements Theorem)

27. $4w + 10 + 13w = 180$

$17w + 10 = 180$

$17w = 170$

$w = 10$

$2(x + 25) + 2x - 30 = 180$

$2x + 50 + 2x - 30 = 180$

$4x + 20 = 180$

$4x = 160$

$x = 40$

29. Yes; $\angle 2 \cong \angle 3$ and $\angle 1$ and $\angle 4$ are supplementary to congruent angles. $\angle 1 \cong \angle 4$ by the Congruent Supplements Theorem.

2.6 MIXED REVIEW (p. 116) **39.** 172° **41.** All definitions are true biconditionals. So the conditionals If two lines are perpendicular, then they intersect to form a right angle and If two lines intersect to form a right angle, then the two lines are perpendicular are both true.

43. $x = \dfrac{1}{2}$ **45.** $z = \dfrac{1}{3}$

QUIZ 2 (p. 116)

1. $x - 3 = 7$ (Given)
$x = 10$ (Addition prop. of equality)

2. $x + 8 = 27$ (Given)
$x = 19$ (Subtraction prop. of equality)

3. $2x - 5 = 13$ (Given)
$2x = 18$ (Addition prop. of equality)
$x = 9$ (Division prop. of equality)

4. $2x + 20 = 4x - 12$ (Given)
$-2x + 20 = -12$ (Subtraction prop. of equality)
$-2x = -32$ (Subtraction prop. of equality)
$x = 16$ (Division prop. of equality)

5. $3(3x - 7) = 6$ (Given)
$9x - 21 = 6$ (Distributive prop.)
$9x = 27$ (Addition prop. of equality)
$x = \dfrac{27}{9}$, or 3 (Division prop. of equality)

6. $-2(-2x + 4) = 16$ (Given)
$4x - 8 = 16$ (Distributive prop.)
$4x = 24$ (Addition prop. of equality)
$x = 6$ (Division prop. of equality)

7. $\overline{BA} \cong \overline{BC}$, $\overline{BC} \cong \overline{CD}$ (Given)
$\overline{BA} \cong \overline{CD}$ (Transitive Prop. of Segment Cong.)
$\overline{AE} \cong \overline{DF}$ (Given)
$BA + AE = BE$ (Segment Addition Post.)
$BA = CD$ (Definition of congruent segments)
$AE = DF$ (Definition of congruent segments)
$CD + DF = BE$ (Substitution prop. of equality)
$CD + DF = CF$ (Segment Addition Post.)
$BE = CF$ (Transitive prop. of equality)
$\overline{BE} \cong \overline{CF}$ (Definition of congruent segments)

8. $\overline{EH} \cong \overline{GH}$, $\overline{FG} \cong \overline{GH}$ (Given)
$\overline{EH} \cong \overline{FG}$ (Transitive Prop. of Segment Cong.) **9.** 38°

CHAPTER 2 REVIEW (pp. 118–120)

1. if-then form: If there is a teacher's meeting, then we are dismissed early; hypothesis: there is a teacher's meeting; conclusion: we are dismissed early; inverse: If there is not a teacher's meeting, then we are not dismissed early; converse: If we are dismissed early, then there is a teacher's meeting; contrapositive: If we are not dismissed early, then there is not a teacher's meeting. **3.** exactly one
5. No; $x^2 = 25$ does not necessarily mean that $x = 5$. x could also $= -5$. **7.** If the measure of $\angle A$ is 90°, then $\angle A$ is a right angle. **9.** $\angle A$ is not a right angle. **11.** If there is a nice breeze, then we will sail to Dunkirk. **13.** C **15.** D

17. $5(3y + 2) = 25$ (Given)
$15y + 10 = 25$ (Distributive prop.)
$15y = 15$ (Subtraction prop. of equality)
$y = 1$ (Division prop. of equality)

19. $23 + 11d - 2c = 12 - 2c$ (Given)
$23 + 11d = 12$ (Addition prop. of equality)
$11d = -11$ (Subtraction prop. of equality)
$d = -1$ (Division prop. of equality)

21. $\angle 1$ and $\angle 2$ are complementary. (Given)
$\angle 3$ and $\angle 4$ are complementary. (Given)
$\angle 1 \cong \angle 3$ (Given)
$\angle 2 \cong \angle 4$ (Congruent Complements Theorem)

ALGEBRA REVIEW (pp. 124–125) **1.** no **2.** yes **3.** yes **4.** no
5. no **6.** yes **7.** no **8.** no **9.** no **10.** yes **11.** yes **12.** yes
13. -5 **14.** $-\dfrac{2}{13}$ **15.** $\dfrac{1}{2}$ **16.** $\dfrac{1}{7}$ **17.** $-\dfrac{11}{2}$ **18.** 2 **19.** -2
20. 0 **21.** $-\dfrac{13}{9}$ **22.** -1 **23.** $-\dfrac{14}{9}$ **24.** $-\dfrac{23}{11}$ **25.** $\dfrac{7}{12}$
26. $-\dfrac{9}{8}$ **27.** $-\dfrac{1}{4}$ **28.** $y = -2x + 5$ **29.** $y = -3x - 12$
30. $y = -\dfrac{2}{3}x + 8$ **31.** $y = -\dfrac{13}{7}x + 13$ **32.** $y = \dfrac{1}{3}x - 2$
33. $y = -12x - 8$ **34.** $y = -2x - 14$ **35.** $y = -x - 2$
36. $y = -3x + 7$ **37.** $y = -2x - 5$ **38.** $y = \dfrac{1}{2}x + 2$
39. $y = -\dfrac{1}{3}x + 1.5$ **40.** $y = -x + 3$ **41.** $y = -3x - 12$
42. $y = 4x - 21$ **43.** $y = -2x$ **44.** $y = 5x + 8$ **45.** $y = 3x - 1$
46. $y = -x + 4$ **47.** $y = -6x - 21$ **48.** $y = 2x + 8$
49. $y = 2x - 29$ **50.** $y = \dfrac{1}{3}x - \dfrac{5}{3}$ **51.** $y = -\dfrac{5}{12}x + \dfrac{3}{2}$

CHAPTER 3

SKILL REVIEW (p. 128) **1.** 133 **2.** 47 **3.** $-\dfrac{1}{4}$ **4.** 18 **5.** 20
6. $\dfrac{77}{2}$ **7.** Definition of a right angle **8.** Vertical angles are congruent. **9.** $\angle 2$ and $\angle 3$ form a linear pair. **10.** Definition of congruent angles **11.** Subtraction property of equality **12.** Distributive property

3.1 PRACTICE (pp. 132–134) **3.** B **5.** A **7.** $\angle 3$ and $\angle 5$, or $\angle 4$ and $\angle 6$ **9.** $\angle 3$ and $\angle 6$, or $\angle 4$ and $\angle 5$
11. perpendicular **13.** parallel **15.** $\overleftrightarrow{QU}$, $\overleftrightarrow{QT}$, $\overleftrightarrow{RV}$, or $\overleftrightarrow{RS}$
17. UVW **19.** 1 **21.** corresponding **23.** consecutive interior
25. alternate exterior **27.** III; 3 **29.** V; 5 **31.** M; 1000
33. yes **35.** no **37.** *Sample answer:* The two lines of intersection are coplanar, since they are both in the third plane. The two lines do not intersect, because they are in parallel planes. Since they are coplanar and do not intersect, they are parallel.
39.

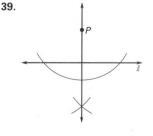

3.1 MIXED REVIEW (p. 134) **47.** $m\angle ABD = 80°$, $m\angle ABC = 160°$ **49.** 77°, 167° **51.** 2°, 92° **53.** 22°, 112° **55.** 30°, 120° **57.** $x + 13 - 13 = 23 - 13$, Subtraction property of equality; $x = 10$, Simplify. **59.** $4x + 11 - 11 = 31 - 11$, Subtraction property of equality; $4x = 20$, Simplify; $\frac{4x}{4} = \frac{20}{4}$, Division property of equality; $x = 5$, Simplify. **61.** *Sample answer:* $2x - 2 + 3 = 17$, Distributive property; $2x + 1 = 17$, Simplify; $2x + 1 - 1 = 17 - 1$, Subtraction property of equality; $2x = 16$, Simplify; $\frac{2x}{2} = \frac{16}{2}$, Division property of equality; $x = 8$, Simplify.

3.2 PRACTICE (pp. 138–141) **3.** Vertical Angles Theorem **5.** Theorem 3.2 **7.** 90 **9.** 20 **11.** 90 **13.** 35 **15.** *Sample answer:* $\angle 1$, $\angle 2$, $\angle 3$, and $\angle 4$ are right angles. **17. a.** right angle **b.** 90° **c.** Angle Addition **d.** $m\angle 3$ **e.** $m\angle 4$ **f.** 90°

19.

Statements	Reasons
2. $\angle 1 \cong \angle 3$	3. If two angles are congruent, then their measures are equal.
5. $m\angle 1 = 90°$	4. Given
6. $90° = m\angle 3$	
7. $\angle 3$ is a right angle.	

21. If $\angle 4 \cong \angle 6$, then $\angle 5 \cong \angle 6$ because $\angle 5 \cong \angle 4$ and because of the Transitive Property of Angle Congruence.

23.

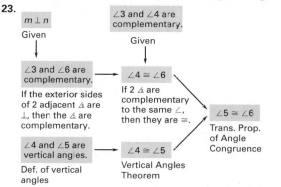

25. No; *Sample answer:* If one of the angles is a right angle, then the crosspieces are perpendicular, so all four angles will be right angles.

3.2 MIXED REVIEW (p. 141) **29.** 38° **31.** 39° **33.** $\angle 1$ and $\angle 5$, $\angle 3$ and $\angle 7$, $\angle 2$ and $\angle 6$, $\angle 4$ and $\angle 8$ **35.** $\angle 1$ and $\angle 8$, $\angle 2$ and $\angle 7$

3.3 PRACTICE (pp. 146–148) **3.** Alternate Exterior Angles Theorem **5.** Consecutive Interior Angles Theorem **7.** 133 **9.** $m\angle 1 = 82°$; *Sample answer:* by the Corresponding Angles Postulate. $m\angle 2 = 98°$; *Sample answer:* $\angle 1$ and $\angle 2$ form a linear pair. **11.** $x = 113$, by the Linear Pair Postulate; $y = 113$, by the Alternate Exterior Angles Theorem. **13.** $x = 90$, $y = 90$; *Sample answer:* by the Perpendicular Transversal Theorem **15.** $x = 100$; *Sample answer:* by the Linear Pair Postulate. $y = 80$; *Sample answer:* by the Alternate Exterior Angles Theorem **17.** $m\angle 2 = m\angle 3 = m\angle 6 = m\angle 7 = 73°$, $m\angle 4 = m\angle 5 = m\angle 8 = 107°$ **19.** 23 **21.** 28 **23.** 12 **25.** 7

27.

Statements	Reasons
1. $p \parallel q$	2. Alternate Interior Angles Theorem
3. $m\angle 1 = m\angle 3$	
4. $\angle 2$ and $\angle 3$ form a linear pair.	5. Linear Pair Postulate
6. $m\angle 1 + m\angle 2 = 180°$	7. Definition of supplementary $\angle$

29. *Sample answer:* It is given that $p \perp q$, so $\angle 1$ is a right angle because perpendicular lines form right angles. It is given that $q \parallel r$, so $\angle 1 \cong \angle 2$ by the Corresponding Angles Postulate. Then, $\angle 2$ is a right angle because it is congruent to a right angle. Finally, $p \perp r$ because the sides of a right angle are perpendicular.

3.3 MIXED REVIEW (p. 149) **33.** 130° **35.** 79° **37.** 69° **39.** If an angle is acute, then the measure of the angle is 19°. **41.** If I go fishing, then I do not have to work. **43.** 21°

QUIZ 1 (p. 149) **1.** $\angle 6$ **2.** $\angle 5$ **3.** $\angle 6$ **4.** $\angle 7$ **5.** *Sample answer:* Since $\angle 1$ and $\angle 2$ are congruent angles that form a linear pair, this shows that $m\angle 1$ and $m\angle 2$ are both 90°. This shows that the two lines are perpendicular so that $\angle 3$ and $\angle 4$ are right angles. **6.** 69 **7.** 75 **8.** 12 **9.** 35°; the top left corner is assumed to be a right angle; $\angle 3$ and $\angle 2$ are complementary, Definition of complementary angles; $m\angle 3 + m\angle 2 = 90°$, Definition of complementary angles; $m\angle 2 = 90° - 55° = 35°$, Substitution; $m\angle 1 = m\angle 2$, Corresponding Angles Postulate

3.4 PRACTICE (pp. 153–156) **3.** yes; Alternate Exterior Angles Converse **5.** no **7.** yes; Corresponding Angles Converse **9.** 45; Consecutive Interior Angles Converse **11.** yes; Alternate Exterior Angles Converse **13.** no **15.** no **17.** 45 **19.** yes; Corresponding Angles Converse **21.** no **23.** yes; Angle Addition Postulate and Alternate Exterior Angles Converse **25.** no **27.** $j \parallel n$ because $31° + 69° = 100°$ and $32° + 68° = 100°$. **29.** 32° **33.** $\angle 1 \cong \angle 4$ and $\angle 2 \cong \angle 3$. *Sample answer:* The angles marked as congruent are alternate interior angles, so $r \parallel s$ by the Alternate Interior Angles Converse. Then $\angle 1 \cong \angle 4$ by the Alternate Interior Angles Theorem and $\angle 2 \cong \angle 3$ by the Vertical Angles Theorem. **35.** *Sample answer:* It is given that $a \parallel b$, so $\angle 1$ and $\angle 3$ are supplementary by the Consecutive Interior Angles Theorem. Then, $m\angle 1 + m\angle 3 = 180°$ by the definition of supplementary angles. Then, $m\angle 2 + m\angle 3 = 180°$ by substitution, and $c \parallel d$ by the Consecutive Interior Angles Converse.

3.4 MIXED REVIEW (p. 156) **41.**

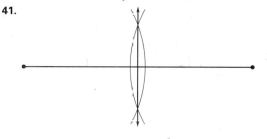

43.

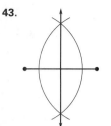

45. $\angle 5$ **47.** $\angle 7$

3.5 PRACTICE (pp. 160–163) **3.** Theorem 3.12 **5.** $\ell_1 \parallel \ell_2$ because of the Alternate Interior Angles Converse.
7. *Sample answer:* Given line ℓ and exterior point P, draw any line n through P that intersects ℓ. Then copy $\angle 1$ at P so that $\angle 1 \cong \angle 2$. Line m will be parallel to line ℓ.
9. Theorem 3.12 **11.** Corresponding Angles Converse
13. Alternate Interior Angles Converse **15.** $85° + 95° = 180°$, so $k \parallel j$ by the Consecutive Interior Angles Converse.
17. *Sample answer:* The measure of the obtuse exterior angle formed by n and k is $90° + \dfrac{90}{2} = 135°$, so $k \parallel j$ by the Alternate Exterior Angles Converse. **19.** *Sample answer:* The measure of the obtuse angle formed by g and the left transversal is $(180 - x)°$. Since $(180 - x)° + x° = 180°$, $g \parallel h$ by the Consecutive Interior Angles Converse. **21.** $p \parallel q$ by the Corresponding Angles Converse; $q \parallel r$ by the Consecutive Interior Angles Converse. Then, because $p \parallel q$ and $q \parallel r$, $p \parallel r$. **23.** a and b are each perpendicular to d, so $a \parallel b$ by Theorem 3.12; c and d are each perpendicular to a, so $c \parallel d$ by Theorem 3.12.
25. *Sample answer:*   **27.** *Sample answer:*

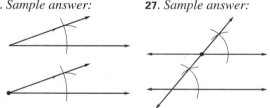

29. *Sample answer:* The two angles that are congruent are corresponding angles, so the two lines are parallel by the Corresponding Angles Converse. **31.** *Sample answer:* Each edge is parallel to the previous edge, so all the strips are parallel by Theorem 3.11. **33.** always **35.** never **37.** $50°$
39. a. *Sample answer:* Hold the straightedge next to each red line and see if the red lines are straight.
b. *Sample answer:* Measure the angles formed by the red lines and the top horizontal line, and see if corresponding angles are congruent.

3.5 MIXED REVIEW (p. 163) **43.** $2\sqrt{58}$, or about 15.23
45. $2\sqrt{34}$, or about 11.66 **47.** $5\sqrt{17}$, or about 20.62
49. Converse: If an angle is acute, then its measure is 42°. Counterexample: a 41° angle (or any acute angle whose measure is not 42°)

51. Converse: If a polygon contains four right angles, then it is a rectangle. Counterexample:

QUIZ 2 (p. 164) **1.** yes; Consecutive Interior Angles Converse **2.** $a \parallel b$ **3.** $a \parallel b$ **4.** $a \parallel b, c \parallel d$ **5.** *Sample answer:* First, it is given that $\angle ABC$ is supplementary to $\angle DEF$. Next, note that $\angle ABC$ and $\angle CBE$ are a linear pair; therefore, by the Linear Pair Postulate, $\angle ABC$ and $\angle CBE$ are supplementary. By the Congruent Supplements Theorem, $\angle CBE \cong \angle DEF$. Finally, the left and right edges of the chimney are parallel by the Corresponding Angles Converse.

3.6 PRACTICE (pp. 168–171) **5.** -2 **7.** parallel; both have slope $\dfrac{1}{3}$. **9.** parallel; both have slope $\dfrac{1}{2}$. **11.** $\dfrac{3}{2}$ **13.** $\dfrac{1}{2}$
15. -1 **17.** $-2, -2$; parallel **19.** 3, 4; not parallel **21.** $\dfrac{5}{6}, \dfrac{5}{7}$; not parallel **23.** about 7.2 feet; *Sample answer:* Using x for the height, a proportion is $\dfrac{3}{5} = \dfrac{x}{12}$. Then, $5x = 36$ and $x = 7.2$. **25.** slope of $\overleftrightarrow{AB}$: $\dfrac{1}{2}$; slope of $\overleftrightarrow{CD}$: $\dfrac{1}{2}$; slope of $\overleftrightarrow{EF}$: $\dfrac{3}{4}$; $\overleftrightarrow{AB} \parallel \overleftrightarrow{CD}$ **27.** $y = 3x + 2$ **29.** $y = -\dfrac{2}{9}x$ **31.** $y = -3$
33. $y = -6x + 3$ **35.** $y = -\dfrac{4}{3}x + 3$ **37.** $y = -x + 6$ **39.** $y = -4$
41. $x = 6$ **43.** $y = \dfrac{5}{4}x - \dfrac{13}{4}$ **45.** *Sample answer:* $y = \dfrac{1}{3}x$
47.

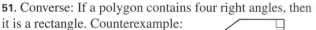

49. 5%; no **51.** 9%; yes
53. $y = x$; 45°

3.6 MIXED REVIEW (p. 171) **59.** $\dfrac{1}{20}$ **61.** $-\dfrac{1}{11}$ **63.** $\dfrac{7}{3}$
65. -2 **67.** -9 **69.** $-11\dfrac{2}{3}$ **71.** yes; Alternate Exterior Angles Converse **73.** no

3.7 PRACTICE (pp. 175–177) **3.** yes; *Sample answer:* The slope of $\overleftrightarrow{AC}$ is -2, and the slope of $\overleftrightarrow{BD}$ is $\dfrac{1}{2}$, and $(-2)\left(\dfrac{1}{2}\right) = -1$. **5.** perpendicular **7.** yes **9.** yes **11.** no
13. $-\dfrac{1}{2}$ **15.** $\dfrac{1}{3}$ **17.** $-\dfrac{3}{2}$ **19.** 3 **21.** slope of $\overleftrightarrow{AC}$: 3; slope of $\overleftrightarrow{BD}$: $-\dfrac{1}{3}$; perpendicular **23.** slope of $\overleftrightarrow{AC}$: $\dfrac{1}{3}$; slope of $\overleftrightarrow{BD}$: $-\dfrac{5}{2}$; not perpendicular **25.** perpendicular
27. perpendicular **29.** perpendicular **31.** not perpendicular
33. slope of $\overleftrightarrow{AB}$: -1; slope of $\overleftrightarrow{PQ}$: $\dfrac{6}{7}$; slope of $\overleftrightarrow{WV}$: -1; $\overleftrightarrow{AB} \parallel \overleftrightarrow{WV}$ **35.** slope of $\overleftrightarrow{AZ}$: $\dfrac{2}{3}$; slope of $\overleftrightarrow{CD}$: $-\dfrac{4}{3}$; slope of $\overleftrightarrow{RS}$: $\dfrac{3}{4}$; $\overleftrightarrow{CD} \perp \overleftrightarrow{RS}$

37. *Sample answer:* The slopes are 2 and $-\frac{1}{2}$, and the product of the two slopes is -1.   **39.** $y = -\frac{3}{5}x + 4$ **41.** $y = \frac{3}{4}x - \frac{7}{4}$
43. $y = -7x + 39$ **45.** $y = \frac{5}{2}x - \frac{35}{2}$ **47.** parallel
49. perpendicular

3.7 MIXED REVIEW (p. 178)
55. $142°$ **57.** $35°$ **59.** $\angle 6$ **61.** $\angle 6$

QUIZ 3 (p. 178)   **1.** $\frac{3}{2}$ **2.** $-\frac{8}{3}$ **3.** $y = 3x + 2$ **4.** $y = \frac{1}{2}x - 5$
5. yes   **6.** no   **7.** 1

CHAPTER 3 REVIEW (pp. 180–182)   **1.** alternate exterior
3. $\overleftrightarrow{BF}$, $\overleftrightarrow{CG}$, or $\overleftrightarrow{AE}$ **5.** Possible answers: $\overleftrightarrow{CG}$, $\overleftrightarrow{AB}$, $\overleftrightarrow{AC}$,
$\overleftrightarrow{AE}$, $\overleftrightarrow{EG}$, $\overleftrightarrow{GH}$ **7.** $m\angle 2 = 105°$; $m\angle 3 = 105°$; $m\angle 4 = 75°$;
$m\angle 5 = 75°$; $m\angle 6 = 105°$ **9.** 22; Alternate Interior Angles
Postulate, $(4x + 4)° = 92°$. So, $x = \frac{92° - 4°}{4} = 22$.
11. Since $m\angle 4 = 60°$ and $m\angle 7 = 120°$, they are
supplementary because their measures add up to $180°$. By
the Consecutive Interior Angles Converse, $\ell \parallel m$.   **13.** $j \parallel k$;
Corresponding Angles Converse
15. $m \parallel n$; Consecutive Interior Angles Converse
17. Slope of $\overleftrightarrow{AB}$ and $\overleftrightarrow{CD}$ is $\frac{1}{2}$; yes.
19. Slope of $\overleftrightarrow{JK} = 3$; slope of $\overleftrightarrow{MN} = \frac{5}{2}$; no   **21.** yes   **23.** yes

CUMULATIVE PRACTICE (pp. 186–187)   **1.** You add 2, then 3,
then 4, and so on: 30.   **3.** $\overleftrightarrow{DT}$ **5.** Exactly 1; through any
three noncollinear points there is exactly one plane.
7. $(-13, 3)$ **9.**
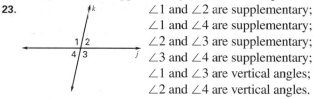
; right   **11.** $x = 6$, $y = 2$
13. $x = 16$, $y = 36$
15. 40 units^2

17. If an angle is a straight angle, then its measure is $180°$. If
an angle is not a straight angle, then its measure is not $180°$.
If an angle measure is $180°$, then it is a straight angle. If an
angle measure is not $180°$, then it is not a straight angle.
19. Two lines can intersect to form acute and obtuse angles.
21. If the angles are same side interior angles of two parallel
lines, they would be supplementary but not a linear pair.
23.
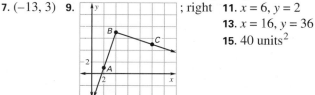
$\angle 1$ and $\angle 2$ are supplementary;
$\angle 1$ and $\angle 4$ are supplementary;
$\angle 2$ and $\angle 3$ are supplementary;
$\angle 3$ and $\angle 4$ are supplementary;
$\angle 1$ and $\angle 3$ are vertical angles;
$\angle 2$ and $\angle 4$ are vertical angles.

25. Yes; by the Law of Detachment   **27.** $55°$
29. $\overleftrightarrow{DE} \parallel \overleftrightarrow{AC}$ by the Consecutive Interior Angles Converse.
31. slope of $\overleftrightarrow{AD} = -\frac{11}{23}$, slope of $\overleftrightarrow{BC} = -\frac{11}{23}$ **33.** $y = -\frac{3}{4}x + \frac{21}{4}$
35. a. 6 in. by 9 in.   **b.** $\angle 1$ and $\angle 3$ are complementary.
c. $\angle 1$ and $\angle 2$ are supplementary.

CHAPTER 4

7.

8.
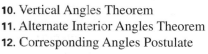

9.
10. Vertical Angles Theorem
11. Alternate Interior Angles Theorem
12. Corresponding Angles Postulate

4.1 PRACTICE (pp. 198–200)   **7.** right scalene   **9.** $77.5°$
11. E   **13.** D   **15.** C   **17.** right isosceles   **19.** right scalene
21. acute scalene   **23.** sometimes   **25.** always   **27.** (Ex. 17)
legs: $\overline{DE}$, $\overline{DF}$, hypotenuse: $\overline{EF}$; (Ex. 19) legs: $\overline{RP}$, $\overline{RQ}$,
hypotenuse: $\overline{PQ}$ **29.** $C(5, 5)$ **31.** $48°$ **33.** $m\angle 1 = 79°$,
$m\angle 2 = 51°$, $m\angle 3 = 39°$ **35.** $m\angle R = 20°$, $m\angle S = 140°$,
$m\angle T = 20°$; obtuse   **37.** $70°$ **39.** $143°$ **41.** $120°$, $24°$
43. Yes; the total length needed is 3×33.5, or 100.5 cm.
45. $\overline{MN}$ and $\overline{LN}$; $\overline{ML}$

47.

Statements	Reasons
4. $m\angle A + m\angle B +$ $m\angle ACB = 180°$	3. Linear Pair Postulate 5. Substitution property of equality 6. Subtraction property of equality

4.1 MIXED REVIEW (p. 201)   **53.** true   **55.** false
57. yes; Alternate Interior Angles Converse   **59.** yes;
Corresponding Angles Converse   **61.** $y = x + 3$
63. $y = \frac{2}{3}x - 7$ **65.** $y = -\frac{7}{2}x - 10$ **67.** $y = -\frac{3}{2}x + 15$

4.2 PRACTICE (pp. 205–208)   **5.** $45°$ **7.** $30°$ **9.** $\overline{PR}$ **11.** $\overline{CA}$
13. $\overline{UV}$ **15.** B, C, D   **17.** triangles FGH and JKH; $\angle FHG \cong$
$\angle JHK$ by the Vertical Angles Theorem, so the triangles
are congruent by the definition of congruence; $\triangle FGH$ and
$\triangle JKH$.   **19.** pentagons $VWXYZ$ and $MNJKL$; definition of
congruence; $VWXYZ \cong MNJKL$ **21.** triangles LKR and
NMQ and quadrilaterals $LKQS$ and $NMRS$; $\overline{LR}$ and $\overline{NQ}$ are
congruent by the addition property of equality, the Segment
Addition Postulate, and the definition of congruence and
$\angle NQM$ and $\angle LRK$ are congruent by the Third Angles
Theorem, so the triangles are congruent by the definition of
congruence; $\angle LSQ \cong \angle NSR$ by the Vertical Angles Theorem
and $\angle KQS \cong \angle MRS$ by the Congruent Supplements
Theorem, so the quadrilaterals are congruent by the
definition of congruence; $\triangle LKR \cong \triangle NMQ$, $LKQS \cong NMRS$.
25. $a = 13$, $b = 13$ **27.** 12   **29.** 65   **31.** $120°$
33. The measure of each of the congruent angles in each
small triangle is $30°$. By the Angle Addition Postulate, the
measure of each angle of $\triangle ABC$ is $60°$.

35.

Statements	Reasons
7. $\angle C \cong \angle F$	1. Given
	2. A, D, B, E; Definition of congruent angles
	3. Triangle Sum Theorem
	4. Substitution property of equality or transitive property of equality
	5. Substitution property of equality
	6. Subtraction property of equality

37. $\triangle ABF$ and $\triangle EBF$; $\overline{BF} \cong \overline{BF}$ by the Reflexive Property of Congruence, and $\angle A$ and $\angle BEF$ are congruent by the Third Angles Theorem, so the triangles are congruent by the definition of congruence.

4.2 MIXED REVIEW (p. 209) **41.** $4\sqrt{10}$ **43.** $\sqrt{26}$ **45.** $3\sqrt{13}$ **47.** $(-2, -2)$ **49.** $(1, 0)$ **51.** $(10, 3)$ **53.** $82°$ **55.** $28°$ **57.** $-\frac{5}{2}$ and -2; no

QUIZ 1 (p. 210) **1.** acute isosceles **2.** acute isosceles **3.** obtuse scalene **4.** 7; $m\angle F = 77°$, $m\angle E = 55°$, $m\angle EDF = 48°$, $m\angle CDF = 132°$ **5.** $\triangle MNP \cong \triangle QPN$; $\angle M$ and $\angle Q$, $\angle MNP$ and $\angle QPN$, $\angle MPN$ and $\angle QNP$, $\overline{MN}$ and $\overline{QP}$, $\overline{NP}$ and $\overline{PN}$, $\overline{MP}$ and $\overline{QN}$ **6.** $107°$

4.3 PRACTICE (pp. 216–219) **3.** yes; SAS Congruence Postulate **5.** yes; SSS Congruence Postulate **7.** $\angle LKP$ **9.** $\angle KJL$ **11.** $\angle KPL$ **13.** yes; SAS Congruence Postulate **15.** yes; SAS Congruence Postulate **17.** yes; SSS Congruence Postulate **19.** $\angle ACB \cong \angle CED$

21.

Statements	Reasons
1. $\overline{NP} \cong \overline{QN} \cong \overline{RS} \cong \overline{TR}$; $\overline{PQ} \cong \overline{ST}$	1. Given
2. $\triangle NPQ \cong \triangle RST$	2. SSS Congruence Postulate

23. It is given that $\overline{SP} \cong \overline{TP}$ and that $\overline{PQ}$ bisects $\angle SPT$. Then, by the definition of angle bisector, $\angle SPQ \cong \angle TPQ$. $\overline{PQ} \cong \overline{PQ}$ by the Reflexive Property of Congruence, so $\triangle SPQ \cong \triangle TPQ$ by the SAS Congruence Postulate.

25.

Statements	Reasons
1. $\overline{AC} \cong \overline{BC}$; M is the midpoint of $\overline{AB}$.	1. Given
2. $\overline{AM} \cong \overline{BM}$	2. Definition of midpoint
3. $\overline{CM} \cong \overline{CM}$	3. Reflexive Property of Congruence
4. $\triangle ACM \cong \triangle BCM$	4. SSS Congruence Postulate

27. Since it is given that $\overline{PA} \cong \overline{PB} \cong \overline{PC}$ and $\overline{AB} \cong \overline{BC}$, $\triangle PAB \cong \triangle PBC$ by the SSS Congruence Postulate.
29. The new triangle and the original triangle are congruent.
35. $AB = DE = 3$, $BC = EF = \sqrt{13}$, and $AC = DF = \sqrt{10}$, so all three pairs of sides are congruent and $\triangle ABC \cong \triangle DEF$ by the SSS Congruence Postulate.

4.3 MIXED REVIEW (p. 219) **39.** *Sample answer:* The measure of each of the angles formed by two adjacent "spokes" is about $60°$.

41. $m\angle 2 = 57°$ (Vertical Angles Theorem)
$m\angle 1 = 180° - m\angle 2 = 123°$
(Consecutive Interior Angles Theorem)
43. $m\angle 1 = 90°$ (Corresponding Angles Postulate)
$m\angle 2 = 90°$ (Alternate Interior Angles Theorem or Vertical Angles Theorem)
45. slope of $\overleftrightarrow{EF} = -2$, slope of $\overleftrightarrow{GH} = -2$, $\overleftrightarrow{EF} \parallel \overleftrightarrow{GH}$

4.4 PRACTICE (pp. 223–226) **5.** $\overline{AB} \cong \overline{DE}$ **7.** By the Right Angle Congruence Theorem, $\angle B \cong \angle D$. Since $\overline{AD} \parallel \overline{BC}$, $\angle CAD \cong \angle ACB$ by the Alternate Interior Angles Theorem. By the Reflexive Property of Congruence, $\overline{AC} \cong \overline{AC}$, so $\triangle ACD \cong \triangle CAB$ by the AAS Congruence Theorem. Then, all three pairs of corresponding sides are congruent; that is, they have the same length. So, $AB + BC + CA = CD + DA + AC$ and the two courses are the same length. **9.** Yes; SAS Congruence Postulate; two pairs of corresponding sides and the corresponding included angles are congruent.
11. No; two pairs of corresponding sides are congruent and corresponding nonincluded angles $\angle EGF$ and $\angle JGH$ are congruent by the Vertical Angles Theorem; that is insufficient to prove triangle congruence. **13.** Yes; SSS Congruence Postulate; $\overline{XY} \cong \overline{XY}$ by the Reflexive Property of Congruence, so all three pairs of corresponding sides are congruent. **15.** $\angle P \cong \angle S$ **17.** $\overline{QR} \cong \overline{TU}$

19.

Statements	Reasons
1. $\overline{FH} \parallel \overline{LK}$, $\overline{GF} \cong \overline{GL}$	1. Given
2. $\angle F \cong \angle L$, $\angle H \cong \angle K$	2. Alternate Interior Angles Theorem
3. $\triangle FGH \cong \triangle LGK$	3. AAS Congruence Theorem

21. It is given that $\overline{VX} \cong \overline{XY}$, $\overline{XW} \cong \overline{YZ}$, and that $\overline{XW} \parallel \overline{YZ}$. Then, $\angle VXW \cong \angle Y$ by the Corresponding Angles Postulate and $\triangle VXW \cong \triangle XYZ$ by the SAS Congruence Postulate. **23.** Yes; two sides of the triangle are north-south and east-west lines, which are perpendicular, so the measures of two angles and the length of a nonincluded side are known and only one such triangle is possible.

25.

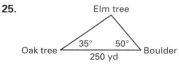

Yes; the measures of two angles and the length of the included side are known and only one such triangle is possible.

27.

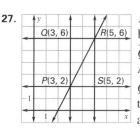

$\angle PQR \cong \angle RSP$ since they are both right angles, and since $\overline{QR} \parallel \overline{PS}$, $\angle PRQ \cong \angle RPS$ by the Alternate Interior Angles Theorem. $QR = SP = 2$, so $\overline{QR} \cong \overline{SP}$. Then, two pairs of corresponding angles and a pair of included sides are congruent, so $\triangle PQR \cong \triangle RSP$ by the ASA Congruence Postulate.

4.4 MIXED REVIEW (p. 227) **33.** (12, −13) **35.** $m\angle DBC =$ 42°, $m\angle ABC = 84°$ **37.** $m\angle ABD = 75°$, $m\angle ABC = 150°$

QUIZ 2 (p. 227) **1.** Yes; SAS Congruence Postulate; $\overline{BD} \cong \overline{BD}$ by the Reflexive Property of Congruence, so two pairs of corresponding sides and the corresponding included angles are congruent. **2.** Yes; SSS Congruence Postulate; $\overline{SQ} \cong \overline{SQ}$ by the Reflexive Property of Congruence, so three pairs of corresponding sides are congruent. **3.** No; two pairs of corresponding sides and one pair of corresponding nonincluded angles are congruent; that is insufficient to prove triangle congruence. **4.** Yes; ASA Congruence Postulate; $\overline{MK} \cong \overline{MK}$ by the Reflexive Property of Congruence, so two pairs of corresponding angles and the corresponding included sides are congruent. **5.** No; $\overline{ZB} \cong \overline{ZB}$ by the Reflexive Property of Congruence, so two pairs of corresponding sides are congruent; that is insufficient to prove triangle congruence. **6.** Yes; AAS Congruence Theorem; $\angle STR \cong \angle VTU$ by the Vertical Angles Theorem, so two pairs of corresponding angles and corresponding nonincluded sides are congruent.

7.

Statements	Reasons
1. M is the midpoint of $\overline{NL}$, $\overline{NL} \perp \overline{NQ}$, $\overline{NL} \perp \overline{MP}$, $\overline{QM} \parallel \overline{PL}$.	1. Given
2. $\angle N$ and $\angle PML$ are right angles.	2. If two lines are perpendicular, they form four right angles.
3. $\angle N \cong \angle PML$	3. Right Angle Congruence Theorem
4. $\overline{NM} \cong \overline{ML}$	4. Definition of midpoint
5. $\angle QMN \cong \angle PLM$	5. Corresponding Angles Postulate
6. $\triangle NQM \cong \triangle MPL$	6. ASA Congruence Postulate

4.5 PRACTICE (pp. 232–235)
3. *Sample answer:* A, G, C, F, E, B, D

Statements	Reasons
1. $\overline{QS} \perp \overline{RP}$	1. Given
2. $\angle PTS$ and $\angle RTS$ are right angles.	2. If two lines are perpendicular, then they form four right angles.
3. $\angle PTS \cong \angle RTS$	3. Right Angle Congruence Theorem
4. $\overline{TS} \cong \overline{TS}$	4. Reflexive Property of Congruence
5. $\overline{PT} \cong \overline{RT}$	5. Given
6. $\triangle PTS \cong \triangle RTS$	6. SAS Congruence Postulate
7. $\overline{PS} \cong \overline{RS}$	7. Corresp. parts of $\cong$ $\triangle$ are $\cong$.

5. You can use the method in the answer to Ex. 4 to show that $\triangle QUR \cong \triangle PUQ$, so by the Transitive Property of Congruent Triangles, $\triangle NUP \cong \triangle QUR$. (You could instead use the Transitive Property of Congruence to show that $\overline{UN} \cong \overline{UP} \cong \overline{UQ} \cong \overline{UR}$.)

7. $\triangle NUP$ and $\triangle PUQ$ are congruent by Ex. 4 above. Since corresponding parts of congruent triangles are congruent, $\angle UNP \cong \angle UPQ$. **9.** SSS Congruence Postulate; if $\triangle STV \cong \triangle UVT$, then $\angle STV \cong \angle UVT$ because corresponding parts of congruent triangles are congruent.

11.

Statements	Reasons
1. $\triangle AGD \cong \triangle FHC$	1. Given
2. $\overline{GD} \cong \overline{HC}$	2. Corresp. parts of $\cong$ $\triangle$ are $\cong$.

13.

Statements	Reasons
1. $\triangle EDA \cong \triangle BCF$	1. Given
2. $\overline{AE} \cong \overline{FB}$	2. Corresp. parts of $\cong$ $\triangle$ are $\cong$.

15.

Statements	Reasons
3. $\overline{CF} \cong \overline{CF}$	1. Given
6. $\angle AFB \cong \angle EFD$	2. Given
	4. AAS Congruence Theorem
	5. Corresp. parts of $\cong$ $\triangle$ are $\cong$.
	7. ASA Congruence Postulate

17.

Statements	Reasons
1. $\overline{UR} \parallel \overline{ST}$, $\angle R$ and $\angle T$ are right angles.	1. Given
2. $\angle R \cong \angle T$	2. Right Angle Congruence Theorem
3. $\angle RUS \cong \angle TSU$	3. Alternate Interior Angles Theorem
4. $\overline{US} \cong \overline{US}$	4. Reflexive Property of Congruence
5. $\triangle RSU \cong \triangle TUS$	5. AAS Congruence Theorem
6. $\angle RSU \cong \angle TUS$	6. Corresp. parts of $\cong$ $\triangle$ are $\cong$.

19. It is given that $\overline{AB} \cong \overline{AC}$ and $\overline{BD} \cong \overline{CD}$. By the Reflexive Property of Congruence, $\overline{AD} \cong \overline{AD}$. So, $\triangle ACD \cong \triangle ABD$ by the SSS Congruence Postulate. Then, since corresponding parts of congruent triangles are congruent, $\angle CAD \cong \angle BAD$. Then, by definition, $\overrightarrow{AD}$ bisects $\angle A$.

21.

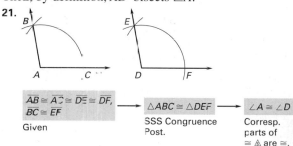

4.5 MIXED REVIEW (p. 235) **25.** 170 m; 1650 m^2
27. 75.36 cm; 452 16 cm^2
29. $x + 11 = 21$
$x = 10$ Subtraction property of equality
31. $8x + 13 = 3x + 38$
$5x + 13 = 38$ Subtraction property of equality
$5x = 25$ Subtraction property of equality
$x = 5$ Division property of equality

33. $6(2x - 1) + 15 = 69$

$6(2x - 1) = 54$	Subtraction property of equality
$2x - 1 = 9$	Division property of equality
$2x = 10$	Addition property of equality
$x = 5$	Division property of equality

35. right scalene; legs: $\overline{MN}$ and $\overline{MP}$, hypotenuse: $\overline{NP}$

4.6 PRACTICE (pp. 239–242) **5.** Yes; the hypotenuse and one leg of one right triangle are congruent to the hypotenuse and one leg of the other. **7.** No; it cannot be shown that $\triangle ABC$ is equilateral. **9.** $x = 70$, $y = 70$ **11.** Yes; the triangles can be proved congruent using the SSS Congruence Postulate. **13.** Yes; the triangles can be proved congruent using the ASA Congruence Postulate, the SSS Congruence Postulate, the SAS Congruence Postulate, or the AAS Congruence Theorem. **15.** Yes; the triangles can be proved congruent using the HL Congruence Theorem. **17.** 11 **19.** 7 **21.** $x = 52.5$, $y = 75$ **23.** $x = 30$, $y = 120$ **25.** $x = 60$, $y = 30$ **27.** GIVEN: $\overline{AB} \cong \overline{AC} \cong \overline{BC}$; PROVE: $\angle A \cong \angle B \cong \angle C$; Since $\overline{AB} \cong \overline{AC}$, $\angle B \cong \angle C$ by the Base Angles Theorem. Since $\overline{AB} \cong \overline{BC}$, $\angle A \cong \angle C$ by the Base Angles Theorem. Then, by the Transitive Property of Congruence, $\angle A \cong \angle B \cong \angle C$ and $\triangle ABC$ is equiangular. **29.** $\triangle ABD$ and $\triangle CBD$ are congruent equilateral triangles, so $\overline{AB} \cong \overline{CB}$ and $\triangle ABC$ is isosceles by definition. **31.** Since $\triangle ABD$ and $\triangle CBD$ are congruent equilateral triangles, $\overline{AB} \cong \overline{BC}$ and $\angle ABD \cong \angle CBD$. By the Base Angles Theorem, $\angle BAE \cong \angle BCE$. Then, $\triangle ABE \cong \triangle CBE$ by the AAS Congruence Theorem. Moreover, by the Linear Pair Postulate, $m\angle AEB + m\angle CEB = 180°$. But $\angle AEB$ and $\angle CEB$ are corresponding parts of congruent triangles, so they are congruent, that is, $m\angle AEB = m\angle CEB$. Then, by the Substitution Property, $2m\angle AEB = 180°$ and $m\angle AEB = 90°$. So, $\angle AEB$ and $\angle CEB$ are both right angles, and $\triangle AEB$ and $\triangle CEB$ are congruent right triangles.

33.

Statements	Reasons
1. D is the midpoint of $\overline{CE}$, $\angle BCD$ and $\angle FED$ are rt. $\angle s$.	1. Given
2. $\angle BCD \cong \angle FED$	2. Right Angle Congruence Theorem
3. $\overline{CD} \cong \overline{ED}$	3. Definition of midpoint
4. $\overline{BD} \cong \overline{FD}$	4. Given
5. $\triangle BCD \cong \triangle FED$	5. HL Congruence Theorem

35. Each of the triangles is isosceles and every pair of adjacent triangles have a common side, so the legs of all the triangles are congruent by the Transitive Property of Congruence. The common vertex angles are congruent, so any two of the triangles are congruent by the SAS Congruence Postulate. **37.** equilateral **39.** It is given that $\angle CDB \cong \angle ADB$ and that $\overline{DB} \perp \overline{AC}$. Since perpendicular lines form right angles, $\angle ABD$ and $\angle CBD$ are right angles. By the Right Angle Congruence Theorem, $\angle ABD \cong \angle CBD$.

By the Reflexive Property of Congruence, $\overline{DB} \cong \overline{DB}$, so $\triangle ABD \cong \triangle CBD$ by the ASA Congruence Postulate. **41.** No; the measure of $\angle ADB$ will decrease, as will the measure of $\angle CDB$ and the amount of reflection will remain the same.

4.6 MIXED REVIEW (p. 242)

45. congruent **47.** not congruent **49.** $(4, 4)$ **51.** $\left(1\frac{1}{2}, 4\frac{1}{2}\right)$ **53.** $\left(-1\frac{1}{2}, -12\frac{1}{2}\right)$ **55.** $y = -x$ **57.** $y = -\frac{3}{2}x - \frac{1}{2}$

4.7 PRACTICE (pp. 246–249) **3.** $(4, 0)$, $(4, 7)$, $(-4, 7)$, $(-4, 0)$ **5.** Use the Distance Formula to show that $\overline{AB} \cong \overline{AC}$. **7.** *Sample figure:*

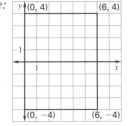

9, 11. Good placements should include vertices for which at least one coordinate is 0.

9. *Sample figure:*   **11.** *Sample figure:*

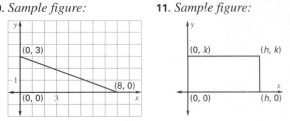

13. 58.31 **15.** $\sqrt{41}$ **17.** $3\sqrt{2}$ **19.** $(45, 35)$ **21.** Show that, since $\overline{HJ}$ and $\overline{OF}$ both have slope 0, they are parallel, so that alternate interior angles $\angle H$ and $\angle F$ are congruent. $\overline{HG} \cong \overline{FG}$ by the definition of midpoint. Then use the Distance Formula to show that $\overline{HJ} \cong \overline{OF}$ so that $\triangle GHJ \cong \triangle GFO$ by the SAS Congruence Postulate. **23.** $F(2h, 0)$, $E(2h, h)$; $h\sqrt{5}$ **25.** $O(0, 0)$, $R(k, k)$, $S(k, 2k)$, $T(2k, 2k)$, $U(k, 0)$; $2k\sqrt{2}$ **27.** Since $OC = \sqrt{h^2 + k^2}$ and $EC = \sqrt{h^2 + k^2}$, $\overline{OC} \cong \overline{EC}$, and since $BC = k$ and $DC = k$, $\overline{BC} \cong \overline{DC}$. Then, since vertical angles $\angle OCB$ and $\angle ECD$ are congruent, $\triangle OBC \cong \triangle EDC$ by the SAS Congruence Postulate. **29.** isosceles; no; no **31.** The triangle in Exercise 5 has vertices which can be used to describe $\triangle ABC$. Point A is on the y-axis and points B and C are on the x-axis, equidistant from the origin. The proof shows that any such triangle is isosceles.

4.7 MIXED REVIEW (p. 250) **35.** 5 **37.** true **39.** true **41.** If two triangles are congruent, then the corresponding angles of the triangles are congruent; true. **43.** If two triangles are not congruent, then the corresponding angles of the triangles are not congruent; false.

QUIZ 3 (p. 250)

1.

Statements	Reasons
1. $\overline{DF} \cong \overline{DG}, \overline{ED} \cong \overline{HD}$	1. Given
2. $\angle EDF \cong \angle HDG$	2. Vertical Angles Theorem
3. $\triangle EDF \cong \triangle HDG$	3. SAS Congruence Postulate
4. $\angle EFD \cong \angle HGD$	4. Corresp. parts of $\cong$ $\triangle$ are $\cong$.

2.

Statements	Reasons
1. $\overline{ST} \cong \overline{UT} \cong \overline{VU}$, $\overline{SU} \parallel \overline{TV}$	1. Given
2. $\angle S \cong \angle SUT$, $\angle UTV \cong \angle V$	2. Base Angles Theorem
3. $\angle SUT \cong \angle UTV$	3. Alternate Interior Angles Theorem
4. $\angle S \cong \angle SUT \cong \angle UTV \cong \angle V$	4. Transitive Property of Congruence
5. $\triangle STU \cong \triangle TUV$	5. AAS Congruence Theorem

3. Use the Distance Formula to show that OP, PM, NM, and ON are all equal, so that $\overline{OP} \cong \overline{PM} \cong \overline{NM} \cong \overline{ON}$. Since $\overline{OM} \cong \overline{OM}$ by the Reflexive Property of Congruence, $\triangle OPM \cong \triangle ONM$ by the SSS Congruence Postulate and both triangles are isosceles by definition.

CHAPTER 4 REVIEW (pp. 252–254) **1.** isosceles right **3.** obtuse isosceles **5.** 53° **7.** $\angle A$ and $\angle X$, $\angle B$ and $\angle Y$, $\angle C$ and $\angle Z$, $\overline{AB}$ and $\overline{XY}$, $\overline{BC}$ and $\overline{YZ}$, $\overline{AC}$ and $\overline{XZ}$ **9.** Yes; ASA Congruence Postulate; two pairs of corresponding angles are congruent and the corresponding included sides are congruent. **11.** Yes; AAS Congruence Theorem; because $\overline{HF} \parallel \overline{JE}$, $\angle HFG \cong \angle E$ (Corresponding Angles Postulate), so two pairs of corresponding angles are congruent and two nonincluded sides are congruent. **13.** $\overline{PQ}$ **15.** 54 **17.** 110

ALGEBRA REVIEW (pp. 258–259) **1.** $\sqrt{73}$ **2.** $\sqrt{170}$ **3.** 4 **4.** 5 **5.** $\sqrt{137}$ **6.** $\sqrt{65}$ **7.** $2x + 12y$ **8.** $-m + 2q$ **9.** $-5p - 9t$ **10.** $27x - 25y$ **11.** $9x^2 y - 5xy^2$ **12.** $-2x^2 + 3xy$ **13.** 6 **14.** 6 **15.** -10 **16.** -5 **17.** 0 **18.** 0 **19.** 10 **20.** no solution **21.** 2 **22.** $x < -5$ **23.** $c < 28$ **24.** $m < 26$ **25.** $x < 9$ **26.** $z > -8$ **27.** $x \geq 3$ **28.** $x < -11$ **29.** $m \geq 1$ **30.** $b > \frac{3}{5}$ **31.** $x < \frac{3}{10}$ **32.** $z \leq 1$ **33.** $t \leq -\frac{14}{5}$ **34.** $r > -6$ **35.** $x \geq -1$ **36.** $x \leq -7$ **37.** $x = 7$ or -17 **38.** $x = 12$ or -8 **39.** $x = 2$ or 8 **40.** $x = 7$ or -5 **41.** $x = 14$ or -20 **42.** $x = -1$ or $\frac{9}{5}$ **43.** $x = 7$ or -4 **44.** $x = \frac{12}{7}$ or -4 **45.** $x = -2$ or $\frac{9}{2}$ **46.** $x = -\frac{4}{3}$ or -4 **47.** $x \geq 10$ or $x \leq -36$ **48.** $x > 14$ or $x < -2$ **49.** $-6 \leq x \leq 10$ **50.** $x \leq 8$ or $x \geq 22$ **51.** $12 < x < 20$ **52.** $-\frac{2}{3} < x < 2$ **53.** $-3 \leq x \leq 7$ **54.** $-\frac{5}{3} \leq x \leq 3$ **55.** $x \leq -2$ or $x \geq 4$ **56.** $x < -8$ or $x > 5$ **57.** $-6 < x < 2$ **58.** $x < -2$ or $x > 5$ **59.** $x \leq -6$ or $x \geq 2$ **60.** $-1 < x < \frac{23}{5}$ **61.** $x < -2$ or $x > \frac{20}{11}$ **62.** no solution **63.** $x < -\frac{8}{3}$ or $x > 4$ **64.** $-3 \leq x \leq \frac{1}{3}$ **65.** all real numbers **66.** $-2 \leq x \leq 0$

CHAPTER 5

SKILL REVIEW (p. 262) **3.** $(-1, 2)$ **4.** 5 **5.** 2 **6.** $-\frac{1}{2}$

5.1 PRACTICE (pp. 267–271) **3.** $\overline{AD} \cong \overline{BD}$ **5.** $\overline{AC} \cong \overline{BC}$; C is on the $\perp$ bisector of $\overline{AB}$. **7.** The distance from M to $\overrightarrow{PL}$ is equal to the distance from M to $\overrightarrow{PN}$. **9.** No; the diagram does not show that $CA = CB$. **11.** No; since P is not equidistant from the sides of $\angle A$, P is not on the bisector of $\angle A$. **13.** No; the diagram does not show that the segments with equal length are perpendicular segments. **15.** D is 1.5 in. from each side of $\angle A$. **17.** 17 **19.** 2 **21.** 3 **23.** C **25.** D **27.** $\overline{PA} \cong \overline{AB}$ and $\overline{CA} \cong \overline{CB}$ by construction. By the Reflexive Prop. of Cong., $\overline{CP} \cong \overline{CP}$. Then, $\triangle CPA \cong \triangle CPB$ by the SSS Cong. Post. Corresp. angles $\angle CPA$ and $\angle CPB$ are $\cong$. Then, $\overleftrightarrow{CP} \perp \overleftrightarrow{AB}$. (If 2 lines form a linear pair of $\cong$ $\angle$s, then the lines are $\perp$.)

29.

Statements	Reasons
1. Draw a line through $C \perp$ to $\overline{AB}$ intersecting $\overline{AB}$ at P.	1. Through a point not on a line there is exactly one line $\perp$ to a given line.
2. $\angle CPA$ and $\angle CPB$ are right $\angle$s.	2. Def. of $\perp$ lines
3. $\triangle CPA$ and $\triangle CPB$ are right $\triangle$s.	3. Def. of right $\triangle$
4. $CA = CB$, or $\overline{CA} \cong \overline{CB}$	4. Given; def. of cong.
5. $\overline{CP} \cong \overline{CP}$	5. Reflexive Prop. of Cong.
6. $\triangle CPA \cong \triangle CPB$	6. HL Cong. Thm.
7. $\overline{PA} \cong \overline{PB}$	7. Corresp. parts of $\cong$ $\triangle$ are $\cong$.
8. $\overleftrightarrow{CP}$ is the $\perp$ bisector of $\overline{AB}$ and C is on the $\perp$ bisector of $\overline{AB}$.	8. Def. of $\perp$ bisector

31. The post is the $\perp$ bisector of the segment between the ends of the wires. **33.** ℓ is the $\perp$ bisector of $\overline{AB}$. **35.** $m\angle APB$ increases; more difficult; the goalie has a greater area to defend because the distances from the goalie to the sides of $\angle APB$ (the shooting angle) increase.

5.1 MIXED REVIEW (p. 271) **41.** 6 cm **43.** about 113.04 cm^2 **45.** $-\frac{4}{5}$ **47.** $\frac{8}{7}$ **49.** 0 **51.** 34

5.2 PRACTICE (pp. 275–278) **3.** 7 **5.** outside **7.** on **9.** The segments are $\cong$; Thm. 5.6. **11.** always **13.** sometimes **15.** 20 **17.** 25 **19.** The $\angle$ bisectors of a $\triangle$ intersect in a point that is equidistant from the sides of the $\triangle$, but MC and MN are not necessarily distances to the sides; M is equidistant from $\overline{JK}$, $\overline{KL}$, and $\overline{JL}$.

21.

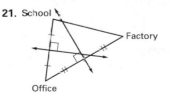

25. about $2\frac{1}{2}$ feet

5.2 MIXED REVIEW (p. 278) **33.** 77 square units
35. $y = \frac{1}{2}x + \frac{5}{2}$ **37.** $y = -\frac{11}{10}x - \frac{56}{5}$ **39.** no

5.3 PRACTICE (pp. 282–284) **3.** median **5.** angle bisector
7. $\perp$ bisector, $\angle$ bisector, median, altitude
9. 12 **11.** 48 **15.** yes **17.** (5, 0) **19.** (5, 2) **21.** (4, 4)
23. $\frac{JP}{JM} = \frac{2\sqrt{5}}{3\sqrt{5}} = \frac{2}{3}$, so $JP = \frac{2}{3}JM$.
29. Measure GH. Because $GH = 0$, G and H must be the
same point; therefore, the lines containing the three
altitudes intersect at one point.

30–32. 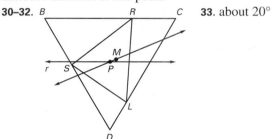 **33.** about 20°

5.3 MIXED REVIEW (p. 284) **39.** $y = -x + 8$ **41.** $y = 3x - 21$
43. $\angle E \cong \angle H$ **45.** $5\sqrt{10}$

QUIZ 1 (p. 285) **1.** 16 **2.** 12 **3.** 10 **4.** 10; the $\perp$ bisectors
intersect at a point equidistant from the vertices of the $\triangle$.
5. at G, the intersection of the medians of $\triangle ABC$,
8 in. from C on $\overline{CF}$

5.4 PRACTICE (pp. 290–293) **3.** $\overline{DF}$ **5.** 21.2 **7.** 16 **9.** 30.6
11. about 54 yd **13.** $\overline{MN}$ **15.** 14 **17.** 31 **19.** $\angle BLN$, $\angle A$,
and $\angle NMC$ are $\cong$ by the Corresp. Angles Post., as are
$\angle BNL$, $\angle C$, and $\angle LMA$. By the Alternate Interior Angles
Thm., $\angle LNM \cong \angle NMC$ and $\angle NLM \cong \angle LMA$, so by the
Transitive Prop. of Cong., $\angle BLN$, $\angle A$, $\angle NMC$, and
$\angle LNM$ are $\cong$, as are $\angle BNL$, $\angle C$, $\angle LMA$, and $\angle NLM$.
Then, $\angle B$, $\angle ALM$, $\angle LMN$, and $\angle MNC$ are all $\cong$ by the
Third Angles Thm. and the Transitive Prop. of Cong.
21. $D\left(2\frac{1}{2}, 0\right)$, $E\left(7\frac{1}{2}, 2\right)$, $F(5, 4)$ **23.** $(c, 0)$

25. $DF = \sqrt{(a-c)^2 + (b-0)^2} = \sqrt{(a-c)^2 + b^2}$ and
$CB = \sqrt{(2a-2c)^2 + (2b-0)^2} = 2\sqrt{(a-c)^2 + b^2}$, so
$DF = \frac{1}{2}CB$; $EF = \sqrt{(a+c-c)^2 + (b-0)^2} = \sqrt{a^2 + b^2}$
and $CA = \sqrt{(2a-0)^2 + (2b-0)^2} = 2\sqrt{a^2 + b^2}$, so
$EF = \frac{1}{2}CA$. **27.** (3, −1), (11, 3), (7, 9) **29.** 31 **31.** $\frac{1}{2}$; $1\frac{1}{4}$; $2\frac{3}{8}$
33. $\overline{DE}$ is a midsegment of $\triangle ABC$, so D is the midpoint of
$\overline{AB}$ and $\overline{AD} \cong \overline{DB}$. $\overline{DE}$ is also a midsegment of $\triangle ABC$, so
by the Midsegment Thm., $\overline{DE} \parallel \overline{BC}$ and $DE = \frac{1}{2}BC$. But F
is the midpoint of $\overline{BC}$, so $BF = \frac{1}{2}BC$. Then by the transitive
prop. of equality and the def. of cong., $\overline{DE} \cong \overline{BF}$. Corresp.
angles $\angle ADE$ and $\angle ABC$ are $\cong$, so $\triangle ADE \cong \triangle DBF$ by the
SAS Cong. Post.

35. No, no, yes, no; if you imagine "sliding" a segment
parallel to $\overline{RS}$ up the triangle, then its length decreases
as the segment slides upward (as can be shown with a
coordinate argument). So, $MN < PQ < RS$, or $12 < PQ < 24$.

5.4 MIXED REVIEW (p. 293)
39. $x - 3 = 11$
  $x = 14$ (Addition prop. of equality)
41. $8x - 1 = 2x + 17$
  $8x = 2x + 18$ (Addition prop. of equality)
  $6x = 18$ (Subtraction prop. of equality)
  $x = 3$ (Division prop. of equality)
43. $2(4x - 1) = 14$
  $4x - 1 = 7$ (Division prop. of equality)
  $4x = 8$ (Addition prop. of equality)
  $x = 2$ (Division prop. of equality)
45. $-2(x + 1) + 3 = 23$
  $-2(x + 1) = 20$ (Subtraction prop. of equality)
  $x + 1 = -10$ (Division prop. of equality)
  $x = -11$ (Subtraction prop. of equality)
47. 23 **49.** 18 **51.** incenter **53.** 6

5.5 PRACTICE (pp. 298–301) **3.** $\angle D$, $\angle F$ **5.** greater than
66 mi and less than 264 mi **7.** $\overline{RT}$, $\overline{SR}$ and $\overline{ST}$ ($\overline{SR} \cong \overline{ST}$)
9. $\angle C$, $\angle B$ **11.** $\angle H$, $\angle F$ **13.** $x > y$, $x > z$ **15.** $\overline{DF}$, $\overline{DE}$, $\overline{EF}$
17. $\angle L$, $\angle K$, $\angle M$ **19.** $\angle T$, $\angle S$, $\angle R$
21, 23. Sample answers are given.
21. 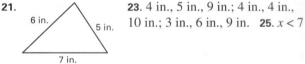 **23.** 4 in., 5 in., 9 in.; 4 in., 4 in.,
10 in.; 3 in., 6 in., 9 in. **25.** $x < 7$

27. The sides and angles could not be positioned as they
are labeled; for example, the longest side is not opposite
the largest angle. **29.** raised **31.** Yes; when the boom is
lowered and $AB > 100$ (and so $AB > BC$), then $\angle ACB$ will
be larger than $\angle BAC$.
33. $\overline{MJ} \perp \overline{JN}$, so $\triangle MJN$ is a right $\triangle$. The largest $\angle$ in a right
$\triangle$ is the right $\angle$, so $m\angle MJN > m\angle MNJ$, so $MN > MJ$.
(If one $\angle$ of a $\triangle$ is larger than another $\angle$, then the side opp.
the larger $\angle$ is longer than the side opp. the smaller $\angle$.)

5.5 MIXED REVIEW (p. 301) **39, 41.** Sample answers are
given. **39.** proof of Theorem 4.1, page 196 **41.** Example 1,
page 136 **43.** $\angle 9$ **45.** $\angle 2$; $\angle 10$ **47.** (−7, 3), (−5, −3),
(1, 7) **49.** (0, 0), (6, −4), (0, −8)

5.6 PRACTICE (p. 305–307) **3.** > **5.** < **7.** < **9.** > **11.** =
13. > **15.** > **17.** B; $AD = AD$, $AB = DC$, and $m\angle 3 < m\angle 5$,
so by the Hinge Thm., $AC > BD$. **19.** $x > 1$ **21.** Given that
$RS + ST \neq 12$ in. and $ST = 5$ in., assume that $RS = 7$ in.
23. Given $\triangle ABC$ with $m\angle A + m\angle B = 90°$, assume $m\angle C \neq$
90°. (That is, assume that either $m\angle C < 90°$ or $m\angle C > 90°$.)
25. Case 1: Assume that $EF < DF$. If one side of a $\triangle$ is
longer than another side, then the $\angle$ opp. the longer side is
larger than the $\angle$ opp. the shorter side, so $m\angle D < m\angle E$.
But this contradicts the given information that $m\angle D > m\angle E$.

Case 2: Assume that $EF = DF$. By the Converse of the Base Angles Thm., $m\angle E = m\angle D$. But this contradicts the given information that $m\angle D > m\angle E$. Since both cases produce a contradiction, the assumption that EF is not greater than DF must be incorrect and $EF > DF$.
27. Assume that $RS > RT$. Then $m\angle T > m\angle S$. But $\triangle RUS \cong \triangle RUT$ by the ASA Congruence Postulate, so $\angle S \cong \angle T$, or $m\angle T = m\angle S$. This is a contradiction, so $RS \leq RT$. We get a similar contradiction if we assume $RT > RS$; therefore, $RS = RT$, and $\triangle RST$ is isosceles by definition.
29. The paths are described by two $\triangle$ in which two sides of one $\triangle$ are $\cong$ to two sides of another $\triangle$, but the included $\angle$ in your friend's $\triangle$ is larger than the included $\angle$ in yours, so the side representing the distance from the airport is longer in your friend's $\triangle$.

5.6 MIXED REVIEW (p. 308) **33.** isosceles, equiangular, equilateral **35.** isosceles **37.** isosceles **39.** 51° **41.** 84°

QUIZ 2 (p. 308) **1.** $\overline{CE}$ **2.** 16 **3.** 21 **4.** $\overline{LQ}$, $\overline{LM}$, $\overline{MQ}$
5. $\overline{QM}$, $\overline{PM}$, $\overline{QP}$ **6.** $\overline{MP}$, $\overline{NP}$, $\overline{MN}$ **7.** $\overline{DE}$
8. the second group

CHAPTER 5 REVIEW (pp. 310–312) **1.** If a point is on the $\perp$ bisector of a segment, then it is equidistant from the endpoints of the segment. **3.** Q is on the bisector of $\angle RST$. **5.** 6 **7.** $\perp$ bisectors; circumcenter **9.** altitudes; orthocenter **11.** (0, 0) **13.** Let L be the midpoint of $\overline{HJ}$, M the midpoint of $\overline{JK}$, and N the midpoint of $\overline{HK}$; slope of $\overline{LM} = 0 =$ slope of $\overline{HK}$, so $\overline{LM} \mid \overline{HK}$; slope of $\overline{LN} = -1 =$ slope of $\overline{JK}$, so $\overline{LN} \parallel \overline{JK}$; slope of $\overline{MN} = 1 =$ slope of $\overline{HJ}$, so $\overline{MN} \parallel \overline{HJ}$.
15. 31 **17.** $m\angle D$, $m\angle E$, $m\angle F$; EF, DF, DE **19.** $m\angle L$, $m\angle K$, $m\angle M$; KM, LM, KL **21.** < **23.** = **25.** Assume that there is a $\triangle ABC$ with 2 right $\angle$, say $m\angle A = 90°$ and $m\angle B = 90°$. Then, $m\angle A + m\angle B = 180°$ and, since $m\angle C > 0°$, $m\angle A + m\angle B + m\angle C > 180°$. This contradicts the $\triangle$ Sum Theorem. Then the assumption that there is such a $\triangle ABC$ must be incorrect and no $\triangle$ has 2 right $\angle$.

CHAPTER 6

SKILL REVIEW (p. 320) **1.** If two $\parallel$ lines are cut by a transversal, consecutive interior angles are supplementary. **2.** If two $\parallel$ lines are cut by a transversal, alternate interior angles are congruent. **3.** AAS Cong. Theorem
4. SSS Cong. Postulate **5.** 13, $-\dfrac{12}{5}$; $\left(-\dfrac{1}{2}, -2\right)$

6.1 PRACTICE (pp. 325–328) **5.** Not a polygon; one side is not a segment. **7.** equilateral **9.** regular **11.** 67°
13. not a polygon **15.** not a polygon **17.** not a polygon
19. heptagon; concave **21.** octagon **23.** $\overline{MP}$, $\overline{MQ}$, $\overline{MR}$, $\overline{MS}$, $\overline{MT}$ **25.** equilateral **27.** quadrilateral; regular
29. triangle; regular

31–33. Sample figures are given.
31. 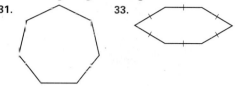 **33.**

35. Yes; *Sample answer:* A polygon that is concave must include an $\angle$ with measure greater than 180°. By the Triangle Sum Theorem, every $\triangle$ must be convex. **37.** 75°
39. 125° **41.** 67 **43.** 44 **45.** 4 **47.** three; *Sample answers:* triangle (a polygon with three sides), trilateral (having three sides), tricycle (a vehicle with three wheels), trio (a group of three) **49.** octagon; concave, equilateral **51.** 17-gon; concave; none of these

6.1 MIXED REVIEW (p. 328) **55.** 63 **57.** 6 **59.** 5
61. (1, 13), (5, −1), (−9, −15) **63.** (2, 15), (−4, −9), (10, −1)

6.2 PRACTICE (pp. 333–337) **5.** $\overline{KN}$; diags. of a $\square$ bisect each other. **7.** $\angle LMJ$; opp. $\angle$ of a $\square$ are $\cong$. **9.** $\overline{JM}$; opp. sides of a $\square$ are $\cong$. **11.** $\angle KMJ$; if 2 $\parallel$ lines are cut by a transversal, then alt. int. $\angle$ are $\cong$. **13.** 7; since the diags. of a $\square$ bisect each other, $LP = NP = 7$. **15.** 8.2°; since the diags. of a $\square$ bisect each other, $QP = MP = 8.2$. **17.** 80°; since consec. $\angle$ of a $\square$ are supplementary, $m\angle NQL = 180° - m\angle QLM = 80°$.
19. 29°; opp. sides of a $\square$ are $\parallel$, so $m\angle LMQ \cong m\angle MQN$ since they are alt. int. $\angle$. **21.** 11; since opp. sides of a $\square$ are $\cong$, $BA = CD = 11$. **23.** 60°; since consec. $\angle$ of a $\square$ are supplementary, $m\angle CDA = 180° - m\angle BAD = 60°$.
25. 120°; since opp. $\angle$ of a $\square$ are $\cong$, $m\angle BCD = m\angle BAD = 120°$. **27.** $a = 79$, $b = 101$ **29.** $p = 5$, $q = 9$ **31.** $k = 7$, $m = 8$ **33.** $u = 4$, $v = 18$ **35.** $b = 90$, $c = 80$, $d = 100$
37. $r = 30$, $s = 40$, $t = 25$

39.

Statements	Reasons
1. $JKLM$ is a $\square$.	2. Opp. $\angle$ of a $\square$ are $\cong$.
3. 360°	4. Substitution prop. of equality
5. $m\angle J$; $m\angle K$	6. Division
	7. Def. of supplementary $\angle$

41. $(a + c, b)$ **43.** $\left(\dfrac{a+c}{2}, \dfrac{b}{2}\right)$ **45.** $\angle 3$ and $\angle 7$ are supplementary by the Linear Pair Postulate, so $m\angle 3 + m\angle 7 = 180°$. Opp. $\angle$ of a $\square$ are $\cong$, so $\angle 6 \cong \angle 7$, or $m\angle 6 = m\angle 7$. Then by the substitution prop. of equality, $m\angle 3 + m\angle 6 = 180°$ and $\angle 3$ and $\angle 6$ are supplementary.
47. $\angle 4$ **49.** Corresp. $\angle$ Postulate (If 2 $\parallel$ lines are cut by a transv., then corresp. $\angle$ are $\cong$.) **51.** 60° **53.** AD increases.

55.

Statements	Reasons
1. $ABCD$ and $CEFD$ are $\square$s.	1. Given
2. $\overline{AB} \cong \overline{CD}$; $\overline{CD} \cong \overline{EF}$	2. Opp. sides of a $\square$ are $\cong$.
3. $\overline{AB} \cong \overline{EF}$	3. Transitive Prop. of Cong.

57.

Statements	Reasons
1. $WXYZ$ is a $\square$.	1. Given
2. $\overline{WZ} \cong \overline{XY}$	2. Opp. sides of a $\square$ are $\cong$.
3. $\overline{WM} \cong \overline{YM}$; $\overline{ZM} \cong \overline{XM}$	3. The diags. of a $\square$ bisect each other.
4. $\triangle WMZ \cong \triangle YMX$	4. SSS Cong. Postulate

6.2 MIXED REVIEW (p. 337) **65.** $4\sqrt{5}$ **67.** $5\sqrt{2}$ **69.** $-\frac{1}{2}$

71. Yes; in a plane, 2 lines $\perp$ to the same line are $\parallel$.
73. $\overline{EF}$, $\overline{DF}$; $m\angle D = 180° - (90° + 55°) = 35°$, so $\angle D$ is the smallest $\angle$ of $\triangle DEF$ and $\angle E$ is the largest. If 1 $\angle$ of a $\triangle$ is larger than another $\angle$, then the side opp. the larger $\angle$ is longer than the side opp. the smaller $\angle$.

6.3 PRACTICE (pp. 342–344) **3.** Yes; if an $\angle$ of a quad. is supplementary to both of its consec. $\angle$s, then the quad. is a $\square$. **5.** Show that since alt. int. $\angle$s BCA and DAC are $\cong$, $\overline{BC} \parallel \overline{AD}$. Then, since one pair of opp. sides of $ABCD$ is both $\parallel$ and $\cong$, $ABCD$ is a $\square$. **7.** Use the Corresponding Angles Converse to show that $\overline{BC} \parallel \overline{AD}$ and the Alternate Interior Angles Converse to show that $\overline{AB} \parallel \overline{DC}$. Then, $ABCD$ is a $\square$ by the def. of a $\square$. **9.** Yes; if opp. sides of a quad. are $\cong$, then it is a $\square$. **11.** No; according to the Vertical Angles Theorem, the given information is true for the diags. of any quad. **13.** No; the fact that two opp. sides and one diag. are $\cong$ is insufficient to prove that the quad. is a $\square$. **15.** *Sample answer:* Since corresp. parts of $\cong$ $\triangle$s are $\cong$, both pairs of opp. sides of $ABCD$ are $\cong$, so $ABCD$ is a $\square$.
17. 70 **19.** 90 **21.** $AB = CD = \sqrt{17}$, so $\overline{AB} \cong \overline{CD}$. $AD = BC = 2\sqrt{17}$, so $\overline{AD} \cong \overline{BC}$. Since opp. sides of $ABCD$ are $\cong$, $ABCD$ is a $\square$. **23.** Slope of $\overline{AB}$ = slope of $\overline{CD}$ = $-\frac{1}{4}$ and slope of $\overline{AD}$ = slope of $\overline{BC}$ = -4, so $\overline{AB} \parallel \overline{CD}$ and $\overline{AD} \parallel \overline{BC}$. Then, $ABCD$ is a $\square$ by the def. of a $\square$.
25. *Sample answer:* Slope of $\overline{JK}$ = slope of $\overline{LM}$ = $\frac{1}{5}$ and slope of $\overline{JM}$ = slope of $\overline{KL}$ = -2, so $\overline{JK} \parallel \overline{LM}$ and $\overline{JM} \parallel \overline{KL}$. Then, $JKLM$ is a $\square$ by the def. of a $\square$.
27. Since opp. sides of $ABCD$ are $\cong$, $ABCD$ is a $\square$, so opp. sides $\overline{AB}$ and $\overline{CD}$ are $\parallel$. **29.** The diags. of the figure that is drawn were drawn to bisect each other. Therefore, the figure is a $\square$. **31.** *Sample answer:* Design the mount so that $\overline{AD} \cong \overline{BC}$ and $\overline{AB} \cong \overline{DC}$, making $ABCD$ a $\square$. Then, as long as the support containing $\overline{AD}$ is vertical, $\overline{BC}$ will be vertical, because opp. sides of a $\square$ are $\parallel$. **33.** Since $\angle P$ is supplementary to $\angle Q$, $\overline{QR} \parallel \overline{PS}$ by the Consecutive Interior Angles Converse. Similarly, $\overline{QP} \parallel \overline{RS}$ by the same theorem. Then, $PQRS$ is a $\square$ by the def. of a $\square$.

35. $(-b, -c)$; the diags. of a $\square$ bisect each other, so $(0, 0)$ is the midpoint of $\overline{QN}$. Let $Q = (x, y)$. By the Midpoint Formula, $(0, 0) = \left(\dfrac{x + b}{2}, \dfrac{y + c}{2}\right)$, so $x = -b$ and $y = -c$.

6.3 MIXED REVIEW (p. 345) **39.** If $x^2 + 2 = 2$, then $x = 0$. If $x = 0$, then $x^2 + 2 = 2$. **41.** If each pair of opp. sides of a quad. are $\parallel$, then the quad. is a $\square$. If a quad. is a $\square$, then each pair of opp. sides are $\parallel$. **43.** A point is on the bisector of an $\angle$ if and only if the point is equidistant from the two sides of the $\angle$. **45.** 60 **47.** 35

QUIZ 1 (p. 346) **1.** convex, equilateral, equiangular, regular **2.** 35; the sum of the measures of the interior $\angle$s of a quad. is $360°$, so $2x + 2x + 110 + 110 = 360$, $4x = 140$, and $x = 35$. **3.** $ABCG$ and $CDEF$ are $\square$, so $\angle A \cong \angle BCG$ and $\angle DCF \cong \angle E$. (Opp. $\angle$s of a $\square$ are $\cong$.) $\angle BCG \cong \angle DCF$ by the Vert. $\angle$s Thm. Then, $\angle A \cong \angle E$ by the Transitive Prop. of Cong. **4.** *Sample answers:* Use slopes to show that both pairs of opp. sides are $\parallel$, use the Distance Formula to show that both pairs of opp. sides are $\cong$, use slope and the Distance Formula to show that one pair of opp. sides are both $\parallel$ and $\cong$, use the Midpoint Formula to show that the diags. bisect each other.

6.4 PRACTICE (pp. 351–354) **3.** always **5.** sometimes **7.** C, D **9.** B, D **11.** 45 **13.** Sometimes; if rectangle $ABCD$ is also a rhombus (a square), then $\overline{AB} \cong \overline{BC}$. **15.** Sometimes; if rectangle $ABCD$ is also a rhombus (a square), then the diags. of $ABCD$ are $\perp$. **17.** square **19.** $\square$, rectangle, rhombus, square **21.** rhombus, square **23.** $\overline{PQ} \parallel \overline{RS}$, $\overline{PS} \parallel \overline{QR}$, $\overline{PQ} \cong \overline{QR} \cong \overline{RS} \cong \overline{PS}$, $\angle P \cong \angle R$, $\angle Q \cong \angle S$, $\overline{PR}$ and $\overline{QS}$ bisect each other, $\overline{PR} \perp \overline{QS}$, $\overline{PR}$ bisects $\angle SPQ$ and $\angle SRQ$, $\overline{QS}$ bisects $\angle PSR$ and $\angle PQR$. **25.** rectangle **27.** Always; opp. $\angle$s of a $\square$ are $\cong$. **29.** Always; each diag. of a rhombus bisects a pair of opp. $\angle$s. **31.** Sometimes; if a rhombus is also a rectangle (a square), then its diagonals are $\cong$. **33.** 18 **35.** 50 **37.** 1 **39.** $2\sqrt{2}$ **41.** $45°$ **43.** 10 **45.** Assume temporarily that $\overline{MN} \parallel \overline{PQ}$, $\angle 1 \not\cong \angle 2$, and that $\overline{MQ} \parallel \overline{NP}$. By the def. of a $\square$, $MNPQ$ is a $\square$. This contradicts the given information that $\angle 1 \not\cong \angle 2$. It follows that $\overline{MQ}$ is not $\parallel$ to $\overline{NP}$. **47.** If a $\square$ is a rectangle, then its diags. are $\cong$; if the diags. of a $\square$ are $\cong$, then the $\square$ is a rectangle; $\overline{JL} \cong \overline{KM}$.

49. If a quad. is a rectangle, then it has 4 right $\angle$s (def. of rectangle); if a quad. has 4 right $\angle$s, then it is a rectangle. (Both pairs of opp. $\angle$s are $\cong$, so the quad. is a $\square$. Since all 4 $\angle$s are $\cong$ and the sum of the measures of the int. $\angle$s of a quad. is $360°$, the measure of each $\angle$ is $90°$, and the quad. is a rectangle.)

51.

Statements	Reasons
1. $PQRT$ is a rhombus.	1. Given
2. $\overline{PQ} \cong \overline{QR} \cong \overline{RT} \cong \overline{PT}$	2. A quad. is a rhombus if and only if it has 4 $\cong$ sides.
3. $\overline{PR} \cong \overline{PR}$, $\overline{QT} \cong \overline{QT}$	3. Reflexive Prop. of Cong.
4. $\triangle PRQ \cong \triangle PRT$; $\triangle PTQ \cong \triangle RTQ$	4. SSS Cong. Postulate
5. $\angle TPR \cong \angle QPR$, $\angle TRP \cong \angle QRP$ $\angle PTQ \cong \angle RTQ$, $\angle PQT \cong \angle RQT$	5. Corresp. parts of $\cong$ $\triangle$ are $\cong$.
6. $\overline{PR}$ bisects $\angle TPQ$ and $\angle QRT$, $\overline{QT}$ bisects $\angle PTR$ and $\angle RQP$.	6. Def. of $\angle$ bisector

53. *Sample answer:* Draw $\overline{AB}$ and a line j $\left(\text{not} \perp \text{to } \overline{AB}\right)$ intersecting $\overline{AB}$ at B. Construct $\overline{BC}$ on j so that $\overline{BC} \cong \overline{AB}$. Construct two arcs with radius AB and centers A and C, intersecting at D. Draw $\overline{AD}$ and $\overline{CD}$. Since all 4 sides of $ABCD$ are $\cong$, $ABCD$ is a rhombus. Since $\overline{AB}$ and $\overline{BC}$ are not $\perp$, $ABCD$ is not a rectangle, and thus not a square. **55.** Rectangle; $PR = QS = \sqrt{41}$; since the diags. of $PQRS$ are $\cong$, $PQRS$ is a rectangle. **57.** Rectangle; $PR = QS = \sqrt{58}$; since the diags. of $PQRS$ are $\cong$, $PQRS$ is a rectangle. **59.** (b, a); $\overline{KM} \cong \overline{ON}$, so $KM = b$ and $\overline{MN} \cong \overline{KO}$, so $MN = a$. **61.** *Sample answer:* Since cross braces $\overline{AD}$ and $\overline{BC}$ bisect each other, $ABDC$ is a $\square$. Since cross braces $\overline{AD}$ and $\overline{BC}$ also have the same length, $ABDC$ is a rectangle. Since a rectangle has 4 right $\triangle$, $m\angle BAC = m\angle ABD = 90°$. Then, $m\angle BAC = m\angle BAE$ and $m\angle ABD = m\angle ABF$, so $m\angle BAE = m\angle ABF = 90°$ by substitution. So tabletop $\overline{AB}$ is perpendicular to legs $\overline{AE}$ and $\overline{BF}$ by the def. of perpendicular. **63.** Rhombus; $\overline{AE} \cong \overline{CE} \cong \overline{AF} \cong \overline{CF}$; $AECF$ remains a rhombus. **65.** Each diag. of a rhombus bisects a pair of opp. $\triangle$. (Theorem 6.12)

6.4 MIXED REVIEW (p. 355) **73.** yes **75.** no **77.** yes **79.** $\frac{1}{2}$ **81.** 9 **83.** Assume temporarily that $ABCD$ is a quad. with 4 acute $\triangle$, that is, $m\angle A < 90°$, $m\angle B < 90°$, $m\angle C < 90°$, and $m\angle D < 90°$. Then $m\angle A + m\angle B + m\angle C + m\angle D < 360°$. This contradicts the Interior Angles of a Quadrilateral Theorem. Then no quad. has 4 acute $\triangle$.

6.5 PRACTICE (pp. 359–362) **3.** isosceles trapezoid **5.** trapezoid **7.** 9 **9.** 9.5 **11.** legs **13.** diags. **15.** base $\triangle$ **17.** $m\angle J = 102°$, $m\angle L = 48°$ **19.** 8 **21.** 12 **23.** 10 **25.** Yes; X is equidistant from the vertices of the dodecagon, so $\overline{XA} \cong \overline{XB}$ and $\angle XAB \cong \angle XBA$ by the Base Angles Theorem. Since trapezoid $ABPQ$ has a pair of $\cong$ base $\triangle$, $ABPQ$ is isosceles. **27.** $m\angle A = m\angle B = 75°$, $m\angle P = m\angle Q = 105°$ **29.** $EF = GF \approx 6.40$, $HE = HG \approx 8.60$ **31.** 95° **33.** 90°

37. $ABCD$ is a trapezoid; slope of $\overline{BC}$ = slope of $\overline{AD} = 0$, so $\overline{BC} \parallel \overline{AD}$; slope of $\overline{AB} = 2$ and slope of $\overline{CD} = -\frac{4}{3}$, so $\overline{AB}$ is not $\perp$ to $\overline{CD}$. $ABCD$ is not isosceles; $AB = 2\sqrt{5}$ and $CD = 5$. **39.** 16 in. **41.** $TQRS$ is an isosceles trapezoid, so $\angle QTS \cong \angle RST$ because base $\triangle$ of an isosceles trapezoid are $\cong$. $\overline{TS} \cong \overline{TS}$ by the Reflexive Prop. of Cong. and $\overline{QT} \cong \overline{RS}$, so $\triangle QTS \cong \triangle RST$ by the SAS Cong. Postulate. Then $\overline{TR} \cong \overline{SQ}$ because corresp. parts of $\cong$ $\triangle$ are $\cong$. **43.** If $AC \neq BC$, then $ACBD$ is a kite; $AC = AD$ and $BC = BD$, so the quad. has two pairs of $\cong$ sides, but opp. sides are not $\cong$. (If $AC = BC$, then $ACBD$ is a rhombus.); $ABCD$ remains a kite in all three cases. **45.** If a quad. is a kite, then exactly 1 pair of opp. $\triangle$ are $\cong$. **47.** Draw $\overline{BD}$. (Through any 2 points, there is exactly 1 line.) Since $\overline{AB} \cong \overline{CB}$ and $\overline{AD} \cong \overline{CD}$, $\triangle BCD \cong \triangle BAD$ by the SSS Cong. Postulate. Then corresp. $\triangle$ A and C are $\cong$. Assume temporarily that $\angle B \cong \angle D$. Then both pairs of opp. $\triangle$ of $ABCD$ are $\cong$, so $ABCD$ is a $\square$ and opp. sides are $\cong$. This contradicts the definition of a kite. It follows that $\angle B \not\cong \angle D$.

49. Yes; $ABCD$ has one pair of $\parallel$ sides and the diagonals are $\cong$. $ABCD$ is not a $\square$ because opp. $\triangle$ are not $\cong$.

6.5 MIXED REVIEW (p. 363) **55.** If a quad. is a kite, then its diags. are $\perp$ **57.** 5.6 **59.** 7 **61.** 80° **63.** Yes; *Sample answer:* slope of $\overline{AB}$ = slope of $\overline{CD} = 0$, so $\overline{AB} \parallel \overline{CD}$ and $AB = CD = 7$. Then one pair of opp. sides are both $\cong$ and $\parallel$, so $ABCD$ is a $\square$.

QUIZ 2 (p. 363) **1.** *Sample answer:* Opposite sides of $EBFJ$ are $\cong$ so $EBFJ$ is a $\square$. Opposite $\triangle$ of a $\square$ are $\cong$, so $\angle BEJ \cong \angle BFJ$. By the Cong. Supplements Theorem, $\angle HEJ \cong \angle KFJ$. Since $\overline{HE} \cong \overline{JE} \cong \overline{JF} \cong \overline{KF}$, $\triangle HEJ \cong \triangle JFK$ by the SAS Cong. Postulate and, since corresp. sides of $\cong$ $\triangle$ are $\cong$, $\overline{HJ} \cong \overline{JK}$. **2.** rectangle **3.** kite **4.** square **5.** trapezoid

6.

Statements	Reasons
1. $\overline{AB} \parallel \overline{DC}$, $\angle D \cong \angle C$	1. Given
2. Draw $\overline{AE} \parallel \overline{BC}$.	2. Parallel Postulate
3. $ABCE$ is a $\square$.	3. Def. of a $\square$
4. $\overline{AE} \cong \overline{BC}$	4. Opp. sides of a $\square$ are $\cong$.
5. $\angle AED \cong \angle C$	5. Corresp. Angles Postulate
6. $\angle AED \cong \angle D$	6. Transitive Prop. of Cong.
7. $\overline{AD} \cong \overline{AE}$	7. Converse of the Base Angles Theorem
8. $\overline{AD} \cong \overline{BC}$	8. Transitive Prop. of Cong.

6.6 PRACTICE (pp. 367–369)

3.

Property	$\square$	Rect.	Rhom.	Sq.	Kite	Trap.
Exactly 1 pr. of opp. sides are $\parallel$.						X
Diags. are $\cong$.		X		X		

7. $\square$, rectangle, rhombus, square

Property	$\square$	Rect.	Rhom.	Sq.	Kite	Trap.
9. Exactly 1 pr. of opp. sides are $\cong$.						
11. Both pairs of opp. $\angle$s are $\cong$.	X	X	X	X		
13. All $\angle$s are $\cong$.		X		X		

15. isosceles trapezoid **17.** square **19.** $\square$, rectangle, rhombus, square, kite **21.** rhombus, square **23.** rectangle, square **25.** Show that the quad. has 2 pairs of consec. $\cong$ sides, but opp. sides are not $\cong$ (def. of kite).
27. Show that the quad. has 4 right $\angle$s; show that the quad. is a $\square$ and that its diags. are $\cong$.
29. Show that exactly 2 sides are $\parallel$ and that the nonparallel sides are $\cong$ (def. of trapezoid); show that the quad. is a trapezoid and that one pair of base $\angle$s are $\cong$; show that the quad. is a trapezoid and that its diags. are $\cong$. **31.** $\overline{BE}$ and $\overline{DE}$
33. $\overline{AE}$ and $\overline{BE}$ or $\overline{DE}$ (and so on), $\overline{AC}$ and $\overline{BD}$ **35.** any two consecutive sides of $ABCD$ **37.** Isosceles trapezoid; $\overline{PQ} \parallel \overline{RS}$, and $\overline{PS}$ and $\overline{QR}$ are $\cong$ but not $\parallel$. **39.** $\square$; *Sample answer:* $\overline{PQ} \parallel \overline{RS}$ and $\overline{PS} \parallel \overline{QR}$. **41.** Rhombus: *Sample answer:* $\overline{PQ} \cong \overline{QR} \cong \overline{RS} \cong \overline{PS}$. **43.** isosceles trapezoid
45. $\square$; if the diags. of a quad. bisect each other, the quad. is a $\square$. Since the diags. are not $\perp$, the $\square$ is not a rhombus and since the diags. are not $\cong$, the $\square$ is not a rectangle.
47. Kite; $\overline{AC} \perp \overline{BD}$ and $\overline{AC}$ bisects $\overline{BD}$, so $\cong$ $\triangle$ can be used to show that $\overline{AB} \cong \overline{AD}$ and then that $\overline{CB} \cong \overline{CD}$. $\overline{BD}$ does not bisect $\overline{AC}$, so $ABCD$ is not a $\square$. Then opp. sides are not $\cong$ and $ABCD$ is a kite. **49.** Draw a line through $C \parallel$ to $\overline{DF}$ and a line through $E \parallel$ to $\overline{CD}$. Label the intersection F. $CDEF$ is a $\square$ by the def. of a $\square$. $\angle DCF$ and $\angle DEF$ are right $\angle$s because consec. $\angle$s of a $\square$ are supplementary. Then $\angle CFE$ is also a right $\angle$ and $CDEF$ is a rectangle. The diags. of a $\square$ bisect each other, so $DM = \frac{1}{2}DF$ and $CM = \frac{1}{2}CE$. The diags. of a rectangle are $\cong$, so $DF = CE$, $\frac{1}{2}DF = \frac{1}{2}CE$, and $DM = CM$. By the def. of cong., $\overline{DM} \cong \overline{CM}$.

6.6 MIXED REVIEW (p. 370) **55.** 16 sq. units **57.** 15 sq. units **59.** 30 sq. units **61.** 1.75 **63.** 7 **65.** 5

6.7 PRACTICE (pp. 376–379) **3.** A **5.** C **7.** D **9.** 25 sq. units **11.** 40 sq. units **13.** 36 sq. units **15.** 49 sq. units **17.** 120 sq. units **19.** 10 sq. units **21.** 361 sq. units **23.** 240 sq. units **25.** 70 sq. units **27.** 12 ft **29.** $b = \dfrac{2A}{h}$
31. $b_1 = \dfrac{2A}{h} - b_2$ **33.** 4 sq. units **35.** 3 ft^2 **37.** 552 in.^{2}
39. No; such a $\square$ has base 6 ft and height 4 ft; two such $\square$s that have $\angle$s with different measures are not $\cong$.
41. 24 sq. units **43.** 192 sq. units **45.** about 480 carnations

47. about 432 chrysanthemums **49.** about 6023 shakes
51. blue: 96 sq. units; yellow: 96 sq. units **53.** Square; square; *Sample answer:* In quad. $EBFJ$, $\angle E$, $\angle J$, and $\angle F$ are right $\angle$s by the Linear Pair Postulate and $\angle B$ is a right $\angle$ by the Interior Angles of a Quadrilateral Theorem. Then $EBFJ$ is a rectangle by the Rectangle Corollary. $\overline{EJ} \cong \overline{FJ}$ because they are corresp. parts of $\cong$ $\square$s. Then, by the def. of a $\square$ and the Transitive Prop. of Cong., $EBFJ$ is a rhombus and, therefore, a square. Similarly, $HJGD$ is a square.
55. $b + h$; $(b + h)^2$ **57.** $(b + h)^2 = b^2 + h^2 + 2A$; $A = bh$
59. Show that the area of $AEGH = \frac{1}{2}h(b_1 + b_2)$. Then, since $EBCF$ and $GHDF$ are $\cong$, Area of $ABCD$ = Area of $AEFD$ + area of $EBCF$ = area of $AEFD$ + area of $GHDF$ = area of $AEGH = \frac{1}{2}h(b_1 + b_2)$.

6.7 MIXED REVIEW (p. 380)
63. obtuse; about 140° **65.** acute; about 15°
67. *Sample answer:* 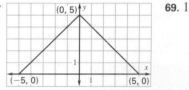 **69.** 1

QUIZ 3 (p. 380) **1.** Kite; $\overline{ON} \cong \overline{OP}$ and $\overline{MN} \cong \overline{MP}$, but opp. sides are not $\cong$. **2.** Trapezoid; $\overline{QR} \parallel \overline{TS}$, but $\overline{QT}$ and $\overline{RS}$ are not $\parallel$. **3.** $\square$; *Sample answer:* $\overline{ZY} \cong \overline{WX}$ and $\overline{ZY} \parallel \overline{WX}$.
4. 5 in. **5.** 12 in. **6.** 8 in. **7.** 52.11 cm^2

CHAPTER 6 REVIEW (pp. 382–384)
1. *Sample answer:* **3.** 115 **5.** 13 **7.** 65°, 115°
9. No; you are not given information about opp. sides. **11.** Yes; you can prove $\triangle$ PQT and SRT are $\cong$ and opp. sides are $\cong$. **13.** rhombus, square

15. rhombus, square **17.** $m\angle ABC = 112°$, $m\angle ADC = m\angle BCD = 68°$ **19.** Square; *Sample answer:* $PQ = QR = RS = PS = \sqrt{34}$, so $PQRS$ is a rhombus; $QS = PR = 2\sqrt{17}$, so the diags. of $PQRS$ are $\cong$ and $PQRS$ is a rectangle. A quad. that is both a rhombus and a rectangle is a square.
21. Rhombus; $PQ = QR = RS = PS = 2\sqrt{5}$
23. $29\frac{3}{4}$ in.^{2} **25.** 12 sq. units

CUMULATIVE PRACTICE (pp. 388–389)
1. 0.040404..., 0.181818..., 0.353535..., 0.898989...
3. 135°; 45° **5.** *Sample answer:* $\triangle QPR \cong \triangle QPS$ and $\triangle QPR \cong \triangle TPS$; show that $\angle 1 \cong \angle 2$, $\overline{QP} \cong \overline{QP}$, and $m\angle QPS = m\angle QPR$, so the $\triangle$s are $\cong$ by the ASA Cong. Postulate. Then show that $\overline{PR} \cong \overline{PS}$, $\angle 2 \cong \angle T$, and $\angle QRP \cong \angle TSP$, so $\triangle QPR \cong \triangle TPS$ by the AAS Cong. Theorem. **7.** P is equidistant from $\overrightarrow{QS}$ and $\overrightarrow{QR}$ by the Angle Bisector Theorem. **9.** 53°, 95°, 32°; obtuse
11. no **13.** yes; HL Congruence Theorem

15. $AB = AC = \sqrt{89}$ **17.** $y = -\dfrac{8}{5}x + \dfrac{97}{10}$ **19.** $\left(\dfrac{17}{3}, 1\right)$

21. If 2 $\angle$ are supplementary, then they form a linear pair; false; *Sample answer:* two consec. $\angle$ of a $\square$ are supplementary, but they do not form a linear pair.
23. $m\angle X > m\angle Z$; the $\angle$ opp. the longer side is larger than the $\angle$ opp. the shorter side. **25.** rhombus **27.** Yes; *Sample answer:* The diags. share a common midpoint, (4.5, 6), which means they bisect each other. Thus, *PQRS* is a $\square$.
29. a. square, rhombus, kite **b.** square, rectangle, isosceles trapezoid **31.** $AC = DF$, $m\angle ACB = 65° = \angle DFE$, and $m\angle ABC = 90° = \angle DEF$, so $\triangle ABC \cong \triangle DEF$ by the AAS Cong. Theorem. **33.** $69°$ **35.** 438.75 in.^{2}

ALGEBRA REVIEW (pp. 390–391) **1.** $\dfrac{4}{5}$ **2.** $\dfrac{7}{4}$ **3.** $\dfrac{25}{27}$ **4.** $\dfrac{11}{4}$
5. $\dfrac{103}{45}$ **6.** $\dfrac{11}{9}$ **7.** $\dfrac{4}{1}$ **8.** $\dfrac{5}{4}$ **9.** $\dfrac{1}{1}$ **10.** 3 **11.** -3 **12.** 6 **13.** -4
14. $\dfrac{13}{4}$ **15.** $\dfrac{7}{6}$ **16.** -1 **17.** 2 **18.** $\dfrac{7}{9}$ **19.** $\dfrac{27}{2}$ **20.** -2 **21.** 8
22. 4 **23.** 9 **24.** 200 **25.** 12 **26.** $\dfrac{24}{5}$ **27.** $\dfrac{42}{17}$ **28.** $\dfrac{5}{9}$ **29.** $\dfrac{3}{2}$
30. 30 **31.** 4 **32.** 5 **33.** $\dfrac{95}{9}$ **34.** 5 **35.** -4 **36.** 9 **37.** -29
38. $-\dfrac{43}{2}$ **39.** $\dfrac{2}{3}$ **40.** -3 **41.** $-\dfrac{2}{3}$ **42.** ± 6

CHAPTER 7

SKILL REVIEW (p. 394) **1.** congruent **2.** not congruent
3. congruent **4.** 10 **5.** $35°$ **6.** $55°$ **7.** $90°$ **8.** $\overline{QR}$
9. about 7

7.1 PRACTICE (pp. 399–402) **5.** translation **7.** rotation
9. $\overline{VW}$ **11.** $\triangle WXY$ **13.** rotation about the origin; a turn about the origin **15.** $\angle A$ and $\angle J$, $\angle B$ and $\angle K$, $\angle C$ and $\angle L$, $\angle D$ and $\angle M$, or $\angle E$ and $\angle N$
17. *Sample answer:* $JK = \sqrt{(-3 - (-1))^2 + (2 - 1)^2} = \sqrt{5}$; $AB = \sqrt{(2 - 1)^2 + (3 - 1)^2} = \sqrt{5}$ **19.** false **21.** reflection in the line $x = 1$; a flip over the line $x = 1$; $A'(6, 2)$, $B'(3, 4)$, $C'(3, -1)$, $D'(6, -1)$ **23.** Yes; the preimage and image appear to be $\cong$. **25.** No; the preimage and image are not $\cong$.
27. LKJ **29.** PRQ **31.** RQP **33.** $AB = XY = 3\sqrt{2}$, $BC = YZ = \sqrt{10}$, $AC = XZ = 4$ **35.** $w = 35$, $x = 4\dfrac{1}{3}$, $y = 3$
37. translation **39.** rotation **41.** reflection; reflection; rotation (or two reflections) **43.** *Sample answer:* Flip the plan vertically to lay the upper left corner, then horizontally to lay the lower left corner, then vertically again to lay the lower right corner.

7.1 MIXED REVIEW (p. 402) **47.** 13 **49.** $\sqrt{89}$ **51.** polygon
53. not a polygon; one side not a segment **55.** not a polygon; two of the sides intersect only one other side.

57. (1) Since slope of $\overline{PQ}$ = slope of $\overline{SR} = \dfrac{2}{7}$ and slope of $\overline{PS}$ = slope of $\overline{QR} = -8$, both pairs of opposite sides are $\parallel$ and *PQRS* is a parallelogram. (2) Since $PQ = SR = \sqrt{53}$ and $PS = QR = \sqrt{65}$, both pairs of opposite sides are $\cong$ and *PQRS* is a parallelogram.

7.2 PRACTICE (pp. 407–410) **3.** not a reflection **5.** reflection
7. $\angle DAB$ **9.** D **11.** $\overline{DC}$ **13.** 4
15. 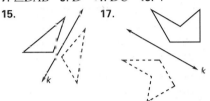 **17.** **19.** True; M is 3 units to the right of the line $x = 3$, so its image is 3 units to the left of the line.

21. True; U is 4 units to the right of the line $x = 1$, so its image is 4 units to the left of the line. **23.** $\overline{CD}$ **25.** $\overline{EF}$ **27.** $(3, -8)$ **29.** $(-7, -2)$
31.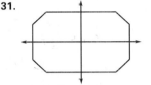

33. Draw $\overleftrightarrow{PP'}$ and $\overleftrightarrow{QQ'}$ intersecting line m at points S and T. By the def. of reflection, $\overline{P'S} \cong \overline{PS}$ and $\overline{RS} \perp \overline{PP'}$, and $\overline{Q'T} \cong \overline{QT}$ and $\overline{RT} \perp \overline{QQ'}$. It follows that $\triangle P'SR \cong \triangle PSR$ and $\triangle Q'TR \cong \triangle QTR$ by the SAS Congruence Postulate. Since corresp. parts of $\cong \triangle$ are $\cong$, $\overline{P'R} \cong \overline{PR}$ and $\overline{Q'R} \cong \overline{QR}$. So, $P'R = PR$ and $Q'R = QR$. Since $P'Q' = P'R + Q'R$ and $PQ = PR + QR$ by the Segment Addition Postulate, we get by substitution $PQ = P'Q'$, or $\overline{PQ} \cong \overline{P'Q'}$.
35. Q is on line m, so $Q = Q'$. By the def. of reflection, $\overline{PQ} \cong \overline{P'Q} \left(\overline{P'Q'}\right)$. **37.** $(6, 0)$ **39.** $(3, 0)$ **41.** Each structure is a reflection of the other. **43.** Triangles 2 and 3 are reflections of triangle 1; triangle 4 is rotation of triangle 1 **45.** $90°$ **47.** The distance between each vertex of the preimage and line m is equal to the distance between the corresponding vertex of the image and line m. **49.** $u = 6$, $v = 5\dfrac{4}{5}$, $w = 5$

7.2 MIXED REVIEW (p. 410) **57.** $\angle P$ **59.** $\overline{BC}$ **61.** $101°$
63. $10 < c < 24$ **65.** $21 < c < 45$ **67.** $25.7 < c < 56.7$
69. $m\angle A = m\angle B = 119°$, $m\angle C = 61°$ **71.** $m\angle A = 106°$, $m\angle C = 61°$

7.3 PRACTICE (pp. 416–419) **7.** P **9.** R **11.** yes; a rotation of $180°$ clockwise or counterclockwise about its center
13. $\overline{CD}$ **15.** $\overline{GE}$ **17.** $\triangle MAB$ **19.** $\triangle CPA$ **21.** By the def. of a rotation, $\overline{QP} \cong \overline{Q'P}$. Since P and R are the same point, as are R and R', $\overline{QR} \cong \overline{Q'R'}$.

23.

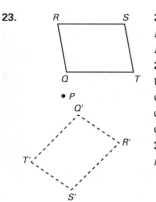

25. $J'(1, 2)$, $K'(4, 1)$, $L'(4, -3)$, $M'(1, -3)$ **27.** $D'(4, 1)$, $E'(0, 2)$, $F'(2, 5)$
29. $X'(2, 3)$, $O'(0, 0)$, $Z'(-3, 4)$; the coordinates of the image of the point (x, y) after a 180° clockwise rotation about the origin are $(-x, -y)$.
31. 30° **33.** 81° **35.** $q = 30$, $r = 5$, $s = 11$, $t = 1$, $u = 2$

37. The wheel hub can be mapped onto itself by a clockwise or counterclockwise rotation of $51\frac{3}{7}°$, $102\frac{6}{7}°$, or $154\frac{2}{7}°$ about its center. **39.** Yes; the image can be mapped onto itself by a clockwise or counterclockwise rotation of 180° about its center. **41.** the center of the square, that is, the intersection of the diagonals

7.3 MIXED REVIEW (p. 419) **45.** 82° **47.** 82° **49.** 98°
51. any obtuse triangle **53.** any acute triangle

QUIZ 1 (p. 420) **1.** *RSTQ* **2.** Reflection in line *m*; the figure is flipped over line *m*. **3.** Yes; the transformation preserves lengths. **4.** $(2, -3)$ **5.** $(2, -4)$ **6.** $(-4, 0)$ **7.** $(-8.2, -3)$
8. rotations by multiples of 120° clockwise or counterclockwise about the center of the knot where the rope starts to unravel

7.4 PRACTICE (pp. 425–428) **3.** $(x, y) \rightarrow (x + 6, y - 2)$
5. $(x, y) \rightarrow (x - 7, y + 1)$ **7.** 8; 3 **9.** 5; −2
11. *Sample figure:*

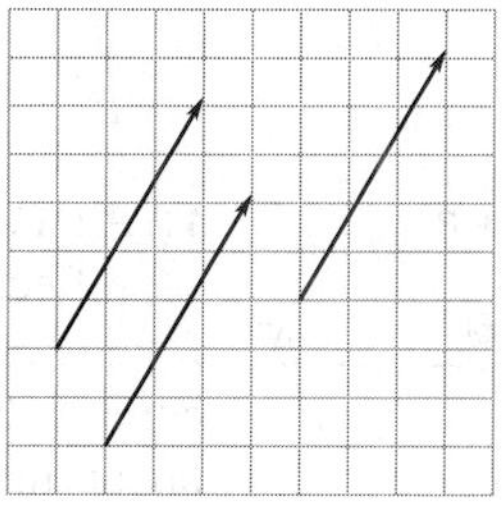

13. *Sample figure:*

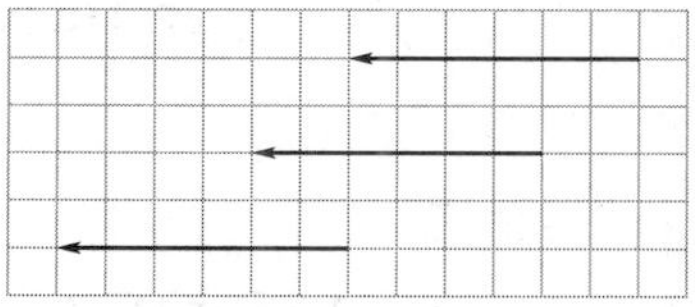

15. $(x, y) \rightarrow (x - 3, y - 4)$; $\langle -3, -4 \rangle$ **17.** $\overrightarrow{HJ}$; $\langle 4, 2 \rangle$
19. $\overrightarrow{MN}$; $\langle 5, 0 \rangle$ **21.** *k* and *m* **23.** 2.8 in. **25.** $(17, -4)$
27. $(-14, 8)$ **29.** $(12.5, -4.5)$

31.

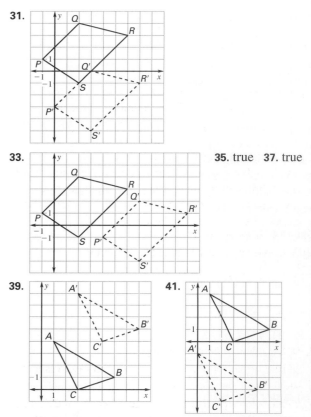

33.

35. true **37.** true

39. **41.**

43. We are given $P(a, b)$ and $Q(c, d)$. Suppose P' has coordinates $(a + r, b + s)$. Then $PP' = \sqrt{r^2 + s^2}$ and the slope of $\overline{PP'} = \frac{s}{r}$. If $PP' = QQ'$ and $\overline{PP'} \parallel \overline{QQ'}$ as given, then $QQ' = \sqrt{r^2 + s^2}$ and the slope of $\overline{QQ'} = \frac{s}{r}$. So, the coordinates of Q' are $(c + r, d + s)$. By the Distance Formula, $PQ = \sqrt{(a - c)^2 + (b - d)^2}$ and $P'Q' = \sqrt{[(a + r) - (c + r)]^2 + [(b + s) - (d + s)]^2} = \sqrt{(a - c)^2 + (b - d)^2}$. Thus, by the substitution prop. of equality, $PQ = P'Q'$. **45.** D **47.** B **49.** no **51.** Samples might include photographs of floor tiles or of fabric patterns. **53.** $\langle 6, 4 \rangle$, $\langle 4, 6 \rangle$ **55.** $\langle 18, 12 \rangle$

7.4 MIXED REVIEW (p. 428) **63.** −5 **65.** −6 **67.** $\frac{3}{4}$ **69.** 12
71. true **73.** false

7.5 PRACTICE (pp. 433–436) **5.** $\overline{A'B'}$ **7.** the *y*-axis **9.** A
11. B **13.** $(1, -10)$ **15.** $(2, -6)$

17. **19.**

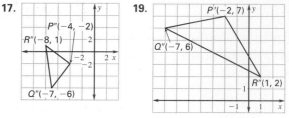

21.

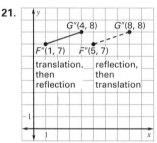

; The order does affect the final image.
23. reflection in the line $y = 2$, followed by reflection in the line $x = -2$
25. 90° counterclockwise rotation about the point $(0, 1)$, followed by the translation $(x, y) \rightarrow (x + 2, y + 3)$
27. A, B, C **31.** After each part was painted, the stencil was moved through a glide reflection (reflection in a horizontal line through its center and translation to the right) to paint the next part. **33.** 1, 4, 5, 6 **35.** The pattern can be created by horizontal translation, 180° rotation, vertical line reflection, or horizontal glide reflection. **37.** The pattern can be created by translation or 180° rotation.

7.5 MIXED REVIEW (p. 436)
41. **43.**

45, 47. Sample explanations are given.
45. Square; $PQ = QR = RS = PS = \sqrt{17}$, so $PQRS$ is a rhombus. Also, since $PR = QS = \sqrt{34}$, the diagonals of $PQRS$ are $\cong$, so $PQRS$ is a rectangle. Then, by the Square Corollary, $PQRS$ is a square. **47.** Rhombus; $PQ = QR = RS = PS = \sqrt{13}$, so $PQRS$ is a rhombus. Since $PR = 6$ and $SQ = 4$, the diagonals are not congruent, so $PQRS$ is not a rectangle or a square. **49.** $A'(-6, 9)$, $B'(-6, 3)$, $C'(-2, 8)$
51. $A'(-3, 7)$, $B'(-3, 1)$, $C'(1, 6)$ **53.** $A'(-9, 9.5)$, $B'(-9, 3.5)$, $C'(-5, 8.5)$

7.6 PRACTICE (pp. 440–443) **3.** translation, vertical line reflection **5.** translation, rotation, vertical line reflection, horizontal glide reflection **7.** translation (T), 180° rotation (R), horizontal glide reflection (G), vertical line reflection (V), horizontal line reflection (H) **9.** D **11.** B
13. translation, 180° rotation **15.** translation, 180° rotation, horizontal line reflection, vertical line reflection, horizontal glide reflection **17.** yes; reflection in the x-axis
19. 180° rotation about the point $(8, 0)$ **21.** TRHVG **23.** T
27, 29, 31. Sample patterns are given.

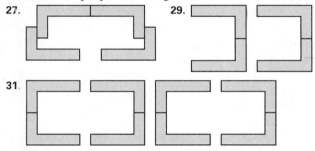

27. **29.** **31.**

33. TRHVG **35.** There are three bands of frieze patterns visible. **39.** just under 3 in.

41. *Sample pattern:*

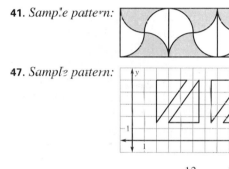

47. *Sample pattern:*

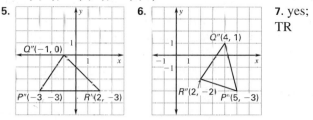

7.6 MIXED REVIEW (p. 444) **55.** $\frac{13}{8}$ **57.** $\frac{16}{19}$ **59.** 1
61. $w = 8$, $y = 2$ **63.** 288 sq. units

QUIZ 2 (p. 144) **1.** $A'(0, 5)$, $B'(5, 6)$, $C'(2, 4)$ **2.** $A'(-4, 6)$, $B'(1, 7)$, $C'(-2, 5)$ **3.** $A'(-3, -2)$, $B'(2, -1)$, $C'(-1, -3)$
4. $A'(4, 4)$, $B'(9, 5)$, $C'(6, 3)$

5. **6.** **7.** yes; TR

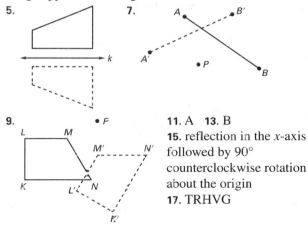

CHAPTER 7 REVIEW (pp. 446–448) **1.** Yes; the figure and its image appear to be congruent. **3.** Yes; the figure and its image appear to be congruent.

5. **7.**

9. **11.** A **13.** B
15. reflection in the x-axis followed by 90° counterclockwise rotation about the origin
17. TRHVG

CHAPTER 8

SKILL REVIEW (p. 456) **1.** 32 units **2.** 31 units **3.** 91 units
4. $\frac{1}{2}$ **5.** $\frac{3}{7}$ **6.** $\frac{11}{4}$

8.1 PRACTICE (pp. 461–464) **5.** 4 : 5 **7.** $\frac{48}{5}$ **9.** 6 **11.** $\frac{6}{1}$
13. $\frac{2}{3}$ **15.** $\frac{7.5 \text{ cm}}{10 \text{ cm}}$; $\frac{3}{4}$ **17.** $\frac{36 \text{ in.}}{12 \text{ in.}}$ or $\frac{3 \text{ ft}}{1 \text{ ft}}$; $\frac{3}{1}$ **19.** $\frac{350 \text{ g}}{1000 \text{ g}}$; $\frac{7}{20}$
21. $\frac{18 \text{ ft}}{10 \text{ ft}}$; $\frac{9}{5}$ **23.** $\frac{400 \text{ m}}{500 \text{ m}}$; $\frac{4}{5}$ **25.** $\frac{2}{3}$ **27.** $\frac{11}{9}$ **29.** 30 ft, 12 ft
31. 15°, 60°, 105° **33.** $\frac{20}{7}$ **35.** $\frac{35}{2}$ **37.** $\frac{7}{3}$ **39.** 12 **41.** 15
43. $-\frac{48}{5}$ **45.** 16 **47.** 21 **49.** Venus: 126 lb; Mars: 53 lb; Jupiter: 330 lb; Pluto 10 lb **51.** 1440 in. **53.** about 1.0 in.

55. 6 **57.** $RQ = 12$, $PQ = 13$, $SU = 15$, $ST = 39$ **59.** $12:1$
61. $144:1$ **63.** $EF = 20$, $DF = 24$

8.1 MIXED REVIEW (p. 464) **69.** $95°$ **71.** $95°$
73. $\left(-1\frac{1}{2}, 3\right)$ and $(1, 3)$ **75.** $\left(-\frac{1}{2}, 3\frac{1}{2}\right)$ and $\left(1\frac{1}{2}, 1\right)$

8.2 PRACTICE (pp. 468–470) **5.** 6 **7.** 11.4 ft **9.** $\frac{x}{y}$ **11.** $\frac{y+12}{12}$
13. true **15.** true **17.** 9 **19.** 14 **21.** $4\sqrt{10}$ **23.** 11.25
25. $6\frac{2}{3}$ **27.** $6\frac{6}{7}$ **29.** about 25 ft **31.** 198 hits **33.** 11
37. Let $\frac{a}{b} = \frac{c}{d}$ and show that $\frac{a+b}{b} = \frac{c+d}{d}$.

$\frac{a}{b} = \frac{c}{d}$ (Given)

$\frac{a}{b} + 1 = \frac{c}{d} + 1$ (Addition prop. of equality)

$\frac{a}{b} + \frac{b}{b} = \frac{c}{d} + \frac{d}{d}$ (Inverse prop. of multiplication)

$\frac{a+b}{b} = \frac{c+d}{d}$ (Addition of fractions)

39. 24 ft **41.** about $\frac{3}{8}$ in.; about $2\frac{1}{2}$ mi

8.2 MIXED REVIEW (p. 471) **47.** 12 m^2 **49.** 26 cm^2
51. $m\angle C = 115°$, $m\angle A = m\angle D = 65°$ **53.** $m\angle A = m\angle B = 100°$, $m\angle C = 80°$ **55.** $m\angle B = 41°$, $m\angle C = m\angle D = 139°$
57. A regular pentagon has 5 lines of symmetry (one from each vertex to the midpoint of the opposite side) and rotational symmetries of $72°$ and $144°$, clockwise and counterclockwise about the center of the pentagon.

8.3 PRACTICE (pp. 475–478) **5.** $5:3$ **7.** $110°$ **9.** $\angle J \cong \angle W$, $\angle K \cong \angle X$, $\angle L \cong \angle Y$, $\angle M \cong \angle Z$; $\frac{JK}{WX} = \frac{KL}{XY} = \frac{LM}{YZ} = \frac{JM}{WZ}$
11. Yes; both figures are rectangles, so all 4 $\angle$ are $\cong$ and $\frac{AB}{FG} = \frac{BC}{GH} = \frac{CD}{HE} = \frac{AD}{FE} = \frac{7}{4}$. **13.** No; $m\angle B = 90°$ and $m\angle Q = 88°$, so corresp. $\angle$ are not $\cong$.
15. yes; *Sample answers: ABCD ~ EFGH, ABCD ~ FEHG*
17. yes; $\triangle XYZ \sim \triangle CAB$ **19.** $4:5$ **21.** 20, 12.5, 20 **23.** $\frac{4}{5}$
25. 2 **27.** 10 **29.** no **31.** sometimes **33.** sometimes
35. always **37.** always **39.** 11, 9 **41.** $39\frac{3}{7}$, $23\frac{1}{7}$
43. analog TV: 21.6 in. by 16.2 in., digital TV: about 23.5 in. by 13.2 in. **45.** *ABCD ~ EFGH* with scale factor $1:k$, so
$\frac{AB}{EF} = \frac{BC}{FG} = \frac{CD}{GH} = \frac{AD}{EH} = \frac{1}{k}$. Then, $EF = k \cdot AB$, $FG = k \cdot BC$, $GH = k \cdot CD$, and $EH = k \cdot AD$, so $\frac{\text{perimeter of } ABCD}{\text{perimeter of } EFGH} =$
$\frac{AB + BC + CD + AD}{EF + FG + GH + EH} = \frac{AB + BC + CD + AD}{k \cdot AB + k \cdot BC + k \cdot CD + k \cdot AD} =$
$\frac{AB + BC + CD + AD}{k(AB + BC + CD + AD)} = \frac{1}{k} = \frac{AB}{EF}$. **47.** 11.2 in.

8.3 MIXED REVIEW (p. 479) **53.** 1 **55.** $-\frac{1}{7}$ **57.** $-\frac{7}{6}$ **59.** 49
61. 9 **63.** 38 **65.** $\frac{32}{13}$ **67.** 21

QUIZ 1 (p. 479) **1.** 10 **2.** 28 **3.** $\frac{24}{7}$ **4.** 21 **5.** $\sqrt{55} \approx 7.42$
6. $\sqrt{70} \approx 8.37$ **7.** 3; $1:2$; $\frac{1}{2}$ **8.** 30; $3:2$; $\frac{3}{2}$ **9.** None are exactly similar, but the 5×7 and wallet sizes are very nearly similar. $\left(\frac{5}{2.25} \approx 2.22, \frac{7}{3.25} \approx 2.15\right)$ **10.** $3\frac{1}{8}$ in.

8.4 PRACTICE (pp. 483–486) **5.** yes **7.** 10, 6 **9.** $\angle J$ and $\angle F$, $\angle K$ and $\angle G$, $\angle L$ and $\angle H$, $\frac{JK}{FG} = \frac{KL}{GH} = \frac{JL}{FH}$
11. $\angle L$ and $\angle Q$, $\angle M$ and $\angle P$, $\angle N$ and $\angle N$, $\frac{LM}{QP} = \frac{MN}{PN} = \frac{LN}{QN}$ **13.** LM; MN; NL **15.** 15; x **17.** 24
19. yes; $\triangle PQR \sim \triangle WPV$ **21.** yes; $\triangle XYZ \sim \triangle GFH$
23. yes; $\triangle JMN \sim \triangle JLK$ **25.** yes; $\triangle VWX \sim \triangle VYZ$
27. $-\frac{2}{5}$ **29.** $(10, 0)$ **31.** $(30, 0)$ **33.** CDE **35.** 15; x
37. 20 **39.** 14 **41.** 27 **43.** 100 **45.** 12 **47.** 25

49.

Statements	Reasons
1. $\angle ECD$ and $\angle EAB$ are right $\angle$s.	1. Given
2. $\overline{AB} \perp \overline{AE}$, $\overline{CD} \perp \overline{AE}$	2. Def. of $\perp$ lines
3. $\overline{AB} \parallel \overline{CD}$	3. In a plane, 2 lines $\perp$ to the same line are $\parallel$.
4. $\angle EDC \cong \angle B$	4. If 2 $\parallel$ lines are cut by a transversal, corresp. $\angle$ are $\cong$.
5. $\triangle ABE \sim \triangle CDE$	5. AA Similarity Post.

51. False; all $\angle$ of any 2 equilateral $\triangle$ are $\cong$, so the $\triangle$ are $\sim$ by the AA Similarity Post. (Note, also, that if one $\triangle$ has sides of length x and the other has sides of length y, then the ratio of any two side lengths is $\frac{x}{y}$. Then, all corresp. side lengths are in proportion, so the def. of $\sim$ $\triangle$ can also be used to show that any 2 equilateral $\triangle$ are $\sim$.) **53.** 1.5 m
55. $\overline{PQ} \perp \overline{QT}$ and $\overline{SR} \perp \overline{QT}$, so $\angle Q$ and $\angle SRT$ are right $\angle$s. Since all right $\angle$ are $\cong$, $\angle Q \cong \angle SRT$. $\overline{PR} \parallel \overline{ST}$ so corresp. $\angle PRQ$ and STR are $\cong$. Then, $\triangle PQR \sim \triangle SRT$ by the AA Similarity Post., so $\frac{PQ}{QR} = \frac{SR}{RT}$. That is, $\frac{PQ}{780} = \frac{4}{6.5}$ and $PQ = 480$ ft.

8.4 MIXED REVIEW (p. 487) **61.** $5\sqrt{82}$ **63.** 46 **65.** 12
67. 8 **69.** $\frac{36}{11}$ **71.** $-16, 16$

8.5 PRACTICE (pp. 492–494) **5.** $\frac{1}{6}$; yes; SSS Similarity Thm. **7.** $\triangle DEF \sim \triangle GHJ$; 2:5 **9.** yes; $\triangle JKL \sim \triangle XYZ$ (or $\triangle XZY$); SSS Similarity Thm. **11.** no **13.** yes; $\triangle PQR \sim \triangle DEF$; SSS or SAS Similarity Thm. **15.** SSS Similarity Thm. **17.** SAS Similarity Thm. **19.** 53° **21.** 82° **23.** 15 **25.** $4\sqrt{2}$ **27.** $\triangle ABC \sim \triangle BDC$; 18 **29.** 140 ft **31.** Locate G on $\overline{AB}$ so that $GB = DE$ and draw $\overline{GH}$ through $G \parallel$ to $\overline{AC}$. Corresp. $\angle A$ and BGH are $\cong$ as are corresp. $\angle C$ and BHG, so $\triangle ABC \sim \triangle GBH$. Then $\frac{AB}{GB} = \frac{AC}{GH}$. But $\frac{AB}{DE} = \frac{AC}{DF}$ and $GB = DE$, so $\frac{AC}{GH} = \frac{AC}{DF}$ and $GH = DF$. By the SAS Cong. Post., $\triangle BGH \cong \triangle EDF$. Corresp. $\angle F$ and BHG are $\cong$, so $\angle F \cong \angle C$ by the Transitive Prop. of Cong. $\triangle ABC \sim \triangle DEF$ by the AA Similarity Post. **33.** 18 ft **35.** Julia and the flagpole are both perpendicular to the ground and the two $\triangle$ formed (one by Julia's head, feet, and the tip of the shadow, and the other by the top and bottom of the flag pole and the tip of the shadow) have a shared angle. Then, the $\triangle$ are $\sim$ by the AA Similarity Post.

8.5 MIXED REVIEW (p. 495) **39.** $m\angle ABD = m\angle DBC = 38.5°$ **41.** $m\angle ABD = 64°$, $m\angle ABC = 128°$ **43.** $\angle 10$ **45.** $\angle 5$ **47.** (2, 7) **49.** (−5, 1)

QUIZ 2 (p. 496) **1.** yes; $m\angle B = m\angle E = 81°$, $m\angle ANB = 46°$, $m\angle A = 53°$ **2.** yes; $m\angle VSU = m\angle P = 47°$, $m\angle U = 101°$, $m\angle V = 32°$ **3.** no; $m\angle J = m\angle H = 42°$, $m\angle A = 43°$, $m\angle P = 94°$ **4.** no **5.** yes **6.** yes **7.** 10 mi

8.6 PRACTICE (pp. 502–505) **7.** CE **9.** GE
11. Yes; $\overline{QS}$ divides two sides of $\triangle PRT$ proportionally.
13. No; $\overline{QS}$ does not divide $\overline{TR}$ and $\overline{PR}$ proportionally.
15. Yes; $\triangle$ Proportionality Converse
17. yes; Corresponding Angles Converse
19. no **21.** 3 **23.** 6 **25.** 14 **27.** 29.4
29. A: 47.8 m, B: 40.2 m, C: 34.0 m
31.

Statements	Reasons
1. $\overline{DE} \parallel \overline{AC}$	1. Given
2. $\angle BDE \cong \angle A$, $\angle BED \cong \angle C$	2. If 2 $\parallel$ lines are cut by a transversal, corresp. $\angle$ are $\cong$.
3. $\triangle DBE \sim \triangle ABC$	3. AA Similarity Post.
4. $\frac{BA}{BD} = \frac{BC}{BE}$	4. Def. of $\sim \triangle$
5. $\frac{BD + DA}{BD} = \frac{BE + EC}{BE}$	5. Segment Addition Post.
6. $\frac{BD}{BD} + \frac{DA}{BD} = \frac{BE}{BE} + \frac{EC}{BE}$	6. Addition of fractions
7. $1 + \frac{DA}{BD} = 1 + \frac{EC}{BE}$	7. Inverse prop. of multiplication
8. $\frac{DA}{BD} = \frac{EC}{BE}$	8. Subtraction prop. of equality

33. Draw a $\parallel$ to $\overline{XW}$ through Z ($\parallel$ Post.) and extend $\overline{XY}$ to intersect the $\parallel$ at A. ($\overline{XY}$ is not $\parallel$ to $\overline{AZ}$ because it would also

have to be $\parallel$ to $\overline{XW}$.) Then, $\frac{YW}{WZ} = \frac{XY}{XA}$. Also, corresp. $\angle YXW$ and A are $\cong$, as are alternate interior $\angle WXZ$ and AZX. Since $\angle YXW \cong \angle WXZ$, $\angle A \cong \angle AZX$ by the Transitive Prop. of Cong. By the Converse of the Base Angles Thm., $\overline{XA} \cong \overline{XZ}$ or $XA = XZ$. Then, by the substitution prop. of equality, $\frac{YW}{WZ} = \frac{XY}{XZ}$. **35.** $MT = 8.4$, $LN = 8$, $SN = 8$, $PR = 27$, $UR = 21$ **37.** about 1040 ft

8.6 MIXED REVIEW (p. 505) **41.** $\sqrt{337}$ **43.** $7\sqrt{2}$ **45.** $\sqrt{305}$ **47.** 15 units **49.** $6\sqrt{2}$ units **51.** reflection **53.** rotation

8.7 PRACTICE (pp. 509–512) **5.** larger; enlargement **7.** Yes; *Sample answer:* a preimage and its image after a dilation are $\sim$. **9.** Enlargement; the dilation has center C and scale factor $\frac{8}{3}$ **11.** Reduction; the dilation has center C and scale factor $\frac{2}{5}$; $x = y = 20$, $z = 25$. **13.** $P'(6, 10)$, $Q'(8, 0)$, $R'(2, 2)$ **15.** $S'(-20, 8)$, $T'(-12, 16)$, $U'(-4, 4)$, $V'(-12, -4)$ **21.** $x = 72$, $y = 63$; 3:4 **23.** enlargement; $k = 4$; 9, 28 **25.** about 9.2 cm **27.** 7:1 **29.** 4.8 in. **31.** 1.7 in.

8.7 MIXED REVIEW (p. 513) **39.** $b = 14$ **41.** $a = 7$ **43.** Yes; *Sample answer:* $\angle C \cong \angle L$ and $\frac{CA}{LJ} = \frac{CB}{LK}$, so the $\triangle$ are $\sim$ by the SAS Similarity Thm.

QUIZ 3 (p. 513) **1.** BD **2.** CE **3.** AF **4.** FA **5.** The dilation is an enlargement with center C and scale factor 2. **6.** The dilation is a reduction with center C and scale factor $\frac{1}{3}$. **7.** reduction, larger **8.** $\frac{9}{4}$

CHAPTER 8 REVIEW (pp. 516–518) **1.** $\frac{21}{2}$ **3.** 4 **5.** 39 in. **7.** $\frac{5}{3}$ **9.** $\frac{3}{5}$ **11.** no **13.** no **15.** 22 **17.** $16\frac{16}{59}$

ALGEBRA REVIEW (pp. 522–523) **1.** 11 **2.** $2\sqrt{13}$ **3.** $3\sqrt{5}$ **4.** $6\sqrt{2}$ **5.** $2\sqrt{10}$ **6.** $3\sqrt{3}$ **7.** $4\sqrt{5}$ **8.** $5\sqrt{2}$ **9.** $9\sqrt{3}$ **10.** $12\sqrt{2}$ **11.** $8\sqrt{5}$ **12.** 15 **13.** $6\sqrt{3}$ **14.** $2\sqrt{2}$ **15.** $8 - 2\sqrt{7}$ **16.** $4\sqrt{11}$ **17.** $\sqrt{5}$ **18.** $21\sqrt{2}$ **19.** $-16\sqrt{3}$ **20.** $5\sqrt{7}$ **21.** $4\sqrt{5}$ **22.** $13\sqrt{2}$ **23.** $21\sqrt{10}$ **24.** 330 **25.** 24 **26.** 36 **27.** $6\sqrt{14}$ **28.** 8 **29.** 112 **30.** 40 **31.** 180 **32.** 32 **33.** 192 **34.** 12 **35.** 125 **36.** 1100 **37.** $\frac{4\sqrt{3}}{3}$ **38.** $\frac{5\sqrt{7}}{7}$ **39.** $\sqrt{2}$ **40.** $\frac{2\sqrt{15}}{5}$ **41.** 1 **42.** $\sqrt{2}$ **43.** $\frac{4\sqrt{6}}{3}$ **44.** $\frac{\sqrt{2}}{2}$ **45.** $\frac{2\sqrt{3}}{3}$ **46.** $\frac{3}{2}$ **47.** $\frac{9\sqrt{13}}{26}$ **48.** $\frac{\sqrt{2}}{2}$ **49.** $\frac{3\sqrt{5}}{5}$ **50.** $\frac{4\sqrt{10}}{5}$ **51.** $\frac{\sqrt{15}}{5}$ **52.** $\frac{\sqrt{6}}{3}$ **53.** ±3 **54.** ±25 **55.** ±17 **56.** $\pm\sqrt{10}$ **57.** ±4 **58.** $\pm\sqrt{13}$ **59.** ±6 **60.** ±8 **61.** ±7 **62.** $\pm\sqrt{10}$ **63.** ±3 **64.** $\pm\sqrt{5}$ **65.** ±2 **66.** $\pm\sqrt{2}$ **67.** ±1 **68.** $\pm\sqrt{7}$ **69.** $\pm\sqrt{6}$ **70.** ±5 **71.** ±4 **72.** ±24 **73.** ±13

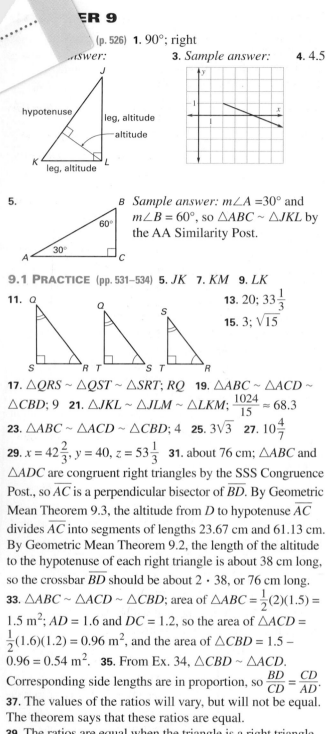

ER 9

(p. 526) **1.** 90°; right

answer: **3.** *Sample answer:* **4.** 4.5

J

hypotenuse — leg, altitude

— altitude

K — leg, altitude — L

5.

B *Sample answer:* $m\angle A =30°$ and
$m\angle B = 60°$, so $\triangle ABC \sim \triangle JKL$ by
the AA Similarity Post.

60°

30°

A — C

9.1 PRACTICE (pp. 531–534) **5.** *JK* **7.** *KM* **9.** *LK*

11.

Q

S — R

Q

T — S

S

T — R

13. 20; $33\frac{1}{3}$

15. 3; $\sqrt{15}$

17. $\triangle QRS \sim \triangle QST \sim \triangle SRT$; *RQ* **19.** $\triangle ABC \sim \triangle ACD \sim$ $\triangle CBD$; 9 **21.** $\triangle JKL \sim \triangle JLM \sim \triangle LKM$; $\frac{1024}{15} \approx 68.3$ **23.** $\triangle ABC \sim \triangle ACD \sim \triangle CBD$; 4 **25.** $3\sqrt{3}$ **27.** $10\frac{4}{7}$ **29.** $x = 42\frac{2}{3}$, $y = 40$, $z = 53\frac{1}{3}$ **31.** about 76 cm; $\triangle ABC$ and $\triangle ADC$ are congruent right triangles by the SSS Congruence Post., so $\overline{AC}$ is a perpendicular bisector of $\overline{BD}$. By Geometric Mean Theorem 9.3, the altitude from *D* to hypotenuse $\overline{AC}$ divides $\overline{AC}$ into segments of lengths 23.67 cm and 61.13 cm. By Geometric Mean Theorem 9.2, the length of the altitude to the hypotenuse of each right triangle is about 38 cm long, so the crossbar $\overline{BD}$ should be about 2 · 38, or 76 cm long. **33.** $\triangle ABC \sim \triangle ACD \sim \triangle CBD$; area of $\triangle ABC = \frac{1}{2}(2)(1.5) =$ 1.5 m²; *AD* = 1.6 and *DC* = 1.2, so the area of $\triangle ACD =$ $\frac{1}{2}(1.6)(1.2) = 0.96$ m², and the area of $\triangle CBD = 1.5 -$ 0.96 = 0.54 m². **35.** From Ex. 34, $\triangle CBD \sim \triangle ACD$. Corresponding side lengths are in proportion, so $\frac{BD}{CD} = \frac{CD}{AD}$. **37.** The values of the ratios will vary, but will not be equal. The theorem says that these ratios are equal. **39.** The ratios are equal when the triangle is a right triangle but are not equal when the triangle is not a right triangle.

9.1 MIXED REVIEW (p. 534) **45.** 8, −8 **47.** If the measure of one of the angles of a triangle is greater that 90°, then the triangle is obtuse; true. **49.** 36 in.² **51.** 62.5 m²

9.2 PRACTICE (pp. 538–541) **3.** $\sqrt{5}$; no **5.** $4\sqrt{3}$; no **7.** 97; yes **9.** 80; yes **11.** $4\sqrt{2}$; no **13.** $8\sqrt{3}$; no

15. $14\sqrt{2}$; no **17.** $2\sqrt{13}$ **19.** $t = 20$ **21.** $s = 24$ **23.** $s = 12$ **25.** 35.7 cm² **27.** 25.2 cm² **29.** 104 cm² **31.** about 41.9 ft; the distance from home plate to second base is about 91.9 ft, so the distance from the pitcher's plate to second base is about 91.9 – 50, or about 41.9 ft. **33.** 94 in., or 7 ft 10 in. **35.** 48 in. **37.** The area of the large square is $(a + b)^2$. Also, the area of the large square is the sum of the areas of the four congruent right triangles plus the area of the small square, or $4\left(\frac{1}{2} \cdot a \cdot b\right) + c^2$. Thus, $(a + b)^2 =$ $4\left(\frac{1}{2} \cdot a \cdot b\right) + c^2$, and so $a^2 + 2ab + b^2 = 2ab + c^2$. Subtracting $2ab$ from each side gives $a^2 + b^2 = c^2$.

9.2 MIXED REVIEW (p. 541) **43.** 9 **45.** 8 **47.** −1225 **49.** 147 **51.** no **53.** no **55.** *Sample answer:* slope of $\overline{PQ} = -\frac{11}{2} =$ slope of $\overline{RS}$; slope of $\overline{QR} = \frac{5}{4} =$ slope of $\overline{PS}$. Both pairs of opposite sides are parallel, so *PQRS* is a □ by the definition of a □.

9.3 PRACTICE (pp. 545–548) **3.** C **5.** D **7.** The crossbars are not perpendicular: $45^2 > 22^2 + 38^2$, so the smaller triangles formed by the crossbars are obtuse. **9.** yes **11.** yes **13.** no **15.** yes; right **17.** no **19.** yes; right **21.** yes; acute **23.** yes; right **25.** yes; obtuse **27.** Square; the diagonals bisect each other, so the quad. is a □; the diagonals are ≅, so the □ is a rectangle. $1^2 + 1^2 = \left(\sqrt{2}\right)^2$, so the diagonals intersect at rt. ∡ to form ⊥ lines; thus, the □ is also a rhombus. A quad. that is both a rectangle and a rhombus must be a square. **29.** $\frac{3}{4}$; $-\frac{4}{3}$; since $\left(\frac{3}{4}\right)\left(-\frac{4}{3}\right) = -1$, $\overline{AC} \perp \overline{BC}$, so $\angle ACB$ is a rt. ∠. Therefore, $\triangle ABC$ is a rt. △ by the definition of rt. △. **31.** *Sample answer:* I prefer to use slopes, because I have two computations rather than three, and computing slopes doesn't involve square roots. **33.** acute **35.** Since $\left(\sqrt{10}\right)^2 + 2^2 < 4^2$, $\triangle ABC$ is obtuse and $\angle C$ is obtuse. By the Triangle Sum Thm., $m\angle A +$ $m\angle ABC + m\angle C = 180°$. $\angle C$ is obtuse, so $m\angle C > 90°$. It follows that $m\angle ABC < 90°$. Vertical angles are ≅, so $m\angle ABC = m\angle 1$. By substitution, $m\angle 1 < 90°$. By the definition of an acute ∠, ∠1 is acute. **37.** A, C, and D **39.** $120^2 + 119^2 = 169^2$, $4800^2 + 4601^2 = 6649^2$, and $(13,500)^2 + (12,709)^2 = (18,541)^2$.

41. Reasons

1. Pythagorean Thm.
2. Given
3. Substitution prop. of equality
5. Converse of the Hinge Thm.
6. Given, def. of right angle, def. of acute angle, and substitution prop. of equality
7. Def. of acute triangle (∠*C* is the largest angle of $\triangle ABC$.)

43. Draw rt. $\triangle PQR$ with side lengths a, b, and hypotenuse x. $x^2 = a^2 + b^2$ by the Pythagorean Thm. It is given that $c^2 = a^2 + b^2$, so by the substitution prop. of equality, $x^2 = c^2$. By a prop. of square roots, $x = c$. $\triangle PQR \cong \triangle LMN$ by the SSS Congruence Post. Corresp. parts of $\cong \triangle$ are $\cong$, so $m\angle R = 90° = m\angle N$. By def., $\angle N$ is a rt. $\angle$, and so $\triangle LNM$ is a right triangle.

9.3 MIXED REVIEW (p. 549) **47.** $2\sqrt{11}$ **49.** $2\sqrt{21}$

51. $\dfrac{3\sqrt{11}}{11}$ **53.** $2\sqrt{2}$ **55.** an enlargement with center C and scale factor $\dfrac{7}{4}$ **57.** $x = 9, y = 11$

QUIZ 1 (p. 549) **1.** $\triangle ABC \sim \triangle ADB \sim \triangle BDC$ **2.** $\overline{BD}$ **3.** 25 **4.** 12 **5.** $2\sqrt{10}$ **6.** $6\sqrt{5}$ **7.** $12\sqrt{2}$ **8.** no; $219^2 \neq 168^2 + 140^2$

9.4 PRACTICE (pp. 554–556) **9.** $4\sqrt{2}$ **11.** $h = k = \dfrac{9\sqrt{2}}{2}$

13. $a = 12\sqrt{3}, b = 24$ **15.** $c = d = 4\sqrt{2}$ **17.** $q = 16\sqrt{2}, r = 16$ **19.** $f = \dfrac{8\sqrt{3}}{3}, h = \dfrac{16\sqrt{3}}{3}$ **21.** 4.3 cm **23.** 18.4 in.

25. 31.2 ft^2 **27.** $24\sqrt{3} \approx 41.6$ ft^2 **29.** about 2 cm
31. $r = \sqrt{2}$; $s = \sqrt{3}$; $t = 2$; $u = \sqrt{5}$; $v = \sqrt{6}$; $w = \sqrt{7}$; I used the Pythagorean Theorem in each right triangle in turn, working from left to right. **33.** the right triangle with legs of lengths 1 and $s = \sqrt{3}$, and hypotenuse $t = 2$
35. Let $DF = x$. Then $EF = x$. By the Pythagorean Theorem, $x^2 + x^2 = (DE)^2$; $2x^2 = (DE)^2$; $DE = \sqrt{2x^2} = \sqrt{2} \cdot x$ by a property of square roots. Thus, the hypotenuse is $\sqrt{2}$ times as long as a leg.

9.4 MIXED REVIEW (p. 557) **43.** $Q'(-1, 2)$ **45.** $A'(-4, -5)$ **47.** AA Similarity Post. **49.** SSS Similarity Thm.

9.5 PRACTICE (pp. 562–565) **3.** $\dfrac{4}{5} = 0.8$ **5.** $\dfrac{4}{3} \approx 1.3333$

7. $\dfrac{4}{5} = 0.8$ **9.** about 17 ft **11.** $\sin A = 0.8$; $\cos A = 0.6$; $\tan A \approx 1.3333$; $\sin B = 0.6$; $\cos B = 0.8$; $\tan B = 0.75$
13. $\sin D = 0.28$; $\cos D = 0.96$; $\tan D \approx 0.2917$; $\sin F = 0.96$; $\cos F = 0.28$; $\tan F \approx 3.4286$ **15.** $\sin J = 0.8575$; $\cos J = 0.5145$; $\tan J = 1.6667$; $\sin K = 0.5145$; $\cos K = 0.8575$; $\tan K = 0.6$ **17.** 0.9744 **19.** 0.4540
21. 0.0349 **23.** 0.8090 **25.** 0.4540 **27.** 2.2460 **29.** $s \approx 31.3$; $t \approx 13.3$ **31.** $t \approx 7.3$; $u \approx 3.4$ **33.** $x \approx 16.0$; $y \approx 14.9$
35. 41.6 m^2 **37.** about 13.4 m **39.** 482 ft; about 1409 ft
41. about 16.4 in. **45.** Procedures may vary. One method is to reason that since the tangent ratio is equal to the ratio of the lengths of the legs, the tangent is equal to 1 when the legs are equal in length, that is, when the triangle is a 45°-45°-90° triangle. Tan $A > 1$ when $m\angle A > 45°$, and $\tan A < 1$ when $m\angle A < 45°$, since increasing the measure of $\angle A$ increases the length of the opposite leg and decreasing the measure of $\angle A$ decreases the length of the opposite leg.

47. Reasons
1. Given
2. Pythagorean Thm.
3. Division prop. of equality
5. Substitution prop. of equality

49. $(\sin 45°)^2 + (\cos 45°)^2 = \left(\dfrac{\sqrt{2}}{2}\right)^2 + \left(\dfrac{\sqrt{2}}{2}\right)^2 = \dfrac{2}{4} + \dfrac{2}{4} = 1$ ✔

51. $(\sin 13°)^2 + (\cos 13°)^2 \approx (0.2250)^2 + (0.9744)^2 \approx 1$ ✔

9.5 MIXED REVIEW (p. 566) **57.** $\triangle MNP \sim \triangle MQN \sim \triangle NQP$; $QP \approx 3.3$; $NP \approx 7.8$ **59.** $5\sqrt{69}$; no

QUIZ 2 (p. 566) **1.** 3.5 m **2.** 5.7 in. **3.** 3.9 in.^{2} **4.** $x \approx 15.6$; $y \approx 11.9$ **5.** $x \approx 8.5$; $y \approx 15.9$ **6.** $x \approx 9.3$; $y \approx 22.1$
7. about 4887 ft

9.6 PRACTICE (pp. 570–572) **5.** 79.5° **7.** 84.3° **9.** $d = 60$, $m\angle D = 33.4°$, $m\angle E = 56.6°$ **11.** 73 **13.** 41.1° **15.** 45°
17. 20.5° **19.** 50.2° **21.** 6.3° **23.** side lengths: 7, 7, and 9.9; angle measures: 90°, 45°, and 45° **25.** side lengths: 4.5, 8, and 9.2; angle measures: 90°, 29.6°, and 60.4°
27. side lengths: 6, 11.0, and 12.5; angle measures: 90°, 28.7°, and 61.3° **29.** $s = 4.1, t = 11.3, m\angle T = 70°$
31. $a = 7.4, c = 8.9, m\angle B = 34°$ **33.** $\ell = 5.9, m = 7.2, m\angle L = 56°$ **35.** 62.4° **37.** 0.4626 **39.** about 239.4 in., or about 19 ft 11 in.; about 4.1°

9.6 MIXED REVIEW (p. 572) **47.** $\langle 3, 2 \rangle$ **49.** $\langle -1, -3 \rangle$
51. $\langle 1, -2 \rangle$ **53.** 25 **55.** 12.6 **57.** 14 **59.** no **61.** yes; right
63. yes; right

9.7 PRACTICE (pp. 576–579) **5.** $\langle 4, 5 \rangle$; 6.4 **7.** $\langle 2, -5 \rangle$; 5.4
9. $\langle 0, 3 \rangle$ **11.** $\langle -3, 6 \rangle$; 6.7 **13.** $\langle 2, 7 \rangle$; 7.3 **15.** $\langle 10, 4 \rangle$; 10.8
17. $\langle -6, -4 \rangle$; 7.2 **19.** $\langle 1, -4 \rangle$; 4.1 **21.** about 61 mi/h; about 9° north of east **23.** about 57 mi/h; 45° north of west
25. $\overrightarrow{EF}$, $\overrightarrow{CD}$, and $\overrightarrow{AB}$ **27.** $\overrightarrow{EF}$ and $\overrightarrow{CD}$ **29.** yes; no
31. $\overrightarrow{u} = \langle 4, 1 \rangle$; $\overrightarrow{v} = \langle 2, 4 \rangle$; $\overrightarrow{u} + \overrightarrow{v} = \langle 6, 5 \rangle$ **33.** $\overrightarrow{u} = \langle 2, -4 \rangle$; $\overrightarrow{v} = \langle 3, 6 \rangle$; $\overrightarrow{u} + \overrightarrow{v} = \langle 5, 2 \rangle$ **35.** $\langle 4, 11 \rangle$ **37.** $\langle 10, 10 \rangle$
39. $\langle 4, -4 \rangle$ **41.** $\overrightarrow{u} = \langle 0, -120 \rangle$; $\overrightarrow{v} = \langle 40, 0 \rangle$
43. about 126 mi/h; the speed at which the skydiver is falling, taking into account the breeze

45.

; The new velocity is $s = \langle -30, -120 \rangle$.

47. When $k > 0$, the magnitude of $\overrightarrow{v}$ is k times the magnitude of $\overrightarrow{u}$ and the directions are the same. When $k < 0$, the magnitude of $\overrightarrow{v}$ is $|k|$ times the magnitude of $\overrightarrow{u}$ and the direction of $\overrightarrow{v}$ is opposite the direction of $\overrightarrow{u}$. Justifications may vary.

IEW (p. 580) **53.** Since $\angle D$ and $\angle E$ are
are $\cong$, $\angle D \cong \angle E$. Since $\triangle ABC$ is
C. $\overline{DE} \parallel \overline{AC}$, so $\angle DBA \cong \angle BAC$ and
the Alternate Interior Angles Thm.
ngle is also equiangular, so $m\angle BAC =$
$0°$. By the def. of $\cong$ $\underline{\triangle}$ and the substitution
op. of equality, $\angle DBA \cong \angle EBC$. $\triangle ADB \cong \triangle CEB$ by the
AAS Congruence Thm. Corresponding parts of $\cong$ $\triangle$ are $\cong$,
so $\overline{DB} \cong \overline{EB}$. By the def. of midpoint, B is the midpoint of
$\overline{DE}$. **55.** $x = 120$, $y = 30$ **57.** $x^2 + 2x + 1$ **59.** $x^2 + 22x + 121$

QUIZ 3 (p. 580) **1.** $a = 41.7$, $b = 19.4$, $m\angle A = 65°$
2. $y = 12$, $z = 17.0$, $m\angle Y = 45°$ **3.** $m = 13.4$, $q = 20.9$,
$m\angle N = 50°$ **4.** $p = 7.7$, $q = 2.1$, $m\angle Q = 15°$
5. $f = 4.7$, $m\angle F = 37.9°$, $m\angle G = 52.1°$
6. $\ell = 12.0$, $m\angle K = 14.0°$, $m\angle L = 76.0°$ **7.** $\langle -5, -1 \rangle$; 5.1
8. $\langle 6, -5 \rangle$; 7.8 **9.** $\langle 3, 5 \rangle$; 5.8 **10.** $\langle -7, -11 \rangle$; 13.0
11. ; about 69° north of east
12. $\langle 4, 2 \rangle$ **13.** $\langle 2, 4 \rangle$ **14.** $\langle -2, -8 \rangle$
15. $\langle 2, 1 \rangle$ **16.** $\langle 6, 13 \rangle$ **17.** $\langle 0, 3 \rangle$

CHAPTER 9 REVIEW (pp. 582–584) **1.** $x = 4$, $y = 3\sqrt{5}$
3. $x = 48$, $y = 21$, $z = 9\sqrt{7}$ **5.** $s = 4\sqrt{5}$; no **7.** $t = 2\sqrt{13}$; no
9. yes; right **11.** yes; acute **13.** $12\sqrt{2} \approx 17.0$ in.; 18 in.^{2}
15. $9\sqrt{3}$ cm; $81\sqrt{3} \approx 140.3$ cm^2 **17.** $\sin P \approx 0.9459$;
$\cos P \approx 0.3243$; $\tan P \approx 2.9167$; $\sin N \approx 0.3243$;
$\cos N \approx 0.9459$; $\tan N \approx 0.3429$ **19.** $x = 8.9$, $m\angle X = 48.2°$,
$m\angle Z = 41.8°$ **21.** $s = 17$, $m\angle R = 28.1°$, $m\angle T = 61.9°$
23. $\langle 12, -5 \rangle$; 13 **25.** $\langle 14, 9 \rangle$; about 16.6; about 32.7° north
of east

CUMULATIVE PRACTICE (pp. 588–589) **1.** No; if two planes
intersect, then their intersection is a line. The three points
must be collinear, so they cannot be the vertices of a
triangle. **3.** never **5.** Paragraph proof: $\overline{BD}$ is the median
from point B, $\overline{AD} \cong \overline{CD}$, $\overline{BD} \cong \overline{BD}$, and it is given that
$\overline{AB} \cong \overline{CB}$. Thus, $\triangle ABD \cong \triangle CBD$ by the SSS Congruence
Post. Also, $\angle ABD \cong \angle CBD$ since corresponding parts of
$\cong$ $\triangle$ are $\cong$. By the def. of an angle bisector, $\overline{BD}$ bisects
$\angle ABC$. **7.** yes; clockwise and counterclockwise rotational
symmetry of 120° **9.** $x = 24$, $y = 113$ **11.** $y = \frac{3}{4}x + \frac{7}{2}$
13. $A'(-1, -2)$, $B'(3, -5)$, $C'(5, 6)$ **15.** $A'(-3, 6)$,
$B'(-7, 9)$, $C'(-9, -2)$ **17.** $3\frac{3}{7}$ **19.** No; in $ABCD$, the ratio
of the length to width is 8:6, or 4:3. In $APQD$, the ratio of
the length to width is 6:4, or 3:2. Since these ratios are
not equal, the rectangles are not similar.
21. Yes; the ratios $\frac{6}{9}$, $\frac{8}{12}$, and $\frac{12}{18}$ all equal $\frac{2}{3}$, so the
triangles are similar by the SSS Similarity Theorem.

23. The image with scale factor $\frac{1}{3}$ has endpoints $\left(2, -\frac{4}{3}\right)$
and $(4, 3)$; its slope is $\frac{\frac{13}{3}}{2} = \frac{13}{6}$. The image with scale factor
$\frac{1}{2}$ has endpoints $(3, -2)$ and $(6, 4.5)$; its slope is $\frac{13}{6}$.
The two image segments are parallel. **25.** 4 **27.** acute
29. Let $\angle A$ be the smaller acute angle; $\sin A = \frac{8}{17}$,
$\cos A = \frac{15}{17}$, and $\tan A = \frac{8}{15}$. **31.** $\langle 2, 16 \rangle$; about 16.1;
about 83° north of east **33.** 20 gal **35.** 189.4 mi

CHAPTER 10

SKILL REVIEW (p. 594) **1.** $2\frac{1}{2}$ **2.** 48 **3.** 23.4 **4.** $-\sqrt{6}$, $\sqrt{6}$
5. -16, 4 **6.** $(8, 10)$ **7.** $JL = \sqrt{145}$, $m\angle J \approx 48.4°$,
$m\angle L \approx 41.6°$ **8. a.** 15 **b.** $\left(3, -4\frac{1}{2}\right)$ **c.** $y = -\frac{3}{4}x - \frac{9}{4}$
d. the segment with endpoints $A'(-7, 0)$ and $B'(5, -9)$

10.1 PRACTICE (pp. 599–602) **5.** No; $5^2 + 5^2 \neq 7^2$, so by the
the Converse of the Pythagorean Thm., $\triangle ABD$ is not a
right $\triangle$, so $\overline{BD}$ is not $\perp$ to $\overline{AB}$. If $\overleftrightarrow{BD}$ were tangent to $\odot C$,
$\angle B$ would be a right angle. Thus, $\overleftrightarrow{BD}$ is not tangent to $\odot C$.
7. 2 **9.** 7.5 cm **11.** 1.5 ft **13.** 52 in. **15.** 17.4 in.
17. C and G; the diameter of $\odot G$ is 45, so the radius is
$\frac{45}{2} = 22.5$, which is the radius of $\odot C$.
19. E **21.** D **23.** C **25.** G **27.** internal
29. 2 internal, 2 external; **31.** 2 external;

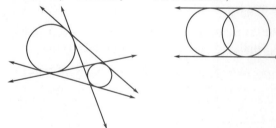

33. $(6, 2)$, 2 **35.** the lines with equations $y = 0$, $y = 4$, and
$x = 4$ **37.** No; $5^2 + 15^2 \neq 17^2$, so by the Converse of the
Pythagorean Thm., $\triangle ABC$ is not a right $\triangle$, so $\overline{AB}$ is not $\perp$
to $\overline{AC}$. Then, $\overleftrightarrow{AB}$ is not tangent to $\odot C$. **39.** Yes; $BD = 10 +$
$10 = 20$ and $20^2 + 21^2 = 29^2$, so by the Converse of the
Pythagorean Thm., $\triangle ABD$ is a right $\triangle$, and $\overline{AB} \perp \overline{BD}$.
Then, $\overleftrightarrow{AB}$ is tangent to $\odot C$. **41.** 53 ft **43.** any two of $\overline{GD}$,
$\overline{HC}$, $\overline{FA}$, and $\overline{EB}$ **45.** $\overrightarrow{JK}$ **47.** -1, 1 **49.** $\overleftrightarrow{PS}$ is tangent to
$\odot X$ at P, $\overleftrightarrow{PS}$ is tangent to $\odot Y$ at S, $\overleftrightarrow{RT}$ is tangent to $\odot X$ at T,
and $\overleftrightarrow{RT}$ is tangent to $\odot Y$ at R. Then, $\overline{PQ} \cong \overline{TQ}$ and $\overline{QS} \cong \overline{QR}$.
(2 tangent segments with the same ext. endpoint are $\cong$.)
By the def. of cong., $PQ = TQ$ and $QS = QR$, so $PQ + QS =$
$TQ + QR$ by the addition prop. of equality. Then, by the
Segment Addition Post. and the Substitution Prop., $PS = RT$
or $\overline{PS} \cong \overline{RT}$. **51.** $QR < QP$

53. *Sample answer:* Assume that ℓ is not tangent to P, that is, there is another point X on ℓ that is also on $\odot Q$. X is on $\odot Q$, so $QX = QP$. But the $\perp$ segment from Q to ℓ is the shortest such segment, so $QX > QP$. QX cannot be both equal to and greater than QP. The assumption that such a point X exists must be false. Then, ℓ is tangent to P.

55. Square; $\overline{BD}$ and $\overline{AD}$ are tangent to $\odot C$ at A and B, respectively, so $\angle A$ and $\angle B$ are right $\angle s$. Then, by the Interior Angles of a Quadrilateral Thm., $\angle D$ is also a right $\angle$. Then, $CABD$ is a rectangle. Opp. sides of a $\square$ are $\cong$, so $\overline{CA} \cong \overline{BD}$ and $\overline{AD} \cong \overline{CB}$. But $\overline{CA}$ and $\overline{CB}$ are radii, so $\overline{CA} \cong \overline{CB}$ and by the Transitive Prop. of Cong., all 4 sides of $CABD$ are $\cong$. $CABD$ is both a rectangle and a rhombus, so it is a square by the Square Corollary.

10.1 MIXED REVIEW (p. 602) **59.** *Sample answer:* Since slope of $\overline{PS} = \dfrac{3}{8} =$ slope of $\overline{QR}$, $\overline{PS} \parallel \overline{QR}$. Since slope of $\overline{PQ} = -3 =$ slope of $\overline{SR}$, $\overline{PQ} \parallel \overline{SR}$. Then, $PQRS$ is a $\square$ by def.
61. $6\dfrac{3}{5}$ **63.** 28 **65.** $2\dfrac{2}{5}$ **67.** 9 **69.** $m\angle A \approx 23.2°$, $m\angle C \approx 66.8°$, $AC \approx 15.2$ **71.** $BC \approx 11.5$, $m\angle A \approx 55.2°$, $m\angle B \approx 34.8°$

10.2 PRACTICE (pp. 607–611) **3.** 60° **5.** 180° **7.** 220°
9. $\overline{BC}$ is a diameter; a chord that is the $\perp$ bisector of another chord is a diameter. **11.** $\overline{AC} \cong \overline{BC}$ and $\widehat{AD} \cong \widehat{BD}$; a diameter $\perp$ to a chord bisects the chord and its arc.
13. minor arc **15.** minor arc **17.** semicircle **19.** major arc
21. 55° **23.** 305° **25.** 180° **27.** 65° **29.** 65° **31.** 120°
33. 145° **35.** $\widehat{AC} \cong \widehat{KL}$ and $\widehat{ABC} \cong \widehat{KML}$; $\odot D$ and $\odot N$ are $\cong$ (both have radius 4). By the Arc Add. Post., $m\widehat{AC} = m\widehat{AE} + m\widehat{EC} = 70° + 75° = 145°$. $m\widehat{KL} = 145°$ and since $\odot D \cong \odot N$, $\widehat{AC} \cong \widehat{KL}$; $m\widehat{ABC} = 360° - m\widehat{AC} = 360° - 145° = 215°$. $m\widehat{KML} = m\widehat{KM} + m\widehat{ML} = 130° + 85° = 215°$ by the Arc Add. Post. Since $\odot D \cong \odot N$, $\widehat{ABC} \cong \widehat{KML}$. **37.** 36; 144°
39. $\widehat{AB} \cong \widehat{CB}$; 2 arcs are $\cong$ if and only if their corresp. chords are $\cong$. **41.** $\overline{AB} \cong \overline{AC}$; in a $\odot$, 2 chords are $\cong$ if and only if they are equidistant from the center. **43.** 40°; a diameter that is $\perp$ to a chord bisects the chord and its arc. **45.** 15; in a $\odot$, 2 chords are $\cong$ if and only if they are equidistant from the center. **47.** 40°; Vertical Angles Thm., def. of minor arc **49.** 15° **51.** 3:00 A.M. **53.** This follows from the definition of the measure of a minor arc. (The measure of a minor arc is the measure of its central $\angle$.) If 2 minor arcs in the same $\odot$ or $\cong \odot$s are $\cong$, then their central $\angle s$ are $\cong$. Conversely, if 2 central $\angle s$ of the same $\odot$ or $\cong \odot$s are $\cong$, then the measures of the associated arcs are $\cong$.
55. Yes; construct the $\perp$s from the center of the $\odot$ to each chord. Use a compass to compare the lengths of the segments. **57.** Since $\widehat{AB} \cong \widehat{DC}$, $\angle APB \cong \angle CPD$ by the def. of $\cong$ arcs. $\overline{PA}$, $\overline{PB}$, $\overline{PC}$, and $\overline{PD}$ are all radii of $\odot P$, so $\overline{PA} \cong \overline{PB} \cong \overline{PC} \cong \overline{PD}$. Then $\triangle APB \cong \triangle CPD$ by the SAS Cong. Post., so corresp. sides $\overline{AB}$ and $\overline{DC}$ are $\cong$.

59. Draw radii $\overline{LG}$ and $\overline{LH}$. $\overline{LG} \cong \overline{LH}$, $\overline{LJ} \cong \overline{LJ}$, and since $\overline{EF} \perp \overline{GH}$, $\triangle LGJ \cong \triangle LHJ$ by the HL Cong. Thm. Then, corresp. sides $\overline{GJ}$ and $\overline{JH}$ are $\cong$, as are corresp. $\angle s$ GLJ and HLJ. By the def. of arcs, $\widehat{GE} \cong \widehat{EH}$. **61.** Draw radii $\overline{PB}$ and $\overline{PC}$. $\overline{PB} \cong \overline{PC}$ and $\overline{PE} \cong \overline{PF}$. Also, since $\overline{PE} \perp \overline{AB}$ and $\overline{PF} \perp \overline{CD}$, $\triangle PEB$ and $\triangle PFC$ are right $\angle s$ and are $\cong$ by the HL Cong. Thm. Corresp. sides $\overline{BE}$ and $\overline{CF}$ are $\cong$, so $BE = CF$ and. by the multiplication prop. of equality, $2BE = 2CE$. By Thm. 10.5, $\overline{PE}$ bisects $\overline{AB}$ and $\overline{PF}$ bisects $\overline{CD}$, so $AB = 2BE$ and $CD = 2CF$. Then, by the Substitution Prop., $AB = CD$ or $\overline{AB} \cong \overline{CD}$.

63.

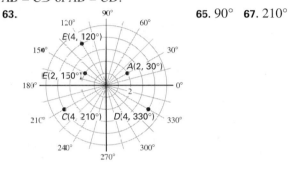

65. 90° **67.** 210°

10.2 MIXED REVIEW (p. 611)
71, 73. Coordinates of sample points are given.

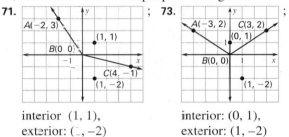

71. interior (1, 1), exterior: (1, −2)
73. interior: (0, 1), exterior: (1, −2)

75. Square; $PQ = QR = RS = PS = 3\sqrt{2}$, so $PQRS$ is a rhombus by the Rhombus Corollary; $PR = QS = 6$, so $PQRS$ is a rectangle. (A $\square$ is a rectangle if and only if its diagonals are $\cong$.) Then, $PQRS$ is a square by the Square Corollary. **77.** 16 **79.** 18

10.3 PRACTICE (pp. 616–619) **3.** 40° **5.** 210° **7.** $y = 150$, $z = 75$ **9.** 64° **11.** 228° **13.** 109° **15.** 47; inscribed $\angle$ that intercept the same arc have the same measure. **17.** $x = 45$, $y = 40$, inscribed $\angle$ that intercept the same arc have the same measure. **19.** $x = 80$, $y = 78$, $z = 160$ **21.** $x = 30$, $y = 20$, $m\angle A = m\angle B = m\angle C = 60°$ **23.** $x = 9$, $y = 6$; $m\angle A = 54°$, $m\angle B = 36°$, $m\angle C = 126°$, $m\angle D = 144°$ **25.** Yes; both pairs of opp. $\angle s$ are right $\angle s$ and, so, are supplementary. **27.** No; both pairs of opp. $\angle s$ of a kite may be, but are not always, supplementary. **29.** Yes; both pairs of opp. $\angle s$ of an isosceles trapezoid are supplementary. **31.** diameter **33.** $\overline{AB}$; a line $\perp$ to a radius of a $\odot$ at its endpoint is tangent to the $\odot$. **35.** $\overline{QB}$; isosceles; base $\angle s$; $\angle A \cong \angle B$; Exterior Angle; $2x°$; $2x°$; 2; $\dfrac{1}{2}m\widehat{AC}$; $\dfrac{1}{2}m\widehat{AC}$

37. Draw the diameter containing $\overline{QB}$, intersecting the $\odot$ at point D. By the proof in Ex. 35, $m\angle ABD = \frac{1}{2}m\widehat{AD}$ and $m\angle DBC = \frac{1}{2}m\widehat{DC}$. By the Arc Addition Post., $m\widehat{AD} = m\widehat{AC} + m\widehat{CD}$, so $m\widehat{AC} = m\widehat{AD} - m\widehat{CD}$ by the subtraction prop. of equality. By the Angle Addition Post., $m\angle ABD = m\angle ABC + m\angle CBD$, so $m\angle ABC = m\angle ABD - m\angle CBD$ by the subtraction prop. of equality. Then, by repeated application of the Substitution Prop., $m\angle ABC = \frac{1}{2}m\widehat{AC}$.

39. GIVEN: $\odot O$ with inscribed $\triangle ABC$, $\overline{AC}$ is a diameter of circle $\odot O$.
PROVE: $\triangle ABC$ is a right $\triangle$.
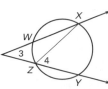
Use the Arc Addition Postulate to show that $m\widehat{AEC} = m\widehat{ABC}$ and thus $m\widehat{ABC} = 180°$. Then use the Measure of an Incribed Angle Thm. to show $m\angle B = 90°$, so that $\angle B$ is a right $\angle$ and $\triangle ABC$ is a right $\triangle$.
GIVEN: $\odot O$ with inscribed $\triangle ABC$, $\angle B$ is a right $\angle$.
PROVE: $\overline{AC}$ is a diameter of circle $\odot O$.
Use the Measure of an Incribed Angle Thm. to show the inscribed right $\angle$ intercepts an arc with measure $2(90°) = 180°$. Since $\overline{AC}$ intercepts an arc that is half of the measure of the circle, it must be a diameter. **41.** *Sample answer:* Use the carpenter's square to draw two diameters of the circle. (Position the vertex of the tool on the circle and mark the 2 points where the sides intersect the $\odot$. Repeat, placing the vertex at a different point on the $\odot$. The center is the point where the diameters intersect.)

10.3 MIXED REVIEW (p. 620)

49. $y = 2x - 9$ **51.** $y = \frac{4}{3}x + 7$ **53.** $y = -\frac{4}{5}x - 16$

55.
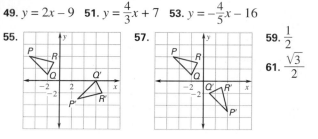
57.

59. $\frac{1}{2}$

61. $\frac{\sqrt{3}}{2}$

QUIZ 1 (p. 620) **1.** 90; a tangent line is $\perp$ to the radius drawn to the point of tangency. **2.** 12; 2 tangent segs. with the same ext. endpoint are $\cong$. **3.** 47° **4.** 133° **5.** 227° **6.** 313° **7.** 180° **8.** 47° **9.** 85.2°

10.4 PRACTICE (pp. 624–627) **3.** 60° **5.** 90° **7.** 88° **9.** 280° **11.** 72° **13.** 110° **15.** 25.4 **17.** 112.5° **19.** 103° **21.** 26° **23.** 37° **25.** 55° **27.** 5 **29.** 60° **31.** 30° **33.** 30° **35.** 0.7° **37.** Diameter; 90°; a tangent line is $\perp$ to the radius drawn to the point of tangency. **39.** The proof would be similar, using the Angle Addition and Arc Addition Postulates, but you would be subtracting $m\angle PBC$ and $m\widehat{PC}$ instead of adding.

41.
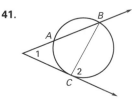
Case 1: Draw $\overline{BC}$. Use the Exterior Angle Thm. to show that $m\angle 2 = m\angle 1 + m\angle ABC$, so that $m\angle 1 = m\angle 2 - m\angle ABC$. Then use Thm. 10.12 to show that $m\angle 2 = \frac{1}{2}m\widehat{BC}$ and the Measure of an Inscribed Angle Thm. to show that $m\angle ABC = \frac{1}{2}m\widehat{AC}$. Then, $m\angle 1 = \frac{1}{2}\left(m\widehat{BC} - m\widehat{AC}\right)$.

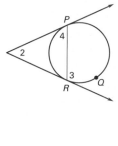
Case 2: Draw $\overline{PR}$. Use the Exterior Angle Thm. to show that $m\angle 3 = m\angle 2 + m\angle 4$, so that $m\angle 2 = m\angle 3 - m\angle 4$. Then use Thm. 10.12 to show that $m\angle 3 = \frac{1}{2}m\widehat{PQR}$ and $m\angle 4 = \frac{1}{2}m\widehat{PR}$. Then, $m\angle 2 = \frac{1}{2}\left(m\widehat{PQR} - m\widehat{PR}\right)$.

Case 3: Draw $\overline{XZ}$. Use the Exterior Angle Thm. to show that $m\angle 4 = m\angle 3 + m\angle WXZ$, so that $m\angle 3 = m\angle 4 - m\angle WXZ$. Then use the Measure of an Inscribed Angle Thm. to show that $m\angle 4 = \frac{1}{2}m\widehat{XY}$ and $m\angle WXZ = \frac{1}{2}m\widehat{WZ}$. Then, $m\angle 3 = \frac{1}{2}\left(m\widehat{XY} - m\widehat{WZ}\right)$.

10.4 MIXED REVIEW (p. 627) **47.** 6 **49.** 25 **51.** 2

10.5 PRACTICE (pp. 632–634) **3.** 15; 18; 12 **5.** 16; $x + 8$; 4 **7.** 9; 6 **9.** The segment from you to the center of the aviary is a secant segment that shares an endpoint with the segment that is tangent to the aviary. Let x be the length of the internal secant segment (twice the radius of the aviary) and use Thm. 10.17. Since $40(40 + x) \approx 60^2$, the radius is about $\frac{50}{2}$, or 25 ft. **11.** 45; 27; 30 **13.** 13 **15.** 8.5 **17.** 6 **19.** $8\frac{2}{3}$ **21.** 4 **23.** $\frac{-9 + \sqrt{565}}{2} \approx 7.38$ **25.** $x = 42, y = 10$ **27.** $x = 7, y = \frac{-13 + 5\sqrt{17}}{2} \approx 3.81$ **29.** 4.875 ft; the diameter through A bisects the chord into two 4.5 ft segments. Use Thm. 10.15 to find the length of the part of the diameter containing A. Add this length to 3 and divide by 2 to get the radius. **31.** $\angle B$ and $\angle D$ intercept the same arc, so $\angle B \cong \angle D$. $\angle E \cong \angle E$ by the Reflexive Prop. of Cong., so $\triangle BCE \sim \triangle DAE$ by the AA Similarity Thm. Then, since lengths of corresp. sides of $\sim \triangle$ are proportional, $\frac{EA}{EC} = \frac{ED}{EB}$. By the Cross Product Prop., $EA \cdot EB = EC \cdot ED$.

10.5 MIXED REVIEW (p. 635) **41.** 10; (3, 0) **43.** 15; $\left(-\frac{11}{2}, 1\right)$

45. 14; (−2, −2) **47.** $y = -\frac{3}{2}x + 17$ **49.** $y = -\frac{1}{3}x - \frac{10}{3}$

SA28 *Selected Answers*

51. $y = \frac{3}{7}x + \frac{81}{7}$ **53.**

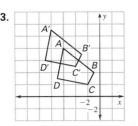

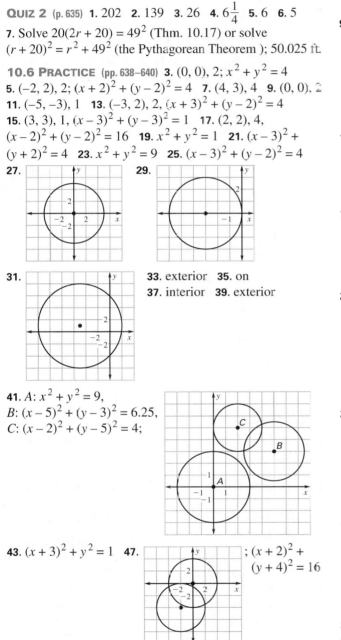

QUIZ 2 (p. 635) **1.** 202 **2.** 139 **3.** 26 **4.** $6\frac{1}{4}$ **5.** 6 **6.** 5
7. Solve $20(2r + 20) = 49^2$ (Thm. 10.17) or solve
$(r + 20)^2 = r^2 + 49^2$ (the Pythagorean Theorem); 50.025 ft

10.6 PRACTICE (pp. 638–640) **3.** (0, 0), 2; $x^2 + y^2 = 4$
5. (–2, 2), 2; $(x + 2)^2 + (y - 2)^2 = 4$ **7.** (4, 3), 4 **9.** (0, 0), 2
11. (–5, –3), 1 **13.** (–3, 2), 2, $(x + 3)^2 + (y - 2)^2 = 4$
15. (3, 3), 1, $(x - 3)^2 + (y - 3)^2 = 1$ **17.** (2, 2), 4,
$(x - 2)^2 + (y - 2)^2 = 16$ **19.** $x^2 + y^2 = 1$ **21.** $(x - 3)^2 +$
$(y + 2)^2 = 4$ **23.** $x^2 + y^2 = 9$ **25.** $(x - 3)^2 + (y - 2)^2 = 4$

27.   **29.**

31.   **33.** exterior **35.** on
37. interior **39.** exterior

41. $A: x^2 + y^2 = 9$,
$B: (x - 5)^2 + (y - 3)^2 = 6.25$,
$C: (x - 2)^2 + (y - 5)^2 = 4$;

43. $(x + 3)^2 + y^2 = 1$ **47.**   ; $(x + 2)^2 +$
$(y + 4)^2 = 16$

10.6 MIXED REVIEW (p. 640) **55.** ▱, rectangle, rhombus,
kite, isosceles trapezoid **57.** ⟨–6, 7⟩; 9.2 **59.** ⟨15, 1⟩; 15.0
61. No; P is not equidistant from the sides of $\angle A$.

10.7 PRACTICE (pp. 645–647) **3.** B **5.** D **7.** the two points
on the intersection of the ⊥ bisector of $\overline{AB}$ and ⊙A with
radius 5;

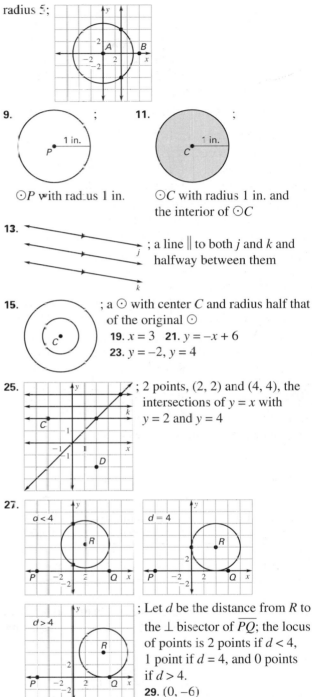

9.   ; **11.**   ;

⊙P with radius 1 in.   ⊙C with radius 1 in. and
the interior of ⊙C

13.   ; a line ‖ to both j and k and
halfway between them

15.   ; a ⊙ with center C and radius half that
of the original ⊙
19. $x = 3$ **21.** $y = -x + 6$
23. $y = -2$, $y = 4$

25.   ; 2 points, (2, 2) and (4, 4), the
intersections of $y = x$ with
$y = 2$ and $y = 4$

27.   ; Let d be the distance from R to
the ⊥ bisector of $\overline{PQ}$; the locus
of points is 2 points if $d < 4$,
1 point if $d = 4$, and 0 points
if $d > 4$.
29. (0, –6)

31. Let d be the distance from P to k. If $0 < d < 4$, then
the locus is 2 points. If $d = 4$, then the locus is 1 point.
If $d > 4$, then the locus is 0 points.

43. **45.**

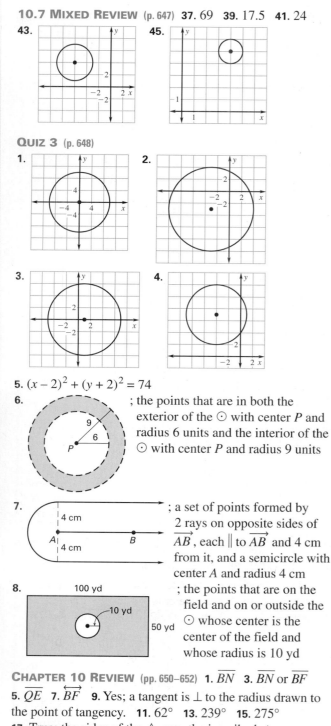

QUIZ 3 (p. 648)

1. **2.**

3. **4.**

5. $(x - 2)^2 + (y + 2)^2 = 74$

6. ; the points that are in both the exterior of the $\odot$ with center P and radius 6 units and the interior of the $\odot$ with center P and radius 9 units

7. ; a set of points formed by 2 rays on opposite sides of $\overrightarrow{AB}$, each $\parallel$ to $\overrightarrow{AB}$ and 4 cm from it, and a semicircle with center A and radius 4 cm

8. ; the points that are on the field and on or outside the $\odot$ whose center is the center of the field and whose radius is 10 yd

CHAPTER 10 REVIEW (pp. 650–652) **1.** $\overline{BN}$ **3.** $\overline{BN}$ or $\overrightarrow{BF}$
5. $\overline{QE}$ **7.** $\overleftrightarrow{BF}$ **9.** Yes; a tangent is $\perp$ to the radius drawn to the point of tangency. **11.** 62° **13.** 239° **15.** 275°
17. True; the sides of the $\triangle$ opp. the inscribed $\angle$s are diameters, so the inscribed $\angle$s are right $\angle$s. **19.** True; $ABCD$ is inscribed in a $\odot$, so opp. $\angle$s are supplementary.
21. 55 **23.** 94 **25.** 34.4

27. $(x - 2)^2 + (y - 5)^2 = 81$; **29.** $(x + 6)^2 + y^2 = 10$;

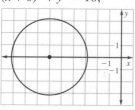
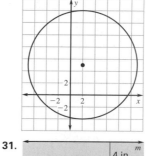

31. ; 2 lines, m and n, on opp. sides of ℓ, each $\parallel$ to ℓ and 4 in. from ℓ, and all the points between m and n

ALGEBRA REVIEW (pp. 656–657) **1.** $\dfrac{A}{\ell}$ **2.** $\dfrac{\sqrt[3]{6\pi^2 V}}{2\pi}$ **3.** $\dfrac{2A}{b}$

4. $\dfrac{2A}{h} - b_2$ **5.** $\sqrt{\dfrac{A}{\pi}}$ or $\dfrac{\sqrt{A\pi}}{\pi}$ **6.** $\dfrac{C}{2\pi}$ **7.** $\sqrt[3]{V}$ **8.** $\dfrac{P - 2w}{2}$ **9.** $\dfrac{V}{\ell w}$

10. $\dfrac{V}{\pi r^2}$ **11.** $\sqrt{\dfrac{S}{6}}$ or $\dfrac{\sqrt{6S}}{6}$ **12.** $\sqrt{c^2 - a^2}$ **13.** $5 + x$

14. $x^2 + \sqrt{2}$ **15.** $2x - 14$ **16.** $3x - 6$ **17.** $x + 2 - 9x$

18. $\dfrac{x}{2} + 3x$ **19.** $5x - 7 = 13$; 4 **20.** $2x - 16 = 10$; 13

21. $2x + 14x = 48$; 3 **22.** $\dfrac{x}{2} = 3(x + 5)$; –6 **23.** 36

24. 51 miles **25.** 142 **26.** $12.50 **27.** 25% **28.** 22%
29. 400% **30.** about 15% **31.** 10 **32.** 25 meters **33.** $2.08

34. about 17% **35.** $\dfrac{1}{2x}$ **36.** $2a^2$ **37.** x **38.** 3 **39.** $\dfrac{a + 2}{a - 8}$

40. $\dfrac{x + 3}{6x - 1}$ **41.** $\dfrac{7d - 1}{3d + 4}$ **42.** $\dfrac{y - 6}{12 - y}$ **43.** $\dfrac{9s - 1}{s - 3}$ **44.** $\dfrac{-5h + 1}{h + 1}$

45. $\dfrac{t - 1}{t + 1}$ **46.** $\dfrac{m - 2}{m + 2}$

CHAPTER 11

SKILL REVIEW (p. 660) **1.** 48 in.^{2} **2.** 44°; 123°, 101°, 136°
3. a. $\dfrac{3}{2}$ **b.** $\dfrac{2}{3}$ **4.** 43.6°, 46.4°

11.1 PRACTICE (pp. 665–668) **3.** 95 **5.** 45 **7.** 1800°
9. 2880° **11.** 5040° **13.** 17,640° **15.** 101 **17.** 108 **19.** 135
21. 140° **23.** 6 **25.** 16 **29.** 30° **31.** about 17.1° **33.** 6
35. 5 **37.** 75° **39.** The yellow hexagon is regular with interior angles measuring 120° each; the yellow pentagons each have two interior angles that measure 90° and three interior angles that measure 120°; the triangles are equilateral with all interior angles measuring 60°.
41. $\angle 3$ and $\angle 8$ are a linear pair, so $m\angle 3 = 140°$; $\angle 2$ and $\angle 7$ are a linear pair, so $m\angle 7 = 80°$; $m\angle 1 = 80°$ by the Polygon Interior Angles Thm.; $\angle 1$ and $\angle 6$ are a linear pair, so $m\angle 6 = 100°$; $\angle 4$ and $\angle 9$ are a linear pair, as are $\angle 5$ and $\angle 10$, so $m\angle 9 = m\angle 10 = 70°$. **43.** Draw all the diagonals of $ABCDE$ that have A as one endpoint. The diagonals, $\overline{AC}$ and $\overline{AD}$, divide $ABCDE$ into 3 $\triangle$. By the Angle Addition Post., $m\angle BAE = m\angle BAC + m\angle CAD + m\angle DAE$.

SELECTED ANSWERS

Similarly, $m\angle BCD = m\angle BCA + m\angle ACD$ and $m\angle CDE = m\angle CDA + m\angle ADE$. Then, the sum of the measures of the interior $\angle$ of $ABCDE$ is equal to the sum of the measures of the $\angle$ of $\triangle ABC$, $\triangle ACD$, and $\triangle ADE$. By the $\triangle$ Sum Thm., the sum of the measures of each $\triangle$ is 180°, so the sum of the measures of the interior $\angle$ of $ABCDE$ is $3 \cdot 180° = (5-2) \cdot 180°$. **45.** Let A be a convex n-gon. Each interior $\angle$ and one of the exterior $\angle$ at that vertex form a linear pair, so the sum of their measures is 180°. Then, the sum of the measures of the interior $\angle$ and one exterior $\angle$ at each vertex is $n \cdot 180°$. By the Polygon Interior Angles Thm., the sum of the measures of the interior $\angle$ of A is $(n-2) \cdot 180°$. So, the sum of the measures of the exterior $\angle$ of A, one at each vertex, is $n \cdot 180° - (n-2) \cdot 180° = n \cdot 180° - n \cdot 180° + 360° = 360°$. **49.** $m\angle A = m\angle E = 90°$, $m\angle B = m\angle C = m\angle D = 120°$. **51.** Yes; if $\dfrac{(n-2) \cdot 180°}{n} = 150°$, then $n = 12$. A regular 12-gon (dodecagon) has interior $\angle$ with measure 150°. **53.** No; if $\dfrac{(n-2) \cdot 180°}{n} = 72°$, then $n = 3\frac{1}{3}$. It is not possible for a polygon to have $3\frac{1}{3}$ sides. **55.** $f(n)$ is the measure of each interior $\angle$ of a regular n-gon; as n gets larger and larger, $f(n)$ increases, becoming closer and closer to 180°. **57.** 10

11.1 MIXED REVIEW (p. 668) **63.** 27.5 in.² **65.** 37.5 sq. units **67.** no **69.** no **71.** 65° **73.** 245°

11.2 PRACTICE (pp. 672–675) **7.** 45°
9. $\dfrac{25\sqrt{3}}{4} \approx 10.8$ sq. units **11.** $\dfrac{245\sqrt{3}}{4} \approx 106.1$ sq. units
13. 30° **15.** 2° **17.** $108\sqrt{3} \approx 187.1$ sq. units **19.** $30\sqrt{3} \approx 52.0$ units; $75\sqrt{3} \approx 129.9$ sq. units **21.** $150 \tan 36° \approx 109.0$ units; $1125 \tan 36° \approx 817.36$ sq. units
23. $176 \sin 22.5° \approx 67.35$ units; $968(\sin 22.5°)(\cos 22.5°) \approx 342.24$ sq. units **25.** $75\sqrt{3} \approx 129.9$ in.² **27.** True; let θ be the central angle, n the number of sides, r the radius, and P the perimeter. As n grows bigger θ will become smaller, so the apothem, which is given by $r\cos\dfrac{\theta}{2}$ will get larger. The perimeter of the polygon, which is given by $n\left(2\sin\dfrac{\theta}{2}\right)$ will grow larger, too. Although the factor involving the sine will get smaller, the increase in n more than makes up for it. Consequently, the area, which is given by $\frac{1}{2}aP$ will increase. **29.** False; for example, the radius of a regular hexagon is equal to the side length. **31.** $32 \tan 67.5° \approx 77.3$ **33.** Let $s =$ the length of a side of the hexagon and of the equilateral triangle. The apothem of the hexagon is $\frac{1}{2}\sqrt{3}\,s$ and the perimeter of the hexagon is $6s$. The area of the hexagon, then, is $A = \frac{1}{2}aP = \frac{1}{2}\left(\frac{1}{2}\sqrt{3}\,s\right) \cdot 6s$, or $\frac{3}{2}\sqrt{3}\,s^2$. The area of an equilateral triangle with side length s is $A = \frac{1}{4}\sqrt{3}\,s^2$. Six of these equilateral triangles together (forming the hexagon), then, would have

area $6 \cdot \dfrac{s^2\sqrt{3}}{4} = \dfrac{3s^2\sqrt{3}}{2}$. The two results are the same.
45. $\dfrac{1}{4}\sqrt{3} \approx 0.43$ m **47.** 3 colors **49.** about 25 tiles

11.2 MIXED REVIEW (p. 675)
55. 3 **57.** −33 **59.** true **61.** false **63.** 7

11.3 PRACTICE (pp. 679–681) **5.** $3:2$, $9:4$ **7.** $2:1$, $4:1$
9. $5:6$, $25:36$ **11.** sometimes **13.** always **15.** $7:10$
17. Since $\overline{AB}$ is parallel to $\overline{DC}$, $\angle A \cong \angle C$ and $\angle B \cong \angle D$ by the Alternate Interior Angles Thm. So, $\triangle CDE \sim \triangle ABE$ by the AA Similarity Postulate; 98 square units. **19.** $3\sqrt{5}:4$
21. $3\sqrt{10}:5$ **23.** 1363 in.² and 5452 in.²; $1:4$ **25.** 820 ft²
27. about 1385.8 ft²; about 565.8 ft²

11.3 MIXED REVIEW (p. 681)
35. 145° **37.** 215° **39.** 80° **41.** 43°

QUIZ 1 (p. 682) **1.** 3240° **2.** 14.4° **3.** $\dfrac{289\sqrt{3}}{4} \approx 125.1$ in.²
4. $729 \tan 20° \approx 265.3$ cm² **5.** $\dfrac{4}{3}$; $\dfrac{16}{9}$ **6.** $\dfrac{13}{20}$; $\dfrac{169}{400}$
7. about $2613

11.4 PRACTICE (pp. 686–688) **3.** F **5.** C **7.** A
9. False; the arcs must be arcs of the same $\odot$ or of $\cong \odot$s.
11. False; the arcs must be arcs of the same $\odot$ or of $\cong \odot$s.
13. about 31.0 cm **15.** 31.42 in. **17.** 25.13 m
19. 5.09 yd **21.** 7.33 in.

23.

Radius	12	3	0.6	3.5	5.1	$3\sqrt{3}$
$m\widehat{AB}$	45°	30°	120°	192°	90°	about 107°
Length of $\widehat{AB}$	3π	0.5π	0.4π	about 3.73π	2.55π	3.09π

25. 36 **27.** $\dfrac{9971\pi}{1500} \approx 20.88$ **29.** $\dfrac{798}{25\pi} \approx 10.16$ **31.** $5\pi + 15 \approx 30.71$ **33.** 60, 9 **35.** $2\frac{1}{2}$, $\dfrac{19}{56}$ **37.** $4\pi\sqrt{7}$ **39.** A: 24.2 in., B: 24.9 in., C: 25.7 in. **41.** The sidewall width must be added twice to the rim diameter to get the tire diameter.
43. about 9.8 laps **45.** about 47.62 in. **47.** about 37.70 ft

11.4 MIXED REVIEW (p. 689) **53.** $10.89\pi \approx 34.21$ in.²
55. $176\pi \approx 552.92$ m² **57.** $2\frac{11}{12}$ **59.** 96° **61.** 258°

11.5 PRACTICE (pp. 695–698) **3.** $81\pi \approx 254.47$ in.²
5. $36\pi \approx 113.10$ ft² **7.** $\dfrac{175\pi}{9} \approx 61.09$ m² **9.** $8\pi \approx 25.13$ in.²
11. $0.16\pi \approx 0.50$ cm² **13.** $100\pi \approx 314.16$ in.² **15.** $\dfrac{49\pi}{18} \approx 8.55$ in.² **17.** $\dfrac{529\pi}{75} \approx 22.16$ m² **19.** $100\pi \approx 314.16$ ft²
21. 13.00 in. **23.** $540\pi \approx 1696.46$ m²
25. $16\pi - 80 \cos 36° \sin 36° \approx 12.22$ ft²
27. $324 - 81\pi \approx 69.53$ in.² **29.** 2.4, 4.7, 7.1, 9.4, 11.8, 14.1
31. Yes; it appears that the points lie along a line. You can also write a linear equation, $y = \dfrac{\pi}{40}x$.
33. 692.72 mi² **35.** $6\pi - 9\sqrt{3} \approx 3.26$ cm²

37. $768\pi - 576\sqrt{3} \approx 1415.08$ cm^2 **41.** No; the area of the $\odot$ is quadrupled and the circumference is doubled. $A = \pi r^2$ and $C = 2\pi r$; $\pi(2r)^2 = 4\pi r^2 = 4A$ and $2\pi(2r) = 2(2\pi r) = 2C$.

11.5 MIXED REVIEW (p. 698) **47.** $\frac{3}{16}$ **49.** $\frac{4}{11}$ **51.** 19.4 cm **53.** 68° **55.** $(x + 2)^2 + (y + 7)^2 = 36$ **57.** $(x + 4)^2 + (y - 5)^2 = 10.24$ **59.** $25\pi \approx 78.5$ in. **61.** $\frac{1896}{43\pi} \approx 14.0$ m

11.6 PRACTICE (pp. 701–704) **5.** $\frac{1}{2} = 50\%$ **7.** $\overline{AB}$ and $\overline{BF}$ do not overlap and $\overline{AB} + \overline{BF} = \overline{AF}$. So, any point K on $\overline{AF}$ must be on one of the two parts. Therefore, the sum of the two probabilities is 1. **9.** about 14% **11.** about 57% **13.** 25% **15.** about 42% **17.** $\frac{4 - \pi}{4} \approx 21.5\%$ **19.** $\frac{1}{4} = 25\%$ **21.** $\frac{3\pi}{392\sqrt{3}} \approx 1.4\%$ **23.** $\frac{3\pi}{98\sqrt{3}} \approx 5.6\%$ **25.** $\frac{\pi - 2}{\pi} \approx 36\%$ **27.** $\frac{1}{6} \approx 16.7\%$ **29.** 10,000,000 yd^2 **31.** 1% **33.** 36% **37.** 60° **39.** 30° **41.** The probability is doubled.

11.6 MIXED REVIEW (p. 705) **45.** No; since $11^2 = 121 \neq 100 + 16$, $\triangle ABC$ is not a right $\triangle$. Then, $\overline{CB}$ is not $\perp$ to $\overleftrightarrow{AB}$ and $\overleftrightarrow{AB}$ is not tangent to the $\odot$. **47.** Yes; $25^2 = 625 = 49 + 576$, so $\triangle ABC$ is a right $\triangle$ and $\overline{CA} \perp \overleftrightarrow{AB}$. Then, $\overleftrightarrow{AB}$ is tangent to the $\odot$.

49. 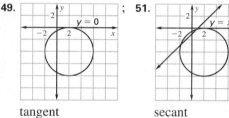   **51.**

tangent   secant

QUIZ 2 (p. 705) **1.** $\frac{738}{17} \approx 43.4$ m **2.** $\frac{286\pi}{45} \approx 20.0$ in. **3.** $\frac{738}{23\pi} \approx 10.2$ ft **4.** $2500\pi \approx 7854.0$ mi^2 **5.** $\frac{343\pi}{24} \approx 44.9$ cm^2 **6.** $\frac{725\pi}{9} \approx 253.1$ ft^2 **7.** $\frac{\sqrt{3}}{64} \approx 2.7\%$

CHAPTER 11 REVIEW (pp. 708–710) **1.** 140°, 40° **3.** 157.5°, 22.5° **5.** 45 **7.** 12 **9.** $36\sqrt{3} \approx 62.4$ cm^2 **11.** $\frac{75\sqrt{3}}{2} \approx 65.0$ m^2 **13.** sometimes **15.** always **17.** 5:3, 25:9 **19.** about 47.8 m, about 21.5 m **21.** about 1.91 in. **23.** $50\pi \approx 157.1$ in.^{2} **25.** $161\pi \approx 505.8$ cm^2 **27.** $196\pi \approx 615.75$ ft^2 **29.** $\frac{3}{10} = 30\%$ **31.** $\frac{3}{5} = 60\%$ **33.** $\frac{1}{4} = 25\%$

CHAPTER 12

SKILL REVIEW (p. 718) **1.** 2:1 **2.** 3:4 **3.** $4\sqrt{3} \approx 6.9$ in.^{2} **4.** $54\sqrt{3} \approx 93.5$ m^2 **5.** 4.8 ft^2

12.1 PRACTICE (pp. 723–726) **3.** Yes; the figure is a solid

that is bounded by polygons that enclose a single region of space. **5.** No; it does not have faces that are polygons. **7.** 6 **9.** 30 **11.** Yes; the figure is a solid that is bounded by polygons that enclose a single region of space. **13.** 5, 5, 8 **15.** 10, 16, 24 **17.** Not regular, convex; the faces of the polyhedron are not congruent (2 are hexagons and 6 are squares); any 2 points on the surface of the polyhedron can be connected by a line segment that lies entirely inside or on the polyhedron. **19.** False; see the octahedron in part (b) of Example 2 on page 720. **21.** True; the faces are $\cong$ squares. **23.** False; it does not have polygonal faces. **25.** circle **27.** pentagon **29.** circle **31.** rectangle **33.** yes;   **35.** yes;

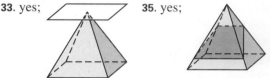

37. octahedron **39.** dodecahedron **41.** cube **43.** 5 faces, 6 vertices, 9 edges; $5 + 6 = 9 + 2$ **45.** 5 faces, 6 vertices, 9 edges; $5 + 6 = 9 + 2$ **47.** 12 vertices **49.** 24 vertices **51.** 12 vertices **53.** 6 molecules

12.1 MIXED REVIEW (p. 726) **61.** 280 ft^2 **63.** 110.40 m^2 **65.** 27.71 cm^2 **67.** 2866.22 in.^{2} **69.** 5808.80 ft^2

12.2 PRACTICE (pp. 731–734) **3.** cylinder **5.** rectangular prism **7, 9.** Three answers are given. The first considers the top and bottom as the bases, the second, the front and back, and the third, the right and left sides. **7.** 5 cm; 8 cm; 3 cm **9.** 24 cm^2; 15 cm^2; 40 cm^2

11. 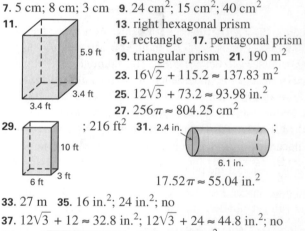 **13.** right hexagonal prism **15.** rectangle **17.** pentagonal prism **19.** triangular prism **21.** 190 m^2 **23.** $16\sqrt{2} + 115.2 \approx 137.83$ m^2 **25.** $12\sqrt{3} + 73.2 \approx 93.98$ in.^{2} **27.** $256\pi \approx 804.25$ cm^2 **29.** ; 216 ft^2 **31.** 2.4 in. ; $17.52\pi \approx 55.04$ in.^{2}

33. 27 m **35.** 16 in.^{2}; 24 in.^{2}; no **37.** $12\sqrt{3} + 12 \approx 32.8$ in.^{2}; $12\sqrt{3} + 24 \approx 44.8$ in.^{2}; no **39.**   **43.** $8\pi \approx 25$ in.^{2}

12.2 MIXED REVIEW (p. 734) **51.** $m\angle A = 58°$, $BC \approx 16.80$, $AB \approx 19.81$ **53.** $1805 \cos 36° \sin 36° \approx 858.33$ m^2 **55.** $96\sqrt{3} \approx 166.28$ in.^{2} **57.** $\frac{8}{11} \approx 73\%$ **59.** $\frac{4}{11} \approx 36\%$

12.3 PRACTICE (pp. 738–741) **3.** C **5.** B **7.** D **9.** about 7.62 ft **11.** about 100.09 ft^2 **13.** $25\sqrt{3} + 180 \approx 223.30$ in.^{2} **15.** 270.6 in.^{2} **17.** 506.24 mm^2 **19.** 219.99 cm^2 **21.** $2\sqrt{29} \approx 10.8$ cm **23.** 138.84π m^2 **25.** 73.73π in.^{2} **27.** right cone; 50.3 cm^2

29.

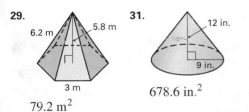

79.2 m²

31. 678.6 in.²

33. 101.1 sq. units **35.** $p = 9$ cm, $q = 15$ cm **37.** $\ell \approx 9.8$ m, $h \approx 7.7$ m **39.** about 1,334,817 ft² **41.** about 302 in.²
43. The surface area of the cup is $\frac{1}{4}$ the surface area of the original paper $\odot$; about 29°.

12.3 MIXED REVIEW (p. 741)
51. 82.84 sq. units **53.** about 11 in.

QUIZ 1 (p. 742) **1.** regular, convex; 4 vertices
2. not regular, convex; 8 vertices **3.** not regular, not convex; 12 vertices **4.** 336.44 ft² **5.** 305.91 m²
6. 773.52 mm²

12.4 PRACTICE (pp. 746–749) **3.** 255 **5.** 5.5 **7.** $540\pi \approx$ 1696 in.³ **9.** 840 in.³ **11.** 100 unit cubes; 4 layers of 5 rows of 5 cubes each **13.** 512 in.³ **15.** $\frac{735\sqrt{3}}{4} \approx 318.26$ in.³
17. 288.40 ft³ **19.** 240 m³ **21.** 310.38 cm³
23. 48,484.99 ft³ **25.** 924 m³ **27.** $\frac{135\sqrt{3}}{2} \approx 116.91$ cm³
29. $3\sqrt[3]{100} \approx 13.92$ yd **31.** $\frac{1211\sqrt{3}}{300} \approx 6.99$ in.
33. $\sqrt{\frac{1131}{10\pi}} \approx 6.00$ m **35.** 150 ft³ **37.** $605\pi \approx 1900.66$ in.³
39. about 92.6 yd **41.** No; the circumference of the base of the shorter cylinder is 11 in., so the radius is about 1.75 in. and the volume is about 82 in.³. The circumference of the base of the taller cylinder is 8.5 in., so the radius is about 1.35 in. and the volume is about 63 in.³. **43.** 7 candles
45. Prism: volume = 36 in.³, surface area = 66 in.²; cylinder: volume ≈ 36 in.³, surface area ≈ 62.2 in.²; the cylinder and the prism hold about the same amount. The cylinder has smaller surface area, so less metal would be needed and it would be cheaper to produce a cylindrical can than one shaped like a prism. **47.** about 1,850,458 lb

12.4 MIXED REVIEW (p. 749) **51.** 30°, 75°, 75°
53. 45°, 60°, 75° **55.** 98 m² **57.** 462 in.² **59.** 144 cm²

12.5 PRACTICE (pp. 755–757) **5. a.** $4\pi \approx 12.6$ ft² **b.** $\frac{16\pi}{3} \approx$ 16.8 ft³ **9.** $\frac{3721\pi}{100} \approx 116.9$ ft² **11.** 400 cm³
13. $\frac{67,183\sqrt{3}}{750} \approx 155.2$ ft³ **15.** $710\sqrt{3} \approx 1229.8$ mm³
17. 48.97 ft³ **19.** 667.06 in.³ **21.** 5 in. **23.** 288 ft³
25. 97.92 m³ **27.** yes **29.** about 17.5 sec
31. 301.59 cm³ **33.** $16\pi \approx 50.3$ m³

12.5 MIXED REVIEW (p. 758) **41.** 144°, 36°
43. $163\frac{7}{11}°$, $16\frac{4}{11}°$ **45.** 168°, 12° **47.** $\frac{26,569\pi}{100} \approx 834.69$ cm²

49. $100\pi \approx 314.16$ m² **51.** 24 vertices

QUIZ 2 (p. 758) **1.** 1080 in.³ **2.** 1020 ft³
3. $350\pi \approx 1099.56$ cm³ **4.** $\frac{243\pi}{4} \approx 190.85$ m³
5. 21.168 mm³ **6.** $\frac{147\sqrt{3}}{4} \approx 63.65$ in.³ **7.** about 5633 ft³

12.6 PRACTICE (pp. 762–765) **3.** *Sample answers:* $\overline{QS}$, $\overline{FT}$, or $\overline{TS}$ **5.** $\overline{QS}$ **7.** $36\pi \approx 113.10$ sq. units
9. about 5.24×10^{-25} cm³ **11.** 4071.50 cm²
13. a hemisphere **15.** 7.4 in. **17.** about 45.4 in.²
19. The diameters of Neptune and its moons Triton and Nereid are, respectively, about 30,775 mi, about 1680 mi, and about 211 mi. Then, the surface areas are about 2,975,404,400 mi², about 8,866,800 m², and 139,900 mi².
21. 6545 in.³ **23.** 14π mm, 196π mm², $\frac{1372\pi}{3}$ mm³
25. 5 cm, 100π cm², $\frac{500\pi}{3}$ cm³ **27. a.** 488.58 in.²
b. 419.82 in.³ **29. a.** 375.29 ft² **b.** 610.12 ft³
31. $\frac{1}{3}$; $\frac{2}{3}$; 1; $\frac{4}{3}$; $\frac{5}{3}$ **35.** $y = 2$; $4\pi \approx 12.57$ sq. units
39. about 257,300 ft² **41, 43.** Answers are rounded to 2 decimal places. **41.** 3.43 cm **43.** 10.42 cm

12.6 MIXED REVIEW (p. 765) **51.** translation, vertical line reflection, 180° rotation, glide reflection
53. translation, 180° rotation **55.** yes; 36 sq. units
57. about 14.4 revolutions

12.7 PRACTICE (pp. 769–771) **5.** C **7.** 6:11 **9.** not similar
11. similar **13.** always **15.** always **17.** 112π cm², 160π cm³ **19.** 384π ft², 768π ft³ **21.** 1:2 **23.** 2:3
25. 88 in. **27.** 8192 in.³ **31.** about 4032 ft²
33. about 34,051 ft³, about 67 in.³

12.7 MIXED REVIEW (p. 772) **39.** $\overline{LK}$ **41.** $\overline{CA}$ **43.** $\angle BAC$
45. $\frac{225\sqrt{3}}{2} + 765 \approx 959.86$ ft² **47.** $\frac{26,896\pi}{25} \approx 3379.85$ in.²
49. about 74.3 in.

QUIZ 3 (p. 772) **1.** 1256.64 cm², 4188.79 cm³
2. 44.41 in.², 27.83 in.³ **3.** 366.44 ft², 659.58 ft³
4. 14,137.17 m², 158,058.33 m³ **5.** 6.5 cm; larger prism: 460 cm², 624 cm³; smaller prism: 115 cm², 78 cm³
6. 3 ft; smaller cone: $9\pi + 3\pi\sqrt{73} \approx 108.80$ ft², $24\pi \approx$ 75.40 ft³; larger cone: $\frac{81\pi + 27\pi\sqrt{73}}{4} \approx 244.80$ ft², $81\pi \approx$ 254.47 ft³
7. $40,000\pi \approx 125,663.71$ ft², $\frac{4,000,000\pi}{3} \approx 4,188,790.21$ ft³
8. 5 ft, $100\pi \approx 314.16$ ft², $\frac{500\pi}{3} \approx 523.60$ ft³

CHAPTER 12 REVIEW (pp. 774–776) **1.** 60 **3.** 8 **5.** 414.69 ft²
7. 96 cm² **9.** 124.71 in.² **11.** $\frac{123,039\sqrt{3}}{5} \approx 42,621.96$ m³
13. 10,500 in.³ **15.** $320\pi \approx 1005.31$ ft³ **17.** $\pi \approx 3.14$ in.², $\frac{\pi}{6} \approx 0.52$ in.³ **19.** no

CUMULATIVE PRACTICE (pp. 780–781) **1.** 30°, 30°, 150°, 150° **3.** Let M be the midpoint of $\overline{TS}$. By the Midpoint Formula, $M = (h, k)$. Then $RM = \sqrt{(h-0)^2 + (k-0)^2} = \sqrt{h^2 + k^2}$. Since $TS = \sqrt{(2h-0)^2 + (0-2k)^2} = 2\sqrt{h^2 + k^2}$, $RM = \frac{1}{2}TS$. **5.** right; $\angle Z$, $\angle Y$

7.

Statements	Reasons
1. $ABDE$ and $CDEF$ are parallelograms.	1. Given
2. $\overline{AB} \parallel \overline{DE}$ and $\overline{CF} \parallel \overline{DE}$	2. Definition of parallelogram
3. $\overline{AB} \parallel \overline{CF}$	3. Two lines $\parallel$ to the same line are $\parallel$.
4. $\angle 4 \cong \angle 5$	4. Corresponding $\angle$ Postulate
5. $m\angle 4 = m\angle 5$	5. Def. of congruent $\angle$
6. $\overline{BD} \parallel \overline{AE}$	6. Definition of parallelogram
7. $\angle 5$ and $\angle 6$ are supplements.	7. Consecutive Interior Angles Theorem
8. $m\angle 5 + m\angle 6 = 180°$	8. Def. of supplementary $\angle$
9. $m\angle 4 + m\angle 6 = 180°$	9. Substitution prop. of =
10. $\angle 4$ and $\angle 6$ are supplements.	10. Def. of supplementary $\angle$

9. never **11.** *Sample answer:* $\overline{BC} \parallel \overline{DE}$, so corresp. angles $\angle ABC$ and $\angle D$ are $\cong$, as are corresp. angles $\angle ACB$ and $\angle E$. Then, $\triangle ABC \sim \triangle ADE$ by the AA Similarity Postulate. **13.** 5 : 8; 25 : 64 **15.** about 73.7°, about 16.3° **17.** 25° **19.** 90° **21.** 100° **23.** 230° **25.** They are supplementary angles; $ABPC$ is a quadrilateral with two right angles, so the sum of the other two angles is 180°. **27.** 12 **29.** 20 **31.** 31.4 **33.** the bisectors of the right $\angle$ formed **35.** 1800 tan 67.5° ≈ 4345.58 cm^2 **37.** $\frac{49\pi}{2} \approx 76.97$ ft^3 **39.** $8\pi \approx 25.13$ ft^2 **41.** 7.1 in.^{2}

SKILLS REVIEW HANDBOOK

PROBLEM SOLVING (p. 784) **1.** $197.46 **3.** 32 kinds **5.** 10 33¢ stamps and 6 20¢ stamps **7.** not enough information (You need to know how much area a can of paint will cover.)

POSITIVE AND NEGATIVE NUMBERS (p. 785)
1. -3.3 **3.** 2.7 **5.** $-1\frac{1}{12}$ **7.** 0 **9.** -1 **11.** -8 **13.** 9 **15.** 0
17. -1 **19.** -0.156 **21.** -3 **23.** -9 **25.** -2.88 **27.** $\frac{1}{30}$

EVALUATING EXPRESSIONS (p. 786) **1.** 100 **3.** -8 **5.** 225 **7.** 47 **9.** 64 **11.** $\frac{1}{8}$ **13.** -48 **15.** $\frac{1}{3}$ **17.** -12 **19.** 25 **21.** 12 **23.** -23

THE DISTRIBUTIVE PROPERTY (p. 787) **1.** $2a + 8$ **3.** $3x - 2$ **5.** $y^2 - 9y$ **7.** $4n - 7$ **9.** $4b^2 + 8b$ **11.** $16x^2 - 72xy$ **13.** $2rs + 2rt$ **15.** $-7x^2 + 21x - 14$ **17.** $6m + 4$ **19.** -1 **21.** $19g^3 + 9g^2$ **23.** $xy + 2x - 3y$ **25.** $3h - 3h^2$ **27.** $3y - 4$ **29.** $4r + 8$ **31.** $3n^2 - 13n + 16$

RECIPROCALS (p. 788) **1.** $\frac{1}{12}$ **3.** 4 **5.** -10 **7.** $\frac{13}{6}$ **9.** 5

RATIOS (p. 788) **1.** $\frac{2}{5}$ **3.** $\frac{9}{5}$ **5.** $\frac{1}{1}$ **7.** $\frac{80}{1}$ **9.** $\frac{13}{15}$ **11.** $\frac{2}{3}$

SOLVING LINEAR EQUATIONS (SINGLE–STEP) (p. 789)
1. 13 **3.** 4 **5.** $-\frac{1}{8}$ **7.** -32 **9.** -8 **11.** -10 **13.** $\frac{21}{2}$ **15.** -80
17. 18 **19.** -23 **21.** $\frac{3}{4}$ **23.** -1

SOLVING LINEAR EQUATIONS (MULTI–STEP) (p. 790)
1. 8 **3.** 8 **5.** -0.6, or $-\frac{3}{5}$ **7.** -15 **9.** 4 **11.** $\frac{7}{8}$ **13.** -18
15. 3 **17.** $-\frac{1}{3}$ **19.** 56 **21.** -10 **23.** 25 **25.** $\frac{13}{6}$ **27.** 29
29. 76 **31.** 6.6 **33.** $-\frac{25}{6}$ **35.** -11

SOLVING INEQUALITIES (p. 791) **1.** $x < 56$ **3.** $x > 7.3$ **5.** $x < 2$ **7.** $x > 3$ **9.** $x > 4$ **11.** yes **13.** yes **15.** no **17.** yes **19.** *Sample answers:* 4, 4.5, and 10; no; when $x = 3$, $(2x - 3) + (x + 5) = x + 8$.

PLOTTING POINTS (p. 792) **1.** $(-1, 0)$ **3.** $(2, -2)$ **5.** $(-5, 3)$ **7.** $(5, -2)$ **9.** $(-2, 5)$ **11.** $(1, 1)$

13–27 odd:

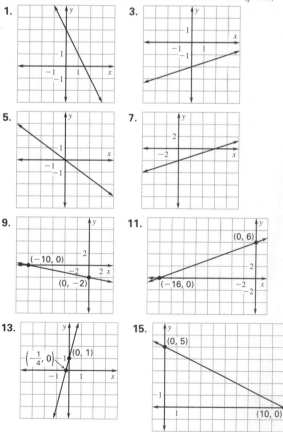

LINEAR EQUATIONS AND THEIR GRAPHS (p. 793)

SLOPE–INTERCEPT FORM (p. 794)

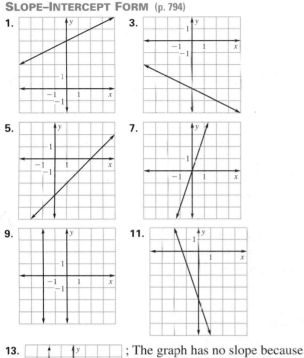

1. graph **3.** graph **5.** graph **7.** graph **9.** graph **11.** graph

13. ; The graph has no slope because a vertical line has the same x-coordinate for every point on the line. If you try to evaluate the slope using any two points, you get zero in the denominator, and division by zero is undefined. The graph has no y-intercept because it does not intersect the y-axis.

WRITING LINEAR EQUATIONS (p. 795)
1. $y = x - 4$
3. $y = \frac{5}{2}x - \frac{3}{4}$ **5.** $y = 0.7x$ **7.** $y = 2x - 7$ **9.** $y = 12x + 66$
11. $y = -11$ **13.** $y = \frac{1}{6}x + \frac{17}{6}$ **15.** $y = 8x + 41$ **17.** $y = \frac{5}{8}x - \frac{5}{4}$
19. $y = -x - 1$ **21.** $y = -0.64x + 3.596$ **23.** $y = \frac{6}{7}x + \frac{11}{7}$

SOLVING SYSTEMS OF EQUATIONS (p. 796) **1.** $(1, 6)$
3. $(-2, -14)$ **5.** $\left(0, \frac{3}{4}\right)$ **7.** $\left(\frac{104}{9}, \frac{100}{9}\right)$ **9.** $(3, -1.2)$
11. $(-15, -19.5)$ **13.** $\left(\frac{3}{8}, -\frac{7}{8}\right)$ **15.** $(2.35, 0.95)$

PROPERTIES OF EXPONENTS (p. 797) **1.** $-\frac{8}{27}$ **3.** $\frac{1}{32}a^5b^5$
5. 1 **7.** $\frac{4}{x^3y^6}$ **9.** 262,144 **11.** $\frac{125}{m^3}$ **13.** $8b^4$ **15.** x^2 **17.** a^4
19. $\frac{a^2}{2bc^3}$ **21.** $-175a^2b^8c$ **23.** $32z^4$

MULTIPLYING BINOMIALS (p. 798) **1.** $x^2 + 2x + 1$
3. $3c^2 - 3$ **5.** $4a^2 + 13a - 35$ **7.** $4f^2 - 16$ **9.** $6h^2 + 9h + 3$

SQUARING BINOMIALS (p. 798)
1. $x^2 + 4x + 4$ **3.** $x^2 + 16x + 64$ **5.** $n^2 - 10n + 25$
7. $225 - 30x + x^2$, or $x^2 - 30x + 225$

RADICAL EXPRESSIONS (p. 799) **1.** 8 and -8 **3.** $\frac{7}{9}$ and $-\frac{7}{9}$
5. 0.3 and -0.3 **7.** $\sqrt{13} \approx 3.61$ **9.** $5\sqrt{2} \approx 7.07$ **11.** -14
13. $2\sqrt{15} \approx 7.75$ **15.** $6\sqrt{2} \approx 8.49$ **17.** $30\sqrt{14} \approx 112.25$
19. $\frac{1}{5} = 0.2$ **21.** $\frac{1}{4} = 0.25$ **23.** $3\sqrt{2} \approx 4.24$ **25.** $\frac{4\sqrt{3}}{9} \approx 0.77$

SOLVING $AX^2 + C = 0$ (p. 800) **1.** 25, -25 **3.** $\sqrt{5} \approx 2.24$,
$-\sqrt{5} \approx -2.24$ **5.** 2, -2 **7.** no solution **9.** 2.4 **11.** 13

SOLVING $AX^2 + BX + C = 0$ (p. 801) **1.** $-4, -1$ **3.** $0, -6$
5. $\frac{9 + \sqrt{77}}{2} \approx 8.89$, $\frac{9 - \sqrt{77}}{2} \approx 0.11$ **7.** $\frac{-2 + \sqrt{2}}{2} \approx -0.29$,
$\frac{-2 - \sqrt{2}}{2} \approx -1.71$ **9.** $\frac{4 + \sqrt{13}}{3} \approx 2.54$, $\frac{4 - \sqrt{13}}{3} \approx 0.13$
11. $\frac{5 + 3\sqrt{5}}{10} \approx 1.17$, $\frac{5 - 3\sqrt{5}}{10} \approx -0.17$

13. 1, 2; The solutions of the quadratic equation are the same as the x-intercepts of the graph.

SOLVING FORMULAS (p. 802) **1.** $b = \frac{A}{h}$ **3.** $b = P - a - c$
5. $a = \frac{P - 2b}{2}$ **7.** $\ell = \frac{S - 2wh}{2w + 2h}$ **9.** $\ell = \frac{S - \pi r^2}{\pi r}$ **11.** $y = 9 - 3x$
13. $y = -\frac{1}{2}x - \frac{3}{2}$ **15.** $y = \frac{6}{7}x - 6$ **17.** $y = \frac{c - ax}{b}$

EXTRA PRACTICE

CHAPTER 1 (pp. 803–804) **1.** Multiply by $\frac{1}{2}$; $\frac{1}{2}$. **3.** powers
of 5; 625 **5.** Multiply by 1.5; 162. **7.** negative **15.** 19
17. 12 **19.** 16 **21.** yes **23.** Q; $\overrightarrow{QP}$, $\overrightarrow{QR}$; $\angle PQR$, $\angle RQP$
25. B; $\overrightarrow{BA}$, $\overrightarrow{BC}$; $\angle ABC$, $\angle CBA$ **27.** $65°$ **29.** obtuse; $\approx 150°$
31. acute; $\approx 25°$ **33.** $(3, -1)$ **35.** $42°$ **37.** $74°$ **39.** $45°$, $135°$
41. 28; 49 **43.** 36; 60 **45.** 31.4; 78.5 **47.** 33; 67.0625

CHAPTER 2 (pp. 805–806) **1.** If you read it in a newspaper, then it must be true. **3.** If a number is odd, then its square is odd. **5.** If you are not indoors, then you are caught in a rainstorm; If you are not caught in a rainstorm, then you are indoors; If you are caught in a rainstorm, then you are not indoors. **7.** If two angles are not vertical angles, then they are not congruent; If two angles are congruent, then they are vertical angles; If two angles are not congruent, then they are not vertical angles. **9.** If $x = 6$, then $2x - 5 = 7$; true. **11.** If two angles are right angles, then they are supplementary; If two angles are supplementary, then they are right angles. **13.** yes **15.** no **17.** If we don't stop at the bank, then we won't see our friends.
19. We go shopping if and only if we need a shopping list.
21. We go shopping if and only if we stop at the bank.

23. *p*: The hockey teams wins the game tonight. *q*: They will play in the championship. $\sim p \rightarrow \sim q$; If the hockey team doesn't win the game tonight, they won't play in the championship. $\sim q \rightarrow \sim p$; If the hockey team doesn't play in the championship, then they didn't win the game tonight. **25.** *AB* **27.** *AB = DF* **29.** $6 - 4$ (or 2) **31.** $\angle 6$ **33.** $\angle 3 \cong \angle 5$ by the Congruent Complements Theorem. **35.** $b = 8$; $c = 27$

37.

Statements	Reasons
1. $\angle 1 \cong \angle 3$	1. Vertical angles are $\cong$.
2. $\angle 4 \cong \angle 2$	2. Vertical angles are $\cong$.
3. $\angle 1$ and $\angle 4$ are complementary.	3. Given
4. $m\angle 1 + m\angle 4 = 90°$	4. Definition of complementary
5. $m\angle 1 = m\angle 3$	5. Definition of congruence
6. $m\angle 4 = m\angle 2$	6. Definition of congruence
7. $m\angle 3 + m\angle 2 = 90°$	7. Substitution property of equality
8. $\angle 3$ and $\angle 2$ are complementary.	8. Definition of complementary

CHAPTER 3 (pp. 807–808) **1.** parallel **3.** skew
5. *Sample answers:* $\overleftrightarrow{AB}, \overleftrightarrow{BC}, \overleftrightarrow{GE}, \overleftrightarrow{HG}$
7. *Sample answers: HAD, ADF, DFH, FHA*
9. alternate interior **11.** consecutive interior

13.

Statements	Reasons
2. $\angle ABC$ is a right angle.	1. Given
	3. Def. of a right $\angle$
7. $m\angle ABD$	4. Given
	5. Def. of $\angle$ bisector
	6. If 2 sides of 2 adj. acute $\angle$s are $\perp$, then the $\angle$s are complementary.
	8. Distributive prop.
	9. Division prop. of equality

15. $x = 30$; $y = 150$ **17.** $x = 125$; $y = 125$ **19.** $x = 118$; $y = 118$ **21.** $\overleftrightarrow{CG} \parallel \overleftrightarrow{DE}$ **23.** Corresponding angles are congruent. **25.** Alternate interior angles are congruent. **27.** $\overleftrightarrow{AB}$: 0; $\overleftrightarrow{CD}$: $-\frac{1}{3}$; $\overleftrightarrow{EF}$: $-\frac{11}{14}$; none **29.** $y = 6x + 19$ **31.** $x = -9$ **33.** yes **35.** $y = \frac{1}{2}x - 3$ **37.** $y = -2x - 11$

CHAPTER 4 (pp. 809–810) **1.** 20, 60, 100; obtuse
3. 40, 90, 50; right **5.** 90°, 45°, 45° **7.** $ABGH \cong BEFG \cong CDEB$; $AEFH \cong CGFD$ **9.** $\angle A, \angle F$; $\angle B, \angle E$; $\angle C, \angle D$; $\overline{AB}, \overline{FE}$; $\overline{BC}, \overline{ED}$; $\overline{AC}, \overline{FD}$ **11.** 13 **13.** SSS **15.** SAS **17.** yes; AAS **19.** no **21.** ASA; corresp. parts of $\cong$ $\triangle$ are $\cong$. **23.** SSS; corresponding parts of $\cong$ $\triangle$ are $\cong$. **25.** Paragraph proof: Given that $\triangle CBD \cong \triangle BAF$, $\overline{BC} \cong \overline{AB}$ by corresp. parts of $\cong$ $\triangle$ are $\cong$. **27.** $x = 60$; $y = 60$ **29.** $x = 45$; $y = 45$

31. *Sample answer:*

Coordinate grid with points $C(-3, 2)$, $D(3, 2)$, $B(-3, -4)$, $A(3, -4)$.

33. 100 **35.** $7\sqrt{2}$

CHAPTER 5 (pp. 811–812) **1.** 12 **3.** *E* is on $\overrightarrow{DB}$.
5. *K* is on $\overrightarrow{EH}$. **7.** 9 **9.** 10 **11.** 8 **15.** The orthocenter should be at the vertex of the right angle of the triangle.
17. $\overline{AC}$ **19.** 5 **21.** 9 **23.** $\overline{BC}, \overline{AC}$ **25.** $\overline{GJ}, \overline{GH}$
27. $\angle Q, \angle P$ **29.** < **31.** = **33.** = **35.** = **37.** <

CHAPTER 6 (pp. 813–814) **1.** no **3.** yes; hexagon; convex
5. no **7.** 25 **9.** 13 **11.** $\angle VYX$; If a quadrilateral is a parallelogram, then its opposite angles are congruent.
13. $\overline{TX}$; If a quadrilateral is a parallelogram, then its diagonals bisect each other. **15.** $\overline{VY}$; If a quadrilateral is a parallelogram, then its opposite sides are parallel.
17. $\overline{VX}$ and $\overline{YW}$; If a quadrilateral is a parallelogram, then its diagonals bisect each other. **19.** Yes; opposite angles are congruent. **21.** *Sample answer:* The slope of $\overline{AD}$ = slope of $\overline{BC} = -\frac{3}{5}$ and the slope of $\overline{AB}$ = slope of $\overline{DC} = -\frac{7}{2}$. If opposite sides of a quadrilateral are parallel, then it is a parallelogram. **23.** *Sample answer:* The slope of $\overline{RS}$ = slope of $\overline{UT} = -\frac{1}{11}$. Since $RS = UT = \sqrt{122}$, $\overline{RS} \cong \overline{UT}$ by definition of congruence. If one pair of opposite sides of a quadrilateral are congruent and parallel, then the quadrilateral is a parallelogram. **25.** parallelogram, rhombus, rectangle, square **27.** rectangle, square **29.** rhombus, square **31.** rhombus **33.** square **35.** $m\angle A = 70°$; $m\angle B = 110°$; $m\angle D = 70°$ **37.** $m\angle G = 115°$; $m\angle E = 115°$ **39.** 23 **41.** $AB = 25$, $BC = 25$, $AD = 39$, $CD = 39$ **43.** $KM = 8\sqrt{10}$, $KP = 8\sqrt{10}$, $MN = 10$, $NP = 10$ **45.** rectangle or parallelogram **47.** 160 **49.** 55

CHAPTER 7 (pp. 815–816) **1.** Z **3.** *Sample answers:* $\overline{QR} \cong \overline{ZY}$; $\overline{RP} \cong \overline{YX}$; $\overline{PQ} \cong \overline{XZ}$ **5.** $(-7, 3)$ **7.** translation; slide 8 units to the right; $E(3, 1)$, $F(3, 3)$, $G(6, 3)$, $H(6, 1)$ **9.** $\triangle GHJ$ **11.** $\triangle FED$ **13.** $\triangle GFE$ **15.** $\triangle NPM$ **17.** $(2, 4)$ **19.** $(1, -12)$ **21.** $(7, 0)$ **23.** $H'(2, 0)$, $E'(5, -2)$, $F'(5, -5)$, $G'(2, -7)$ **25.** $J'(4, -4)$, $K'(1, -2)$, $M'(4, 0)$, $N'(7, -2)$ **27.** *a, b* **29.** $\langle -3, 5 \rangle$ **31.** $\langle -7, 7 \rangle$ **33.** $(-5, -1)$

35.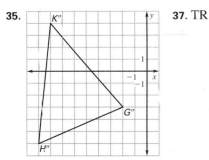

37. TR

CHAPTER 8 (pp. 817–818) **1.** $\frac{2}{1}$ **3.** $\frac{5}{8}$ **5.** 60°, 80°, 100°, 120°
7. 7 **9.** 3 **11.** 1 **13.** $\frac{10}{y}$ **15.** $\frac{x}{y}$ **17.** 6 **19.** 5 **21.** 32 **23.** 6.25
25. 3:2 **27.** $u = 9$, $y = 4$, $z = 10$ **29.** yes; $\triangle ABC \sim \triangle DEF$
31. no **33.** (0, 12.5) **35.** (0, –12) **37.** no **39.** yes; $\triangle ACE \sim$
$\triangle BCD$; 12 **41.** yes; $\triangle EFG \sim \triangle HJK$; 8 **43.** yes; $\frac{4}{8} = \frac{1}{2}$
45. 20 **47.** $A'(10, 0)$, $B'(25, 15)$, $C'(20, 25)$, $D'(5, 15)$
49. $A'(1, –1)$, $B'(1.5, 1)$, $C'(0.5, 2)$, $D'(–2, –1)$

CHAPTER 9 (pp. 819–820) **1.** $\triangle ABC \sim \triangle ACD \sim \triangle CBD$; AC
3. $\triangle JLK \sim \triangle JKM \sim \triangle KLM$; JL **5.** 10 **7.** $\sqrt{61}$; no
9. 50; yes **11.** 13 **13.** 175 **15.** 28 **17.** about 91.2 cm^2
19. yes **21.** yes **23.** yes; right **25.** yes; obtuse
27. yes; obtuse **29.** $x = 16$; $y = 8\sqrt{3}$
31. $\sin S = 0.8615$, $\cos S = 0.5077$, $\tan S = 1.6970$;
$\sin T = 0.5077$, $\cos T = 0.8615$, $\tan T = 0.5893$
33. $\sin X = 0.7241$, $\cos X = 0.6897$, $\tan X = 1.05$;
$\sin Z = 0.6897$, $\cos Z = 0.7241$, $\tan Z = 0.9524$
35. $x = 8.8$; $y = 3.7$ **37.** $AC = 9$, $m\angle A = 53.1°$, $m\angle B = 36.9°$
39. $MP = 171$, $m\angle N = 50.7°$, $m\angle M = 39.3°$
41. $\langle 4, 11 \rangle$; 11.7 **43.** $\langle –4, 7 \rangle$ **45.** $\langle 3, 3 \rangle$

CHAPTER 10 (pp. 821–822) **1.** D **3.** G **5.** H **7.** A **9.** internal
11. internal **13.** D; 2 **15.** $y = 3$, $x = 5$, $y = –1$ **17.** 55°
19. 35° **21.** 145° **23.** 270° **25.** 70 **27.** 240 **29.** 80
31. 70 **33.** 4 **35.** 10 **37.** 4 **39.** (12, –3); 7 **41.** (–3.8, 4.9);
0.9 **43.** $(x – 5)^2 + (y – 8)^2 = 36$ **45.** $(x – 2)^2 + (y – 2)^2 = 4$
47. $x = 4$ **49.** $y = –2$, $y = 6$

CHAPTER 11 (pp. 823–824) **1.** 6120° **3.** 10,440° **5.** 140
7. 120 **9.** 15° **11.** 10° **13.** 20 **15.** 4 **17.** 20° **9.** 4°
21. 16.97; 18 **23.** 48.50; 169.74 **25.** 25.98; 32.48
27. 3:1; 9:1 **29.** 125 square inches **31.** about 9.07
33. about 147 **35.** about 11.78 **37.** about 95.49
39. about 452.39 **41.** about 41.89 **43.** about 19.63
45. about 67% **47.** about 83% **49.** about 68%

CHAPTER 12 (pp. 825–826) **1.** polyhedron; not regular;
convex **3.** polyhedron; regular; convex **5.** $F = 7$, $V = 7$,
$E = 12$; $7 + 7 = 12 + 2$ **7.** square **9.** 220 cm^2 **11.** 120 in.^{2}
13. 339.29 cm^2 **15.** 85 in.^{2} **17.** 282.74 cm^2
19. about 1060.29 ft^3 **21.** about 2001.19 in.^{3}
23. about 247.59 ft^3 **25.** 701.48 cm^3 **27.** about 513.13 in.^{3}
29. about 871.27 ft^3 **31.** 2123.72 m^2; 9202.77 m^3
33. 216 m^2; 216 m^3 **35.** 196π cm^2; $457\frac{1}{3}\pi$ cm^3